1992
AMA
Educators'
Proceedings

Enhancing Knowledge
Development
in
Marketing

1992 AMA Educators' Proceedings

Enhancing Knowledge Development in Marketing

EDITORS

Robert P. Leone   University of Texas, Austin
V. Kumar   University of Houston

MANAGING EDITORS

Peter J. Gordon   Southeast Missouri State University
Bert J. Kellerman   Southeast Missouri State University

TRACK CHAIRS

Robert W. Shoemaker   New York University
George Zinkhan   University of Houston
S. Tamer Cavusgil   Michigan State University
Roger Calantone   Michigan State University
Margery Steinberg   University of Hartford
Ajay Kohli   University of Texas, Austin
Wagner A. Kamakura   Vanderbilt University
Raymond Fisk   University of Central Florida

 AMERICAN MARKETING ASSOCIATION

Volume 3

250 S. Wacker Drive • Chicago, Illinois 60606 • (312) 648-0536

The Library of Congress has cataloged this serial as follows:
  AMA educators'proceedings—1983-   —Chicago, IL:
    American Marketing Association,

    v.;ill.; 28cm.—(Series)

    Annual.
    ''Represents a compilation of the papers presented at the...American
Marketing Association Educators' Conference.''
    Continues: American Marketing Association. Educators' Conference.
Educators' conference proceedings.
    ISSN 0888-1839 = AMA educators' proceedings.
    ISBN 0-87757-231-3

    1. Marketing—Congresses. I. American Marketing Association.
Educators' Conference. II. Title: Educators' proceedings. III. Series: Series
(American Marketing Association)

HF5410.A45   86-643031
                    658.8'007'15—dc19
                                          AACR 2 MARC-S

Library of Congress   [8606]

PREFACE AND ACKNOWLEDGEMENTS

The papers and abstracts compiled here were presented at the 1992 Summer Educators' Conference held in Chicago on August 8-11 at the Hyatt Regency Hotel. One hundred and fifty manuscripts were selected for presentation from a total of 281 manuscripts submitted to seven competitive tracks. The conference also featured 16 special sessions selected from over 20 submitted proposals.

We wish to convey our sincere thanks to the authors and special session participants who took the time to share their ideas and findings. By sparking discussion, stretching our understanding, and challenging the status quo agenda, they maintain the vitality of the discipline. We also would like to thank the session chairs for keeping the speakers on track and the discussants who took the time to review the papers and give their valuable feedback to the authors.

Our sincere thanks go to the track chairs for their outstanding job. The track chairs are: Robert W. Shoemaker (Advertising and Sales Promotion), George Zinkhan (Buyer Behavior), S. Tamer Cavusgil and Roger Calantone (Global/International Marketing), Margery Steinberg (Marketing Education), Ajay Kohli (Marketing Management and Strategy), Wagner A. Kamakura (Marketing Research/Research Methodology), and Raymond Fisk (Retailing/Services). Their combined expertise and unselfish dedication made it possible for us to achieve the mammoth task of processing over 300 submittals in less than five months.

Each of these track chairs, in turn, credit much of their task to the prompt and professional feedback they received from the reviewers. Although we never interacted with the reviewers directly during the process, we sincerely thank them for lending their time, insight, and critical recommendations to the process.

The Blue Ribbon Panel Members Ed Blair, Paul Busch, Wagner Kamakura, Ajay Kohli, Frank Mulhern, and Gerard Tellis had one of the toughest assignments in selecting the overall best paper awards for the conference. We sincerely thank them for their excellent job.

The professionals at AMA International Headquarters brought their rich program experience to the task of staging this conference. We appreciate the support we received from Ann Pellegrini, Maria Cardenas, Francesca Van Gorp, Jackie Whitmer, and Cherylyn Costello.

Bill Bearden, AMA Education Division Vice President, was encouraging and helpful. He patiently shared AMA goals and conference protocol while welcoming program innovations. We are also thankful to marketing departments at Northwestern University, University of Chicago, DePaul University, University of Illinois at Chicago, and Loyola University for the gracious gesture to co-sponsor the Sunday reception.

We also thank Peter Gordon and Bert Kellerman for their help in producing the final copy.

A final word of thanks goes to Jaishankar Ganesh (Houston) and S. Srinivasan (Texas), who were "fortunate" enough to be our research assistants, for their administrative and clerical support over the past year.

Robert P. Leone
University of Texas, Austin

V. Kumar (VK)
University of Houston

Program Co-Chairs
1992 Summer Educators' Conference

Manuscript Reviewers for 1992 Summer Educators' Conference

Nils-Erik Aaby
University of Colorado

David Aaker
University of California, Berkeley

Manoj K. Agarwal
State University of New York

Joseph W. Alba
University of Florida

Dana L. Alden
University of Hawaii

Costas Alexandrides
Georgia State Universtity

Chris T. Allen
University of Cincinnati

Jeff Allen
University of Central Florida

Mark I. Alpert
University of Texas

Eugene Anderson
University of Michigan

Craig Andrews
Marquette University

Eric J. Arnould
California State University, Long Beach

Nancy Arts
University of Southern Maine

Henrey Assael
New York University

Gert Assmus
Dartmouth College

Jill S. Attaway
Illinois State University

Preetmohinder Aulakh
University of Texas, Austin

Catherine Axinn
Ohio University

Kenneth D. Bahn
University of Texas, Arlington

Julie Baker
University of Texas, Arlington

Thomas L. Baker
University of Akron

Siva K. Balasubramanian
University of Iowa

Rajeev Batra
University of Michigan

Kapil Bawa
New York University

Barry L. Bayus
Cornell University

William O. Bearden
University of South Carolina

Sharon E Beatty
University of Alabama

Boris W. Becker
Oregon State University

George A. Belch
San Diego State University

Daniel C. Bello
Georgia State University

Bruce Vanden Bergh
Michigan State University

Leonard L. Berry
Texas A&M University

Mukesh Bhargava
University of Alberta

Abhijit Biswas
Lousiana State University

Mary Jo Bitner
Arizona State University

Peter Bloch
University of Massachusetts

Paul N. Bloom
University of North Carolina

Jean J. Boddewyn
Baruch College

Claire Bolfing
James Madison University

Ruth N. Bolton
University of Delaware

Michael R. Bowers
University of Alabama, Birmingham

V. Carter Broach, Jr.
University of Delaware

Steve Brown
University of Georgia

Bill Browne
Oregon State University

James A. Brunner
University of Toledo

Lauranne Buchannan
University of Florida

Randolph E. Bucklin
University of California, Los Angeles

William P. Burgers
University of New Orleans

Scot Burton
Lousiana State University

Paul Busch
Texas A&M University

Alan J. Bush
Memphis State University

John C. Busterna
University of Minnesota

Charles Canedy
University of Hartford

Les Carlson
Clemson University

Frank J. Carmone Jr.
Florida International University

Greg Carpenter
Northwestern University

Mary Carsky
University of Hartford

Clarke Caywood
Northwestern University

Frank Cespedes
Harvard Business School

Dipankar Chakravarti
University of Arizona

Amitava Chattopadhyay
McGill University

Joel B. Cohen
University of Florida

Eli Cox
University of Texas, Austin

Samuel Craig
Stern School of Business

Betsey Creyer
Stern School of Business

William L. Cron
Southern Methodist University

John A. Czepiel
New York University

Michael R. Czinkota
Georgetown University

Pratibha Dabholkar
University of Tennessee, Knoxville

William Darden
Lousiana State University

Sayeste A. Daser
Wake Forest University

Patricia J. Daugherty
University of Georgia

Krishnakumar S. Davey
Opinion Research Corporation

William H. Davidson
University of Southern California

Duane Davis
University of Central Florida

Kathleen Debevec
University of Massachusetts

Rohit Deshpande
Dartmouth College

Peter R. Dickson
Ohio State University

Attila Dicle
Rhode Island College

James H. Donnelly
University of Kentucky

Naveen Donthu
Georgia State University

Dale F. Duhan
Texas Tech University

Calvin P. Duncan
University of Colorado

Richard M. Durand
University of Maryland

F. Robert Dwyer
University of Cincinnati

Terry Elrod
University of Alberta

Dogan Eroglu
Georgia State University

Sevgin Eroglu
Georgia State University

Michael J. Etzel
University of Notre Dame

Kenneth R. Evans
University of Missouri

Charles Farris
University of Virginia

Stan Fawcett
Michigan State University

Edward F. Fern
Virginia Tech

Adam Finn
University of Alberta

Sarah Fisher Gardial
University of Tennessee

Irene R. Foster
Vanderbilt University

Karen F.A. Fox
University of Santa Clara

Bobby Friedmann
University of Georgia

Charles Futrell
Texas A&M University

David M. Gardner
University of Illinois

Meryl P. Gardner
University of Delaware

Thomas W. Garsombke
University of Wisconsin, Superior

Hubert Gatignon
University of Pennsylvania

Esra Gencturk
University of Texas, Austin

Jim Gentry
University of Nebraska

William R. George
Villanova University

Peter Gillett
University of Central Florida

Linda L. Golden
University of Texas

Roger Gomes
Clemson University

Cathy Goodwin
University of Manitoba

Jerry R. Goolsby
University of South Florida

Jerry B. Gotlieb
Universtity of Miami

Donald H. Granbois
Indiana University

David Griffith
University of Oklahoma

Stephen J. Grove
Clemson University

Sunil Gupta
Columbia University

Dennis Guseman
California State, Bakersville

Joe Hair
Lousiana State University

Gerald Hampton
San Francisco State University

Amy Handlin
Monmouth College

Nancy L. Hansen
University of New Hampshire

Hari S. Hariharan
University of Wisconsin, Madison

Bari Harlam
Columbia University

Jon M. Hawes
University of Akron

Susan E. Heckler
University of Arizona

Caroline Henderson
Dartmouth College

Robin Ann Higie
University of Connecticut

Ron Hill
Villanova University

Elizabeth C. Hirschman
Rutgers University

Charles Hofackler
Florida State University

Richard Holton
University of California

Pamela Homer
California State University, Long Beach

Ralph C. Hook, Jr.
University of Hawaii

Daniel J. Howard
Southern Methodist University

Mariea G. Hoy
University of Tennessee, Knoxville

Wayne D. Hoyer
University of Texas, Austin

Michael R. Hyman
University of North Texas

Subbash Jain
University of Connecticut

Chris Janifzowsky
University of Florida

Lance Jarvis
UCF Brevard Area Campus

Bernard J. Jaworski
University of Arizona

Joby John
Bentley College

Wesley Johnston
Georgia State University

Marilyn Jones
University of Houston, Clear Lake

Mary L. Joyce
San Francisco State University

Barbara Kahn
University of Pennsylvania

Terence J. Kearney
Marquette University

Jerome B. Kernan
George Mason University

Tina Kessler
New York University

Noreen Klein
Virginia Tech

Saul Klein
Northeastern University

Patricia Knowles
Clemson University

Pradeep Korgaonkar
Florida Atlantic University

Bruce S. Kossar
University of Texas, Austin

Mike Kotabe
University of Texas, Austin

Aradhna Krishna
Columbia University

Priscilla LaBabera
New York University

Duncan G. LaBay
University of Massachusetts at Lowell

Raymond W. LaForge
University of Louisville

Charles W. Lamb
Texas Christian University

Zarrel V. Lambert
Auburn University

H. Bruce Lammers
California State University, Northbridge

Michael Larec
University of Baltimore

Dana Lascu
University of Richmond

John Lastovicka
University of Kansas

Myung-Soo Lee
Baruch College, Cuny

Donald R. Lehmann
Columbia University

James H. Leigh
Texas A&M University

Thomas Leigh
University of Georgia

Lance Leuthesser
California State University, Fullerton

Sidney J. Levy
Northwestern University

Donald Lichtenstein
University of Colorado

James E. Littlefield
Virginia Tech

William B. Locander
University of Tennessee

Dolly Loyd
University of Southern Mississippi

Mushtaq Luqmani
Western Michigan University

Karen Machleitt
University of Cincinnati

Scott B. MacKenzie
Indiana University

M. Carole Macklin
University of Cincinnati

Stanley Madden
Baylor University

Jayashree Mahajan
University of Arizona

Vijay Mahajan
University of Texas, Austin

D. Maheswaran
New York University

Naresh K. Malhotra
Georgia Tech

Ajay Manrai
University of Delaware

David Mazursky
New York University

H. Lee Meadow
Northern Illinois University

Robert Meyer
University of Pennsylvania

Joan Meyers-Levy
University of Chicago

Ronald Michaels
Indiana University

Andrew Mitchell
University of Toronto

Banwari Mittal
Northern Kentucky University

Robert Mittelstaedt
University of Nebraska

Michael Mokwa
Arizona State University

Christine Moorman
University of Wisconsin, Madison

Michael Morris
University of Central Florida

George Moschis
Georgia State University

Mike Mullen
Michigan State University

Mantrala Murali
University of Florida

Gene W. Murdock
University of Wyoming

Patrick E. Murphy
University of Notre Dame

Kent Nakamoto
University of Arizona

James Narus
Wake Forest University

Robert Nason
Michigan State University

Thomas P. Novak
Southern Methodist University

Carl Obermiller
Seattle University

Gina O'Connor
Rensselaer Polytechnic Institute

Thomas C. O'Guinn
University of Illinois

Richard Olshavsky
Indiana University

Glen Omura
Michigan State University

Joseph Orsini
California State University, Sacramento

Julie Ozanne
Virginia Tech

Thomas J. Page
Michigan State University

A. Parasuraman
Texas A&M University

Leonard J. Parsons
Georgia Institute of Tech.

Cornelia Pechmann
University of California

Robert Peterson
University of Texas, Austin

Robin Peterson
New Mexico State University

Gregory Pickett
Clemson University

Carol Pluzinski
New York University

Christopher P. Puto
University of Arizona

S.P. Raj
Syracuse University

Daniel Rajaratnam
Baylor University

Sridhar Ramaswami
Iowa State University

Venkatram Ramaswamy
University of Michigan

Vithala Rao
Cornell University

Peter H. Reingen
Arizona State University

Marsha L. Richins
University of Massachusetts

Nancy M. Ridgway
University of Colorado

John R. Ronchetto, Jr.
University of San Diego

Martin S. Roth
Boston College

Robert Ruekert
University of Minnesota

Ronald Rubin
University of Central Florida

Gary J. Russell
Vanderbilt University

Rolan T. Rust
Vanderbilt University

John Ryans
Kent State University

Ben Sackmary
Buffalo State College

Paul L. Sauer
Canisius College

Alan G. Sawer
University of Florida

Leon Schiffman
Baruch College

Robert Schindler
Rutgers University

Sandra Schmidt
University of Virginia

David Schmittlein
University of Pennsylvania

Sanjit Sengupta
University of Maryland

Arun Sharma
University of Miami

Subhash Sharma
University of South Carolina

Subhash Sharma
University of Southern California

Elaine Sherman
Hofstra University

Daniel Sherrell
Lousiana State University

John Sherry
Northwestern University

Tassu Shervani
University of Texas, Austin

Jagdish Sheth
Emory University

Terry Shimp
University of South Carolina

Itamar Simonson
University of California, Berkeley

Jagdip Singh
Case Western Reserve University

Stanley F. Slater
University of Colorado, Colorado Springs

Daniel C. Smith
University of Wisconsin, Madison

Ruth Belk Smith
University of Baltimore

Michael Soloman
Rutgers University

Robert Spekman
University of Virginia

Susan Spiggle
University of Connecticut

Krishnakumar Srinivasan
Georgia Institute of Technology

Narasimhan Srinivasan
University of Connecticut

T. C. Srinivasan
Virginia Poly. Institute & State Univ.

Rajendra Srivastava
University of Texas, Austin

Vlasis Stathakopoulous
University of Hartford

Roxanne Stell
Northern Arizona University

Debra Stephens
University of Maryland

Barbara Stern
Rutgers University

Devanathan Sudharshan
University of Illinois

Harish Sujan
Pennsylvania State University

R. Sukmar
University of Houston

Carol R. Surprenant
University of Rhode Island

Theresa Swartz
California Polytechnic

Dave Szymanski
Texas A&M University

Ronald Taylor
Mississippi State University

Bernard J. Tellis
University of Southern California

Gerard Tellis
University of Southern California

Donald Thompson
Georgia Southern University

Minakshi K. Trivedi
SUNY at Buffalo

Lewis Tucker
University of Hartford

Jacquelyn L. Twible
University of South Florida

Alice Tybout
Northwestern University

Bruce Vanden Bergh
Michigan State University

Alladi Venkatesh
University of California, Irvine

Meera Venkatraman
Sufflok University

Beth Walker
Arizona State University

Orville C. Walker Jr.
University of Minnesota

Fredercik E. Webster Jr.
Dartmouth College

Charles B. Weinberg
University of British Columbia

Doyle L. Weiss
University of Iowa

Albert R. Wildt
University of Missouri, Columbia

James Wiley
University of Alberta

William Wilkie
University of Notre Dame

David Wilson
PennsylvaniaState University

Russell Winer
University of California, Berkley

Arch Woodside
Tulane University

Richard Yalch
University of Washington

Attila Yaprak
Wayne State University

Ugar Yavas
East Tennessee State University

Youjai Yi
University of Michigan

Judy Zaichkowsky
Simon Frazer University

Michael J. Zenor
University of Texas, Austin

William Zikmund
Oklahoma State University

Mary Zimmer
University of Georgia

TABLE OF CONTENTS

MANAGERIAL DECISION MAKING AND INFORMATION USE

DECISION SUPPORT/EXPERT SYSTEMS IN INTERNATIONAL MARKETING: A WORKSHOP

METHODOLOGICAL ISSUES IN MANAGEMENT AND STRATEGY RESEARCH

SALES MANAGEMENT IN SERVICE INDUSTRIES

ADVERTISING TO CHILDREN, ETHICS AND QUESTIONS OF DECEPTION

GROUP BUYER BEHAVIOR: ENVIRONMENTAL AND PROCESSING INFLUENCES

INTERNATIONAL MARKETING METHODOLOGY

MODELS FOR SCALE DEVELOPMENT AND TESTING

ISSUES IN ADVERTISING AND PROMOTION

INNOVATIONS AND CONSUMER INNOVATIVENESS

COMPARATIVE MARKETING STUDIES

IN SEARCH OF COMPETITIVE ADVANTAGE

RESEARCH IN MARKETING: A POTPOURRI

RETAILING

MARKETING CHANNELS ISSUES

CROSS CULTURAL PERSPECTIVES ON BUYER BEHAVIOR

EXPORT MARKETING

STYLE AND SUBSTANCE IN THE MARKETING CURRICULUM

THE STRUCTURE AND GOVERNANCE OF CHANNELS

THE IMPACT OF INTERVIEWER-RESPONDENT INTERACTIONS ON DATA QUALITY

HEALTH CARE AND NON-PROFIT MARKETING

Addendum

Author Index

FEAR APPEAL RESEARCH: PERSPECTIVE AND APPLICATION

Ken Chapman, University of Colorado at Boulder

ABSTRACT

This paper summarizes past fear-appeal studies and theories and synthesizes them into a parsimonious model that will enable message design practitioners to work more intelligently and efficiently. The Recommended Fear Model (RFM) presents a paradigm, consistent with past literature, that illustrates some of the more salient variables that should be considered when developing a message that incorporates a fear-appeal.

INTRODUCTION

Fear appeals have been used for decades in a variety of mass media campaigns, including a plethora of public service announcements: the AIDS (Acquired Immune Deficiency Syndrome) awareness and prevention campaign (Bush and Boller 1991; Edgar, Freimuth, and Hammond 1988; Struckman-Johnson, Gilland, Struckman-Johnson, and North 1990); several anti-smoking promotions (O'Keefe 1971; Insko, Arkoff, and Insko 1965; Leventhal and Watts 1966); safety belt usage campaigns (Robertson 1976); dental hygiene promotions (Evans, Rozzelle, Lasater, Dembroski, and Allen 1970); and anti-drunk driving messages (King and Reid 1989). Messages that utilize a fear stimuli to enhance persuasion are also evident in politics (the cold war, the defense budget, recession/depression), religious conformity (sin and repentance), and commercial products (insurance, home security systems). All these "fear messages" use some noxious or threatening stimuli (death, mutilation, disease) to heighten an individuals' receptivity to establishing or changing an attitude and/or behavior to include the fear reducing recommendation (not to drink and drive, to use a condom, to use American Express travelers checks, etc.).

As important and ubiquitous as fear-appeals are in commercial and societal messages, they are not thoroughly understood, and a comprehensive model that is useful to message design practitioners still does not exist. This paper will summarize past fear-appeal studies and theories and present a conceptual model consistent with this literature. Although there is still an abundance of work that needs to be undertaken regarding the underlying theoretical psychological/cognitive principles of a fear-appeal, it is time to synthesize some of the available data and theories and begin developing a model that will assist message design practitioners in their decision to employ a fear stimuli.

The first part of the paper will briefly discuss the general relationship between fear messages and persuasion. The subsequent section will address some of the most prevalent theories that have been postulated to explain the effects of a fear appeal on persuasion. Next, the several variables that have been explicated as being relevant to a fear message will be considered. These variables have been categorized as either preconditional or implementational in the context of the Recommended Fear Model (RFM). The preconditional factors being characteristics or traits of the target audience, the implementational factors describing some of the salient variables that the message designer can manipulate to enhance the effectiveness of the message. The final section will present the Recommended Fear Model and discuss its application to message development, its limitations, and directions for future research.

HIGH FEAR, LOW FEAR OR NO FEAR: WHICH IS MOST EFFECTIVE?

The seminal work of Janis and Feshbach (1953) concluded that a minimal amount of fear was more effective in attitude change than a high fear message. This proposition was supported by numerous studies in the 1950's and 60's (DeWolfe and Governdale 1964; Goldstein 1959; Haefner 1965; Insko, Arkoff, and Insko 1965; Janis and Feshbach 1953, 1954; Janis and Terwilliger 1962). There also have been studies that have found no relationship between fear and persuasion (Frandsen 1963; Millman 1968) and others that reported mixed findings (Leventhal and Watts 1966). However, a majority of the fear-appeal studies and reviews since Janis and Feshbach's work have documented a positive fear-persuasion relationship (Dabbs and Leventhal 1966; Higbee 1969; Leventhal 1970; Miller and Hewgill 1966; Rogers 1983; Sternthal and Craig 1974; Sutton 1982). A myriad of studies have demonstrated that a persuasive message containing a strong fear appeal is more effective than a message with a low or no fear stimuli (Burnett and Oliver 1979; Chu 1966; Hass, Bagely, and Rogers 1975; Hewgill and Miller 1965; Leventhal 1970, 1971; Leventhal and Niles 1965; Leventhal, Singer, and Jones 1965; Leventhal and Watts 1966; Miller and Hewgill 1966; Powell 1965; Rogers 1975, 1985; Schwartz, Wolfgang, and Kumf 1985; Sutton and Hallett 1988; Wheatley 1971). Sutton (1982) carried out a meta-analysis on twenty-one past studies (1953-1980) and found statistically significant results suggesting that the higher the level of fear in a message, the greater the messages acceptance. Sutton noted that this relationship was stronger for intention than for actual behavior.

In a majority of the aforementioned studies, it has been acknowledged that the mediating variables, not the absolute levels of fear, have been found to be important in elucidating the relationship between the message's effectiveness and the level of fear used. Most current work details that this relationship is moderated by several variables endogenous to the message's audience (Burnett and Oliver 1979; Burnett and Wilkes 1980; Maddux and Rogers 1983; Ray and Wilkie 1970; Rogers 1975, 1985; Rogers and Mewborn 1976; Rotfeld 1988).

THEORETICAL PERSPECTIVES

The Fear Drive Model

The basic assumption in the fear drive model is adapted from the drive reduction theories used by animal behavior theorists in the 1950's (Hovland 1953; Miller 1951; Sutton 1982). The drive reduction theories postulate that fear acts as a drive mechanism and that individuals will be motivated to reduce this drive. This model is applicable to fear arousing messages in the sense that when a communication arouses fear in an individual, this leads to a heightened emotional state (the drive aroused by fear), which in turn, motivates the person to find a means to alleviate the sense of drive. Lessening the fear arousal can essentially occur in two fashions. The individual can adopt the recommendation suggested in the message or introspectively search for some means to reduce the level of fear. The internal search is likely to lead to some form of defensive behavior. Defensive behaviors can take the shape of either denying the threat or avoiding the communication, both negating the effectiveness of the message.

Janis and Feshback (1954) reported that high fear messages are less effective than low fear messages due to the high fear/anxiety felt by the recipient. This high state of emotional arousal tends to stimulate a defensive response (e.g. avoidance, denial, distortion of the message, strong subvocal counteragruments) which interferes with the acceptance of the message (Insko, Arkoff, and Insko 1965; Janis and Feshbach 1953, 1954). High levels of fear were postulated to be less effective than moderate levels, and moderate levels more effective than low levels, which lead to the fear drive model being associated with an inverted 'U' (nonmonotonic) relationship between fear and persuasion. A moderate level of fear created enough drive to facilitate persuasion, yet not such and overwhelming sense of drive as to cause interference with the message's recommendations. Thus, a moderate level of fear was believed to be the "optimal" level. Janis (1967) proposed a family of curves to account for the relationship between persuasion and fear, however, theses curvilinear functions have been strongly criticized as having very little validity (Leventhal 1970).

A number of scholars have found logical and theoretical problems with the fear drive model (Boster and Mongeau 1984; Leventhal 1970, 1971; Sutton 1982; Sutton and Hallett 1988), which led to it being usurped by Leventhal's (1970) parallel response model. Most denunciations of the fear drive model are that: (1) the model is so flexible it can accommodate nearly any findings, yet doesn't lend itself to rigorous testing, (2) what is the nature of the fear that evokes this sense of drive, and (3) the manner is which fear (as a drive) influences persuasion is not specified (Beck and Frankel 1981; Boster and Mongeau 1984; Leventhal 1970).

The Parallel Response Model

The parallel response model moved away from the fear drive model's premise that fear was the central explanation for the effects in past experiments toward a model that suggests that fear interacts with other variables to affect attitudes and behavior (Boster and Mongeau 1984; Leventhal 1970; Leventhal and Niles 1965). The parallel response model began focusing on the individual responses that people may have to a fear arousing message and some of the cognitive processes involved. Proposed by Leventhal (1970), the parallel response model hypothesizes danger control and fear control processes that operate in parallel in response to a fear arousing situation. Danger control directs adaptive behaviors extracted from the environment (using the recommendations suggested in the message), while fear control guides the emotional responses (denying the threat or avoiding the message). The two processes are postulated to work in parallel, however, in some situations they may interfere with one another, for example, in extremely high fear situations, the fear control process (a defensive reaction) being so strong as to overcome the danger control process.

As discussed in Beck and Frankel (1981), a health related fear-appeal may make the audience fearful, but protective actions result from a desire to control the danger, not to reduce the fear. When individuals focus on the controlling of danger (a cognitive response), there is a greater probability of accepting the message's recommendation. Focusing on fear control (an emotional response) however, can undermine the message's effectiveness. The parallel response model differs from the fear drive model in that it makes a distinction between danger motivation and fear motivation, whereas the drive model focuses on fear control (the emotional response).

The parallel response model has many of the same drawbacks as the fear drive model, especially in that it doesn't make specific predictions that can be tested. Other criticisms (Boster and Mongeau 1984; Sutton 1982; Rogers 1975) of the model have been the ambiguity of the two constructs, no clear definition as to which construct takes precedence (danger or fear), and no demarcation as to when the constructs are acting independent of one another or when they begin to overlap.

The Protection Motivation Model

Like Leventhal's parallel response model, Rogers' (1975, 1983) protection motivation theory assumes that emotional arousal is less important than the individual's cognitive appraisal of the fear stimuli, and thus emphasizes the cognitive factors that mediate the effects of a fear appeal. Rogers proposed that when attempting to understand the persuasive mechanisms underlying a fear appeal, attitude change is not mediated by the emotional state of fear, but is a function of the mediating variables and cognitive processes that motivate a protection motivation response. The greater the level of protection motivation aroused, the higher the probability of conformity to the recommendations in the message.

Rogers focused on three crucial components that mediate a fear appeal: (1) the magnitude of the noxiousness of a depicted event, (2) the probability of that event's occurrence, and (3) the efficacy of a protective response. Maddux and Rogers (1983) added a fourth mediating cognitive process to the model in an attempt to make the model more comprehensive. The revised theory incorporates a self-efficacy cognitive process (Bandura 1977; Beck and Frankel 1981). The self-efficacy process is viewed as the individual's assessment/belief (expectancy-value) that s/he is capable of performing a given behavior (the recommendation in the message). In a study by Maddux and Rogers (1983) the self-efficacy expectancy component of the protection motivation model was shown to significantly influence an individual's probability of conforming to a recommended coping behavior, and proved to be the most powerful mediating variable in the model.

Rogers states that these variables interact in a multiplicative fashion, thus if one of them equals zero then no protection motivation (no attitude change) occurs. For example, if a message (targeting 18-24 year olds) communicates the deaths, injuries and mutilations that occur due to drunk driving (the noxious stimuli=high), that drunk driving is the leading cause of death for people in this age group (probability of occurrence=high), yet, no specific recommendation is made that can easily be carried out by the individual (efficacy of protective response=0), then the message would not facilitate attitude or behavioral change.

The protection motivation model has not undergone numerous empirical tests, however, conceptually it is well accepted and a review of the limited studies involving protection motivation has provided support for the model (Maddux and Rogers 1983; Rogers 1983; Tanner, Day, and Crask 1989).

FACTORS WHICH MEDIATE THE STRENGTH OF THE FEAR APPEAL

Several researchers have stated that many of the ambiguous findings in the myriad of past studies are due to a failure to understand the subjects predisposed characteristics and a lack of control and/or definition of mediating stimuli in the message itself (Dabbs and

Leventhal 1966; Katz 1960; Leventhal 1970; Rogers 1975). The following section examines several of these moderating variables. The variables are categorized as implementational or preconditional factors.

Preconditional Factors

The preconditional factors are various characteristics of the target audience that can mediate the effectiveness of the message. If a message designer is considering a fear appeal communication, understanding the importance of these variables will lead to the development of a more effective message.

Self-esteem

According to a number of studies, self-esteem contributes to the differential effects of fear on persuasion. Most studies that have addressed self-esteem and its influence on a fear arousing message have found a positive relationship between self-esteem and the level of fear and the message's effectiveness (Dabbs and Leventhal 1966; Higbee 1969; Leventhal and Trembly 1968; Rosen, Terry, and Leventhal 1982). Subjects that rate as having high self-esteem tend to be more persuaded by high levels of fear in a message, whereas, low self-esteem individuals tend to be more persuaded by messages that use low levels of fear. Dabbs and Leventhal (1966) noted that conceivably, high self-esteem individuals are more active and aggressive in dealing with their environment and are thus more adroit in their reaction to a state of high fear. On the other hand, the low self-esteem individual is most capable of adapting to a situation of low fear.

As in much of the fear literature conflicting results abound. Leventhal and Perloe (1962) showed that self-esteem was negatively related to the acceptance of a message using fear. Subjects in the low self-esteem category were influenced more by a threatening message than were subjects in the high self-esteem group. The problem with this study was that the level of fear was not manipulated, and subsequent research has not substantiated these findings. The RFM will adhere to the positive relationship between self-esteem and effectiveness of a fear arousing message.

Perceived Threat Control

Perceived threat control is a factor that essentially combines the self-esteem and efficacy of the recommendation variables into one factor. As discussed in Beck and Frankel (1981), perceived threat control involves two processes, response efficacy and personal efficacy. Response efficacy is the perceived probability that the recommended response will actually reduce and/or prevent the fear stimuli's occurrence, e.g. quitting smoking will lessen one's chance of getting lung cancer. Personal efficacy is very similar to the self-efficacy term that Maddux and Rogers (1983) added to the protection motivation model. Personal efficacy is defined as the person's perceived ability to carry out the actions recommended in the message. This is related to a person's self-esteem in that it corresponds to the individual's belief in his/her ability to master his/her environment.

Very little empirical evidence exists to illustrate the relationship between an individual's level of perceived threat control and his/her corresponding fear-persuasion relationship. However, when a person's perceived threat control is low s/he is more likely to operate on a fear control mode, rather than a danger control mode, and would thus be less likely to initiate the cognitive process of acknowledging and acting upon the actions recommended in the communication (Beck and Frankel 1981). Given the perceived threat control's links to self-esteem (personal efficacy), efficacy of the coping response (discussed below), and its logical connection to fear and danger controls, a positive fear persuasion relationship will be used in the RFM. A message that utilizes a high level of fear will be more effective on a person who has a high level of perceived threat control

Risk Aversion or Avoiding/Coping Behavior

A topic closely related to an individual's level of self-esteem is how he/she cognitively "handles" the fear that has been stimulated by the message, i.e. is the person a "coper" or an "avoider." Goldstein (1959) referred to subject's "coping" and "avoidance" characteristics and found that low fear was more persuasive on "avoiders" than on "copers." In a state of high fear, as the term connotes, "avoiders" would possibly avoid the message either on a cognitive level or in the physical sense (turning the channel or skipping the page). Thus, a negative relationship between risk aversion and fear is stipulated.

A person who is highly risk averse (an "avoider") will be persuaded more by a low or no fear message than by a high fear message. A highly fearful message directed at a person that is risk averse (an "avoider") will likely lead to very little message acceptance and trigger emotional and cognitive defensive reactions. This risk aversion-fear relationship reinforces the positive relationship between self-esteem and the level of fear in a message. The ability to "cope" (low risk aversion) with fear has been show to be a facet of a high self-esteem individual (Leventhal and Trembly 1968; Rosen, Terry, and Leventhal 1982).

Perceived Vulnerability

Another variable which is related to an individual's level of self-esteem and avoiding/coping behavior is the subject's perceived vulnerability to the fear stimuli used in the message. It could be argued that an individual who rates as having a high self-esteem is a "coper" and would consider him/herself not very vulnerable to the threat used in the message, thus low-vulnerability individuals tend to be more influenced by messages that contain a high level

of fear. On the other hand, some studies (Leventhal and Watts 1966; Watts 1967) have found that individuals who tend to feel highly vulnerable to the fear stimuli may actually reduce their desire to take the action recommended in the high fear message.

Overall, most of the literature suggests that vulnerability and level of fear in a persuasive message have a negative relationship. Low or no fear is best suited for subjects who feel highly vulnerable to the threat, and high fear is most persuasive on individuals who do not feel very vulnerable (Sternthal and Craig 1974). Individuals who do not feel vulnerable, need a stronger message to get them to acknowledge that they may be susceptible to the issue addressed in the communication (e.g. disease, death, theft).

Perceived Familiarity and Prior Knowledge of the Subject Matter

It has been suggested that when individuals are more familiar with the subject matter in the communication, lower levels of fear would be more persuasive. On the other hand, when the audience is unfamiliar with a message, a higher level of fear may be more persuasive (Greenwald and Sakumura 1967; Higbee 1969). High familiarity with a topic may allow the individual to generate strong subvocal counterarguments to the message or distort the information based on their prior knowledge. This would decrease the chance that the recommendation suggested in the message would be utilized.

This factor has not been researched thoroughly, however, when using a high level of fear in a message it should be noted that the audience's prior knowledge of the subject may influence the effectiveness of the communication. A high level of fear may be being used in a message, however, the audience may be quite familiar with the subject matter (e.g. lung cancer and smoking, the use of safety belts, AIDS) which could lead the them taking a position contrary to the communication's message. By pretesting the audiences' familiarity and knowledge of the subject matter the message can be designed in such a manner as to control and circumvent counterarguments and information distortion.

Implementational Factors

The implementational factors are variables which the message designer can manipulate to increase the effectiveness of the fear appeal, such as controlling the magnitude of the threat stimuli or refuting erroneous beliefs held by the audience.

Specificity and Efficacy of Recommendations

The hypotheses regarding message efficacy and specificity is that when a recommendation is extremely specific and highly efficacious, this will facilitate conformity to the suggested recommendation. Leventhal and Niles (1964) noted that the easier the recommendation can be carried out (higher efficacy), the greater the message's effectiveness. Leventhal (1965) concluded that when the recommendations in the message are clearly effective, attitude and behavior change is more likely to take place. In these studies however, the specificity and efficacy of the recommendations were found to be main effects and not directly contingent on the level of fear used.

In general, research on the nature of the recommendations used in a message have generally found that the more specific and efficacious the recommendation the greater the message's persuasion, this being more important in high fear appeal messages than in low fear messages (Leventhal 1971; Leventhal and Niles 1965; Higbee 1969; Rogers 1975).

Source Credibility

There is an abundance of evidence that suggests that source credibility does influence the fear-persuasion relationship and is an important variable to consider when using a fear appeal (Hewgill and Miller 1965; Insko, Arkoff, and Insko 1965; Powell and Miller 1967). The study by Hewgill and Miller (1965) found that when they tried to persuade PTA members of the importance of fallout shelters, messages that contained high levels of fear combined with a highly credible source were the most persuasive. Source credibility may be an important issue in any type of message, however, it is more salient in fear arousing messages. If the fear appeal uses a spokesperson or makes references to a source, it is critical that both of these be perceived as highly credible to the audience. When a source is considered to be an authority, or is viewed with respect and/or admiration by the audience, the probability that the audience will believe the information and act upon the recommendation will be increased (Hewgill and Miller, 1965). On the contrary, low source credibility can lead to message rebuttal.

Magnitude of Threat Stimuli

As stated in Rogers (1975) several studies (Dabbs and Leventhal 1966; Leventhal, Singer, and Jones 1965) have found that manipulations of fear affect the individual's perceived seriousness of the threat and that increases in the magnitude of the threat stimuli can facilitate attitude change. The magnitude of the threat stimuli is varied by manipulating the vividness and/or graphical nature of the pictorial or rhetorical nature of the threatening stimuli. A problem that seems to arise when researchers are studying fear appeals is that many do not check to ensure that they have either manipulated the level of the fear appeal or have even elicited a certain level of fear in their subjects. This illustrates the importance of pretesting a message to ensure it elicits the

desired response. This becomes exceptionally important when using a fear appeal strategy in a message. If a fear appeal is found to be an appropriate vehicle, then it behooves the message designer to pretest various threat stimuli to obtain the desired level of fear for maximum message effectiveness.

RECOMMENDED FEAR MODEL

A Recommended Fear Model (RFM) for message development is proposed that could assist message design practitioners in their decision to use a fear appeal strategy and aid in the effective implementation of that decision (see Figure 1). In addition to incorporating the aforementioned preconditional and implementational factors, an information refutation factor has been added to the implementational factors, producing a comprehensive message development paradigm. The information refutation factor explicates that if the audience has preconceived misconceptions that could hinder the acceptance of the recommendations, these need to be dispelled. Recognizing and pretesting the target audience for the preconditional variables combined with understanding and utilizing the implementational factors will facilitate the development of a message with optimal effectiveness.

The preconditional variables are individual differences which dictate what level of fear will improve the message's effectiveness. As illustrated in Figure 1, the first group of preconditional factors, which includes self-esteem and perceived threat control ability, have a positive relationship with the recommended level of fear. When self-esteem is high, a high level of fear is recommended to maximize the message's effectiveness. Similarly, if the audience's perceived threat control ability is low, a low level of fear is recommended in the message. The lower set of preconditional variables, which includes risk aversion behavior, perceived vulnerability, perceived probability of occurrence, and familiarity/prior knowledge, all exhibit a negative relationship with the recommended fear level. When the target audience scores low in these areas, the best strategy for the message designer is to use a high level of fear. It is the combination of all the preconditional factors that will ultimately suggest what level of fear will be most effective on this audience.

The two sets of preconditional factors are not mutually exclusive. Many of the variables will influence one another, thus the linkage in the model. Self-esteem has been shown to be an especially important factor in mediating a fear appeal's persuasiveness in that it interacts with a person's coping and avoiding behavior, their perceived threat control ability, their perceived vulnerability, and their perceived probability of occurrence (Dabbs and Leventhal 1966; Goldstein 1959; Higbee 1969; Leventhal and Trembly 1968; Rosen, Terry, and Leventhal 1982). It should be noted that familiarity and

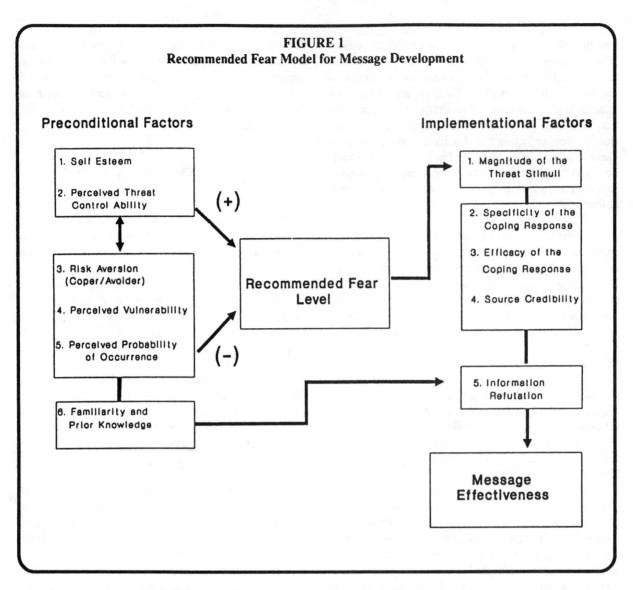

FIGURE 1
Recommended Fear Model for Message Development

Preconditional Factors

1. Self Esteem
2. Perceived Threat Control Ability

(+)

3. Risk Aversion (Coper/Avoider)
4. Perceived Vulnerability
5. Perceived Probability of Occurrence

(−)

6. Familiarity and Prior Knowledge

Recommended Fear Level

Implementational Factors

1. Magnitude of the Threat Stimuli
2. Specificity of the Coping Response
3. Efficacy of the Coping Response
4. Source Credibility
5. Information Refutation

Message Effectiveness

prior knowledge will not likely interact with self esteem or a person's risk aversion behavior, but may interact with the other preconditional factors in the model as well as have a direct bearing on whether or not information refutation is necessitated.

The RFM can help message designers effectively reach their goals and objectives. Essentially the model is stipulating a cluster of variables that would be useful to segment and target a market. People have different reactions to a fear appeal and an effective targeting strategy can match a fear message to an audience that will be most persuaded by it.

Burnett and Oliver (1979) found a segmentational and targeted strategy to be an appropriate means in which a health maintenance organization (HMO) could most effectively use a fear message in its mailings. They conducted a field experiment designed to "..assess the effect of a fear promotion on attitudinal and behavioral responses to a new group health plan...." Their cluster analysis, from a questionnaire included in the HMO's brochure mailings, revealed that higher levels of fear produced greater acceptance of the message in two specific populations of their study. The HMO used this information to target those groups with a high fear message. The number of inquires to the HMO increased nearly 90 percent during this targeted mailing, which was the desired affect of the brochure. Although this dramatic increase in inquires could have been due to a variety of factors, it does suggest that a targeted fear message can be highly effective.

Once the preconditional factors have been analyzed, and a target audience has been designated, a decision can be made as to what level of fear (if any) would be most influential. This level of fear dictates the magnitude of the threat stimuli that should be used in the message. If a high level of fear is suggested, then the threat stimuli (language and/or pictures) should be graphic and explicit, whereas, if a low level of fear is implied, more subdued language and/or pictures would be more appropriate. The other implementational factors (#'s 2,3,4 in the model) are main effects in any message design and are not influenced by the level of fear is used. It should be noted that although these three implementational factors are influential in any message, they are exceptionally important in a message that uses a high level of fear.

Finally, if the information the audience is using to counterargue or distort the message and its recommendations is inaccurate, then a mechanism needs to be in place to rectify these misconceptions. This mechanism has been termed "information refutation". Information refutation will not only make the message more effective, but can lead to a better understanding of the perceived threat control ability, perceived probability of occurrence, and perceived vulnerability measures.

To address the model's applicability, a hypothetical AIDS message (in a simplified environment) will be analyzed in the context of the RFM. The target audience for the AIDS message is heterosexual males, ages 18-35. A sample was taken from this population and the preconditional factors were tested. A majority of the subjects rated as having a high self-esteem (self-esteem=high), felt very adept at handling any problem that came their way (perceived threat control ability=high) and would take on any problem that should arise in their life (risk aversion=low, risk behavior=coper). A majority felt that AIDS was a disease that affected solely homosexuals and IV drug users so they really didn't have to worry about it (perceived vulnerability=low, perceived probability of occurrence=low). All the men knew something about the disease, although their facts were not all correct, and nearly all had heard about Magic Johnson's revelation that he is infected with the Human Immunodeficiency Virus (HIV) (familiarity and prior knowledge=high, information refutation=necessary).

Except for the familiarity and prior knowledge factor, the preconditional factors suggest that a high fear message would be most effective on this audience. The magnitude of the threat stimuli needs to be high, as dictated by the recommended fear level. With a high level of fear it is exceptionally important that the coping responses be extremely specific and easy to execute. Without these, as discussed in the parallel response model, the fear control mechanism will predominate and the high level of fear will not improve the message's effectiveness. With highly specific and efficacious coping responses, the danger control process will dictate the behavioral actions, which should be greater acknowledgment and acceptance of the recommendations suggested in the message.

We know that the audience has some preexisting views of the subject matter thus they could distort or counterargue the message, therefore, the message needs to be designed in such a fashion as to address these potential distractions (information refutation). For example, if it was revealed from the tests regarding familiarity and prior knowledge that a majority of the men believed that AIDS could be transmitted by perspiration, then the message should include information directly refuting the perspiration transmittal myth. Finally, if a spokesperson is used or facts are presented, both would need to be highly credible.

This simple example has exemplified how a message designer could utilize the RFM to ensure that s/he has considered many of the important factors that dictate which level of fear, if any, should be used and how to best implement the fear message.

LIMITATIONS AND FUTURE RESEARCH

It is hoped that this train of thought will facilitate further work in this area to develop useful tools for message design practitioners. Given that billions of dollars are spent on advertising, and millions of these dollars involve messages that use fear ($18 million in air time was used on the 1987-1988 AIDS television campaign, Bush and Boller 1991.) tools that can improve a message's effectiveness are a worthwhile pursuit. The RFM in its current form should not be used as a black-and-white decision making tool, however, it is useful in highlighting some of the more salient variables that should be considered when deciding to design a message that may incorporate a fear appeal.

Certainly the greatest limitation and simultaneously the principal area for future research is the fact that the RFM has not been tested. Chances are quite high that upon measuring the preconditional factors some will suggest using a high level of fear, while others will suggest using a low or medium level. The model needs some weighted coefficients which would assist the message designer in determining which variables would have the most affect. An empirical test of the model could resolve this issue.

A prerequisite of the RFM is that the message designer must first and foremost understand the target audience. By screening the market, on the basis of the preconditional factors, the message designer can decide if a high fear message will be more effective than a low or no fear message, however, this research will by no means will be an easy task and may not uncover any absolutes.

One of the problems encountered when trying to assimilate the information from past research is that the nature of the fear is different in each case. Fear is a very state/context dependent variable. Fear in one situation may not be fear in another. The message designer needs to be aware of this and regularly test his/her audience and message to ensure that the desired conditions still exist.

The positioning of the threat stimuli has received little attention. Where is the best position to place the threatening stimuli relative to the recommended coping response? Research in this area could be quite beneficial to the message designer and easy to implement into the message. Another area of research that has had very little attention is whether a positive message is more effective than a fear message, both containing the same information and recommendations.

ENDNOTE

Acknowlegements: I would like to thank Dr. Sandy Moriarty for her comments and review, and Bonnie Scher for her review and editorial prowess.

REFERENCES

Bandura, Albert (1977), "Self-Efficacy: Toward a Unifying Theory of Behavioral Change," *Psychological Review,* 84, 191-215.

Beck, Kenneth H. and Arthur Frankel (1981), "A Conceptualization of Threat Communications and Protective Health Behavior," *Social Psychology Quarterly,* 44 (September), 204-217.

Boster, F. J. and P. Mongeau (1984) " Fear-Arousing Persuasive Messages," *Communication Yearbook,* Robert N. Bostrom, ed. Beverly Hills: Sage Publications, 8, 330-375.

Burnett, John and Richard Oliver (1979), "Fear Appeal Effects in the Field: A Segmentation Approach," *Journal of Marketing Research* 16 (May), 181-190.

Burnett, John J. and Robert E. Wilkes (1980), "Fear Appeals to Segments Only," *Journal of Advertising Research,* 20 (5), (October), 21-24.

Bush, Alan J. and Gregory W. Boller (1991), "Rethinking the Role of Television Advertising During Health Crises: A Rhetorical Analysis of the Federal AIDS Campaign," *Journal of Advertising,* 20 (1), 28-37.

Chu, C. C. (1966), "Fear Arousal, Efficacy, and Imminency," *Journal of Personality and Psychology,* 4, 517-524.

Dabbs, J. M., Jr. and H. Leventhal (1966), "Effects of Varying the Recommendations in a Fear-Arousing Communication," *Journal of Personality and Social Psychology,* 4, 525-531.

DeWolfe, A. S. and C. N. Governdale (1964), "Fear and Attitude Change," *Journal of Abnormal and Social Psychology,* 69, 119-123.

Edgar, Timothy, Vicki S. Freimuth, and Sharo L. Hammond (1988), "Communicating the AIDS Risk to College Students: The Problem of motivating Change," *Health Education Research,* 3 (1), 59-65.

Evans, Richard I., Richard M. Rozzelle, Thomas M. Lasater, Theodore M. Dembroski, and Ben P. Allen (1970), "Fear Arousal, Persuasion and Actual Versus Implied Behavior Change: New Perspective Utilizing a Real-Life Dental Hygiene Program," *Journal of Personality and Social Psychology,* 16 (2), 220-227.

Frandsen, K. (1963), "Effects of Threat Appeals and Media of Transmission," *Speech Monographs,* 30, 101-104.

Goldstein, Micheal J. (1959), "The Relationship Between Coping and Avoiding Behavior and Response to Fear Arousing Propaganda," *Journal of Abnormal and Social Psychology,* 58, 247-252.

Greenwald, A. G. and J. S. Sakumura (1967), "Attitude and Selective Learning: Where are the Phenomena of Yesteryear?," *Journal of Personality and Social Psychology,* 7, 387-397.

Haefner, D. P. (1965), "Arousing Fear in Dental Health Education," *Journal of Public Health Dentistry,* 25, 140-146.

Hass, Jane W., Gerrold S. Bagely, and Ronald W. Rogers (1975), "Coping with the Energy Crisis: Effects of Fear Appeals Upon Attitudes Towards Energy Consumption," *Journal of Applied Psychology,* 60 (December), 754-756.

Hewgill, Murray A. and Gerald R. Miller (1965), " Source Credibility and Response to Fear-Arousing Communications," *Speech Monographs,* 32 (June), 95-101.

Higbee, Kenneth L. (1969), "Fifteen Years of Fear Arousal: Research on Threat Appeals: 1953-1968," *Psychological Bulletin,* 72 (6), 426-444.

Hovland, Carl, Irving L. Janis and Harold H. Kelly (1953), *Communication and Persuasion,* New Haven: Yale Press.

Insko, C. A., A. Arkoff, and V. M. Insko (1965), "Effects of High and Low Fear-Arousing Communications Upon Opinions Toward Smoking," *Journal of Experimental Social Psychology,* 1, 256-266.

Janis, Irving L. (1967), Effects of Fear Arousal on Attitude: Recent Development in Theory and Research," *Advances in Experimental Psychology,* 4, 166-224.

Janis, Irving L. and Seymour Feshbach (1953), "Effects of Fear Arousing Communications," *Journal of Abnormal and Social Psychology,* 48, 78-92.

_____ and Seymour Feshbach (1954), "Personality Differences Associated with Responsiveness to Fear-Arousing Communications," *Journal of Personality,* 23, 154-166.

_____ and R. Terwilliger (1962), "An Experimental Study of Psycholological Resistance to Fear Arousing Communications," *Journal of Abnormal and Social Psychology,* 65, 403-410.

Katz, D. (1960), "The Functional Approach to the Study of Attitudes," *Public Opinion Quarterly,* 24, 163-204.

King, Karen Whitehill and Leonard N. Reid (1989), "Fear Arousing Anti-Drinking and Driving PSA's: Do Physical Injury and Death Threats Influence Young Adults," *Current Issues and Research in Advertising,* 12, (1/2), 155-175.

Leventhal, Howard (1971), "Fear Appeals and Persuasion: The Differentiation of a Motivational Construct," *American Journal of Public Health,* 61 (June), 1208-1225.

_____(1970), "Findings and Theory in the Study of Fear Communications," *Advances in Experimental Social Psychology,* L. Berkowitz, ed. New York: Academic Press, 5, 119-186.

_____, R. P. Singer and S. Jones (1965), "Effects of Fear and Specificity of Recommendations Upon Attitudes and Behavior," *Journal of Personality and Social Psychology,* 2, 20-29.

_____and J. C. Watts (1966), "Sources of Resistance to Fear-Arousing Communications on Smoking and Lung Cancer," *Journal of Personality,* 34, 155-175.

_____and Patricia N.Niles (1965), "Persistence of Influence for Varying Durations of Exposure to Threat Stimuli," *Psychological Reports,* 16, 223-233.

_____and G. Trembly (1968) "Negative Emotion and Persuasion," *Journal of Personality,* 36, 154-168.

_____and Sidney Perloe (1962), "A Relationship Between Self-Esteem and Persuasibility," *Journal of Abnormal and Social Psychology,* 64, 385-388.

Maddux, James E. and Ronald W. Rogers (1983), "Protection Motivation and Self-Efficacy: A Revised Theory of Fear Appeals and Attitude Change," *Journal of Experimental Social Psychology,* 19 (September), 469-479.

Miller, N. E. (1951), "Learnable Drives and Rewards," *Handbook of Experimental Psychology,* S.S.Stevens, ed. New York: Wiley.

Miller, G. R. and M. A. Hewgill (1966), "Some Recent Research on Fear-Arousing Message Appeals," *Speech Monographs,* 33, 377-391.

Millman, S. (1968), "Anxiety, Comprehension, and Susceptibility to Social Influence," *Journal of Personality and Social Psychology,* 9, 251-256.

O'Keefe, M. Timothy (1971), "The Anti-Smoking Commercials: A Study of Televisions Impact on Behavior," *Journal of Communication,* 26 (Autumn), 41-45.

Powell, Frederic A. (1965), "The Effects of Anxiety Arousing Messages When Related to Personal, Familial, and Impersonal Referents," *Speech Monographs,* 32 (June), 102-106.

_____and G. Miller (1967), "The Effects of Anxiety-Arousing Messages When Related to Personal, Familial and Impersal Referents," *Speech Monographs,* 32 (June), 102-106.

Ray, Michael L. and William Wilkie (1970), "Fear: The Potential of an Appeal neglected by Marketing," *Journal of Marketing,* 34, 54-62.

Robertson, Leon S. (1976), "The Great Seat Belt Campaign Flop," *Journal of Communication,* 26 (Autumn), 41-45.

Rogers, Ronald W. and C. Ronald Mewborn (1976), "Fear Appeals and Attitude Change: Effects of a Threat's Noxiousness, Probability of Occurrence, and the Efficacy of Coping Responses," *Journal of Personality and Social Psychology,* 34 (1), 54-61.

_____(1975), "A Protection Motivation Theory of Fear Appeals and Attitude Change," *The Journal of Psychology,* 91, 93-114.

_____(1985), "Attitude Change and Information Integration in Fear Appeals," *Psychological Reports,* 56, 179-182

Rogers, Ronald W. (1983), "Cognitive and Physiological Processes in Fear Appeals and Attitude Change: A Revised Theory of Protection Motivation," *Social Psychophysiology,* J. Cacioppo and R. Petty, eds. New York: The Gilford Press, 153-174.

Rosen, John T., Nathaniel S. Terry and Howard Leventhal (1982), "The Role of Esteem and Coping in Response to a Threat Communication," *Journal of Research in Personality,* 16, 90-107.

Rotfeld, Herbert J. (1988), "Fear Appeals and Persuasion: Assumptions and Errors in Advertising Research," *Current Issues and Research in Advertising,* 11 (1), 21-40.

Schwartz, Norbet, Servay Wolfgang and Martin Kumf (1985), "Attribution of Arousal as a Mediator of Effectiveness of Fear-Arousing Communications," *Journal of Applied Social Psychology,* 15 (2), 178-188.

Sternthal, Brian and C. Samuel Craig (1974), "Fear Appeals: Revisited and Revised," *Journal of Consumer Research,* 1 (December), 22-34.

Struckman-Johnson, Cindy, Roy C. Gilland, Davis L. Struckman-Johnson, and Terry C. North (1990), "The Effects of Fear of AIDS and Gender on Responses to Fear-Arousing Condom Advertisements," *Journal of Applied Social Psychology,* 20 (17), 1396-1410.

Sutton, S. R. (1982), "Fear-Arousing Communications: A Critical Examination of Theory and Research," *Social Psychology and Behavioral Medicine,* J. Richard Eiser, ed. John Wiley and Sons Ltd., 303-337.

Sutton, Stephen and Robert Hallett (1988), "Understanding the Effects of Fear-Arousing Communications: The Role of Cognitive Factors and Amount of Fear Aroused," *Journal of Behavioral Science,* 11 (4), 353-360.

Tanner, John F., Jr., Ellen Day and Melvin R. Crask (1989), "Protection Motivation Theory: An Extension of Fear Appeals Theory in Communication," *Journal of Business Research,* 19, 267-276.

Watts, J. C. (1967), "The Role of Vulnerability in Resistance to Fear-Arousing Communications," Unpublished doctoral disseration, Bryn Mawr College.

Wheatley, John J. (1971), "Marketing and the Use of Fear or Anxiety-Arousing Appeals," *Journal of Marketing,* 35 (April), 62-64.

VICTIMS' RIGHTS, FEAR APPEALS, AND AROUSAL

Dianne Eppler, Old Dominion University
Tony L. Henthorne, University of Southern Mississippi
Michael S. LaTour, Auburn University
Kathy Micken, Old Dominion University

ABSTRACT

Victims' rights and the allocation of funds to support victims' rights programs are now riding high on the agenda of public policy makers nationwide. The victims' rights movement has grown not in an effort to lessen the rights of defendants, rather to ensure that the victims of crime are afforded the dignity and respect they deserve (Siegelman 1988).

The issues surrounding the rights of crime victims, and the importance of those issues, must be effectively communicated to the public. One method of communication frequently utilized in the forwarding of victims' rights issues is the fear appeal. However, the use of fear appeals (an advertising message designed to influence individual behavior through the threat of danger [Tanner, Day, and Crask 1989]) often has been associated with failure in social marketing efforts. Kotler and Andreasen (1982) suggest that many of these campaigns did not succeed due to inadequate testing of the fear appeal messages.

Although many researchers have attempted to evaluate the effectiveness of fear appeals, the results of their work have been inconsistent. The "optimal" level of fear stimulation has remained an elusive target (Rotfeld 1988; Wheatley and Oshikawa 1970). Other components of the individual's thought process are believed to make fear and subsequent reaction to fear unique to the individual (Rotfeld 1988).

This paper will examine the use of the fear appeal as message content to support victims' rights awareness. More specifically, this study addresses the individualistic, or idiosyncratic, nature of fear by evaluating the underlying multiple dimensions of fear arousal (Thayer 1978) produced by victims' rights advertising and the resulting impact of this stimuli on attitudinal impressions.

The Thayer model of arousal contends that for some individuals, when encountering unusually high levels of stimulation, an energy arousal dimension dominates that is associated with positive feelings about the stimulus (e.g., advertisement). Other individuals, experiencing the same high levels of stimulation, will find a tension arousal dimension dominating that is associated with negative feelings toward the stimulus. The present study examines whether the use of a "strong fear appeal" victims' rights advertisement elicits sufficient stimula-

tion of tension arousal to produce negative impressions of the ad.

Method

Data were collected via mall intercept in a large regional shopping mall in a culturally and demographically diverse SMSA in the mid-Atlantic region. The experimental manipulation was accomplished by the use of a print ad treatment. The ad treatment was an actual black and white print advertisement run several years ago in a different city than the location of this study. The control ad was the same ad, minus the picture. Assignment to "groups" was random in the sense that the questionnaires were shuffled prior to distribution.

Arousal was measured through the use of the AD-ACL checklist (Thayer 1978). The instruments' reliability has been substantiated by several replications (Thayer 1978). Validity of the measures has been determined through an evaluation of the AD-ACL scores correlations with electrophysiological measures (see Clements, Hafer and Vermillion 1976) for a detailed discussion of this research).

Results

Overall MANOVA test for treatment effects was significant at the $p < .01$ level ($F = 3.88$) and for gender effects at the $p < .066$ level ($F = 2.11$). Treatment/gender interactions were non-significant ($F = .745, p < .59$). It is evident that significantly more tension occurred in the fear treatment group. The current results also indicate the attitude toward the ad (A_{ad}) was significantly more negative for the treatment group. So, rather surprisingly and somewhat contrary to part of Thayer's (1978) theory, we find that insufficient tension was generated to drive energy down, but the impact of the treatment indicates a more negative ad response.

While very little Deactivation Sleep (fatigue) was generated by the advertisements, the treatment group did experience less fatigue than the control group. The results also indicate that the treatment ad was significantly less calming than the control ad. This is not surprising given the nature of the stimulus. No other impact on attitude toward victims' rights or behavioral intention measures was found for the treatment effects. Women were found to be significantly more tense and less calm than the males in the sample. Women also expressed a significantly stronger desire to be more vigilant and to vote to increase funding for victim's rights programs.

Limitations

Ideally, a larger, more costly sample and application of a four "video ad" manipulation with "high tension/low energy, moderate tension/moderate energy, high energy/low tension, and low tension/low energy" ads would have produced a greater range of arousal and a more robust study. An extention of the present study would be served by such an approach. Another limitation of the current study may also be attributed to the two print ad manipulation. Specifically, some interaction between the picture and the copy could be a confound not accounted for. Future research extentions may also consider the application of a multiple indicator LISREL model incorporating arousal dimensions as intervening variables between the ad treatment (effects coded) and various dependent variables such as attitude towards the ad.

For further information please contact:
Michael LaTour
Auburn University
Dept. of Marketing and Transportation
Auburn University, AL. 36849

American Marketing Association / Summer 1992   *11*

SEMANTIC CUES AND BUYER EVALUATION OF PROMOTIONAL COMMUNICATION

Priya Raghubir Das, New York University

ABSTRACT

This paper postulates that the way a deal is phrased impacts deal evaluations and purchase intent for economically and informationally equivalent deals. This "semantic effect" is moderated by the product price level. An empirical test across eight products using a mixed Latin Square design support the hypotheses.

INTRODUCTION

Semantic cues are expressions within the message that facilitate the buyers ability to evaluate the offer (Berkowitz and Walton 1980). Semantic cues in a promotional message are distinct from the intrinsic economic value of the deal. They deal with how one says something, rather than with what is said.

The question of whether deal semantics affect deal evaluation and purchase intent is not a new one (Berkowitz and Walton 1980). Research in the area of deal phrasing has primarily focussed on reference price effects (e.g., Blair and Landon 1981) demonstrating semantic effects using the absence or presence of a variety of reference prices (e.g., Lichtenstein, Burton, and Karson 1991). An alternative explanation for these semantic effects is that they are due to the differential information content of the message rather than the pure semantic effect of how one phrases the deal. Little research has been conducted to examine the "pure" effects of deal semantics, holding economic value, information content and reference price effects constant.

In this paper we investigate such effects in terms of organic effects[1] rather than as contextual effects (Lichtenstein, Burton and Karson 1991). We assess whether the way an offer is phrased (i.e., its semantics) will influence deal evaluations and purchase intent when (1) the economic value of the deal is held constant at a 25 percent discount level, (2) the reference price effect is held constant, using list price as the reference price for all messages. The generalizability of the above effects are investigated for eight products under two price conditions. The four semantic cues investigated are "25 percent off total when you purchase 2," "Buy 1, Get 1 at 1/2 price," "Save $__ on purchase of 2" and "2 for $__." The dollar value of the offer is constant across different messages in the same price condition ($1 and $5 for the low and high price conditions respectively). A constant reference price format, the original list price ($3.99 and $19.99), is used for all message types.

In the following sections relevant literature is re-viewed, hypotheses are presented, the methodology is detailed and results are discussed.

LITERATURE REVIEW

Reference Price Effects

A central issue in promotional advertisements has been the effect the inclusion of a reference price (e.g., prior price, competitive price, manufacturer suggested retail price) on perceptions of deal value. Lichtenstein et al. (1991) argue that in a comparative pricing context, the reference price and offering price are focal cues, i.e., they occupy the focus of attention in a perceptual situation. The semantic phrase is classified as a contextual cue (Lichtenstein et al. 1991), which includes all other behaviorally based stimuli. A third type of cue, organic cues are defined as those "cues that pertain to the inner physiological and psychological processes that affect behavior" (p. 381). The reference price semantic effect literature reviewed below has focussed on the contextual cue explanation of semantic effects.

The classic reference price effect is that promotional advertisements which cite some comparison increase consumers' estimates of the savings offered by advertised prices (Blair and Landon 1981; Della Bitta et al. 1981; Urbany, Bearden, and Weilbaker 1988; Lichtenstein and Bearden 1989) though the full claims made by the advertisement are not accepted (Liefeld and Heslop 1985).

Lichtenstein, Burton and Karson (1991) found that semantic cues of the type "Seen elsewhere $___, Our Price $____" influenced favorability of purchase evaluations in advertisements more than semantic cues like "Was $___, Now Only $___." These two reference price formats prime different reference prices: comparative prices vs. past prices. Lichtenstein et al. (1991) explained their results in terms of the distinctiveness of the deal vs. its consistency across time. However, it can be argued that the two formats are different in more than just semantics. The first contains information about comparative pricing and the latter contains information about past prices. Thus, it may be that the differential information content, rather than the way the offer is phrased that could lead to the semantic effects found.

Framing Effects

Kahneman and Tversky (1979) demonstrated how choices are affected by the decision frame made salient in a judgment task, holding information content equal.

When a choice is framed in terms of gains (from a natural reference point) people show risk aversion, whereas when the same choice is framed in terms of a loss, people show risk seeking preferences. In this paper we focus on how different judgmental frames are activated by different semantics.

HYPOTHESES

Main Effect of Semantics

Deals can be valued in terms of the amount saved or the amount to be spent. They can also be thought of in terms of discount percentages, or packages where you need to buy something to get something on deal. Each of these decision frames can be activated using different message formats. When a decision criteria is made salient it exerts an involuntary, almost automatic effect on evaluation (Taylor and Fiske 1978).

When a promotion is phrased as a dollar saving ("$__ off..."), then the total amount of the saving becomes salient. When the same promotion is framed as a total outlay ("2 for $___"), the total expense is the salient decision frame. Likewise, when a promotion is framed as a percentage off ("25% off ..."), the discount percentage is the most salient aspect of the deal and when it is framed as a package (e.g., "Buy 1, get 1 at 1/2 price"), then the decision criteria is in terms of number to be bought (e.g., "1") to avail of the promotional offer, and the promotional offer itself ("1 at 1/2 price"). It is hypothesized that these different judgmental frames activated by deal semantics lead to differences in deal evaluations and purchase intent.

H1: Deal semantics affect deal evaluation and purchase intent.

Main Effect of Price Level

Intuitively the greater the amount of the savings, the better the deal. Weber's Law applied to price perceptions suggests that the width of the acceptable price range is directly proportional to the level of price acceptability (Monroe 1973). As prices are higher, the width of acceptable prices increases (Lichtenstein, Bloch, and Black 1988). If a deal on a higher priced product is compared to the maximum of the acceptable price level, then the higher the price level, the greater the perception of deal value[2].

Price level is a focal cue (Lichtenstein et al. 1991), the effect of which is greater than that of semantics (a contextual cue). Accordingly, the price effect is expected to be greater than the semantic effect.

Further, deals are typically valued in terms of what one pays vs. the value of what one gets, or "value for money" (Berkowitz and Walton 1980). The greater the

difference in value received for amount paid, the greater the perceived value of the deal. Thus, for every message, deal value and purchase intent are hypothesized to be higher for high priced vs. low priced products.

H2: Deal Evaluation and Purchase Intent will be greater for higher priced items, given the same percentage off.

Semantic x Price Level Interaction

Different judgmental criteria (e.g., total savings vs. total expense) affect deal value perceptions differently. Take for example a product with initial price $3.99 and a "25 percent off purchase of 2" deal. The total savings are $2 and the total expense is $5.99. A total savings of $2 may be viewed as less attractive than a total outlay of $5.98. Accordingly, for a low priced product, the message making the savings amount salient may not be as well perceived as the message making the total outlay salient. The superiority of the 'total expense' frame may be less true for a product with an initial price of $19.99. Here the total savings are $10 and the total expense is $29.98. A saving of $10 may be perceived as no less valuable as a deal which requires a $29.98 total expense. The total savings frame has a greater effect on deal valuations as the amount of the savings rise. Thus,

H3a: Product Price level and semantic cues will interact such that: a 'dollar off' frame will be rated higher than a 'total expense' frame for high priced products but not for low priced products.

Contrast the above with a frame which makes only the percentage off salient ("25% off..."), or frames the deal as a "Buy 1, Get 1 ..." offer. The greater the initial price, the greater will be the value of either of these deals for a given percentage off or total promotional offer. However, the price level will not make a difference to their relative evaluation.

H3b: Product Price level and semantic cues will not interact for the "25 percent off ..." and "Buy 1, Get 1..." frames.

Relative Effect Size

Product price also impacts deal evaluation through its effect on motivation to process message content vs. message semantics. Semantics work through activating decision frames which then are most accessible in short term memory. The most accessible information may be used as a decision frame automatically (Fiske and Taylor 1991). However, a larger dollar value saved increases the motivation of the subject to analytically evaluate messages (Petty and Cacioppo 1986). The greater the original price, the greater the value the deal would offer and accordingly the less the effect of the most available decision frame. Thus, a larger semantic effect is hypothesized for low vs. high priced products.

H4: Semantics have a greater effect for lower priced products.

To test these hypotheses a mixed 4 x 2 Latin Square experimental design was developed where subjects were presented with eight products advertised on different deals. Each deal was rated and purchase intentions measured. The procedure took 10 minutes.

METHOD

Choice of Messages

A pretest was conducted to see whether the way a deal is phrased affects the purchase ranking of a single product (Green Giant tinned peas). The messages used were (a) "2 for the price of $1," (b) "Buy one, Get one at 1/2 price," and (c) "25 percent off the purchase of 2" (identical at the list price of 67 cents). Students were asked to rank order deals. The sample was drawn from a doctoral student population (n=20). In so far as this sample is well aware of framing effects[3], and less likely to fall prey to them, this sample provides a strong test of the existence of semantic effects. Prior to debriefing, only 2/20 showed suspicion of the hypothesis.

The ANOVA results showed that semantics significantly impacted deal ranks (F= 8.86. p<.0002). The rank orders were "2 for $1;" "Buy 1, Get 1 at 1/2 price" and "25 percent off purchase of two." Forty-five percent (9/20) of the subjects expressed preferences in this rank order. A fourth message type "$___ off,..." was added after perusal of supermarket flyers over a two week period.

Selection of Products and Price Levels

Criteria for choice of products included those products which were likely to be (a) purchased by a student population, (b) independent of gender, (c) bought in pairs, and(d) approximately available at the experimental price. The two price levels were chosen such that (a) they were significantly different, (b) buying two items at the higher price level was within a student budget, and (c) at least four products at each price level ($3.99 and $19.99). 20 products were pretested on a student sample of 5 for adherence to the above criteria. From this list, eight products were chosen, four each at the two price levels. These were further pretested on a sample of 9 students. The low priced products chosen were wine, underwear, cookies and socks. The high priced products chosen were CDs, video cassettes, t-shirts and jeans.

Dependent Variables

Subjects recorded deal evaluations and purchase intent on multiple 7 point scales. The standard deal valuation operationalisation: "perceived worth," "price acceptability," "perceived savings" and "value for the money" (Berkowitz and Walton 1980) was found difficult to understand and interpret during pretesting. Accordingly, three commonly used semantic differential scales anchored by "Valuable-Worthless," "Attractive-Unattractive" and "Good-Bad" were used. The scale for purchase intent was anchored by "Definitely will buy" to "Definitely will not buy" (Aaker and Day 1990).

The eight deal valuation scales had Cronbach's alphas of .94 (range = .93 to .96). The average correlation between deal value (DV) measures and purchase intent (PI) was .86 (range from .77 to .90, p<.01 for all).

Design & Sample

The design was a mixed Latin Square experimental design with 4 messages x 4 products x 2 price levels requiring 4 treatment groups (see Chart 1). Each of the four products at the two price levels received one of the four promotional messages, in a fully counter balanced manner. Different groups rated a given product on a different promotional message. The four groups received repeated measures of different product-message combinations. Price was manipulated within subjects. Product and message type were manipulated both between and across subjects. Subjects were randomly assigned to groups and groups were randomly assigned to treatments using a randomized block design (Fleiss 1986). The Latin Square is designed to provide an internal replication of the results. The square itself was replicated over 16 times (Fleiss 1986). Order of deal statement in the questionnaire was randomized and controlled across subjects by using four permutations of order of presentation.

Undergraduate and graduate students at Long Island University were the subjects for the study (n=73).

DATA ANALYSIS AND RESULTS

Measures on deal proneness and average purchase quantity were collected for potential use as covariates. However, these were non-significant and were not used for further analysis. The random effect of the products chosen was not significant after adjusting for the price effects (for deal value F(3,207)=.21, p=.889; for purchase intent F(3,210)=.68, p=.566). The product effects were not analyzed further.

Semantic Message Effect

Hypothesis 1 which predicted a main effect of message type, was marginally supported (F(3,207)=2.46, p<.064) for perceptions of DV, but not for PI (F(3,210)=1.30, p=.277). Table 1 summarizes the mean DV and PI scores for the different messages across the two price conditions.

CHART 1
Experimental Design

Semantic Messages	Low Priced Prod. (@ $3.99)				High Priced Prod. (@ $19.99)			
	Wine	Under Wear	Cookie	Socks	CDs	Video	T-Shirt	Jeans
25% off,..	I	IV	III	II	I	IV	III	II
Buy 1,...	II	I	IV	III	II	I	IV	III
Save $...	III	II	I	IV	III	II	I	IV
2 for $...	IV	III	II	I	IV	III	II	I

1. Numbers in the matrix from I to IV denote the 4 experimental groups.

2. Rows represent the main effects of semantics.

3. Columns are the Price effects, with products nested in price.

TABLE 1
Means of Deal Evaluation and Purchase Intentby Message Type and Price Level

Dependent Measures & Price levels	Messages			
	25% off...	Buy 1, ...	Save $...	2 for $...
Deal Evaluation				
Low Price	3.7 a	4.1 b,e	3.8 a,b	4.3 c,d,e
High Price	4.1 b,e	4,5 c,e	4.4 c,e	4.3 c,e
Purchase Intent				
Low Price	3.6 f	3.9	3.6 f,g	4.1 h
High price	3.9	4.1	4.0 h	4.0

1 Means are on a scale of 1 to 7, where higher numbers denote more favorable evaluations and higher intentions. Numbers which do not share a common subscript are significant at the .05 level.

Price Effect

Hypothesis 2 which predicted a main effect of price was strongly supported for DV perceptions $(F(1,69)=8.27, p<.005)$ as well as for PI $(F(1,69)=4.15, p<.045)$. The effect size was greater than the semantic effect size as expected. Thus, the same percentage off is valued more for higher priced products vs. lower priced products. This was directionally true of all the message types except the "2 for $__" message $(t(73)=.10, p=.922)$. It was significant for the "25 percent off,.." message $(t(73)=2.04, p<.045)$ and strongly significant for the "Save $__,..."

message $(t(73)=2.71, p<.008)$. Similarly, for PI, the message was valued more highly at a higher price level than at a lower price for most messages (see Table 1).

Message x Price Interaction

Hypothesis 3 predicted a significant interaction for message with price. This was not supported overall for either perceptions of DV $(F(3,207)=1.47, p=.224)$ or for PI $(F(3,210)=.88, p=.452)$. Separate ANOVAS were done for the two types of messages where interactions were expected and for the two messages where these were not

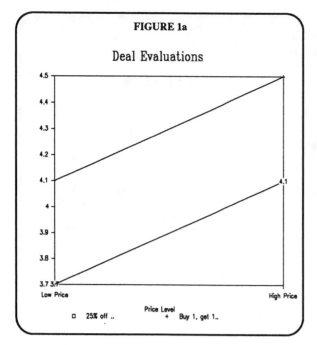

FIGURE 1a

Deal Evaluations

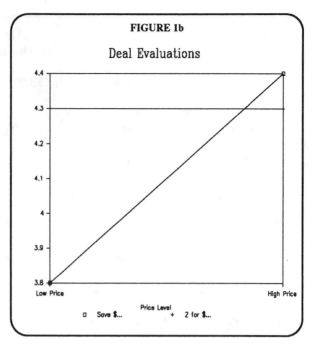

FIGURE 1b

Deal Evaluations

expected. There was no interaction for "25 percent off,...," and "Buy 1,..." as expected (F(1,69)=.16, p=.687 for DV; and F(1,70)=.21, p=.647 for PI). However, for the `total expense' frame and the `total savings' frame, interactions were significant as expected (F(1,70)=4.21, p<.044 for DV; and F(1,70)=4.05, p<.048 for PI; Figures 1a and 1b). As conjectured, the `savings' frame led to greater perceptions of DV as total savings increased (t(73)=2.71, p<.008). Perceived DV in the `savings' frame equalled or overtook the perception of DV for the `total expense' frame in the high price condition. On the other hand, the perceived DV in the `total expense' frame stayed approximately constant across the two price conditions (t(73)=0.10, p=.922).

Effect Size

Hypothesis 4 argued that the semantic effect size would be larger in the low price condition as compared to the high price condition. Separate ANOVAs were done for the low price condition and the high price condition to assess the differential effect sizes. In the low price condition the message effect was significant for DV (F(3,210)=3.15, p<.026) but did not reach significance for PI (F(3,210)=2.04, p=.110). In the high price condition, on the other hand, the message effect was non-significant for DV (F(3,207)=.95, p=.417) and for PI (F(3,210)=.33, p=.807). The eta square for semantics in the low price condition is.0431 whereas in the high price condition it is .0136. The same pattern is apparent in the number of significant mean differences in the two conditions (Table 1), and the range of the means for DV and PI in the two conditions.

While not hypothesized, a smaller effect was found for PI vs. DV across all measures (main and interaction effects).

DISCUSSION

To summarize, we have demonstrated that "pure" semantic effects of promotional advertisements exist beyond the well researched reference price effects. The mere phrasing of a deal affects deal evaluation and purchase intent. Overall the "2 for $.." and "Buy 1, get 1 at 1/2 price" frames were most effective across price levels. Their effect is moderated by the price of the product. For example the "Save $.." frame is particularly effective at high price levels, but not at low price levels. These results are consistent with the "organic effects" explanation, i.e., can be explained in terms of the different judgmental frames semantics make salient. Further as suggested by the literature on involvement (Fiske and Taylor 1991), as price of a product increases, the semantic effect reduces. Semantic effects were also found to be stronger for deal evaluation than purchase intent.

The major limitations of this research is its use of a laboratory experiment with limited external validity. These findings need to be replicated in a field study before any strong conclusions can be drawn. They also need to be tested on different products at varying price levels. Only four different message types have been studied in this study. Generalizability would require the study of a larger set of message types.

Caution needs to be used in generalizing these results to choice situations. Given the dilution of the effect from evaluations to purchase intentions, a further dilution of the semantic effect for actual purchase may be expected. The moderating effects of distinctiveness and consistency (Lichtenstein and Bearden 1989), price consciousness (Lichtenstein, Bloch, and Black 1988) and reference price formats (Lichtenstein, Burton, and Karson 1991) need to be studied to draw the boundary conditions of these findings.

The main contribution of this study is to demonstrate that "pure" semantic effects exist which cannot be explained by inclusion or exclusion of a reference price or differential information contained in the message. These effects are moderated by the price level of the product. These results have implications for differential promotional communication of a range of consumer products.

ENDNOTES

[1] Thanks are due to an anonymous reviewer for this suggestion.
[2] Thanks are due to an anonymous reviewer for pointing this out.
[3] Two anonymous reviewers pointed this out.

Thanks are due to George Siomkos and Gaura Narayan for their assistance in data collection. I would further like to thank Robert Shoemaker and participants at the Marketing Models seminar at New York University, Fall 1991, for their comments and suggestions throughout this research. Thanks are due to Vicki Morowitz, Elizabeth Creyer and Gita Johar at NYU for their comments on earlier drafts, and to Gordon Moskowitz and Prof Geeta Menon for their assistance with data analysis. Finally, thanks are due to three anonymous reviewers for their comments.

REFERENCES

Aaker, A. and George S. Day (1990), *Marketing Research*. New York: John Wiley.

Berkowitz, Eric N. and John R. Walton (1980), "Contextual Influences on Consumer Price Responses: An Experimental Analysis," *Journal of Marketing Research*, 17, 349-358.

Blair, Edward A. and E. Laird Landon (1981), "The Effectiveness of Reference Prices is Retail Advertisements," *Journal of Marketing*, 45, 61-69.

Della Bitta, Albert J., Kent B. Monroe, and John M. Mcginnis (1981), "Consumer Perceptions of Comparative Price Advertisements," *Journal of Marketing Research*, 18, 416-427.

Fleiss, Joseph L. (1986), *The Design and Analysis of Clinical Experiments*. New York: Wiley.

Fiske, Susan T. and Shelley E. Taylor (1991), *Social Cognition*. New York: McGraw Hill.

Kahneman, Daniel and Amos Tversky (1979), "Prospect Theory: An Analysis of Decision Under Risk," *Econometrica*, 47, 263-291.

Lichtenstein, Donald R., Peter H. Bloch, and William C. Black (1988), "Correlates of Price Acceptability," *Journal of Consumer Research*, 15 (3), 243-252.

_____and William O. Bearden (1989), "Contextual Influences on Perceptions of Merchant-Supplied Reference Prices," *Journal of Consumer Research*, 16 (1), 55-66.

_____, Scot Burton, and Eric J. Karson (1991), "The Effect of Semantic Cues on Consumer Perceptions of Reference Price Ads," *Journal of Consumer Research*, 18 (3), 380-391.

Liefeld, John and Louise A. Heslop (1985), "Reference Prices and Deception in Newspaper Advertising," *Journal of Consumer Research*, 11 (4), 868-876.

Monroe, Kent B. (1973)," Buyers' Subjective Perceptions of Price," *Journal of Marketing Research*, 10 (February), 70-80.

Petty, Richard E. and John T. Cacioppo (1986), *Communication and Persuasion: Central and Peripheral Routes to Attitude Change*. New York: Springer-Verlag.

Taylor, Shelley E. and Susan T. Fiske (1978), "Salience, Attention and Attribution: Top of the Head phenomena," in L. Berkowitz, ed. *Advances in Experimental Social Psychology*, New York: Academic Press, 11, 249-288.

Urbany, Joel E., William O. Bearden, and Dan C. Weilbaker (1988), "The Effect of Plausible and Exaggerated Reference Prices on Consumer Perceptions and Price Search," *Journal of Consumer Research*, 15 (1), 95-110.

THE INTERACTIVE EFFECTS OF INTERNAL AND EXTERNAL REFERENCE PRICES ON BRAND CHOICE

Tung-Zong Chang, National Chengchi University

ABSTRACT

A frame of reference is instrumental in facilitating the buying task by serving as a stimulus, or a *referent*, to which other stimuli are related. Referents can be classified into *internal referents*, those stored in one's memory system, or *external referents*, those from external environments, such as marketing stimuli. Frames of reference can be in various levels also. For example, a referent may be a brand or a product attribute. When facing new or unfamiliar alternatives, a familiar brand in a product category is often used as a basis of comparison, i.e., a *reference brand*. Also, multiple attributes are usually used in brand evaluations and each product attribute may be a referent, or a *reference attribute*. Among many conceivable important reference attributes, reference price is frequently cited as an influential frame of reference in product evaluations and purchase decisions.

Alternative theories, such as the adaptation level theory and the assimilation-contrast theory, have been used to predict and describe the possible effects of reference prices. As a referent could be either internal or external, two types of reference prices can be recognized: *internal reference prices* and *external reference prices*. While the latter has traditionally been viewed as merchant-supplied reference prices, external reference prices may also be provided by other third independent parties such as consumer union.

Previous literature did not fully consider that consumers often have to make a judgment about two prices, a list price and a discount (actual) price. The present study proposes to investigate how consumers' internal and external reference prices jointly affect brand choice behavior. In particular, how the perceived acceptable price range (internal), list price (external), and discount price (external) interact and affect brand acceptance is scrutinized. As consumers often have prior price perceptions on the product category and are exposed to a marketer-provided list price and a discount price, an investigation of the result of such joint effect is very important.

Based on the assimilation/contrast theory, a consumer's response to a brand depends on whether or not its price is within a certain latitude of acceptance. Holding other things constant, if the list price or discount price is outside the acceptable range, consumers should judge it as unacceptable. If the price is too low to be acceptable, the brand is rejected because of its **questionable quality**. On the other hand, if a price is unacceptably high, the denial is because of its **affordability**. If these underlying difficulties, questionable quality or affordability, can be overcome, the brand may be acceptable based on the assumption of compensatory effect. Hypotheses are developed based on this line of reasoning.

A 2 (list price) x 3 (discount price) between-subject experiment was employed. The price manipulations were to create various positions of the list price and discount price on the perceived acceptable price range. Two hundred seventy-five subjects were recruited from various upper-level undergraduate business classes in a midwest state university and randomly and evenly assigned to one of the six experimental conditions. Results of the manipulation checks indicate that the list price manipulation and other aspects of experimental control are successful. The brand one would consider buying for personal use was used as the dependent variable in the analysis. All hypotheses are supported ($p < 0.05$).

The results indicate that, brand choices are significantly influenced by the positions of external reference prices relative to the internal reference prices in a compensatory manner. Specifically, an inadmissable high external reference price may be compensated by an acceptable or an unacceptably low discount price, and vice versa. The conclusions offer important implications for marketing researchers and practitioners in pricing decisions.

The major contribution of this paper is to show that the acceptable price range is a valuable concept which may help predict the degree of brand acceptance. The relative positions of the list price and discount price on the acceptable price range jointly affect brand choice. Prior research has suggested that if the offering price falls below the acceptable range, bargain perceptions may not be enhanced. The present study shows otherwise. That is, it is possible for an offering price below the acceptable range to enhance the bargain perception if the offering price is framed as a discount from an acceptable or an unacceptably high list price. This difference in results may be due to the fact that the list price in this study is not exaggerated and the sponsor is credible.

For further information contact: Professor Tung-Zong Chang
Department of Business Administration
National Chengchi University
Taipei, Taiwan 11623

ADVERTISING VARIABLES THAT PREDICT CONSUMER RESPONSES

Arjun Chaudhuri, University of Connecticut
Ross Buck, University of Connecticut

ABSTRACT

This paper develops hypotheses concerning the relationship of advertising variables to psychological outcomes. It is postulated that interactions between media, product and advertising appeals may predict two different types of outcomes. The first, arises from spontaneous communication and results in syncretic cognition; the second, arises from symbolic communication and results in analytic cognitions.

INTRODUCTION

Most theory and research on attitudes has been directed towards explaining rational outcomes: emotion has been conceptualized rather simplistically in positive - negative terms, and it has been assumed that rational considerations determine the emotional response. However, recent research suggests that emotion is complex and may actually influence rational processing (Ray and Batra 1983). This paper postulates that emotional (syncretic cognitions) and rational (analytic cognitions) outcomes vary in their <u>relative</u> importance according to the nature of the advertising characteristics (media, product and advertising strategy) that are used.

Although these advertising characteristics have been studied separately and in a piecemeal fashion, their combined effects have not generally been considered in a systematic manner. As advocated by Pechmann and Stewart (1989), this paper investigates the interactions between the advertising variables and thereby addresses the need to understand the circumstances under which each of these variables contributes to consumer responses.

THEORETICAL FRAMEWORK

Developmental - interactionist theory (Buck 1988) presents a theoretical framework for understanding the psychological processes that are generated by advertising stimuli. According to Buck (1988), human motivation is "the potential for activation and behavior that is inherent in a system of behavior control" (p.5) and emotion is "the process by which motivational potential is realized or read out when activated by challenging stimuli" (p.9). Thus, emotion is a readout mechanism that carries information about motivational systems and is a continuous and ever present expression of motivational states.

Buck (1988) views cognition as knowledge and defines it as "a more or less complex and organized internal representation of reality, acquired by means of the individual's cognitive skills and through experience with reality" (p. 6). Two types of cognition are described of which the first is <u>syncretic cognition</u> or "knowledge by acquaintance," which cannot be described but is "known" immediately by the person and may consist of sensations, bodily symptoms, drives and primary affects, such as happiness, sadness, fear, anger, surprise and disgust (Ekman and Friesen 1975). This is the same process of immediate and subjective experience which William James (1890) wrote about: "I know the color blue when I see it, and the flavor of a pear when I taste it....but <u>about</u> the inner nature of these facts or what makes them what they are I can say nothing at all" (p. 22).

In contrast to syncretic cognition, which is holistic, synthetic and right brain oriented, <u>analytic cognition</u> or "knowledge by description" is sequential, analytic and left brain oriented. While syncretic cognition is derived from direct sensory awareness, analytic cognition results from the interpretation of sensory data and involves judgements about phenomena. As Bertrand Russell (1912) observed, "My knowledge of a table as a physical object....is not direct knowledge. Such as it is, it is obtained through acquaintance with the sense-data that make up the appearance of the table" (p.73-74). Further, analytic cognition can be symbolically communicated, while syncretic cognition is spontaneously communicated.

Thus, communication also has two aspects - spontaneous and symbolic. <u>Spontaneous communication</u> is biologically shared, non - intentional or automatic and non propositional. It requires only knowledge by acquaintance and is expressed through signs which make motivational - emotional states externally accessible. <u>Symbolic communication</u> is learned, socially shared, intentional and propositional. It requires knowledge by description and is based upon learned symbols, which have a learned and arbitrary relationship with their referents. Two simultaneous streams of communication are envisaged, therefore, which are equal in importance and which interact and modify one another. However, while "pure" spontaneous communication is possible, "pure" symbolic communication is not. In other words, symbolic communication is always accompanied by spontaneous communication (Buck 1984).

These two types of communication involve two different systems of information processing and behavior control - one biological, the other learned. Buck (1988) argues that a hierarchy of biologically based <u>special</u>

purpose processing systems (SPPS) - reflexes, instincts, drives, primary affects, effectance motivation and curiosity - evolved and are "hard - wired" into the structure of the nervous system. As one travels up the hierarchy, these special purpose systems increasingly interact with the general purpose processing systems (GPPS) of learning and cognition, which are shaped by the individual's experiences over the course of development and which serve to control behavior so as to adapt to changes in the environment. Figure 1 illustrates this.

This interaction between the two systems of behavior control is fundamental to the developmental - interactionist perspective. For example, the primary affects, in spite of their biological basis, are open to influence from the individual's past experiences, learning and analytic cognition in order for affective behavior to be more flexible in response to changes in the environment. Similarly, analytic cognitions, are also acquired, in part, through the individual's affective experiences with reality. Thus, these systems of behavior control interact and inform each other in a given situation, leading to goal directed behavior. In that sense, neither can be thought to have "primacy."

Consonant with the above, it is suggested that there are two primary types of psychological outcomes as a result of advertising. The first arises from spontaneous communication and results in syncretic cognition (knowledge by acquaintance); the second arises from symbolic communication and results in analytic cognition (knowledge by description). The stimulus antecedents in the advertising domain have been suggested by Zaichkowsky (1986) to be: the choice of media, the nature of the product category advertised and the advertising strategy adopted. These three elements, arising from the nature of the advertisement itself, will be examined in this paper as the sources of explained variance in syncretic and analytic cognitions.

MEDIA

According to the uses and gratification approach to mass media (Katz, Blumer, and Gurevitch 1973), people use the mass media to gratify different emotional and rational needs. It is postulated that print media generate a higher relative level of analytic cognition than broadcast media, whereas broadcast media elicit higher relative levels of syncretic cognitions including affective responses such as happiness, fear, etc. According to McLuhan (1964), print media emphasize the visual aspect of the senses leading to an analytic cognitive style of information processing that is logical and sequential. Electronic media, on the other hand, encourage a holistic style of processing that is synthetic and involves all of the senses. This is akin to the concepts of spontaneous and symbolic communication. Some spontaneous cues, such as music, are available only in the broadcast media and thus it is suggested that relative to print media, broadcast

media emphasize SPPS and syncretic cognition.

On the other hand, Park and Young (1986) found that music in television commercials had a distracting effect during analytic cognitive situations. The lack of such cues as music in print media may thus encourage analytic cognitive responses, in comparison to broadcast media. Further, Wright (1974) showed that, in comparison to broadcast, print media moderate greater analytic cognitive responses to advertising, such as source derogation and counterarguing and he suggested that this was so, because print allows more opportunity to process information than broadcast. Figure 2 illustrates the relative importance of the GPPS and SPPS systems with regard to two broad classes of media - broadcast (television, radio, etc.) and print (magazines, newspapers, etc.).

H1: The mean syncretic cognitive response will be significantly higher for broadcast ads than for print ads.

H2: The mean analytic cognitive response will be significantly higher for print ads than for broadcast ads.

PRODUCT CATEGORY

In Krugman's (1965) view, it is the medium or format of an ad that determines the level of involvement. This has been disputed by Preston (1970) who claims that it is the content of the ad, specifically the product category advertised, that accounts for differences in the level of involvement. According to Preston, products advertised on television have less differentiation between brands than products advertised in magazines and this creates less involvement with television ads, since there is less risk associated with the products advertised.

Thus, certain products may be viewed as high in analytic value since they are risky. On the other hand, certain products may be high in syncretic value. This would apply to products, such as beer, chocolate, liquor, sodas, etc., where brand differences are imperceptible to most consumers but where the hedonic component is high. Additionally, for certain product classes (automobiles, televisions) consumers may process information in both highly analytic and syncretic ways and for other categories evaluation may be low in both. This is well supported by past research on product involvement (Laurent and Kapferer 1985).

Involvement with the product category is thus, arguably a function of both syncretic and analytic values and certain products are high in product involvement because they are high in either or both analytic and syncretic value. Consequently, the depiction of such products in an advertisement may evoke both analytic and syncretic cognitions. Figure 3 illustrates, for some product categories, the relative importance of the SPPS/GPPS systems.

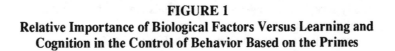

FIGURE 1
**Relative Importance of Biological Factors Versus Learning and
Cognition in the Control of Behavior Based on the Primes**

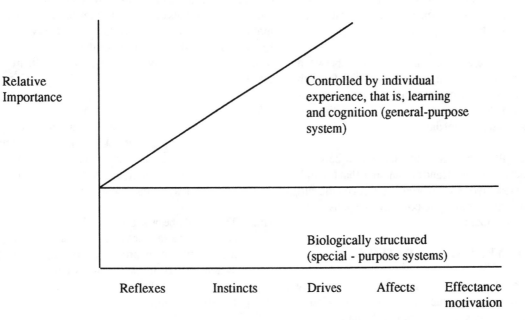

Relative
Importance

Controlled by individual
experience, that is, learning
and cognition (general-purpose
system)

Biologically structured
(special - purpose systems)

| Reflexes | Instincts | Drives | Affects | Effectance motivation |

From Buck, R. (1988), *Human Motivation and Emotion.* New York: John Wiley.

FIGURE 2
**Relative Importance of GPPS/SPPS Systems
With Regard to Print and Broadcast Media**

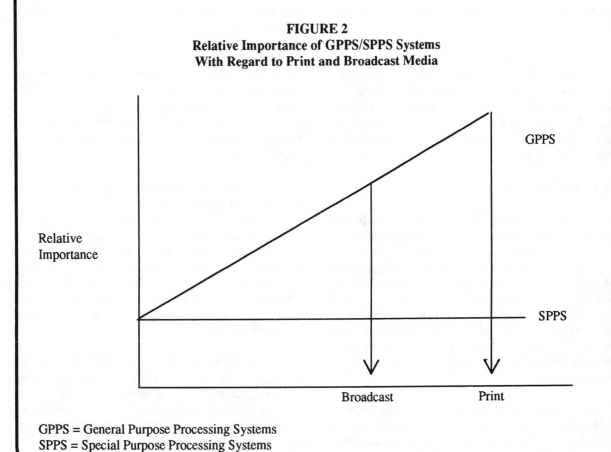

Relative
Importance

GPPS

SPPS

Broadcast   Print

GPPS = General Purpose Processing Systems
SPPS = Special Purpose Processing Systems

Further, the advertising of products high in analytic value in _print_ media especially serves to engender _analytic_ cognitions, since print allows readers the opportunity to process information that reduces the inherent risk in such product categories. Similarly, the advertising of products high in syncretic value in _broadcast_ media, especially television, elicits _syncretic_ cognition by delineating the pleasure, or relief from displeasure, that can be derived from the advertised product.

H3:   There will be a significant interaction between product involvement and media, such that for high but not low involvement products, broadcast media will produce greater syncretic cognitive response than print media.

H4:   There will be a significant interaction between product involvement and media, such that for high but not low involvement products, print media will produce greater analytic cognitive response than broadcast media.

ADVERTISING STRATEGY

Although advertising stimuli may simultaneously elicit syncretic and analytic cognitions, the relative amounts of these may vary according to the nature of the stimuli. For instance, Figure 4 suggests how different advertising treatments may fall along the hierarchy of special purpose processing systems and the relative importance of general purpose processing systems in each of these cases.

Three broad classes of theories of advertising strategy have been identified: systematic, heuristic and affective (Pechmann and Stewart 1989). Affective theories can be further divided into theories of classical conditioning and vicarious learning. These four theories of advertising strategy are examined below in terms of their relationships to analytic and syncretic cognitions.

Systematic Learning

Systematic learning theories, under the traditional information processing paradigm in consumer behavior (Bettman 1979), view the consumer as an active processor of information. Lavidge and Steiner (1961) proposed a hierarchy of advertising effects in which attitude formation for a brand starts with beliefs, leads to overall evaluation and, finally, leads to behavior. This process of the creation of beliefs and judgements about brands on the basis of symbolic advertising communication is also the process of knowledge by description, which produces analytic cognitions.

Industrial products, services like banking and household appliances are low in syncretic value and high in analytic value. The advertising of such products emphasizes brand information and analytic cognitive response.

Consequently, the main effects of advertising message appeals may, in fact, be due to the interaction between product category and advertising appeals. Bowen and Chaffee (1974) found that ad appeals, in which objective brand information was given, were more effective under conditions of _high involvement_ with the product category. Thus, a greater level of involvement motivates the consumer to process brand information. Product information is also likely to generate greater analytic cognitive responses when it is used in the print media, since print allows greater opportunity to process such information (Wright 1974).

H5:   There will be a significant interaction between product involvement and advertising strategies, such that for high but not low involvement products, ads high in systematic learning strategies will produce greater analytic cognitive response than ads low in systematic learning.

H6:   There will be a significant interaction between advertising strategies and media, such that in print media but not in broadcast media, ads high in systematic learning strategies will produce greater analytic cognitive response than ads low in systematic learning.

Heuristic Learning

According to Chaiken (1980) persons process information in both systematic and heuristic ways. While systematic processing involves thoughtful, "mindful" analysis of the content of the ad, heuristic processing involves the use of simple heuristic cues in order to arrive at a conclusion (brand preferences, etc.). Thus, spontaneous affective cues may elicit heuristic processing and generate syncretic cognition. Ray and Batra (1983) state that emotion laden stimuli in ads may create better message acceptance, since in a positive affective state, people tend to make speedier, less complex judgements.

Such spontaneous communication is also more likely to take place in television, due to its capacity for greater vividness in the images presented. Chaiken and Eagly (1983) associate heuristic processing with broadcast and systematic processing with print media, since print media are better used for presenting difficult messages, while broadcast is better for simple messages. Krugman's (1965) theory of low involvement also deals with the importance of heuristics (repetition of the brand name, etc.) via television.

Further, Petty and Cacioppo (1986) suggest that emotional ad appeals are effective via the peripheral (heuristic) route when motivation to think about the message is low. Pechmann and Stewart (1989) treat heuristic processing as the antithesis of analytic processing, since this process is used when consumers wish to avoid detailed consideration of the merits of a brand. The

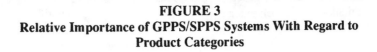

FIGURE 3
Relative Importance of GPPS/SPPS Systems With Regard to
Product Categories

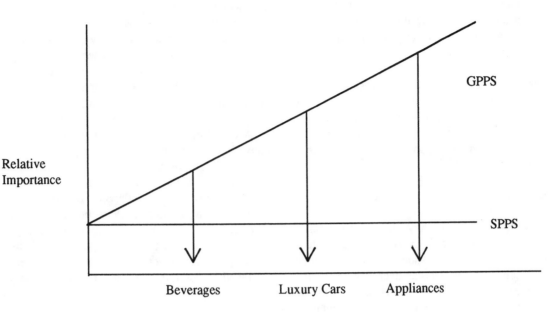

GPPS

Relative
Importance

SPPS

Beverages   Luxury Cars   Appliances

GPPS = General Purpose Processing Systems
SPPS = Special Purpose Processing Systems

FIGURE 4
Relative Importance of GPPS/SPPS Systems With Regard to
Advertising Strategies

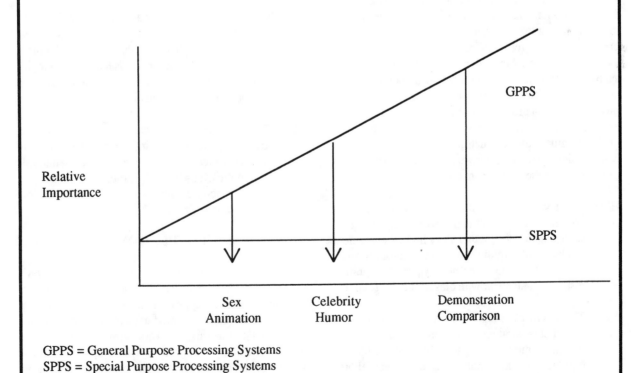

GPPS

Relative
Importance

SPPS

Sex   Celebrity   Demonstration
Animation   Humor   Comparison

GPPS = General Purpose Processing Systems
SPPS = Special Purpose Processing Systems

implication may then be made that heuristic processing is more likely under conditions of low involvement.

H7: There will be a significant interaction between product involvement and advertising strategies, such that for low but not high involvement products, ads high in heuristic learning strategies will produce greater syncretic cognitive response than ads low in heuristic learning.

H8: There will be a significant interaction between advertising strategies and media, such that for broadcast media but not for print media, ads high in heuristic learning strategies will produce greater syncretic cognitive response than ads low in heuristic learning.

Classical Conditioning

Pavlov (1927) and others have demonstrated that if two dissimilar objects are repetitively associated in close contiguity to each other, the response originally elicited by the unconditioned stimulus can over time be elicited by the conditioned stimulus alone. When conditioning has taken place, there is knowledge by acquaintance, which cannot be described by subjects, since it has been structured by experience alone. This can take place vicariously via the process of spontaneous communication, which results in syncretic cognition through the use of spontaneous cues in the advertisement. Involvement is created with the ad by using affect-laden symbols, such as trade characters.

Of particular interest is the interaction, if any, between such thematic elements and different media. For instance, it is entirely possible that humor on broadcast media produces greater affect than in print due to the "vividness" effect. Also, spontaneous advertising cues, such as symbols and music may lead to associations with syncretic cognitions, particularly in low involvement products. Certain products, such as tissues, fabric softeners and gasoline are low in syncretic value and low in analytic value. Ads for such products utilize classical conditioning strategies to derive ad induced affect, thereby differentiating the brand from competition.

H9: There will be a significant interaction between product involvement and advertising strategies, such that for low rather than high involvement products, ads high in classical conditioning strategies will produce greater syncretic cognitive response than ads low in classical conditioning.

H10: There will be a significant interaction between advertising strategies and media, such that in broadcast media rather than in print media, ads high in classical conditioning strategies will produce greater syncretic cognitive response than ads low in classical conditioning.

Vicarious Learning

Pechmann and Stewart (1989) describe the process of vicarious learning through advertising. The rewards/punishments meted out to the model in the ad are exemplified in the model's expressive behavior, such as facial expressions etc. The process of observing such emotional expression results in arousal and a vicarious sharing of the same subjective experience as undergone by the model in the ad. The consumer comes to associate the brand with the emotion generated and sees the brand as the social instrument that obtains rewards and stays punishment.

Accordingly, it is suggested that spontaneous nonverbal cues, such as the facial expressions of advertising models represent vicarious learning strategies that result in syncretic cognitions concerning the emotional benefits of advertised brands. Such observational learning is apt to be greater in television, due to its lifelike representation of human interaction. McLuhan (1964) considered television to be a "re-action" (p.320) medium in the sense that viewers tend to pay greater attention to the facial expressions of the actors than to the action in progress.

Further, it may be conceived that products high in inherent risk, or high involvement products, are likely to be most conducive to the depiction of such strategies on television. The rewards or punishments vicariously experienced by the consumer are more meaningful in the context of socially visible products, such as clothing, in which the sanction or approval provided by other people is most relevant.

H11: There will be a significant interaction between product involvement and advertising strategies, such that for high rather than low involvement products, ads high in vicarious learning strategies will produce greater syncretic cognitive response than ads low in vicarious learning.

H12: There will be a significant interaction between advertising strategies and media, such that in broadcast media rather than in print media, ads high in vicarious learning strategies will produce greater syncretic cognitive response than ads low in vicarious learning.

CONCLUSION

The introduction of both syncretic and analytic cognitions as dependent variables allows for a comprehensive theoretical approach to our understanding of advertising effects. There has been a long standing debate (Zajonc 1980; Lazarus 1984) concerning the primacy of emotion and analytic cognition. The perspective utilized in this paper reconciles the opposing viewpoints by considering emotion as a kind of cognition as well (syncretic cognition), that is far more complex than simplistic positive - negative conceptualizations. Instead of asking whether syncretic or analytic cognition is "primary," we have argued that they differ in their relative importance in different media, products and advertising strategies.

REFERENCES

Bettman, James R. (1979), *An Information Processing Theory of Consumer Choice.* Reading, MA: Addison-Wesley.

Bowen, Lawrence and Steven H. Chaffee (1974), "Product Involvement and Pertinent Advertising Appeals," *Journalism Quarterly,* 51 (Winter), 613-621.

Buck, Ross (1984), *The Communication of Emotion.* New York: Guilford Press.

_____(1988), *Human Motivation and Emotion.* New York: John Wiley.

Chaiken, Shelly (1980), "Heuristic Versus Systematic Information Processing and the Use of Source Versus Message Cues in Persuasion," *Journal of Personality and Social Psychology,* 39 (5), 752-766.

_____and Alice H. Eagly (1983), "Communicator Modality as a Determinant of Persuasion: The Role of Communicator Salience," *Journal of Personality and Social Psychology,* 45 (2), 241-256.

Ekman, Paul and Wallace V. Friesen (1975), *Unmasking the Face.* Engelwood Cliffs, NJ: Prentice-Hall.

James, William (1890), *The Principles of Psychology.* New York: Henry Holt and Co.

Katz, Elihu, Jay. G. Blumler and Michael Gurevitch (1973), "Uses of Mass Communication By the Individual," *Public Opinion Quarterly,* 37 (Winter), 504-516.

Krugman, Herbert E. (1965), "The Impact of Television Advertising: Learning Without Involvement," *Public Opinion Quarterly,* 29 (Fall), 349-356.

Laurent, Gilles and Jean-Noel Kapferer (1985), "Measuring Consumer Involvement Profiles," *Journal of Marketing Research,* 22 (February), 41-53.

Lavidge, R. J. and Gary A. Steiner (1961), "A Model for Predictive Measurements of Advertising Effectiveness," *Journal of Marketing,* 25 (3), 59-62.

Lazarus, R. S. (1984), "On the Primacy of Cognition," *American Psychologist,* 39, 124-129.

McLuhan, Marshall H. (1964), *Understanding Media:* *The Extension of Man.* New York: McGraw Hill.

Park, C. Whan and S. Mark Young (1986), "Consumer Response to Television Commercials: The Impact of Involvement and Background Music on Brand Attitude Formation," *Journal of Marketing Research,* 23 (February), 11-24.

Pavlov, Ivan (1927), *Conditioned Reflexes. An Investigation of the Physiological Activity of the Cerebral Cortex.* London: Oxford University Press.

Pechmann, Cornelia and David W. Stewart (1989), "The Multidimensionality of Persuasive Communications: Theoretical and Empirical Foundations," in *Cognitive and Affective Responses to Advertising,* Patricia Cafferata and Alice M. Tybout, eds. Lexington, MA: Lexington Books.

Petty, Richard E. and John T. Cacioppo (1986), *Communication and Persuasion: Central and Peripheral Routes to Attitude Change.* New York: Springer-Verlag.

Preston, Ivan L. (1970), "A Reinterpretation of the Meaning of Involvement in Krugman's Models of Advertising Communication," *Journalism Quarterly,* 47, 287-95.

Ray, Michael L. and Rajeev Batra (1983), "Emotion and Persuasion in Advertising: What We Do and Don't Know About Affect," in *Advances in Consumer Research,* Richard P. Bagozzi and Alice M. Tybout, eds. Ann Arbor, MI: Association for Consumer Research, 10, 543-548.

Russell, Bertrand (1912), *Problems of Philosophy.* New York: Oxford University Press.

Wright, Peter L. (1974), "Analyzing Media Effects on Advertising Responses," *Public Opinion Quarterly,* 38 (Summer), 195-205.

Zaichkowsky, Judith L. (1986), "Conceptualizing Involvement," *Journal of Advertising,* 15 (2), 4-14.

Zajonc, Robert B. (1980), "Feeling and Thinking: Preferences Need No Inferences," *American Psychologist,* 35, 151-175.

EFFECTS OF PRICE UNCERTAINTY ON CONSUMER REFERENCE PRICE AND PRICE THRESHOLDS

Tridib Mazumdar, Syracuse University
Sung Youl Jun, Syracuse University

ABSTRACT

Reference price is a central concept in pricing research. Research has shown that consumers use reference price for price judgments and brand choice decisions. It is also argued that there is a zone of indifference around the reference price where consumers are insensitive to price differences. That is, unless a purchase price exceeds or falls below certain thresholds, consumers do not perceive a "loss" or a "gain" respectively.

Despite the recognized role of reference price in price judgments, consumers are often found to exhibit considerable uncertainty about the reference point they should use to evaluate purchase prices. This research examines how price uncertainty may influence consumer reference price estimates. Recognizing that consumers may have a zone of indifference around the chosen reference point, we also investigate whether the locations of the loss and gain thresholds are symmetric around the reference point and how price uncertainty influences the locations of these thresholds.

In an experimental setting, uncertain subjects were provided with a uniform distribution of probable prices within a fairly wide range and were to asked to provide a point estimate of reference price of a to-be-purchased product. Based on a pretest, reference price was operationalized by the amount of money subjects would allocate for the proposed purchase. Subjects also indicated their loss and gain thresholds. Certain subjects were provided with a stable price which was set at the midpoint of the above uncertain price range and were asked to provide similar estimates.

Uncertain subjects provided a higher reference price estimate than certain subjects. Moreover, the absolute magnitudes of both loss and gain thresholds for uncertain subjects were higher, indicating an upward shift in the entire range of acceptable prices. The results also show that the loss threshold was closer to the reference price estimate than the gain threshold, implying an asymmetry in the locations of the thresholds. Price uncertainty influenced the two thresholds differently. The zone of indifference in the domain of loss was wider for uncertain subjects than for certain subjects. However, no such effect was found in the domain of gains. Implications of these findings for consumer price judgments are discussed.

For further information contact:
Tridib Mazumdar
Department of Marketing
School of Management
Syracuse University
Syracuse, NY 13244-2130.

THE INFLUENCE OF ORIGIN EVALUATION AND ORIGIN IDENTIFICATION ON RETAIL SALES

Pamela Kiecker, Texas Tech University
Dale F. Duhan, Texas Tech University

ABSTRACT

Johansson's (1988) model examined consumers' propensity to use a product's region of origin as a cue in their product evaluation and purchase decision. The research reported here was designed to test Johansson's conceptualization of the influence of origin cues on sales. Specifically, the research (1) measured the predictive value of origin information in a particular market, then (2) used the measured predictive value to forecast the impact of origin information on sales and, finally, (3) tested the forecast in a field experiment.

The test involved two research phases. In the first phase, the market was surveyed to determine the relative evaluation of region of origin as a source for the products used in the study. In the second phase, a field experiment manipulated the presentation of origin information in a retail setting to determine the relative effect of origin information on retail sales for products from a specific region.

To control for potential difficulties presented by brand origin and product origin ambiguities, table wines were selected as the product category for this research. The selection of this product category, in which both the products and the brands are unique, eliminates both product and brand ambiguity and also makes each product/brand combination unique, thus simplifying the research design. Within the table wine category, Texas was chosen as the region of origin.

The data collection instrument used in the first phase of the study surveyed wine "enthusiasts" regarding a variety of general issues related to wine purchase and consumption. Specific items were included to determine the respondents' evaluations of Texas wines compared to other domestic and imported wines. A total of 928 mail questionnaires were completed and returned, resulting in a response rate of 31 percent.

Results of the survey demonstrated the predictive value of the Texas origin information and the lower evaluation of Texas as an origin for wines. Following Johansson's conceptualization, these findings allowed us to predict that emphasizing the origin of Texas wines via the retail setting would negatively affect the sales and market position of those wines.

The field experiment used to test this prediction involved an in-store manipulation of the presentation of origin information. The manipulations involved three display alternatives in each of three retail stores: (1) the "Texas Set" treatment in which all Texas wines were presented exclusively in a Texas wine display, (2) the "Varietal" treatment in which Texas wines were displayed with other domestic and imported wines by variety (e.g., cabernet, chardonnay, etc.), and (3) the "Combo" treatment which was the combination of both the Texas display and the Varietal display.

The results of the field experiment confirmed the predictions regarding market position for the Texas wines. The "Texas Set" treatment resulted in the lowest share for Texas wines (2.8% of all wine sales). The "Varietal" treatment resulted in the highest share (9.5%). The third treatment, "Combo," resulted in a share level between the other two treatments (5.5%). The differences among these share levels were examined with two-way analysis of variance using "store" as a second factor.

The overall model indicates that both the display treatment and store are significant factors. The significance of the store factor indicates that differences among the stores (other than size which was controlled by using market share rather than absolute sales levels), such as store layout, geographic location of store, type of clientele, were useful in accounting for the variance in market share. Treatment means were further analyzed by t-tests (least significant differences). All of the means were found to be significantly different from one another.

The results of this study also illustrate that the use of a special retail display does not always have a positive (or even a neutral) effect on the sales of the products featured in the display. In this case, the research not only illustrates this potential effect, but also provides an explanation for the effect. It would appear that retail managers that are faced with decisions about the use of origin information should first identify whether the image of the origin to be featured is positive or negative within that product category.

For further informaiton please contact: Pamela Kiecker or Dale Duhan
Texas Tech University
P.O. Box 4320
Lubbock, Texas 79409

COUNTRY OF ORIGIN EFFECT: THE NEW CONCEPTUALIZATION AND ALTERNATIVE MODELS

Yangjin Yoo, University of South Carolina-Columbia

ABSTRACT

This study provides an alternative view of country of origin effect by decomposing the country of origin (CO) construct into two separate constructs: country of origin information and attitude toward a country (A_c). The four alternative mediating roles of A_c on attitude toward foreign products are proposed with other constructs.

INTRODUCTION

Since Schooler (1965) reported the effect of country of origin on the evaluation of products, controversy has surrounded the saliency of the construct. For example, Bilkey and Nes (1982) summarized the empirical findings of the country of origin effect (COE), and concluded that "within the limits of the methodologies employed, all of the studies reviewed indicate that the country of origin does influence buyer perceptions of the products involved" (p. 94). On the other hand, the salience of country of origin effect has been challenged by others (Erickson, Johansson, and Chao 1984; Johansson, Douglas, and Nonaka 1985). For example, Johansson et al. (1985 p. 395) asserted that "country of origin effects may be less significant than has generally been believed."

The conflicting views regarding the importance of COE led the author to review the empirical CO studies reported (Yoo 1989)[1]. Yoo concluded that 22 of the 25 studies reviewed found significant COEs and that advancements in methodology and new approaches had been made in CO studies. However, due to the various specification levels of products used and various operationalizations of the COE construct (discussed later) definite conclusions could not be reached by simply reviewing the reported research of others. The lack of a coherent theory or framework for COE studies also indicates that additional work in this area is necessary. Hence, the purpose of this paper is to provide an alternative view of country of origin by decomposing the country of origin construct into two separate constructs: country of origin information (COI) and attitude toward a country (A_c). Alternative causal models incorporating the new construct A_c and the refined construct of COI, together with other salient attributes and attitude toward *foreign* products (A_{fp}), is proposed. The mediator role of A_c is used to develop the causal relationship with A_{fp}.

CONCEPTUAL AND METHODOLOGICAL ISSUES OF PREVIOUS STUDIES

The theoretical perspectives of country of origin effects are limited and the empirical results of CO studies lack solid theoretical grounding for the relationships posited among the constructs. Even though more than half of the studies reviewed by Yoo used attitudinal measures for either dependent or independent variables, only a few studies provided a clear conceptual/theoretical basis for COE. These studies included image variables as part of the belief-attitude model (Erickson, et al. 1984), belief-attitude relationship (Johansson et al. 1985), and causal modeling of country image, belief, and attitude (Han 1989). Hong and Wyer (1989, 1990) used an information processing perspective and product-attribute information on product evaluation to explain COEs. Johansson (1989) used country stereotype as one of salient attributes in his integrative framework of determinants and effects on the propensity to use "Made-In" labels.

Yoo's review also suggested that some of the methodological limitations raised by Bilkey and Nes (1982) remain: namely, the use of intangible product, use of survey, and a tendency to use single cues. Most studies used intangible cues when the product was being evaluated. Only one study used tangible product by intercepting and asking subjects whether they were aware of the country of origin of the product just purchased (Hester and Yuen 1987). Two studies used visual cues by providing pictures of the products involved in addition to questionnaires (Brown et al. 1987; Thorelli et al. 1989). Most of the studies used the survey method and only about 20% of the studies used experimental design (Jaffe and Nebenzahl 1984; Johansson and Nebenzahl 1986; Ettenson et al. 1988; Thorelli et al. 1989; Hong and Wyer 1989). Nine of the 25 studies reviewed (7/25 in Bilkey and Nes' review) used multiple cues in their investigation of the relative effects of CO.

Most studies found significant COEs. However, three studies did not. Erickson et al. (1984) found that the CO does have a direct effect on beliefs, but not on attitudes (indirectly through beliefs). Johansson et al. (1985) found that the CO has a less significant effect than other variables such as familiarity and knowledge about product class; COEs occur predominantly in relation to the evaluation of specific attributes rather than overall evaluations. Ettenson, Wagner and Gaeth (1988) found that CO information accounted for little of the explained variance (Effect size: $\omega^2 = 3\%$). The results of Ettenson et al. (1988) study suggest that the COE may diminish as the amount of information available to the consumer increases. Since methodological issues and limitations tend to remain, along with limited use of theory to justify the relationship among the constructs, the closer examination of the theoretical and methodological issues raised by multi-cue studies and problems of specification level of products used and operationalization of CO is provided in the following section.

Multi-Cue Studies and Relative Importance of COE

For the multi-cue studies of CO, it is difficult to judge which cue is more effective without a measure of relative importance among the variables involved. To evaluate the relative importance of the variables included in multi-cue studies, comparisons of the coefficients among variables in structural equations were used in three studies (Erickson et al. 1984; Johansson et al. 1985; Han 1989). The measure of effect size was used in two studies that use experimental designs (Ettenson et al. 1988; Thorelli et al. 1989). Ettenson et al. (1988) used omega squared (ω^2) to assess the relative importance of the six attributes to participants in each group. They found that fiber content and price were the most important attributes for both males and females in the purchase of apparel products. However, COE accounted for only a small percent (4 percent for female and 3 percent for male) of the variance in the apparel purchase decision. Thorelli et al. (1989) found significant main effects of CO on their dependent variables (quality perception, overall attitude, and purchase intention) with a small effect size $(\omega^2 = .02 \text{ to } .04)$ for the CO variable. The *small effect size* of CO in experimental studies (or the small coefficient in structural equations in surveys) might be due to the dominance of the major variables chosen in multi-cue settings, which vary from product to product (familiarity, ownership, and attribute of a car: Erickson et al. 1984; Johansson et al. 1985, warranty of product and store image: Thorelli et al. 1989, and style and price for apparel: Ettenson et al. 1988).

Problem of Specification Level of Products Used and Operationalizations of CO

Various levels of products specifications and different operationalizations of constructs in the CO studies were used in the studies reviewed. For example, even in the single category of a product, such as a car, a variety of specifications were used for eliciting the image or the COE; from the full specification level such as brand and model of car to nearly zero specification level. These different levels of product specification used in previous studies might cause confounding with other variables (brand, familiarity or knowledge of product, experience, etc.) or lack of control over the subjects' cognitive processing. When a very specific cue (e.g., Toyota Celica in Erickson et al. 1984; Johansson et al. 1985) was used to evaluate multiple attributes of the product, the major role of the other factors, such as the familiarity and ownership of specific car, could be the reason for the small effect size of CO. On the other hand, the lack of product specification ("Cars from _____ Country" in Brown et al. 1987) could be the reason for the overestimation/underestimation the COE. For example, Brown

et al. (1987) asked subjects to rate cars from six countries to measure attitude toward European, Japanese, and U.S. cars. Those subjects actually owned cars from seven different countries and twenty-one different car makers. Therefore, actual ownership of a car would inflate or deflate the effects of CO in the attribute-attitude model. Thus, when insufficient specification of the cue (car) is provided, it is difficult to examine what is being elaborated in the subjects' cognition processes.

A more serious problem of specification of cue is encountered by three image studies that did not specify the product category (Narayana 1981; Jaffe and Nebenzahl 1984; Darling and Arnold 1988). In such situations, the subjects can process any information related to the specified country, if they have it. Thus, it is difficult to control what has been encoded and what is being retrieved by the subjects when asked to evaluate country image or product attributes. To evaluate the relative importance of COE in multi-cue studies, whether effect size is small or not, the relevant level of product specification when operationalizing CO construct need to be used. The following section offers an alternative operationalization of CO construct by decomposing COE into country of origin information or indicator[2] (COI) and attitude toward country (A_C).

AN ALTERNATIVE CONCEPTUALIZATION OF CO AND MODELS FOR COE

Country of Origin as A_C and COI

Since the CO affect product evaluations either solely or with other attributes, the separation of COE from other product related attributes is the first step toward developing an A_C construct. This approach is supported by the results of multi-cue studies which show that the COE, when treated separately from other product relevant attributes (Erickson et al. 1984; Johansson et al. 1985; Han 1989 etc.), was small or non existent. When the CO construct is operationalized as an image construct, the COE could be confounded with brand image. For example, when a well known brand name is exposed (e.g., Sony) with known country (Japan), the COE may be small or non-existent given the dominant role of brand image in product evaluation. However, when the unknown brand name with a well known country (e.g., "brand X from Japan") is exposed, the CO could be used as a cue for product quality. Therefore, CO, when it is operationalized as either a country image ("consumers' general perception of quality for products made in a given country," Bilkey and Nes 1982) or a simple manifestation of CO (Made In _____) is not sufficient to represent the CO construct. Hence, an alternative conceptualization of CO as A_C and COI is proposed.

Attitude toward the country (A_C) *is defined here as a predisposition to respond in a consistently favorable or unfavorable manner to a particular country.* This definition of A_c implies that it is a more precise construct than country image, country stereotype, or a simple manifestation of CO, since the A_c could be acquired by either product or non-product related prior experiences. The non-product related experience could be obtained from any *direct* prior experience or involvement with a specific country (travel, being an employee of a foreign subsidiary in home country, culture or language learning, etc.) or any *indirect* prior experience or concurrent exposure to any information or news regarding a specific country (human rights reports, reports of demonstrations regarding political issues, economic performance of a foreign county, especially trade conflict to the home country, etc.).

Obviously, the A_c formed through direct experience is stronger than that of indirect experience (i.e., in terms of intensity). Notice that A_c, as defined here, is similar to the attitude toward an ad A_{ad}, (MacKenzie, Lutz, and Belch 1986, pp. 130-131), since the purpose of developing an A_c construct is to find the causal relationship, if any, with the attitude toward foreign products (A_{fp}) by substituting A_c with A_{ad}. If the role of A_c is assumed to behave similarly to the role of A_{ad} in its causal relationship with attitude toward a brand (A_b) as suggested by others (Mitchell and Olson 1981; MacKenzie et al. 1986; Homer 1990, etc.), then A_c could be viewed as a mediator to A_{fp}. Some of previous studies indicates CO has direct effect on A_b and/or indirect effect on A_b through belief (Erickson et al. 1984; Han 1989). Hence, the mediator role of CO (A_c in this study) allows using the similar assumption of A_{ad} in role of mediator. Therefore, the mediator effects models of A_c on A_{fp} that are proposed are similar to the mediator effects models of A_{ad} on A_b (Mitchell and Olson 1981; MacKenzie et al. 1986; Homer 1990).

The country of origin information/indicator (COI) is defined as *manufactured or assembled in ____ country*. Thus, COI provides more specific information than a "Made In" label. The relationships between COI and other product related salient attributes (b_i) seems to be enduring, as previous studies using "Made In" labels suggest. For example, Johansson asserts that "the country of origin label provides a brief summary of the actual attributes of a product" in his simplified information processing perspective of the use of the "Made In" label (Johansson 1989, p. 51). Further, this "Made In" label, as an extrinsic summary cue, could be used for inference or as a proxy: "The cue might be used by the customer to guess the attributes of a product (a cognitive "inference" effect); to simplify information processing (a cognitive "proxy" effect) . . ." Johansson (1989 p. 55). This cognitive inference effect of the "Made In" label shows how COI in the proposed models is related to beliefs concerning other intrinsic product attributes (b_i) of foreign made products, hence COI is related to cognition of foreign products (C_{fp}).

Hong and Wyer (1990) also found that CO (as "Made In" label) can affect interpretation of information about specific product attributes. However, these effects are likely to be pronounced only when CO is conveyed sometime *before* the attribute descriptions, allowing a separate concept of the product to be formed. When presented the day before (24 hours), CO not only influenced product evaluation but also affected the interpretation of the attribute description. The existence of an *order effect* of CO supports the use of COI as an *antecedent to* other intrinsic attributes.

Alternative Models (Hypotheses) for Country of Origin Effect

The country image, which can be incorporated by A_c[3], has been used an antecedent to attitude toward *foreign* brands (A_b) in previous studies either *indirectly* through beliefs (Erickson et al. 1984 and the halo model of Han 1989) or *directly* (summary construct model of Han 1989) to brand attitude. Erickson et al. (1984) found that the CO, operationalized as an image variable, does have a direct effect on belief formation and not on attitude (only an *indirect effect* on attitude through belief). Similar to the four alternative structural specifications of the mediating role of A_{ad} (MacKenzie et al. 1986 and Homer 1990), four alternative structural specifications (hypotheses) of the mediating role of A_c are proposed here (see Figure 1). Furthermore, Mittal (1990) showed that when image attributes are added to the usual utilitarian attributes of A_{ad}, the role of beliefs as predictors is enhanced. Since the definition of A_c includes country image, the findings of Mittal (1990) provide the logic for the models presented in Figure 1.

The *affect transfer hypothesis* (ATH) posits a direct one-way casual flow from A_c to A_{fp}. This relationship is inferred by a significant *direct effect* of country image (A_c in this study) on A_b (A_{fp} in this study) explained by the coefficient of ß$_1$ in summary construct model of Han (1989). Based on this finding and the affective transfer hypothesis of A_{ad} literature (Mitchell and Olson 1981 etc.), the affective transfer hypothesis of A_c to A_{fp} is proposed in Figure 1.

The *dual mediation hypothesis* (DMH) specifies an indirect flow of causation form A_c through cognition (beliefs) of foreign product (C_{fp}) to A_{fp}, in addition to the direct effect postulated by ATH. This indirect effect (A_c --> C_{fp} --> A_{fp}) is implied by the halo model (country image --> beliefs --> brand attitude) of Han (1989). Han's two alternative causal models (the halo and the summary construct model) are especially useful to DMH since his models explain two casual paths depending on the familiarity with a country's products.

The *reciprocal mediation hypothesis* (RMH) portrays a reciprocal relationship between A_c and A_{fp}, with

FIGURE 1
Four Alternative Structural Specifications of Mediating Role of A_c

A. Affect Transfer Hypothesis

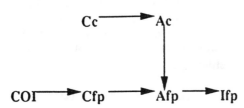

B. Dual Mediation Hypothesis

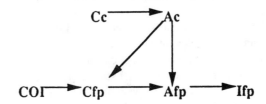

C. Reciprocal Mediation Hypothesis

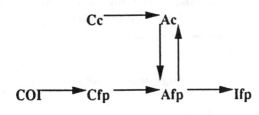

D. Independent Influences Hypothesis

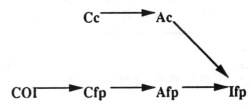

COI : Country of Origin Information/ Indicator
Cc   : Cognition of (Foreign) Country
Cfp : Cognition of Foreign Products
Ac   : Attitude Toward the Country
Afp : Attittude Toward the Foreign Products
Ifp : Intention to Purchase Foreign Products

causation flowing in both directions, as suggested by balance theory. Balance theory predicts that the consumer will attempt to achieve a balanced configuration by either liking both the country and the product from that country or disliking both. The application of balance theory to RMH can be explained by the example: if you love (hate) French wine, you might have a good (bad) attitude toward France (or *vice versa*).

The *independent inference hypothesis* (IIH) assumes no causal relationship between A_c and A_{fp}. Instead, A_c and A_{fp} are postulated to be independent determinants of purchase intention of foreign product(I_{fp}). The partial support for IIH can be found in most previous single-cue studies with purchase intention as the dependent variable, which have shown causation from CO (A_c in this study) to intention to purchase foreign products.

Each causal structure, shown in Figure 1, can be regraded *in its entirety* as a hypothesis about the role of A_c. Devising alternative hypotheses or using the "method of multiple hypotheses" was suggested by Platt (1964) for strong inference. However, due to the exploratory nature of theorizing concerning the mediating role of A_c, selecting a single hypothesis as the "best" explanation without empirical tests might prematurely eliminate viable information provided by the alternative models or theories. Rather, an effort to develop an overall model that could incorporate multiple hypotheses (or theories) may be the more fruitful approach to an understanding of COE. Hence, the overall model (as a full model for an incremental test) is derived by including all paths from the four alternative hypotheses (as restricted models) and by including consumer ethnocentrism (see Figure 2).

Consumer ethnocentrism is included in the overall model since it is a relevant construct for CO studies. The consumer ethnocentrism concept can be applied to "a predictor variable in correlational studies [*like the proposed model*]...potentially relevant predictors of attitude [*such as cognition of country and cognition of foreign product in the proposed model*] and buying intention and purchase behavior" (Shimp and Sharma 1987, p. 287). Their finding provides evidence of nomological validity in using theoretically related constructs such as "Attitudes toward foreign-made products" (*like* A_{fp} *in the model*) and "General feeling toward foreign-made products" (Shimp and Sharma 1987, p. 286).

By conceptualizing the CO construct as two sperate constructs such as COI and A_c, the proposed model could resolve the conflicting research findings of CO studies. Also, by incorporating information processing perspectives and cue utilization perspectives (Eroglu and Machleit 1989) and by the developing an A_c construct--which is similar to but more precise than country image construct--and by relating it to A_{fp}, the proposed model (Figure 2) explains all but one causal relationship. This path, between COI and A_c, is due to the decomposition of the country of origin construct. Notice that no causal relationship is hypothesized in the model between the two constructs. However, the COI could be used as a cue for retrieving A_c, if present.

DISCUSSION AND IMPLICATIONS

When the CO construct is decomposed into COI as a cue and A_c, we could find their causal relationships with other related constructs, especially A_{fp}. Then the distinctive nature of A_c could serve as a mediator to A_{fp} and attitude toward purchase of foreign products (Aact$_{fp}$), as the proposed models suggest. However, the nomological validity of the proposed model depends on empirical

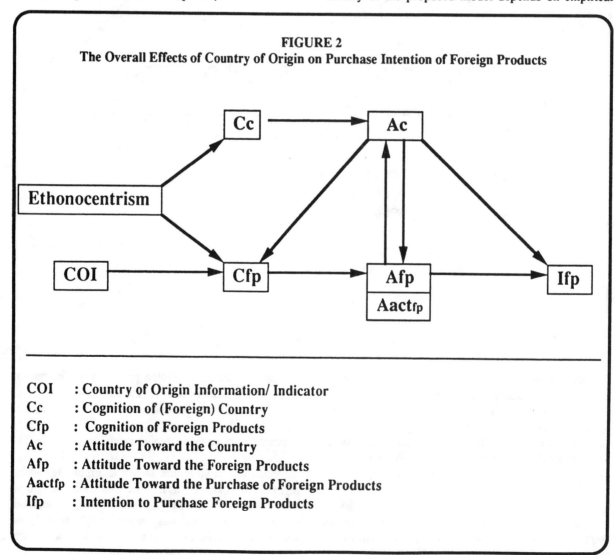

FIGURE 2
The Overall Effects of Country of Origin on Purchase Intention of Foreign Products

COI   : Country of Origin Information/ Indicator
Cc   : Cognition of (Foreign) Country
Cfp   : Cognition of Foreign Products
Ac   : Attitude Toward the Country
Afp   : Attitude Toward the Foreign Products
Aactfp : Attitude Toward the Purchase of Foreign Products
Ifp   : Intention to Purchase Foreign Products

testing in the future. To validate the model, the first step is to develop reliable and valid measures for the A_c construct. Then, using a structural modeling approach, discriminant validity of A_c can be evaluated. If A_c is a separable construct from the CO construct, then the decomposition of CO would reconcile the controversial issue of the salience of the COE.

The existence of A_c tests four alternative mediator roles of A_c on A_{fp} and $Aact_{fp}$ in the proposed models. If A_{fp} and $Aact_{fp}$ prove to be distinct constructs and behave differently from those of domestically produced products (A_{dp} and $Aact_{dp}$), these constructs might be quite useful to foreign marketers and domestic marketers. Since the implicit assumption that consumers behave differently toward home made products from foreign made products (due to negative attitude[4] in some cases) seem to be true, the implications of this study will be highly relevant to managers. Also previous studies comparing the (quality) images and buying intentions of domestic and foreign made products (I_{dp} vs. I_{fp}) showed that consumers tend to evaluate domestically produced brands or products favorably. The fact that "the perceived quality of imported brand is sagging in the aftermath of national fit of Japanese-bashing,......, U.S. car brands, meanwhile, are riding a wave of positive perceptions" (*The Wall Street Journal* 1992) clearly shows that county of origin effect is working in consumers and is therefore important to managers. Also the finding of Netemeyer et al. (1991), the testing of the reliability and validity of CETSCALE in European countries, implies that consumer ethnocentrism may be a universal phenomenon. These findings suggest that the decomposing of the CO construct into A_c and COI is more meaningful than using the CO construct confoundedly as "Made In" label, country images, and stereotyping of previous studies.

The COI, operationalized as "Assembled or Manufactured In" in this study, could retrieve an attitude toward *multiple*[5] countries. When multiple attitudes toward countries are retrieved and are conflicting in favorability, this conflict might *discount* the favorable brand attitude. For example, if a favorable attitude toward the brand origin country (Japan for Sony) and an unfavorable attitude toward the "assembled in" country (e.g., Malaysia) are retrieved simultaneously, this tension might affect on already established favorable attitude toward brand and therefore lower the purchase intention of "Sony assembled in a third country."

On the other hand, when the product is "assembled or manufactured" in the consumers' home country (e.g., Honda Accura), the favorable brand attitude (A_b) combined with the favorable attitude toward domestically produced foreign branded product[6] (A_{fp} with no or less negative effect of consumer ethnocentrism) would *elevate* the purchase intention of a foreign product (I_{fp}). Hence, the proper conceptualization of CO (as A_{fp} and COI) would provide the rationale for American firms using "Made in U.S.A. with imported (fabric) materials" label and for foreign firms using "Assembled in U.S.A. using Japanese parts" or "Sony made in U.S.A." As a firm globalizes its operations to reduce costs (move plant to low labor cost country or use global souring) the possible negative or positive effects of CO can and should be considered. For instance, the effect of CO indicating the use of components from less developed country than the brand origin country (e.g., Japanese brand assembled in South Asian countries, use of Mexican automobile parts by U.S. firms) should be considered by the firms. For another instance, when foreign firms use a lot of local components, either required by the "Local Content Law" or other reasons, this information (COI) could be used for promotional purpose designed to reduce any negative effect of consumer ethnocentric tendency.

ENDNOTES

[1] The same review format of Bilkey and Nes (1982), as a sequel to their review, and other evaluative criteria were used to investigate whether methodological limitations and remaining issues suggested by Bilkey and Nes (1982) were still existing and unresolved. Tables and the list of references (published 1980 - 1989) are available upon request to the author.

[2] The term 'indicator' will be used interchangeably with information. However, "indicator" implies visible information disclosed in label such as "Made In," "Assembled In," and "Manufactured In."

[3] Notice that the definition of A_c is assumed to be positively correlated with country image, hence A_c would have the same causal relationship with b_i and A_b as country image.

[4] The findings of Shimp and Sharma (1987, p. 286) shows that consumer ethnocentric tendency is *negatively* related to "attitude toward foreign-made product" (r = -.44 to -.59) and "general feeling toward foreign-made product" (r = -. 45 to -.69).

[5] As companies become globalized, it is common practice to assemble products in target (local) countries or to assemble in a third country and to export to target countries. For example, when the information regarding "Sony assembled in Malaysia" is exposed to consumers either from the label or from the other information sources, they are expected to retrieve an attitude toward Malaysia in addition to an attitude toward Japan.

[6] This is the case of "foreign-branded/US-made products" in Han and Terpstra's (1988) study of bi-national products. However, their definition of bi-national product does not include the example of "Sony assembled in Malaysia."

REFERENCES

Bilkey, W. J. and Erik Nes (1982), "Country of Origin Effect on Product Evaluation," *Journal of International Business Studies,* 13 (Spring/Summer), 89-99.

Brown, Jacqueline J., David C. Light and Gregory M. Gazda (1987), "Attitudes toward European, Japanese and US Cars," *European Journal of Marketing,* 21 (5), 90-100.

Darling John R. and Danny R, Arnold (1988), "Foreign Consumers' Perspective of the Products and Marketing Practices of the United States versus Selected European Countries," *Journal of Business Research,* 17, 237-248.

Erickson, Gary M., Johny K. Johansson, and Paul Chao (1984), "Image Variables in Multi-Attribute Product Evaluations: Country-of-Origin Effects," *Journal of Consumer Research,* 11 (September), 694-699.

Eroglu, Sevgin A. and Karen A. Machleit (1989), "Effect of Individual and Product-specific Variables on Utilizing Country of Origin as a Product Quality Cue," *International Marketing Review,* 6 (6), 27-41.

Ettenson, Richard, Janet Wagner, and Gary Gaeth (1988), "Evaluating the Effect of Country of Origin and the `Made in USA' Campaign: A Conjoint Approach," *Journal of Retailing,* 64 (Spring), 85-100.

Han, Min C. (1989), "Country Image: Halo or Summary Construct?" *Journal of Marketing Research,* 26 (May), 222-229.

_____ and Vern Terpstra (1988), "Country of Origin Effects for Uni-National and Bi-National Products," *Journal of International Business Studies,* (Summer), 235-255.

Hester, Susan B. and Mary Yuen (1987), "The Influence of Country of Origin on Consumer Attitude and Buying Behavior in the United States and Canada," in *Advances in Consumer Research,* Melanie Wallendorf and Paul Anderson, eds. Provo, UT: Association for Consumer Research, 14, 538-542.

Homer (1990), "The Mediating Role of Attitude Toward the Ad: Some Additional Evidence," *Journal of Marketing Research,* 28 (February), 78-86.

Hong, Sung-Tai and Robert S. Wyer, Jr. (1989), "Effects of Country-of-Origin and Product-Attribute Information on Product Evaluation: An Information Processing Perspective," *Journal of Consumer Research,* 16 (September), 175-187.

_____ and _____ (1990), "Determinants of Product Evaluation: Effects of Time Interval between Knowledge of a Product's Country of Origin and Informational about Its Specific Attributes," *Journal of Consumer Research,* 17 (December), 277-288.

Jaffe, Eugne D. and Israel D. Nebenzahl (1984), "Alternative Questionnaire Formats for Country of Image Studies," *Journal of Marketing Research,* 21 (November), 463-471.

Johansson, Johny K. (1989), "Determinants and Effects of the Use of 'Made in' Labels," *International Marketing Review,* 6 (1), 47-58.

_____ and Israel D. Nebenzahl (1986), "Multinational Production: Effects on Brand Value," *Journal of International Business Studies,* 17 (3), 101-126.

_____, Susan P. Douglas, and Ikujiro Nonaka (1985), "Assessing the Impact of Country Origin on Product Evaluations: A New Methodological Perspectives," *Journal of Marketing Research,* 22 (November), 388-396.

MacKenzie, Scott B., Richard J. Lutz, and George E. Belch (1986), "The Role of Attitude Toward the Ad as a Mediator of Advertising Effectiveness: A Test of Competing Explanations," *Journal of Marketing Research,* 23 (May), 130-143.

Mitchell, Andrew A. and Jerry C. Olson (1981), "Are Product Attribute Beliefs the Only Mediator of Advertising Effects on Brand Attitude?" *Journal of Marketing Research,* 18 (August), 318-332.

Mittal, Banwari (1990), "The Relative Role of Brand Beliefs and Attitude Toward the Ad as Mediators of Brand Attitude: A Second Look," *Journal of Marketing Research,* 27 (May), 209-219.

Narayana, Chem L. (1981), "Aggregate Images of American and Japanese Products: Implication on International Marketing," *Columbia Journal of World Business,* 16 (Summer), 31-35.

Netemeyer, Richard G., Srinivas Durvasula, and Donald R. Lichenstein (1991), "A Cross-National Assessment of the Reliability and Validity of the CETSCALE," *Journal of Marketing Research,* 28 (August), 320-327.

Platt, John R. (1964), "Strong Inference," *Science,* 146 (October 16), 347-353.

Schooler, Robert D. (1965), "Product Bias in the Central American Common Market," *Journal of Marketing Research,* 2 (November), 394-397.

Shimp, Terence A. and Subhash Sharma (1987), "Consumer Ethnocentrism: Construction and Validation of the CETSCALE," *Journal of Marketing Research,* 24 (August), 280-289.

The Wall Street Journal (1992), "Imports' Image Sag," (March 13), B8.

Thorelli, Hans B., Jeen-Su Lim and Jongsuk Ye (1989), "Relative Importance of Country of Origin, Warranty and Retail Store Image on Product Evaluations," *International Marketing Review,* 6 (1), 35-46.

Yoo, Yangjin (1989), "Country or Origin: Update and Future," *Working Paper,* University of South Carolina.

EFFECTS OF BRAND IMAGE AND MULTIPLE COUNTRY ORIGINS ON PRODUCT EVALUATION

Tiger Li, Michigan State University

ABSTRACT

The effects of brand image and multiple country origins on product evaluation are examined. The results show that in between-brand evaluation, buyers prefer the product with superior brand image to the product with inferior brand image regardless of country origin. In within-brand evaluation, buyers prefer the product with superior image of country origin to the product with inferior image of country origin regardless of brand name.

INTRODUCTION

International buyer behavior researchers assume that buyers' attitudes to a product are influenced by two information factors: brand image and country origin. Over the past two decades two streams of research have been formed to study the effects of the two factors on product evaluation. However, for a long time the two research streams were fairly independent of each other. As observed by Johansson (1989) research on brand image rarely brought effects of country of origin into consideration while study of country image seldom mentioned brand name impact.

In recent years, a number of researchers have made considerable efforts to integrate the two streams of research. Johansson, Douglas and Nonaka (1985) constructed a conceptual model to synthesize the effects of country origin, brand name and other product information. Han (1989) suggested that both brand image and country image may serve as a summary construct.

New developments in international business call for further integration of the two research streams. For the past decade, many corporations have shifted part of their manufacturing capacity abroad to reduce costs in labor and raw materials. As a result, one can observe an interesting phenomenon in the market: the emergence of one brand with multiple country origins. For example, Nike shoes, a brand with high reputation among young buyers, are made not only in the U.S. but also in South Korea and China. Sony stereos, another favorable consumer product, are manufactured in Japan, Singapore and Malaysia.

A number of questions arise from this multiple country origin phenomenon. How do buyers evaluate a product with multiple origins? Do they differentiate products with the same brand name but different origins? If it is a product with a well-known brand name, will buyers still refer to country image for evaluation?

OBJECTIVE

This study intends to explore the above issues by examining effects of brand image and multiple country origins on product evaluations. In particular, we will focus on two types of evaluations: between-brand evaluation and within-brand evaluation. Between-brand evaluation involves evaluation of products of different brands, e.g. Sony vs. GE. Within-brand evaluation refers to evaluation of products with the same brand name but different country origins, e.g. Sony made-in Japan vs. Sony made in Taiwan.

BETWEEN-BRAND EVALUATION

In between-brand evaluation we are mainly concerned with products with different brand images. We propose that when products have different brand images buyers are more favorable to the product with a superior brand image than the product with an inferior brand image regardless of country of origin. Buyers would prefer the product with a superior brand image because a superior image conveys information of better qualities and buyers are able to differentiate the two products based on brand image alone. Therefore:

H1: When products have different brand images, buyers are more favorable to the product with a superior brand image than the product with an inferior brand image, regardless of country of origin.

WITHIN-BRAND EVALUATION

In within-brand evaluation, buyers evaluate products with the same brand but different country origins. We propose that in such evaluation buyers are more favorable to the product with a superior country image than the product with an inferior country image. Brand image will not affect evaluation since buyers evaluate products with the same brand name. Country image becomes the determinant since products can be differentiated only from country image.

In within-brand evaluation there exist two different cases: evaluation of products with the same superior brand and evaluation of products with the same inferior brand. Country Image plays different roles in each case.

In the case of products with the same superior brand, buyers would prefer the product with a superior country image because such a country image reinforces the brand image. The effect of reinforcement arises from the fact that a good brand is often associated with a favorable country of origin. For example, Rolex always reminds people of Switzerland. By the same token, an inferior country image would cause buyers to underrate the product with the same brand since such a country image is inconsistent with the brand name. For instance, what would consumer think about Rolex made in Hongkong?

In the case of products with the same inferior brand name, buyers would offer higher scores for the product with a superior country image since such an image may compensate for the poor brand name. On the other hand, a poor country image would further downgrade the product with a poor brand image.

H2: In within-brand evaluation, buyers are more favorable to the product with a superior country image than the product with an inferior country image. Brand image will not affect evaluation since buyers evaluate products with the same brand.

EXPERIMENT DESIGN

One product category - mid-priced stereo receiver is selected as the object of product evaluation. This product is chosen for two reasons. First, same brands with different made-in labels can be found in large numbers in this product category. Second, this product category has been found to offer more personal relevance to college students who would be chosen to evaluate the products (Hong and Wyer 1989).

Two brands, Sony and Realistic, are selected. Sony brand represents superior brand image and Realistic inferior brand image. The selection of these two brands was based on 1990 Consumer Report's ratings of mid-priced receivers and a pilot study conducted among college students.

Two countries, Japan and Malaysia, are used to represent different country origins. While Japan stands for superior image of country origin, Malaysia represents inferior image of country origin. Over the past 15 years products made-in Japan, particularly electronic products, have continuously won consumers' preference in regard to product quality. Malaysia, along with some other developing countries, is considered to have inferior country image concerning product quality (Bilkey and Nes 1982). In addition, Sony and Realistic electronic products can be found produced in both of these two countries.

The stimulus list was designed in the form of product brochure. Four lists were developed introducing four stereo receivers: Sony Made in Japan (SonyJ), Sony Made in Malaysia (SonyM), Realistic Made in Japan (RealJ), Realistic Made in Malaysia (RealM).

Two hundred nine college students were selected to evaluate each of the four products on a ten-point scale. They were chosen as the subjects because of their familiarity with stereos and their interest in purchasing such products.

RESULT

The mean evaluation scores of the four products were 8.291 (SonyJ), 7.004 (SonyM), 6.090 (RealJ), and 4.990 (RealM) respectively. ANOVA was applied to test the equality of the four means. The F test statistic was 220.66 at .0001 significance level, thus rejecting the null hypothesis that the means of the four products were equal.

Then, Fisher's Least Significant Difference was used to test our hypotheses. In between-brand evaluation, we observed that the mean scores of the two Sony products (SonyJ and SonyM) were significantly higher than those of the two Realistic products (RealJ) and (RealM), indicating the first hypothesis was supported. In within-brand evaluation, we found that the mean score of Sony made in Japan (SonyJ) was significantly higher than that of Sony made in Malaysia, and the mean score of Realistic made in Japan (RealJ) was significantly higher than that of Realistic Made in Malaysia (RealM), thus supporting the second hypothesis.

MANAGERIAL IMPLICATION

Our analysis shows that in between brand evaluation buyers appear to rely more on brand image than on country origin. This further confirms that building brand reputation should continue to be a priority for firms that wish to market their products successfully in the ever competitive markets.

However, the effect of country origin should not be ignored. Our findings demonstrate that the product with a better country origin outperformed that with an inferior country origin when the two products share similar brand image. Therefore, a company may be benefitted by emphasizing a good country origin while downplaying a poor one in product promotion.

For further information please contact:
Tiger Li
Department of Marketing and Transportation
Michigan State University
East Lansing, MI 48824

AN EXPLORATORY STUDY OF THE NEW PRODUCT INVESTMENT DECISION BY U.S. AND FINNISH MANAGERS

Stanley Slater, University of Colorado at Colorado Springs
Nils-Erik Aaby, University of Colorado at Colorado Springs

ABSTRACT

New products are essential to the long-term health and success of all businesses. A great deal of research has been done on the characteristics of successful new products but very little has been done on how managers actually make new product investment decisions. In this exploratory study we analyze similarities and differences in the decison making styles of U.S. and Finnish managers.

INTRODUCTION

New product development is one of business's most important activities. At 3M, products less than 5 years old account for 25% of sales. During the 1980's, profits from new products grew from one-fifth of corporate profits to one-third (Takeuchi and Nonaka 1986). Booz, Allen, and Hamilton (1982) found that new products have similar importance in a study of 700 firms competing in industrial and consumer markets.

However, several studies have shown that U.S. firms trail foreign competition in many aspects of the new product development process. To be successful, companies must make decisions faster, develop new products more rapidly, and deliver them more quickly than their competitors (Bower and Hout 1980). Stalk (1988) though, found that U.S. businesses often take twice as long as foreign competitors to get products to market. And while the U.S. is undoubtedly the world leader in new products from product line extensions (e.g., Honey Nut Cheerios), our leadership in innovative new products has slipped substantially as evidenced by the fact that since 1983, "the U.S. has lost share in total patents in 38 of 48 product categories, particularly in office computers, electronics, transportation equipment, and shipbuilding," (Dumaine 1991, p. 6).

The new product development and management process has been studied extensively for over 20 years. The most common approach has been to study the characteristics of new product successes and failures (e.g., Rothwell 1972; Cooper 1979; Calantone and Cooper 1981; Zirger and Maidique 1990). Characteristics of successful new product introductions include: (1) customer orientation (Rothwell 1972; von Hippel 1986); (2) unique and/or superior product (Cooper 1979; Cooper and Kleinschmidt 1987; Zirger and Maidique 1990); (3) marketing and technical proficiency (Cooper 1979; Zirger and Maidique 1990); (4) managerial excellence and commitment (Zirger and Maidique 1990; and (5) col-laboration and cooperation among all groups involved in product development (Quinn 1985; Labich 1988; Zirger and Maidique 1990).

An aspect of the new product development process that has received relatively little attention though, is the new product investment decision itself. In other words, what factors do managers use to determine the attractiveness of a new product opportunity? This issue is important for two reasons. First, given the large number of studies of characteristics of successful and unsuccessful new products, we now have a fairly clear concept of the desired attributes of a new product program. Are these the characteristics that managers value most highly? Second, evidence suggests that U.S. managers use information cues differently than their Japanese and European counterparts (e.g., Kotabe, Duhan, Smith and Wilson 1991). Are U.S. managers more or less risk averse than their foreign counterparts? Does the same cue have different implications for U.S. and foreign managers.

Characteristics of Successful New Products

Product Cues: Attractive new product opportunities are defined by specific company/product and market characteristics. In most new product development studies the most important determinant of success is buyers' perception of product superiority (e,g., Cooper 1979; Cooper and Kleinschmidt 1987; Zirger and Maidique 1990). This finding is substantiated by the product diffusion research that points out the importance of incremental value to buyers in the new product adoption process (e.g., Mahajan, Muller, and Bass 1990).

Familiarity Cues: A second critical internal characteristic is "strategic focus" (Zirger and Maidique 1990). It is well accepted that familiarity with either the technology or the market reduces risk and increases the likelihood of success (e.g., Roberts and Berry 1985; Sykes 1986). Market and technological familiarity enable firms to utilize existing internal and external information sources and networks. Familiarity also allows the firm to build on existing capabilities and resources.

Market Sturcture Cues: Influential market characteristics include rate of market growth, competitive intensity, and buyer power, among others. While market structure generally influences a business's performance (e.g., Porter 1980) and market growth provides the best opportunity for new product success (Lambkin and Day 1989; Lieberman and Montgomery 1988), it seems that market characteristics have a lesser influence on new product success than do internal characteristics (Zirger and Maidique 1990). This is because, even in the early stages of a market's development, buyers must be induced to switch from an old "solution" to a new "solution", or technology (Cooper and Schendel 1976). This inducement must take the form of added value for the buyer through product or service superiority.

Thus in this study we examine the following propositions:

P1 Managers weight product superiority cues most heavily in the new product investment decision.

P2 Managers utilize market and technological familiarity cues more than market structure cues but less than product superiority cues in the new product investment decision.

P3 Managers place the lowest emphasis on market structure cues in the new product investment decision.

Cross Cultural Comparisons of the New Product Investment Decision

The popular business press (e.g., Dumaine 1991) regularly castigates U.S. business for losing its edge in product development and innovation to foreign competition. A common reason cited for this is the preoccupation with current earnings, and consequent risk aversion, of U.S. managers (Hayes and Wheelwright 1984). This is not purely an American problem though, as a recent study (Kotabe 1990) found that Japanese managers emphasize both product and process innovation more than European managers. We therefore also examine the following proposition:

P4 Managers from different cultures have different perceptions of the overall attractiveness and risk of the same set of new product investment opportunities.

It also seems that managers from different cultures have a different perspective on the importance of different cues. This may be the result of valuing different objectives as in the case of a Japanese preference for market share and a U.S. preference for profitability or because structural conditions in home markets (e.g., regulation, taxation, collusion) make certain characteristics more or less important. For example, Kotabe et al. (1991) found that Japanese and U.S. managers differed in the perceived veracity of a number of the PIMS Principles, therefore:

P5 Managers from different cultures utilize information cues differently in reaching new product investment decisions.

RESEARCH DESIGN

New Product Decision Cues

After an extensive review of the literature on the new product investment decision, we decided to use as our predictor variables the eight factors that Roure and Maidique (1986) identified as the most important factors in the new venture funding decision. These variables effectively represent the variety of factors discussed in the literature and are few enough in number for respondents to cognitively process the information in them.

The general cues and specific variables used are: **Product Superiority:** (1) performance superiority of the product; (2) cost superiority of the product; **Market/ Technological Familiarity:** (3) market familiarity; (4) technology familiarity; **Projected Performance:** (5) projected profitability; (6) target market share; **Market Structure:** (7) buyer power, and (8) market growth. Each variable has either 2 or 3 possible states. For example, compared to competitive products, this product represents either a minor performance improvement or a substantial performance improvement.

Design and Measurement

The eight predictor cues were combined into a factorial design which yielded a possible total of 576 unique information profiles. Bretton-Clark's Conjoint Designer program (c.f. Green and Srinivasan 1990) was used to establish an orthogonal fractional factorial design. This produced a set of 16 profiles which adequately represents the 576 possible combinations of the predictor variables. Each of the sixteen profiles describes a unique new product investment project.

For the dependent measure, respondents were asked to rank-order the 16 profiles from most attractive to least attractive. Except for the experimentally manipulated content on the 8 information cues, all other information on the profile was identical for all the profiles. For each of the 16 profiles, the order of the information cues was randomized to reduce order bias and to discourage respondents from simply sorting on one particular cue. This should produce more extensive cognitive involvement by respondents and lead to the evaluation of each new product investment profile based on its unique characteristics. Each respondent was also asked to rate (on a 1 to 7 scale) each profile in terms of attractiveness, riskiness, and probability of investment. In addition to the above a number of demographic characteristics were measured.

Pretest of Instrument

In order to test the instrument and the instructions, 12 MBA students completed the ranking and rating of each profile. The students were enrolled in an evening MBA program and all were part-time students, with full-time jobs and had 6-8 years of industrial experience. The pretest showed that the instructions were clear and that the cognitive task of rank-ordering the 16 new product investment profiles was manageable. Upon completion of the pre-test, the students' input was solicited.

Sample and Data Collection

To test the 5 propositions stated above, two convenience samples of Executive MBA students were used. One set of data was collected in the U.S.A. (N=55) and one in Finland (N=21). All respondents were middle level managers in large firms or senior managers in smaller firms. The average age of the respondents was 36 with 10 years of industrial experience. Their educational background was distributed equally among engineering and science, business, and liberal arts. All but 7 of the 76 respondents were employed full-time at the time of the study. A statistical comparison of personal and work related demographics showed no statistically significant differences between the two samples.

The data were collected at the beginning of two executive MBA seminars in marketing strategy. Each manager was given a questionnaire with an instruction sheet, the 16 product investment profiles and a page requesting demographic information. For each respondent, the order of the 16 new product investment profiles was randomized to reduce order bias. The respondents were asked to evaluate the information on each of the 16 new product investment profiles and to rank order the profiles in the order of preference. Subjects were then asked to provide a rating for each profile on a scale from 1 to 7 (from low to high) for attractiveness, risk, and probability of investment.

ANALYSIS AND RESULTS

Bretton-Clark's Conjoint Analyser was used to develop the information cue utilization profile for each of the samples. The results from this analysis are shown in Figure 1. Each of the bars in the figure shows the relative importance of each cue for the U.S. and the Finnish sample. The numbers in Figure 1 are index numbers indicate the relative importance of the 8 cues.

Use of New Product Cues

Based on prior research on the importance of new product characteristics to the success of the project, we expected product performance and cost reduction to be the most important cues in the decision process. While product performance seems to be one of the most important cues, along with market growth and technological familiarity, it does not carry a disproportionate weight in the decision. Furthermore, cost reduction appears to be of average importance only.

As expected, market familiarity and technology

familiarity seem to be important cues, particularly to U.S. managers. However, technology that is "new to us" seems to be a favorable cue. In another seeming contradiction to earlier research, the structural factor of market growth appears to be one of the most important influences on the new product investment decision. Thus, while we do not statistically analyze the relationships among the cues, judgementally it appears that both U.S. and Finnish managers utilize cues somewhat differently from what we expected.

Comparison of U.S. and Finnish Decision Making

In examining differences between the U.S. and Finnish samples, we analyzed whether the 2 groups, on average, perceived the portfolio of 16 profiles to be different in terms of overall attractiveness, perceived risk, or probability of investment. To assess proposition P4, simple t-tests were conducted. No differences were found between the groups of managers.

From the analysis of individual cues, market growth and product performance appear important to both Finnish and U.S. managers. The Finnish managers seem to prefer high performing products products that yield high market growth, perhaps reflecting the limitations of their small domestic market. The U.S. managers do also, but to a lesser extent. The U.S. managers appeared to rely heavily on new product investment projects that involve technology that is "new to us", confirming an American preoccupation with technology. This leads us to think that our propositions P1 and P2 are too simplistic. Perhaps in some markets, cultures, and/or industries, product cues are most important (i.e. U.S. with product performance and technology) while in other (perhaps smaller home markets) markets, market growth potential is more important. It is interesting to note that type of buyer appears to be of little importance to either sample while the U.S. managers appear to put more emphasis of target market selection, reflecting an objective of market penetration rather than market expansion.

DISCUSSION AND CONCLUSION

While this study can only be described as exploratory and suggestive, we believe that its results are interesting and warrant additional work in this area. First, while there is a large body of research on determinants of new product success, investment decisions do not seem to utilize the suggested cues. Why does it seem that managers' decision making frameworks do not incorporate the cues as the research indicates they should? One possible explanation for our findings is that while our sample consists of experienced managers, they are not necessarily involved with the new product management process. Future research should focus on new product investment decision participants.

Also, it has been suggested (e.g., Gupta 1984; Szilagyi

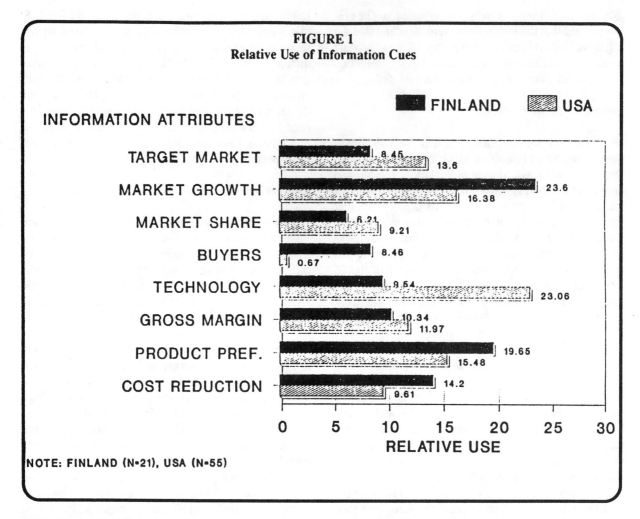

FIGURE 1
Relative Use of Information Cues

INFORMATION ATTRIBUTES

FINLAND   USA

Attribute	Finland	USA
TARGET MARKET	8.46	13.6
MARKET GROWTH	23.6	16.38
MARKET SHARE	6.21	9.21
BUYERS	8.46	0.67
TECHNOLOGY	9.54	23.06
GROSS MARGIN	10.34	11.97
PRODUCT PREF.	19.65	15.48
COST REDUCTION	14.2	9.61

RELATIVE USE

NOTE: FINLAND (N=21), USA (N=55)

and Schweiger 1984) that a manager's personal characteristics including personality traits such as propensity for risk, biographical background including functional and industry experience, and managerial style such as a preference for entrepreneurial or administrative behaviors, will influence the type of decisions that a manager will make. It may be that individual decisions are based more on a manager's personal style and less on rational analysis of a particular situation. Future research on managers' decision making styles should consider these theoretically important personal influences.

Another important issue is whether new product success research that has been conducted in the major industrialized countries can be generalized to smaller or lesser developed countries. Are the determinants for success dependent on the market structure of the target economy? This could have major implications for companies that are looking to export for growth and profit opportunities and could explain differences in the managerial importance of cues from country to country. Finally, this type of study should be conducted in other major economies such as the U.K., Germany, and Japan. Only then can we develop any confidence in findings of cross-cultural similarity or difference.

It is premature to offer real "conclusions" about the new product investment decision-making process. In fact, the only conclusion that we can offer is that this work should be built upon. By better understanding the decision-making process, we can understand its shortcomings and suggest ways that businesses might improve the process. Given the importance of new products to business performance, this is a topic that should receive substantial attention.

REFERENCES

Booz Allen and Hamilton (1982), *New Products Management for the 1980s,* New York: Booz Allen and Hamilton.

Bower, Joseph L. and Thomas M. Hout (1988), "Fast-cycle Capability for Competitive Power," *Harvard Business Review,* (November/December), 110-118.

Calatone, Roger and Robert G. Cooper (1981), "New Product Scenarios: Prospects for Success," *Journal of Marketing,* 45 (Spring), 48-60.

Cooper, A. C. and D. Schendel (1976), "Strategic Responses to Technical Threats," *Business Horizons,* (February), 61-69.

Cooper, R. G. (1979), "The Dimensions of Industrial New Product Success and Failure," *Journal of Marketing,* 43 (Summer), 93-103.

_____and E. J. Kleinschmidt (1987), "New Products: What Separate Winners from Losers?," *Journal of Product Innovation Management,* 4, 169-184.

Dumaine, B. (1991), "Closing the Innovation Gap," *Fortune,* (December 2), 56-62.

Green, Paul E. and V. Srinivasan (1990), "Conjoint Analysis in Marketing Research: New Developments and Directions," *Journal of Marketing,* 54 (October), 3-19.

Gupta, Anil (1984), "Contingency Linkages Between Strategy and General Manager Characteristics: A Conceptual Examination," *Academy of Management Review,* 9 (3), 399-412.

Hayes, R. and S. Wheelwright (1984), *Restoring our Competitive Edge: Competing Through Manufacturing,* New York: John Wiley and Sons.

Kotabe, Masaaki (1990), "Corporate Product Policy and Innovative Behavior of European and Japanese Multinationals: An Empirical Investigation," *Journal of Marketing,* 54 (April), 19-33.

_____and Dale F. Duhan with David K. Smith, Jr. and R. Dale Wilson (1991), "The Perceived Veracity of PIMS Strategy Principles in Japan: An Empirical Inquiry," *Journal of Marketing,* 55 (January), 26-41.

Labich, K. (1988), "The Innovators," *Fortune,* (June 6), 49-64.

Lambkin, Mary and George Day (1989), "Evolutionary Processes in Competitive Markets: Beyond the Product Life Cycle," *Journal of Marketing,* 53 (July), 4-20.

Lieberman, Marvin, and David Montgomery (1989), "First-Mover Advantages," *Strategic Management Journal,* 9, 41-58.

Mahajan, Vijay, Eitan Muller, and Frank M. Bass (1990), "New Product Diffusion Models in Marketing: A Review and Directions for Research," *Journal of Marketing,* 54 (January), 1-26.

Porter, M. (1980), *Competitive Strategy.* New York: Free Press.

Quinn, J. B. (1985), "Innovation and Corporate Strategy: Managed Chaos," in *Technology in the Modern Corporation: a Strategic Perspective,* Mel Horwitch., ed. Pergamon Press, Inc.

Roberts E. B. and C. A. Berry (1985), "Entering New Businesses: Selecting Strategies for Success," *Sloan Management Review,* 26 (3), 3-17.

Rothwell, R. (1972), "Factors for Success in Industrial Innovations," *Project SAPPHO--A Commparative Study of Success and Failure in Industrial Innovation,* S.P.R.U.

Roure, J. B. and M. A. Maidique (1986), "Linking Prefunding Factors and High-Technology Venture Success: An Exploratory Study," *Journal of Business Venturing,* 3 (August).

Stalk, George, Jr. (1988), "Time - The Next Source of Competitive Advantage," *Harvard Business Review* 88 (July/August), 41-51.

Sykes, Hollister B. (1986), "Lessons From a New Venture Program," *Harvard Business Review,* (May/June), 69-74.

Szilagyi, A. D. and D. M. Schweiger (1984), "Matching Managers to Strategies: A Review and Suggested Framework," *Academy of Management Review,* 9 (4), 626-637.

Takeuchi, H. and I. Nonaka (1986), "The New New Product Development Game," *Harvard Business Review,* (January/February), 137-146.

Von Hippel, E. (1986), "Lead Users: A Source of Novel Product Concepts," *Management Science,* 32, (7) (July), 791-805.

Zirger, Billie Jo and Modesto A. Maidique (1990), "A Model of New Product Development: An Empirical Test," *Management Science,* 36 (7) (July), 867-883.

A PATENT BASED STUDY OF THE RELATIONSHIP BETWEEN INDUSTRY RESEARCH STRUCTURE AND RESEARCH ACTIVITY

William W. Keep, University of Kentucky
Glenn S. Omura, Michigan State University

ABSTRACT

New products and the technological changes that make them possible are increasingly important to both marketing academics and practitioners. Identifying factors that affect the technological change process is important because it is change at this level that makes future product introductions possible. Yet previous new product development studies often mix factors that influence the technological change process with those that affect the product introduction process.

Researchers in industrial organization (IO) economics have complimented marketing research by demonstrating the importance of including competitive relationships in models of industry innovation. However, various studies have reported inconsistent findings because of a lack of agreement regarding what constitutes the relevant industry.

The current paper has two purposes. First, the present research identifies factors that specifically influence the technological change process within a competitive environment. Factors that affect technological change prior to the launch of a new product or innovation are modelled and the relevant industry is narrowly defined to include only those firms actively researching in a specific technological area. This approach addresses two major weaknesses of previous research.

The second purpose of this paper is to demonstrate the use of a rich, publicly accessible, but underexploited database of competitor activities. The data for this study are patent filings in the U.S. Patent Office. Patent data is historical, objective, systematically collected, and readily available. Thus far this database has not been fully exploited by contributors to marketing literature. The current paper demonstrates how theory can be used to generate a managerially useful model for monitoring technological change via the patenting process.

Using the industrial organization (IO) approach from economics, the current research develops and tests a model of five variables hypothesized to influence the technological change process. The variables modelled are: the number of competing firms, the level of research concentration, competitor lead time, technological focus, and technological complexity. A sixth variable, the interaction between technological focus and technological complexity is also tested.

Each variable is operationalized in a manner that is both consistent with previous studies and unique to the nature of the patent classification scheme. The variables are operationalized at the patent subclass level. Technological change, the dependent variable, is measured as the amount of research activity observed in specific patent subclass from 1969 until 1990.

The model was tested using multiple regression with ordinary least squares (OLS) estimation and Pearson correlations. Analysis confirms that an industry's total research activity increases as the number of competitors increases or as technological complexity decreases. An industry's total research activity decreases when the aforementioned variables are in the opposite direction and when both technological complexity and technological focus are high. As originally tested the industry concentration variable was unstable. The variable was redefined as a dummy variable and was also found to be positively related to research activity at concentration levels below 40 percent.

The technological focus variable was removed because of high correlation between it and the interaction term. The lead time variable was not found to be significant.

The promising results provide ample opportunity to further refine the technological change model. The rich market information represented in the patent database argues for its greater utilization in emphasizing the technology core of the new product development strategy literature.

For further information please contact:
William W. Keep
University of Kentucky
Department of Marketing
345 Business & Economics Building
Lexington, KY 40506-0034

SOURCES OF GLOBAL COMPETITIVENESS IN THE U.S. PHARMACEUTICAL INDUSTRY: AN EQS APPLICATION

Poh-Lin Yeoh, Michigan State University

ABSTRACT

A critical issue in the study of multinational pharmaceutical competition is understanding the factors that are critical for global success. Global success in the industry is defined as the ability of a firm to develop and introduce fast moving new chemical entities (NCEs). For example, Barral (1990) defines an innovative NCE as a global product that is marketed in at least seven industrialized countries which include Japan, France, Germany, Italy, Switzerland, the U.S., and the U.K. Similarly, Grabowski (1989, 1990) argues that drugs which are marketed in a limited number of countries are not innovative drugs. In this study, the classification by Hass and Coppinger (1987) is used, that is, global NCEs are defined as drugs that demonstrate substantial multinational acceptance by six major countries. More appropriately, they call this the "6/4" rule.

Two major research questions that drive this study are:

1. What factors influence a firm's ability to develop and market drugs that are fast movers?

2. Are there any differences between early and late entrants in their ability to develop and market "fast-movers"?

Based on a critical analysis of the new product development and innovation literature, the following factors are identified to be critical dimensions of product success in the pharmaceutical industry: (a) therapeutic differentiation; (b) functional resource commitments in R&D and marketing; (c) source of innovation; (d) therapeutic market diversification; and (e) new product development efforts. The timing of entry variable was used to differentiated firms as early and late entrants. This similar classification scheme was also used by Urban et al. (1986) who suggested that entry order can best (parsimoniously, at least) be considered a dichotomy: early and late. The relationships among the variables are shown in Figure 1.

EQS, developed by Bentler (1985) is used to estimate this structural equation model across both groups -- early and late entrants. Overall, while findings from this study suggest that the choice to enter as an early or late entrant has important consequences for global competitiveness, there are also fundamental sources of global competitiveness in the pharmaceutical industry.

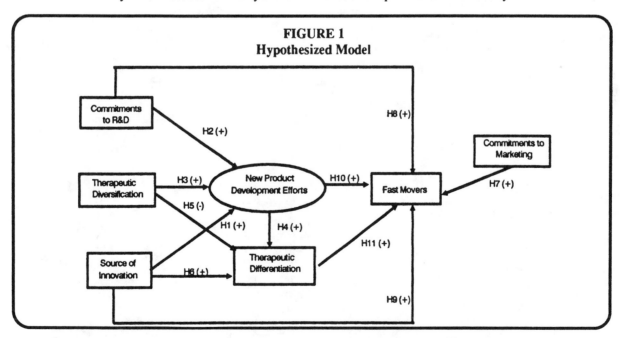

FIGURE 1
Hypothesized Model

REFERENCES

Bentler, P. M. (1985), *Theory and Implementation of EQS : A Structural Equations Program*. Los Angeles: BMDP Statistical Software.

Barral, P. E. (1990), Fifteen Years of Pharmaceutical Research Results Throughout the World (1975-1989). Paris: Foundation Rhone-Poulenc Sante.

Grabowski, Henry (1989), "An Analysis of U.S. International Competitiveness in Pharmaceuticals," *Managerial and Decision Economics*, 27-33.

_____(1990), "Innovation and International Competitiveness in Pharmaceuticals," in The *Proceedings of the 2nd International Joseph Schumpeter Society Meetings*, Ann Arbor, MI: University of Michigan Press, 167-185.

Hass, A. E. and P. Coppinger (1987), "USA Still Tops in New Chemical Entities," *Medical Marketing and Media*, (September), 45-48.

Urban, G. L., T. Carter, S. Gaskin, and Z. Mucha (1986), "Market Share Rewards to Pioneering Brands: An Empirical Analysis and Strategic Implications, *Management Science*, 32 (6), 645-659.

For more information contact:
Poh-Lin Yeoh
International Business Centers
Michigan State University
6 Kellogg Center
East Lansing, MI 48824

GAP ANALYSIS OF CUSTOMER SERVICE PERCEPTIONS WITHIN A CHANNEL DYAD

R. Mohan Pisharodi, Oakland University

ABSTRACT

The majority of customer service evaluation models in published literature are based on the measurement of <u>customer perceptions</u> of customer service variables and are founded in the implicit assumption that if supplier perceptions of customer service can be brought closer to customer perceptions of the same, the supplier will be able to provide service packages which will result in the desired customer response (such as more purchases, more customer satisfaction, etc.). While this assumption appears logical, it has not yet been validated through empirical research. The research reported in this paper seeks to empirically test this crucial assumption in the context of physical distribution customer service.

As a part of this research, the relationship between market response and supplier perceptions as well as customer perceptions of customer service was conceptualized in the form of a descriptive model based on three "gaps." In this model, market response (consisting of various attitudinal and purchase responses of the customer) is portrayed as the dependent variable. Market response is determined, to a great extent, by the gap between the customer's perceptions of actual service levels received and corresponding normative/comparison levels which the customer uses to evaluate service levels. This gap, in turn, is influenced by supplier-customer differences (or the gap) in the perception of comparison levels as well as parallel differences (or the gap) in the perception of actual service levels. In order to test the conceptualized relationships linking market response and the above mentioned gaps in customer service perceptions, four research hypotheses were developed and tested.

MEASUREMENT

Responses were collected through mail questionnaires from supplier-customer dyads (i.e., manufacturer-wholesaler/super-market chain pairs) in the grocery industry. While market response was measured directly, the three "gaps" were measured using computed measures. To facilitate the subtraction of scale values during the computation of differences in perception, only items which measured responses on ratio scales or on interval scales (e.g., time in days) were included. Usable responses were obtained from 52.63 percent of the manufacturers to whom questionnaires were mailed and from 64.47 percent of the customers to whom questionnaires were mailed. Data collection resulted in 91 usable units of analysis (supplier-customer pairs).

DATA ANALYSIS AND RESULTS

The analysis of the measurement model closely followed the updated procedure for scale development recommended by Gerbing and Anderson (1988). The measurement model was analyzed for unidimensionality using oblique multiple group factor analysis and for reliability using coefficient alpha. The values of standardized coefficient alpha for the indicator sets finally selected through this process ranged from 0.83 to 0.94.

The research hypotheses were tested using LISREL 7 on a variance-covariance matrix generated from the collected data. The results of statistical analysis provided support for the existence of a strong relationship between market response and the gap between customer perceptions of actual service levels and normative/comparison levels. This relationship was found to be positive in direction when normative levels are subtracted from actual levels during the computation of the gap. The results of data analysis also provided partial support for the relationships linking the above mentioned gap with the two gaps (normative and actual) between supplier and customer perceptions.

CONCLUSIONS AND IMPLICATIONS

The results of this research provide empirical support for the importance of supplier-customer differences in the perception of customer service levels. Moreover, the direction of difference (i.e., whose perception was higher) was found to be critical in ultimately determining the customer's evaluation of a supplier's customer service package. The results also highlighted the importance of monitoring normative and actual levels of customer service as perceived by both the customer and the supplier in a channel dyad. The findings of this research stress the need to pay more attention to the communication of customer service quality.

For further information please contact:
R. Mohan Pisharodi
Oakland University
School of Business Administration
Rochester, Michigan 48309-4401

SERVICE QUALITY IN A HIGH-TECH INDUSTRIAL MARKET: AN APPLICATION OF SERVQUAL

Leyland F. Pitt, University of Cape Town
Pierre Oosthuizen, University of Cape Town
Michael H. Morris, University of Central Florida

ABSTRACT

Literature relating to quality stresses the importance of measurement as a prerequisite to the attainment of quality. This study investigates the applicability of the SERVQUAL instrument for measuring the quality of high-tech industrial services. The results indicate that the model on which SERVQUAL is based is valid for the mainframe software industry, and that the SERVQUAL instrument, with some modification, is applicable.

INTRODUCTION

Schonberger and Knod (1988) indicate that quality has historically been the most undermanaged of customer wants. However, there is a growing recognition that quality can be used strategically in the marketplace, as it represents a key source of differentiation and competitive advantage. Luchs (1986) expounds on this theme by identifying quality as the most potent strategic weapon available to most businesses, citing data from the PIMS studies. The PIMS data suggest that there is a strong positive correlation between offering high quality products and services and profitability within industries.

While discussions of quality have historically focused on companies that make and sell products, recent years have witnessed increased emphasis on service quality. A key factor driving this interest in service quality was the development of the SERVQUAL scale (Parasuraman, Zeithaml, and Berry 1986). Clearly, the management of service quality is heavily dependent on the ability to conceptualize and measure quality in a service context, and SERVQUAL has made a significant contribution in this regard.

The expanding body of research on services has primarily been concerned with consumer services. Much less attention has been devoted to services within industrial markets. And yet, the market for industrial services has grown much more rapidly over the past decade than that for industrial products, with a growth rate exceeding 10 percent annually (Statistical Abstract 1990). Further, a number of researchers have suggested that indus-trial services are different than consumer services, and that quality is the over-riding concern among purchasers of industrial services (Jackson and Cooper 1988; Singh 1990).

The purpose of this paper is to assess the applicability

of SERVQUAL in an industrial context. The unique aspects of industrial services are first examined. Results are reported of a cross-sectional survey directed at customers of a mainframe software company in South Africa. An attempt is made to evaluate reliability as well as content, convergent, nomological, and discriminant validity.

THE DISTINCT NATURE OF INDUSTRIAL SERVICES

Considerable attention has been devoted to establishing differences between products and services, and identifying the corresponding marketing implications (e.g., Lovelock 1983; Uhl and Upah 1983). Implicit in such discussions is the assumption that services tend to have a fairly common set of characteristics. And yet, differences among types of services can often be as great or greater than differences between products and services. The distinction between industrial and consumer services represents a case in point.

Industrial services have a number of characteristics which create unique challenges for managers. Compared to consumer services, industrial services:

· Tend to be non-convenience type services;
· Are transportable and usually taken to the customer;
· Involve extensive customer contact in delivery;
· Are not as conducive to mass-production or mass-marketing;
· Often do not involve the customer becoming part of the service, i.e., the service is directed at things, not people;
· Frequently involve expensive equipment, but also tend to be people intensive, with an emphasis on people's capabilities, experience, background;
· Involve customers with more precise service level expectations, which are more clearly communicated to the vendor;
· Involve a fairly formal buying process, with a heavy emphasis on the tangible evidence of seller's ability to provide the service;
· Involve longer term, ongoing relationships with service provider;
· Demonstrate demand patterns that are somewhat more stable and predictable.

Characterizations such as these are generalizations,

and there certainly are exceptions. However, they would seem helpful in distinguishing such industrial services as software development, architectural design, or machine tool refinishing from traditional consumer services.

SERVICE QUALITY IN INDUSTRIAL MARKETS

Like product quality, service quality is concerned with conformance of the relevant features and characteristics of a service to customer needs. Arguably, service providers face a more difficult challenge in defining and managing quality levels when compared to product providers. This difficulty can be traced to the intangible, customized, and simultaneous production-consumption properties of industrial services. These services contain few search properties and are high in experience and credence properties. Levitt (1981) alludes to this difficulty when he explains that the less tangible the essence of product, the more powerfully and persistently the judgement about it gets shaped by how it is presented and who presents it.

To manage service quality, firms must set formal service standards. Typical product quality standards, such as conformance to design specifications or the number of defective items produced, do not really apply. Standards can be identified, however, by focusing on the major components of the service experience, including the people and equipment used to deliver the service, as well as any supporting tangible evidence.

Gronroos (1983) has suggested that services be evaluated based on their technical quality and functional quality. Technical quality refers to what the customer receives, such as the audit report provided by a CPA firm, or the transportation of goods provided by a trucking firm. Concerns here include the firm's general know-how, technical abilities of employees, ability to generate effective technical solutions to problems, physical equipment, and the computer support system, among others. Functional quality concentrates on how the customer receives a service, such as the professionalism of the accountant or the cleanliness of the truck. Management of functional quality emphasizes the attitudes and behaviors of those employees in contact with customers, the internal relationships between these and other employees, the appearance of personnel and equipment to which customers are exposed, the accessibility of the firm's services, and the maintenance of communication/contact with customers. These two quality dimensions work in tandem. A well-trained accountant who is rude to customers, or a fully equipped state-of-the-art truck that is routinely late with deliveries both represent quality problems. It does appear, though, that customers will sometimes excuse minor technical quality problems if functional quality is excellent.

Parasuraman, Zeithaml, and Berry (1985) identify three themes relevant to service quality: (a) Service quality is more difficult for the customer to evaluate than goods quality; (b) Service quality perceptions result from a comparison of customer expectations with actual service performance; and (c) Quality evaluations are not made solely on the outcome of a service, but also involve evaluations of the process of service delivery. They propose a model of service quality that can be summarized as follows: *Service quality as perceived by a customer depends on the size and direction of the gap between expected service and perceived service, which, in turn, depends on the nature of the gaps on the service provider's side, associated with the design, marketing, and delivery of services.*

These authors clarify the term 'expectations' by noting that it differs from the consumer satisfaction literature definition of expectations. The latter generally views expectations as predictions made by consumers about what is likely to happen during an impending transaction or exchange, while the former views expectations as desires or wants of the customer, that is, what he or she feels a service provider should offer, rather than would offer. Their research also revealed that, regardless of the type of service, customers used basically similar criteria in evaluating service quality. These criteria fell into ten key categories, labelled 'service quality determinants:' reliability, responsiveness, competence, accessibility, courtesy, communication, credibility, security, understanding/knowing the customer, and tangibles.

MEASURING SERVICE QUALITY

Parasuraman, Zeithaml, and Berry (1988) operationalized their conceptual model of service quality by employing Churchill's (1979) framework for developing measures of marketing constructs. This resulted in a 22-item instrument (SERVQUAL) for assessing customer perceptions of service quality. Underlying the 22 items are five dimensions distilled from the original 10 service quality criteria, used by customers when evaluating service quality, regardless of the type of service. These dimensions are: (1) Tangibles--physical facilities, equipment, and appearance of personnel; (2) Reliability--ability to perform the promised service dependably and accurately; (3) Responsiveness--willingness to help customers and provide prompt service; (4) Assurance--knowledge and courtesy of employees and their ability to inspire trust and confidence; (5) Empathy--caring, individualized attention the firm provides its customers.

The developers conceded that items that may be relevant to the discussion of service quality for one particular industry/firm may not be reflected in their generalized instrument. The instrument may, they explain, need to be reworded or augmented when applied in specific applications. Subsequent research has generally produced support for the use of SERVQUAL, with some notable exceptions. For instance, Carman (1990) partially replicated Parasuraman, Zeithaml, and Berry's (1988) work, and found *inter alia*: (a) that SERVQUAL did a 'fair job' in terms of construct validity; (b) in terms of discriminant validity, most of the dimensions recommended by Parasuraman, Zeithaml, and Berry were found. Validity checks, however, suggested that the dimensions were not so generic as to exclude the addition of items or new factors in specific applications of SERVQUAL; and (c) minor customizing of wording will often be required. However, Babakus (1990) has raised serious validity questions based on his own replication in a consumer services context.

Industrial services were not included in the development or testing of SERVQUAL. As we have seen, these services can differ quite significantly from those in consumer markets. While the SERVQUAL scale should be applicable, regardless of the type of service, Brensinger and Lambert (1990) have suggested SERVQUAL may be of limited managerial value in an industrial context. This brings us to the current study.

THE STUDY

The formal objective of this research was to determine the applicability of the SERVQUAL model for measuring service quality in an industrial environment. This was achieved by assessing the validity of the service quality construct and its operationalization in a mainframe software environment. The following criteria were employed:

Instrument Reliability: *Is SERVQUAL consistent in its measurement of the variables by which the service quality construct is operationalized?*

Content Validity: *Does the scale appear to measure what it is supposed to?*

Convergent Validity: *Does a measure of service quality determined by SERVQUAL correspond with other measures of service quality?*

Nomological Validity: *Does this study produce the same factor structure found by Parasuraman, Zeithaml, and Berry (1988)?*

Discriminant Validity: *Are the dimensions that emerge from the study truly different from one another?*

The Research Instrument

The questionnaire developed by Parasuraman, Zeithaml, and Berry (1988) was used with minor modification. Of the twenty-two questions in the original SERVQUAL instrument, four questions were modified to be more appropriate to the industrial environment. Respondents were required to answer the twenty-two

items in terms of their expectations of an ideal mainframe software vendor, followed by their perceptions of the participating software company with respect to the same items. Participants would then give an indication of their position within their respective companies as well as their overall impression of service provided by the software company. To encourage an open expression of views, no attempt was made to obtain information that would reveal identities or the companies with whom individuals were associated.

Sampling and Data Analysis

The participating software company supplied a database of the addresses of 118 of its customers, as well as the names of people that filled various posts at these companies. A marketing manager at each of the customer firms was identified and sent a pack containing five or ten questionnaires depending on the company size, together with self-addressed, stamped return envelopes. In addition, a personally addressed cover letter, explaining the objective of the research and requesting that the recipient distribute the enclosed question-naires among a specified group of people within the company, was sent. A total of 118 packets containing 664 questionnaires were prepared.

Questionnaire packs were mailed to the respondents, with a specified cutoff date of five weeks from the date of mailing. Three weeks after the packs had been mailed, follow-up telephone calls were made to fifty of the companies. These calls were made to verify packet receipt, to reassure the companies of response anonymity, and to encourage further responses. By the final cutoff date, a total of 211 responses had been received, for a response rate of 31.78 percent.

Samples of two hundred were used in the development of the SERVQUAL instrument (Parasuraman, Zeithaml, and Berry 1988), and the achieved sample size should therefore be considered comparable. In the following discussion, items and gap scores on the individual items are referred to by the prefix G. Thus, item 4 is referred to as G4, and so forth.

RESULTS

Instrument Reliability

A measure is said to be reliable if it consistently obtains the same result. The recommended measure of the internal consistency of a set of items is provided by coefficient alpha, and it should be the first measure one calculates to assess the quality of an instrument (Churchill 1979). Coefficient alphas for the five SERVQUAL dimensions can be found in Table 1.

The high coefficient alphas for the reliability, responsiveness, and empathy dimensions, as well as the

TABLE 1
Coefficient Alphas for the SERVQUAL Dimensions.

Dimensions	Cronbach Alpha	Dimensions	Cronbach Alpha
TANGIBLES	0.575	ASSURANCE	0.661
RELIABILITY	0.876	EMPATHY	0.839
RESPONSIVENESS	0.852		

low alpha for tangibles, compare favorably with the results obtained by both Parasuraman, Zeithaml, and Berry (1988) and Carman (1990). The comparatively low scores for both the tangibles and assurance dimensions indicate, however, that the sample of items did not perform that well in capturing the construct which motivated the measure. The tangible and assurance scores may also indicate that the particular operationalization of the underlying constructs may not be suitable in the setting of this study. An analysis of item-to-total correlations and revised alphas indicated that some items could be dropped from individual dimensions to give improved alphas (G9,G19) or very slightly reduced alphas (G3).

A total service quality score is obtained by summing and averaging the scores for the individual dimensions. The reliability of the total construct would not be measured by coefficient alpha, but rather by using the formula for reliability of linear combinations (Nunnally 1978). The high total-scale reliability achieved in this study (0.93) offers support for the reliability of the SERVQUAL instrument in a high-tech environment.

Content Validity

Content validity refers to the logical appropriateness of the measure. After completing the expectations and perceptions sections in the questionnaire, respondents were asked to give an indication of their overall impression of service provided by the participating software vendor. Table 2 shows the mean SERVQUAL scores for respondents grouped by their overall impression of service.

These results indicate support for the content validity of the SERVQUAL instrument for measuring service quality in an industrial environment. SERVQUAL scores clearly become more negative as overall service impressions change from excellent to poor.

TABLE 2
SERVQUAL Scores Compared With Service Impression.

	EXCELLENT	GOOD	ADEQUATE	POOR
OVERALL	-0.1318	-0.7213	-1.4785	-2.5175
TAN	0.3696	0.0062	-0.1912	-0.2826
REL	-0.6182	-1.6154	-2.6031	-4.0273
RES	-0.3370	-1.0923	-2.0294	-3.6196
ASS	-0.0326	-0.4938	-1.0485	-2.1932
EMP	0.0522	-0.4843	-1.4841	-2.5524
# of responses	24	85	71	23

Convergent Validity

Evidence of the convergent validity of a measure is provided by the extent to which it correlates highly with other methods designed to measure the same construct (Churchill 1979). Table 2 presents superficial support for SERVQUAL in this respect. Regression of overall service impressions with an overall SERVQUAL score yielded the results in Table 3.

TABLE 3
Regression of Overall Service Impression and Overall SERVQUAL Score.

Regression model R-square = .532	Sign. of Model (f) = .0001
Parameter est. for SERVQUAL score = 0.678	Sign. of parameter estimate (t) = .0001

The results of a correlation analysis of overall service impression with overall SERVQUAL score also indicated a high correlation (-0.7291) between the two measures, that is statistically significant (Prob > |R| = 0.0001). Both of these results provide support for convergent validity of the SERVQUAL instrument for measuring service quality in a high-tech environment.

Nomological and Discriminant Validity

Nomological validity exists if items in the SERVQUAL model that are expected to load together in a factor analysis actually do so (Carman 1990). Discriminant validity is indicated if the factors, and their items, are truly different from each other (Carman 1990). The initial factor analysis used the principal components methods. The number of factors retained were those with eigenvalues greater than one. Although items that were expected to load together largely did so, the only postulated dimension that was clearly distinguishable was the tangibles factor. Both the Parasuraman, Zeithaml, and Berry (1988) and Carman (1990) studies obtained more satisfactory results following oblique rotation.
The results of the initial factor analysis were then subjected to a PROMAX rotation, as suggested by Carman (1990), yielding the rotated factor structure in Table 4. Once again, items that were expected to load together did so to a large extent. Five factors emerged, but were not exactly as predicted by the Parasuraman, Zeithaml, and Berry (1988) study, nor as clearly differentiable as might be expected.

Factor 4 and factor 5 were notable by the small number of items loading on them. These factors relate to the tangible dimension posited by the SERVQUAL model. The original tangible factor appears to be split into two separately identifiable factors. Of the two factors, one relates to the physical manifestation of the company (factor 5) and the second relates to contact personnel or instances of customer - company interaction (factor 4).

TABLE 4
PROMAX Rotated Factor Solution*

	FAC.1	FAC.2	FAC.3	FAC.4	FAC.5
G1					0.80
G2				0.44	0.64
G3				0.78	
G4	0.36		0.34	0.48	0.38
G5	0.86	0.34			
G6	0.81	0.60			
G7	0.80	0.47	0.39		
G8	0.91	0.43	0.35		
G9	0.63	0.51	0.46		
G10	0.69	0.50	0.39		
G11	0.80	0.62	0.50		
G12	0.68	0.72	0.53		
G13	0.65	0.64	0.59		
G14	0.40	0.43	0.77		
G15			0.81		
G16	0.33	0.55	0.50	0.61	
G17	0.65	0.57	0.47		
G18	0.52	0.84	0.37		
G19	0.34	0.67			0.31
G20	0.45	0.81	0.38	0.30	
G21	0.64	0.69	0.67		
G22	0.66	0.76	0.50		

*(Loadings less than 0. 0 are not reflected)

This is particularly significant in the setting of the study as it is quite possible that certain customers dealing with a software company might very seldom, if ever, actually visit the premises. Customers at remote geographic locations might never see the software company premises, and only deal with contact personnel on site, or telephonically. This rationale would explain the relatively high loading of item G16 (relating to employee courtesy) on factor 4. The remaining factors can be related to the SERVQUAL model. Factor 1 corresponds with the reliability dimension of the model. Factor 2 relates to the empathy dimension, while factor 3 most closely resembles the assurance dimension. The responsiveness factor proposed by Parasuraman, Zeithaml, and Berry loads along with the reliability items as factor 1.

These results indicate support for the nomological validity of SERVQUAL for measuring service quality in a high-tech industrial environment, but cast some doubt on its discriminant validity. An indication of the weakness of the instrument in this area is provided by reference axis correlations, which indicate a high (-0.437) partial correlation between factors 1 and 2. An additional point in this regard is the high coefficient alpha (0.9188) obtained by a correlation analysis of reliability and responsiveness items. A further correlation analysis on all 22 items in the instrument yielded a final indication of its questionable discriminant capability in terms of the five dimensions proposed by Parasuraman, Zeithaml, and Berry (1988). This analysis yielded a coefficient alpha of 0.919. Parasuraman, Zeithaml, and Berry (1988), used similar analyses to purify the instrument, where items with low corrected item-to-total correlations were deleted. This approach resulted in the removal of items G1 - G4 and G15 in this study. A factor analysis on the reduced set of items yielded the two factor solution presented in Table 5. Once again, the reference axis correlations indicated a high (-0.56) partial correlation between factors 1 and 2, casting some doubt on the discriminant validity of the instrument in this study.

The factor labelled Performance is a combination of the reliability and responsiveness dimensions in the original SERVQUAL model. The items loading on this factor all seem to relate to the actual performance of the service. G17, which corresponds to competence in the ten dimension conception of service quality, is not out of place in this factor. It is difficult to imagine a service provider (particularly in a high-tech industry) being reliable, but incompetent. The inclusion of G12 (employees will always be willing to help customers) in the empathy factor does not seem inconsistent. G14 and G15 represent two of the original four dimensions that were collapsed into the assurance dimension. G3, G4, and G16 all relate to customer - service provider interaction (neatness, courtesy, quality of documentation), and have been labelled Interaction Cues. The items loading on the final factor do not necessarily involve any interaction between customer and service provider and can therefore be seen as solely physical or tangible cues.

Expectations Versus Perceptions

Examination of the responses for individual perception items indicated that questions 9 (error free records) and 15 (feeling safe in transactions) had more missing values than other questions (192 and 198 responses respectively, out of a possible 211). The response pattern for question 9 indicates that in an industrial marketing setting, not all the customers of a company will experience all facets of its service. Question 15 responses indicate support for the concept that there are credence properties associated with goods and services in a high-tech industry that customers might find difficult to evaluate even after a purchase has been made.

Descriptive statistics of customers expectations, perceptions and service quality gaps indicated that, in this study, areas where customers have the highest expectations are those that the service provider finds the most difficult to meet. Gaps 8, 5, 6 and 17 rank among the

TABLE 5
PROMAX Rotated Factor Solution - Reduced Item Set.

ITEM	FACTOR1	FACTOR2	ITEM	FACTOR1	FACTOR2
G5	.87	.32	G14	.40	.57
G6	.78	.55	G16		.67
G7	.80	.48	G17	.66	.56
G8	.91	.43	G18	.49	.82
G9	.61	.54	G19	.35	.56
G10	.67	.56	G20	.40	.82
G11	.79	.64	G21	.66	.71
G12	.66	.75	G22	.68	.74
G13	.61	.73			

These analyses led to the final interpretation indicated in Table 6.

TABLE 6
Final Factor Interpretation.

Factor Description	Items	Alpha
Performance	G5 G6 G7 G8 G9 G10 G11 G13 G17	0.9158
Empathy	G12 G18 G19 G20 G21 G22	0.866
Security/Credibility	G14 G15	0.6244
Interaction Cues	G3 G4 G16	0.5175
Physical Cues	G1 G2	0.5160

highest in terms of both expectations and gap perceived. The final interpretation of the factor analyses indicated that these items related to the SERVQUAL reliability factor (G7 relates to competence, but was included in the first factor). The standard deviations of the high expectations items indicated that there is relative consensus among customers with respect to these expectations. Conversely, the standard deviation of the highest gap items indicate that customers may not be as consistent in their perceptions of the service provider's shortfalling. The latter result may be an indicator of the heterogeneous nature of service provided, as well as signalling the possibility of being able to segment customers on the basis of their service quality perceptions.

Parasuraman, Zeithaml, and Berry (1988) used a regression analysis to obtain an indication of the relative importance of the SERVQUAL dimensions. Since the factors in this study did not correspond to the postulated factors, a stepwise regression was performed using the overall quality measure as a dependent variable and individual gaps as independent variables.

TABLE 7
Stepwise Regression of Overall Service Impression and 22 SERVQUAL Gaps.

Variable	Estimate	F	Prob>F
INTERCEPT	1.34556897	255.00	0.0001
G5	-0.12327606	11.93	0.0007
G6	-0.10407687	7.10	0.0085
G13	-0.07397150	5.95	0.0158
G17	-0.12571826	15.33	0.0001
G22	-0.08496525	6.51	0.0116

Model R-square = .632, F = 47.09, f < .0001

The results of the stepwise regression concur with the ratings accorded to individual items in the expectations part of the questionnaire. Items found to be significant in the regression model largely had high mean expectation scores. The significant items belonged to two of the five factors identified earlier. Items G5, G6, G13, and G17 belong to the Performance factor (a combination of reliability, responsiveness, and competence). This finding concurs with Parasuraman, Zeithaml, and Berry (1988), who consistently found reliability to be the most critical dimension. Item G22 relates to the empathy factor, which Parasuraman, Zeithaml, and Berry (1988) found to be less important in all their samples.

This is not surprising in the setting of this study. Shaw, Giglierano, and Kallis (1989) have noted the importance of intangible attributes in the marketing of complex technical products. Reliability, competence, and understanding the customers' specific service requirements can be seen as intangible product features that meet risk reduction needs in the customers' minds. Moriarty and Kosnik (1989) have identified uncertainty about suppliers being able to provide prompt, effective service as one of the characteristics of high-tech markets.

In the mainframe software industry, the service provider may deal with several customers who all belong to the same company. The original development of SERVQUAL involved individual customers evaluating essentially singular customer-service provider interactions. A comparison of mean expectations of respondents grouped according to a manager/non-manager category as well as a software support/application development personnel category was therefore also made. The significant differences are shown in Tables 8 and 9.

The results indicate that in several cases the means of the expectations of the tested groups were found to be significantly different. The implication is that service providers in high-tech industrial markets may find themselves catering to groups with different service expectations within individual customer companies. Research along the lines of the new expectation model proposed by Parasuraman, Berry and Zeithaml (1991) will almost certainly shed more light on this.

CONCLUSIONS AND RECOMMENDATIONS

The results of this study indicate that the ten dimensions of service quality identified by Parasuraman, Zeithaml, and Berry (1985) are valid for the mainframe software industry. Of the five factors proposed by Parasuraman, Zeithaml, and Berry (1988), Reliability, Empathy, and Tangibles were identified in this study. Carman's (1990) questioning of the stability of the relationship between individual items and their expected

TABLE 8 and 9 Comparison of Expectation Means					
a) for managers/non-managers			b) for software spt./application dev.		
Variable	T	Prob>|T|	Variable	T	Prob.>|T|
E1	-2.4217	0.0163	E1	-1.9311	0.0560
E2	-2.9291	0.0038	E11	2.0993	0.0381
E3	-2.2772	0.0238	E20	2.3398	0.0211
E4	-4.5010	0.0000			

HO: The means of the two groups are equal   HO: The means of the two groups are equal

factors is supported. These findings indicate that the factor structure of SERVQUAL is perhaps not as generic as first conceived, and the interpretation of factors is likely to be situation dependent. Parasuraman, Zeithaml, and Berry (1988) indeed indicated that this might be the case by suggesting that modification and supplementation of the basic SERVQUAL instrument might be desirable where only a single service was concerned.

The SERVQUAL instrument is applicable in the mainframe software environment, and can be modified to include items that users of the instrument feel are particular to the environment. Research into the validity of SERVQUAL has dealt mainly with individual, independent consumers and their interactions with service providers. This study has investigated SERVQUAL in an industrial, and more specifically, a high-tech setting. There might be different groups within the same company that interact with the service provider. The application of SERVQUAL might need to be modified to take into account the different service quality expectations and different service bundles offered to corporate customers.

Absolute SERVQUAL scores for individual items do not seem to be meaningful in isolation. The relative importance of items and dimensions can be determined by comparison with one another. A logical extension of this comparative approach would be for SERVQUAL to include questions relating to a company's competitors, given the competitive dimension of quality suggested by Luchs (1986) and De Souza (1989). Interpretation of such results could indicate to companies how they compare with major competitors, as well as highlight areas that need to be addressed to be successful in a competitive high-tech market.

REFERENCES

Abratt, R. (1986), "Industrial Buying in High-Tech Markets," *Industrial Marketing Management*, 15, 293-298.

Babakus, E. (1990), "Dimensions of Service Quality: Method Artifacts," *Proceedings*, Summer Educator's Conference, Chicago: American Marketing Association, 290.

Brensinger, R. P. and D. M. Lambert (1990), "Can the SERVQUAL Scale be Generalized to Business-to-Busienss Services?," *Proceedings*, Summer

Educator's Conference, Chicago: American Marketing Association, 289.

Carman, J. M. (1990), "Consumer Perceptions of Service Quality: An Assessment of the SERVQUAL Dimensions," *Journal of Retailing,* 66 (Spring), 33-55.

Churchill, G. A. (1979), "A Paradigm for Developing Better Measures of Marketing Constructs," *Journal of Marketing Research,* 16 (February), 64-73.

De Souza, G. (1989), "Now Service Businesses Must Manage Quality," *The Journal of Business Strategy,* (May/June), 21-25.

Jackson, R. W. and P. D. Cooper (1988), "Unique Aspects of Marketing Industrial Services," *Industrial Marketing Management,* 17 (May), 111-118.

Gronroos, C. (1983), *Strategic Management and Marketing in the Service Sector.* Cambridge, MA: Marketing Science Institute.

Lambert, D. M. and M. C. Lewis (1990), *"A Comparison of Attribute Importance and Expectation Scales for Measuring Serivce Quality, Proceedings,* Summer Educator's Conference, Chicago: American Marketing Association, 291.

Levitt, T. (1981), "Marketing Intangible Products and Product Intangibles," *Harvard Business Review,* (May/June), 94-102.

Lovelock, C. H. (1983), "Classifying Services to Gain Strategic Marketing Insights," *Journal of Marketing,* 47 (Summer), 9-20.

Luchs, R. (1986), "Successful Businesses Compete on Quality - not Costs," *Long Range Planning,* 19 (February), 12-17.

Moriarty, R. T. and T. J. Kosnik (1989), "High-Tech Marketing: Concepts, Continuity, and Change, *Sloan Management Review,* (Summer), 7-17.

Nunnally, J. (1978), *Psychometric Theory,* New York: McGraw-Hill, Inc.

Parasuraman, A., L. L. Berry, and V. A. Zeithaml (1991), "The Nature and Determinants of Customer Expectations of Service, *Report No. 91-113,* Cambridge, MA: The Marketing Science Institute.

Parasuraman, A., V. A. Zeithaml, and L. L. Berry (1985), "A Conceptual Model of Service Quality and its Implications for Future Research, *Journal of Marketing,* 49 (Fall), 41-50.

Parasuraman, A., V. A. Zeithaml, and L. L. Berry (1988), *SERVQUAL: A Multiple Item Scale for Measuring Consumer Perceptions of Service Quality, Journal of Retailing,* 64 (Spring), 12-37.

Schonberger, R. J. and E. M. Knod, Jr. (1988), "Operations Management Serving the Customer," Third Edition, Plano, TX: Business Publications, Inc.

Shaw, J., J. Giglierano, and J. Kallis (1989), "Marketing Complex Technical Products: The Importance of Intangible Attributes," *Industrial Marketing Management,* 18, 45-53.

Singh, M. P. (1990), "Service as a Marketing Strategy: A Case Study of Reliance Electric," *Industrial Marketing Management,* 19 (August), 193-200.

Uhl, K. P. and G. D. Upah (1983), *"The Marketing of Services: Why and How It Is Different*, in *Research in Marketing,* 6, JAI Press, Inc., 237-57.

U.S. Bureau of Census (1990), *Statistical Abstract of the United States,* 108th ed. Washington, DC: U.S. Government Printing Office.

Zeithaml, V. A. (1981), "How Consumers Evaluation Processes Differ between Goods and Services," in *Marketing of Services,* J.H. Donnelly and W.R. George, eds. Chicago: American Marketing Association, 186-190.

Zeithaml, V. A., A. Parasuraman, and L. L. Berry (1990), *Delivering Service Quality,* New York: The Free Press.

THE FRANCHISED DISTRIBUTION OF SERVICES AND SERVICE QUALITY

Irfan Ahmed, Texas A&M University

ABSTRACT

The aspect of distribution of services is an under-researched area both in the channels of distribution and services marketing literatures. However, the distribution of services is distinctive in that due to the lack of separation of production and delivery, the distributor may manufacture part of the service in addition to performing the normally considered channel functions. This paper approaches the franchised distribution of services and attempts to relate channel dynamics and structure to the nature of the service and delivered service quality, based on research in channels, services, and organizational economics.

A franchise involves two independent parties with investments, channel roles, and expectations of rewards, with inherent conflict and cooperative behavior, sources of power and mutual dependence. Transaction-specific assets of franchisees imply a source of power and opportunism for franchisors through a dependence of the franchisee on the franchisor. Due to a need for dependence balancing and an inability to do this through alternative measures, it is expected that franchisees will develop offsetting investments through close bonding with customers, with a view to making themselves indispensable in the transaction.

Bonding with customers, while ideally in the interests of both franchisor and franchisee, is also viewed here from a dependence perspective as a source of power for the franchisee, and a source of dependence for the franchisor. It is expected that, allowing for market structure, franchisors will opt for higher levels of integration in services where franchisees can make themselves indispensable due to an entrenched customer preference for particular service providers.

The use of institutional and contractual structures, especially 'covenants not to compete' are also expected to be used by franchisors to reduce the possibility of being held hostage by franchisees, by reducing the transferability of the franchisee's investment in bonding with customers. The use of restrictive contractual structures is expected in such situations. However, in light of research on the effects of restrictive, formalized systems governing transactions on channel member perceptions of control and autonomy and consequent commitment to the relationship, the use of arrangements considered restrictive could have an adverse effect on the quality of service delivered by the franchisee. The existing market competitiveness, purchase cycle, and image of the service brand are expected to moderate occurrence of such service defaults. Dissatisfaction with arrangements with franchisors may cause franchisees to underperform on service quality if it does not have an adverse effect on their profitability or if the default can escape detection by the franchisor. Despite the use of contract governed requirements and performance standards, delivery on components such as responsiveness, assurance and empathy are expected to suffer, with overall service quality not exceeding levels of adequacy.

The delivery of barely adequate levels of service by some franchisees is likely to be detrimental to the long term competitive position of the franchise system. The use of negatively perceived dependence balancing measures by franchisors is recommended against, in light of the demonstrated superiority of non-coercive sources of power over coercive sources of power. An alternative means, franchisors' independent and parallel investment in bonding with customers to undermine part of the indispensability of franchisees, is suggested as a course of action for the franchisor to balance its dependence on franchisees for maintaining relationships with customers.

For further information contact:
Irfan Ahmed
Texas A&M University
Department of Marketing
College Station, TX 77843-4112

TANGIBLE VERSUS INTANGIBLE COPY IN INDUSTRIAL PRINT ADVERTISING

Joseph A. Bellizzi, Arizona State University West
Lauri Minas, Intel Corporation
Wayne Norvell, Kansas State University

ABSTRACT

Introduction and Methods

Industrial print advertising is used primarily to enhance the productivity of a sales force or the reputation of a supplier. Some researchers and practitioners believe that industrial ad copy should be less product specific and more intangible, describing vendor attributes rather than specific product attributes. In this study, two alternate ads were designed. One contained tangible and specific wording about product attributes while the other used more general and less specific terms to describe the firm and its products. Copy length, headline, lead-in, close, and logo were the same for both versions. A computer network was selected as the product. The advertiser was a fictitious company, Advanced Business Computer Corporation. A total of 336 MIS managers and 313 computer dealers comprised the sample.

The questionnaire included 32 Likert-type items to assess subjects' reaction to the ads in addition to a few questions concerning personal and company characteristics. The 32 items were factor analyzed using principle component analysis with VARIMAX rotation. Five factors were extracted using the eigenvalue of 1 rule. The five factors represent (1) a product information dimension, (2) a sponsoring firm reliability/experience/longevity dimension, (3) readers' willingness dimension to seek additional information or make inquiries for more information, (4) overall appeal and reader enjoyment of the ad dimension, and (5) a quantity and clarity dimension regarding information included in the ads. Factor scores on these items were used as the dependent variables. The independent variables were type ad with two levels (tangible copy or intangible copy) and type reader (MIS manager or computer dealer). Analysis of variance was used to analyze the results.

Results and Discussion

No interaction effects were found between type ad and type reader using factor scores as dependent variables. As might be expected, the intangible ad was seen as being associated with a more reliable and experienced sponsor (factor 2, $F = 9.1$, $p < .003$). On the other hand, the tangible ad was perceived as including adequate quantity and clarity of information (factor 5, $F = 5.0$, $p < .026$). No other main effects for type ad or type reader were found. Univariate tests of the 32 individual Likert-type items provided additional insight.

The intangible as was seen a being associated with a company likely to be around for a long time; a company most likely to have good product support, service, and training; a company that probably understands computer network needs; an advertised product that is probably easy to use; and a more enjoyable ad to read ($p < .05$). The intangible ad was also viewed to be marginally associated with a company most likely to be a leader, with extensive experience in computer networks, whose product is probably the best on the market and reliable, and more likely to influence a reader to call the listed phone number for more information ($.10 > p > .05$). The tangible ad was seen as being associated with a product with a good upgrade path and competitively priced ($p < .05$).

Not surprisingly, the two ads produced different results and it may be difficult to say which one produced superior results. However, the intangible ad copy appears to have some merit especially regarding reader perceptions of reliability, experience, and service which may be particularly important in the computer industry where product technology advances very rapidly making it difficult for customers to assess the merit of tangible product claims.

For further information please contact:
Professor Joseph A. Bellizzi
Business Programs
Arizona State University West
P.O. Box 37100
4701 W. Thunderbird Road
Phoenix, Arizona 85069

RESPONDING TO A PRODUCT CRISIS: A COMPARISON OF MEMORY RETRIEVAL VS. REFUTATIONAL STRATEGIES

Richard F. Yalch, *University of Washington*
John E. Butler, *University of Washington*
Jeremiah J. Sullivan, *University of Washington*
Phillip H. Phan, *University of Washington*

ABSTRACT

A product crisis initiated by publicized claims that apples were dangerous because of Alar served as the context for comparing advertising responses. Information processing theory and research suggested a memory-retrieval message as an alternative to the apple industry's approach of directly refuting the crisis information. Shoppers were intercepted entering a grocery store, made aware of the crisis and then exposed to a crisis response message. The results showed that stimulating individuals to retrieve positive product thoughts effectively countered the crisis information. Continuing to focus on the crisis even when the crisis could be credibly refuted did not. Other methods for responding to crises are evaluated using information processing theory.

INTRODUCTION

The severe negative consequences of product crises have led many firms to develop crisis response plans (Reinhardt 1987; Stanton 1989). A key element in many of these plans is to use advertising and public relations to respond to the unfavorable information about the firm's products. To date, crisis research has studied the sales effects (Holak and Reddy 1986), stock market reactions (Jarrell and Peltzman 1985), and legal ramifications (Morgan 1988) but little is available on the use of communications. This paper describes ways to use information processing theory to develop crisis control messages. One such message is tested in a field study involving a major product crisis.

Advertising and Crisis Management

In a crisis, organizations must cope with the sudden exposure of consumers to unfavorable product information, usually linking their products to undesirable health and safety problems. For example, firms have seen the demand for their products altered because consumers became aware of dangers related to product tampering (e.g., Tylenol and Sudafed) and product safety (e.g., Suzuki Samurai and NutriSystem). Sometimes, the crisis involves how a firm conducts its business not its specific products. For example, Nordstrom faced negative publicity in the *Wall Street Journal* and "Sixty Minutes" because of its employee relations and Star-Kist had to defend the way its suppliers caught tuna.

Crises are particularly difficult to manage because they occur with little or no prior warning, attract unwanted media attention, and negatively affect sales. Often, the source of the problem is not under the marketer's control (Tylenol tampering) and, occasionally, is based on falsehoods (rumors linking Corona beer to unsanitary brewing facilities; Hume 1987). Although the source and truthfulness of the problem affect the long-term response to a crisis, they may be irrelevant to the immediate communication problem. That is, although tampering may occur only once or a product may not be contaminated, consumer concerns may reduce sales unless the firm adopts an effective communication program.

Firms react to a product crisis in different ways. Some firms ignore it, hoping it is short-lived and without sales impact. They continue promotional communications as usual to draw attention from the crisis to the positive aspects of their product. Other firms cease promotions trying not to stimulate thinking about the product at a time when thoughts spontaneously turn to the crisis. For example, consumers might react to Tylenol advertising during a tampering by thinking about the tampering. Alternatively, firms acknowledge the accusations and try to refute them. Nutri/System ran a series of ads disputing law suits claiming that its diet program caused gall bladder problems. At an extreme level, a firm can launch a counterattack, trying to disparage and discredit its accusers. For example, facing rumors that the company's logo containing a sorcerer's head and thirteen stars could be interpreted as a sign of Satan, Procter & Gamble filed lawsuits against several individuals it suspected of spreading the rumor that the company supported Satanism (*Advertising Age* 1982).

This paper considers ways to develop a short-term communication strategy for firms facing a public relations crisis. It does not address the underlying issues causing the crisis or long-run effects. That is, we do not consider whether a firm should withdraw a product that has been tampered with or how a firm should treat its employees. The focus is on short-term mass media strategies for dealing with the negative publicity. This is achieved by reviewing relevant literature on responding to rumors and other forms of negative information, developing communication strategies based on information processing research, and reporting on an experiment testing one proposed strategy against a widely used method, a direct refutation of the negative information.

LITERATURE REVIEW

Crisis management continues to attract interest (see special issue of *Public Relations Journal* devoted to it in Spring 1991). However, a literature review failed to locate any empirical study that specifically dealt with product crises similar to the Tylenol/Sudafed tamperings or Suzuki Samurai safety warnings. However, two relevant studies were identified. One concerned a test of how a politician might respond to negative campaign charges (Calantone and Warshaw 1985). In this study, *Time* magazine accused a hypothetical candidate for the U. S. Congress of contributing to a water pollution problem by not supporting a new sewage treatment system. Without crisis control messages, this candidate's share of the vote dropped from 50 percent to 13 percent. Two response approaches were tested individually and in combination. A message denying the validity of the charges effectively restored the candidate's share to 55 percent. The other message did not deny the charges but countered with charges against the opposing candidate. In this condition, the candidate's vote share rose to 46 percent. A third condition, combining the denial and counterattack approaches was the most effective one with the vote share rising to 65 percent. These results support the use of a refutational approach in a product crisis. For example, a firm could deny unfavorable claims against it and suggest that competing products have their own problems.

Although Calantone and Warshaw's research favored a refutational approach with a counterattack, a study by Tybout, Calder and Sternthal (1981) suggests that other approaches may be more effective than a refutational approach. This study tested four possible responses to untruthful rumors. Rumors do not have the credibility associated with many crisis creating events but often alter consumers' buying behavior. In New York City, consumption of several brands of soft drinks in minority communities (especially Tropical Fantasy) declined sharply when unknown individuals spread untrue charges that the Ku Klux Klan produced the products and they contained ingredients designed to sterilize black males (Levinson 1991).

In 1980, the McDonald's corporation was plagued with a persistent rumor that its hamburgers were made with worms. Efforts to ignore or refute the rumor were unsuccessful and research was undertaken to develop an effective response. Tybout, et al. (1981) tested several different approaches. One was to refute the rumor by pointing out the higher cost of worms relative to hamburger meat and the government inspection of meat (labeled by the authors as the refutational approach). Another was to attempt to distract consumers away from the rumor and to minimize its negative associations (referred to as the storage approach by the authors). For

the McDonald's worm rumor, this entailed linking the rumor to French cooking. This created both positive associations for worms and reduced the strength of the association between worms and McDonald's hamburgers. The third approach allowed the rumor to be learned but immediately before the consumers evaluated McDonald's, they were asked to retrieve experiences involving McDonald's that were expected to be more positive than beliefs involving the worm rumor. The authors named this the retrieval approach.

In the study, a confederate exposed consumers to the worm rumor while they viewed a television program containing McDonald's advertising. Then they were exposed either to a refutational, a storage, or a retrieval message. Control groups consisted of consumers not exposed to the rumor or exposed to the rumor but no countering message. At the end of the procedure, consumers evaluated McDonald's. These evaluations revealed that the rumor unfavorably affected attitudes: consumers exposed to the worm rumor were less favorable toward McDonald's than individuals not exposed to the rumor. The storage and retrieval approaches were successful in undoing this harm (consumers exposed to the rumor and one of these messages were as favorable toward McDonald's as those who were not exposed to the rumor), but the refutational approach was not effective (these individuals were as unfavorable toward McDonald's as those exposed to the rumor without a response).

AN INFORMATION PROCESSING VIEW OF RUMORS AND PRODUCT CRISES

The relative superiority of the retrieval method to the refutational method may be explained using information processing theory and the schema concept. Schemas are knowledge structures resulting from an individual's experiences with an object. For McDonald's, a consumer's schema would include all information related to McDonald's. This would be the integration of exposures to advertising, personal experiences in eating at McDonald's, word of mouth communications, and all other references to McDonald's. Answers to open-ended survey questions ("tell me what you know about McDonald's"), sentence completion ("I was about to go to McDonald's when . . ."), and brand image tasks ("describe a typical patron of McDonald's") reflect a McDonald's schema.

In this framework, it is possible to model the effect of a rumor. Exposure to the rumor creates a link between the brand (McDonald's) and an undesirable object (worms), which is later activated (brought to conscious awareness) when references are made to the brand. This causes the negative feelings associated with the undesirable object to become transferred to the brand. The failure of the refutational message may be explained by the activation of beliefs linking the worm to McDonald's hamburgers. Exposure to this information reminds consumers of McDonald's alleged use of worms in its hamburger meat and maintains the association of these two thoughts in long-term memory. This association is detrimental to evaluative judgments because of the unfavorableness of the thought of eating worms. On the other hand, a retrieval strategy is effective because it focuses consumers' thoughts on attributes besides hamburgers and worms (e.g., French Fries and Milk Shakes), making it less likely that consumers retrieve the worm association when making their evaluative judgments of McDonald's. The storage strategy also reduces the likelihood of retrieving the rumor by discouraging consumers from associating the worm rumor with McDonald's when they are exposed to it.

Tybout et al. (1981) study supports an information processing view of attitude development and change. In this view, overall attitudes are considered to be based on what consumers believe about a product and the favorableness or unfavorableness of these beliefs. Thus, individuals believing that Crest contains fluoride and that fluoride is effective in preventing cavities should have a favorable opinion of Crest. Exposing these individuals to rumors and product crisis information may alter their beliefs, (e.g., purchasing Star-Kist tuna is bad because dolphins are caught in the tuna fishing nets), leading to less favorable attitudes toward the product. Alternatively, the favorableness of existing beliefs (fiber is good for you) may change because of crisis publicity (e.g., the fiber in Horizon bread is not good for you because it comes from wood chips not wheat bran).
Information processing research has determined that individuals rarely use all of their knowledge in making evaluative judgments (Seamon, Marsh and Brody 1984). Instead, a subset of this knowledge is used. An item's use depends on its accessibility or ease of being remembered and its association with the retrieval cues present at the point of choice. For example, it is more likely that individuals' attitudinal judgments will be influenced by Chevrolet's being made in America (a long-time theme of its advertising) than by its EPA gas mileage ratings. However, the EPA rating's influence may be enhanced by requiring car dealers to put a sticker with the mileage information (a retrieval cue) on every car.

The power of many rumors and product crisis information to alter consumer attitudes and behavior may be explained by the ability of events with extreme consequences (e.g., death, sterilization) and bizarre causes (e.g., Ku Klux Klan producing soft drinks and devil worshippers owning Procter & Gamble) to stand out in consumer's memories. Consumers may easily retrieve these associations to the brand and be influenced by them — even when they do not believe the rumor is true.

Although the Tybout et al. (1981) study provides conceptual and empirical guidance for developing communication strategies for combating rumors and other types of unfavorable product information, there are some unanswered questions justifying additional research. For example, their study concerned a rumor with little scientific or rational basis. Would the same results be true if the negative information was based on scientific research? The worm rumor was communicated using word of mouth by an individual who was part of the experiment. Would the same findings be true if the information was communicated by a respected television news organization? Further, their study was conducted with graduate students in a university setting and examined changes in attitudes. Would the results change if the behavioral intentions of consumers were studied in a natural shopping environment? These and other questions stimulated our interest in conducting an experiment to study crisis communications in a different context.

THE FIELD EXPERIMENT

Crisis

It was decided to use a recent product crisis as the context for studying crisis response messages. Artificially creating a crisis was considered but rejected because of concerns that subjects would not find an artificial crisis to be credible. The crisis selected involved publicity about potential harmful effects of Alar (Daminozide UDMH), a growth and color enhancer that was developed by the Uniroyal Chemical company in 1963. On February 26, 1989, the "Sixty Minutes" television show aired a segment entitled "A is for Apples" (Phan and Chong 1990). This show focused on a study done by the Natural Resources Defense Council, which purported to show that Alar caused cancer. Although the risks associated with Alar had been raised before, the earlier publicity had not affected sales. The highly viewed Sixty Minutes show created instant media attention, resulting in a dramatic sales decline. Uniroyal ceased the sale of Alar and sales of red delicious apples ultimately returned to their pre-crisis levels. Although the crisis was over, informal discussions with consumers indicated that they were still aware of the Alar health warnings and that reminders about the crisis would have a negative impact on attitudes and behavior toward apples. Thus, the crisis provided an appropriate setting for evaluating alternative advertising approaches to respond to a product crisis.

Design

A field experiment was conducted to evaluate two types of crisis response advertising. A refutational approach, which is the most common response, was compared to a schema-activation (retrieval) message. In addition, a no-message control group was used to assess the absolute as well as the relative effectiveness of each approach. Consumers were classified on several dimensions to determine if the effectiveness of the crisis management responses varied depending on consumer characteristics. The dimensions included initial favorableness toward the product, level of thinking about the

58

product, and understanding of the crisis. Behavioral reactions to the crisis and crisis response messages were assessed using the consumers' shopping intentions.

Measures of Consumer Characteristics

Three methods of classifying consumers were taken. Given the context for the study, intercept interviewing in a grocery store, the measures had to be simple to administer. The consumers' product schema was assessed using two open-ended questions. Subjects were asked to "list as many adjectives as you can to describe apples (for example, 'juicy')." Next, they were asked to "list as many specific types of apples, apple uses, and apple products as you can (for example, 'apple pie')." The number of items listed in response to the two questions were summed to form an overall measure of their level of knowledge about apples. The range of responses was from zero to 35. Using a median split, individuals reporting nine or more responses were classified as having a high level of product knowledge (44 percent of the sample). Individuals reporting eight or fewer responses were classified as having a low level of product knowledge (56 percent of the sample).

The individual's crisis schema was assessed using five multiple choice questions about Alar's impact. These questions were developed using the transcript of the "60 Minutes" show of February 26, 1989 and from subsequent national news media stories (e.g., "Alar is sprayed on apple to (a) make them last longer in the store, (b) make them look shinier and more colorful, (c) don't know)"). The responses were coded one if correct and zero if no response or incorrect. The total number of correct responses to the five questions served as the measure of level of understanding of the rumor prior to being reexposed to it.

The third measure was the consumer's overall liking of apples. This was assessed by a question asking consumers how much they liked apples (very little to very much). Individuals were later classified as favorable if they responded that they liked apples or liked apples very much (69 per cent of the sample), otherwise they were considered unfavorable (31 per cent).

Dependent Measure

Five measures of behavioral intentions were taken at the end of the survey. These assessed the likelihood that shoppers would visit the apple (produce) section, examine apples, purchase apples, purchase in quantities more or less than usual, and the specific number to be purchased. Analysis of the responses suggested that only two decisions — to buy or not to buy and whether this represented a change from normal behavior — were relevant to concerns about Alar being used in apples. Thus, responses to these two items were summed to measure changes in shopping behavior following expo-

sure to the negative product information and countering advertising response.

Hypotheses

Five hypotheses were developed based on the results of the McDonald's worm rumor study and other information processing research.

Hypothesis 1: After exposure to crisis-related information, consumers exposed to a retrieval-type response message will have a more favorable purchase intention than consumers not exposed to a crisis response message.

Hypothesis 2: After exposure to crisis-related information, consumers exposed to a refutational-type crisis response message will not have a more favorable purchase intentions than consumers not exposed to a crisis response message.

The first hypothesis predicts that exposure to the health dangers associated with the use of Alar in apple growing will cause a short-term avoidance of apples but that a message designed to focus attention on the positive aspects of apples will counter this shift. On the other hand, a message designed to refute the danger claims is not expected to counter the unfavorable health claims. Both predictions are based on the McDonald's study. The refutational message is predicted to be ineffective because it maintains attention on the Alar scare whereas the memory retrieval message is predicted to be effective because it distracts consumers from thinking about Alar.

Hypothesis 3: Consumers with a high level of product knowledge will have more favorable purchase intentions after exposure to a retrieval-type message than consumers with a low level of product knowledge. The effectiveness of the refutational message will not depend on the level of product knowledge.

A key aspect of a retrieval strategy is the activation of product thoughts unrelated to the crisis that interfere with activation of the crisis information. Consumers who have a well-developed knowledge structure should be better able to generate interfering product thoughts than consumers with little product knowledge. Therefore, a retrieval strategy should be more effective with knowledgeable consumers. On the other hand, because the refutational message focuses on the crisis not the product, its effectiveness should not depend on the level of product knowledge.

Hypothesis 4: Consumers with a high level of crisis awareness will have more favorable purchase intentions after exposure to a retrieval-type message than to a refutational message. Consumers with a low level of crisis awareness will respond equally well to a refutational and retrieval message.

Individuals with an accurate understanding of the crisis were expected to respond as the McDonald's consumers did in Tybout et al. (1981). Thus, the refutational message was expected to remind them of the crisis and be less effective than a message that focused on product features not related to the crisis. On the other hand, individuals with little understanding of the crisis would not activate crisis thoughts when exposed to the refutational message. Therefore, they should respond as well to the refutational message as to the memory retrieval message.

Hypothesis 5: Consumers who are favorably disposed toward the product will have more favorable purchase intentions after exposure to a memory retrieval message than consumers who are unfavorably disposed toward the product. The favorableness of prior attitudes toward the product will not affect the effectiveness of the refutational-type message.

The rationale for this hypothesis is straightforward. Individuals who are favorably disposed toward the product will have many positive thoughts to retrieve when stimulated to do so, making the memory retrieval message effective. On the other hand, those who are not favorably disposed will retrieve unfavorable product thoughts and these will not counter the crisis information. Chattopadya and Basu (1990) found that message elaboration stimulated by a humorous advertisement was effective only when the audience was favorably disposed to the product prior to message exposure.

Procedure

Shortly after the Alar scare became publicized, two-person teams of researchers visited thirty supermarkets in urban and suburban areas of Western Washington State. No apples are commercially grown in Western Washington, which is separated by a large mountain range from the region that contains apple orchards. Thus, respondents were not presumed to have any unusual biases towards apples. The supermarkets were located in upper, middle, and lower income neighborhoods. Each team intercepted shoppers about to enter the store and offered a dollar to participate in a study of apples. A total of 302 consumers participated. They were assigned randomly to message conditions by a prior sorting of the questionnaire booklets.

The first page of the questionnaire contained items measuring the consumer's product schema and liking for apples. The second page consisted of distractor questions designed to reduce the schema-invoking impact of the first page. The third page contained a five-item measure of the crisis schema. Then, the fourth page re-introduced respondents to the Alar controversy with a description of the Natural Resources Defense Council claims made on "60 Minutes." On the next page was either the refutational advertisement actually used by the industry, the memory

retrieval advertisement developed by the researchers, or nothing. The refutational approach was developed by the International Apple Institute and the Washington State Apple Commission as part of a $1,000,000 campaign to refute the health warnings made by the Natural Resources Defense Council on Sixty Minutes. It acknowledged a recent report that Alar was used on apples. It then stated that, contrary to the report, Alar was actually used sparingly, it was highly unlikely to be consumed in dangerous quantities, and respected scientific authorities endorsed apples as a safe and healthy food. The memory-retrieval message acknowledged that a public advocacy group was claiming that apples were bad but did not elaborate on the claims. It then asked consumers to retrieve past experiences with apples, especially those involving childhood and referred to slogans such as "an apple a day keeps the doctor away." The last page contained a five-item test of purchase intentions.

ANALYSIS AND RESULTS

A summary of the responses to the three consumer classification measures (product schema, crisis schema, and product attitudes) and dependent measure of purchase intentions are provided in Table 1. The last two columns of the table show the buying intentions of the consumers based on whether they were high or low in the particular characteristic. Individuals who reported liking apples had significantly higher purchase intentions than individuals who indicated no strong liking of apples, suggesting that the median split on this measure was meaningful. There were no significant differences in intentions depending on whether consumers were knowledgeable about apples or the Alar scare. Interestingly, the correlation between product knowledge and crisis knowledge was only .08, indicating that two different types of knowledge were being assessed.

Effects of counter crisis messages

The two messages designed to minimize the impact of negative product information on buying intentions were compared against the no message control group using analysis of variance. The results showed a main effect indicating a difference in intentions depending on whether a message was used and the specific type of message $(F(2,284) = 3.08, p < .05)$. Further analysis using the Student Neuman-Kuels test revealed a significant difference between the memory-retrieval message (mean = 5.8) and the no-message control group (4.6) and an insignificant difference between the refutational message (mean = 5.5) and the control group. This supports hypothesis one. However, the difference between the memory-retrieval message and the refutational message was not statistically significant.

Next, additional analyses were conducted to determine if there were any differences in message effectiveness for consumers based on their knowledge about

TABLE 1
Responses to Survey Questions About Consumer Characteristics and Purchase Intentions

Measure	Mean	Std Dev	Range	Buying Intentions* Low (n=)	High (n=)
Product Schema	8.9	4.5	0-35	5.4 (162)	5.7 (128)
Crisis Schema	2.8	1.5	0-5	5.6 (118)	5.5 (184)
Product Attitude	4.0	1.0	1-5	4.8 (89)	5.9 (198)
Purchase Intentions	5.5	2.3	2-10		

*Last two columns report the mean buying intentions for individuals who are low and high in the characteristic presented in the row.

TABLE 2
Mean Buying Intentions by Type of Message and Audience Characteristics

Audience Characteristics	Type of Message Refutational	Retrieval	No Message
High Product Schema	5.9 (.29)	5.8 (.30)	4.9 (.69)
Low Product Schema	5.2 (.29)	5.8 (.27)	4.4 (.70)
High Crisis Schema	5.3 (.26)	5.9 (.25)	4.7 (.58)
Low Crisis Schema	5.8 (.32)	5.5 (.34)	4.4 (.82)
High Product Attitude	6.0 (.26)	6.1 (.22)	4.8 (.57)
Low Product Attitude	4.9 (.31)	5.0 (.41)	4.3 (.86)

Note: standard errors in parentheses.

and the audience characteristics. None of the hypotheses was supported by statistically significant results (p > .1). Interestingly, the memory-retrieval message was equal to or slightly more effective than the refutational message in all cases except when individuals had little knowledge about the Alar crisis. The latter may be attributable to the fact that many of these individuals held beliefs that Alar was even more dangerous than claimed by those opposing its use.

DISCUSSION

The results of this study provide evidence in support of using information processing theory to develop crisis control messages. A message-retrieval message designed to stimulate individuals to retrieve positive product thoughts rather than to focus on the crisis was effective in countering the crisis information. However, it was not significantly more effective than a message designed to refute the crisis. Efforts to provide additional support for an information processing explanation for the effectiveness of the retrieval message by examining the relative effectiveness of the two types of messages across individuals varying in their knowledge about the product, knowledge about the crisis, and prior attitude toward the product was not successful.

The failure to find significant interactions between the messages and audience characteristics may be somewhat attributable to the choice of product, crisis and research setting. For example, most individuals are familiar with apples, and their apple schemas are probably easily accessed. Similarly, the crisis had received widespread coverage and appeared to be over. Consequently, variations in product and crisis thoughts across consum-

apples, knowledge of the crisis, and prior attitudes toward apples (see Table 2). Separate analyses of variance were conducted using the message treatments and how individuals were classified to test hypotheses three, four and five, which predicted interactions between the messages

ers may have been narrower than would be true of other crises. In addition, the field setting limited the length and complexity of the questionnaire. These factors would tend to work against finding significant interactions between the measures and the messages. Nevertheless, the results of this study combined with other information processing research are sufficiently compelling to justify analyzing various advertising approaches in response to crises.

MANAGERIAL IMPLICATIONS

Product crises are among the most dreaded events facing product managers. They appear without warning and immediately affect sales. However, several possible courses of action are suggested by Tybout et al. (1981). Let's review them in the context of information processing theory and the experiment reported in this paper.

1. Do nothing. The rationale for this is that without repeated exposure, the negative information will gradually fade from memory. In addition, individuals are discouraged from spontaneously retrieving the crisis information by not exposing them to any product references. This is equivalent to a celebrity's going into seclusion to escape media attention. This should be an effective strategy if the media and public allow the crisis to pass. However, Procter & Gamble's experience with its Satanic ownership rumor demonstrates the staying power of many crises. P&G ultimately changed its logo. Firms must also consider the cost of being quiet while waiting for a crisis to pass. The public will be exposed to only one side of the crisis and competitors are free to actively woo the firm's customers.

2. Refutation. Although the McDonald's experiment found that a refutational approach was unsuccessful in combating the negative product judgments resulting from exposure to a rumor linking the product to worms, the present experiment showed that it was somewhat successful. One reason for the difference might be that few consumers believed the McDonald's worm rumor, whereas many consumers were concerned about Alar. Also, the Alar health allegations had been more widely publicized than the McDonald's worm rumor. Hence, it was likely that this information was more credible and accessible than the worm rumor.

The dangers in adopting a refutational approach are that they may lend credence to the claims ("If there wasn't some truth to it, why would the company bother to respond?"). Also, they may cause consumers to learn more about the crisis increasing its accessibility. Thirdly, by merely reminding consumers that there have been allegations about the organization or its products, consumers may access their existing repertoire of crisis information. This will make it more elaborate, increasing

the likelihood that it will come to mind later on. The principle is similar to the effect of practice on learning. By continuing to practice, one inhibits forgetting. If a refutational approach is chosen, the firm should try to provide as little information as possible about the problem, provide substantial information that refutes the allegations, use credible sources for the information, and do so in a vivid manner to insure that the refutational information is well-learned.

3. Storage Approaches. These strategies entail reducing the negative information's link to the organization and/or minimizing its unfavorableness. In a recent incident in Seattle, Sudafed caplets were poisoned resulting in several deaths. The public relations firm responsible for the problem tried to focus attention on "tampering" and the deaths and not on "Sudafed" and the poisonings. This is consistent with information processing research as this inhibits the development of a strong association between Sudafed and the deaths. Similarly, NutriSystem had to cope with allegations that its dieting efforts resulted in gall bladder problems. The initial effort to refute the charges were not effective in countering the allegation resulting in a continued loss of business. A more effective program involved linking gall bladder problems to obesity and not to NutriSystem's diet recommendations.

An alternative to the redirection of associations with unfavorable product information is to minimize the danger inherent in the negative characteristic. For example, in the McDonald's experiment, the unpleasantness of eating worms was countered by pointing out that worms are used in gourmet French cooking. This approach is based on creating positive associations to counter the unfavorableness of the negative product information. A good approach might be to use humor, though the organization must be careful not to belittle legitimate public concerns. President Ronald Reagan used humor effectively in countering efforts to focus public attention on his negative characteristics. For examples, concerns about his age were alleviated by jokes that people should not worry that he might be "too young" for the job.

4. Retrieval approaches. In both the McDonald's worm rumor study and the study reported in this paper, retrieval approaches were effective methods to combat unfavorable product information. The underlying rationale is that when making evaluative judgments, consumers typically use less than their full complement of associations about the product. For example, when judging automobiles, consumers would be overwhelmed if they tried to consider every automobile on every possible characteristic. With just ten automobiles and ten characteristics, this would involve 100 bits of information. Most consumers simplify the task by focusing on a few characteristics (such as styling and reliability), and

clustering the automobiles into groups (definitely acceptable, definitely unacceptable, and those in between). Only ten of the hundred possible items of information might be used to make a decision. If consumers are actively thinking about product crisis information, it is likely that the organization's product will be relegated to the unacceptable category. On the other hand, by focusing attention on other attributes, the negative information will not be used in making product judgments.

Retrieval can be influenced through mass communications. For example, the spreading of a rumor linking worms to hamburgers might be countered by advertising fish and chicken rather than hamburgers. This would minimize the chances that consumers would spontaneously retrieve the rumor information. Before selecting a retrieval approach, the organization should conduct research to determine which thoughts can be easily retrieved by consumers susceptible to the crisis information, the valence or relative favorableness of these thoughts, and what information would be most likely to trigger retrieval of favorable product thoughts. In the present study, it was relatively easy to get individuals to retrieve the many positive associations to apples (e.g., Grandma's Apple Pie).

CONCLUSION

Product crises can potentially occur for every organization at any point in time. Consequently, organizations should be prepared to deal with them. This paper has reviewed the literature addressing product crises and identified several strategies for coping with them. Two approaches, directly refuting the crisis and focusing attention on information not related to the crisis, were compared against no response in a field experiment. Consistent with other research, a retrieval approach was successful in restoring buying intentions. A direct refutation also restored intentions but not to a statistically significant level. An interesting observation in support of a limitation of a refutational approach is the anecdotal evidence provided to us by representatives of the apple industry that fewer apples were sold when labeled "Alar free" than when unlabeled.

REFERENCES

Advertising Age (1982), "Procter & Gamble Rumor Blitz Looks Like a Bomb," (August 9), 1, 68-69.

Calantone, Roger J. and Paul R. Warshaw (1985), "Negating the Effects of Fear Appeals in Election Campaigns," *Journal of Applied Psychology,* 70 (August), 627-633.

Chattopadyay, Amitava and Kunal Basu (1990), "Humor in Advertising: The Moderating Role of Prior Brand Evaluation," *Journal of Marketing Research,* 27 (November), 466-476.

Holak, Susan L. and Srinivas K. Reddy (1986), "Effects of a Television and Radio Advertising Ban: A Study of the Cigarette Industry," *Journal of Marketing,* 50 (October), 219-227.

Hume, Scott (1987), "Corona Fights Bad-Beer Rumors," *Advertising Age,* (August 3), 6.

Jarrell, G. and S. Peltzman (1985), "The Impact of Product Recalls on the Wealth of Sellers," *Journal of Political Economy,* 77.

Levinson, Arlene (1991), "Wild Sterilization Rumor Nearly Killed Soda Brand," *Seattle Times,* (July 7), 16.

Morgan, Fred W. (1988), "Tampered Goods: Legal Developments and Marketing Guidelines," *Journal of Marketing,* 52 (April), 86-96

Phan, Phillip and R. Chong (1990), "Crisis Management: A Second Look at The Alar Scare," *Pacific Northwest Executive,* (April), 19-21.

Reinhardt, Claudia (1987), "How to Handle a Crisis," *Public Relations Journal,* (November), 43-44.

Stanton, Alex (1989), "On the Home Front," *Public Relations Journal,* 45 (September), 15-16.

Seamon, J. G., R. L. Marsh, and N. Brody (1984), "Critical Importance of Exposure Duration for Affective Discrimination of Stimuli that are not Recognized," *Journal of Experimental Psychology, Learning, Memory and Cognition,* 10 465-469.

Tybout, Alice, Bobby Calder, and Brian Sternthal (1981), "Using Information Processing Theory to Design Marketing Strategies," *Journal of Marketing Research,* 18 (February) 73-79.

ADVERTISING AND THE SELF: IS NEGATIVE AFFECT EFFECTIVE?

Maureen Morrin, New York University

ABSTRACT

This study suggests that advertising can reduce the level of satisfaction with the self yet create favorable attitudes toward the ad. Such advertising does not appear to produce greater levels of negative affect among consumers with large self-concept discrepancies.

INTRODUCTION

Can advertising change how we feel about ourselves? Is it capable of making us dissatisfied with who we think we are or anxious about who we think we ought to be? What types of consumers are most vulnerable to advertising that produces negative emotions? And is such advertising effective at creating favorable attitudes toward the ad and toward the advertised product? The purpose of this paper is to extend our knowledge of the relationship between consumers' self-concepts and advertising that produces negative emotions.

LITERATURE REVIEW

There is no generally accepted definition of the self (or self-concept), even among researchers in the basic disciplines. Rosenberg describes the self as "the totality of the individual's thoughts and feelings having reference to himself as an object" (Rosenberg 1979, p. 7). Generally speaking, psychological researchers have conceived of the development of the self as an internal or mental process, while sociological researchers have examined the external or situational influences on the development of the self. James (1892) provided one of the first definitive conceptualizations of the self. He suggested that each of us has multiple social selves, one for each person or group of persons that has a particular image of us.

Symbolic interactionists stress the importance of social context in defining the self (e.g. Mead 1934). Their research suggests we are able to step out of our own shoes, so to speak, and see ourselves from others' perspectives. Cooley (1902) labeled this the "looking glass self." Our self-concept, then, is a function not only of what we think of ourselves, but of what others think of us, or more precisely, what we think others think of us.

Self-esteem is a construct closely related to that of the self. James defined self-esteem as a ratio of "successes" to "pretensions." The fundamental idea, which continues to this day, is that self-esteem is a function of one's actual (or perceived) accomplishments compared to one's goals and aspirations. These two elements are now generally referred to as the "actual" and "ideal" selves. It is believed that a significant discrepancy between one's actual and ideal selves reduces one's self-esteem. While a considerable body of work has utilized the self-esteem construct, much less attention has been directed to other types of self-concept discrepancies such as the discrepancy between what one actually is and what one believes one ought to be (e.g. Higgins 1987), discussed later in this paper.

The Self in Marketing

The precursor to marketing studies involving the self-concept were those which attempted to link product preference to consumer personality traits (Dittmar 1990). Evans (1959), for example, compared owners of Ford and Chevrolet autos but failed to find any systematic differences in the personalities of these two groups. Other attempts to link personality to product purchase found similarly weak results (e.g. Tucker and Painter 1961). It was largely due to the disappointing results of studies based on personality that alternatives emerged, including studies based on the self-concept.

The marketing literature began to report on the link between self-concept and consumer behavior at least as early as 1959. Levy (1959) argued that consumer behavior is motivated not just by the functional value of goods but also by their symbolic value. Levy's work stimulated research on the relation between consumer self-image and product image. The basic hypothesis for much of this work in the 1960's was that a high degree of congruity between consumer self-image and product image would lead to higher levels of product preference and purchase (e.g. Grubb and Grathwohl 1967). Birdwell (1968) found support for the congruity hypothesis based on car ownership. Consumers' self-images were found to be more congruent with the brand of car they owned than with several other brands not owned. Dolich (1969) provided additional support for the congruity hypothesis by showing that self-image/product image congruity was just as effective for "private" products such as bar soap and toothpaste as for "social" products such as beer and cigarettes. Sommers showed that consumers perceive their own self-images and those of reference groups in terms of products (e.g. Sommers 1964).

Although motivation research fell out of favor among researchers in the 1970's (Hirschman and Holbrook 1982), work continued on the subject of the self. It can be argued that there was room for improvement concerning theories about the self since up until the late 1960's almost none of the studies conducted took into account the impact of social context (Lee 1990). The psychological component of the self had been investigated but not the sociological component. The early studies were also criticized (e.g. by Evans 1968) for their reliance on post-purchase data. Such studies could not prove causality between congruity and product purchase, since the reported congruity could have developed after product purchase. (See Landon 1974 for a review.)

By the 1980's, the concept of the self had become a multifaceted construct that included elements such as the actual, ideal, and social selves. Sirgy's 1982 review paper lamented the proliferation of and lack of agreement on self-concept constructs as well as the atheoretical approach utilized by many researchers in the field. In the late 1980's, the concept of the "extended self" was proposed by Belk (1988). Belk suggested that the self-concept extended beyond one's own mind and body to include material possessions. Individuals, according to Belk, perceive and define themselves, at least in part, based on what they own.

Cognitive psychologists conceive of the self as a schema, or an organized system of knowledge structures stored in memory (Markus 1977). A person's self schema is thought to impact one's behavior in the marketplace via the level of involvement. Consumers are thought to be more cognitively involved in processing stimuli which are relevant to their self schemata. One recent theory based on a cognitive conceptualization of the self is self-discrepancy theory (e.g. Higgins, Klein, and Strauman 1985). Self-discrepancy theory, like many other social psychological theories involving emotion, assumes that cognition largely precedes and determines affective response (Fiske and Taylor 1991). (See Zajonc 1980 for an alternative view.)

Affect is an all-encompassing term that can include emotions, moods, evaluations, and preferences (Fiske and Taylor 1991). In this study, affect is defined as an emotional response which is assessed by means of verbal reports. Two emotions are examined in this study: dejection and anxiety. Dejection-related emotions are defined as those which describe a sad, unmotivated, or dissatisfied state. Agitation-related emotions are defined as those which describe a frightened, threatened, or nervous state. These definitions are consistent with clinical psychological usage (Higgins et al. 1986).

Affect types can be characterized along two dimensions: pleasantness/unpleasantness and high/low arousal (Russell 1978). In this typology, dejection-related and agitation-related emotions would both be classified as unpleasant, but the agitation-related emotions would be classified at a higher level of arousal. Dejection and agitation, therefore, while not mutually exclusive constructs, can be considered distinct.

Self-Discrepancy Theory

Higgins' self-discrepancy theory (e.g. Higgins et al. 1985) extends our understanding of the self by categorizing the various 'selves' that compose our self-concept and by linking discrepancies between these selves to distinct, negative affective states. Higgins proposes that there are two major cognitive dimensions of the self which he calls *domains of the self* and *standpoints on the self*. Higgins distinguishes among three domains of the self: the *actual* self, the *ideal* self, and the *ought* self.

The actual self refers to the representation of attributes that one currently believes one possesses. The ideal self refers to the representation of attributes which one ideally would like to possess. These can be thought of as one's hopes, dreams and goals for oneself. The ought self refers to the representation of attributes that one believes one ought to possess. These attributes include one's sense of duty, obligations, and conscience. Higgins et al. explain that "the difference between the `ideal' and the `ought' self is reflected in the classic conflict between one's `personal desires' and one's `sense of duty'" (Higgins et al. 1985, p. 53). The second cognitive dimension of the self, standpoints on the self, refers to the person from whose standpoint a judgement about the self is being made. The standpoints on the self consist of: *own* and *other* (e.g. parent or friend). For the purposes of the research reported here, only the "own" standpoint is utilized.

Higgins et al. propose that discrepancies between actual and ideal self-concepts (A/I discrepancies) produce dejection-related emotions and symptoms such as dissatisfaction and disappointment. Discrepancies between actual and ought self-concepts (A/O discrepancies), on the other hand, produce agitation-related emotions and symptoms such as anxiety and fear. Higgins et al. (1986, Study 2) examined the effect of contextual priming on subjects who had both large actual/ideal and large actual/ought discrepancies versus those who had small discrepancies. Ideal priming (i.e. describing various aspects associated with the ideal self) increased feelings of dejection among subjects with large discrepancies while slightly decreasing feelings of dejection among subjects without large discrepancies. Similarly, ought priming increased feelings of agitation among subjects with large discrepancies while slightly decreasing such feelings among subjects without large discrepancies.

The fact that contextual priming can temporarily increase the accessibility or salience of a particular self-concept discrepancy is key in applying self-discrepancy theory in an advertising context. The study hypothesizes that advertising can act as a contextual prime for consumers' actual/ideal and actual/ought self-concept discrepancies. Evidence exists (Richins 1991) to support the notion that advertising can raise the ideal standard by which consumers compare themselves, thereby causing an affective reaction of dissatisfaction with the self. Richins (1991) conducted several studies among female college students and found that those exposed to magazine advertisements containing attractive models reported less satisfaction with their own physical appearance, compared to those exposed to ads without such models.

The primary theoretical foundation for Richins' study lies in Festinger's (1954) social comparison theory. Festinger proposed that individuals are motivated to compare themselves to similar others in order to have a standard against which they can evaluate their own abilities and opinions. Comparison others may also be simply those who are salient or accessible in memory, for example, people in advertisements. In Richins' study advertising acts as a temporary contextual cue. The attractive models in the print ads have the effect of raising the subjects' standards of attractiveness and, in Higgins' terminology, increasing the discrepancy between actual versus ideal attractiveness levels, resulting in lowered satisfaction with the self. Interestingly, Richins (1991) found that the increased gap between actual and ideal self-concepts resulted not from a reduction in subjects' evaluations of their own attractiveness, but rather solely from an increase in the standard of comparison. This finding, she states, is consistent with previous theories that suggest one's actual self-concept is fairly stable by adulthood.

HYPOTHESES

The first set of hypotheses seeks to confirm Richins' findings that exposure to "ideal" advertising reduces subjects' satisfaction with the relevant self-concept attribute (i.e. attractiveness) but does not alter their self-ratings on that attribute. That is, the dissatisfaction with self stems solely from an increase in comparison standards rather than from a change in one's actual self-concept.

H1a: Ideal advertising will reduce subjects' satisfaction with the relevant self-concept attribute (attractiveness).

H1b: Ideal advertising will not reduce subjects' self ratings on the relevant attribute (attractiveness).

The next set of hypotheses seeks to extend Richins' findings to the area of "ought" advertising, or advertising which acts as a contextual prime for subjects' sense of duty, obligation or conscience.

H2a: Ought advertising will reduce subjects' satisfaction with the relevant self-concept attribute (dutifulness).

H2b: Ought advertising will not reduce subjects' self

ratings on the relevant attribute (dutifulness).

The next set of hypotheses tests whether self-concept discrepancies moderate advertising's ability to produce negative affective responses. Ideal and ought ads are not expected to affect all subjects equally. It is hypothesized that ideal and ought advertising will create higher levels of negative affect only among subjects who have large self-concept discrepancies. This expectation is based on similar findings by Higgins et al. (1986, Study 2) in a non-advertising context.

H3a: Among subjects exposed to ideal advertising, those with larger actual/ideal self-concept discrepancies will exhibit higher dejection scores.

H3b: Among subjects exposed to ought advertising, those with larger actual/ought self-concept discrepancies will exhibit higher agitation scores.

The last set of hypotheses concerns the relationship between advertising condition and consumers' attitudes toward the ad and toward the product. It is hypothesized that subjects in the ideal and ought conditions will rate both the ads and products more favorably than will subjects in the control condition. These hypotheses suggest that advertising which primes consumers' ideal or ought self-concepts is more successful at generating favorable attitudes than is advertising that is unrelated to consumers' self-concepts.

H4a: Subjects in the ideal and ought advertising conditions will exhibit more favorable attitudes toward the ads than will control subjects.

H4b: Subjects in the ideal and ought advertising conditions will exhibit more favorable attitudes toward the advertised products than will control subjects.

METHOD

The experiment consisted of two parts: (1) the measurement of subjects' self-concept discrepancies (independent variable), and (2) exposure to one of three advertising manipulations (independent variable) followed by an assessment of several dependent measures including attitude toward the ad, attitude toward the product, self rating of attractiveness and dutifulness, satisfaction with attractiveness and dutifulness, and affective response.

Subjects' self-concept discrepancies were measured using the Selves questionnaire (Higgins et al. 1985). This instrument was completed one to two weeks prior to the experimental manipulation so as to minimize possible carry-over effects. On this questionnaire, subjects are asked to list attributes associated with each of their own self-concepts: actual, ideal and ought. After listing the attributes for a self-concept, subjects are asked to rate the extent to which they believe they possess (or would like to possess or ought to possess) each attribute on a scale of 1 (=slightly) to 4 (=extremely).

An actual/ideal discrepancy score is calculated for each subject by comparing the two relevant lists of attributes. Exact matches (e.g. friendly 3, friendly (3) are given a weight of the sum of the two ratings (e.g. +6). Other exact or synonymous matches (operationally defined by Roget's Thesaurus) are given a weight equal to the negative of the distance in ratings (e.g. wealthy 1, rich 4 results in a weight of -3). Opposites or antonymous mismatches (defined by Roget's Thesaurus) are given a weight equal to the negative of the sum of the ratings (e.g. depressed 3, happy 4 results in a weight of -7). Finally, items in the ideal self-concept which have neither a synonymous or antonymous match are given a weight equal to the negative of its rating (e.g. married 3 results in a weight of -3). The weights are summed for a total actual/ideal discrepancy score. The same procedure was carried out for the actual/ought discrepancies.

Subjects were exposed to one of three advertising manipulations: ideal, ought, or control. The ideal and ought advertising manipulations were designed to act as contextual primes for subjects' ideal and ought self-concepts, respectively. Each of the three conditions (ideal, ought, control) were operationalized by exposing subjects to photographic slides of print ads from national magazines such as *Glamour* and *GQ*. Subjects in each condition were exposed to a total of five advertisements. A photographic slide of each ad was projected for 30 seconds, followed by a brief pause during which subjects answered six closed-ended questions evaluating the ad and the advertised product.

Approximately 20 ads per condition were initially chosen for consideration. These were narrowed down to 5 ads per condition based on a small pre-test (n=4) and subjective judgement. The ideal priming was operationalized on the basis of physical appearance (similar to Richins 1991 study). This self-concept attribute will be referred to as "attractiveness" in this paper. Since approximately 20 percent of subjects included a reference to attractiveness in the ideal section of the Selves questionnaire, this attribute was considered sufficiently important for investigation. Ads for the ideal condition featured attractive models (either full face or full body) for personal care items and clothing. Separate sets of ads were in the ideal condition: one set targeted towards males (such as male cologne) and one set targeted towards females (such as cosmetics).

The ought priming was operationalized on the basis of donating behavior to international charity organizations for children. This self-concept attribute is referred to as "dutifulness" in the paper. Since approximately 40 percent of subjects included a reference related to dutifulness to others in the ought section of the Selves question-

naire, this attribute was considered sufficiently important for investigation. Print ads featuring disadvantaged children were featured in ads for relief organizations such as Plan International (formerly Foster Parents Plan).

The control condition, which is designed not to evoke significant negative affective responses, was operationalized using print ads for laundry detergents such as Tide and Cheer. It was believed that laundry detergents would be relatively unrelated to subjects' ideal and ought self-concepts and hence produce minimal affective responses of dejection and agitation.

A sample of undergraduate marketing students at a private, suburban college was used. The subjects were asked to voluntarily participate in the experiment during the end of two class sessions (one used to administer the Selves questionnaire and a subsequent session used to conduct the advertising manipulation and administer the dependent measures). Subjects were told that the purpose of the experiment was to understand how people evaluate print ads. Subjects were randomly assigned to each treatment in groups of 12 to 20 students (classes or large groups within a class) so as to minimize disruption to their regular classroom routine. At the end of the experiment subjects were verbally debriefed and told of the true experimental hypotheses. A total of 68 completed sets of questionnaires were obtained. Two subjects whose answers to the Selves questionnaire indicated that they did not take the task seriously were eliminated from the sample.

Attitudes toward each ad were assessed using three 5-point semantic differential scale items (convincing/ unconvincing, appealing/unappealing, interesting/boring). These three items were summed for each subject over all five advertisement exposures for an advertisement rating. Attitudes toward the product were assessed with a scale that consisted of three Likert items (i.e., "I like the advertised product." "The ad made me feel this product is right for me." "I will definitely buy the product in this ad."). Each item was rated on a five point scale from "Strongly Agree" to "Strongly Disagree." These three items were summed for each subject over all five advertisement exposures for a product rating. The anchoring of the semantic differential and Likert items was reversed for half of the subjects to minimize positive or negative answer biases.

Following exposure to the ads, subjects' affective responses were measured using the Emotions scale (Higgins et al. 1985; Higgins et al. 1986). This scale asks subjects to rate how often they have felt each of 62 emotions (e.g. listless, happy, panicky) in the past week on a scale from 0 (=almost never) to 4 (=almost always). The order of items on the Emotions scale was reversed for half of the subjects to minimize order effects. Sixteen of the items are agitation-related, 14 of the items are dejection-related, and the 32 remaining items are fillers. For each subject, the 16 agitation-related items were summed for an agitation score, and the 14 dejection-related items were summed for a dejection score.

Finally, subjects rated their own level of attractiveness and satisfaction with attractiveness on five point scales from "Not at all" to "Very." Subjects also rated the extent to which they fulfilled obligations to those less fortunate than themselves ('dutifulness') from "Not well at all" to "Very well" as well as their satisfaction with how well they fulfilled such obligations from "Not at all" to "Very." The anchors for each of these four items were reversed for half of the sample. We attempted to minimize the potential for social desirability biases by informing subjects that their answers to the questionnaire would be kept "anonymous and completely confidential."

RESULTS AND DISCUSSION

The first set of hypotheses concern the effect of advertising on subjects' self ratings and their satisfaction with the relevant self-concept attributes. It was hypothesized that the ideal and ought ads would reduce subjects' satisfaction with but not their self-ratings of the relevant attributes.

Interestingly, exposure to ideal ads did not reduce subjects' satisfaction with their own physical attractiveness as was hypothesized (H1a) (see Table 1). This finding runs counter to Richins' (1991) study. Since Richins used only female subjects, it was hypothesized that the divergent findings could be a function of gender. Individual analyses were conducted for females and males (see Table 2), but the differences did not approach significance (due largely to the small cell sizes).

It is interesting to note that for the entire student sample, females exhibit significantly lower ratings of and levels of satisfaction with their own attractiveness than do males (see Table 3). Additional work seems warranted here, to examine gender effects in advertising's ability to create dissatisfaction with the self.

Importantly, the ability of advertising to reduce subjects' satisfaction with an ought self-concept attribute (dutifulness) was supported (H2a) (see Table 4). Subjects exposed to the ought advertising were significantly less satisfied with their own level of dutifulness than were subjects exposed to the control ads. Subjects' self-ratings of dutifulness were not significantly different between the two groups, as hypothesized (H2b) (see Table 4). In

---

TABLE 1
Effect of Ideal Advertising

Satisfaction With Attractiveness (H1a)				Self Rating of Attractiveness (H1b)			
Condition:		Diff:	p:	Condition:		Diff:	p:
Ideal	Control			Ideal	Control		
3.22	3.29	-0.07	0.84	3.51	3.36	0.15	0.54
(n=40)	(n=14)			(n=40)	(n=14)		
(1.01)	(0.75)			(0.77)	(0.91)		

TABLE 2
Effect of Ideal Advertising (Female/Male)

Satisfaction With Attractiveness (F)				Satisfaction With Attractiveness (M)			
Condition:		Diff:	p:	Condition:		Diff:	p:
Ideal	Control			Ideal	Control		
3.05	3.12	-0.07	0.90	3.40	3.35	0.05	0.88
(n=20)	(n=4)			(n=20)	(n=10)		
(1.16)	(0.63)			(0.84)	(0.82)		

TABLE 3
Gender Differences on Attractiveness Attribute

Satisfaction With Attractiveness				Self Rating of Attractiveness			
Female:	Male:	Diff:	p:	Female:	Male:	Diff:	p:
3.10	3.51	-0.41	0.07	3.30	3.71	-0.41	0.04
(n=30)	(n=36)			(n=30)	(n=36)		
(1.01)	(0.81)			(0.74)	(0.84)		

TABLE 4*
Effect of Ought Advertising

Satisfaction With Dutifulness (H2a)				Self Rating of Dutifulness (H2b)			
Condition:		Diff:	p:	Condition:		Diff:	p:
Ought	Control			Ought	Control		
2.54	3.36	-0.82	0.03	2.62	3.14	-0.52	0.18
(n=12)	(n=14)			(n=12)	(n=14)		
(0.81)	(0.93)			(0.88)	(1.03)		

*Note: "p" = probability that the difference in means occurred due to chance. Cell sizes are in the first set of parentheses; standard deviations are in the second set of parentheses. Items are measured on 5-point scales from 1 (=Not at all) to 5 (=Very).

TABLE 5
Effect of Self-Concept Discrepancy on Negative Affective Response to Ads

Linear Regression of Dejection Score on Actual/Ideal Discrepancy Among Subjects Exposed to Ideal Advertisements (H3a)			Linear Regression of Agitation Score on Actual/Ought Discrepancy Among Subjects Exposed to Ought Advertisements (H3b)		
Predictor Variable:	Student's t:	p:	Predictor Variable:	Student's t:	p:
Constant	6.52	0.0000	Constant	6.66	0.0001
A/I Gap	-0.16	0.8757	A/O Gap	-0.08	0.9386
n=40			n=12		
Overall F<1			Overall F<1		
R-squared=0.0007			R-squared=0.0006		

Note: "p" = probability that the estimated parameter is zero. A/I=actual/ideal discrepancy, A/O=actual/ought discrepancy. Discrepancies measured by Selves questionnaire.

TABLE 6
Effect of Advertising on Attitudes Toward Ad and Product

Advertisement Ad Ratings (H4a)					Product Ratings (H4b)				
Condition:			F:	p:	Condition:			F:	p:
Ideal	Ought	Control			Ideal	Ought	Control		
42.75	50.67	44.86	2.34	0.10	38.13	44.46	45.18	5.18	0.01
(n=40)	(n=12)	(n=14)			(n=40)	(n=12)	(n=14)		
(142.3)	(107.7)	(82.13)			(75.97)	(45.93)	(68.06)		

Note: "p" = probability that the difference in means occurred due to chance. (for one-way ANOVA). Cell sizes are in the first set of parentheses; standard deviations are in the second set of parentheses. Scores are sums of three 5-point closed ended items across five ads/products.

other words, the advertising appears to have caused the dissatisfaction with self as a result of an increased standard of comparison rather than a reduction in self-rating.

The next set of hypotheses tests whether self-concept discrepancies moderate advertising's ability to produce negative affect. Ordinary least squares regressions of negative affective response (dejection, anxiety) on size of self-concept discrepancy (actual/ideal, actual/ought) did not achieve significance and hence do not support hypotheses 3a and 3b (see Table 5). It is believed that these hypotheses were not confirmed because the research attempted to link too broad of a construct (i.e. ideal and ought self-concepts) to very specific self-concept attributes (i.e. attractiveness and dutifulness). Future attempts to confirm self-concept discrepancy theory in an advertising context might be more successful if the Selves questionnaire were revised to focus on the self-concept attributes of interest to the researcher i.e., those to be subsequently primed by advertising manipulations.

The last set of hypotheses predicted that subjects in the ideal and ought conditions would rate the ads and products to which they were exposed more favorably than would subjects in the control condition. In regard to attitudes toward the ad (H4a), subjects in the ought condition rated the ads significantly higher than did subjects in the ideal and control conditions (see Table 6). This result is not surprising since the ought treatment was the only treatment successful at reducing subjects' satisfaction with the self. With regard to product rating (H4b), subjects in the ought and control conditions rated the products significantly higher than did those in the ideal condition. The high product rating in the ought condition was expected, given the ads' effectiveness at reducing subjects' satisfaction with self. However, the high product rating in the control condition was not predicted.

CONCLUSIONS AND LIMITATIONS

This study has shown that advertising can act as a contextual prime for consumers' ought self-concepts. Such advertising reduces subjects' satisfaction with the self without significantly altering subjects' self-ratings on the relevant self-concept attribute. These results occurred for both males and females. However, directional evidence suggests that gender differences may be more likely to exist with regard to ideal self-concepts. The evidence also indicates that advertising which is effective at reducing consumers' satisfaction with the self may be effective at producing more favorable attitudes toward the ad. It should be noted that since this research was conducted on a relatively small scale with uneven cell sizes, the results can be considered only preliminary. However, the results seem encouraging enough to warrant further research.

ENDNOTE

Special thanks to Professor Ralph Gallay and his students at Rider College for providing the data for this study, and to Professors Robert Shoemaker, Betsy Creyer, and Jacob Jacoby at New York University and Professor E. Tory Higgins at Columbia University for helpful comments on an earlier draft.

REFERENCES

Belk, R. W. (1988), "Possessions and the Extended Self," *Journal of Consumer Research,* 15 (September), 139-168.

Birdwell, A. E. (1968), "A Study of the Influence of Image Congruence on Consumer Choice," *Journal of Business,* 41 (January), 76-88.

Cooley, C. H. (1902), *Human Nature and the Social Order.* New York: Scribner's.

Dittmar, H. (1990), *Material Possessions and Identity.* Uunpublished Dissertation, University of Sussex.

Dolich, I. J. (1969), "Congruence Relationship Between Self-Image and Product Brands," *Journal of Marketing Research,* 6 (February), 80-84.

Evans, F. B. (1959), "Psychological and Objective Factors in the Prediction of Brand Choice," *Journal of Business,* 32, 340-369.

Evans, F. (1968), "Automobiles and Self-Imagery: Comment," *Journal of Business,* 41 (October), 445-459.

Festinger, Leon (1954), "A Theory of Social Comparison Processes," *Human Relations,* 7 (May), 117-140.

Fiske, Susan T. and Shelley E. Taylor (1991), "Social Cognition and the Self," *Social Cognition,* 2nd edition, New York: McGraw-Hill, Chapter 6, 180-242.

Grubb, E. L. and H. L. Grathwohl (1967), "Consumer Self-Concept, Symbolism and Market Behavior: A Theoretical Approach," *Journal of Marketing,* 31 (October), 22-27.

Higgins, E. T. (1987), "Self-Discrepancy: A Theory Relating Self and Affect," *Psychological Review,* 94, 319-340.

_____, R. Klein, and T. Strauman (1985), "Self-Concept Discrepancy Theory: A Psychological Model for Distinguishing Among Different Aspects of Depression and Anxiety," *Social Cognition,* 3 (1), 51-76.

_____, T. Strauman, and R. Klein (1986), "Standards and the Process of Self-Evaluation: Multiple Affects from Multiple Stages," in *Handbook of Motivation and Cognition: Foundations of Social Behavior,* Richard M. Sorrentino and E. Tory Higgins, eds. New York: Guilford, 23-63.

Hirschman, E. C. and M. B. Holbrook (1982), "Hedonic Consumption: Emerging Concepts, Methods and Propositions," *Journal of Marketing,* 46 (Summer), 92-101.

James, W. (1892), *Psychology: The Briefer Course.* New York: Holt.

Landon, E. L. (1974), "Self Concept, Ideal Self Concept, and Consumer Purchase Intentions," *Journal of Consumer Research,* 1 (September), 44-51.

Lee, D. H. (1990), "Symbolic Interactionism: Some Implications for Consumer Self-Concept and Product Symbolism Research," *Advances in Consumer Research,* 17, 386-393.

Levy, S. J. (1959), "Symbols for Sale," *Harvard Business Review,* 37 (July/August), 117-124.

Markus, H. (1977), "Self Schemata and Processing Information About the Self," *Journal of Personality and Social Psychology,* 35, (February), 63-78.

Mead, G. H. (1934), *Mind, Self and Society.* Chicago: University of Chicago Press.

Richins, Marsha L. (1991), "Social Comparison and the

Idealized Images of Advertising," *Journal of Consumer Research,* 18, 71-83.

Rosenberg, M. (1979), *Conceiving the Self.* New York: Basic.

Russell, J. A. (1978), "Evidence of Convergent Validity on the Dimensions of Affect," *Journal of Personality and Social Psychology,* 36, 1152-1168.

Sirgy, M. J. (1982), "Self-Concept in Consumer Behavior: A Critical Review," *Journal of Consumer Research,* 9 (December), 287-300.

Sommers, M. S. (1964), "Product Symbolism and the Perception of Social Strata," *Proceedings of the American Marketing Association,* 22, 200-216.

Tucker, W. T. and J. J. Painter (1961), "Personality and Product Use," *Journal of Applied Psychology,* 45 (5), 325-329.

Zajonc, R. B. (1980), "Feeling and Thinking: Preferences Need No Inferences, *American Psychologist,* 35, 151-175.

SEGMENTING THE MATURE MARKET BY CHARACTERISTICS OF ORGANIZATIONAL RESPONSE TO COMPLAINT BEHAVIOR

Jeff Allen, University of Central Florida
Duane Davis, University of Central Florida
Garland Keesling, Towson State University
William Grazer, Towson State University

ABSTRACT

A composite of 17 weighted items regarding preferences of the mature market for organizational response to registered complaints is used to identify four distinct market segments. The segments are constructed using a sample of 306 mature consumers in Central Florida. Managerial implications for the actionability of the segments to response characteristics are discussed and strategies for business redress suggested.

INTRODUCTION

There has been considerable research over the past fifteen years on the consumption preferences of what has frequently been referred to as the 'mature' (i.e. 55-plus years of age) market (Lazer 1986). Many different studies have characterized it as heterogeneous and a full range of marketing strategies has been suggested for effectively serving this market. For instance, Lazer (1985) suggests viewing the mature market as a composite of four distinct age groups; 55 to 64, 65 to 74, 75 to 85, and 86 and over. Others have recommended transgenerational strategies where products may be marketed across age segments (Bone 1991; Underhill and Francheille 1984; Louden 1976).

Some (Visvabharathy and Rink 1985) suggest combining age breakdowns with such factors as income, education, and personality. Others (Gollub and Javitz 1988; Day 1987-88; Keane 1984) recommend the use of lifestyles or psychographic variables to enhance the understanding of mature segments. Still others have applied additional factors to segment the mature market including: behavioral and attitudinal similarities (French and Fox 1985; Bartos 1980), information processing and self-concept (Greco 1987), and physical and psychological dimensions (Doyle 1989; Schewe 1988; Lazer 1986; Lumpkin and Greenburg 1982).

The mature market has grown substantially in size, activity, and economic strength. According to the 1980 Census, the number of elderly consumers (65 and over) constituted 12 percent of the population. Based on these figures, projections for the year 2030 indicate an increase to 63.3 million elders, or about 21 percent of the U.S. population. The number of persons 55 and over is expected to grow from 52.2 million in 1988 to 75.9 million in the year 2030 representing over 25 percent of the population (U.S. Census Bureau 1989).

While size alone does not suggest a viable market segment, mature consumers represent an attractive market when income data are taken into account. Mature consumers typically possess greater discretionary income dollars than their younger counterparts (Van der Merne 1987; Brown 1986; Petre 1986). Moreover, much of this analysis does not consider that many own their own homes outright, have fewer big-ticket purchases, no longer support children, and have access to more methods of home equity (e.g., reverse, rollover mortgages). One source even notes that people over 50 years of age control 75 percent of the nation's wealth and 50 percent of its discretionary income (Konrad and DeGeorge 1988).

The needs of mature consumers vary greatly by product category given changes in age and income (Lazer and Shaw 1987; Visvabharathy and Rink 1984). Numerous studies have been conducted on various elements in the marketing mix. For example, promotional studies have focused on media choice, copy design, and advertising content (Day et al. 1987-88; Gilly and Zeithaml 1985; Keane 1984; Bartos 1980). Pricing studies suggest that differences exist in the use of unit pricing, coupon redemption, willingness to shop, and utilization of senior-citizen discounts (Beardon and Mason 1979; Lambert 1979). Distribution related studies indicate that store choice and brand loyalty may be a function of consumer mobility (Lumpkin and Hunt 1989; Gelb 1978). Product studies also clearly support the notion that the mature market is not monolithic (Moschis 1991).

Quality/price attributes of the store (Lumpkin et al. 1985), and the availability of in-store information sources (Lumpkin and Festervand 1988; Beardon and Mason 1979) have also been suggested as a means of segmenting the mature market. Greco (1987), Schewe (1985), and Visvabharathy and Rink (1984) summarize much of the research concerning the mature consumers' demand for products, as well as, their responses to other marketing mix variables. These and other investigations yield meaningful strategic implications for the study of mature market behavior.

COMPLAINT BEHAVIOR

Studies attempting to examine the complaint behavior of elderly consumers have frequently found mature consumers to complain less than their younger counterparts (Beardon and Mason 1979; Pfaff and Blivice 1977; Valle and Koeske 1977; Wall et al. 1977). Elderly consumers are said to largely refrain from complaint behavior (Lawther 1978) and perceive fewer complaint alternatives when dissatisfied (Moyer 1984). Furthermore, high levels of purchase satisfaction have been attributed to elderly consumers (Warland 1984; Westbrook 1977; Mason and Himes 1973).

However, contrary to previous findings, Bernhardt (1981) found the elderly to be equally as likely to complain in response to dissatisfaction. In addition, the elderly were generally more dissatisfied with products and services than the overall population. Contradictory findings such as these, suggest that the mature market is comprised of multiple segments exhibiting a variety of complaint characteristics. If this is the case, an understanding of the mature market and related complaint behavior cannot be complete on an aggregate level.

It may be preferable to study consumer complaints from a process perspective (Landon 1979) where a complaint is registered with an organization and some type of response is provided. By understanding the expectations of complainants, organizations can provide types of responses that enhance consumer satisfaction and continued patronage (Goodwin and Ross 1990).

As the number of studies on consumer complaint behavior continues to increase, it is useful for researchers to define complaints and categorize them across segments of the mature market (Landon 1979). To date, survey researchers have not provided a thorough or sophisticated analysis of complaint behavior in this important area. As a result, this study is an attempt to identify distinct segments within the mature market based upon consumer preferences for characteristics of business response to customer complaints.

METHODOLOGY

A three-part mail survey was employed to collect data on the preferences and complaint behavior of mature consumers. The questionnaire was pretested on a convenience sample (n=20) of mature individuals from a local organization within the geographic area of interest. Consequently, the questionnaire was modified in wording and scale composition to increase reader clarity. Content validity was established according to the guidelines set forth by Nunnally (1978) including an extensive search of the literature, expert opinion, and a pretest on similar study units.

Questionnaire Development

In Part I of the questionnaire, a set of questions was presented which assessed a wide range of respondents' personal experience with complaint behavior involving:

the frequency and form of their past complaints, the frequency and form of past organizational responses to their complaints, the recipients of their complaints, and the types of organizations that subsequently provided redress action. These questions were developed from previous complaint experiences and expert opinion.

Part II of the survey provided a battery of seventeen (17) items that represented different types and characteristics of business response. The composite of items was developed from a search of the literature (Resnik and Harmon 1983; Gilly and Gelb 1982; Cosenza and Wilson 1981; Grantzin 1975) and from pretest interviews conducted with frequent complainers. Content validity was established by ensuring that the items included were representative of the characteristics of business response used by organizations in responding to consumer complaints.

To assess respondents' overall preferences for each of these characteristics, a weighted attribute measure was utilized (Torgerson 1958). The likelihood that each respondent "would be satisfied" with a specific characteristic was measured on a 5-point scale with anchors of 1 = "No Chance" and 5 = "For Certain" with a midpoint of 3 = "50-50 Chance." The importance of each specific characteristic was also measured on a 5-point Likert scale ranging from 1 = "Very Unimportant" to 5 = "Very Important." Each likelihood score was multiplied by its corresponding importance measure to produce a weighted index for each of the seventeen items used in the analysis.

The final section of the measurement instrument consisted of a series of demographic questions for classification purposes. Scales were developed to characterize each mature respondent's sex, age, education, household status, previous occupation, and income.

Data Collection

Data for the study were collected from a sample of 1,000 current members of the American Association of Retired Persons (AARP) in the Central Florida market area. This area has experienced tremendous growth in the retirement age group and the mature market is aggressively targeted by marketers for a variety of products and services.

To establish the representativeness of the current sample, survey results were compared with known values for the population on demographic characteristics of sex, age, education, and income (Armstrong and Overton 1977). Current estimates of the population parameters in the Central Florida area were obtained from *Florida Estimates of the Population '90* and the *Statistical Abstract of The United States '91*. No significant differences were found on the demographics tested at the .05 level, suggesting that the sample is reasonably representative of the mature population. In all, a total of 319 questionnaires were returned, from which 306 were deemed usable. This represents a response rate of 30.6 percent.

Analytic Procedures

The data were initially subjected to the SPSSX Cluster Analysis for case procedures. Utilizing the squared Euclidean distance criteria, four distinct clusters were identified from the weighted indices on the seventeen response characteristics. Cluster procedures are commonly used for classifying respondents according to similarities for further analysis (Punji and Stewart 1983).

Validation of the identified clusters was accomplished using a split-sample approach to ensure the homogeneity and discriminating ability of the cluster solution. A four cluster solution was selected because of the interpretability and consistency of the clusters obtained in the validation procedure. Analysis of Variance (ANOVA) performed on the composite of classification items revealed that all seventeen items were significantly (p's .001) related to cluster membership.

To classify each of the clusters by their respondent members and to facilitate comparison, scores on the indices were standardized. Those respondents that possessed a Z-score of greater than zero were classified as having positive preferences toward the response characteristic and were included in the percentage calculations. The range of means on the unweighted seventeen items was between 2.96 and 3.82 with an average of 3.36. When weighted, the indices tended to report a preference that is even more positive (i.e. a 50-50 chance times its importance). Further analysis developed cluster profiles using the scores on these items for cross-tabulation and ANOVA procedures.

RESULTS

Empirical Clusters

From the empirical cluster solution in the previous analysis, profiles of the four distinct clusters identified are presented in Table 1. The table displays the percentage of complainants, by cluster, who demonstrated a preference for the seventeen characteristics of redress action offered by firms. The names assigned to the clusters are: (1) "Assentors", (2) "Credibles", (3) "Suspecters", and (4) "Agnostics." These labels are descriptive of their overall preferences regarding alternative organizational responses to registered complaints.

ASSENTORS

The smallest of the clusters, which constitutes only 8 percent (n=25) of the total sample, was labeled the "Assentors." In comparison to other clusters, this segment exhibits a strong preference for most alternative redress actions offered by a firm. In fact, this cluster

reports the highest percentages on all but 5 of the 17 items. Large percentages of this group report that they would be satisfied with a response that is: prompt (82%), courteous or friendly (77%), personal (91%), and apologetic (96%), even if it questions the veracity of their complaint (96%).

It is interesting to note that some apprehension appears to exist on items that pertain to the directness and efficacy of the firm's response. For example, only half (50%) of the Assentors would be satisfied if a firm's response claimed to solve all of their problems, or if the response was verbal, or addressed from someone important in the firm. Fifty-five percent (55%) of the Assentors preferred a written letter from the organization and 46 percent a response in the form of a telephone call.

CREDIBLES

The largest of the clusters, representing 49 percent of the sample (n=149), was dubbed the "Credibles." In contrast to the Assentors, members of this cluster reported that they would more likely prefer a firm's response that was either written (62%) or verbal (54%), and if it was made by someone in an important position in the firm (58%).

Similar to the Assentors, members of this cluster have a relatively strong preference for most other redress actions. For example, 70 percent would be satisfied if a firm's response is prompt, 76 percent if the response is courteous, and 82 percent if it is personal. Additionally, if the response is in writing, this group reports the highest overall level of satisfaction (62%).

SUSPECTERS

"Suspecters" which account for 17 percent of the sample (n=53), appear to be suspicious of most characteristics of redress action. Regardless of whether the action is courteous or brief (38%), friendly (30%), personal (8%), apologetic (28%), or is a 'form letter' (15%), this group reports low levels of satisfaction. Low satisfaction is also indicated if a firm challenged the complaint legitimacy or denied responsibility for the complaint (17% and 21%), respectively.

Relative to the previous groups described, the Suspecters display only moderate satisfaction on many of the seventeen items, but tend to prefer responses that either solve (76%) or provide a means of solving the problem (51%). They would be more satisfied with a firm's response that is by telephone (51%), verbal ((61%), and by a person in an important position in the firm (62%).

AGNOSTICS

The fourth cluster, the "Agnostics," show a strong skepticism by reporting the lowest percentage of overall

TABLE 1
Cluster Profiles of Preferences for Redress to Complaint

BEHAVIOR

	Cluster			
	1	2	3	4
	Assentors	Credibles	Suspecters	Agnostics
Statement	n=25 (8%)	n=149 (49%)	n=53 (17%)	n=79(26%)
1. If a firm responds promptly.	82%	58%	49%	10%
2. If a firm's response is courteous.	77	70	38	14
3. If a firm's response is friendly.	77	76	30	14
4. If the tone of a firm's response is personal.	91	82	8	17
5. If the response solved all of my problems.	50	62	76	23
6. If the firm's response provided a means of solving my problem.	86	61	51	47
7. If a firm's response questioned the truthfulness of my complaint.	96	36	17	33
8. If the firm denied responsibility for the complaint.	59	25	21	38
9. If the firm provided an apology.	96	54	28	10
10. If the response referred me to another person in the firm.	59	44	23	14
11. If a firm's response was brief.	50	45	38	19
12. If a firm's response is sincere.	64	40	53	5
13. If a firm's response is written.	55	62	40	10
14. If a written response is a 'form letter'.	41	30	15	19
15. If a firm's response is a telephone call.	46	35	51	3
16. If a firm's response is verbal.	50	54	61	11
17. If the response is made by a person with an important position	50	58	62	23

satisfaction for 13 of the 17 redress characteristics. Only the Suspecters scored lower on the remaining four items of whether the response was personal (17%), questioned the truthfulness of the complaint (33%), denied responsibility for the complaint (38%), or is a computerized `form letter' (19%).

In contrast to members of the other three clusters, preferences for response characteristics were noted as typically low on the majority of items. For example, members in this cluster would not be satisfied with a firm's response that is sincere (5%) or in the form of a telephone call (3%). Only 10 percent of the members would be satisfied if a firm responds promptly, provides an apology, or the response is in writing. Similarly, 14 percent tended to prefer a response that is courteous, friendly, or referred them to another person in the firm. In essence, this cluster appears to be inherently negative in reaction to commonly accepted characteristics of complaint redress.

DISCUSSION

Four distinctly identifiable segments of mature consumers appear to exist with respect to their preferences for specific characteristics of business response to complaint behavior. To further describe the nature and composition of the clusters, a number of classifying variables (sex, age, education, household status, previous occupation, and income) were tested for differences in cluster membership.

Two of the attributes, education and income, were found to be significantly different across clusters. As illustrated in Table 2, the Suspecters contain the largest percentage (79%) of those with some college or more. While a large majority of members in three of the clusters indicate incomes of $25,000 or more, only 52 percent of the Assentors report a current income equal to or exceeding that amount.

The final attributes by which the clusters were profiled focused on the respondents' propensity to complain and satisfaction with the subsequent redress action. When asked if "you usually complain to firms when you experience problems with products or services," affirmative responses were frequent among the Credibles and Suspecters (84% and 90%), and common among the Assentors and Agnostics (67% and 70%). Responding to the question "Are you usually satisfied with the response (whatever form) that you receive from firms that you complain to," 72 percent of the Assentors and Credibles replied "Yes," but only 63 percent and 52 percent of the Suspecters and Agnostics were satisfied.

IMPLICATIONS

The findings of the study suggest a number of managerial implications regarding the actionability of the identified segments to types of redress offered by organizations. From the results, it appears that the market is composed of four distinct segments whose preferences for characteristics of redress action differ. Also, substantial precentages of consumers in these groups indicate a strong propensity to complain and a relatively low level of complaint satisfaction. Given the emphasis that business is placing on retaining existing customers, a better understanding of the preferences of these segments for types of redress action is essential to develop an effective redress strategy.

From a strategic standpoint, it would be desirable to tailor redress actions to each segment according to their preferences. Yet, varying redress strategies for each mature segment would be difficult to implement and cost prohibitive for most organizations. Alternatively, study findings suggest a single redress strategy that combines similar preferences across segments to be practical and cost effective.

The Credibles and Suspecters combined represent nearly two-thirds (66%) of the mature market. While different preferences between these two groups exist, certain similarities may be instrumental in determining a redress strategy. For example, both segments exhibit a preference for a business response that either solves or provides a means of solving their problems. A preferred response is one that is prompt and verbal, especially if it comes from someone important in the firm. This set of preferences is consistent because an important person in the firm would be perceived as having the means available to quickly solve consumer problems as they arise.

A smaller portion of the market, the Assentors, are

TABLE 2
Attribute Profile of Mature Complainants

		Clusters			
		1	2	3	4
		Assentors	Credibles	Suspecters	Agnostics
	Attribute	(8%)	(49%)	(17%)	(26%)
1.	Education (some college or above)	43%	59%	79%	49%
2.	Income ($25,000. or over)	52%	85%	81%	79%
3.	Complaint Propensity	67%	84%	90%	70%
4.	Complaint Satisfaction	72%	72%	63%	52%

1. P .09807
2. P .01404
3. P .02173
4. P .01732

similarly disposed to complain when they encounter problems, but show a relatively high level of preference for most characteristics of redress action taken. This would suggest that the preferences of this segment are fairly consistent with types of organizational response that are currently employed. In general, members of this segment do not expect the redress action to solve all of the problems encountered, but are receptive if the response is personal and apologetic, even if there is some doubt expressed about the truthfulness of their complaint.

The Agnostics, who represent almost a quarter of the overall market, are prone to complain and evince a low level of satisfaction with most characteristics of redress offered by a firm. However, they also are mildly receptive if a response to their complaint provides a means for solving the problem and is made by someone important in the firm. Even though this segment may be difficult to satisfy, a truly customer-oriented firm would be responsive to all legitimate complaints. These complainants have received promises to which the firm should be accountable.

CONCLUSION

This study suggests that the mature market may be segmented according to preferences for characteristics of business redress to consumer complaints. To date, the literature has few studies that pursue this line of research. Most previous efforts have been limited to segmentation by demographics. The segments discovered here may be useful in designing a redress strategy to better serve the burgeoning mature market.

Congruent with Bernhardt (1981), the findings of this study are inconsistent with earlier works (e.g., Beardon and Mason 1979; Lawther 1978; Wall et al. 1977) which have characterized the mature market as relatively complacent when experiencing dissatisfaction with purchases. Results here indicate that, on average, 80 percent of all mature consumers complain. In general, the preferred response to complaint behavior across segments is to have someone important in the firm, who is courteous and prompt, attempt to solve the problem.

The mature market is an increasingly important consuming segment that expresses only moderate satisfaction with current organizational response to registered complaints. If organizations are to better serve this market, an understanding of the preferred redress characteristics desired by each segment should help to alleviate existing dissatisfaction and retain these consumers as customers. This study has hopefully provided the initial foundation for addressing such a problem.

REFERENCES

Armstrong, J. S. and T. S. Overton (1977),"Estimating NonResponse Bias in Mail Surveys," *Journal of Marketing Research,* XIV, (August), 396-402.

Bartos, Rena (1980), "Over 49: The Invisible Consumer," *Harvard Business Review,* (January/February), 140-148.

Beardon, William 0., and J. Barry Mason (1979), "Elderly Use of In-store Information Resources and Dimensions of Product Satisfaction Dissatisfaction," *Journal of Retailing,* 55, (Spring), 79-91.

Bernhardt, Kenneth L. (1981), "Consumer Problems and Complaint Actions of Older Americans: A National View," *Journal of Retailing,* 57, 3 (Fall), 107-123.

Bone, Paula F. (1991), "Identifying Mature Segments," *The Journal of Consumer Marketing,* 8, 4 (Fall), 19-32.

Brown, Paul D., (1986) "Last Year it was Yuppies-This Year Its Their Parents," *Business Week,* (March 10), 68-74.

Cosenza, Robert M. and J. W. Wilson (1981), "How to Handle Your Customers," *Public Relations Journal,* 37 (December), 20-22.

Day, Ellen, et al. (1987-88), "Reaching the Senior Citizen Market(s)," *Journal of Advertising Research,* 28, (December/January) 23-30.

Doyle, Thomas B. (1989), "Survival of the Fittest," *American Demographics,* (May), 38-41.

Florida Estimates of the Population '90 (1990), Prepared by the Population Program Bureau of Economic

Research, University of Florida.

French, William J. and R. Fox (1985), "Segmenting the Senior Market," *Journal of Consumer Marketing,* 2, 1 (Winter), 61-72.

Gelb, Betsy D. (1978), "Exploring the Gray Market Segment," *MSU Business Topics,* 26, (Spring), 41-6.

Gilly, Mary and Betsy Gelb (1982), "Post-Purchase Consumer Processes and the Complaining Consumer," *Journal of Consumer Research,* 9 (December), 353-357.

_____and Valerie A. Zeithaml (1985), "The Elderly Consumer and Adoption Technologies," *Journal of Consumer Research,* 12, (December), 353-357.

Gollub, James and Harold Javitz (1988), "Six Ways to Age," *American Demographics* (June), 28+...

Goodwin, Cathy and Ivan Ross (1990), "Consumer Evaluations of Responses to Complaints: What's Fair and Why," *Journal of Consumer Marketing,* 7, 2 (Spring), 39-47.

Grantzin, Kent L. (1975), "Two-Way Communication in the Marketing Channel: The Case of Consumer Complaint Letter, *Proceedings,* Southern Marketing Association, 222-224.

Greco, Alan J. (1987), "Linking Dimensions of the Elderly Market to Market Planning," *Journal of Consumer Marketing,* 4 (Spring), 2, 47-55.

Keane, John G. (1984), "Our Aging Population: Advertising Implications," *Journal of Advertising Research,* 24, 10-12.

Konrad, Walecia and Gail DeGeorge (1988), "U.S. Companies Go For the Gray," *Business Week,* (April 3), 64-67.

Lambert, Zarrel V. (1979), "An Investigation of Older Consumers' Unmet Needs and Wants at the Retail Level," *Journal of Retailing,* 55, 4 (Winter), 35-57.

Landon, Edwin L. (1979), "The Direction of Consumer Complaint Research," *Advances in Consumer Research,* 7, 335-337.

Lawther, Karen (1978), "Social Integration and the Elderly Consumer: Unfairness, Complaint Actions, and Information Usage," *1978 AMA Educators' Conference Proceedings,* American Marketing Association, 341-345.

Lazer, William and Eric H. Shaw (1987), "How Older Americans Spend Their Money," *American Demographics,* 9, 9 (September), 36-41.

_____(1986), "Dimensions of the Mature Market," *Journal of Consumer Marketing,* 3 (Summer), 3, 23-34.

_____(1985), "Looking Inside the Mature Market," *American Demographics,* 7, 3 (March), 22-25...49.

Louden, David L. (1986), "Senior Citizens: An Underdeveloped Market Segment," *Southern Marketing Association Proceedings,* 124-126.

Lumpkin, James R. and Barnett A. Greenberg (1982), "Apparel-Shopping Patterns of the Elderly Market," *Journal of Retailing,* 4 (Winter), 68-89.

_____and James B. Hunt (1989), "Mobility as an Influence on Retail Patronage Behavior of the Elderly: Testing Conventional Wisdom," *Journal of the Academy of Marketing Sciences,* 17, 1 (Winter), 1-12.

_____and Troy A. Festervand (1988), "Purchase Information Sources of the Elderly," *Journal of Advertising Research,* 27, 6 (December/January), 31-43.

_____Barnett A. Greenberg and Jac L. Goldtucker (1985), "Marketplace Needs of the Elderly: Determinant Attributes and Store Choice," *Journal of Retailing,* 61, 2 (Summer), 75-105.

Mason, J. Barry and Samuel Himes (1973), "An Exploratory Behavioral and Socioeconomic Profile of Consumer Action About Dissatisfaction with Selected Household Appliances," *Journal of Consumer Affairs,* (Winter), 121-127.

Moyer, Mel (1984), "Characteristics of Consumer Complaints: Implications for Marketing and Public Policy," *Journal of Public Policy and Marketing,* 3, 67-84.

Moschis, George P. (1991), "Marketing to Older Adults," *The Journal of Consumer Marketing,* 8, 4 (Fall), 33-42.

Nunnally, J. C. (1978), *Psychometric Theory.* New York: McGraw-Hill Book Company.

Petre, Peter (1986), "Marketers Mine Gold in the Old," *Fortune,* (March 31), 70-78.

Pfaff, Martin and Sheldon Blivice (1977), "Socioeco-

nomic Correlates of Consumer and Citizen Dissatisfaction and Activism" in Ralph L. Day, ed. *Consumer Satisfaction, Dissatisfaction and Complaining Behavior,* Bloomington: Indiana University, School of Business, 115-123.

Punji, G. and D. W. Stewart (1983), "Cluster Analysis in Marketing Research: Review and Suggestions for Application," *Journal of Marketing Research,* 17, 134-148.

Resnik, Alan and Robert Harmon (1983), "Consumer Complaints and Managerial Response: A Holistic Approach," *Journal of Marketing,* 47 (Winter) 86-97.

Schewe, Charles D. (1985), "Gray America Goes to Market," *Business,* 3 (April/June), 3-9.

_____(1988), "Marketing to Our Aging Population: Responding to Physiological Changes," *Journal of Consumer Marketing,* 5, 3 (Summer) 61-73.

Torgerson, Warren (1958), *Theory and Methods of Scaling.* New York: John Wiley and Sons.

Underhill, Lois and Caldwell Francheille (1984), "What Age Do You Feel - Age Perception Study," *Journal of Consumer Marketing,* 1, 18-27.

United States Bureau of the Census (1989), "Projections of the Population of the United States, by Age, Sex and Race: 1948 to 2080," *Current Populations Reports: Population Estimates and Projections,* Series p. 25, (January), 1018, 38-39 and 104-105.

_____(1991), *Statistical Abstract of the United States,* Washington, D.C.: U.S. Government Printing Office, 128 and 450.

Valle, Valerie A. and Randi Koeske (1977), "Elderly Consumer Problems: Action, Sources of Information and Attributions of Blame," Paper presented at the Annual Meeting of the American Psychological Association (August).

Van der Merne, Sandra (1987), "GRAMPIES: A New Breed of Consumers Comes of Age," *Business Horizons,* (November/December), 14-19.

Visvabharathy, Ganesan and David R. Rink (1984), "The Elderly: Neglected Business Opportunities," *Journal of Consumer Marketing,* 1, 4 (Fall), 35-46.

Wall, Marjorie, Lois E. Dickey and W. Wayne Talarzyk (1977), "Predicting and Profiling Consumer Satisfaction and Propensity to Complain" in Ralph L. Day, ed. *Consumer Satisfaction, Dissatisfaction, and Complaining,* Bloomington: Indiana University, School or Business, 91-101.

Warland, Rex H. (1984), "Consumer Complaining and Community Involvement," *Journal of Consumer Affairs,* 18 (Summer), 64-78.

Westbrook, Robert A. (1977), "Correlates of Post Purchase Satisfaction with Major Household Appliances" in Ralph L. Day ed. *Consumer Satisfaction, Dissatisfaction, and Complaining Behavior,* Bloomington: Indiana University, School of Business, 85-90.

EXPLAINING DIFFERENCES IN INDIVIDUALS' PROPENSITY TO COMPLAIN

Nancy Ryan McClure, Texas Tech University
Pamela Kiecker, Texas Tech University

ABSTRACT

Research investigating the potential causes and effects of consumer dissatisfaction suggests that consumers' responses to a dissatisfying experience depend upon the type of industry, characteristics of the situation, and demographic and psychographic characteristics of consumers involved. This research uses a highly structured design to test a series of hypotheses with respect to consumer complaining behavior. Findings regarding the influence of industry, situational, demographic, and psychographic characteristics are presented.

INTRODUCTION

The majority of the research conducted in the field of consumer behavior has focused on consumers' decision making processes for the potential purchase of goods and services. Over the last decade, there has been a growing interest in the post-purchase reactions and behaviors of consumers. This has led to the formation of a subset of consumer researchers concentrating their study in the area of Consumer Satisfaction/Dissatisfaction. Specifically, the reactions and behaviors of consumers due to dissatisfying experiences are being extensively researched. It is in this area of study that consumer complaining behavior (CCB) is specifically investigated (Singh 1988, 1989, 1990a 1990b; Gilly 1985, 1987; Richins 1983, 1987).

The study of CCB is important for several reasons. First, satisfied consumers are more likely than dissatisfied consumers to be loyal to an individual firm or store, product, brand, or manufacturer. Second, satisfied consumers are likely to tell their families and friends about their positive experiences, which may stimulate further business for the organization. Dissatisfied consumers, in contrast, may discontinue use of the product or service, complain about the situation to their families and friends (reducing potential new business), or even pursue litigation.

While marketing professionals generally acknowledge that the primary goal of their activities in the marketplace is to satisfy consumers' wants and needs, it has been estimated that one in five shopping experiences results in consumer dissatisfaction (Andreasen and Best 1978). Furthermore, in the majority of these cases of dissatisfaction, the consumer does not take any action toward remedying the situation. These facts pose a considerable challenge to marketers and should motivate

consumer researchers to achieve a better and more complete understanding of the consumer complaining phenomenon.

To enhance the current status of research in the area of CCB, investigation of the determinants of consumer responses to dissatisfaction is necessary. To aid in this investigation, the research reported here considers the influence of industry, situational, and consumer demographic and psychographic characteristics on CCB.

BACKGROUND

Consumer complaining behavior begins when a consumer evaluates a purchase or consumption experience in terms of whether or not prior expectations regarding the good or service are met (Day 1980). When these evaluations produce negative evaluations, the consumer is dissatisfied. According to Day and Landon (1977), the two broad-based options available to dissatisfied consumers are (1) to take no action or (2) to take some action. Consumers who do not take action may choose not to do so for several reasons. One potential reason for not taking action is that, while consumers may desire to resolve the problem, they do not know how to do so. Another potential reason for not taking action is that consumers may think it is not worth their time and/or effort to pursue the issue. Other potential reasons might include consumers' beliefs that no one could or would do anything about the problem, time pressures (no time to correct the problem), and feelings of embarrassment about speaking out regarding a negative aspect of an organization. Under conditions of high store and/or brand loyalty, consumers also may not take action. Because the consumer has patronized the store or bought the product many times in the past, s/he benevolently accepts the current dissatisfying situation as "unusual" and gives the store and/or product another chance. Finally, the type of industry involved also may explain why consumers do not take action. Consumers may feel as if they have no recourse in industries in which the level of concentration is high. Considering this rather extensive list of potential explanations for consumers' failure to take action in dissatisfying situations, it is important to note that a consumer's decision to not take action does not imply that she/he has been satisfied.

When a consumer elects to take some action in response to a dissatisfying experience, the action may be either public or private. One form of private action is warning family and friends, or employing negative word-of-mouth (WOM). It has been estimated that 85 percent of those consumers who are dissatisfied tell their friends and members of their families about the negative experience. In turn, each informed person tells an average of five others the same negative information (Richins 1983). This phenomenon can have considerable ill effect on the firm or product and can lead to loss of current and future business. An alternate form of private action is to boycott the manufacturer or seller. This private action is commonly known as brand or store "switching."

If consumers opt for a more public form of action, one of the responses they may choose is to complain to a third party agency, such as the Better Business Bureau or the Federal Trade Commission. Another form of public action is to seek legal action for purposes of resolving dissatisfaction. Examples of legal actions include malpractice and product liability suits. A third form of public action is to seek redress directly from the firm. Public complaining of this type may involve seeking a cash refund, a product exchange or refund, or an explanation or apology from the firm. Compared to other public forms of complaining behavior, this alternative represents the optimal condition for the firm. In seeking redress directly from the firm, consumers give valuable feedback to the firm and provide it with an opportunity to rectify the problem without the ramifications of the alternative response choices. Ideally the firm should seek to maximize seller-directed complaints while minimizing other types of action, both public and private.

Given the goal of maximizing seller-directed complaints (hereafter designated simply by "complaints"), it is necessary to understand what motivates individuals to choose this response option over the alternatives. The marketing literature suggests four general areas of influence, namely, industry characteristics, situational characteristics, and consumers' demographic and psychographic characteristics. Each is briefly reviewed in the following sections.

Industry Characteristics

It has been suggested that industry characteristics impact consumers' tendencies to complain (e.g., Singh 1990b; Hirschman 1970; Andreasen 1985). Four key characteristics of industries have been identified. Each contributes to the level of industry concentration. The first is the *availability of alternate products/sellers* (when concentration is high, availability of alternate products is low). Because it would do little good to threaten switching patronage if the product is "necessary" to the consumer and the offending firm is the only one available to satisfy the needs of the consumer, it has been suggested that consumers are less likely to complain under conditions of few alternatives (Singh 1990b). A more appropriate consumer response might take the form of a letter registering the complaint with a regulating agency, for example.

The second industry characteristic is *restricted information* (when concentration is high, information is highly restricted). Some industries discourage the practice of comparison shopping and advertising. For this reason, consumers may be unable to judge the practices of the firm (a health care provider, for example). Therefore, the more information is restricted, the less likely consumers are to complain (Andreasen 1985).

The third industry characteristic is *consumer knowledge* (when concentration is high, consumer knowledge is low). Consumers differ in their abilities to assess goods or service quality. In general, the higher consumers' knowledge, the more likely they are to complain (Singh 1990b). For example, one individual may assume that he is responsible for a program failure on the computer and, therefore, elect not to complain. Another, more savvy individual, may be able to diagnose a faulty motherboard and, consequently, seek redress by complaining.

The fourth characteristic of industries impacting CCB is the *length of the purchase cycle* (when concentration is high, the purchase cycle is long). If purchase cycles are long, the seller may not concentrate much effort on establishing store or brand loyalty (Singh 1990b). In car sales, for example, the salesperson may merely attempt to gain the one-time sale, knowing that it may be 3-10 years before the customer buys another car. Therefore, the longer the purchase cycle, the less likely consumers are to complain.

While the theoretical perspective offered above seems intuitively appealing, the diversity of industry characteristics coming to bear on any classificational schema makes it difficult to clearly delineate meaningful distinctions. Contrary to findings reported by Singh (1990b), Hirschman originally hypothesized that the consumers within industries with few options of goods and service providers do not have the opportunity to switch and, instead, are confronted with a situation with only the opportunity to voice a complaint.

Situational Characteristics

Previous research has included *problem severity* and *problem attribution* as dominant situational characteristics affecting CCB (Richins 1983, 1987, Folkes 1984). Problem severity is determined by the price of the product, the time and effort consumers believe are required to correct the problem, issues of health, and usability (whether the problem is merely cosmetic or actually impedes use of the product). For example, although a consumer may be dissatisfied with an inexpensive pair of scissors that do not cut cleanly, she/he is not likely to complain to the retailer. However, if a $500 transmission does not work correctly, the consumer is more likely to complain and insist that the problem be resolved. It follows that the greater the perceived problem severity, the more likely consumers are to complain

(Richins 1983). With regard to the influence of problem attribution on CCB, it has been found that consumers attributing the source of their dissatisfaction to the seller or manufacturer of the product are more likely to complain than consumers attributing the source of their dissatisfaction to their own behaviors (Folkes 1984).

Demographic Characteristics

Studies examining the impact of consumers' demographic characteristics on response choice have investigated the influence of income, education, sex, and age on consumers' propensity to complain. Consumers at higher income levels generally possess more highly developed market skills than those at lower income levels. Such market skills are likely to assist consumers in their efforts to satisfactorily resolve their problems (Bearden and Oliver 1985). The more highly developed market skills of higher income consumers make these individuals more likely to complain than lower income consumers. Similarly, consumers with higher levels of education are more likely to be aware of alternatives to problem resolution than consumers with lower levels of education. As a result of their higher education levels, they possess more resources in the form of information and confidence to deal with problems in the marketplace (Singh 1990a). Therefore, consumers with higher levels of education are more likely to complain than those with lower levels of education. And, both age and gender are likely to influence CCB. There is evidence that younger consumers are more likely to complain than older consumers and that men are more likely to complain than women (Warland, Hermann, and Willits 1975; Andreasen 1985).

While the explanatory power of industry, situational, and demographic characteristics is acknowledged, none of them individually nor collectively has been shown to explain why two or more individuals under *identical conditions* will choose different responses to the same dissatisfactory experience. It is possible, for example, that two consumers with strikingly similar demographic characteristics go to dinner together. They are at the same restaurant, have the same waiter, and order the same meal, which, naturally, is priced the same. Both meals are cold. One consumer complains and the other does not. To explain the differences in complaining behavior in this scenario requires examination of characteristics other than those already outlined, namely consumers' psychographic characteristics.

Psychographic Characteristics

A variety of psychographic characteristics of consumers is likely to influence the likelihood of their complaining. Examples include personality characteristics--confidence, self-esteem, compliance, tolerance of risk--of consumers. One such characteristic, assertiveness, has been examined in previous research on CCB. Assertiveness is defined as a characteristic enabling individuals to act in their own best interests, to stand up for themselves without undue anxiety and to comfortably express their honest feelings (Alberti and Emmons 1974). Richins (1983) and Singh (1989) suggested a positive correlation between consumers' assertiveness and their complaining behavior. Richins (1983) concluded that assertive consumers are more likely to complain than non-assertive consumers primarily because they are more likely to perceive business organizations to be generally responsive to consumer complaints. The positive attitude toward business held by assertive consumers results in their expectation that the offending business will react in a way to help resolve their problems.

The preceding discussion suggests the following hypotheses:

H1: *Industry characteristics* will impact the likelihood of CCB.

The lesser the industry concentration, the more likely consumers are to complain.

H2: *Situational characteristics* will impact the likelihood of CCB.

a: The more severe the problem, the more likely consumers are to complain.

b: If cause for dissatisfaction is attributed to the seller or manufacturer of the product (rather than the individual consumer), consumers are more likely to complain.

H3: *Demographic characteristics* will impact the likelihood of CCB.

a: Consumers with higher income levels are more likely to complain than consumers with lower income levels.

b: Consumers with higher educational levels are more likely to complain than consumers with lower educational levels.

c: Younger consumers are more likely to complain than older consumers.

d: Men are more likely to complain than women.

H4: *Psychographic characteristics* will impact the likelihood of CCB.

Consumers who are more assertive are more likely to complain than consumers who are less assertive.

RESEARCH METHODS AND RESULTS

Many of the criticisms of past research have been

directed at the method of data collection. Generally, previous studies in this area have involved asking respondents to recall a dissatisfying experience and to answer questions regarding that experience. The primary drawbacks to this method are that (1) respondents may be unable to accurately recall the situation, and (2) individuals are very likely to have differing opinions as to what constitutes "dissatisfaction." A scenario format was used here to redress some of the methodological limitations of previous work in this area.

Scenarios were presented via a survey instrument administered to undergraduate business students. Each participating student received "bonus" points only if the instrument were completed in full. A total of 150 completed surveys was used. The scenarios manipulated three factors--industry concentration, problem severity, and problem attribution. The manipulation of industry concentration involved the use of three scenarios, each reflecting consumer experiences in a different industry. Consistent with previous research (e.g., Singh 1990b), consumer experiences within the grocery (low concentration), automobile repair (moderate concentration), and health care (high concentration) industries were included. Each of the three scenarios included one of three levels of problem severity (low, moderate, and high). A repeated measures design was used for the manipulation of problem attribution. For each respondent, the original presentation of the scenarios presented the information in such a way that a reasonable person would conclude that the blame for the dissatisfying experience should be attributed to the firm. Modified versions of the scenarios, presenting the information in such a way that a reasonable person would conclude that the consumer was at fault, were then presented to each respondent. The scenarios

FIGURE 1

PROBLEM SEVERITY	INDUSTRY		
	Grocery	Auto Repair	Health Care
Low	C	B	A
Moderate	B	A	C
High	A	C	B

were pretested to assure that they represented believable, "real-world" situations for the subjects. A Latin Squares design reflecting the manipulations received by each of three groups of respondents is shown in the Figure.

In addition to the scenarios, the data collection instrument had two other components. The first component included a measure of the psychographic variable of interest. Assertiveness was measured by the Rathus Assertiveness scale, consisting of 30, seven-point Likert format items, for which respondents indicate the extent to which the behaviors (both assertive and unassertive) described by the items are characteristic of themselves. Consumers' assertiveness "scores" were a sum of their responses to all 30 items (with a range of -90 to +90). The Rathus scale has been validated on undergraduate populations and shown strong test/retest reliability (Rathus 1973). The second component included demographic information, namely age, sex, income, and education.

Data Analysis and Results

An analysis of covariance (ANCOVA) procedure was used to test the significance of each of the variables as predictors of CCB. As the measure of CCB, respondents were asked (after reading each scenario) to indicate how likely they were to mention the problem to the seller (where 1 = "very likely" and 4 = "not at all likely"). Assertiveness and income were used as covariates. ANCOVA results and least square cell means and standard errors are presented in Tables 1 and 2. Findings with respect to each of the hypothesized relationships are discussed in the following paragraphs.

The test of H1 regarding industry concentration was significant (F = 16.19, p < .0001). However, means comparisons indicate that consumers are most likely to complain within the high concentration condition and least likely to complain within the low concentration condition. These findings are opposite of the hypothesized relationship. The significant interactions between industry concentration and both problem severity and problem attribution may contribute to this finding. In hindsight, it seems logical that the industry concentration effect is contingent upon consumers' perceptions of both problem severity and attribution.

Tests of H2a and H2b supported the hypotheses regarding situational characteristics. Problem severity (F = 105.62, p < .0001) and problem attribution (F = 247.00, p < .0001) are both significant. Means comparisons indicate significant differences in consumers' likelihood of complaining between all three levels of problem severity, with likelihood of complaining increasing with each greater level of problem severity. Means comparisons for problem attribution showed that consumers were more likely to complain when the cause for dissatisfaction is attributed to the seller or manufacturer of the product (rather than themselves). Again, the significant interaction between these situational characteristics seems reasonable. The consumers' likelihood of complaining for each of the three severity levels will depend upon the attribution.

Not surprising given the homogeneity of the student sample, hypotheses with respect to consumers' income, educational level, and age (H3a-c) were not supported. In addition, H3d--that men are more likely to complain than women--was not supported. This result could be attribut-

TABLE 1
Results for General Linear Models Procedure

Source of Variation	Degrees of Freedom	Type III Sum of Squares	F Value	Prob. > F
Industry Concentration (IC)	2	22.64	16.19	0.0001
Problem Attribution (PA)	1	172.68	247.00	0.0001
Problem Severity (PS)	2	147.68	105.62	0.0001
Assertiveness	1	13.00	18.72	0.0001
Gender	1	1.39	1.99	0.1588
Income	1	0.03	0.04	0.8427
PS x IC	4	33.15	11.85	0.0001
PS x PA	2	4.16	2.98	0.0515
IC x PA	2	3.95	2.83	0.0598
PS x IC x PA	4	32.92	11.77	0.0001
Model	20	438.80	31.87	0.0001
Error	872	609.62		
TOTAL	892	1048.42		

TABLE 2
Least Square Cell Means and Standard Errors

	Least Square Means	Standard Errors	Sample Size
Industry Concentration			
low (grocery)	2.45	.05	150
moderate (auto repair)	2.30	.05	150
high (health care)	2.07	.05	150
Problem Attribution			
self	2.71	.04	450
other	1.84	.04	450
Problem Severity			
low	2.79	.05	150
moderate	2.23	.05	150
high	1.80	.05	150

able to the fact that women who enter college (and especially those who major in business) are not representative of women in the general population.

As hypothesized, the test of H4 showed that consumers who are more assertive are more likely to complain than consumers who are less assertive ($F = 18.72$, $p < .0001$). This finding lends support to the notion that characteristics unique to individuals also contribute to consumers' likelihood to complain.

DISCUSSION

This study was designed to empirically test a theoretical model of consumer complaining behavior, specifically that of seller-directed complaints. The model that is proposed and tested draws from the CCB literature and adds to the growing number of studies that go beyond simple descriptive analysis. It provides support of hypotheses regarding problem severity, problem attribution, and assertiveness as predictors of CCB. It calls into question some of the previously hypothesized relationships with respect to industry characteristics. By its identification of significant interactions, it also suggests the importance of simultaneously examining multiple constructs in future investigations of CCB.

Findings also indicate that there are differences in CCB unique to individuals due to their varying degrees of assertiveness. This result suggests that other personality characteristics also may influence CCB. Future research might consider expanding this model to include characteristics such as consumers' perceived risk, compliance, self-esteem, and/or aggression, as examples.

While the explanatory power of the model tested here is encouraging, further research is needed. The sample used in this study, due to its homogeneity, was inappropriate for tests of some demographic variables. Little variance was expected in terms of respondents' age and educational level, for example. In addition, there was little variance found in respondents' reported incomes.

Since these demographic characteristics have been found to be significant predictors of CCB in previous research, it would be worthwhile to test the model proposed here with samples possessing more diverse demographic profiles.

Another interesting extension of this research would be to include an analysis of response options other than seller-directed complaints. Future research might include exit, switching, third party redress, and negative WOM as alternative consumer responses to dissatisfaction.

Customer satisfaction clearly is a major objective of organizations wanting to succeed in the 90s and beyond. Being able to recognize elements of the environment (customer, situation, industry) that may inhibit or promote CCB will help these organizations better serve their customers and seek the important feedback they need to provide the best possible service. Toward this end, further research is this area is encouraged.

REFERENCES

Alberti, Robert E. and Michael L. Emmons (1974), *Your Perfect Right: A Guide to Assertive Behavior*. San Luis Obispo, CA: Impact.

Andreasen, Alan and Arthur Best (1977), "Consumers Complain--Does Business Respond?" *Harvard Business Review*, 55 (July/August), 93-101.

_____(1985), "Consumer Responses to Dissatisfaction in Loose Monopolies," *Journal of Consumer Research*, 12 (September), 135-41.

Bearden, William O. and Jesse E. Teel (1980), "An Investigation of Personal Influences on Consumer Complaining," *Journal of Retailing*, 56 (Fall), 3-20.

_____and Richard L. Oliver (1985), "The Role of Public and Private Complaining in Satisfaction with Problem Resolution," *Journal of Consumer Affairs*, 19 (Winter), 222-240.

Day, Ralph L. and E. Laird Landon, Jr. (1977), "Towards a Theory of Consumer Complaining Behavior," in *Consumer and Industrial Buying Behavior*, Arch Woodside, Jagdish Sheth, and Peter Bennett, eds. Amsterdam: North Holland Publishing Company.

_____(1980), "Research Perspectives on Consumer Complaining Behavior," in *Theoretical Developments in Marketing Proceedings*, Charles W. Lamb and Patrick M. Dunne, eds. Chicago: American Marketing Association.

Folkes, Valerie S. (1984), "Consumer Reactions to Product Failure: An Attributional Approach," *Journal of Consumer Research*, 10 (March), 398-409.

Gilly, Mary C. (1985), "Consumer Complaint Handling as a Strategic Marketing Tool," *Journal of Consumer Marketing*, 2 (Fall), 5-16.

_____(1987), "Postcomplaint Processes: From Organizational Response to Repurchase Behavior," *Journal of Consumer Affairs*, 21 (Winter), 293-313.

Hirschman, Albert O. (1970), *Exit, Voice, and Loyalty: Responses to Decline in Firms, Organizations, and States*. Cambridge, MA: Harvard University Press.

Rathus, S.A. (1973), "A 30-Item Schedule for Assessing Behavior," *Behavior Therapy*, 39 (1), 181-186.

Richins, Marsha L. (1983), "An Analysis of Consumer Interaction Styles in the Marketplace," *Journal of Consumer Research*, 10 (June), 73-82.

_____(1987), "A Multivariate Analysis of Responses to Dissatisfaction," *Journal of the Academy of Marketing Science*, 15 (Fall), 24-31.

Singh, Jagdip (1988), "Consumer Complaint Intentions and Behavior: Definitional and Taxonomical Issues," *Journal of Marketing*, 52 (January), 93-107.

_____(1989), "Determinants of Consumers' Decisions to Seek Third Party Redress: An Empirical Study of Dissatisfied Patients," *Journal of Consumer Affairs*, 23 (Winter), 329-363.

_____(1990a), "A Typology of Consumer Dissatisfaction Response Styles," *Journal of Retailing*, 66 (Spring), 57-99.

_____(1990b), "Voice, Exit, and Negative Word-of-Mouth Behaviors: An Investigation Across Three Service Categories," *Journal of the Academy of Marketing Science*, 18 (Winter), 1-15.

Warland, Robert H., Robert O. Hermann, and Jane Willits (1975), "Dissatisfied Consumers: Who Gets Upset and Who Takes Action," *Journal of Consumer Affairs*, 9, 148-163.

ALTERNATIVE COMPARISON STANDARDS IN THE FORMATION OF CONSUMER SATISFACTION/DISSATISFACTION

Richard A. Spreng, Michigan State University
Andrea L. Dixon, Indiana University

ABSTRACT

While expectations have been utilized as the comparison standard for many studies of consumer satisfaction/dissatisfaction, a number of alternative comparison standards have also been suggested. After briefly reviewing expectations as a standard, these comparison standards are defined and examples of each are presented. A framework for classifying these standards is proposed.

INTRODUCTION

The disconfirmation of expectations model (Oliver 1980) has dominated the research literature on consumer satisfaction and dissatisfaction. This model suggests that satisfaction is formed through the process of disconfirmation, which is the cognitive comparison of pre-use expectations and post-use perceptions of product performance. In studies based on this model, expectations represent the standard against which performance is compared.

In recent years, however, researchers have questioned the appropriateness of expectations as the standard (e.g., Olshavsky and Spreng 1989; Sirgy 1984; Tse and Wilton 1988; Westbrook and Reilly 1983; Woodruff, Cadotte, and Jenkins 1983). A number of alternative standards have been suggested, and most of these comparison standards generally performed well in explaining satisfaction (e.g., Barbeau 1985; Cadotte, Woodruff, and Jenkins 1987). However, only a few of the standards that have been proposed have been empirically tested, and our knowledge of these standards is somewhat limited (Woodruff, Clemons, Schumann, Gardial, and Burns 1991; Woodruff, Schumann, and Clemons 1989).

The purpose of this paper is to further develop the standards literature. After discussing expectations as a standard, a framework will be introduced to provide a structure for the various standards that have been suggested. These standards will be illustrated by direct quotes from consumers.

EXPECTATIONS AS THE STANDARD

Expectations as the standard has dominated the study of consumer satisfaction. In fact, the completeness of this domination is evident in that some writers <u>define</u> satisfaction in terms of expectations. For example, Engel, Blackwell, and Miniard (1990, p. 545) state, "Satisfaction is defined here as a post consumption evaluation that a chosen alternative at least meets or exceeds expecta-

tions." Since they suggest that disconfirmation, which is the assessment of the degree to which the product meets expectations, is an antecedent of satisfaction, it is apparent that satisfaction is defined in terms of expectations.

Generally, expectations have been conceptualized in two ways. Expectations have been operationalized in terms of the probability of occurrence (e.g. Westbrook 1987; Westbrook and Reilly 1983; Bearden and Teel 1983), or in terms of an evaluative aspect that assesses how good/bad the occurrence is (e.g., Churchill and Surprenant 1982; Oliver 1980; Tse and Wilton 1988). An example of this latter approach is taken by Oliver (1981, pp.33-34) when he states:

> "Expectations have two components: a probability of occurrence (e.g., the likelihood that a clerk will be available to wait on customers) and an evaluation of the occurrence (e.g., the degree to which the clerk's attention is desirable or undesirable, good or bad, etc.)."

Oliver suggests that when these components are properly combined, "high expectations" means that the shopper anticipates that desirable events will occur, and undesirable events will not occur; "low expectations" means that desirable events will not occur, and undesirable events will occur. It is clear that when conceptualized in this way, expectations are confounded with desires. To illustrate this, asking a consumer to rate "This store has attentive salespeople: likely/unlikely" will provide a measure of what the consumer believes about this store, and the consumer's desires about this can be measured separately (e.g. "Attentive salespeople are: desirable/un-desirable"). Measured in terms of belief and evaluation, the question would read "In terms of attentiveness of the salespeople, I expect that this store will be: good/bad." If a certain store is measured in this way, and the consumer says that this store is bad, we do not know whether this store has (a) attentive salespeople, and the consumer does not want attentive salespeople, or has (b) inattentive salespeople, and the consumer wants attentive salespeople. Oliver (1980; 1981) has suggested measuring expectations as a belief-times-evaluation, as in a Fishbein and Ajzen (1975) attitude model. But again, when measured in this way, it is unclear whether the standard that is impacting satisfaction is what the subject expects (the belief component) or what the subject desires (the evaluation component).

The position taken here is that expectations should be conceptualized as beliefs and not as evaluations, since this is more in line with normal uses of this term (Olson and Dover 1979). Therefore, expectations will be defined as: Beliefs (i.e., the subjective probability of association between two entities) about product attributes or performance at some time in the future.

Possibly an even greater problem has to do with the meaning people attach to the term "expect." For example, one of the authors was recently talking to a woman who was very dissatisfied with the treatment she received at a retail store. When asked why this dissatisfied her she replied, "I just expect to be treated better than that." However, when probed further ("You mean you anticipate being treated better than that when you go to a retail store?"), she replied, "No, you never get decent service anymore. I just don't expect to be treated like this." Clearly, this consumer is not using the term "expectations" to refer to beliefs about the future, but rather in terms of some other standard.

An additional example of the imprecise use of the term expectation is from Zeithaml, Parasuraman, and Berry. In their early work (e.g., Parasuraman, Zeithaml, and Berry 1985) they suggested that quality "...involves a comparison of expectations with performance." While they do not explicitly define expectations, from the examples they provide (e.g., see page 46), it seems they are talking about beliefs about product performance. In a later study (Parasuraman, Zeithaml, and Berry 1988), they refined their definition when they say "...service quality, as perceived by consumers, stems from a comparison of what they feel service firms should offer (i.e., from their expectations) with their perceptions of the performance of firms providing the services." They go on to suggest that in the service quality literature "expectations" doesn't mean predictions, but rather "...expectations are viewed as desires or wants of consumers, i.e., what they feel a service provider *should* rather than *would* offer." The measures of their "expectations" used the word "should," (e.g., "These firms should be dependable."). Later still (Zeithaml, Parasuraman, and Berry 1990), they use "expectations" and "wants or desires" interchangeably. Yet when measuring "expectations" they now use the word "excellent" (e.g., "Employees at excellent companies will be neat appearing."). Thus, even within one research program by the same authors we see several different standards used (i.e., predictive expectations, desires or wants, and excellence), all ostensibly referring to "expectations."

ALTERNATIVE COMPARISON STANDARDS

This section will attempt to identify and define various standards that have been suggested in the satisfaction literature, and propose a classification system for standards. Four classes of standards are proposed: expectations, experience-based norms, desires, and equity. The Table summarizes these standards and definitions.

After defining each standard, an example will be provided as an illustration of the standard. The examples are from a project conducted by undergraduate marketing students as part of a consumer behavior course. Each student interviewed two consumers, one who had had a very satisfying experience, and the other a very dissatisfying experience. There were a total of 49 students, and 98 interviews. The students simply asked the subject to talk about the experience while being recorded on audiotape. The students were instructed to be careful to avoid using a standard in their instructions, as this could bias the response. For example, in conducting focus groups on service quality, Zeithaml, Berry, and Parasuraman (1991) asked questions such as "What do you expect from a service provider?" When consumers are asked about what they "expected," these instructions are likely to direct subjects' responses toward expectations as the standard. The experiences dealt with many kinds of products (e.g., cars, stereos, bicycles, shampoo) and services (e.g., restaurants, retail stores, hair care, car repairs).

There are a number of obvious limitations of data such as this that preclude any type of quantitative/ systematic analysis of the protocols. For example, since the interviews were conducted by a large number of relatively untrained interviewers, there was a great deal of variability in the quality of the interviews. However, the verbatim comments do provide at least preliminary evidence of the use of various standards. Thus, these protocols are presented simply as <u>illustrations</u> of the various standards. They are, none-the-less, real consumers talking about actual product experiences.

Expectations Standards

The first classification is based on expectations, and includes traditional expectations, as well as persuasion-based expectations or promises (Woodruff et al. 1991). Expectations were defined above as beliefs. As an example of this standard, a consumer who was dissatisfied with his mountain bike said, "They showed in the advertisements people riding on trails and being rough. Just jumping off a curb once completely bent my back rim." In essence, this example represents a consumer's beliefs about the performance that were developed by the implicit promise of performance in the advertisement.

Persuasion-based expectations are defined as explicit statements from the seller regarding the performance of the product, and seem to develop very strong expectations. An example of a promise that was broken is provided by one subject: "The manager promised that the engine would be looked at while the car was in, and it wasn't." This consumer used the word "promised" several times and stated she was dissatisfied because "They didn't do what they promised." As pointed out by Woodruff, et al. (1991), expectations and promises may

TABLE

STANDARD	DEFINITION
EXPECTATIONS	
Expectations	Beliefs (i.e., the subjective probability of association between two entities) about product attributes or performance at some time in the future.
Persuasion-Based Expectations	Explicit statements from the seller regarding the performance of the product.
EXPERIENCE BASED	
Last Received	The most recent experience the consumer had with the brand or product category.
Average Performance	The performance the consumer believes the typical (or average) product or service of this type provides.
Favorite	The performance one gets from one's most preferred brand.
Best Available	The performance one believes is the best performance that is available.
Best on Attributes	The performance one believes one can receive from the best brand on each attribute, even though no one brand is best on all the attributes at the same time.
DESIRES	
Desires	The performance of a product or service that the consumer judges will lead to higher level values.
Ideal	The performance that is the best one can imagine, an abstract "ideal."
Excellence	Product performance that is what the consumer desires or wants.
EQUITY	
Fairness	The performance that the consumer thinks he or she should receive, given what was put into the exchange.
What Others Have Received	The performance that others have received, and therefore the performance the consumer believes he/she should receive.

diverge. For example, a retailer may promise short lines, but past experience with that retailer leads one to expect long lines. When subsequent lines are long, and thus match expectations, the consumer may still be dissatisfied since the persuasion-based expectation was not met.

Experience-Based Standards

This group of standards is based on Woodruff, Cadotte and Jenkins (1983). They suggested that consumers utilize standards based on past experiences with products, and are constrained by what "can be."

Last experience as a standard is based on the most recent experience the consumer had with the brand or product category. For example, in describing his satisfaction with a car dealer, one consumer said, "I went to another dealer several weeks before, and the minute the guy knew I wasn't going to buy a car soon he just seemed to turn off to me." While this is certainly a viable satisfaction standard, empirical tests are not reported in the literature.

A second experience-based standard is average performance, which deals with the performance the consumer believes a typical product or service of this type provides. A consumer discussing a satisfying experience with a fast food place stated, "It was clean, and there were no crumbs on the tables. And that's kind of unique in a fast food place. The manager smiled at me, and usually they don't do that at a fast food place." Cadotte, et al. (1987) tested this standard and found that for two restaurant types this standard explained the most variation in satisfaction.

A third experience-based standard is favorite brand, which is the performance one gets from one's most preferred brand. One subject, who was dissatisfied with how long a transaction took at a large building supply store, compared this attribute to his favorite hardware store, "...where you can get out of your car, park right next to the store, walk right into the store, there's almost always someone there to help you out. You bring your stuff up to the front, you pay for it and you're gone." Cadotte, et al. (1987) found the favorite brand standard explained the most variance for one restaurant type.

A fourth standard based on past experience is best available, which refers to the performance one believes is the best performance that is available. For example, a subject stated, "Dollar for dollar, it's the best computer you can buy." This is another standard which has not been empirically tested.

Finally, best on each attribute is a standard by which a consumer compares an experience with the performance he/she believes one can receive from the best brand on each attribute, even though no one brand is best on all the attributes at the same time. For example, one fast food restaurant may be the standard for quickness of service, another may be the standard for quality of food, while still another is the standard for atmosphere. One subject reported being satisfied at a retail store: "[The salespeople] gave me the kind of individual attention you get at a really nice specialty store, but the prices were like a discount store."

Desires as Standards

This class of standards deals with the performance that is desired or wanted, and is not necessarily constrained by past performance or even reality. This group includes desires, ideal, and excellence as standards.

Spreng and Olshavsky (1991), based on the means-end chain model, defined desires as "the aspects and levels of aspects of a product or service that the consumer judges will lead to higher-level values." As an example of this standard, one consumer said, "I really needed to talk to someone who knew what they were doing and really help me, but these girls didn't know what they were doing. I had a goal here and I couldn't accomplish it, and this really aggravated me."

Empirical tests of desires have been somewhat limited. Swan, Trawick, and Carroll (1981) measured both expectations and desires, and found that when perfor-

mance was greater than or equal to desires, satisfaction was higher. Westbrook and Reilly (1983) did not actually measure a comparison standard (i.e., values), but rather the comparison process (i.e., similar to measuring disconfirmation without measuring expectations or perceived performance). They found a very poor fit of their model, but as they concede, measurement problems probably account for much of their results. In a study of student satisfaction with a course, Barbeau (1984) found desires disconfirmation to have the strongest effect (β =.46), past experience disconfirmation next strongest (β=.34) and expectation disconfirmation was non-significant (β =.005). Also, see Myers (1988) for the use of desires in segmentation.

A second standard that is included in the desires category is ideal performance. A number of researchers have explored this standard, and it often deals with the performance that is the best one can imagine, an abstract "ideal." Few attempts have been made to empirically test ideals as a standard. Tse and Wilton (1988) found that "ideal performance" did not have a direct effect on satisfaction, although their measurement of ideal resulted in a measure that was skewed and had very little variance. In the present study none of the subjects made statements that appeared to be an example of ideal as a standard. Research is required to explicitly probe if, in fact, this standard is actually used by consumers.

Finally, excellence is included in this group, although it is not altogether clear that this standard is markedly different from several other standards. As previously discussed, Zeithaml et al. (1990) utilize excellence as their standard in identifying service quality, and define it in terms of what the consumer wants or needs. However, from their usage it is not clear whether this is anchored to consumer values, or to past experience. For example, if a consumer defines "excellence" as what the best firm provides, then this is clearly an experience based norm. An example of this type of usage may be indicated by a consumer who was dissatisfied with the service in a restaurant and stated "...this was supposed to be one of the finer restaurants [in town]." While it appears that the standard is some level of excellence, there is also the element of comparison among other restaurants in town. Within the satisfaction literature, this standard has not been empirically tested.

Equity Standards

Two standards are classified in this group. Fairness deals with the performance that the consumer thinks he or she should receive, given what was put into the exchange. Based on equity theory, this standard suggests that consumers calculate the ratio of their inputs to their outputs in an exchange. If the consumer receives what they "deserve" or "ought" to receive, given what they put into the exchange, they should be satisfied. For example, one consumer here said, "I left my calculator unprotected in a book bag, and it was damaged; I sent it in and they sent me a new one." In this case the consumer thought he got a better deal than he really deserved. Tse and Wilton (1988) did not find a significant relationship between equity and satisfaction. Oliver and DeSarbo (1988), however, did find that equity impacted satisfaction.

The second Equity standard is more specific, in that it uses as a standard the performance that others have received. For example, one consumer was dissatisfied with the speed of service in a restaurant and stated, "Another waitress was better. Her customers came in after us, but they got their food before us, and were out before us." This standard has not been empirically tested.

Combinations of Standards

As suggested by several authors (e.g., Woodruff et al. 1987; Tse and Wilton 1988) consumers may use multiple standards. For example, one consumer, describing his satisfaction with his stereo speakers stated, "My speakers sound better than most other speakers I've heard. Some of my friends have speakers that cost hundreds of dollars more, and I think mine sound better." This consumer seems to be using both the standard of average performance and the standard of what others have received. Since the performance he received is high relative to what he paid, fairness also might be a standard here.

DISCUSSION

As indicated from the verbatim comments, there is evidence that consumers use a wide variety of standards in determining their satisfaction. These results bring up a number of questions and directions for future research regarding the use of standards in the determination of satisfaction.

The first question that must be addressed is whether the standard used in forming satisfaction judgments matters. As suggested by Woodruff, et al.(1990), changing the standard used in satisfaction measures can change the results of satisfaction measures. Therefore, in measuring satisfaction it is important to correctly specify the standards that are actually being used.

Second, diagnostically it is valuable to know the standard being used. For example, if the standard of reference is desires, then it will be important to ascertain what consumers desire from the product, rather than what they expect to receive. This is particularly important given the dominance of expectations in current thinking on consumer satisfaction. For example, some are suggesting that businesses "manage expectations" by promising less than can be delivered. This advice may be very dangerous in a competitive environment in which one's competitors promise — and deliver — more.

Future Research

A first priority is to conduct a rigorous qualitative study in which the standards used are identified. Protocol analysis with a trained interviewer could be useful in exploring the standards consumers use in determining their satisfaction or dissatisfaction (Woodruff, et al. 1990).

A second direction is to compare various standards in their ability to explain satisfaction. While several standards may be used, even within one experience, a few standards may prove to be much better at accounting for the variation in satisfaction. This process has already begun (Cadotte, et al. 1987; Tse and Wilton 1988; Barbeau 1985), but the number of standards tested has been limited.

Future research should also explore the situational or dispositional aspects that influence the use of various standards. It is possible that people tend to use different standards in different situations. Consumer differences, such as consumer knowledge, might also impact the standard used. Below are examples of potential moderators of standard choice along with the standards that might be used. If there is variation in standard choice, managers must be aware of the factors that impact which standard is used.

New Product versus Old Product. When utilizing a product or brand for the first time, a consumer may use a standard such as desires, based on values or consequences they want fulfilled. Also, consumers may rely on promises of what a product will do. When using an "old" product, the consumer may use an experience-based norm, such as last performance.

Dependence on Others for Information. When a consumer is dependent upon others, such as a salesperson, for information, expectations or promises might be important standards. This would be true for technically complex products, or products that have experience or credence attributes.

Consumer Knowledge. Consumers high in product knowledge may have stored in memory clearly defined attributes and levels of attributes that are sought, and use desires, excellence, or best on each attribute standards. Those low in knowledge would be more likely to use an experience-based norm or expectations.

Consumer Experience. Consumers high in experience with the product category might use average performance, favorite, or last used as a standard, while those who have little experience may use what others have received, what is promised, or their expectations. In fact, consumers with little experience may have nothing other than expectations formed from persuasive messages as a basis for a standard.

Consumer Involvement. Consumers with a high level of felt involvement may be likely to use desires (based on values) as a standard, since the product domain has a high degree of self-relevance. Those with a low level of involvement may use an experience-based norm, such as last used.

Product Type. Churchill and Surprenant (1982) suggested that there may be differences in the determinants of satisfaction based on whether the product is a durable or a non-durable. Other product dimensions might be tangibility and goods type (convenience, shopping, and specialty).

Usage Situation. If the product is used in a public situation (e.g., serving wine to guests), the standard may be excellence, while if used in a private situation (e.g., drinking wine with just family present) a standard such as favorite may be used.

Role in the Purchase Process. The standard used may depend upon whether the purchaser is buying the product for his/her own use, or for someone else. For example, in

giving a gift a consumer may use ideal or excellence as a standard.

Hedonic versus Functional Goods. If the product is purchased to fulfill a hedonic need, "desires" based on values may play a strong role as the reference standard. However, products purchased to fulfill functional needs may utilize experience-based standards of last received or average performance.

CONCLUSION

Standards research appears to be an important and promising direction for satisfaction research. It is important theoretically because the problems and limitations of the disconfirmation of expectations model (LaTour and Peat 1979; Westbrook and Reilly 1983; Spreng and Olshavsky 1991) indicate that much is yet to be discovered about the processes of consumer satisfaction. From a practitioner's standpoint, reliance on expectations has resulted in an incomplete, and possibly incorrect, emphasis on consumer expectations. A greater understanding of the standards actually used by consumers in determining their satisfaction will improve the ability of business firms to provide satisfaction.

REFERENCES

Barbeau, J. Bradley (1985), "Predictive and Normative Expectations in Consumer Satisfaction: A Utilization of Adaption and Comparison Levels in a Unified Framework," in *Consumer Satisfaction, Dissatisfaction and Complaining Behavior*, H. Keith Hunt and Ralph L. Day, eds. Indiana University, 27-32.

Bearden, W. O. and J. E. Teel (1983), "Some Determinants of Consumer Satisfaction and Complaint Reports," *Journal of Marketing Research*, 20 (February), 21-28.

Cadotte, Ernest R., Robert B. Woodruff, and Roger L. Jenkins (1987), "Expectations and Norms in Models of Consumer Satisfaction," *Journal of Marketing Research*, 24, (August), 305-314.

Churchill, G. A. and C. Surprenant (1982), "An Investigation into the Determinants of Consumer Satisfaction," *Journal of Marketing Research*, 19 (November), 491-504.

Engel, James F., Roger D. Blackwell, and Paul W. Miniard (1990), *Consumer Behavior*. 6th ed., Chicago, IL: The Dryden Press.

Fishbein, Martin and Icek Ajzen (1975), *Belief, Attitude, Intention and Behavior: An Introduction to Theory and Research*. Reading, MA: Addison-Wesley Publishing Co.

LaTour, Steven A. and Nancy C. Peat (1979), "Conceptual and Methodological Issues in Consumer Satisfaction Research," in *Advances in Consumer Research*, William L. Wilkie, ed. Ann Arbor, MI:

Association for Consumer Research, 6, 431-437.

Myers, James H. (1988), "Attribute Deficiency Segmentation: Measuring Unmet Wants," in *Advances in Consumer Research*, Michael J. Houston, ed. Provo, UT: Association for Consumer Research, 15, 108-113.

Oliver, Richard L. (1980), "A Cognitive Model of the Antecedents and Consequences of Satisfaction Decisions," *Journal of Marketing Research*, 17 (November), 460-469.

_____(1981), "Measurement and Evaluation of Satisfaction Processes in Retail Settings," *Journal of Retailing*, 57, 3 (Fall), 25-48.

_____and Wayne S. DeSarbo (1988), "Response Determinants in Satisfaction Judgments," *Journal of Consumer Research*, 14 (March), 495-507.

Olshavsky, Richard W. and Richard A. Spreng (1989), "A `Desires as Standard' Model of Consumer Satisfaction," *Journal of Consumer Satisfaction, Dissatisfaction and Complaining Behavior*, 2, 49-54.

Olson, Jerry C. and Philip A. Dover (1979), "Disconfirmation of Consumer Expectations Through Product Trial," *Journal of Applied Psychology*, 64 (2), 179-189.

Parasuraman, A., Valarie A. Zeithaml, and Leonard L. Berry (1985), "A Conceptual Model of Service Quality and Its Implications for Future Research," *Journal of Marketing*, 49 (Fall), 41-50.

_____, _____, and _____(1988), "SERVQUAL: A Scale for Measuring Consumer Perceptions of Service Quality," *Journal of Retail-*

ing, 64 (Spring), 13-40.

Sirgy, Joseph M. (1984), "A Social Cognition Model of Consumer Satisfaction/ Dissatisfaction," *Psychology and Marketing,* 1 (2), 27-43.

Spreng, Richard A. and Richard W. Olshavsky (1991), "A Desires-as-Standard Model of Consumer Satisfaction: Implications for Measuring Satisfaction," *Journal of Consumer Satisfaction, Dissatisfaction and Complaining Behavior* (in press).

Swan, John E., I. Frederick Trawick, and Carroll G. Maxwell (1981), "Satisfaction Related to Predictive, Desired Expectations: A Field Study," in *New Findings on Consumer Satisfaction and Complaining Behavior,* Ralph S. Day and H. Keith Hunt, eds. Bloomington, IN: School of Business, Indiana University, 15-22.

Tse, David K. and Peter C. Wilton (1988), "Models of Consumer Satisfaction Formation: An Extension," *Journal of Marketing Research,* 25 (May), 204-212.

Westbrook, Robert A. (1987), "Product/Consumption-Based Affective Responses and Postpurchase Processes," *Journal of Marketing Research,* 24 (August), 258-70.

_____and Michael D. Reilly (1983), "Value-Percept Disparity: An Alternative to the Disconfirmation of Expectations Theory of Consumer Satisfaction," in *Advances in Consumer Research,* Richard P. Bagozzi and Alice M. Tybout, eds. Ann Arbor, MI: Association for Consumer Research, 10, 256-61.

Woodruff, Robert B., Ernest R. Cadotte, and Roger L. Jenkins (1983), "Modeling Consumer Satisfaction Processes Using Experience-Based Norms," *Journal of Marketing Research,* 20 (August), 296-304.

_____, David W. Schumann, and D. Scott Clemons (1990), "Consumers' Reactions to Product Use Experiences: A Study of the Meaning of Consumer Satisfaction and Dissatisfaction," *Proceedings of the Society for Consumer Psychology,* Washington: American Psychological Association, 26-30.

_____, D. Scott Clemons, David W. Schumann, Sarah F. Gardial, and Mary Jane Burns (1991), "The Standards Issue in CS/D Research: A Historical Perspective," *Journal of Consumer Satisfaction, Dissatisfaction and Complaining Behavior,* (in press).

Zeithaml, Valarie A., A. Parasuraman, and Leonard L. Berry (1990), *Delivering Quality Service.* New York: Free Press.

_____, Leonard L. Berry, and A. Parasuraman (1991), "The Nature and Determinants of Customer Expectations of Service," Marketing Science Institute working paper 91-113.

BUYER-SELLER ENCOUNTERS: A COMPARATIVE ASSESSMENT

Angela da Rocha, COPPEAD, University Federal do Rio de Janeiro
Carl H. Christensen, CR Consultores Associados, Rio de Janeiro

ABSTRACT

This paper is directed at understanding why certain patterns of buyer-seller relationships prevail in given societies. It provides a preliminary framework to analyze the factors influencing the ways these relationships are developed.

INTRODUCTION

Terms such as "exchange" and "relationships" are at the very heart of the marketing concept. Yet their use is often confusing and the research on exchange relationships is scarce and fragmentary. This paper attempts to contribute to the clarification of this issue by: (1) reviewing existing theories and empirical evidence on buyer-seller relationships; (2) identifying a list of factors to analyze why certain patterns of buyer-seller relationships prevail under given environmental conditions.

THEORETICAL BACKGROUND

During recent years, increased attention in the business literature has been devoted to the process of interaction of buyers and sellers in the marketplace. This is by no means surprising because this interaction, by which some sort of exchange is produced, is a necessary condition for the survival and growth of business organizations.

However, the result is that we are faced with two different models of buyer-seller interactions that coexist in the Western business literature. The first one, the "marketing concept approach," is mainly the product of the American experience and of other Western countries and is directly associated with the marketing literature. It deals with issues such as societal marketing and consumerism. The other model arises out of theoretical developments by a group of European researchers combined with models developed on buyer-seller relationships in Japan. It appears under the labels of networking, buyer-seller interactions, partnership, strategic alliances etc.

THE MARKETING CONCEPT APPROACH

Buyer-Seller Relationships in the U.S.

Despite some consumer activism in the first half of the 1900's, it was only after the Second World War that criticism towards marketing and other business practices left the ivory tower and started to permeate the American society. During the sixties and the seventies, growing social discontent gave birth to an organized social movement, called "consumerism."

Consumerism has been defined as "...the organized efforts of consumers seeking redress, restitution and remedy for dissatisfaction they have accumulated in the acquisition of their standard of living" (Buskirk and Rothe 1972, p.112) or "...a social movement seeking to augment the rights and power of buyers in relation to sellers" (Kotler 1972, p.49). These and other definitions are quite revealing of the ways producers and consumers interacted in the U.S. They suggest that: (1) buyers were dissatisfied with sellers; (2) buyers perceived themselves in a comparatively weaker position to sellers; (3) buyers perceived an information/communication gap between sellers and buyers. The figure below shows a list of traditional buyers' and sellers' rights as well as of additional rights wanted by American consumers in the early seventies.

Commenting on the sellers' rights, Kotler observed that they were "...among the essential core rights of businessmen in the United States. Any radical change in these would make U.S. business a different kind of game." He added however that "...in looking over these traditional sellers' and buyers' rights, I believe that the balance of power lies with the seller" (p. 49). Kotler also suggested that "the real issue" was not "vocal consumer protest" but its "legacy... regarding the balance of buyers' rights and sellers' rights" (p. 52).

The above comments suggest that the relationship between customers and sellers in the U.S. was openly antagonistic and unfavorably balanced towards sellers' interests. It also suggests that social forces emerged and continue to act in order to establish, or re-establish, what was then considered an adequate balance of rights.

Theories Based on U.S. Buyer-Seller Relationships: The Societal Marketing, Macromarketing and Consumerism

At first look, it is amazing to the distanced observer that a social movement such as consumerism would even appear in the U.S. The marketing concept, which claimed "customer satisfaction" to be the major business goal, was supposedly widely accepted by business organizations. However, according to Kotler (1972), it was not necessarily practiced. This is why Drucker (1973) suggested that consumerism was "the shame of marketing."

The principle of "customer satisfaction" has been a core concept in marketing since after the Second World War as the American market moved from a seller's to a

Traditional Rights of:	
Sellers	**Buyers**
* Introduce any product of any size and style in the marketplace so long it is not hazardous to personal health or with proper warnings and controls if it is.	* Refuse to buy any product that is offered to them.
	* Know that the product is safe.
	* Know that the product is essentially as represented by the seller.
* Set any price if not discriminatory between similar classes of buyers.	
	Additional Rights Desired
* Spend any amount on promotion as long as it is not defined as unfair competition.	* Receive adequate information about the product.
* Formulate any message provided it is not mis leading in content or execution.	* Be protected against questionable products and marketing practices.
* Introduce any buying incentive schemes they wish.	* Have an influence on products and marketing practices to increase the "quality of life."
Adapted from Kotler (1972)	

buyer's market (Buskirk and Rothe 1970). However, the meaning of "customer satisfaction" was associated to only a very limited understanding of customer "needs," which were not viewed in a long-term perspective but rather as more or less immediate individual desires to be served by competing firms.

Earlier marketing thought saw each firm's permanent search for differential advantage to gain customer preference as the major force of competition in the marketplace. As the dynamics of innovation would permit a given firm to better serve customer needs at a certain point in time, consumer preference would shift from one to another competitor (e.g. Alderson 1957). The potential conflict between short and long-term needs was not contemplated by those theories, nor was the impact of business practices on societal needs including environmental preservation.

Kotler (1972) saw the problem as one of confusing "customer satisfaction" and "customer desires." He observed that "catering to customer satisfaction does not necessarily create satisfied consumers" (p. 54) but offered a rather optimistic perspective of the impact of consumerism a being "beneficial, pro marketing, and ultimately profitable" (p. 57).

Webster (1974) affirmed that the old marketing concept focused on the immediate "desires" of the individual consumer but did not consider his long-term "interests" as a citizen. He believed that the "old marketing concept" was dead. From a later point in time, Bloom and Greyser (1981) supported the view of the compatibility of the marketing concept with consumerism when affirming that "consumerism remains an opportunity rather than a threat" (p. 133).

The question of the social implications of marketing practices was at the center of a major upheaval in the way scholars of marketing defined its boundaries as Kotler and Levy (1969) advanced the idea of "broadening the concept of marketing" and Lazer (1969) called for the recognition of the societal dimensions of marketing. This theoretical debate gained momentum with other academicians such as Ferber (1970) predicting a growing importance of marketing for social and public policy issues and Lavidge (1971) calling for the use of societal criteria in marketing decisions.

Kotler (1972) suggested the change of the original marketing concept to a "societal marketing concept" by the inclusion of a long-term view of consumer welfare. Bartels and Jenkins (1977) went further proposing a distinction between micro and macromarketing where the first would encompass the original marketing concept while the second would deal with the means of "optimizing overall social benefit from the entire marketing process" (p. 19). Although these proposals did not receive immediate universal acceptance by the academic community (see, for example, Luck 1969, 1974), Hunt (1976) reported empirical evidence that "at least among marketing educators, the broadened concept of marketing is a fait accompli" (p. 19).

THE INTERACTION APPROACH

Theories Based on European Buyer-Seller Relationships: Interaction and Networks

Early developments of European theories on buyer-seller relationships came from the IMP Group (The International Marketing and Research Group). According to Cunningham (1985), one of the original founders of the research group, there was a perception that American marketing theory was not applicable to their reality.

The group focused initially on organizational buying behavior and developed the "Interaction Approach" to study dyadic supplier-customer relationships in the context of industrial marketing (e.g. Hakansson 1982; Turnbull 1987). The following figure presents a comparison between U.S and North European based theories of buyer-seller relationships, as proposed by the IMP Group.

According to the IMP Group, the interaction approach, as opposed to the traditional marketing concept approach, was based on a view of buyers and suppliers as engaged in long-term, active, interdependent relationships.

consisting of 'nodes' or positions... and links manifested by interaction between the positions" points much more to a structural than to a relational model. In many ways, his re-creation of the interaction model reflects an adaptation to a more competitive, individualistic environment in the US than in Northern Europe where those theories originally appeared. He does, however, call the attention of business practitioners to the long-term strategic implications of networking.

Commenting on the concept of networks, Jarillo (1988) observes that "the construct of networks is difficult to fit within the basic paradigm of competitive strategy" (p. 31) and indicates that most research on this topic continues to come from European scholars.

The Marketing Concept Approach	The Interaction Approach
* focus on discrete purchasing decisions	* focus on relationships between buyers and sellers
* view of suppliers as making their offers to a passive market	* idea of interaction between two active parties
* perception of low risk in changing suppliers	* emphasis on high cost of changing suppliers
* assumption of independence of buyers and suppliers	* assumption of interdependence of buyers and suppliers
* separation of organizational buying behavior and marketing	* interplay between purchasing strategies and marketing strategies
Adapted from Cunningham (1985)	

Subsequent research efforts emphasized related issues such as "portfolio theory" and "networks" (e.g. Mattson 1984; Campbell 1985a), extending the analysis of interactions from dyadic buyer-supplier relationships to the multiple connections of organizations in one or various markets. Portfolio theory is an extension of the interaction approach to a company's multiple relationships in several markets and network theory refers to the links among many organizations that participate in a given market. It assumes that it is only possible to talk about a network when a certain quantity and quality of relationships are established.

The concepts of "interaction" and "networks" have been adopted by U.S scholars and adapted to the specific context of American buyer-seller relationships (e.g. Thorelli 1986; Thomas and Soldow 1988). Thorelli, in particular, developed a theory of networking which, in some aspects, differs from the initial IMP Group propositions since it does not emphasize long-term relationships though it does recognize them. It is much more a systemic view of markets where different competitors, customers, etc. interact. His definition of a network "as

Buyer-Seller Relationships in Japan

A major shock to the prevailing understanding of buyer-seller relationships came from Japan in the form of striking differences between American and Japanese buyer-seller relationships. Personal relationships are the very essence of the Japanese culture (Nakane 1970). Japanese marketing systems are based on long-term relationships between firms in a group, between manufacturers and suppliers, between manufacturers and distributors, etc. The groups, or networks, to use the European terms, form what is called "keiretsu," where the members are linked by financial, managerial, or other kinds of ties (Ross 1983; Campbell 1985b; Murray and Blenkhorn 1985; Cusumano and Takeishi 1991).

Interaction with consumers is also a major element of the Japanese marketing system (Czinkota 1985) where long-term relationships are established between customers and retailers. Because in Japan "the customer is king," it is an important function of retailers to choose the best products for their customers as well as to provide superior and personalized service. The retailer, due to his personal ties to the manufacturer, is able to provide strong assurance of product quality to the customer (Johansson 1986). The customer, on the other side, offers loyal patronage to the retailer (Rosenberg 1986).

A natural consequence of personal relationships is the rivalry among different groupings or "networks" (Campbell 1985b). Leading companies in the same industry, each one supporting and supported by its network, compete fiercely in the Japanese marketplace (Smothers 1990).

Japanese buyer-seller relationships, either when we look to individual consumers or to organizational buyers, can be defined as personal, cooperative, harmonious and long-term.

Theories Based on Japanese Buyer-Seller Relationships: Strategic Alliances

The Japanese experience has had a major impact on American management and marketing theory. Jorde and Teece (1989) suggest that "two somewhat independent shifts are causing academics, businessmen and policy makers to rethink fundamental ideas about competition and cooperation. The first is the increased level of international competition, particularly from Japan... the second and more subtle shift... concerns the role of interfirm agreements" (p. 25). Lodge and Walton (1990) go so far as to propose the establishment of a new way for American corporations to compete. American companies should "change relationships both at their perimeter, or `boundary,' and internally at the core where person is bound to person in work of the firm. They [should] change... away from the adversarial, arm's length, short-term, contractual, and rigid relationships of the past towards ones which are more cooperative, intimate, long-term, consensual, and flexible." The new idea is to form "a coalition of rivals cooperating for R&D," "a partnership of manufacturers, suppliers and customers" and "a consortium of capital and labor" (p. 10). The authors recognize the difficulty of such a change since "it faces profound obstacles rooted in fundamental premises about the proper roles and relationships of government, business and labor.... some of our deeply rooted American traditions..." (p. 10).

These recommendations show that the Japanese experience has been noticed, that there is a clear awareness of the differences from US practices and that there are attempts towards including the concepts into American business practices. The difficulty comes, however, as Jarillo (1988) mentioned when discussing networking, in trying to combine cooperative views with competitive strategy. The research on "strategic alliances" aims exactly at achieving this match.

Most theory on strategic alliances appears in the late 80s and early 90s and emphasizes certain forms of alliances, such as "technology alliances" (Nueno and Oosterveld 1988), "logistics alliances" (Bowersox 1990), "information partnerships" (Konsynski and McFarlan 1990), "alliances in industrial purchasing" (Heide and John 1990) and "global strategic alliances" (Devlin and Bleackley 1988; Ohmae 1989; Nohria and Garcia-Pont 1991).

A major issue in this research stream is defining exactly what are strategic alliances and linkages. To Devlin and Bleackley (1988) "strategic alliances are specifically concerned with securing, maintaining or enhancing a company's competitive advantage." They affirm that strategic alliances differ from old style cooperative agreements because they are oriented towards the long-term and strategic in nature while these other relationships are "casual" and "unlikely to dramatically change a company's competitive position" (p. 18).

Ohmae (1989) points out that "managers have been slow to experiment with genuinely strategic alliances." He explains why such behavior exists among American managers: "A real alliance compromises the fundamental independence of economic actors, and managers don't like that" (p. 143). In the same vein, Bowersox (1990) indicates that one of the major limitations to implement strategic alliances is the ability of American managers to develop trust. According to the author, "this attitude is not easy for managers schooled in an adversarial tradition" (p. 44).

BRIDGING THE MARKETING CONCEPT AND INTERACTION APPROACHES

The question to be addressed is the applicability of these two approaches to other environments. In order to answer the question, it is necessary to understand the environmental factors that affect the interaction of buyers and sellers in different societies. We propose the following list of factors that may influence the way these relationships develop: (see list on following page).
We shall now analyze the cases of the U.S and Japan choosing the appropriate factors to explain why buyer-seller relationships are the way they are in each society.

Environmental Factors in U.S. Buyer-Seller Relationships

The United States can be described as a society that emphasizes individual goals over collective ones. In fact, for many social scientists since Alexis de Tocqueville in the 1800s, no other society has ascribed such importance to individual welfare based on the belief that the sum of individual welfares will produce society's welfare. Such an individualistic orientation tends to favor competition. Competition is emphasized as a necessary condition for the vitality of the economic system.

In American society, direct conflict is accepted as a

Type	Variable	Possibilities
Cultural	Goal achievement	as individual or through groups
	Norms of interacting	competitive or cooperative
	Conflict management	regulated or avoided
	Trust	institutionalized suspicion vs generalized trust
	Time horizons	short or long-term perspective
Social	Structure	equalitarian or hierarchical
	Education level	high or low
Economic	System	laissez-faire or state control
	Market regulation	free or protected
	Change rate	rapid or slow
Political	Government	democratic or autocratic
	Responsibility	citizens or government
	Citizen involvement	high or low
Legal	Litigation	third entities(court) or interpersonal
	Effectiveness	fair or unfair
	Efficiency	fast or slow resolution

natural part of human interaction. Therefore, it is not avoided but it is regulated. On the other side, agreements are not based on trust but on what is commonly called "institutionalized suspicion;" whatever is in a written contract has legal value and obligations are limited to the specific contractual rules. Consumers and manufacturers in the United States tend to use formal and complete contractual forms to regulate their relationships.

Equalitarianism is another basic American value which finds its roots in the early days of colonization. It does not mean the absence of difference but that all citizens should have the same basic rights. Although some groups might be more privileged than others, there is a conscious agreement that the political and legal systems should give equal rights to the less privileged. Economic abuse of buyers by sellers is against basic American cultural values.

The dominant time perspective in the U.S. is, at least at this point in its history, short-term. This implies that decisions taken by individuals within organizations will tend to have a limited time horizon in terms of implications. Long-term consumer welfare or even long-term organizational welfare are not a major consideration.

On the other side, the exercise of democracy and citizenship in the United States stimulates the expression by various segments of the population of their opinions about political, economic and social affairs. Because citizens are also consumers, any dissatisfactions can be communicated through the same channels. Finally, the

legal system in the United States is prepared to respond efficiently and effectively to legal actions on behalf of consumer interests.

Environmental Factors in Japanese Buyer-Seller Relationships

Japan can be described as a holistic or collective society where individual interests are subordinated to group goals. These groups are established through personal ties between individuals and organizations in such a way as to form an intricate social fabric. The establishment of these networks is associated with a certain collapse of the boundaries of individuals or organizations within the group. The resulting network becomes an unit in itself. Separations between firms that belong to the same "keiretsu" are not always clear with employees of one company working at the other, cross participation in each firm's capital, debt lines extending between the companies, etc. Moreover, there is an overall concern for each member group's welfare as well as welfare of the system.

Since relationships are long term, cooperation and conflict avoidance are essential for their maintenance. In addition, a generalized reciprocity, that is, a permanent system of mutual obligations that is not limited to specific obligations or to a specific period of time, is part of the relational environment.

Relationships in Japan are defined according to a series of very precise societal rules of relative hierarchical position. In fact, the Japanese have an extreme need to rank themselves and their organizations, so that each person's or firm's proper social place is precisely defined. These hierarchical rules are rooted in the cultural and historical development of Japan, particularly to the Confucian division of society in classes. In the case of consumers' relationships to distributors or to manufacturers, the interests and preferences of consumers are considered as more important than the sellers.' One reason for that comes from the way social hierarchy was defined during the Tokugawa era which placed sellers below buyers in terms of social status.

The economic system is a combination of controlled competition in certain areas and free competition in others. The fierce competition in Japanese domestic market has favored the Japanese consumer with excellent products if not low prices. Cooperation among companies and between companies and the government has also served the consumer's interest. As to the political system, Japan has been, throughout its history, governed by autocracies. The Japanese people have not exercised, as much as the Americans, the responsibilities of citizenship. In the paternalistic Japanese society, citizens' welfare is a major responsibility of government but this is balanced with the collective orientation which, in turn, makes each person an active participant in society's common goals. Thus, there seems to be little incentive for consumer movements in Japan, at least under the forms that appeared in American society. Finally, the legal system is much less used in Japan than in the United States because disputes are typically dealt with at the interpersonal level rather than using detailed contracts and litigation involving third parties to resolve uncertainties.

CONCLUDING REMARKS

It was not by accident that consumerism appeared in the United States; it is clearly the result of historical developments and cultural values found in the American society related mainly to the ways buyers and sellers interact. As an academic response to these social phenomena, the concept of "societal marketing" and of "macromarketing" were developed to substitute the original marketing concept which did not incorporate long-run consumer welfare and a broader perspective of social needs. Because the U.S. was the environment and major source for marketing theory and, up to the 80s, the only

prominent model of economic success, American marketing theory was universally recognized and adopted by marketers and marketing scholars all over the world. It must be understood, however, that the original marketing concept as well as the new one with societal dimensions are products of the unique U.S. historical experience.

On the other side, the theories associated with networking, interaction and strategic alliances were partly a North European theoretical development and partly developed in the U.S. as a recent outcome of the observation of Japanese management practices. They emphasize a cooperative rather than competitive view of customer-firm encounters. Yet these theories are based on different sets of realities from those previously examined. They also are the result of unique cultural and historical experiences.

A final question to be raised is why have the North European and Japanese experiences combined so well as to permit the development of similar theories of buyer-seller interaction? Although there is no space here to fully develop the argument, we believe that both North European (particularly Scandinavian) and Japanese societies have favored cooperation rather than competition in buyer-seller relationships. In fact, it should be noted that the Scandinavian socialist experience is based on a collectivist (although not holistic) approach to social organization; it was not by accident that cooperativism has been specially successful in these countries. As to Japan, the holistic view of society has also been conducive to long-term cooperative interactions. But it has been its economic success and present position as a world power that have drawn the world's attention to the ways Japanese buyers and sellers interact in the marketplace.

The two theoretical approaches to buyer-seller relationships, the Marketing Concept Approach and the Interaction Approach, are clearly products of distinct environments and should be seen in this light. Researchers should be aware of the impact of environmental factors on buyer-seller relationships. This is one type of interpersonal relationship among many different kinds created by a society and it is forged by very complex cultural forces, as well as other environmental influences (such as economic, social and legal) that also tend to be culture-specific.

REFERENCES

Alderson, W. (1957), *Marketing Behavior and Executive Action.* Homewood, IL: Irwin.

Bartels, R. and R. L. Jenkins (1977), "Macromarketing," *Journal of Marketing,* 41 (4), 17-20.

Bloom, P. and S. A. Greyser (1981), "The Maturity of Consumerism," *Harvard Business Review,* 59 (6), 130-139.

Bowersox, D. J. (1990), "The Strategic Benefits of Logistics Alliances," *Harvard Business Review,* 4 (July/August), 36-45.

Buskirk, R. H. and J. T. Rothe (1970), "Consumerism - An Interpretation," *Journal of Marketing,* 34 (4), 61-65.

Campbell, N. C. G. (1985a), "Network Analysis of a Global Capital Equipment Industry," *Proceedings of the 2nd Open International IMP Research Semi-*

nar, Uppsala: University of Uppsala, (September), 4-6.

_____(1985b), "Buyer/Seller Relationships in Japan and Germany: An Interaction Approach," *European Journal of Marketing*, 19 (3), 57-66.

Cunningham, M. T. (1985), "Interaction and Networks: A Review of the Evolution and Development of the IMP Group's Research Activities from 1976-1985," *Proceedings of the 2nd Open International IMP Research Seminar*, Uppsala: University of Uppsala, (September), 4-6.

Cusumano, M. A. and A. Takeishi (1991), "Supplier Relations and Management: A Survey of Japanese, Japanese-Transplant and U.S. Auto Plants," *Strategic Management Journal*, 12, 563-588.

Czinkota, M. R. (1985), "Distribution in Japan: Problems and Changes," *The Columbia Journal of World Business*, 20 (3), 65-70.

Devlin, G. and M. Bleackley (1988), "Strategic Alliances - Guidelines for Success," *Long Range Planning*, 21 (5), 18-25.

Drucker, P. (1973), "The Shame of Marketing," in W. T. Kelley, ed. *New Consumerism, Selected Readings*, Columbus: Grid, chapter 15.

Ferber, R. (1970), "The Expanding Role of Marketing in the 1970's," *Journal of Marketing*, 34 (1), 29-30.

Hakansson, H. (1982), *International Marketing and Purchasing of Industrial Goods: An Interaction Approach*. Chicago: Wiley.

Heide, J. and G. John (1990), "Alliances in Industrial Purchasing: The Determinants of Joint Action in Buyer-Seller Relationships," *Journal of Marketing Research*, 27 (1), 24-36.

Hunt, S. D. (1976), "The Nature and Scope of Marketing," *Journal of Marketing*, 40 (3), 17-28.

Jarillo, J. C. (1988), "On Strategic Networks," *Strategic Management Journal*, 9 (October), 31-41.

Johansson, J. K. (1986), "Japanese Consumers: What Foreign Marketers Should Know," *International Marketing Review*, 3 (2), 37-43.

Jorde, T. M. and D. T. Teece (1989), "Competition and Cooperation: Striking the Right Balance," *California Management Review*, 31 (3), 25-37.

Konsynski, B. and F. McFarlan (1990), "Information Partnerships: Shared Data, Shared Scale," *Harvard Business Review*, (September/October), 114-120.

Kotler, P. (1972), "What Consumerism Means for Marketers," *Harvard Business Review*, 50 (3), 48-57.

_____and S. Levy (1969), "Broadening the Concept of Marketing," *Journal of Marketing*, 33 (1), 10-15.

Lavidge, R. (1970), "The Growing Responsibilities of Marketing," *Journal of Marketing*, 34 (1), 26-28.

Lazer, W. (1969), "Marketing's Changing Social Relationships," *Journal of Marketing*, 33 (1), 3-9.

Lodge, G. and R. Walton (1989), "The American Corporation and its New Relationships," *California Management Review*, 31 (3), 9-24.

Luck, D. (1969),"Broadening the Concept of Marketing - Too Far," *Journal of Marketing*, 33 (3), 53-55.

_____(1974), "Social Marketing: Confusion Compounded," *Journal of Marketing*, 38 (4), 70-72.

Mattson, L. G. (1984), "An Application of a Network Approach to Marketing: Defending and Changing Market Positions," in N. Dhokalia and J. Arndt, eds. *Changing the Course of Marketing: Alternative Paradigms for Widening Marketing Theory*, Greenwich: JAI.

Murray, J. A. and D. L. Blenkhorn (1985), "Organizational Buying Processes in North America and Japan," *International Marketing Review*, 2 (4), 55-63.

Nakane, C. (1970), *Japanese Society*. Berkeley: University of California Press.

Nohria, N. and C. Garcia-Pont (1991), "Global Strategic Linkages and Industry Structure," *Strategic Management Journal*, 12, 105-124.

Nueno, P. and J. Oosterveld (1988), "Managing Technology Alliances," *Long Range Planning*, 21 (3), 11-17.

Ohmae, K. (1989),"The Global Logic of Strategic Alliances," *Harvard Business Review*, (March/April), 143-154.

Rosenberg, L. J. (1986), "Deciphering the Japanese Cultural Code," *International Marketing Review*, 3 (3), 47-57.

Ross, R. E. (1983), "Understanding the Japanese Distribution System: An Explanatory Framework," *European Journal of Marketing*, 17 (1), 5-13.

Smothers, Norman P. (1990), "Patterns of Japanese Strategy: Strategic Combinations of Strategies," *Strategic Management Journal*, 11, 521-533.

Thomas, G. P. and G. Soldow (1988), "A Rules-Based Approach to Competitive Interaction," *Journal of Marketing*, 52 (2), 63-74.

Thorelli, H. B. (1986), "Networks: Between Markets and Hierarchies," *Strategic Management Journal*, 7, 37-51.

Turnbull, P. W. (1987), "Interaction and International Marketing: An Investment Process," *International Marketing Review*, 4 (4), 7-19.

Webster, F. E. Jr. (1974), *Social Aspects of Marketing*. Englewood Cliffs, NJ: Prentice-Hall.

AN EMPIRICAL EXAMINATION OF THE EXPERIENCES OF NON-JAPANESE FIRMS WITH THE JAPANESE DISTRIBUTION SYSTEM

Daniel Rajaratnam, Baylor University
Joseph A. McKinney, Baylor University

ABSTRACT

The Japanese distribution system (JDS) has been described as ancient and complex (Glazer 1968), uneconomic and cumbersome (Adams and Kobayashi 1969), inefficient, and costly (Hartley 1972), archaic, and old fashioned (Schmuckli and Tajima 1973), an invisible barrier to market entry (Shimaguchi and Lazer 1979), long, complicated, confusing, unintelligible, and an impossible maze (Lazer, Murata and Kosaka 1985). In the 1960s, 1970s and 1980s new forms of retailing and distribution began to make their appearance in Japan (Brooks 1989, USITC 1990) resulting in a decline in the traditional forms of distribution (JEI Report 1989). However, in the Structural Impediments Initiative (SII) talks with Japan, the U.S. government targeted the JDS as the greatest barrier to market entry there (KKC Brief 1990).

These accusations about the JDS as a trade barrier were investigated by two surveys of non-Japanese firms operating in Japan. The initial survey was conducted in 1979 and was mailed to members of the American Chamber of Commerce in Japan. The 1986 survey was mailed to members of the American, Australian, British, and New Zealand Chambers of Commerce in Japan. The surveys excluded members not representing business firms. The questions used in both surveys were the same. In the 1979 survey, 306 questionnaires were mailed and 92 usable replies were received, for a response rate of 30 percent. In the 1986 survey, 449 questionnaires were mailed and 203 usable replies were received, for a response rate of 45 percent. In both surveys, respondents were permitted to respond without revealing the identity of their firm.

Six hypotheses which are consistent with or supported by the literature on the JDS, were formulated and tested. The first hypothesis stated that non-Japanese firms operating in Japan in 1986 are less dependant upon distribution entirely by wholesalers than in 1979. This hypothesis was supported. The second hypothesis stated that distribution apart from the traditional JDS is possible to a greater extent in 1986 than in 1979 for non-Japanese firms operating in Japan. This hypothesis was also supported. The third hypothesis stated that the JDS in 1986 increased the cost of products of non-Japanese firms to a smaller extent than in 1979. This hypothesis was also supported. The fourth hypothesis stated that the JDS in 1986 insulates non-Japanese firms from their customers to a lesser extent than in 1979. This hypothesis was also supported. The fifth hypothesis stated that services of Japanese trading companies are utilized to a lesser extent by non-Japanese firms operating in Japan in 1986 than in 1979. This hypothesis was not supported. The last hypothesis stated that non-Japanese firms operating in Japan in 1986 are more satisfied with the marketing of their products by Japanese trading companies than in 1979. This hypothesis was supported for firms selling consumer products only.

The results of this study indicate that in the opinion of executives of non-Japanese firms operating in Japan, the JDS was less formidable in 1986 than it was in 1979. This was true for both consumer and industrial products. On the basis of these findings, several conclusions can be drawn. First, it is possible for non-Japanese firms to distribute their products directly to customers in Japan without being entirely dependent upon Japanese wholesalers. Second, distribution apart from the traditional Japanese distribution channels is possible but not without some difficulty. Third, the JDS increases the cost of products of non-Japanese firms to some extent. Fourth, the JDS is more likely to insulate firms selling industrial products from their customers, than firms selling consumer products. Fifth, services of Japanese trading companies are likely to be utilized either occasionally or not at all by non-Japanese firms operating in Japan. Finally, firms that utilize the services of Japanese trading companies are usually satisfied with the marketing of their products by these organizations.

For further information and references please contact:
Daniel Rajaratnam
Hankamer School of Business
Baylor University
Waco, TX 76798-8007

THE EFFECTS OF CULTURE ON INTERFIRM COMMUNICATIONS

Soumava Bandyopadhyay, The University of Alabama
Robert A. Robicheaux, The University of Alabama

ABSTRACT

This paper presents a theoretical framework to study the impact of the cultural environment on the nature of communication strategies between firms in channels of distribution. Most interfirm communication and influence strategy empirical research has been conducted in channels of distribution in the United States. This might have led to a possible cultural bias in the inferences that have been made regarding the use of communication strategies. The choice of communication strategies depends partly on organizational culture of the firm which is bound by the business culture of the host environment. The business culture is in turn conditioned by the wider national culture. Therefore, the effects of the cultural environment on all aspects of interfirm communication warrant a closer investigation by marketing researchers.

The major dimensions of national culture are language, religion, politics, law, education, social organization, aesthetic systems, technology and material culture, and values and attitudes. Changes in the cultural variables have a close relationship with economic development. Most aspects of culture vary along a continuum between two extremes, one usually found in underdeveloped and developing economies, and the other usually found in modern, industrialized economies of the West. The former type of cultural environment can be called traditional and the latter type can be called modern.

In the proposed framework, the governance structure of marketing channels interacts with culture to affect communication strategies. Based on the Political Economy and Relational Exchange paradigms, two extreme types of governance structures, markets (characterized by discrete transactions between firms) and hierarchies (characterized by relational exchanges), are considered.

We thus conceptualize an interorganizational marketing environment in two dimensions: culture (traditional and modern) an structure (markets and hierarchies). Testable propositions are developed regarding communication strategy use in all four environments.

The facets of interfirm communication that are considered include direction, frequency, modality, and content. Direction refers to the vertical movement of communication between channel member organizations. Frequency indicates the amount of contact between organizational members. Modality refers to the method (formal or informal) used to transmit information. Content refers to the nature of influence strategies (direct or indirect) that channel members use to persuade other channel members.

The research propositions state that distribution channels in traditional cultures are characterized by (a) more unidirectional communications, (b) less frequent communications, (c) more use of formal communication modes, and (d) more use of direct influence strategies compared to distribution channels in modern cultures. Also, legal pleas are used less frequently and promises are used more frequently in traditional cultures than in modern cultures. When indirect influence strategies are used in traditional cultures, recommendations are used more frequently than information exchange. In addition, there is a positive relationship among the uses of request, promise, and threat strategies in a traditional cultural environment. In discussing the effect of governance structure, it is proposed that in terms of direction, frequency, modality, and content of interfirm communication, channels characterized by hierarchical structures in traditional cultures are more similar to channels characterized by hierarchical structures in modern cultures than to channels characterized by market structures in traditional cultures.

This paper is a first step toward a greater understanding of the impact of the cultural environment on interfirm communication strategies. The propositions need to be validated by rigorous empirical testing. American businesses need to realize that they must be able to understand and appreciate overseas cultural environments in order to motivate their foreign channel partners and build continuing relationships with them. U.S. businesses must use communication strategies which are compatible with local practices and expectations. This would make for more effective international trade.

For further information contact:
Robert A. Robicheaux, Ph.D.
The University of Alabama
Department of Management and Marketing
P.O. Box 870225
Tuscaloosa, AL 35487-0225

IMPLICATIONS OF STRATEGIC ALLIANCE STRUCTURE: A COOPERATIVE STRATEGY/RELATIONAL EXCHANGE FRAMEWORK

Edwin R. Stafford, Arizona State University

ABSTRACT

A framework is proposed and illustrated that attempts to bring better understanding of the competitive implications associated with specific types of strategic alliances based upon two structural dimensions, cooperative strategies and exchange relationships. Combining specific forms of cooperation with exchange impacts the trade-offs between partner flexibility and cooperative synergy.

INTRODUCTION

The recent partnership joining computer rivals Apple and IBM reflects a growing inclination among organizations to collaborate (O'Connor 1991). Driving the trend are the increasing risks in developing new technologies, market globalization, and powerful foreign competitors (Chipello 1989). Surprisingly, the U.S. Justice Department is encouraging alliances, particularly for research and development (Chipello 1989), and one-on-one competition among firms is increasingly being replaced by competition among constellations of firms that routinely venture together (cf. Arndt 1979; Harrigan 1986). Interorganizational collaboration is already a recognized force behind Japanese corporations (Gerlach 1987; Jarillo 1988).

"Strategic alliances" are commonly described as interorganizational relationships where partners make substantial investments toward developing long-term collaborative efforts for meeting their individual goals (Mattsson 1988). While research has delineated when competitive verses cooperative activities between organizations may be appropriate (cf. Campbell 1985), implications associated with specific forms of cooperative ventures vary, depending upon how interorganizational alliances are structured. At present, the marketing and strategic management literatures are split into largely independent research streams on various forms and conceptualizations of alliances, ranging from symbiotic marketing (cf. Adler 1966; Varadarajan and Rajaratnam 1986) to joint ventures (cf. Harrigan 1986; Tyebjee 1988) to coalitions (cf. Porter and Fuller 1986) to strategic networks (cf. Jarillo 1988; Thorelli 1986) to various marketing channel systems (cf. Stern and El-Ansary 1988). Some of this research is splintered even further through definition controversies regarding various conceptualizations. For instance, Varadarajan and Rajaratnam (1986) have taken issue with Adler (1966) concerning whether symbiotic marketing includes merg-

ers, and Tyebjee (1988) has contended that joint ventures do not necessarily require the creation of a new separate entity as advocated by Harrigan (1986). Thus, current understanding about certain types of partnerships may not be readily applicable across differing conceptualizations.

A unified framework is needed that better articulates various structures of strategic alliances to more readily understand underlying strategic considerations. Often, researchers have not clearly distinguished two dimensions that affect inter-partner relationship management and competitive strategy, (1) inter-partner cooperative activities, and (2) exchange relationships bonding partners together. It is proposed that the combined interaction of an alliance's cooperative strategy and exchange relationship determines the implications associated with that partnership. Figure 1 presents the proposed framework.

FRAMEWORK OVERVIEW

Cooperative Strategies

Astley and Fombrun (1983) have described market environments as ecological communities to illuminate collective organizational adaptation, reflecting a growing consensus that organizations do not act as autonomous agents within their respective markets, but rather organizations jointly create the parameters of how they collectively survive (cf. Arndt 1979). Interorganizational adaptation occurs both unintentionally and voluntarily (Bresser 1988). Unintended adaptations may be exemplified by strategic groups, where firms within a group tend to follow similar strategies (Porter 1980), and informal cooperation takes place between groups where each pursues a different marketing orientation without challenging other groups. Within strategic groups, however, competition may be fierce. Voluntary cooperative adaptations are reflective of strategic alliances, where organizations deliberately establish formal ties for collaboration. Borys and Jemison (1989) have identified three generic "value creations" (integrated activities) implicit among partnerships: sequential, reciprocal, and pool. These cooperative activities parallel Thompson's (1967) interdependency framework of functional departments within organizations.

A sequential strategy involves a one-way transfer of a resource or value chain activity between partners where one "hands off" to the other (Borys and Jemison 1989), like the Nippon Chemi-Con/Data Ray partnership de-

FIGURE 1
A Cooperative Strategy/Relational Exchange Framework
Of Strategic Alliance Structures with Illustrations

	Relational Exchanges		
Cooperative Strategies	Contractual Arrangement	Procreational Venture	Acquisitional Venture
Sequential	A	B	C
Reciprocal	D	E	F
Pool	G	H	I

(A) **Sequential/Contractual Arrangement:** To guarantee suitable sourcing of auto parts and raw materials, Chrysler has maintained hundreds of multi-year purchasing contracts with its best suppliers (Stundza 1985).

(B) **Sequential/Procreational Venture:** To obtain better control over a source of electro-deposited copper foil critical to Oak Industries' manufacturing process, Oak-Mitsui was established as a new entity joint venture by Oak Industries and Mitsui (Tyebjee 1988).

(C) **Sequential/Acquisitional Venture:** As a means of entering the electronic component business, Nippon Chemi-Con, a Japanese capacitor manufacturer, acquired a 75 percent stake in Data Ray, an American concern. The venture resulted in Nippon Chemi-Con handling virtually all the manufacturing functions with Data Ray overseeing the marketing functions (Tyebjee 1988).

(D) **Reciprocal/Contractual Arrangement:** In a contractual agreement with DuPont, Merck traded marketing rights of some of its pharmaceutical drugs in exchange for development rights to DuPont's heart drugs (*Business Week* 1989).

(E) **Reciprocal/Procreational Venture:** Prior to Sony's acquisition of CBS, the two concerns maintained a 50-50 joint venture called the Digital Audio Disc Corporation, which manufactured pre-recorded compact discs. CBS contributed its music recording experience, vast catalogue of recorded music, and distribution while Sony offered its state-of-the-art technology in production and entertainment hardware (Tyebjee 1988).

(F) **Reciprocal/Acquisitional Venture:** The Ebara Group, a large Japanese pump manufacturer, infused a substantial amount of capital into Cryodynamics. The joint venture involved Ebara contributing manufacturing skills and a worldwide sales network in exchange for Cryodynamics' design experience and product testing capabilities (Tyebjee 1988).

(G) **Pool/Contractual Arrangement:** To better serve their mutual customers, Apple Computer and Digital Equipment pooled RandD resources to jointly develop technology and products to link Apple's popular Macintosh personal computers with Digital's VAX mini-computers (Schlender 1988).

(H) **Pool/Procreational Venture:** As a means of improving the efficiency of the two companies, Pacific Mutual Life Insurance of California and Mutual Life Insurance of New York pooled their administration and claims-service management functions into a new jointly-owned company called the Employee Benefits America Administration Co. (*Wall Street Journal* 1988).

(I) **Pool/Acquisitional Venture:** In order to pool efforts in cancer drug research in 1983, Bristol-Myers invested into Oncogen, an existing therapeutics research firm (Hamilton 1986).

scribed in Figure 1-C. A sequential strategy is common among vertically-linked alliances (Bresser and Harl 1986), and many manufacturing firms use this strategy to secure sourcing as in the Chrysler (Figure 1-A) and Oak/Mitsui (Figure 1-B) alliances. Just-in-time supplier arrangements and licensing agreements are common manifestations of this strategy. Sequential strategies allow partners to specialize in distinctive competencies and reduce inter-partner duplication. Among cooperative strategies, sequential may be the most flexible because the partner ties will focus primarily on the point of operational contact (Borys and Jemison 1989). As such, the partners' activities will be less complexly linked and may be less interdependent, allowing for better opportunity to change partners when necessary. An inherent pitfall with a sequential strategy is that because partners specialize in specific tasks, partners attain virtually no enjoyment of inter-partner economies of scale. Furthermore, with the exception of licensing, inter-partner learning is also restricted. A sequential strategy's less complex nature facilitates relatively easier partnership dissolution, which could more readily paralyze ex-partners with losses of sourcing, customers, or important value-chain activities.

A reciprocal cooperative strategy consists of a two-way interchange between partners trading complementary outputs or value chain activities with one another (Borys and Jemison 1989). Reciprocal strategies result from complementary dissimilarity between partners (Porter and Fuller 1986). Examples of this strategy include trading distribution of one product for development rights of another as in the Merck/DuPont agreement (Figure 1-D), or the exchange of various value chain activities for joint-products as with the Sony/CBS (Figure 1-E) and Ebara/Cryodynamics (Figure 1-F) ventures. Like a sequential strategy, a reciprocal strategy allows partners to capitalize on value chain strengths to minimize redundancy. However, a reciprocal relationship is more complex, necessitating adaptation between a wider range of partnering operations. Inter-partner fit is less precisely specified a priori, requiring the relationship to evolve through partner interaction and making reciprocal relationships the most difficult to administer (Borys and Jemison 1989). Interorganizational slack and flexibility are key start-up considerations. This initial slack, however, can facilitate inter-partner learning. The complexity of a reciprocal strategy may be very difficult to adjust in dynamic market conditions. Moreover, depending upon how many activities are being traded among partners, reciprocal strategies make partnership dissolution troublesome.

A pool strategy entails partners sharing one or more of the same activities or drawing from a common resource (Borys and Jemison 1989; Nielsen 1988; Porter and Fuller 1986). Although partners may not necessarily be competitors, a pool strategy tends to evolve when partners are more similar in strengths, weaknesses, and marketing objectives, and the partners are unable to perform the pooled activity as effectively alone (Porter and Fuller 1986). Because pool partners tend to face common threats and opportunities, pooling seems more stable than other cooperative strategies (Porter and Fuller 1986). Examples of pool strategies include the sharing of RandD expenses as in the Apple/Digital (Figure 1-G) and Bristol-Myers/Oncogen (Figure 1-I) alliances or the combining of service facilities as in the Pacific Mutual Life/ Mutual Life partnership (Figure 1-H). The primary benefits of pooling include scale economies, excess capacity reductions, knowledge transfers, and risk sharing (Nielsen 1988; Porter and Fuller 1986). However, pooling may be the least flexible of all the cooperative strategies (Porter and Fuller 1986). Integration of like activities among partners hampers strategy adaptation within a dynamic environment, and termination is also less easily facilitated (Porter and Fuller 1986). Dissolution may require ex-partners to start the once pooled activity from scratch, relying only upon what has been learned through the alliance.

Commitment to more than one competitive strategy can be self-defeating (Porter 1980); pursuing an "overall cost leadership" strategy, for instance, can diffuse the effectiveness of a simultaneous "differentiation" strategy. However, unlike competitive strategies, Nielsen (1988) has noted "combining cooperative strategies does not necessarily mean that any one of the cooperative strategies is weakened or made ineffective" (p. 480). Cooperative strategies have an "additivity effect" in that a sequential strategy of one activity can be combined with a pool strategy in another and bring a partnership two benefit mechanisms; expenses can be reduced by a sequential strategy through the elimination of inter-partner duplication of one activity, and combined with a pool strategy of another activity, expenses can be reduced even further through scale economies. Hence, pursuing different forms of cooperative strategy simultaneously can bring appended advantages. Bresser (1988) has proposed that combined collective and competitive strategies can be beneficial, provided that an organization maintain secrecy of competitive plans. This, however, is often jeopardized by interorganizational information links. The next section describes exchange relationships used to initiate cooperation.

Exchange Relationships

Exchange relationships between firms may be visualized as a continuum (Dwyer, Schurr, and Oh 1987), ranging from discrete one-time exchanges to relational exchanges, which involve long-term relationships, to integrated exchanges of full mergers and acquisitions. Although Dwyer et al. (1987) have only regarded contractual vertical ties within their conceptualization of relational exchange, the framework described here refers to equity relationships along with horizontal and diagonal ties as forms of relational exchange as well. This seems appropriate because Dwyer et al. (1987) have described relational exchanges as "marriages," and other researchers have commonly characterized horizontal and diagonal equity relationships between organizations as "marriages" also (cf. Harrigan 1986; Tyebjee 1988). The interorganizational cooperation literature implicitly describes three types of bonds between partners: contractual arrangements, procreational ventures, and acquisitional ventures.

Contractual arrangements reflect non-equity long-term agreements between partners. The relationship is consummated by a legal document specifying the cooperative contributions and power base of each partner. Technology development agreements, exemplified by the Merck/DuPont (Figure 1-D) and the Apple/Digital (Figure 1-G) partnerships as well as sourcing pacts as depicted by the Chrysler example (Figure 1-A) are common illustrations of this form of exchange. Of the three exchanges, contractual arrangements are the most flexible. Because no equity is involved, investment in the partnership is substantially less. Moreover, within the bounds of the contractual arrangement, partners are able to afford greater autonomy from each other. Should the partnership fail to meet objectives, break up is better facilitated. Consequently, because the commitment to the partnership may be perceived as less permanent than equity arrangements, contracts provide the least control over important assets and skills that organizations may seek from their partners (Harrigan 1986). Thus, contractual arrangements seem feasible when the strategic necessity of the relationship is no more than moderately important.

Procreational ventures involve partners contributing to the creation of a new separate entity to facilitate long-term cooperation (Harrigan 1986). Although the new entity may have its own assets and management team, the new entity's "parents" usually take an active role in its strategic decisions. Examples of procreational ventures include Oak-Mitsui (Figure 1-B), the Digital Audio Disc Corporation (Figure 1-E), and the Employee Benefits America Administration Company (Figure 1-H); each is a separate entity jointly-owned by two partners. The establishment of a new entity requires intensive capital and resources from the partners. Inter-partner relations as well as the new entity's autonomy and relations with its owners must be considered. Partners must agree which resources and technologies will be shared among owners and the new entity, how transactions will be channeled among owners and the new entity, and other issues relating to cooperative synergies. Moreover, markets must be carefully allotted among the partners and the new entity as it is not uncommon for firms to find that they are competing in markets with their own joint ventures (Harrigan 1986). While jointly operating a separate entity creates a stronger commitment for interorganizational cooperation, should the arrangement grow ineffective, dissolution of the partnership is difficult. Break-up may require one partner buying out the other's interest in the procreated entity.

Acquisitional ventures involve one partner acquiring partial interest of another and is forged through the voluntary consent of the partners to collaborate with joint-management teams and jointly-owned assets (cf. Tyebjee 1988). The Nippon Chemi-Con/Data Ray (Figure 1-C), the Ebara/Cryodynamics (Figure 1-F), and the Bristol-Myers/Oncogen (Figure 1-I) alliances all incorporate acquisitional exchanges. Sometimes partners take cross-shareholding positions with each other as in the recent alliance between AT&T and Italtel, an Italian telecommunications concern (*Mergers and Acquisitions* 1990). Acquisitional ventures are distinguished from other forms of minority investments, where the objective of the investing organization is either to make a passive investment or exploit the other party's resources perhaps for ultimate takeover, because such situations do not involve mutual party motives to cooperate.

Like the procreational venture, an acquisitional venture requires an intensive resource commitment to establish, creating a stronger obligation for partners to cooperate and strengthening the acquired partner's competitive posture. Depending upon the level of involvement of shared activities, there may be some enjoyment of inter-partner learning. One primary concern of acquisitional ventures, however, is the delicate balance of power established between partners (Harrigan 1986). Unlike the joint management of a separate entity, acquisitional ventures require a far more intimate setting for partners to operate. Depending upon how much of the acquired partner is assumed, the investing partner may afford great bargaining power over its partner, threatening the autonomy of the acquired partner. Issues concerning marketing orientation, the appropriate level of joint-owner intervention, management of intra-firm relationships, and what capabilities (other than cash) the investing partner will provide to the partnership must be resolved for success (Harrigan 1986). Ineffective handling of power can lead to the resignation of key personnel from within the partially acquired partner, jeopardizing the partnership's competitive advantage. For instance, Tyebjee (1988) has illustrated such a case where Nippon Chemi-Con acquired a 75 percent stake in Data Ray, restricting much of Data Ray's decision-making autonomy. The original founders of Data Ray eventually left the company, forcing the company to shift away from hi-tech manufacturing to focus on marketing functions for Nippon Chemi-Con (Figure 1-C).

In sum, the strategic alliance literature describes three types of interorganizational ties, which may be viewed as delineations of "relational exchange." The integrated cooperation/exchange framework in Figure 1 may be viewed as a typology of components underlying strategic alliances. While some alliances can be categorized within one cooperation/exchange cell presented in the framework (as the selected examples illustrate), many partnerships are multi-component structures, encompassing several cooperative strategies and exchange relationships. For example, the Apple-IBM alliance involves a contractual arrangement to pool technologies for joint-products to network their computers as well as two procreational ventures to pool RandD in creating software and standards for future jointly-produced computers (O'Connor 1991). By isolating cooperation/exchange structural options within alliances, however, key relationship management and strategic marketing implications emerge.

DISCUSSION

The framework suggests that as alliances move from sequential strategies to reciprocal and pool strategies, integrated activities become progressively more intricate with increasing partner interdependency and cooperative inflexibility. Simultaneously, as alliances move from contractual arrangements to equity ties, relationship administration becomes progressively more complex with increasing start-up, interface, and exit costs. Together, risks and benefits associated with cooperative strategies can be enhanced or moderated by the forms of exchange used to consummate the alliance. For alliances forged under contractual arrangements with sequential cooperative strategies, the benefits include limited capital expenditures to implement, more flexibility in adapting strategy to meet partners' needs, and better facilitated partnership dissolution. However, under such conditions, there is virtually no enjoyment of inter-partner economies of scale or learning, and the low switching costs can endanger partnership stability. In contrast, for equity exchange relationships with more complex forms of cooperation, such as reciprocal and pool strategies, the benefits are more likely to include inter-partner economies of scale and learning, but at the expense of more intense capital outlay, strategic inflexibility, and greater impediments toward partnership termination.

Strategically combining forms of cooperation with exchange can affect a partnership's adaptive flexibility while administering integrated activities. For instance, within a pool/contractual arrangement, the pool strategy's inflexibility within a volatile environment may be moderated under the contract's lower switching costs. Thus, partners can enjoy inter-partner learning and economies of scale with the added benefit of lowered exit costs. In contrast, within a sequential/procreational venture or a sequential/acquisitional venture, the sequential strategy's relative benefit of limited inter-partner complexity may be nullified by the higher exit and relationship management costs of maintaining an equity tie.

Because many interorganizational partnerships encompass several cooperation/exchange components presented in Figure 1, specific implications associated with one cooperation/exchange component involving some inter-partner activity may affect benefits and risks associated with other cooperation/exchange components within the same partnership. In the Apple-IBM alliance, the moderate strategic flexibility of the pool/contractual arrangement within the partnership may be deemed less flexible when linked with the two pool/procreational ventures being instigated simultaneously. Instability or termination of one cooperation/exchange component within the partnership could trigger instability among other cooperation/exchange components. As such, multi-cooperation/exchange activities between partners are likely to further restrict autonomy and flexibility between partners.

Harrigan (1986) has cautioned that the need for some partner autonomy and flexibility within alliances will be greatest when market competition is volatile, requiring rapid responses to change. This may suggest that contractual arrangements employing less intricate forms of cooperation (i.e., sequential) may be most feasible. However, such alliances may be inappropriate when there is need to pool resources to lower costs or secure channel access through equity. Bresser and Harl (1986) have offered recommendations on how potentially inflexible partnerships can protect themselves from threatening market factors. For instance, the erection of entry barriers moderates competitive volatility fueled by new participants. Organizations can also insulate themselves through the diversification of cooperative and competitive strategies and by choosing to operate in resource rich environments where the problems of market-share maintenance and survival are relatively less urgent. Despite these options, Bresser and Harl (1986) note that actual implementation may be infeasible or, at best, offer only short-lived advantages. Moreover, partner complacency can result if organizations place too much faith on such mechanisms. In sum, attempts to curb market threats may not be effective in off-setting risks associated with strategic alliances.

RESEARCH IMPLICATIONS

A framework has been proposed toward better understanding strategic alliances by distinguishing their inherent cooperation and exchange dimensions. Depicting alliances from a cooperation/exchange perspective rather than other more general conceptualizations unveils strategic differences associated with specific partnership structures. The cooperation/exchange interaction affects trade-offs between partner autonomy and switching costs with cooperative synergies and flexibility.

Directions for future study include examination of organizational culture and cognition (Deshpande and Webster 1989), which may impact alliance stability (Borys and Jemison 1989). Corporate culture establishes employee expectations and trust in authority. When partners lack compatible cultures or "thought worlds," expectations and trust between partner employees may not readily materialize. Thus, organizations with vastly different cultures (as Apple and IBM had a decade ago) may find pooling partnerships involving equity precarious due to the different partner expectations; the less complex interface of a sequential/contractual arrangement, on the other hand, may be more conducive for two opposing cultures to collaborate. Discernment of how organizational culture and cognition impact an alliance structure's stability is needed.

Anderson and Narus (1990) have recognized the importance of trust within partnerships. Swan, Trawick, Rink, and Roberts (1988) have defined five dimensions of trust: dependability, honesty, competency, customer-orientation, and likability. Cooperation/exchange structure may moderate how these dimensions impact alliances. For instance, likability and honesty between partners may be more of a concern within pool strategies involving equity due to the greater complexity and permanence of the partnership. Competency, on the other hand, may be less of a concern among sequential/contractual arrangements because of the lower exit costs. The role of trust within alliances needs to be better articulated.

There is also need to better explain how market forces influence partnership design. Harrigan (1986) has noted that vertical ties (sequential strategies) are useful under rapidly growing markets to reduce supply bottlenecks; however, horizontal ties (pooling activities) are more feasible when markets slow down to consolidate industry capacity. In addition, equity relationships are more practical when product demand uncertainty is high to better secure competitive positions, while non-equity relationships are preferable when product demand is more certain. Harrigan's observations are generally compatible with market evolution frameworks by Porter (1980) and Lambkin and Day (1989), which suggest organizational flexibility is crucial in volatile embryonic markets whereas scale efficiencies and cost reductions grow important in more stable maturing markets. This may provide a foundation for better determining which alliance structures best accommodate specific market factors.

ACKNOWLEDGEMENT

The author wishes to thank Michael D. Hutt of Arizona State University for his comments on earlier drafts of this paper.

REFERENCES

Adler, Lee (1966), "Symbiotic Marketing," *Harvard Business Review,* (November/December) 59-71.

Anderson, James C. and James A. Narus (1990), "A Model of Distributor Firm and Manufacturer Firm Working Partnerships," *Journal of Marketing,* 54, 42-58.

Arndt, Johan (1979), "Toward a Concept of Domesticated Markets," *Journal of Marketing,* 43 (Fall), 69-75.

Astley, W. Graham and Charles J. Fombrun (1983), "Collective Strategy: Social Ecology of Organizational Environments," *Academy of Management Review,* 8 (4), 576-587.

Borys, Bryan and David B. Jemison (1989), "Hybrid Arrangements as Strategic Alliances: Theoretical Issues in Organizational Combinations," *Academy of Management Review,* 14, 234-249.

Bresser, Rudi K. (1988), "Matching Collective and Competitive Strategies," *Strategic Management Journal,* 9, 375-385.

_____ and Johannes E. Harl (1986), "Collective Strategy: Vice or Virtue?," *Academy of Management Review,* 11, 408-427.

Business Week (1989), "Merck Wants to be Alone -- But With Lots of Friends," (October 23), 62.

Campbell, N. C. G. (1985), "An Interaction Approach to Organizational Buying Behavior," *Journal of Business Research,* 13, 35-48.

Chipello, Christopher J. (1989), "More Competitors Turn to Cooperation," *Wall Street Journal,* (June 23), B1.

Deshpande, Rohit and Frederick E. Webster, Jr. (1989), "Organizational Culture and Marketing: Defining the Research Agenda," *Journal of Marketing,* 53, 3-15.

Dwyer, F. Robert, Paul H. Schurr, and Sejo Oh (1987), "Developing Buyer-Seller Relationships," *Journal of Marketing,* 51, 11-27.

Gerlach, Michael (1987), "Business Alliances and the Strategy of the Japanese Firm," *California Management Review,* (Fall), 126-142.

Hamilton, Joan O'C. (1986), "Jealousy, Money, Power: A Biotech Marriage Breaks Up," *Business Week,* (July 21), 103.

Harrigan, Kathryn Rudie (1986), *Managing for Joint Venture Success,* Lexington, MA: Lexington Books.

Jarillo, J. Carlos (1988), "On Strategic Networks," *Strategic Management Journal,* 9, 31-41.

Lambkin, Mary and George S. Day (1989), "Evolutionary Processes in Competitive Markets: Beyond the Product Life Cycle," *Journal of Marketing,* 53, 4-20.

Mattsson, Lars-Gunnar (1988), "Interaction Strategies: A Network Approach," in *American Marketing Association Summer Educators' Conference Proceedings,* Chicago, IL: American Marketing Association.

Mergers and Acquisitions (1990), "The Strategic Alliance of AT&T and Italtel," (January/February) 70-71.

Nielsen, Richard P. (1988), "Cooperative Strategy," *Strategic Management Journal,* 9, 475-492.

O'Connor, Rory J. (1991), "Apple-IBM Ship Sets its Course," *San Jose Mercury News,* (October 3), E1, E8.

Porter, Michael E. (1980), *Competitive Strategy,* New York: Free Press.

_____ and Mark B. Fuller (1986), "Coalitions and Global Strategy," in *Competition in Global Industries,* Michael E. Porter, ed. Boston, MA: Harvard Press.

Schlender, Brenton R. (1988), "Apple, Digital Equipment Outline Pact to Devise Ways to Link Their Computers," *Wall Street Journal,* (January 8) 6.

Stern, Louis W. and Adel I. El-Ansary (1988), *Marketing Channels,* 3rd ed., Englewood Cliffs, NJ: Prentice-Hall.

Stundza, T. (1985), "Chrysler: The Purchasing Story That Hasn't Been Told Yet," *Purchasing,* (July 25) 42-49.

Swan, John E., I. Frederick Trawick, David R. Rink, and Jenny J. Roberts (1988), "Measuring Dimensions of Purchaser Trust in Industrial Salespeople," *Journal of Personal Selling,* 8 (May), 1-9.

Thompson, James D. (1967), *Organizations in Action,* New York, NY: McGraw-Hill.

Thorelli, Hans B. (1986), "Networks: Between Markets and Hierarchies," *Strategic Management Journal,* 7, 37-51.

Tyebjee, Tyzoon T. (1988), "A Typology of Joint Ventures: Japanese Strategies in the United States," *California Management Review,* (Fall) 75-86.

Varadarajan, P. "Rajan" and Daniel Rajaratnam (1986), "Symbiotic Marketing Revisited," *Journal of Marketing,* 50, 7-17.

Wall Street Journal (1988), "Administrative Joint Venture to be Formed by 2 Insurers," (January 8) 9.

BUILDING BRIDGES: A MODEL OF PARTNERSHIP BETWEEN BUYERS AND SELLERS

Syed Saad Andaleeb, Pennsylvania State University-Erie
Wonsick Lee, Pennsylvania State University-Erie
Daniel U. Gruneisen, Pennsylvania State University-Erie

ABSTRACT

What factors contribute to the formation of partnership agreements or strategic alliances, in buyer-seller contexts? The need for a better understanding of these interorganizational linkages led Anderson and Narus (1990) to propose a model of working partnerships between manufacturers and their distributor firms. Heidi and John (1990) also examined alliances in industrial purchasing to enhance our understanding of the factors that foster working relationships. Dwyer, Schurr and OH (1987) provided a comprehensive framework for analyzing buyer-seller relationships. In this paper, we propose a model in which partnership is viewed in terms of desire to continue a relationship and satisfaction with the business relationship. Coupled with the traditional model, which explains interorganizational relationships from an economic need or resource dependence perspective (e.g., Aldrich 1979; Blau 1964; Dwyer and Welsh 1985; Emerson 1962; Kotter 1979; Pfeffer and Salancik 1978) we attempt to broaden our focus by including an important meta-construct, psychological commitment to examine partnership relations.

Psychological commitment in the partnership relation is promoted by co-destiny, relationship durability, and trust. Co-destiny in the buyer-seller context is defined as a mutual understanding that the supplier and its OEM customer view the end user as the only customer to serve. Both parties are keenly aware of the final customer's needs and are driven by the mission to fulfill these needs. Relationship durability is defined as that aspect of a working relationship characterized by a long-term horizon, not as a relationship involving a single transaction (cf., Jackson 1985). It promotes a sense of stability in the context of a turbulent environment to engender future commitment to the relationship. Trust of A in B is defined as A's willingness to risk involvement and vulnerability in the relationship with B, in which responsibility is vested in B to act on behalf of A in the belief that the decision will produce positive outcomes or not produce negative outcomes for A.

Since an organization will seek to build relationships with other organizations when it perceives a need for resources and support, resource dependence is also a crucial determinant of partnership relations. We define dependence as the degree to which a target firm needs the source firm to achieve its goals.

Methodology

A survey was conducted in the commercial area of north-west Pennsylvania. One hundred questionnaire packets were distributed to suppliers of OEMs and 88 completed responses were returned. Guided by theory and the relevant concepts, a pool of questionnaire items was generated for the target variables. These questions were individually reviewed by the present researchers and managers at the preliminary stages. Prior to the major survey for this study, the completed questionnaire was tested on a small pilot sample.

Results and Discussions

Desire to continue the relationship as a dependent variable was significantly accounted for by dependence (R-Squared $= .31$, $F = 18.6$, p, $< .00$). Additional variance accounted for by adding three other predictor variables (co-destiny, trust, and relationship durability) in the regression equation was marginal (R-Squared $= .39$, R-Squared increase of $.08$). However, adding these three predictor variables in the regression equation to account for satisfaction in the partnership relationship substantially increased the R-square value (increase of R-Squared $= .36$).

Positive associations were predicted between the two sub-constructs of partnership and between the predictor variables. The results showed moderate to high correlations among these variables. Due to multicollinearity, multiple regression was supplemented by canonical analyses to test the model. An elaborate discussion is omitted here due to space limitations. However, we found that desire to continue the business relationship was closely tied to resource dependence and that satisfaction in the relationship was closely tied to feelings of co-destiny, relationship durability, and trust.

For further information please contact:
Syed Saad Andaleeb
School of Business
Pennsylvania State University-Erie
Station Road, Erie PA 16563

EFFECT OF CORPORATE TAKEOVERS AND LEVERAGED BUYOUTS: AN EXTENSION OF STRATEGIC MODELS IN MARKETING

A. N. M. Waheeduzzaman, Kent State University

ABSTRACT

This paper proposes a conceptual model that intends to capture the effect of corporate takeovers and leveraged buyouts in marketing. Previous conceptualization suggested that the outcome of mergers and acquisitions depends on strategic and organizational fit of the two firms and the takeover process. The proposed model recognizes the suggestions of the previous research and applies that in explaining a few marketing response variables.

BACKGROUND

Mergers and acquisitions are a reflection of the ongoing corporate restructuring process in American business. The recent history of corporate restructuring reveals that the style of corporate growth has gone through many phases. In the 1950s, corporations were reorganizing themselves from the shocks of World War II. Corporate growth in the 1960s was aimed at achieving diversity. It was believed that diversity would bring vitality and would reduce the risk in economic downturns. Most of the diversifications that took place during this period were concentric, i.e., were in the same or similar product lines or businesses.

In the 1970s, a different type of diversification occured. Diversification into unrelated businesses started taking place, resulting huge conglomerates. These conglomerates had extensive market and financial power, but their performance was poor. The average return of these conglomerates has been lower than the *Fortune* 500 companies (Hopkins 1987, p. 1). Such performance came under criticism in the 1980s. It was argued that the corporations had grown so large that they could no longer take care of themselves. They needed to be trimmed to be efficient. Thus the process of a new type of restructuring began in the 1980s. This instigated what the popular press called hostile takeovers and leveraged buyouts.

The hostile takeovers and leveraged buyouts of the 1980s were antithesis to the unrelated diversifications that created large conglomerates. They were also a threat to the incumbent management whose efficiency in running the organization was challenged (Vedder 1988). Some of these takeovers were carried out through increased use of debts, high-yield junk bonds, and leveraging of company assets. This style of takeover was different from those takeovers of the 1960s or before. In those days, the takeovers were usually friendly in nature. Hostility was not so common. In the 1980s, many buyouts were hostile in nature and the larger ones received the attention of the media and the public.

In general, the number of mergers and acquisitions has been increasing in the post-depression era. However, in the 1980s a sharp increase was observed. For example, in total 1558 deals were concluded in 1980. This increased by 285 percent to 4446 deals in 1986. Then the growth leveled off a bit, coming down to 3415 in 1989 (see Table 1). Such a decrease may be attributed to the heavy criticisms that hostile takeovers and leveraged buyouts were receiving in popular press. Perhaps, some sort of "ceiling effect" was there too, suggesting that there was no further room for growth. Increases in the compeletion of LBOs and divestitures were also observed in the 1980s. In 1980, only 0.7 percent deals were LBOs and 6.8 percent were divestitures. This increased to 11 percent and 33 percent in 1989. In terms of value, the increase in the deals was even more noticeable (see Table 2).

FOCUS OF THIS PAPER

While the pace of mergers and acquisitions was quite fast, the pace of research in the area was rather slow (Walsh 1989; Jemison and Sitkin 1986). Academic investigations and theoretical inquiry into the topic are increasing, however. This paper proposes a conceptual model that is intended to capture the effect of corporate takeovers and leveraged buyouts in marketing. It uses strategic and management frameworks (Lubatkin 1983; Jensen and Ruback 1983; Jemison and Sitkin 1986; Easterwood, Seth, and Singer 1989) as the underlying theoretical schema, applying them in explaining various marketing response variables.

The management frameworks mentioned above suggested that the outcome of mergers and acquisitions depends on the strategic and organizational fit of the two firms and the takeover process. In the following discussion, a model is developed based on earlier literature and then its specifications are described. The model specification section elaborates the schematic presentation and the functional relationships of the variables involved. Testable hypotheses are presented in the next section. Finally, suggestions regarding the implementation of the model and conclusion are presented.

MODEL DEVELOPMENT

The process of mergers and acquisitions has been studied by people from various disciplines. Economists

TABLE 1

Mergers and Acquisitions, LBOs, and Divestitures: 1980-1989

Year	Total Mergers		LBOs		Divestitures	
	No. of Deals	Value ($ bil)	No. of Deals	Value ($ bil)	No. of Deals	Value ($ bil)
1980	1558	32.8	11	0.24	104	5.1
1981	2328	69.5	100	3.87	476	10.2
1982	2298	60.7	164	3.45	562	8.4
1983	2393	52.7	231	4.52	661	12.9
1984	3175	126.1	254	18.72	793	30.6
1985	3484	146.0	255	19.67	1039	43.5
1986	4446	205.8	337	45.16	1419	72.4
1987	4015	178.3	279	36.23	1219	57.7
1988	4000	236.4	377	46.56	1273	83.2
1989	3415	231.4	388	61.58	1119	60.8

Note: Prepared from "Decade in Review," *Megers and Acquisitions*, (March-April), 1990.

TABLE 2

LBOs and Divestitures as a Percentage of Total Mergers and Acquisitions in Number and Value: 1980-89

Year	Divestitures		LBOs	
	Number	Value	Number	Value
1980	6.8	15.6	0.7	0.7
1981	20.4	14.6	4.3	5.6
1982	24.5	13.8	7.1	5.7
1983	27.6	24.5	9.7	8.6
1984	25.0	2.4	8.0	14.9
1985	29.8	29.8	7.3	13.5
1986	31.9	35.2	7.6	21.9
1987	30.4	32.4	7.0	20.3
1988	31.8	35.2	9.4	19.7
1989	32.7	26.3	11.4	26.6

Note: Prepared from data given in Table 1. Original data were collected from "Decade in Review," *Megers and Acquisitions*, (March-April), 1990.

studied it from the industrial organization and market competition perspective. To them, this was a part of the competitive process and should be allowed to continue unless it unfairly restricted competition or free trade. Competition and trust-antitrust issues were also the concerns of legal studies in the area. Mangement scholars looked into the process from the strategic and organizational fit perspective and tried to relate that to efficiency and performance. Both short and long term productivity and performance were considered. The finance literature dealt with the role of mergers and acquisitions in changing the value of the firm, profitability, cash flow, and return. Behavioral scientists focused on the morale/

motivation of managers and employees, turnover, leadership and post-merger acculturation. In marketing, the effect of mergers and acquisitions was not pursued seriously. Except for a few cursory remarks about marketing responses (see Rumelt 1974; Ansoff et al. 1971) no specific study was found to be undertaken.

In this paper, an effort is made to determine the effect of mergers and acquisitions in marketing with the help of a conceptual model. The model is developed from various studies in the strategy and management area. Although there are numerous management studies dealing with the effect of mergers and acquisitions on organizational performance, only a few specifically relate to the devlopment of this model. Among these, the notable ones are, Lubatkin's (1983) and Kusewitt's (1985) suggestions regarding the contingency framework, Jemison and Sitkin's (1986) strategic, organizational and acquisition process framework, Jensen and Ruback's (1983) conceptualization of market for corporate control, and Easterwood, Seth and Singer's (1989) proposition of the strategic impact model. The contribution of these studies in the conceptual development of the model is discussed below.

In a review of theoretical and empirical studies on management, Lubatkin (1983) noted the existence of a contingency framework determining the effect of mergers and acquisitions. According to him (Lubatkin 1983, p. 218), "whether a firm gains or loses from merger is contingent upon a number of conditions. These are its competitive strengths, the growth rate of its markets, and the degree to which these two achieve a logical or strategic fit with competitive strengths and market growth rates of its acquired firm." Similar views were also held by Kusewitt (1985). The logical compatibility or strategic fit of competitive strengths and market growth helps in achieving synergy. Synergy augments the overall strength of the merged firms. It is an outcome of the strategic fit that positively contributes to organizational performance through technical economies (involving marketing, production, experience, scheduling, banking and compensation), pecuniary economies (gained through monopoly and monopsony), and diversification economies (achieved in portfolio management and risk reduction) (Lubatkin 1983). The spillover effect of synergy and its impact in other functional areas including production and marketing were also noted in other studies (Rumelt 1974; Ansoff et al. 1971).

The concept of strategic fit and its contribution in synergy propounded by Lubatkin (1983) was well taken by Jemison and Sitkin (1986). Theoretically, they accepted his arguments but preferred to call it organizational fit. They felt that strategic fit was embedded in the overall organizational fit. Conceptually, their organizational fit overlaps Lubatkin's strategic fit. They also added a new dimension, i.e., the acquisition process to explain the outcome of mergers and acquisitions. Using the suggestions of Lubatkin (1983), Kusewitt (1985), and Jemison and Sitkin (1986), it can be argued that, the choice and outcome of acquisition depends simultaneously on the strategic fit, the organizational fit, and the process of acquisition.

Lately, due to the recent growth of takeovers and buyouts and the subsequent response of management in such deals, the importance of the acquisition process has been emphasized. This paper recognizes the need for capturing the effect of the process itself. Three specific aspects of the takeover process that affect the performance of the merged companies were noted in previous literature. They were, management's interest in the deal (Maupin 1987; Easterwood, Seth, and Singer 1989), the amount of hostility in the buying process (Fowler and Schmidt 1989), and the debt-structure of the corporations (Easterwood, Seth, and Singer 1989). The conceptual model, elaborated in the next section, attempts to capture the effect of these three aspects of the takeover process in marketing.

MODEL SPECIFICATION

The model (shown diagrammatically in Figure 1) proposes that the impact of takeovers and buyouts in marketing is a function of strategic fit, organizational fit and the takeover process. Mathematically, this can be shown as: Response Variables = f (Strategic fit, Organizational fit, Takeover Process)

As the model intends to capture the outcome of takeovers pertaining to marketing only, the choice of the response variables becomes limited. Among the marketing variables, specific concerns were raised about the effect of takeovers on product lines (addition or deletion of lines; Ansoff et al. 1971), price (change in price due to changed competitive scenario, oligopoly or monopoly; FTC 1981), expansion and coverage of market (Ansoff et al. 1971), market share (Christensen and Montgomery 1981), and innovation and productivity (Jensen 1983; Kaplan 1989). The marketing functions are also likely to be affected by the takeover process. However, to keep the model simple, in this paper, only three dependent variables viz. change in market share, change in innovation, and change in distribution efficiency, were used as marketing response variables. Strategic fit is the degree to which the target firm augments or complements the parents' strategy and thus makes identifiable contributions to the financial and nonfinancial goals of the parent. The extent to which the target firm (or parent firm) would contribute to the goals of the parent (or the target firm) depends on the relatedness of the businesses of the two firms in terms of products, markets and technology. The contribution of relatedness of business in developing scale economy and synergy was extensively discussed in the literature (see Rumelt 1974). Relatedness in businesses can be observed if the two merged firms use similar production technologies (Salter and Weinhold 1979), serve similar markets or have similar distribution channels (Didrechsen 1972; Howell 1970), or share the transfer of functional skills i.e., production, R & D, marketing, and distribution in their day to day operations (Salter and Weinhold 1979).

Organizational fit refers to the degree of possible integration between the two merged firms. This depends on the match between their administrative, cultural and personnel characteristics (Jemison and Sitkin 1986). Specifically, the matching of the sizes of the firms, age of the firms (Greiner 1972), leadership style (Kitching 1967), management control system (Leighton and Tod

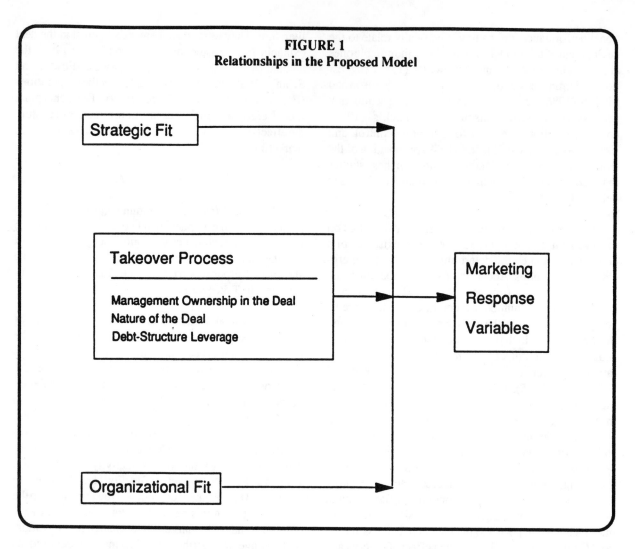

FIGURE 1
Relationships in the Proposed Model

Strategic Fit

Takeover Process
─────────────────
Management Ownership in the Deal
Nature of the Deal
Debt-Structure Leverage

Marketing
Response
Variables

Organizational Fit

1969), and individual motivation and productivity (Graves 1981; Marks 1982; Walsh 1988; 1989) have been mentioned in the literature.

The process of acquisition refers to the purchasing process involving the participation of management, stockholders, and financial intermediaries. In the literature, various characteristics of the process were studied. Notable among these were the attributes mentioned by Walsh (1989). Seven attributes of the transaction that may affect the personnel performance were: the approach of the acquirer (i.e., merger or tender offer), the nature of bargaining (i.e., the number of counter offers and the days to settlement), explicit talk of management retention, the press characterization of the nature of transaction (i.e., friendly, neutral or hostile), the nature of payment (i.e., cash, stock or combination), and premium paid for the company. In a recent paper, Easterwood, Seth, and Singer (1989) limited the process variables (specially of LBOs) to corporate ownership and debt structure. Ownership and debt-structure were also found to be relevant for friendly and hostile takeovers (Morck et al. 1988). And again, to keep the model simple, only three independent variables were included as process variables. They were: the ownership stake of the management in the deal, the debt-structure (to capture the presence of leverage) and

the overall response of the management to the deal (i.e., friendly or hostile). The effect of these three variables in marketing with other strategic and organizational fit variables were considered in the model.

The delineation of specific varaiables of the model is given in Table 3. The extent to which the process variables affect the marketing response variables can be formally captured with the help of a few hypotheses. Specific hypotheses pertaining to the takeover process, and the rationale that lead to the formulations of these hypotheses are presented below.

HYPOTHESES

As mentioned in the previous section, three specific aspects of the takeover process were considered in the model. Hypotheses concerning each of these aspects, viz. the nature of the deal (friendly or hostile), the debt-structure (degree of equity leveraged) of the corporations, and management's ownership in the deal are presented below.

Nature of the Deal: Friendly or Hostile

Takeovers or buyouts can be carried out through

TABLE 3
Variables Involved in the Proposed Model

Variable Group	Description of Variables
Marketing Response Variables	Change in Market Share Change in Innovation Change in Distribution Efficiency
Strategic Fit Variables	Relatedness in Production Relatedness in Marketing Relatedness in Technology
Organizational Fit Variables	Matching of Size of Firms Matching of Age of Firms Similarity in Leadership Style Similarity of Organizational Structure
Takeover Process Variables	Management Ownership in the Deal Nature of the Deal (Friendly or Hostile) Debt-structure (Equity Leveraged or Not)

mergers, tender offers, and proxy fights, or a mix of all of three. They usually begin with what is called a "friendly" merger offer from the bidder to the target management. If turned down (as is often seen), the bidder directly goes to the shareholders with a tender offer with higher share value. Depending on the response of the management to counter the bidder (commonly called raider) the transaction may be friendly or hostile. Hostility in the takeover process is believed to have harmful effect on the performance of the management and the corporation (Greenspan 1987; Wheat 1987; Drucker 1986; Shad 1985). Wheat (1987) summarized these arguments and noted, (1) hostile takeovers focus the attention of management on short term consequences, (2) many takeovers are carried by bidders whose debt-payment capability is questionable, (3) as a defense to hostile takeovers the corporate management have moved away from "one man one vote" principle and concentrated power, making them victim in their own hands, and (4) the process of recapitalization through going public after the takeovers benefited only a few, leaving the company debt-ridden.

Contrary to this notion, many (e.g., Jensen 1983, 1989; Vedder 1988) believe that hostility is a part of the process and that it should not be viewed negatively. Rather they appreciated the role of corporate raiders in the restructuring process. Historically, raiders are engaged in what Shumpeter calls "the creative destruction" process (*Wall Street Journal,* June 5, 1985; Jensen 1989). This is seen as eventually being beneficial to the society (Jensen and Ruback 1983, p. 47). Thus, the impact of takeovers remains to be a controversial issue. Based on the discussion above, the following testable hypotheses are proposed:

H1: Hostility in the takeover process will have no effect on the market share of specific products.

H2: Hostility in the takeover process will not decrease the innovation capability of the corporation.

H3: Hostility in the takeover process will have no effect on the corporation's distribution efficiency.

Debt and Leveraged Buyouts

The second aspect of the takeover process considered in the model, was the debt-structure of the corporations, especially in terms of leveraged buyouts. It has been argued that LBOs have generated excess burdens of debt on corporations. This added liquidity to corporate assets. Former SEC Chairman John Shad called this the "leveraging of America" and warned about its consequences (Shad 1985). LBOs increased because, in the short run everyone in the LBO deals gains. However, in the long run, the company's cushion against adversity, its continuity, and its capacity to endure shocks are diminished. Debt-ridden companies are not likely to be able to create new products, innovate, or grow to meet the future market needs. Thus the long term competitiveness of the corporation suffers.

The extent to which the arguments for and against the LBOs are true needs evaluation. It is observed that a majority of the LBOs has taken place in mature industries, which have shown stable growth and maintained steady cashflow. They were better equipped to support the debts undertaken. These industries (four-digit SIC classification) include stone, clay, and glass, textile, apparel, food, primary retailing, commercial printing, electrical and on-electrical machinery, paper, and fabricated products (Waite and Fridson 1989). Taggert (1986) has also noted the favorable debt-financing capability of the taken-over corporations, a majority of whom were LBOs. He did not find their capital structure to be more risky than average. Kaplan (1989) found that the average operating earnings of the LBOs increased by 42 percent from the year prior to the buyout to the third year after the buyout. Cashflows increased by 96 percent over the same period. Other studies also show significant improvement in profit margin, sales per employee, working capital, inventories, and receivables (Lichtenberg and Siegel 1989). A few examples of successful leveraged buyout companies include Levi Strauss, A.O. Scott, Safeway, and Weirton Steel. Based on the controversy regarding the effect of leveraged buyouts, the following hypotheses are proposed.

H4: Leveraged buyouts will negatively affect the market share of specific products of the corporation.

H5: Leveraged buyouts will negatively affect the distribution efficiency of the corporation.

There is a great concern about the effect of takeovers and buyouts on capital investment and R & D. It is argued that, being debt-ridden, these companies will not have enough capital to invest for product innovation and future growth. This argument needs evaluation. First, evidences show that the present debt-finacing capability of the LBO corportaions is not bad. In a majority of the cases their economic performance was better than average (Jensen 1989). Second, the industries in which the LBOs have taken place are the mature industries, chracterized by low growth and smaller R & D investment (Kaplan 1989; Lichtenberg and Siegel 1989). Hall (1988) did not find evidence to show that leveraged acquisition reduces R & D. Jensen (1983), argues in favor of LBOs and notes, "those who make the argument that takeovers are reducing R & D spending also have come to grips with aggregate data on such spending, which is inconsistent with the argument. Total spending on R & D in 1984, a year of record acquisition activity, increased by 14 percent according to *Business Week's* annual survey of 820 companies." Given the above discussion the following hypothesis is presented:

H6: Leveraged buyouts will decrease the innovation capability of the corporation.

Management Ownership In the Deal

The last but not the least important aspect of the takeover process is the management's ownership in the deal. Their personal interest in the deal is likely to affect the performance of the corporations. Favorable buyouts carried through ESOP (employee stock ownership plan) may increase motivation/productivity and unfavorable buyouts may decrease motivation/productivity. Bohl (1989) observed productivity loss, Paulus and Gay (1987) observed productivity gain, and mixed evidences were observed by Pitts (1976) and Walsh (1988) in LBO deals. Motivation of the management in a deal is likely to affect the innovation capability of the corporation. This can be tested with the help of the following hypothesis.

H7: Management's ownership in the deal positively affects the innovation capability of the corporation.

IMPLEMENTATION

Most of the variables in the model were operationalized in the studies mentioned. A detailed discussion of this seems redundant (space limitations also preclude that). In order to implement the model both strategic and organizational fit may be used as two seperate independent variables whose composite score may be determined from the variables defining them (see Table 3). Among the process variables, management's stake in the deal is given by the percentage of ownership of management in the total stock. The degree of debt-structure or leveraging may be measured by the percentage of assets (or equity) being leveraged. The nature of the deal may have three levels viz. friendly, hostile, or neutral. Among the dependent variables market share can be measured by actual market share, innovation capability can be measured by R & D expenditure, and a distribution efficiency index may be taken from the literature in the area. Using the above operationalization of the dependent and independent variables a multiple regression analysis may be used to capture the effect of the takeover process in marketing and to test the hypotheses proposed.

CONCLUSION

Based on previous studies in management and strategy area, this paper proposed a conceptual model intended to capture the effect of takeovers and buyouts in marketing. The delineation of the model reveals that the effect of takeovers and buyouts depends on the strategic and organizational fit of the two merged firms, and the takeover process. Like any other conceptual model this model has its limitations. One of them pertains to the choice of the variables. In the model specification, both at the dependent and independent level, only the major variables were included to keep the model simple and implementable. Given the broad and general nature of the framework, more variables could be added in each variable grouping. Especially, more marketing variables may be added to consider the effect of the takeover process in various other areas in marketing. However, with the inclusion of more variables in the model, multicollinearity may be a problem in implementation. Factor analysis or other data reduction techniques may need to be used in such cases. Secondly, the effect of leveraged buyouts and takeovers can be captured for both the target and the parent firm. The purpose of the study will determine which one will have to be chosen. Finally, the model is yet to be implemented. Real life data may require the change of specification and operationalization of the model.

Inspite of these limitaions, the model endeavors to focus the attention of the marketers to an important area that should have received attention much earlier. Extending the conceptualization from strategy and management area, the model makes useful suggestions in capturing the effect of takeovers and leveraged buyouts in marketing.

GLOSSARY

Acquisition refers to the purchase one company (target firm) by another company (parent firm). Through acquisition the parent company gains control over the functions of the target company.

Buyouts or **Takeovers** are the words of the 1980s. Both refer to the purchase of one company by another. The terms gained attention in the 1980s because of the nature of hostility in the purchase deals.

Corporate Restructuring is the process by which a company attempts to change its present operation with the help of a better organizational structure, formed through some kind of merger, acquisition, or similar modes of purchase.

Leveraged Buyout (LBO) involves the purchasing of a company with small amount of equity and large amount of debt. The small equity works as a leverage in the purchase of a target company whose own assets and cashflows are used to finance the purchase (acquisition).

Merger refers to the integration of two or more companies to consolidate market or financial power for present or future gain.

REFERENCES

Ansoff, Igor, Richard G. Brandenburg, Fred E. Porter, and Raymond Radosevich (1971), *Acquisition Behavior of U. S. Manufacturing Firms: 1945-1965.* Nashville: Vanderbuilt University Press.

Bohl, Don Lee (1989), *Tying the Corporate Knot.* An American Management Association's Research Report on the Effects of Mergers and Acquisitions, New York: American Management Association, 13.

Cristensen, H. K. and C. A. Montgomery (1981), "Corporate Economic Performance: Diversification Strategy vs. Market Structure," *Strategic Management Journal,* (October/December), 327-343.

Didrechsen, J. (1972), "The Development of Diversified and Conglomerate Firms in the United States: 1920-1970," *Business History Review,* (Fall), 202-219.

Drucker, Peter (1986), "Hostile Talkeover and Its Discontents," *The Frontiers of Management,* (October 1986), Reprinted in *Hostile Takeovers,* Hearings before the Committee on Banking, Housing and Urban Affairs, 682-707.

Easterwood, John C., Anju Seth, and Ronald F. Singer (1989), "The Impact of Leveraged Buyouts on Strategic Direction," *California Management Review,* (Fall), 30-43.

Federal Trade Commission (FTC) (1981), *Statistical Report on Mergers and Acquisitions.* Washington, DC: Government Printing Office.

Fowler, Karen L. and Dennis R. Schmidt (1989), "Determinants of Tender Offer Post-Acquisition Financial Performance," *Strategic Management Journal,* 10, 339-350.

Graves, D. (1981), "Indvidual Reactions to a Merger of Two Small Firms of Brokers in the Re-Insurance Industry: A Total Population Survey," *Journal of Management Studies,* 18, 89-113.

Greenspan, Alan (1987), "Excerpts from the Testimony of Alan Greenspan before the U.S. Committee on Banking, Housing and Urban Affairs, *Hostile Takeovers,* Hearings before the Committee on Banking, Housing and Urban Affairs, 22.

Greiner, Larry E. (1972), "Evolution and Revolution as Organaziations Grow," *Harvard Business Review,* (July/August), 41.

Hall, Bronwyn H. (1988), "The Effect of Takeover Activity on Corporate Research and Development," in *Corporate Takeovers: Causes and Consequences,* Alan J. Auerbach, ed. Chicago: University of Chicago Press, 69-100.

Hopkins, Donald H. (1987), "Acquisition Strategy and the Market Position of Acquiring Firms," *Strategic Management Journal,* 8, 535-547.

Howell, R. A. (1970), "Plan to Integrate Your Acquisitions," *Harvard Business Review,* (November/December), 66-76.

Jemison, David B. and Sim B. Sitkin (1986), "Corporate Acquisitions: A Process Perspective," *Academy of Management Review,* 11 (1), 145-163.

Jensen, Michael C. (1983), "The Takeover Controversy: Analysis and Evidence," *Journal of Finanacial Economics,* (April).

_____and Richard Ruback (1983), "The Market for Corporate Control: The Scientific Evidence," *Journal of Financial Economics,* 11 (April), 3-50.

_____(1989), "Eclipse of the Public Corporation," *Harvard Business Review,* (September/October), 61-74.

Kaplan, Steven (1989), as quoted by Michael Jensen in "Eclipse of the Public Corporation," *Harvard Business Review,* (September/October) 1989, 61-74.

Kaufman, Henry (1989), "Bush's First Priority: Stopping the Buyout Mania," *Washington Post,* (January 1).

Kitching, J. (1967), "Why do Mergers Miscarry," *Harvard Business Review,* 45 (Novemeber/December), 84-102.

Kusewitt, Jr., J. B. (1985), "An Exploratory Study of Strategic Acquisitions Factors Relating to Performance," *Strategic Management Journal,* 6, 151-169.

Leighton, C. M. and G. R. Tod (1969), "After Acquisition: Continuing Challenge," *Harvard Business Review,* 47 (March/April), 90-102.

Lichtenberg, Frank and Donald Siegel (1989), *The Effects of Leveraged Buyouts on Productivity and Related Aspects of Firm Behavior.* Washington, DC: National Bureau of Economic Research.

Lubatkin, Michael (1983), "Mergers and Performances: A Review of Current Research," *Academy of Management Review,* 8, 218-225.

Marks, M. L. (1982), "Merging Human Resources: A Review of Current Research," *Mergers and Acquisitions,* 17, 38-44.

Maupin, Rebekah J. (1987), "Financial and Stock Market Variables as Predictors of Management Buyouts," *Strategic Management Journal,* 8, 319-327.

Morck, Randall, Andrei Shleifer, and Robert W. Vishnay (1987), "Characteristics of Targets of Hostile and Friendly Takeovers," in *Corporate Takeovers: Causes and Consequences,* Alan J. Auerbach, ed. Chicago: The University of Chicago Press.

Paulus, John D. and Robert S. Gay (1987), "Is America Helping Herself: Corporate Restructuring and Global Competitiveness," *World Economic Outlook,* New York: Morgan and Stanley.

Pitts, R. A. (1976), "Diversification Strategies and Organizational Policies of Large Diversified Firms," *Journal of Economics and Business,* 28, 181-188.

Rumelt, R. P. (1974), *Strategy, Structure and Economic Performnace,* Boston, MA: Harvard Business School.

Salter Malcom S. and Wolf A. Weinhold (1979), *Diversification Through Acquisitions: Strategies for Creating Economic Value.* New York: The Free Press.

Shad, John (1985), "Securities and Exchange Commission Staff Report in Response to Senate Proximere's Requests for the Record at April 4, 1985," Hearings on Tender Offers before the Subcommittee on Securities of the Senate Committe on Banking, Housing and Urban Affairs, *Impact of Corporate Takeovers,* 99th Congress, 283-295.

Taggert, Robert A. Jr. (1986), "Corporate Financing: Too Much Debt?" *Financial Analysis Journal,* (May/June), 35-42.

Vedder, Richard K. (1988) "Three Cheers for the Corporate Raider," in *Hostile Takeovers: Issues in Public and Corporate Policy,* David L. McKee, ed. New York: Praeger Publications, 3-15.

Waite, Stephen and Martin S. Fridson (1989), "Do Leveraged Buyouts Pose Major Credit Risks?" *Mergers and Acquisitions,* (July/August), 43-47.

Walsh, James P. (1988), "Top Management Turnover Following Mergers and Acquisitions," *Strategic Management Journal,* 9, 173-183.

_____(1989), "Doing a Deal: Merger and Acquisition Negotiations and Their Impact Upon Target Company Top Management Turnover," *Strategic Management Journal,* 10, 307-322.

Wheat, Francis (1987), "Testimony of Francis Wheat before the U.S. Committee on Banking, Housing and Urban Affairs," *Hostile Takeovers,* Hearings before the Committee on Banking, Housing and Urban Affairs, 106.

WHEN MEN AND WOMEN BUY CARS

Robin Widgery, University of Michigan
Jack McGaugh, University of Michigan

ABSTRACT

Gender differences in the salience of automobile purchase motivations were examined in five metropolitan markets. A significant gender effect was found, indicating that females report significantly higher salience scores for purchase motivation. Support was also found for a gender X age interaction effect - an historical hypothesis. These effects were found in each of the five market samples.

RESEARCH METHOD

In these five markets telephone interviews were conducted among 1,740 randomly selected households. The purpose for gathering this information was to examine automobile purchasing intentions and motivations. In each market household selection was based on whether it was situated within the trading area of a client automobile dealer.

Dependent variables included 28 items measuring the importance (salience) of various purchase motivations - how important each was as a directive influence in the vehicle purchase decision. The importance score of each motivation was anchored on a three point scale: 1 = not important; 2 = important; 3 = very important.

There were three types of purchase motivations measured - **product attributes**; (11 items), **dealership attributes** (10 items), and **purchase incentives** (7 items). Respondents were asked how important the 11 product attributes were in their decisions to purchase a particular vehicle, how important the ten dealership attributes were in selecting a dealer, and how important the seven incentives were in choosing the best deal.

Independent variables were gender and age of respondents. To test the traditional hypothesis predicting differences between male and female respondents, motivation scores were compared by gender. To test the consistency of this hypothesis among all five markets in the sample, a two-way ANOVA was examined to assess any interaction between gender and market. No such interaction effect was found for any of the three types of purchase motivations. Scores for males and females were compared using multiple student t tests for each of the 28 items. Moreover, global comparison scores were calculated for each of the three types of purchase motivations (product attributes, dealer attributes and purchase incentives).

To test the Age X Gender interaction (historical) hypothesis, respondents were classified by age group, using six categories, ranging from 18-24 to 65-plus years. To test the consistency between age and each of the five markets, a two-way ANOVA was used to test for any interaction effect for each of the three types of purchase motivation. No significant interaction effect was found.

RESULTS

In testing the gender difference hypothesis, multiple t tests were used for each of the three groups of purchase motivations. Only four of the 11 **product attribute** items showed significant differences: freedom from repairs, length of warranty, fuel economy, and pick-up and acceleration. An analysis of all product attribute items combined showed that females reported significantly higher importance scores than males ($t = -3.42$; $p < .001$).

Eight of the ten **dealership attribute** items showed significant differences supportive of the gender hypothesis: dealership's reputation, quality of service department, dealer's willingness to deal, experience with the dealership, selection available, convenience of location, convenience of hours open, and experience with salesman. An analysis of all dealership attribute items combined showed that females scored significantly higher than males ($t = -6.30$; $p < .0001$).

All seven of the **purchase incentive** items showed significant differences, supporting the gender hypothesis: total overall price, dealer offering best deal, best trade-in allowance, interest rate of loan, special price discount, monthly payment, and special rebate offer. An analysis of all incentive items combined showed that females scored significantly higher than makes ($t = -5.45$; $p < .0001$).

A test of the Age X Gender interaction effect was supported for two of the three groups of purchase motivators - **product** motivations ($F = 2.99$; $p < .01$) AND **dealer** motivations ($F = 2.47$; $p < .02$). While there was no significant Age X Gender interaction effect for incentive motivations, there was significance for **all motivations** combined ($F = 2.90$; $p < .01$). (Plots of the gender centoids for the salience scores across all age groups is available upon request.) Generally these figures illustrate the consistent interaction between age and gender on the salience measures. In all, the differences between males and females in the youngest age group are not significant, while the differences generally increase for older groups. This is strong support for the interaction hypothesis - that differences between males and females will be greater among older respondents than for the young.

DISCUSSION

These findings give substantial support to the Gender hypothesis, that females score higher than males on the importance of various decisional considerations related to the purchase of an automobile. Nineteen of the 28 purchase considerations had significantly higher salience scores for females than males. (In no case were scores significantly higher for males.)

When examining the gender differences that occur for each of the 28 purchase motivations, it is noteworthy that the fewest significant differences are found for the **product attribute** scores. With the **product attributes** women show greater concern for pocketbook issues than men: freedom from repairs, fuel economy, and length of warranty. Greater concern for economic matters is also punctuated by the higher scores reported for women among **all** the **incentive** items.

Income Differences. This greater concern with economic issues may be explained by a generally lower income among single, working women who are likely to purchase a vehicle for themselves. To test this notion that working women are more sensitive to the importance of monetary issues, married women were compared to single working women, using multiple t-tests. While incomes were significantly lower among single, working women, no significant differences were found between the various economic and monetary concerns for the two groups. Moreover, it was found that differences were not significant between married and single women generally.

The Gender X Age Interaction Effect. An alternative explanation for the gender X age interaction effect may not be related to the difference between the traditional and contemporary socialization of females and males during formative years. Instead, the similar salience scores in the lower age groups may be attributable to female respondents in the 18-24 years group being less likely than older female groups to be ready to purchase a new vehicle. This argument assumes that <u>imminent purchase</u> may heighten consumer interest in various purchase motivations. Those who do not foresee a purchase in their immediate future may evaluate as less important the various purchase motivations.

To test the <u>imminent purchase</u> alternative explanation a two-way ANOVA was performed using **gender** and **timing** of the next vehicle purchase as independent variables and salience scores as dependent variables. Respondents were asked when they expected to purchase their next vehicle: within six months, 12 months, 18 months, 24 months, or not planning a purchase within the next two years. While a significant gender effect was found, there was no significant purchase timing effect, nor a gender X timing interaction effect. These findings frustrate the <u>imminent purchase</u> explanation.

Another possible reason for the gender X age interaction effect might be found in the assumption that there is a higher proportion of single women in the youngest age group. The argument can be made that this female group is less likely to be in the market for a vehicle purchase, thus being less concerned with the various purchase motivations. To test this notion a two-way ANOVA examined **age** and **marital status** among all females in the sample. While a significant **age** effect was found for each of the three categories of purchase motivation (**dealer attributes,** F = 6.50; p < .001; **product attributes,** F = 3.70; p < .01; **purchase incentives,** F = 4.26, p < .001), no significant gender **X marital status** interaction effect was found. In fact, among the females in the youngest age category, single respondents actually had higher salience scores for **dealer attributes** and **purchase incentives than those who were married.**

Marketing Implications. The strongest findings from this research is the fundamental difference between males and females in their perceptions of the importance of various motivations related to the purchase of automobiles. It implies that females consider the purchase of an automobile more seriously than do males. There is a message in this research for automotive advertisers. Today, females care more than males about the various message appeals used to persuade consumers. Tomorrow this may not be true. If the historical hypothesis is sound, these gender differences may be temporal, washing out in the coming years.

For further information please contact:
Robin Widgery
Professor of Marketing
University of Michigan
Flint, MI 48502

THE PORTRAYAL OF WOMEN IN CANADIAN ADVERTISING: PERPETUATING THE STEREOTYPES?

Nan Zhou, Acadia University

ABSTRACT

Since the advent of the women's movement in the 1960s, much attention has focused on the image of women in advertising in Canada (Advertising Advisory Board 1977; Canadian Radio-television and Telecommunications Commission 1978, 1982, 1990a, 1990b; ERIN Research 1990; Pasold 1976; Rotenberg 1986; Royal Commission on the Status of Women in Canada 1970). Advertisers have often been criticized for assigning stereotypical roles to female characters in ads. This practice is believed to have undesirable social effects (Courtney and Whipple 1983; Darman and Laroche 1991).

One study (Kindra 1982), using a sample of ads in both Canadian and U.S. magazines published in 1981, reported that the use of female characters as sex objects was "at an all-time high" (p. 114). It also found that women were shown as dependent on men and as low income earners. The study concluded that "although the portrayal of women in traditional roles had declined, their projected image continues to be narrow and limited" (p. 109). A limitation of the study was that separate analysis for Canadian ads was not provided.

Under public pressure and threat of government regulation, the Canadian advertising industry began self-regulation in 1981 (Wyckham 1987). Guidelines on sex-role stereotyping published by the Canadian Advertising Foundation have now been endorsed by major advertising organizations in the country (Darman and Laroche 1991).

Has the image of women in advertising improved since then? This paper reports the results of a content analysis of the portrayal of women in Canadian advertising through a comparison with the portrayal of men, using a national magazine ad sample published in 1990.

The results showed that the frequency of male and female characters used as sex objects was low and there was no significant gender difference. Although males were more often than women shown in higher level occpuations and in business settings, women were cast as often as men in important roles.

While direct comparison between the results of the present study and Kindra's was not possible, it appeared that ads in 1990 gave a more favorable and realistic presentation of female characters in Canadian advertising than in 1981.

REFERENCES

Advertising Advisory Board (1977), *Women and Advertising, Today's Message - Yesterday's Images?* Report of the CAAB Task Force on Women and Advertising, Toronto: CAAB.

Canadian Radio-television and Telecommunications Commission (1978), *Attitudes of Canadians Toward Advertising on Television.* Hull, Quebec: Supply and Services Canada.

_____(1982), *Images of Women.* Cat. BC92-26/1982E, Ottawa: Minister of Supply and Services.

_____(1990a), "News Release - CRTC Calls for Comments on Sex-Role Portrayal in Broadcast Media," (December 28).

_____(1990b), "Public Notice, CRTC 1990-114," (December 28).

Courtney, Alice E. and Thomas W. Whipple (1983), *Sex Stereotyping in Advertising,* Lexington, MA: Lexington Books.

Darmon, Rene Y. and Michel LaRoche (1991), *Advertising in Canada: A Managerial Approach.* Toronto: McGraw-Hill Ryerson.

ERIN Research (1990), *The Portrayal of Gender in Canadian Broadcasting - Summary Report 1984-1988.* Cat. BC92-46, Ottawa: Minister of Supply and Services.

Kindra, Gurprit S. (1982), "Comparative Study of the Roles Portrayed by Women in Print Advertising," in *Marketing: Proceedings of the Annual Conference of the Administrative Sciences Association of Canada,* Michel LaRoche, ed. Montreal: Concordia University, 3, 109-16.

Pasold, Peter W. (1976), "Role Stereotyping in Magazine Advertising of Different Countries", in *Marketing: Proceedings of the Annual Conference of the Administrative sciences Association of Canada,* J.R.B. Ritchie and P. Filiatrault, eds. Quebec: Universite Laval, 41-60.

Rotenberg, Ronald H. (1986), *Advertising: A Canadian Perspective.* Toronto: Allyn and Bacon.

Royal Commission on the Status of Women in Canada (1970), *Report,* Ottawa: Information Canada.

Wyckham, Robert G. (1987), "Self-Regulation of Sex Role Stereotyping in Advertising: The Canadian Experience," *Journal of Public Policy and Marketing,* 6, 76-92.

For further information contact:
Nan Zhou
School of Business Administration
Acadia University
Wolfville, Nova Scotia B0P 1X0

CHANGING PATTERN OF CAR ADVERTISEMENTS IN MAGAZINES: THE PAST 30 YEARS

A. N. M. Waheeduzzaman, Kent State University

ABSTRACT

This study attempts to capture the changing pattern of car advertisements during last 30 years. Specifically, it focuses on the changes in themes, the use of product attributes and the appeals in magazine advertisements through content analysis of magazine ads. In total, 694 advertisements of *Time* published in 1955, 1970, and 1985 were analyzed. Findings show that (confirmed by Chi-square tests), there was a significant variation in themes, attributes, and appeals used in advertisements in these three years.

INTRODUCTION

"Old magazines provide a fascinating window onto our social history, and it is the advertisements that comprise the most interesting pages, displaying behaviors, styles, and roles for diverse objects of our culture." (Pollay 1985, p.24)

Pollay is right. Advertising is an important historical record. It is like a family album of our society. This is especially true when it comes to print media. Being one of the oldest, print media have captured the history of our society better than any other medium. Using content analysis research techniques, historians and marketers are increasingly delving into print media advertisements to understand the changing values of society (Pollay 1985), culture and consumption patterns (McCracken 1986), and images of ourselves (Belk and Pollay 1985). A list of studies that have used advertisements as their primary unit for content analysis in the marketing/advertising area is given in Table 1 (Page limitation precludes a detailed description of these studies).

The studies listed in the table mostly focused on broad issues in marketing and advertising. They have investigated a variety of issues in marketing including the portrayal of blacks, women and the elderly in advertising; the content, copy, layout and design of advertisements; and the use of humor, sex, and animation in advertisements. These studies have also looked at social responsibility issues, consumer and cultural issues and cross-cultural comparison of ads. None of these studies specifically investigated the trend in advertising of any particular product or product class. Product specific content analysis can be useful in showing the changes in the themes in advertsing, the image-appeals being used, and/or the emphasis palced on various product attributes on a longitudinal basis. The current study attempts to fill this gap in product-specific content analysis. It focuses on the trends in the advertising of a particular product (cars) over a 30-year period.

STUDY FOCUS AND OBJECTIVES

During last 30 years, the needs and preferences of the American consumers regarding the purchase of various products including cars have changed substantially. The car manufacturers have responded to this by changing/adapting their overall offering. They changed the designs and features of the cars (added new attributes), pricing (made affordable cars and offered financing), and distribution (made cars available at the doorsteps of the consumers through a wide network of distributors). In advertising and promotion, the basic theme or purpose of the ads changed, and changes were also observed in the use of product attributes and the type of appeals in advertising content. The analysis of advertising content should reveal the changes that have taken place in the basic offering of the product over time. This study was primarily an attempt to capture these historic trends with the following specific objectives.

1. Determine the changes in the themes in car advertising over thirty years.

2. Determine the trend in the use of product attributes in the content of the advertisements.

3. Determine the trend in the type of appeals used in the advertisements to create product imagery.

4. Study the changes in the characteristics of advertisements (e.g., size and location of ads, use of human portrayal, and sex representation) during these years.

METHODOLOGY

Definition of Major Content Categories

Three types of content categories, advertising theme, product attributes, and type of appeals were the main focus of the study. Theme is defined as the major motif of the advertisement around which the manifest copy of the ad is built (Berelson 1952, p.18). It may be a single assertion about the subject matter or referant being analyzed (Kassarjian 1977). For the purpose of this study, the themes of the advertisements were grouped into eight different categories. This was similar to a categorization presented by Schmalensee (1983). Categorization was done based on the language, wording of the message, expressions, and major slogans contained in the advertisement.

TABLE 1
Content Analysis Studies That Used Advertisements As Their Unit of Analysis

Issues	Studies
Portrayal, stereotyping, and role of blacks in advertising	Boyenton 1965; Kassarjian 1969; Roberts 1970; Cox 1969; Dominick and Greenberg 1970; Greizer 1971; Bush, Solomon, and Hair 1977; Berkman 1963
Portrayal and role of women, sex differentiation, use of women as sex objects, and related issues	Courtney and Lockeretz 1971; Dominick and Rauch 1972; Wagner and Banos 1973; Sexton and Haberman 1974; Venkatesan and Losco 1975; McArthur and Resko 1975; Poe 1976; Belakaoui and Belakaoui 1976; Kerin, Lundstrom, and Sciglimpgalia 1979; Scheibe 1979; Whipple and Courtney 1985
Portrayal and role of elderly Americans in advertising	Harris and Feinberg 1977; Swayne and Greco 1987
Comparative advertisements	Shimp 1975; Brown and Jackson 1977; Jackson, Brown and Harmon 1979; Harmon, Razzouk and Stern 1983; Bergh, Adler and Oliver 1987
Information content of advertisements	Resnik and Stern 1977; Laczniack 1979; Dowling 1980; Stern, Krugman and Resnik 1981; Harmon, Razzouk and Stern 1983; Madden, Caballero and Matsukubo 1986
Ad copy, layout and design	Lord, Eastlack, and Stanton 1987; Feasley and Stuart 1987; Shimp, Urbany and Camlin 1988
Social responsibility and related issues	Healey and Kassarjian 1983; Healey, Fisher and Healey 1987; Lill, Gross and Peterson 1986; Pollay 1986
Humor in advertising	Kelly and Solomon, 1975 Weinberger and Spotts, 1989
Sex in advertising	Soley and Kurzbard 1986
Animation in advertising	Bush, Hair and Bush, 1983
Cross-cultural comparisons	Dowling 1980; Madden, Caballero and Matsukubo, 1986; Hong, Moderrisoglu and Zinkhan, 1987; Mueller 1987; Tse, Belk and Zhou, 1989
Culture, consumption, social and values	Belk and Pollay 1985; Pollay 1985; McCracken 1986; Gross and Sheth 1989

Note: This list contains only those studies that have analyzed the contents of advertisements in different media. Content analysis studies of journal articles, comic strips, and other items are not included here. For a content analysis of journal articles see Yale and Gilly (1988).

Product attributes refer to those innate features and characteristics that define the product. Usually, advertisements focused on these attributes in their manifest content to sell the product. An ad may emphasize one or more specific attributes of the product. For example, Volkswagon was promoted with the help of one product attribute, i.e., superiority of its product engineering. Because of changes over time in consumers needs and preferences, the frequency of various product attributes used in advertisements is expected to be different in the three years investigated.

Type of appeals used in the advertisement refers to those aspects of the advertisements that are used to create an image of the product. They are not a part of the physical product, as are the attributes, but they are associated with the product to build an image. For example, Roll Royce, Mercedes, or Cadillac has always been promoted with a status or prestige appeal. The appeal is created by the illustration, headline, expressions, and overall layout and design of the advertisement.

Magazine and Adverstisement Selection

To meet the study objectives, it was necessary to find magazines that were aimed at general audience and not focused to any particular audience group (e.g., women, black, specific social class, etc.), contained many car advertisements, and had a long publication record. From the magazines that met these criteria, *Time* was chosen. It is a widely read magazine with a long publication record (since 1923), and contains many automobile ads. Since at any given point in time, the advertisements in the same medium for a particular product are likely to contain same or similar messages (the car ads of a particular brand in ABC television station don't differ from the car ads in CBS television in terms of message content), for a longitudinal study like this, a single particular source should serve the purpose. This approach was used by Gross and Sheth (1989). They too, used only one source (*Ladies Home Journal*) for their content analysis.

To determine the changes in car advertisements during last 30 years, a sample of 3 years, 1955, 1970, and 1985 (at an interval of 15 years) was taken. Car advertisements of all the issues of *Time* in each year were coded through a predesigned and pretested form. This resulted in an analysis of 694 advertisements: 155 in 1955, 205 in 1970, and 334 in 1985.

Reliability

The reliability test for this study was done in the light of a recent study done in this area (Gross and Sheth 1989). A "different coder consistency" test was conducted with the help of a doctoral student from a U.S. business school who had familiarity with content analysis techniques. Before actual coding, individual differences were dis-

cussed and irrelevant noises were removed to bring consistency in coding. A total sample of 68 advertisements, distributed proportionately in the three years (15 for 1955, 20 for 1970, and 33 for 1985), were chosen for the test. The sample size was determined on the assumption that about 85 percent of time the intercoder agreement would be reached with 95 percent confidence and 10 percent margin of error (see Churchill, Jr. 1987, p. 485, for sample size determination). A commonly used measure of reliability in this area is given by the ratio of coding agreements to the total number of coding decisions, and an 80 percent intercoder agreement is considered to be acceptable (Kassarjian 1977). The percentage of intercoder aggreement for different categories is given below. The intercoder agreements for the content categories (mostly above 85 percent agreement) show that the coding was reliable.

Category	1955	1970	1985
Theme	91%	82%	85%
Attribute	79%	86%	86%
Appeal	88%	88%	92%

FINDINGS OF THE STUDY

Characteristics of Advertisements and Trend

In this study, a total of 694 advertiments were analyzed. In 1985, 334 ads were published compared to 155 in 1955 (see Table 2). Thus, during last 30 years the yearly publication rate of car advertisements in *Time* has nearly doubled. Today, readers of *Time* would likely be exposed to at least six different car advertisements per issue. Most of the 694 ads (95%) were not repetitive in nature. Repetition of ads was almost absent in 1955 and was infrequent in 1970. In 1985, more repetitive ads (about 7%) were seen. The repeat advertisements were included in the study. Although they have increased the frequency of some of the items under study, they did not in essence affect the findings.

About 90 percent of the ads were placed inside the magazine (no specific part was preferred) in the years selected. Full page ads were frequent in 1955 and two-folded pages in 1970. The use of the front inside cover was highest (10%) in 1955 and lowest (2.4%) in 1985. The portrayal or presentation of people in ads was high in 1955 (55%), lower in 1970 (22%), and in 1985, only 16 percent of ads contained human models. In general, the decline in the use of human models in advertisements is consistent with earlier studies in the area (Feasley and Stuart 1987; Pollay 1985). Couples in their mid-thirties were the age group represented the most often in the three years examined.

Qualitatively, car advertisements appear to have moved toward simplification, with fewer headlines, fewer sentences in the ad copy, fewer illustrations, and fewer

TABLE 2
Changes in Advertisement Characteristics

		1955	1970	1985
Publication rate				
Advertisement/ year		155	205	334
Advertisement/ issue		3.0	3.9	6.4
Advertisement/ month		12.9	17.1	27.8
Size				
Half page		2.0	4.4	2.4
Full page		69.0	24.4	58.1
Two folded pages		29.0	70.7	34.1
More than two pages		—	0.5	4.2
Advertising supplement		—	—	1.2
	Total	100.0	100.0	100.0
Location				
Front outside cover		10.3	5.4	2.4
Inside page		89.7	94.1	97.0
Back inside cover		—	0.5	0.6
	Total	100.0	100.0	100.0
Human Portrayal				
Children and family		3.8	2.4	6.4
Youth		45.8	15.6	9.0
Middle aged		5.2	3.9	0.6
	Total	54.8	21.9	15.6
Sex representation				
Male		5.4	2.9	2.4
Female		6.3	5.9	4.2
Both		43.1	13.1	9.0
	Total	54.8	21.9	15.6

Note: Except publication rate, all figures are in percentages.

use of human models. The overall quality of ads, their presentation, layout and design have also changed significantly. In 1985, most of the advertisements were attractive, well-designed, and reflected a professional approach in communication. Compared to 1955 ads, the ads of 1970 and 1985 show more novelty in the layout and design of the ad. The organization and presentation of messages in the copy of the ad also looks more professional in the later years. Similar observations were made by Pollay (1985) in a decade-by-decade descriptive study of print ads.

A summary of the findings about the types of themes, use of attributes, and appeals is presented in Table 3. The table shows that about two-thirds of the advertisements were aimed at creating brand image. They focused on specific brands in the advertising copy. The use of product attributes dominated the 1985 ads, and the use of appeals was more observed in 1985. These are elaborated in the following sections.

Types of Themes

In each of the three years, "establishing brand image" was the major theme. About two-thirds of the ads were brand-specific. They focused on only one brand. In 1955, about 66 percent of the ads contained "establishing brand image" as the principal theme, compared to 56 percent in 1970, and 55 percent in 1985 (see Table 4).

TABLE 3
Summary Table: Themes, Attributes, and Appeals

	1955	1970	1985
Two most featured themes	Establishing brand image	Establishing brand image	Establishing brand image
	Establishing company image	Establishing competitive superiority	Informing about product attributes
Exposure of product attributes	54% ads contained	48% ads contained	82% ads contained
Two most featured attributes	Machine/engine power, Price/ purchase economy	Price/purchase economy, engineering	Product engineering, Driving comfort and performance
Use of appeals	57% ads contained	37% ads contained	32% ads contained
Three most featured appeals	Style, Performance, Elegance, Thrill	Sportiness, Performance, Thrill	Sportiness, Aspiration, Style
Brands featured	Mostly American	Mostly Foreign	American and Foreign
Two most featured brands	Buick, Chrysler, Pontiac	Toyota, Renault, Audi, Volvo	Oldsmobile, Buick

Note: 1. Thrill and elegance had equal score in 1955, and style and smartness had equal scores in 1985.

2. Chrysler and Pontiac had equal scores and ranked second in 1955. In 1970, both Toyota and Renault ranked first, and Audi and Volvo ranked second.

In 1955, besides promoting the brand image, establishment of a corporate image was also a major concern of the manufacturers. Such ads were necessary for the automobile manufacturers who were trying to establish their corporate image in a fast growing mass market for automobiles. This was reflected in the content of the advertisements, where 13 percent of the advertisements were devoted to "establishing company image." These ads focused on the company as a whole, and no specific brand was mentioned in the content. Typical slogans used to build company image include, "GM Leads the Way" and "Chrysler: The Forward Look."

The themes showed a different pattern in 1970. In

that year, next to "establishing brand image," the most frequent themes were "establishing competitive superiority" (17%) and "informing about product attributes" (12%). This was a period when small and sporty cars were abundant in the market. To gain share in such a competitive market it was necesssary for companies to establish the comparative superiority of their brands against others. Typical slogans that were used to establish competitive superiority include:

o   How a car uses gas. How Audi used gas (Audi).

o   Read yourself out of a Chevy, Volkswagen or Volvo (Renault).

o   The predictable winner whenever excellence is

TABLE 4
Type of Themes

Themes	1955	1970	1985
Arousal of a specific need	1.9	—	—
Informing about product attributes	5.8	11.7	16.8
Motivating a direct purchase	2.6	4.4	11.4
Establishing competitive superiority	6.5	16.6	6.6
Introducing a new product	3.9	9.3	4.2
Establishing brand image	65.8	56.1	54.5
Estabilishing company image	12.9	2.0	6.6
Creating specific product difference	0.7	—	—
Percentage total =	100.0	100.0	100.0
Total response =	155	205	334

Note: A chi-square test at .05 significance level showed that the distribution of various categories of themes of the advertisements were different in these three years.

All figures are in percentages.

a way of life (Cadillac).

o Some cars have it some cars don't (Saab).

Recent advertisements, as evident from the types of themes used, are more focused on consumers' purchase decision process. In 1985, next to "establishing brand image," the two other most frequent themes were "informing about product attributes" (17%) and "motivating a direct purchase" (11%). Both themes were aimed at influencing the later stages of consumers' purchase decision process, with "informing about product attributes" influencing the evaluation stage and "motivating a direct purchase" affecting the action stage.

Use of Product Attributes

The use of product attributes in the content of the advertisements, as a whole, has been on the rise. About 82 percent of the advertisements in 1985 contained product attributes compared to 48 percent in 1970 and 54 percent in 1955 (see Table 5). Increasing use of product attributes were also observed by Pollay (1985) in a historical analysis of advertisements.

In 1955, engine power was the most featured product attribute (23%), compared to price or purchase economy (19%) in 1970, and product engineering and craftmanship (26%) in 1985. The emphasis on engine power in 1955 was a reflection of the car as a whole. The emphasis on price or purchase economy in the 1970s was due to the introduction of compact cars, especially the less expensive brands from Japan. In 1985, the engineering or craftmanship of the product was used more frequently, reflecting consumers' interest in physical product. Some car ads contained blue prints of cars, or their architectural

designs to reflect technological superiority. Volkswagon ads were the pioneer in advertising the engineering aspects of the product.

The price or economy of purchase was always a concern of the manufacturers. In all the three years, it was one of the three most frequently advertised attributes. Perhaps because of the fall in the price of oil in the 1980s, fuel economy was less frequently featured in 1985 than in 1970. The other commonly featured attributes were driving comfort and performance, interior design and spaciousness, and credit facility and financing.

Type of Appeals Used

While the use of product attributes was increasing, the use of image appeals in the content of the advertisements was decreasing. Image appeals were used in 57 percent of the advertisements in 1955, compared to 37 percent 1970, and 31 percent in 1985 (see Table 6). This suggests that, in today's information conscious society, the product and product attributes are of more importance to the consumers than imagery.

An analysis of the advertisements that contained image appeals shows that the most frequent appeals in 1955 were style, performance, thrill and elegance. In 1970, a new appeal, "sportiness," was included to build a different image of the car. Sportiness remained the most featured appeal in 1985 also. About one-third of the ads of 1970 and 1985 that contained appeals featured sportiness. With sportiness, in 1970, performance and thrill were also used. In 1985, with sportiness, a new appeal, "aspiration/success" was included in the content. Possibly, these ads were directed to the rising groups of

TABLE 5
Use of Product Attributes

Attributes	1955	1970	1985
Engine power	22.6	2.0	2.0
Driving comfort & performance	3.2	8.8	15.0
Interior design & spaciousness	3.2	3.9	7.2
Product engineering	9.7	11.9	38.7
Product extension/services	——	——	2.6
Fuel economy	1.3	3.4	2.0
Price/purchase economy	13.6	18.5	6.6
Credit facility	——	——	7.8
Percentage of ads that contained attributes =	53.6	48.5	81.9

Note: A chi-square test at .05 significance level showed that the use of various product attributes in the content of advertisements was different in these three years.

All figures are in percentages.

Table 6
Type of Appeals Used

Appeals	1955	1970	1985
Status	1.9	1.5	0.6
Style/beauty/fashion	10.3	2.0	3.3
Performance	8.4	5.4	1.8
Thrill/excitement	8.4	5.4	1.8
Elegance/sophistication	7.7	2.4	0.6
Smartness	6.5	3.9	3.3
Richness/luxury	5.2	3.9	2.1
Aspiration/success	7.7	1.0	5.1
Sportiness/liveliness	——	10.2	9.9
Sensuality/sex	——	1.0	0.6
Family life	1.3	0.5	2.7
Percentage of advertisements that used appeals =	57.4	37.1	31.7

Note: A chi-square test at .05 significance level showed that the type of appeals used in the advertisements were different in these three years.

All figures are in percentages.

successful young professionals, commonly known as "yuppies."

LIMITATIONS AND CONCLUSION

Although the study reveals the variation in ad contents on a historical basis, the findings have their limitations. The contents of advertisements could depend on the brands being marketed during a particular period. This is especially true in 1970 when foreign brands were introduced in this country. Being at the introductory stage of the product life cycle, they were advertised heavily and were mainly aimed at establishing brand name.

It has been argued that, at any specific time period, within medium variations in ad contents for a particular product may not be drastically different if audience differences are not substantial. However, this is a limitation also. Future research may be directed to determine the inter-media variation in ad contents. That would substantiate the generalizability of this research.

In spite of these limitations, the study has revealed that there is a difference in advertising themes, use of product attributes and appeals during the period of study. In 1955, when bigness was in demand, manufacturers produced big cars and marketed them with appeals like style, performance, thrill. In 1970, when the need was for smaller sporty cars, manufacturers flooded the market with smaller varieties of compact sporty cars, and promoted them with appeals like sportiness, performance, and thrill. The outdoor lifestyles of Americans were highlighted during this period. In 1985, aspiration and success were added to the creation of images. The changes in the contents of car advertisements reflect the changing needs and preferences of consumers at different time periods.

REFERENCES

Belakaoui, A. and J. M. Belakaoui (1976), "A Comparative Analysis of the Roles Portrayed by Women in Print Adverstisements: 1958, 1970, 1972," *Journal of Marketing Research,* 13 (May), 168-172.

Belk, Russell W. and Richard W. Pollay (1985), "Images of Ourselves: The Good Life in Twentieth Century Advertising," *Journal of Consumer Research,* 11 (March), 887-897.

Berelson, B. (1952), *Content Analysis in Communication Research.* New York: Free Press.

Bergh, Bruce V., Keith Adler, and Lauren Oliver (1987), "Linguistic Distinction Among Top Brand Names," *Journal of Advertising Research,* (August/September), 39-44.

Berkman, D. (1963), "Advertising in *Ebony* and *Life*: Negro Aspiration vs. Reality," *Journalism Quaterly,* 40, 53-64.

Boyenton, W. H. (1965), "The Negro Turns to Advertising," *Journalism Quarterly,* 42, 227-35.

Brown, Stephen W. and Donald W. Jackson (1977), "Comparative Television Advertising: Examining Its Nature and Frequency," *Journal of Advertising,* 6 (4), 15-18.

Bush, R. F., P. J. Solomon, and J. F. Hair, Jr. (1977), "A Content Analysis of the Portrayal of Black Models in Television Commercials," *Proccedings of American Marketing Association,* 427-430.

Bush, Alan J., Joseph F. Hair, Jr., Robert P. Bush (1983), "A Content Analysis of Animation in Television Advertising," *Journal of Advertising,* 12 (4).

Churchill. Jr., Gilbert A. (1987), *Marketing Research.* 4th edition, New York: Dryden Press.

Courtney, A. E. and S. W. Lockeretz (1971), "An Analysis of the Roles Portrayed by Women in Magazine Advertisements," *Journal of Marketing Research,* 8 (February), 92-95.

Cox, K. K. (1969), "Changes in Stereotyping of Negros and Whites in Magazine Advertisements," *Public Opinion Quarterly,* 33, 603-606.

Dominick, J. R. and B. S. Greenberg (1970), "Three Seasons of Blacks on Television," *Journal of Advertising Research,* 10, 21-27.

_____ and G. E. Rauch (1972), "The Image of Women's Network TV Commercials," *Journal of Broadcasting,* 16 (Summer), 259-265.

Dowling, Frahame R. (1980), "Information Content in U.S. and Australian Television Advertising," *Journal of Marketing,* 44 (Fall), 34-37.

Feasley, Florence G. and Elnora W. Stuart (1987), "Magazine Advertising Layout and Design: 1932-1982," *Journal of Advertising,* 16 (2), 20-25.

Geizer, R. (1971), "Advertising in Ebony: 1960 and 1969," *Journalism Quarterly,* 48, 131-134.

Gross, Barbara J. and Jagdish N. Sheth (1989), "Time-Oriented Advertising: A Content Analysis of United States Magazine Advertising, 1980-1988," *Journal of Marketing,* 53 (October), 76-83.

Harmon, Robert R., Nabil Y. Razzouk, and Bruce Stern (1983), "Information Content of Comparative Magazine Advertisements," *Journal of Advertising,* 12 (4), 10-19

Harris, Adella J. and Jonathan F. Feinberg (1977), "Televison and Aging: Is What You See What You Get?" *The Gerontologist,* 17 (October), 464-468.

Healey, John S. and Harold H. Kassarjian (1983), "Advertising Substantiation and Advertising Response: A Content Analysis of Magazine Advertisements," *Journal of Marketing,* 47 (1), 107-117.

_____, Melvyn E. Fisher, and Grace F. Healey (1987), "Advertising Screamers vs. Hummers," *Journal of Advertising Research,* 43-49.

Hong, Jae W., Aydin Muderrisoglu, and Geroge M. Zinkhan (1987), "Cultural Differences and Advertising Expression: A Comparative Content Analysis of Japanese and U.S. Magazine Advertising," *Journal of Advertising,* 16 (1), 55-68.

Jackson, Donald W., Stephen W. Brown, and Robert R. Harmon (1979), "Comparative Magazine Advertisements," *Journal of Advertising Research,* 19, 6 (December), 21-26.

Kassarjian, H. H. (1969), "The Negro and American Advertising," *Journal of Marketing Research,* 29-39.

_____ (1977), "Content Analysis in Consumer Research," *Journal of Consumer Research,* (June), 8-18.

Kelly, Patrick, and Paul J. Solomon (1975), "Humor in Television Advertising," *Journal of Advertising,* 4 (3), 31-35.

Kerin, Roger A., William J. Lundstrom, and Donald Sciglimpaglia (1979), "Women in Advertisement: Retrospect and Prospect," *Journal of Advertising,* 8,

3 (Summer), 37-42.

Laczniack, Gene R. (1979), "Information Content in Print Advertising," *Journalism Quarterly,* 56 (Summer), 324-345

Lill, David, Charles Gross, and Robin Peterson (1986), "The Inclusion of Social Responsibility Themes by Magazine Advertisers: A Longitudinal Study," *Journal of Advertising,* 15 (2), 35-41.

Lord, John B., Joseph O. Eastlack, Jr., and John S. Stanton, Jr. (1987), "Health Claims in Food Advertising: Is There a Bandwagon Effect?" *Journal of Advertising Research,* (April/May), 9-15.

Madden, Charles S., Majorie J. Caballero, and Shinya Matsukubo (1986), "Analysis of Information Content in U.S. and Japanese Magazine Advertising," *Journal of Advertising,* 15 (3), 38-45.

McArthur, Leslie Z., and Beth G. Resko (1975), "The Portrayal of Men and Women in American Television Commercials," *Journal of Social Psychology,* 97 (December), 209-220.

McCracken, Grant (1986), "Culture and Consumption: A Theoretical Account of the Structure and Movement of the Cultural Meaning of Consumer Goods," *Journal of Consumer Research,* 13 (June), 71-84.

Mueller, Barbara (1987), "Reflections of Culture: An Analysis of Japanese and American Advertising Appeals," *Journal of Advertising Research,* (June/July), 51-59.

Poe, Alison (1976), "Active Women in Ads," *Journal of Communication,* 26 (Autumn), 185-192.

Pollay, Richard W. (1985), "The Subsiding Sizzle: A Descriptive History of Print Advertising, 1900-1980," *Journal of Marketing,* 49 (Summer), 24-37.

_____ (1986), "The Distorted Mirror: Reflections on the Unintended Consequences of Advertising," *Journal of Marketing,* 50 (April), 18-36.

Resnik, A. and B. L. Stern (1977), "An Analysis of Information Content in Television Advertising," *Journal of Marketing,* 41, 50-53.

Roberts, C. (1970), "The Portrayal of Blacks on Network Television," *Journal of Broadcasting,* 15, 45-53.

Scheibe, Cyndy (1979), "Sex Roles in TV Commercials," *Journal of Advertising Research,* 19, 1 (February), 23-27.

Schmalensee, D. (1983), "Today's Top Priority Advertising Research Questions," *Journal of Advertising Research,* (April/May), 49-60.

Sexton, Donald E. and Phyllis Haberman (1974), "Women in Magazine Advertisements," *Journal of Advertis-*

ing Research, 14 (August), 41-46.

Shimp, Terence A. (1975), "Comparison Advertising in National Television Commercials: A Content Analysis with Specific Emphasis Devoted to the Issue os Incomplete Comparative Assertions," *Marketing in Turbulant Times: AMA Combined Proceedings,* Chicago.

_____, Joel E. Urbany, and Sarah E. Camlin (1988), "The Use of Framing and Characterization for Magazine Advertising of Mass-Marketed Products," *Journal of Advertising,* 17 (1), 23-30.

Shuman, Ronald B. (1937), "Identification Elements of Advertising Slogans," *Southwestern Social Science Quarterly,* 17, 342-52.

Soley, Lawrence, and Gary Kurzbard (1986), "Sex in Advertising: A Comparison of 1964 and 1984 Magazine Advertisements," *Journal of Advertising,* 15 (3), 46-54.

Stern, Bruce, Dean Krugman, and Alan Resnik (1981), "Magazine Advertising: An Analysis of Its Information Content," *Journal of Advertising Research,* 21 (April), 39-44.

Swayne, Linda E. and Alan J. Greco (1987), "The Portrayal of Older Americans in Television," *Journal of Advertising,* 16 (1), 47-54.

Tse, David K., Russell W. Belk, and Nan Zhou (1989), "Becoming a Consumer Society: A Longitudinal and Cross-cultural Content Analysis of Print Ads from Hong Kong, The Peoples Republic of China, and Taiwan," *Journal of Consumer Research,* 15, (March).

Venkatesan, M. and J. Losco (1975), "Women in Magazine Ads: 1959-1971," *Journal of Advertising Research,* 5, 49-54.

Wagner, L. C. and J. B. Banos (1973), "A Women's Place: A Follow-up Analysis of the Roles Portrayed by Women in Magazine Advertisements," *Journal of Marketing Research,* 10, 213-214.

Weinberger, Marc G. and Harlan E. Spotts (1989), "Humor in U.S. versus U.K. TV Commercials: A Comparison," *Journal of Advertsing,* 18 (2), 39-44.

Whipple, Thomas W. and Carole M. Courtney (1985), "Female Role Portrayal in Advertising and Communication Effectiveness," *Journal of Advertising,* 14 (3), 4-8, 17.

Yale, Laura and Mary C. Gilly (1988), "Trends In Advertising Research: A Look at the Content of Marketing-Oriented Journals from 1976 to 1985," *Journal of Advertising,* 17 (1), 12-22.

SOME COMMENTS ON THE ROLE OF EMOTIONS IN CONSUMER BEHAVIOR

Barry J. Babin, University of Southern Mississippi
William R. Darden, Louisiana State University
Mitch Griffin, Bradley University

ABSTRACT

Emotion is gaining increasing recognition as a variable important to the explanation of many consumer variables. This paper reviews recent research into human emotion as it pertains to consumer behavior. In doing so, an attempt is made to synthesize the diverse literature as it pertains to (1) discriminating between various emotive terms, (2) the interrelationship between cognition and affect, and (3) the measurement of emotion.

INTRODUCTION

A growing number of scholars have acknowledged the paucity of consideration extended to emotional, or affective, aspects of consumer behavior (e.g., Hirschman and Holbrook 1982; Ray and Batra 1983; Peterson and Sauber 1983; Ahtola 1985; Cacioppo, Losch, Tassinary, and Petty 1986; Burke and Edell 1989; Holbrook and Westwood 1989). The move of emotions toward epistemic prominence is far from surprising as it appears to parallel similar movements in social psychology (Russell 1978), cognitive psychology (Bower and Cohen 1982); and sociology (Swanson 1983). The decade of the 80s produced few topics which aroused as much sparked debate and controversy among social scientists as did the role of emotion (affect) in explaining human behavior (e.g., Lazarus 1982; Tsal 1985; Zajonc and Markus 1985; Russell and Woudzia 1986).

A great deal of this controversy can be traced to a number of difficult, and sometimes unresolved, issues surrounding the study of emotion. (1) Primary among these issues is defining and discriminating between the myriad of terms which fall under the emotive umbrella (Fehr and Russell 1984). (2) A closely related issue concerns the interrelationship between cognition and emotion; or to what extent are they related at all (Allen and Janiszewski 1989)? (3) Perhaps the issue that has developed the most attention concerns the measurement of experiential and/or emotive dimensions of behavior (Winton, Putnam, and Krauss 1984). Although controversies surrounding the study of emotion appear to be relatively enduring, a great deal of insight can be gained from the existing body of empirical and conceptual evidence. This paper attempts to bring together previous literature from marketing and psychology as it relates to these three important issues.

AFFECT, EMOTIONS, MOODS AND OTHER TEMPERAMENTAL DESCRIPTORS

Three terms often used interchangeably in the consumer behavior literature are affect, emotion, and mood. Although it often becomes clear that these terms have many commonalities, the indiscretion with which terms describing emotion and/or affect, and the wide range of phenomena which they are used to describe, can be a source of confusion (Cacioppo and Petty 1989). Of these three descriptors, affect appears most often in the marketing and consumer research literature.

Affect

While many authors have stated that the role of "affect" in consumer behavior has been neglected, there appears to be no shortage of studies employing "affect" as a construct. The fact that many feel affect has been neglected in no way stems from its frequent use as a synonym for attitude (Cacioppo et al. 1986). However, this view basically reflects a cognitive orientation in keeping with computer-like analogies of human information processing (Batra 1986). Thus, it appears that affect as a construct has been many things to many people.

The introduction of the construct of affect in the marketing research literature may well be the result of Osgood, Suci, and Tannenbaum's (1957) seminal work. These authors proposed affect as a primary basis for providing meaning to objects, both physical and psychological. In addition, Osgood et al. (1957) provide semantic differentials to measure affect consisting of bipolar adjectives like good - bad, pleasing - annoying, favorable - unfavorable, etc. This orientation captures the evaluative aspects of affect, and is consistent with the traditional tripartite (C-A-B) view of affect (Cacioppo and Petty 1989; Cohen and Areni 1991). The majority of applications of affect in marketing and consumer research have been under this guise of affect as a predisposition. Common applications have often found affect employed in multiattribute studies of affect toward some act (Bagozzi 1982), or as a measurement of ad-based affect, or attitude toward an ad (Mitchell and Olson 1981).

However, an attitudinal operationalization of the construct affect is subject to criticism as overly simplistic and narrow (Holbrook and Westwood 1989). Ahtola

(1985) specifically points to the inability of traditional operationalizations of affect to capture its hedonic, or nonutilitarian, aspects. As an alternative, a multidimensional representation of affect is proposed which explicitly accounts for a utilitarian and hedonic aspect, each capable of directly influencing behavior. Batra (1986) has proposed a four-dimensional structure to account for affect associated with exposure to ads. The four dimensions consist of (1) SEVA (surgency, elation, vigor, or activation), (2) deactivation or sensuousness, (3) social affection and tenderness, and (4) "sizzle" which induces "appetitive" desires to purchase or consume. While affect is still seen as a basis for preferences, Batra (1986) points out how it can promote information processing (through SEVA) and trigger purchasing behavior.

Likewise, others have taken a broader view of affect than an attitudinal perspective allows. For example, affect has been hypothesized as an important peripheral element in information processing (Petty, Cacioppo, and Schumann 1983) distinguished from attitudes based on its relative *transiency* and *specificity*. The authors suggest, for instance, how a pleasant luncheon environment can make an argument more effective. Also, Westbrook (1980) has noted the affective nature of satisfaction. In a later study, measures of Izard's 10 fundamental affects are used to predict postpurchase consumer responses (Westbrook 1987). In doing so, affect is defined as a mental phenomena characterized by conscious feeling states, accompanying both emotions and moods. Also, Westbrook (1987) takes the stand that positive and negative affect are separate dimensions, rather than bipolar ends of a single continuum.

In sum, it appears that there are several inescapable facets surrounding the construct of affect. Based on previous applications in marketing and consumer research, affect appears to be related to evaluations, is multidimensional, interacts with cognition to affect behavior, and is generally accompanied by emotions and moods.

Emotion

Specific references to "emotion" in the marketing literature are found far less often than are applications of "affect." Although Copeland (1923) mentioned emotion as a major motivation behind a large portion of consumer behavior, its use as a descriptive term useful in explaining consumption is only recently reemerging as authors begin to increasingly accept the notion that consumption is often undertaken "in direct pursuit of fun, feelings, and fantasies" (Holbrook and Hirschman 1982, p. 132).

In a number of previous applications in consumer behavior, emotion has been treated similarly to affect as a simple bipolar unidimensional construct (Holbrook and Westwood 1989). Such a simplistic view seems inappro-

priate considering the wide ranging nature of emotions and their importance as primary motivators of consumer behavior (Grossbart et al. 1975) capable of overriding utilitarian concerns (Ahtola 1985; Hudson and Murray 1986). Fonberg (1986) notes the motivational aspects of emotions by pointing out the term's latin origins.

Spiritus movens, derived from *emovere*, literally means to push or move.
Emotions are fuels for drives, for all motion, every performance, and any behavioral act . . . [t]his hedonistically bidirectional feature of emotion seems to be of great importance . . . In sum, emotions are the fuel for drives (p. 302).

Not all attempts at studying emotion and its influence on consumer behavior are subject to criticism based on a simplistic treatment. These multifaceted studies have either adapted a multidimensional perspective as developed in environmental psychology (Mehrabian and Russell 1974) or have measured a number of emotions without making any ascriptions concerning the dimensionality or polarity of the resulting emotional space or circumplex (Conte and Plutchik 1981; Izard 1977).

As an example of the latter approach, Holbrook and Westwood (1989) examined emotional responses of television commercial viewers. Using three-item scales representing each of Plutchik's (1980) eight basic emotions, (1) acceptance, (2) fear, (3) surprise, (4) sadness, (5) disgust, (6) anger, (7) anticipation, and (8) joy, a reasonable facsimile of the proposed circumplex was uncovered by plotting emotional vectors in commercial space using regression scores. These findings basically support additional research indicating the ability of Plutchik's circumplex to measure emotions elicited from advertising stimuli. This conceptualization assumes that any attempt to define dimensions of emotion is arbitrary due to the circular arrangement of basic emotions within emotion space.

In contrast, a greater number of studies involving emotions in consumer research have adapted a conceptual development of emotion grounded mainly in environmental psychology (Mehrabian and Russell 1974). Rather than assuming arbitrary axes as in a circumplex, this approach theorizes the existence of three basic bipolar dimensions which can be used to define a diversity of emotional reactions, including the range encompassed by Plutchik's eight basic emotions.

In an attempt to establish the convergent validity of these three dimensions, Russell (1978) used a variety of techniques, including multidimensional scaling and canonical correlation, to demonstrate the relatedness of various authors' (Bush 1972; Averill 1975) proposed emotional schemes and his own. Based on results of this study, Russell (1978) concludes there is strong evidence of convergent validity for a three dimensional schema with the dimensions of pleasure and arousal being particularly ubiquitous. In addition, support was found for a third dimension which defines emotions in terms of their control, dominance, or potency. This third dimension, generally referred to as dominance, is related to both pleasure and arousal.

This three dimensional perspective, pleasure, arousal, and dominance (PAD), has been employed to study a number of varying consumption situations. As previously discussed, Donovan and Rossiter (1982), as well as Anderson (1986), have employed "the PAD paradigm" in explaining a number of approach-withdrawal behaviors in retail environments. This approach has also been employed in a study of playful consumption involving subjects' emotional responses based on interacting with a video game (Holbrook et al. 1984). Pleasure, Arousal, and Dominance were found to correlate with subjects' preferred cognitive style and format, as well as game performance.

Havlena and Holbrook (1986) directly compare the ability of PAD dimensions with Plutchik's psychoevolutionary framework to account for emotions arising during consumption experiences. Multiple item semantic differential scales representing PAD and 3-item scales representing each of the eight basic emotions listed above were used by two separate groups of judges rating the emotionality of 149 consumption experience descriptions. Each PAD dimension achieved an interjudge reliability exceeding .90 as measured by Cronbach α. Based on these reliabilities, and PAD's superiority in reproducing the hypothesized structure of emotional space, the authors conclude that the Mehrabian-Russell (1974) model (PAD) appears preferable to Plutchik's (1980) model in accounting for emotions arising from consumption experiences.

A more recent study (Havlena, Holbrook, and Lehmann 1989) verifies these findings. However, the linguistic nature of Plutchik's (1980) eight basic dimensions is noted, leading to a potential advantage when studying advertising content. For advertising, words may be more important, and thus, Plutchik's (1980) conceptualization may be superior. In contrast, actions are central in describing consumption experiences, making PAD a superior conceptual basis for studying these types of emotions. As an aside, it is interesting to note that Havlena et al. (1989) recover "dimensions" of the space defined by Plutchik's eight basic emotions. These "dimensions" show a striking similarity to pleasure and arousal as defined by Mehrabian and Russell (1974).

The superiority of PAD in accounting for consumption related emotions may be more than coincidental considering both its underpinnings in environmental psychology and the environmental nature of emotions as pointed out by numerous scholars (e.g., Ittleson 1973;

Russell 1983; Brewin 1989). For example, Lazarus (1975) points out how emotional activity arises from evaluation and appraisal of "moment to moment encounters" with one's environment. Put differently, emotions are seen as mediating relationships between a person and an environment (Lazarus 1982; Holbrook and Batra 1987). Influenced greatly by Darwin (1872), Plutchik (1983) defines emotions similarly as appropriate responses to unforseen events in the environment. In large part, it is the environmental nature of emotion which makes it appropriate to serve a role as a major mediator of behavior in a comprehensive (Consiousness-Emotion-Value) model of consumer behavior (Holbrook 1986).

The importance of emotion in explaining behavior emanating from person-environment interactions is made even more clear when its motivational aspects are considered. The words of Fonberg (1986) above clearly point this out. In addition, others have included motivation as an important component of emotion (Grossbart et al. 1979; Izard 1977; Brewin 1989; Anderson 1990). A motivational conceptualization of emotion also places it as a plausible candidate to fill the role of the "missing mediating construct" needed within comprehensive models of patronage and consumer behavior as alluded to by Sheth (1983).

Several points can be made to summarize this brief review of research specifically dealing with "emotion." First, emotions appear relevant for studying consumption experiences. Second, environmental psychology provides an appropriate conceptualization of emotion when considering consumption experiences. Third, emotions have both an environmental and a motivational aspect. Finally, emotion may deserve explicit recognition in comprehensive models of consumer behavior.

Mood

The term "mood" has also appeared in the marketing literature. Belk (1975) has listed mood as an important situational variable pervasive through many consumption phenomena. Gardner (1985) has provided a detailed review of mood research as it pertains to consumer behavior and defines mood as a subjectively felt feeling state. Following this definition, a number of appropriate consumption phenomena are hypothesized as being affected by a consumer's mood. Gardner (1985) concludes by calling for more research on mood in four specific areas: (1) the effects of mood on basic decisions like, when to shop, where to shop, and whether to shop alone or with others; (2) the **mediation** of behavior at point-of-purchase; (3) comparisons of marketer induced moods and other moods; and (4) the interaction of marketer environments with pre-existing mood states.

Peterson and Sauber (1983) have developed a parsimonious verbal report scale to measure a person's global mood-state. They define mood as a state of mind, or feeling, associated with a temporary internal state within a particular environment. They also adapt the perspective of mood as an intervening variable capable of influencing predispositions, and thus, affecting the probability of occurrence of various responses to consumer situations. So one explicit use of this scale would be to partial out potential confounding effects due to significantly high positive or negative mood-states to enable a more precise examination of relationships between other variables.

A stream of research relevant to consumer behavior which deals with the effects of mood on behavior is the study of helping behavior or charitability (e.g., Gaertner and Dovidioi 1977). Cialdini and Fultz (1990) report the results of a "mega-analysis" of previous literature dealing with the impact of negative mood-states on helping behavior which has obvious marketing implications. They conclude that negative moods lead to a significant and nontrivial increase in helping behavior. Likewise, Isen (1987) reports evidence of similar effects on charitability from subtle increases in the level of positive mood experienced by a subject. Studies such as these point out the relevance of "mood" to studies of decision processes like those common to consumer behavior, however, more work is needed to define precisely the nature of these relationships.

To conduct studies of mood's effects, it often becomes necessary to manipulate subject mood. Hill and Ward (1989) have investigated possible confounding effects due to changes in subject mood. Using an experimental design, subjects' moods were manipulated by informing them that they had won a certain game of chance (*Mutant Robots from Outer Space*). Half of the subjects were told they won because of "luck," while the others were led to attribute their success to "skill." The results of the experiment revealed improved moods in both groups of subjects, however, "lucky" subjects experienced relatively lower levels of self-efficacy and an increased latency in decision-making than did "skillful" subjects. Thus, the precise effects of various mood manipulation techniques may vary.

Synthesis

To sum, there are many similarities between the concepts of "affect," "emotion," and "mood." First, it appears that each of these terms can be represented as a multidimensional phenomenon. Second, moods and emotions are both seen as a result of a person interacting within some environment. However, mood can be distinguished from emotion as mood as typically a antecedent state, whereas emotion is a response to the particular environment. Third, each term has been operationalized in some manner which has proved capable of impacting decision processes and behavior. Often this impact has been hypothesized as a mediating effect (between the self and an environment). It is not surprising, based on their similarities, that a number of authors have concluded that

various "feeling" terms are virtually indistinguishable and can be used interchangeably (Ray and Batra 1983; Izard 1977; Batra 1986; Holbrook and Batra 1987; Burke and Edell 1989; Ellis 1990). In noting that emotions are sometimes referred to as affects, Fehr and Russell (1984) discuss the difficulty of establishing definitions for emotion and related terms. They conclude that a classical definition of emotion, and other feeling-laden terms, appears unlikely. Rather, emotions are recognized based on their prototypicality with what we perceive to be *ideal* cases of emotion.

If pressed then, a fine distinction between affect, emotion, and mood may be possible. Of the three, emotion appears to be the more encompassing term, with affect and mood being particular types or examples of emotion (Batra 1986; Russell and Snodgrass 1987). It is the sum of all the components that make up a central construct of emotion (Holbrook 1986). To be more precise, affect has been distinguished from emotion linguistically, as it refers to "emotion as expressed in language" (Russell 1978, p. 1152), and by order of magnitude as being less intense than full blown emotions (Isen 1987). Further, the concept of attitude is not interchangeable with affect. Moods are distinguished from affect emotion in that they are generally not directed toward any particular object and are generally referred to with a temporal respect (Russell and Snodgrass 1987).

COGNITION AND EMOTION

A vigorous and sometimes *emotional* debate has arisen over the past decade concerning the relatedness or independence of emotions and cognition. During the early part of this debate a wave of consumer researchers adapted the perspective of feelings formed without thinking, and carrying the idea further, concluded that consumer decisions were often completely thoughtless (Olshavsky and Granbois 1979). However, recent evidence tends to be less supportive of this view. Regardless, the relationship between cognition and emotion is central to consumer behavior because it strikes at the heart of issues encompassing consumer sovereignty.

Preferences Need No Inferences

This was the issue raised by Zajonc (1980) in a well-cited and influential article which outlines evidence supporting his *independence hypothesis*. The idea that emotion can be formed in the complete absence of cognition is supported by evidence demonstrating an attachment of affect toward some stimulus in the absence of its recognition. The *mere exposure effect*, or objective familiarity, is said to occur when subjects show increased liking for an object to which they have previously been exposed despite reporting no recollection of having ever seen that particular object (Zajonc 1986). Zajonc and Markus (1982) report evidence of a mere exposure effect for novel objects as innocuous as polygons, Chinese ideographs, photographs of faces, and tonal patterns.

Zajonc, Pietromonaco and Bargh (1982) report neurological evidence for an independence hypothesis based on the varying roles of each hemisphere of the brain in processing cognitions and emotions. The lateralized valence effect predicts better performance on recognition (cognitive) tasks among subjects when a visual shape is first presented to the right hemisphere but predicts greater preference when shapes are first presented to the left side of a brain. The basic premise of lateralized valence is that things processed on the left side of the brian are evaluated more positively. However, each study cited by Zajonc et al. (1982) involved only visual stimuli, and therefore, they suffer from a potential confounding factor.

Zajonc's work spawned numerous replies reasserting a role for cognition in emotional experiences. Lazarus (1982) reacted to the independence hypothesis by announcing the rediscovery of a recognition of emotions as a consequence of cognitions. He explains the full range of emotional experience as a sequence proceeding from (1) thoughts, to (2) action impulses, to (3) somatic disturbances. He criticizes Zajonc for mistaking rationality with cognition. In addition, empirical evidence supporting cognitive primacy is provided by Lazarus (1982) in an experiment showing that subjects' can react emotionally to a stimulus even if only a small part of it is recognized. Additionally, Lazarus (1975) demonstrates how emotional disorders can be cognitively controlled through self-regulation. A simple example would be a compulsive buyer tearing up their credit cards. Later evidence also supports cognitive treatment of emotional disorders (Brewin 1989).

Other authors appear critical of affective primacy or independence as well. Tsal (1985) replied to Zajonc and Markus (1982) by asserting that all affective reactions are affected by some form of cognitive representation, even though that representation may be less than conscious. Similarly, Plutchik (1983) argues that the first step in triggering an emotion is a belief that a stimulus is related to one's well being. This cognitive activity is followed by an action impulse. Similarly stated, emotion presupposes the existence of a cognition or evaluation and provides a basis for learning through S->R type models (Plutchik 1980). Likewise Weiner (1982) conceptualizes an attributional basis for affects and/or emotions involving a *cognitive* evaluation of a stimulus based on three dimensions of causation: locus, stability, and control.

Perhaps most poignant among retorts of the independence hypothesis is provided by Russell and Woudzia (1986). In this interesting paper, Zajonc is criticized for failing to provide his conceptualization of affect, but as he centered mostly on preferences, they assume affective judgments as a more precise term to describe Zajonc's affect. They also extract both a broad (affect always independent) and a narrow (in at least one case there is

independence) version of the independence hypothesis and provide substantial evidence against a broad version. For example, they point out that a mere exposure effect equates a lack of recognition with a total lack of memory and cognition. Empirical evidence demonstrating subjects' cued recall ability fails to substantiate this assumption (Tulving 1974). Similarly, this conjecture could be refuted by demonstrating an ability to retrieve information from sensory memory. Second, a mere exposure effect ignores evidence demonstrating that people form prototypes for unfamiliar stimuli which are elaborated to various degrees. Thus they conclude, cognitive processes other than familiarity and recognition can lead to affective judgments.

Other empirical evidence demonstrating a cognitive basis for a mere exposure effect exists. In an experiment involving Norwegian words as stimuli, Allen and Janiszewski (1989) demonstrate that an effect due to mere exposure depends upon subjects' contingency awareness. Similarly, Anand et al. (1988) show how affective evaluations in a mere exposure type experiment can be mediated by levels of uncertainty associated with an objects recognition. This study also provided evidence refuting a lateralized valence effect by demonstrating enhanced preference of verbal versus nonverbal stimuli when processed in an efficient manner (verbal to left hemisphere nonverbal to right hemisphere).

In response to criticisms like these, a weak form of the independence hypothesis was adapted. Zajonc and Markus (1985), in a reply to Tsal (1985) state, "we propose that there exist instances where affect is independent of cognitive influences" (p. 363). Using this form of their hypothesis, it would be necessary to show only one case of affective primacy to support the independence hypothesis. However, this proposition appears unfalsifiable on close inspection because it would be impossible to test every instantiation of affect. Thus, the weight of evidence appears to continue to support some relation between cognition and affect or emotion.

Distinguishing Cognition and Emotion

Increasingly, distinguishing between cognition and emotion (affect) is becoming difficult (Burke and Edell 1989). Kuhl (1986) describes how some cognitive psychologists now include emotions as nodes in propositional networks right along with other cognitive representations. In other instances, authors fail to draw a distinction between cognition and affect at all (Bower 1981; Mandler 1983). Kroonenberg and Snyder (1989), in an application of three-mode factor analysis, demonstrate how subjects consistently use both affective and cognitive factors (pleasant, complex, and interesting) to provide bases for problem solving. They conclude that affect and cognition are inseparable, although distinct. In the future, more applications involving emotion and affect as forms of information may be observed.

To conclude this section on the cognition-affect debate, several points can be summarized. First, it appears that a stronger conceptual and empirical argument can be made supporting an important and primary role for cognition in forming affective judgments and emotions. Second, emotion and cognition appear to have many similarities with a primary difference lying in each's relative latency and decay rate. Third, and most important, thought is probably never completely free of feeling and feeling is never completely free of thought (Lazarus 1982).

MEASUREMENT ISSUES

As mentioned earlier, emotion is multifaceted and difficult to define. One pervasive aspect of emotion is that it consists of both physiological and psychological components. Thus, any attempt to measure an emotion by virtue of only one component or the other would depend upon interrelationships between physiological and psychological aspects.

Psychobiological Measures

A division of brain functioning consisting of assignment of affective functions to the right brain and cognitive functions to the left has become increasingly popular (Ray and Batra 1983). As more is learned about psychobiology, such a division seems overly simplistic, and a substantial body of psychobiological evidence indicates that the physiology and psychology of emotion are inevitably intertwined.

For instance, a number of studies provide evidence of repression of certain emotions due to lesions in certain parts of the brain. For example, the amygdala forms hedonistic evaluations of information stored in the hippocampus. When the amygdala is damaged, people recognize physical features of objects, but are unable to place an hedonic value on it. Accordingly, it appears "the amygdala is more involved in emotional regulation and in converting sensory inputs into subjective feelings and directing behavior according to their hedonic value" (Fonberg 1986, p. 324). Likewise, lesions of the amygdala can lead to suppression of somatic and visceral displays, as well as autonomic processing (Kaada 1972). On the other hand, the neocortex appears to provide a capability to inhibit emotions (Fonberg 1984). As a consequence, a great deal of "irrational" thinking has been associated with a disproportionate influence of the amygdala over the neocortex.

Leading directly from this research are attempts to measure emotions based on activation of various portions of the brain. For example, Ekman, Davidson, and Friesen (1990) have recently demonstrated that smiles associated with true positive emotion, or joy (Duchenne Smile), appear to be associated with increased activation within the left anterior portion of the brain. In contrast, forced smiles, or smiles associated with less positive emotions,

appear to produce relatively more activity in the right anterior region. Kroeber-Riel (1979) provides an example of how arousal due to a marketing stimulus can be measured by activation within the brain as indicated electronically. He indicates that marketers are able to evoke increased levels of phasic activation (temporary disturbances), which can be measured, leading to increased energy expenditure while processing a stimulus (like a store window for example) (Kroeber-Riel 1980).

Somativisceral Measurements

A key advantage to psychobiological and somativisceral measurements of emotion is that these types of responses are relatively inescapable and ubiquitous (Cacioppo et al. 1986). Repressing a visceral display of joy or anger (turning red, heating up, etc.) is extremely difficult. Thus, physiological types of measures have an advantage in objectivity over various introspective techniques.

The most common visceral measure of emotion is based on observation of facial expressions. Ekman et al. (1971) have developed a scoring technique (FAST) which allows judges to reliably code emotional expressions of individuals as viewed on videotapes. FAST centers on various visceral indicants of emotion categories as displayed in one of three facial areas (top, middle, bottom). In the present study, three judges used FAST to accurately predict the emotion displayed in 45 out of 51 faces. Izard (1977) provides similar instruction on gaging emotions through facial expressions. More recently, the Emotional Measurement Service has employed facial expressions as scale indicators to judge consumer responses to advertising (*Marketing News* 1990). However, caution may need to be taken when using "modeled" rather than actual facial expressions as representations of emotion as Ekman et al. (1990) have demonstrated how electrically induced smiles, as well as other artificial smiles, differ from true smiles resulting from real emotion.

Psychobiological measurement alternatives such as these have lead some to criticize attempts to account for consumer hedonism and emotion through verbal methods (Hudson and Murray 1986). However, cognitive activity has also been shown to have physiological correlates. Jennings, Nebes, and Yovetich (1990) have demonstrated that increased heart-rates, galvanic skin responses, and other visceral measures can all be *cognitively* induced. Thus, many traditional cognitive variables may be subject to the same criticism as are self-reports of consumer emotion.

Verbal Reports

It is not surprising that self-reports of emotion would be subject to criticism. The validity of self-report measures of emotion suffer from problems due to language limitations, a possibility of deception, and difficulties dealing with parallel experiences of numerous emotions (Plutchik 1983). Considering these problems, does any justification exist for using verbal self-report measures of emotive states and experiences?

A number of studies provide evidence concerning the convergence of multiple methods of emotional measurement. The weight of the evidence concerning verbal reports indicates that they show substantial concomitance with psychobiological and somativisceral indicants of emotion (Ekman et al. 1971; Gaertner and Dovidioi 1977). Lazarus (1968) has previously studied the effectiveness of arousal manipulations and demonstrated that polygraph (GSR) measures correlated significantly with subjective reports of arousal. Ekman et al. (1990) has shown that left anterior brain activity, as measured with alpha power, is associated with smiles indicative of true positive emotions and subject self-reports of joy.

Clearly, in the best of all worlds, measures of emotions would include multiple devices including each type discussed above. However, the weight of empirical evidence tends to support self-report measures of emotions (Brewin 1989). At best, they correspond directly with physiological changes which accompany emotions, and at worst, they are "rough indices" of true emotions (Plutchik 1980). In addition, there are some relative advantages of verbal self-reports. For example, although psychobiological and somativisceral measures are difficult to argue with from an objective viewpoint, they suffer from several inherent disadvantages. Specifically, they are often obtrusive, expensive, and are not suffi-ciently developed to be indicative of any particular affective category (with the possible exception of facial expressions). In contrast, self-reports are relatively unobtrusive, inexpensive, and provide evidence of specific categories of emotional experience. Thus, until many of the shortcomings of physiological measures are overcome, verbal reports provide a suitable alternative in studying emotions (Ray and Batra 1983).

SUMMARY AND CONCLUSIONS

The amount of energy devoted to the study of emotions in consumer behavior is currently increasing in an attempt to make up for past neglect. However, many basic issues concerning emotions remain unresolved. Based on this brief review of emotion research, which can not possibly address every related topic area, a few suppositions can be made which are relevant to research into consumer emotion. These include:

* Affect is not synonymous with attitude.
* Emotion is a more encompassing term which can generally serve as a synonym for affect and mood.
* Emotions are evoked as the result of person-environment interactions.
* Emotions resulting from consumption experiences can be described along three basic dimensions (PAD).
* Emotions are a mediating variable, intervening between the person and subsequent actions.
* Emotions have a motivational component.
* Cognition and emotion are related concepts.
* Verbal measurements of emotion can be supported by previous research.

REFERENCES

Ahtola, Olli T. (1985), "Hedonic and Utilitarian Aspects of Consumer Behavior," in *Advances in Consumer Research*, Elizabeth Hirschman and Morris Holbrook eds. Ann Arbor, MI: ACR, 12.

Allen, Chris T. and Chris A. Janiszewski (1989), "Assessing the Role of Contingency Awareness in Attitudinal Conditioning with Implications for Advertising Research," *Journal of Marketing Research*, 26 (February), 30-43.

Anand, Punam, Morris B. Holbrook, and Debra Stephens (1988), "The Formation of Affective Judgments: The Cognitive-Affective Model Versus the Independence Hypothesis," *Journal of Consumer Research*, 15 (December), 386-391.

Anderson, Patricia M. (1986), "Personality, Perception and Emotional-State Factors in Approach-Avoidance Behavior in the Store Environment," in *Proceedings* of the American Marketing Association, Summer Educators Conference. Chicago, IL: American Marketing Association.

Anderson, Joan Kristen (1990), "Arousal and the In-verted-U Hypothesis: A Critique of Neiss's 'Reconceptualizing Arousal,'" *Psychological Bulletin*, 107 (1), 96-100.

Averill, J.R. (1975), "A Semantic Atlas of Emotional Concepts," *JSAS Catalog of Selected Documents in Psychology*, 5, 330.

Bagozzi, Richard P. (1982), "A Field Investigation of Causal Relations Among Cognitions, Affect, and Cognition," *Journal of Marketing Research*, 21 (November), 562-584.

Batra, Rajeev (1986), "Affective Advertising: Role, Processes, and Measurement," in *The Role of Affect in Consumer Behavior*, Robert A. Peterson, Wayne D. Hoyer, and William R. Wilson eds. Lexington, MA: Lexington Books.

Belk, Russell (1975), "Situational Variables and Consumer Behavior," *Journal of Consumer Research*, 2 (December), 157-164.

Bower, Gordon H. (1981), "Mood and Memory," *American Psychologist*, 36, 129-148.

_____ and Paul R. Cohen (1982), "Emotional Influences in Memory and Thinking: Data and Theory," in *Affect and Cognition*, Margaret S. Clark and

Susan T. Fiske, eds. Hillsdale, NJ: Lawrence Erlbaum Associates.

Brewin, Chris P. (1989), "Cognitive Change Processes in Psychotherapy," *Psychological Review*, 96 (3), 379-394.

Burke, Marian Chapman and Julie A. Edell (1989), "The Impact of Feelings on Ad-Based Affect and Cognition," *Journal of Marketing Research*, 26 (February), 69-83.

Bush, L. E. (1972), "Successive-Intervals Scaling of Adjectives Denoting Feelings," *JSAS Catalog of Selected Documents in Psychology*, 2, 140.

Cacioppo, John T., Mary E. Losch, Louis G. Tassinary, and Richard E. Petty (1986), "Properties of Affect and Affect-laden Information Processing As Viewed through the Facial Response System," in *The Role of Affect in Consumer Behavior*, Robert A. Peterson, Wayne D. Hoyer, and William R. Wilson eds. Lexingon, MA: Lexington Books.

_____ and Richard E. Petty (1989), "The Elaboration Likelihood Model: The Role of Affect and Affect-Laden Information Processing in Persuasion," in *Cognitive and Affective Responses to Advertising*, Patricia Cafferata and Alice M. Tybout eds., Lexington, MA: Lexington Books.

Cialdini, Robert B. and Jim Fultz (1990), "Interpreting the Negative Mood-Helping Literature via "Mega"-Analysis: A Contrary View," *Psychological Bulletin*, 107 (February), 210-4.

Cohen, Joel B. and Charles S. Areni (1991), "Affect and Consumer Behavior," in *Handbook of Consumer Theory and Research*, Thomas S. Robertson and Harold Kassarjin, eds. Englewood Cliffs, NJ: Prentice-Hall, 188-240.

Conte, Hope R. and Robert Plutchik (1981), "A Circumplex Model for Interpersonal Personality Traits," *Journal of Personality and Social Psychology*, 40 (April), 701-711.

Copeland, Melvin (1923), "What Motivates Consumers?" *Harvard Business Review*, 2 (October/July), 139-153.

Darwin, Charles (1872), *The Expression of the Emotions in Man and Animals*. Chicago, IL: University of Chicago Press.

Donovan, Robert J. and John R. Rossiter (1982), "Store Atmosphere: An Environmental Psychology Approach," *Journal of Retailing*, 58 (Spring), 34-57.

Ekman, Paul, Wallace V. Friesen, and Silvan S. Tomkins (1971), "Facial Affect Scoring Technique: A First Validity Study," *Semiotica*, 3 (1), 37-58.

_____, Wallace V. Friesen and Richard J. Davidson (1990), "The Duchenne Smile: Emotional Expressions and Brain Physiology II," *Journal of Personality and Social Psychology*, 58 (February), 342-353.

Ellis, Henry C. (1990), "Depressive Deficits in Memory: Processing Initiative and Resource Allocation," *Journal of Experimental Psychology: General*, 119 (January), 60-62.

Fehr, Beverley and James A. Russell (1984), "Concept of Emotion Viewed From a Prototype Perspective," *Journal of Personality and Social Psychology*, 113 (March), 464-486.

Fonberg, Elzbieta (1984), "Amygdala Functions Within the Alimentary System," *Acta Neurobiologica Experimentalis*, 34, 435-466.

_____ (1986), "Amygdala, Emotions, Motivation, and Depressive States," in *Emotion: Theory, Research, and Experience*, Robert Plutchik et al. eds. New York: Academic Press.

Gaertner, Samuel L. and John F. Dovidioi (1977), "The Subtlety of White Racism, Arousal, and Helping Behavior," *Journal of Personality and Social Psychology*, 35 (October), 691-707.

Gardner, Meryl Paula (1985), "Mood States and Consumer Behavior: A Critical Review," *Journal of Consumer Research*, 12 (December), 281-300.

Grossbart, Sanford L., Robert A. Mittelstaedt, William W. Curtis, and Robert D. Rogers (1975), "Environmental Sensitivity and Shopping Behavior," *Journal of Business Research*, 3 (October), 281-94.

_____, Douglas Amedeo, and David Chinchen (1979), "The Influence of Retail Environments on Customer Cognitions and Feelings," in *Proceedings of the Marketing Educators' Conference*, Beckwith et al. eds. Chicago: American Marketing Aassociation, 268-273.

Havlena, William J., Morris B. Holbrook, and Donald R. Lehmann (1989), "Assessing the Validity of Emotional Typologies," *Psychology and Marketing*, 6 (Summer), 97-112.

_____ and _____ (1986), "The Varieties of Consumption Experience: Comparing Two Typologies of Emotion in Consumer Behavior," *Journal of Consumer Research*, 13 (December), 394-404.

Hill, Ronald Paul and James C. Ward (1989), "Mood Manipulation in Marketing Research: An Examination of Potential Confounding Effects," *Journal of Marketing Research*, 26 (February), 97-104.

Hirschman, Elizabeth C. and Morris B. Holbrook (1982), "Hedonic Consumption: Emerging Concepts, Methods and Propositions," *Journal of Marketing*, 46 (Summer), 92-101

Holbrook, Morris B. and Elizabeth C. Hirschman (1982), "The Experiential Aspects of Consumption: Consumer Fantasies, Feelings, and Fun," *Journal of Consumer Research*, 9 (September), 132-140.

_____, Robert W. Chestnut, Terence A. Oliva, and Eric A. Greenleaf (1984), "Play as a Consumption Experience: The Roles of Emotions, Performance, and Personality in the Enjoyment of Games," *Journal of Consumer Research*, 11 (September), 728-739.

_____ (1986), "Emotion in the Consumption Experience: Toward a New Model of the Human Consumer," in *The Role of Affect in Consumer Behavior*,

Robert A. Peterson, Wayne D. Hoyer, and William R. Wilson eds. Lexington, MA: Lexington Books.

_____ and Rajeev Batra (1987), "Assessing the Role of Emotions as Mediators of Consumer Responses to Advertising," *Journal of Consumer Research,* 14 (December), 404-420.

_____ and Richard A. Westwood (1989), "The Role of Emotion in Advertising Revisited: Testing a Typology of Emotional Responses," in *Cognitive and Affective Responses to Advertising,* Patricia Cafferata and Alice M. Tybout eds. Lexington, MA: Lexington Books.

Hudson, Larel A. and Jeff B. Murray (1986), "Methodological Limitations of the Hedonic Consumption Paradigm and a Possible Alternative: A Subjectivist Approach," in *Advances in Consumer Research,* Vol. 13, Ann Harbor, MI: ACR.

Isen, Alice M. (1987), "Positive Affect, Cognitive Processes, and Social Behavior, in *Advances in Experimental Social Psychology,* L. Berkowitz ed. New York: Academic Press.

Ittleson, William H. (1973), "Environmental Perception and Contemporary Perceptual Theory," in *Environment and Cognition,* W.H. Ittelson, ed. New York: Seminar Press.

Izard, Carroll E. (1977), *Human Emotion.* New York: Plenum Press.

Jennings, J. Richard, Robert D. Nebes, and Nancy A. Yovetich (1990), "Aging Increases the Energetic Demands of Episodic Memory: A Cardiovascular Analysis," *Journal of Experimental Psychology: General,* 119 (January), 77-91.

Kaada, B.R. (1972), "Stimulation and Regional Ablation of the Amygdaloid Complex with Reference of Functional Representations," in *The Neurobiology of the Amygdala,* B.E. Eleftheriou, ed. New York: Plenum Press.

Kroeber-Riel, Werner (1979), "Activation Research: Psychobiological Approaches in Consumer Research," *Journal of Consumer Research,* 5 (March), 240-250.

Kroonenberg, Pieter M. and Conrad W. Snyder, Jr. (1989), "Individual Differences in Assimilation Resistance and Affective Responses in Problem Solving," *Multivariate Behavioral Research,* 24 (July), 257-284.

Kuhl, Julius (1986), "Motivation and Information Processing: A New Look at Decision Making, Dynamic Change, and Action Control," in *Handbook of Motivation and Cognition: Foundations of Social Behavior,* Richard M. Sorrentino and Tory Higgins, eds. New York: The Guilford Press.

Lazarus, Richard S. (1968), "The Principle of Shor-Circuiting of Threat: Further Evidence," *Journal of Personality,* 33, 622-635.

_____ (1975), "The Self-Regulation of Emotion," in *Emotions-Their Parameters and Measurement,* ed. Lennart Levi. New York: Raven Press.

_____ (1982), "Thoughts on the Relations Between Emotion and Cognition," *American Psychologist,* 37 (September), 1019-1024.

Mandler, George (1983), *Consciousness: Its Function and Construction.* LaJolla, CA: Center for Human Information Processing.

Marketing News (1990), "Ad-testing Technique Measures Emotions," 24 (April 16), 9.

Mehrabian, Albert and James A. Russell (1974), *An Approach to Environmental Psychology.* Cambridge, Massachusetts: MIT Press.

Mitchell, Andrew A. and Jerry C. Olson (1981), "Are Product Attribute Beliefs the Only Mediator of Advertising Effects on Brand Attitude?," *Journal of Marketing Research,* 28 (August), 318-332.

Olshavsky, Richard W. and Donald H. Granbois (1979), "Consumer Decision Making - Fact or Fiction," *Journal of Consumer Research,* 6 (September), 93-100.

Osgood, C., G. J. Suci, and P. Tannenbaum (1957), *The Measurement of Meaning.* Urbana, IL: University of Illinois Press.

Peterson, Robert A. and Matthew Sauber (1983), "A Mood Scale for Survey Research," in *Proceedings* of the American Marketing Association's Summer Educators Conference, Chicago: American Marketing Association.

Petty, Richard E., John T. Cacioppo, and David Schumann (1983), "Central and Peripheral Routes to Advertising Effectiveness: The Moderating Role of Involvement," *Journal of Consumer Research,* 10 (September), 135-146.

Plutchik, Robert (1980), "A General Psychoevolutionary Theory of Emotion," in *Emotion: Theory, Research, and Experience,* Robert Plutchik et al. eds. New York: Academic Press.

_____ (1983), "Emotions in Early Development: A Psychoevolutionary Approach," in *Emotion: Theory, Research, and Experience,* Robert Plutchik et al. eds., New York: Academic Press.

Ray, Michael L. and Rajeev Batra (1983), "Emotion and Persuasion in Advertising: What We Do and Don't Know About Affect," in *Advances in Consumer Research,* Vol. 9, R. P. Bagozzi and A. M. Tybout eds. Ann Harbor, MI: ACR.

Russell, James A. (1978), "Evidence of Convergent Validity on the Dimensions of Affect," *Journal of Personality and Social Psychology,* 36 (October), 1152- 1168.

_____ (1983), "Pancultural Aspects of the Human Conceptual Organization of Emotions," *Journal of Personality and Social Psychology,* 45 (June), 1281-1288.

_____ and Lisa Woudzia (1986), "Affective Judgments, Common Sense, and Zajonc's Thesis of Independence," *Motivation and Emotion,* 10 (2), 169- 183.

_____ and Jacalyn Snodgrass (1987), "Emotion

and the Environment," in *Handbook of Environmental Psychology,* D. Stokols and I. Altman eds. New York: John Wiley and Sons, 245-280.

Sheth, Jagdish N. (1983), "An Integrative Theory of Patronage Preference and Behavior," in *Retail Management and Patronage Behavior,* W. R. Darden and R. Lusch eds. New York: Elsevier Science, 9-28.

Swanson, Gue E. (1983), "Travels Through Inner Space: Family Structure and Openness to Absorbing Experiences," *American Journal of Sociology,* 83 (4), 890-919.

Tsal, Yehoshua (1985), "On the Relationship Between Cognitive and Affective Processes: A Critique of Zajonc and Markus," *Journal of Consumer Research,* 12 (December), 358-362.

Tulving, Endel (1974), "Cue-Dependent Forgetting," *American Scientist,* 62, 74-82.

Weiner, Bernard (1982), "The Emotional Consequences of Causal Attributions," in *Affect and Cognition,* Margaret S. Clark and Susan T. Fiske, eds. Hillsdale, NJ: Lawrence Erlebaum Associates.

Westbrook, Robert A. (1980), "Intrapersonal Affective Influences on Consumer Satisfaction with Products," *Journal of Consumer Research,* 7 (June), 49-54.

_____ (1987), "Product/Consumption-Based Affective Responses and Postpurchase Processes," *Journal of Marketing Research,* 24 (August), 258- 70.

Winton, Ward M., Lois E. Putnam, and Robert M. Krauss (1984), "Facial and Autonomic Manifestations of the Dimensional Structure of Emotion," *Journal of Experimental and Social Psychology,* 20 (May), 195-216.

Zajonc, Robert B. (1980), "Feeling and Thinking: Preferences Need No Inferences," *American Psychologist,* 35 (2), 151-175.

_____, Paula Pietromonaco and John Bargh (1982), "Independence and Interaction of Affect and Cognition," in *Affect and Cognition,* M. S. Clark and S. T. Fiske, eds. Hillsdale: Lawrence Erlbaum Associates.

_____ and Hazel Markus (1982), "Affective and Cognitive Factors in Preferences," *Journal of Consumer Research,* 12 (December), 363-364.

_____ and _____ (1985), "Must All Affect Be Mediated By Cognition?," *Journal of Consumer Research,* 12 (December), 363-4.

_____ (1986), "Basic Mechanisms of Preference Formation," in *The Role of Affect in Consumer Behavior,* Robert A. Peterson, Wayne D. Hoyer, and William R. Wilson eds. Lexington, MA: Lexington Books.

ASSESSING THE ROLE OF GUILT IN SERVICE MARKETING EVALUATIONS

Claire Bolfing, James Madison University
Andrew M. Forman, Hofstra University

ABSTRACT

The study examines the role of guilt in consumer evaluations of on-going service relationships. Two forms of guilt, self-induced and marketer-induced, are studied from the standpoint of their relationship to each other and their impact on satisfaction evaluations of the overall service and with the service provider. The results indicate that each of the two forms of guilt impacts on consumer evaluations albeit in a manner independent of one another. Marketer-induced guilt affected consumer evaluation with the service itself, whereas self-induced guilt impacted on evaluations of the service provider. Implications for marketing marketing researchers and practitioners are discussed.

INTRODUCTION

The ability of consumers to develop complex pre- and post-purchase consumption evaluations is widely accepted. Indeed, the emphasis on creating customer satisfaction as a competitive strategy highlights the importance industry places on the understanding and influence of consumer evaluations. In order to more fully understand these evaluation processes, research on evaluation models has broadened to include many antecedent constructs that can affect the development of customer satisfaction. In general, studies have focused on antecedent states that are traditional information processing constructs and are cognitive mediators of evaluation differences. There is growing recognition, however, of the importance of emotional or affective responses as major contributors to consumption evaluations (Cohen and Areni 1991; Gardner 1985; Holbrook et al. 1984; Westbrook 1980, 1983, 1987; Westbrook and Oliver 1991). Questions regarding which affects or feelings are most influential and the nature of the relationships between feelings and evaluation constructs attest to the importance of relevant conceptualizations. Even more problematic is the recognition that product and service evaluations may necessitate unique affect-evaluation models for these consumption experiences (Czepiel 1990; Zeithaml, Parasuraman, and Berry 1985; Zeithaml, Berry, and Parasuraman 1988). Most of the studies just listed on antecedent states focus on product/brand evaluations, so there is little research on affect in service strategies. The growth of the services section presents a need and offers an opportunity to test affect relationships across many different service encounters.

Many service encounters are ongoing relationships, where consumers and service providers build and maintain interactions to achieve long-term benefits. Repeated encounters cement the personal and professional bonds between service provider and client (Czepiel 1990). More importantly, if these relationships require the active participation of the customer, e.g. patient-dentist visits and weight loss programs, the service delivery requires that the service provider and client depend on each other to make the service experience a positive one. The customer's evaluation of this experience is likely to be built on both cognitive and affective phenomena, since ongoing co-dependent encounters require trust and an "opening up" to each other that transcends mere functional evaluations (Dwyer, Schurr, and Oh 1987).

This provider-client co-dependency obviously can generate strong feelings of trust, happiness, etc. But there may be negative affective repercussions to these relationships as well. When consumers are expected to actively participate in a service delivery, such as performing ongoing dental hygiene and maintaining dietary or exercise programs, their failure to do so can create guilt and anxiety. Guilt over their own shortcomings may impact seriously customer evaluations of the service provider, the service experience, and the outcomes from a satisfactory or dissatisfactory evaluation.

The concept of guilt has long been dominant in such diverse fields as theology, philosophy, and counseling and psychiatry -- disciplines in which guilt and guilt arousal are viewed as effective agents of attitude and behavior change (Stein 1968). Only recently have marketing researchers begun to examine guilt's effectiveness in marketing strategies (Bozinoff and Ghingold 1983; Lascu 1991). The purpose of this article is threefold. First, we review the formation of guilt in ongoing service encounters and present a conceptual framework for the inclusion of guilt in evaluation processes. Then, we investigate the extent of guilt and its relationship to post-consumption constructs, namely satisfaction and behavioral outcomes, in a service encounter where "customers" must contribute to the delivery or reception of the desired service experience. Finally, implications are discussed for better conceptualizations of constructs and for more sophisticated analyses in service environments.

CONCEPTUAL BACKGROUND

The Nature of Guilt

Guilt is one of many affective states that are common to the human experience. A typical list of feeling states includes shame, guilt, surprise, joy, distress, disgust, fear, anger, contempt, and interest (Izard 1977). This short list of feeling states indicates that there are both positive and negative affects influencing human processes.

Guilt is defined as the feeling that one has violated some rule of conduct to which one attaches value (Miller 1985). Guilt requires not only a perception that one has violated the moral order, but also the taking of responsibility for that violation, with the understanding that one *could and should have* done something differently to keep the violation from having occurred (Frijda 1986; Lindsay-Hartz 1984). The transgression can create concern because the violation is perceived as disturbing the sense of equity with others or with the self (Izard 1977).

The creation of guilt does not presuppose that rational assessment of one's actions was undertaken. One may feel profoundly guilty and thus responsible for a wish, a feeling, or an action even though objectively, there was no possibility of personal control. All that is required is the feeling -- not the rational evaluation -- that one could have done differently had one wished to do so.

There is general agreement that all positive and negative affect states may vary in stability, specificity, and intensity (For review, see Gardner 1985; Isen 1984; Westbrook 1980). A general feeling or affect is characterized as a consciously experienced, stable, subjective state, either personality traits or ongoing feelings toward concepts (Westbrook 1987). A mood is transient, particularized to a specific time and situation, and may or may not be consciously experienced (Gardner 1985). An emotion is an intense, conscious, attention-getting personal affect (Westbrook and Oliver 1991).

Several researchers contend that guilt may fall into more than one of the above affect categories (Ghingold 1980; Miller 1985; Mosher 1980; Otterbacher and Munz 1973). Consider the case where an individual seems to feel perennially guilty. This person may go through life assuming responsibility for all manner of shortcomings. On the other hand, specific consumption occasions can lead to guilt feelings which can be quite strong but of limited duration. Otterbacher and Munz (1973) label the general and transient guilt feelings G-Trait and G-State, respectively, while Ghingold (1980) identifies the two guilt categories as inherent guilt and aroused guilt, respectively.

Lascu (1991) develops a number of propositions which elaborate on the differences as well as relationships between inherent and aroused guilt. Inherent guilt is self-induced, and reflects a tendency for self blame. True, marketing communications can contribute to inherent guilt, but these messages are assimilated into prior experience and used accordingly to influence a consumer's propensity to attach self-blame to a future undesirable consumption experience. Aroused guilt is marketer-induced and represents immediate communications during

a consumption experience. Marketer-induced feelings are the results of strategic and tactical marketing actions that occur at the point-of-purchase or service delivery. A setting is created, a procedure is initiated or an interaction is controlled that tells the customer in some fashion that she/he has failed to fulfill the customer role in an ongoing service encounter. The service provider thus is able to evoke an affective response or mood because of the marketing action.

In addition, marketer-induced or aroused guilt and pre-existing, inherent guilt states may interact. Lascu (1991) hypothesizes that individuals who tend to attach self-blame easily are more influenced by marketer-induced guilt messages and thus, will exhibit more pronounced attitudinal and behavioral changes than individuals who do not have high levels of inherent guilt. Certainly, the roles of both guilt constructs need to be examined in an evaluation process model of ongoing service encounters. The next sections describe selected evaluation constructs and hypothesized guilt effects on these constructs.

Guilt and Usage Evaluation Concepts

Guilt and Pre-usage performance norms. Consumers quickly learn to script service encounters as a mechanism for anticipating what actions will occur, the order in which the actions will take place, the role of the service provider who performs the actions, and the setting in which the event unfolds (Smith and Houston 1983; Solomon et al. 1985). Thus, all aspects of the consumption experience, e.g., players, occasions, setting, etc., comprise this "cognitive script." Scripts are particularly useful in service encounters, given the variability of service experiences. The scripts based on experience across a number of service encounters give a better feel for what should be occurring in a particular service encounter. These scripts are the conceptual equivalent of the experience-based performance norm construct in the Woodruff, Cadotte, and Jenkins (1983) evaluation model.

Additionally, the service provider has expectations regarding actions on the part of the client. These expectations of client performance may be extremely relevant to successful service delivery. Expectations may refer to behavior during the service encounter (e.g., sitting still in the dentist chair, with mouth opened wide) or behaviors that were to have occurred between encounters (e.g., practicing prescribed dental hygiene measures). The customer learns from previous interpersonal encounters that failure to conform to prescribed behaviors can evoke personal feelings of guilt.

Two issues are of concern here. First, the customer is capable of using self-induced or inherent guilt to shape any subsequent pre-usage performance norms, which in turn can be used as standards for evaluating the post-usage service performance. Second, marketer-controlled guilt is unlikely to have any effect on normative standards, given the timing of the delivered marketing communication. Performance norms are composites of all the learning that has preceded the evaluation process in question, so it is not possible for an immediate marketing tactic to affect this construct to any great extent.

Guilt and Post-usage Evaluations

Following service delivery and consumption, customers evaluate the service experience in comparison to the evaluative standard. Disconfirmation beliefs produce satisfaction judgements, which in turn influence behavioral intentions and post-usage actions, such as complaining/complimenting. The simultaneous production and consumption of a service experience suggests that services must be conceptualized as the interaction of actors (service personnel), customers, and the service environment (Bitner 1990; Garland and Westbrook 1989; Surprenant and Solomon 1987). Consequently, pre- and post-usage performance beliefs are multiattribute in nature to capture the diverse elements at work in a service experience.

There is growing support for the creation of satisfaction judgements based on consumption-related affective responses, e.g. guilt, joy, surprise, etc., and disconfirmation beliefs (Westbrook 1987; Westbrook and Oliver 1991). Moreover, satisfaction implies a hedonic continuum ranging from a terrible experience to a delightful event, and is usually conceptualized as an affective, situation-specific evaluation (Oliver 1981; Westbrook and Oliver 1991; Woodruff, Cadotte, and Jenkins 1983). Following satisfaction, outcomes such as post-usage brand/service attitudes, behavioral intentions, and overt actions are likely to occur.

A growing body of literature now indicates that affective states, including guilt, can influence thoughts, cognitive processing, and social behavior (Isen 1984). Marketing studies report a direct relationship between positive and negative feelings and subsequent shifts in affective and cognitive evaluations (Axelrod 1963; Westbrook 1980, 1983, 1987; Westbrook and Oliver 1991). The Westbrook studies used both stable and transient negative affect states as precursors of attitudinal, cognitive, and behavioral change.

When guilt for failure to uphold a service role is high, whether self-induced or marketer-induced, the client can counterbalance the guilt by adjusting the evaluation of the service provider and the overall service experience downwards. This denial mechanism tries to shift some of the blame from the client to the service provider, i.e., counterarguing, so the client does not feel overwhelmed by the transgression. The result is likely to be more negative beliefs and attitudes about the service provider and aspects of the service delivery, as well as refusal to follow behavior modification recommendations for the

future. The ultimate outcome possibility in the face of denial may be a strong disinclination to use that service provider again or to recommend either the provider or the service experience to others in the future.

Research Questions

This research will attempt to explore two questions dealing with guilt and the ongoing service encounter evaluation. First, are there two sources of guilt, inherent or self-induced guilt and aroused or marketer-induced guilt, which can affect the interactions between service providers and clients of ongoing service experiences? Second, do the two types of guilt create negative judgments for post-usage satisfaction and behavioral intentions?

METHODOLOGY

The research design for this study was a field experiment using students enrolled in several sections of a marketing management course at a mid-sized northeastern university. Classes were randomly assigned in a 2 (marketer-induced guilt or MIG) X 2 (self-induced guilt or SIG) between-subjects design. A total of 168 students participated in the experiment. Students were upper classman (junior and senior undergraduates) and represented a cross-section of business administration majors. The course was required for all students participating in the study. Virtually all students agreed to participate, but due to absences during the follow-up phases, the usable sample consisted of 155 subjects.

Procedure

Given the nature of the experimental design, whereby students were given different messages about their effort to induce guilt and the instructor was subsequently evaluated following these manipulations, permission from university administration for this test was crucial. Many of the questions regarding instructor/course performance were patterned after the course evaluation instrument typically used for teacher evaluations. Subjects completed three questionnaires during the semester, the first administered early in the semester, the second approximately halfway through the course, and the third two weeks before the end of the term. Students' identities were closely guarded and kept from the instructor by having each subject write down an identification code in his/her notebook and then using only this code on the three questionnaires.

The first questionnaire measured: (1) students' performance norms regarding course dimensions, the instructor, and the usefulness/worth of the course overall[1]; (2) the independent variable SIG; and (3) some basic student demographics. Over the next few weeks, students in the MIG group heard several communications from the instructor on their failure to prepare adequately for the course, while students in the control group did not hear any overly harsh criticisms regarding preparation and effort expended in the course. The second questionnaire again measured SIG and students' post-consumption performance ratings for the instructor and course. In addition, they completed other questions on the existence of MIG (manipulation check), the dependent measures of satisfaction feelings about the instructor and the course, and demographics. The third questionnaire repeated the questions from the second instrument and also assessed some dependent measures of behavioral outcomes. Upon completion of the third questionnaire the subjects were debriefed regarding the nature of the study. Additionally, they were informed that they could obtain a summary of the findings, upon request.

Independent Variables

As mentioned, students either heard strong criticisms of the amount of effort they were expending in the class, thus creating a sense of failure on their part to contribute to the service experience, or they received no unusually strong messages of violation of rules of conduct. These communications (or lack thereof) represented marketer-induced guilt. Self-induced guilt, a stable affective trait, could not be manipulated but instead was measured as a general and consistent inner predisposition or trait of responding with a class of behaviors which may be described as guilty (Mosher 1980).

We wish to review the construction of guilt scales for MIG and SIG that will serve as manipulation checks at this point. Scale construction was based on past scale development efforts (Bozinoff and Ghingold 1983; Haefner 1956; Mosher 1980; Otterbacher and Munz 1973). A series of semantic differential scales describing how subjects felt about their preparation and readiness <u>at the moment for this particular marketing class</u> were used to convey marketer-induced guilt. Students answered 21 sets of five-point, bipolar adjectives in all; however, some scales were included for discriminant validity. Self-induced guilt was measured as agreement with statements describing one's concern about accountability <u>for school preparation in general</u>.

Dependent Measures

Satisfaction feelings toward both the instructor and toward the course overall were measured using five-point, emotional/affective, bipolar rating scales (derived from Cadotte, Woodruff, and Jenkins 1987). identical seven-item satisfaction inventories were used for both and consisted of the following bipolar sets: happy-unhappy, delighted-terrible, relaxed-tense, pleased-troubled, calm-nervous, content-frustrated, and satisfied-dissatisfied (recoded for directional consistency). Subjects indicated their likelihood of recommending both the course and the instructor (behavioral outcomes) using single-item, five-interval, bipolar rating scales (very likely-very

unlikely). All four dependent measures were coded with high scores indicating less satisfaction and less positive future behavior with respect to the instructor and the overall course.

RESULTS

Three questionnaires were needed to measure all antecedent and evaluation constructs in sequence over the course of this experiment, but some variables, e.g. self-induced guilt, marketer-induced manipulations, and instructor and course satisfaction were included in more than one instrument. First, a repeated measures test for any change in the above variables was conducted. There were no significant differences in students' consecutive scores for SIG, MIG, and satisfaction feelings. Thus, this study will report only the scores from the third questionnaire for all variables of interest.

Validation of Constructs

The measurement scales were subjected to several tests to assess their quality. First, the multi-item measures were evaluated for unidimensionality with the use of a principal component factor analysis. In the case of each scale, only one factor could be extracted, providing evidence of unidimensionality. Secondly, Cronbach alpha reliability values indicated all scales were reliable (all α's > 0.70).

Sample Equivalence and Manipulation Checks

The two groups were first examined to ensure equivalence. In terms of demographic backgrounds, an examination of the results of chi-square analyses revealed no significant differences in gender, class year, or major. A t-test reveled no significant differences based on grade-point average. Importantly, no differences were found in the level of SIG across the two experimental groups. Hence, there is no reason to believe that any differences ultimately found were due to pre-existing systematic variation between the groups.

Subjects exposed to marketer-induced guilt messages were expected to record more guilt with respect to this specific marketing course than those who did not receive performance criticism. In keeping with this, MIG subjects ($x = 2.35$) reported different guilt levels (t = 2.63, p < .0.01; d.f.=109) than the control group ($x = 2.65$).

Subjects were assigned to one of two groups based on their score on the self-induced guilt scale. Those scoring in the top one-third were designated as a "high-guilt" group, while those in the bottom third were classified as belonging to a "low-guilt" group. Thus, subjects can be categorized or segmented by their amount of inherent guilt. The next section reviews whether or not these guilt conditions mediate the evaluation process.

Guilt and Service Evaluation Relationships

The research questions were addressed with the use of an Analysis of Variance procedure. The results indicate an across-the-board absence of a significant interaction between MIG and SIG, in apparent contradiction to the relationship hypothesized by Lascu (1991). The results of the ANOVA are presented in Table 1. Group means and standard deviations are presented in Table 2.

In terms of the main effects, the ANOVA results reveal that subjects in the high MIG group did, indeed, indicate significantly lower levels of satisfaction with the course (F = 2.70; p < 0.05), and were less likely to recommend the course to others (F = 3.87; p < 0.05) than their counterparts in the low MIG group. They were, however, apparently unaffected in their evaluations of the service provider. No significant differences were uncovered in the satisfaction levels or willingness to recommend the instructor to others.

On the other hand, subjects that possessed a high level of SIG expressed lower levels of satisfaction with the instructor (F = 2.70; p < 0.05) and were less likely to recommend the instructor to others (F = 3.99; p < 0.01). Here, however, their evaluations of the overall course was not affected. No significant differences were found between the high and low SIG groups in their expressed satisfaction with the course or their willingness to recommend the course to others.

Overall, the results indicate that MIG and SIG do not significantly interact. Furthermore, they seem to play very different roles in the consumer post-use evaluation process. Whereas MIG impacts on satisfaction with the only the service itself, SIG seemingly affects only the evaluation of the service provider.

DISCUSSION

As an initial attempt to relate the negative affect guilt to service encounters requiring both service provider and client activity, this study suggests that guilt does have the ability to affect post-consumption evaluation judgements. Some possible limitations of the study should be noted, however. The sample consisted of undergraduate students whose evaluation reactions might not generalize to other groups of customers. Second, guilt conceptualizations in the marketing discipline are fairly novel and there is limited information on construct measurement. More research is needed on guilt construct validation and comparisons between various measures is urgent. In fact, different measures may yield different patterns and relationships to evaluation judgments. Finally, it is important to reiterate that this study deals only with <u>ongoing</u> service relationships.

Nevertheless, there is evidence that guilt may take two different forms -- an inherent, self-induced and more long-lived trait form as well as a situation-specific, marketer-induced, transitory pattern. Service clients can bring guilt "baggage" to a service interaction and they can respond to more immediate criticisms of failure to meet service expectations. Service providers must be aware of the nature of guilt, and they need to distinguish between the impact of antecedent levels of inherent guilt and their own ability to create guilt on the spot. Each guilt form plays a different role in service evaluations.

For the most part, marketer-induced guilt played little role in the determination of more negative post-consumption evaluation decisions. Only satisfaction judgments regarding the overall course were affected negatively by service provider rebukes. Judgments about the service provider or instructor and intentions to recommend the instructor and even the course to others were not seriously eroded. There are several possible reasons for this limited influence. One rationale for this selective effect may be that customers will not give up on all aspects of a service experience just because they are "taken to task." They received an unacceptable level of service delivery (hence the negative course judgments) but they also know that they have not held up the client end of the service encounter and so must accept the consequences. The customer (a student in this study) is to blame, not the service provider. In fact, the customer may feel that the service provider was right all along and become more attentive to his/her role in the service experience. Ultimately, satisfactory evaluations of the service provider (here, the instructor) remain intact and the client is still in favor of recommending the provider and the service experience to others.

Consider a weight loss program experience. Weight loss clinics operate on the notion that clients will lose a certain number of pounds each week by following a specified regimen. Marketer-induced guilt messages during weigh-ins at which no progress has been shown can motivate better performance in subsequent weeks and even create better evaluations of the clinic operators who must have been correct in their assessment of weight loss dynamics. The tendency would be to spread the news of the providers' expertise and the program's efficacy to others.

Service strategies can take advantage of the above findings. If service firms offering ongoing service encounters can use internal marketing to expertly staff and train service providers, these providers in turn gain credibility, establish customer loyalty, and have the ability to make themselves the service experience. With this strength, providers can use more powerful guilt messages during service delivery to influence client behavior and still reap future business.

Bozinoff and Ghingold (1983) propose a second rationale for limited marketer-induced guilt influence.

TABLE 1
ANOVA Results

Source of Variation	Adjusted SS	df	MS	F
Instructor Satisfaction				
MIG	0.22	1	0.22	0.43
SIG	2.73	2	1.38	2.70[a]
2-Way Interaction	0.25	2	0.12	0.24
Residual	52.25	103	0.51	
Course Satisfaction				
MIG	1.69	1	1.69	3.02[a]
SIG	1.71	2	0.86	1.54
2-Way Interaction	0.88	2	0.44	0.79
Residual	57.57	103	0.56	
Recommend Course				
MIG	0.83	1	0.83	0.75
SIG	8.55	2	4.28	3.87[a]
2-Way Interaction	2.80	2	1.40	1.27
Residual	113.73	103	1.10	
Recommend Instructor				
MIG	0.20	1	0.20	0.18
SIG	9.05	2	4.53	3.99[b]
2-Way Interaction	2.51	2	1.26	1.11
Residual	116.76	103	1.13	

N.B. all main effect probabilities are based on one-tail tests
[a] $p < 0.05$
[b] $p < 0.01$

TABLE 2
Group Means[a] and Standard Deviations By Treatment Condition

Measure	Low MIG n=65		High MIG n=103	
	Low SIG n=18	High SIG n=22	Low SIG n=33	High SIG n=35
Instructor Satisfaction	3.55 (0.55)	3.94 (0.79)	3.49 (0.73)	3.93 (0.76)
Course Satisfaction	3.36 (0.62)	3.98 (0.85)	3.44 (0.83)	3.57 (0.77)
Instructor Recommendation	2.63 (1.41)	1.43 (0.90)	2.23 (1.31)	1.71 (1.06)
Course Recommendation	2.25 (1.16)	1.74 (1.25)	2.27 (1.28)	1.33 (0.66)

[a] Items reverse scored

They suggest that it may be unrealistic to expect a brief, even single presentation of a guilt arousing communication to have an effect on attitudes and intentions. However, the procedure in this study did not limit the MIG manipulation to a single communication. The instructor gave repeated reminders of the students' shortfalls. This rationale may be true for some experimental procedures, but MIG probably had the potential for more influence in this study, and yet little change was evoked.

A more serious reason for limited MIG influence is the possibility that mood manipulation created a confound which obfuscated the true relationship between aroused guilt and service evaluation. Hill and Ward (1989) suggest that both success and failure mood manipulations contribute to the confound of self-efficacy. In our study, the instructor's guilt messages may have reduced subjects' willingness to believe they have the ability to achieve desired results. If students do not feel strongly about their role in the learning process, they will have lower levels of perceived guilt and thus less negative service evaluations. More research is needed on the use of failure in mood manipulations to assess the threat of a self-efficacy confound.

Self-induced guilt or inherent guilt was much more influential in the determination of satisfaction feelings and word-of-mouth communications. Whenever students registered high SIG, they gave less favorable satisfaction ratings to the instructor and felt more disinclined to recommend the course or the instructor than students with low SIG. SIG poses a serious threat, therefore, to service providers and future business. Service providers must learn how to "read" their customers early in a service interaction to know if clients tend toward self-blame. These negative and persistent feelings color every aspect of a service evaluation. While marketers obviously cannot control levels of SIG in their consumers, future research should seek to uncover effective strategic means by which marketers can accommodate high-guilt consumers and can attenuate the impact of their self-induced guilt on service provider evaluations. As one suggestion, service providers may be able to provide education early in an interaction to redirect these customers' attribution tendencies.

For ongoing service experiences where customers must play an active part, the message is clear. Guilt arousal can be an effective strategy, but persistent guilty feelings cloud all judgments. Service marketers must be careful when trying to build marketing strategies around this negative affect.

ENDNOTE

[1] Performance norms were assessed with a series of 7-point scales that asked subjects about their bases for comparison for judging this course. The scale ranged from the best course they have had or could imagine to the worst course they have had or could imagine.

REFERENCES

Axelrod, Joel N. (1963), "Induced Moods and Attitudes Towards Products," *Journal of Advertising Research,* 3, 19-24.

Bitner, Mary Jo (1990), "Evaluating Service Encounters: The Effects of Physical Surroundings and Employee Responses," *Journal of Marketing,* 54 (April), 69-82.

Bozinoff, Lorne and Morry Ghingold (1983), "Evaluating Guilt Arousing Marketing Communications," *Journal of Business Research,* 11, 243-255.

Cadotte, Ernest R., Robert B. Woodruff, and Roger L. Jenkins (1987), "Expectations and Norms in Models of Consumer Satisfaction," *Journal of Marketing Research,* 24 (August), 305-314.

Cohen, Joel B. and Charles S. Areni (1991), "Affect and Consumer Behavior," in *Handbook of Consumer Theory and Research,* Thomas S. Robertson and Harold H. Kassarjian, eds. Englewood Cliffs, NJ: Prentice-Hall, 188-240.

Czepiel, John A. (1990), "Service Encounters and Service Relationships: Implications for Research," *Journal of Business Research,* 20, 18-21.

Dwyer, F. Robert, Paul H. Schurr, and Sejo Oh (1987), "Developing Buyer-Seller Relationships, *Journal of Marketing,* 51 (April), 11-27.

Frijda, Nico H. (1986), *The Emotions.* Cambridge, England: Cambridge University Press.

Gardner, Meryl P. (1985), "Mood States and Consumer Behavior: A Critical Review," *Journal of Consumer Research,* 12 (December), 281-300.

Garland, Barbara C. and Robert A. Westbrook (1989), "An Exploration of Client Satisfaction in a Nonprofit Context," *Journal of the Academy of Marketing Science,* 17 (Fall), 297-303.

Ghingold, Morry (1980), "Guilt Arousing Marketing Communications: An Unexplored Variable, "in *Advances in Consumer Research,* Vol. VIII, Kent Monroe, ed. Ann Arbor, MI: Association for Consumer Research, 442-448.

Haefner, D. P. (1956), "Some Effects of Guilt Arousing and Fear Arousing Communications on Opinion Change," unpublished technical report.

Hill, Ronald Paul and James C. Ward (1989), "Mood Manipulation in Marketing Research: An Examination of Potential Confounding Effects," *Journal of Marketing Research,* 26 (February), 97-104.

Holbrook, Morris, B., Robert W. Chestnut, Terence A. Oliva, and Eric A. Greenleaf (1984), "Play as a Consumption Experience: The Roles of Emotion, Performance and Personality in the Enjoyment of Games," *Journal of Consumer Research,* 11 (September), 728-739.

Isen, Alice M. (1984), "Toward Understanding the Role of Affect in Cognition," in *Handbook of Social Cognition,* Robert S. Wyer and Thomas K. Srull, eds., Hillsdale, NJ: Lawrence Erlbaum Associates, 179-236.

Izard, Carroll E. (1977), *Human Emotions.* New York: Plenum Press.

Lascu, Dana-Nicoleta (1991), "Consumer Guilt: Examining the Potential of a New Consumer Construct," in *Advances in Consumer Research,* Vol. XVII, Rebecca H. Holman and Michael R. Solomon, eds., Ann Arbor, MI: Association for Consumer Research, 290-295.

Lindsay-Hartz, Janice (1984), "Contrasting Experiences of Shame and Guilt," *American Behavioral Scientist,* 27 (July/August), 689-704.

Miller, Susan (1985), *The Shame Experience.* Hillsdale, NJ: The Analytic Press.

Mosher, Donald L. (1980), "Guilt," in *Encyclopaedia of Clinical Assessment,* R. H. Woody, ed., Washington, DC: Bass, 602-613.

Oliver, Richard L. (1981), "Measurement and Evaluation of Satisfaction Processes in Retail Settings," *Journal of Retailing,* 57 (Fall), 25-48.

Otterbacher, John R. and David C. Munz (1973), "State-Trait Measure of Experiential Guilt," *Journal of Consulting and Clinical Psychology,* 40, 115-121.

Smith, Ruth A. and Michael J. Houston (1983), "Script-Based Evaluations of Satisfaction with Services," in *Emerging Perspectives in Services Marketing,* Leonard L. Berry, G. Lynn Shostack, and Gregory D. Upah, eds. Chicago: American Marketing Association, 59-62.

Solomon, Michael R., Carol Surprenant, John A. Czepiel, and Evelyn G. Gutman (1985), "A Role Theory Perspective on Dyadic Interactions: The Service Encounter," *Journal of Marketing,* 49 (Winter), 99-111.

Stein, E. V. (1968), *Guilt: Theory and Therapy.* Philadelphia: The Westminster Press.

Surprenant, Carol F. and Michael R. Solomon (1987), "Predictability and Personalization in the Services Encounter," *Journal of Marketing,* 51 (April), 86-96.

Westbrook, Robert A. (1980), "Intrapersonal Affective Influences Upon Consumer Satisfaction," *Journal of Consumer Research,* 7 (June), 49-54.

_____ (1983), "Consumer Satisfaction and the Phenomenology of Emotions During Automobile Ownership Experiences," in *International Fare in Consumer Satisfaction and Complaining Behavior,* Ralph L. Day and H. Keith Hunt, eds. Bloomington, IN: Indiana University, 2-9.

_____ (1987), "Product/Consumption-Based Affective Responses and Postpurchase Processes," *Journal of Marketing Research,* 24 (August), 258-270.

_____ and Richard L. Oliver (1991), "The Dimensionality of Consumption Emotion Patterns and Consumer Satisfaction," *Journal of Consumer Research,* 18 (June), 84-91.

Woodruff, Robert B., Ernest R. Cadotte, and Roger L. Jenkins (1983), "Modeling Consumer Satisfaction Processes Using Experience-Based Norms," *Journal of Marketing Research,* 20 (August), 296-304.

Zeithaml, Valarie A., A. Parasuraman, and Leonard L. Berry (1985), "Problems and Strategies in Services Marketing," *Journal of Marketing,* 49 (Spring), 33-46.

_____, Leonard L. Berry and A. Parasuraman (1988), "Communication and Control Processes in the Delivery of Service Quality," *Journal of Marketing,* 52 (April), 35-48.

MOOD STATES AND CONSUMER COMPLAINT BEHAVIORS

Ved Prakash, Morgan State University

ABSTRACT

Although the effects of mood states have been studied in a variety of contexts, as yet no specific studies have been published on their effects on a particular aspect of post-purchase evaluation i.e. consumer complaint behavior (CCB). The major objective of this paper is to partially fill this gap by drawing from the mood literature in psychology and consumer behavior and by suggesting some hypotheses of the relationship between the two constructs. I will also try to discuss some of the problems involved in testing these hypotheses.

We may look into the literature and draw some conclusions about the effects of mood states. For this purpose, I found Gardner (1985), Gardner and Hill (1989) and Prakash (1985) to be extremely useful sources. It may be useful to define mood states to be different from emotions, and being transient and specific to a time and a situation. First, mood states may bias judgements in mood congruent directions as mood congruent items are more accessible from memory (Hill and Gardner 1986). Second, positive moods increase the probability that individuals will engage in behaviors with expected positive outcomes, and decrease the probability that individuals will engage in behaviors with expected negative outcomes (Hill and Gardner 1986). Third, positive moods may increase the likelihood that positive associations to a particular behavior will be accessible in memory, and therefore increase the probability that the behavior will be performed (Hill and Gardner 1986; Gardner 1985; Clark and Isen 1982). Fourth, in contrast to positive moods, the behavioral effects of negative moods are more complex because negative moods themselves are more heterogenous. Moderately negative moods may be helpful in retrieving information about product/services that are accessible to sales due to negative moods (e.g. insurance). Finally, Gardner (1985) wisely summarizes the effects of moods in other situations as follows: "Effects of mood states may be greatest in those consumer behavior situations where stimuli are ambiguous, consumers are somewhat aroused, induction and actions are temporally contiguous, perceived benefits of being precise are low, and moods are positive" (p. 290). Next, as suggested by Gardner (1985), I will discuss the relevance of mood effects in three specific situational contexts: service encounters, point of purchase stimuli, and communication stimuli as they might relate to consumer complaint behavior.

Service Encounters

The main conclusion is that the type of treatment consumers receive, will have an effect on their recall of mood congruent items. Gardner (1985) gives several examples: (a) when opening a bank account, consumers in a good mood are more likely to recall positive information about their accounts; (b) patients admitted to hospitals in bad moods may retrieve more negative information about past hospital experiences than those in good moods and thus are more likely to presume the worst about an impending hospital stay. The main implication for consumer complaint behavior is that a satisfactory handling of consumers during the service encounter is likely to reduce the severity of complaint behavior and consumers are more likely to recall positive experiences during the encounter.

Some examples of techniques of appropriate mood induction during service encounters are as follows: (a) an overall pleasant design of providers' physical settings could have an effect on mood and subsequently may lead to positive evaluation; (b) provision of clear user-friendly systems and positive feedback throughout the task during monadic transactions; (c) service providers may train their own employees to appropriately handle and manage their own moods during interaction with customers to better manage consumer moods; (d) appropriate positive moods inductions contiguous to the service encounter could have positive effects on the transaction.

Point of Purchase Stimuli

The implications for consumer complaint behavior are similar to the ones discussed under the previous heading. Shoppers in positive moods are more likely to retrieve positive information later. Some methods of appropriate mood induction include the use of special personnel, events, colors and lighting. Mood states induced by retail environment may affect purchase intentions. Interactions with sales personnel, tone set by sales personnel may set an upbeat mood, and thus reduce the subsequent probability of consumer complaint behavior.

Communication Stimuli: Context

There is a general advantage to placing advertisements in contexts that induce positive moods. Positive moods induced by an advertisement may lead to higher purchase probability. The effects of negative moods are more complex. Mildly negative moods may be an effective marketing tool for such products as insurance or drought relief. Advertisements that induce positive moods may facilitate learning, integration, and acquisition of favorable material and may enhance the evaluation of advertised brands. Advertisements may be used to elicit a certain mood. The elicited mood may then be the key to the retrieval of advertisements associated with those moods. More research is needed into the central role of advertising and the range of moods and the range of usage experiences associated with these moods created.

MOOD STATES AND CONSUMER COMPLAINT BEHAVIORS

Thus far, I have mainly summarized from the mood related literature. Prakash (1985) was perhaps the only study conceptualizing on the relationship between mood states and post-purchase evaluation. That study visualized a longitudinal design involving the measurement of mood at three different times i.e. pre-purchase expectations formation, during the actual purchase, and at post purchase evaluation. The net result would the be either satisfaction, or dissatisfaction leading to consumer complaint behavior. These effects would be moderated by the level of prior familiarity, such that mood effects would have minimal influence on subjects with higher level of familiarity as they would be guided more by cognitive evaluation. The operational model proposed by Prakash (1985) was 3x3 factorial design with repeated measures. He suggested measurement of 3 mood states (Positive, neutral and negative) at two stages: pre-purchase and post-purchase evaluation. This model has not been yet been empirically tested and results have not yet been published.

In this paper, I wish to go a step further and focus on consumer complaint behavior and discuss how mood states may influence this behavior. I propose some hypotheses for testing this relationship and discuss some of the problems involved. The literature on the subject shows that CCB is a multidimensional construct and there are three major types of CCB i.e. voice, private party action and third party action (Singh 1988). The type of a CCB a consumer might undertake depends upon four major mediators/moderators e.g., intensity of dissatisfaction, expectancy-value of the CCB, attitude toward the act of complaining and prior experience of undertaking the CCB (Day 1984; Singh and Wilkes 1991; Prakash 1991). It may be hypothesized that mood states may play the role of an additional moderator between the intensity of dissatisfaction and the intention to undertake a CCB. Gardner (1985) discussed mood induction techniques during the time the customer is in store or while businesses are advertising the product in media, but she did not discuss mood management at the post-purchase level and its effects in containing consumer complaining behavior, which is the objective of the next section where some hypotheses are presented.

SOME HYPOTHESES

Based on what I have drawn from Gardner (1985) on service encounters, point of purchase stimuli and communication context, I propose the following hypotheses on effects of mood states on CCB:

H1: That consumers experiencing a positive mood during a service encounter are less likely to complain than consumers experiencing a negative mood during a service encounter.

H2: Consumers experiencing a positive environment during either a service encounter or during a point of purchase stimuli are less likely to complain than consumers experiencing a negative environment during either a service encounter or a point of purchase stimuli.

H3: Consumers experiencing a positive mood or a positive environment during either a service encounter or during a point of purchase stimuli are more likely to recall more positive aspects of the product/service during the post purchase evaluation than consumers experiencing negative mood or negative environment during these aforesaid stages.

H4: Conversely, consumers experiencing negative mood or negative environment during the service encounter or point of purchase stimuli are more likely to recall more negative aspects of the product/service during the post purchase evaluation.

H5: Services or businesses training their employees in positive mood management of their own moods while dealing with consumers during the encounter would experience lower level of complaints than businesses not training their employees in positive mood management.

H6: Services or businesses that train their employees in mood management while dealing with consumers at the post-purchase level will experience lower level of complaints than businesses not training their employees in positive mood management at the post-purchase level.

H7: Positive moods induced by advertisements in appropriate context or programs would lead to a lower frequency of consumer complaint behavior than advertisements inducing negative moods.

H8: Advertisements inducing positive moods may facilitate better recall of favorable aspects of the product than advertisements inducing negative moods in the advertisement

Based on the CCB literature (i.e. moderating role of mood states), the following hypotheses may be proposed:

H9: Dissatisfied consumers in a positive mood at the postpurchase evaluation level are more likely to undertake voice CCB than consumers in a negative mood.

H10: Dissatisfied consumers in a negative mood at the postpurchase evaluation level are more likely to undertake either private party action or third party action (e.g. Better Business Bureau) than those in a positive mood at the postpurchase level.

H11: Dissatisfied consumers deciding to undertake legal action in a court of law would not be influenced by mood states but by other mediators/moderators such as expectancy-value of the CCB and prior experience of complaining.

Problems in Testing the Mood Effects Hypotheses

Serious difficulties remain in operationalizing and testing these hypotheses. First, the mood induction techniques present serious problems. The mood created in experimental settings may last only for a short duration, thus creating problems for a longitudinal study. Secondly, even if a longitudinal design is undertaken as suggested by Prakash (1985), it may require a large sample size because of the large number of cells and the need to have adequate number of subjects in each cell. Thirdly, there are a wide variety of moods especially of the negative type and studying their effects involves much more complexity than a study of positive moods. Fourthly, mood effects studies involving dyadic interactions between salesperson/buyer or between service provider and complainant present horrendous problems of control of noise from extraneous variables.

Marketing Strategy Implications

The purpose of this research paper has been to stimulate thinking on the effects of mood states on consumer complaint behaviors. The implications for marketing strategy are enormous. A judicious management of consumer mood especially the induction of positive mood during the point of purchase encounters may not only lead to a higher level of customer satisfaction but may also help reduce consumer complaint behavior after the purchase. Also, an appropriate training of the company representatives in managing their own reactions in dealing with consumers during the purchase, or at the time of consumers expressing grievances after the purchase, can play a significant role in minimizing the severity of the CCB. A good mood management by the company representatives may lead to an assimilation effect where consumers may forgive the company or its product deficiencies. On the other hand, a poor mood management may lead to a contrast effect where consumers may exaggerate the deficiencies in the product. Finally, as we have seen that at the postpurchase level if consumers are in a positive mood, their anger is contained at the local level and they tend to seek a constructive resolution of their grievances. On the other hand consumers in a negative mood are more likely to spread negative word of mouth and/or undertake some type of third party action, both of which can be extremely damaging to the businesses. The challenge for researchers is the study of consumer (and company) mood management at the postpurchase level.

REFERENCES

Day, R. (1984), "Modeling Choices Among Alternative Responses to Dissatisfaction," in *Advances in Consumer Research*, Thomas C. Kinnear, ed. Provo: UT: Association for Consumer Research, 11, 496-499.

Clark, Margaret and Alice Isen (1982), "Toward Understanding the Relationship Between Feeling States and Social Behavior," in *Cognitive Social Psychology*, Albert Hastorf and Alice Isen, eds. New York: Elsevier/North-Holland, 73-108.

Gardner Meryl, P. (1985), "Mood States and Consumer Behavior: A Critical Review," *Journal of Consumer Research*, 12 (3), 281-300.

_____ and Ronald Paul Hill (1989), "Consumers' Mood States and the Decision-Making Process," *Marketing Letters*, 1 (3), 229-238.

Hill, Ronald Paul and Meryl P. Gardner (1986), "The Buying Process: Effects of and on Consumer Mood States," in *Advances in Consumer Research*, M. Wallendorf and P. Anderson, eds. Provo, UT: Association for Consumer Research, 14, 408-410

Isen, Alice M. (1984), "Toward Understanding the Role of Affect in Cognition," in *Handbook of Social Cognition*, Robert Wyer Jr. and Thomas Srull, eds. Hillsdale, NJ: Lawrence Erlbaum, 179-236.

Prakash, Ved (1985), "Mood States and Consumer Satisfaction: A Conceptual Framework," in *Consumer Satisfaction, Dissatisfaction and Complaining Behavior*, the ninth conference, H. Keith Hunt and Ralph L. Day, eds. Bloomington, IN: Indiana University Press, 33-39.

_____ (1985), "Intensity of Dissatisfaction and Consumer Complaint Behaviors," *Journal of Consumer Satisfaction, Dissatisfaction and Complaining Behavior*, 4, 110-122.

Singh, Jagdip (1988), "Consumer Complaint Intentions and Behavior: Definitional and Taxonomical Issues," *Journal of Marketing*, 52 (1), 93-107.

_____ and Robert E. Wilkes (1991), "A Theoretical Framework for Modeling Consumers' Response to Marketplace Dissatisfaction," *Journal of Consumer Satisfaction, Dissatisfaction and Complaining Behavior*, 4, 1-12.

MANAGING THE TRANSITION FROM A R & D TO A MARKETING DRIVEN ORGANIZATION

Linda Shea, University of Massachusetts at Amherst
Bill Wooldridge, University of Massachusetts at Amherst

ABSTRACT

This paper describes the transition to a team-based marketing organization in a large consumer products firm. Based on interviews, we identify three stages in the evolution. Each stage is characterized by structural changes, unique managerial techniques, product management skills, and conflict resolution mechanisms. Implications and questions for research are discussed.

INTRODUCTION

This paper examines the management of organizational transition. In recent years many firms have attempted to move from functionally based organizations towards "team" structures. Perhaps the most common form of this evolution involves marketing departments developing product teams headed by marketing-based product managers. The research reported here investigates the process through which a major consumer products firm accomplished such a transition. The ensuing changes significantly altered power relationships within the firm and created unavoidable organizational conflict.

While substantial literatures on organizational change (Lewin 1951; Daft 1982; Kanter 1983) and conflict (Pondy 1969; 1972; Cosier and Ruble 1981; Smith 1989; Pinkley 1990) exist, neither fully explain the processes of long term organizational transition. Ruekert and Walker (1987), for example, focus on the inherent tension between marketing and R&D and the apparent effects of organizational characteristics on the frequency and degree of these interdepartmental conflicts. Similarly, much of the change literature focuses on the importance of change agents and identifies various change strategies.

Closer to the present study, Gersick (1991) explores how new theories from a variety of fields are challenging traditional assumptions about how change occurs. These "punctuated equilibrium" theories describe how various forces promote stability over long periods of time which are, only occasionally, interrupted by brief periods of revolutionary change. Tushman and Romanelli (1985), for example, describe how organizations move through periods of relative stability (convergence) and upheaval. They observe that while most organizations remain stable over long periods of time, identifiable forces elicit dramatic changes all at once.

Given this framework, the purpose of this study was to examine a particular type of organizational upheaval-the shift from a functionally based to a team based marketing organization. While previous work has, for the most part, focused on the role of top management in these transformations (Tushman, Newman and Romanelli (1986), here the concern is primarily with the functioning of the new teams and their team leaders. After describing stages in the development of the teams we discuss implications and develop a set of research propositions.

The Research Context

The research was conducted in a large consumer products firm that began developing a product management organization when it was acquired six years earlier. Prior to the acquisition the firm had been experiencing decreasing revenues and was losing market share. Six years later, the firm is back on track having had steady sales increases over the last three years. Not surprisingly, management attributes the turnaround to the product management organization and the changes reported here.

Before the merger, primary responsibility for new product development rested within Research and Development and the emergence of product management resulted in a permanent shift in intraorganizational power away from R&D to marketing. Overtime, resources, rewards, prestige, and power all shifted from R&D to marketing.

Several considerations make this an exceptionally representative form of organizational change. First, from the perspective of the evolution of firms from a production to a marketing orientation (Keith 1960), our interviews were conducted in an organization that was just completing such a transition. Second, the team orientation commonly practiced in product management make it an appropriate example of the general trend toward autonomous work groups in all facets of industry. As organizations continue to "delayer," coordination is achieved less through hierarchical power and more from the cross-functional communications of "knowledge based" workers (Drucker 1988). Finally, in organizations where new product development is emphasized, the product manager and the product management team may play instrumental roles in the formation of strategy.

In sum, the adoption of product management teams by the organization studied here is representative of changes occurring throughout industry. While this type of change is widely acknowledged to be taking place, there is little documentation regarding the processes that underlie these changes. The ideas presented here, therefore, are likely to have wide applicability and relevance as organizations continue to move away from functionally-based hierarchical arrangements towards cross-functional teams.

Research Method

Since the study was exploratory and had the objective of developing testable propositions from new insights, we utilized a qualitative research approach (Glasser and Strauss 1967). Our primary data sources were semi-structured interviews with three different levels of product managers, the vice president of marketing and several other product team members. In addition, secondary data sources, industry reports, and internal documents helped provide a context for the study.

Since our goal was to describe "as yet incompletely documented phenomena" (Burgelman 1983, p. 224), our concerns differed from those of hypothesis testing research (Eisenhardt and Bourgeois 1988). Specifically, rather than issues of external validity, this research focused on gathering qualitative data that added new information about the transition process. Our method was iterative, therefore, evolving as we went along.

We began with a semi-structured interview of the first product manager asking questions about the organization, who the players were, their backgrounds, etc. As with all of the interviews, this interview was conducted by both authors, one having primary responsibility for asking questions and the other for taking detailed notes. After receiving permission from respondents, the sessions were also tape recorded.

After the initial interview, the authors "regrouped," transcribed the interview notes, and discussed what had been said. From this, "working hypotheses" were developed and used to generate a new set of interview questions for the second respondent. This iterative process continued throughout the interviews so that each respondent both confirmed earlier statements and contributed additional information. The process continued, adding new informants until a point of diminishing returns was met. That is, it evolved to the point where respondents were merely confirming what had been said earlier.

What emerged is a description of how one firm managed the process of moving from a functionally based, R&D driven organization to a product management team organization over a period of six years. Based on the experiences of this firm, we develop a stage model of the process. Our purpose is to move toward the development and testing of new theory by uncovering apparent relationships and patterns.

Stages of Organizational Transition

Prior to the period studied, marketing in the firm had primarily "facilitated," having "no control over final decisions." Sales and marketing functions were fragmented and efforts were focused on supporting individual products. Research and Development had overall responsibility for new product development and dealt directly with top management on product related issues.

The acquisition of the firm by a competitor represents the beginning of the transitionary period studied. After the merger, the firm remained relatively autonomous, operating as a distinct division and retaining its own brand names. A distinct and much noticed difference, however, was that marketing, not R&D, began "getting the calls" from headquarters.

Three stages of organizational transition unfolded as the research progressed - confrontational, transitional, and auto-resolving. Each of these periods lasted several years and was marked by key events and milestones.

Confrontational. Early in this period a new vice president of marketing was brought in from outside the firm. Aside from being an outsider several issues surrounding this appointment stand out. First, the new vice president had an extensive background in product management, having held comparable and higher level positions elsewhere. Second, the existing senior marketing staff not only remained, but maintained their current titles and responsibilities. Thus, the appointment created an additional hierarchical level and the senior marketing manager now "outranked" other functional heads.

This period was also marked by widespread turnover, especially in marketing. Fifteen new people were hired to fill four levels of product management positions: senior product manager, product manager, associate product manager and assistant product manager. Within 3 years only 5 of the 15 remained. A few long term R&D employees left as well.

Several factors apparently contributed to the significant turnover of this period. For the most part, the marketing people didn't like the pressure of "being the bad guy." The new vice president, who now outranked the head of R&D, created and "taught" the product manager role. The new product managers who had to implement the function were told, "Make it happen!"

"There were people who could not live with his management style. ... because he was a tremendously demanding individual and you either subscribed to that philosophy and survived or you didn't."

"You had a 23 year old downstairs telling a 50 year old director of R&D, 'look your designer has really dropped the ball, I've tried to work with him, now we're 3 weeks behind and my boss is giving me hell.' The R&D manager turns his back and walks away without even acknowledging, and refuses to. Now, if they came back with their tail between their legs, they were usually sent back. The idea was - this is going to happen to you your entire career unless you go back down there. Leadership isn't given, its taken."

Indeed, this strategy appears to be a critical element in the successful establishment of the product management system. While the marketing V.P. could have intervened on his subordinates' behalf, his tendency was to resist, leaving the new product managers to establish their own credibility. The successful ones apparently did this through sheer backbone and stubbornness.

"Relationships were damaged back then. Relationships were destroyed." "Anything you tell a creative person about 'their baby' is so personal. No matter how gentle you are, all they see is a sledgehammer. I didn't go home feeling good about what I did. It was a very difficult period for a lot of us."

To a lesser degree, people also left if they weren't successful. "While you were generally backed up when you made a hard decision, you had to be right more than wrong." Again, this appears to be a critical way individuals, and the product management system in general, began to establish credibility. In an earlier case study , Gemmill and Wilemon (1972) identified sources of social power evidenced by product managers in their role as influence agents. They suggested that the use of expert power (gaining cooperation by demonstrating knowledge and expertise) was more effective in the long run than the use of reward or coercive power (gaining cooperation through the promise of certain rewards or through the threat of punishment). In our case, it proved beneficial for the product managers to achieve some (product) successes to gain support from other team members; however, in the short run, the threat of going to one's boss was avoided, yet used if necessary.

"Early on there were several key successes that became very visible ,... (where) the 'glory' was widely shared... A mutual respect was developed over time. If you hit someone over the head with a club and you do repeatedly, to work into a relationship where they respect you wasn't easy. It was out of our professionalism and being right a lot more than we were wrong that brought the respect."

In sum, three factors emerged as keys to success during this initial period. First, the strong leadership of the newly appointed V.P. provided substance for the general product management notion. Several respondents described this person as a "great teacher" who brought "us from infancy to toddlerhood." Further, somewhat due to hierarchical position but more because of personal expertise and presence, he tended to "dominate" colleagues in other functions. Second, the limited use of hierarchical authority allowed product managers to es-

tablish themselves and gain the respect of other team members. "Everybody knew that ultimately the product manager could force the issue (use the hierarchy). The game was not having to." Finally, the strategic use of successes and the sharing of rewards began to weaken entrenched positions and create support for the new arrangements.

Transitional. If the initial period was marked by confrontation, the second stage was characterized by an evolving empathy. The beginning of this period is symbolized by a second change in marketing leadership. Around year four, the senior V.P. of marketing left for a prestigious position at another firm. All indications suggest that this departure was at his initiative. He was "certainly in the good graces of upper management" and "liked and respected by the marketing staff." Still, the appointment of a new marketing V.P. created the opportunity for the organization to evolve to its next stage.

The succeeding head of marketing was a long time company employee who had been in the marketing department prior to the merger. Perhaps as noteworthy, this individual began his career as an engineer and had worked in the firm's R&D department. Thus, he had "seen both sides of the fence." While the new manager's style in all likelihood differed from his predecessor, this did not seem to be a primary issue. Rather, as an insider he was seen more as "one of us," and while relationships between the predecessor and other V.P.s were not considered poor, the appointment of the successor to a large degree put arrangements back on an "equal footing." Thus began an era where individuals at all levels began to think in terms of teams as much as functions.

Related to the above, was a growing perception of equality among product managers and R&D personnel. In the previous period, the new found power and visibility of product managers was resented by R&D personnel and they were generally viewed as "primadonnas." In contrast, during this era product managers began to be seen as problem solvers, performing critical "leg work" to coordinate the overall effort. Effective product managers made use of this and "made it very visible that they were serving team members." In addition, product managers consistently recognized the contributions of individual team members when presenting a team's work to upper management. Thus, as one manager put it, "the glory began to be shared."

Finally, it became important for product managers to change their management style. While in the first period, it was critical for managers to establish credibility, in this period managers seemed to maintain respect through give and take. For example, as one product manager noted, "It's important that people know I genuinely want their input. In the end, though, they know its my decision." On this point another manager noted,

"As a designer I put an element of myself into everything I did,...you know, with creatives, its ego. So now I let them put their 'signature' on what they do. Everything's not that important. Giving in on small things and listening can make a big difference."

In short, product managers became less authoritarian during this period. One manager noted, " A good product manager uses everything from the iron fist to being a virtual schmooz artist. But today it's less iron fist and more canvas gloves." On a more subtle level, rivalries between functions began to be better understood and accepted. In marketing, for example, product managers began to accept being the brunt of "marketing jokes."

"Quite frankly, a lot of it is on the level of schoolyard harassment. It can be childish, but its also sort of release. ... that's the adversarial part and there will always be a natural confrontation. If we don't take it personally and maybe even share in the humor ... most people accept that and it helps us reach the common goal."

Thus, three factors seem to have facilitated the emergence of this period of evolving understanding and mutual respect. New management reduced perceptions of inequalities between marketing and other functions. Product managers used opportunities to demonstrate their contribution to the overall effort. Finally, and perhaps most important, conflicts began to be resolved in a less authoritarian manner.

Autonomous. To this point our stage model has described the chronological development of the product management concept within the firm. To a certain degree this is deceptive in that it does not recognize that product teams and relationships among individuals vary. While for the most part, the firm has transcended the confrontational stage, some pockets persist. In general, the firm remains in the transitional stage. There are, however, indications that it is evolving toward a third stage, one characterized by autonomous communications. Managers reported that some teams communicated at a "higher level" and is was clear that this was the primary objective for the future.

"My objective in the next two years ... is communication. Graphics working with engineering, so that when there's a minor change to the package dimensions ... we're not cutting off the logo."

It is important to distinguish the nature of communication within each period. During the confrontational stage, managers reported mostly one-way directional communications. Individual contributors rarely communicated with one another and lacked an overall perspective. Product managers forced marketplace consider-

ations onto the product development team. During the transitional stage, communications became more structured through coordinating meetings. Communications across functions increased, but were primarily limited to structured settings. Input from management was often resented and product managers spent "countless hours" smoothing ruffled egos. On this last point, one manager offered the following:

"There's a lot of manipulating. It's usually my judgment, but I'll drop names if I have to. I might, for instance, say ...'I personally like what you're doing here, but I'll tell you for a fact there's no way in the world we'll get it by Pete. We can try it, I'll back you up, but there's no way in hell we're going to get it past Pete, let alone Tom or Mike.'... so its always a struggle. You just can't go down there and say what you need. Everything's so personal."

Presently, the product management organization seems to be evolving to a point where communications between team members occur naturally. Product managers report spending less time relaying information, and interpreting how changes in one area affect other functions. Further, the nature of conflicts and their resolution also appears to be changing. "Coordination across functions and cost considerations ...(etc.), are increasingly anticipated."

Ideally, management maintains that product managers will remain central to the process, "the one person representing the overall product to upper management," but communications across functions will (should) happen automatically.

"There should be fewer team meetings. Less management from the minutes ... holding people accountable and follow-up."

"One area where there's still resentment is the feeling that someone's looking over your shoulder, ... breathing down your neck, ... and there's less need for it today."

Thus, as teams continue to evolve, the role of the product manager appears to be changing again. They are spending less time coordinating activities across functions and are increasingly using their marketing skills to "establish a vision and keep priorities centered."

Interestingly, the formalization of the product team structure seems to be facilitating a less structured approach in the management of the product teams. Formal documentation of the product team concept, its functioning, and designation of the product manager as the team leader was not completed until year six. For several years, a committee composed of representatives from all affected functions was charged with the task of formally documenting responsibilities, tasks, and relationships within and across teams. The culmination of this effort represents a new level of maturity for the organization. In a formal sense, the transition from a functionally based to team based structure has taken place. The ambiguity that characterized earlier interactions has, to a large degree, passed and there is a growing recognition, among all parties, of the primacy of marketplace considerations.

DISCUSSION AND PROPOSITIONS

Consistent with established theory, the case reported here confirms that radical change occurs in compact periods of upheaval followed by longer periods of relative stability and incremental adjustment. The case also demonstrates, however, that factors in the transition back to stability and incremental adjustments made after the period of upheaval have important implications for how the organization develops and functions.

Table 1 summarizes key distinguishing features of each period. As shown, each period is marked by a significant structural event. In the first two periods, a change of management facilitated the transition to a new era. In the last period, the formalization of the product team structure seemed to coincide with an increasingly ingrained product management ideology.

Like previous studies (Tushman, et al. 1986), the period of upheaval reported in this case was associated with confrontation and changes in leadership. New leaders "arrive with a strong belief in the new mission. Moreover, they are unfettered by prior commitments .." (Tushman, et al. 1986, p. 42). The marketing V.P. brought in during the confrontational stage fits this description well. What is perhaps more interesting is that the departure of this individual may have been necessary for continued evolution of the product teams. Previous research suggests that new leaders replace existing management. In the present study, however, the new leadership only temporarily supplanted existing management. In fact, the resurrection of prior management seems to mark the beginning of a less confrontational, more stable era where incremental adjustments and fine tuning of the system could take place. Thus, the following proposition is suggested.

P1: Leaders that facilitate radical change inhibit the transition back to stability. Thus, timely leadership changes following periods of upheaval facilitate the continued development and fine tuning of new arrangements.

The formal documentation of the product management structure marking the beginning of the autonomous era is also of interest. Prior to year six, there were no official structural changes documenting the transformation taking place within the organization. Product managers were left to organize product teams as they saw fit

and there was a lot of trial and error as personalities got to know one another. In many cases, this lead to "over-control" by product managers. As these experiences became ingrained within the organization, a sense of what worked, what didn't, and what was ideal developed among team members. Thus, rather than being an edict of management, the system's formal documentation represents the organization's collective experience and wisdom and, as such, has facilitated more autonomous arrangements.

Stated differently, while the shift from a functionally-based to a team-based structure represents less hierarchical control, the organization had to get tighter before it could get looser. Thus, the following propositions are suggested.

P2: During the transition to a team-based structure, managers will seek to solidify new arrangements by developing a variety of relatively rigid ad hoc structures.

P3: As the organization gains experience with the new arrangements, team-based values will supplant the need for formal controls and relatively few of the ad hoc structures will be formally selected.

Finally, also shown on Table 1, each period appears to be characterized by a unique set of product manager attributes and these appear to have important marketing management implications. In the initial period, marketing management trained new product managers through what one respondent characterized as "trial by fire," and since conflicts were often "bloody," success for a product manager was determined largely by the individual's fortitude and strength of character. During the second stage, product managers "served" the team by structuring the overall effort and containing conflicts. Organizational and interpersonal skills, therefore, were critical. Finally, the last period appears to be characterized by autonomous mutual adjustment and team problem solving. Key product manager skills, therefore, may shift once more. Specifically, managers, will need to exercise keen judgment in determining the amount of autonomy appropriate within various team settings. Further, as teams become increasingly self-managing, the managerial contributions of product managers will diminish. The quality of their marketing skills, therefore, will likely become more apparent. Thus, the following proposition is suggested.

P4: During the transition to a team-based product management structure, the requisite skills of product managers change overtime. Early in the transition, product managers' success will be determined largely by their organizational and managerial skills. Later in the transition, marketing skills will become predominate.

TABLE 1
Key Distinguishing Features Within Each Period

Stage	Structural Indicator	Key Managerial Techniques	Product Manager Attributes	Conflict Resolution
Confrontational	New V.P of Mkting	Limited use of hierarchy	Fortitude	Coercive Power
		Showcasing success	Strength of character	Forced
		Trial by fire		
Transitional	Departure of Marketing VP	Demonstration of value	Organizational skills	Expert power
	Appointment of long-term insider as mktg head	Concessionary behavior		Smoothing
		Structured coordination		
Autonomous	Product team structure officially documented	Autonomous mutual adjustment	Judgment	
			Marketing knowledge	Problem-solving
	Product Mgr. designated team leader			

CONCLUSION

The study reported here was exploratory and is merely suggestive of how the transition from a functional to a team-based marketing organization occurs. It would be unrealistic to assume that the description above fully describes all the important events taking place during this firm's transition. The purpose was to examine this period of dramatic change in order to gain insights that could guide future research.

Importantly, the study suggests that evolution from one stage of marketing development to another is not a smooth, incremental process. Rather it is better characterized as "frame-breaking" upheaval (Tushman, et al, 1986). Thus, that all firms do not undergo such "evolution" is not surprising. Change of this nature is painful and generally must be precipitated by crises. In this case, declining market share and a merger acted as catalysts for change that were then supported by top management commitment symbolized by the appointment of a powerful marketing leader.

For research on organizational change and marketing management the study raises significant questions. Are there identifiable stages in the change from one stage of marketing development to the next? Is the evolution of marketing in a firm necessarily characterized by frame-breaking change? If so, what factors generally precipitate these changes? What is the role of top management and marketing leadership in various stages of the process? And finally, do product managers need different sets of skills to be successful at various stages in the development of a product management structure?

REFERENCES

Burgelman, R. A. (1983), "A Process Model of Internal Corporate Venturing in the Diversified Major Firm," *Administrative Science Quarterly*, 28 (June), 223-244.

Cosier, R. A. and T. L. Ruble (1981), "Research on Conflict-Handling Behavior: An Experimental Approach," *Academy of Management Journal*, 24 (December), 816-831.

Daft, Richard L, (1982), "Bureaucratic Versus Nonbureaucratic Structure and the Process of Innovation and Change," in *Research in the Sociology of Organizations,* Samuel B. Bacharach, ed. 1, 132.

Drucker, P. (1988), "The New Organization," *Harvard Business Review,* 66 (September/October), 65-76.

Eisenhardt, K.M. and L.J. Bourgeois (1988), "Politics of Strategic Decision Making in High-Velocity Environments: Toward a Midrange Theory," *Academy of Management Journal,* 31, (December), 737-770.

Gemmill, Gary R. and David L. Wilemon (1972), "The Product Manager as an Influence Agent," *Journal of Marketing,* 36 (January), 26-30.

Gersick, Connie J.G. (1991) "Revolutionary Change Theories: A Multilevel Exploration of the Punctuated Equilibrium Paradigm," *Academy of Management Review,* 16 (January), 10-36.

Glasser, B. J. and A. L. Strauss (1967), *The Discovery of Grounded Theory.* Chicago: Aldine.

Kanter, R. M. (1983), *The Change Masters.* New York: Basic Books.

Keith, Robert J. (1960), "The Marketing Revolution," *Journal of Marketing,* (January), 35-38.

Lewin, Kurt (1951), *Field Theory in Social Science.* New York: Harper & Row.

Miles, Raymond E. and Charles C. Snow (1978), *Organizational Strategy, Structure and Process.* New York: McGraw-Hill Company.

Narver, John C. and Stanley F. Slater (1990), "The Effect of a Market Orientation on Business Profitability," *Journal of Marketing,* 54 (October), 20-33.

Pinkley, R. L. (1990), "Dimensions of Conflict Frame: Disputant Interpretations of Conflict," *Journal of Applied Psyhchology,* 75 (2), 117-126.

Pondy, L. R. (1969), "Organizational Conflict: Concepts and Models," *Administrative Science Quarterly,* 14, 296-320.

_____ (1972), "Varieties of Organizational Conflict," *Administrative Science Quarterly,* 17, 499-505.

Ruekert, Robert W. and Orville C. Walker, Jr. (1987). "Interactions Between Marketing and R&D Departments in Implementing Different Business Strategies," *Strategic Management Journal,* 8 (May/June), 233-248.

Smith, K. (1989), "The Movement of Conflict in Organizations: The Joint Dynamics of Splitting and Triangulation," *Administrative Science Quarterly,* 34 (March), 1-20.

Tushman, M. and E. Romanelli (1985), "Organizational Evolution: A Metamorphosis Model of Convergence and Reorientation," in *Research in Organizational Behavior,* L. L. Cummings and B. M. Straw, eds. Greenwich, CT: JAI Press, 7, 171-222.

_____, W. H. Newman, and Elaine Romanelli (1986), "Managing the Unsteady Pace of Organizational Evolution," *California Management Review,* 29 (Fall), 29-44.

MARKET ORIENTATION, INFORMATION, AND MARKETING STRATEGIES

John C. Narver, University of Washington
Seong Y. Park, University of Washington
Stanley F. Slater, University of Colorado at Colorado Springs

ABSTRACT

A market orientation is a business culture in which all employees are committed to the continuous creation of superior value for customers. Previous research has shown a strong positive relationship between market orientation and business performance. However, to date, the relationship between market orientation and marketing strategies has not been tested.

In a theoretical and empirical analysis the present paper examines the linkage between market orientation and marketing strategies. Consisting of the three behavioral components of customer orientation, competitor orientation, and interfunctional coordination, market orientation comprises a very effective means for the gathering and utilizing of market information. Thus, a market orientation is expected to be strongly associated with a business's strategies to create superior value for customers and thereby to create superior value for the business.

Competitive-advantage strategies can be divided into two types: Those that are related to creating customer value and those that are not. The former we label "customer-value" strategies, and the latter we label "internal strategies." Customer-value strategies include focus strategies, market-information strategies, and differentiation strategies. Internal strategies include low cost strategies and mark-up (arbitrary) price strategies. We would expect a market orientation to manifest the customer-value strategies.

We divide the fifteen strategies into the four subgroups. "Focus strategies" include the strategies to segment markets; target offerings to markets with specialized needs; increase sales of existing products in existing markets; introduce existing products into new markets; develop new products for existing markets, and introduce new products into new markets. "Market-information strategies" include strategies to use marketing research and to systematically monitor opportunities and threats in a business's market(s). "Differentiation strategies" include strategies to differentiate products; price products on a value-to-customer basis; improve product quality; provide high levels of customer services; and emphasize a business's brand names. "Internal strategies" include the strategies to offer a low price relative to competitors' prices and to price products on a standard mark-up.

The present research investigates the relationship of market orientation to each of the customer-value and internal strategies. We hypothesize that market orientation is positively related to the customer-value strategies and is negatively related to the internal strategies.

We conducted empirical investigations in two Fortune 500 companies. The first, completed in 1990 in a diversified manufacturing company, was an investigation of six of the above-described fifteen strategies. The second, completed in 1991 in a forest products company, was an investigation of the entire fifteen strategies. The sample sizes of the first and second study are 36 SBUs and 38 SBUs respectively. The respondents were one or more members of the top-management team of each SBU.

Regression analysis using an independent-effects model was applied. Nine situational variables, each of which could affect the use of the subject strategies, were used as controls in the two analyses. The nine variables are: (1) the SBU's relative costs; (2) the SBU's relative size; (3) the power of the SBU's buyers; (4) the power of the SBU's suppliers; (5) the rate of growth of the SBU's market; (6) the rate of technological change in the SBU's market; (7) the concentration of sellers in the SBU's market; (8) the ease of entry of new sellers into the SBU's market; and (9) the intensity of competition in the SBU's market. With the small sample sizes, we used a step-wise regression (with a criterion of $p < .30$) in order to obtain a parsimonious model in the two studies.

In the diversified manufacturing company, the data directly support three of the six hypotheses. The data suggest that the strategies of segmenting markets, differentiating products, and tracking market opportunities and threats are strongly related to market orientation ($p < .02$). With respect to the three hypotheses not supported (marketing research, emphasize brand name, and offer low price), the sign on the regression coefficient of market orientation in all three cases is in the direction hypothesized, but the coefficient is not statistically significant.

In the forest products company the data directly support the 13 strategies in which we hypothesized a positive relation. Neither of the other two strategies, the internal strategies of pricing low and using a mark-up approach to pricing in which we hypothesized a negative relationship to market orientation, is statistically significant. In addition to demonstrating a linkage to the customer-value strategies, market orientation provides the strongest explanation for these strategies.

Why are the findings in the forest products company stronger than those in the diversified manufacturing company? The forest products businesses are on average lower in technology and their products are more highly interchangeable with competitors' products than is true in the diversified manufacturing company. Therefore, the forest products businesses at the margin may benefit more from the competitive strategies inherent in a market orientation. This is a plausible reason for why we observe in the forest products company the larger relationship between market orientation and the use of such strategies.

The present research provides initial, strong evidence for the expected linkage between market orientation and strategies designed to contribute to the creation of value for customers. This research comprises a beginning in the development of a body of theory and evidence relating market orientation to marketing strategy, a research focus that complements the theory and mounting evidence on market orientation and business performance.

For further information please contact :
John C. Narver
School of Business Administration
University of Washington
Seattle, WA

THE R & D - MARKETING INTERFACE: AUTHORITY AND TRUST DIMENSIONS OF INTERDEPARTMENTAL EXCHANGE

Doug Ayers, University of Kentucky
Robert Dahlstrom, University of Kentucky

ABSTRACT

Increasingly turbulent environments demand integrative product development processes (Gupta and Wilemon 1990). Such integrative approaches require effective relationships between functional units, particularly R&D and marketing. The effectiveness of the interaction between R&D and marketing has been shown to be positively related to the success of new product development (NPD) efforts (Gupta et al. 1985; Souder 1988). Accordingly, we utilize contemporary institutional economics in proposing a model for effective working relationships between R&D and marketing. Our discussion focuses on bureaucratic and trust-based antecedents to effectiveness. Effectiveness is characterized as the perception that the interdepartmental relationship is worthwhile, equitable, productive, and satisfying (cf. Ruekert and Walker 1987; Van de Ven 1976).

Bureaucratic Structuring and Effectiveness

The interaction between R&D and marketing in the (NPD) process is an organized form of collective behavior where: (1) behavior among members is aimed at attaining collective and self-interested goals; and (2) interdependent processes emerge through the division of tasks and responsibilities among members (cf. Van de Ven 1976). Because members may have self-interested goals which conflict with collective goals of the system, bureaucratic structures can be utilized to ensure the effective pursuit of collective goals. Two important structural variables are centralization and formalization (Van de Ven 1976). Centralization reflects the extent to which decisions are shared in the social system. Formalization refers to the degree to which activities and relationships are governed by rules, procedures, and contracts (Ruekert et al. 1985). With regard to the development of new products, an organic structure is thought to be more effective than a mechanistic one (Gupta, et al. 1986; Ruekert et al. 1985). An organic structure is characterized by low levels of centralization and formalization (Burns and Stalker 1961). Centralization has been found to be negatively related to the effectiveness of the R&D - marketing relationship (Gupta et al. 1987; Ruekert and Walker 1987). Therefore, the following is proposed:

P1: The effectiveness of the R&D-marketing interface is negatively related to the degree of centralized decision making.

Empirical analyses of the relationship between formalization and effectiveness offer contradictory findings. Gupta, et al.(1986) state that formalization appears to be both a facilitator and barrier to effective integration between R&D and marketing. We propose splitting the formalization construct into two separate but related constructs. The first construct is task formalization, and the second is role formalization. Because the NPD process is very imprecise, flexibility is required to develop innovative solutions to customers' problems. As posited by innovation theory, the NPD process is not amenable to highly formalized policies and procedures (cf. Zaltman et al. 1973). Requiring R&D and marketing personnel to operate "strictly by the book" is likely to stifle innovation and lead to the perceived loss of autonomy. Accordingly, the following proposition is presented.

P2: The effectiveness of the R&D-marketing interface is negatively related to the degree of task formalization.

Gupta et al. (1987) demonstrate a positive relationship between formalization and the level of integration achieved between R&D and marketing. This relationship is based on defining formalization as clarity of roles. Here the responsibilities of R&D and marketing managers were explicitly articulated through job descriptions. We argue that roles can be formalized while tasks may be less formalized. For example, a manager may be responsible for generating a new product idea, but the tasks necessary to derive such an idea may be left to the discretion of the manager. Saghafi et al. (1990) found that both R&D and marketing managers felt that their relationship would be enhanced if senior management clarified each party's roles and responsibilities in the NPD process. Accordingly, the third proposition is as follows.

P3: The effectiveness of the R&D-marketing interface is positively related to the degree of role formalization.

Trust and Effectiveness

Just as bureaucratic structures can secure control and desirable outcomes, trust can serve as a powerful governance mechanism (Bradach and Eccles 1989). The presence and adherence to norms can result in trust, and it is these norms that serve as a governance mechanism by guiding behavior. The nature of the tasks associated with NPD make trust an appropriate governance mechanism for the R&D-marketing interface. According to Ouchi (1981), norms are most effective for tasks which are highly unique, completely integrated or ambiguous for other reasons. Norms of relevance to the R&D-marketing interface are solidarity, conflict harmonization and role integrity.

Solidarity addresses the level of commitment to the preservation and continuation of the relationship. Effective R&D-marketing interfaces have been characterized as those in which all parties are mutually committed to the relationship (cf. Souder 1988)

As the number of transactions between R&D and marketing increases, so does the level of conflict between the two parties (Ruekert and Walker 1987). Effective R&D-marketing interfaces are characterized by extensive interaction and thus conflict is inevitable. Ruekert and Walker (1987) found that when conflicts between R&D and marketing were actively resolved, the relationship was perceived to be more effective.

Role integrity refers to the maintenance of roles in a relationship. While role formalization addresses the extent to which roles are defined, integrity addresses whether individuals conform to expectations. When individuals fulfill role expectations their exchange partners should experience lower levels of frustration, thus enhancing relational effectiveness. Therefore, the following is proposed:

P4: The effectiveness of the R&D-marketing interface is enhanced through relational norms.

Increasingly turbulent environments require extensive interaction between R&D and marketing in the development of successful new products. Understanding the bureaucratic and trust-based antecedents to effective interaction will enhance the ability of management to appropriately organize the R&D/marketing interface.

For further information contact:
Doug Ayers
University of Kentucky
Department of Marketing
Lexington, KY 40506-0034

IDENTIFICATION OF DETERMINANT OBJECTIVE ATTRIBUTES OF NEW AUTOMOBILES USING KELLY'S REPERTORY GRID TEST

Pola B. Gupta, University of Northern Iowa
Brian T. Ratchford, State University of New York at Buffalo

ABSTRACT

This paper presents a methodology for identifying the determinant objective attributes of new automobiles using the subjective perceptual constructs elicited through Kelly's repertory grid test. Based on the methodology presented in this paper, this study identifies nine determinant objective attributes for new automobiles. The knowledge of determinant objective attributes of a product is useful in measuring utilities, objective quality, attitudes etc. This information is also beneficial to the manufacturers for product design considerations.

LITERATURE REVIEW

In order to compute correct utilities for cross-selectional analyses, it is desirable to use objective measures rather than perceptual measures because the perceptual measures are affected by the lack of information. Furthermore, there is a considerable amount of agreement for using determinant attributes of products, because not all attributes are important for all consumers. The utilization of determinant attributes not only results in parsimony but also a desirable feature for cross sectional analysis.

One method of obtaining determinant attributes of a product is by direct questioning, where the researcher gives the respondents a list of all objective attributes and asks them which attributes determined their choice. One problem with such an approach is that respondents may not be able to respond accurately because of the difficulty in translating objective attributes into the corresponding perceived benefits. For a comparison of traditional methods (direct questioning, indirect questioning, and observation and experimentation) readers may refer to Alpert (1971).

This study presents an alternative methodology for identifying determinant objective attributes of new automobiles. In brief, this is a achieved in two steps. First step involves generating determinant perceptual constructs of a chosen product using Kelly's repertory grid technique. The second step involves developing an analytical procedure for translating the determinant perceptual constructs into their corresponding determinant objective attributes. A similar study was conducted by Agarwal (1978) to link perceptual constructs and objective attributes. Though the first step in both studies is similar, they differ in terms of the analytical procedures used for translating percep-

tual constructs into their corresponding objective attributes. Agarwal (1978) used multidimensional scaling technique in order to identify the perceptual dimensions utilized by consumers in evaluating the automobiles.

METHODOLOGY AND RESULTS

Data were collected from a sample of twenty nine new car buyers in the Buffalo SMSA. Using the Kelly Repertory Grid Test (KRGT), a total of sixteen salient perceptual constructs were identified. The Kelly Grid has the advantage of enabling the researcher to generate constructs in the language of the consumer. To uncover dimensions underlying these sixteen salient constructs, they were factor analyzed and factor scores were computed. Based on a scree test, five factors which explained 80 percent of the variation were selected.

In order to identify the objective attributes corresponding to the five factors, an exhaustive list of ratings of each of the 37 cars on 51 objective attributes available in *Consumer Reports* was collected. Each of the 51 objective attributes was regressed on factor scores from the five perceptual factors. Eliminating all objective attributes which were not significantly related to at least one perceptual dimension, and eliminating redundant attributes, led to a total of nine determinant attributes for which objective data were readily available, and which were significantly related to one or more of the perceptual constructs. The following is the list of nine determinant objective attributes identified in our study: price, reliability gas mileage, rear leg room, acceleration, routing handling, ride, front seat comfort, and luggage capacity. A problem is that these attributes may not adequately capture differences in sportiness and style, which were identified as salient constructs in the KRGT. Unfortunately, there is no clean objective analog for these two attributes. Ideally, the attributes 'sportiness' and 'styling' should be added to the list of nine determinant attributes mentioned above. If these two attributes are to be included, one could obtain information about 'sportiness' and 'styling' of cars by asking the experts in the car industry to rate each of the cars on these two attributes and taking the average ratings of each car as the measures on those dimensions.

Finally, in order to validate the above procedure canonical correlation analysis was performed with the sixteen perceptual constructs as the criterion set and the determinant objective attributes as the predictor set.

Results of the canonical correlation suggest that the perceptual constructs are significantly related to the determinant objective attributes.

The procedure suggested in this paper is more appropriate for products where most perceptual constructs can be represented in terms of their objective physical dimensions. For example, this methodology is less useful for food products as it is very difficult to translate constructs such as 'tasty' and 'spicy' into more meaningful physical ingredients of the products.

In sum, the proposed methodology for identifying the determinant objective attributes of products seems to be a valuable tool. The authors do not claim that this method is better than the existing methods for identifying determinant objective attributes of a product. As concluded by Alpert (1971), comparing methods of identifying determinant attributes is not an easy task because there is no standard for measuring their relative merits. In conclusion, the proposed methodology may only be considered as an alternative method for identifying determinant objective characteristics of certain type of products.

For further information please contact:
Pola B. Gupta
Department of Marketing
College of Business Administration
University of Norther Iowa
Cedar Falls, IA 50614-0126

TOWARD A SCENARIO DEVELOPMENT METHODOLOGY FOR THE STUDY OF TIME USE: EXPLORATORY STEPS

Jay D. Lindquist, Western Michigan University
Carol F. Kaufman, Rutgers University
Paul M. Lane, Western Michigan University

ABSTRACT

Extensive work in the area of how individuals use their time has been done by a number of scholars including Gramm (1987), Hall (1983), Harris (1987), Hendrix, Kinnear and Taylor (1979), Lane, Kaufman and Lindquist (1989), Lane and Lindquist (1988, 1990), Robinson (1983) and Shaw (1986). However, considerable discussion has surfaced regarding the ability of existing methodologies to represent the perceptual, subjective experiences of time use (Hirschman 1987). In response to such concerns, Lane and Lindquist (1988) proposed a time/use commitment taxonomy which they argued could reflect a broader spectrum of time use perceptions, such as time committed to activities which must be done, obligations of that time to scheduled activities, and planned versus spontaneous time use. The taxonomy was subsequently preliminarily verified across a broad spectrum of individuals from the U.S. and some Far Eastern countries (1990).

However, the work to date in the area of time/use commitment has primarily been descriptive in nature with little or no investigation as to why people use their time as they do. Traditional time log approaches chart how much time has been used in certain activities, but do not take the further step of determining why time was used in the ways reported. This paper contains a methodology that deals with an initial step toward producing a research design to determine the underlying reasons for why people use time the way they do. This initial step is the proposal of an exploratory method that will lead to the development of scenarios that reflect the underlying pool of reasons for time use behavior.

According to Kahn and Wiener (1967), "scenarios are hypothetical sequences of events constructed for the purpose of focussing attention on causal processes and decision points." Scenarios, then, are descriptions of situations or conditions that commonly undergird various decision or behavior patterns. Situational influences have been found to be of significant importance in understanding consumer behavior (Belk 1975), and they are seen as key in understanding time use by individuals.

The focus of this piece is on the initial development steps of a procedure for scenario construction that is based on those things in a person's life that either "influence" or "affect" the way he or she uses his or her time. This is of importance as one tries to go beyond the study of time use behavior patterns, which is essentially descriptive, to an understanding of why people use their time as they do. Once a usable scenario development procedure is properly framed the opportunity to put together situations meaningful to consumers with respect to their time use will be realized. A series of common or unique time use situation scenarios may then be constructed for various market segments.

The study of time use situational influences can be carried out initially by having members of potential target market groups indicate their level of identification with the various scenarios presented to them. From this, individuals and groups may be sorted into more clearly defined time use segments. These data may then be helpful in the development and positioning of products and services that have important time use dimensions. Arguably one of the keys to all of this is the ability to construct the appropriate scenarios.

The authors suggest a set of initial steps that are seen as more systematic than those typically found in the scenario design related literature. The proposed steps include segment identification, instrument preparation, instrument pretest, data collection, content analysis and Likert-type scale construction, pretesting, data collection, correlations among items, clustering related items, factor analyze clusters, develop scenarios based on clustering and validate scenarios.

The methodology was tested through all steps short of scenario construction and found workable. More extensive verification is currently underway.

For further information contact:
Jay D. Lindquist, Ph.D.
Department of Marketing
Western Michigan University
Kalamazoo, MI 49008-3812

TWO MEASURES OF CONSUMER INVOLVEMENT: A COMPARATIVE ANALYSIS

Emin Babakus, Memphis State University

ABSTRACT

Two comprehensive measures of involvement-the Personal Involvement Inventory (PII) and the Consumer Involvement Profiles (CIP) were evaluated. The instruments were assessed comparatively using samples of U.S. consumers. The study sought to extend the involvement concept into services area by examining the measures within personal banking services context as well as using a tangible product (TV sets).

Conceptualization efforts with regard to consumer involvement reached a peak during the middle of the past decade. Two major studies were published the following year, both with strong conceptual basis and empirical evidence, and both claiming to have developed a reliable and valid measure of consumer involvement (Laurent and Kapferer 1985; Zaichkowsky 1985). However, the theoretical and operational underpinnings of these measures were materially different, leaving potential users of the measures in a difficult choice situation. In fact, the net impact of these two studies has been an increased debate over the nature and the measurement of the involvement concept (e.g., Higie and Feick 1989; Jain and Srinivasan 1990; Mittal 1989; Mittal and Lee 1988, 1989).

There have been attempts to revise the PII scale to make it more compatible with the CIP (McQuarrie and Munson 1987), and to redefine the concept by adding an emotional component (Zaichkowsky 1987). Additional efforts have been devoted to provide a unified model of involvement (Mittal and Lee 1988, 1989). However, efforts to reconcile these two measures of involvement have yet to lead to conclusive results.

The 16-item CIP scale was received (Laurent 1989) both in French and English (an initial translation). The French version was translated into English again and back to French to insure item contents were preserved. The PII scale was reduced to a 14-item by eliminating six items that are indicators an attitude as opposed to involvement. The remaining 14 items were then classified into a rational-emotional scheme. TV sets and bank services were chosen as two product/service categories.

Data were gathered via a mail survey from members of a consumer research panel. The 600 members of the household research panel were randomly divided into two equal groups. One group received the questionnaire designed for the TV sets, and the other for the personal bank services. Five additional items were included for construct validation purposes.

The measures were subjected to maximum likelihood exploratory factor analysis followed by reliability analysis. In the case of the 14-item PII scale, an oblique two-dimensional solution emerged as expected. The CIP scale generated four-factor solutions for both samples. Contrary to a priori expectations, items representing the "interest" and "pleasure" dimensions converged on a single factor in both cases. However, this result is not unique to this study as similar results have been reported elsewhere (Roehrich and Valette-Florence 1990). Other items consistently loaded on their designated factors in a meaningful way. The two involvement measures were also subjected to confirmatory factor analysis using LISREL. Overall fit measures suggested the two-dimensional PII and four-dimensional CIP models as viable characterizations of the data.

Further validation efforts were carried out using summated scores of the two-dimensional PII and the four-dimensional CIP scales. These measures were correlated among themselves as well as with five outcome variables. The pattern of correlations between various outcome variables and the rational and emotional dimensions of PII revealed close similarities. On the other hand, the "interest & pleasure" component of the CIP scale showed a pattern of correlations similar to the PII dimensions with the outcome variables. The "sign" and "risk 1" (importance of negative consequences) dimensions also produced results similar to those provided by the PII components. The "risk 2" dimension of CIP had much weaker correlations with the outcome variables.

Findings suggest that there is a relatively strong overlap between the PII dimensions and only the "interest & pleasure" dimension of CIP. Beyond that, these two scales may not be used as alternative measures of involvement. Results also suggest the PII scale has a clearer conceptual and empirical foundation as a measure of enduring involvement with a product category.

For further information contact:
Emin Babakus
Department of Marketing
Memphis State University
Memphis, TN 38152

AN EMPIRICAL EXAMINATION OF THE INFORMATIONAL CONTENT OF SERVICES ADVERTISEMENTS

David N. LaBand, Clemson University
Gregory M. Pickett, Clemson University
Stephen J. Grove, Clemson University

ABSTRACT

While the area of services marketing has grown remarkably over the past two decades, the exploration of some specific services phenomena has lagged noticeably (Fisk, Tansuhaj, and Crosby 1988). One marketing area which has received relatively little emphasis from services researchers is services advertising (Kenney and Fisk 1990). While a few studies which investigate how specific service providers might best devise their communication effort do exist, little empirical research of how services advertising in general differs from physical goods advertising has been conducted. The fundamental question of whether advertisers of services are approaching their communication task in a manner that accommodates the special nature of the service product remains.

For some time, various services marketing experts have suggested that services advertising should be different than physical goods advertising (Shostack 1977; Berry 1980; George and Berry 1981; Legg and Baker 1987). A basic proposition found throughout the literature argues that consumers have more difficulty evaluating the quality of service products prior to, during and after consumption (Zeithaml 1981; Parasuraman, Zeithaml and Berry 1985; Legg and Baker 1987) because services are less tangible and subjectively experienced (Shostack 1977; Berry 1980; Gronroos 1990). This ultimately contributes to a greater sense of perceived risk (Gussman 1981; Murray and Schlacter 1990) that should compel consumers to seek more factual information about services prior to purchase. Information like price (Berry 1980; Zeithaml 1981), guarantees and warranties (Hart 1988; Zeithaml 1981), documentation of service excellence (Berry and Clark 1988; George and Berry 1981) and service capacity (Blackman 1985; Rathmell 1974) have all been suggested as viable cues to provide "far in advance of the services offering in the marketplace. Failure to do so will cause disastrous results for the unsuspecting service provider" (Johnson, Scheuing and Gaida 1981, p. 68). These factual stimuli meet the criteria established by Puto and Wells (1982) for informational ads. Our research represents an empirical exploration of the proposition that services advertisers emphasize such factual information in their messages.

To accomplish our task, over 17,000 newspaper ads and nearly 10,000 TV ads placed by sellers of both physical goods and service products were content analyzed for the presence of the four cues noted above. The newspaper ads appeared during one year period in a large, mid-atlantic daily newspaper, while the TV advertisements were broadcast over a ten month span in the same market. Along with the presence (absence) of the four informational cues, information regarding the size of the print ad in square inches and TV ads' national, regional or local focus were recorded. The product categorization (goods vs services) was based upon Shostack's (1977) and Zeithaml's (1981) continua and classifications were purified through total agreement among the three authors and a fourth independent judge. Tangible-dominant products were categorized as goods, while intangible-dominant products were categorized as services. Overall, there were 36 service and 113 physical goods offerings among our final set of TV ads and 34 service and 89 physical goods offerings among the newspaper ads.

The empirical analysis was performed through a sense of ordinary least squares regressions, the first of which explored a smaller set of products at the extremes of a goods vs service continuum; the second of which augmented the first set by including those products not as clearly tangible or intangible dominant, and a third analysis which viewed all products that the judges could discern as goods or services. Analyses were performed for both media, controlling for ad-size (print ads) and, product market (TV ads) since such factors may influence an ads informational content. Results indicated (1) that the service advertisements in both media possess significantly more of the four informational cues than do ads for physical goods, and (2) that, in general, the mean number of these cues becomes less across the services vs goods continuum as the products examined become more and more tangible-dominant.

In sum, services advertisers are clearly emphasizing factual informational content of a type suggested by various service experts and are emphasizing these cues more than those promoting physical goods. Whether or not a conscious effort is being made, it appears that services marketers are indeed attempting to compensate for services' lack of tangibility through the provision of factual information.

For further information contact:
Stephen J. Grove
Clemson University
College of Commerce and Industry
Clemson, SC 29634-1325

MISINFORMATION PROVIDED BY RETAIL SALESPEOPLE: AN OVERLOOKED ASPECT OF THE INFORMATION ENVIRONMENT

Nancy M. Ridgway, University of Colorado at Boulder
Scott A. Dawson, Portland State University

ABSTRACT

A small scale study was conducted looking at the provision of misinformation by retail salespeople. Possible sources of the provision of misinformation were hypothesized, including characteristics of the salespeople themselves and perceived characteristics of management. It was discovered that personal characteristics such as attitudes and goals are related to the provision of misinformation.

INTRODUCTION

Beginning in the early 1970s, an extensive stream of research has explored the information environment. These issues can be organized in terms of the provision and the consumption of information. Work on the provision of product and service information has focused on designing information environments so that the "right" information is provided in the "right" manner leading to consumers making "better" decisions (Bettman 1975; Scammon 1977; Bettman, Payne, and Staelin 1986). Topics investigated from the perspective of information consumption include the extent of external and internal search (Newman and Staelin 1972; Newman 1977; Punj and Staelin 1983), the effects of information overload on decision making (Jacoby, Speller, and Kohn 1974; Best and Williams 1980; Malhotra 1982; Malhotra, Jain, and Lagakos 1982) and the effects of incomplete information on decision-making (Johnson and Levin 1985).

Retail salespeople play a very important role in the provision of consumer information. Consumer choice decisions may be influenced by the accuracy, extent, style and content of the information provided. Although research has shown the importance of retail salespeople as providers of information, a largely neglected consideration is the degree to which that information is valid and correct. Apparently, many consumers rely heavily on retail salespeople for product information. For instance, one study found that many buyers totally abdicated the decision of brand choice for refrigerators to retail salespeople (Claxton and Anderson 1980). Thus, while consumers may rely on retail salespeople for help in making purchase decisions, it is unknown whether accurate information is provided. In a retail marketplace in where supply exceeds demand by perhaps a factor of two, store managers cannot afford lost patronage, possible legal action, and negative word-of-mouth caused by misleading statements of salespeople (Boedecker, Morgan, and Stoltman 1991).

The purpose of the present paper is to examine the reasons for salesperson misinformation. Toward that end, the next section defines salesperson misinformation and highlights its importance in terms of consumers' need for information, manufacturers' marketing programs, and retailers' responsibility. Then, a series of hypotheses suggesting factors believed to affect the provision of salesperson misinformation are presented. Next, a small-scale study that provides preliminary testing of possible correlates of misinformation is described. Finally, suggested directions for future research into the area of salesperson misinformation are discussed.

THE IMPORTANCE OF SALESPERSON MISINFORMATION

In this paper, salesperson misinformation is defined as **the intentional or unintentional communication of incorrect product, service or store information by a retail salesperson.** This includes not only information provided, but also information intentionally or unintentionally withheld—i.e., errors of omission as well as comission. Retail salesperson misinformation impacts at least three important areas: the information needs of consumers, manufacturers' marketing programs, and retailers' social and legal responsibility to consumers. Each of these areas is briefly discussed below.

First, because of the minimal effort expended by most consumers in prepurchase search, salesperson misinformation is extremely important to consumer decision making. Results of early studies found that many consumers exerted minimal search effort, even when shopping for major durable products. For instance, two studies reported that most consumers visited only one retail outlet prior to purchasing durables such as automobiles or appliances (Newman and Staelin 1972; Westbrook and Fornell 1979). In addition, another study found that nearly 30 percent of consumers may totally depend on salespeople for brand decisions (Claxton and Anderson 1980). Importantly, when compared to other respondents, these individuals were also found to be the least educated and least likely to have considered more than one brand. Thus, a picture begins to emerge whereby the individuals most in need of reliable salesperson information may be the least prepared to discern the credibility of that information.

Second, manufacturers depend on retail salespeople for promotion of many goods. While advertising and public relations efforts create brand awareness and a limited amount of product knowledge, consumers may require additional information from salespersons. In a study of appliance purchases, for example, it was found that in most cases the salesperson, not the consumer, determined the extent of search and evaluation of alternatives (Olshavsky 1973). Another study indicated that disclosure of test information for products (such as *Consumer Reports'* evaluations) increases the probability of purchase (Crosby and Grossbart 1982). In sum, manufacturers (and especially producers of shopping goods, such as appliances) rely on retail salespeople to consummate sales and to promote consumer satisfaction. Salesperson misinformation (commision and omission) will negatively affect the successful transmission of complete and correct product information to consumers.

Finally, many responsible retailers have long-run consumer satisfaction and well-being as a goal (Weitz 1981). However, the limited amount of research on this topic reveals a lack of practice of this doctrine. For instance, one study found that 75 percent of the retail managers argued that an advertisement should be run even though most merchandise in the ad was sold, while 80 percent suggested that discontinuation information should not be provided to consumers unless specifically requested (Dornoff and Tankersley 1975-76). To the extent that misinformation leads to negative word-of-mouth by consumers, salesperson misinformation could be detrimental to a store. Additionally, salesperson misinformation (whether intentional or unintentional) can lead to legal liability for the store (fraud, deceit, or the creation of unintended warranties) (cf., Boedecker, Morgan, and Stoltman 1991).

HYPOTHESES RELATING TO PROVISION OF MISINFORMATION BY RETAIL SALESPEOPLE

This section develops hypotheses for study that are believed to impact the provision of misinformation, centering on characteristics of the salesperson and the store management. A near theoretical and empirical void exists as to the provision of misinformation by retail salespeople. Therefore, no previous research can be summoned to provide support for these hypotheses. Thus, these hypotheses must be viewed as preliminary. In addition, this study must be viewed as the first of many that are needed to examine the causes of salesperson misinformation. It should also be noted that characteristics of the shopper may influence the provision of misinformation. For instance, salespeople may perceive some shoppers to be a "pain-in-the-neck" (Furse, Punj, and Stewart 1984), and when faced with such a consumer may alter the amount or correctness of information provided. Consumer characteristics, however, are beyond the scope of the present investigation.

Characteristics of the Salesperson

It is believed that in general, a salesperson who is

more committed to the retailing profession will provide less misinformation. A review of salesperson literature supports this contention (cf., Kohli 1989, Leigh and McGraw 1989; Teas 1981). Specifically, the extent of misinformation given may be a function of the salesperson's: (1) perceived professionalism, (2) perceived importance of providing correct information, (3) reported job satisfaction, (4) aspirations for a higher position in the retailing profession and (5) total selling experience. First, the amount of professionalism that an individual perceives in his or her role as a salesperson may impact the accuracy of information communicated to consumers. If an individual does not take the job seriously, she/he may not feel that being informed and conveying accurate information is an important part of the job. Second, if the salesperson believes that the provision of accurate information is important, and feels a personal responsibility to provide good information, misinformation (including withholding of relevant information) should be lower. Third, if job satisfaction is low, the salesperson may be more likely to convey inaccurate information because they do not enjoy what they do. That enjoyment (or lack thereof) should carry over into how the salesperson treats his/her customers. Fourth, if the salesperson does not have a goal of reaching a higher position in retailing (i.e., compared to viewing the job as temporary and/or as a dead end), she/he may be less motivated to stay informed and convey accurate information to consumers. In this instance, the salesperson may view the provision of correct information as a key to consumer satisfaction and important to future career goals. Fifth, salespersons who have less sales experience may be less committed to the profession and thus convey more misinformation to consumers. In sum, the following characteristics of salespeople are hypothesized to be positively associated with the provision of misinformation. The hypotheses are stated such that their acceptance signifies **higher** reported levels of misinformation provided.

H1: The lower the level of perceived professionalism, the higher the reported level of misinformation provided.

H2: The less a salesperson feels that providing correct information is important, the higher the reported level of misinformation provided.

H3: The lower the reported job satisfaction, the higher the level of misinformation provided.

H4: The lower the aspirations for a retail career, the higher the level of misinformation provided.

H5: The fewer the number of years of retail experience, the higher the level of misinformation provided.

Perceived Characteristics of Store Management

A store's policies and the perceived attitudes of store management may also have an important impact on the existence and degree of misinformation generated by salespersons. First, the more a salesperson believes the store's management is adequate and supportive (in terms of competence, availability of training, commitment to excellence, etc.), the more likely the employee will convey correct product information to consumers. Confidence that a store's management is competent and that a store is well run should translate into greater commitment on the part of sales personnel. Conversely, to the extent a salesperson does not believe the store management to be competent and supportive, the more likely she/he may be to provide misinformation. Second, as a direct corrollary of the previous hypothesis, it is proposed that the less training a salesperson receives, the more misinformation will be conveyed by sales staff. Finally, if the salesperson feels that she/he is not adequately compensated monetarily for the job, more misinformation will be given to consumers. Collectively, the following perceived management characteristics are hypothesized to be positively related to provision of misinformation.

H6: The less a salesperson perceives management as adequate, the higher the reported level of misinformation provided.

H7: The less training received by the salesperson, the higher the reported level of misinformation provided.

H8: The less the salesperson perceives his/her compensation to be fair, the higher the reported level of misinformation provided.

METHOD—SAMPLE AND MEASUREMENT

Generating a sample of retail salespeople and a reasonable response rate for the study faced three major hurdles. First, the tremendous turnover of retail salespeople—reaching 100 percent per year at some retailers—makes it nearly impossible to obtain an accurate mailing list. Numerous list vendors were contacted and all maintained that turnover in the industry prohibited constructing a reasonably current mailing list. This problem led to contacting individual stores and soliciting participation of salespeople through store managers. Here, the second problem surfaced. The sensitive nature of the primary dependent variable—provision of misinformation—caused an unwillingness to participate among the majority of store managers contacted. A total of five stores—one discount, two mass merchandise and two department—in two major metropolitan areas on the West Coast eventually agreed to participate. For participating stores, surveys and return envelopes were provided to all of each stores' salespeople. The managers would agree to only a single wave of the survey. The single-page questionnaire (front and back of one legal-sized sheet) included a short introductory letter that requested participation and assured anonymity. Here, the third problem (not unanticipated, of course) evidenced itself. Perhaps due to the fear of being identified and the fact that sales clerks were contacted through their employers, the response rate was low. Of the 635 surveys

sent, a total of 125 were returned in usable form. While the overall response rate was 19.7 percent, rates varied from 38.5 percent from a department store to 6.5 percent from a mass merchandise store. The sample breakdown in number of salespeople by store type is: department store—71; mass merchandiser—24; and discount—25 (the origin of five surveys could not be identified). The overall response rate, while low, is acceptable, and understandable given the sensitive nature of the questions (Ridgway and Price 1982; Peterson and Ridgway 1985).

Where possible, multi-item scales were constructed to measure the attitudinal constructs necessary for testing the study's hypotheses. The retailing literature provided a number of items for measuring job satisfaction and professionalism (Bagozzi 1978; Churchill, Ford, and Oliver 1974; Dubinsky and Matson 1979; Teas 1981). The items culled from these studies were the starting point for these scales. After some deletion and re-wording by the authors, these items were subjected to the pre-test described below. The remainder of items were generated by the authors with consultation from store employees and managers and from the conceptual definitions of the attitudinal variables (i.e., provision of misinformation, importance of correct information, and managerial adequacy/support). All items were pre-tested in two ways. First, the initial pool of items was refined based on the assessments of a number of store managers who provided evaluations of the appropriateness of the items. In addition, the items were reduced based on a pre-test whereby retail salespeople responded to the items (these managers and salespeople were not part of the eventual sample). All attitudinal items were measured using a 5-point, Strongly Agree/Strongly Disagree Likert-type scale. The scales were purified using the procedures suggested by Churchill (1979) and Nunnally (1978). Items with factor loadings of more than .40 on more than one factor were excluded and with the exception of one item, only items with item-total correlations above .35 were included in the final measures. The resultant multi-item scales are described in Table 1. All measures had suitable levels of reliability. Though more is needed to improve the reliability of the Provision of Misinformation measure, the level achieved here (a = .63) is acceptable for initial stages of research (Nunnally 1978).

To measure years of retail experience, respondents were asked for the number of years they had worked as a retail salesperson. Aspirations for a career in retailing, amount of training received, and fairness of compensation were all measured on a 5-point Strongly Agree/Strongly Disagree Likert-type scale.

ANALYSIS AND RESULTS

The first analysis looked for possible differences in provision of misinformation between store types. Previous research suggests that specialty stores have the highest committment to social responsibility, followed

TABLE 1
Description of Measures

	ITEM TOTAL	FACTOR LOADING
PROVISION OF MISINFORMATION (Alpha = .63)		
I have on occasion withheld some information when a customer has asked me a question.	.51	.72
I do not feel obligated to tell customers all I know about a product.	.40	.61
On a few occasions, I have answered a customer's question with information that I knew was not right.	.36	.52
I am sometimes just too busy to provide the answers to all the questions customers ask.	.38	.48
PROFESSIONALISM (Alpha = .77)		
I am more professional than the majority of sales associates where I work.	.55	.73
I feel my performance is near the top in comparison to other salespeople where I work.	.63	.71
I feel I know the correct answers to most customer's questions.	.49	.65
Most customers probably feel that I am more professional than other retail salespeople.	.57	.65
I know enough about the products I sell in order to help customers make good purchase decisions.	.48	.63
Customers are satisfied with the quality of services that I provide.	.41	.48
IMPORTANCE OF CORRECT INFORMATION (Alpha = .76)		
Customers depend on me for information to help them make their purchases.	.63	.76
Providing correct and current information to customers is one of the most important aspects of my job.	.56	.75
I try to keep current with the positive and negative features of the brands in my department.	.51	.59
Quality customer service is an important goal where I work.	.53	.58
Salespeople do not need to know their products as well as they did in the past.	.39	.52
JOB SATISFACTION (Alpha = .72)		
I find my work very challenging.	.58	.79
I plan to continue with a career as a retail salesperson.	.53	.70

TABLE 1 (continued)	ITEM TOTAL	FACTOR LOADING
I find my work very interesting.	.57	.68
I am fairly compensated for the work I do as a retail salesperson.	.30	.51
Because of some of the products I sell, I go out of my way to read certain publications.	.42	.50
MANAGERIAL ADEQUACY/SUPPORT (Alpha = .77)		
The amount of product training provided by store management has not been adequate.	.62	.77
The majority of my associates are competent salespeople.	.55	.68
Product knowledge among the management at my store is extensive.	.59	.67
Management at my store cares about the quality of salespeople they are hiring.	.55	.65
I feel comfortable asking my superior(s) for further information about products in my department.	.50	.64
I wish store management would provide more training about the products I sell.	.31	.52

by department stores and, lastly, discount stores (Dornoff and Tankersley 1975-76). Thus, before data from store types were pooled, it was deemed important to determine if this research finding would apply to the provision of misinformation. Analysis of variance, treating reported provision of misinformation as the dependent variable, was performed. The mean levels of misinformation across the three types showed little variation and no statistically significant differences. All other measures in the study involve metrically scaled variables. Thus, correlational analysis was the method used to test the study's hypotheses.

Regarding characteristics of the salesperson, the results concerning perceived professionalism are supportive of H1. Salespeople with lower levels of perceived professionalism tend to report that they provide greater amounts of misinformation (r = -.22, p < .01). Providing incorrect (and correct) information seems to be associated with the degree to which a salesperson perceives him/herself as a professional. As hypothesized by H2, the less a salesperson perceives that providing correct information is important, the more s/he tends to report providing misinformation (r = -.33, p < .001). Providing correct information seems closely tied to a high customer service orientation. As the item descriptions in Table 1 show, the importance of correct information includes items capturing perceptions that customers depend on the salesperson for informatin, that providing correct and current infor-

mation to customers is one of the most important aspects of the salesperson's job, and that quality customer service is an important goal of the salesperson's company.

The results also support H3 and H4. Provision of misinformation is significantly and negatively related to job satisfaction (r = -.26, p < .003) and aspirations for a career in retailing (r = -.22, p < .01). Finally, H5 explores the relationship between years of retail experience and provision of misinformation. In this study, the relationship was negative but weak (r = -.12, p < .09), so while fewer years as a sales clerk may be related to provision of misinformation, the relationship found here is not statistically significant.

The hypotheses involving perceived characteristics of store management (adequacy of store management, amount of training provided by management and adequacy of compensation) were not supported by this data. Although adequacy of store management was negatively related to provision of misinformation (r = -.14, p < .07), the correlation was not statistically significant.

DISCUSSION AND DIRECTIONS FOR FUTURE RESEARCH

This study sought to provide an initial framework, possible correlates and preliminary findings for studying an important aspect of the salesperson's job—the provi-

TABLE 2
Correlations Between the Provision of Misinformation
and the Hypothesized Concepts

HYPOTHESIS	CONCEPT	RELATIONSHIP WITH PROVISION OF MISINFORMATION	
		CORRELATION	P
	Characteristics of Salesperson		
1	Perceived Professionalism	-.22	.01
2	Importance of Correct Information	-.33	.001
3	Job Satisfaction	-.26	.001
4	Aspirations for Retail Career	-.22	.01
5	Years of Retail Experience	-.12	.09
	Perceived Characteristics of Store Management		
6	Adequacy of Store Management	-.14	.07
7	Amount of Training Provided	-.09	NS
8	Fairness of Compensation	-.06	NS

sion of accurate information. While researchers have verified the salient role that retail salespeople serve as providers of consumer information for products and services, the literature has not yet attempted to determine the overall accuracy of this information or what factors may affect that accuracy. The empirical research reported here was concerned with the latter; determining which salesperson and perceived store characteristics might be associated with the provision of misinformation. Though the measures used in the study were suitably reliable, the results are limited by a relatively small sample of salespeople and store types. Thus, the findings may be thought of as a starting point for developing an understanding of the provision of retail misinformation.

Overall, the results suggest that the provision of misinformation by salespeople is largely a function of individual attitudes and goals. The salesperson who will go out of his/her way to provide correct information has the self-perception of being professional, concerned about customer service and desirous for a career in retailing. Moreover, the provision of correct information to consumers appears to be asociated with higher levels of job satisfaction. Though misinformation provision was not related to the perceived store management characteristics in this study, additional research involving these

variables is warranted. The stores from which the sample was drawn in this study were large. Smaller, specialty store employees should be surveyed before the notions of perceived adequacy of management, adequacy of training and monetary compensation are dismissed as important in the provision of misinformation.

Many opportunities exist for future research on the provision of misinformation by salespeople. A first step would be a replication of this study with a larger, nationwide sample. Future work should also seek to add items to the core multi-item scale developed here to measure the provision of misinformation and establish higher reliability. In addition, salespeople should be sampled from a greater variety of institutions in order to discern whether perceived store management characteristics impact the provision of misinformation. Other potential causes of misinformation exist and need to be examined. For example, the provision of misinformation could be affected by an employee's liking of his/her immediate supervisor, the employee's transient mood on a given day or customer characteristics ("pain in the neck" customers versus troublefree customers).

Although beyond the scope of the present study, a number of factors associated with products could also affect the provision of misinformation. For example, products that change frequently in terms of features and methods of operation could increase misinformation. In addition, products that are inherently more difficult to understand and learn about (i.e., technical products) could increase misinformation. Another product-related situation is the proliferation of brands in a product category. The existence of many alternative brands, each with assumed advantages and disadvantages, can confuse salespersons and consumers alike.

The results reported here, though somewhat preliminary, can help to inform the hiring, training and incentive practices of retail managers. Providing timely and correct information is a salient aspect of fulfilling customer expectations and, in an over-saturated retail environment in which customer expectations continue to be matured by the likes of Nordstrom store managers must excel at motivating and training their salespeople to be credible sources of product information. Furthermore, incorrect product information that leads to purchase and dissatisfaction can at the least result in negative word-of-mouth, and at the most legal challenges by consumers in an increasingly litigious society. The results suggest that managers should hire individuals who seek a career in retailing. Previous experience could be an asset as well. Training programs must provide thorough and continuously updated product and/or service knowledge.

REFERENCES

Bagozzi, Richard P. (1978), "Salesforce Performance and Satisfaction as a Function of Individual Differences, Interpersonal, and Situational Factors," *Journal of Marketing Research,* 15 (November), 517-531.

Best, Roger J. and Daniel B. Williams (1980), "Structural Properties of Consumer Information and Perceptions of Informativeness," in *Advances in Consumer Research,* Vol. 7, J. C. Olsen, ed. Ann Arbor, MI: Association for Consumer Research, 501-506.

Bettman, James R. (1975), "Issues in Designing Consumer Informaiton Environments," *Journal of Consumer Research,* 2 (December), 169-177.

_____, John W. Payne, and Richard Staelin (1986), "Cognitive Considerations in Designing Effective Labels for Presenting Risk Information," *Journal of Public Policy and Marketing,* 5, 1-28.

Boedecker, Karl, Fred Morgan, and Jeffrey Stoltman (1991), "Legal Dimensions of Salespersons' Statements: A Review and Managerial Suggestions," *Journal of Marketing,* 55, 1 (January), 70-80.

Churchill, Gilbert A. (1979), "A Paradigm for Developing Better Measures of Marketing Constructs," *Journal of Marketing Research,* 16 (February), 64-73.

_____, Neil M. Ford, and Orville C. Walker, Jr. (1974), "Measuring Job Satisfaction of Industrial Salesmen," *Journal of Marketing Research,* 11 (August), 254-260.

Claxton, John D. and Dennis Anderson (1980), "Energy Information at the Point of Sale: A Field Experiment," in *Advances in Consumer Research,* J. C. Olsen, ed. Ann Arbor, MI: Association for Consumer Research, 7, 277-282.

Crosby, Lawrence A. and Sanford L. Grossbart (1982), "Voluntary Performance Information Disclosures: Economic Perspectives and an Experimental Test," in *Advances in Consumer Research,* A. Mitchell, ed. Ann Arbor, MI: Association for Consumer Research, 9, 321-326.

Dornoff, Ronald J. and Clint B. Tankersley (1975-76),

"Do Retailers Practice Social Responsibility?," *Journal of Retailing,* 51 (Winter), 33-42.

Dubinsky, Alan J. and Bruce E. Mattson (1979), "Consequences of Role Conflict and Ambiguity Experienced by Retail Salespeople," *Journal of Retailing,* 55 (Winter), 70-86.

Furse, David H., Girish N. Punj, and David Stewart (1984), "A Typology of Individual Search Strategies Among Purchasers of New Automobiles," *Journal of Consumer Research,* 10 (March), 417-431.

Jacoby, J., D. E. Speller, and C. A. Kohn (1974), "Brand Choice Behavior as a Function of Information Load," *Journal of Marketing Research,* 11 (February), 63-69.

Johnson, Richard D. and Irwin P. Levin (1985), "More than Meets Eye: The Effect of Missing Information on Purchase Evaluations," *Journal of Consumer Research,* 12 (September), 169-177.

Kohli, Ajay K. (1989), "Effects of Supervisory Behavior: The Role of Individual Differences Among Salespeople," *Journal of Marketing,* 53, 4 (October), 40-50.

Leigh, Thomas W. and Patrick F. McGraw (1989), "Mapping the Procedural Knowledge of Industrial Sales Personnel: A Script-Theoretic Investigation," *Journal of Marketing,* 53, 1 (January), 16-34.

Malhotra, Naresh K. (1982), "Information Load and Consumer Decision Making," *Journal of Consumer Research,* 8 (March), 419-430.

_____, Arun K. Jain, and Stephen W. Lagakos (1982), "The Information Overload Controversy: An Alternative Viewpoint," *Journal of Marketing,* 46 (Spring), 27-37.

Newman, Joseph (1977), "Consumer External Search: Amount and Determinants," in *Consumer and Industrial Buying Behavior,* A. Woodside, ed. New York: North-Holland, 79-94.

_____ and Richard Staelin (1972), "Prepurchase Information Seeking for New Cars and Major Household Appliances," *Journal of Marketing Research,* 9 (August), 249-257.

Nunnally, Jum C. (1978), *Psychometric Theory.* New

York: McGraw-Hill Book Company.

Olshavsky, Richard W. (1973), "Customer-Salesman Interaction in Appliance Retailing," *Journal of Marketing Research,* 10 (May), 208-212.

Peterson, Robert A. and Nancy M. Ridgway (1985), "A Note on the Perception of Threatening Question," *Proceedings of the American Statistical Association,* 443-447.

Punj, Girish H. and Richard Staelin (1983), "A Model of Consumer Information Search Behavior for New Automobiles," *Journal of Consumer Research,* 9 (March), 366-380.

Ridgway, Nancy M. and Linda L. Price (1982), "The Effects of Respondent Identification in a Mail Survey," *Proceedings of the AMA Educators Confer-*ence, Series 48, 410-413.

Scammon, Debra L. (1977), "Information Load and Consumers," *Journal of Consumer Research,* 4 (December), 148-155.

Teas, Kenneth R. (1981), "A Test of a Model of Department Store Salespeoples' Job Satisfaction," *Journal of Retailing,* 57 (Spring), 3-26.

Weitz, Barton A. (1981), "Effectiveness in Sales Interactions: A Contingency Framework," *Journal of Marketing,* 45 (Winter), 85-103.

Westbrook, Robert A. and Claes Fornell (1979), "Patterns of Information Source Usage Among Durable Goods Buyers," *Journal of Marketing Research,* 16 (August), 303-312.

MANAGING THE EVIDENCE FOR THE INEXPERIENCED SERVICE CUSTOMER

Kathleen Seiders, Texas A&M University

ABSTRACT

The effects of tangible representations of a service on the inexperienced firm customer are examined. A conceptual model shows the impact of managed evidence as it differs among experienced and inexperienced customers. Literature focusing on both consumer evaluation processes and service sector strategy is reviewed and propositions are presented.

INTRODUCTION

Intangibility is a well-documented aspect of the majority of services. This characteristic defines a fundamental difference between the marketing of goods and services. A service is, essentially, a performance which customers must purchase in advance of consumption (Berry 1980; Berry, Parasuraman, and Zeithaml 1985; Gronroos 1983; Grove and Fisk 1983).

Although services are deficient in physical attributes conveying information about the product form (Howard 1989), every service has some minimum number of tangible factors which serve to express its identity. Tangibles associated with the service function as "clues" about the service; a marketer who manipulates these clues is "managing the evidence" about the service (Shostack 1977).

The necessity for marketers to manage service tangibles effectively arises because services are more difficult for consumers to imagine and desire than goods (Berry and Parasuraman 1991). Most services lack standardization, which adds to consumer uncertainty. Tangible clues play a key role in promoting a service, both preceding and during a service experience (Booms and Bitner 1981). Relevant communication targets for the promotion effort include prospective buyers, current customers, the general public, and the employment market (Flipo 1986).

Tangibles associated with services include physical facilities, contact personnel, equipment, advertising, correspondence, promotion materials, other customers, and price lists. Customers are attentive to these pre-purchase clues as input for future buying decisions. Service-related cues leading to inferences about what the service experience will be like may be regarded as implicit service promises (Zeithaml, Berry, and Parasuraman 1991).

TANGIBLES IN SERVICES MARKETING

Characteristics of service firms are problematic for customers to process and formulate mentally. Special challenges are inherent in the consumer evaluation of service performance. Three non-discrete categories of tangibles which customers utilize for better understanding of services have been delineated (Berry and Parasuraman 1991). In proposing a fourth category--social environment--we divide physical and social components for individual consideration. This distinction follows the separation of services marketing mix variables physical evidence and participants. As antecedents of service encounter satisfaction, these variables affect both expectations and perceived service performance (Bitner 1990).

Types of Evidence

* Physical environment, including facilities' exteriors and interiors; expressing both aesthetic and functional design.
* Social environment, determined by employees and other customers, through appearances and behavior.
* Communications, encompassing all forms of media including advertising, promotional and educational materials, signage, billing statements, instructions, uniforms, and trucks.
* Price information, expressed as price data in a visible form, signaling the positioning of the company and influencing customers' expectations.

Perceptions influenced by presented tangibles affect beliefs about the tangibles themselves in addition to other less apparent service characteristics. Evaluating tangibles is a more simple task than evaluating more abstract service attributes. When associated representations of a service have been emphasized to enhance its benefits, the service has been "tangibilized" (Berry and Clark 1986).

Vitalizing the Marketing Strategy

The manipulation of tangible clues provides the services marketer an opportunity to position and differentiate a business. A firm's marketing strategy may be efficiently conveyed to both customers and employees when tangibles are used to reinforce the desired service image.

Network service companies are especially dependent on managed evidence to project a consistent and coherent position. The Body Shop International, the British cosmetics retailer with stores in 37 countries, is an example of a firm successfully using tangibles to support an overall marketing strategy of environmental leadership. Store interiors feature graphics highlighting ecological activism, products are packaged in recycled containers, and forest green trucks bear environmental slogans in giant white letters.

A variety of subroles employ evidence management and contribute to the support of the overall marketing strategy. These subroles are not mutually exclusive; they include shaping first impressions; managing trust; facilitating quality service; changing an image; providing sensory stimulation; and socializing employees (Berry and Parasuraman 1991).

The purpose of this paper is to examine the subrole of shaping first impressions. Within the context of services marketing, this involves attracting the inexperienced customer: the customer who has had little or no interaction with a particular firm.

Treatment of evidence management in the marketing literature has primarily focused on service facilities (Kotler 1973; Upah and Fulton 1985; Bitner 1986, 1992). Evidence management is inherent in the dramaturgy model of impression management (Grove and Fisk 1983) and the molecular model of market entities (Shostack 1977). Minimal research has been dedicated to examining consumer responses to marketing which integrates the entire range of evidence types.

The potential for strategic segmentation and positioning by service firms using tangibles-oriented marketing has not yet been thoroughly investigated. We attempt to begin a process of integrating existing knowledge about evidence management into a framework which describes the function of tangibles in affecting the inexperienced customer.

TANGIBLES AND THE INEXPERIENCED CUSTOMER

Among individual reactions to a particular physical environment are approach or avoidance behaviors (Mehrabian and Russell 1974). All types of evidence may influence an initial decision to purchase a service. Tangibles reinforce the verbal promises of a service firm, enabling it to create a first impression which underscores important dimensions of reliability, responsiveness, and competence (Parasuraman, Zeithaml, and Berry 1984). Because consumers rely heavily on visible clues in the absence of other information, individuals inexperienced with a firm will be especially attentive to presented tangibles.

A Model

Figure 1 offers a summary view of the elements which influence the service customer relative to his/her experience level with the firm. For input to the evaluation process, the inexperienced customer relies on tangibles associated with the service offering. The experienced customer's perception of the firm results from more intangible qualities conveyed through the consumption experience. In the following sections, elements of the framework are described and developed through the use of existing literature. Research propositions are offered and managerial implications are discussed.

The Inexperienced Consumer

Behavior of the inexperienced or novice consumer has been studied and analyzed within the realm of goods marketing. Certain concepts and findings from this area of research are likely to be applicable to a services setting. A consideration of the relevant literature requires comparing consumer experience with goods product classes to customer experience with service firms.

Qualitatively different types of choice processes are conducted by consumers who have varying degrees of prior knowledge and experience (Howard and Sheth 1969). An important factor is the consumer's confidence or level of certainty that his/her evaluative judgment will be correct. Inexperienced consumers often perform a more heavy weighting of attributes which are easily comprehended or made salient by promotional efforts. Reliance on simplified rather than complete information is greater for novice consumers than for experts (Alba and Hutchinson 1987). "Simple rules" of information processing are used more by consumers with minimal prior knowledge and experience (Bettman and Park 1980).

In complex settings, inexperienced customers may engage in more lengthy evaluations of attribute levels, striving to develop choice criteria which experienced customers have already established (Bettman and Park 1980). Although many researchers have found product experience to diminish external search, some have discovered experienced consumers to engage in more elaborate problem solving. Knowledgable individuals may reduce external search because their expertise enables them to search more efficiently (Brucks 1985). Situational complexity and consequences of choice decisions are important variables in the evaluative processes of consumers. Despite certain variations in research findings from investigation of the two consumer segments, distinctions between the novice and the expert are significant and central to the future study of service expectation antecedents.

Perceived Risk

As consumers typically purchase services prior to consumption, they must trust service companies to deliver on whatever promises have been implied. Risk is intrinsic to this arrangement because promises may not be accurate reflections of services as they are actually performed. Consumers perceive greater risk in services purchases than goods due to intangibility and limited information; lack of standardization; absence of guarantees or warranties; and an often specialized nature which is very difficult to evaluate (Zeithaml 1981). Variability in service delivery makes quality judgments problem-

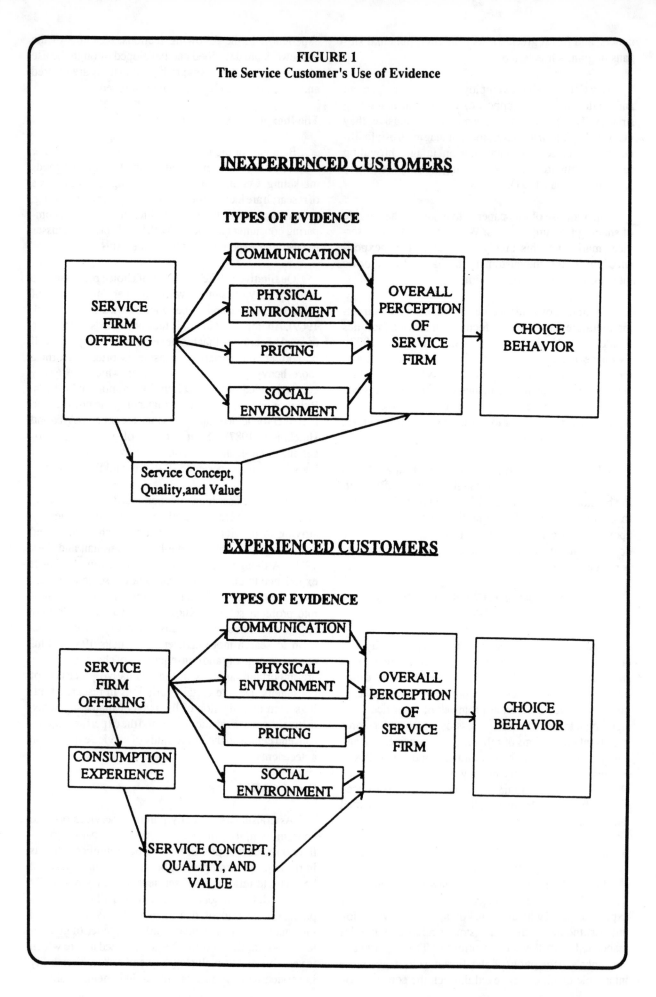

FIGURE 1
The Service Customer's Use of Evidence

INEXPERIENCED CUSTOMERS

TYPES OF EVIDENCE

SERVICE FIRM OFFERING → COMMUNICATION, PHYSICAL ENVIRONMENT, PRICING, SOCIAL ENVIRONMENT → OVERALL PERCEPTION OF SERVICE FIRM → CHOICE BEHAVIOR

Service Concept, Quality, and Value

EXPERIENCED CUSTOMERS

TYPES OF EVIDENCE

SERVICE FIRM OFFERING → COMMUNICATION, PHYSICAL ENVIRONMENT, PRICING, SOCIAL ENVIRONMENT → OVERALL PERCEPTION OF SERVICE FIRM → CHOICE BEHAVIOR

CONSUMPTION EXPERIENCE → SERVICE CONCEPT, QUALITY, AND VALUE

atic, bringing uncertainty to the purchasing process. This uncertainty, combined with imagined consequences of choosing the wrong service provider, creates perceived risk (Guseman 1981).

The service purchase and usage process often has complex demands which involve a sequence of steps requiring negotiation (Lovelock 1981). Accompanying this higher level of customer involvement is an increase in acknowledged risk. A potential customer with no experience of a particular service faces magnified uncertainty with regard to both financial and social risk.

Proposition 1a: Perceived risk is greater for the customer having little or no experience with the service firm.

When perceived risk is a prominent influence, consumers search for personal sources of information which are believed to be credible and unbiased. Novice consumers are more likely than expert to assume the opinions of those who have engaged in the consumption experience. Using this vicarious knowledge, the inexperienced customer is able to add conceptualizations of quality and value to his/her overall perception of the firm, as shown in Figure 1.

The importance of the service for the consumer, the strength of the service provider's image, and the nature and scope of purchase decision implications all impact the level of imagined risk. Most service purchase choices cannot be reversed (Booms and Nyquist 1981); therefore, if a firm's reputation is unclear, customers will pay more attention to tangibles (Flipo 1986).

Proposition 1b: The greater the perceived risk associated with a service, the more likely is the customer to search for tangible clues.

RELIANCE ON TANGIBLE CLUES

Tangible representations allow consumers to recognize the purpose and positioning of a service firm within its market. Visible cues are used as mnemonic devices which permit customers to mentally categorize and discriminate among types of service provider (Bitner 1992). This ability to categorize enables an individual to make finer distinctions with stronger reliability.

Movement towards greater specificity in categorization is significant, as it drives the consumer to make higher level evaluations and prompts the marketer to communicate more specific information (Alba and Hutchinson 1987). While experienced customers draw categorization abilities from the consumption experience, the inexperienced are dependent on evidence offered by the firm.

Proposition 2: The less experienced in using a service, the more a customer will rely on tangible

cues for mental categorization.

Evaluation of Quality

A method of differentiation used by the prospective service customer is the determination of firm quality. Although structurally similar to satisfaction, service quality goes beyond assessment of specific transactions to define a global appraisal of excellence (Parasuraman, Zeithaml, and Berry 1986). The evaluative process may be more complex for the service consumer, as it is difficult for providers to control for quality and offer a consistent product (Lovelock 1981).

Attributes which signal quality may be intrinsic, relating to a product's physical make-up, or extrinsic, apart from the actual product (Olson 1977). Intrinsic attributes of an insurance agency, for example, include comprehensiveness of policy offerings and efficiency of claim processing. Extrinsic cues to the service include office location and design and printed informational materials. Because service customers have fewer intrinsic cues on which to base beliefs, they will typically use extrinsic cues to infer quality (Zeithaml 1988).

Visible symbols which convey a complete image of product quality are sought by prospective customers. The major extrinsic cues to service quality are price, brand name, level of advertising, and physical facility. Inexperienced customers, lacking in consumption process information, are even more dependent on external cues for quality evaluation purposes.

Proposition 3: The less experienced in using a service, the more a customer will rely on tangible cues to deduce quality.

SURROGATE EVIDENCE IN THE DECISION PROCESS

A classification of qualities of goods proposes search qualities, which are determined prior to purchase, and experience qualities, which are determined only after purchase or during consumption (Nelson 1970). Credence qualities are those which are impossible to evaluate at any time (Darby and Karni 1973).

Services, due to their inherent intangibility and simultaneity of production and consumption, are rich in experience qualities. Few search qualities are relevant to most services; credence qualities are prominent in certain specialized, professional services (Zeithaml 1981). Of ten established service quality determinants, only two--tangibles and credibility--can be known before purchase (Parasuraman, Zeithaml, and Berry 1985).

The inexperienced services customer has no direct information about experience qualities, but can only receive it vicariously. As shown by Figure 1, informational cues are used to assist with task response, or the choice decision. Operating without intrinsic cues, without adequate information, services customers require tangible clues from potential providers.

Surrogates for intrinsic cues are "packages of evidence" which guide the customer's deductive process of evaluation (Shostack 1977). A company brand is a surrogate for intrinsic cues: customer response to the strongest presented brand is a mediation factor in the choice decision. For example, American Express presents "the card" as a symbol or icon; advertisements display a giant AmEx card as the tail of the Concorde, as part of the New York City skyline, and as a monolith on Easter Island. Problem solving by novices is characterized by a more pronounced use of readily understood external factors. The more cohesive and focused the presentation of service firm tangibles, the more inclined is the novice to accept such evidence as surrogates for service product identity.

Both cognitive and affective qualities influence consumer response to tangibles. With the proportional increase in experience attributes, affective judgments begin to predominate (Lutz 1986). Affective response encourages more generalized attitudes, entailing a willingness to accept service tangibles as surrogates for other unexperienced dimensions.

Proposition 4: Because a customer must buy a service before experiencing it, he/she seeks surrogate evidence to guide his/her initial purchase decision.

Experience-Based Approaches

Predictive value is higher for intrinsic cues than extrinsic cues, proving more effective use in the quality evaluation process (Zeithaml 1988). For the inexperienced service consumer, tangibles influence both the expected and the perceived service (Flipo 1986). As Figure 1 shows, once the service is experienced, tangibles are reduced to being just one element of the overall perception.

Experienced service users may reduce their time investment, relying more on their actual interactions with the firm rather than external cues (Booms and Nyquist 1981). As the customer becomes more expert, the tangible dimensions of a service are consistently disregarded.

Novices are likely to select information for processing based on expediency in order to avoid becoming overwhelmed (Alba and Hutchinson 1987). In a complex decision situation, the expert may choose more elaborate information which is probably not based on tangible clues. When making an investment decision, a consumer would more readily obtain objective-source financial data than rely on institutional advertising. In the selection of information for processing, the expert customer is

likely to discount the messages conveyed by tangibles associated with the service.

Proposition 5: The more experienced the customer, the less important are tangible clues for purchase decisions.

The potency of managed evidence is strongest in the initial cultivation of a relationship: the attraction of the new service customer. Tangibles may not impact the choice decision of an experienced customer, or compensate for an unsuccessful service encounter. Nevertheless, reinforcing the firm's image with the use of managed evidence remains a valuable marketing objective throughout the relationship.

Service Classifications

The potential to attract an inexperienced customer to a service firm varies with the particular characteristics of the service business. Variability among types of services is substantial; it may be appropriate for some analyses to segment services into clusters which share certain relevant marketing features (Lovelock 1983). A service which requires the customer to enter the service "factory", such as a restaurant, theatre, or hair salon, will utilize different strategic elements than one whose customer relates at arm's length, such as a mail order business or a long-distance telephone company.

Shostack (1977) presented service businesses on a spectrum ranging from "tangible dominant" to "intangible dominant". The more intangible the position, the greater the necessity to differentiate the invisible qualities through the positioning of tangible clues. A series of two-dimensional classifications were offered by Lovelock (1983) for application to various service industries. A firm's position on a particular matrix will affect both the strategy and tactics of tangibles manipulation. For example, a people-based operation whose service facilities are unseen by customers must focus on effective tangible communications. Allied Van Lines equips its sales associates with a package of graphic materials to use in presenting estimates to prospective clients for interstate residential moves. Included are attractive magazines and brochures, left with the client in a folder picturing a sparkling Allied van at the foot of a snow-capped peak.

A typology offered by Bitner (1992) is designed for the analysis of the "servicescape", or physical environment associated with a service organization. Dimensions are primary actor identification and complexity of the service environment. Aspects of this framework are salient for marketers selecting strategic messages to be directed to the inexperienced customer.

Proposition 6: The importance of tangibles for the inexperienced firm customer is affected by particular service industry characteristics.

Evidence Management for Employees

Due to the prevalence of direct human contact in service delivery, firms benefit from simultaneously supporting customers and employees (Berry, Parasuraman, and Zeithaml 1988). Tangibles will affect the employees of the firm in addition to the customers: employee satisfaction, motivation, and productivity may be positively reinforced. Such variables, reflected in employee behavior, directly influence the social environment which cues the inexperienced customer.

An employee's positive internal response to a service environment prompts expressions of commitment and purpose for belonging to the organization. The physical environment and other tangible representations of the service will affect the quality of the social interactions between and among employees and customers (Bitner 1992).

Proposition 7: The same tangible clues used as surrogate evidence by inexperienced customers will serve to enhance performance by a firm's contact personnel.

MANAGERIAL IMPLICATIONS

In order to give form to abstract qualities and transform risk into benefit, the services marketer must effectively select and utilize the appropriate signals as evidence. An inexperienced customer will often have either an ongoing or periodic desire for a service. When this customer is in control of supplier selection, the choice will likely be made on the basis of perceived relationship benefits (Berry 1989). The marketer's need to elicit customer trust is paramount.

Marketers who research and understand the value perceptions of consumers are better able to position the organization, address specific market segments, and differentiate their service along chosen dimensions. The segmentation process will be enhanced when marketers are capable of distinguishing the differences in evaluation processes among experienced and inexperienced customers. Tangibles management may then allow the customer to estimate an appropriate level of service expectation, avoiding a gap in what is promised and what is delivered.

SUMMARY AND CONCLUSIONS

The service characteristic of intangibility defines the importance of the role of managing evidence in services marketing. In the absence of other experiences to counterbalance the service firm image, tangible clues assume disproportionate influence for the inexperienced customer. Representations of the service adopt a surrogate role when the consumption experience is missing.

A model of the relationships integral to the consumer evaluation of managed evidence, focusing on customer experience, was presented. Relevant marketing literature was discussed and specific propositions were offered. This consideration of these phenomena is intended to suggest a direction for future empirical study. A need exists within the services sector for further investigation of the strategic potential inherent in tangibles-oriented marketing.

REFERENCES

Alba, Joseph W. and J. Wesley Hutchinson (1987), "Dimensions of Consumer Expertise, *Journal of Consumer Research,* 14 (March), 411-54.

Berry, Leonard L. (1980), "Services Marketing is Different," *Business,* (May/June), 24-49.

_____(1983), "Services Marketing is Different," in *Services Marketing,* Christopher H. Lovelock, ed. Englewood Cliffs, NJ: Prentice-Hall, 29-36.

_____and Terry Clark (1986), "Four Ways to Make Services More Tangible," *Business,* (October/December), 53-54.

_____(1989), "Relationship Marketing," in *Emerging Perspectives on Services Marketing,* Leonard L. Berry, G. Lynn Shostack, and Gregory D. Upah, eds. Chicago: American Marketing Association.

_____(1989), "How to Sell Services," *American Demographics,* (October), 42,43.

_____and A. Parasuraman (1991), *Marketing Services: Competing Through Quality,* New York: The Free Press.

_____, _____, and Valarie A. Zeithaml (1985), "Quality Counts in Services, Too," *Business Horizons,* (May/June), 44-52.

_____, _____, and _____(1988), "The Service Quality Puzzle," *Business Horizons,* (September/October), 35-43.

Bettman, James R. and C. Whan Park (1980), "Effects of Prior Knowledge and Experience and Phase of the Choice Process on Consumer Decision Processes," *Journal of Consumer Research,* (December), 234-48.

Bitner, Mary Jo (1986), "Consumer Responses to the Physical Environment in Service Settings," in *Creativity in Services Marketing,* M. Venkatesan, Diane M. Schmalensee, and Claudia Marshall, eds. Chicago: American Marketing Association, 89-93.

_____(1990), "Evaluating Service Encounters: The Effects of Physical Surroundings and Employee Responses," *Journal of Marketing,* 54 (April), 69-82.

_____(1992), "Servicescapes: The Impact of Physical Surroundings on Customers and Employees," *Journal of Marketing,* 56 (April), 57-71.

_____, Bernard H. Booms and Mary Stanfield Tetrault (1990), "The Service Encounter: Diagnosing Favorable and Unfavorable Incidents," *Journal of Marketing,* 54 (January), 71-84.

Booms, Bernard H. and Mary Jo Bitner (1981), "Marketing Strategies and Organization Structures for Service Firms," in *Marketing of Services,* James H. Donnelly and William R. George, eds. Chicago: American Marketing Aassociation.

_____and Jody L. Nyquist (1981), "Analyzing the Customer/Firm Communication Component of the Services Marketing Mix," in *Marketing of Services,* James H. Donnelly and William R. George, eds. Chicago: American Marketing Association.

Brucks, Merrie (1985), "The Effects of Product Class Knowledge on Information Search Behavior," *Journal of Consumer Research,* 12 (1), 1-16.

Darby, M. R. and E. Karni (1973), "Free Competition and the Optimal Amount of Fraud," *Journal of Law and Economics,* 16 (april), 67-86.

Flipo, Jean-Paul (1986), "Service Firms: Interdependence of External and Internal Marketing Strategies," *European Journal of Marketing,* 5-14.

George, William R. and Leonard L. Berry (1983), "Guidelines for the Advertising of Services," in *Service Marketing,* Christopher H. Lovelock, ed. Englewood Cliffs, NJ: Prentice-Hall, 407-412.

Gronroos, Christian (1983), "Innovative Marketing Strategies and Organization Structures for Service Firms," in *Emerging Perspectives on Services Marketing,* Leonard L. Berry, G. Lynn Shostack and Gregory D. Upah, eds. Chicago: American Marketing Association.

Grove, Stephen J. and Raymond P. Fisk (1983), "The Dramaturgy of Services Exchange: An Analytical Framework for Services Marketing," in *Emerging Perspectives in Services Marketing,* Leonard L. Berry, G. Lynn Shostack, and Gregory D. Upah, eds. Chicago: American Marketing Association.

Guseman, Dennis (1981), "Risk Reduction and Risk Perception in Consumer Services," in *Marketing of Services,* James H. Donnelly and William R. George, eds. Chicago: American Marketing Association.

Howard, John A. (1989), *Consumer Behavior in Marketing Strategy.* Englewood Cliffs, NJ: Prentice Hall.

_____and Jagdish N. Sheth (1969), *The Theory of Buyer Behavior.* New York: McGraw Hill.

Kotler, Phillip (1973), "Atmospherics as a Marketing Tool," *Journal of Retailing,* 49 (Winter), 48-64.

Lovelock, Christopher H. (1981), "Why Marketing Management Needs to be Different for Services," in *Marketing of Services,* James H. Donnelly and William R. George, eds. Chicago: American Marketing Association.

_____(1983), "Classifying Services to Gain Strategic Marketing Insights," *Journal of Marketing,* 47 (Summer), 9-20.

_____(1983), "Think Before You Leap," in *Emerging Perspectives on Services Marketing,* Leonard L. Berry, G. Lynn Shostack, and Gregory D. Upah, eds.

Chicago: American Marketing Association.

Lutz, Richard (1986), "Quality is as Quality Does: An Attitudinal Perspective," presentation to MSI, Cambridge, MA.

Mehrabian, Albert and James Russell (1974), *An Approach to Environmental Psychology,* Cambridge, MA: MIT.

Nelson, Philip (1970), "Information and Consumer Behavior," *Journal of Political Economy,* 78 (20), 311-329.

Olson, Jerry C. (1977), "Price as an Informational Cue: Effects in Product Evaluation," *Consumer and Industrial Buying Behavior,* A. Woodside, J. Sheth, and P. Bennet, eds. New York: North Holland Co., 267-286.

Parasuraman, A., Leonard L. Berry, and Valarie A. Zeithaml (1984), "Synchronizing Demand and Supply in Service Businesses," *Business,* (October/December), 35-37.

_____, _____, and_____(1985), "A Conceptual Model of Service Quality and It's Implications for Future Research," *Journal of Marketing,* 49 (Fall), 41-50.

_____, Valarie A. Zeithaml, and Leonard L. Berry (1986), "Servqual: A Multiple Item Scale for Measuring Customer Perceptions of Service Quality," MSI: Research Program.

_____, _____, and_____(1991), "Understanding Consumer Expectations of Service," *Sloan Management Review,* 32, 39-48.

Shostack, G. Lynn (1977), "Breaking Free From Product Marketing," in *Services Marketing,* Christopher H. Lovelock, ed. Englewood Cliffs, NJ: Prentice-Hall.

Upah, Gregory. and James N. Fulton (1985), "Situation Creation in Services Marketing," in *The Service Encounter,* John Czepiel, Michael Solomon, and Carol Suprenant, eds. Lexington, MA: Lexington Books, 255-264.

Zeithaml, Valarie A. (1981), "How Consumer Evaluation Processes Differ Between Goods and Services," in *Marketing of Services,* James H. Donnelly and William R. George, eds. Chicago: American Marketing Association.

_____, A. Parasuraman and Leonard L. Berry (1986), "Communication and Control Processes in the Delivery of Service Quality," *Journal of Marketing,* (April), 35-48.

_____(1988), "Consumer Perceptions of Price, Quality, and Value: A Means End Model and Synthesis of Evidence," *Journal of Marketing,* 52 (July), 2-22.

_____, A. Parasuraman, and Leonard L. Berry (1990), *Delivering Service Quality.* New York: The Free Press, McMillan.

_____, Leonard L. Berry, and A. Parasuraman (1991), "The Nature and Determinants of Customer Expectations of Service," MSI: Report, 91-113.

VALUE-DRIVEN MARKETING: BEYOND SOCIAL RESPONSIBILITY

Peter S. Carusone, Wright State University
Paula M. Saunders, Wright State University
Herbert E. Brown, Wright State University

ABSTRACT

A value-driven marketing approach comprised of (1) proactive marketing statesmanship, (2) humanistic values, and (3) alternative marketing is advocated as a moral imperative for providing products which will be good for both the consumer and society. This revolutionary concept represents the next level of evolution toward higher standards of business conduct.

INTRODUCTION

The need to inject humanistic values into the marketing of every type of product and service sold in America has never been greater. The nation is already living with physical carnage from toxic and unhealthy products, not to mention the economic and social chaos such products produce. These outcomes are being effected by sellers who truly believe they are "consumer-oriented." For example, General Motors spent years and billions of dollars developing its new import-fighting automobile, the Saturn, and, from early indications, has produced a profit and import-fighting winner. Unfortunately, for a large number of its early buyers, the car was introduced without airbags--a decision perhaps driven by consumer research indicating consumer lack of interest in airbags, or consumer unwillingness to pay the price. The Saturn airbag decision is a visible expression of an underlying social, economic, and political perspective that permeates virtually the entire American marketing landscape. It is a debilitation equivalent to that expressed by the U.S. Congress when its members play the politics of re-election--giving "customers" what research shows they want, will pay for, etc., rather than offering and voting for what is good for the republic, even if it means loss of "business," i.e., votes. Better yet, what the political system needs is statesman-politicians who will educate the citizen to the implications and alternatives of actions so that citizen involvement can produce a more informed choice. Similarly, what the marketing system needs is more statesman-executives who do right things because they are the right things to do, not because they are forced to do them, and who have a proactive interest in educating and selling consumers on positive alternatives. Such executives are willing to exercise moral leadership; they are individuals who think like Phil Sokolof (Hamlin 1990), a highly motivated millionaire industrialist who personally financed a two and one-half million dollar campaign which called attention to the need for Value-Driven Marketing.

VALUE-DRIVEN MARKETING

Value-Driven Marketing is *a managerial philosophy that represents a proactive commitment to the highest known (exemplar) standards of human, societal, and environmental well being, subject to the fulfillment of profit and customer need satisfaction objectives.* It is not running to get ahead of a crowd, especially after the damage has already been done--ala McDonald's which took eight years to get the animal fat out of its French fries, and only then after pressure and extensive publicity generated by Phil Sokolof. After suffering a heart attack when only 43 and losing his wife to cancer, Sokolof personally converted to a low-fat diet and began a campaign to food companies about their use of highly saturated oils. But the really noteworthy aspect of Sokolof's crusade is that he was motivated by personal conviction and values, not by the prospect of monetary gain. His actions were based on a personalized belief that the use of highly saturated oils can cause high cholesterol and heart attacks, and it would, therefore, be in the public interest to remove the saturated fat. McDonald's handling of this problem was an all-too-common approach--offering more positive alternatives grudgingly and only after being pressured.

If an approach based on proactive marketing statesmanship, humanistic values, and alternative marketing strategies is to occur, some new thinking is needed. It is no doubt unreasonable to expect food executives to be as passionate about the availability of positive food choices as was Phil Sokolof, but one could argue that if business executives in the food industry had practiced cultivating a high degree of social and ethical responsibility, guided by a sense of what is in the public interest, they would have taken the initiative rather than waiting to be prodded. Unfortunately, the evidence indicates that the Sokolofs of the world are needed because business tends to be both defensive and slow to respond (Kotler 1972). In contrast, the response of a Value-Driven Marketing executive would be neither defensive nor slow. Instead, promotion of the public good would be linked directly to the firm's core business and its economic self-interest. Value-Driven Marketing recognizes and revives the concept of noblesse oblige (the idea of honorable behavior, a responsibility of those in privileged positions) within a humanistic paradigm (Kotler 1987).

CEOs and other executives who accept this responsibility will take a giant step forward for the benefit of their firms as well as for society. In so doing, they will have risen above the marketing standards of the illicit drug industry whose dealers "give'em what they want" without regard to negative consequences to the buyer.

CONSUMER SOVEREIGNTY AND MARKETING STATESMANSHIP

Consumer sovereignty, and choice, are central to the marketing concept. But how much consumer sovereignty exists if meaningful and positive alternative choices are not available? One telling commentary in this regard is the recurring notion to add "None of the Above" to the slate of candidates in every election as voters increasingly question whether or not the politicians they are being "sold" represent adequate, "healthy," or long-run best-interest choices. Consider, also, that until the late 1980s, product quality was not even offered as an option by the American auto industry, and then only after foreign producers forced the issue.

Pseudo-sovereignty was also evident during the 1980s when American car companies were offering car buyers up to 75,000 possible combinations per car line (*Wall Street Journal* 1983; *Car and Driver* 1989). Unfortunately, this mind-boggling array of largely superficial alternatives did little to satisfy real customer needs (Meyer 1979). However, it did drive up costs, cause confusion in the marketplace, restrict the boundaries of real choice, and detract from more important issues such as finding viable alternatives to the petroleum-driven internal combustion engine. As Dholakia and Dholakia so aptly observe, the significant lack of choice is at the macro not the micro level.

> In the United States, micro or brand choices are very abundant, but the degree of choice drops sharply as we move to macro levels such as product choice and choice of alternative consumption patterns. By degree of choice, we are not referring merely to the existence of an alternative but to its accessibility and comparability to other alternatives (1985).

In almost every arena, the range of choice readily available in society is restricted by the lowest common denominator. In vending machines, it's Coke or Pepsi, leaving those who prefer something other than sugarwater, chemicals and carbonation without a choice. Hard rock and rap-dominated music pervades the airwaves, TV, shopping centers, and even the phone lines for callers put on hold. Violence has become so prevalent in the movies that a whole generation is desensitized to it. Fortunately, there's a small ray of hope in education, where consumers are crying out for more and better choices. In response, a small cadre of "alternative" schools are seeking to apply Deming's principles of quality management as a remedy for the educational pablum that has passed for education for too many years (Tribus 1990). In so doing, they are expanding consumer choice so as to include positive and healthy "alternatives."

The time has undoubtedly arrived for proactive involvement by all elements of society to ensure that American consumers have meaningful choices in every important aspect of their lives, a perspective also implied by the Dholakias' notion of using choice creatively for increasing human welfare (1985). This will require marketing statesmanship to inspire alternative approaches to the market. This notion is not totally new and, in fact, is consistent with Dawson's early model of "The Human Concept."

> A consumer-orientation directs attention of the firm only to some fraction of the population of the society which supports it...and only with the individual's role as buyer/consumer of a particular product or service...A broader human concept can provide...the commitment of a business organization to the service of an internal and an external social purpose concurrent with the service of profit. Profit may become the necessary, but not sufficient, condition for the survival of the firm (1969).

THE NEED TO ADOPT VALUE-DRIVEN MARKETING IS URGENT

The need to rethink and redefine the implicit moral values which guide the day-to-day decisions of American business is urgent. According to Maziarz, there is an urgent call to resolve "those issues that prevent men from having value-freedom instead of value-bondage (1979)." Ken Boulding speaks to this issue when he argues that:

> The ultimate product of economics is people of high moral worth. Unless it produces these, the whole system is worthless. And unless we have some vision of infinite moral worth, we tend to reach an equilibrium and be satisfied with what we have achieved (1979).

Marketing's interest in values, unfortunately, has been limited primarily to analysis and understanding of consumer attitudes and beliefs which influence buyer behavior and permit the marketer to sell more, rather than to proactively influence (and sell) consumers to buy what is good for them. The essence of a business is the value system which underlies its corporate culture and guides management's sense of what is in the public interest relative to its target market(s). This includes interests of which the firm's customers may not even be aware and which the business knows more about than the consumer, for example: product ingredients, safety, performance, maintenance and service requirements, long-term and cumulative (and often hidden) effects, etc. Accordingly, a firm that is driven by both a customer and a society best-interest value system (as it makes product and service, and especially, communications decisions) will continuously and proactively pursue profits, through satisfying the consumer's long-term best interests, with the same alacrity with which it pursues profits through satisfying the consumer's perceived short-term needs.

The study and use of values as an extension of business ethics, personal values of corporate leaders versus corporate cultural values, and moral values as the basis of corporate conduct have been sorely neglected. In fact, traditional customer-driven marketing has led to the dead-end conclusion that the only way to make money is to give consumers what they want, or what is most readily sold to them. This encourages modern marketers to act like indulgent parents who are oblivious to their parental guidance duties and hide behind the apologia of consumer satisfaction--no matter that the consumer's knowledge base about products and the consequences of their use is often extremely limited and ill-formed. This is a traditional Theory X view of customers as opposed to the more humanistic Theory Y view, which credits consumers with intelligent decision making abilities (Kotler 1987).

Clearly, it is time for widespread adoption and promotion of positive values where consumer choice is concerned. But can such values lead to profitability? Under Value-Driven Marketing, they can, though it is difficult to find examples in firms--because there are not that many around. But enough examples do exist to illustrate that it can be done. "Fast food restaurants should be places that serve healthy, unprocessed foods," says Ken Raffel, who, along with his brother operates one of the nation's most successful Arby's. The Raffels' restaurant, in Portland, Maine, offers organically grown vegetables, locally-baked whole wheat buns, fresh crab meat supplied by local fishermen, and preservative-free apple cider from some of Maine's best orchards (Gunst 1987). Cheese & Stuff, a five million dollar-a-year, natural-food, no-chemical-additives store in Hartford, Connecticut, also illustrates the point. The highly profitable store carries anywhere from 250 to 400 kinds of cheeses and forty different olive oils (Carlson 1988). Another company that has chosen to exceed industry quality standards in the production of its product is Stride-Rite, a company that puts a leather lining inside its children's shoes, even though the industry standard is plastic lining, which costs less. The company does this because management believes that it is better, in the long term, for the children. In sum, combining business ethics and profitability is largely a question of corporate character (Lewin 1983).

Unfortunately, the decision to become a value-driven marketer is all too often motivated less by statesmanship than by tragedy or bad luck. For example, Paul Buxman converted his forty-acre table grape farm in Dinuba, California, to organic agriculture in 1981, shortly after his son was diagnosed as having leukemia and the farm's well water was found to contain ten times the state's proposed maximum level of a dangerous pesticide (Street 1990). Similarly, Stephen Pavich became a large-scale organic grower only after being overcome by fumes while cleaning a mechanism inside an agri-chemical spray tank (Street 1990).

RIGHT TO INFLUENCE EVOKES RESPONSIBILITY FOR VALUE DRIVEN MARKETING

Whether planned or incidental, Value-Driven Marketing involves a shift in responsibility for insuring that the consumer knows what is best. But, to say that the marketer is responsible for insuring that the consumer is fully informed is simply too much for some to swallow, e.g.,:

...the view that marketing has a greater social responsibility than just satisfying customers at a profit, is an erroneous and counterproductive idea. For marketers to attempt to serve the best interests of society is not only undemocratic but dangerous as well (Gaski 1985). ... By whose say-so are boards of directors authorized to play God (Heilbroner 1972)?

Though this viewpoint sounds and is logical, as far as it goes, it fails to recognize the tremendous formative influence that marketing activity already exerts on society, i.e.:

...a strong case can be made for the point that marketing is more of a formative factor and less of an adaptive aspect of culture than it once was. This proposition may be supported in a variety of ways including mergers and consolidations, which have increased the marketing skill and power of many firms; the influence that advertisers and the advertising industry have over media of mass communications; concentration of buying power among a smaller number of corporations or purchasing groups in general merchandise retailing...the atmosphere of department stores, shopping centers, supermarkets, and other institutions in which many people spend much time and which must be viewed as at least partial determinants of some of the values and viewpoints of their patrons (Beckman, Davidson, and Talarzyk 1973).

It may be argued, in fact, that a consumer-oriented marketing concept only serves to act as a kind of Gresham's law that caters to the lowest common denominator of needs and wants and, in the process, further cultivates, inculcates, and promotes the values which those needs and wants represent. Thus, this democratic approach to marketing too often results in solidification of the lowest level of consumption values. It also results in gross neglect of what is truly best for individual consumers, and collectively, for society.

The well established concept of social responsibility attempts to address this issue by requiring the firm to pay attention to long-run consumer and stakeholder interests, as well as to customer wants and the firm's financial goals. There is no question that this represents a broadening of the marketing concept to encompass socially responsible action, but what precisely does that mean? According to one authority:

> ...it means something, but not always the same thing, to everybody. To some it conveys the idea of legal responsibility or liability; to others it means socially responsible behavior in an ethical sense; to still others the meaning transmitted is that of 'responsible for,' in a causal mode; many simply equate it with 'charitable contributions'; some take it to mean socially 'conscious' or 'aware'; many of those who embrace it most fervently see it as a mere synonym for 'legitimacy,' in the context of 'belonging' or being proper or valid; a few see it as a sort of fiduciary duty imposing higher standards of behavior on businessmen at large (Votaw 1978).

Despite its ambiguities, the social responsibility notion strongly suggests that unbridled consumer orientation has severe negative side effects. The concept also represents a higher level of consciousness and sensitivity about the role of business and the impact of marketing on society than what has been traditionally inferred by the consumer-driven marketing concept (Halcomb 1986). In this sense, social responsibility represents an advancement from previous orientations and, indeed, may well be a prelude to an emerging era of value-driven strategic thinking.

Unfortunately, even the concept of societal marketing is impotently and peripherally positioned outside the core of the business. Drucker forcefully notes this very point:

> Because our society is rapidly becoming a society of organizations, all institutions, including business, will have to hold themselves accountable for the 'quality of life' and will have to make fulfillment of basic social values, beliefs, and purposes a major objective (Drucker 1970).

Whatever the case, the societal marketing concept is either not working, or does not go far enough. In the food industry, for example, despite increasing concern about nutrition, consumers at-large still choose products which are high in fat, sugar, sodium, MSG and other chemicals. Why don't they choose foods which are obviously more wholesome (natural, high in fiber, organic, etc.)? Reasons include:

1. Lack of Interest--Unappetizing, incompatible with culture, habit, etc.

2. Lack of Awareness--Of problem and/or alternatives

3. Confusion--Due to conflicting expert and commercial claims

4. Lack of Choices--Inconvenient and/or unavailable alternatives

5. Consumers are "Hostages"--Thomas Bonoma says it is his confirmed belief that ...much of today's marketing manages to convert suspects and prospects not into customers, but hostages...My definition of a hostage is a regular buyer of your products or services who wishes he or she weren't, but can't switch because nothing better is available (1989).

The question can also be asked of business. Why don't organizations choose to do the "right thing" where their customers are concerned and make positive alternative products available to them? Barriers which have inhibited business from doing the right thing include some very real and troublesome constraints:

1. The belief that the only responsibility of business is making profits.

2. The obligation of a business to its stockholders.

3. The belief that although humanism sometimes pays, forsaking it often pays more (Firat, Dholakia and Bagozzi 1987).

4. Bureaucratic effects such as the prevalence of situational ethics, a short-run orientation, industry orientation and cronyism. "...the puzzle for many individual managers becomes: How does one act in such a world and maintain a sense of personal integrity (Jackall 1988)?"

ALTERNATIVE MARKETING--THE TIME HAS COME

A necessary conclusion of those who study marketing from a value-oriented perspective is that what is in the short-term good for General Motors, or McDonald's, is not necessarily good for individuals or the country, in either the short or long-term. Perhaps the next lesson to be learned is that what is good for society is also good for business, in other words, the time has come for Alternative Marketing.

Alternative Marketing is *the process of cultivating mass markets for nontraditional products by designing profitable strategies to increase awareness, desirability, and availability of products that promise to enhance the human condition.* It is a new way of thinking about the identification and realization of strategic profit opportunities. It is based on a firm commitment to statesmanship-like ethical behavior arising from a higher value system. The net effect is to expand consumer sovereignty by giving consumers more meaningful alternatives from which to choose, better information about the consequences of choices, and an environment more conducive to consumer habit modification--for those who are inclined to move away from deleterious consumption habits.

The Alternative Marketing concept is revolutionary. It goes much further than the societal concept while answering the decision-maker's profitability (how to keep score) quandary. If not guided by profit maximization, how is a decision-maker to know how to act (Abratt and Sacks 1988)? Value-driven marketers do not have this problem because social objectives become imbedded in the mission, and decisions, of the firm. As a result, social values are internalized and related explicitly to the markets and technologies participated in by the firm.

THE FOCUS, MEANS, AND ENDS OF VALUE DRIVEN/ALTERNATIVE MARKETING

Under consumer-driven marketing, "Pleasing" products[1] are sold by consumer-driven marketers seeking to satisfy targeted customers' needs and wants by developing and selling products that are high in immediate satisfaction but which may ultimately hurt the consumer's long-term interest (Kotler 1972). More "Salutary" products are sold under societal marketing as the firm makes incremental changes designed to achieve a degree of social legitimacy, or validation. Such changes are likely to be viewed as lying outside of the normal main function of the business, and are likely to be undertaken primarily to obtain more favorable press and ward off the wrath of pressure groups and legislators. The firm's products and its marketing posture may begin to reflect greater emphasis on issues of public concern such as the "green" revolution (*Consumer Reports* 1991) or recycling or health and safety, but only in ways that do not threaten to disrupt the core business and its allied industries.

In contrast, the modern, value-driven marketer is proactively committed to the realization of profits through both customer satisfaction and social benefit by means of products which are high in both immediate satisfaction and long-run consumer welfare. Under Value Driven Alternative Marketing, leadership comes from statesman-like CEOs who recognize that though consumers want appealing and conveniently available products, they also want products that are good for them, and they want business to act responsibly regarding the long-term welfare of society. Furthermore, they need information to understand the difference. The goal--which is the task and challenge of Alternative Marketing--is to address the hostage syndrome and give the consumer both more information and more meaningful choices.

AN IDEA WHOSE TIME HAS COME FOR BOTH BUSINESS AND GOVERNMENT

What has to be accomplished to realize the potential of Alternative Marketing? Initiatives must come from the private sector, of course, but public leadership may also be needed. Almost certainly, government will have to become involved to promote private sector initiatives. Virtually every industrialized nation now accepts the notion that business and government cooperation adds to the competitive effectiveness of a nation and is socially beneficial. The United States is not a total exception to this, but acceptance of business-government cooperation in the U.S. is minimal and grudging. If we are to become a "kinder, gentler" society, as well as remain a healthy and competitive one, the time may well have come for the U.S. government to become more proactively involved in the encouragement of the practice of Alternative Marketing--through both advocacy and action.

Political advocacy speaks for itself, and some is already being done. But clearly, much more is needed. More effort is also needed to pull socially beneficial products into the marketplace, not by legislative mandate, but by government action like that taken when the computer industry was literally breathed into existence by government purchases of thousands of computers for its missile program. This action built an industrial infrastructure that could proceed on its own to produce computers for the commercial market. Government action relative to "unsought" but socially beneficial products could have a similar effect in stimulating and quickening the private sector's willingness to embrace the far-reaching concept of Value-Driven Alternative Marketing.

SUMMARY

The propositions set forth in this paper are based on a reasoned approach to the restructuring of marketing thinking and practice, and are consistent, the authors believe, with the values of the capitalistic market system in which managers must operate. Making profits, in the long-run, is seen as contingent on the survival and advancement of human civilization which is, after all, the paramount objective of value-driven alternative marketing.

Some will interpret these ideas as a form of naive utopianism and radical thought, perhaps failing to fully appreciate the spirit described by Dholakia, Firat, and Bagozzi (1987) of critical inquiry and creative conceptualization. It is in this spirit of inquiry and conceptualization that the concept of Value-Driven Alternative Marketing is offered.

Further research and critical analysis of the Alternative Marketing concept are needed to substantiate its viability and to design specific operational blueprints for increasing awareness, desirability, and availability of more beneficial alternative consumption choices, particularly at the macro level.

ENDNOTE

[1] This is based on Kotler's classification of products according to immediate satisfaction (IS) versus long-run consumer welfare (LW): **Deficient** products are low in both IS and LW; **Pleasing** products are high in IS, low in LW; **Salutary** products are low in IS, high in LW; and **Desirable** products are high in both IS and LW.

REFERENCES

Abratt, Russell and Diane Sacks (1988), "The Marketing Challenge: Towards Being Profitable and Socially Responsible," *Journal of Business Ethics,* (July), 497-507.

Beckman, Theodore N., William R. Davidson, and W. Wayne Talarzyk (1973), *Marketing,* Ninth Edition, New York: The Ronald Press Company, 44-45.

Bonoma, Thomas V. (1989), "Strategic Marketing: Marketing Has a Legacy of Unfinished Business," *Marketing News,* (December 12), 15.

Boulding, Kenneth E., "Prices and Values: Infinite Worth in a Finite World," in *Value and Values in Evolution,* Edward A. Maziarz, ed. New York: Gordon and Breach, 37, 46.

Car and Driver (1989), "Eye On The Road: Mass Production or Messy Production?"(February), 7.

Carlson, Barbara (1988), "Peace & Profits," *New England Business,* (September), 55-59, 89

Consumer Reports (1991), "Selling Green," (October), 687-692.

Dawson, L.M. (1969), "The Human Concept: New Philosophy for Business," *Business Horizons,* (December), 29-38.

Dholakia, Nikhilesh, A. Fuat Firat, and Richard P. Bagozzi (1987), "Rethinking Marketing," in *Philosophical and Radical Thought in Marketing,* A. Fuat Firat, Nikhilesh Dholakia, and Richard P. Bagozzi, ed. Lexington, MA: Lexington Books.

_____, and Ruby Roy Dholakia (1985), "Choice and Choicelessness in the Paradigm of Marketing," in *Changing the Course of Marketing: Alternative Paradigms for Widening Marketing Theory,* Nikhilesh Dholakia and Johan Arndt, eds. Greenwich, CT: JAI Press, 180-183.

Drucker, Peter (1970), *Technology, Management and Society.* New York: Harper and Row.

Firat, A. Fuat, Nikhilesh Dholakia, and Richard P. Bagozzi, eds. (1987), *Philosophical and Radical Thought in Marketing.* Lexington, MA: Lexington Books.

Gaski, J. F. (1985), "Dangerous Territory: The Societal Marketing Concept Revisited," *Business Horizon,* 28, 42-47.

Gunst, Kathy (1987), "Down East, They Eat Organically Grown Food at Arby's," *The New York Times,* (March 4).

Halcomb, Ruth (1968), "Incentives and Ethics," *Incentive Marketing,* (October), 36-39, 67.

Hamlin, Suzanne (1990), "Health on the Run," *Dayton Daily News,* (August 29).

Heilbroner, Robert L. (1972), "Controlling the Corporation," in *In the Name of Profit,* Heilbroner et al. New York: Doubleday, 237-238.

Jackall, Robert (1988), *Moral Mazes.* New York: Oxford University Press.

Kotler, Philip (1987), "Humanistic Marketing: Beyond the Marketing Concept," in *Philosophical and Radical Thought in Marketing,* A. Fuat Firat, Nikhilesh Dholakia, and Richard P. Bagozzi, eds. Lexington, MA: Lexington Books, 287.

_____ (1972), "What Consumerism Means for Marketers," *Harvard Business Review,* (May/June), 48-57.

Lewin, T. (1983), "Business Ethics' New Appeal," *New York Times,* (December 11), Section 3, 4.

Maziarz, Edward A. (1979), *Value and Values in Evolution.* New York: Gordon and Breach.

Meyer, Leonard B. (1979), "The Dilemma of Choosing: Speculations about Contemporary Culture," in *Value and Values in Evolution,* Edward A. Maziarz, ed. New York: Gordon and Breach, 119-127.

Stoneback, Tom, Vice President and Chief Administrative Officer of Rodale Research Center (1990), in "Publisher Who Devoted Life to Good Health, Food, Dies," *Dayton Daily News,* (September 23), 17-A.

Street, Richard Steven (1990), "The Clean Revolution: Local Heroes," *California,* (June 1990), 74.

The Wall Street Journal (1983), "Giving Buyers Wide Choices May Be Hurting Auto Makers," (December 15), 33

Tribus, Myron (1990), "The Application of Quality Management Principles in Education at Mt. Edgecumbe High School, Sitka, Alaska," Unpublished paper, (November).

Votaw, Dow (1978), quoted in Michael Beesley and Tom Evans, *Corporate Social Responsibility: A Reassessment,* London: Croom Helm, 33.

THE INFLUENCE OF PERSONAL AND ORGANIZATIONAL VALUES ON MARKETING PROFESSIONALS' ETHICAL BEHAVIOR

Ishmael P. Akaah, Wayne State University
Daulatram B. Lund, University of Nevada-Reno

ABSTRACT

Introduction

To date, the thrust of marketing ethics studies has been the delineation of practices that pose ethical problems and/or the assessment of ethicality of these practices (Akaah and Riordan 1989; Chonko and Hunt 1985). More recently, the thrust of ethics studies has shifted to the examination and modeling of the factors that underlie unethical marketing behavior. In these emerging models of ethical decision making in organizations, (e.g., Ferrell, Gresham, and Fraedrich 1989; Hunt and Vitell 1986; Trevino 1986), personal and organizational values have been among the most widely mentioned variables.

Conceptually, personal and organizational values as ethics correlates derive from the fact that they are at the heart of individuals' personality and cognitive structure (Parsons and Shils 1951; Pitts and Woodside 1991; Rokeach 1973). The literature reflects some attention to this topic (Barnett and Karson 1987; Fritzche 1989; Harris 1990; Lincoln, Pressley, and Little 1982). But, given the fragmented nature of past findings, the potential of personal and organizational values as correlates of ethical behavior remains to be established empirically (Fritzche 1989). To this end, the present study was undertaken. More specifically, the study examined the influence of personal and organizational values on marketing professionals' ethical behavior.

Methodology

The data for this study were obtained by self-administered questionnaires mailed to a sample of 1,500 marketing professionals drawn from the 1989 American Marketing Association directory. Of the 477 completed returns, 407 were used in the present analysis. Apart from the usual background information of the respondents, multi-items data for personal values, organizational values, and ethical behavior constructs were generated on 7-point scales with descriptive bipolar anchors.

The personal values construct was operationalized by four personal value subscales (intellectualism, honesty, self-control, and religiousness) developed by Scott (1965). The organizational values construct was operationalized based on the eleven-item scale developed by England (1967). Based on the results of principal factor analysis, these items were reduced to three organi-

zational value subscales: service, productivity, and leadership. Similarly, the ethical behavior construct was operationalized by Newstrom and Ruch's (1975) seventeen-items scale. Principal factor analysis of these items resulted in six ethical behavior subscales: personal use, passing blame, bribery, padding of expenses, falsification, and deception. The simultaneous influence of personal and organizational values on marketing professionals' ethical behavior was examined using structural equation modeling. The structural model expressed ethical behavior as the endogenous construct and personal values and organizational values, as the exogenous constructs. All model parameters were estimated via LISREL VI (Joreskog and Sorbom 1983).

Results and Discussions

Prior to testing the model, reliability coefficient alpha was estimated for each subconstruct. While most coefficient alphas were in the acceptable range (alpha > .7), coefficients for ethical behavior subconstructs were generally low. The LISREL estimated maximum likelihood parameters suggested a good fit between the data and the proposed model (Chi-square = 71.82, df = 59, p < 0.122). A good data-model fit was further supported by the goodness-of-fit index of 0.974 and the root mean square residual of 0.042. The total coefficient of determination figures for the exogenous constructs (personal and organizational variables) and the endogenous construct (ethical behavior) were 0.740 and 0.763, respectively. Similarly, the gamma parameter estimates indicated the relationship between organizational values and ethical behavior to be statistically significant (gamma = 0.310, t = 2.54), while the relationship between personal values and ethical behavior was not significant (gamma = 0.286, t = 1.26). Results also showed the correlation between organizational values and personal values to be statistically significant (phi = 0.363, t = 3.35). The total coefficient of determination for the structural equation was 0.148.

The study finding that organizational values were more important than personal values as ethics correlates represents a potentially important issue. While a few past studies (e.g., Barnett and Karson 1987; Lincoln, Pressley, and Little 1982) lend support to this, additional research is needed for more conclusive results. Such research studies will need to (1) include more correlates of ethical behavior to increase the explanatory power of the structural model; (2) develop improved measures and measurement scales for ethical behavior and other constructs; and (3) reflect sample respondents stratified by organizational hierarchy, industry, and geography.

For and further information please contact:
Daulatram B. Lund
University of Nevada-Reno
College of Business /028
Reno, NV 89557

TOWARD A MULTIPARADIGMATIC OVERVIEW OF MARKETING DURING PRODUCT-HARM CRISES

Gary Kurzbard, Long Island University
George J. Siomkos, Industrial Crisis Institute and Long Island University
Srikumar S. Rao, Long Island University

ABSTRACT

This paper uses Thomas Kuhn's paradigmatic framework to analyze the perceptions of the general public, corporations and governmental agencies during a product-harm crisis. Differing viewpoints lead to conflict which can rapidly intensify. Methods are suggested to reconcile perceptions and defuse crises.

INTRODUCTION

One of the aspects of marketing that has been sorely neglected is the area of product-harm (p-h) crises. The new interest in p-h crisis and its ramifications is due to public concern that products may not be as safe as manufacturers' claims would lead them to believe. So new in fact and so complex are the dynamics of p-h crisis marketing, that the discipline of marketing itself has yet to incorporate it with any degree of specificity within the discipline of marketing proper. This paper examines the necessity of providing a critical-theoretical framework to allow this neoteric aspect of marketing to gain smooth access within the corpus of knowledge generally recognized to be marketing's domain.

Perhaps the most striking example of a discipline's examination of its own foundations can be found in the work of Thomas Kuhn (1970) in his now legendary *The Structure of Scientific Revolutions*. It is a work widely regarded in Philosophy of Science as a seminal influence in our understanding of the dynamics of scientific change. Every field reaches a point at which meta-theoretical considerations are used to analyze its own structures, limitations, and possibilities.

Kuhn's work can be instrumental in assisting scholars of product-harm (p-h) crisis in their explorations to discover both the causes of crises and the means for their control. Several such scholars have pointed to the need for an examination of the perceptual contexts in which crisis emerge (Starbuck and Hedberg 1977; Billings et al. 1980; Dyson 1983; Milburn, Schuler and Watman 1983). This paper will examine the implications and some of the consequences of the opposition of conflicting perceptual structures during p-h crises. Following Kuhn, it is argued that corporate managers and the consumer public often develop "incommensurable" perceptual frameworks so that although the facts of a p-h crisis are the same for both managers and consumers, the perception of the unfolding events within that crisis may be diametrically opposed.

What is most unfortunate for crisis marketing is that since corporate managers share many of the perceptual frameworks of consumers, being products of the same society and culture, those frameworks which they do not share are presumed by them to be insignificant, and are often overlooked. A process of masking is developed within corporate strategy when dealing with crisis that becomes ever more aggravated as the various planning stages for crisis control become more complex and require greater levels of authority to implement. Each level of marketing control may introduce a new dimension to handling a crisis unnoticed by the level of management below it. In addition to the incommensurability of perceptions between a corporation and a public it serves, there are levels of incommensurability within the hierarchical structure of the corporation itself. Corporate CEO's, for example, are trained to glean an overall view of the crisis situation. Their criteria of judgment as to whether the crisis is handled well or ill will likely be far different from those marketing managers who are responsible for dealing with a single aspect of crisis control. Crisis "incommensurability" may be said to include three main types: intra-corporate, external-consumer, and government-official. The first is characterized by a structural-organizational perspective; the second, by the interrelationship between corporate structure and public perception. Should those perceptions be negative, the public may demand government intervention by insisting on an investigation of corporate practices. Government regulatory agencies having oversight of specific industries may feel compelled to exert their authority as a result of public outcry. The goals of such agencies may not be the elimination of crises, as in the cases of corporate crisis perspectives, but rather in demonstrating to the public that it is performing in the public interest, thereby justifying its own existence. The third dimension of incommensurability emanates from a government-official perspective on corporate crisis planning. What emerges from the three incommensurable perspectives is a triad of incommensurability which militates against the successful resolution of crises.

This paper examines some of the implications for the resolution of conflict among the various elements that manifest themselves in p-h crisis situations, and offers suggestions for the reduction of the inevitable friction developed by the interplay among them. In the midst of a p-h crisis, an irate public may bring to bear latent animosities and suspicions about the motives of a particular corporation. These suspicions may be irrelevant to the specific crisis at hand and yet the crisis itself may act as a spur to reviving ancient resentments. If the public believes that a particular p-h crisis could have been avoided but was overlooked because of cost cutting measures, the concept of profits, for example, may become the bellows stoking the coals of public outcry. Since no one has ever defined what a fair profit is, the public's perception of it and the corporate perception of it provide a clear framework from which to view countervailing perceptions.

PROFITS: OPPOSING PERCEPTUAL GRIDS

At a meeting of the shareholders of United States Steel, its president told an enthusiastic audience "We don't make steel, we make money." From the perspective of outsiders, the conflation of product with profit is rather cynical. But the shareholders of U.S. Steel applauded the statement to indicate not only their approval but also their recognition that the president of the company knew his priorities. As Milton Friedman held (1970), "The social responsibility of business is to increase its profit." The idea of profit as central to business is part of a paradigm instilled early in business education. Profits enable corporations to prosper, to judge their relative worth with respect to other corporations, allow for research and development of new techniques and products to enrich the nation as a whole, generate contacts and associations with foreign companies and governments, provide salaries and remunerations for employees, among a host of other attributes. Among the corporate *Weltanschauung* profits are therefore multifaceted indicators of the well being of the corporation. The general public, however, may view profits as indices of corporate rapacity. The perception may be that profits have come directly from their own pockets, and that they represent a gouging allowable only by the public need for products or services. The corporation within the public framework can be depicted as a ravenous, impersonal, faceless entity, with little concern for those whom it devours. In one of the most famous cartoons of the 19th century, businessmen in the form of vultures are depicted dripping with blood. The caption reads "Let us prey." This image of the denizens of the corporate world has been developed and refined throughout the present century. The essential problem is that within the framework of modern business practices, no adequate definition of "fair" profit has yet emerged. The governmental-official sector may view profit as a source of revenue and as a dimension of the general health of the economy. Government agencies use profits as stochastic indices in assessing and monitoring the overall economy. National profits may thereby be used by the government-official sector as gatekeepers in determining who will be allowed into the G-7 or excluded from it. Profits are, therefore, inextricably intertwined with national prestige.

It is important to note that although profits presented in an absolute dollar amount would be identical to the three sectors, the perception of what those profits mean is vastly different. The idea of profits is merely illustrative of a whole host of perceptual conflicts which can emerge as a result of different perceptual grids superimposed on them. Within the ordinary course of business events, these perceptual differences lie dormant and unobtrusive. It is only in the midst of p-h crisis that they present a formidable obstacle to normal marketing practices and a potential threat to corporate autonomy. The opposing perceptual frameworks may create a paroxysm of outrage so intense as to interfere directly with corporate survival. Strategies for dealing with these different perceptual frameworks are neglected by Crisis Management Teams (CMTs) to the detriment of their efforts. Corporate pronouncements in the midst of a p-h crisis must pay due regard not only to what they wish to say but also how what they say can influence public perceptions.

The case of Perrier's recent p-h crisis is illustrative of the preceding discussion. Despite the fact that Perrier had a CMT in place in London, and was earnestly seeking to find the reason for the benzine contamination of its product, the public still harbored resentments and suspicions that the company's cost-cutting measures may have resulted in a relaxing of safety controls. Profits, therefore, were seen by many in the general public as being more important to the corporation than supplying a safe beverage to the market. Perrier became so flushed by public perceptions that it gave three reasons, all contradictory, as to the cause of the crisis. What is worse, is that these conflicting messages came directly from the president of the corporation (Kurzbard and Siomkos 1992).

PUBLIC EXPECTATIONS, PRIVATE GRIFF AND OFFICIAL REFEREES: CONFLICTING PERCEPTIONS

Public Expectations

One of the chief difficulties corporations must overcome when trying to persuade the general public of any position that they take is that of impersonality. Corporations have the status of persons only within courts of law, not within the consciousness of individual consumers. Even individuals who are purchasers of corporate products may not readily associate those products with the corporation that manufactures them. Few consumers indeed know the corporation that manufactures a brand, and fewer still that the brands they use regularly may be under the same corporate umbrella. Their loyalty is brand loyalty and not corporate loyalty. The result of this is that often when a brand is shown to have a defect, the corporation's name comes into their range of awareness usually for the first time. Since there is no initial loyalty to the corporation, no loyalty can be expected in time of crisis. As the defective product begins to lose its market share, as a result of increasing press coverage, any residual brand loyalty may begin to erode, and the distancing between a brand and its public may solidify into a degree of impersonality equal to that shown to the corporation. The modern corporation seems to have taken Greiner (1972) to heart when he suggests that crises are inevitable in light of the increasing complexity of corporate operations. It is much easier for marketing organizations to overcome p-h crises when they have public sympathy. That sympathy can be most powerfully engendered when consumers think of corporations as comprising large groups of people very much like themselves, not as amorphous giants devouring everything in their wake. Such images gain mythic proportions in time of p-h crises. Media attention given to products during crises can not only illuminate the nature of the crises, but can also lend somber shadows to them as well. As long as consumers tend to hold an incommensurable model of corporations directly in conflict with the model of the corporations themselves, an insurmountable but unnecessary barrier may be erected thwarting all attempts at effective communication between corporations and consumers. While not all consumers have identical, and negative, perceptions of the corporation embroiled in a p-h crisis, focused media attention does tend to engender uniformity of views in "active" consumers. These are the ones who typically initiate legal action, solicit government intervention, organize protests or boycotts or otherwise take measures that contribute to the continuing unfoldment of the p-h crises. Dissenting opinions are generally privately held and not accorded media attention.

Corporate Grief

Within the paradigmatic framework taught in our most prestigious business schools, the idea of business as *bonum in se*, or good in itself, is widely promulgated. The diffusion of this idea is not so much explicit as implicit in the coursework and the attitudes displayed within the campus environment. Student attitudes undergo an osmotic transformation in that their values and personal identities become united with those of the institution that is educating them. This common ethos is sorely tested at the time of crisis. Corporate executives may feel beset by a public which does not understand the benefits business is providing them. They seem to be saying "If only we could get our message out, if only we could make the public see what we see, the crisis will be over." Yet, the very public the corporations are trying to reach, may tend to disregard corporate pronouncements as the verbal embodiments of vested interests. Suspicion, not sympathy, is developed. Corporations remain faceless and their actions are regarded as inimical to the consumer public. Although executives share many cultural views with the general public by virtue of similar acculturation dynamics inherent within a specific society, those views tend to diverge as graduate business education inculcates its own frame-of-reference. Corporate executives can do "everything right" within that frame-of-reference and still communicate messages directly contrary to their intent. While managers worldviews in this area are not monolithic,

there does exist a general unanimity. Jackall (1988) points out, "Organizational proximity to actual production processes, for instance, shapes managers' attitudes in distinctive ways, providing, say, plant managers, even those in entirely different industries, with beliefs more in common with each other than with their own organizational colleagues in, say, sales and marketing. But, as a general rule, managers familiarity with and pragmatic acceptance of inevitable industrial mishaps breeds in them a certain cavalier attitude toward them that outsiders, especially those who adopt the ideology of Godly purity, might see as grave peril."

Official Referees

Official government agencies often take the perspective *sub specie eternatatus*, with an eye toward eternity. Since governments are presumed to serve both the private and the public sectors, they often act to reconcile frictions when they emerge between them. Their perspective is meta-confrontational in their attempts to lessen the intensity of crisis situations. The official perspective mandates seeing a particular p-h crisis as not merely delimited to corporations and consumers at the time of crisis but the impact of crises on the national economy. Crises affecting entire major industries will impact directly on rates of unemployment, the diminution of the GNP and loss of status within the industrialized communities of the globe. Official interventions in crisis management situations, however, is fraught with many dangers due to the inextricable complexities inherent in satisfying the reasonable demands of conflicting constituencies. Governments may be charged with whitewashing when the public disapproves of their actions in a p-h crisis, or being overzealous when their actions conflict with corporate desires, and charged with political pandering rather than effectuating a viable solution to a crisis. Official institutions themselves may share a degree of impersonality as do the corporations they are empowered to oversee, so that the public may well perceive a uniting of forces against them. Governments like corporations are impersonal and, as like goes with like in the public perception, so will official institutions naturally gravitate toward the side of large corporations.

Government agencies instituted to oversee industry-wide corporate operations might be seen by the public as actually attempting to protect the corporation at the public expense. It was widely reported at the time, for example, by the Yankelovich Organization that the public held the FDA as responsible as the corporations that manufactured the Dalkon Shield I.U.D. and Thalidomide. The automobile industry, specifically Ford Motor Co. and its Pinto model were seen as culpable by providing the public with an unsafe vehicle. Sharing that culpability, however, in the public mind, was the NHTSA (National Highway Traffic Safety Administration), a government agency mandated to protect the general public from unnecessary hazards. The pharmaceutical industry likewise, was brought to the public spotlight with the Tylenol recalls initiated by Johnson & Johnson. The FDA shared in the public's initial suspicions that Johnson & Johnson may not have taken all the precautions necessary to prevent contamination of its products.

A CRITICAL GRID OF DIFFERENT PERSPECTIVES

Kuhn's early work demonstrates how conflicting perspectives are generated within scientific community, and how some perspectives supplant others. In effect, Kuhn provides a sociology of scientific change in which entire world views and their assumptions are removed from the arena of empirical conflict. The corpus of his work has highlighted those points of conflict between the content of science, and the process by which facts are ascertained through its methodologies. The gravamen of Kuhn's argument is that the process of scientific inquiry and the facts determined to be extent from that process come into direct conflict when the data remain recalcitrant. Under those conditions, in which an anomalous datum directly contradicts long established scientific practices and theories, a new model may emerge that will explain it, at the same time as it incorporates preexisting content.

What Kuhn is discussing is nothing less than a scientific convulsion to the established world view. Should all efforts prove fruitless at the incorporation of the anomaly, a new perspective, or in Kuhn's terms, a "revolutionary" perspective will come into play. What is important is that new perspectives and models are heard over the death knells of their discarded progenitors. The coming to birth of any new scientific perspective is replete with the dedicated opposition of those with a vested interest in maintaining them. Careers have been made and reputations established on the basis of paradigms long since agreed upon. What can replace them, therefore, is the persistence of the recalcitrants of the data despite the best efforts for their incorporation in the old model. Kuhn's insight is that the real conflict within a scientific community is two-fold: (a) facts not fitting with other facts, and (b) facts not fitting within the social fabric of the scientific community, and the subsequent dislodgements of elements within the scientific social order. Perhaps the Copernican revolution supplies the best example of both elements. Another famous example is the clock-work mechanism model of Isaac Newton yielding to the relativity perspective of Albert Einstein. The social element of scientific research is undervalued at our peril, as witness the controversies currently argued by the various constituencies for different models in quantum physics. Kuhn's highlighting of the social dimensions of scientific change stresses his awareness of the relationships of different paradigmatic perspectives in direct conflict.

THE RELATIONSHIP BETWEEN THE SCIENTIFIC RECONCILIATION OF CONFLICTING PARADIGMS WITH THE IMPLICIT PARADIGMS WITHIN PRODUCT-HARM CRISES

The essential difference between the scientific paradigm shifts that Kuhn discusses and the same phenomenon within p-h crises is that the paradigms of the scientific world are common knowledge to those within the scientific community. Within p-h crises, however, the dimensions of each paradigm carried by the public, private, and official sectors, are often implicit and ill defined. Product-harm crisis, is therefore, more opaque and problematic in terms of immediate reconciliation than other forms of crises. The battleground for scientific exchange is usually professional journals which use mathematics as a common language. No such language exists in the area of p-h crisis. At best, scholars engaged in p-h crisis marketing can speak to each other in a common language. This language, however, has neither the precision nor the richness of its mathematical counterpart. Moreover, it is filled with the pitfalls and ambiguities common to the vernacular. But since language is the only common medium available to p-h crisis managers, how can effective measures be taken to counteract the ill effects of conflicting perspectives?

Another dimension that must be considered is the timeframe in which a reconciliation of conflicting paradigmatic imperatives can be resolved. Product-harm crisis managers have as one of their chief considerations, an increasing erosion in market share brought about by the harmful product. Product-harm crisis managers do not have the luxury of waiting a millennium for Copernicus to supplant Ptolemy. Given the limitations of the timeframe within which crisis managers operate, and given their historical inability to see perspectives other than their own, it is not surprising that many p-h crises are dealt with unsuccessfully. Organizational imperatives can make a rush to judgment inevitable, the results of which may be more devastating to the corporation than the initial crisis itself. Another difference between the scientific community and the tripartite nature of p-h crisis situations is that the former is homogeneous and works within commonly held perspectives. Product-harm crisis marketers, however, labor within heterogeneous communities which share little common ground except for a general sociocultural foundation. When a crisis emerges among the three, there are few general rules to ascertain the success or failure of the crisis except in terms understandable to crisis managers. Since these managers set the goals of success using their own perspectives and backgrounds, their determination of whether their managerial skills were effective or not will be predicated on the goals they themselves set. The very criteria that they bring to bear to evaluate their own performance are themselves a product of the paradigm from which they work.

Should a CMT decide that success represents a return to pre-crisis market share levels within a carefully delimited time framework, and should their efforts prove "successful," they may terminate their activities with a good deal of satisfaction. As time passes, however, they may discover that the erosion in market share has continued to a point never previously envisioned by them, and that their initial success in stemming the crisis was a will-o'-the-wisp. Any number of factors could account for the temporary cessation of market erosion. Market demand for the entire product category may have risen, or the public may have taken an initial wait-and-see attitude, or the press may have paid scant attention to the p-h crisis amid an entire panoply of other possibilities. Given the perspective of p-h crisis marketers, it may be that they would believe it was their ministrations which resulted in their success. The public's perspective has no regard for the goal set by the CMT. They may be waiting for the corporation to put on a human face, thereby justifying the confidence they showed in purchasing its products. The official-governmental sector bides its time in the hope that its intervention will not be necessary. It, too, is relying on the CMTs to come up with a solution that would be acceptable to the public. Its security, therefore, may often rest with the assurances of the CMTs that the crisis can be managed internally. What has emerged is a dynamic interplay of expectations predicated on a single corporate paradigm. Should those expectations not be satisfactorily dealt with in each sector, the entire p-h crisis management operation may be counterproductive. In such situations, residual animosities may be fomented that bring about multiple crises of increasing severity based on unfulfilled expectations. The dynamics of interplay between the three constituencies varies depending on whether the p-h crisis was clearly caused by external factors unforeseeable by competent managers acting prudently or whether it could or should have been anticipated as a possible occurrence during the regular conduct of business.

INCOMMENSURABILITY AND PARADIGM SHIFTS WITHIN PRODUCT-HARM CRISIS MARKETING

One of the signal advantages p-h crisis marketing has when dealing with multiple conflicting perspectives, that is lacked by the scientific world, is that reconciliations among perspectives are possible, not the supplantation of one perspective for another as in scientific revolutions. In every paradigm shift, cited by Kuhn, one paradigm emerged as clearly the victor over another. No such conditions appertain within p-h crises. In order to bring about this reconciliation, however, the different perspectives must be ascertained to exist as external to the corporate perspective and the official-governmental perspective. In the absence of such strategic separations, CMTs will be talking to themselves, they will be converting the converted and completely misunderstand an irate public clamoring for satisfaction. When Kuhn discussed incommensurability of paradigms in his *The Essential Tension* (1977), he was describing the various perspectives of physicists and chemists in analyzing the same problem. He demonstrated conclusively that scientists within specific disciplines see problems as they have been trained to see problems, namely, within a critical grid supplied by their respective sciences. He claimed and substantiated the view that these critical grids were entirely incommensurable and not translatable from one scientific discipline to another. Suggestions that the principles of chemistry could be reduced to the laws of physics, resulted in violent fulminations emanating from many societies of chemistry. Marketers face even greater eruptions since they face a heterogeneous community with a common language as the only medium of reconciliation. The first order of business of CMTs, therefore, is the development of strategies for seeing the reflections of public and official expectations as the determinants of long lasting and successful p-h crisis management operations. In the absence of such perspectives, no real managerial initiatives can be said to have taken place. The ultimate goal, therefore, of p-h crisis management is not the short range aim of reversion to the *status quo ante*, but the active reconciliation of the multiple perspectives about a crisis within each sphere which can influence it. Before such reconciliations can occur, they must be seen to be present in every crisis situation although with differing degrees of intensity. *Product-harm crisis management is a dynamic process for the reconciliation of conflicting paradigms brought to bear within any crisis situation.*

SUGGESTIONS FOR THE REDUCTION OF PARADIGMATIC INCONSISTENCIES AND ELIMINATION OF INCOMMENSURABLE P-H CRISIS ELEMENTS

There is an implicit assumption in the determination that p-h crises within business contexts involve multiplicities of forces that sometimes merge and sometimes come into conflict. Crisis by its nature is a dynamic event, or series of events, with social, political and economic ramifications. Scholars in crisis management theory have suggested as much by bringing such concepts prominently into the field (Shrivastava et al. 1988; Pauchant et al. 1990, to cite just two examples). In order to understand the constituent elements of complexity, however, it is necessary to provide a framework for the analysis of the constituent elements so that the dynamic interaction can be clearly elucidated. That analysis is most profitably pursued when the presuppositions of the inquiry are opened for inspection. This paper has attempted to show that an understanding of Kuhn's work will enable researchers to pursue their analysis with an eye toward the different perspectives of multiple stakeholders. In the broadest sense, those stakeholders comprise a private sector, the public-consumer sector and the official-governmental sector. Each sector has its own presuppositions, requirements and expectations as a result of the effective resolution of the p-h crisis. It is been argued that CMTs by virtue of their education, background and predispositions, tend to see p-h crises within their own perspective to the neglect of other perspectives which may have a bearing directly related to the success or failure of the most carefully conceived p-h crisis marketing strategies. When other perspectives are considered at all, it is through a filtration and transformation process understandable to p-h crisis marketers. What develops as a result of this is a procrustean bed of uncertainties and ambiguities. This process involves a stretching or a lopping of inconsistent or undesirable data to fit the preconceived notions of p-h crisis marketers. These notions, taken as a group, comprise a paradigm for the resolution of crises, which is both insufficient and tendentious. As a remedy, we suggest that every CMT have in place market research teams to assess the values, attitudes and expectations of the public in any p-h crisis. The focus should not be generalized attitude studies, or purchase intent research, but specific instruments designed to determine current attitudes within the specifiable confines of unique crisis events. Product-harm crises, by their nature, are different from the normal course of events. They are upheavals of those events, and must be treated as discrete functions within crisis management assessments.

Researchers have indicated that successfully handled p-h crises can provide new opportunities as well as dangers (Siomkos 1989; David 1990). Once the perceptual barriers of conflicting perceptual frameworks have been removed, new alliances and allegiances between the public and corporations can be developed. A public inclined to see a corporate position is much more amenable to identification with that position than a public perpetually kept as outsiders. The public can be a natural ally to corporations since those corporations provide jobs and economic security to millions. But the current framework within p-h crisis marketing thinking regards the public sector as a group to be assuaged and pacified rather than what they really are, groups of individuals for whom products may pose some harm to themselves or their families. Given the consumer perspective, such concerns are justified. Given traditional management perspectives, such concerns are transformed into threats. As a result, conflicts persist and over time may actually augment the intensity of the initial stages of a p-h crisis. Once those barriers are removed, however, effective liaisons between the consumer and the corporation can be developed, thereby rendering the official-governmental sector's intervention unnecessary. The subsumption of consumer attitudes to those already held by the CMT itself will thereby be reduced or eliminated. The question will no longer be "Why are we beset by so many enemies?" but rather, "Why do so many others perceive us as enemies?" The answer to this essential question lies in the active adoption of the consumer-public's perceptions by CMTs. This can only be effectuated by a breaking down of perceptual barriers to reduce the incommensurability of the various perspectives. This is the heart and soul of effective p-h crisis marketing.

REFERENCES

Billings, R. S., Milburn, T. W., and Schaalman, M. L. (1980), "A Model of Crisis Perception: A Theoretical and Empirical Analysis," *Administrative Science Quarterly*, 25, 300-316.

David, R. (1990), "Damage Limitation," *Business*, (April), 88-91.

Dyson, K. (1983), "The Cultural, Ideological and Structural Context," in *Industrial Crisis: A Comparative Study of the State and Industry*, K. Dyson and S. Wilks, eds. Oxford: Martin Robertson, 26-66.

Friedman, Milton (1970), "The Social Responsibility of Business Is to Increase Its Profits," *New York Times Magazine*, (September 13).

Greiner, L.E. (1972), "Evolution and Revolution as Organisations Grow," *Harvard Business Review*, (July/August), Reprinted in *Readings in Strategic Managementt*, D. Asch and C. Bowman, eds. London: Macmillan, (1989), 373-387.

Jackall, Robert (1988), *Moral Mazes: The World of Corporate Managers*. New York: Oxford University Press.

Kuhn, Thomas (1970), "The Structure of Scientific Revolutions," *International Encyclopedia of Unified Science*, Chicago: The University of Chicago Press, 2 (2).

Kuhn, Thomas (1977), *The Essential Tension*. Chicago: The University of Chicago Press.

Kurzbard, Gary and George J. Siomkos (1992), "Crafting a Damage Control Plan: Lessons from Perrier," *Journal of Business Strategy*, 13, 2 (March/April), 39-43.

Milburn, T.W., Schuler, R.S. and Watman, K.H. (1983), "Organizational Crisis. Part I: Definition and Conceptualization;" and "...Part II: Strategies and Responses," *Human Relations*, 36 (12), 1141-1180.

Pauchant, Thierry C., Ian Mitroff, D.N. Weldon, and G.F. Ventolo (1990), "The Ever-Expanding Scope of Industrial Crises: A Systemic Study of The Hinsdale Telecommunications Outage," *Industrial Crisis Quarterly*, 4, 243-261.

Shrivastava, Paul, Ian Mitroff, Miller, D. and Migliani, A. (1988), "Understanding Industrial Crises," *Journal of Management Studies*, 25, 283-303.

Siomkos, George J. (1989), "Managing Product-Harm Crises," *Industrial Crisis Quarterly*, 3 (1), 41-60.

Starbuck, William H. and Hedberg, B.L.T. (1977), "Saving an Organization From a Stagnating Environment," in *Strategy + Structure = Performance / The Strategic Planning Imperative*. H.B. Thorelli, ed. Bloomington, IN: Indiana University Press, 249-258.

EVALUATION AND USE OF MARKET RESEARCH BY MANAGERS: THE ROLE OF ANTECEDENT AND MEDIATING FACTORS

Sundar G. Bharadwaj, Texas A&M University

ABSTRACT

The adoption of the marketing concept and a customer driven focus has been recommended for better economic performance of organizations for over three decades. One of the main tenets of the marketing concept is *customer orientation*. A key aspect of Levitt's conceptualization is the emphasis it places on satisfaction of customer needs. Thus, the customer is the central focus of all marketing activity (Kotler 1988). A market driven strategy requires product ideas to flow from detailed market analysis (i.e., the customer is a major source of new product ideas for firms). However, researchers have criticized this approach by pointing out that it predisposes managers towards developing products for existing markets, catering to consumers' current needs, but being incapable of determining their future wants and needs (Hayes and Abernathy 1980; Anderson 1982). In other words, they suggest that since customers tend to talk in terms of the familiar (about what is around them at a particular moment), they are extremely poor sources of innovative product ideas (Bennet and Cooper 1981).

The limitations of the customer as a source of new product ideas is only one part of the story. Conducting market research does not mean it will be utilized. A survey by the American Marketing Association and the Marketing Science Institute focussing on the contribution of 25 years of marketing's "R&D" pointed out that line managers have adopted surprisingly little of the knowledge generated from decades of market research (Myers, Greyser, and Massey 1979). This paper views managers as consumers of research information and examines the role of antecedent and mediating factors in the evaluation and use of market research by managers to explain this discrepancy. The paper draws on the consumer information processing paradigm, cognitive biases literature from psychology, and social judgement theory to offer twelve propositions pairing individual characteristics and a manager's use of market research information.

Prior research examining factors affecting the use of marketing knowledge have focused on organizational factors that are major determinants of effective use of marketing research and knowledge (Menon and Varadarajan 1989; Moorman, Zaltman and Deshpande 1990). However, with few exceptions (Lee, Acito and Day 1987; Perkins and Rao 1990) little research has focussed on how the characteristics of the individual manager moderate the use of market research.

MODEL

In the proposed conceptual model of the knowledge utilization process, factors antecedent to knowledge utilization are identified. The prior knowledge and beliefs of managers, and heuristics (employed) and biases of managers are posited as antecedent factors. Evaluation of the information is expected to mediate the relationship between the market research information collected and the market research information utilized in decision making. In the evaluation stage, a disconfirmation process occurs, and market research results that are confirming and more likely to fall in the latitude of acceptance are more likely to be utilized. On the other hand, market research results that are disconfirming, and more likely to fall in the latitude of rejection are less likely to be utilized. The likelihood of results in the latitude of noncommitment being utilized is an empirical issue. Social judgement theory (Sherif and Hovland 1961; Sherif and Sherif 1967) is used as one source of theoretical support for the model.

DISCUSSION AND CONCLUSION

Increasing knowledge (market research) utilization has been an ongoing concern. The fact that Marketing Science Institute (MSI) has listed this issue as the first of its top ten priorities for the period 1990-1992 reflects the importance. An examination of literature suggests that certain facilitating factors enhance knowledge utilization. These include credibility of the source of the report (Fishbein and Ajzen 1975; Petty, Cacioppo, and Schumann 1983; Root and Kinnear 1991; and Sherif and Sherif 1967), increasing latitude of acceptance (Deshpande and Zaltman 1982; Huber, Payne, and Puto 1982; Huber and Puto 1983), and increasing the vividness of the report presented (Kahneman and Tversky 1979).

In conclusion, this is one of the first attempts to develop a behavioral approach to knowledge utilization; i.e., examining a manager as a consumer of market research information. The goal of the paper was to examine whether certain kinds of buyer behavior research could be used to explain managerial phenomena. Overall, it appears that this micro approach is a fruitful direction to take and it at least provides a partial explanation for the phenomena of market research utilization by managers.

For further information contact:
Sundar G. Bharadwaj
Department of Marketing
Texas A&M University
College Station, Texas 77843-4112

IMPROVING MANAGERIAL DECISION MAKING THROUGH AN EXTENDED MODEL OF THE INNOVATION-DECISION PROCESS INCORPORATING RESISTANCE CONCEPTS

Terri L. Rittenburg, University of Wyoming
Gene W. Murdock, University of Wyoming

ABSTRACT

Decision making by marketing managers frequently relies on basic models of the consumer decision-making process. One model that holds promise for improving managerial decision making is the Klonglan and Coward (1970) model of the adoption process for innovations. This model has not realized its full potential, however, partially because it does not reflect recent thoughts on resistance behavior. This paper extends the Klonglan and Coward model to include concepts and models which incorporate resistance behavior. The extended model then is used to develop both managerial decision-making implications and research propositions. In addition, the literature on resistance behavior and on the Klonglan and Coward model is reviewed.

INTRODUCTION

Recently there has been an increased concern with the role resisters and resistance play in the diffusion of innovations (Murdock 1990; Ram 1987, 1989; Sheth 1981). The general thrust of these writings has been to point out the need to better understand resisters and resistance behavior in order to better understand the innovation-decision process. This need has arisen largely because of the pro-innovation, pro-adopter, pro-diffusion bias in the literature (Rogers 1983; Sheth 1981).

Anticipating and understanding the behavioral processes used by consumers in their decisions to adopt or reject an innovation are enhanced by modeling the behavior to the extent such behavior can be captured in a figure. Models provide guidance for marketers who are attempting to influence the consumer's decision. The Klonglan and Coward (1970) model has been particularly helpful in this regard; however, the model stops short and does not incorporate current thoughts on the importance and nature of resistance and resisters.

The purpose of this paper is two-fold. First, the Klonglan and Coward (1970) model is extended by incorporating important concepts from the recent writings on resisters and resistance behaviors. Second, a series of research propositions, which are implied by the extended model, are set forth. The accomplishment of these two objectives should allow marketers a greater understanding of both the processes that underpin consumer decisions to adopt or not adopt innovations and the directions future research should take in testing the modeled relationships.

THE LITERATURE REVIEWED

The relevant literature consists of two topical areas. First, literature on resistance/resisters to innovations is reviewed, followed by literature on Klonglan and Coward's model.

Resistance to the Diffusion of Innovations

The literature on resistance to the diffusion of innovations is best characterized as sparse, but increasing. While much of the research on diffusion of innovations can be indirectly tied to resistance behavior, only a few studies directly address resistance behavior.

It has been argued that resistance may be more important than innovativeness in understanding why innovations fail (Murdock, Franz, and Rammohan 1980; Ellen, Bearden, and Sharma 1991). It has also been suggested that resisters can be categorized and incorporated into existing models of the innovation decision process (Murdock, Franz, and Rammohan 1980; Murdock 1990). Habit, perceived risk, self-efficacy, performance satisfaction, innovation characteristics, consumer characteristics, and propagation mechanisms have all been shown to influence resistance to the diffusion of innovations (Sheth 1981; Ellen, Bearden and Sharma 1991; Ram 1989). Tansuhaj, et al. (forthcoming) establish that fatalism and traditionalism are generally associated with resistance even in different cultures. The literature on resistance generally supports the position best stated by Sheth (1981) that resistance and resistance behavior needs further study as the emphasis to date has been on innovativeness and innovative behavior. The resistance research that has been done appears to be following one of two paths: first, a number of studies have attempted to relate consumer, product, and situational characteristics to resistance similar to the research on innovativeness (Murdock and Franz 1983; Tansuhaj, et al. (forthcoming), Ram 1987 and 1989; Sheth 1981; Ellen, Bearden and Sharma 1991) and second, a few studies have attempted to define and categorize resisters and model resistance behavior (Murdock, Franz, and Rammohon 1980; Murdock 1990).

More extensive literature reviews which incorporate the general literature on adoption and diffusion of innovations are available in Murdock (1990) and Goff and

Nataraajan (1991). This paper's purpose is to extend Murdock's (1990) modification of the Rogers and Shoemaker model by incorporating the Klonglan and Coward (1970) model.

The Importance of Modeling Resistance Behavior

If market researchers want to understand the adoption/rejection process, it is important that they be able to anticipate the behavioral processes used by consumers in their decisions to adopt/reject an innovation. Models aid researchers in anticipating and understanding these processes. However, the existing models are deficient because they do not explicitly incorporate the concept of resistance.

Incorporating resistance may help researchers understand the sources of post purchase dissonance. Additionally, the roles opinion leaders play in the diffusion process may be better understood. Because of the risk involved with discontinuous innovations and the influence of negative word-of-mouth, opinion leaders may be a more important source of communications in resisting than in adopting innovations. The need to communicate with resisters and to understand their reasons for resistance is also emphasized by modeling their behavior. Certainly, different communication strategies and perhaps product modification will be necessary for resisters to become adopters. The positive aspects of resistance also might be highlighted by incorporating resistance into existing models. In short, the first step in overcoming the pro-innovation/pro-diffusion bias is to recognize resistance by incorporating it into existing decision process models. Symbolic adoption (adoption of the idea, but not the product) and symbolic rejection (adoption of the product, but not the idea) can be particularly important because they imply dissonance. A large number of either symbolic adopters or symbolic rejecters might portend future problems for an innovation.

The Klonglan and Coward Model

Klonglan and Coward's (1970) symbolic adoption process model (Figure 1) is based on the notion that all innovations include an idea component, and some include a material component as well. In other words, the idea upon which the innovation is based must be mentally accepted before use adoption and physical use of the innovation can occur. Klonglan and Coward's use of the term 'symbolic adoption' is distinguished from the use of this term by Bohlen (1968) and Rogers (1968), who refer to symbolic adoption as adoption of an idea without a material parallel, or of Hirschman (1982), who defines symbolic adoption as assignment of social meaning to an existing product. In this paper, Klonglan and Coward's (1970) definition of 'symbolic adoption' will be used, meaning the mental acceptance of the idea component of an innovation (for which there may or may not be a material component).

A number of researchers have found support for Klonglan and Coward's (1970) adoption process model. Davis (1979) applies the model to changing the instructional practices of college faculty. He demonstrates, as the Klonglan and Coward (1970) model implies, that it is necessary to get faculty to accept the idea prior to accepting the actual change. An extension and application of the Klonglan and Coward model to food products is provided by Herrmann, Warland, and Carpenter (1972). This study develops a set of adoption categories based on the model and applies the model and the developed categories by successfully describing adopters and nonadopters of several food products. They conclude that still more categories of "nontriers" need to be developed and provide support for the studying of resistance behavior (particularly symbolic rejecters) (Herrmann, Warland, and Carpenter 1972, pp. 27-28).

Other studies that support the basic process outlined in the Klonglan and Coward (1970) model include Mittelstaedt, Grossbart, Curtis and DeVere (1976) who use the stages developed by Herrmann, Warland, and Carpenter (1972) to illustrate that high and low sensation seekers will differ in their propensities to follow the stages. High sensation seekers may tend to move through the process faster and substitute trial for evaluation. Yetley and Roderuck (1980) apply the Klonglan and Coward model to assess and provide guidelines for a study on the adoption of nutritional practices. They were not able to clearly identify the relationships among the steps in Phase A of the model and adoption behavior. Weber, McCray, and Claypool (1985) use the theoretical framework of Klonglan and Coward model to validate the propensity to adopt alternative housing. Specifically, they focus on the need for acceptance of the idea. They found that propensity to adopt alternative housing increased with increased knowledge of the housing types as the model would predict. The basis for the model is supported also by Lionberger (1963), who stated that diffusion of an idea and diffusion of a practice are not synonymous; the idea may be accepted, but intervening variables could determine whether or not the practice actually is used.

The Klonglan and Coward model may be particularly useful in considering consumer resistance to innovations because of its separation of acceptance of the idea of the innovation and actual use adoption. As Murdock, Franz and Rammohan (1980) point out, there may be different categories of resisters; part of this categorization scheme is based on symbolic adoption or rejection and use adoption or rejection. For example, symbolic resisters are described as people who physically adopt an innovation but symbolically resist. Symbolic adopters are those who adopt the idea of the innovation but reject physical adoption. Murdock (1990) presents a paradigm of the innovation-decision process, incorporating resister categories. While the symbolic adoption stage is implicit in these resister categories, it is not explicit in Murdock's

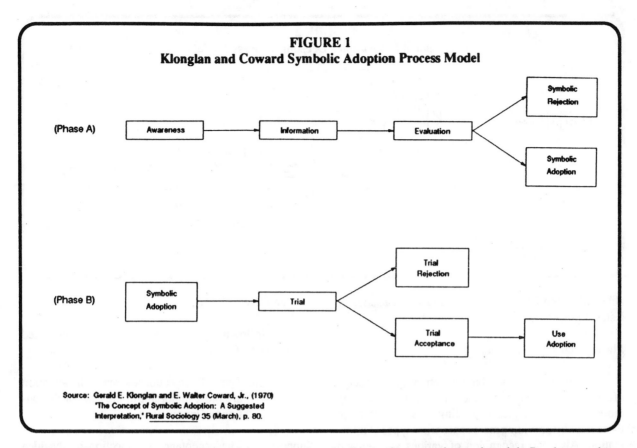

FIGURE 1
Klonglan and Coward Symbolic Adoption Process Model

Source: Gerald E. Klonglan and E. Walter Coward, Jr., (1970)
"The Concept of Symbolic Adoption: A Suggested
Interpretation," Rural Sociology 35 (March), p. 80.

paradigm. Therefore, an extended model is proposed combining Klonglan and Coward's (1970) model, Rogers and Shoemaker's (1971) model, and Murdock's (1990) resistance model.

EXTENDED MODEL OF THE INNOVATION-DECISION PROCESS

A proposed model of the innovation-decision process, incorporating resister categories, is included in Figure 2. The first three stages, Knowledge, Persuasion, and Decision, are drawn from Rogers and Shoemaker (1971). The Symbolic Adoption vs. Symbolic Rejection stage represents acceptance or rejection of the idea component of the innovation.

Klonglan and Coward (1970) suggest that Incomplete Adoption occurs in cases where Symbolic Adoption does not result in Use Adoption. Forms of Incomplete Adoption are Constrained Adoption, in which the adoption unit is unable to use the idea which has been accepted because action or inaction by some relevant group makes the use of the innovation unavailable (such as use of fluoridated water), and Anticipatory Adoption, in which the adoption unit does not move beyond Symbolic Adoption because the situational context is presently not appropriate for use of the innovation (such as use of public fallout shelters). More often though, it is assumed that those who Symbolically Adopt engage in a Trial, which is either accepted or rejected. Trial Acceptance would lead to Use Adoption; Use Adoption could result in Continued Adoption by Adopters, or Discontinuance

by Discontinuers or those who might Readopt at a later point in time. Later Adopters are suggested as those who engage in Trial but delay Adoption for some reason. Those who Symbolically Adopt but reject after Trial would be categorized as Symbolic Adopters; they have accepted the idea of the innovation but not its physical usage.

Symbolic Rejection would result in Use Adoption, perhaps preceded by Trial, or Use Rejection. According to the Murdock, Franz and Rammohan (1980) classification scheme, those who Symbolically Reject but Adopt for Use are Symbolic Resisters, and those who Symbolically Reject and Reject for Use are Aware Nonadopters.

This extended model allows the decision process for each resister category to be seen clearly with respect to acceptance or resistance of both the idea component of an innovation and physical use of that innovation. Explicitly delineating this process enhances understanding of the decision process taking place for individuals in different categories. In addition, it should aid researchers in exploring issues related to innovation resistance and marketers in developing more effective strategies for various market segments.

IMPLICATIONS OF THE EXTENDED MODEL

The extended model of the innovation-decision process presented here has implications for marketing managers and researchers. Managerial implications relate to market segmentation strategies and marketing mix vari-

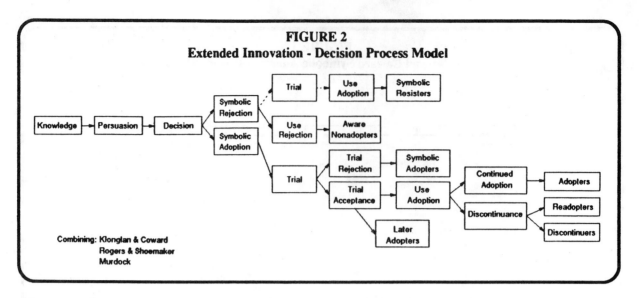

FIGURE 2
Extended Innovation - Decision Process Model

Combining: Klonglan & Coward
Rogers & Shoemaker
Murdock

ables. Research implications are included as a series of testable propositions.

Managerial Implications

By considering the symbolic adoption/rejection stage of this decision process, marketers may be able to develop more effective strategies for guiding consumers through these steps by providing more appropriate types of information. Also, the recognition of various adopter and resister categories may aid marketers in identifying market segments. Targeted strategies could be developed to reach these various segments more effectively.

There may be implications regarding post purchase dissonance, particularly for those categories where the symbolic and use stages are in disagreement. Marketers might develop specific strategies to relieve dissonance; in the case of symbolic resisters, reinforcement of use of the innovation might be the most appropriate approach. Sheth and Frazier (1982) present a model which could be adapted for these particular segments.

Assuming that consumers can anticipate the consumption process and outcomes more easily for continuous than for discontinuous innovations, symbolic adoption should be greater for continuous innovations. Further, the types of resistance might differ for continuous versus discontinuous innovations. Robertson (1967) describes continuous innovations as those which have the least disruptive influence on established behavior patterns, dynamically continuous innovations as those with more disrupting effects than continuous innovations without altering established patterns, and discontinuous innovations as those which involve the establishment of new behavior patterns. Resistance has been found to be higher for discontinuous innovations (Ram 1987). Marketing implications for this extended model may be most relevant for discontinuous innovations, for which resistance and resister categories may have the most significance to marketers.

Future Research Implications

The following research propositions are suggested by the extended model:

Proposition: Symbolic rejection and symbolic adoption are most important in the case of discontinuous innovations.

Support: The acceptance or rejection of the idea component is key to use adoption for discontinuous innovations because the consumer has little previous cognitive experience with the innovation. In addition, decisions regarding discontinuous innovations would be more likely to require cognition prior to use because of the importance of the decision to the consumer and the related behavior change required for its adoption.

Proposition: Sociological variables will be more important than economic variables in explaining symbolic adoption or rejection, while economic variables will be more important than sociological in explaining use adoption or rejection.

Support: This is an extension of Klonglan and Coward's (1970) thoughts to include the concept of rejection or resistance.

Proposition: Word-of-mouth communications are most important in the decision for use adoption or rejection, and mass media communications are most important for symbolic adoption or rejection.

Support: Particularly for discontinuous innovations, word-of-mouth communications are important in reducing perceived risk, and such risk is increased in use adoption over symbolic adoption. Trial and the resulting experience as communicated by word-of-mouth most likely will influence use adoption while mass media may be able to stimulate symbolic adoption, but not overcome habit and perceived risk.

Proposition: The most difficult and potentially detrimental market segments in the successful diffusion of innovations are aware nonadopters and discontinuers.

Support: Both aware nonadopters and discontinuers have made the decision to reject both the idea and the innovation's use. Because of this, they are most likely to negatively influence other potential adopters via word-of-mouth and least likely to be influenced by mass communications.

Proposition: The adoption or rejection of discontinuous innovations will be most influenced by symbolic adoption/rejection, while continuous innovations will be most influenced by trial.

Support: The decision-making process is more likely to include the step of symbolic adoption/rejection when the innovation is discontinuous. Continuous innovations imply some consumer knowledge of the idea and thus, trial and a less extensive decision-making process.

Proposition: Symbolic resisters, who have symbolically rejected the innovation but engage in use adoption, should experience higher levels of post purchase dissonance that most other groups. The same may be true of symbolic adopters, who adopted the idea of the innovation but rejected after trial.

Support: Both symbolic resisters and symbolic adopters experience an inconsistency between cognition and/or affect and behavior. This disequilibrating effect would be expected to produce the psychological tension of post purchase dissonance. Post purchase dissonance for these two groups would be expected to be greater than among other groups for whom cognition, affect and behavior are consistent. The rationale for this expected outcome is that these two groups, more so than other groups, are acting inconsistently with their beliefs.

Proposition: Individuals with more highly developed cognitive scripts will exhibit greater resistance toward discontinuous innovations than those with less developed cognitive scripts.

Support: There is some evidence that level of cognitive script development may be related to resistance toward an innovation (Rittenburg 1988). This resistance should be greater for discontinuous innovations, which call for a new script or major modification of an existing script, than for continuous innovations, which may call for minor adaptation of an existing script. For those with less developed scripts, the existing script (if any) would not be as firmly entrenched and should be more adaptable.

CONCLUSIONS

Although a greater understanding of adopter and resister categories, based on reasons for resistance, should aid in shedding light on the nature of resistance to innovation, the model of the innovation-decision process which is proposed here may have raised more questions than it answers. Questions might include: Is innovativeness the opposite of resistance? Is resistance a scripted behavior (Subramanian and Mittelstaedt 1991)? The model's primary contributions are in matching the symbolic adoption/rejection stage to the cognitive process(es) experienced by many consumers and in clarifying the process(es) engaged in by various categories of resisters to innovations.

A greater understanding of resister segments should aid marketers in developing more effective strategies to reach these segments. It is hoped that these strategies include not only more targeted appeals based on reasons for resistance, but also acknowledgment of and respect for the legitimate reasons for nonadoption and more efficient targeting to those segments most suited to adopt a given innovation. If marketers are truly to implement the marketing concept, the focus must shift from an emphasis on overcoming resistance to an understanding of that resistance and a genuine attempt to meet consumers' real underlying needs.

REFERENCES

Bohlen, Joe M. (1968), "Research Needed on Adoption Models," in *Diffusion Research Needs,* North Central Regional Research Bulletin 186, Columbia, MO: University of Missouri Agricultural Experiment Station, 15-21.

Davis, Robert H. (1979), "A Behavioral Change Model with Implications for Faculty Development," *Higher Education,* 8 (2), 123-140.

Ellen, Pam Scholder, William O. Bearden, and Subhash Sharma (1991), "Resistance to Technological Innovations: An Examination of the Role of Self-Efficacy and Performance Satisfaction," *Journal of the Academy of Marketing Science,* 19 (Fall), 297-307.

Goff, Brent G. and Rajan Nataraajan (1991), "Exploring Resistance to Mortgage Refinancing: A Consumer Policy Perspective," Working Paper, Auburn, AL: Auburn University.

Herrmann, R. O., R. H. Warland, and E. H. Carpenter (1972), "Consumer Adoption and Rejection of Imitation Food Products," University Park, PA: The Pennsylvania State University, College of Agriculture, Agricultural Experiment Station, Bulletin 779 (January).

Hirschman, Elizabeth C. (1982), "Symbolism and Technology as Sources for the Generation of Innovations," in Andrew Mitchell, ed. *Advances in Consumer Research IX,* Ann Arbor, MI: Association for Consumer Research, 537-541.

Klonglan, Gerald E. and E. Walter Coward, Jr. (1970), "The Concept of Symbolic Adoption: A Suggested Interpretation," *Rural Sociology,* 35 (March), 77-83.

Lionberger, Herbert F. (1963), "Individual Adoption Behavior, Applications from Diffusion Research - Part I," *Journal of Cooperative Extension,* 1 (Fall), 157-166.

Mittelstaedt, R. A., S. L. Grossbart, W. W. Curtis, and S. P. DeVere (1976), "Optimal Stimulation Level and the Adoption Decision Process," *Journal of Consumer Research,* 3 (September), 84-94.

Murdock, Gene W. (1990) "Resisters to Innovations: Overcoming the Consumer Innovation Bias to Resisters," in William Bearden et al. eds. *AMA Summer Educator Conference Proceedings,* Chicago: American Marketing Association, 68-73.

_____and Lori Franz (1983), "Habit and Perceived Risk as Factors in the Resistance to the Use of ATMS," *Journal of Retail Banking,* 5 (2), 20-29.

_____, _____, and Balusu Rammohan (1980), "Resistance to Innovations: A Review, Classification Scheme, and Potential Application to Electronic Funds Transfer Systems," in Ronald L. Vaughn et al. eds. *Proceedings of the 1980 Midwest Marketing Association,* Carbondale, IL: Bradley University and Southern Illinois University, 131-137.

Ram, S. (1987), "A Model of Innovation Resistance," in Melanie Wallendorf and Paul Anderson, eds. *Advances in Consumer Research XIV,* Provo, UT: Association for Consumer Research, 208-212.

_____(1989), "Successful Innovation Using Strategies to Reduce Consumer Resistance: An Empirical Test," *Journal of Product Innovation Management,* 6 (20), 20-34.

Rittenburg, Terri L. (1988), "Anticipated Behavioral Change in the Innovation Decision Process," unpublished doctoral dissertation, University of Nebraska-Lincoln.

Robertson, Thomas S. (1967), "The Process of Innovation and the Diffusion of Innovation," *Journal of Marketing,* 31 (January), 14-19.

Rogers, Everett M. (1968), "A Communication Research Approach to the Diffusion of Innovations," in North Central Regional Research Bulletin 186, Columbia, MO: University of Missouri Agricultural Experiment Station, 27-30.

_____(1983), *Diffusion of Innovations.* 3rd ed., New York: The Free Press.

_____and F. Floyd Shoemaker, F. Floyd (1971), *Communication of Innovations.* New York: The Free Press.

Ruttan, V. W. and Yujiro Hayami (1973), "Technology Transfer and Agricultural Development," *Technology and Culture,* 14 (2), 119-151.

Sheth, Jagdish N. (1981), "Psychology of Innovation Resistance: The Less Developed Concept (LDC) in Diffusion Research," in *Research in Marketing,* 4, 273-282.

_____and Gary L. Frazier (1982), "A Model of Strategy Mix Choice for Planned Social Change," *Journal of Marketing,* 46 (Winter), 15-26.

Subramanian, Suresh and Robert A. Mittelstaedt (1991), "Conceptualizing Innovativeness as a Consumer Trait: Consequences and Alternatives," in Mary C. Gilly et al. eds. *1991 AMA Educators' Proceedings,* Chicago: American Marketing Association, 2, 352-360.

Tansuhaj, Patriya, James W. Gentry, Joby John, L. Lee Manzer, and Bong Jin Cho (1991), "A Cross-National Examination of Innovation Resistance," *International Marketing Review,* forthcoming.

Weber, Margaret J., Jacquelyn W. McCray, and P. L. Claypool (1985), "Propensity to Adopt Innovative Housing: Development of Knowledge Indexes," *Social Indicators Research,* 17 (November), 401-421.

Yetley, Elizabeth A. and Charlotte Roderuck (1980), "Nutritional Knowledge and Health Goals of Young Spouses," *Journal of the American Dietetic Association,* 77 (July), 31-41.

THE ADE SCALES: MEASURES OF ACCURACY, DIFFICULTY, AND EFFORT FOR EVALUATING DECISION AIDS AND INFORMATION FORMATS

Robert E. Widing II, Case Western Reserve University
Erik Olson, Norwegian School of Management, Oslo
W. Wayne Talarzyk, The Ohio State University

ABSTRACT

Introduction

No validated and reliable measures of decision maker evaluations of information formats and/or decision aids have been reported in the literature. Instead, single items or scales that have not been subjected to psychometric analyses have been used in previous research (e.g., Widing, et al. 1986; Keller and Staelin 1987; Russo, et al. 1986; Bettman and Zins 1979). The goal of this research is the development of valid and reliable scales for this purpose. The scales should provide a useful tool for decision aid researchers to evaluate the promise of information acquisition and decision aids.

Two dimensions have been identified in past research as being of key importance in evaluating a decision process. These include the quality of the decision and the effort expended in making the decision. Indeed, these dimensions are interrelated as a tradeoff has been assumed to exist between them. We contend, however, that a third dimension, the difficulty encountered in making a decision is also key, especially in the case of aided decision making. To be effective, decision aids should help reduce the difficulty experienced during choice, thereby reducing the effort expended and enhancing decision accuracy; that is, reducing effort and improving accuracy might be simultaneously attained through the reduction of difficulty. Hence, this third dimension is particularly important to add in the study of decision aids.

Scale Development

An experimental setting using three computer assisted decision aids was utilized to test the validity and reliability of the scale items. Student subjects (n=215), from a large midwestern university, were randomly assigned to one of the three decision aids. The three formats were: (1) the LINEAR, in which the brands were ranked based upon a weighted average using user specified attribute importance weights; (2) the CUTOFF, a non-compensatory format in which the user set minimum attribute scores and only brands exceeding each specified cutoff were presented; and (3) the EQUAL WEIGHT, a non-interactive format in which brands were ranked based on a summary score from an equal importance

weight model. All formats presented the attribute scores in a brand by attribute matrix.

The items used to assess "difficulty" measured confusion, frustration, and difficulty experienced during the choice process. The "accuracy" items measured accuracy, confidence the best choice was made and certainty the best choice was made. The "effort" items measured the amount of "thinking", "mental effort" and "thought" required to complete the choice task. The items were first subjected to a common factor analysis, using a maximum likelihood extraction with an oblique rotation (oblimin). The pattern matrix indicated that the items for each factor loaded strongly on the hypothesized dimensions, with the lowest loading being .66. The cross loadings were also reasonably low, with the highest cross load being .25, and 16 of 18 cross loadings being .10 or below. The eigenvalues (accuracy = 4.64; effort = 1.96; difficulty = .70) and variance explained (accuracy = 51.6%; effort = 21.7%; difficulty = 7.7%) were acceptable and the scree plot showed a dropoff and flattening after the third factor. Since no items were found to be deficient using the common factor analysis, all were retained for a confirmatory factor analysis.

A three factor restricted (confirmatory) analysis was performed using EQS. The correlation matrix was analyzed using a maximum likelihood solution. Each item was set to load only on its own factor and the factors were allowed to correlate. The overall chi-square was significant at $p < .05$ (chi square = 37.95, 24 degrees of freedom, $p = .035$). Due to the fairly large sample size (n = 215), however, this was not unexpected; further, the moderate chi-square relative to the degrees of freedom suggest an acceptable fit to the data. The Bentler-Bonett (B-B) non-normed fit index is .983, and the B-B normed fit is .970, which indicate the model fits the data very well. The error is low, as indicated by the average absolute standardized residuals (ASR) of .027 and the average off-diagonal ASR of .034. The largest individual standardized residual was .089, again indicating low error. The loadings for each item ranged from .76 to .88, with all T values exceeding 12 ($p < .001$). These results are consistent with those required for establishing that the constructs were well measured (Bagozzi and Yi 1988). The reliability of the scales, assessed using Cronbach's alpha, was .898 for Effort, .846 for Difficulty, and .890 for Accuracy. In addition, the individual Alpha's for each decision aid were high for every dimension, as the lowest was .823. These reliabilities are considered to be quite acceptable (Nunnally 1978).

Conclusion

In this study, a set of scales measuring three key aspects of decision making have been tested. The scales, measuring user evaluations of effort, difficulty, and accuracy, were shown to possess elements of construct validity and reliability. They should prove useful to both decision aid researchers and information providers. The promise of decision aids is that they might increase decision quality, while simultaneously making the task less difficult and effortful. By using valid and reliable scales which measure these dimensions, researchers and information providers will be able to determine the degree to which decision aids/formats perform from the users' perspective.

For further information contact:
Robert E. Widing II
Weatherhead School of Management
Case Western Reserve University
Cleveland, OH 44106

THE CEVAL VALIDATION METHODOLOGY: A FRAMEWORK FOR VALIDATING EXPERT SYSTEMS

Aysegül Özsomer, Michigan State University
Cüneyt Evirgen, Michigan State University
Michel Mitri, Michigan State University

ABSTRACT

In the last few years, there has been increased interest in the application of expert systems (ES) to a variety of domains, international marketing (IM) being one of them (See Rangaswamy, et al. 1989 and Cavusgil 1990 for a discussion of applications of ES in IM). ES are quickly being applied to a wide variety of problems in IM, such as international collaborative venture selection, foreign distributor selection and international freight forwarder selection to name a few (Mitri, et al. 1991a).

No matter to which domain applied, ES have an impact on the organization's ability to achieve its objectives as well as on overall performance. Consequently, the design and implementation of a rigorous and scientific validation methodology is necessary, if not crucial, for the effective use of ES in respective domains. This type of validation is especially important when ES have the potential of enhancing the competitiveness of organizations through facilitating better and quicker decision making.

Up to now, most attention has centered on the potential applications (Cavusgil 1990) and development processes of ES in IM. Formal validations of ES are rarely published, if done at all. This paper presents a formal, systematic methodology for the validation of ES called the CEVAL Validation Methodology. The methodology suggested is suitable for evaluating ES that a) perform tasks requiring evaluative reasoning and b) are developed and implemented using the Candidate Evaluation shell. (See Mitri 1991, for a theoretical analysis of the Candidate Evaluation problem solving method).

DIMENSIONS TO EVALUATE EXPERT SYSTEMS: A PROPOSED METHODOLOGY

If the objective of ES is to facilitate better and quicker decision making, a set of criteria must be established against which to evaluate the system. Hence, a formal methodology must be capable of first defining the criteria that the validation process will use and then evaluating the ES on those criteria. The Ceval Validation Method-

ology consists of four criterion that are sequentially interrelated:(1) Correctness of the reasoning techniques, (2) Quality of the decision made or advice given by the ES, (3) Efficiency, and (4) Effectiveness.

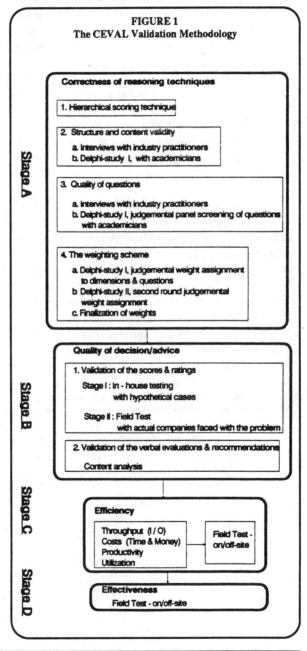

FIGURE 1
The CEVAL Validation Methodology

Correctness of reasoning techniques
1. Hierarchical scoring technique
2. Structure and content validity
   a. Interviews with industry practitioners
   b. Delphi-study I, with academicians
3. Quality of questions
   a. Interviews with industry practitioners
   b. Delphi-study I, judgemental panel screening of questions with academicians
4. The weighting scheme
   a. Delphi-study I, judgemental weight assignment to dimensions & questions
   b. Delphi-study II, second round judgemental weight assignment
   c. Finalization of weights

Quality of decision/advice
1. Validation of the scores & ratings
   Stage I : In - house testing with hypothetical cases
   Stage II : Field Test with actual companies faced with the problem
2. Validation of the verbal evaluations & recommendations
   Content analysis

Efficiency
Throughput (I / O)
Costs (Time & Money)
Productivity
Utilization
Field Test - on/off-site

Effectiveness
Field Test - on/off-site

Stage A
Stage B
Stage C
Stage D

For further information contact:
Aysegül Özsomer
Michigan State University
6 Kellogg Center,
E. Lansing, MI 48824-1022

A CAUSAL MODEL FOR FOREIGN MARKET ATTRACTIVENESS: USE OF A DECISION SUPPORT TOOL AS THE KNOWLEDGE BASE

Cuneyt Evirgen, Michigan State University

ABSTRACT

Evaluation and assessment of foreign market entry attractiveness is a critical marketing decision. A poor assessment generally leads to poor decisions and irrecoverable financial losses. Thus, one must know the critical dimensions for evaluating foreign market attractiveness and deduce the information categories relevant to foreign market selection.

This presentation will develop a causal model of informational requirements in identifying attractive foreign markets, and test the external validity of the data provided by the decision support tool, the Country Consultant. Empirical testing of the model is currently under way.

Information reduces the uncertainty which pervades the foreign environment entry decision. The need for information in determining and assessing foreign market opportunities is well supported in the literature (Johanson and Vahlne 1977; Walters 1983; Daser 1984; Cavusgil 1985; Bodur 1986; Keng and Jivan 1989). Cavusgil (1987) notes that international marketers have difficulty in sorting out the relevant, reliable, and timely pieces of information. Information on demographic, political, economic, cultural, and legal environments, as well as market entry conditions and market structure (in aggregate or disaggregate form) are identified in the literature as the principal information requirements in the evalua-

tion of foreign market attractiveness.

To address these difficulties, a decision support tool is developed by a research team at a major Midwestern university to serve as a knowledge base for the international manager. This decision support tool, the Country Consultant, brings international business and artificial intelligence (AI) expertise together. This expert system aids the international business executive in decision making, particularly with respect to target market evaluation and selection. It incorporates both business executive insights and market research findings.

In this study, a causal model for the evaluation of foreign market attractiveness is proposed. The model is presented using LISREL notation (Joreskog and Sorbom 1989) and is presented in Figure 1.

The Country Consultant, is a unique application of the AI techniques to the field of international marketing. Such an "intelligent" system whose "intelligence" arises from its inferencing capabilities when explicit information is scarce or not available (just as an expert would do) is highly likely to be beneficial for anyone who needs reliable, relevant and timely information on foreign markets. Furthermore, it contains uniquely processed information rather than raw data. "In addition, it uses an indexing schema that accounts for the various decision models cited in the literature" (Mitri, et al. 1991, p.31).

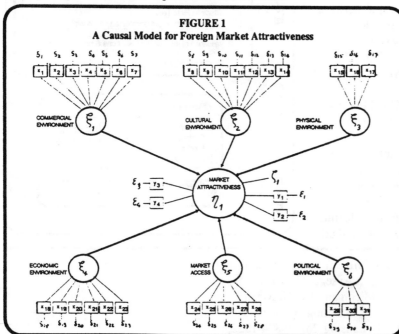

FIGURE 1
A Causal Model for Foreign Market Attractiveness

For further information please contact:
Cuneyt Evirgen
6 Kellogg Center
Michigan State University
East Lansing, MI 48824-1022

CONSTRUCT MEASUREMENT IN MARKETING STRATEGY RESEARCH: TOWARD DEVELOPING BETTER MEASURES OF MARKETING STRATEGY CONSTRUCTS

Gordon T. Gray, Oklahoma City University

ABSTRACT

This paper examines the role of construct measurement in marketing strategy research, especially in relation to the measurement of marketing strategy constructs. Both the importance of construct measurement and the timeliness of measurement issues in developing the marketing strategy field are addressed. Following a review of previous marketing strategy measures, three recommendations for developing better measures of marketing strategy constructs are discussed.

Wind and Robertson (1983) and others (e.g., Lunsford and LaForge 1987) have suggested the need for a measurement stream of marketing strategy research. It is evident, however, that researchers have largely failed to respond to this recommendation. Marketing strategy constructs continue to suffer from both inadequate conceptualization and poor measurement (Greenley 1989; Thomas and Gardner 1985).

This paper maintains that greater attention to measurement issues and improved measures of marketing strategy constructs would provide researchers with many benefits. These include: providing a stronger basis for interpreting results from large-scale, quantitative research; increasing both academic and managerial understanding of marketing phenomena and thereby reducing the tendency toward premature prescription in marketing strategy research; and providing for more rigorous analyses of relationships among marketing strategy and non-strategy constructs (including environmental and performance constructs).

MEASURING MARKETING STRATEGY

In an effort to assess the state-of-the-art in marketing strategy measurement, a review of marketing strategy research studies was completed. This review focused on those studies which specifically sought to operationalize and measure marketing strategy through observable indicators reflecting theoretical constructs. Although not completely comprehensive, the review covered most of the significant studies of the past decade. Three major weaknesses of current measurement approaches were identified: (1) inadequate attention to specifying the conceptual domain and dimensionality of marketing strategy constructs; (2) widespread use of nominal and single-item scales in measuring marketing strategy constructs; and (3) inadequate attention to formally assessing the reliability and validity of marketing strategy measures.

RECOMMENDATIONS FOR IMPROVING MARKETING STRATEGY MEASUREMENT

In many cases, the linkages between marketing strategy constructs and their measures have been left unspecified or else described in relatively loose (unverifiable) ways. In striving for better measures, a set of three recommendations (based on the weaknesses identified in the above review) were developed. First, attention must be given to conceptual aspects of construct development and validity. This includes clearly defining each marketing strategy construct, specifying the construct's dimensionality, and developing appropriate measures for the construct (or for each dimension of a multi-dimensional construct) based on the specified conceptual domain.

The second and third recommendations move research emphasis from the conceptual to the analytic domain. A second recommendation is the use of multi-item scales to measure marketing strategy constructs. Nominal categorizations and single-item scales are generally limited in that they cannot adequately capture the latent variables being measured (Nunnally 1978). Since marketing researchers continue to propose and employ measures of marketing strategy without formally assessing the validity of their measures, a third recommendation is assessment of key construct validity components for all marketing strategy measures.

SUMMARY

Testing relationships between marketing strategy and other variables depends ultimately on the quality of marketing strategy measures. Researchers must therefore focus greater attention on the development and assessment of those measures. Without such attention, confidence in research results is eroded, which implies that the managerial prescriptions derived from such research may be questionable.

For further information please contact:
Gordon T. Gray
Oklahoma City University
Oklahoma City, OK 73106

EVENT STUDY METHODOLOGY: APPLICATIONS IN MARKETING

Steven W. Pharr, University of Idaho
Mario G.C. Reyes, University of Idaho
Linda J. Morris, University of Idaho

ABSTRACT

The development, execution, and evaluation of changes in marketing strategy have employed a number of pre and post-test activities to assess the likelihood of success. These efforts often include concept tests, field tests, experimental designs, survey research, and sales response modeling. These traditional approaches have attempted to enhance the development of new marketing strategies and tactics or to evaluate efforts after implementation is underway. The current research proposes the Event Study methodology as an *additional* source of information for assessing the *potential* impact of changes in marketing strategy. This approach provides an indication of market/industry response at an *intermediate point* at the time strategic change is *announced*.

The basic premise behind Event Study methodology is the efficient market hypothesis (Chaney, et al. 1991). The occurrence of an event represents new information in the financial market. The anticipated response to a change in marketing strategy and the expected affect upon future stockholder returns will be reflected by changes in stock price. The ability of new information about future activities to influence current stock price is consistent with the basic anticipatory nature of financial markets (Soros 1987). Whether it is the individual investor that makes the assessment and behaves accordingly, or if the investor simply acts as a "conduit" for the assessment of industry experts is much less of an issue so long as the basis of the stock price adjustment is a thorough understanding of the target market's buyer behavior.

The Event Study methodology is a multi-step procedure. It involves, first, the identification of an information event and the date of occurrence. Next, stock price data are collected for the period surrounding the event date. This observation period is broken down into two subperiods: the pre-event period and event window. The 'normal' rate of return for the firm's common stock is estimated for the pre-event period and abnormal returns (AR) are calculated for the event window. Hypotheses testing involves analysis of the abnormal returns during the event window. By analyzing the pattern of AR, the researcher gains insights into the stock market's reaction to the information event. The following schematic representation and equations illustrate the model:

$$1\underline{\hspace{3cm}}T\underline{\hspace{3cm}}T+N$$

Pre-event Period	Event Window

Estimate the parameters for the normal return

$$R_{i,t} = a + bR_{m,t} + e_t,$$

where

Calculate the abnormal return, AR_t, as the difference between actual and predicted

$R_{i,t}$ = normal return for firm i's stock at day/week/month t during the estimation (pre-event) period.

$R_{m,t}$ = return on the S&P 500 stock index at day/week/month t during the estimation period.

a, b = are the parameters to be estimated and e_t = the error term

AR_t = the difference between the actual return and predicted return ($R_{i,t}$), given $R_{m,t}$ during the event window. That is,

$$AR_t = R_{i,t} - E[R_{i,t}|R_{m,t}], \text{ when } t = \text{event window}$$

During the week of December 24-30, 1986, McDonald's Corporation announced a promotional campaign emphasizing the nutritional value of selected menu items (*Nation's Restaurant News*, 1/1/1987). An event analysis indicated mixed, yet nonsignificant abnormal returns following the event date. This might represent a luke-warm response at best. In April and May of 1987, a number of groups criticized the McDonald's campaign and initiated legal action for false and misleading nutritional content (*Business Week* 5/11/1987). The new K-Mart logo was unveiled during the week of September 10-14, 1990 (Sullivan 1990). Subsequent analysis showed significant abnormal returns following the event date. This was supported by K-Mart's positive evaluation in the fall of 1991 (*Discount Store News* 10/7/91).

For further information contact:
Steven W Pharr
College of Business and Economics
University of Idaho
Moscow, ID 83843

COMMUNICATION STYLE: AN ASSESSMENT OF PSYCHOMETRIC PROPERTIES

John E. Weiss, University of Colorado at Boulder
Jakki Mohr, University of Colorado at Boulder

ABSTRACT

The psychometric properties of a scale for communication style are examined by using a sample of 113 salespeople from a diverse group of industries. Measurement of salespeople's perception of their communication style in interactions with customers suggests two dimensions (affiliative and controlling). Additionally, reliability analyses indicate good internal consistency. Evidence of convergent and discriminant validity is presented. Finally, relationships of the communication style dimensions to communication satisfaction, manifest influence, and relationship effectiveness are used to assess nomological validity. The series of nomological validity hypothesis tests show that the affiliative communication style has stronger relationships than a controlling style with all of the theoretically related constructs.

INTRODUCTION

One of the key social processes affecting any interpersonal relationship is communication. Certainly this holds true in any business relationship as well. In inter-firm communication the salespeople or other boundary spanning personnel are the vehicle through which the communication interaction occurs. In both the sales and channels literatures, communication has been examined extensively (e.g., Miles, Arnold, and Nash 1990; Mohr and Nevin 1990; Wiener and Doescher 1991; Williams, Spiro, and Fine 1990). Much research has focused on the content of the communication and how message content can be designed to achieve greater influence in the target[1] (e.g., Angelmar and Stern 1978; Frazier 1990; Frazier and Summers 1984).

The focus on content is understandable since content is the most explicit element of persuasive communication. However, this focus on content does not provide a complete picture of the interpersonal communication interaction. While a concern with the content of communication interactions is important, research to date has not well-integrated other aspects of communication.

An element of communication that may also be important in designing effective influence strategies is communication style (e.g., Williams and Spiro 1985). Communication style is not what is said, but *how* it is said. By adjusting the manner in which a message is communicated, the source may be able to change the target's perceptions of the content of the message. In fact, Frazier (1990) indicates that targets' perceptions of communication play a role in affecting their behaviors.

Thus, in a marketing context, salespeople may have an opportunity to develop and implement an influence strategy by tailoring both the content and the style of the message to needs or requirements of individual customers. A change in communication style may also be a way for salespeople to make rapid adjustments in the message in response to the reactions of the customer. By recognizing how one's communication style might impact the target's perception of the message in a communicative effort, salespeople add a potentially powerful means to their ability to influence customers.

Weiss and Mohr (1991) addressed this notion and explored the communication style construct at a conceptual level. They defined the construct, reviewed and synthesized the literature, and presented possible theoretical and managerial implications for marketers.

Building on the work of Weiss and Mohr (1991), the objective of this research is to develop and validate a measure of communication style for marketers in an inter-firm context. This measure of communication style focuses on *how* salespeople tend to communicate with their customers. After a brief review of communication style, several related outcome variables are discussed. Then a paper-and-pencil, self-report measure of communication style is developed and implemented to a sample of 113 salespeople. The reliability and validity of this scale is assessed. This paper concludes with a discussion of managerial and theoretical implications, limitations of the present research, and directions for future research.

COMMUNICATION STYLE

This section briefly reviews prior conceptualizations of communication style. It also examines dimensions of communication style that have been proposed in both the marketing and communication literature. (See Weiss and Mohr 1991 for a more thorough review.)

Definition

Williams and Spiro (1985) proposed that communication style "is the synthesis of content, code and communication rules into unique and infinite combinations" (p. 434). More simply, the essence of style is an individual's particular patten of communication. For example, some individuals are very loud and controlling in expressing themselves, while others can be more friendly or quiet in communication. While Williams and Spiro (1985) based their framework on a theory of leadership style (Bass 1967; Schul, Pride, and Little 1983; Sheth 1976), they did not explore the communications theory behind communication style. However, the communications field has a history of exploring communication style. Norton (1978, 1983) defines communication style as "the way one verbally, nonverbally, and paraverbally interacts to signal how literal meaning should be taken, interpreted, filtered, or understood" (1978, p. 99).

Dimensions of Communication Style

The marketing research exploring communication style is limited. Williams and Spiro (1985) found three style dimensions in their research. Those dimensions were: task, self, and interaction-oriented communication styles. Each of these dimensions relates to an outcome that the source of the communication desires. *A task-oriented style is* one in which the salesperson is concerned with efficiency and the business goal of the interaction. The *self-oriented style is* one in which the salesperson or source is preoccupied with his/her own welfare and less empathetic towards the target. An *interaction-oriented style is* one where the focus of the communicator is more personal or social, to the extent of ignoring the business task at hand.

Communication style has been examined in more detail in the communications literature. The research on communication style in the communications literature reveals a variety of dimensions including: dominant, dramatic, animated, open, contentious, relaxed, friendly, attentive, intimate, and impression leaving (cf. Buller and Buller 1987; Miller 1977; Norton 1978; Norton and Miller 1975). However, two key dimensions appear consistently across studies and appear to explain the majority of variance in the communication style construct (Weiss and Mohr 1991). These two dimensions are control or dominance and affiliation or socialness (see also O'Connor 1990).

The controlling style includes behaviors that establish and maintain control in the influence interaction (Buller and Buller 1987). For a respondent to be characterized as having a controlling or dominant communication style, he or she would be described as dominant and forceful, coming on strong, directing the course of conversation, and trying to take charge (Norton and Miller 1975). Williams and Spiro's (1985) self-oriented style appears to be somewhat similar to the dominance style in the communications literature. Individuals who exhibit a self-oriented style do not exhibit empathy towards others in influence interactions. In fact, this individual is likely preoccupied with himself and is concerned most with his or her own welfare (Sheth 1976).

The affiliative style is composed of behaviors designed to establish and maintain a positive relationship. Individuals who exhibit an affiliative style would be described as friendly, open, and interested in the positive outcome of relational development attempts. The interaction style in Williams and Spiro's (1985) work relates to the affiliative style. Their interaction-oriented person was characterized as social and personal, even to the extent of ignoring the task at hand. This interactive oriented style is described by Sheth (1976) as one where the interactant considers personalizing and socializing as an important part of the process. In fact, it may be considered the most important element in the communication process.

Parenthetically, one may note the tendency to label controlling styles as "bad" and affiliative styles as "good," however, such labeling is likely premature. Such a labeling would preclude the notion that a controlling style might be appropriately used under certain circumstances. For example, Soldow and Thomas (1984) suggest that, if members of an interaction agree on a relational stance (i.e. style), then one member can be dominant and such a stance can actually be beneficial to the interaction. (Because this paper focuses on measurement, such a contingency framework of communication style is not explored in this particular research.)

Although the affiliation and the controlling communication style dimensions appear most frequently in the literature, a number of other possible dimensions have been identified. As mentioned above, Williams and Spiro (1985) identify and measure three distinct dimensions (self, task, and interaction-oriented). Norton (1978) argues that there may be as many as nine different dimensions of communication style. The measurement instrument developed for this research includes items adapted from both of these studies and was designed to measure the multiple dimensions identified by this previous research.

VARIABLES RELATED TO COMMUNICATION STYLE

In this section, we discuss three variables that we expect to be related conceptually to the communication style construct. The hypotheses developed in this section will form the basis from which the nomological validity of the measure is examined.

The following variables reflect possible outcomes of communication encounters: (1) communication satisfaction (Hecht 1978), (2) manifest influence (Kohli 1989), and (3) relationship effectiveness (Ruekert and Walker 1987). These specific outcome variables have been investigated in previous marketing and communication research and are expected to be related conceptually to the communication encounter.

Communication Satisfaction

Hecht (1978) argues that communicators need to assess the results of communication encounters. This is necessary so that the source can adjust aspects of his/her communicative efforts, such as communication style. The ability of the source to assess the results of his/her communication may then lead to increased effectiveness in one's communication. One such result is communication satisfaction (Hecht 1978). Communication satisfaction is thought of as the general intrinsic satisfaction and positive affect which is derived from the actual communication encounter.

Hecht's (1978) theory argues that one way to assess the results of actual communication encounters is to look at the communication satisfaction exhibited by the source in the interpersonal interaction. He maintains that satisfaction with communication is related to the fulfillment of the source's expectations about the communicative episode, as well as the reinforcement that the source receives from the target during and after a communicative episode. Hecht (1978) proposes that for satisfaction to occur in the context of communication, the source must receive reinforcement (or punishment in the case of dissatisfaction) from the target of the communication.

We expect that the source's choice of communication style may be associated with the source's communication satisfaction.[2] A source using an affiliative communication style is likely to feel higher levels of communication satisfaction than a source using a controlling communication style. Using an affiliative communication style means using communication behaviors that encourage positive relations and consider personalization as an important part of the process. It is much more likely that a source will receive reinforcement of this behavior than a source using a controlling communication style. Such positive reinforcement then leads to higher levels of communication satisfaction in the source.

H1: An affiliative communication style is associated with higher levels of communication satisfaction than a controlling communication style.

Manifest Influence

Manifest influence refers to changes in opinions and behavior in the target that result from the influence attempt of the source (Kohli 1989). Consistent with the argument that the interaction of the source's behaviors and resources determines influence (Weitz 1981; Kohli 1989), communication style may impact manifest influence. Specifically, a controlling communication style may be associated with higher levels of manifest influence. The source may choose to use a controlling style to demonstrate that the primary concern of the interaction is to disseminate information; as such, the target may accede influence to the source or comply with his/her

wishes. By using a controlling style, the source may be seen as more confident and frank, and therefore, more likely to be concerned with the behavioral decision at hand rather than the interpersonal relationship between the interactants.

H2: A controlling communication style is associated with higher levels of manifest influence than an affiliative communication style.

Effectiveness of the Relationship

Relationship effectiveness can be thought of as the extent to which the relationship between the source and the target is productive. Ruekert and Walker (1987) use relationship effectiveness as an outcome variable that combines a functional outcome with a psychosocial outcome. This construct may be useful in examining how respondents view the relative worth of maintaining the business relationship based on an assessment of how the relationship has functioned from a business perspective. Communication style may be one element upon which such a judgement is made.

In an unexpected finding, Ruekert and Walker (1987) found that both difficulty in two-way communication and the amount of conflict related positively to the effectiveness of the relationship. In terms of communication style choice, these results have interesting implications. Since a controlling style of communication is one that likely limits the amount of feedback asked for or allowed from the target by the source, it is not a style that encourages two-way communication. In fact, it tends to discourage such. A source using a controlling style may be perceived by the target as one who is more concerned about operational aspects of the relationship and not unduly concerned with the social or interactional aspects of the relationship. It is possible that a source may personally like to have a more social relationship with target personnel, but at the same time the source may realize that such a relationship might interfere with sound business decision making. Hence:

H3: A controlling communication style is associated with higher levels of perceived effectiveness in the relationship than an affiliative style.

METHOD

In this section, we describe the development of the communication style scale and the data collection process. In addition, we present the other measures used in this study, including those for the three variables related to communication style and covariates used to help control for alternative explanations of our hypotheses.

Scale Development

Following Churchill's (1979) recommendations,

multi-item measures were developed for each of the measures. (A full listing of items is available from the authors.)

Communication Style. The items for communication style were designed to measure the controlling and affiliative dimensions, as well as to tap other dimensions which have appeared in previous communication style work. The initial pool of items was generated from available existing measures as ascertained by an extensive literature search. Many items were drawn from Norton's (1978) Communication Style Measure and from Williams and Spiro (1985). Items are included to represent the eight dimensions identified by Norton (1978) (dominant, dramatic, contentious, animated, impression leaving, relaxed, attentive, open, and friendly) and the three dimensions given by Williams and Spiro (1985) (task-oriented, self-oriented, and interaction-oriented). Additionally, items were created specifically for this study. All items were adapted to describe communication style in the domain of salespeople interacting with customers. Each item used a 7-point Likert-type response format ranging from "strongly disagree" to "strongly agree," and several items were reverse scored. These items were revised based on the comments of field salespeople and several marketing academics. An original group of 44 items was reduced to 35 usable items based on comments from these individuals. For example, items for communication style included "I had a tendency to dominate the conversation with this customer" and "I verbally acknowledged the contributions of this customer."

The survey instrument was pretested using a convenience sample of salespeople and sales managers. Each pretest informant was asked to reveal difficulties or ambiguities that arose while reading the instructions or filling out the questionnaire. On the basis of comments from these individuals, the survey was revised until it was clear and easy to respond to. Additionally, it was deemed to be general enough to be applicable in a wide variety of industry and sales situations.

Other Variable Measures. Multi-item scales were used to measure each of the three outcome variables. Each of these scales used a seven-point Likert scale format and the anchor/labels on the items are specified below. In most cases, the items were adapted to reflect the environment of a salesperson/customer interaction. Details as to the initial construction of these scales follows:

Communication Satisfaction - This seven item scale focused on the feeling of the source towards the communication encounter with the target and is based on the Hecht (1978) scale of communication satisfaction. These items used anchors from "strongly disagree" to "strongly agree," and included such items as "I was satisfied with how I presented my

thoughts to this customer."

Manifest Influence - Eight items, taken from Kohli's (1989) manifest influence scale, were used for this measure of the degree to which the salesperson perceived they influence the thinking or opinions of the customer. These items all used anchors ranging from "very small" to "very large," and included such items as "To what extent did your participation in the sales interaction influence the decision eventually reached?"

Relationship Effectiveness - This is a six item measure taken from the Ruekert and Walker (1987) measure of effectiveness in intraorganizational relationships. The items used anchors ranging from "to no extent" to "to great extent," and included such items as "To what extent have you had an effective working relationship with this customer?"

Covariates. In addition to the outcome variables, several other variables were measured as control variables:

Industry - Industry was assessed to control for variance attributable to the multi-industry context (discussed subsequently).

Social Desirability Bias - A measure of social desirability bias (Spector 1987; Luthans and Thomas 1989) was taken to partial out effects from the salesperson's tendency to possibly respond more positively to the affiliative items than the controlling items.

Salesperson Characteristics - Measures for gender, years of experience, and length of association with customer firm were also taken.

Data Collection

Before distributing the questionnaire, several issues needed to be addressed. First, the issue of respondent (salesperson, customer, or both) needed to be addressed. While, ideally, measures would be collected from both sides of the dyad, we chose to examine salesperson responses only. This choice was made for several reasons. Since the salesperson is the member of the communication dyad that is more likely than the customer to make alterations in communication style, salespeople were chosen as respondents. Also, more variance in communication style is expected in the response of salespeople for the same reason, that is, they are the ones making more changes in style. In addition, this choice is made because of the preliminary nature of this study. Salespeople, rather than customers, represent the side of the dyad which is under the control of marketing managers. Thus, examining the responses of salespeople gives insight into present marketing/sales practices and seems an appropriate first step in studying the communication style construct. An important aspect of this decision was to include the measure of social desirability of responses as a control for response bias. The limitations of this choice will be addressed in the limitations section.

Second, the issue of context needed to be addressed -- either single or multiple industries. Multiple industries were selected for the sample. In developing and validating this measurement instrument, we wanted it to be generalizable to multiple contexts. Additionally, in a single-industry context, there might be a tendency to use one style versus another. Hence, we have opted for external validity at the expense of some internal validity. Note, however, that we included a measure for industry context in order to control for any error variance that the multiple-industry context may have introduced.

Third, we needed to ensure variation on the communication style scale. We did this by asking half of the respondents to provide information on the most recent interaction with their worst customer; and the other half, on the most recent interaction with their best customer (see for example, similar manipulations in Smith 1991). Pretesting indicated that respondents were willing and able to follow these instructions.

Survey questionnaires were mailed or delivered to sample of 192 salespeople and sales managers representing 13 industries. The sample was drawn primarily from sales professionals in the Rocky Mountain region, although some respondents were from other regions of the country. The industries represented in the sample include both industrial and consumer goods categories, and involve transactions at both the wholesale and retail level. (A listing of the different industries sampled and the number of responses collected from each industry is available from the authors.) Each member of the sample was given a survey questionnaire, a letter detailing instructions for completing and returning the survey, and a postage paid return envelope.

A total of 113 usable responses was received for a response rate of 58.9 percent, which is higher than response rates typical in organizational marketing research. Using a technique suggested by Armstrong and Overton (1977), the effects of nonresponse bias were analyzed by comparing early and late responses. Eighty-four percent of the questionnaires were received well before the last 16 percent and two groups were formed based on this criterion. The group's responses on the summed scales of the communication style dimensions and the three outcome variables were compared using t-tests. This comparison revealed no significant differences in the constructs under examination in this study, suggesting that nonresponse bias is not a significant issue. A stronger test of nonresponse bias would have been to contact the nonrespondents.

RESULTS

Reliability

A high internal consistency estimate can provide us with some support for the construct validity of our measure (Peter 1981). Assessing the internal consistency of a scale is one step in the reliability assessment process. Both factor analysis[3] and item-to-correlations were used to purify the communication style scale (Churchill 1979). An item is included on a factor if its primary loading was greater than .40 on that factor and less than or equal to .30 on any other factor. Items with high cross-loadings were eliminated. Items which showed low item-to-total correlations were deleted from the scales. This purification process based on the item-to-total correlations and the factor analysis resulted in a final communication style scale consisting of 26 items. (See Table 1 for summary statistics.)

In examining the dimensionality of the communication style scale, a screen test (Dillon and Goldstein 1984) indicated a two-factor solution. The eigenvalues of the first two factors ($\lambda 1 = 6.73, \lambda 2 = 3.26$) accounted for 37 percent of the variance in the subjects' responses.

The first factor (24.9 % of the variance), comprised of 17 items, measured the perceived *affiliativeness* of the salespersons' communication style. The 17 items were summed to create an affiliative communication style scale (alpha = .89).

The second factor (12.1% of the variance), consisting of nine items, was related to the perceived dominance or *controllingness* of the salespersons' communication style. A controlling communication style scale was created by summing these nine items (alpha = .72). Interestingly, the two dimensions of communication style are not significantly correlated with each other and the correlation coefficient is quite low (r = .11, p > .10).

These results are generally consistent with previous work. Norton (1978) suggested that his eight dimensions would form two clusters or subconstructs. These clusters were based on either the sender orientation (more dominant) or the receiver orientation (more passive) of the communicator. Our results also suggest that the three dimensions found by Williams and Spiro (1985) load primarily on the two factors of control and affiliation. It appears that the task and self-oriented dimensions are more controlling styles, while the interaction-oriented dimension is a more affiliative style.

The other measures (communication satisfaction, manifest influence, and relationship effectiveness) each exhibited a unidimensional solution and acceptable reliability coefficients after purification (see Table 1). Three items were deleted from the scale for communication

TABLE 1
Measurement Properties of Final Scales

Scales	Number of Items	Range	Mean[a]	Standard Deviation	Cronbach Alpha
Communication Style (Affiliative)	17	36-116	93.27	14.31	.89
Communication Style (Controlling)	9	12-60	31.51	8.65	.72
Communication Satisfaction	4	11-28	22.42	3.71	.84
Manifest Influence	8	12-56	38.24	9.59	.93
Relationship Effectiveness	4	9-28	21.57	4.99	.90

[a]7-point scales

satisfaction and two items were deleted from the scale for relationship effectiveness.

Validity

Discriminant validity is the extent to which a measure is unique and not simply a reflection of another variable (Campbell and Fiske 1959; Churchill 1979; Peter 1981). Convergent validity refers to the extent to which alternative measures correlate highly with other measures of the same construct (Campbell and Fiske 1959; Churchill 1979; Peter 1981). Factor analysis was used to assess discriminant and convergent validity of the constructs. Since each item represents an independent attempt to measure a particular dimension of the construct, all items of a scale should load strongly on one factor to satisfy requirements of convergent validity, and weakly on all other factors to satisfy requirements of discriminant validity (e.g., Kohli 1989). Table 2 shows the results of the factor analysis as evidence of convergent and discriminant validity for the communication style and outcome variable scales. While the affiliative dimension and the communication satisfaction scale exhibited some cross loadings, it was not deemed severe enough to be a serious problem.

To assess nomological validity (H1 - H3), we examined the simple correlations between the control and affiliation communication style scales and measures of the three outcome variables (communication satisfaction, manifest influence, and relationship effectiveness). The correlation matrix in Table 3 summarizes the results relevant to the hypotheses regarding the outcome variables.[4]

Hypothesis I suggested that affiliative styles are associated with higher levels of communication satisfac-

tion than controlling styles. The zero-order correlation between affiliative communication style and communication satisfaction was positive and significant ($r = .46$, $p < .01$); the correlation between the controlling communication style and communication satisfaction was negative and insignificant ($r = -.03$, $p > .10$).[5] These results tend to support Hypothesis 1.

The test of Hypothesis 2 produced some unexpected findings. This hypothesis proposed that the use of a controlling style would be related to higher levels of manifest influence than the use of an affiliative style. The correlation coefficient between controlling style and manifest influence is positive and significant ($r = .28$, $p < .01$) for the hypothesized association. However, the correlation is even larger for the relationship between an affiliative style and manifest influence ($r = .53$, $p < .01$). Such a result suggests that Hypothesis 2 is given mixed support.

The results from Hypothesis 3 are more easily interpretable. The hypothesized relationship was that a controlling style would be more strongly related to the effectiveness of the relationship than would an affiliative style. This hypothesis is clearly rejected. The correlation between the controlling dimension and relationship effectiveness was insignificant ($r = -.01$, $p > .10$). However, a very strong relationship exists between effectiveness and an affiliative style ($r = .60$, $p < .01$).

Overall, these results provide some support for the nomological validity of the communication style scale. Hypothesis 1 (communication satisfaction) was supported and indicates that the dimensions of communication style move in the expected direction. Hypothesis 3, while rejected, might still be interpreted as supporting the nomological validity of the communication style scale.

TABLE 2
Factor Analysis (Varimax Rotation) of Final Scale Items

Scale	Item No.	1	2	3	4	5
				Factor		
Communication Style (Affiliative)	5	.71				
	8	.62				
	9	.49		.45		
	10	.51				
	11	.59				
	12	.57		.42		
	14	.48				
	15	.44				
	17	.70				
	20	.75				
	21	.40				
	22	.60				
	26	.47				
	28	.70		.44		
	29	.47				
	34	.52			.51	
	35	.62				
Communication Style (Controlling)	1		.56			
	2		.65			
	3		.51			
	4		.40			
	6		.73			
	16		.51			
	18		.54			
	19		.45			.44
	30		.56			
Communication Satisfaction	2			.71		
	4			.77		
	6			.78		
	7			.72		
Manifest Influence	1				.53	
	2				.76	
	3	.41			.57	
	4				.70	
	5				.77	
	6	.52			.62	
	7	.46			.74	
	8				.53	
Relationship Effectivenesss	1					.74
	2					.75
	3					.41
	4					.79

TABLE 3
Pearson Correlations Between Communication Style Dimensions and Outcome Variables

Measures	1	2	3	4	5
1. Communication Style (Affiliative)	1.00				
2. Communication Style (Controlling)	.11	1.00			
3. Communication Satisfaction	.46[a]	-.03	1.00		
4. Manifest Influence	.53[a]	.28[a]	.43[a]	1.00	
5. Relationship Effectiveness	.60[a]	-.01	.36[a]	.58[a]	1.00

[a]p<.01

Hypothesis 3 is based on the rather counterintuitive findings advanced by Ruekert and Walker (1987) that difficulty and conflict in communication were positively related to the effectiveness of relations. Their study was concerned with intraorganizational communication and may not accurately reflect the different communication environment that likely exists in interpersonal contact between organizations. Our results appear to suggest that more perishable relationships, such as those between salesperson and customer, may behave differently. As such, the strong positive relationship between an affiliative communication style and relationship effectiveness cannot be viewed with complete surprise.

Hypothesis 2 (manifest influence) provides mixed support for nomological validity. The correlation coefficients are significant and positive for both relationships between the controlling dimension and manifest influence (r = .28), and between the affiliative dimension and manifest influence (r = .53), with the latter coefficient being stronger.

Interestingly, these results taken together show a consistently high positive relationship between the affiliative dimension and the three outcome variables. This may suggest that it is more normal for salespeople to use an affiliative communication style in all of their sales interactions, without regard to type of customer or sales situation. Moreover, it may also suggest that a controlling style is one that must be leaned, whereas an affiliative style may be one that is more natural to salespeople.

DISCUSSION

The communication style scale developed here assessed the dimensions and psychometric properties of the scale. Evidence of reliability, and convergent and discriminant validity were provided. Before concluding that the measure exhibits construct validity, additional evidence of nomological validity would be useful.

Perhaps the most interesting finding to emerge from the tests of hypotheses on the outcome variables is that the affiliative style of communication is more highly associated with all of these variables. One simple normative interpretation of these results would be that the choice of an affiliative communication style by salespeople is "good," while the choice of a controlling style is "bad." Although the correlational analysis used in this study cannot be used to infer that choice of communication style "leads to" the outcome variables examined, it does give us a glimpse of the association between them. These results give us some basis to start considering more normative implications of studying the communication style construct.

The role of a controlling communication style in sales interactions seems somewhat limited based on the findings given here. However, a positive relationship is shown between the controlling style and manifest influence. This suggests that it may be premature to argue that a controlling style has limited usefulness in sales interactions. Perhaps in sales environments, where the buyer or target firm shows high levels of indecision, a controlling style is beneficial in that it helps to influence or move the target to a decision point in a more expeditious manner. This is not to say that salespeople are "forcing" the target into making decisions that are not appropriate for them, but rather that they are helping the target move to a decision point more confidently. The target may feel that the salesperson who uses a controlling style is more sure about him/herself and the ideas that they are presenting, thus making it easier for the target to make a buying decision favorable to the source.

Communication style appears to be a variable that would be useful in both sales and channels studies of influence strategy. Potential applications include using the communication style scale as (1) a covariate in studies that manipulate communication content variables and (2) a predictor variable in correlational studies along with other communication and influence measures. Companies could administer this scale as part of a periodic tracking of sales and other boundary personnel. With additional assessment of its predictive validity, this scale could become useful as a diagnostic tool for sales managers. For example, if it is found that using an affiliative style is preferable in many cases, these measures could be used to indicate whether a salesperson is using an inappropriate communication style. Performance may be enhanced by using the appropriate communication style. Further investigation of the construct may suggest that style norms can be established for salespeople to give them guidance in dealing with different types of customers.

There are several limitations inherent in this study. All of the data collected for this research is from only the salesperson side of the dyad. This means that the responses reflect only the perceptions of the salespeople surveyed. Although the salespeople may feel that they are capable of accurately assessing their own style of communication in a particular interaction, it is possible that customers may perceive a different style being used. This is also a problematic issue when the outcome variables are being measured. For example, a salesperson's perception of his/her levels manifest influence may be quite different from the levels of influence that the customer perceives. Obviously, future work in this area must examine responses from both sides of the dyad. Limitations in resources and access to customers contributed to this decision to sample only one side of the dyad. In addition, the measurement of the variables examined in this project were taken after the particular sales interaction occurred. Therefore, the results of the sales transaction between salesperson and customer may bias the respondents answers. Consequently, the results of this study must be interpreted with caution.

Using multiple industries for data in this study may also be viewed as a limitation. While this choice is congruent with our goal of generalizability, it is harmful to the internal validity of the results. Using a large sample of respondents from one industry is one way to help

control variance attributable to using a sample of different industries, and is the next step in our examination of communication style.

The choice of variables related to communication style might be seen as a limitation as well. The outcome variables used in this study were strongly conceptually related to the communication style construct. Still, the hypotheses tests showed relationships that were not as clearly interpretable as expected. Therefore it seems appropriate that additional outcome variables must be examined to better understand the usefulness of communication style and to help substantiate the nomological validity of the communication style scale.

This research must be viewed as a preliminary step in understanding what the communication style construct is and how it might be used in sales interactions. Since the salesperson/customer interaction is fundamental to all businesses, a better understanding of the communication link between these individuals is of relevant and primary concern to managers as well as researchers.

Future research of the communication style construct may also be warranted to more closely examine the dimensions suggested by previous researchers. Although our results suggest that two general communication styles emerge, it may be interesting to further explore the relationship that these other style dimensions have with the dimensions found in this research. Perhaps some of the other style dimensions seen in previous work are subconstructs or merely building blocks of the affiliative and controlling dimensions.

Further study of antecedents and consequences of communication style would appear to be a promising direction for future research. This would help give us further insight into the role that this construct plays in the interpersonal influence process. Additionally, the notion of a contingency approach to communication style could be further explored; it is possible that one style is more appropriate, under certain circumstances, than another. With this communication style scale, such propositions can be explored empirically.

ENDNOTES

[1] The terms source and target will be used to describe the relationship of the two parties in the communication process. The source refers to the individual or organization engaging in the influence attempt, while the target indicates the person or organization that is the focus of the communication or influence attempt.

[2] Rather than detailing expected relationships between all possible dimensions of communication style and the outcome variables, we specify relationships between

only the two major dimensions (controlling and affiliative) and outcomes

[3] Gerbing and Anderson (1988) suggest that confirmatory factor analysis is the technique of choice in scale development. However, they also report that exploratory factor analysis can be useful as a scale development technique to reduce a large number of indicators to a more manageable set and as a preliminary analysis technique in the absence of detailed or sufficiently established theory. Therefore, since this examination of communication style is somewhat

preliminary, exploratory factor analysis (principal components/varimax rotation) was chosen.

[4] The partial correlations produced when controlling for the effects of the variables used as covariates in this study were similar in sign and magnitude to the correlations presented in Table 3.

[5] Implicit here in the tests of the hypotheses is that each person has a score on both dimensions of communication style.

REFERENCES

Angelmar, Reinhard and Louis Stem (1978), "Development of a Content Analytic System for Analysis of Bargaining Communication in Marketing," *Journal of Marketing Research,* 15 (February), 93-105.

Armstrong, J. Scott and Terry S. Overton (1977), "Estimating Nonresponse Bias in Mail Surveys," *Journal of Marketing Research,* 14 (August), 396-402.

Bales, R. F. (1970), *Personality and Interpersonal Behavior.* New York: Holt Rinehart and Winston.

Bass, Bernard M. (1967), "Social Behavior and the Orientation Inventory," *Psychological Bulletin,* 68 (October), 260-292.

Buller, Mary Klein and David B. Buller (1987), "Physicians' Communication Style and Patient Satisfaction," *Journal of Health and Social Behavior,* 28 (December), 375-388.

Campbell, Donald T. and Donald W. Fiske (1959), "Convergent and Discriminant Validity by the Multitrait-Multimethod Matrix," *Psychological Bulletin,* 56 (March), 81-105.

Churchill, Gilbert A., Jr. (1979)," A Paradigm for Developing Better Measures of Marketing Constructs," *Journal of Marketing Research,* 16 (February), 64-73.

Dillon, William R. and Matthew Goldstein (1984), *Multivariate Analysis: Methods and Applications.* New York: John Wiley and Sons.

Frazier, Gary L. and John O. Summers (1984), "Interfirm Influence Strategies and Their Application within Distribution Channels," *Journal of Marketing,* 48 (Summer), 43-55.

_____ (1990), "The Design and Management of Channels of Distribution," in *The Interface of Marketing and Strategy,* George Day, Barton Weitz, and Robin Wensley, eds. Greenwich, CN: JAI Press, Inc., 255-304.

Gerbing, David W. and James C. Anderson (1988), "An Updated Paradigm for Scale Development Incorporating Unidimensionality and Its Assessment," *Journal of Marketing Research,* 25 (May), 186-192.

Hecht, Michael L. (1978), "The Conceptualization and Measurement of Interpersonal Communication Satisfaction," *Human Communication Research,* 4 (Spring), 253-264.

Kohli, Ajay (1989), "Determinants of Influence in Organizational Buying: A Contingency Approach," *Journal of Marketing,* 53 (July), 50-65.

Luthans, Fred and Linda Thomas (1989), "The Relationship Between Age and Job Satisfaction: Curvilinear Results from an Empirical Study," *Personnel Review,* 18 (1), 23-26.

Miles, Morgan P., Danny R. Arnold, and Henry W. Nash (1990), "Adaptive Communication: The Adaptation of the Seller's Interpersonal Style to the Stage of the Dyad's Relationship and the Buyer's Communication Style," *Journal of Personal Selling and Sales Management,* 10 (Winter), 21-27.

Miller, Larry D. (1977), "Dyadic Perception of Communicator Style, Replication and Confirmation," *Communication Research,* 4 (January), 87-112.

Mohr, Jakki and John R. Nevin (1990), "Communication Strategies in Marketing Channels: A Theoretical Perspective," *Journal of Marketing,* 54 (October), 36-51.

Norton, Robert W. and Larry D. Miller (1975), "Dyadic Perception of Communication Style," *Communication Research,* 2 (January), 50-67.

_____ (1978), "Foundation of a Communicator Style Construct," *Human Communication Research,* 4 (Winter), 99-112.

_____ (1983), *Communicator Style: Theory, Applications, and Measures.* Beverly Hills, CA: Sage Publications.

O'Connor, Patrick J. (1990), *Personal Selling.* New York: Macmillan Publishing Co.

Peter, J. Paul (1981), "Construct Validity: A Review of Basic Issues and Marketing Practices," *Journal of Marketing Research,* 18 (May), 133-145.

Ruekert, Robert W. and Orville C. Walker (1987), "Marketing's Interaction with Other Functional Units: A Conceptual Framework and Empirical Evidence," *Journal of Marketing,* 51 (January), 1-19.

Schul, Patrick L., William M. Pride, and Taylor L. Little (1983), "The Impact of Channel Leadership Behavior on Intrachannel Conflict," *Journal of Marketing,* 47 (Summer), 21-34.

Sheth, Jagdish M. (1976), "Buyer-Seller Interaction: A Conceptual Framework," *Proceedings for the Association for Consumer Research,* Cincinnati, OH: Association for Consumer Research, 382-386.

Smith, Daniel C. (1991), "An Examination of Product and Market Characteristics That Affect the Financial Outcomes of Brand Extensions," *Marketing Science Institute,* Working Paper No. 91-103.

Soldow, Gary F. and Gloria Penn Thomas (1984), "Relational Communication: Form Versus Content in the Sales Interaction," *Journal of Marketing,* 48 (Winter), 84-93.

Spector, Paul E. (1987), "Method Variance as an Artifact in Self-Reported Affect and Perceptions at Work: Myth or Significant Problem?," *Journal of Applied Psychology,* 72 (August), 438-443.

Weiss, John E. and Jakki Mohr (1991), "Communication Style: Looking Beyond Content in Designing Influence Strategies," in Gilly, Mary C. and F. Robert Dwyer, eds. 1991 *AMA Educators' Conference: Enhancing Knowledge Development in Marketing,* Chicago: American Marketing Association, 33-45.

Weitz, Barton A. (1981), "Effectiveness in Sales Interactions: A Contingency Framework," *Journal of Marketing,* 45 (Winter), 85-103.

Wiener, Joshua Lyle and Tabitha A. Doescher (1991), "A Framework for Promoting Cooperation," *Journal of Marketing,* 55 (April), 38-47.

Williams, Kaylene C. and Rosann L. Spiro (1985), "Communication Style in the Salesperson-Customer Dyad," *Journal of Marketing Research,* 22 (November), 434-442.

_____, _____, and Leslie M. Fine (1990), "The Customer-Salesperson Dyad: An Interaction/ Communication Model and Review," *Journal of Personal Selling and Sales Management,* 10, (Summer), 29-43.

ORGANIZATIONAL BEHAVIOR DETERMINANTS OF SALES EMPOWERED SERVICE PROVIDER JOB PERFORMANCE

Kenneth R. Evans, University of Missouri-Columbia
John A. Grant, Southern Illinois University at Carbondale

ABSTRACT

Introduction

The purpose of this paper is to enhance conceptual understanding of the implications in expanding service provider role responsibilities to include sales expectations. Sales and service performance expectations serve as criterion variables which are proposed to be influenced by employee perceptions of role ambiguity, job characteristics, centralization, job satisfaction, stress and service delivery. A theoretical model is advanced and tested which attempts to explain variability in service and sales performance.

Methodology

The study employed a dyadic multi-stage survey methodology designed to assess critical features believed to be consistent with relevant sales and services marketing literatures. Participants were 84 service provider/salespeople (called "personal bankers") recently empowered to perform sales tasks in addition to their normal service tasks; and 1003 of their customers.

A customer questionnaire and a corresponding service provider questionnaire were designed to measure the quality of a recent banking transaction. The customer's perception of the service transaction was measured using a modified version of the SERVQUAL instrument. Individual questions were developed to provide a multiple measure for each of five dimensions of service quality. The service provider/salesperson questionnaire included additional modified scales that assessed (1) the degree of perceived stress, (2) employee satisfaction, (3) perceived centralization, (4) role ambiguity, and (5) perception of core job characteristics.

Results

A path analysis was conducted to test the tenability of the proposed conceptual model. All customer responses of each service provider/salesperson were averaged and served to establish the measures of accuracy in service provider perception. The initial test of the model using LISREL VII with maximum likelihood estimation, indicated a number of potential modifications to the structural specification of the proposed model. As no previous study was available to provide clear guidance, it was deemed appropriate to selectively modify the model where both fit and theory warranted. The adjustments resulted in a structural model which achieved a goodness of fit index of .934.

Of the fifteen relationships advanced in the hypothesized model, ten were found to be significant. Key results include: positive relationships between perceived job characteristics and sales performance, job satisfaction and service perception accuracy; a negative relationship between role ambiguity and job satisfaction; a positive relationship between centralized power distribution within the service provider's organization and job stress; a positive relationship between perception of centralized power distribution and job stress; a positive relationship between centralization and sales performance; a negative relationship between stress and job satisfaction; and a negative relationship between service perception accuracy and job related stress.

Discussion

Employee perceptions of job characteristics were found to contribute to inaccurate perceptions of the customer service experience and positively correlated to customer transaction rate. In addition, sales empowered service personnel were more effective cross-sellers when they viewed decision making authority as relatively centralized. Thus, there did not appear to be a consistent set or configuration of organizational behavior and transaction reltated perceptions which served to determine sales empowered service provider job satisfaction, transaction rate and/or cross-sell.

The apparent role of stress and service perception accuracy is particularly interesting. Stress is elevated by role ambiguity and negatively influences job satisfaction. However, increased accuracy in the service provider's understanding of the customer's transaction experience came at the cost of higher levels of stress.

Variability in service perception accuracy among sales empowered service providers is in part directly explained by employee perceptions of job charcteristics and job related stress and indirectly by role ambiguity and perceived centralization. Thus, getting close to the customer was counter intuitive to the sales empowered, service provider setting. This is in contrast to the evidence that closeness to the customer was more likely to contribute to sales success.

For further information please contact:
Kenneth R. Evans
Department of Marketing
University of Missouri
214-C Middlebush Hall
Columbia, Missouri 65211

ADAPTING TO WHAT?: A CONTINGENCY APPROACH TO SALES INTERACTIONS BASED ON A COMPREHENSIVE MODEL OF CONSUMER CHOICE

Dong Hwan Lee, State University of New York at Albany
Richard W. Olshavsky, Indiana University

ABSTRACT

A comprehensive model of consumer choice is applied to the contingency approach to the salesperson-consumer interaction to permit more detailed investigations of adaptive sales strategies. Protocol analysis, applied in a unique way, is suggested to overcome the measurement difficulties that characterize past contingency research.

INTRODUCTION

Past research on personal selling centered on the effects of salespersons' various sales behaviors (Capon 1975; Jolson 1975), behavioral predispositions (Bagozzi 1978; Scheibelhurt and Albaum 1973; Mattheiss et al. 1977), and capabilities (Lamont and Lundstrom 1977; Weaver 1969) on performance. Although some studies found relationships between the construct of interest and performance, overall results of this line of research are inconsistent and equivocal. The main limitation of this research is in its attempt to uncover factors or behaviors that determine effective performance across all sales situations. The disappointing results of this line of research led researchers to adopt a dyadic research approach. The dyadic approach focused on the relationship between the similarities between the salesperson and the customer and their impact on effectiveness (Busch and Wilson 1976; Riordan, Oliver, and Donnelly 1977; Woodside and Davenport 1974). While some studies found a relationship between similarity and performance, other dyadic studies failed to demonstrate meaningful relationships between the two constructs. Dyadic similarity studies focused on static properties of the customer-salesperson dyad and thus failed to consider the interactions between sales behavior and dyadic characteristics. (For a more detailed review of this research, see Weitz 1981.) The mixed results of dyadic research led researchers to propose an alternative, "contingent" approach (Weitz 1978, 1981; Weitz, Sujan, and Sujan 1986). The fundamental idea behind the contingent approach is that effectiveness in sales interactions is dependent upon the salesperson's "adaptability" to sales situations. Behavior of the salesperson can be characterized by the degree to which behavior is adapted to each specific sales interaction. At one extreme, salespeople are nonadaptive when they deliver the same "canned" presentation to all customers. At the other extreme, salespeople formulate and deliver an individualized presentation to each customer.

We believe that the contingent framework proposed by Weitz has considerable merit and promises to greatly increase our understanding of the determinants of sales effectiveness. However, as presented to date, the contingent framework has serious limitations. The central theme of the contingent approach is that adaptive strategies should be determined by the behaviors and characteristics associated with the salesperson and the customer. Although the framework (Weitz 1978, 1981; Weitz et al. 1986) embraced this notion at a conceptual level, it has largely neglected the great variety of consumer behaviors that may actually occur during a sales transaction and the highly adaptive manner in which some of these consumer behaviors may appear within a sales transaction. For example, in applying his model, Weitz (1978) assumed that all of the consumers in his study made choices using a linear additive rule. While a linear additive rule adequately predicts consumer choice behavior at the outcome level, consumer choice processes can occur in a variety of ways (Bettman 1979; Johnson and Puto 1987). The specific choice processes consumers use not only varies greatly but may be determined, at least in part, by the behavior of the salesperson (Olshavsky 1973). Additionally, some behaviors that are only indirectly related to choice, although potentially important determinants of consumer choice processes, can be (in fact *are*) easily neglected by researchers.

The purpose of this paper is to introduce a comprehensive model of consumer choice to the contingent approach to sales interaction research. The model identifies a broad range of behaviors that consumers may actually go through during the choice process. Some of these behaviors are directly related to choice while others are only indirectly related. Then the implications of this model for the contingency approach to sales effectiveness are identified. These implications are intended to alert researchers not only to the many possible types of behaviors exhibited by consumers (any of which salespeople may be adapting) but also to the possible adaptations consumers may be making (in part to the salesperson's behaviors) over the course of a sales transaction. Some suggestions for future research on sales interactions are advanced, in the form of testable propositions, that identify and measure not only the relevant adaptive behaviors of the salesperson but also the determinants of the behaviors of the consumer during the interactions. Finally, some suggestions are made concerning the manner in which the protocol analysis technique must be modified for use in sales transaction.

A COMPREHENSIVE DESCRIPTION OF CONSUMER CHOICE

Since the lack of consideration of the many types of consumer behaviors that actually occur during the sales interaction is identified as the major shortcoming of current contingency models of adaptive selling, we first introduce a comprehensive model of consumer choice. This section is based upon the comprehensive description of consumer choice proposed by Olshavsky (1985).[1]

Consumer Behavior with Respect to Goods

Olshavsky describes four major types of consumer behavior with respect to goods: Goal Formation, Acquisition, Consumption, and Disposition. For the purposes of this paper, only those behaviors relating to goal formation are considered.[2] *Goal formation* encompasses four subtypes of behavior: desire formation, priority formation, preference formation, and intentions formation. Typically, these behaviors are assumed to occur in this sequence. However, it must be noted that these behaviors may actually occur in a highly intertwined manner. Since preference formation is synonymous with brand (and store) choice, it is addressed first.

Preference Formation. Preference formation pertains only to those behaviors *directly* involved in the identification of the most preferred brand. Preference formation may not occur on some occasions (e.g., affect referral). If it does occur, preference formation can occur in a variety of ways -- other-based, own-based, or some combination of these two. Other-based preference formation refers to the strategy whereby the choice is subcontracted to another person or organization (e.g., following the recommendation of Consumers Reports or imitation of a friend). Own-based preference formation refers to the strategy whereby the consumer personally evaluates his or her image of the alternatives in the consideration set using one or more evaluative criteria according to some rule. The rule may be compensatory (e.g., linear additive) or noncompensatory (e.g., lexicographic). If a great many alternatives are involved, the consumer may use a phased strategy; e.g., a noncompensatory rule is used to screen alternatives and then the remaining alternatives are evaluated by a compensatory rule. Alternatively, an own-based strategy may involve the use of a heuristic (e.g., using price as an index of quality). Finally, a consumer may combine other-based and own-based preference formation strategies; e.g., an own-based choice is made among recommended alternatives only (Rosen and Olshavsky 1987).

Behaviors Preceding Preference Formation. **Desire formation** is the first of two types of behaviors that precede preference formation and are involved in "setting up" for the preference formation task. Assuming that the consumer desires to utilize an own-based preference formation strategy, setting up for preference formation involves at least five types of behaviors (not necessarily in this sequence): establishing salient evaluative criteria and the intensity of desire for each criterion (e.g., the specific attributes desired in the car must be established as a basis for deciding among alternative brands), establishing the consideration set (e.g., which cars or models to evaluate), forming an image of each of the alternative brands in the consideration set (e.g., the consumer's perception of each brand on each of the evaluative criteria), selecting a choice rule (e.g., conjunctive), and selecting a procedure for the execution of that rule (e.g., by-brand or by-attribute, if applicable). The second important type of behavior that occurs prior to preference formation is **priority formation**. Priority formation involves the establishment of the *relative importance* of all evaluative criteria. For example, "acceleration" may be considered more important than "styling" and "styling" may be judged to be more important than "reliability." The relative importance of evaluative criteria is based on the relative intensity of desire established for each evaluative criterion during desire formation.[3]

Behaviors Following Preference Formation. Preference formation is followed by **intentions formation**. At this stage, the consumer develops a plan to purchase a specific brand (and/or to patronize a specific store) during a specific time period. The brand that is most preferred may not necessarily be the brand that a customer intends to purchase because of financial or temporal considerations. (This stage may involve associated financial costs, such as finance charges and operating costs, as well as price.)

Consumer Behavior with Respect to Information.

Olshavsky (1985) treats behaviors directed toward goods as <u>conceptually distinct</u> from behaviors directed toward information (it is recognized however that considerable overlap occurs between these two types of behaviors in actual choice). Consumer behaviors with respect to information are viewed as a *subgoal* to desire formation with respect to goods. For example, a consumer who desires to engage in own-based preference formation may want to obtain information about the specific brands included in the consideration set. Hence, all consumer behaviors directed toward information are viewed as being *indirectly* related to preference formation (or to desire formation or priority formation or intentions formation). As to be discussed, these behaviors have separate implications for adaptive sales interactions. Although behavior with respect to information involves many different types of behaviors, the terminology that has been applied to goods can be applied to information because information is itself a type of economic good.

Desire Formation. Before a consumer can execute the desired preference formation strategy, information appropriate to that strategy must be available. Behaviors that establish which *types of information* are desired are referred to as desire formation with respect to information. When a customer desires information (e.g., to establish evaluative criteria, to establish a consideration set, or to establish an image of each brand included in the consideration set), his or her prior knowledge with respect to the product will influence the extent and the intensity of desire for new information from external sources. For example, when the desired information is readily available in memory or when it can be inferred using prior knowledge, the desire for information will be low. However, when the information is unavailable in memory, inaccessible, or inadequate (e.g., it may be out of date), a desire for the information from external sources (e.g., salesperson or friend) will be formed.[4]

Priority Formation. The desire for different types of information can be *prioritized* based upon the relative intensity of desire for each type of information desired. For example, a consumer who forms a more intense desire for "acceleration" than for "reliability" during desire formation related to goods may also form a more intense desire for information about "acceleration" than for information about "reliability" during desire formation with respect to information. Subsequently, during priority formation with respect to information, information about acceleration may be relatively more important than information about reliability.

Preference Formation. Preference formation involves those behaviors that establish which of several specific *sources of information* within each desired type of information source is most preferred. As with goods, preference can be established by an other-based strategy, an own-based strategy, or some combination of these two. For example, a salesperson may be recommended to a consumer by another consumer. Or, if the consumer uses an own-based strategy, he or she may form a preference for a particular salesperson on the basis of evaluative criteria such as trust, expertise, and the similarity of the salesperson to the consumer.

Intentions Formation. Intentions formation refers to the stage wherein the consumer establishes a *plan* to obtain specific types of information from specific sources. As with goods, financial and temporal constraints may lead to a discrepancy between the desired amount, type, and sources of information and the amount, type, and sources of information that the consumer actually plans to utilize.

Acquisition. Acquisition involves the transportation of the consumer to the source of the information (if necessary), the "purchase" or taking possession of the information (if it is in hard copy form), and the transportation of the information to the consumer's place of residence (if it is in hard copy form and if transportation is appropriate). For example, to obtain a brochure about

a particular brand/model of an automobile a consumer may travel to the dealer, take physical possession of the brochure, and then transport that brochure to his/her home where the brochure is read in preparation for the brand choice.

Consumption. Consumption pertains to the storage (hard copy only), preparation (hard copy only), and use of information. Use of information refers to cognitive processes involved in sensation, perception, and integration. Sensation involves the transfer of information from an external source to the central nervous system through a sensory modality. Perception refers to all behaviors relating to the encoding of information -- specifically, pattern recognition, categorization, and comprehension. Integration pertains to at least six basic types of cognition: learning, judgment, reasoning, concept formation, decision making, and problem solving.

Disposition. Disposition refers to the fate of the information that has been sensed, perceived, and integrated. Information that has been learned (i.e., available in long term memory) may or may not be "accessible" when it is later required for preference formation with respect to goods (Burke and Srull 1988).

IMPLICATIONS FOR THE CONTINGENCY APPROACH TO SALES INTERACTIONS

This comprehensive description of consumer choice behaviors suggests that a salesperson may adapt to a consumer's behavior in a variety of ways depending upon the general type of behavior (i.e., consumer behavior concerning goods or concerning information), depending upon the specific stage (e.g, desire formation or preference formation) that emerges, and depending upon the specific type of behavior that transpires within each stage (e.g., an own-based or other-based preference formation strategy). In addition, the consumer may adapt his or her behavior to the behaviors of the salesperson. Some specific illustrative implications are discussed below.[5]

Consumer Behavior with respect to Goods

Preference Formation. If preference formation does not occur on a particular occasion due to prior preference formation behaviors (i.e., the customer already knows which brand and store is most preferred), then what type of adaptation is necessary? The salesman can be effective simply by expediting the customer's "purchase" of the good (i.e., handling the exchange of goods and payment). To attempt to do otherwise could disrupt a purchase planned for that salesperson's brand and store or possibly cause the customer to delay the purchase, to purchase a different (possibly less profitable) brand or even to purchase the good at another store. In this case, the consumer's choice behavior is contingent upon the actions of the salesperson; in effect the salesperson's behavior could prompt the consumer into engaging in a choice process when no choice process would have occurred otherwise.

If preference formation does occur and it is other-based, the consumer may simply follow the salesperson's recommendation (Formisano, Olshavsky, and Tapp 1982; Olshavsky 1973) or the consumer may imitate the salesperson's behavior (i.e., the consumer prefers the brand that the salesperson states he/she owns). If the consumer uses an own-based strategy, the salesperson could facilitate the execution of the choice process in various ways depending on the customer's specific strategy (e.g., if the consumer is executing a conjunctive rule, the salesperson can help the consumer to locate each of the alternative brands in the consumer's consideration set).

Desire Formation. The salesperson could attempt to influence the customer's desire formation strategy (e.g., change it from a noncompensatory rule to a compensatory rule). If the customer desires to use a compensatory rule, the salesperson can attempt to influence the customer's choice processes in various ways. The salesperson can attempt to influence the customer's evaluative criteria (by adding or deleting criteria) or the intensity of desire for various attributes (i.e., the importance weights, Lutz 1975; Weitz 1978). If the customer desires to use an own-based preference formation strategy involving some heuristic, the salesperson could attempt to influence which heuristic is to be used (e.g., switch the consumer from using price as an index of quality to using manufacturer's reputation as an index of quality). Depending upon the salesperson's behavior, the consumer may modify his or her planned desire formation behaviors; e.g., a salesperson judged to be trustworthy and knowledgeable may greatly influence or even be the sole basis for the formation of the consumer's evaluative criteria and their importance weights.

Priority Formation. The salesperson could attempt to influence the customer's perception of the relative importance of evaluative criteria. If two or more evaluative criteria of equal intensity of desire are involved or if the consumer is not certain of the intensity of desire, the salesperson could attempt to influence the relative importance of evaluative criteria (e.g., to emphasize the relative importance of reliability over acceleration).

Intentions Formation. Because financial or temporal considerations may be as important as the preference itself, a salesperson's adaptive strategies after the preference formation could be critical to close the transaction. The salesperson could attempt to influence the intentions formation process by acquainting the consumer with the store's financing policies or by influencing the customer's perception of the total cost of a good (i.e., price plus savings in operating costs or trade-in value).

Consumer Behavior with respect to Information

Desire Formation. The salesperson could attempt to influence the customer to form a desire for new information from external sources. For example, the salesperson could state that a new model of a car is completely redesigned and therefore the consumer's current knowledge should be updated.

Priority Formation. The salesperson could attempt to influence the perceived relative importance of different types of information (e.g., driving the car is more important than reading published reviews).

Preference Formation. If the consumer uses an own-based preference formation strategy, the salesperson could attempt to make himself/herself the preferred salesperson (e.g., by persuading the consumer of his/her expertise).

Intentions Formation. The salesperson could attempt to influence the perceived costs (in terms of money and/or time) of obtaining information from various sources. For example, the salesperson could emphasize the high additional time costs associated with continued search at other stores.

Acquisition. The salesperson could expedite the consumer's acquisition of information. For example, a car salesperson could mail a brochure to a consumer to save the consumer the time and effort of traveling to the dealer (i.e., if the salesperson judges this to be an effective move for this particular consumer).

Consumption. The salesperson could attempt to influence the consumer's comprehension of information (e.g., by helping the consumer to understand certain technical terms) or could attempt to influence the integration of information (e.g., by changing the consumer's image of one or more of the attributes of each of the brands in the consideration set).

Disposition. The salesperson could attempt to influence the consumer's ability to retrieve processed information. For example, at a critical point in the preference formation process, the salesperson could "remind" the consumer concerning those positive attributes of the salesperson's brand the consumer may have forgotten.

Sources of Complication

If two or more consumers are involved in the transaction (e.g., husband and wife; husband, wife, and children), investigating the adaptive behavior of the salesperson (and of the consumers) becomes even more complex because the salesperson must decide which member(s) of the decision making group is (are) relevant. A further complication arises when the salesperson does not have the information desired by the consumer. In this case, the salesperson knows what the customer desires to know but is unable to provide the information. Finally, in order to maintain control over the choice process (Wright 1986), a consumer may alter his/her choice strategy.

SOME PROPOSITIONS

Research in personal selling has suggested that a salesperson's knowledge and experience are positively related to sales performance (Weitz et al. 1986). Weitz (1978) suggested that effective and ineffective salespeople differ in terms of amount of knowledge, whereas the strategy formation skill is associated with procedural knowledge. Several other studies have found that a salesperson's ability moderated the relationship between effectiveness and the practice of customer-oriented behavior (Grikscheit and Crissey 1973). Salespeople accumulate a base of knowledge and experience and organize them into categories of selling situations so that they can be readily applied when the salesperson encounters new customers and new selling situations rather than reacting to each new situation uniquely (Weitz et al. 1986).

Thus, it is proposed that a salesperson's level of *expertise* (or experience) is positively related to his or her ability to *recognize correctly* the different stages that transpire over the entire choice process. It is also proposed that a salesperson's level of expertise (in terms of declarative and procedural knowledge) is critically important for adaptive strategy formation when the consumer is in the stage of preference formation with respect to information. That is, the adaptability and the performance of salespeople at this stage is positively related to his or her level of expertise. Taken together, the expert salesperson is expected to formulate and deliver adaptive sales strategies more effectively than the salesperson who lacks such expertise.

However, existing personal selling research suggests that sales approaches interact with consumer characteristics (Hakansson, Johansson, and Wootz 1977; Spiro, Perreault, and Reynolds 1976). Thus, it is our premise that the effectiveness of any adaptive strategies will be determined by the interaction between consumer factors and salesperson factors. Incorporating consumer characteristics into the framework is consistent with the contingency approach which suggests that effectiveness in sales interactions is moderated by both the salesperson and the consumer (Weitz 1981). Among many consumer factors, *prior knowledge* has been recognized as an important factor to influence various information processing activities (Alba and Hutchinson 1988; Bettman 1986). Although past studies examined the impact of various consumer factors on the sales outcome (see Weitz 1981 for a review), no research has investigated how the level of consumer knowledge operates in conjunction with salesperson expertise in dyadic relations from an adaptive selling perspective.

The consumer's prior knowledge about the product category such as evaluative criteria, attribute-specific values, and image of the alternatives in the consideration set should be an important factor for salespeople in formulating adaptive influence strategies. For example, the consumer who lacks knowledge may seek various types of input such as what the relevant evaluative criteria should be and the specific values of different attributes for different brands. Because the "novice" consumer may be unable to define his or her information desires accurately for each evaluative criterion, the amount and the range of information required will be large and broad. The novice consumer may also follow the standard (prototypical) sequence in the preference formation process. For this type of customer, a relatively straightforward selling technique or even a canned presentation may be effective. The "expert" consumer, on the other hand, may have enough attribute-specific information (i.e., image of alternatives) and will define evaluative criteria precisely based on prior knowledge and experience. For this type of customer, more selective, situation-specific, and in-depth selling strategies are likely to be more effective. This implies that not all salesperson are knowledgeable enough to effectively adapt their sales strategies to high knowledge consumers. Unexperienced and less knowledgeable salespeople will not be able to form accurate perceptions of the consumer, formulate appropriate strategies, and revise strategies appropriately. The foregone discussion can be summarized as the following contingency propositions:

P1: A salesperson's level of expertise will be positively related to his or her ability to correctly *recognize* the many stages and types of consumer behaviors that actually occur during sales interaction.

P2: A salesperson's level of expertise will be positively related to his or her ability to *formulate and adjust* adaptive sales strategies in response to the many types of behaviors that actually occur during a sales interaction.

P3: A salesperson's level of expertise will be critically important to implement the adaptive strategy effectively when the consumer is in the stage of *preference formation with respect to information.*

P4: A consumer's level of knowledge will *interact* with the salesperson's level of expertise to affect the salesperson's ability to *recognize* the many stages and types of consumer behaviors that actually occur during a sales interaction.

P5: A consumer's level of knowledge will *interact* with the salesperson's level of expertise to affect the salesperson's ability to *formulate and adjust* adaptive sales strategies in response to the many types of consumer behaviors that actually occur during a sales interaction.

SOME METHODOLOGICAL SUGGESTIONS

Although the importance of a contingency approach has been recognized by researchers, our understanding of this topic remains very limited. One of the reasons concerns the lack of a good theory to guide investigations of these very complex behaviors. But another reason concerns the enormous difficulties associated with the empirical study of sales transactions. As shown in the comprehensive description of choice behavior just presented, most of the important behaviors may occur during dynamic interactions between the salesperson and the consumer over time, thus these behaviors cannot be properly captured by outcome-oriented measurement approaches.

We believe that the constructive view of consumer choice advanced in consumer research can be fruitfully applied to the contingency approach to sales interactions. According to the constructive view, consumers construct the rules they use on the spot, during the actual course of selecting an alternative rather than use rules or heuristics which have been already developed and stored in memory (Bettman and Zins 1977). Thus the focus of research on constructive processes has been on *process* and specifically on the use of *elements* of choice of rules, rather than on overall choice rules (Bettman and Park 1980).

There are striking similarities between the constructive view of consumer choice and the contingency approach to salesperson-customer interactions. Because the salesperson-consumer interaction is a dynamic process, each party influences and is influenced by the other during the interactive process; some of this influence may take the form of partial strategies or elements of strategies being exhibited by both the consumer and the salesperson. Moreover, although the consumer preference formation strategy may actually follow a sequence of stages, the transition between stages, and the duration of each stage, and the amount and the type of input (e.g., concerning goods and concerning information) the consumer desires and the salesperson delivers at each stage may be partial or incomplete.

Just as the study of constructive choice processes has been advanced by the adoption of protocol analysis (see Johnson and Puto 1987 for references), so may the contingency approach to sales interactions benefit. A major advantage of protocol analysis is that a great deal of data on underlying "processes" may be exposed for inspection by the researcher. It has been proposed that retrospective protocols could be collected directly after the transaction (Weitz 1981). However, the time delay that unavoidably occurs could lead to various types of retrieval errors or interpretation problems (e.g., theorizing by the consumer and by the salesperson) that might distort the data in unknown ways (Ericsson and Simon 1984). The retrieval problems can be offset somewhat by

various procedures such as exposing the consumer and the salesperson separately to a videotaped recording of the transaction, as suggested by Olshavsky (1976). But the interpretation problems may still remain.

Concurrent protocol analysis has the potential to identify emerging stages, changes of behaviors and strategies, and possibly the determinants of the changes that occur during the interaction process for both the customer and the salesperson without the danger of participant theorizing about their behaviors. However, the personal selling situation poses a unique problem for the application of concurrent protocol analysis (Olshavsky 1976). Specifically, "thinking aloud" by either the salesperson or the consumer may provide the other party with information as to that person's "private" motives, strategies, and reactions which would normally not be transmitted during the interaction. Thus, a modified version of concurrent protocol analysis must be developed that avoids this problem if concurrent protocol analysis is to be used at all.

In thinking of a solution to this seemingly impossible problem, it is crucial to prevent the consumer from learning of the salesperson's private thoughts (i.e., thoughts other than what the salesperson would normally transmit to the consumer) and vice versa. This could be accomplished if the researcher arranges for the sales transaction to occur entirely by phone (or fax or teletype). (This procedure is obviously more appropriate for certain types of products or services.) The "public" conversation could be recorded straightforwardly. The "private" thought processes of the consumer (and of the salesperson) could be recorded with the phone mouth piece covered immediately after each "public" utterance to the salesperson (consumer). Of course, problems may arise due to the delays that will occur between the public and the private thoughts; but these delays will be considerably shorter than those associated with protocols that are collected after the entire transaction has been completed. And the procedure will produce unnatural "interruptions" in the thought processes; but it is an empirical question as to just how serious these interruptions are relative to the benefits that this suggested procedure may provide. (Contrary to expectation, empirical research has demonstrated that the protocol analysis procedure itself is not disruptive to the thought processes (Ericsson and Simon 1984)).

If this modified concurrent protocol analysis were adopted, the analysis of these data could be guided by a new coding scheme proposed by Olshavsky and Kumar (1992). Their coding scheme is more *comprehensive* and *detailed* than past schemes (e.g., Bettman and Park 1980) in that it encompasses all of the behaviors that are discussed in this paper and it has the potential to include a comparably comprehensive coding scheme for all of the salesperson's behavior as well.

CONCLUSIONS

Personal selling is a complex and dynamic influence process. Effective salespeople can adapt their sales techniques both within and across sales interactions. Consumers form preferences in a variety of ways and experienced and successful salespeople probably already know this and adapt to each accordingly. Likewise, a great many important behaviors that are only indirectly related to choice are exhibited by consumers and are reacted to by salespeople. A contingency approach to the customer-salesperson interaction promises to enhance our knowledge about the sales effectiveness. However, if we are to make progress in learning how salespeople adapt their strategies to a consumer's choice processes effectively, we need to increase our understanding about the consumer's behaviors in preference formation process in terms of scope and depth. Our comprehensive model of consumer choice processes is intended to complement the limitations of the existing contingency framework of sales effectiveness.

We also need to overcome the methodological limitations of outcome-oriented measures that do not serve the purpose of the contingency approach. The measures adopted to operationalize the contingency model should not be limited by a single, static model of how consumers make choices. The measures must be able to capture the varied, dynamic, and interactive behaviors. With proper modifications, concurrent protocol analysis may allow us to obtain detailed measures not only of the relevant adaptive behaviors of the salesperson but also the behaviors of the consumer.

Future research should test the contingency propositions by operationalizing them as testable hypotheses. Suggestions for developing testable contingency propositions are discussed by Weitz (1981). The measures of consumer knowledge (e.g., Brucks 1985; Sujan 1985) and salesperson knowledge (e.g., Leigh and McGraw 1987; Sujan, Sujan, and Bettman 1988) have been improved. Concurrent process tracing method in conjunction with knowledge measures should facilitate future research in this important area.

ENDNOTES

[1] While the description presented here pertains only to the behavior of final consumers, with a little effort the basic ideas can be extended to the behavior of industrial buyers. For this reason, the term "consumer" is used throughout; but "customer" would apply as well.

[2] The acquisition, consumption, and dispositions of goods are not discussed here because these behaviors occur *after* choice. It is recognized, however, that a salesperson typically plays a crucial role in the "acquisition" of a good. And it is recognized that a salesperson may play a crucial role in all three of these types of behaviors in repeat purchase situations. However, in the interest of brevity, these complications are not considered here.

[3] Priority formation, in a broader sense, also involves the establishment of the relative importance of all goods desired at a particular point in time. For example, a college education may be more important than a new automobile. This aspect of priority formation is less important for the study of preference formation in the context of salesperson-customer interaction, because the consumer typically enters the interaction with the salesperson when the intensity of desire for the specific good under consideration is higher than other goods. Still, in some circumstances, the broader behaviors involved should be considered.

[4] It should be noted that desire formation with respect to information may be highly influenced by the preference formation with respect to goods process. For example, a consumer using a lexicographic rule may only require information concerning the most important attribute if there are no "ties."

[5] The types of adaptive selling considered here are primarily concerned with the interaction between the salesperson and the final consumer in the transaction related situations (i.e., one transaction). The situations involving relationship-oriented transactions are not considered.

REFERENCES

Alba, Joseph W. and J. Wesley Hutchinson (1987), "Dimensions of Consumer Expertise," *Journal of Consumer Research,* 13 (December), 441-454.

Bagozzi, Richard P. (1978), "Salesforce Performance and Satisfaction as a Function of Individual Difference, Interpersonal, and Situational Factors," *Journal of Marketing Research,* 15 (November), 517-531.

Bettman, James R. (1979), *An Information Processing Theory of Consumer Choice.* Reading, Massachusetts, Addison-Wesley Publishing Co.

_____and Michael A. Zins (1977), "Constructive Processes in Consumer Choice," *Journal of Consumer Research,* 4 (September), 75-85.

_____and C. W. Park (1980), "Effects of Prior Knowledge and Experience and Phase of Choice Process on Consumer Decision Processes: A Protocol Analysis," *Journal of Consumer Research,* 7 (December), 234-248.

Brucks, Merrie (1985), "The Effects of Product Class Knowledge on Information Search Behavior," *Journal of Consumer Research,* 12 (June), 1-16.

Burke, Raymond R. and Thomas K. Srull (1988), "Competitive Interference and Consumer Memory for Advertising," *Journal of Consumer Research,* 15 (June), 55-68.

Busch, Paul and David T. Wilson (1976), "An Experimental Analysis of a Salesman's Expert and Referent Bases of Social Power in the Buyer-Seller Dyad," *Journal of Marketing Research,* 13 (February), 3-11.

Capon, Noel (1975), "Persuasive Effects of Sales Messages Developed from Interaction Process Analysis," *Journal of Business Administration,* 60 (April), 238-244.

Ericsson, K. Anders and Herbert A. Simon (1984), *Protocol Analysis - Verbal Reports as Data.* Cambridge, Massachusetts: MIT Press.

Formisano, Roger A., Richard W. Olshavsky, and Shelley Tapp (1982), "Purchase Strategy in a Very Difficult Task Environment," *Journal of Consumer Research,* 8 (March), 370-380.

Grikscheit, Gary M. and William J. E. Crissey (1973), "Improving Interpersonal Communication Skill," *MSU Business Topics,* 21 (Autumn), 63-68.

Hakansson, Hakan, Jan Johanson, and Bjorn Wootz (1977), "Influence Tactics in Buyer-Seller Processes," *Industrial Marketing Management,* 5 (Fall), 319-332.

Johnson, Michael D. and Christopher Puto (1987), "A Review of Consumer Judgment and Choice," in *Review of Marketing,* Michael J. Houston, ed. American Marketing Association, Chicago, 236-292.

Jolson, Marvin A. (1975), "The Underestimated Potential of the Canned Sales Presentation," *Journal of Marketing,* 39 (January), 75-78.

Lamont, Lawrence M. and William J. Lundstrom (1977), "Identifying Successful Industrial Salesmen by Personality and Personal Characteristics," *Journal of Marketing Research,* 14 (November), 517-529.

Leigh, Thomas W. and Patrick F. McGraw (1989), "Mapping the Procedural Knowledge of Industrial Sales Personnel: A Scrip-Theoretic Investigation," *Journal of Marketing,* 53 (January), 16-34.

Lutz, Richard J. (1975), "Changing Brand Attitudes Through Modification of Cognitive Structure," *Journal of Consumer Research,* 1 (March), 49-59.

Mattheiss, T. H., Richard M. Durand, Jan R. Muczyk, and Myron Gable (1977), "Personality and the Prediction of Salesmen's Success," in *Contemporary Marketing Thought,* B. Greenberg and D. Bellenger, eds. Chicago: American Marketing Association, 499-502.

Olshavsky, Richard W. (1973), "Customer-Salesman Interaction in Appliance Retailing," *Journal of Marketing Research,* 10 (May), 208-212.

_____(1976), "Consumer Decision Making in Naturalistic Settings: Salesman-Prospect Interactions," in Beverlee B. Anderson, ed. *Advances in Consumer Research,* 3, 379-381.

_____(1985), "Toward a More Comprehensive Theory of Choice," in *Advances in Consumer Research,* Hirschman, Elizabeth and Morris Holbrook, eds. Provo, UT: Association for Consumer Research, 12, 465-470.

_____and Anand Kumar (1992), "Toward a More Comprehensive Coding Scheme for the Analysis of Protocol Data in Studies of Brand Choice," in *Proceedings* of the 1992 American Marketing Association Winter Educator's Conference, 3, 122-131.

Riorden, Edward A., Richard Oliver, and James H. Donnelly, Jr. (1977), "The Unsold Prospect: Dyadic and Attitudinal Determinants," *Journal of Marketing Research,* 14 (November), 530-537.

Rosen, Dennis and Richard W. Olshavsky (1987), "A Protocol Analysis of Brand Choice Strategies Involving Recommendations," *Journal of Consumer Research,* 14 (December), 440-444.

Scheibelhurt, John H. and Gerald Albaum (1973), "Self-Other Orientations Among Salesmen and Non-salesmen," *Journal of Marketing Research,* 10 (February), 97-99.

Spiro, Rosann L., William D. Perreault, Jr., Fred D. Reynolds (1976), "The Selling Process: A Critical Review and Model," *Industrial Marketing Management,* 5 (December), 351-363.

Sujan, Mita (1985), "Consumer Knowledge: Effects on Evaluation Strategies Mediating Consumer Judgments," *Journal of Consumer Research,* 12 (June), 31-46.

_____, Harish Sujan, and James Bettman (1988), "Knowledge Structure Differences Between More Effective and Less Effective Salespeople," *Journal of Marketing Research,* 25 (February), 81-86.

Weaver, Charles N. (1969), "An Empirical Study to Aid in the Selection of Retail Salesclerks," *Journal of Retailing,* 45 (Fall), 22-26.

Weitz, Barton A. (1978), "Relationship Between Salesperson Performance and Understanding of Customer Decision Making," *Journal of Marketing Research,* 15 (November), 501-516.

_____(1981), "Effectiveness in Sales Interactions: A Contingency Framework," *Journal of Marketing,* 45 (Winter), 85-103.

_____, Harish Sujan, and Mita Sujan (1986), "Knowledge, Motivation, and Adaptive Behavior: A Framework for Improving Selling Effectiveness," *Journal of Marketing,* 50 (October), 174-191.

Willet, Ronald P. and Allen Pennington (1966), "Customer and Salesman: The Anatomy of Choice and Influence in a Retailing Setting," in *Science, Mar-*

keting and Technology, Raymond M. Hass, ed. Chicago: American Marketing Association, 598-616.

Woodside, Arch G. and William J. Davenport (1974), "The Effect of Salesman Similarity and Expertise on Consumer Purchasing Behavior," *Journal of Mar-* *keting Research,* 11 (May), 198-202.

Wright, Peter (1986), "Schemer Schema: Consumers' Intuitive Theories about Marketers Influence Tactics," *Advances in Consumer Research,* Richard J. Lutz, ed. Association for Consumer Research, 1-3.

THE EFFECT OF VALUE CONGRUENCE ON SALESPERSON PERFORMANCE IN THE LIFE INSURANCE INDUSTRY

Anne L. Balazs, University of Oklahoma

ABSTRACT

The focus of management theory and practice since the early Eighties has been on organizational culture. Popular business literature has presented many examples of economic turnaround and prosperity once the organizational culture has been recognized, harnessed, and properly managed. Analogous to the anthropological term, the organizational culture is composed of shared values, beliefs, and norms in an organization. Values are an integral part of a culture, forming the behavioral patterns of its members. The sharing of values between the corporate organization and its members is assumed to be necessary for effective and profitable performance. The focus of this research was on **how** organizational values affect the performance of salespeople.

A combined ethnographic/survey research methodology was used to thoroughly investigate the impact of organizational values. Two firms within the life insurance industry were the setting for this research. The first phase of the research was spent in agencies and the home offices of these two companies for observation and interviewing. The second phase involved the administration of a questionnaire to a national sample of life insurance agents and their sales managers. The third phase investigated the level of value congruency in the companies and the possibility of value exchange. The fourth phase integrated the influence of organizational and personal values into the Churchill, Ford, and Walker Model of Salesperson Performance. The influence of value congruency on performance and its determinants was addressed through causal modeling.

Depending upon how congruency between organizational and personal values was measured, the results of this study differ. Using an index to determine specific value differences between agents and their managers led to the conclusion that value congruency had no significant effect on performance and its determinants. Using the Shared Values Scale as an indicator of value congruency led to the support of most of the study's hypotheses regarding a positive influence on the determinants of salesperson performance. Neither measure provided support for value congruency having a significantly positive effect on performance.

The implications of these results are that caution should be used in measuring values and congruency between individuals and an organizational value system; however measured, value congruency does not imply greater productivity on the part of the salesperson; increased satisfaction and organizational commitment and more accurate role perceptions were found among those with greater value congruency.

For further information please contact:
Anne L. Balazs
University of Oklahoma
College of Business Administration
Norman, OK 73019-0450

American Marketing Association / Summer 1992

233

ANTECEDENTS OF MOTHERS' PERCEPTIONS OF TOY-BASED PROGRAMMING: AN EMPIRICAL INVESTIGATION

Les Carlson, Clemson University
Russell N. Laczniak, Iowa State University
Darrel D. Muehling, Washington State University

ABSTRACT

Previous research (Muehling, Carlson, and Laczniak 1991) suggests that parents are concerned with certain aspects of toy-based programs (TBP—television programs which have been developed primarily to promote toys). Yet, little is known about why parents hold specific beliefs regarding TBP. This study focused on determining if structural (parental socialization tendencies) and content (media usage patterns) aspects of parent/child interactions serve as potential bases for mothers' beliefs about TBP.

Research dealing with TBP is a logical extension to work which identified parental concerns about television advertising directed at children (e.g., Atkin 1975; Yankelovich 1970). Yet, parents are likely to believe that TBP affects kids differently than advertising, since TBP are 30 minute shows rather than 30 second commercials. Other authors (e.g., Grossbart and Crosby 1984) have identified aspects of relationships between parents and children which serve as bases for parental reactions to child-directed food advertising. Such research also functions as a framework for this investigation of mothers' beliefs about TBP. Specifically, to the extent mothers perceive that TBP interferes with structural- and content-based aspects of the parent-child relationship, they may formulate specific beliefs regarding TBP.

Consumer and advocacy groups have aired a multitude of concerns regarding TBP. The American Academy of Pediatrics suggested that TBP could promote violent and aggressive behavior in children (*Marketing News* 1988). The now disbanded Action for Children's Television has expressed skepticism about the ethical fairness of TBP and noted the overcommercialization of children's television (*Marketing News* 1991). In addition, TBP has been criticized because of its potential to impact children while their advertising defenses have not been initiated (Charren 1988). Concern about TBP is not limited to advocacy groups; congress passed a bill that requested the FCC to define "program length commercials" and study their effects on children (Gamarekian 1990).

Previous research has shown that parental beliefs about TBP reflect sentiments voiced by advocacy groups (Muehling, Carlson, and Laczniak 1991), possibly reflecting the highly publicized nature of these claims. Specifically, parental concerns are likely to deal with beliefs that TBP: (1) lead children to behave in an anti-social manner, (2) exploit children as consumers, and (3) replace more creative shows designed for children.

Data analyzed included responses from 318 mothers in three geographic locations in the U.S., i.e., Northwest, South and Midwest. Indices tapping anti-social behaviors and negative consumer behavior outcomes in children, and beliefs that TBP represent less than optimal children's programming were developed to measure maternal perceptions about TBP. These were then linked to parenting orientation, media usage and demographic variables via canonical correlation.

Results suggest that two bases for specific TBP concerns are both structural and content in nature and exhibit certain demographic characteristics. Specifically, mothers find some aspects of TBP relatively more troubling than others (i.e., TBP takes advantage of children as consumers). They may be able to deal with such uncertainties about the influence of the marketplace on children by resorting to parenting tendencies that have proven to be useful in the past (controlling children's exposure to the media). However, findings also suggest deeper concerns (i.e., TBP leads to anti-social behaviors in children) that may not be as amenable to current parenting practices. Thus, concerns about TBP are not simply related to their impact on marketplace aspects involving children, but also on how TBP may influence and contribute to a deterioration of the overall relation between parents and children.

This suggests avenues for the development of specific programs and policies that might address maternal concerns. Public service announcements, during TBP and/or using TBP characters, could be targeted at providing suggestions for consumer behaviors that children could learn. Deeper fears about the effect of TBP on parent/child interactions might be assuaged by endorsements from parent- teacher organizations and child development/parenting experts.

For further information contact:
Les Carlson
Department of Marketing
Clemson University
Clemson, SC 29634-1325

A GRICEAN PRAGMATIC APPROACH TO ADVERTISING COMPREHENSION AND DECEPTION IN ADVERTISING

John Richardson, University of Chicago
Judy Cohen, Rider College

ABSTRACT

Researchers in deception in advertising have often expressed a desire for a theory of non-literal inferences. Linguistic pragmatics, as developed by H. P. Grice, can provide just such a theory. After arguing that deception through implication must be studied at the comprehension stage, we offer a brief but thorough introduction to Gricean theory, using several real and fictional advertising claims to exemplify Gricean principles. We show that pragmatic implication does not arise only in the context of deception, but is a common feature of efficient communication, a fact with hitherto unappreciated research and policy implications.

INTRODUCTION

The detection of deception in advertising has long been of major concern to consumer behavior researchers, practitioners, and public policy officials. The recent renaissance of activity at the FDA and FTC promises to bring the issue of deception in advertising back to the forefront. Furthermore, as we will show in this paper, certain concepts that are crucial to understanding deceptive communication are in fact crucial to understanding nondeceptive communication as well.

LOCATING DECEPTION IN THE HIERARCHY OF COMMUNICATION EFFECTS

According to Richards (1990, p. 109), deceptive advertising by definition includes "an explicit or implicit claim ... [that] conveys a belief about a product/service attribute which is demonstrably false or unsubstantiated as true ...." The process which leads up to the creation of this false or unsubstantiated belief has been described by Armstrong and Russ (1975) roughly as follows: When the consumer is exposed to an advertisement, s/he perceives the advertisement as making certain claims. We will call this the comprehension or perception stage. The consumer then goes on to believe or not believe the claims. We will call this the persuasion or belief stage. The consumer is then said to be deceived if and only if (1) the consumer perceives the advertisement as making a certain claim; (2) the consumer believes the perceived claim; (3) the perceived and believed claim is false.

In this paper, we will focus on the comprehension stage, since the issue of comprehension is logically prior to the issues of belief or factuality. Moreover, from a public policy perspective, the FTC is concerned with whether advertising content has the capacity to result in false beliefs (Preston and Richards 1986; Richards 1990). Clearly, any advertisement that is perceived to make claims that are at variance with the facts has the capacity to create false beliefs about the product. Finally, from a consumer research perspective, the theoretical machinery necessary for understanding consumers' comprehension of deceptive advertisements will, as we mentioned above, give us insights into how consumers comprehend all ads, regardless of whether they are deceptive or not.

Several researchers have taken a different tack and have focused on the belief stage (for example, Burke et al. 1988; Gunert and Dedler 1985; Barbour and Gardner 1982). Even Armstrong and Russ, in a later paper (Armstrong, Gurol, and Russ 1979), shifted their focus to the belief stage and post-belief stages of the deception process, and ignored the comprehension stage. While the belief and post-belief stages are important, it is also important to know where these beliefs are coming from; i.e., are the believed claims the result of comprehending the advertisement itself or are they background beliefs at best evoked by the ad? It is not obvious that evoked beliefs, however erroneous, are evidence of deception. Hence, it is important to include tests of comprehension in any test of beliefs. This is particularly true when experimental designs include known brand names or particularly familiar product categories.

A more critical problem arises when subjects are asked questions regarding their beliefs about a product in order to gauge their comprehension of an advertisement about that product (Burke, et al. 1988). Since comprehending an advertisement as making a certain claim is neither necessary nor sufficient to believing the content of that claim, tests of belief simply cannot be used to gauge comprehension. Once again, this problem is particularly severe when known brands or highly familiar product categories are employed in the research design. In general, it is important to break deception down into its component effects and measure each effect separately, using only those measuring instruments that are genuinely appropriate to the effect in question.

LITERALLY FALSE VERSUS MISLEADING ADVERTISING

A popular typology of deceptive advertisements has been suggested by D. Cohen (1974). This typology distinguishes between advertisements which are factually incorrect and those which are literally true, but which create a false impression. This distinction is somewhat off the mark. The question of factuality arises for all claims and only after questions relating to comprehension and belief have been raised and answered. The question of literality, on the other hand, is a comprehension-related issue. Therefore, a more cogent typology should distinguish between claims that are literally conveyed and those that are conveyed or implied in some non-literal way. Then any claim that is literally conveyed, believed, but factually incorrect can be classified as literally false. On the other hand, any claim that is conveyed or implied in some non-literal way, is believed, but is factually incorrect can be classified as misleading.

Shimp (1979) observed that as the FTC cracked down on deceptive advertising, blatantly false advertising did indeed decrease, though only to be replaced by more subtle forms of deception. Generally speaking, misleading advertisements are more subtle in their deception than are literally false ads. Moreover, increasingly many studies have focused explicitly on advertisements that deceive through implication (Burke et al. 1988; Gaeth and Heath 1987; Harris 1977; Preston 1967; Preston and Scharbach 1971; Shimp 1978; Snyder 1989). The sheer scope of these studies show that deception through implication has been and still is a major concern. Moreover, the robustness of some of the effects studied in these papers has shown that implication can be a powerful and effective method of communication, a point we will emphasize below.

While these studies offer many interesting specific cases of deception through implication, they lack an overall framework in which to understand the mechanics of non-literal implication. The closest anyone has come in the advertising to proposing a theory of how non-literal implications arise was in Preston (1967). Preston examined several cases in which an ad's claim "invited" the respondent to draw a fallacious inference. For instance, the inference "if y then x" is commonly drawn from the premise "if x then y" even though the latter does not logically entail the former. Preston found that subjects did indeed commit such fallacies when exposed to advertising claims of the relevant form.

Otherwise, advertising researchers have examined only individual cases, or at best, classes of intuitively similar cases (e.g., Preston 1977; Grunert and Dedler 1985). Grunert and Dedler went so far as to suggest that developing a simple typology of misleading claims is the best general framework one could hope for. Although we agree that typology-building is and will continue to be an important part of framework-building, we will offer an explanatory framework for studying non-literal meanings. This framework is based on Gricean pragmatics, which has been developed by linguists and philosophers of language over the last 25 years. This framework has its typological aspects but also offers some deep theoretical insight into how and why non-literal meanings arise. Indeed, Grice's (1967) original work was devoted largely to explaining the origins of many of the same classical fallacies that Preston (1967) simply assumed as givens.[1]

LINGUISTIC PRAGMATICS

An understanding of Gricean pragmatics should begin with a definition of pragmatics. The classical semiotic definition of pragmatics calls it the study of the relation between signs and their users. A more straightforward definition in the classical spirit would call pragmatics the study of language use. However, pragmatics has come to be viewed in the linguistic and philosophy of language literatures as the study of those aspects of the meaning of a linguistic form that are not part of its literal content . The link between the classical and modern conceptions of pragmatics is that non-literal meanings are assumed to arise from rules governing language use. Gricean pragmatics is the most well-articulated theory of what these rules are and how these rules give rise to non-literal meaning.

Before reviewing Gricean theory, we would like to rectify two misconceptions that seem to have arisen in the advertising literature regarding what pragmatics is. First, in a paper widely cited in the deception literature, Harris (1977) suggests that most pragmatic implications arise "through the interaction of the linguistic input and the hearer's stored knowledge" (p. 604). It is clear from Harris' examples that by "stored knowledge" he means real world knowledge, such as inferring from the statement "the python caught the mouse" that the python ate the mouse. While this sort of inference from real world knowledge may (or may not) be the most common sort of implication at the level of individual examples, it is only one type of implication studied in the linguistic literature. (Nor is inference from real world knowledge as idiosyncratic a matter as suggested by Grunert and Dedler 1985. See Atlas and Levinson 1981; Prince 1981.)

Most work on pragmatic implications in the linguistic literature focuses not on inference from real world knowledge but on what might be called inference from linguistic knowledge. What exactly we mean by this will be made clearer below. However, an example might help clarify things a bit. For instance, people will quite generally infer from the statement "some coelenterates are sessile" that not all coelenterates are sessile, despite the fact that the latter proposition does not logically imply the former. Needless to say, this common inference is not driven by people's common knowledge of coelenterates and sessility. Rather, as we will explain in detail below, it is driven by (1) people's linguistic knowledge that 'all' is semantically a stronger quantifier than 'some' and (2) the pragmatic rule that says, in essense, that speakers should always use the strongest appropriate quantifier. These two bits of linguistic knowledge lead speakers to conclude that the speaker feels that saying 'all coelenterates are sessile' is too strong, which suggests, simply, that not all coelenterates are sessile. Hence, people can and commonly do use linguistic knowledge to draw non-literal inferences about subject matters about which they have little to no real world knowledge at all. It is this sort of inference that has most interested linguistic pragmaticians, especially those of the Gricean persuasion.

Now, it just so happens that indeed, not all coelenterates are sessile. This points up another misconception that seems to have occured in the advertising literature (Preston 1967; Grunert and Dedler 1985). In these works, the suggestion seems to be that the use of implication in advertising is an inherently deceptive practice. Evidence that this is a widespread belief is that all of the research on implication in advertising is also research on deception in advertising. This might suggest to some that implications are always false. But, as the example just given shows, it is clearly not true that implications are always false. Indeed, implications are a ubiquitous means of efficiently conveying more than what is literally said. So, for instance, a perfectly honest advertiser could claim "Some beers are more expensive than Splatz, but only Splatz is made with Muehlhuegel spring water", realizing full well that consumers will draw the inference that not all beers are more expensive than Splatz. As long as some beers are more expensive and some beers are less expensive than Splatz, this implication is simply true, and therefore obviously not deceptive.

Note that this last misconception concerning the nature of implications is in part due to a conflation of the levels of comprehension and factuality. Pragmatic implication occurs at the level of comprehension, and implicated propositions, like all propositions, can be either factual or nonfactual. However, it remains true that deceptive advertisements would be more likely to be deceptive through implications than through literal falsehood if the legal system only prosecuted literal falsehoods or was strongly biased towards prosecuting literal falsehoods. This may in fact be the case, especially since systematic theories of implication have been lacking. Just such a needed theory of implication has been offered by Grice (1967).

GRICEAN PRAGMATICS

Gricean pragmatics offers several benefits to researchers interested in deception in advertising at the comprehension stage, as well as comprehension of advertisements in general. First, the theory and practice of Gricean pragmatics has yielded a rich and multifaceted typology of non-literal meanings. Second, for several of the classes of non-literal meanings in this typology, Gricean theory offers a deeper understanding into how and why these non-literal meanings arise. We will consider both of these contributions of Gricean pragmatics. Since, however, these two strands of Gricean research are highly intertwined, we will not discuss them sequentially, but in relation to each other. We will begin by defining a few basic concepts, and then present Grice's theory of the logic of language use, including his celebrated maxims. We will then give examples of several kinds of non-literal meanings that have yielded in part or whole to Gricean explanation.

Basic Concepts in Gricean Pragmatics

Gricean theory is a theory of utterance meaning. (An utterance is simply a sentence or other meaningful linguistic form that is actually used in an act of communication.) Grice recognized a three-way distinction: (1) what an utterance conveys; (2) what an utterance literally says; and (3) what an utterance implicates. With a few exceptions, to be noted below (in our discussion of the maxim of quality), what an utterance conveys is the sum of what it says and what it implicates. The literal meaning of an utterance is, by definition, what the utterance says. Hence, any non-literal meaning conveyed by the utterance is, by theorem, what the utterance implicates. These non-literal meanings are commonly called implicatures in the linguistic literature. We, however, will call them implications, since this term has become standard in the advertising literature (and since Grice himself used the term 'implicature' to refer to the phenomenon of non-literal meanings, not instances of the phenomenon, a practice we will follow.)

Grice distinguished among several different kinds of implications. The most important distinction, and the only one we will discuss here, is that between generalized and particularized implications. A particularized implicature is one that is crucially dependent on context. A famous example is shown in the following exchange:

Speaker A: "Is there a telephone around here?"

Speaker B: "There is a gas station on the corner."

In the context of Speaker A's question, Speaker B's statement is generally perceived to convey that there is a telephone at the gas station. This however is clearly not part of the literal meaning of this utterance. Hence it must be an implication. But note that this implication is itself crucially dependent on context. If Speaker A had asked where she/he could buy cigarettes, the implication of Speaker B's answer would have been quite different.

A generalized implication is one that tends to arise regardless of context (unless it is specifically cancelled or suspended.) We have already given an example of generalized implicature above in our discussion of the fact that "some" implicates "not all". We will discuss this example, and others like it, below in our discussion of quantity implicature. Simply note for now that this implication is not dependent on context.

General Gricean Framework

The Gricean framework is predicated on two premises. The first premise is that communication is a rational goal-directed process. The second is that communication is an inherently cooperative enterprise, i.e., speaker and hearer cooperate to maximize mutual understanding. Both of these premises, but especially the latter, led Grice to formulate the Cooperative Principle as the central postulate of his framework. According to the Cooperative Principle, a communicator is to make his/her utterance "such as is required, at the stage at which it occurs, by the accepted purpose ... of the [enterprise] in which [the communicator] is engaged" (Grice 1975, p. 45).

The question, then, is what does it take for an utterance to count as being "such as is required." As a first step towards answering this question, Grice formulated (p. 45-46) the following Maxims of Conversation (which we will rename the Maxims of Communication, as they readily relate to utterances that are not intuitively "conversational"):

The Gricean Maxims of Communication

1. The Maxims of Quality
   A.   Do not say that which you believe is false.
   B.   Do not say that for which you lack sufficient evidence.

2. The Maxims of Quantity
   A.   Make your contribution as informative as is required.
   B.   Do not make your contribution more informative than is required.

3. The Maxim of Relation
   A.   Be relevant.

4. The Maxims of Manner
   A.   Avoid obscurity of expression.
   B.   Avoid ambiguity.
   C.   Be brief.
   D.   Be orderly.

With these Maxims of Communication in hand, one can reconceive the Cooperative Principle as the following Basic Rule for Communicators: Communicators, in order to maximize mutual understanding, must obey the Maxims of Communication. To this, we can then add the following Basic Rule for Audiences: Assume that the communicator intends to maximize mutual understanding and therefore that she/he is following the Maxims of Communication.

But this much still does not explain how, why or when non-literal meanings will arise. To bridge this gap, Grice proposed a mechanism that we will paraphrase and call the Extended Rule for Audiences: If the literal meaning of a communicator's utterance seems to place that utterance in violation of one or more of the maxims,

search for a non-literal interpretation that would place the utterance in compliance with those maxims. Finally, coming full circle, one must assume that the following Extended Rule for Communicators is also in effect: Choose your utterances with careful regard to the non-literal interpretations they are likely to evoke in the minds of audiences obeying the Extended Rule for Audiences. As we will show in the last section, this Extended Rule for Communicators can help policymakers devise a coherent doctrine for dealing fairly with alleged cases of deception by implication.

Now, the precise nature of the non-literal meanings that audiences will seek out in order to "square" an utterance with the Maxims of Communication will, of course, be largely determined by which specific maxim would otherwise be violated and, more precisely, by how that maxim would be violated. This suggests that non-literal interpretations will tend to organize themselves into a natural typology according to which maxim the literal meaning of the utterance would otherwise violate, and how. This has, in fact, been found to be the case, as emphasized especially by Horn (1984, 1989). We will follow this natural typology below as we introduce and discuss several of the classes of implications that have been most thoroughly researched in the linguistic literature.

Quality-Based Implications

According to the first maxim of quality, communicators must try to be truthful. There are, however, several circumstances in which the literal meaning of an utterance is clearly false and yet the utterance can be said to convey something that is true. These include utterances which can be taken to be ironic, metaphoric, hyperbolic or fictional. For instance, the maker of a dowdy old reliable product can effectively reinforce that image by ironically claiming to be hip or luxurious. Metaphorically true literal falsehoods are extremely common in advertising. One particularly well known example was Esso gasoline's slogan, "Put a tiger in your tank." Hyperbole is closely related to puffery. Car advertisements that superficially appear to suggest that certain automobiles are technologically on a par with modern fighting jets or even space vehicles fit into this category. Finally, transparently fictional claims such as "harvested in the moonlight by the Jolly Green Giant" are undoubtedly meant to convey an atmosphere, not a fact.

Precisely because quality-based implications "play loose" with the maxim of truthfulness, advertisers should bear the burden of showing that their claims are transparently ironical, metaphorical, hyperbolic or fictional to the average consumer in the target audience. There have been several cases over the years in which advertisers have taken quality-based implications beyond the bounds of the readily defensible. For example, the Rubic's Cube was called a "magic toy" on the (obviously fictional) cartoon program that was used to promote the product to children. This could be considered an indefensible use of fiction, since children may not realize that claims made about a real world product within a fictional setting are not to be taken as literally true. For another example, advertisements for courses that promise to teach foreign languages in an unreasonably short amount of time (e.g. "Kick the subtitle habit in just ten weeks") could conceivably be defended as hyperbole, but are undoubtedly most accurately viewed as simple deceptions.[2]

Quantity Based Implications

As noted above, one of the original objectives of Gricean pragmatics was to explain many of the same logical fallacies that Preston (1967) investigated in his pioneering work. If these fallacious inferences can be explained as reasonable pragmatic implications that arise from the Cooperative Principle and the Maxims of Communication, those who attempt to exploit them can no longer so readily disavow their potentially deceptive effects as the unforseeable consequences of attempting to communicate with a logically inept audience. Hence any success that Gricean theory may have in demonstrating that the classical logical fallacies arise as reasonable pragmatic implications of cooperative communication would clearly have important public policy implications. As it turns out, Griceans have, in fact, been quite successful in demonstrating that the classical logical fallacies obey a sort of pragmatic logic and are therefore eminently predictable and not the unforeseeable product of an audience whose logical abilities are lacking. Indeed, the work that has been done in this area (especially Horn 1972, 1984, 1989; Gazdar 1979) is generally considered to be exemplary of Gricean thinking at its finest and most successful.

The maxim that has been far and away the most useful in explaining the pragmatic logic behind logical fallacies has been the first quantity maxim as constrained by the first quality maxim. According to the first quantity maxim, one is to say as much as necessary. According to the first quality maxim, one must be truthful. Combining these, one can derive the following pragmatic rule: Make the strongest statement possible that is consistent with the facts. If, then, a communicator utters something that is pointedly weaker than what s/he might have uttered, the audience is free to infer that the unuttered stronger statement is false.

The basic method for explaining generalized quantity implicature has involved: (1) selecting a semantically coherent portion of the vocabulary of whatever language is being investigated, for instance, the quantifiers or the connectives; (2) rank ordering the elements of this portion of the vocabulary according to their semantic strength, for instance, 'all' is stronger than 'some;' 'and' is stronger than 'or;' (3) deriving from the Maxims of Communication a rule that says, in essence, that a cooperative

speaker, in order to say as much as is required, must use the strongest element in the scale that does not give rise to a violation of the quality maxims; and (4) making the simple inference from (1) through (3) that a speaker who uses the weaker of two elements in an utterance thereby implicates that an otherwise identical utterance that contained the stronger of the two elements would have been false, or at least not clearly true. A few examples should make this clear.

Let us consider the case of the connectives. People commonly deduce a proposition of the form "not (P and Q)" from a proposition of the form "P or Q." For example, a well-known advertisement said, roughly, "pay me now [alluding to a simple, inexpensive purchase] or pay me later [alluding to an expensive repair job]." This strongly suggests that paying a little now is an effective means of avoiding paying a lot later. But this inference is by no means entailed by what was literally said, since the statement "(you) pay me now or (you) pay me later" is logically consistent with "you pay me both now and later." This, however, is (roughly speaking) the proposition whose negation has been inferred.

Instead of dismissing this inference as illogic plain and simple, however, Griceans have attempted to explain this inference as based on a reasonable pragmatic implication derived from the first quantity maxim. Briefly put, since 'and' is intutively stronger than 'or' (this intuition can be backed up by logic, but see Richardson & Richardson 1990 for a discussion of some of the complexities involved), a speaker who uses 'or' thereby implicates that a minimally different utterance in which 'and' replaced 'or' would have run afoul of the quality maxims. In other words, uttering "(you) pay me now OR (you) pay me later" is predicted to implicate that "(you) pay me now AND (you) pay me later" is false (or at least of significantly diminished likelihood), which is precisely the inference we set out to explain.

Perhaps the most celebrated of these strength scales is the one according to which the quantifier 'all' is stronger than the quantifier 'some.' Uttering 'some' is therefore predicted to implicate 'not all,' which, as we have already shown above, is indeed the case. There are several other classes of implications that have yielded to explantion based on similar strength scales. These include: "I believe that P" implicating "I don't know that P;" "I like X" implicating "I don't love X;" "it is possible that P" implicating "it is not certain that P;" and, as argued in Richardson and Richardson (1990) to some extent against Gricean mainstream opinion, the famous inference from "if P, then Q" to "if not P, then not Q."

Relevance and Manner Based Implications

Quantity and quality based implications clearly differ from each other substantially. Recall however that the first quality maxim was crucially invoked in the explanation of the quantity based implications given above. Although the matter is somewhat controversial (see Sperber and Wilson 1986; Horn 1989; Atlas and Levinson 1981; and Richardson and Richardson 1990), it seems that the maxims of relevance and manner do not single-handedly give rise to any "free standing" implications, but rather act, like the first maxim of quality, as a constraint on quantity implications. The maxim of relevance can be most straightforwardly interpreted as directing communicators to stick to a given topic and to ensure that all comments made about that topic are of at least some potential importance to the audience. To see how these relevance rules can interact with quantity to give rise to another kind of implication, consider the following exchange:

Young woman: "I really like coffee, but caffeine makes me so irritable."

Older man: "I always drink Orange Label coffee."

Assuming that the older man is obeying the maxim of relevance, his utterance must be viewed as being on the same topic as the younger woman's and as contributing some information of potential importance. Further assuming that the older man is obeying the quantity maxims, his utterance must be viewed as saying no more or less than needs to be said to convey his message. From these premises, one can infer that the older man considers his utterance as conveying useful advice for solving the younger woman's dilemma. The most straightforward interpretation in light of common background knowledge is that Orange Label coffee is caffeine free, but note that this dialogue could also be used to announce a new brand of coffee that contains valium.

The various manner maxims have nothing per se to do with content but rather with form; that is, they direct communicators to express their messages as coherently but as succinctly as possible. The maxim of order is an especially potent source of interesting implications. Although 'order' should be taken to refer to all facets of good organization, the simple linear order of the words, phrases and sentences in an utterance can and often is exploited to create pragmatic implications. The most famous example of this is the different interpretations given to logically equivalent pairs of sentences, such as: "Mary won the lottery and moved to Belize" versus "Mary moved to Belize and won the lottery." The first sentence suggests not only that winning the lottery preceded the move to Belize, but that winning the lottery was what made the move to Belize feasible. The second sentence, on the other hand, reverses the assumed order of events and therefore strongly suggests that there is national lottery in Belize (which Mary won after moving

there).

This general effect can be, and often is, employed by advertisers. A benign example might be: "Install our storm windows and save energy." In this example, this general pragmatic order effect is used to efficiently and naturally convey a reasonable claim. A less benign example might be: "Drink Weight-Off and lose 20 pounds a week!" An advertiser, confronted with the objection that no diet drink by itself could achieve the promised results, might defend the advertisement by pointing out, quite correctly, that the advertisement makes no such literal claim. However, since the pragmatic effect arises naturally from the rules governing cooperative language use, this defense rings hollow.

SUMMARY

In this paper, we have argued that Gricean pragmatics can be a useful tool for understanding the role of non-literal meaning in the comprehension of advertisements and especially useful for developing a coherent approach to deceptive advertising. First, the application of Gricean theory in linguistics has led to the discovery of several broad classes of pragmatic implications which can be systematically studied as they relate to deceptive advertising. (That is, we need no longer approach deception by implication on a case by case basis.) Second, Gricean theory has led to a respectably deep understanding of several of these classes of implications. This is of great scientific value to anyone interested in any aspect of non-literal meaning in advertising or any form of marketing communication.

It is also, however, of great philosophical interest to anyone interested in policing deception. In short, the success of Gricean theory in predicting and explaining several classes of pragmatic implication disproves the claim that pragmatic implications are idiosyncratic and/ or random occurrences that advertisers can not be expected to anticipate. At the same time, Gricean theory predicts, and the linguistic evidence confirms, that conveying information through pragmatic implications is neither a rare nor an inherently deceptive practice, but a common and efficient use of language. Given the severe time and space constraints that advertisers operate under, advertisers have an unusually acute need for efficient communication. So pragmatic implication is a perfectly reasonable tool for honest advertisers to employ. Indeed, precisely because pragmatic implicature is such an effective tool for efficient communication, honest advertisers have a genuine interest in not allowing pragmatic implicature to become synonymous with deception in advertising.

FOOTNOTES

[1] The linguist Michael Geis (1982) has applied Gricean

theory to deception in advertising. Although his extended exegesis of Grice is useful, several of his own analyses are linguistically questionable. Furthermore, his failure to take the existing advertising literature into account and the relentlessly adversarial pose he struck throughout his work considerably diminishes its value to advertising researchers.

[2] These phenomena are interesting to Griceans as examples in which non-literal meanings arise that "save" utterances from violating the first maxim of quality. Unlike in the case of quantity, relevance and manner based implicatures to be discussed below, however, Gricean theory itself has done little to explain how irony, hyperbole, metaphor and other "figurative" meanings actually arise. See Stern (1988a, 1988b) for attempts to explain the inner workings of these phenomena within the framework of literary analysis, a framework in which phenomena like these have long been of central concern.

REFERENCES

Armstrong, Gary M., Metin N. Gurol and Frederick A. Russ (1979), "Detecting and Correcting Deceptive Advertising," *Journal of Consumer Research,* 6 (December), 237-246.

_____ and Frederick A. Russ (1975), "Detecting Deception in Advertising," *MSU Business Topics,* (Spring), 21-31.

Atlas, J. and S. Levinson (1981), "It-clefts, Informativeness and Logical Form," in Peter Cole, ed. *Radical Pragmatics,* New York: Academic Press.

Barbour, Frederic and David M. Gardner (1982), "Deceptive Advertising: A Practical Approach to Measurement," *Journal of Advertising,* 11 (1), 21-30.

Burke, Raymond, Wayne DeSarbo, Richard Oliver, and Thomas Robertson (1988), "Deception by Implication: An Experimental Investigation," *Journal of Consumer Research,* 14 (March), 483-94.

Cohen, Dorothy (1974), "The Concept of Unfairness as it Relates to Advertising," *Journal of Marketing,* 38 (July), 8-13.

Gaeth, Gary J. and Timothy B. Heath (1987), "The Cognitive Processing of Misleadning Advertising in Young and Old Adults," *Journal of Consumer Research,* 14 (June), 43-54.

Geis, M. (1982), *The Language of Television Advertising.* New York: Academic Press.

Grice, H. P. (1967), *The William James Lectures.* Published in part as Grice (1975) and Grice (1989).

_____ (1975), "Logic and Conversation," in P. Cole and J. Morgan, eds. *Syntax and Semantics 3: Speech Acts,* New York: Academic Press.

_____ (1989), *Studies in the Way of Words.* Cambridge: Harvard University Press.

Grunert, Klaus G. and Konrad Dedler (1985), "Misleading Advertising: In Search of a Measurement Methodology," *Journal of Public Policy and Marketing,* 4, 153-165.

Harris, Richard (1977), "Comprehension of Pragmatic Implications in Advertising," *Journal of Applied Psychology,* 62 (5), 603-7.

Horn, Larry (1972), *On the Semantic Properties of Logical Operators in English.* Bloomington: Indiana University Linguistics Club.

_____ (1984), "Toward a New Taxonomy for Pragmatic Inference: Q-Based and R-Based Implicature," in Schiffrin, ed. *Meaning, Form and Use in Context: Linguistic Applications,* Georgetown University Roundtable 84, Washington: Georgetown University Press, 11-42.

_____ (1989), *A Natural History of Negation.* Chicago: University of Chicago Press.

Preston, Ivan (1967), "Logic and Illogic in the Advertising Process," *Journalism Quarterly,* 44, 231-9.

_____ (1977), "The FTC's Handling of Puffery and Other Selling Claims Maide 'By Implication'," *Journal of Business Research,* 5 (June), 155-181.

_____ and Jef I. Richards (1986), "The Relationship of Miscomprehension to Deceptiveness in FTC Cases," in *Advances in Consumer Research,* Richard J. Lutz, ed. Provo, UT: Association for Consumer Research, 13, 138-142.

_____ and Steven E. Scharbach (1971), "Advertising: More Than Meets the Eye?" *Journal of Advertising Research,* 11 (June), 19-24.

Prince, Ellen F. (1981), "Toward a Taxonomy of Given-New Information," in Peter Cole, ed. *Radical Pragmatics,* New York: Academic Press.

Richards, Jef I. (1990), *Deceptive Advertising.* Hillsdale, NJ: Erlbaum.

Richardson, John and Alan Richardson (1990), "On Predicting Pragmatic Relations," *Proceedings of the 16th annual meeting of the Berkeley Linguistic Society.*

Shimp, Terence (1978), "Do Incomplete Comparisons Mislead?" *Journal of Advertising Research,* 18 (December), 21-27.

_____ (1979), "Social-Psycological (Mis) Representations in Television Advertising," *Journal of Consumer Affairs,* 13 (Summer), 28-40.

_____ and I. Preston (1981), "Deceptive and Nondeceptive Consequences of Evaluative Advertising," *Journal of Marketing,* 45 (Winter), 22-32.

Snyder, R. (1989), "Misleading Characteristics of Implied Superiority Claims," *Journal of Advertising,* 18 (4), 54-61.

Sperber, D. and D. Wilson (1986), *Relevance.* Cambridge: Harvard University Press.

Stern, Barbara (1988a), "How Does an Ad Mean?," *Journal of Advertising,* 17 (2), 3 - 14.

_____ (1988b), "Figurative Language in Services Advertising: The Nature and Uses of Imagery," in *Advances in Consumer Research,* Michael J. Houston, ed. Provo: UT: Association for Consumer Research, 15.

CONSIDERATIONS IN ADVERTISING DIRECTED TO CHILDREN

Srivatsa Seshadri, University of Arkansas
C.P. Rao, University of Arkansas

ABSTRACT

Advertising related to children's products has always drawn the attention of marketing practitioners, academicians, and consumer groups. This paper substantively reviews the literature to identify the issues that have concerned all alike. Implications for corporate communications are discussed and suggestions made to enhance the perceptions of the social responsiveness of corporations.

INTRODUCTION

Few business issues raise more important ethical considerations than the subject of advertising directed to children. Society and business institutions seem to be at perpetual opposition on this issue. This stems from their differing perspectives about the ethics involved, and their respective beliefs on the 'cause and effect' relationships between the ads and their effects on children. ". . . Both business and government believe in a special welfare for children, but only one side (i.e. government) will let a personal ethic dictate strategy. For the other (i.e. business), the situational ethic is predominant and it demands little or no action. Specifically, marketers and broadcasters admit the need for reform, but bow to compulsion to sustain competitive advantage," (Turk 1979).

The power of advertising flows from the potential of the mass-media to influence its audience. Children, as a sizeable proportion of the viewers, and with appreciable leverage on family purchases, are the focus of many advertisements, much to the chagrin of their parents. It must in all fairness be said that the public does not denounce advertisements per se. And businesses acknowledge that children are a special target market and need to be handled cautiously. The core of the matter for businesses and society alike therefore translates to resolving what and how to advertise to this target market.

Children's Growing Economic Power

Four to twelve year old children's buying power has grown from around $2 billion in 1968 to about $5 billion in 1988 to $9 billion now, (McNeal 1988, 1990). The market power of children below 12 years of age is as much as $50 billion a year. Children also have about $130 Billion influence in most of the family purchases (*Wall Street Journal*, June 28, 1991). About 57 percent of children between 13 to 19 years of age had some voice in the choice of a personal computer, 49 percent in a family car, 69 percent in planning a vacation and 42 percent in choosing a television (Williams 1990). Such high influence and involvement in family purchases is enough to lure businesses to attempt to influence children and in turn infuriate parents. This $130 billion influence on household purchases serves to cause the great divide between business and the public. To aggravate things "We are witnessing an increasingly aggressive children's market place characterized by new media (i.e. cable T.V., print etc.), new advertisers, new products and tie-in between children's products and children's entertainment vehicles" (Weisskoff 1985).

Present Focus

In spite of its importance to marketers and public alike one witnesses a declining focus on various aspects of advertising directed toward children. From the literature it is evident that active research work in this area took place in the preceding decades (60's and 70's), probably induced by the establishment of **NAD** (National Advertising Division) of the Council for Better Business Bureau Inc. and **ACT** (Action for Children's T.V.), but has since waned. This is all the more surprising in light of the fact that (1) there is a sharp focus on the issue in Western Europe as can be inferred by the amount of research being done in the area, particularly in U.K. and France, (2) the activities of corporations are coming under some heavy scrutiny and their ethics constantly debated, and (3) the children's market is growing at a phenomenal pace.

Given the sensitive nature of the subject, work in the area can help suggest appropriate corporate marketing communications to target this market keeping the ethical perspectives in view. The subject of advertising directed to children appears to be misleadingly simple. But a whole range of sub-issues crop up. Deceptive advertising, false claims, and use of sophisticated visual techniques, are some of them. This paper does not attempt to deliberate on these sub-issues. Nor are we advocating the desirability or otherwise of targeting children in advertising. The major purposes of this paper are:

1. To review the related literature and research findings on the effects of advertising on children and the associated social concerns,

2. To derive a set of conclusions on the social concerns, and

3. To explore and pinpoint the implications for corporate marketing communications.

GENERAL EFFECTS OF ADVERTISING

In his powerful exposition of advertising's consequences Pollay (1986) reviewed the work of scholars in humanities and social sciences on advertising's social and cultural consequences, and found that most view its effects as "inescapable and profound. ... The Advertising man in some respects is as much a brain alterer as a brain surgeon, but his tools and instruments are different." Possibly an exaggeration then, it is no more so today. The tremendous leaps in communication technology and the strides made by applied behaviorists give the advertiser the power to play with viewers' minds.

Most scholars see advertising as "reinforcing materialism, cynicism, irrationality, selfishness, anxiety, social competitiveness, sexual preoccupation, powerlessness, and/or loss of self-respect" (Pollay 1986). Few would disagree that this is being unfair to advertising, but few would disagree that advertising is all pervasive and affects its audience in subtle ways. With its main objective to persuade, it is a process of changing viewers' behaviors, cognition, attitudes, beliefs, and thus values. It is this process, with its attended consequences, that is the cause of much debate on the subject of advertising, more so in the context of children.

Consumer Socialization

A brief review of the socialization aspect of consumer behavior is appropriate in understanding the relevancy of the opposition to ads directed toward children. Consumer socialization can be summarized as (Ward 1974) "the process by which young people acquire skills, knowledge, and attitudes relevant to their functioning as (prudent) consumers in the market place" (parenthesis added). This process begins in childhood and continues through-out an individual's life-span.

Researchers indicate two kinds of learning processes in children in the course of their consumer socialization:

(1) The cognitive learning process based on Piaget's (1928) theory of the stages of cognitive development, and

(2) The social learning process which proceeds by observation, imitation, and through the influences of the socialization agents.

Five socialization agents - family, peers, mass-media, religion and education, individually and collectively, impact on the child. Parental influence decreases with age (Fauman 1966) while peers and mass-media influence the consumer socialization process significantly, but education is the least influential (Moschis and Churchill 1978). The findings indicate the predominant role of the mass-media, and advertising by extension, on a child's socialization process. This strong influence in the child's developmental process deeply worries parents and consumer protection activists.

EFFECTS OF ADVERTISING ON CHILDREN -- RESEARCH FINDINGS

Children and young adolescents exhibit information processing deficits (John and Cole 1986; Gaeth and Heath 1987). They lack understanding of advertising's persuasive intent (Blatt, Spencer, and Ward 1972; Robertson and Rossiter 1974; Ward, Reale, and Levinson 1972; Ward, Wackman, and Wartella 1977; Macklin 1985; Macklin 1987), and show deficiencies in recall (Blatt et al. 1972; Hendon, McGann, and Hendon 1978; Rubin 1974; Ward et al. 1972; Ward et al. 1977). It has also been demonstrated that young children use less information than older ones in making product-choice decisions (Capon and Kuhn 1980; Ward et al. 1977; Wartella et al. 1978). Finally, they have been found unable to use cognitive defenses, or do so only if cued (Brucks, Armstrong and Goldberg 1988). The fear among parents and consumer groups alike is that these deficiencies make children an easy target for persuasion.

Children's susceptibility to external influences, particularly advertising, especially during their formative years, prejudices parents and consumer protection activists to focus on advertising directed to children so intensely. Miscomprehension of advertisements is high even among adults (Jacoby, Hoyer, and Sheluga 1980; Jacoby, Hoyer, and Zimmer 1981; Jacoby, Nelson, and Hoyer 1982; Russo, Metcalf, and Stephens 1981; Jacoby and Hoyer 1989) underscoring children's vulnerability to ads in general. Advertisements could therefore, unintentionally, affect the process of psychological growth thus causing negative sociological, attitudinal, and behavioral responses as already discussed. It is also suspected that their food-habits are affected to the detriment of their health and parent-child relationships deteriorate, because of its influence. A brief review of the research findings, supporting or refuting these fears would help gain a clearer perspective of the issues involved. Effects of advertisements on children can be broadly classified into six groups, which are not necessarily mutually-exclusive.

Attitudinal Effects

Two types of effects are indicated by studies. The first is the long-term effects on children's general attitudes. The second is the effect on the development of their attitudes toward commercials and, consequently, toward businesses in general.

Most parents claim that materialism is detrimental to a child's mental growth and that advertisements develop materialistic attitudes in children (A.C.T. 1971). Goldberg and Gorn (1978) found that T.V. advertisements directed to children (a) lead the child to select material objects over socially-oriented objects, and (b) lead to more disappointed, unhappy child due to parent-child conflict, corroborating the results of Atkin (1975) who recorded considerable unhappiness in children denied products advertised on T.V. Hawkins and Pingree (1981) also reported similar findings stating that advertising impacted negatively on children by encouraging antisocial tendencies, excessive materialism, parent-child conflict, and cynicism or false-view of the real world. Moschis and Churchill (1978) report that children watching T.V. ads developed materialistic attitudes and social motivations of consumption. In the same study they further found a negative relationship between their exposure to T.V. ads and their economic motivations.

Children have been found to articulate that "Advertisers fake well" (Bever et al. 1975) and conclude "All products lie" (ibid.). This negative response among children was also found by Brucks et al (1988). Eventually, the child's faith in the products and advertisements may be effected. "False and misleading advertisements leave an indelible mark on (a child) and destroy completely his faith in (advertised) products" (O.E.C.D. 1982).

Behavioral Effects

Ward, Wackman, and Wartella (1979) showed that more than two-thirds of the children surveyed confirmed that commercials "made them want to have things" a finding replicated by Brucks et al (1988). Besides Ward et al (1979) also found that the frequency of requests for products was a function of age and the product itself. A Michigan State University study in 1978 found that only 52 percent of the mothers of 5-7 year-old acquiesced to their children's request for advertised products, while 77 percent of the mothers of 11-12 year old did so suggesting the probable increase in nagging behavior with age, partly attributed to the effect of commercials. Many other studies support the inference. Goldberg (1990) researched on the consequence of a Quebec law banning advertising to children on T.V. The results showed that, with US television stations as the sole source for T.V. commercials, product awareness, persistent requests and use of toys and cereals among English speaking children of Quebec was higher when compared to the French speaking children. Another study by C.M.R. (Children's Market Research), New York, investigating 9 to 12 year-old girls (*Advertising Age,* February 29, 1988) found the girls demonstrated begging techniques for use on reluctant parents, for advertised products. Strong correlations have been found between products that children request persistently and those advertised on T.V. (Galst and White 1976; Caron and Ward 1975; Sheik and Moleski 1977; Atkin 1975) suggesting ad induced nagging behavior among children.

Aitken (1989) found a positive relationship between television advertising and under-age drinking. Results showed that T.V. commercials for alcoholic drinks be-

came increasingly salient and attractive over years 10-14. By the age of 14, children perceive beer commercials as promoting macho-masculinity, sociability, and working-class values. These results suggest claims that advertising does not promote or reinforce underage drinking are questionable.

Contrary to the above finding, Smith (1990), in a study sponsored by tobacco industry's international organization (INFOTAB), found that juvenile smoking was highest in Norway with total ban on advertising tobacco products, and lowest in Hong Kong with fewer restrictions on tobacco advertising. Finding that the major influence on smoking among the young was smoking by friends and family he inferred that advertising lacked negative effects on juveniles' smoking habits. Corroborating this finding was Jenkins' (1988) study in Canada evidencing no relationship between juvenile smoking and tobacco advertising and a strong positive relationship was found with peer pressure and family smoking behavior.

Food Habits

In 1974 the National Nutrition Policy Study stated that " . . . Persuasive commercial forces work unremittingly to encourage unwise eating habits. . . Most promote over-sugared, over-salted snack foods that distort diets." Things may not have changed much since then, according to some reports. A survey eight years after the above statement (O.E.C.D. 1982) found 8-12 year-old children spent about half their allowances on snacks, 72 percent of which were sugared. These snacks were purchased repeatedly and sometimes substituted for meals. While no research has been done to link advertisements directly to this behavior, critics feel that advertisements portray snack food products as appropriate and desirable for consumption. This message is taken literally by children, thereby affecting their intake of wholesome food. Galst and White (1976) found that, in the context of the strong correlation between products advertised and those requested by children, the leading products advertised and requested were candies and sugared cereals. They concluded that the media was a vehicle of unhealthy persuasion.

Wiman and Newman (1989) found negative effects of television advertising on children's nutritional awareness. Exposure to T.V. advertisements and nutritional knowledge were inversely related supporting Galst and White's (1976) conclusions. Other research results, by inference, also implicate T.V. advertisements on the undesirable food choices of children (Atkin 1975; Clancy-Hepburn, Hickey, and Nevill 1974; Leaman 1973; Robertson and Rossiter 1977).

Parental Tensions

Advertising has the ability to interject itself and

intrude in family interactions (National Science Foundation 1977; Culley, Lazer, and Atkin 1976; Foote and Mnookin 1980; Goldberg and Gorn 1978; Pollay 1986) and most parents feel powerless to deal with the situation and the associated family frictions. Parents and children often argue over ad related request denials (Atkin 1975) leading to family conflicts (National Science Foundation 1977). Parents aren't alone in implicating advertising. School guidance counsellors regard advertising as a source of family conflicts (Barry 1978; LeRoux 1979), leading to suggestions that parents should regulate media exposure and children's behavior (Council of Better Business Bureaus 1975; Gordon 1981) to avoid strife in the family.

It is inferred that ad induced consumption requests strain parent child relationship. This is more so in the economically disadvantaged families, who presumably must deny most requests (National Science Foundation 1977). Denial, and the consequent feelings of guilt and resentment, is frustrating to both the child and the parent (ibid.). These complicate family consumption patterns, leading to maladaptive practices, especially among the poor, according to some.

The effectiveness of ads toward children can be seen by the ability of children to persuade their parent in buying the advertised products. Parents have been found to pay 25 percent more for an advertised product even when a less expensive non-advertised product is available (O.E.C.D 1982).

Psychological Effects

Children are believed to become cynical about other social institutions, judging them to be riddled with hypocrisy (Bever et al. 1975). In the same study Bever also found children "adopt a rigid moral stance and an overgeneralized view of the world by assuming that like advertising, all aspects of adult life "always lie".... They are confused about what adult reality is". This over generalization may eventually make them defensive, when cued (Brucks, Armstrong, and Goldberg 1988).

Advertisements generally have personal enhancement appeals and social status appeals which affect a child's self-concept (National Science Foundation 1977). Unfortunately limited empirical studies have been done to understand these issues, though studies indicate the formation of social motivations in the socialization process, through mass-media (Moschis and Churchill 1978).

Socio-cultural Effects

The only such effect predominantly discussed and to some extent researched is the stereo-typed perception inculcated in children by advertisements. It has been argued that ads have a high percentage of whites compared to blacks, and males compared to females, affect-

ing children's belief about the real world ratios (National Science Foundation 1977). A similar study (Buttle 1989) evidences the stereo-typing effect with regard to role of sexes and recommends some form of regulatory control to reverse the trend.

SOCIAL CONCERNS

From these findings and perspectives one discerns two major issues that the ad related social concerns center on:

1. Advertisement's impact on a child's attitudes, behaviors, and development,

2. The repercussions of this development on parent-child relationships.

Ads directed to children are seen to bring pressure on parents to purchase products through children, strain family budgets, effect eating habits of the children causing parents to be frustrated, and finally resulting in parent-child conflicts (Grossbart and Crosby 1984). Hite and Randy (1987) in examining and comparing the attitudes of business and consumers concerning advertising directed toward children found consumers more concerned and more negatively disposed toward such advertising. They often viewed it as being manipulative, promoting materialism, stifling creativity, and disrupting parent-child relationships. These results are not surprising, given the findings of other researchers.

RECOMMENDATIONS FOR CORPORATE COMMUNICATIONS

The forgoing discussions indicate the seriousness of the problem of advertisements directed to children. The social concerns are genuine and indications are that children's advertising may have some detrimental effects. Suggestions for controlling such effects have ranged from outright banning of all ads directed to children, to adoption of self-regulation by all the agencies involved in the development of such advertisements. We believe that it would be too simplistic to take an extreme stance of banning advertisements directed to children. Economical and legal considerations preclude it. As the National Association of Broadcasting succinctly put it "Free, competitive American system of broadcasting which offers programs of entertainment, news, general information, education, and culture is supported by advertisements." This is true of the print media too. The social justification for the advertisements directed toward children is summed up by Howard et al. (1973) as arising "From the process of consumer socialization -- experience as a consumer -- both in it's own right and as a training ground for other types of decision making. ... As the child grows, he attains greater discretion which gives him the basis of making more selective choices and drawing inferences from the consequences of making those choices."

We believe that self-regulations by the marketing corporations would be the best choice. Such self-imposed discipline is a direct consequence of adopting the marketing concept and the obligation to be socially responsive. As Bloom and Kotler (1975) indicate, such high levels of public concern also provide a defence against inimical environmental forces through increased customer loyalty, better image, etc.

Considerations and Suggestions

Some considerations for formulating and implementing corporate communications could be:

* Children are extremely vulnerable to manipulations.

* Children are imaginative and therefore can easily fall prey to deceptive advertising.
* Advertisements are an educational medium for children and play an important part in the psychological development of the child.

* Advertisements play a great role in the socialization of children.

* Parent-child relationships can be impacted by the effects of advertisements on the child.

Corporations, particularly those that cater to the children's market, must weigh these considerations while developing their promotional programs, more specifically while creating advertisements. We acknowledge that this is no easy task. But the seriousness of the issue on one hand and the demands of the marketing concept on the other call for such an approach.

Some specific actions that can be taken to address these issues could be:

* Avoid social stereotyping in advertisements.

* Project positive social values of friendship, kindness, honesty, justice, generosity, and resect for others.

* Consider the knowledge, sophistication, maturity, and vulnerability of the children to whom the ad is directed.

* Contribute constructively to parent-child relationship.

* Handle self-concept representations carefully and constructively, specially ensuring projection of documented evidences of such promised benefits as strength, growth, physical progress, and growing up.
* Avoid implication that a parent who purchases a product is more generous than one who does not.

* Adhere, to the extent possible, the guidelines laid down by The National Advertising Division of the Council for Better Business Bureau, Inc., New York and the National Association of Broadcasters.

These call for voluntary abdication by corporations of certain freedoms such as the freedom of expression and, to an extent, laissez-faire. Both social and firm related benefits of such self-imposed restrictions in the production and presentation of children related ads will far outweigh the sacrifices entailed by the firms. This utilitarian perspective will best reflect the organization's commitment to the marketing concept and its social responsibilities.

Corporations have already shunned products and advertising that are detrimental to health (such as sugared candies, tobacco products etc) in response to market demands. Many have embraced cause marketing, making contributions to such causes as environmental protection, literacy programs, etc. having done this, and earned kudos from all their constituencies as also a temporary competitive advantage. Thus the suggestions proposed here are not too difficult to adopt. Unfair though it seems to single out corporations for corrective actions, it does seem the best way to achieve the utilitarian objective. The suggestions take on more credibility when corporations realize that they would also be serving another of their most important assets - their employees, who are also parents and have family responsibilities in the larger context of the society.

REFERENCES

A.C.T. - Action for Children's Television (1971), "General Comments on Television Advertising to Children," Testimony before the FTC (November), 10.

Aitken, P. P. (1989), "Television Alcohol Commercials and Under-age Drinking," *International Journal of Advertising (UK)*, 8 (2), 133-150.

Atkin, Charles K. (1975), "The Effects of Television Advertising on Children: Summary Abstracts of Eight Research Investigations," *Working Paper*, Michigan State University.

Bandura, A., and Walters R. H. (1963), *Social Learning and Personality Development*. New York: Holt, Rinehart and Winston, Inc.

Barry, Thomas E. (1978), "Children's Television Advertising: The Attitudes and Opinions of Elementary School Guidance Counselors," *Journal of Advertising*, 7 (4), 9-16.

Bever, Thomas G., Martin L. Smith, Barbara Bengen,

and Thomas G. Johnson (1975), "Young Viewers Troubling Response to TV Ads," *Harvard Business Review*, 53 (6), 119-121.

Blatt, J.,Lyle Spencer, and Scott Ward (1972), "A Cognitive Development Study of Children's Reactions to Television Advertising," in *Television and Social Behavior, Vol. 3: Television in Day to Day Life: Patterns of Use*, E.A. Rubinstein, G.A. Comstock, and John P. Murray, eds. Washington: U.S. Department of Health, Education and Welfare, 452-468.

Bloom, Paul E. and Philip Kotler (1975), "Strategies for High Market Share Companies," *Harvard Business Review*, 53 (November/December), 63-72.

Brucks, Merrie, Gary M. Armstrong and Marvin E. Goldberg (1988), "Children's Use of Cognitive Defenses Against Television Advertising: A Cognitive Response Approach," *Journal of Consumer Research*, 14 (March), 471-482.

Buttle, Francis (1989), "Sex-Role Stereotyping in Advertising: Social and Public Policy Issues," *Quarterly Review of Marketing*, 14 (Summer), 9-14.

Capon, Noeland and Deanna Kuhn (1980), "A Developmental study of Consumer Information-Processing Strategies," *Journal of Consumer Research*, 7 (December), 225-233.

Caron, Andre and S. Ward (1975), "Gift Decisions by Kids and Parents," *Journal of Advertising Research*, 15 (August), 15-20.

Clancy-Hepburn, Katherine, Anthony A. Hickey, and Gayle Nevill (1974), "Children's Behavior Responses to TV Food Advertisements," *Journal of Nutrition Education*, 6 (3), 93-96.

Council of Better Business Bureaus, Children's Review Unit, National Advertising Division (1975), *Children's Advertising Guidelines*. New York: The Council.

Culley, James D., William Lazer, and C. K. Atkin (1976), "The Experts Look at Children's Advertising," *Journal of Broadcasting*, 20 (Winter), 3-21.

Fauman, B.C. (1966), "Determinant's of Adolescents' Brand Preferences," *Masters Thesis*, Sloan School of Management, MIT.

Foote, Susan Barlett and Robert H. Mnookin (1980), "The 'Kid Vid' Crusade," *Public Interest*, 61 (Fall), 90-105.

Gaeth and Heath (1987) ,"The Cognitive Processing of Misleading Advertising in Young and Old Adults: Assessment and Training," *Journal of Consumer Research*, 14 (June), 43-54.

Galst, Joann and Mary White (1976), "The Unhealthy Persuader: The Reinforcing Value of Television and Children's Purchase Influencing Attempts at the Supermarket," *Child Development*, 47, 1089-96.

Goldberg, Marvin E. (1990), "A Quasi-Experiment Assessing the Effectiveness of TV Advertising Directed to Children," *Journal of Marketing Research*, 27 (November), 445-454.

_____ and Gerald J. Gorn (1978), "Some Unin- tended Consequences of TV Advertising to Children," *Journal of Consumer Research*, 5 (March), 22-29.

_____ and _____ (1974), "Children's Reactions to Television Advertising: An Experimental Approach," *Journal of Consumer Research*, 1 (September), 69-75.

Gordon, Richard L. (1981), "Children's TV Ad Rule Dying," *Advertising Age*, 6 (April), 1.0

Gorn, Gerald J. and Goldberg, Marvin E. (1977), "The Impact of Television advertising on Children from Low Income Families," *Journal of Consumer Research*, 4 (September), 86-88.

Grossbart, Sanford L. and Lawrence A. Crosby (1984), "Understanding the Basis of Parental Concern and Reaction to Children's Food Advertising," *Journal of Marketing*, 48 (3), 79-92.

Hawkins R. P. and Suzanne Pingree (1981), "Using TV to Construct Social Reality," *Journal of Broadcasting*, 25 (4), 347-364.

Hendon, Donald W., Anthony F. McGann, and Brenda L. Hendon (1978), "Children's Age Intelligence, and Sex as Variables Mediating Reactions to TV Commercials: Repetition and Context Complexity Implications for Advertisers," *Journal of Advertising*, 17 (Summer), 4-12.

Hite Robert E. and Randy Eck (1987), "Advertising to Children: Attitudes of Business vs. Consumers," *Journal of Advertising Research*, 27 (October/November), 40-53.

Howard, John et al. (1973), "Advertising and Public Concern: An FTC Staff Report," Chicago: Crain Communications.

Jacoby, J., W. D. Hoyer, and D. A. Sheluga (1980), *The Miscomprehension of Televised Communication*. New York: American Association of Advertising Agencies.

_____, _____, and M.R. Zimmer (1981), "To Read, View, or Listen? A Cross-Media Comparison of Comprehension," New York University, Graduate School of Business Administration, *Working Paper* no. 81-72.

_____, M.C. Nelson and W.D. Hoyer (1982), "Corrective Advertising and Affirmative Disclosure Statements: Their Potential for Confusing and Misleading the Consumer," *Journal of Marketing*, 46 (Winter), 61-72.

_____ and W.D. Hoyer (1989), "The Comprehension / Miscomprehension of Print Communications: Selected Findings," *Journal of Consumer Research*, 15 (March), 434-443.

Jenkins, John (1988), "Tobacco Advertising and Children: Some Canadian Findings," *International Journal of Advertising (UK)*, 7 (4), 357-367.

John, Deborah and Catherine Cole (1986), "Age Differences in Information Processing: Understanding Deficits in Young and Elderly Consumers," *Journal of Consumer Research*, 13 (December), 297-315.

Leaman F.A. (1973), "Nutrition: Television's Fruitless Image; A Cultivation Analysis of Children's Nutritional Knowledge and Behavior," *Master's Thesis,* Annenberg School of Communication, University of Pennsylvania.

LeRoux, Margaret (1979), "Children's Ad Hearings Underway," *Advertising Age,* 50 (4), 1,81.

Macklin, M. Carole (1985), "Do Young Children Understand the Selling Intent of Commercials?," *Journal of Consumer Affairs,* 19 (Winter), 293-304.

_____ (1987), "Preschoolers' Understanding of the Informational Function of Television Advertising," *Journal of Consumer Research,* 14 (September), 229-239.

McNeal, James (1988), "The Children's Market," *Incentive,* 162 (September), 87-96.

_____ (1990), "Children as Customers," *American Demographics,* 12 (September), 36-39.

Moschis, P. George and Gilbert A. Churchill (1978), "Consumer Socialization: A Theoretical and Empirical Analysis," *Journal of Marketing Research,* 15 (November), 599-609.

National Science Foundation (1977), *Research on the Effects of Television Advertising on Children: A Review of the Literature of Recommendations for Future Research.* Washington, DC: NSF, RANN Program, Division of Advanced Productivity Research and Technology.

O.E.C.D. - Organization for Economic Cooperation and Development (1982), *Advertising Directed to Children.* Paris: Organization for Economic Cooperation Development.

Piaget, J. (1928), *The Child's Conception of the World.* New York: Harcourt, Brace.

Pollay, W. Richard (1986), "The Distorted Mirror: Reflections on the Unintended Consequences of Advertising," *Journal of Marketing,* 50 (April), 18-36.

Robertson, Thomas S. and John R. Rossiter (1974), "Children and Commercial Persuasion: An Attribution Theory Analysis," *Journal of Consumer Research,* 1 (June), 13-20.

_____ and _____ (1977), "Children's Responsiveness to Commercials," *Journal of Communication,* 27 (1), 101-106.

Rubin, Ronald S. (1974), "The Effects of Cognitive Development on Children's Responses to Television Advertising," *Journal of Business Research,* 2 (4), 409-419.

Russo, J. E., B. L. Metcalf, and D. Stephens (1981), "Toward an Empirical Technology for Identifying Misleading Advertising," *Journal of Consumer Research,* 8 (September), 119-131.

Sheik, Arnes A. and Martin L. Moleski (1977), "Conflict in Family Over Commercials," *Journal of Communication,* 27 (Winter), 152-157.

Smith, Glen (1990), "The Effect of Advertising on Juvenile Smoking," *International Journal of Advertising (UK),* 9 (1), 57-79.

Turk, Peter (1979), "Children's Television Advertising: An Ethical Morass for Business and Government," *Journal of Advertising,* 8 (1), 4-8.

Ward, Scott, Greg Reale, and David Levinson (1972), "Children's Perceptions, Explanations, and Judgements of Television Advertising: A Further Exploration," in *Television and Social Behavior,* E. A. Rubinstein, G. A. Comstock, John P. Murray, eds. Washington: U.S. Department of Health, Education and Welfare, 468-490.

_____ and Daniel B. Wackman (1972) "Children's Purchase Influence Attempts and Parental Yielding," *Journal of Marketing Research,* 9 (3), 316-319.

_____ (1974), "Consumer Socialization," *Journal of Consumer Research.* 1 (June) 1-14.

_____, Daniel B. Wackman, and Ellen Wartella (1979), *How Children Learn to Buy.* Beverly Hills, CA: Sage.

Wartella, Ellen, Daniel B. Wackman, and Scott Ward (1978), "Children's Consumer information Processing: Representation of Information from Television Advertisements," in *Advances in Consumer Research,* H. Kieth Hunt, ed. Ann Arbor: ACR, 5, 535-539.

Weisskoff, Rita (1985), "Current Trends in Children's Advertising," *Journal of Advertising Research,* 25 (1), RC-12-14.

Williams, Monte (1990), "'Parental Guidance' Lost on this Crop," *Advertising Age,* 31 (July), 26 and 28.

Wiman, Alan R. (1980), "Parental Influence and Children's Responses to Television Advertising," *Journal of Advertising,* 12 (1), 12-18.

_____ and Larry M. Newman (1989), "Television Advertising Exposure and Children's Nutritional Awareness," *Journal of Academy of Science,* 17 (Spring), 179-188.

INCOMPLETELY - LAUNCHED AND RETURNING YOUNG ADULTS: SOCIAL CHANGE, CONSUMPTION, AND FAMILY ENVIRONMENT

KerenAmi Johnson, Old Dominion University
Scott D. Roberts, Old Dominion University

ABSTRACT

This paper discusses the growing phenomenon of economically dependent adult children. Four historical value shifts related to this phenomenon are identified and discussed in terms of their marketing importance. The relationship between these family arrangements and segmentation opportunities are explored. The authors conclude by suggesting that marketing academics and practitioners must become more socio-historically aware

INTRODUCTION

In a column that surely foreshadows a major issue of the 1990s, Ann Landers offered her syndicated newspaper advice to a woman plagued by the boorish habits of two able-bodied adult sons (aged twenty-six and twenty-seven) who lived with her. In the same week that a Virginia newspaper ran the Landers column, it also carried a local writer's suggestion for young couples who wished to accumulate the down payment for a home mortgage: the entire family - mom, dad, and the kids - should move in with the parents of either spouse for a prearranged period of time. As for more systematic advice, *Letitia Baldridge's Complete Guide to the New Manners for the 90s* includes a section entitled "When Adult Children Want to Move Back Home." These are just a few examples of a growing family phenomenon called the "returning young adult syndrome" (RYA).

The RYA, however, is only one subset of a more prevalent and general tendency: the economically dependent adult child or "incompletely-launched young adult" (ILYA). A young adult who is incompletely-launched is defined as one who is ill-prepared to become financially independent of his or her parents. A returning young adult is defined as one who returns to the household of the parent for any number of reasons, one of which is the inability to remain financially independent. Thus an ILYA may or may not become an RYA, and an RYA may return for reasons other than that s/he was incompletely-launched (Schnaiberg and Goldenberg 1989).

Recently, scholars in marketing have become interested in the structural origins and intrafamilial dynamics of arrangements which support the prolonged economic dependence of adult children. Roberts, Voli, and Johnson (1992) discuss the impact of ILYAs and RYAs on the notion of determinate stages in the family life cycle, and Burnett and Smart (1991) attempt to isolate RYAs from an aggregate database and ascertain the extent to which

their media habits differ from their peers who live independently. While these publications have focused upon the phenomena of RYA/ILYAs from both conceptual and empirical perspectives, and have discussed their potential importance to marketing, neither has dealt with the specific products and services which may be impacted by these family changes.

The purpose of this paper is to link marketing literature and practice to historical consumption patterns associated with value change. The major argument of this paper is that some of the fundamental assumptions that underlie market segmentation, especially as related to the family-as-consumption-unit, derive from taken for granted assumptions about family life of the 1950s. This period (one in which many of today's marketing managers grew up) was an atypical one. Post-war family life in the United States was shaped by a huge baby boom, strict role boundaries exhibited by men and women, an increase in the rate of marriage accompanied by a decrease in the age of marriage and the birth of first children (Goldscheider and Waite 1991), low divorce rates, and significant advances in life-extending medical technology.

We have two specific objectives: (1) To trace four cultural shifts in family values which have generally influenced consumption patterns, and (2) To discuss the managerial implications of these changes, especially in terms of market segmentation and product positioning. Having defined the ILYA-RYA concept in the preceding section, the following section locates this phenomenon as part of an ongoing process of consumption-related value change originating in the nineteenth century.

RYAs AND ILYAs: STUMBLING TOWARD ADULTHOOD

RYA/ILYA Family Milieu: Level I (Individual)

Members of an RYA family, by definition, share space for "the second time around." According to Riche (1990), 22-24 is the most common age at which people begin to live independently. Most people aged 20-21 are still in their parents home, while most people ages 22-24 have left. There are, however, a significant number of "false starts:" about 40 percent of young adults return to live with their parents at least once.

Schnaiberg and Goldenberg (1989) address the emotional complications which attend such an unanticipated return. They present the social-psychological dynamics of the RYA syndrome as a system of responses to disconfirmed expectations regarding the shared meanings of adulthood. According to these authors the RYA syndrome is, at one level, a family milieu characterized by the following:

(1) children's unanticipated economic dependency and/or failures to launch careers and become successfully autonomous adults;

(2) deviance from parental expectations that children will physically separate from parents in "young adulthood" (college or post-college years);

(3) one or more "attempts" by these children to fulfill these expectations, followed by a return to a parental home for varying periods of time; and

(4) anomic context for household labor organization and allocation of family resources when there is a returning young adult in the household; anger of parents (and often of children), and substantial conflict over these issues.

Because of the highly individualistic orientation prevalent in modern culture, a child's unplanned return is in some way considered a deviation from the norm of good parenting instead of as a normal response to circumstances beyond one's control. Many RYA/ILYA parents thus interpret this milieu as evidence of personal failure in child-rearing. Mounting evidence, including census data, suggest, however, that this is not the case. The following section locates the RYA/ILYA phenomenon in terms of social forces, a collective arena which transcends the purely personal.

Level II: Sociocultural Milieu (Collective)

From a sociological perspective, the RYA phenomenon is not simply an aggregation of private disappointments. Rather, it is seen as the enactment of shared values in the context of a change in opportunity structures which were previously taken for granted. First, some aggregate evidence to document the existence and magnitude of RYA/ILYA living arrangements:

* Between 1960 and 1990 the proportion of persons 18 to 24 years old who lived in the home of their parents increased from around 43 percent to nearly 55 percent (Riche 1990).

* One third of never married persons 25 to 29 years old lived at home with their parents in 1990 (Saluter 1991).

The tendency to interpret these data as deviance from the norm turns upon the source of shared expectations these RYAs violate: the nature and cultural availability of standards for "good parents" and "successful children."

As far as the RYA phenomenon is concerned, the critical ideological norms of parenting are embodied in a predominantly middle-class "postwar parenting model" (Schnaiberg and Goldenberg 1989). This model specifies a set of child-rearing goals and the means by which they can be reached. In particular, the ideology of post-war parenting demands an intense - though time-limited - commitment of emotional and financial resources to one's offspring. This same model also delimits expectations for the education (e.g., college attendance away from home), living arrangements (e.g., dorms, apartments, or fraternity/sorority houses away from home), and family of procreation one's son or daughter will eventually establish (e.g., early marriage and early childbearing in the context of a marriage expected to be permanent).

If the standard for parenting is intense involvement, the measure of parental success is, ironically, the separation or independence of the child at the "proper" time. The RYA phenomenon thus embodies a variety of individual responses to a set of widely-held values and expectations gone awry. Both represent taken-for-granted assumptions regarding the availability and continued expansion of material means. However, the range of opportunities for education and employment congruent with goals of the post-war parenting model has narrowed significantly in the last decade (Woodward 1990). Unfortunately, expectations regarding one's "right" to a particular level of discretionary spending persist. These widely held expectations on the part of young adult consumers come as no surprise in the context of an emergent structure of child-centered values which has affected consumer lifestyles for at least the last century. These value shifts are detailed in the next section.

CULTURAL SHIFTS AND CONSUMPTION PATTERNS

Because expectations regarding specific material and status achievements persist despite recent changes in the economic opportunity structure, the RYA syndrome cannot be dismissed as merely an aggregation of personal troubles. The significance of family consumption in coping with reduced opportunities is also a public issue, seen to arise from a structural change in society (Mills 1959). Under these circumstances, the relationship between the RYA phenomenon and the post-war parenting model must be considered in the macro-context of a public issue as well as in the micro-context of a personal problem. Accordingly, this section examines public aspects of the RYA phenomenon - the culturally available antecedents of shared expectations presently violated by RYAs and ILYAs - by tracing four historical shifts in value which also have influenced family consumption patterns. The shifts are as follows:

(1) a transformation in the economic and sentimental value of children (Zelizer 1985);

(2) a rise in consumerism and mass advertising (McCracken 1988);

(3) recent cultural emphases on individualistic norms of adult development (Belk 1988; Roberts and Dant 1991); and,

(4) newly-constricted opportunities for certain types of education and employment (Woodward 1990).

First, we discuss each shift in terms of its cultural and historical meaning, then review the marketing of selected products and services associated with these changed contexts.

The Transformed Value of Children

Between 1870-1930 the value of an American child to his or her parents was socially transformed from that of a potentially useful worker to an "economically worthless" but "emotionally priceless" being (Zelizer 1985, p. 3). This sharply contrasts with the way children were previously regarded, that is, as miniature adults who were often expected to work alongside older laborers (Leslie 1967). Certain conditions facilitated increased emotional investment in children: a reduction in infant mortality, definitions of middle-class motherhood as a full-time and totally fulfilling pursuit (Ehrenreich and English 1979), and more recently, reliable and comparatively safe means of birth control. Additionally, social reforms like compulsory education and child labor laws legitimated the special status and "rights" of childhood. As a result, children were simultaneously removed from the labor force and socially defined as "the leading figure in the family" (Ehrenreich and English 1979, p. 185).

Certain products and services logically accompanied this transformation. Once motherhood was properly viewed as a full-time occupation, the "correct" set of tools became important. For example, childbirth - the biological beginning of motherhood - became an appropriate focus for progressive technology. By the end of the nineteenth century, growing numbers of physicians had claimed the right to attend childbirth and, by the middle of the twentieth century, hospital (versus home) deliveries among the middle class had become the norm.

Also, emerging "experts" in child rearing wrote books and delivered lectures, consumer product companies introduced infant formulas and special foods, and pharmaceutical firms manufactured preventive vaccines for previously fatal childhood diseases. There was an attendant growth in the service industry, specifically in home health and public health nursing, and elementary and secondary school teachers. Around the same time that the notion of childhood as a separate state became a central family concern, a rise in consumerism and mass advertising infused spending with new cultural meaning. In the next section, we discuss the relationship between the new meanings associated with childhood and the changed value assigned to consumption activities.

Rise in Consumerism[1] and Mass Advertising

During the first half of the 20th century, the legally-defined rights of children were extended in the popular imagination to include culturally defined "rights" to "a separate consumption agenda [products and services], separate institutions [schools, summer camps, scouts], and the material means to support these entitlements [allowances, gifts]" (Schnaiberg and Goldenberg 1989). The consumption agenda associated with childhood (further discussed below) was just one part of the growth in consumption as a general means of personal fulfillment (McCracken 1988).

By the 1920s, growth in the marketplace for consumer goods had increased to a point where the socialization of young consumers became a new issue. The parents' task - to teach wise consumer habits - was aided by volumes of expert advice regarding allowances, child-oriented savings accounts, and family training in "proper" childhood spending habits (Zelizer 1985). These prescriptions coexisted with a wide range of culturally available injunctions for "correct" self-definition and personal fulfillment through the acquisitions of goods and services (Ewen and Ewen 1982).

Moschis discusses the many aspects and effects of consumer socialization (Moschis 1985; Moschis and Moore 1979). However, an important, but unanticipated consequence of contemporary consumer socialization is the following: consumption patterns established in childhood in effect teach children how to spend their parents' money. Such consumption activities reflect what one writer recently called "premature affluence" (Woodward 1990, p. 54) - a persistent, and not altogether realistic, set of spending habits based exclusively on discretionary income. These habits came about partly because of increased options presented in advertising and in the media, and partly because of parental and cultural tolerance (and even encouragement) for such behavior.

It is now not uncommon for adolescents to exhibit ownership and/or control over various role-related product clusters. For example, the material requirements for the role of "child" in a middle class family often include having one's own bedroom, often with a private television set and VCR. For the pursuit of excellence during one's leisure hours, youth-oriented product and service clusters include sports equipment and publicly organized opportunities for competition (school athletic teams, city leagues, etc.). The number of automobiles that Americans own is directly related to the number of licensed drivers, suggesting that the role of "teenager" in a middle class home often commands a private automobile - an important consumption tool in its own right.

Over time, certain consumption habits and expectations for products and services came to serve as signals for "adulthood." In middle-class America, the role of a "normal" adult is often signaled in terms of a career and the acquisition of certain possessions (Belk 1988; Csikszentmihalyi and Rochberg-Halton 1981). Markers of the life transition to adulthood might include the expectation of a college degree with its product and service cluster (clothing, special tools and equipment, education loans, credit cards and career-related charge accounts), an apartment away from parents, a car, and a job which provides sufficient income to live independently. This "consumption agenda" has become a near expectation for many, and has been consistently and heavily reinforced by media portrayals both with advertising and in the popular images provided by half-hour television programming. The next section describes a third value shift, the move and acceptance over time that adults have a right to their own personal development and the consumption that entails.

Individualism and Adult Development

As the sentimental value of children increased during the first half of this century, parallel developments in psychology established the concept of a "self" that was fully formed by the chronological end of adolescence (Allport 1937; Piaget 1932). Erikson (1959), however, extended the idea that one continues to grow socially and emotionally beyond adolescence. Erikson's most influential research appeared after World War II, a time when statistical evidence for increased life expectancy had begun to accumulate. Increased life expectancy, coupled with a new focus on adult development, legitimated the "rights" of parents to define personal fulfillment apart from the parameters of career and child-rearing.

The pursuit of personal development by adults of all ages simultaneously shaped and was shaped by a booming "self-help" industry. If Erikson described the stages of adult development, Maslow's work (1956) could be interpreted to mean that the pinnacle of self-actualization was a reasonable pursuit in each stage. Given the culture of the time, it is not surprising that self-actualization and consumption were considered co-equal. Promotions for product and service areas such as gourmet foods, recreational facilities and sporting equipment, and leisure travel experiences grew as popular perceptions of the possibilities of adult development changed. However, when adult entitlements to increasingly elaborate self development "bump up" against an adult child's entitlement to a previously-established standard of living - as often happens in the RYA/ILYA syndrome - there may be growth in another market: family counseling and mental health services.

Change in the Opportunity Structure

The years that elapsed between watching one's

parents spend and the point at which today's RYAs would be able to spend as adults was a period in which the world changed: opportunities for employment contracted (and continue to do so) along with real income, but expectations have remained high and, in fact, may have increased (Schiller 1983). The 1991-92 recession provides inescapable evidence that many of the high paying jobs that once existed in management, manufacturing, and assembly may be gone forever. The only job real growth in the last decade has been in (generally) lower paying service jobs and in small, start-up entrepreneurial firms (Weber 1992).

As jobs become more difficult to find, members of the new cohort of labor force entrants are confronted by increasingly rigid qualifications, often entailing college, graduate school, and the accompanying loans payments that follow. Expenses for professional training, along with the growing cost of independent living, have forced growing numbers of young adults to return to their parents' household. This problem is particularly acute in the northeast United States, where a two-bedroom apartment can easily rent for more than $1000 per month.

Discrepancies in what parents and children believe that young adults can/should achieve and what is actually possible in light of long-term economic constraints may lead to tensions within the family. Some of this tension can be attributed to opportunity costs for parents. That is, resources - time, money, emotional energy - parents had planned to invest in themselves after the children's departure are now re-allocated to support their RYAs and ILYAs. Tensions arise because parents usually must revise their consumption expectations downward in order to provide continued support for the RYA/ILYA. This re-allocation flies in the face of conventional wisdom that households will have more discretionary income once their youngest child reaches the age of eighteen - the "empty-nest" stage (see Roberts, Voli, and Johnson 1992 for a discussion of the inadequacies of the traditional Family Life Cycle model) .

DISCUSSION AND CONCLUSIONS

We have argued that the chronological age of individuals and the age of one's children have become relatively poor predictors of the link between life events and consumption patterns. As far as marketing managers are concerned, the central question of the RYA/ILYA phenomenon is one of segmentation opportunities. Key to this issue are the following: How enduring is the RYA/ILYA phenomenon likely to be? Is it a fad in child-rearing - a momentary response to a poor economy - or do these arrangements reflect deeper, long-term structural tendencies meriting a strategic response? While there is no way to answer these questions definitively, the demographic and historical evidence suggests that these arrangements are not momentary aberrations but are likely to persist for some time.

There are several reasons for this position. First, what we have learned to regard as "normal" living arrangements for families and "appropriate" expectations for the onset of adulthood are grounded in the peculiar distortions of the United States in the 1950s. These taken-for-granted assumptions are thus influenced by a very particular conjunction of social, demographic, and economic forces not likely to recur.

It is also important to remember that what we call "normal" behavior at any point in recent history has always been heavily biased toward the habits and preferences of the white middle class (Ewen and Ewen 1982). Even before the turn of the century, middle class women were those most likely to remain home and cultivate the domestic arts in a home free of boarders. The earnings of a middle class male also allowed children to attend school full time without working in farms or factories. Because this new standard of living was based on scientific progress, faith in the benefits of science extended to conclusions reached by a growing body of experts prepared to advise the middle class regarding "correct" practices and experiences (Johnson and Roberts 1992).

Marketing - as a relatively new, elite profession - took the middle class biases of the 1950s for granted when developing the family life cycle as a basis for segmentation. The fact that the RYA/ILYA phenomenon is so large should force marketers to rethink segmentation strategies related to family consumption units. While some may interpret the rise in financially and emotionally dependent young adults as momentary deviance from the norm of correct child rearing, it is equally viable to interpret the living arrangements associated with RYAs as a long term rational response to macroenvironmental changes in our society and economy. This interpretation can lead to more forward-thinking marketing strategies aimed at identifying and meeting the needs of consumers who experience these types of resource sharing situations.

Certain products and services seem particularly useful to this segment of consumers. Relevant examples include, but are not limited to, the following:

Housing:

Inexpensive modular-type furniture for the RYA's room.

Repair services for shared consumer durables like family-size appliances which are less likely to be replaced with new downsized versions in the near future.

The need to have either more space, comfort, or privacy, or use current space more efficiently (e.g., closet organizers, acoustical tile, storage units, remodeling services, etc.).

Health:

Mental health/crisis intervention, counseling.

Flexible health insurance benefits, including options to include adult children in coverage.

Education:

Increased adult education offerings at the community level.

Family-life skills and personal growth courses, including practical issues such as cooking, home gardening, family conflict resolution, communication skills, and personal management.

We urge marketers to broaden their comparative and historical knowledge of the historically-based structures of (normal) family life. There is a tendency to apply unexamined assumptions to a market like the American family because it is easy to assume familiar things have always been so. In an era sensitive to global marketing, it is common to teach the awareness of and tolerance for exotic family structures. But we sometimes forget to examine the biases inherent in what is most familiar, and thus we may lose important marketing opportunities.

Research in the future should include not only the effects of the RYA/ILYAs on demand for product and service categories, but also the influence of this phenomenon on the consumer decision process itself. For example, how is family decision making affected by the addition of a second, third, or fourth adult participant? Which roles in the joint decision making process - gatekeeping, influencer, etc. - are accessible to the RYA/ILYA? How do preexisting family structure and product categories influence the number and types of decision making roles assumed by RYA/ILYAs? These are just a few of the provocative issues that merit the scholarly attention of researchers concerned with the relationship between family issues and marketing practices.

ENDNOTE

[1] The term consumerism is used in the anthropological context, and should not be confused with the consumer movement associated in marketing with figures like Ralph Nader and President Kennedy (the rights of consumers).

REFERENCES

Allport, Gordon W. (1937), *Personality: A Psychological Interpretation.* New York: Henry Holt.

Baldridge, Letitia (1990), *Letitia Baldridge's Complete Guide to the New Manners for the 90s.* New York: Rawson.

Belk, Russell W. (1988), "Possessions and the Extended Self," *Journal of Consumer Research,* 15 (September), 139-168.

Burnett, John and Denise Smart (1991), "Returning Young Adults: Implications for Marketers," *Psychology and Marketing,* (forthcoming).

Csikszentmihalyi, Mihaly and Eugene Rochberg-Halton (1981), *The Meaning of Things: Domestic Symbols and the Self.* Cambridge, MA: Cambridge University Press.

Ehrenreich, Barbara and Deirdre English (1979), *For Her Own Good: 150 Years of Experts' Advice to Women.* Garden City, NY: Anchor Press/Doubleday.

Erikson, Erik (1959), "Identity and the Life Cycle," *Psychological Issues,* 1 (1), 1-171.

Ewen, Stuart and Elizabeth Ewen (1982), *Channels of Desire: Mass Images and the Shaping of American Consciousness.* New York: McGraw Hill.

Goldscheider, Frances K. and Linda J. Waite (1991), *New Families, No Families?: The Transformation of the American Home.* Berkeley: University of California Press.

Johnson, Keren Ami and Scott D. Roberts (1992), "Habits of the Heart: Postmodern Aspects of Viable Organ Transplantation," Working Paper, Old Dominion University, Norfolk, VA 23529-0220.

Leslie, Gerald R. (1967), *The Family in Social Context.* New York: Oxford University Press.

Maslow, Abraham H. (1954), *Motivation and Personality.* New York: Harper Brothers.

McCracken, Grant (1988), *Culture and Consumption: New Approaches to the Symbolic Character of Consumer Goods and Activities,* Bloomington: Indiana University Press.

Mills, C. Wright (1959), *The Sociological Imagination.* Glencoe, IL: The Free Press.

Moschis, George P. (1985), "The Role of Family Communication in Consumer Socialization of Children and Adolescents," *Journal of Consumer Research,* 11 (March), 898-913.

Moschis, George and Roy Moore (1979), "Decision-Making Among the Young: A Socialization Perspective," *Journal of Consumer Research,* 6 (September), 101-112.

Piaget, Jean (1932), *The Moral Judgement of the Child.* London: Routlege and Kegan Paul.

Riche, Martha F. (1990), "The Boomerang Age," *American Demographics,* (May), 24-30, 52-53.

Roberts, Scott D. and Rajiv P. Dant (1991), "Rethinking Resource Allocation in Modern Society: A Meanings-Based Approach," *Journal of Economic Psychology,* 12, 411-429.

Roberts, Scott D., Patricia K. Voli, and Keren Ami Johnson (1992), "Beyond the Family Life Cycle: An Inventory of Variables for Defining the Family as a Consumption Unit," in *Developments in Marketing Science,* Vol. 15, Victoria Crittenden, ed. Miami: Academy of Marketing Science, 71-75.

Saluter, Arlene F. (1991), *Marital Status and Living Arrangements: March 1990.* Washington, DC: Bureau of the Census, U.S. Government Printing Office.

Schiller, Bradley R. (1983), *The Economy Today.* New York: Random House.

Schnaiberg, Allan and Sheldon Goldenberg (1989), "From Empty Nest to Crowded Nest: The Dynamics of Incompletely-Launched Young Adults," *Social Problems,* 36 (June), 251-269.

Weber, Joseph (1992), "Seizing the Dark Day: Recession can Bring Unexpected Opportunities," *Business Week,* (January 13), 26-28.

Woodward, Kenneth L. (1990), "Young Beyond Their Years," *Newsweek Special Edition: The 21st Century Family,* (Winter/Spring), 54-60.

Zelizer, Viviana I. (1985), *Pricing the Priceless Child: The Changing Social Value of Children.* New York: Basic Books.

AN INFORMATION PROCESSING FRAMEWORK FOR INDUSTRIAL BUYING BEHAVIOR

Mitzi M. Montoya, Michigan State University
Glenn S. Omura, Michigan State University
Roger Calantone, Michigan State University

ABSTRACT

Insufficient research is available on industrial buyers as "consumers of information." The value of the abundant information available to decision makers is dependent upon managers' recognition that they need information, are motivated to acquire it, and properly use it. This perspective requires viewing the marketing manager as a "consumer of information." The purpose of this paper is to develop a foundation of theory-based propositions that integrates industrial buying behavior (IBB) literature and information processing with the goal of stimulating theory-driven, information assisted, decision making research. The explicit propositions give specific directions and an organized framework to guide research streams. This re-classification and integration of IBB models with information processing theory demonstrates that the buying process is a form of contingent information processing. The contingency approach specifies task, environment, and person variables that mediate the information need, acquisition, and utilization process of industrial information consumers. The extensive specification of propositions serves to stimulate further theory development and empirical testing.

Information processing has been a dominant research stream in the consumer behavior field in the last decade (Arndt 1986). While information processing has been applied to many marketing areas, this paper draws primarily from choice models, information search and acquisition, and information overload research. This unification of the industrial buying process and information processing provides an in-depth understanding and specification of the <u>relationships</u> between the subprocess and specific contingency elements of the proposed framework.

Consistent with current research on decision processes, the three phases of the proposed information processing framework are: (1) problem recognition and information need, (2) information search and acquisition, (3) information use and evaluation, (cf. Newell and Simon, 1972; Einhorn and Hogarth, 1981). This three phase process is iterative in nature. It is dependent, overall and at each phase, upon task, environment and person contingency factors. A contingent view of the buying process is supported by the well-known, complex buying process models (e.g., Robinson, Faris, and Wind, 1967) as well as the individual decision making literature (e.g., Payne 1982; Beach and Mitchell, 1978). A review of information processing research supports the three general categories of contingent factors - task, person, and environment - as well as the specific variables within each category. Characteristics unique to organizational decision environments, such as social and political factors, can be considered in the context of the three general categories. An integrated framework of these characteristics, relationships, and effects is proposed.

The consequence of the proposed phase and variable interdependency is the recognition that the buying process is dynamic, highly contingent, and distinctively iterative. The value to marketers of understanding this process is that specific contingent factors could be managed to most effectively and efficiently achieve a desired result. The propositions offered in this paper provide a foundation for the development of very specific and integrated hypotheses regarding the industrial buying process.

REFERENCES

Arndt, Johan (1986), "Paradigms in Consumer Research: A Review of Perspectives and Approaches," *European Journal of Marketing*, 20 (8), 23-40.

Beach, Lee Roy and Terence R. Mitchell (1978), "A Contingency Model for the Selection of Decision Strategies," *Academy of Management Review*, 3, 439-449.

Einhorn, H. J. and R. M. Hogarth (1981), "Behavioral Decision Theory: Processes of Judgment and Choice," *Annual Review of Psychology*, 32, 53-88.

Newell, Allen and Herbert A. Simon (1972), *Human Problem Solving*. Englewood Cliffs, NJ: Prentice-Hall.

Payne, John W. (1982), "Contingent Decision Behavior," *Psychological Bulletin*, 92, 382-402.

Robinson, P. J., C. W. Faris, and Y. Wind (1967), *Industrial Buying and Creative Marketing*. Boston, MA: Allyn and Bacon.

ENDNOTE

*   A complete list of references and the formal propositions is available from the authors. Also, the authors gratefully acknowledge the funding support for this paper by the Edward Lowe Foundation.

For further information contact:
Mitzi M. Montoya
Michigan State University
Eli Broad Graduate School of Management
Department of Marketing and Logistics
East Lansing, Michigan 48824

USING FOCUS GROUPS TO STUDY HOUSEHOLD DECISION PROCESSES AND CHOICES

Jeffrey J. Stoltman, Wayne State University
James W. Gentry, University of Nebraska-Lincoln

ABSTRACT

This paper discusses the application and benefits of the focus group method to the study of household decision processes and choices. The conventional wisdom regarding focus groups cannot be simply extended and applied to this research setting. We recommend integrating the family therapy literature. While consumer researchers are unlikely to encounter the same type or level as a therapist, one must be equipped to deal with the "hostilities" that may surface during household groups.

INTRODUCTION

Wroe Alderson's (1957) discussion of consumer behavior focused on the household. Despite this auspicious start and the many subsequent calls for a focus on family/household decision processes and choices, the cumulative body of knowledge is far from adequate. Compared to other substantive research topics, the total number of studies focused on the household is small, and the extant literature is largely comprised of studies focused on individual behavior as opposed to household consumption. Studies of the family have often dealt with only one (key) informant from the household, despite consistent evidence that household members differ greatly in their preferences and in their perceptions of each other and the decision process (cf. Corfman 1991; Corfman and Lehmann 1987; Davis, Hoch, and Ragsdale 1986).

Although the need is compelling, there has been very little work done in consumer research that has involved more than two members of the household. The Foxman, Tansuhaj, and Ekstrom (1989) study is noteworthy because of the effort made to study perceptions of the father, mother, and child, but even this study ignores other household members (i.e., other children and other extended household members). The pursuit of the "heads of household" approach to conducting household research appears to have limited potential, and attempts to examine household consumption should seek to include all members of the unit of analysis whenever possible.

Several necessary augmentations to the present approach to studying household phenomena can be identified. First, as recently suggested by Lutz (1991), we need research methods that will obtain data from all household members. Second, we must develop methods which can be used to examine the full spectrum of household types and which allow us to consider whether observations generalize or suggest conditions, processes, and/or out-

comes unique to certain types of households (e.g., unique to single parent households). Third, we need methods that will allow us to explore the range of decisions and choices contained within the household. This step will make our understanding less dependent on "major event" phenomena (e.g., purchasing a home or buying a car). It should also afford an opportunity to explore the continuities present in household consumption. Indeed, the household presents a unique opportunity to explore extended, rather than neatly contained, forms of consumption. In addressing this need, a fourth need becomes apparent: Researchers need to observe households over several occasions, rather than in just a one-shot fashion. In the process of obtaining multiple observations, we must be concerned with the resulting effect on the validity of the measures, particularly where conventional quantitative measures are being used (see Cook and Campbell 1979). Fifth, and finally, we need to gain a deeper appreciation for and understanding of the many levels of interaction and the many subtle ways in which households communicate, influence, and make choices. We need to develop methods that will put us in closer proximity to the phenomena. The purpose of this paper is to encourage researchers to develop and apply the focus group method as a means of addressing these needs.

One logical explanation for our failure to make significant inroads dealing with the range of issues identified here is the complexity and difficulty of obtaining the necessary data. As noted by Moore-Shay and Wilkie (1988) in their recent review, a number of barriers are encountered by the researcher. Household decisions are made over an extended period of time, even continuously in many circumstances. Many of these decisions are interdependent, and the fact that several (often all) household members may be involved in a decision further complicates the measurement task, as does the subtlety of the social phenomena that are often operative.

A number of methodological approaches have been applied in this setting (Burns and Gentry 1991; Miller, Rollins, and Thomas 1982). Quantitatively-oriented, or so-called "paper and pencil" techniques, are more seriously challenged by the circumstances noted above. Notwithstanding the significant advances being made in this area (see Corfman 1991), the shared perception that conducting research in this setting is particularly difficult may stem from a reliance on techniques that are not well suited to meet the challenge. By comparison, qualitatively-oriented techniques appear to offer a useful way to begin addressing these needs. Recent developments regarding ethnographic/naturalistic inquiry methods provide evidence that interesting insights can be obtained (cf. Arnould and Wallendorf 1991; Hill 1991; Krugman and Gopal 1991; Meyer and O'Guinn 1991; Thompson, Locander, and Pollio 1990; Wallendorf 1991), and the general capabilities of the qualitative techniques have not been adequately tested in this capacity. Perhaps the most important benefit of pursuing this particular path of inquiry is the ability to engage in discovery-oriented activity that will assist in the development and refinement of measures of key constructs (see Calder 1977; Hirschman 1989; Marshall and Rossman 1989).

We see a methodological continuum ranging from single-participant surveys and case studies, through household focus groups, to ongoing particpant-observer approaches. The household focus group richer information than surveys because family dynamics can be observed and explored at length. While this may be a more costly approach (both in terms of time and fees), focus groups offer may be a viable compromise compared to the continuous observation (i.e., ethnographic) approach. As Suen and Awry (1989) note, "continuous observations over an extended period of time are expensive, intrusive, and impractical." In advocating the use of focus group methods in this context we note that the focus group methods generally enjoy favorable status in the practitioner camp. While focus groups are seldom used in academic settings, there is no good reason to continue along this path. Wells (1991, p. 9) has criticized academe for showing little interest in some very good methods, with focus groups being at the top of the list: "focus groups are used all of the time in real research on consumer behavior but rarely in academic research." We also note that the focus group methods share the same general features and thus the benefits associated with the naturalistic inquiry or qualitative/ethnographic techniques which are gaining acceptance. Foremost among the benefits is the capability to discover previously overlooked phenomena. We wish to emphasize that the goal of household focus group research discussed here is not to gain insight about a particular product or service, but rather insight about household consumption phenomena. As such, the application of the general technique is compatible with and seeks to contribute to the body of scholarly research.

This remainder of this paper provides a brief examination the potential strengths and weaknesses of focus group research in the household context. Both the advantages and the problems stem from the fact that the household is a unique unit of observation. Previous discussions of focus group research have not dealt with households per se, and certainly not with a focus on decision processes and communication styles within the household. Next we will review the literature in Family Therapy, as the roots of the focus group technique intersect with the clinical concept of group therapy. The final section of the paper provides general guidance for the conduct of household focus groups adapting procedures identified in the family psychotherapy literature. These guidelines provide a useful starting point for gaining unique perspective on household consumption without creating or adding to any existing problems within the household. We propose that the household focus group will be especially fruitful when investigating decision sequences (compared to a retrospective or hypothetical approach), communication processes, and verbal versus non-verbal interactions.

HOUSEHOLD FOCUS GROUPS

While there is an extensive literature on focus groups (Fern 1982; Greenbaum 1988; Hayes and Tathum 1989; Langer 1991; McQuarrie and McIntyre 1988; Nelson and Frontczak 1988; Stewart and Shamadasani 1990; Stiansen 1988; Wells 1974), the literature does not deal with the family or the household as the unit of observation. There is a fairly strong belief that focus group participants should not be acquaintances. Bellenger, Bernhardt, and Goldstucker (1976, p. 10) state: *Many researchers believe that an individual should not be allowed to participate in a group containing a friend, neighbor, or relative; they will tend to talk to each other and not to the group as a whole. For that same reason, church groups or organizations should not be asked to send people. The people that arrive in these groups have already established relationships, some being leaders and some being followers.* Wells (1974, p. 134), provides a more neutral view, agreeing that friends may be "less than candid in the presence of people they see every day," but notes that a group of acquaintances may show greater productivity than a group of strangers because of the "naturalness and ease of conversation."

There have been investigations of the acquaintance issue. For example, Fern (1982) found that groups of strangers produced an average of 26.7 more relevant ideas than groups of acquaintances (but this difference was not statistically significant). Nelson and Frontczak (1988) conducted a study of three types of groups: strangers, acquaintances (members of a small club), and spouses. They found no differences in terms of the quantitative nor qualitative (quality of ideas generated) measures of output from the various groups. As this example suggests, the application of the focus group method to this setting will not be a matter of simply extending existing procedures and guidelines. The focus group literature is primarily focused on the tasks of forming, moderating, and analyzing the remarks made by groups of unaffiliated individuals. Little direction is likely to be provided on many issues. Moreover, many issues may be irrelevant as the purpose of the focus group changes from one of substance (reaction to old/new stimuli in the marketplace) to one of process (interactions within the household). Table 1 provides an overview of the strengths and weaknesses associated with the use of the focus group method in this context.

Focus groups provide a means of tapping into the phenomenology of the household. We should obtain rich insights into communication patterns and modes of expression within the household. One clear strength of the focus group method is that the researcher can learn not just from what is said, but also from facial expressions and tone of voice. Focus group procedures directly confront the researcher with breadth and depth of a consumers' feelings, thoughts, and reactions (cf. Langer 1991). Given that nonverbal communication is relatively more important among families (Noller and Fitzpatrick 1990), this opportunity to observe glances, knowing smiles, gestures, grimaces, etc. is a critical advantage for the focus group methodology. This approach also provides a unique way to explore certain manifestations of intergenerational influences systematically (see Lutz 1991). Other benefits noted are generally associated with focus groups (cf. Bellenger, Bernhardt, and Goldstucker 1976; Stewart and Shamadasani 1990).

Stiansen (1988) mentions the common problem with scheduling, and this will probably be exacerbated in this setting. The problem of dominant group members (cf. Barabba 1990; Stiansen 1988), may be heightened in this context because of existing instrumental and expressive roles and the differences in age and accessibility to resources (cf. Leik 1963). Extant groups pose other challenges. The "normal routine" of the focus group moderator may not apply. Issues such as "framing the group dynamic" and "legitimizing the opinions of group members" (cf. Whatley and Flexner 1988) take on a fundamentally different meaning in this context. The dictum that a vocal participant can spoil a focus group session (cf. Barabba 1990) takes on a different meaning: A vocal household member may, in fact, act that way in the home, and this behavior may thus reflect important and valid information. The onus is clearly on the researcher to establish a working communication system with the members of the household, and the diverse age ranges and perspective can pose another problem. While a group moderator needs to be encouraging, different skills are needed to encourage simultaneously an eight-year old, eighteen-year old, and two adults, all of whom disagree about an issue that is important to each of them

both individually and collectively. Also, encouraging one member can easily offend others in the household as "side-taking" is a common family phenomenon (see Kaslow 1990a, 1990b).

The focus on consumption and production issues may allow the group to recount very positive memories, but at the same time issues may be raised that normally are allowed to remain dormant. Belk's (1988) work on the extended self shows clearly the relevance of possessions to the self-concept/esteem of persons, and they can be symbolic of larger problems within a household. There is strong evidence that household members usually hold conflicting opinions as to what transpired in any given situation (Foxman, Tansuhaj, and Ekstrom 1989; Spiro 1983). The mere act of posing questions to members of the household raises the potential for conflict, and any conflict that is resurrected or created must be controlled. The issue of household conflict and the need for moderators to be prepared to exert control is of such importance that a look at the Family Therapy literature is warranted.

FAMILY THERAPY

Because of the existing social system, family therapists observe a higher, often more intense degree of interaction, and a greater sense of immediacy compared to what goes on in heterogeneous group settings or in one-on-one settings. For these reasons, the family therapist must possess or acquire a different set of skills. As noted by Bednar, Burlingame, and Masters (1988), there are multiple levels and types of influence present in the family's social system, which is an amalgam of personal, interpersonal, group, and systemic influences that must be considered (see also Bradbury and Fincham 1990; Kaslow 1990a, 1990b). There is also a "reciprocal determinism" involved in the actions of individuals in this system which creates an increasingly complex situation affecting the interaction between therapist (information gatherer) and client (respondent). As noted by Korchin (1976, p. 384), compared to group therapies, family therapy: *does not start from the shared base of mutual ignorance. The family members come in with a mass of common experience; the therapist is the outsider, in his own office. In order even to make sense out of their allusions to shared experience, he has to learn the family culture, rules, and language. Why does everyone laugh when Johnny says that Dad is getting to be more like Uncle Joe? The therapist has to get within the family system to understand and work with it. Yet he cannot become a 'regulated part of the system,' caught up in its cliques and power struggles, for he must also stand apart from it in order to understand its workings and guide its changes. Thus, the balance between involvement and detachment becomes more critical in family therapy than in other forms of psychotherapy.* With the exception of the stated interest in guiding changes in the family/client, this general orientation is similar to the observations offered in the qualitative research literature (cf. Calder 1977; Marshall and Rossman 1989; Thompson, Locander, and Pollio 1989). Both the therapist and the family consumer researcher share an interest in devising methods to define, probe, and analyze various manifestations of family interaction. In this respect, the "data-gathering" stages of the family therapies are of the greatest use.

The guidelines provided in Table 2 represent an adaptation of Korchin's (1976) prescriptions for the conduct of family therapy sessions. While an ordering of events is implied, all phases should be considered to be of equal importance and should be regarded as necessary steps to take. Because of the probability that conflict and hostility may emerge, it is incumbent upon the academic researcher to have cleared the study with a Human Subjects' Committee and to be certain to use the informed consent process with the group participants. In the event of hostilities, the researcher should be prepared to discontinue the data collection effort and implement a control plan that will either shift the discussion to the goal of reducing conflict instead of one of monitoring the inter-

actions, or a control plan that directs participants to qualified professional assistance. The direct participation of trained family therapist or counselor would serve this purpose, though some additional expense may be involved and the theoretical emphasis (e.g., Freudian strategy) of this individual must be considered. It will often be easier to take this route than for the consumer researcher to acquire the training necessary to cope with the possibility of hostility.

The first session or two should be spent with the heads of the household in order to secure cooperation, schedule sessions, and to begin to develop a relationship with the household. These initial sessions provide a two-way street where you can get to know them, and they can get to know you. An extensive household history should be taken and focused on getting a sense of the cast of relevant characters, the milestones, continuities, the symbols and rituals, and a sense of the possible antecedents and precedents under which the household may be operating. This has obvious phenomenological overtones and also makes good sense from the standpoint of establishing rapport. Beyond improving the manageability and conduct of subsequent sessions, this action is an explicit recognition of, and an opportunity to observe, the importance of intergenerational influences on consumption behaviors.

The initial full-group sessions should be used to establish the ground rules and to clarify the mosaic of motives and perceptions. The ground rules should establish that each household member must speak for himself/herself, and that there will be an effort to intervene in situations where one person tries to represent the views of another. This helps create an atmosphere where recollections and viewpoints have equal status and it will facili-

---

TABLE 2
Guidelines for Conduction Household Focus Groups

_ Clear the study with University Human Subjects Committee because of the likelihood of conflict.

_ Discontinue data collection immediately if hostility emerges.

_ Have a control plan ready to implement if hostilities emerge—Retain the services of a properly trained counselor or therapist. Consider having this individual conduct the sessions.

_ Conduct initial meetings with heads of household to secure cooperation and take a family history.

_ During first full-household session, review history with entire household and revise and extend that history based on input received.

_ Make an effort to discover the household decision style and rules. Consider a comparative study of the rules based on the observations of the household itself (e.g., "How do you think your neighbors, the Smiths,...").

_ First session should establish the ground rules: each member speaks for themselves, all points of view have validity, if there questions please ask, etc.

_ It is recommended that children's views are solicited first.

_ Go beyond apparent consensus to probe, compare and contrast recollections and opinions of events.

_ Maintain objective observer status at all times. Do not take sides.

_ Have a plan for dealing with possible after-effects. This group will remain intact after you have accomplished your task.

tate participation. This will be a difficult task in families with well-defined hierarchies. In this case, it is advisable to start with questions to children. In the initial sessions, extant household rules must also be discovered and discussed openly. These can be compared to the rules that exist within the general culture, or within subcultures, and the comparison process could easily include the solicited views of household members. The examination of these rules will be a time consuming and difficult task, as "many such rules are less than clear and they may be inconsistently applied or interpreted" (Korchin 1976, p. 386). Special attention should be given to nuances and shades of meaning, as well as to the more obvious differences of opinion or recollection. Further, much of the communication may be nonverbal, and the communication pattern may be directed by a dominant member without any verbal record being created. Coding schemes such as that proposed by Bales (1950) may provide a useful basis for encoding the interactions observed (see also Solomon et al. 1985). Throughout the data collection effort, the researcher should go beyond apparent consensus and several attempts should be made to probe, compare and contrast different recollections and interpretations of events. The moderator must be prepared to avoid being drawn in by the predictable household dynamics of scapegoating and coalition formation. The researcher must maximize interaction by avoiding the alienation of household members and protect their own objective observer status. While this is a challenge in most focus group settings, the dynamics of the household provide a real test (particularly when children are involved). Finally, we emphasize that specific attention must be given to the after-effects of participation in a study. There is a unique ethical responsibility because the household group remains together long after the researcher has accomplished his/her task. The meddling of the researcher, particularly an inept one, may do lasting damage to household ties. One solution is to direct any emergent hostility toward yourself, but, at a minimum, a researcher should line up the necessary professional resources and leave household members with clear instructions as to where to turn if help is needed.

CAVEATS AND FINAL THOUGHTS

There are differences between the agenda of the therapist and the agenda of the consumer researcher that should be considered. Notwitshstanding Belk's (1988) observations regarding the importance of possessions, the conflicts associated with most household consumption choices are probably rather tame compared to the psychological pathologies confronted by family therapists. Therapists are often challenged by painful life experiences (both latent and manifest) and deep rooted problems with destructive potential. The family therapy literature understandably deals with issues pertaining to the role of discovery and intervention, and these subjects are not easily disentangled. The general procedure and the interrogatory style of the clinical approach is based on

the fact that the therapist is a willing agent for change. Assuming consumer researchers will not be interested in changing the behavior of the household, one should cautiously adapt or adopt the therapeutic protocols reported in the therapy literature.

A related reason for such caution is the fact that the techniques employed in family group therapy are deeply rooted in theoretical frameworks, e.g., a Rogerian therapist would approach the basic task quite differently than an Adlerian or Freudian therapist (see Corsini 1973). There is no consensus as to which framework provides the most effective treatment, and there is little at this juncture to suggest one orientation over the other. Though it seems that the non-directive and non-judgmental approach of the Rogerian protocol has advantages, each of the options should be explored. Though this complicates the task of identifying and adapting techniques or strategies that may be used, consumer researchers need to consider the conjunction of the subject phenomena and the various theoretical frameworks before committing to a course of action (e.g., exploration of compulsiveness or addiction within the household may benefit more from a Freudian approach).

There is a concern that many of intervention strategies are rigorless and ambiguous, partially because of these theoretical frameworks (see Bednar, Burlingame, and Masters 1988). As a means of addressing this persistent problem, Mahrer (1988) recently proposed the adoption of a "discovery-oriented" psychotherapy research perspective, and significant potential is likely to stem from the adoption of his recommendations. Both the concern regarding the encroachment of theoretical perspective and the useful role to be played by discovery-oriented approaches are reminiscent of the cautions voiced by Calder (1977) in his discussion of the clinical/judgmental form of qualitative research and of the current debate regarding the advantage of interpretivist procedures (Hirschman 1989). Thus, despite the important differences, there are many parallels and there are important contributions that can be gleaned from this literature. It is important to remember that the agenda of the household researcher and the family therapist will overlap in one fundamental respect: Both are interested in developing strategies and techniques which help to reveal the familial relationships and behaviors of relevance to the presenting issue, whether it is pathology or consumption.

In the application and refinement of the household focus group, many of the findings reported in the household decision process literature will be strengthened and fresh insights will emerge. While the relative absence of qualitative data in the household choice literature is a critical shortcoming, it is being remedied (Arnould and Wallendorf 1991; Hill 1991; Krugman and Gopal 1991; Meyer and O'Guinn 1991; Thompson, Locander, and Pollio 1990). Ethnographic techniques generally, and the household focus group technique in particular, can provide a legitimate and unique basis for investigating many of the dynamic properties of household decision making and choice processes. A number of behavioral issues will be confronted which have thus far been dealt with at arm's length, if at all. Indeed, a reliance on only certain methodologies leads to the proposition that household consumption conflicts are not very severe and probably do not persist (cf. Peter and Olson 1990). Yet, there is evidence that families literally dissolve because of financial, or, more broadly, consumption-related matters (Bradbury and Fincham 1990; Kaslow 1990a,b). This "dark side" of household consumer behavior could easily be confronted in focus group settings because the research may touch upon the underlying reasons and the manifestations of such problems. Obviously, these gains come at some cost. If one is prepared to confront areas of deep-seated conflict, one must also be prepared to contain them. The paper and pencil method is "safe" by comparison, but by being safe, an open question remains: Have we fully explored the phenomenon of interest by remaining at a safe distance?

REFERENCES

Alderson, Wroe (1957), "The Motivation of Consumer Buying," Chapter 7 of *Marketing Behavior and Executive Action*, Homewood, IL: Irwin.

Arnould, Eric and Melanie Wallendorf (1991), "Domestic Consumption Rituals and the Reproduction of American Households," *Proceedings*, Conference on Household Consumption and Production, Irvine, CA.

Bales, Robert F. (1950), "A Set of Categories for the Analysis of Small Group Interaction," *American Sociological Review*, (April).

Barabba, Vincent P. (1990), "The Market Research Encyclopedia," *Harvard Business Review*, 90 (1), 105-116.

Bednar, Richard, Gary Burlingame, and Kevin Masters (1988), "Systems of Family Treatment: Substance or Semantics?" *Annual Review of Psychology*, 39, 401-434.

Belk, Russell (1988), "Possessions and the Extended Self," *Journal of Consumer Research*, 15 (September), 139-168.

Bellenger, Danny N., Kenneth L. Bernhardt, and Jac L. Goldstucker (1976), "Qualitative Research Techniques: Focus Group Interviews," *Qualitative Research in Marketing*, Chicago: American Marketing Association, 7-28.

Bradbury, Thomas N. and Frank D. Fincham (1990), "Attributions in Marriage: Review and Critique," *Psychological Bulletin*, 107 (1), 3-33.

Burns, Alvin and James Gentry (1990), "Toward Improving Household Consumption Behavior Research: Avoidance of Pitfalls Using Alternative Household Data Collection Procedures," *Advances in Consumer Research*, 17, 518-530.

Calder, Bobby J. (1977), "Focus Groups and the Nature of Qualitative Marketing Research," *Journal of Marketing Research*, 14, 353-364.

Cook, Thomas D. and Donald T. Campbell (1979), *Quasi-Experimentation: Design and Analysis Issues for Field Settings*. Chicago: Rand McNally.

Corfman, Kim P. (1991), "Perceptions of Relative Influence: Formation and Measurement," *Journal of Marketing Research*, 28 (May), 125-136.

_____ and Donald R. Lehmann (1987), "Models of Cooperative Group Decision-Making and Relative Influences: An Experimental Investigation of Family Purchase Decisions," *Journal of Consumer Research*, 14 (June), 1-13.

Corsini, Richard (1973), *Current Psychotherapies*. Itasca, IL: F. E. Peacock, Inc.

Davis, Harry L., Stephen J. Hoch, and E. K. Easton Ragsdale (1986), "An Anchoring and Adjustment Model of Spousal Predictions," *Journal of Consumer Research*, 13 (June), 25-37.

Fern, Edward F. (1982), "The Use of Focus Groups for Idea Generation: The Effects of Group Size, Acquaintanceship, and Moderator on Response Quantity and Quality," *Journal of Marketing Research*, 19, 1-13.

Foxman, Ellen, Patriya Tansuhaj, and Karin Ekstrom (1989), "Family Members' Perceptions of Adolescents' Influence in Family Decision Making," *Journal of Consumer Research*, 17 (March), 482-491.

Greenbaum, Thomas L. (1988), *The Practical Handbook and Guide to Focus Group Research*, Lexington, MA: D. C. Heath.

Hayes, Thomas J. and Carol Tathum (1989), *Focus Group Interviews: A Reader*. Chicago, IL: American Marketing Association.

Hill, Ronald Paul (1991), "Homeless Women, Special Possessions, and Meaning of Home," *Proceedings*, Conference on Household Consumption and Production, Irvine, CA.

Hirschman, Elizabeth C. (1991), "Secular Mortality and the Dark Side of Consumer Behavior: Or How Semiotics Saved My Life," *Advances in Consumer Research*, 18, 1-4.

_____ (1989), *Interpretive Consumer Research*. Provo, UT: Association for Consumer Research.

Kaslow, Florence W. (1990a), *Voices in Family Psychology. Vol. 1*, Beverly Hills, CA: Sage Publications.

_____ (1990b), *Voices in Family Psychology. Vol. 2*, Beverly Hills, CA: Sage Publications.

Korchin, Sheldon J. (1976), *Modern Clinical Psychology: Principles of Intervention in the Clinic and Community*. New York: Basic Books.

Krugman, Dean M. and Yasmin Gopal (1991), "In-Home Observation of Television and VCR Movie Rental Viewing," *Advances in Consumer Research*, 18, 143-149.

Langer, Judith (1991), "Focus Groups," *American Demographics*, (February), 38-39.

Leik, R. K. (1963), "Instrumentality and Emotionality in Family Interaction," *Sociometry*, 26, 131-145.

Lutz, Richard J. (1991), "Editorial," *Journal of Consumer Research*, 17 (March).

Mahrer, Alvin R. (1988), "Discovery-Oriented Psychotherapy Research," *American Psychologist*, 43 (September), 694-702.

Marshall, Catherine and Gretchen Rossman (1989), *Designing Qualitative Research*. Beverly Hills, CA: Sage Publications.

McQuarrie, Edward and Shelby McIntyre (1988), "Conceptual Underpinnings for the Use of Group Interviews in Consumer Research," *Advances Consumer Research*, 580-586.

Meyer, Timothy and Thomas O'Guinn (1991), "The Videocassette Recorder and the Family," in *Proceedings*, Conference on Household Consumption and Production, Irvine, CA.

Miller, Brent C., Boyd C. Rollins, and Darwin L. Thomas (1982), "On Methods of Studying Marriages and Families," *Journal of Marriage and the Family*, 44 (November), 851-873.

Moore-Shay, Elizabeth and William Wilkie (1988), "Recent Developments in Research on Family Decisions," *Advances in Consumer Research*, 15, 454-460.

Nelson, James E. and Nancy T. Frontczak (1988), "How Acquaintanceship and Analyst Can Influence Focus Group Results," *Journal of Advertising*, 17 (1), 41-48.

Noller, Patricia and Mary Anne Fitzpatrick (1990), "Marital Communication in the Eighties," *Journal of Marriage and the Family*, 52 (November), 832-843.

Peter, J. Paul and Jerry Olson (1990), *Consumer Behavior: Marketing Strategy Perspectives*, Second Edition, Homewood, IL: Irwin.

Solomon, Michael R., Carol Suprenant, John A. Czepiel, and Evelyn A. Antman (1985), "A Role Theory Perpsective on Dyadic Interactions: The Service Encounter," *Journal of Marketing*, 49 (Winter), 99-111.

Spiro, Rosann (1983), "Persuasion in Family Decision-Making," *Journal of Consumer Research*, 9, 393-402.

Stewart, David and Prem Shamadasani (1990), *Focus Groups: Theory and Practice*, Beverly Hills, CA: Sage Publications.

Stiansen, Sarah (1988), "How Focus Groups Can Go Astray," *Adweek*, (December) 5, 4-6.

Suen, Hoi K. and Donald Awry (1989), *Analyzing Qualitative Observational Data*. Hillsdale, NJ: Lawrence Erlbaum Associates.

Thompson, Craig, William Locander, and Howard Pollio (1989), "Putting Consumer Experience Back into Consumer Research: The Philosophy and Method of Existential Phenomenology," *Journal of Consumer Research*, 16, 133-146.

_____ (1990), "The Lived Meaning of Free Choice: An Existential- Phenomenological Description of Everyday Experience of Contemporary Married Women," *Journal of Consumer Research*, 17 (December), 346-361.

Wallendorf, Melanie (1991), "Ethnographic Techniques for Household Research," in *Proceedings*, Conference on Household Consumption and Production, Irvine, CA.

Walters, Lynda Henley (1982), "Are Families Different From Other Groups?" *Journal of Marriage and the Family*, 44 (November), 841-850.

Wells, William D. (1974), "Group Interviewing," in *Handbook of Marketing Research*, Robert Ferber, ed. New York: McGraw-Hill Book Co., 2-133—2-146.

_____ (1991), "How to be Useful," *The Communicator*, (January), 9-10.

RESEARCHING INTERNATIONAL BUSINESS MARKETS: THE ROLE OF FOLLOW-UP

Robin N. Shaw, Griffith University
Florence Ling, Monash University

ABSTRACT

The effectiveness and efficiency of utilizing follow-up techniques in international mail survey research were questioned, in the context of a comprehensive survey of Singapore travel agents related to the outbound Singapore-to-Australia travel market.

To examine the assertion that earlier respondents tend to have a special interest in the subject under inquiry, various operational definitions of "special interest" could be formulated, but they would all probably emphasize elements such as those often incorporated in the consumer behavior concept of "involvement". That is, importance and relevance would be essential criteria, and in the organizational context of the travel agent, these would be manifest in aspects such as the share of business related to a particular destination, and the growth trend and satisfaction level associated with the destination. Four questions on the questionnaire addressed these aspects explicitly, but no significant differences were found between the NFU ("no follow-up") and WFU ("with follow-up") respondents.

In terms of demographics, the organizational analogs of age, occupation, expenditure, family size and composition, etc., may be dimensions such as years in business, customer profile by segment served, expenditure on advertising and sales promotion, number of staff by category and number of offices. No significant differences were found between the NFU and WFU respondents on these variables.

Regarding organizational psychographics (activities, interests, and opinions), which may be extended to include the nature of the experiences undergone and hence the attitudes likely to have been formed, the remaining questions addressed a wide variety of issues, including customer segments served, perceived attractiveness of various characteristics of Australia, perceived roles of travel agents, experience with Australia, etc. With very few exceptions, no significant differences were found between the NFU and WFU respondents.

When it is recognized that the significant exceptions mentioned above were in the context of approximately ten times as many instances of no difference in responses on the questionnaire, it is clear that the NFU and WFU groups were, on average, much more similar to each other than different.

However, it could be argued that a more qualitative examination of the differences is warranted, to ensure that differences of importance and relevance to the researcher (and the sponsor of the research) are not overlooked because of the sheer weight of numbers apparently operating against them. For example, key issues might be the extent to which the group of travel agents would recommend Australia as a destination, taking this as a summary expression of the favorability of predisposition towards Australia. However, no significant differences were found between the NFU and WFU respondents on this variable.

Therefore, in the confines of the present study, it appears that substantial time (if not money) could have been saved by not engaging in any follow-up at all. The implications for international business research may be provocative, if replications under varying circumstances support the results obtained in this study. Apart from generating a larger quantum of responses, and hence allowing finer distinctions to be drawn with greater confidence from the data analysis, there may be little justification for devoting scarce resources to the follow-up stage. Perhaps resources could be diverted into larger initial sample sizes, or more intensive pretesting, or monetary or other incentives, thereby enhancing the productivity of the survey while condensing the time frame for the total study.

For further information contact:
Robin N. Shaw
Commerce and Administration
Griffith University
Nathan, Queensland 4111
Australia

INTERNATIONAL MARKET ASSESSMENT: THE "DEMAND-SIDE" EFFECTS OF INFRASTRUCTURE

Brian D. Ottum, University of Utah
Richard J. Semenik, University of Utah

ABSTRACT

This paper argues that traditional approaches to international market assessment tend to focus on *economic* infrastructure—roads, telephone lines, energy supply—and not the *social* and *intangible* infrastructure—education and health systems, etc. Though the former has a well known effect on the "supply-side" aspects of international marketing, like the firm's production, distribution and promotion, the paper demonstrates that there are "demand-side" effects as well.

INTRODUCTION

Infrastructure is the aggregate of all facilities that allow a society to function. Traditionally, the amount and condition of a country's economic infrastructure—transportation, communications, water, waste treatment, and energy—have been considered key factors in international market assessment because of the impact such factors have on marketing operations. These economic infrastructure factors are important to the "supply-side" aspects of marketing transactions: what products and services can be effectively and efficiently produced, distributed, and promoted. However, less recognition has been given to the fact that other forms of infrastructure impact the "demand-side" of marketing transactions: consumers will seek those products and services that are relevant to their local lifestyles which are fostered by the **social** and **intangible** infrastructure of a country. Social and intangible infrastructure includes education, health, public welfare, information and technology systems in a society. Poor conditions in social and intangible infrastructure can limit economic growth, purchasing power, standard of living, and hence market attractiveness in much the same way that poor economic infrastructure can.

This article provides an overview of the role and importance of infrastructure in international market assessment. First, the nature of infrastructure in its many forms—economic, social and intangible—is discussed. Next, the importance of all forms of infrastructure to economic development and market activities is described. The recognition of economic infrastructure in current methods used by marketers to assess market attractiveness is then considered. Finally, a broader view of infrastructure that includes its social and intangible components is proposed for international market assessment which highlights both the supply-side and demand-side effects of these factors on market transactions.

What Is Infrastructure?

The term "infrastructure" has broad meaning. The most general definition of infrastructure identifies underlying systems which facilitate societal function (Rainer 1989). These systems can have a multitude of components, depending on the type of societal function supported. Some specific definitions are:

"Core infrastructure [is defined as] streets, highways, airports, mass transit, water systems, etc" (Aschauer 1989, p. 177).

"The public works [include] roads, streets, bridges, water treatment and distribution systems, irrigation, waterways, airports, and mass transit installations and facilities that are basic to the growth and functioning of an economy. The term public infrastructure includes a range of investments broader than public works investment" (Eberts 1990, p. 16).

"Public overhead capital [all infrastructure] is divided into two components: social (SOC) and economic (EOC). Projects of the latter type are specifically aimed at supporting directly productive activities, and include roads, bridges, harbors, power projects, and similar undertakings. SOC projects, on the other hand, are more concerned with what has been termed 'investment in human beings,' i.e., education, welfare, and health undertakings" (Hansen 1965, p. 5).

"The term 'infrastructure' has been coined to describe the network of public works which are basic to the economic and social life of any nation state" (Webley 1985).

These descriptions of infrastructure, taken collectively, suggest that infrastructure factors affect very basic elements of the production and supply of goods and services. Transportation facilities, communications capability, and energy resources are needed for the supply of goods and services: not only for production but also for efficient distribution. These definitions also identify a **social** facilitation which is manifest by the level of infrastructure. It can be argued that this social facilitation impacts the nature of goods and services which will ultimately be in demand. If the level of infrastructure development is so low that a standard of living barely beyond subsistence is being provided, then the range and level of demand for goods and services will also be low.

At this point, approaches to international market assessment recognize the production and supply effects of infrastructure, but do not explicitly consider the potential impact of social facilitation.

A Broader View of Infrastructure

To fully appreciate the potential impact of infrastructure on markets, a broader view of infrastructure is needed. A taxonomy for all classes of infrastructure is provided in Table 1. The three major infrastructure categories--economic, social and intangible--and the components associated with each are listed in Table 1. The most commonly discussed category of infrastructure in marketing contexts is **economic infrastructure**. This is the public capital that is used to directly support a society's economy. Some synonyms for economic infrastructure are economic overhead capital, public works, core infrastructure, and physical capital. The categories of economic infrastructure displayed in Table 1 identify factors typically included in market assessments. Transportation capabilities related to the acquisition of materials for production and the distribution of output. Telecommunications infrastructure facilitates all forms of communication including those needed for promotion. Finally, water, waste and energy infrastructure primarily affect a firm's ability to run production operations.

It is the other two classes of infrastructure which receive little attention in international market assessments, however. **Social infrastructure** represents public investment in the human aspects of economic activity. Synonyms for this class are social overhead capital and human capital. All forms of education, health care and public welfare are included in this category. The components of social infrastructure have a pervasive affect on the standard of living of citizens in a country. The education system impacts literacy and skill development. Health infrastructure enhances the physical well being of citizens. The public welfare system provides for the safety and aesthetic needs of a society. The last of the three classes of infrastructure, **intangible infrastructure**, is the most recent addition to the mechanisms classified as infrastructure. It covers the networks which are needed to support modern information-based economies. The information, technology, and research/development components of this class support not only economic activities of businesses but also the use of information and technology by citizens in their daily lives which affects both standard of living and lifestyle. We will demonstrate that the components of social and intangible infrastructure and their effects on citizens impact the "demand-side" of economic activity in a market. As such, they represent an important consideration in overall market assessment.

THE IMPORTANCE OF INFRASTRUCTURE

This broader view of infrastructure is important. In its many forms, infrastructure influences the economic and social health of a country and ultimately the marketplace behavior of its citizens. A short digression into very basic economic theory is needed to illustrate infrastructure's importance to the characteristics and potential health of a market.

Infrastructure and Economic Theory

Productivity is the key element of basic economic theory related to infrastructure. In the 1950s, economists began to realize that infrastructure played a key role in determining the productivity of a nation and consequently, the productivity of individual firms. On the micro-level, a classic essay on external economies showed how infrastructure can increase an individual firm's productivity in two different ways: creation of atmosphere and unpaid factors of production (Meade 1952). In the first effect, "creation of atmosphere," a firm's productivity is enhanced by increasing the efficiency of public inputs. This exemplifies the concept of a perfect public good—one that is free and cannot be "used up." Air and sunshine are (nearly) perfect public goods. Any firm entering a region with good infrastructure immediately benefits without infringing on the benefits received by other firms. A second way infrastructure can increase firm productivity is through "unpaid factors of production." An example is free access roads. They are not paid for directly by firms (although they are indirectly and partially paid for through fuel taxes), but are definitely used by firms in the conduct of their business.

Beyond the micro-level effect on the productivity of firms stemming from infrastructure, modern productivity theory posits a macro-effect in what is known as "agglomeration" theory (Carlino 1987). Agglomeration theory links a firm's ability to realize the benefits of economies of scale to two "agglomeration" factors—the concentration of a firm's industry in a region (or city) and the size of the region (or city) itself. The concentration of the firm's industry in a region is important because as more firms locate in a region, each firm's productivity increases due to support firms clustering near the primary producers. This effect creates "localization economies." Similarly, the size of the region effects productivity because as there are a greater number of customers to serve, firms can be more efficient in serving a larger number of customers in close proximity. Again, there is a positive effect on the productivity of each firm. This is an agglomeration effect referred to as "urbanization economies."

Modern agglomeration theory is important because it includes infrastructure as an "unpaid" input in the production function, which is the second of Meade's (Meade 1952) effects of infrastructure on productivity. Thus, it is viewed as important as the factors from classical economics (i.e., land, labor and capital) in determining the productivity and thus the supply-side

TABLE 1
A Taxonomy of Infrastructure

Economic Infrastructure
Transportation infrastructure
  ·roads, highways, bridges, tunnels
  ·railway systems

  ·waterway systems, ports, harbors
   ·airports
  ·pipelines

Telecommunications infrastructure
  ·telephone lines, systems and exchanges
  ·radio and television broadcast stations
  · satellites
  · fiber optic networks

Water infrastructure
·water distribution system, pipes,
·dams and reservoirs; irrigation
and drainage
·water purification plants

Waste infrastructure
  ·waste treatment plants, sewage fields
  ·incinerators, composting, landfills
  ·coastal and soil protection
  ·pollution control

Energy infrastructure
  ·electricity subsystem and network
  ·electrical power stations and transformers
  ·natural gas subsystem and pipelines
  ·oil subsystem, refineries, tanks, pipelines
  ·alternative energy sources

Social Infrastructure
Education Infrastructure
  ·day care and preschools
  ·primary and secondary schools

  ·universities
  ·training centers

Health Infrastructure
  ·hospitals and clinics
  ·emergency services
  ·rehabilitation centers
  ·elderly/disabled facilities

Public Welfare Infrastructure
  ·fire and police protection systems
  tanks
  ·support services
  ·libraries, museums, theaters,
  concert halls
  ·community centers
  ·homeless shelters

Intangible Infrastructure
Information Infrastructure
  ·computer networks
  ·information processing

  •Information dissemination
  ·information access

Technology Infrastructure
  ·technological development
  ·technological expertise
  ·technology transfer mechanisms
  ·technology access

R&D Infrastructure
  ·research parks
  ·conservation/historic/artistic
  preservation
  ·business incubator systems
  ·parks, forests, beaches,
  campgrounds

---

potential of a city, region or nation. The benefits of economies from urbanization are important because as population size increases, it costs less per resident to provide, maintain and operate infrastructure. Adequate public infrastructure—water, sewer, power, and streets—and the potential for economic agglomeration serve to attract firms and private investment. Improvements in infrastructure should attract businesses thus benefiting existing business and potential entrepreneurs (Davidson 1989). Similarly, as social infrastructure can be used to improve the standard of living in a society, firms will discover a better educated and more qualified workforce which also relate directly to productivity.

Leading theorists in agglomeration theory are now incorporating the newer, intangible forms of infrastructure—like information and research and development—in their analyses (Nijkamp 1988). "Information centers," which represent spatial concentrations of communication, knowledge, and research infrastructure to transfer results from scientific research to users elsewhere, are being recognized as vital to the advancement of economies. These intangible forms of infrastructure must be included as factors of production in the same fashion that economic forms of infrastructure are.

Empirical Support for Infrastructure Effects on Economies

Aside from this basic theoretical support for the effect of infrastructure on productivity, the last ten years have been marked by an increase in the number of empirical studies which have shown that infrastructure impacts productivity, private investment and other aspects of economic activity. Researchers have identified that infrastructure effects a broad range of economic factors at the city, state, regional, and national. Most studies have identified infrastructure effects on economic activity in the United States although major empirical efforts have been undertaken in six foreign countries.

Several researchers have reaffirmed that spending on economic infrastructure (mostly in the form of public works projects like highways and utilities) has had a significant and positive effect on **private** capital investment and productivity in U. S. cities. In a study of thirty-six U. S. cities, Deno (1988) found that each dollar spent on sewers and highways resulted in a thirty-cent increase in net private spending. Eberts (1986) supported Hansen's (1986) theory of development by identifying that investment in core infrastructure in U. S. cities has a positive and statistically significant relationship to levels of manufacturing output. This effect found by Eberts varied across cities in the United States with public capital spending having a greater effect in southern cities than in northern cities. This same study suggested that core infrastructure investment had greater impact in cities with a rather low base level of infrastructure. Eberts (1986) and others (Dallenberg 1987; Deno 1986) argue that infrastructure and private capital are complements in that investment in either helps stimulate investment in the other. The proposed causal relationship was studied further by Eberts and Fogerty (1987). In this study, data on public outlays and manufacturing investment from 1904 to 1978 in forty U. S. cities were used to identify a significant (and argued to be causal) relationship between public and private spending in thirty-three of the forty cities. Specifically, public investment in core infrastructure stimulated private investment in older cities and private investment stimulated infrastructure investment in younger cities in the southern United States.

At the next economic level, data have been gathered to show how investment in infrastructure can affect a state's prosperity. In the state of Missouri, a large study suggested that investment in public works infrastructure accounted for thirty percent of the gain in real income in the state from 1963 to 1966 (CONSAD 1969). Two separate studies found that business location decisions were made in part on the basis of the amount and condition of state roads (Bartik 1985; Fox and Murray 1988). Similarly, two additional studies found that the combination of state spending on highways and schools had a positive and significant effect on total output and personal income (Garcia-Mila 1987; Helms 1985).

Eberts' (1990) recent review of regional studies reveals that public capital stock investment significantly stimulates economic activity either by augmenting the productivity of private inputs or more directly by enhancing "unpaid" factors of production which accrue to private firms. Furthermore, by enhancing a region's amenities, public infrastructure may also be related to household and corporate formation which contributes to a region's economic growth. In Eberts 1990 summary, private capital and public capital appear to complement each other with private capital seeming to have a larger effect on productivity (Hulton and Schwab 1984; Martin 1979; Mera 1975).

The effects of infrastructure at the national level have only recently received scholarly attention. The work done by economist David Aschauer is the most significant to date (Aschauer 1987, 1988, 1989). Aschauer

used U. S. Government infrastructure spending figures and national productivity data from 1949 through 1985 to demonstrate that a decline in net capital stock has caused the slowdown in U.S. productivity of the last fifteen years. His research has three critical findings: nonmilitary public capital stock is dramatically more important in determining productivity than the flow of either nonmilitary or military spending; military capital bears little relation to productivity; and core infrastructure spending has the most explanatory power for changes in national productivity. Aschauer has developed statistical support for the assertion that infrastructure spending causes productivity increases. Other authors have supported these results on both the national level (Munnell 1990) and the regional level (Eberts 1990). In recent popular press, Aschauer has claimed that for every dollar spent on roads, bridges, and sewers GNP in the United States will ultimately be increased by four dollars (Friedman and Black 1991).

Finally, empirical studies undertaken outside the U. S. have shown that infrastructure has various economic effects. A nine nation study undertaken by the European Economic Community from 1979 to 1985 (reported by Biehl 1986) was the first comprehensive study of all aspects of infrastructure—social, economic and intangible. Although effects differ between the categories, the results support the hypothesis that infrastructure impacts regional development. The study concludes that the better the infrastructure endowment of a region, the higher its development potential defined in terms of income, productivity and employment. Outside of Europe, Looney and Frederiksen (1981) used Mexican state data to support the contention that economic infrastructure was significant in explaining the variations in gross domestic product (GDP) in moderately healthy states but not in lagging states. Conversely, social infrastructure was significant in explaining income differences between lagging states but not healthy states. Findings similar to the Mexican results were found using Japanese data where infrastructure was judged to have a positive but varying effect depending on the region (Mera 1973). Data from India were used to argue that the slowdown in infrastructure investment from 1956 through 1980 caused stagnation in both heavy and consumer goods industries (Ahluwalia 1986). Nijkamp (1988) used data from the Netherlands to show that "information centers" (concentrations of knowledge and research and development infrastructure) have had a significant impact on industrial innovation and hence, productivity. Finally, a recent analysis of regions in Sweden has been used to show that total production in an information-driven economy is significantly influenced by road, airport and research and development capacity (Andersson, Anderstig and Harsman 1990).

The results of the studies discussed here are summarized in Table 2. There are several important implications from the results of these studies. First, ample evidence is provided that infrastructure effects economic activity at various levels—city, state, regional, and national. Second, **all** classes of infrastructure—economic, social, and intangible—have been identified to effect various kinds of economic activity from productivity through industrial innovation. The studies conducted in international settings are the most important to the premise of this paper, however. Not only do they focus on international markets, but more importantly, these studies highlight the effects of social and intangible infrastructure. Further, the social and intangible infrastructure effects identified in these studies relate to demand-side aspects of economic activity. In the Mexican study, income differences were associated with the level of social infrastructure (Looney and Frederiksen 1981). The Andersson, Anderstig, and Harsman (1990) study, links research and development capacity to economic productivity in Sweden. As discussed earlier, productivity plays an important role in the agglomeration effect of urbanization economies. This, in turn, increases the breadth and depth of demand for goods and services in a market. The Dutch study verified a similar effect on productivity for intangible infrastructure, but the effect in that case was related to industrial innovation (Nijkamp 1988).

INFRASTRUCTURE IN INTERNATIONAL MARKET ASSESSMENT

Current approaches to international market assessment concentrate exclusively on the supply-side effects of infrastructure (for example, see treatments in Cateora 1990; Dahringer and Muhlbacher 1991; Toyne and Walters 1989). These traditional treatments focus on infrastructure factors related to marketing infrastructure such as market research firms and retail options; transportation infrastructure which includes roads, seaports, and storage facilities; communications infrastructure which assesses media availability; and commercial infrastructure associated with such facilitators as banks and advertising agencies. Aside from focusing on supply-side factors, these traditional treatments concentrate solely on economic infrastructure to the exclusion of social and intangible infrastructure. Education and health systems, public welfare programs, computer networks, and research and development will all affect the environment within which demand will be manifest. Yet, they remain unaccounted for in approaches to market assessment. The point is not that these factors represent markets for goods and services themselves, which they do, but rather that business and consumer demand is affected by these factors. Just as the factors of economic infrastructure can impact the standard of living within a market, so too do the social and intangible infrastructure variables. Further, the productivity effects of infrastructure discussed earlier create an environment for carrying out marketing activities that impact the marketing operations of the firm. Recall the effect of urbanization economies on productivity. Urbanization is fostered by the social and intangible infrastructure and thus the breadth and depth

of demand for goods and services is affected. What is needed, therefore, is a broader perspective on infrastructure which recognizes both the supply-side and demand-side effects it has on the process of market transactions and thus market attractiveness.

Recognizing Supply-Side and Demand-Side Effects of Infrastructure in International Market Assessment

To fully incorporate the impact of infrastructure in foreign market assessment, both supply-side and demand-side effects must be recognized. This entails a determination of the ways in which infrastructure can affect a market transaction from both the supply and demand sides. Figure 1 offers such a perspective. This figure graphically represents that all three categories of infrastructure are related to the culmination of market transactions.

Infrastructure Impacts the Supply-Side of Market Transactions

This is the traditional view of the effect of infrastructure which is typically represented in even the most cursory assessment of international markets. Each link in the chain of activities carried out to supply goods and services to a market is effected by infrastructure. Here, we have added to the traditional perspective, how the social and intangible infrastructure factors are relevant to the supply-side of market transactions as well.

Overall Market Strategy. Strategic market management holds that firms must assess the demographic, economic, competitive, political, and regulatory environments of prospective markets. This is a traditional "environmental scan" that would rely mostly on secondary data. From such a scan, a standardized versus customized market approach will be determined. In addition, the more highly developed all forms of infrastructure are in a country, the more standardized (with some cultural variations) the overall market strategy can be. High levels of social and intangible infrastructure normally warrant a high standard of living and products and services suited to that standard of living.

Product Development and R&D. The firm will assess opportunities for existing products as well as the need to develop new products to match market conditions and opportunities. Social infrastructure (education) will determine the supply of trained development personnel. Intangible infrastructure will relate to technological, information and domestic research and development capabilities which will impact productivity. Communication infrastructures contribute to determining consumer needs and also how fast the development process can proceed.

Production. This factor is most directly affected by core infrastructure factors. Transportation infrastructure

TABLE 2
Empirical Findings Relating Infrastructure to Productivity and Private Investment

Level of Analysis	Infrastructure Factors	Effect
City (United States)		
Deno 1988	sewers and highways	private investment
Eberts 1986	core infrastructure	manufacturing output
Eberts and Fogarty 1987	core infrastructure	private investment
Hansen 1965	core infrastructure	manufacturing output
State (United States)		
Bartik 1985	state roads	business location decisions
CONSAD 1969	public works infrastructure	real income gains
Fox and Murray 1988	state roads	business location decisions
Garcia-Mila 1987	highways and schools	total output and personal income
Helms 1985	"	"
McGuire 1987	"	"
Regional (United States)		
Eberts 1990	public works infrastructure	household and corporate formation
Hulton and Schwab 1984	"	"
Martin 1979	"	"
Mera 1975	"	"
National (United States)		
Aschauer 1987, 1988, 1989	nonmilitary public capital stock	productivity/GNP
	core infrastructure	productivity/GNP
International		
Ahluwalia 1986	core infrastructure	India consumer and heavy industry growth
Andersson, et. al 1990	road, airport, R&D capacity	economic productivity in Sweden
Biehl 1986	social, economic, intangible	EEC regional development
Looney and Frederiksen 1981	economic, social infrastructure	Mexican state GDP and income differences
Mera 1973	core infrastructure	Japanese regional development
Nijkamp 1988	intangible infrastructure	Dutch industrial innovation

(economic) will determine how and how fast raw materials will reach the production facility. Energy and water infrastructure will determine where a production facility can be located, and what its capacity will be. Intangible infrastructure related to technological, information and R&D capabilities will again determine the technologies that can be used to produce the product. Social infrastructure will determine the supply of trained technical and non technical labor availability.

Distribution. In traditional supply-side analyses, transportation infrastructure is a primary assessment due to the need to distribute goods. Ports, railroads, air-transport and roadways will all impact supply--both for carrying out production and delivering finished goods to the next link in the channel. The level of development of the retail system is considered here as well.

Advertising and Promotion. Critical to bringing about a transaction from the supply-side perspective are advertising and promotion. Telecommunications infra-structure will determine the mode, content and reach of

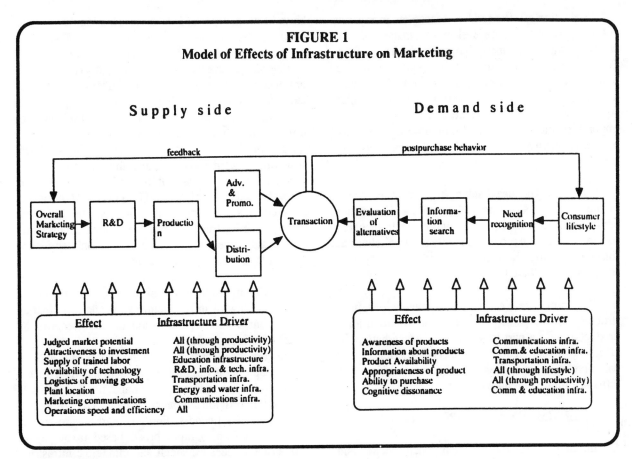

FIGURE 1
Model of Effects of Infrastructure on Marketing

Supply side   Demand side

marketing communications. If there are few televisions in households, radio or newspaper may be used. Newspapers are not used in most Third World nations due to the low literacy rate, which can be traced to a poor social infrastructure. Placards, posters and billboards suffer from the same problem. Promotion is also sensitive to infrastructure; direct mail requires an effective communications infrastructure (Douglas and Wind 1987). In Third World nations with poor development of all classes of infrastructure, firms must resort to in-store demonstrations of new goods for promotion because there are no other reliable means for reaching the consumer.

Infrastructure Impacts the Demand-Side of Market Transactions

Normally, firms will assess demand in a potential market with the same environmental scan that was cited in the supply-side assessment. Market potential is defined by demographics, cultural values, technological development, competitive intensity and other traditional measures. It has been argued from the outset, that while such an approach to demand assessment is necessary and useful, the effects of infrastructure, especially social and intangible factors, can add richness and breadth to such an evaluation. The demand-side effects of infrastructure can be incorporated by establishing the factor as a weighted component in market assessment approaches like the GE or Boston Consulting Group approach. Alternatively, demand-side effects of infrastructure can be examined by using a simple portrayal of consumer

decision making as illustrated in Figure 1. With such a portrayal, all classes of infrastructure, with particular emphasis on social and intangible infrastructure, can be considered.

Consumer Lifestyle. As the discussion of economic theory provided earlier emphasized, infrastructure indirectly determines consumer lifestyle through its effect on productivity and economic prosperity—disposable income and standard of living are affected by investment in infrastructure. Further, the empirical evidence of infrastructure effects suggested that social and intangible infrastructure relate to income and impact the prosperity in a society. Higher quality of life will, again, increase the breadth and depth of goods and services demanded.

Need Recognition. This level of behavior is a product of the lifestyle factor just discussed. One point that has not yet been raised is the extent to which a highly developed social infrastructure contributes to quality of life. High quality and accessible educational, health care, and social welfare systems allow citizens to pursue a higher level of human existence. Similarly, as the intangible infrastructure develops, information based societies will access and process information, including marketing information, in ways which must be understood and accommodated by firms hoping to cultivate demand within those markets.

Information Search. This constitutes the collection of relevant data available to the consumer. The education

Evaluation of Alternatives. Consumers in any market economy will, at some level, engage in the process of comparison and evaluation of products which meet needs. For consumer products, this often takes place in the shop or roadside stand. The local transportation infrastructure determines the variety and type of products on display. Again, education infrastructure and reading ability is important in the comparisons. Communication and information infrastructures will facilitate the evaluation process.

Purchase. The local banking/finance system as part of the core infrastructure will determine if currency, credit cards, debit cards, checks, or other instruments are part the transaction process. Equally as important as the financial system is the information and technology infrastructure to facilitate the process.

Post purchase Behavior. Communications infrastructure (in the form of available information about products) plays a part in soothing or exacerbating this effect and education does as well. The experiences from past purchases are fed back to Consumer Lifestyle to influence future purchases.

SUMMARY AND IMPLICATIONS

Infrastructure factors have traditionally been considered quite narrowly in the assessment of international markets. Normally, only *economic* infrastructure factors have been incorporated in the evaluation of markets. Further, these approaches to assessment have tended to concentrate on supply-side aspects of marketing goods and services. Effects on production, distribution, and promotion have been the primary concern of firms contemplating foreign market entry. Such a perspective on infrastructure, however, underplays the full range of infrastructure variables and subsequent demand-side effects on market transactions. *Social* and *intangible* infrastructure affect markets because they have effects on productivity and standard of living in a region. In turn, the width and depth of demand for goods and services is affected by these infrastructure factors. The social and intangible infrastructure can have as great an affect on market attractiveness as the more commonly employed economic factors of infrastructure.

Marketing strategists would be well served by taking a broader view of infrastructure as it relates to market assessment. A conceptualization of the effects of all forms of infrastructure has been proposed which offers a framework for identifying both the supply-side and demand-side effects on market transactions. With such a framework, type and level of demand, not just ability to supply, will provide a broader basis for a determination of market attractiveness. Further, market assessments will benefit from a more broad based taxonomy of infrastructure because social and intangible infrastructure are explicitly recognized as affecting demand.

REFERENCES

Andersson, Ake E., Christer Anderstig and Bjorn Harsman (1990), "Knowledge and Communications Infrastructure and Regional Economic Change," *Regional Science and Urban Economics,* 20 (November), 350-376.

Ahluwalia, Isher Judge (1986), "Industrial Growth in India: Performance and Prospects," *Journal of Development Economics*, 23 (September), 1-18.

Aschauer, David A. (1989), "Is Public Expenditure Productive?," *Journal of Monetary Economics*, 23 (March), 177-200.

_____(1987), "Is the Public Capital Too Low?," *Chicago Fed Letter*, 4 (2), 1-5.

_____(1988), "Rx for Productivity: Build Infrastructure," *Chicago Fed Letter*, 5 (13), 1-3.

Bartik, Timothy J. (1985), "Business Location Decisions in the United States: Estimates of the Effects of Unionization, Taxes and Other Characteristics of States," *Journal of Business and Economic Statistics*, 3 (January), 14-22.

Biehl, Dieter (1986), *The Contribution of Infrastructure to Regional Development.* Luxembourg: Office for Official Publications of the European Communities.

Carlino, Gerald A. (1987), "Productivity in Cities: Does City Size Matter?," *Business Review (Federal Reserve Bank of Philadelphia)*, (November/December), 3-12.

Cateora, Philip R. (1990), *International Marketing,* Seventh Edition (Homewood, IL: Richard D. Irwin, Inc.)

CONSAD, Research Corporation. (1969). "A Study of the Effects of Public Investment." Office of Economic Research, Economic Development Administration.

Costa, Jose da Silva, Richard W. Ellson and Randolph C. Martin (1987), "Public Capital, Regional Output, and Development: Some Empirical Evidence," *Journal of Regional Science*, 27 (August), 419-430.

Dallenberg, Douglas (1987), "Estimates of Elasticities of Substitution Between Public and Private Inputs in the Manufacturing Sector of Metropolitan Areas," unpublished PhD dissertation, University of Oregon.

Dahringer, Lee and Hans Muhlbacher (1991), *International Marketing: A Global Perspective,* Reading, MA: Addison-Wesley Publishing Company, Inc..

Davidson, Pamela J. (1989), "Growth Centers and Rural Development," *Economic Development Review*, 7 (Fall), 46-50.

Douglas, Susan and Yoram Wind (1987), "The Myth of Globalization," *Columbia Journal of World Business,* 22, 4 (Winter), 19-30.

Deno, Kevin T. (1986), "The Short Run Relationship Between Investment in Public Infrastructure and the Formation of Private Capital," unpublished PhD dissertation, University of Oregon.

_____(1988), "The Effect of Public Capital on U.S. Manufacturing Activity: 1970-1978," *Southern Economic Journal*, 55 (October), 400-411.

Eberts, Randall W. (1986). "Estimating the Contribution of Urban Public Infrastructure to Regional Growth," Working Paper 8610, Federal Reserve Bank of Cleveland.

_____(1990), "Public Infrastructure and Regional Economic Development," *Economic Review (by the Federal Reserve Bank of Cleveland)*, 26 (1), 15-27.

_____and Michael S. Fogarty. (1987). "Estimating the Relationship Between Local Public and Private Investment," Working Paper 8703, Federal Reserve of Cleveland.

Fox, William F. and Matthew N. Murray (1988). "Local Public Policies and Interregional Business Development," report, University of Tennessee.

Garcia-Mila, Teresa and Therese J. McGuire (1987). "The Contribution of Publicly Provided Inputs to States' Economies," report # 292. State University of New York at Stony Brook.

Hansen, Niles M. (1965), "Unbalanced Growth and Regional Development," *Western Economic Journal*, 4 (Fall), 3-14.

Helms, L. Jay (1985), "The Effect of State and Local Taxes on Economic Growth: A Time-Series Cross Section Approach," *Review of Economics and Statistics*, 67 (November), 574-582.

Hulton, Charles R. and Robert M. Schwab (1984), "Regional Productivity Growth," *American Economic Review*, 74 (March), 152-162.

Looney, Robert and Peter Frederiksen (1981), "The Regional Impact of Infrastructure Investment in Mexico," *Regional Studies*, 14 (4), 285-296.

Martin, Randolph C. (1979), "Federal Regional Development Programs and U.S. Problem Areas," *Journal of Regional Science*, 19 (May), 157-170.

Meade, J.E. (1952), "External Economies and Diseconomies in a Competitive Situation," *Economic Journal*, 62 (March), 54-67.

Mera, Koichi (1973), "Regional Production Functions and Social Overhead Capital: An Analysis of the Japanese Case," *Regional and Urban Economics*, 3 (May), 157-185.

_____(1975), *Income Distribution and Regional Development*. Tokyo: University of Tokyo Press.

Munnell, Alicia (1990), "Why Has Productivity Growth Declined? Productivity and Public Investment," *New England Economic Review (Federal Reserve Bank of Boston)*, (January/February), 3-22.

Nijkamp, Peter (1988), "Information Center Policy in a Spatial Development," *Economic Development & Cultural Change*, 37, 173-193.

Rainer, George (1989), *Understanding Infrastructure-A Guide for Architects and Planners*. New York: John Wiley and Sons.

Reich, Robert B. (1991), "The REAL Economy," *The Atlantic Monthly*, 35-41.

Tobin, James, Alan S. Blinder, Jack A. Meyer, et al. (1989), "A Warning About America's Third Deficit From 327 Prominent Economists," in *Public Investment in Human and Physical Infrastructure: a Hearing before the Joint Economic Committee of the Congress of the United States*, Washington, DC: U.S. Government Printing Office.

Toyne, Brian and Peter G. P. Walters (1989), *Global Marketing Management: A Strategic Perspective*, Boston, MA: Allyn and Bacon.

Webley, Simon (1985), *Stiffening the Sinews of the Nations: Economic Infrastructure in the US, UK and Canada*. London: Contemprint Limited.

THE ROLE OF COUNTRY OF ORIGIN INFORMATION ON BUYERS' PRODUCT EVALUATION: AN IN-DEPTH INTERVIEW APPROACH

Wai-kwan Li, *University Of Illinois at Urbana-Champaign*
Kent B. Monroe, *University Of Illinois at Urbana-Champaign*

ABSTRACT

Although survey studies have suggested consumers use country-of-origin cues to *signal* product quality, experimental studies have found that consumers perceived country of origin as a product *attribute*. However, this study using in-depth interviews provides evidence that supports both signalling and attribute roles, depending on the technology level of the product.

INTRODUCTION

Recent globalization of business has brought about important changes in manufacturing locations of products. With these changes, marketing managers need to consider whether buyers' evaluations of a product are influenced by knowing the country in which it is made. Although previous research has provided evidence of country-of-origin effects on product evaluations, there is no converging conclusion about how country of origin (COO) affects buyers' product evaluations (Bilkey and Nes 1982; Ozsomer and Cavusgil 1991).

Johansson (1989, p. 55) argued that COO may function as a "summary cue" that is used by consumers to guess the attributes of a product (a cognitive "inference" effect); or, to simplify information processing (a cognitive "proxy" effect)". Parallel to Johansson's (1989) propositions, Han (1989), using telephone interviews, found that COO may function as a "halo" or a "summary construct". Essentially, the "halo" model describes how buyers infer beliefs from the country image, whereas the "summary construct" model is used to abstract product information into a country image, which is the same as Johansson's cognitive "inference" and "proxy" effects, respectively. Finally, using conjoint analysis, Havlena and DeSarbo (1991) found that COO (together with newness of brand) functioned as an "indicator" of perceived risk. In short, these three conceptualizations suggest similar effects: COO may indicate perceived quality in product evaluations. This tentative conclusion parallels findings in the pricing literature that price (another extrinsic attribute) may serve as a signal of perceived quality (Rao and Monroe 1989; Zeithaml 1988). However, what the COO cue actually indicates to buyers remains unexplored. Does this cue signify overall product quality, the quality of intrinsic attributes, performance risk, or something else? The present study, therefore, attempts to determine what is the specific signalling effect of the COO cue on buyers' product evaluations.

On the other hand, four experimental studies that focus on how consumers use COO information consistently report that COO was used as a product attribute in product evaluations (Hong and Wyer 1989, 1990; Li, Leung and Wyer 1991; Li and Wyer 1991). This finding is consistent with Johansson's (1989) point that COO may also be regarded as a salient product attribute, implying that COO may provide some unique perceived benefits to consumers. The present study tries to provide some insights into what these unique perceived benefits are.

The divergent findings between experimental and survey research may be due to their methodological differences. Moreover, as suggested by Johansson's (1989) integrative framework, it is possible, at least theoretically, for COO to play both a signalling and an attribute role. However, no previous research has provided support for this dual effect on product evaluations. Therefore, we will investigate the effects that COO may have on product evaluations by a different approach, in-depth interviews. One of the advantages of this method is its power for attaining an in-depth understanding of another person's experiences (Kvale 1983; Thompson, Locander, and Pollio 1989). By trying to understand buyers' actual experiences related to the effect of COO information, we should be able to determine whether the signalling and attribute roles can be observed simultaneously, if they do exist.

Therefore, the purposes of this study are: (1) specify what COO signals to consumers; (2) reveal what perceived benefits COO provides; and (3) investigate whether COO can play both signalling and attribute roles in product evaluations.

COO as a Signal of Product Quality

Scitovszky (1945) postulated that consumers might not be able to assess product quality directly, and, therefore, use surrogate measures, such as company size, market success and price. Hence, when consumers have difficulties in understanding the benefits of its intrinsic attributes, such as evaluating an unfamiliar product, they may use the product's extrinsic attributes as an indicator of product quality (Rao and Monroe 1989).

Although Johansson (1989) postulated that COO may be used by customers to infer product quality, it is unclear whether he referred to overall product quality, or the quality of some attributes. Similarly, Han (1989) proposed that COO can be used to infer the beliefs about a product, but which beliefs are to be inferred has not been specified. In another framework, Ozsomer and Cavusgil (1991) posed that COO can affect buyers' beliefs, as well as their attitudes toward a brand. However, they have not specified what beliefs would be affected. If COO influences only some beliefs, then the interesting question is: What are these beliefs?

COO as a Product Attribute

COO usually appears as a "made in" label on a product. It is difficult to imagine what benefits it can provide to consumers as a product attribute. Nevertheless, four experimental studies reported that this cue, just like other product attributes, was used as an attribute in product evaluations (Hong and Wyer 1989, 1990; Li et al. 1991; Li and Wyer 1991). This finding implies that COO, per se, may provide some benefits to consumers. Although no empirical data has reported what benefits COO may provide, Johansson (1989) proposed two possibilities, namely, affect (i.e. like or dislike) and norms.

First, COO can be a salient product attribute that can influence liking directly. For example, Americans may like American cars because of patriotism. Second, COO can be incorporated into the social norms directly. Specifically, the social norms may impose what are the "acceptable" and "unacceptable" COOs for a product. Therefore, the COO cue can be expected to exert its influence on product evaluations apart from any influence on quality perceptions. Although these two possibilities seem plausible, they need to be verified.

METHOD

The research process employed was basically iterative and flexible. A pilot in-depth interview was conducted to obtain some responses and comments. Based on that, some essential issues were identified and were organized into an initial interview framework. After interviewing five informants, the initial framework was revised to focus on four emerging themes. The revised framework was used for interviewing the next thirteen interviewees. Overall, nine male and nine female students enrolled in an introductory business course at a major mid-western university were interviewed.

The Initial Interview Framework

Interviewees were first asked to name a set of countries that could manufacture products of good quality, and then another set of countries that manufacture products of inferior quality. The objective of these two questions was to activate the schemata (a mental representation of linkages among different COOs) of "good" COOs and "bad" COOs. They were then asked to suggest some quality products from a "good" COO, and inferior

products from a "bad" COO. The objective was to determine what products might be familiar to the subjects, so as to facilitate subsequent inquiry. Informants then were invited to select a product that they would like to discuss in detail and to reveal what made them believe some countries could manufacture quality products but some countries could not. To obtain reliable and rich information, subjects were asked to talk about two to three different products. The respondents were then asked whether they agreed a "bad" country could also manufacture some quality products. If the response was positive, they were asked to provide some examples, and elaborate what made them believe so. At this stage, informants would have had two groups of countries in mind: the "good" and "bad" countries. They would also have two categories of products in mind: the quality products from "good" countries that "bad" countries could not manufacture in good quality, and the quality products that a "bad" country could manufacture or produce. They were asked to provide labels to these two groups of countries, as well as to the two categories of products, and to contrast the differences between them. The reason for asking informants to suggest labels is to capture a higher level of abstractions than the specific countries and products (Zeithaml 1988).

Revision of Initial Framework

A rough idea about the signalling role of COO emerged after interviewing the first five informants. It seems that both the "good" and "bad" country schemata did exist. Interesting enough, an informant said there were some products which any country could manufacture in equally good quality. Therefore, one more product category was added to the framework (quality products from "good" and "bad" countries). Furthermore, informants believed that in manufacturing the three categories of products, different types of skills were required. They believed that unless workers could master a particular type of skills, a country would not be able to manufacture that category of products in high quality. It seems that the beliefs about the possession of necessary manufacturing skills is a critical factor in product evaluations; therefore, it is necessary to uncover what these beliefs are.

One informant confirmed that COO could function as an attribute.

I like American clothing, I can't explain...I like Mexican rugs and blankets, their color is more bright, lively, and cheerful, that makes you happy. (S1)

Given this initial information, the interview framework was revised to focus on four emergent themes:

(1) The specific characteristics of the "good" and "bad" countries;

(2) The specific characteristics of the three categories of products;

(3) The skills required to manufacture the three categories of products;

(4) The perceived benefits provided by a COO.

The first three themes address a COO's role as a signal for product quality, whereas the fourth theme deals with a COO's role as a product attribute.

The Framework

First, subjects were asked to suggest some "good" and "bad" countries for producing quality products. Then, they were asked to provide labels for these two groups of countries. Second, they were asked to name (a) some products that only the "good" countries could manufacture in good quality, (b) some products that only the "bad" countries could manufacture in good quality, and (c) some products that any country could manufacture in high quality. They were then asked to label each category of products, and to compare the major differences of the three categories of products. Third, they were asked to specify, and suggest a label for, the skills and resources that would be involved in manufacturing these three categories of products.

To understand how the name of a country may function as a product attribute, some products that some particular countries are famous for were suggested by the interviewer (e.g., Swiss watch, Mexican poncho, Mexican tequila). Subjects were asked whether they would prefer that product from that specific country, from another country, or whether they would be indifferent, provided that everything is about the same. After they had stated their preferences, they were asked to explain why they made such choices.

RESULTS

COO as a Signal

Information obtained from the interviews was very consistent. Informants had similar opinions about what were the "good" and "bad" COOs. They also had convergent perceptions about what are the quality products from "good" and "bad" COOs. Furthermore, all informants agreed that different type of skills are required for manufacturing different categories of products.

Country Classification. All eighteen informants said Japan can manufacture quality products, twelve of them believed that Germany can, and ten thought the United States can also. Subjects gave similar labels to this group of "good" countries, which implies that the meaning abstracted from this group of countries is similar, although the specific countries mentioned might differ.

Typical examples of labels include advanced countries, industrial countries, and developed countries. They described this group of countries as wealthy, developed, industrialized, and with a high technological level. In these countries people have more education and higher living standards, and generally do not have to worry about basic needs (such as food). Workers are well trained and efficient, have sufficient manufacturing experiences and good work attitudes. The manufacturing processes are automated and scientific.

Informants' suggestions about "bad" COOs were much more diversified. Nine informants mentioned at least one South East Asian country (e.g., Taiwan, Korea), eight suggested Mexico, five said Central or South American countries. Other countries mentioned include African countries, the Soviet Union, Eastern European countries, and India. Three informants gave a general category of countries, such as, less developed countries, third world countries. Despite the diversified nature of the countries they named, they gave similar labels to them. Typical examples were undeveloped countries, and underdeveloped countries. They described this group of countries as poor, less developed, not industrialized, and have little technology. People have little education, poor living conditions and worry about food. Workers have little training or production experience. Although labor is cheap, the quality is low, and inefficient. The manufacturing processes are labor intensive and chaotic.

To sum up, interviewees had "good" and "bad" COO schemata in their minds. In general, they classified countries as industrialized or undeveloped countries. They perceived the industrialized countries as having high technology, well-trained and educated workers, with state-of-the-art manufacturing processes. In contrast, undeveloped countries have little technology, workers have little training and education, and manufacturing processes are primitive.

Product Categorization. Informants agreed that there are some products that only industrialized countries can manufacture in high quality. On the other hand, they believed there are some products that people in undeveloped countries can make, with a quality better than those from industrialized countries. However, only some interviewees reported that there are some products people in different countries produce equally well.

The major examples of the first category of products include cars, electronic products, computers. Examples of these labels include: hi-tech products, technical advanced products, and complex products. It seems appropriate to label this category of products as high-technology products. The informants described these products as of high complexity and high technology. These products require much research and development, and a large amount of processing is involved. One subject mentioned that the certainty of quality of these products is important.

The examples of the second category of products are handicrafts like rugs, blankets, ponchos, hand-made sweaters. Two informants mentioned some agricultural or food products like coffee, bananas, and liquor. Examples of the labels they gave to this category were quite different: handicrafts, hand-made products, and cultural products. It seems appropriate to label this category of products as handicrafts. This label seems to fit with how they described these products. The subjects described this category of products as of low complexity, low technology, requiring little research and development, and little processing is involved. One subject mentioned that the certainty of quality of these products is not so important.

The third category of products was only mentioned by five subjects. In their opinion, either the COO does not affect their evaluations, or they do not care about where they come from. Subjects suggested a variety of products: pen and pencils, tables and chairs, thread, yarn, scissors, pots and pans, hardware, food products, gymnastics shoes. It may be that this category is too diversified, and, therefore, it is difficult to abstract a single label for it. The informants could not suggest a label for these products, even when they were encouraged to do so. An informant said it does not require too many steps to make these products. In order to facilitate the following discussion, this category of products is labelled as "simple" products. It should be noted that the low percentage of mentioning this category of products may reflect that these products were not associated with any country. This speculation is consistent with why they think COO would not affect their evaluations of these products.

In short, subjects identified three categories of products, namely, high-technology products, handicrafts, and "simple" products. While industrialized countries are good at manufacturing high-technology products, undeveloped countries are competent at making handicrafts. There also exists some products that both group of countries can do equally well.

Types of Skills. What leads the informants to categorize the products into these three categories? One of the possible reasons is the products require different skills and resources.

To be able to manufacture high quality high-technology products, informants said the workers should be well-educated, and have sufficient specific training. Manufacturers should have rich capital resources, state of the art technology, advance equipment, and ample industrial knowledge. They labelled this type of skill as technical skill, mental skill, or scientific skill. They believed these skills are difficult to learn and require formal training. It may be suitable to label these skills as technical skills.

To produce handicrafts in high quality, informants said the skills involved are different. Informants said raw

material must be available, like straw for making African baskets, wool for making Mexican ponchos. In addition, rich tradition, heritage, experience, and a lot of time and effort are required for making handicrafts. They labelled these skills as hand skills, culture-related skills, or skills that are traditional. They believed these skills are passed down from one generation to another, which are inside their culture. They can be learned from experience, practice, or just observation, little formal training is required. It seems reasonable to call these necessary skills as traditional skills.

Culture-related skills are something they are born with, they live with, they play with... As they grow up, they will learn. They learn from their parents. (S18)

For manufacturing "simple" products, unlike in manufacturing high-technology products, neither high technology nor much capital would be required. In contrast to handicrafts, not much traditional skills are necessary. Based on the description by an informant, it may be reasonable to label this type of skill as blue-collar skill.

It only requires some basic knowledge, it is a combination of technical and cultural skills. (S18)

To summarize, three different types of skill were believed to be required for manufacturing the three categories of products in good quality. Technical skills are required for manufacturing high-technology products; traditional skills are necessary for making handicrafts; blue-collar skills are associated with "simple" products.

The Signalling Process. As reported above, informants classified different countries as industrialized or undeveloped countries. They believed these two groups of countries are good at manufacturing either high-technological or handicraft products. They also agreed that different skills are required for manufacturing these three categories of products in high quality. It seems that "skills" is the intervening variable between COO and perceived quality of products. It was the belief about whether a country possesses that particular skill or not, that affected the perceived quality of products from that country. For example, consumers may not believe an undeveloped country possesses technical skills:

I don't think they [people in any developing countries] have the industrial knowledge to make good cars. They don't have the capital to set up the factory, ability to transport cars to my country, they don't have the knowledge to run a factory... (S6) I prefer a Honda from Japan or Canada. I doubt about the quality of a Honda from Mexico. It's the stereotype that make me hesitate. The country and people have not manufactured cars before, so I hesitate if they can make it. (S17)

Mexican workers have little education. That makes me difficult to believe they can produce cars of good quality. They always ask for help, food, and money, how can these people who need so much help be able to produce a car? How can they build a car if they can't even build a shelter? (S1)

On the other hand, informants may doubt whether industrialized countries still possess traditional skills:

Education takes away a person's creativity with their hands... that makes them [Americans] have little ability to make good handicrafts. (S1)

Another subject emotionally confessed we do have these beliefs in our mind:

Japanese are mass production, efficient; Swiss are slow, but detail, as a child sees in the cartoon. It's our special beliefs about countries. We assume without any facts. It's illogical! It's wrong! (S11)

It is reasonable to conclude that the signalling process of COO on product evaluations is as follows: The presence of a COO label activates consumers' beliefs schema. They will then consider whether that country has the appropriate type of skill or not. If they believe the country has the necessary skill, they will believe it can manufacture quality products. To sum up, the signalling process suggest the following relationships:

Country Cue --> Beliefs About Possession of Skills --> Perceived Quality

COO as a Product Attribute

Consistent with the earlier experimental studies, informants' responses in the present study also indicate they would consider COO as a product attribute which can lead to different kinds of benefits, namely, authenticity, exoticness, personalization, patriotism, and enhanced social standing. While the first four kinds of benefits can be regarded as different kinds of affect, the last one can be considered as conforming to social norms.

Authenticity. A consumer may prefer a product simply because the product originates from a particular country. Owning a product from the original country may provide a feeling of owning an authentic product.

Italian "Mexican style" clothes should be of better quality, but I think I would lose "something" from that. It's not real. It's not the natural thing. (S6) I prefer Ireland sweater to Italian/French "Irish style" sweater... it roots from Ireland....(S9) I prefer Mexican tequila to California tequila, because it is originated there, ... I appreciate this old fashion, traditional things....(S9) I prefer Mexican tequila to tequila from other countries. More tradition, heritage

inside. A kind of learn and pass down. (S11)

Exoticness. Consumers may prefer a product from a special place just because they want to have something different, or because they feel they can "buy" the culture through purchasing the product.

I like Mexican ponchos, it has some "ethnic". Its exoticness makes me like it more. France and Italy can make good ponchos, but not a Mexican poncho. I would buy a Mexican poncho, but not a France made "mexican" poncho. (S10) I prefer Mexican tequila to California tequila. I want to have something exotic, something different. (S16) I like throw rugs and blankets from Mexico. They have a western and Spanish style. I would like that kind of style in my room... (S1)

Personalization. Consumers may prefer a product from a certain country because they assume products from that original country are hand-made. That hand-made characteristic makes them feel closer to the producer, and they also appreciated the time and effort required to make the product.

You feel closer to the producer, more value. It's an affective feeling. It [Swiss watch] is hand-made, more time and effort is involved, that make me appreciate it more. (S9) I like those [Mexican] blankets, rugs, ponchos. They are hand-made. I like them because someone really put time in it, more "meaning" and effort. (S3) ... Swiss watches is preferred to Japanese watches... not mass-produced. They are hand-crafted... They (Swiss) made watches for church... It has personal, intrinsic meaning, more value, more symbolic meaning,...sentimental value...(S11)

Patriotism. Consumers may prefer to purchase a product made in their home country due to patriotic reasons. First, they want to show support for their home country, and therefore prefer the product from that country to other COOs. Second, they may want to identify with their country. An informant who is a second generation of an Italian immigrated family:

I would always prefer Italian products, because I would like to associate with Italy. (S15)

Enhanced Social Standing. Some consumers may prefer a product that can enhance their social standing. Hence a consumer owning a product from a reputable COO, which is also known for its expensiveness, may feel his/her social standing is enhanced. This observation may explain a common phenomenon why people may prefer Italian shoes or Swiss watches.

I prefer Italian shoes to British shoes. They have better reputation. I may feel better. (S16) I prefer

Swiss watch to Japanese watch. No one heard of a Japanese Rolex, but everybody knows Swiss Rolex. People may buy things based on their status. They will buy more expensive clothes, for better standing. They want to look good, enhance their social standing. (S17)

To sum up, the attribute role suggests the following relationships:

Country Cue --> Perceived Benefits

CONCLUSIONS

Based on the information given by the informants in the present study, there is evidence to believe that COO can serve as a signal for possession of relevant skills, as well as a product attribute for product evaluations.

For a COO label to be able to signal any information, it has to be either categorized as an industrialized country or undeveloped country. For example, if it is categorized as an industrialized country, beliefs about its possession of technical skills will be activated, which implies a country has the ability to manufacture high-technology products. Therefore, consumers will tend to believe that country can manufacture quality high technology products. However, being an industrialized country may also signal it has less traditional skills; hence, consumers will doubt the quality of handicrafts from these countries. Thus, the classification of the COO will signal the possession of the relevant skills, which affects one's evaluation of products.

Besides being a signal, COO can also serve as a product attribute, which may bring in at least five different perceived benefits: authenticity, exoticness, personalization, patriotism, or enhanced one's social standing.

It is worth mentioning that none of the products wherein COO seemed as an attribute were high technology products: Mexican clothes, ponchos, tequila, rugs and blankets, Irish sweaters, Italian shoes, and Swiss watches. We speculate that COO may only function as a product attribute in evaluating non-technical products. This speculation may explain why the non-experimental studies, in which either automobiles or televisions were used (Ozsomer and Cavusgil 1991, p. 274), gave little support for COO to function as an attribute. It seems that when the products are of high technology, COO is more likely to function as a signal of possessing (or not possessing) technical skills. In fact, based on the interview information, when the products are automobiles or electronic products, informants tended to think about whether the COO has the technical skill or not. However, when they talked about handicrafts, they would think about whether the COO has the traditional skills, as well as the perceived benefits. This finding indicates that when the product is a handicraft, subjects use COO as a signal as well as an attribute. Therefore, it seems that the cognitive processes in evaluating high technology products and handicrafts are different.

LIMITATIONS AND DIRECTIONS FOR FUTURE RESEARCH

The present study may generate more questions than answers. First, the proposed signalling process is based on the information provided by 18 introductory business students. Although we believe the sample was not contaminated by the course content, we have to acknowledge that the external validity of our findings is limited. Second, special concern should be paid to the "simple" products and the skills involved. Since only a limited number of informants mentioned this issue, the idea still needs more development. Third, the speculation that product type would lead to different cognitive processes should also be examined in a more careful manner.

REFERENCES

Bilkey, Warren J. and Erik Nes (1982), "Country-Of-Origin Effects on Product Evaluations," *Journal of International Business Studies*, 13 (Spring), 89-99.

Han, C. Min (1989), "Country Image: Halo or Summary Construct?" *Journal of Marketing Research*, 26 (May), 222-229.

Havlena, William J. and Wayne S. Desarbo (1991), "On the Measurement of Perceived Consumer Risk," *Decision Sciences*, 22 (September/October), 927-939.

Hong, Sung-tai and Robert S. Wyer (1989), "Effects of Country-of-Origin and Product-Attribute Information on Product Evaluation: An Information Processing Perspective." *Journal of Consumer Research*, 16 (September), 175-187.

_____ and _____ (1990), "Determinants of Product Evaluation: Effects of the Time Interval Between Knowledge of a Product's CO and Information about its Specific Attributes," *Journal of Consumer Research*, 17 (December), 277-288.

Johansson, Johny K. (1989), "Determinants and Effects of the Use of 'Made in' Labels," *International Marketing Review*, 6 (January), 47-58.

Kvale, Steinar (1983), "The Qualitative Research Interview: A Phenomenological and A Hermeneutical Mode of Understanding," *Journal of Phenomenological Psychology*, 14 (Fall), 171-196.

Li, Wai-kwan, Kwok Leung, and Robert S. Wyer, Jr. (1991), "Country-Of-Origin Effects on Product Evaluations: The Role of Motivation and Information Load," Working paper, University of Illinois at Urbana-Champaign.

_____and Robert S. Wyer, Jr. (1991), "Country-Of-Origin Effects on Product Evaluations: The Role of Information Load, Decision Importance, and Product Familiarity," Working paper, University of Illinois.

Ozsomer, Aysegul and S. Tamer Cavusgil (1991), "Country-Of-Origin Effects on Product Evaluations: A Sequel to Bilkey and Nes Review," in *AMA Educators' Proceedings: Enhancing Knowledge Development in Marketing, Volume 2*, Mary Gilly et al., eds. Chicago: 269-277.

Rao, Akshay R. and Kent B. Monroe (1989), "The Effect of Price, Brand Name, and Store Name on Buyers' Perceptions of Product Quality: An Integrative Review," *Journal of Marketing Research*, 26 (August), 351-357.

Scitovszky, Tibor (1945), "Some Consequences of the Habit of Judging Quality by Price," *Review of Economic Studies*, 12 (Winter), 100-105.

Thompson, Craig J., William B. Locander and Howard R. Pollio (1989), "Putting Consumer Experience Back into Consumer Research: The Philosophy and Method of Existential-Phenomenology," *Journal of Consumer Research*, 16 (September), 133-146.

Zeithaml, Valarie A. (1988), "Consumer Perceptions of Price, Quality, and Value: A Means-End Model and Synthesis of Evidence," *Journal of Marketing*, 52 (July), 2-22.

SCALE DEVELOPMENT, UNIDIMENSIONALITY, AND CONFIRMATORY FACTOR ANALYSIS: AN APPLICATION OF THE GERBING AND ANDERSON PARADIGM

Carl E. Ferguson, Jr., University of Alabama
Robert A. Robicheaux, University of Alabama
Jay U. Sterling, University of Alabama

ABSTRACT

The development and validation of trait and attitude measures has concerned marketing and social science researchers for many years. And, in recent years, considerable attention has also been focused on the testing the unidimensionality of linear summates or composite scale scores. Traditionally, scale development has relied on exploratory factor analysis, item-total correlations, and coefficient alpha. However, Gerbing and Anderson (1988) argue that a "composite score is meaningful only if each of the measures is acceptably unidimensional" and that only a confirmatory factor analysis of a multiple indicator measurement model directly tests unidimensionality. What can one expect from the revised paradigm? This paper reports on one such application.

METHODOLOGY

A national premium pet food manufacturer was interested in measuring performance attributes and criteria. Candidate items were drawn from each of the functional areas of marketing: pricing, product, promotion, and distribution follow extensive focus group sessions with management and veterinarians nationwide. The selected measures were structured as Likert items using a balanced 7 point rating scale. The final questionnaire included 129 performance measures.

A national mailing to 1,000 veterinarians resulted in 512 completed questionnaires. Of these 512, 276 contained complete data on all 129 performance items. Following the traditional scale development paradigm, an exploratory principal components factor analysis with varimax rotation was used to reduce the large number of measures to a more manageable set of latent factors (Churchill 1979).

RESULTS

Twenty-four factors were identified based on eigenvalues greater than 1. The twenty-four factors accounted for 64 percent of the total variance. For the purpose of this illustration, the discussion is limited to the first two factors. Factor 1 was identified as a price and trade discounts factor and accounted for 10.6 percent of the total variance. Factor 2 was interpreted as sales force knowledge and integrity and accounted for 7.4 percent of the total variance. All cross loadings were less than .3 in magnitude. Linear composites were computed for each factor. Standardized Cronbach's alpha for the price and sales force scales were .91 and .90 respectively. Based on traditional scale development criteria, the scales were considered to be theoretically and statistically sound.

Following the updated paradigm, a congeneric multiple indicator confirmatory measurement model was estimated with Lisrel 7 to test the unidimensionality of the scale items. The resulting parameter estimates, t-values, item reliabilities (squared multiple correlations), modification indices, and normalized residuals strongly suggested that the items failed to meet Gerbing and Anderson's criteria for unidimensionality. With 376 degrees of freedom, the model produced a C^2 of 1,146. There were 6 constrained factor loadings with modification indices greater than 5.. And, of the 406 off-diagonal elements of Q_d, 87 were greater than or equal to 5. Twenty-four had a value of 10 or greater.

CONCLUSION

The confirmatory factor model requires that each indicators manifest a single common factor and that the unique variances of each indicant be random. These data are not consistent with this model. Under the revised paradigm, one must conclude that the composite scales constructed from the items are not unidimensional. Most researchers would find this to be an unsettling conclusion given the extraordinarily clean exploratory factor structure and the high item-correlations and reliability coefficients.

While Gerbing and Anderson (1988) suggest this approach to testing for unidimensionality, they did not offer specific criteria for evaluating the confirmatory analysis or revised steps for item selection and scale development. Such criteria and procedures must be developed if this new paradigm is to be fully embraced.

For further information contact:
Carl E. Ferguson, Jr.
The University of Alabama
Box 870225
Tuscaloosa, AL 35487-0225

THE EFFECT OF RESCALING ON THE MEASUREMENT AND FIT STATISTICS OF CAUSAL MODELS: AN EXPLORATORY STUDY

Manjit S. Yadav, Texas A&M University

ABSTRACT

Rescaling procedures quantify qualitative data and have been shown to aid theory testing by improving measures' internal consistency and convergent and discriminant validity. This paper investigates the applicability of rescaling to theory development and testing using causal models. Results of an exploratory empirical study suggest that, as expected, rescaling improves the measurement part of the causal model. Changes in the statistics of overall fit, which may depend on the veracity of the causal model's underlying theory, show no clear pattern. Based on the results of this exploratory study, several directions for future research are identified.

INTRODUCTION

Fully explicating the conceptual content of a construct, carefully selecting multiple items capturing that content, and providing clear instructions to the subjects or respondents, are some standard practices usually recommended for the development of good measures (e.g., Churchill 1979; Nunnally 1978; Peter 1981). To complement such standard practices, rescaling procedures have been presented in the marketing research literature as valuable methodological tools for improving measures' internal consistency and convergent and discriminant validity (Didow, Keller, Barksdale, and Franke 1985; Didow, Perreault, and Williamson 1983; Franke 1985). Some researchers have argued that, in addition to these methodological reasons, there may also be a behavioral rationale for rescaling marketing research data (e.g., Yadav and Franke 1989). Marketing data frequently tend to be qualitative (e.g., ordinal or nominal), although interval-level properties are often assumed. Rescaling procedures are useful because they allow a researcher to explicitly examine such measurement assumptions, and also to improve the internal consistency of the measures.

This paper explores the usefulness of rescaling procedures in theory development and testing using structural equations models. Specifically, the paper examines the effect of rescaling on (1) the measurement and (2) structural equations portions of a causal model. Towards this end, some issues related to measurement and rescaling are first presented followed by details of two commonly-used rescaling procedures. We then provide a brief discussion of the role rescaling procedures can play in the development and testing of causal models. Finally, results of an exploratory study are presented in which the effect of rescaling on the measurement and fit statistics

of a causal model is investigated.

RESCALING: THEORETICAL BACKGROUND

Before the exploratory empirical study is presented, it may be useful to consider the relationship (and distinction) between measurement and rescaling provided by Young (1984).[2] "Measurement is the process that uses rules to assign numbers to attributes of things or events observed in circumstances assumed by the observer to be <u>quantitative</u>," whereas scaling "uses rules to assign numbers to attributes of things or events observed in circumstances assumed by the observer to be <u>qualitative</u>" (pp. 55-56, emphasis added).

The terms quantitative and qualitative, however, are relative (Young 1984). For example, assuming that a measuring tape provides quantitative information, measuring the length of a line with one can be said to provide a measurement of how long that line is. However, one could argue that categories provided on the measuring tape (e.g., 1.0, 1.1, 1.2, etc.) are too broad and thus provide only qualitative assessments of length in that different line lengths (e.g., 1.11, 1.12) may be classified together (e.g., as 1.1). In any case, the variety of measurement circumstances typically encountered in marketing research can be conceptualized to lie along a continuum ranging from qualitative to quantitative. Rescaling procedures can be used to quantify data collected in circumstances which can be (subjectively) characterized as qualitative. For example, reporting one's job satisfaction on a ratings scale (if assumed to provide qualitative data) can <u>eventually</u> be scaled to obtain a measurement. Scaling procedures assign new numerical values to scale points which are consistent with the measurement-level assumptions, and simultaneously attempt to make the multiple items of a construct as homogeneous as possible. Such quantification aids theory testing by improving internal consistency and convergent and discriminant validity of measures (e.g., Didow et al. 1985).

PRINQUAL

In a comparative study of two scaling procedures, PRINQUAL (SAS Institute Inc., 1983) and dual scaling (Nishisato 1980), Liu and Franke (1986) found that both procedures provided similar rescaled results, but PRINQUAL was more efficient (i.e., it required less computer time). Though a dual scaling algorithm can be programmed and used with relative ease, PRINQUAL is provided as a procedure on SAS and is therefore more readily available. In addition, PRINQUAL has the advantage of using different data types (e.g., interval, nominal, ordinal) with greater flexibility. Motivated by these considerations, PRINQUAL was used to rescale the data in the empirical study reported in this paper.

PRINQUAL can be used to rescale interval, ordinal, or nominal data. In fact, this procedure can be used to rescale data in situations where multiple items in a measure represent a mix of nominal, ordinal, and interval scales. PRINQUAL accomplishes scaling using a two-stage iterative procedure. In the first stage, the procedure transforms each variable in a manner consistent with that variable's indicated measurement properties (e.g., interval, ordinal, nominal). Consistency with measurement properties implies that PRINQUAL respects the nominal, ordinal, or interval nature of the scales while transforming the response categories of a particular scale. If an input variable is indicated as ordinal, PRINQUAL's transformations leave relative ranks unchanged. For example, scale points low, medium, and high may be transformed to 1.0, 2.5, and 3.6 to retain the original scale's rank ordering. Similarly, equal intervals are maintained between response categories on an interval scale. A nominal scale simply indicates categorical distinctions, so any transformation that maintains the original categories is permitted.

In the second stage, PRINQUAL uses traditional principal component analysis to maximize the proportion of variance accounted for by a given number of orthogonal components. During a typical application of PRINQUAL, these two stages (i.e., transformation of response categories followed by principal component analysis) are iteratively employed until incremental improvements (in proportion of variance explained) become insignificant or only marginal. In a rescaling application, for example, iterations may be stopped when the original 1 to 5 response categories in a 5-point ratings scale are transformed to 0.7, 1.3, 2.5, 3.5, and 4.3. These rescaled numbers are then referred to as the optimal scale values of the original response categories and employed in all subsequent analyses (e.g., hypothesis testing). Further details on PRINQUAL (and a related procedure called PRINCIPALS) are provided by Didow, Perreault, and Williamson (1983); Didow et al. (1985); Liu and Franke (1985); and Young (1984).

Rescaling and Causal Models

A causal model essentially represents a network of causal relationships between the (1) manifest and latent variables, and (2) between the latent variables themselves (Joreskog and Sorbom 1986) and has numerous applications for theory development and testing in marketing (Bagozzi 1980). Given that rescaling procedures improve measures' internal consistency and convergent and discriminant validity (Didow et al. 1985), what can

be expected about their effect on the measurement and fit statistics of causal models?

First, note that the measurement part of a causal model describes the linkages between the observed or manifest variables and the latent variables they are designed to capture. Because rescaling improves internal consistency, corresponding improvements in the measurement part of a causal model are expected due to rescaling. For example, squared multiple correlations (which measure how effectively individual items separately tap that construct) and coefficients of determination of the indicator variables (which measure how effectively items jointly tap their respective constructs) may improve after rescaling.

However, as far as the effect of rescaling on the structural equations part of the causal model is concerned, no a priori statements can be made. Overall fit of the structural equations part of the causal model depends on the veracity of its underlying theory and on the error inherent in the measurement of the latent constructs. After rescaling, with measurement error reduced and latent variables tapped more effectively, the fit of the structural equations represents a stronger test of the underlying theory (see Calder, Phillips, and Tybout 1981). Under these conditions of reduced measurement error, parameters representing the causal linkages can be measured more precisely (i.e., with less error). But the statistics of overall fit can either improve or deteriorate depending on how well the causal model's underlying theory is (or is not) supported.

STUDY

In this study, two sets of analyses were conducted using LISREL-VI (Joreskog and Sorbom 1986) to estimate a causal model--one with the raw data and another with the rescaled data. To examine the impact of rescaling, we compared the measurement model statistics, overall model fit statistics, and parameter estimates provided by these two analyses.

The Causal Model

The model employed in this investigation (see Figure 1) is from a study reported earlier by Wolfle (1988), where the substantive concern was to examine the effect of postsecondary education on the development of self-esteem. The motivation for using this causal model in the present investigation is, however, primarily methodological. Because several manifest variables in this model are measured with nominal or ordinal scales (but analyzed as interval-scale variables in the original study), we felt that the effects (if any) of rescaling would be more readily apparent. A second consideration was that the original study's author made the necessary raw data readily available to us for this investigation. It is acknowledged that these model selection criteria are rather subjective, but were considered satisfactory for the planned exploratory study.

As shown in Figure 1, the causal model has two exogenous variables: socioeconomic background and ability. Post-secondary education and self-esteem in 1972 and self esteem in 1979 were the endogenous variables. The causal linkages between the exogenous and endogenous variables are as shown. Given the methodological focus of this investigation, the rationale behind the various linkages will not be presented here (see Wolfe (1988) for the theoretical justification of these linkages and the constraints imposed on the model).

Socioeconomic background was measured with these indicator variables: father's education (FaEd), mother's education (MaEd), and father's occupational status (FaOcc). FaEd and MaEd were based on composite scales developed by the National Longitudinal Study (NLS) of the high school class of 1972 (Riccobono et al. 1981) and coded as follows: less than high school (1) high school graduate (2), some college (3), college graduate (4), and masters or Ph.D. (5). Father's occupational status was also based on a composite variable. The second exogenous variable (Ability), was measured with two indicator variables: scores on a reading and mathematics test conducted in 1972 (see Wolfle (1988) for details).

Self-esteem was measured with a four-item scale. Each item had four response categories ranging from "disagree strongly" to "agree strongly." The four items capturing this construct were: (1) I take a positive attitude toward myself; (2) I feel I am a person of worth, on an equal plane with others; (3) I am able to do things as well as most other people; and (4) On the whole, I am satisfied with myself. Self-esteem was measured twice--once in 1972 and again in 1979.

Post-secondary education was measured with a single indicator variable. This was based on responses to a question respondents were asked in a follow-up questionnaire in 1979. The question pertained to college education attainment and responses were coded as follows: none (0), less than two years (1), two years or more (2), finished college (3), masters degree (4), and Ph.D. or professional degree (5).

Rescaling with PRINQUAL

Data from 1000 respondents from the National Longitudinal Study were employed in this exploratory investigation. The indicator variables of the two exogenous and two endogenous variables were rescaled one at a time using PRINQUAL. In each case, a variable-by-variable covariance matrix was analyzed. To illustrate how this procedure was carried out, rescaling of the four indicator variables of self-esteem (1972) is now described.

S1a, S1b, S1c, and S1d are indicated in Figure 1 as

the four indicator variables of the latent variable self-esteem (1972). A covariance matrix of the four indicator variables was analyzed by PRINQUAL. In the R-type principal component analysis used by PRINQUAL, the original four dimensional space (because there are four variables) was reduced to a single dimension by extracting one principal component; the other components individually accounted for only a small proportion of the total variance. The extracted component accounted for 52.6% of the total variance. The rescaled values of the response categories in each of the four items (S1a, S1b, S1c, S1d) are shown in Table 1. Examining the rescaled values indicates that the interval-level assumption of the original scales is violated in several instances. In item S1b, for example, response categories 1 and 2 are collapsed into a single category.

Similar rescaling analyses were performed separately for self-esteem (1979), ability, and socioeconomic background. In each case, the PRINQUAL-extracted single principal component accounted for a moderately large proportion of the total variance (self-esteem (1979) = 64.1%, ability = 84.3%, socioeconomic background = 97.6%). Post-secondary education was not rescaled because it has only one indicator variable (PRINQUAL requires at least two indicator variables).

COMPARISON OF THE UNSCALED AND SCALED RESULTS

To examine the effect of rescaling on the measurement model, overall fit, and parameters of the causal model, two sets of analyses were performed using LISREL--one with the raw data and another with the rescaled data. A covariance matrix was used as input in both analyses. Results based on these analyses are now discussed.

Measurement of the Latent Constructs

As indicated earlier, rescaling procedures increase the internal consistency of measures (e.g., Didow et al. 1985). In the context of the present causal model, rescaling was therefore expected to improve the measurement part of the causal model. That is, after rescaling, the X indicator variables should tap the latent exogenous variables more effectively. The same argument holds for the Y variables and latent endogenous variables as well.

Table 2 shows a comparison of the measurement model with and without rescaling. Squared multiple correlations and measurement errors (s) are reported for both the unscaled and scaled results. Squared multiple correlations increase and measurement errors decrease for all the X and Y indicator variables (except S1a). This evidence appears to support the argument that rescaling improves the measurement parts of the causal model--the indicator variables tap the latent constructs more effectively. Though the improvements obtained in the context of this model are only marginal, the magnitude of such

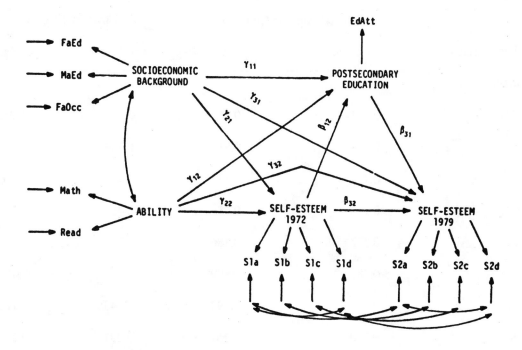

FIGURE 1
Model of Self-Esteem

Source: Adapted from Wolfle (1988)

TABLE 1
Rescaling Performed by Prinqual: An Illustration

CONSTRUCT: Self-Esteem (1972)

Indicator Variable	Original Response Category			
	1	2	3	4
S1a	1.0	1.46	2.40	4.0
S1b	1.0	1.0	2.03	4.0
S1c	1.0	1.26	2.17	4.0
S1d	1.0	1.69	2.15	4.0

Note: The response categories were scaled by PRINQUAL to interval-level values. To show a comparison of the scaled values with the original response categories, the rescaled values are shown linearly transformed to maintain the end points (1 and 4) of the original scale.

improvements obtained in a particular application of rescaling will naturally vary from one modeling context to another.

Fit of the Structural Equations

Overall fit of structural equations depends both on the soundness of the underlying theory and the error inherent in the measurement of the latent exogenous and endogenous constructs. The results discussed above indicate that rescaling appears to improve the measurement part of the causal model. As rescaling simply permits a stronger test of the theory underlying a causal model, the magnitude and direction of changes in the overall fit statistics may vary from one model to another. Hence, as argued in an earlier section, no a priori statements can be made about the effect of rescaling on the overall fit of the model. In fact, one goal of this exploratory study was to

TABLE 2
Comparison of the Measurement Models

Manifest Variable	Squared Multiple Correlations		Measurement Error (θ)	
	Unscaled	Scaled	Unscaled	Scaled
Y variables:				
S1a	0.257	0.251	0.289	0.292
S1b	0.554	0.619	0.153	0.130
S1c	0.480	0.524	0.171	0.156
S1d	0.136	0.156	0.483	0.472
S2a	0.372	0.386	0.212	0.207
S2b	0.781	0.809	0.063	0.055
S2c	0.540	0.593	0.143	0.126
S2d	0.220	0.264	0.291	0.275
X Variables:				
FaEd	0.707	0.762	3.230	2.623
MaEd	0.351	0.367	4.966	4.840
FaOcc	0.409	0.438	330.100	313.700
Math	0.635	0.653	17.030	16.160
Reading	0.564	0.593	9.374	8.730

Note: Squared multiple correlations increase and measurement errors decrease for all manifest variables except S1a.

investigate the magnitude of such changes in overall fit that may result due to rescaling.

Table 3 presents a comparison of the unscaled and scaled results. Squared multiple correlation for the structural equations show a slight decrease for all three endogenous constructs. Hence the total coefficient of determination for the structural equations also shows a slight deterioration (from 0.412 to 0.398). Measures of overall fit, however, show a marginal improvement. The chi-square decreases from 133.31 to 124.35, accompanied by a corresponding improvement in the goodness of fit (GFI) index. But root mean square residual (RMR) increases from 0.292 to 0.331.

Hence, at least for the causal model used in this investigation, rescaling results only in marginal changes in statistics of overall fit. But no clear pattern seems to emerge in these changes. Although some measures of overall fit show a marginal improvement, the structural equations appear to become less effective in explaining variation in the latent endogenous variables. These results naturally pertain only to the casual model used in this exploratory investigation. The magnitude and direction of changes in overall fit statistics may vary considerably from one causal model to another.

Model Parameters

Standardized estimates of the parameters and standard errors of those estimates, with and without scaling, are shown in Table 4. As can be observed, parameter estimates change due to rescaling though the statistical significance (or lack thereof) of most parameter estimates remains unchanged. However, one parameter (γ_{22}) which was significant before scaling, becomes statisti-

TABLE 3
Comparison of the Structural Equations' Models

Criteria	Unscaled	Scaled
A. Squared multiple correlations for structural equations:		
Self-Esteem (1972)	0.025	0.016
Post-Secondary Education	0.406	0.392
Self-Esteem (1979)	0.093	0.090
B. Coefficient of Determination for the Structural Equations	0.412	0.398
C. Measures of Fit:		
Chi-Square (66 df)	133.310	124.350
Goodness of Fit Index	0.981	0.982
Adjusted Goodness of Fit Index	0.970	0.972
Root Mean Square Residual	0.292	0.331

TABLE 4
Comparison of Parameter estimates and Standard Errors

Parameter	Standardized Estimate		Standard Error	
	Unscaled	Scaled	Unscaled	Scaled
γ_{11}	0.224*	0.241*	0.016	0.015[a]
γ_{21}	0.060	0.049	0.005	0.005
γ_{31}	0.053	0.080	0.005	0.005
γ_{12}	0.518*	0.497*	0.010	0.009[a]
γ_{22}	0.228*	0.103	0.003	0.003
γ_{32}	0.013	0.009	0.003	0.003
β_{12}	0.031	0.033	0.131	0.123[a]
β_{31}	0.071	0.062	0.012	0.012
β_{32}	0.267*	0.258*	0.045	0.042[a]

* significant at $p < 0.05$

[a] standard error less after rescaling; others remain unchanged

cally insignificant after rescaling. An examination of the standard errors of the parameter estimates indicates that four out of nine errors decrease in magnitude, though the magnitude of these changes is quite small. But, as noted before, the effect of rescaling on parameter estimates and their respective standard errors can vary considerably from one causal model to another.

CONCLUSIONS AND DIRECTIONS FOR FUTURE RESEARCH

Rescaling procedures quantify qualitative data, and have been shown to improve measures' internal consistency and convergent and discriminant validity. This paper investigates the applicability of rescaling to theory development and testing using causal models. Given the exploratory nature of this investigation, only tentative conclusions can be offered at this point.

Results of the empirical study indicate that, as expected, rescaling improves the measurement part of the causal model. The structural equations part, however, provides mixed results. After rescaling, parameter estimates are characterized by reduced standard errors. But, whereas some measures of overall fit improved, a marginal deterioration was observed in others. Although the interval-level assumption of the rating scales was found to be violated in several instances, accounting for those violations with rescaling produced only slight changes in the overall fit of the model. At least for the causal model employed in this investigation, parameters and measures of fit provided by LISREL were quite stable and rescaling

data produced only marginal changes. However, it is conceivable that this stability may not generalize to all causal modeling situations. In any case, because rescaling procedures are readily available and easy to use (PRINQUAL is available on SAS), their use should be encouraged to at least improve the measurement part of the causal model.

To obtain a better understanding of how rescaling affects the measurement and fit of causal models, the exploratory study reported in this paper can be followed by research in three main directions. First, results from more studies can be rescaled to identify situations where rescaling is effective (or ineffective) in improving the measurement and fit statistics of causal models. A systematic investigation of the effect of methodological factors (e.g., scale characteristics, number of items, number of scale points) may be useful in this regard. LISREL 7, with the PRELIS preprocessor built into the main program, can now conveniently handle a variety of data types by analyzing different types of input matrices (e.g., polychoric correlations for ordinal data). A comparison of these new capabilities with traditional rescaling approaches constitutes a second area of investigation that may yield useful results to guide the development and testing of causal models. The third, and probably the most promising, research direction could involve the use of simulation studies in which the theory and measurement components of a causal model are systematically varied. Such investigations may provide more generalizable guidelines regarding the usefulness of rescaling procedures to aid theory testing using causal models.

ENDNOTES

[1] I would like to thank Lee M. Wolfle, Virginia Tech, for providing access to the data for this study.

[2] The terms scaling and rescaling are used interchangeably in this paper. Both imply a transformation of qualitative data.

REFERENCES

Bagozzi, Richard P. (1980), *Causal Models in Marketing*. New York, NY: John Wiley and Sons,

Churchill, Gilbert A. (1979), "A Paradigm for Developing Better Measures of Marketing Constructs," *Journal of Marketing Research*, 16 (February), 64-73.

Didow, Nicholas M., William D. Perreault, and Nicholas C. Williamson (1983), "A Cross-Sectional Optimal Scaling Analysis of the Index of Consumer Sentiment," *Journal of Consumer Research*, 10 (December), 339-347.

_____, Kevin Lane Keller, Hiram C. Barksdale, Jr., and George R. Franke (1985), "Improving Measures of Quality By Alternating Least Squares Optimal Scaling," *Journal of Consumer Research*, 22

(February), 30-40.

Franke, George R. (1985), "Evaluating Measures Through Data Quantification: Applying Dual Scaling to an Advertising Copytest," *Journal of Business Research*, 13, 61-69.

Joreskog, K.G. and D. Sorbom (1983), *LISREL VI: Analysis of Linear Structural Relationships by Maximum Likelihood and Least Squares Methods*. Chicago, IL: National Educational Resources.

Liu, Scott S. and George R. Franke (1986), "Improving Marketing Measures By Rescaling Variables: A Comparison of Dual Scaling and PRINQUAL," in *Proceedings of the Southern Marketing Association*, Robert L. King, ed. Atlanta, GA: Southern Marketing Association, 246-250.

Nishisato, Shizuhiko (1980), *Analysis of Categorical Data: Dual Scaling and its Applications*. Toronto:

University of Toronto Press.

Nunnally, Jum (1978), *Psychometric Theory*. 2nd ed., New York, NY; McGraw-Hill Book Company.

Peter J. Paul (1981), "Construct Validity: A Review of Basic Issues and Marketing Practices," *Journal of Marketing Research*, 18 (May), 133-145.

Riccobono, J., L. B. Henderson, G. J. Burkheimer, C. Place, and J. R. Levinson (1981), *National Longitudinal Study: Base Year (1972) Through Fourth Follow-Up (1979) Data Files Users Manual*. Washington, DC: National Center for Education Statistics.

SAS Institute Inc. (1983), "Statistical Macros: %PRINQUAL, %CONJOINT, and the OPSCAL MATRIX Function," *SAS Technical Report P-131*, Cary, NC: SAS Institute Inc.

Wolfle, Lee M. (1988), "Effects of Postsecondary Education on Self-Esteem," working paper, Virginia Tech, Blacksburg.

Yadav, Manjit S. and George R. Franke (1989), "Investigating the Behavioral Rationale for Rescaling Marketing Measures," *Proceedings*, Summer Educators' Conference, Chicago, IL: American Marketing Association, 201-205.

Young, Forrest W. (1984), "Scaling," *Annual Review of Psychology*, 35, 55-81.

SAMPLE SIZE EFFECTS ON THE STABILITY OF OPTIMAL SCALING ESTIMATES - A PRELIMINARY INVESTIGATION

Nicholas M. Didow, University of North Carolina
Michael R. Mullen, Michigan State University

ABSTRACT

In a limited, preliminary study using multiple, independent subsamples of 25, 50, 100, 200, and 400 subjects, we find little improvement in the general stability of alternating least squares optimal scaled values estimated from samples of 50 or more subjects in measurement models with response scales commonly used in marketing.

INTRODUCTION

Many of the measures used in marketing research surveys involve response categories of ordinal metric that do not meet the assumptions of statistical applications typically used to analyze the data (Perreault and Young 1980; Srinivasan and Basu 1989). For example, latent variables are often measured with multiple-item five-point or seven-point Likert-type ordinal response scales, then sum scales are developed, and measures of association or mean differences are analyzed. The practice of treating ordinal data as if they were interval or ratio is based upon an implicit assumption that subjects respond to multiple scales and between response categories in similar ways such that the underlying metrics are equivalent. The Alternating Least Squares Optimal Scaling (ALSOS) family of psychometric methods, and in particular PRINCIPALS principal components analysis of nonmetric and mixed metric data, is a promising set of market research techniques that rescale the response starting values to the best estimate of interval data. Hence, subsequent analysis can be based on data that better meet the measurement assumptions of the analytic models.

While ALSOS has had a limited, yet encouraging, introduction in psychometrics in general and marketing in particular, several research questions have emerged concerning the appropriate use of ALSOS. One question is in regard to the number of subjects, or sample size, and the effects of sample size on the stability of optimal scaling estimates. The purpose of this research is to provide a preliminary investigation into this issue. The robustness of the optimal scaling approach will be analyzed by partitioning a data set into mutually exclusive samples of different sizes for separate analysis. Optimal scale value estimates thus derived (from sample sizes of 25, 50, 100, and 200 respondents) will be compared to those estimated from a much larger sample size (sample size of 400 respondents). The results will be presented and implications for using PRINCIPALS and further

research needs will be discussed. The following section summarizes the major marketing literature on ALSOS and provides an intuitive explanation for "optimal scaling".

ALSOS

Alternating least squares optimal scaling procedures are a family of psychometric techniques developed for the quantitative analysis of qualitative or nonmetric data (Young, Takane, and de Leeuw 1978). Perreault and Young (1980) introduced this family of ALSOS procedures to marketing researchers for analysis of metric and non-metric data. They noted (p. 2) that:

> "Conceptually, the approach underlying ALSOS straight forward: consistent with a set of measurement restrictions, nominal or ordinal valued variables in the data are transformed to interval scale values."

Perreault and Young also discussed general marketing applications and provided marketing examples. Young (1981) provided an overview of the methodological and theoretical foundations of ALSOS. He noted that optimal scaling is a data analysis technique which assigns numerical values to observation categories. Young (1981) viewed it as the process of quantifying qualitative data.

PRINCIPALS, a data analysis procedure which is a member of the ALSOS family, is used in this paper. It is a general extension of principal components analysis for use with non-metric or mixed metric data (Young, Takane, and de Leeuw 1978). The PRINCIPALS procedure can be thought of as a process which seeks to linearize all of the bivariate scatter plots of the items in the PRINCIPALS analysis. It produces the best possible estimate of the underlying interval scales, given the measurement characteristics of the data.

Didow, Perreault, and Williamson (1983) and Didow, Keller, Barksdale and Franke (1985) extended and applied the use of PRINCIPALS to marketing problems. Didow, Perreault, and Williamson used PRINCIPALS to empirically investigate the measurement assumptions of the Index of Consumer Sentiment. With PRINCIPALS, they transformed mixed metric data to numerical values so that it was

"possible to examine the estimated optimal scaled

values to provide insights into the structure of the original nonmetric data," (Didow, Perreault, and Williamson 1983, p. 343).

Didow et al. (1985) explained and demonstrated the utility of PRINCIPALS for improving the measurement quality of mixed metric and nonmetric data. They transformed original ordinal and nonmetric response categories to interval level measurement for two tripartite, attitude research examples. The reliability and convergent and discriminate validity of the measures were improved in both cases. Didow and his colleagues also explored the stability of the PRINCIPALS technique, although they were limited by the size of their sample of 214 observations to the use of holdout samples and jackknife analysis. PRINCIPALS was used by Mullen and Didow (1991) to analyze cross-cultural, etic survey data gathered at different times and places. The data were partitioned into mutually exclusive and exhaustive subsets made up of the two separate, known populations from which the data were collected. Independent transformations of the data revealed the structures of the respective underlying metrics. In this way, Mullen and Didow analyzed the measurement comparability, or lack thereof, across the two populations by examining the optimal scaling results.

DATA

The data used in this preliminary analysis of sample size effects on the stability of optimal scaling estimates come from a large survey of Japanese and American employees by Lincoln and Kalleberg (1985). Employees were surveyed in the Indianapolis, Indiana, metropolitan area in the U.S. and in the Atsugi region of Japan. Fifty-two US plants took part in the survey yielding 4,567 employee responses. In Japan, 46 firms cooperated resulting in 3,735 employee responses. Lincoln and Kalleberg compared the samples on many dimensions and found them to be reasonably comparable in terms of participating firms and employees. Their study compared satisfaction, occupational commitment or loyalty, and other constructs for Japanese versus American employees. Marketing researchers might be interested in similar constructs in consumer behavior, sales force motivation, and business to business research. Table 1 reports the six items designed to measure "loyalty" or "occupational commitment" by the original Lincoln and Kalleberg survey instrument. The "commitment" items used 5-category Likert response scales as noted in Table 1.

Much greater detail concerning the sample, the research instrument, and relevant theory are available in Lincoln and Kalleberg (1985). For this research project, however, the Lincoln and Kalleberg study provides a rich and large data base for a preliminary analysis of sample size effects on the stability of optimal scaling estimates.

ANALYSIS

The Japanese and American samples were randomly partitioned into 20 mutually exclusive subsamples. These subsamples are made up of two sets from each country of 25, 50, 100, 200, and 400 subjects.

PRINCIPALS analysis was done using the PRINQUAL procedure generally available for personal computers (SAS 1988). The rescaling used Kruskal's (1964) secondary least squares monotonic transforma-

---

TABLE 1
Survey Items Designed to Measure "Loyalty" or "Occupational Commitment" Construct
(from Lincoln and Kalleberg 1985)

	STRONGLY AGREE				STRONGLY DISAGREE
"I would take any job in order to continue working for this company."	1	2	3	4	5
"I feel very little loyalty to this company."	1	2	3	4	5
"I am proud to work for this company."	1	2	3	4	5
"I would turn down another job for more in order to stay with this company."	1	2	3	4	5
"My values and the values of this company are quite similar."	1	2	3	4	5
"I am willing to work harder than I have to in order to help this company succeed."	1	2	3	4	5

TABLE 2
OPTIMAL SCALED VALUES (OSV) BY INDEPENDENT
SUBSAMPLES AND TWO A PRIORI KNOWN GROUPS

(Item: "I feel very little loyalty to this company.")

| | | A Priori Known Groups | | | | | |
| Sample Size | Original Likert Value | Japanese Respondents | | | American Respondents | | |
		Sample1	Sample2	Average OSV	Sample11	Sample12	Average OSV
n=400	1	.83	-.33	.25	2.65	2.34	2.50
	2	2.25	2.53	2.39	2.65	2.34	2.50
	3	2.84	3.17	3.00	2.65	2.34	2.50
	4	4.07	3.78	3.93	3.20	3.58	3.39
	5	4.95	4.84	4.90	6.00	5.78	5.89
		Sample3	Sample4		Sample13	Sample14	
n=200	1	-.53	-.63		2.49	2.73	
	2	2.97	3.34		2.49	2.73	
	3	3.07	3.53		3.61	3.67	
	5	4.26	4.80		5.64	5.71	
		Sample5	Sample6		Sample15	Sample16	
n=100	1	2.05	-.20		2.77	2.99	
	2	2.26	1.87		2.77	2.99	
	3	2.70	3.06		2.77	2.99	
	4	4.17	3.84		3.54	3.18	
	5	4.89	3.84		5.70	7.09	
		Sample7	Sample8		Sample17	Sample18	
n=50	1	-.21	1.44		-	2.70	
	2	2.42	2.58		3.04	2.70	
	3	3.87	3.30		3.13	2.70	
	4	3.87	3.30		3.21	3.23	
	5	3.87	6.13		5.60	6.25	
		Sample9	Sample10		Sample19	Sample20	
n=25	1	-	-		-	2.60	
	2	3.06	3.11		1.95	2.60	
	3	3.06	3.11		2.86	2.60	
	4	3.28	3.11		4.33	3.12	
	5	6.78	5.56		4.33	6.36	

tion as recommended by Perreault and Young (1980) and Young (1981) for categorical, ordinal level data. For the 20 subsamples, 10 each from the a priori known groups of Japan employees and American employees, the six item "occupational commitment" scale was analyzed separately with the PRINCIPALS algorithm (SAS 1988) resulting in twenty sets of independently derived best estimates of the underlying interval metric for each response category of each item.

The optimal scaled values (OSV) for the 20 subsamples are shown in Table 2 for one of the six items in the "occupational commitment" scale. The estimates are reported for each of the 20 subsamples. The raw or original ordinal categories of from "1" to "5" are shown in the left hand column. The transformed or optimal scaled values are listed across from the originally assigned value. The OSV for each item can now be compared for each raw category. For example, we can examine the OSVs for the first Japanese subsample, Sample1. The response categories of 1, 2, 3, 4, and 5 were rescaled to .83, 2.25, 2.84, 4.07, and 4.95, respectively. Detailed discussions of the general interpretation of OSVs from the PRINCIPALS procedure can be found in

Didow et al (1985) and Didow, Perreault and Williamson (1983). The issue here, however, is the extent to which the OSV estimates are stable across different sample sizes.

We are assuming that the OSV estimates from the four largest subsamples (400 respondents each) are the basis against which smaller sample size based OSV estimates can be compared. Therefore, our analysis will investigate the extent to which OSVs derived from smaller samples deviate from those derived from the large subsamples. Because of space limitations we focus

TABLE 3
Subsample Deviations from Large Sample Size OSV Estimates by Independent Subsamples and Two A Priori Known Groups

Sample Size	Original Likert Value	A Priori Known Groups			
		Japanese Respondents		American Respondents	
		Sample3	Sample4	Sample13	Sample14
n=200	1	.78	.88	.01	-.23
	2	-.58	-.95	.01	-.23
	3	-.07	-.34	.01	-.23
	4	-.13	.40	-.22	-.28
	5	.64	.10	.25	.18
Average Absolute Value of Deviation		.44	.53	.10	.23
Group Average		.49		.17	
Overall Average			.33		
		Sample5	Sample6	Sample15	Sample16
n=100	1	-1.80	.45	-.27	-.49
	2	.13	.52	-.27	-.49
	3	.30	-.06	-.27	-.49
	4	-.24	.09	-.15	.21
	5	.01	1.06	.19	-1.20
Average Absolute Value of Deviation		.50	.44	.23	.58
Group Average		.47		.41	
Overall Average			.44		
		Sample7	Sample8	Sample17	Sample18
n=50	1	-.46	-1.19	-	-.20
	2	-.03	-.19	-.54	-.20
	3	-.87	-.30	-.63	-.20
	4	.06	.63	.18	.16
	5	1.03	-1.23	.29	-.36
Average Absolute Value of Deviation		.49	.71	.41	.22
Group Average		.60		.32	
Overall Average			.46		
		Sample9	Sample10	Sample19	Sample20
n=25	1	-	-	-	-.10
	2	-.67	-.72	.55	-.10
	3	-.06	-.11	-.36	-.10
	4	.65	.82	-.94	.27
	5	-1.88	-.66	1.56	-.47
Average Absolute Value of Deviation		.82	.58	.85	.21
Group Average		.70		.53	
Overall Average			.62		

on the one item from the six item occupational commitment scale. We found the OSV results for this item across the subsamples to be typical of all these items.

Table 3 reports the OSV estimate deviations for each of the remaining sixteen subsamples compared against the average OSVs for both sets of Japanese and American subsamples with n=400.

The Table also notes the average absolute value of deviation for each sample, for similar sized samples within the two a priori known groups, and across all similar sized samples collapsing across the two known groups.

The average absolute value of OSV deviation generally decreases as sample size increases in both the Japanese and American samples. Overall the deviation decrease is from .62 for a sample size of 25, to .46 for a sample size of 50, to .44 for a sample size of 100, to .33 for a sample size of 200.

DISCUSSION

The stability of the results of this rescaling procedure has previously been explored only with the techniques of holdout samples and jackknife analysis in Didow et al (1985). Those techniques indicated a reasonable level of stability for sample sizes of 100 to 200. However, it is problematic to generalize from those findings, because the observations from subsample to subsample were not independent. In addition, the authors of that study did not explore the effects of different sample sizes on the stability of the results.

The large number of subjects in Lincoln and Kalleberg's (1985) survey allow us to examine the stability of rescaling across mutually exclusive samples of the same size and between samples of different sizes.

In general, the results are more consistent for sample sizes of 50 or more subjects. While there is some deterioration in stability for samples with fewer than 50 observations, these OSVs are also rather stable and generally consistent with the OSVs in the larger samples. Alternatively, the deviation of OSVs generally does not markedly improve as independent sample sizes increase from 50 to 100 to 200 subjects, compared to criterion OSVs estimated on samples of 400 subjects. However, the OSVs from the rescaling procedure for the samples with 25 subjects deviate considerably from the OSVs estimated from the larger samples of 400 subjects.

CONCLUSION

This analysis shows that the optimal scaling procedure produced relatively similar results for sample sizes of 50 or more. These values, however, deviate from values estimated from larger samples of 400 subjects. Hence, the stability of ALSOS rescaling of response categories associated with similar multiple item scales should be a general concern to researchers, and of particular concern if the sample size is less than 50. Researchers should look to procedures like holdout samples and jackknife techniques to address optimal scaling stability issues with respect to virtually any sample size, especially those of fewer than 50 to 100 observations.

Additional research is needed to investigate sample size effects on the stability of optimal scaling estimates. This study, exploratory in nature, has used data from one six-item measure, with 5-point Likert response scales. Other research projects need to examine the scaling stability issue with other combinations of questions, items, response scales, and sample sizes. This is also an area where a simulation study might be helpful to model more fully the causal parameters involved herein and look more comprehensively at sample size effects and other scaling issues.

REFERENCES

Didow, Nicholas M., Kevin Lane Keller, Hiram C. Barksdale, Jr., and George R. Franke (1985), "Improving Measure Quality by Alternating Least Squares Optimal Scaling," *Journal of Marketing Research,* 22 (February), 30-40.

_____, William D. Perreault Jr., and Nicholas C. Williamson (1983), "A Cross-Sectional Optimal Scaling Analysis of the Index of Consumer Sentiment," *Journal of Consumer Research,* 10 (December), 339-347.

Kruskal, J. B. (1964), "Multidimensional Scaling by Optimizing Goodness of Fit to a Nonmetric Hypothesis," *Psychometrika,* 29, 1 (March), 1-27.

Lincoln, James R. and Arne L. Kalleberg (1985), "Work Organization and Workforce Commitment: A Study of Plants and Employees in the U.S. and Japan," *American Sociological Review,* 50 (December), 738-760.

Mullen, Michael and Nicholas M. Didow (1991), "Are Cross-Cultural Survey Data Comparable? Optimal Scaling Provides Useful Evidence," in Gilly et al. eds. *Enhancing Knowledge Development in Marketing,* Proceedings of the 1991 American Marketing Association Summer Educators' Conference, 608-609.

Perreault, William D. Jr. and Forrest W. Young (1980), "Alternating Least Squares Optimal Scaling: Analysis of Nonmetric Data in Marketing Research," *Journal of Marketing Research,* 27 (February), 1-13.

SAS (1988), *SAS Technical Report P-179.* Additional SAS/STAT Procedures, Release 6.03, SAS Institute

Inc., SAS Circle Box 8000, Cary, NC: USA 27512-8000.

Srinivasan, V. and Amiya K. Basu (1989), "The Metric Quality of Ordered Categorical Data," *Marketing Science*, 8(3), 205-230.

Young, Forrest W. (1981), "Quantitative Analysis of Qualitative Data," *Psychometrika*, 46, 4 (December), 357-388.

_____, Yoshio Takane and Jan de Leeuw (1978), "The Principal Components of Mixed Measurement Data: An Alternating Least Squares Method with Optimal Scaling Features," *Psychometrika*, 43 (June), 279-282.

INTERNATIONAL ADVERTISING APPEALS AND STRATEGY: A CROSS-CULTURAL ANALYSIS

Venkatapparao Mummalaneni, St. John's University
James P. Neelankavil, Hofstra University

ABSTRACT

Advertising generally reflects a society's culture and advertising appeals further manifest this linkage. Hence, appeals can be revealing of societal values as well as advertiser's goals and strategies. Most previous studies on advertising appeals have either focused on individual types of appeals or on the effectiveness of these appeals. Generally, none of the previous studies have compared the use of varying advertising appeals in a cross-cultural context.

The purpose of this paper is to explore the relative frequency of various advertising appeals used in an international context. We have investigated the type of appeals used in four Asian countries--Hong Kong, Japan, South Korea and Taiwan for both indigenous and imported products.

For several decades now, research on advertising appeals has been undertaken by marketers [Brooke 1981], and by researchers in the field of communication and psychology [Janis and Feshbach 1953]. In the area of international advertising strategies, effects of increased nationalism on advertising [Dunn 1978] and standardization in advertising [Calvin et al. 1980] have been studied. Likewise, effects of international advertising on consumer attitudes and patterns [Hornik 1980]; effectiveness of fear appeals [Ray and Wilkie 1970]; use of humor in advertising [Sternthal and Craig 1973] and impact of sexual appeals [Bellow et al. 1983] have also been explored.

While the trend in recent research has been to examine the types and effectiveness of appeals, the effects of multiple appeals in a multiple country setting have received scant attention. Based upon the propositions found in the literature reviewed, four hypotheses were developed in the present study. The individual hypotheses suggest separately, the influence of four factors, namely, the market country, country of product origin, type of product and finally, the target customer group on the advertising appeals employed in the four Asian countries of interest. Recent reviews indicate extensive usage of content analysis in empirical research focusing on advertising communications (Yale and Gilly 1988; Kolbe and Burnett 1991) and this method is considered appropriate for the purposes of our study. Advertisements were extracted from native language magazines published in the four Asian countries of interest and available in the U.S. While magazines were thus chosen per convenience, care was taken to include multiple issues of each magazine and all the advertisements (except the classifieds) in these magazines were content analyzed.

Content analysis of the 543 advertisements was done by two trained judges. Both the judges analyzed independently the first 100 of the ads and since the reliability as assessed by the coefficient of agreement was satisfactory (>0.80), the rest of the ads were coded by single judges.

Based on our analysis, the most frequently employed appeal among the four countries was product performance. Attributes/ingredients was the next most frequently encountered appeal. Achievement was the least frequently used appeal. The top three and bottom three appeals by rank (in terms of frequency) are similar to the findings of Stewart and Furse [1986] in their study of advertising appeals in television commercials in the United States.

We tested the hypotheses through separate contingency table analyses and found that advertising appeals are not independent of either product type, country of product origin, country in which the product is marketed or the consumer target group. That is, advertising appeals are apparently related to these four factors. For instance, whereas the self-esteem appeal is hardly ever utilized in Japan, it is frequently employed in both Hong Kong and Taiwan. Similarly, the incidence of sexual appeals is greatest in the case of clothing items but low in ads featuring home appliances. Japanese made products tend to emphasize attributes or ingredients more than any other country. It is reasonable to conclude then that in creating appeals, international advertisers take into consideration, the nature of the product, country of origin and other factors in developing their strategy. Further research into the advertiser decision process concerning the creation of advertising appeals for international markets should enhance our understanding of the issue of standardization in advertising strategy.

For further information please contact:
Venkat Mummalaneni
Asst. Professor of Marketing
St. John's University
Jamaica, N. Y. 11439

HISPANIC ADVERTISING: THE IMPORTANCE OF FAMILY AND ETHNIC IDENTIFICATION

Linda C. Ueltschy, Kent State University
Paul J. Albanese, Kent State University

ABSTRACT

Differential strength of ethnic identification has been well documented in sociological research (Sandberg 1974), and has been a topic of interest in the last decade in consumer research (Hirschman 1981; Valencia 1985; Deshpande, Hoyer, and Donthu 1986). Fundamental consumer-related differences between Hispanics who identify strongly with their ethnic group and between those who identify weakly have been postulated in the marketing literature (Deshpande et al. 1986).

This study investigates the strength of ethnic identification of Hispanic consumers in relation to their feelings toward dramatic styles of television commercials. It focuses on the Mexican American segment of Hispanic consumers, recognizing that there are indeed significant cultural differences between and among other groups of Hispanics, such as Cubans or Puerto Ricans.

The importance of family in Latin American culture, especially in Mexico, is so widely accepted that it has become almost stereotypical of Hispanics (Stansifer 1991). The rising ethnic consciousness of Hispanics is also noted in recent studies (Yankelovich, Skelly, and White 1984; Deshpande et al. 1986). This consciousness can be manifested in an empathy with advertising that uses Hispanic models and is directed specifically at Hispanics (Deshpande et al. 1986).

Given that culture affects the consumer behavior of individuals (Walendorf and Reilly 1983), an important moderator of Hispanic consumer behavior would be their degree of "Hispanicness" (Valencia 1985). Ethnicity in this study was operationalized in two ways. Hispanics are divided into Strong and Weak Identifiers based on a self-identification measure. Secondly, a fifteen item ethnic identification scale was utilized, which demonstrated high reliability (Cronbach alpha = .94). The Pearson product moment correlation coefficient between the ethnic identification scale and the self-identification strength of ethnicity was +.7391 (p < .0001), supporting the construct validity of the index.

Additional reliability and validity checks on the ethnicity scale included factor analysis and two types of discriminant analysis to verify the ethnicity scale's ability to explain and predict classification of the respondents into the three groups: non-Hispanics, strong Hispanic Identifiers and Weak Hispanic Identifiers. In the stepwise discriminant analysis, the best discriminators (all successful discriminators using Wilks' Lambda at p < .001), in order of importance, were Hispanic weddings, a Spanish holiday, Spanish mass, Spanish magazines, Spanish TV stations, quincinera, Hispanic friends and Hispanic children should learn to speak Spanish. Facto analysis was used on the variables in the ethnic identification scale, with four factors emerging (mass media usage, religious and social activities, communication activities and education) which explained 98.2 percent of the total variance. Using these factor scores as input into the discriminant analysis, the quadratic discriminant function correctly classified 100 percent of the total respondents.

The sample (N=88, 54 identifying as Hispanics and 34 non-Hispanics) was taken from three locations in the Midwest where settled out migrants of Mexican American descent make up a significant percentage of the residents. Each subject viewed four different television commercials, after which a questionnaire was completed (a Spanish version was available); ordering effects were controlled for by altering the order in which the ads were shown.

Significant differences were found within the Hispanic subgroup, supporting all five hypotheses. Hispanics demonstrated more positive feelings toward ads portraying a family than to non-family ads (p < .001). Hispanics responded more favorably to ads portraying a member of their own ethnic group than to ads in which Hispanics were not present (p < .0001). Strong Hispanic Identifiers demonstrated more positive feelings toward those ads portraying a family (p < .01) and those including a Hispanic member (p < .001) than did Weak Hispanic Identifiers. The comparative importance of the family to Hispanics versus non-Hispanics was supported at p < .10.

For further information please contact:
Linda Ueltschy
Dept. of Marketing
Kent State University
Kent, Ohio 44242

INNOVATOR BUYING OVER TIME AND THE CUMULATIVE EFFECTS OF INNOVATIONS

Frank Alpert, University of Missouri-St. Louis

ABSTRACT

Research on the adoption of innovations has thoroughly investigated the adoption of one innovation in isolation from other innovations. In contrast, this article investigates if, how, and why the buying of earlier innovations relates to the innovator's buying of later innovations within the same product class? For example, does having bought VisiCalc (the original computer spreadsheet) affect the buying of Lotus 1-2-3 (the first integrated spreadsheet)?

Understanding this "cumulative effects of innovations" is more important than ever because the rate of product innovation is higher today than it has ever been. For example, product categories such as computer hardware, computer software, information technology products generally, and consumer electronics have all seen rapid and dramatic change. Furthermore, innovator buying behavior is especially significant because innovators determine the initial success or failure of new-to-the-world products and influence the rate of diffusion of those innovations.

Much has been written about the adoption and diffusion of innovations. For comprehensive reviews of that research see, for example, Rogers (1983), and, more specific to marketing, Gatignon and Robertson (1991). This paper looks at an aspect of this topic that has received little attention. As Robertson and Gatignon (1986) broadened this topic "horizontally," to investigate the effects of competition on the diffusion of an innovation, this paper expands the topic "vertically," to investigate the relationship of prior innovations to the adoption of an innovation. "Few attempts have been made to chart the development of innovativeness within an individual over time" (Hirschman 1980), and likewise little research has focused on the pattern of buying by innovators over time.

It should not be surprising that the cumulative effects of innovations have received little attention. The origin of the diffusion of innovation literature is in the fields of communication (as is the founder of the paradigm, Everett Rogers) and sociology. These early studies dealt with one-time innovations like rural electrification. It should also not be too surprising that marketing has not looked at the issue of cumulative effects. The marketing literature has more of a micro-focus on the buying decision for a particular product than a macro-focus on buying patterns over several years. A perusal of marketing, consumer behavior, and product planning textbooks will show that cumulative innovation effects are rarely touched on.

Figure 1 presents an overview of innovator buying of innovations. This process moves along on its own internal dynamic, given the innovation motivations that drive the process.

FIGURE 1
The Innovator Buying Cycle

EMBRACING INNOVATIONS
Chasing the Advances
Innovation Fascination

↓

INNOVATION SATIATION
Product Accumulation in the Closet
Cumulative Innovation Disappointment
Pace of Innovation Slows Down

↓

INNOVATOR NO MORE
What I've Got is Good Enough Now
Innovator Becomes Extremely Cautious, Careful Buyer
Moving On

The article also examines how the key dimensions of adoption--Rogers' (1983) classic five dimensions (relative advantage, compatibility, trialability, complexity, observability) or Gatignon and Robertson's (1991) four dimensions (value, learning, social, cost)--change over time for innovators.

For further information please contact:
Frank Alpert
School of Business Administration
University of Missouri-St. Louis
8001 Natural Bridge Road
St. Louis, MO 63121

UNDERSTANDING FOLLOWERSHIP AND THE PRIMACY ADVANTAGE: A MODEL OF CONSUMER INNOVATION LEARNING

Brian T. Engelland, Southern Illinois University at Carbondale

ABSTRACT

Introduction

How and under what situations can pioneers be overtaken? Extant strategy literature suggests that followers must offer something extra in order to be successful, but just how a follower does this is unclear. Engineering, management, strategy and marketing literature have focused on distinctly different approaches to the same question.

This paper proposes to take a step toward integrating the major literature dealing with the pioneer and follower relationships, and their impact on adopter preference development. Learning theory is explored as the theoretical underpinnings that explain why primacy has a long term advantage. An innovation learning model is developed, along with nine propositions that flow from the inter-relationships among the two innovation characteristics (complexity and relative advantage); three mediating conditions (receptivity, expertise and familiarity); and one contingency variable (distinctiveness). This research builds on the work of Carpenter (1989) and Carpenter and Nakamoto (1989, 1990) who have examined pioneering advantage in relation to both consumer preference formation and microeconomic theory.

Key Concepts

The *primacy advantage* is a differential advantage accruing to the first innovation in any category which becomes knowledge in the consumer's mind. When an innovation assumes a position as the leader of the class in hierarchical mental storage, that class leader is recalled as the standard of comparison for all other innovations that are subsequently perceived as belonging to that class. The class composition is determined by perceptual associations between innovations. The less two innovations are associated, the more likely they are perceived to be in two different classes.

Model Description

The model defines the perceptual distance between two innovations as the key determinant of primacy advantage, and explicates the necessary conditions that overcome a pioneer's primacy advantage. Strategies are developed that enable followers to obtain a primacy advantage for their product, thus "overtaking" the pioneer in the mind of the consumer.

A general contingency model is proposed to symbolically represent the learning process which leads to the adoption decision. The model assumes that the decision-maker already has stored knowledge about some innovations. When presented with communications regarding a new innovation, the mental processing function is mediated by three endogenous variables, (1) familiarity with any related previous innovation, (2) category expertise, and (3) receptivity to innovation. Mental processing produces some evaluation of the communication, resulting in long term memory storage.

The perceptual location in which the new information is stored is contingent upon the perceived distinctiveness of the new innovation. If the new innovation information is sufficiently indistinct so that it fails to exceed the decision-maker's contrast threshold, the information will not be stored (that is, forgotten). If the new information is marginally distinctive, it will be stored in perceptual proximity to the information for the previous innovation. If the distinctiveness is great, the information will be stored at some degree of perceptual separation. Whether the information is stored separately or in proximity will make a difference upon recall. Information stored together will be recalled together; information stored apart will be recalled apart.

Propositions are developed which relate relative advantage, complexity, familiarity, expertise, receptivity, distinctiveness, association and perceptual distance to primacy advantage. Alternate strategies are explored for followers which may overcome the pioneer's primacy advantage. These include: (1) launch timing, (2) pre-announcing, (3) connection-making communications, (4) communications frequency, and (5) communications distinctiveness.

For further information please contact:
Brian T. Engelland
Department of Marketing
Southern Illinois University
Carbondale, IL 62901-4620

RECONCEPTUALIZING AND MEASURING CONSUMER INNOVATIVENESS

Suresh Subramanian, University of South Dakota
Robert A. Mittelstaedt, University of Nebraska-Lincoln

ABSTRACT

Drawing on the model of adoption decision making proposed by Klonglan and Coward, consumer innovativeness is reconceptualized and a scale based upon this conceptualization is developed. The scale's reliability and validity are assessed and advantages over other conceptualizations are discussed.

INTRODUCTION

Consumer innovativeness continues to attract the interest of researchers in marketing as evidenced by the number of articles and papers that have been presented at conferences and have appeared in journals. A recent review (Subramanian and Mittelstaedt 1990) noted 41 empirical studies of consumer innovativeness reported in the *Journal of Marketing, Journal of Marketing Research, Journal of Consumer Research, Proceedings of the American Marketing Association,* and *Advances in Consumer Research* between 1967 and 1990. Of the 33 demographic, psychological, behavioral and communications variables reported in two or more of those studies, only 8 produced consistent relationships in at least two studies and only one in as many as 4 studies. This seems to reinforce the earlier conclusion of Gatignon and Robertson (1985) that the validity of conclusions about the traits of innovators is "questionable due to the lack of consistent findings in empirical studies" (p. 861). Even earlier, noting equivocal findings, Midgley and Dowling (1978) were led to offer a reconceptualization of the innovativeness concept. Since then, other conceptualizations and operationalizations continue to be advanced.

This paper derives from Midgley and Dowling's (1978) critique but offers a conceptualization which differs from the one presented by those authors. Starting with the distinction between the psychological trait of innovativeness and the behavior of adoption, it is argued that a more promising link between innovativeness and its antecedents may be found between the trait and another psychological variable, the decision to adopt itself. After a review of the relevant literature, a scale based on this distinction is described and a pilot study to assess its reliability and validity is presented.

THE CONCEPT OF INNOVATIVENESS AND ITS MEASUREMENT

The measurement of the innovativeness construct has received both research attention and blame for the equivocal findings mentioned above. Because measurements are based on conceptualizations, they are discussed together in this section.

The older and most of the widely used measures of innovativeness are based upon the Rogers' conceptualization of innovativeness and rely on the time of adoption as the defining criterion for the degree of innovativeness displayed by a single consumer, i.e., innovators are identified as innovators because they adopt early in the diffusion process. With few exceptions (e.g. Ostlund 1972), studies based on the Rogers' conceptualization have operationalized "innovativeness" by looking at purchase (e.g. Lambert 1972; Robertson and Myers 1969), product trial (e.g. Donnelly 1970; Taylor 1977), or ownership (e.g. Darden and Reynolds 1974; Summers 1972).

Midgley (1977) and Midgley and Dowling (1978) criticized the Rogers' conceptualization as tautological and argued that innovativeness is "the degree to which an individual makes innovation decisions independently of the communicated experience of others" (1977, p. 4). The 10 item Independent Judgment Making (IJM) scale of Carlson and Grossbart (1984) is a measurement based on this construct.

Hirschman (1980) reconceptualized innovativeness as a higher order trait stemming from the desire for "novelty seeking." Building on this, Venkatraman and Price (1990) and Venkatraman (1986) draw a distinction between cognitive and sensory innovativeness and have developed measures appropriate to this conceptualization.

Meanwhile, the debate about the domain specificity of innovativeness continues. Foxall and Haskins (1986) argued for the use of a non-product specific scale, the Kirton Adaption Inventory, while Goldsmith and Hofacker (1991) developed a new, product-specific scale.

INNOVATIVE DECISION MAKING

To return to the Midgley and Dowling (1978) critique, they argued that "the construct, innovativeness, only has meaning within the relevant theoretical system, that is, the theory of the diffusion of innovations. . . In the context of any specific innovation, complex situational and communication effects intervene between individuals' innovativeness and their observed time of adoption" (p. 230). A model similar to that of Rogers but different in at least one important respect is that of Klonglan and Coward (1970). Their model is "derived from the widely held view that all innovations include an idea component and that some innovations also include a material component" (p. 77). Accordingly, their model involves two phases (Figure 1).

Phase A comprises the steps that relate to the consumer being aware of the innovation and acquiring knowledge about the same. This is similar to the knowledge stage in the Rogers and Shoemaker model. Phase A concludes with an evaluation of the innovation characteristics resulting in either "symbolic adoption" or "symbolic rejection." Symbolic adoption is the acceptance of the innovation in its ideational form while symbolic rejection is the failure to do so. It should be noted that Klonglan and Coward's usage of the term "symbolic adoption" differs from the definition proffered by Bohlen (1968), who referred to symbolic adoption as "adoption of a nonmaterial idea or position" (p. 20), or Rogers (1968), who described symbolic adoption as "the adoption of symbolic ideas without a direct material parallel" (p. 30), or Hirschman (1981), who defined symbolic innovation as the assignment of social meaning to an existing product.

According to the model, symbolic adoption is a necessary condition to proceed to Phase B, which includes trial and use adoption. Again, the outcome of trial may be either acceptance or rejection. To the extent trial can occur without adoption, trial acceptance is a necessary condition to use adoption. Of course, there is the possibility of trial rejection. Although the model is similar to the Rogers (1983) five stage adoption model in terms of the starting and ending positions, the Klonglan and Coward model permits the consumer to reject the innovation at two points, one of which is prior to trial. Further, there is the possibility of external forces and situational factors acting so as to preclude one from passing beyond either symbolic acceptance or trail acceptance.

It is the first of these two Phases, the point of symbolic acceptance or rejection, upon which the measurement presented in this paper is based. In other words, the approach explored in this paper would define innovators by the time of their decision to accept an innovation rather than by their purchase behavior. In this way, our conceptualization differs from the Rogers approach, although it resembles it more than it does the Midgley, or the Hirschman approaches.

SCALE DEVELOPMENT

A six item scale was developed to measure symbolic adoption with items based on the model of Klonglan and Coward (1970) and research in the marketing literature based on it (Grossbart, et. al. 1975; Mittelstaedt, et. al. 1976). A six point agree-disagree scale was used for each

item. The scale was pretested using a sample of 57 undergraduate junior and senior students for overall readability, comprehensibility, and cohesiveness among the items. The items were found to be fairly well correlated with a Cronbach's alpha of .83. After computing inter-item and item-total correlations, it was found that dropping any of the items did not add to the alpha level; all the six items were retained.

In the second stage, the language of three of the items was modified. The modified scale was then tested with a sample of 51 upper-division undergraduate students and found to have a Cronbach's alpha of .91. Once again item-total and inter-item correlations were computed and it was seen that dropping any of the items did not increase alpha level. Factor analysis generated a single factor with overall 68 percent of the variance being explained by the six items. Scale items appear in the Appendix B.

STIMULI DEVELOPMENT

The stimuli chosen to test and validate the scale were new varieties of computer software. Two reasons supported this decision. First, because the intent of the study was to develop a measure of symbolic adoption, it was important to use innovations that contained a major ideational component and whose adoption would require a significant shift in the way some activity was carried out. Second, research by Lapidus (1991) found that, among college undergraduates, computer products showed moderate to high levels of familiarity and a well defined normal curve in terms of knowledge and involvement levels.

In the first stage, 11 innovative software packages were briefly described and 51 upper-division undergraduates rated the products on the degree of perceived innovativeness, the product's typicality, and their familiarity with similar software. Based on the results, three software packages were chosen for the final study (Appendix A).

VALIDATION

Scale validation is an integral part of scale development process (Churchill 1979; Nunnally 1978). Convergent validity is concerned with confirming that the scale under test is related to constructs that theory suggests are associated with it. To establish convergent validity, two innovativeness related scales were chosen. Since the two major conceptualizations of innovativeness, Rogers (1983) and Midgley and Dowling (1978), are based on the time of adoption and the communicated experiences of others respectively, one scale was chosen to represent each conceptualization. The scale developed by Goldsmith and Hofacker (1991), has demonstrated good scale properties and was chosen to represent the first conceptualization. Because it is product specific and was originally designed for music products, it was altered

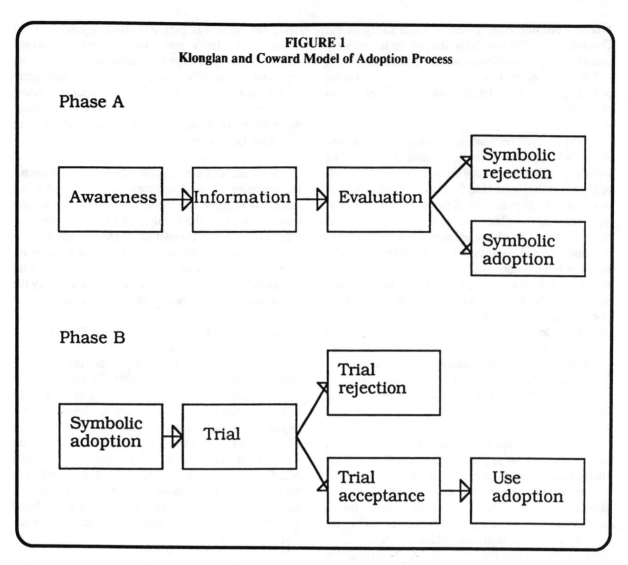

FIGURE 1
Klonglan and Coward Model of Adoption Process

Phase A

Awareness → Information → Evaluation → Symbolic rejection / Symbolic adoption

Phase B

Symbolic adoption → Trial → Trial rejection / Trial acceptance → Use adoption

minimally to make each item specific to computer software. The altered scale was pretested with 51 undergraduates and found to have an alpha of .79. The Independent Judgment Making scale (Carlson and Grossbart 1984) is based upon the second conceptualization of innovativeness. Because it has been shown to have good scale properties and is not product-category specific, no changes were made in it.

Discriminant validity is the confirmation of the fact that the construct being measured by the scale is indeed different from similar constructs, i.e., the scale is not measuring another established construct. Based on the items in the scale, it appeared that discriminant validity would need to be established with the construct Ongoing Search. The Bloch, Sherrel and Ridgway Ongoing Search Scale (1986) developed for computer products was used unchanged to measure this variable.

Nomological validity is confirming the existence of relationships between the construct being measured by the new scale and other constructs that theory suggests are related to it. In the case of symbolic adoption, the consumer innovativeness literature was reviewed to select suitable constructs. An earlier review (Subramanian

and Mittelstaedt 1991) revealed that the relationships between innovativeness and most variables are equivocal. In addition, because most of the other variables in this study are product-category specific, the use of demographic and personality variables was ruled out. Among variables that were product-category specific, two that have demonstrated the most unequivocal relationships are "product category interest" and "product category involvement." However, product category interest appeared to be very similar to product category involvement, and product category knowledge was substituted to be used with product category involvement.

To measure product category knowledge levels, a 46 item computer software knowledge scale was built using the framework laid out by Brucks (1986). The three dimensions of Attribute-related, Terminology-Related, and Purchasing Procedures-related knowledge were used as a guideline for constructing items. Help was sought from faculty computer software experts and a knowledgable salesperson. This scale was pretested using 51 undergraduate students and an alpha of .82 was found. Inter-item and item-total correlations were computed, leading to the deletion of 9 items with corresponding increases in alpha. The final scale of 37 items had a coefficient alpha of .90.

To measure involvement, a number of scales are currently available including those by Zaichowsky (1987), Bloch (1986), and Lastovicka and Gardner (1979). In a recent study Smith (1990) validated 7 existing involvement scales and concluded that the 11 "importance" items of the Gardner and Lastovicka (1979) scale produce the most favorable blend of reliability and validity. The scale is easily adaptable to any product category with no change to any items and, accordingly, was used to measure involvement. Pretested with 51 undergraduates, it was found to be unidimensional with an alpha of .87.

DATA COLLECTION

The final sample comprised 88 university students from two separate campuses of a U. S. university and included 48 males and 40 females, 15 graduate students and 73 undergraduates. All students answered the questionnaire for class credit; one response was unusable.

All subjects studied the three innovative software products, and filled out the symbolic adoption scale for each product. In addition as part of manipulation check, each stimulus contained an item that measured the perceived innovativeness of the product. The other scales - involvement, knowledge, independent judgment making, and innovativeness - were filled out once by each subject. Data collection was carried out in a three day period.

ANALYSIS

The results of the analysis are presented in Table 1. Because the symbolic adoption scale was used 3 times (once for each stimulus), three sets of results are listed. The scale appears to have items that hang together well, as evidenced by the fairly high Cronbach's alpha scores. In addition, it should be noted that in no case could the alpha be increased by deleting any items. The scale was tested for unidimensionality by factor analysis and, in all the three cases, it appeared to be so. In each case, the first factor explained at least 64 percent of the total variance and in no case did the second factor have an Eigen value that approached 1. Thus it appears safe to conclude that the scale, in its current form, demonstrates reliability and unidimensionality.

To establish the several types of validity, symbolic adoption scores were correlated with innovativeness, independent judgment making, product category involvement, ongoing search, and product category knowledge. Because it is generally agreed that an innovation is that which is perceived to be "new" by the potential adopter, the symbolic adoption scores for each subject and product were analyzed using the perceived innovativeness scores for that innovation as a covariate. The results can be viewed as follows.

Convergent Validity

Convergent validity was tested by correlating the symbolic adoption scores with the Goldsmith and Hofacker (1991) innovativeness scores and the Carlson and Grossbart (1984) IJM scores. One of the correlations with the Goldsmith and Hofacker scale was significant at the .05 level and one approached significance (p = .12). This suggests that the symbolic adoption scale does have some amount of convergence with another current measures of innovativeness.

In testing for convergent validity with IJM scores, it was found that while two of the correlations with the IJM scale were significant at the .05 level, they were negative. This was contrary to our original hypotheses, and in the last section of the paper, this finding is discussed in more detail.

Discriminant Validity

Discriminant validity was tested by studying the correlations between the symbolic adoption scores and ongoing search scores. A low correlation between the two would suggest that the scale under construction was indeed measuring a construct distinct from ongoing search. Table 1 shows that in two of the products, there appeared to be no relationship; however for Product 3, the relationship appeared significant. This suggests that while the constructs are largely independent, there is some potential overlap.

Nomological Validity

To establish nomological validity symbolic adoption scores were correlated with two constructs (product category knowledge and involvement with the product category), that theory suggests would be related. In two of the three cases, the relationship between symbolic adoption and product category involvement approached significance; in all cases it was positive. However symbolic adoption scores were found to be unrelated to knowledge scores for any of the products, although it approached significance for one.

DISCUSSION

In summary, the symbolic adoption scale appears to have reliability and unidimensionality. It is moderately related to the innovativeness scale of Goldsmith and Hofacker (GHI), as it should be. It is mostly unrelated to ongoing search, as it should be. It is mostly unrelated to product category involvement and product category knowledge, although it should be. Finally, it is mostly negatively related to IJM, to which it should be positively related.

To interpret these findings, it is necessary to refer to

TABLE 1

Symbolic Adoption scale (Product 1)

Reliability (Cronbach's alpha): .89

Correlations:

	Innovati-veness	IJM	Ongoing Search	Involvement	Knowledge
Symbolic Adoption	.13* (P=.12)	-.23* (P=.01)	.10 (P=.16)	.08 (P=.22)	.09 (P=.21)

Factor Analysis:

Factor	Eigen Value	Pct of Variance
1	4.11	68.5
2	.66	11.0
3	.53	8.9
4	.35	5.9
5	.20	3.5
6	.13	2.2

Symbolic Adoption scale (Product 2)

Reliability (Cronbach's alpha): .89

Correlations:

	Innovati-veness	IJM	Ongoing Search	Involvement	Knowledge
Symbolic Adoption	-.04 (P=.34)	-.22* (P=.02)	-.02 (P=.40)	.13* (P=.10)	-.02 (P=.42)

Factor Analysis:

Factor	Eigen Value	Pct of Variance
1	3.89	64.9
2	.66	11.2
3	.54	9.0
4	.45	7.6
5	.28	4.8
6	.15	2.5

Symbolic Adoption scale (Product 3)

Reliability (Cronbach's alpha): .89

Correlations:

	Innovati-veness	IJM	Ongoing Search	Involvement	Knowledge
Symbolic Adoption	.18* (P=.05)	-.09 (P=.20)	.15* (P=.07)	.11* (P=.14)	.16* (P=.07)

Factor Analysis:

Factor	Eigen Value	Pct of Variance
1	4.09	68.3
2	.63	10.6
3	.47	4.4
6	.19	3.2

Table 2, which presents the correlations among the GHI, IJM, ongoing search, product category involvement, and product category knowledge. Note that each of these scales yielded reasonable levels of alpha, although one would prefer to see higher values for the GHI and the ongoing search scale.

In these data, the GHI and the IJM scale were significantly, inversely related. As noted earlier, these two represent very different conceptualizations of innovativeness. The GHI scale which is product-specific, is based upon ownership and other surrogates of possession, while the product-independent IJM addresses generalized pre-purchase communication and behavior. In addition, the distribution of scores on the IJM scale was seen to be strongly skewed to the lower end of the scale, possibly reflecting the strong wording of the items. In any case, this raises the question of convergence between the various conceptualizations of innovativeness, an issue that may have to be settled if we are to increase our understanding of this construct.

The different nature of these two scales is demonstrated further by the correlations with other variables; IJM was unrelated to each of the others while the GHI was significantly related to all of them. This, coupled with the fact that the symbolic adoption scale is based on a model more like the Rogers' conceptualization (upon which GHI is based) would suggest that symbolic adoption would be differentially related to the GHI and IJM scales, and the negative relationship between symbolic adoption and IJM should not surprising. However, it is to be noted that we did hypothesize a positive relationship between symbolic adoption and the IJM and GHI scales.

Equally puzzling is the relationship between product category involvement and product category knowledge. As can be seen in Table 2, these two variables were independent of one another and differentially related to GHI and ongoing search. The positive correlations between these two scales and product category knowledge is as expected; the negative relationships to product category involvement are most unexpected we can only speculate that a more appropriate measure of involvement should have been selected.

CONCLUSIONS

This paper has presented a measure of innovativeness based on a conceptualization grounded in the model of Klonglan and Coward (1970). While it requires further testing, it appears to have some useful psychometric properties. As the construct of interest, and the one on which the measurement of innovativeness is based, symbolic adoption offers some distinct advantages over the earlier conceptualizations of the adoption construct:

First, it is less likely to be affected by external influences than purchase measures of adoption. For example earlier indicators of adoption which include purchase, trial, ownership, etc., are all affected by a number of external influences such as availability of product and finances. In addition, purchase based measures implicitly assume that the consumer is currently in the market for the product. These are major influences which may keep the person who accepts the idea of the innovation from making a trial which involves purchase or any other activity costing money and/or time. For example, even the most innovative person is likely to be out of the market for cars if he or she has recently purchased one. Symbolic adoption which is concerned with the adoption of the idea of the innovative product

TABLE 2

Correlations	IJM	Ongoing Search	Involvement	Knowledge
Innovativeness	-.23*	.47**	-.24*	.20
IJM		.01	.03	.04
Ongoing-Search			-.28**	.58**
Involvement				-.05
Knowledge				

Innovativeness: Cronbach alpha .79

IJM: Cronbach alpha .94

Ongoing-Search: Cronbach alpha .81

Involvement: Cronbach alpha .87

Knowledge: Cronbach alpha .91

therefore does not require some of the prerequisites for purchase or ownership that other measures of adoption do.

Second, as conceptualized by Klonglan and Coward, symbolic adoption is the output of cognitive processing, a "psychological" phenomenon. Most researchers continue to view innovativeness as a consumer trait (in the sense that extroversion or aggressiveness or shyness are traits) and search for other related, antecedent consumer characteristics. Since many of these other characteristics are also "psychological" in the broadest sense, attempting to relate them to the outcome of a decision process may prove more fruitful than trying to relate them to a purchase behavior.

Finally, and at the managerial level, it might be argued that symbolic adoption is likely to be a less than perfect predictor of eventual adoption. While that is probably true, it seems highly likely that the other outcome of the decision, symbolic rejection, will prove a very reliable predictor of non-adoption. Thus, measuring symbolic adoption and rejection "upstream" may be very useful in determining the "ceiling rate" of eventual adoption for those innovations which do not reach 100% saturation.

REFERENCES

Bloch, Peter H. (1986), "Product Enthusiasts: Many Questions, a Few Answers," XIII, in *Advances in Consumer Research,* Richard J. Lutz, ed. Provo, UT: Association for Consumer Research, 539-544.

_____, Daniel L. Sherrell, and Nancy Ridgway (1986), "Consumer Search: An Extended Framework," *Journal of Consumer Research,* 13 (June), 119-126.

Brucks, Merrie (1985), "The Effects of Product Class Knowledge on Information Search Behavior," *Journal of Consumer Research,* 12 (June), 1-16.

_____ (1986), "A Typology of Consumer Knowledge Content," in *Advances in Consumer Research,* Richard J. Lutz, ed. Provo UT: Association for Consumer Research, 13, 58-63.

Carlson, Les and Sanford L. Grossbart (1984), "Toward a Better Understanding of Inherent Innovativeness," in *AMA Educators' Proceedings,* R.W. Belk et al. eds. Chicago: American Marketing Association, 50, 88-91.

Churchill, Gilbert A., Jr. (1979), "A Paradigm for Developing Better Measures of Marketing Constructs," *Journal of Marketing Research,* 16 (February), 64-73.

Darden, William R., and Fred D. Reynolds (1974), "Backward Profiling of Male Innovators," *Journal of Marketing Research,* 11 (February), 79-85.

Donnelly, James H. (1970), "Social Character and Acceptance of New Products," *Journal of Marketing Research,* 7 (February), 111-113.

Foxall, Gordon and Christopher G. Haskins (1986), "Cognitive Style and Consumer Innovativeness: An Empirical Test of Kirton's Adaption-Innovation Theory in the Context of Food Purchasing," *European Journal of Marketing,* 20 (3/4), 63-80.

Gatignon, Hubert and Thomas S. Robertson (1985), "A Propositional Inventory for New Diffusion Research," *Journal of Consumer Research,* 11 (March), 849-867.

Goldsmith, Ronald E. and Charles F. Hofacker (1991), "Measuring Consumer Innovativeness," *Journal of the Academy of Marketing Science,* 19 (3), 209-221.

Hirschman, Elizabeth C. (1980), "Innovativeness, Novelty Seeking, and Consumer Creativity," *Journal of Consumer Research,* 7 (December), 289-95.

_____ (1981), "Symbolism and Technology as Sources for the Generation of Innovations," in *Advances in Consumer Research,* Andrew Mitchell, ed. St. Louis, MO: Association for Consumer Research, 9, 537-541.

Joachimsthaler, Eric A. and John L. Lastovicka (1984), "Optimal Stimulation Level-Exploratory Behavior Models," *Journal of Consumer Research,* 11 (December), 830-835.

Klonglan, G. E. and E. W. Coward (1970), "The Concept of Symbolic Adoption: A Suggested Interpretation," *Rural Sociology,* 35, (March), 77-83.

Lambert, Zarrel V. (1972), "Perceptual Patterns, Information Handling, and Innovativeness," *Journal of Marketing Research,* 9 (November), 427-31.

Lapidus, Richard (1991), "Visual Information Processing of Print Advertising: Cognitive and Experiential Response to Artistic Style," Unpublished Doctoral Dissertation, University of Nebraska.

Lastovicka, John L. and David M. Gardner (1979), "Components of Involvement," in *Attitude Research Plays for High Stakes,* John C. Maloney and Bernard Silverman, eds. Chicago, IL: American Marketing Association, 53-73.

Midgley, David F. (1977), *Innovation and New Product Marketing.* New York: Halsted Press, John Wiley and Sons.

_____ and Grahame R. Dowling (1978), "Innovativeness: The Concept and Its Measurement," *Journal of Consumer Research,* 4 (March), 229-242.

Mittelstaedt, Robert A., Sanford L. Grossbart, William W. Curtis, and Stephen P. Devere (1976), "Optimal Stimulation Level and the Adoption Decision Process," *Journal of Marketing Research,* 3 (September), 84-94.

Nunnally, Jum C. (1978), *Psychometric Theory,* New York: McGraw-Hill.

Ostlund, (1972), "A Study of Innovativeness Overlap,"

Journal of Marketing Research, 9 (August), 341-343.

Robertson, Thomas S. and James H. Myers (1969), "Personality Correlates of Opinion Leadership and Innovative Buying Behavior," *Journal of Marketing Research,* 6 (May), 164-8.

Rogers, Everett M. (1962), *Diffusion of Innovations.* New York: The Free Press.

_____(1983), *Diffusion of Innovations.* third edition, New York: The Free Press.

_____and F. Floyd Shoemaker (1971), *Communication of Innovations.* New York: The Free Press.

Smith, Laurie P. (1990), " A Validation Study of Selected Involvement Measures Assessing Women's Involvement With Cosmetics," Unpublished Doctoral Dissertation, University of Nebraska.

Subramanian, Suresh and Robert A. Mittelstaedt (1991), "Conceptualizing Innovativeness as a Consumer Trait: Consequences and Alternatives," in *AMA Summer Educators Conference Proceedings.* Mary C. Gilly et al. eds. 352-360.

Summers, John O. (1971), "Generalized Change Agents and Innovativeness," *Journal of Marketing Research,* 8 (August), 313-316.

_____(1972), "Media Exposure Patterns of Consumer Innovators," *Journal of Marketing,* 36 (January), 43-49.

Taylor, James W. (1977), "A Striking Characteristic of Innovators," *Journal of Marketing Research,* 14 (February), 104-107.

Venkatraman, Meera Pandit (1986), "Consumer Innovativeness: The Concept and its Relationship with Innovative Behavior," Unpublished Doctoral Dissertation, The University of Pittsburgh.

_____and Linda Price (1990), "Differentiating Between Cognitive and Sensory Innovativeness, *Journal of Business Research,* 20, 293-315.

Zaichkowsky, Judith L. (1987), "The Personal Involvement Inventory: Reduction, Revision, and Application to Advertising," Working Paper, Simon Fraser University.

APPENDIX A
Stimuli Used in the Study

1. The Encyclopedia: This software contains the entire American Encyclopedia. In addition to written information, the software also includes pictures wherever they appear in the original volumes. The user can search for information in a variety of ways and directly bring text and visual information into other wordprocessing files.

2. Scan Do: The Scan Do software makes keying in of information by hand almost redundant. The software permits you to input any amount of text without keying the material by hand. All that is required is to pass a hand held scanner over the page of text, and it is automatically read into the computer. The scanner can read upto 5 pages per minute.

3. The Highwayman: The Highwayman software contains details on all paved roads in the US. When provided with a starting and destination postal address, it will print out the shortest, the fastest, and the cheapest (taking into account toll-roads) route that one can take. Can accomodate queries relating to multiple stop-overs and other special requests like "scenic route" etc.

APPENDIX B
Items in the Final Scale

1. If this software were availabe at my local store I would consider purchasing it.

2. If I were in the market for some computer software, and this software package was available at my regular place of shopping, I would consider purchasing it.

3. I think this is a software package that I would like to have.

4. I think I would like to try this software package.

5. I am willing to expend the effort to try out this software package.

6. I like the idea of this software package.

AN EXAMINATION OF STRUCTURAL FACTORS AFFECTING PRODUCTIVITY IN JAPANESE RETAILING, 1976 - 1988

Robert Stassen, *University of Arkansas*
Mayuresh Kelkar, *University of Arkansas*
Craig Schulman, *University of Arkansas*

ABSTRACT

Criticisms of the Japanese distribution system have centered on the many small firms which dominate its wholesale and retail markets, arguing that such systems inflate prices of consumer goods through their inefficiency. The existing system supports multiple levels of wholesalers and a retail structure dominated by an abundance of small shops. This paper examines the relationship of this distribution system's structure on retail productivity in an effort to assess its role as an inadvertent trade barrier that limits the affordability of all consumer products.

The study utilizes Census of Commerce data from 1976, 1979, 1982 1985, and 1988 reported by Japan's Ministry of International Trade and Industry, with each of the country's forty-seven prefectures serving as observations in a cross-sectional design. These reports contain three retailing inputs: number of employees, inventory, and selling space. This allowed the productivity measures of sales per employee, sales per square meter, and inventory turnover to be used as in the study to provide a assessment of productivity which includes both capital and labor retailing inputs. Seemingly unrelated regression modeling was used in an attempt to isolate the effects of the number of retailers per person, the proportion of small and family establishments, and population density from the effects of changing macro-economic conditions on the productivity measures. Analysis was confined to five retail types within household furnishings sector.

All independent variables were found to have a consistently significant effect across measures of productivity in at least one of the retail categories. Sales per square meter was the productivity dimension most consistently affected by the variables included in this study, with population density having a consistent positive effect across categories. Sales per employee was negatively affected by the proportion of small and family establishments within a prefecture, however, the number of retailers in a market had an inconsistent effect on this variable in certain categories. Inventory turnover was consistently affected only by the population density of the prefecture. While many consistent relationships were found across categories, several inconsistencies limit the ability to make generalizations about the relationship of productivity and retail structure in Japan, particularly with respect to competitiveness and economies of scale.

For further information contact:
Robert Stassen
Department of Marketing and Transportation
320 College of Business Administration
University of Arkansas
Fayetteville, AR 72701

A CROSS-NATIONAL COMPARISON OF THE DETERMINANTS OF BUSINESS PERFORMANCE: IMPLICATIONS FOR GLOBAL VS. MULTI-DOMESTIC STRATEGIES

David M. Szymanski, Texas A&M University
Sundar G. Bharadwaj, Texas A&M University
P. Rajan Varadarajan, Texas A&M University

ABSTRACT

Successful business performance in foreign and domestic markets depends heavily on developing appropriate strategies for competing effectively in multiple markets. Developing sound multimarket strategies in turn requires that businesses ascertain whether a global (one strategy for all markets) or multidomestic (separate strategies for each market) marketing strategy will maximize returns on their investments, as well as an understanding of factors critical to successful performance in foreign markets. While there seems to be a general consensus that developing sound-international strategies is a function of the quality and quantity of information available on factors conducive to superior business performance in foreign and domestic markets, we find that only a few studies have actually examined the strategic determinants of business performance (in terms of measures such as market share and profitability) in foreign markets (e.g., Douglas and Craig 1983; Douglas, Craig, and Reddy 1987; Kotabe 1990). Thus, the purpose of the study described here is to examine whether global or multidomestic strategies are appropriate when competing in certain markets. Specifically, we examine whether the effects of competitive strategy and market structure variables on business performance generalize across U.S., U.K., Canadian, and Western European markets, and identify factors critical to performance within each of the four markets.

RESULTS

The results suggest that the competitive strategy-performance relationship generalizes across the markets considered, and that the data can be pooled across the U.S., U.K., Canadian, and Western European samples. The findings from the pooled sample suggest that a broad product line, high product quality, high levels of customer service, and competing in more concentrated markets are conducive to enhancing the market share position of a business. Selling high quality goods, relatively lower levels of R&D effort, vertical integration and emphasis on new products, competing in high growth markets, following a strategy of increasing market share, and sharing customers among business units, yet minimizing the degree to which operating facilities are shared across these same units are conducive to enhancing a business' financial performance.

CONCLUSION

A key question for firms competing in multiple national markets is "Whether pursuit of a single strategy in all markets or pursuit of different strategies in different national markets is conducive to superior firm performance?" In an attempt to provide insights into this question, this study examined a number of strategic variables for their effects on business profits in Western markets. The findings reveal that product quality and market share are among the more critical determinants of the business' financial performance. More importantly, the findings reveal that the same competitive strategy can be used with equal effectiveness in U.S., U.K., Canadian, and Western European markets.

For further information please contact:
Dr. David M. Szymanski
Assistant Professor of Marketing
College of Business Administration and
Graduate School of Business
Texas A&M University
College Station, Texas 77843-4112

APPLYING MARKETING CONCEPTS IN THIRD WORLD COUNTRIES: ASSESSING THE EXISTENCE AND IMPLICATIONS OF STAGES OF ORGANIZATIONAL MARKETING DEVELOPMENT

Kofi Q. Dadzie, Georgia State University
Ishmael P. Akaah, Wayne State University
Edward A. Riordan, Wayne State University

ABSTRACT

This paper examines the degree to which the perceived usefulness of marketing concepts and the performance of marketing management activities vary across Third World and developed countries (United States and Japan). The results suggest that the applicability issue does not apply only to Third World countries.

INTRODUCTION

Several arguments have been posited for and against the application of conventional marketing concepts, techniques, and activities in Third World countries. Among the main arguments for the application of marketing concepts in these economies is the contingency argument-- the view that marketing knowhow is applicable in all countries, but the degree of applicability is contingent upon environmental influences. If the "contingency" arguments for the applicability of conventional marketing knowhow in the Third World are valid, then it follows that the level of global applicability of marketing knowhow might vary with country and organizational characteristics. The appeal of the contingency arguments, notwithstanding, the impact of country and organizational factors on the applicability of marketing knowhow, remains to be empirically examined. Although a promising body of literature on Third World marketing has emerged, no study has comprehensively examined the influence of organizational factors on the applicability of modern marketing knowhow. The present study attempts to build on previous studies of Third World marketing, by examining the influence of a selected set of organizational factors on the applicability of marketing knowhow across both developed and developing economies. More specifically, the study examines the extent to which homogeneous groups of firms exist relative to the application of marketing concepts and techniques and whether these groups reflect similar or different stages of economic development.

METHODOLOGY

The target population for the study comprised business organizations from the U.S., Japan and two Third World countries (Kenya and Nigeria). The U.S. and Japan samples were chosen using the Dun and Bradstreet's *Principal International Business - World Marketing Directory* (1990) and the two Third World samples were drawn from the *Owens Directory* (1988). The sampling process yielded a total of 1450 firms, with 650 from the U.S., 400 from Japan, and 200 each from Nigeria and Kenya. A mail questionnaire was sent to the senior marketing executive in each of the sampled firms, after a pretest. In the case of the Japanese sample, the questionnaire was translated into Japanese before its use. Four hundred and fifty questionnaires were returned of which 419 were useable -- representing a net response rate of 28.9 percent.

Country characteristics were operationalized in terms of the level of four economic development factors, i.e., GNP per capita, adult illiteracy rate, annual rate of inflation and life expectancy. Organizational attributes were assessed by using multiple indicators and measurement scales for customer orientation, interfunctional integration, and marketing orientation of senior executives. Applicability of marketing concepts and techniques and marketing management activity performance were also operationalized by using multiple items and scales.

The data were analyzed via cluster analysis. The number of extracted clusters was based on cluster stability and the minimization of within group variance. To test the significance of similarities and differences in study response across the extracted clusters, a canonical correlation analysis was also performed.

RESULTS

The analysis yielded four homogenous clusters. The four clusters were statistically different on 23 of the 25 items examined (p < .01). The first cluster comprised mostly African firms, the second and third, U.S. firms, and the fourth Japanese firms. The extracted clusters reflected varying levels of development and application of marketing concepts and techniques -- thus lending support to the contigency framework.

CONCLUSION

In summary, the study results imply that different environments might call for different degrees and extent of applicability of modern marketing knowhow.

For further information contact:
Kofi Q. Dadzie
Department of Marketing
Georgia State University
University Plaza
Atlanta, GA 30303

PRELIMINARY FINDINGS ON COOPERATIVE RESEARCH EFFORTS BETWEEN BUSINESS SCHOOLS AND THE PRIVATE AND PUBLIC SECTORS

Steven W. Pharr, University of Idaho

ABSTRACT

Recent criticisms of business education suggest that academia has fallen short in the areas of research and service (AACSB and EFMD 1982, Porter and McKibbin 1988). Cooperation between faculty, practitioners and business research bureaus has been suggested as a means to enhance outcomes of the educational process (Lambert and Sterling 1988). Anticipated benefits might include increased faculty research, hands-on student experience with business problems, affordable quality research for businesses, and greater credibility for business schools (Pharr and Stuefen 1991). Although a few cooperative arrangements of this type have been reported, the level of incidence and degree of success in American higher education is not known. This research considered a number of probable causes of the problems cited and the anticipated or experienced benefits associated with cooperative research efforts. In addition, survey research was employed in order to document the incidence of these types of programs, levels of activity and success, and the associated benefits and problems.

This research focused on two separate, yet related populations of interest; University and College based Schools of Business and Business Research Bureaus in the United States. The contact persons for the former were Business School Deans and Research Bureau Directors for the latter. Sample selection was straight forward. In the case of the Research Bureau population, the Association for University Business and Economic Research (AUBER) membership directory was used to identify the members of the population (Still and Stanphill 1989). Since the entire membership totaled only 155, a census was used. In the case of business school deans, the AACSB membership directory was employed (AACSB 1991), from which a random sample of 300 educational members was selected.

Survey execution involved four stages: a prenotification letter; a survey packet including a cover letter, the survey and a postage-paid envelop; a reminder postcard; and finally, a second mailing of the survey packet to those who failed to respond. Response rates were 48 percent and 51 percent for the Dean and Bureau Director samples, respectively. To test for nonresponse bias, respondents and nonrespondents were compared in terms of degrees offered, accreditation status and average number of tenure track faculty members. Both the respondents and nonrespondents were virtually identical regarding degree programs offered. The nonrespondents, however, had a lower accreditation rate and smaller full-time tenure track faculties than responding institutions, however, this might be expected due to the research orientation of the survey. The most likely effect would be a slight overstatement of cooperative research activities at U.S. colleges and universities.

Evaluation of both samples was carried out in the same manner. Institutions were categorized according to their level of research productivity, with productivity operationalized as the number of academic publications resulting from cooperative activities. Similar patterns were observed in both samples. The largest category was the zero publication group while the productive groups were considerably smaller. Some indication of a critical mass is apparent, although the numbers are not overwhelming. Larger faculties tend to be more productive, have lighter teaching loads, and higher rates of accreditation. Somewhat independent from faculty size was the level of faculty involvement. Higher levels of productivity were achieved by those institutions with the greatest faculty participation rates. The most popular areas of inquiry were economics, management and marketing while accounting and POM were the least common. A majority of the most productive institutions were active in two or more areas of inquiry and the most common clients were business firms and government agencies.

Regarding the benefits and problems associated with these efforts, the most frequently mentioned positives were an improved image and an increase in faculty competence and earnings. Increased faculty research and publications were listed less frequently. Drawbacks of these efforts include a lack of funding, faculty support and administrative problems. Consistent with these findings is a less than enthusiastic assessment of the likelihood of generating academic publications. However, cooperative efforts between business and academia **are** taking place in many schools and academic publications have resulted. The key ingredients include high levels of faculty involvement and streamlined coordination of the cooperative effort. Ironically, these are the problems cited most often.

For further information please contact: Steven W. Pharr
University of Idaho
College of Business and Economics
Moscow, Idaho 83843

THE ROLE OF PROCEEDINGS IN THE EVALUATION OF FACULTY RESEARCH STANDARDS IN AACSB-ACCREDITED MARKETING DEPARTMENTS

Jane P. Wayland, Eastern Illinois University
David J. Urban, Virginia Commonwealth Univeristy
Dennis R. McDermott, Virginia Commonwealth University

ABSTRACT

Previous research has not included the role of conference proceedings in the evaluation of faculty research. This paper broadens the current knowledge. A survey of AACSB-accredited marketing department chairs determined that conference proceedings are not considered evidence of faculty research to a significant extent especially among institutions that have a high emphasis on research. The findings also indicate that marketing chairs perceive national conferences to have greater value than regional conferences.

INTRODUCTION

Conferences have long played a major role in the development of marketing educators. Conferences provide the arena for intellectual stimulation among participants, a forum for new ideas, placement services for new employment possibilities, opportunities for personal growth, and an outlet for research endeavors. It is the published proceedings of the marketing conferences that is topic of this paper.

Many different conferences are held each year offering a wide variety of research outlets for the marketing academician. Unlike other research outlets, conference proceedings require additional time and costs. Papers presented at conferences cost the faculty member time to attend the conference and in some cases lost time in the classroom. Monetary costs that include travel, expenses during the conference, and registration fees are important to administration. It is important to balance the time requirements and monetary costs with the perceived value of the published paper. Are articles published in conference proceedings important to faculty members and the universities they serve?

Research is becoming increasingly important in the evaluation of faculty for promotion and tenure. This has prompted researchers to study the function research plays in the evaluation of faculty and to rank journals to determine the importance of journal quality in evaluating research productivity. The current literature provides little insight as to the perceived value of national and regional conference proceedings. This paper presents several objectives in understanding the function of published proceedings in faculty research evaluation. The questions examined include:

a. How do chairs of AACSB-accredited marketing departments view various proceedings as evidence of published faculty research?

b. What are the differences between AACSB-accredited schools that have a greater research emphasis than schools that have less emphasis on research in the evaluation of research published in proceedings?

c. Do chairs view proceedings differently for assistant, associate and full professors?

d. Are there differences between AACSB-accredited schools that offer a Ph.D./D.B.A. and those that do not in the evaluation of proceeding publications?

PREVIOUS RESEARCH

Research is an important activity for faculty members. Several studies of AACSB schools reveal the importance of research. Beltramini, Schlacter, and Kelley (1985) in a study of 69 marketing department chairs, determined that teaching was the most important academic activity overall, with research being a close second. D'Onofrio, Slama and Tashchian (1988) based on a study of marketing and non-marketing department chairs, concluded that research was the major factor in evaluating faculty performance. Teer and Wisdom (1989) found that marketing faculty and department heads stressed research as being the most important criterion. Marketing faculty at AACSB schools placed more emphasis on research than non-AACSB institutions in a study by Tong and Bures (1989). Research is weighted more for schools that have Ph.D. programs and those that do not (Robicheaux and Boya 1989).

The quality of research has often been measured by the assessment of the quality of the journal the article appears. Coe and Weinstock (1983) surveyed 105 marketing department chairs from AACSB-accredited schools and found that the journal in which an article appeared was clearly the most important factor in assessing the article's quality. Bertsch (1986) also reported that 48 of 125 deans at AACSB-accredited institutions responding to his survey used journal rankings to evaluate faculty performance for promotion, tenure, or merit pay. Many schools rate the scholarly impact of an article according to where it is published rather than the content of the article (Motes 1986).

Traditionally, publications in national proceedings have been viewed more positively than publications in academic journal articles outside the marketing discipline by marketing department chairpersons (Beltramini, Schlacter, and Kelley 1985). However, only two studies have included a conference proceeding in their rankings. Browne and Becker (1991) in a study of marketing chairs at AACSB-accredited schools ranked AMA Conference *Proceedings* 39 out of 52 journals. The authors also noted that the AMA Conference *Proceedings* had fallen from 24 to 39 in a twelve year period. Only 2.7 percent of the respondents rated the *Proceedings* as being high quality. Thirty percent rated it as being fairly high quality and 49.3 percent rated the conference *Proceedings* as being fairly low in quality.

Luke and Doke (1987) in a study of faculty members and chairs of members of AACSB found that AMA Conference *Proceedings* were viewed as having low prestige and importance as well as low in popularity and familiarity. However, the *Proceedings* were still considered higher on both dimensions than the *Journal of Business, Industrial Marketing Management,* and *Business Horizons* among others.

Limited research has been conducted on proceedings as evidence of scholarly research. The lack of research suggests a need for exploratory research in this area. This study concentrates on ascertaining the current view of proceedings as evidence of published research at AACSB-accredited schools.

RESEARCH METHODOLOGY

Respondent Selection

Chairs/coordinators of marketing departments of 256 AACSB-accredited schools were surveyed using a mailed questionnaire. A follow-up questionnaire was mailed approximately three weeks after the first questionnaire. The procedure generated 145 replies. Three surveys were returned unanswered, leaving 142 usable responses for a response rate of 55.5 percent. Table 1 presents a profile of respondents by size of faculty and program.

RESULTS

Relative Importance of Published Proceedings

Using a seven point scale, respondents were asked to what extent articles published in the proceedings of nine separate conferences were considered evidence of published faculty research in their departments. A score of one indicated that the articles were considered published research to a very insignificant extent and a seven indicated the articles were considered published research to a great extent. Paired t-tests were used to determine statistical differences between the mean responses of the

TABLE 1
Profile of Respondents

Size of Graduate Program

Not Applicable	3.6%
100 or less	10.9%
101-250	22.5%
251-500	27.5%
501-1000	21.7%
More than 1000	13.8%

Size of Undergraduate Program

Not Applicable	4.3%
500 or less	10.8%
501 - 1000	17.3%
1001 - 2500	31.7%
2501 - 5000	23.7%
More than 5000	12.2%

Total Number of Marketing Faculty

Less than 8	21.9
9 - 15	48.2
16 - 20	15.8
21 - 34	14.0

Faculty Profile	Mean	Mode
Full Professors	3.86	2.00
Associate Professors	2.94	1.00
Assistant Professors	3.27	3.00
Instructors and Part-time faculty	2.96	1.00
Tenured	6.17	4.00
Untenured	4.36	3.00

conferences. Each conference was paired with the conference ranked below it. Table 2 provides the mean values of the respondents and the results of the paired t-tests.

As would be expected, papers in national proceedings were regarded more highly than regional conference proceedings. The Association for Consumer Research and the American Marketing Association Educators' Conference were the only conferences that were rated higher than the scale's midpoint as evidence of published faculty research. Academy of Marketing Science was the third most important proceedings followed by AMA's Services and AMS Retailing Conferences. The mean responses as indicated in Table 2 suggest that papers published at AMA and ACR are considered evidence of published faculty research. However, other conference papers are not necessarily considered significant evidence of faculty research among AACSB-accredited

TABLE 2
Proceedings as Evidence of Faculty Research

Conference	Mean
Assn. for Consumer Research (ACR)	4.46
American Marketing Assn. Educators' (AMA)	4.22
Academy of Marketing Science (AMS)	3.67
American Marketing Assn. Services Conference (AMAS)	3.09
Academy of Marketing Science Retailing Conference (AMSR)	2.82
Southern Marketing Assn. (SMA)	2.75*
Southwestern Marketing Assn. (SWMA)	2.27
Midwest Marketing Assn. (MMA)	2.23*
Western Marketing Assn. (WMA)	2.15**

Question: To what extent are articles published in the proceedings of the following professional meetings considered evidence of published faculty research?
1 = to a very insignificant extent and
7 = a great extent

* not significant compared to the preceding conference
** significant at .04 to the preceding conference other entries p ≤ .01 compared to the preceding conference

marketing departments.

The paired t-tests indicate significant differences between the conferences in most all instances. The Association of Consumer Research was rated significantly higher than the American Marketing Association Educators' which in turn was significantly higher than the Academy of Marketing Science. No differences were found between Academy of Marketing Science Retailing Conference and Southern Marketing Association or between Southwestern Marketing Association and Midwest Marketing Association.

Since responses were confidential, no information was available to determine regional representativeness of AACSB schools. This may have an impact on the perceived value of regional conferences. If more respondents participate in the Southern Marketing Association because of their geographic location, it is plausible that this conference may be rated higher than another regional conference.

Importance of Proceedings Among Research Institutions

Respondents were asked to distribute 100 points

among teaching, research and service according to the relative emphasis placed upon these activities at their institutions for assistant, associate and full professors. Respondents allocating 50 or more points on research were categorized as "high research emphasis" institutions. Respondents ranking research less than 50 were categorized as having a "lower research emphasis". T-tests were utilized to determine if high research institutions viewed proceedings differently than institutions that placed less emphasis on research. Among all conferences, except Advances in Consumer Research, there was a significant difference between the high and low research groups at the assistant, associate and full ranks. Institutions that place more emphasis on research viewed proceedings as less evidence of published faculty research for all ranks than did institutions that place less emphasis on research.

A review of the means also indicates that proceedings are viewed as evidence of faculty research to a greater degree for assistant professors than for associate and full professors. For example, the means for AMS at institutions with a high research emphasis indicates that a paper published in the AMS *Proceedings* is considered stronger evidence of research for assistant professors (3.20). Associate professors (3.17) and full professors (2.82) are given less credit for a paper published at AMS. While there is no statistical significant difference between ranks, this trend generally occurs both in schools that emphasize research and those that have less emphasis on research. Perhaps as faculty members become more senior, higher quality research is expected. Senior faculty have less pressure to "publish and perish" than do assistant professors who may be interested in quantity and quality efforts. Senior faculty have more experience and therefore can make contributions of higher quality. Service activities also increase as faculty advance in rank (AMA Task Force 1988).

Ph.D. Versus Non-Ph.D. Schools

The respondents were further categorized into Ph.D./D.B.A. granting institutions and those that do not offer a doctoral degree. T-tests were again used to determine if there was a significant difference among the two groups in evaluating the conference proceedings. Table 4 indicates the mean responses of the two groups. Again, in all conferences except Advances in Consumer Research, Ph.D. granting institutions viewed proceedings as less evidence of published research than did non-Ph.D. granting institutions. This confirms the previous finding as research is emphasized in doctoral degree granting institutions (Robicheaux and Boya 1989

CONCLUSIONS AND IMPLICATIONS

This study revealed that conference proceedings are not used to a large extent as evidence of published faculty research. However, proceedings are viewed somewhat

TABLE 3
Comparison of Schools in Relation to Research Emphasis

	Assistant Professor		Associate Professor		Full Professor	
	Lo (n=64)	High (n=71)	Lo (n=77)	High (n=59)	Lo (n=96)	High (n=40)
ACR	4.59	4.35	4.54	4.31	4.58	4.07
AMA	4.59	3.82*	4.60	3.68*	4.54	3.41*
AMS	4.09	3.20	4.01	3.17	3.98	2.82
AMAS	3.45	2.67	3.37	2.66	3.33	2.44
AMSR	3.08	2.50	3.01	2.46**	2.95	2.27
SMA	3.20	2.18	3.16	2.07	3.01	1.92
SWMA	2.62	1.91	2.57	1.85	2.49	1.70
MMA	2.59	1.84	2.56	1.75	2.48	1.56
WMA	2.51	1.79	2.44	1.76	2.39	1.57

* not significant
** significant at p = .06
all other entries p < .05

more favorably for assistant professors than associate and full professors. Institutions with a higher emphasis on research regard the proceedings as published research to a lesser degree than other institutions. Findings also indicate that some proceedings are perceived to have a higher value than other conference proceedings. Advances in Consumer Research, AMA Educators', and Academy of Marketing Science were viewed as having more importance than the specialized and regional conferences.

Given that the published proceedings have little

TABLE 4
Comparison of Ph.D. and Non-PH.D. Granting Institutions

	Ph.D. Schools (n=79)	Non-Ph.D. (n=49)
ACR	4.40	4.63*
AMA	3.91	4.53**
AMS	3.21	4.10
AMAS	2.89	3.24*
AMSR	2.44	3.15
SMA	2.24	3.16
SWMA	1.86	2.68
MMA	1.84	2.59
WMA	1.72	2.52

* not significant
** significant at p = .06
all other entries p < .05

impact in the evaluation of faculty research, should marketing faculty ignore publishing in national and especially regional proceedings? There are increasingly more marketing journals which provide additional outlets for faculty. Other research by the authors indicate there are at least 100 journals available to marketing scholars for publication of their research. Many of these journals have begun publication within the last ten years.

With fewer submissions to conferences, proceedings may suffer in terms of quality papers. Less quality research and presentations may not provide interesting and stimulating sessions for participants. This may in turn cause conferences, especially regional conferences, to suffer future membership loss or low attendance. These possibilities, along with tight budgets, may negatively impact the advantages of publishing papers in regional and national proceedings.

The unique nature of proceedings when correctly administered can provide greater benefits for the researcher than a publication in a low quality journal. Presentations at conferences provide feedback for new ideas, the review process provides written critiques, and the proceedings provide outlets for pretests and small samples. Additionally, there are numerous opportunities for interpersonal interaction among colleagues at national and regional conferences which may lead to future research.

It also could be argued that some proceedings require a more rigorous review process than do lower level journals. AMA Educators' Proceedings ranked higher in quality than 13 other journals in the Browne and Becker study (1991). The current study ranked AMA and ACR

Proceedings positively, possibly due to long term visibility of the two conferences.

While this study has provided empirical information on the current function of proceedings in the evaluation of faculty research, it is limited to AACSB-accredited marketing departments. No conclusions can be made about non-accredited institutions. Future research should include these schools and colleges of business as well as information on other advantages that conferences offer their members. Additional empirical information is required to further understand the role of conference proceedings in the research efforts of marketing faculty as well as the long term effects on national and regional proceedings.

REFERENCES

AMA Task Force on the Development of Marketing Thought (1988), "Developing, Disseminating, and Utilizing Marketing Knowledge," *Journal of Marketing*, 52 (4), 1-25.

Beltramini, Richard F., John L. Schlacter, and Craig Kelley (1985), "Marketing Faculty Promotion and Tenure Policies and Practices," *Journal of Marketing Education*, 7 (Summer), 74-80.

Bertsch, Thomas M. (1986),"Journal and Article Ratings: Criteria and Usage in Evaluating Marketing Teachers," in *Marketing in a Dynamic Environment,* Michael H. Morris and Eugene E. Teeple, eds. Orlando, Florida: Atlantic Marketing Association, 270-276.

Browne, William G. and Boris W. Becker (1991), "A Longitudinal Study of Marketing Journal Familiarity and Quality," in *1991 AMA Summer Educators' Conference Proceedings: Enhancing Knowledge Development in Marketing,* Mary C. Gilly et al., eds. Chicago, Illinois: American Marketing Association, 702-710.

Coe, Robert K. and Irwin Weinstock (1983), "Evaluating Journal Publications of Marketing Professors: A Second Look," *Journal of Marketing Education*, 5 (Spring), 37-42

D'Onofrio, Marianne J., Mark E. Slama, and Armen Tashchian (1988), "Faculty Evaluation Perspectives in Colleges of Business: How Marketing Department Heads' Evaluations Differ from Those of Department Heads in Other Business Disciplines," *Journal of Marketing Education*, 10 (Summer), 21-28.

Luke, Robert H. and E. Reed Doke (1987), "Marketing Journal Hierarchies: Faculty Perceptions," *Journal of the Academy of Marketing Science*, 15 (1), 74-77.

Motes, William H. (1989),"What Our Doctoral Students Should Know About the Publishing Game," *Journal of Marketing Education*, 11 (Spring), 22-27.

Robicheaux, Robert A. and Unal O. Boya (1989), "Assessment of Marketing Educators Institutional Evaluation Versus Idealized Work Styles," *Journal of Business Research*, 19, 277-282.

Teer, Harold B. and Barry L. Wisdom (1989), "Differing Perceptions of Job Priorities for Marketing Education," *Journal of Marketing Education*, 11 (Fall), 12-18.

Tong, Hsin-Min and Allen L Bures (1989), "Marketing Faculty Evaluation Systems: A National Survey," *Journal of Marketing Education*, 11 (Spring), 10-13

EVALUATION OF MARKETING PUBLICATIONS: SOME NEW FINDINGS

Peter J. Gordon, *Southeast Missouri State University*
Kenneth A. Heischmidt, *Southeast Missouri State University*

ABSTRACT

This paper reports the findings of a nationwide survey of department chairpersons at AACSB member schools. Those surveyed were asked to rate over 40 publications in the field of marketing. The resultant ratings were then used to develop a ranking of the top journals.

PURPOSE AND METHODOLOGY

The primary purpose of this study was to examine the perceived value of marketing related journals, based on the evaluations of department chairpersons at AACSB member schools, and to develop a ranking based upon these ratings.

Several previous studies have examined the stature of marketing publications. Most notable of these were three studies published in the mid-eighties. Luke and Doke (1987) reported results from the evaluation of thirty marketing related journals, with the *Journal of Marketing* (*JM*) receiving the highest rating. Cox and Weinstock (1983) rated fourteen marketing related journals, while Fry, Walters, and Scheuermann (1985) evaluated fifty business related journals. Both these studies cited the *Journal of Marketing Research* (*JMR*) as the number one journal in the discipline. All three studies rated *JM, JMR* and *Journal of Consumer Research* (*JCR*) as the top three publications.

Despite these findings, no study has been completed which collects evaluation data from department chairpersons. It is the department chairpersons who are the primary evaluator of faculty performance for diverse reasons from promotion and tenure, merit and market pay, professional development funding for existing faculty and also is one of the primary "screeners" in evaluating the background of faculty applicants.

A national mail survey was sent to all 628 US based AACSB member schools during the winter of 1990-91. The questionnaire was addressed to the Marketing Department Chair. A 21.2 percent response rate was achieved with the return of 133 surveys. Five surveys were not useable, leaving a total of 128 from which the following findings were based.

The respondents were asked to rate over 40 journals and other publications in the field of marketing. The other publications included *Marketing News, Marketing Educator,* trade publications (such as *Advertising Age*) and both national and regional proceedings. The *JMR* was used as a base index of 100, with respondents instructed to allocate scores to the other publications. Allocated scores could exceed 100 if the respondent perceived the publication to be better than *JMR*.

RESULTS

The mean scores for each Journal were computed. The journals were then ranked in descending order according to the mean score. Table 1 shows the ranking for the "Top 10."

Consistent with past research, *JMR, JM* and *JCR* were the highest rated three journals. Next came *Harvard Business Review*. These journals were relatively closely

	TABLE 1		
Rank	Journal	Mean	S.D.
1	Journal of Marketing Research (assigned)	100	-
2	Journal of Marketing	97.09	14.54
3	Journal of Consumer Research	87.02	20.61
4	Harvard Business Review	86.85	35.03
5	Marketing Science	73.35	32.50
6	Journal of Retailing	70.71	23.15
7	Journal of Advertising Research	69.78	22.97
8	Journal of Business	69.64	28.00
9	Journal of Academy of Marketing Science	65.51	26.07
10	Journal of Advertising	65.36	24.50
11	Journal of Business Research	64.34	23.26

clustered, and make a clearly identifiable top four.

Next came a relatively closely clustered group of eight journals, which round out the "Top 10 + 1." A relatively large gap of 4 points separated the number 11 and number 12 journals.

Although many of these journals appeared also on the lists prepared by other researchers, a notable addition is *The Journal of the Academy of Marketing Science (JAMS)* and the high ranking of *Marketing Science*.

It should also be noted that the standard deviations were such magnitude so as to make subtle differences in rank somewhat meaningless, particularly as one moves down the list. The pre-eminence of *JMR*, *JM* and *JCR*, however is clearly evidenced. The greatest consistency among respondents was in the rating of *JM*, with the smallest standard deviation of any publication on the list. At the other extreme, *HBR* had the highest standard deviation, reflecting vastly differing opinions. Several respondents rated *HBR* as a "200," indicating they perceived it as twice as good as *JMR*. Others, however, rated it considerably below *JMR*.

CONCLUSIONS

Understanding how the first level of administration perceives the academic status of various journals is important to faculty in developing personal research strategies. By seeking evaluations form department chairpersons, this research substantially provides convergent validity to the other research published in this area. It also provides some indication of the presence of several emerging journals, whose status appears to be ring.

REFERENCES

Coe, Robert K. and Irwin Weinstock (1983) "Evaluating Journal Publications of Marketing Professors: A Second Look," *Journal of Marketing Education*, 5 (Spring), 37-42.

Fry, D. Michael, C. Glenn Walters and Lawrence E. Scheuermann (1985) "Perceived Quality of Fifty Selected Journals: Academicians and Practitioners," *Journal of the Academy of Marketing Science*, 13 (Spring), 352-361.

Luke, Robert H. and E. Reed Doke (1987), "Marketing Journal Hierarchies: Faculty Perceptions, 1986-87," *Journal of the Academy of Marketing Science*, 15 (Spring), 74-78.

A NEW WAY OF GATHERING SURVEY DATA: A VOICE RESPONSE PANEL OF RESPONDENTS

Marcus Schmidt, Southern Denmark Business School at Sonderburg
Morten Jansen, GfK Denmark

Marcus Schmidt, Southern Denmark Business School at Sonderburg
Morten Jansen, GfK Denmark

ABSTRACT

The paper presents a new way of gathering data: A panel of respondents is performing a daily call to a voice response computer (VR) and is listening to a pre-recorded voice which is asking questions regarding opinions, preferences, and behavior. Respondents are then providing answers using the buttons on their push button phones (Table 1 summarizes how a VR-panel approach to data

gathering might be structured, Schmidt 1991 p. 11).

STUDY AND RESULTS

In late 1990 the management of the Danish subsidiary of GfK Denmark - a commercial market research agency (HQ Nuremberg, FRG - approx. 2000 employees worldwide) decided to sponsor a pilot project concerning the establishment of a VR-panel (called ´TelePanel´),

TABLE 1
A Voice-Response-by-Panel Approach to Interviewing

R = Respondent, Q = Questions

Research Design	Voice Response Panel
Where does interview take place ?	Home of R., office, at friends, hotel, phone box, car, street (portable phone), abroad (!) etc.
How is the interview initiated ?	R. is phoning VR-computer
How does interview take place ? keys on press-button phone	R. provides answers to Q. posed by pre-recorded voice using the
Who fills in the questionnaire ?	Respondent
Where are data stored when the interview has been finished ?	On VR-computer at Agency
How does data gathering take place ?	(No need since data are at processing destination)

TABLE 2
Comparison of results between VR-panel and Gallup-poll (CATI):
Three questions with same wording

Comparison of Results

Wording of question	GfK VR-Panel					Gallup Poll				
	Yes	No	?	n	Day	Yes	No	?	n	Day
1. Do you think the liberal party and the conservative p. should merge ?	15	51	34	294	20.3	17	43	40	800	10.3
2. Do you think one should abolish the 13-point scale for marking in primary school ? **)	24	58	18	473	8.5	23	68	9	700	8.4
3. Assume you were forced to choose between a better salary and a better pension - which alternative would you prefer ? (S/P/?)	48	36	16	446	25.6	49	39	12	800	2.4

Rem.: 'n´ of Gallup as published in press, All days in Table 2 refer to 1991
Day of Gallup = day of publication, day(s) of survey were approx. 2-3 week earlier.
**) Difference between the two survey results significant on 1% level.
Two other differences not significant on 5% level !

which had been proposed by the authors.

Table 2 shows the comparison of results between the VR-panel and Gallup polls.

The results of the test-retest reliability evaluation is shown elsewhere. In all cases the response pattern was found to be relatively stable across measurements. More details to follow in final draft.

DISCUSSION

The most important obstacles to the VR-panel approach is cost, management, and maintenance of the panel of respondents, and programming effort regarding computer logic and macros (i.e. links to other kinds of software). The authors conclude that the VR-panel approach provides survey data which are *at least as reliable* as established technologies like CATI and mail-panels. It is hypothesized that it is possible to gather VR-data with *even better validity* than by using other known methods!

REFERENCES

Groves, R. M. and Mathiowetz, N. A. (1984), "Computer Assisted Telephone Interviewing: Effects on Interviewers and Respondents," *Public Opinion Quarterly,* 48, 356-369

Schmidt, M (1991), "Comment on Van Valey and Crull in Doing What We Couldn´t Do Before," *Proceedings from The 1991 Sawtooth Software Conference*, Ketchum, ID

For further information contact:
Marcus Schmidt
Southern Denmark Business School
Grundtvigsallé 150
6400 Sonderburg, Denmark

ASSESSING NONRESPONSE BIAS THE RIGHT WAY: A CUSTOMER SATISFACTION CASE STUDY

Randall G. Chapman, Boston University

ABSTRACT

Sub-sample measurement is used to assess the presence of nonresponse bias in a customer satisfaction survey case study. An "infinite" call-back approach resulted in 100% response to the follow-up sub-sample measurement telephone surveying effort. The results of wave and sub-sample measurement nonresponse bias analyses are compared.

INTRODUCTION

Survey response rates of less than 100 percent always raise the possibility, but not the certainty, of nonresponse bias. The key question in all surveys with less than 100% response rates (which, of course, means all surveys) is: Are survey respondents approximately representative of all target population members? A survey response rate of less than 100 percent — even one of less than 10 percent — does not necessarily imply nonresponse bias exists. However, the potential impact of nonresponse bias, if present, is obviously greater with low survey response rates. This occurs because estimates from respondents are used to represent all target population members when, in actuality, a weighted average of the respondents and non-respondents is "truth." As survey response rates decrease, the impact of differences between respondents and non-respondents is magnified.

Nonresponse bias is, of course, just one component of nonsampling error. Many have called for greater attention to be devoted to documenting, managing, and reducing nonsampling errors. See, for example, Dalenius (1981), Kish (1982), and Groves (1989). The stakes are substantial in nonresponse bias assessment, particularly if the findings of Assael and Keon (1982) regarding the relative size of nonsampling error as a proportion of total survey error are generalizable.

The ideal way to assess nonresponse bias is, not unexpectedly, the most costly: sub-sample measurement. Only by contacting and eliciting survey answers from a sample of non-respondents (or a sample of all population members, if respondents and non-respondents cannot be identified individually) can nonresponse bias be detected unambiguously. Other approaches are only suggestive of the presence of absence of nonresponse bias, since they don't deal with the explicit issue of concern: Do respondents and non-respondents see things and behave in statistically-similar fashions? To address this question, the actual survey answers (opinions, attitudes, and behavior) of respondents and non-respondents must be compared explicitly. Demographic comparisons of respondents and non-respondents and wave analyses (comparisons of early and later respondents, under the assumption that later respondents adequately represent non-respondents) are relatively straightforward to conduct. But, they don't address the fundamental issue of concern. Demographic comparisons and wave analyses are only suggestive rather being definitive as to the comparability of respondents and non-respondents. Even if respondents and non-respondents share similar demographics and even if early and later respondents are similar in their survey answers, this is no absolute guarantee that respondents and non-respondents see things and behave identically. See Armstrong and Overton (1977) for a review of nonresponse bias assessment approaches. See also Ratneshwar and Stewart (1989) for a review of mail survey nonresponse.

This paper describes a current customer satisfaction survey in which sub-sample measurement was conducted. This permits the theoretically-correct sub-sample measurement results to be compared to the results of other nonresponse bias assessment approaches. After describing the customer satisfaction case study context, the nonresponse bias results are presented and interpreted. Concluding remarks complete the paper.

THE CUSTOMER SATISFACTION STUDY

The research objective in this customer satisfaction study was to identify and measure the principal sources of satisfaction and dissatisfaction of current Boston University MBA students. The specific research questions of interest in this study included the following:

* How well is the Boston University MBA program "performing"? What are its perceived strengths and weaknesses?

* How do current MBA students view a range of currently relevant issues facing the MBA program?

At the time of the survey, currently relevant issues such as the following were of particular interest: frequency of use of cases in classes; amount of group work; mix of domestic and international students; possible alternative scheduling of day, evening, and weekend classes; class size; and functioning of the MBA mail file system.

The survey population was all current full-time and part-time Boston University MBA students, excluding

Executive MBA program students. A census of all target population members was conducted. Given the length of the survey instrument (118 closed-ended rating-scale and multiple-choice questions) and budgetary constraints, a mail survey methodology was chosen. A single mailing of the questionnaire was made to students' home addresses. The cover letter was on official Boston University stationery and was signed by the director of the Boston University MBA program. Students could return the questionnaires by mail to the Graduate Programs Office of the Boston University School of Management or, alternatively, drop them off in person. Due to budget constraints, postage on the pre-addressed return envelope was not provided.

The 41 five-point performance rating scales were anchored by "Poor" and "Excellent." An explicit "Don't Know" option was provided. These performance dimensions were grouped explicitly into five categories: Graduate Programs Office (GPO); MBA Curriculum; PC Lab; Career Planning and Placement (CPP); and, Facilities. Sample performance dimensions under the "Graduate Programs Office (GPO)" category included "Pre-Registration Services," "Course Add/Drop Services," "Financial Aid Services," and "Orientation Activities." In addition to individual performance items, overall evaluations on each of the categories were sought (for example, "Overall Quality of Facilities").

Extensive background exploratory research was conducted in developing this questionnaire. Discussions with relevant program managers and informal discussions with 25+ customers were used in developing the questionnaire. Pre-testing resulted in some minor changes in wording and format to the initial questionnaire draft.

The overall survey response rate was 25.4 percent, below original expectations. Whether this was due to the absence of a stamped return envelope, the questionnaire length, or the general disinterest of the current customer base was unknown. However, this low survey response rate obviously raised the issue of nonresponse bias. Were the respondents representative of all customers? Or, were they systematically biased (either positively or negatively)? The normal concern in such circumstances is that the most interested and most positively-inclined customers took the time to respond to the survey. If so, the respondents' answers would present a more positive view than the beliefs of all customers. Based on these concerns, a major nonresponse bias analysis effort seemed warranted.

NONRESPONSE BIAS ANALYSIS

To assess nonresponse bias, several possible approaches exist. The most elaborate one, sub-sample measurement, was the primary basis of the nonresponse bias assessment reported in this paper. In what follows,

the wave analysis and sub-sample measurement methodologies are described, the nonresponse bias results are reported and interpreted, and a number of related and consequent issues are discussed.

Wave Analysis Methodology

Since the returned questionnaires were dated upon receipt, it was a simple matter to identify those that were "early" and those that were "later." A receipt date was chosen to divide the questionnaires into approximately equal early and later groups. The actual date chosen resulted in a 44%/56% split into the early and later groups.

Sub-Sample Measurement Methodology

Since respondents and non-respondents were not identified in the original mail survey, a follow-up survey of all population members was necessary. A telephone surveying approach was adopted so that an "infinite" call-back administrative approach could be used. By telephoning follow-up sample members as many times as necessary to achieve 100 percent response, second-order follow-up nonresponse was avoided.

To be able to promise follow-up respondents that the telephone survey would take only a couple of minutes to complete, only a very few questions could be included in the follow-up survey. Three questions from the original survey were selected for inclusion in the follow-up survey. These performance dimensions were among the most important to these customers, based on an initial analysis of the original respondents' self-reported importance weights. The three performance dimensions included in the follow-up survey were "Quality of Core Courses," "Quality of MBA Faculty," and "Overall Quality of MBA Curriculum."

A total of 74 customers were included in the follow-up survey. This customer satisfaction study was part of an MBA-level marketing research class. Each of the 24 students in the class contacted three randomly chosen population members. One enthusiastic class member chose to contact two additional randomly chosen population members. These 74 customers were randomly selected from the original sample frame. Sufficient telephone calls were made to reach every one of these 74 members of this follow-up group. This "infinite" call-back program took approximately six weeks to complete, no doubt due to the nature of the work habits of the customer population (full-time and part-time MBA students).

Nonresponse Bias Results

The results of the nonresponse bias analysis are reported in Table 1. Results for the three sub-sample measurement scales ("Quality of Core Courses," "Quality of MBA Faculty," and "Overall Quality of MBA Curriculum") are reported for all respondents, early and later respondents, and sub-sample measurement follow-up respondents. As may be noted, there was a small amount of item nonresponse, even among the sub-sample measurement respondents. Incidentally, for five of the survey respondents, a receipt date was not recorded on the questionnaires. Thus, these five respondents could not be included within the wave analysis. This is the reason why the "Early Wave Respondents" and the "Later Wave Respondents" in Table 1 sum to five respondents less than "All Respondents."

Key findings are as follows:

* The wave analysis results suggest that nonresponse bias is not present. Two of the three performance dimensions have virtually identical means (3.59 versus 3.57 and 3.40 versus 3.39), while the later respondents report a somewhat higher level of perceived performance than the early respondents (3.42 for later respondents versus 3.29 for early respondents) for one performance dimension, "Quality of Core Courses." Based only on these wave analysis results, the respondents and non-respondents (or, more precisely, early respondents and later respondents) in this customer satisfaction study would be judged to be approximately equivalent.

* Original survey respondent means for the three performance scales are all less than the sub-sample measurement means (3.37, 3.59, and 3.53 for the sub-sample measurement telephone follow-up respondents). Original respondents appear to hold slightly less favorable perceived performance views than all customers (as represented by the sub-sample measurement group).

* Response variability was somewhat lower among the sub-sample measurement respondents, compared to the other respondent groups.

The directional findings cited above are made without reference to statistical variability. Given the relatively large sample sizes involved here, these differences between the original respondents and the sub-sample measurement respondents may be statistically significant, but exact statistical tests are required. Since the wave analysis yields virtually identical means, statistical testing seems irrelevant for the wave analysis results. Any statistical differences would be overshadowed by the principle of managerial relevance: statistical differences (due just to large sample sizes) that are small in absolute value are of little managerial relevance.

Using a difference of means test, the responses of the original mail survey respondents and the sub-sample measurement telephone follow-up respondents may be compared. The null hypothesis is that there is no difference. The calculated test statistic values for the three questions are -1.34, -1.12, and -1.43, which are distributed normally by the Central Limit Theorem. Given a critical value of 1.645 at the 10 percent level of significance for a two-tailed test, the null hypotheses of equality cannot be rejected. Therefore, these statistical tests sug-

TABLE 1
Results of Nonresponse Bias Analysis

	MBA Performance Ratings		
	"Quality of Core Courses"	"Quality of MBA Faculty"	"Overall Quality of MBA Curriculum"
All Respondents:			
Mean	3.37	3.59	3.40
Standard Deviation	0.88	0.87	0.76
Number of Responses	345	345	345
Early Wave Respondents:			
Mean	3.29	3.59	3.40
Standard Deviation	0.83	0.82	0.72
Number of Responses	154	153	151
Later Wave Respondents:			
Mean	3.42	3.57	3.39
Standard Deviation	0.91	0.92	0.79
Number of Responses	186	187	181
Sub-Sample Measurement:			
Mean	3.50	3.70	3.53
Standard Deviation	0.65	0.68	0.68
Number of Responses	72	74	70

gest that there are no meaningful differences between the original mail survey respondents and the sub-sample measurement telephone follow-up respondents. Nonresponse bias appears not to be present in this customer satisfaction survey. The original respondents are representative of all customers, despite the low survey response rate.

Discussion

This analysis approach is based on the presumption that the best possible estimate of "truth" (in this case, how Boston University MBAs perceive the current performance of the Boston University MBA program) comes from the sub-sample measurement survey, since it contains no nonresponse bias by definition. The question of interest concerns the extent to which the respondents' answers to the original survey approximate, in a statistical sense, the "true" answers from the sub-sample measurement survey. Any differences in results between the sub-sample measurement survey and the original survey are presumed to be due to nonresponse bias.

The difference-of-means tests reported above are based on the assumption of independent samples. And yet, these two groups (original respondents and sub-sample measurement follow-up respondents) are dependent, by definition. Both groups come from the same population — current Boston University MBA students. Since the pattern of dependence is unknown (no questioning was conducted of the follow-up group as to whether they had already responded, so as not to threaten respondent anonymity), any dependence test would be problematic. In addition, there is obviously no way to assess the truthfulness of follow-up respondents' statements as to their response behavior with regard to the original survey. Furthermore, since the follow-up sub-sample measurement survey was conducted after the original survey (by definition), customers' opinions could have changed systematically in the interval between the original and follow-up surveys. Such possible temporal instability is always a problem in sub-sample measurement studies. Sub-sample measurement follow-up studies must, by definition, occur after the original surveying effort. Even with identified non-respondents, the passage of time between the original surveying and the follow-up non-respondent survey could have resulted in changes in the non-respondents' (and even the original respondents') answers.

Since the sub-sample measurement administration procedure was by telephone while the original survey was by mail, a possible method bias exists. Perhaps customers respond differently to questions posed by telephone compared to mail. Sub-sample measurement with a follow-up mail survey might have yielded different results than these telephone results. On the other hand, a follow-up mail survey would have inevitably had further

nonresponse, thus raising additional nonresponse bias questions. Given the relatively low response rate to the original mail survey in this customer satisfaction study, a mail survey follow-up surely would be problematic. The telephone follow-up, with "infinite" callbacks, at least resulted in complete responses, so there was no secondary nonresponse bias issue.

Comparisons of demographics or psychographics of original and sub-sample respondents might have been of some interest if notable, statistically significant differences had been confirmed. These differences might have pointed to patterns that would be useful either in interpreting the current empirical results or in planning future surveying efforts. However, in the absence of such differences, these comparisons are unwarranted since the survey responses are of primary interest, not the characteristics of the respondents. Of course, in any event, such differences would have been specific to the particular empirical setting used in this study.

CONCLUDING REMARKS

Simple nonresponse bias analyses, such as demographic comparisons and wave analysis, do not necessarily solve the nonresponse bias problem. They are suggestive, however, and perhaps represent a minimal level of "insurance" with regard to the representativeness of survey respondents to the broader target population. That which is simple, easy, and inexpensive to do is not necessarily correct, however.

In this customer satisfaction case study, wave analysis indicated the complete absence of nonresponse bias. In directional terms, the sub-sample measurement results suggested that the original mail survey respondents were less positively inclined than the sub-sample measurement telephone follow-up respondents. However, after statistical testing (difference-of-means tests between the original and follow-up respondents), the most theoretically-correct nonresponse bias analysis approach, sub-sample measurement, demonstrated the statistical equivalence of the two groups. Thus, the sub-sample measurement results show (even with a 10% level of statistical significance) that nonresponse bias is absent in this customer satisfaction survey case study. In this case study, survey results based on original respondents may be taken as representative of all target population members.

While this is only a single customer satisfaction survey case study, it is instructive in identifying the potential magnitude of nonresponse bias and the relative quality of alternative approaches to assessing nonresponse bias. Hopefully, other marketing researchers will both conduct similar sub-sample measurement analyses and report the results. Work such as this — and other carefully conducted nonsampling error efforts, such as those by

Assael and Keon (1982) and Swan, O'Connor, and Lee (1991)—needs to be widely replicated. Only by conducting and publishing such research is it possible to establish norms for the relative efficacy of the costly but theoreti-cally-correct sub-sample measurement approach compared to other much less-expensive nonresponse bias approaches.

REFERENCES

Assael, Henry and John Keon (1982), "Nonsampling Vs. Sampling Errors in Survey Research," *Journal of Marketing,* 46 (Spring), 114-123.

Armstrong, J. Scott and Terry S. Overton (1977), "Estimating Nonresponse Bias in Mail Surveys," *Journal of Marketing Research,* 14 (August), 396-403.

Dalenius, T. E. (1981), "The Survey Statistician's Responsibility For Both Sampling and Measurement Errors," in D. Krewski, R. Platek, and J. N. K. Rao, eds. *Current Topics in Survey Sampling,* New York: Academic Press, 17-29.

Groves, Robert M. (1989), *Survey Errors and Survey Costs.* New York: John Wiley and Sons.

Kish, Leslie (1982), "On the Future of Survey Sampling," in N. K. Namboodiri, ed. *Survey Sampling and Measurement,* New York: Academic Press, 13-21.

Swan, John E., Stephen J. O'Connor, and Seung Dong Lee (1991), "A Framework For Testing Sampling Bias and Methods of Bias Reduction in a Telephone Survey," *Marketing Research,* 3 (December), 23-34.

Ratneshwar, Srinivasan and David W. Stewart (1989), "Nonresponse in Mail Surveys: An Integrative Review," *Applied Marketing Research,* 29 (Summer), 37-46.

EFFECTIVE AND COST-FREE REFINEMENTS OF CHARITABLE CONTRIBUTION INCENTIVES FOR MAIL SURVEYS

John R. Dickinson, University of Windsor
A. J. Faria, University of Windsor

ABSTRACT

The effect of three variables on mail survey response rate (number of completed questionnaires returned adjusted for undelivered questionnaires) and response speed (number of days between date of mailing and date completed questionnaire received) was examined. Each variable was operationalized at two levels: early versus late position in the cover letter of the offer of a charitable donation (first vs. third of seven paragraphs), whether a choice of charities was provided or a single charity specified (choice vs. no choice), and the type of charity or charities (health-related vs. social/cultural). The manipulation of these variables does not add to total survey costs, once the decision to utilize an incentive has been made. Response completeness in other studies (and in this one) was negligible and was not investigated.

With early placement the incentive presumably becomes a part of the "evaluation of the request" (Furse and

Stewart 1984) and the evaluation is more likely to be positive. The effect of offering a donation to a charity is contingent on the degree to which the subject is sympathetic to or supportive of the particular charity. This is more likely to occur (1) when a choice of charities is provided and (2) when the charities are popular ones. Six charitable organizations used in this research: Canadian Cancer Society, Canadian Heart and Stroke Foundation, Canadian Lung Association, Canadian Olympic Association, Canadian Foundation for the Literary Arts, and the Heritage Canada Foundation. The single charity condition specified either the Canadian Cancer Society or the Canadian Olympic Association.

Two criteria and three treatment variables manipulated give rise to six main effect hypotheses: Response rate and response speed, respectively, will be enhanced when an incentive is offered early in the cover letter compared to when it is offered late (H1, H2), when a list of charities to receive a donation is provided compared to

TABLE 1
Percentage Response Rates and Average Days to Respond

| | Early Mention | | Late Mention | |
	No Choice	Choice	No Choice	Choice
Health-related	57.0% 6.3 days	52.6% 4.2 days	45.6% 4.4 days	35.8% 3.7 days
Social/cultural	35.0% 3.9 days	34.1% 5.5 days	18.2% 5.0 days	21.6% 4.8 days

TABLE 2
Statistical Tests of Hypotheses

	Treatment	Criterion	Significance (p-value)
H1	Early/late mention main effect	rate	<.001
H2	Early/late mention main effect	speed	<.02, wrong direction
H3	Choice/no choice main effect	rate	>.30
H4	Choice/no choice main effect	speed	<.06
H5	Charity type main effect	rate	<.001
H6	Charity type main effect	speed	>.95
H7	Choice-mention interaction	rate	>.90
H8	Choice-mention interaction	speed	>.70
H9	Charity type-mention interaction	rate	>.90
H10	Charity type-mention interaction	speed	<.03, wrong direction

when a single charity is specified (H3, H4), and when (more popular) health-related charities are utilized compared to when (less popular) social/cultural charities are utilized (H5, H6).

The effects of choice of charity and type of charity may be anticipated to be contingent on the respondent being aware of these inducements yielding four interaction hypotheses: The effect of charity choice (H7, H8) and of charity type (H9, H10) on response rate and response speed, respectively, will be greater when the incentive is presented early in the cover letter.

A commercial list sample of 150 households per cell was selected to ensure proportionate coverage of Canada's provinces and territories. Cover letters were on the letterhead of a research firm and signed by the president. A postage-paid envelope was enclosed. Questionnaires were mailed on the same date. 115 questionnaires were undeliverable, yielding cell sample sizes of 134 to 137. A three-way, fixed-effects factorial analysis of variance was used to test the research hypotheses, response per se being dichotomous (Lunney 1970) and response speed being ratio scaled. Results are presented in Tables 1 and 2.

For further information please contact:
Dr. John R. Dickinson
Faculty of Business Administration
University of Windsor
Windsor, Ontario, Canada N9B 3P4

THE SOCO SCALE REVISITED: AN APPROACH TO ENHANCING ITS MANAGERIAL RELEVANCE

Donald A. McBane, Clemson University
Gregory M. Pickett, Clemson University

ABSTRACT

An ability to determine whether customer-oriented selling is an effective approach in a particular industry is of interest to practitioners wishing to maximize returns from their sales efforts, and the SOCO (Sales-Orientation, Customer-Orientation) scale (Saxe and Weitz 1982) represents an important research tool for those interested in this issue. Unfortunately, the interpretation of the two factors which arise in the SOCO scale has recently been questioned.

Dunlap, Dotson, and Chambers (1988) suggest one factor be considered a customer-oriented factor, while the second factor be considered a "hard-sell" factor. It may be that some salespeople try to push products on prospects, but find it easier to sell when the prospect has first expressed a need for a product. It is also possible that some salespeople want to sell only those products needed by their prospects, but if it appears the opportunity to complete a sale may be lost, they feel pressured to meet company sales quotas and thus try to pressure the prospect to make an unneeded purchase. In either case, a different scoring approach to the SOCO scale is needed to capture these complex relationships.

Figure 1 shows how the customer-orientation and sales-orientation dimensions can be used to accommodate either interpretation. Relaters would focus on learning about prospect needs in a genuine effort to find solutions. Persuaders might focus on these needs in an effort to find solutions, or only to make it easier to sell. Salespeople in the lower quadrants would focus on obtaining orders, with those in the left quadrants attempting to avoid doing anything that would jeopardize their relationship with their customers, while those in the right quadrants would be willing to use high pressure, deceptive, or manipulative tactics to get the sale.

Items used in the revised scoring of the scale were limited to those in the original scale, so as to extend the usefulness of this approach for researchers who have administered the existing scale. Analysis revealed four items for the vertical dimension (question numbers 2, 12, 14 and 23 in the original scale), and four (items 6, 10, 19 and 20) for the horizontal dimension.

Research Agenda

To encourage further use of the SOCO scale, we suggest some propositions regarding the effectiveness of various selling styles. Comparing the information obtained from the matrix approach to that obtained from the unidimensional approach should continue to establish the usefulness of the SOCO scale.

P1: Persuaders will be seen by their sales managers as having greater ability to develop new accounts, because they will spend the time to learn about prospect needs, but will be less likely to take no for an answer.

P2: Hard-sellers will be seen by their sales managers as having greater ability to generate sales of new company products, as they will not be constrained to sell only those products for which prospects have expressed a need, and should be less likely to take no for an answer from their prospects.

P3: Relaters will be seen by their sales managers to have more goodwill with their customers, because they are most likely to be concerned about customer needs while not sacrificing the customer's interest to increase the probability of making a sale.

FIGURE 1			
Interest in Customer Needs	High	Relaters	Persuaders
	Low	Soft-sellers	Hard-sellers

For further information please contact:
Donald A. McBane
Marketing Department
245 Sirrine Hall
Clemson University
Clemson, SC 29634-1325

ON THE DEVELOPMENT OF AN IMPROVED INDICATOR OF TURNOVER INTENTION

Kevin M. McNeilly, Miami University
Frederick A. Russ, University of Cincinnati

ABSTRACT

A "turnover tendency" measure including individual items from measures of other constructs provides better results than a turnover intention measure, but it did not generalize to other data sets. Interviews with reps who left provided insights about reasons for leaving that could be added to the measure in future research.

INTRODUCTION

Sales management continually struggles to develop tactics that will reduce sales rep turnover. Academic researchers continue to seek a better understanding of the causes of turnover that will help managers in their struggle. Recent research has produced promising results, but it has raised a number of questions as well. Although most of the antecedents seem to have been well identified, there are concerns about the quality of the instruments developed to measure them. For example, Howell, Wilcox, Bellenger, and Chonko (1988) have pointed out problems with the dimensionality of standard role stress measures, and Russ and McNeilly (forthcoming), based on insights gained from moderator variable analysis, have pointed out the need to broaden measures of job satisfaction and organizational commitment.

Turnover intention is frequently used as a variable in sales turnover research. It has been criticized, primarily for practical reasons: (1) while it is significantly correlated with actual turnover, those correlations are far from perfect (see Futrell and Parasuraman 1984); and (2) there is reluctance by employers to allow its measurement; they are concerned that asking about turnover intention will cause sales reps to begin thinking about leaving. A turnover intention measure also presumes that sales reps answer accurately. That is, reps are expected to have given this issue some thought and be willing to disclose this information. If the cognitive effort is absent or trust in the researchers is lacking, it is not surprising that turnover intention may not do the best job of predicting actual turnover.

Despite these problems, there is a great need for a subjective measure that tracks turnover well. From a **research** standpoint, such a measure is important because it allows studies to be conducted in a single phase, rather than requiring a survey to measure antecedents and a later survey to capture actual turnover. From a **managerial** perspective, such a measure will allow managers to identify sales reps at risk of leaving in time to try to do something about it.

The <u>purpose</u> of this research is to explore the development of a different measure that tracks turnover better than turnover intention and avoids the criticisms aimed at such measures. This new measure, "turnover tendency," will pull together items from existing instruments. Turnover tendency would differ from turnover intention in that it would reflect attitudes about aspects of the sales rep's firm and his or her job rather than probability estimates about the rep's chances of leaving. As such it should have greater diagnostic value for sales management. Its measurement would also be less obtrusive. To be of any value, however, "turnover tendency" must be an improvement over turnover intention in its ability to predict and explain actual turnover.

The sections that follow describe the data collection plan, the results of our analyses to develop a turnover tendency measure, and the implications of these results.

DATA COLLECTION

Data collection involved three phases. The **first** phase involved mail surveys of two very different sales forces, a total of 218 responses. Details of these two surveys are provided in the next three paragraphs.

Two waves of questionnaires were mailed to the sales reps, the first with a cover letter from top management, the second with a cover letter from the researchers. Each mailing included a stamped return envelope. The response rate for both studies was approximately 85%. Performance evaluation forms for each sales rep were mailed to the sales supervisor to whom they reported, along with a cover letter from management. A 100% response rate for the sales supervisors was achieved.

The sales rep survey measured organizational commitment, job satisfaction, role conflict and role ambiguity, and turnover intention. The sales supervisor survey measured performance of the sales reps, as well as several "demographic" variables including tenure and gender. The survey instruments contain scales used rather widely in the organizational and sales management literature. See to Table 1 for measures and coefficient alphas.

In the first sales force, 21 sales managers provided ratings of 150 sales reps of a publishing firm. The reps called on universities and colleges nationwide. In the second sales force, 20 first-level sales supervisors provided ratings of 68 sales reps. The reps called on supermarket accounts, selling food and non-food products for

---
TABLE 1
Sources of Measures and Reliabilities

Role Conflict: The belief held by an employee that the expectations and demands of two or more partners are incompatible and that he/she cannot simultaneously satisfy the demands being made of him/her. (Rizzo, House, and Lirtzman 1970) Seven of nine items on original scale. (Sales Force 1, alpha=.76) (Sales Force 2, alpha=.79)

Role Ambiguity: Uncertainty occurring from the nature of the expected job behavior. (Rizzo, House, and Lirtzman 1970) Eight of nine items on original scale. (Sales Force 1, alpha=.80) (Sales Force 2, alpha=.74)

Organizational Commitment: One's identification with and loyalty to an organization (Mowday, Steers, and Porter 1979). Fourteen of the original fifteen items, with one of those items modified. (Sales Force 1, alpha=.92) (Sales Force 2, alpha=.87)

Job Satisfaction: The positive emotional state resulting from appraisal of one's job or experience (Gregson 1987). Twenty items from the original thirty item scale, chosen (and occasionally modified) to be the best fit for the situation in the firm being studied. Dimensions include satisfaction with promotion, pay, supervisor, co-workers, and the work itself. This is a scale based on the Job Descriptive Index developed by Smith, Kendall, and Hulin (1969) and called "the most widely used measure of job satisfaction extant today" (Yeager 1981). (Sales Force 1, alphas range from .67 to .89) (Sales Force 2, alphas ranged from .62 to .88)

Intent to Leave: One's behavioral intention to withdraw (Bluedorn 1982). Used chances of staying (three of six items) and different time periods to fit company's situation better. (Sales Force 1, alpha=.95) (Sales Force 2, alpha=.95)

Performance: A multidimensional subjective assessment (by the first level sales manager) of the reps' attitudes, ability, and accomplishments (Futrell and Parasuraman 1984). Used nine items from the scale, dropping "improvement ... over last year," because many sales reps had not been working for that sales manager long enough. (Sales Force 1, alpha=.91) (Sales Force 2, alpha=.89)
---

companies who chose not to sell direct in those markets where the food broker operated. Descriptive information from the two sales forces shows that the first had an almost even split between male and female reps (49%-51%), with most being college educated, and averaging 5 1/2 years with the firm (range: 1 to 22 years). The second had more male reps than female reps (60%-40%), was less educated, and averaged 2 1/3 years with the firm (range: 1 to 13 years).

In the **second** data collection phase we determined the actual turnover behavior in the two sales forces within the first year after the initial survey. This phase, based on information obtained from sales management and company records, identified those who stayed and those who left, providing a criterion item for use in measure development. This phase also provided addresses and telephone numbers so that those who had left could be contacted in the third phase.

The **third** data collection phase involved structured, open ended phone interviews to probe sales reps' reasons for leaving. These interviews were conducted to help understand circumstances surrounding turnover, among those who were not expected to leave on the basis of the original questionnaire responses.

RESULTS

Differences Between Stayers and Leavers

Table 2 shows means for stayers and leavers in the two sales forces. Within each sales force, significant differences between stayers and leavers are indicated.

For the 150-person sales force of Firm 1, there are significant differences in the expected directions for all the variables except some of the satisfaction dimensions, which are in the expected directions, but not significant. Those who left the firm were less loyal and less satisfied. They felt more role ambiguity and conflict and did not perform as well. Finally, they had worked with the firm for a shorter period of time and indicated a greater chance of leaving.

The results for the smaller sales force were generally consistent, except that differences between stayers and leavers were typically smaller. Only the difference in performance ratings was statistically significant.

Predicting Turnover

Discriminant analysis was used to develop classification equations predicting who would stay and who would leave. Three analyses were performed for each sales force. The first analysis used only turnover intention as an independent variable. It is the measure that previous research suggests is most closely related to turnover.

The second analysis, performed in stepwise fashion, added all ten measured variables that we identified as potentially linked to turnover: organizational commitment, five job satisfaction dimensions, role ambiguity and conflict, performance, and job tenure. To the extent that these variables affect turnover directly (rather than indirectly through their impact on turnover intention), adding these should improve the accuracy of the discriminant function.

The third analysis used all sixty-one individual items from the variables in the second analysis. As with the second analysis, a stepwise approach was taken. Although this capitalizes on chance, it helps to capture in an efficient way a parsimonious set of items that may be

included in a measure of turnover tendency. This analysis should do the best job of all at predicting turnover.

Finally, we validated the "best" discriminant function for each sales force by applying the discriminant functions developed for the first sales force to the second sales force, and vice-versa. This is an even more stringent validation test than using a holdout sample.

Statistics for the discriminant analyses are shown in Tables 3 and 4. The classification matrices for each analysis plus the validation test are shown in Tables 5 and 6.

Table 3 provides the results from using only the turnover intention measure as an independent variable to discriminate between stayers and leavers, then adding ten other constructs, and finally using all the individual items. As expected, canonical correlations improve with each analysis. Only Sales Force 1 showed a significant relationship between actual turnover and turnover inten-

	TABLE 2			
	Construct Scores for Stayers and Leavers			
	SALES FORCE 1		SALES FORCE 2	
CONSTRUCT	Left (N=26)	Stayed (N=124)	Left (N=10)	Stayed (N=58)
Role Ambiguity[1]	3.17	2.74*	2.79	2.77
Role Conflict[1]	4.05	3.45**	3.99	3.38
Org. Commitment[2]	4.58	5.14*	5.20	5.56
Overall Satisfaction[1]	3.36	3.72**	3.26	3.38
Sat. w/ Promotion[1]	3.12	3.80**	2.93	3.23
Sat. w/ Supervisor[1]	3.42	3.90	3.65	3.89
Sat. w/ Work Itself[1]	3.95	4.25	3.90	4.01
Sat. w/ Income[1]	2.22	2.51	2.07	2.05
Sat. w/ Coworkers[1]	4.09	4.12	3.75	3.73
Performance[2]	4.80	5.56**	4.42	5.08*
Turnover Intention[3]	0.23	0.15*	0.29	0.22
Job Tenure (years)	3.07	6.05**	1.68	2.44

** p<.01; * p<.05
[1] 5 point scale
[2] 7 point scale
[3] Probability of leaving

TABLE 3
Discriminant Analysis Statistics

Sales Force	Independent Variables	Eigenvalue	Canonical Correlation	Wilks' Lambda	Chi²	DF	P<
1	Turnover Intention	0.03	0.17	0.97	4.13	1	.042
2	Turnover Intention	NS					
1	Constructs	0.19	0.40	0.84	25.25	3	.000
2	Constructs	0.06	0.24	0.94	4.06	1	.044
1	Items	0.32	0.49	0.76	40.09	4	.000
2	Items	0.60	0.61	0.62	29.99	5	.000

TABLE 4
Univariate Statistics and
Standardized Discriminant Function Coefficients (SDFC)

	Sales Force 1				Sales Force 2			
Analysis w/	Independent Variables	Wilks' Lambda	p<	SDFC	Independent Variables	Wilks' Lambda	p<	SDFC
Constructs	Performance	.914	.000	0.60	Performance	.940	.044	1.00
	Sat w/Promo	.867	.000	0.63				
	Job Tenure	.841	.000	0.44				
Items	Orgcommit3	.882	.000	0.56	Performance3	.899	.008	0.57
	Orgcommit13	.825	.000	-0.46	Workitself4	.833	.003	0.73
	Promotion3	.789	.000	0.67	Workitself1	.762	.001	-0.81
	Performance1	.758	.000	0.49	Orgcommit2	.697	.000	0.80
					Orgcommit10	.624	.000	-0.61

tion. Both the second discriminant analysis using eleven constructs and the third analysis using all 61 items showed significant results. Perhaps unexpectedly, it takes only a small number of items to do the best job of all.

Table 4 presents the univariate statistics from the analysis using the constructs and individual items. Unfortunately, there is no match between significant items across the two firms, but both discriminant functions include organizational commitment items, a performance item, and satisfaction items. For Sales Force 1, the significant items included the following: I feel very little loyalty to this organization*; I really care about the fate of this organization; my firm has a fair promotion policy;

and a rating of the sales rep's willingness to work hard. For Sales Force 2, the items included the following: my work is not satisfying*; my work is challenging, I talk up this organization to my friends as a great organization to work for; I am extremely glad that I chose this organization to work for over others I was considering at the time I joined; and a rating of the sales rep's current sales ability. (The * refers to a reverse-scored item.)

Table 5 presents the discriminant classification matrices. Matrix 5(A) shows that the discriminant analysis using turnover intention alone correctly classified 83% (124 reps that actually stayed or left were accurately predicted to do the same) in Sales Force 1. Using the

TABLE 5
Classification Matrices

Sales Force 1   Sales Force 2

(5A)
DISCRIMINANT ANALYSIS WITH TURNOVER INTENTION AS INDEPENDENT VARIABLE

		Predicted					Predicted	
		Leave	Stay				Leave	Stay
Actual	Left	1	25		Actual	Left	NA	NA
	Stayed	1	123			Stayed	NA	NA

Percentage correct: 82.7%   Percentage correct: NA

(5B)
MDA WITH CONSTRUCTS AS INDEPENDENT VARIABLES

		Predicted					Predicted	
		Leave	Stay				Leave	Stay
Actual	Left	8	18		Actual	Left	0	10
	Stayed	3	121			Stayed	0	58

Percentage correct: 86.0%   Percentage correct: 85.3%

(5C)
MDA WITH INDIVIDUAL ITEMS AS INDEPENDENT VARIABLES

		Predicted					Predicted	
		Leave	Stay				Leave	Stay
Actual	Left	12	14		Actual	Left	5	5
	Stayed	5	119			Stayed	1	57

Percentage correct: 87.3%   Percentage correct: 91.2%

eleven constructs (matrix 5B) classified with 86% accuracy (129 reps out of 150 correctly matched) in Sales Force 1 and 85% accuracy (58 reps out of 68) in Sales Force 2. The individual items provided the best multiple discriminant analysis for both sales forces (matrix 5C). In Sales Force 1, 131 reps were correctly matched (87%) and in Sales Force 2, 62 reps were correctly classified (91%).

Because the items and discriminant function coefficients were not the same for each sales force, we tested the classification ability of each discriminant function on the other sales force. Table 6 shows that when the discriminant function using the individual items from one sales force was used in classifying members of the other sales force it did not do as well as the turnover intention measure by itself.

The results suggest that significant constructs or items can be identified, but the discriminant functions do not hold up particularly well across the sales forces. This may be caused "legitimately" by real differences in the situations of the two sales forces -- for example, the differences in the importance of satisfaction dimensions or differences in sales force demographics (age, education). The results also suggest that we may not have

TABLE 6
Validation Analysis

		Predicted					Predicted	
		Leave	Stay				Leave	Stay
Actual	Left	3	23		Actual	Left	5	5
	Stayed	9	115			Stayed	7	51

Percentage correct: 78.7%   Percentage correct: 82.4%

adequately tapped the items or measures that can indicate turnover. Thus, we cannot yet report success in developing a measure of turnover tendency.

There were a number of individuals who were misclassified. To explain this unpredicted turnover and to identify additional reasons for leaving that were not well tapped by our measures, we conducted telephone interviews with those who left (including those correctly predicted to leave). Company policy would not permit interviewing those who stayed even though we might have predicted that they would leave. The results of these interviews are summarized in the next section.

Interviews with leavers

Phone interviews were attempted with everyone who was no longer with each firm a year after the initial questionnaires were administered. Of 36 interviews attempted (26 from Sales Force 1 and 10 from Sales Force 2), 28 were completed, a response rate of 78%.

The interviews began with open ended questions about respondents' reasons for leaving and followed by soliciting importance ratings (major reason, minor reason, not important) from a list of possible reasons for leaving that were read to the sales rep.

The results of these interviews were not intended to be analyzed statistically because of the qualitative nature of the data and the small sample sizes. Impressions gained from these interviews are summarized in the following paragraphs. Only summaries of interviews with unpredicted leavers (from the discriminant analyses with items as independent variables) are included here, because interviews with predicted leavers tended to confirm the reasons identified in the discriminant analysis.

Of the nineteen reps (14 from Sales Force 1 and 5 from Sales Force 2) who left their firm, but were not predicted to leave, interviews were completed with fifteen. Two of these left for reasons that might have been picked up had we used INDSALES (Churchill, Ford and Walker 1974) instead of a version of the JDI (Smith,

Kendall, and Hulin (1969) to measure satisfaction: one disliked the customers; the other disagreed with company policies. For two others it was a matter of pay, but with a different twist from what is usually measured: they felt that they had to work too hard to earn a satisfactory income level. That is, the pay was fine but they had to do too much to earn it. These could presumably be handled by including items that focused on work versus financial rewards.

Four reps left when they took outside opportunities that were more attractive. Availability of opportunities is commonly included in models that explain turnover (Bluedorn 1982, Mobley 1982). It is not clear whether a generalized measure of opportunity availability would have identified these leavers, however. Opportunity availability should be reflected in organizational commitment scores and in turnover intention, but these respondents show no lack of loyalty. Hence, we must presume that (1) the respondents did not know of the opportunities at the time they completed the questionnaire or (2) the respondents were not inclined to admit that they were thinking about leaving. Perhaps significantly, the four who left to take better jobs had greater job tenure than any of the other leavers.

Finally, six reps left for non-job-related reasons: three to start/raise a family, one to attend school, one because of a spouse's job transfer, and one to be closer to home and family members. For the researcher trying to predict turnover, this suggests the need to add items tapping these outside influences.

DISCUSSION AND CONCLUSIONS

What do the data analyses and subsequent interviews show? First, we can predict who will leave with modest success, but the results are far from perfect. Moving to the item level to develop a turnover tendency indicator helped very little. Part of the blame may fall on the measures we chose to use in this research. For example, Churchill et al.'s (1974) INDSALES could have been used instead of the Gregson (1987) adaptation of the JDI scale; or the Mowday et al. (1979) measure of organizational commitment instead of the alternative by Hrebiniak and Alutto (1972). And part of the problem may rest on an underspecified model that did not include other measures possibly affecting turnover, including availability of alternatives, for example.

The results also suggest, however, the potential benefits of adding new items to the scales or new variables to the model. The most obvious new items would focus on satisfaction with the effort and time required to be devoted to the job, which could be added to "the satisfaction with the job itself" variable. A potential new variable for turnover models is the desire to satisfy "personal" (i.e., non-job-related) needs. Items could tap the attitudes toward raising children and interest in furthering one's education. A second variable might focus on a spouse's career plans and opportunities. Managers who sought to measure such variables will risk EEO problems, but researchers presumably can take such measures in an effort to provide a better understanding of the causes of turnover.

Our interviews also had implications for "prevent-

ing" turnover as well as predicting it. If unpredicted leavers are solid performers (and almost all of them appeared to be in our study), then it is costly for the firm to have them leave. Recognizing that some productive reps may leave for more attractive opportunities, managers may be able to identify attractive alternative jobs in their own companies that will at least keep these skilled individuals working for the firm, even if not in a sales job.

Creative firms and managers may also be able to help sales reps meet their personal needs without forcing them to leave the firm to do so. These solutions might include better family or educational leave policies, improved day care options, reduced territory sizes (allowing less travel or shorter working hours), or, for larger companies, reassignment to new territories to match a spouse's new job location.

Thus, providing better measures of turnover intention still needs further exploration. Trying to keep productive sales reps is important. If reps are reluctant or unable to communicate their feeling directly, then less obtrusive or more relevant measures need to be used.

REFERENCES

Bluedorn, Allen C. (1982), "A Unified Model of Turnover from Organizations," *Human Relations,* 35, 135-153.

Churchill, Gilbert A., Jr., Neil M. Ford, and Orville C. Walker, Jr. (1974), "Measuring the Job Satisfaction of Industrial Salesmen," *Journal of Marketing Research,* 11 (August), 254-260.

Futrell, C. M. and A. Parasuraman (1984), "The Relationship of Satisfaction and Performance to Sales Force Turnover," *Journal of Marketing,* 48, 33-40.

Gregson, Terry (1987), "Factor Analysis of a Multiple-Choice Format for Job Satisfaction," *Psychological Reports,* 61, 747-750.

Howell, Roy D., James B. Wilcox, Danny N. Bellenger, and Larry B. Chonko (1988), "An Assessment of the Role Conflict and Role Ambiguity Scales," *AMA Educator's Proceedings,* 54, 314-319.

Hrebiniak, L. G. and J. A. Alutto (1972), "Personal and Role-Related Factors in the Development of Organizational Commitment," *Administrative Science Quarterly,* 17, 555-573.

McNeilly, Kevin M. and Frederick A. Russ (forthcoming), "Organizational Commitment and Job Satisfaction: Their Links to Role Stress, Turnover, and Performance," *Journal of Personal Selling and Sales Management.*

Mobley, W. H. (1982), *Employee Turnover: Causes, Consequences and Control.* Reading, MA: Addison-Wesley.

Mowday, Richard T., Richard M. Steers, and Lyman W. Porter (1979), "The Measurement of Organizational Commitment," *Journal of Vocational Behavior,* 14 (April), 224-247.

Rizzo, John R., Robert J. House, and Sidney I. Lirtzman (1970), "Role Conflict and Ambiguity in Complex Organizations," *Administrative Science Quarterly,* 15 (March), 150-163.

Smith, P. C., L. M. Kendall, and C. L. Hulin (1969), *The Measurement of Satisfaction in Work and Retirement.* Chicago: Rand-McNally.

Yeager, S. J. (1981), "Dimensionality of the Job Descriptive Index," *Academy of Management Journal,* 24, 205-212.

SPECIFICATION OF SALES TRAINING OBJECTIVES: ORGANIZATIONAL PRACTICES AND RECOMMENDATIONS

Earl D. Honeycutt, University of North Carolina at Wilmington
Vince Howe, University of North Carolina at Wilmington
Thomas N. Ingram, Memphis State University

ABSTRACT

The *Wall Street Journal* (March 7, 1989) reported sales training programs are receiving increased emphasis in order to better equip salespersons with new or improved job skills. However, this increased emphasis is not without substantial cost. According to *Sales & Marketing Management* magazine, firms invest an average $11,617, $14,501, and $22,237, respectively, on consumer product, services oriented, and industrial product sales training programs (February 1989, p. 23). Further, the total hours of training delivered to salespeople exceeds the combined training devoted to executive, senior, and middle managers (Gordon 1988).

Given the importance of sales training and the significant allocation of corporate resources to the activity, companies are demanding more accountability for the funds invested in the sales force. In a recent survey, sales and marketing managers rated the need to measure the impact survey, sales and marketing managers rated the need to measure the impact of sales training on performance as mandatory (*Marketing News*, March 13, 1989). This cannot be accomplished unless specific sales training objectives are set in order to gauge effectiveness. As stated by Goldstein (1986):

> "Goals and objectives are the key steps in determining the training environment, and unless they are specified, there is no way to measure success" (p. 26).

Important questions regarding how sales training objectives are set and how these objectives are related to other elements of the sales training process have been virtually ignored by sales researchers. As a result, this study investigated current sales management practices regarding objective setting for sales training programs. In particular, the study addressed the following research questions:

RQ1 What sales training objectives do companies most commonly set?

RQ2 Who is responsible for setting sales training objectives?

RQ3 Is the specific selling domain of the firm being accounted for in the objective setting process? Or, said another way, are different objectives set for consumer, industrial, and service companies?

RQ4 Is the allocation of training time congruent with the stated objectives?

RQ5 Is there agreement between different sales personnel regarding he optimal allocation of time relative to the objectives?

Sample and Administration

Members of the National Society of Sales Training Executives (NSSTE) were selected to provide information for the sales trainer viewpoint. Sales manager subscribing to *Sale and Marketing Management* magazine provided the sampling frame for that group. Finally, the sales managers distributed surveys to two of their firm's sales representatives. Total surveys mailed out to the two groups, sales trainers and managers, were 136 and 500, respectively. After an initial mailing and two follow-up mailings, useable returned questionnaires were 113, 100, and 85, respectively. This represented response rates of 83 percent, 20 percent and 22 percent.

Results and Conclusions

A study of Erffmeyer, Russ and Hair (1991) found that a majority of firms used subjective assessment methods to determine training needs. The authors called for a more systematic approach, including using a variety of input sources, for training needs assessment and objective setting. Our results indicated only 47 percent of the respondents stated that two or more parties (e.g. trainers, managers, and experienced sales representatives) were involved in setting objectives.

The sales training objectives most frequently cited by the total sample were: (1) increase sales volume, (2) decrease turnover, (3) improve use of time, and (4) improve customer relations. Although 72 percent of the trainers and sales managers stated their firms set specific objectives, a majority of those listed "increase sales volume" as their main training objective. Since selling is a process involving many stages with certain skills required at each stage, management must be more attuned to setting specific training objectives for their training programs. This not only allows for more efficient programs but also a greater opportunity for program evaluation.

Few differences were found between the type of firm (industrial, consumer, and service) and the main training program objectives specified. Industrial firms reported a greater percentage of training program time allocated to increasing product knowledge, while consumer and service firms allocated more time to improve specific sales techniques. In general, all respondents indicated more time (37 percent) was devoted to increasing product knowledge.

REFERENCES

Erffmeyer, Robert C, K. Randall Russ, and Joseph F. Hair, Jr. (1991), "Needs Assessment and Evaluation in Sales Training Programs," *Journal of Personal Selling and Sales Management*, XI:1 (Winter), 17-30.

Goldstein, Irving L. (1980), "Training in Work Organizations," *Annual Review of Psychology*, 31, Annual Reviews, Inc., 229-272.

Gordon, Jack (1988), "Who is Being Trained to do What?," *Training*, 25, 51-60.

Marketing News (1989), "Study Reveals Sales-Training Needs of Business Marketers," (March 13), 6.

Sales and Marketing Management, Survey of Selling Costs (1989), "Training Tables," 141 (February), 23.

Wall Street Journal (1989), "Labor Letters," (March 7), A1.

For further information please contact:
Earl D. Honeycutt
Department of Management and Marketing
Cameron School of Business Administration
University of North Carolina at Wilmington
Wilmington, NC 28403

HISPANIC CONSUMPTION: THE IMPACT OF STRONG AND WEAK ETHNIC IDENTIFICATION

Naveen Donthu, Georgia State University
Joseph Cherian, University of Illinois

ABSTRACT

Perhaps as a sign of maturity, the stream of Hispanic consumer research has shown growing disparity in the types of results and recommendations that are reported: At one extreme an author states that Hispanics may not be all that different from Anglos in behavior (Palmeri 1991). At the other end several authors still exhort that Hispanics do differ from Anglos in attitude and behavior (Webster 1991).

The current trend in business strategy when dealing with Hispanics is demassification (Berman 1991; Deshpande, Hoyer, and Donthu 1986). Hispanics are no longer viewed as a monolithic entity; rather the inherent diversity among Hispanics is acknowledged and utilized in the design of marketing mixes. This paper will show that the same differences can be found within Hispanics that were once found between Hispanics and Anglos in the general population.

There are at least two basic causes for the diversity within any ethnic population — the first is the intrinsic difference among sub-cultures, i.e. what they came with; the second is the difference in identification, i.e. what they did with it after they came. In marketing literature related to Hispanic cultures, at least two types of differences in identification have been identified — enduring and episodic. Enduring identification refers to the base-level intensity of affiliation with a parent culture. The strength of this type of identification has been measured either on the basis of self-reports of self-perception (Deshpande, Hoyer, and Donthu 1986; Hirschman 1981), or inferred from the language(s) spoken (Spanish-only, Spanish and English, and English-only) (Webster 1991), or the perceived need to assimilate with the dominant population (Mehta and Belk 1990). These measures enable some groups to be termed Strongly Identified Hispanics or Weakly Identified Hispanics.

Consumption behavior can be divided into two basic classes — the consumption of services and the consumption of products. One characteristic distinguishing consumption of services from consumption of products is the degree of interaction required between the provider and the consumer: services are 'inseparable' (Kotler 1991). Therefore, in the consumption of services the ethnicity of the provider should be crucial to an strongly identified ethnic consumer. This should be more true of low-involvement services. Thus:

H1a: SH will prefer Hispanic service providers more than WH.

H1b: The preference for Hispanic service providers will be higher for low-involvement services than for high-involvement services.

H1a: The difference in preference will be less for high involvement services.

While attitudinal differences between Strong and Weak Hispanics have been shown, and behavioral differences between Hispanics and Anglos have been shown, behavioral differences between Strong and Weak Hispanics has not been shown in literature. Two dimensions are explored here — economic value and external influence; in particular there are two aspects to external influence— personal (i.e., family and friends), and impersonal (i.e., media). The hypothesis related to consumption of products are:

H2a: SH will be less driven by economic value.

H2b: SH will be more brand loyal, especially to brands bought by family and friends.

H2c: SH will be more affected by ads, especially by those targeted towards them.

Using survey response from 240 Hispanics (106 Strong Hispanics and 134 Weak Hispanics) all hypotheses were borne out, at the 0.05 level. In other words, for services, Strong Hispanics do consider it more important to locate Hispanic vendors; this is more true for low-involvement services than for high-involvement services. Further, for products, Strong Hispanics are less driven by value and more driven by personal and media influences.

REFERENCES

Berman, Gary L. (1991), "The Hispanic Market: Getting Down to Cases," *Sales and Marketing Management,* 143, 12 (October), 65-74.

Deshpande, Rohit, Wayne Hoyer and Naveen Donthu (1986), "The Intensity of Ethnic Affiliation: A Study of the Sociology of Hispanic Consumption," *Journal* of *Consumer Research,* 13 (September), 214-220.

Hisrschman, Elizabeth C. (1981), "American Jewish Ethnicity: Its Relationship to Some Selected Aspects of Consumer Behavior," *Journal of Marketing,* 45 (Summer), 102-110.

Kotler, Philip (1991), *Marketing Management: Analysis, Planning, Implementation and Control.* Prentice-Hall, NJ.

Palmeri, Christopher (1991), "No Habla Espanol," *Forbes,* 148, 14 (December), 140.

Webster, Cynthia (1991), "Attitudes Toward Marketing Practices: The Effects of Ethnic Identification," *Journal of Applied Business Research,* (Spring 1990-1991), 7 (2) 107-116.

For further information please contact:
Naveen Donthu
Department of Marketing
Georgia State University
Atlanta, Ga 30303

STATUS CONSUMPTION: THE CONCEPT AND ITS MEASURE

Jacqueline C. Kilsheimer, Florida State University
Ronald E. Goldsmith, Florida State University
Leisa Reinecke Flynn, Florida State University

ABSTRACT

Status consumption can be defined as the motivational process by which individuals strive to improve their social standing through the conspicuous consumption of consumer goods that confer or symbolize status both to the individual and to surrounding significant others. Status consumption can be thought of as a trait-like, individual difference variable that distinguishes people by the degree to which they seek to improve their relative social status through purchasing. As social class and income research has been problematic in the past, the benefit of studying status consumption is that it may provide a valid measure for segmenting markets for consumption differences that transcend social class and income lines. In this paper we describe the concept of status consumption and develop a model and measure to both conceptualize and operationalize this construct.

Given the social science literature discussing status and the need to improve ones' status through consumption, we develop the antecedents, dimensions, and consequences of status consumption. We propose six antecedents of status consumption that give rise to its occurrence: (1) a motivation to consume for status, (2) a desire to improve one's self-concept through the purchase of consumer goods, (3) a desire to improve one's social class, (4) a recognition of objects denoting status in the culture, (5) products symbolizing status and success, and (6) the nonfunctional benefits of status goods. Then we present four dimensions of status consumption: (1) sociability, (2) conspicuous consumption, (3) a desire for status, and (4) not buying only for function. Finally, we suggest six possible consequences of status consumption: (1) purchase of status products, (2) selection of status brands, (3) positive brand attitudes towards status products, (4) differential media use for status products, (5) differential shopping behaviors for status products, and (6) a decrease in price sensitivity for status brands. As the purpose of this paper is the development of a reliable and valid scale, we focus on analyzing the four dimensions of the scale and criterion validity.

In two independent samples of undergraduate business students, we developed and tested a reliable Status Consumption Scale (SCS). In our first study, we created a fifty-five item scale that represented the proposed four dimensions. This initial scale was judged for face validity by a panel of Ph.D business students. This scale was administered to three hundred and ninety-one undergraduate business students. We ran a series of explor-atory factor analyses using oblique rotation. Also we utilized Cronbach's alpha for reliability. Based on this, we condensed the scale to twenty-seven items representing three factors: (1) sociability, (2) an interest in consuming for status (combining the two previous dimensions of a desire for status and conspicuous consumption), and (3) not buying only for function.

For the second study, this revised scale was then combined with an eighteen item measure of status purchase behaviors. The behavior measure, based on an undergraduate focus group, represented a list of six status brands for each of three product categories: clothing, electronics, and personal care items. For this list of eighteen status products, the respondents marked each status good they had purchased within the past year. To illustrate criterion validity, the number of status goods the respondent had purchased should correlate positively with the SCS score.

This revised survey was then administered to two hundred and fifty-one undergraduate business students. A series of exploratory factor analyses and reliabilities were run on the second sample using the same procedures as the first study. This resulted in a three factor nineteen item scale with reliabilities of .83 for the sociability dimension, .85 for the interest in consuming for status dimension, and .85 for the not buying only for function dimension. The entire SCS had a reliability of .86. Then a series of confirmatory factor analysis were run testing the full three factor model and the unidimensionality of each of the three factors. The resulting adjusted goodness-of-fit indexes were: .859 for the overall three factor model, .927 for the sociability dimension, .980 for the interest in consuming for status dimension, and .933 for the not buying only for function dimension. Given the early stage of the SCS development, these results were encouraging. Finally, correlations between the SCS and the purchase illustrated that there was a link between the SCS scores and self-reported purchase of status goods in three product domains; thus there was initial evidence of criterion validity.

In conclusion, in this paper we describe the scale development of a measure representing the construct of status consumption. Data from two studies show the scale is reliable and has good content and criterion validity. An implication of this work is that the SCS may be an additional explanatory variable describing a portion of consumer purchase motivation. For managers, this suggests that markets may be segmented based on a motivation to consume for status. To further investigate this, the relationship between status consumption and marketing mix variables needs to be studied. Finally, research is also needed to illustrate the scale's discriminant and convergent validity along with its ability to be generalized to non-student populations

---

For further information please contact:
Jacqueline C. Kilsheimer
Florida State University
College of Business
Tallahassee, FL 32306-1042

PERSONAL AND INTERPERSONAL INFLUENCES ON ILLICIT CONSUMPTION: THE MODERATING ROLE OF PROTECTIVE SOCIAL COMPARISON

Randall L. Rose, University of South Carolina
William O. Bearden, University of South Carolina

ABSTRACT

One important ongoing task for social influence researchers is the identification of factors that moderate the relative influences of personal and interpersonal considerations on behavioral intentions. As Miniard and Cohen have pointed out, "to the extent [that] consumers' behavior is influenced by concerns over what others might think of them or how others might act toward them as a function of their product choice and usage, the identification and separation of normative from personal reasons for preferring a product would appear to be quite useful" (Miniard and Cohen 1983, p. 171). Toward this objective, this paper reports tests of one such potential moderator of interpersonal influences on intentions to conform in the consumption of marijuana and alcohol.

We propose that it is possible to make predictions concerning the relative importance of personal and interpersonal antecedents of intentions by measuring consumers' predispositions to act on the social cues available at the time a purchase or consumption decision is being made. Lennox and Wolfe (1984) identified such a measure, which they chose to call "protective social comparison" (PSC), in their critique and revision of the original self-monitoring scale (Snyder 1974). Lennox and Wolfe (1984) identified PSC as a factor distinct from the self-monitoring construct because of its relatively strong relationship with social anxiety (Lennox and Wolfe 1984, p. 1363). Their results suggest that PSC might be useful as a measure of predispositions toward conformity and as a potential moderator of the influence of normative pressures on consumer behavior in general, as well as the consumption of illicit substances in particular.

In brief, theory and empirical research suggest that responses to conformity pressures in the consumption of illicit substances by young people may be moderated by individual difference factors such as PSC. In particular, because of their social anxiety, persons scoring high in PSC should assign greater weight to interpersonal influences and should view those interpersonal influences more favorably when making decisions than those with lower PSC scores. Further, PSC should moderate the overall strength of the influence of interpersonal considerations on conformity intentions. That is, interpersonal influences should be a stronger determinant of conformity intentions when PSC is higher that when PSC is lower. Two studies were conducted in which these propositions were tested in the context of marijuana use by college students and alcohol use by high school students.

Students responded first to the key conformity intentions measures on an 11-point scale anchored by "certainty would smoke the marijuana" (11) and "there is no chance that I would smoke the marijuana" (1). Items used to operationalize the global version of the Miniard and Cohen (1983) behavioral intentions model were assessed next. The 13-item PSC scale was operationalized as the sum of responses to 6-place scales labeled "always true" (5) to "always false" (0).

The results of the present research provide support for some of our expectations, but not all, in the context of drug and alcohol conformity settings experienced by young people. That is, both college students (marijuana) and high school students (beer) perceived interpersonal considerations to be more favorable and more important to their conformity decisions when they scored higher on the PSC scale than when their scores were lower. However, the influence on conformity intentions of students' overall evaluation on interpersonal considerations did not differ between high and low PSC groups as expected. Rather, in both studies, the moderating effect of PSC operated through the overall evaluation of personal considerations. That is, the overall effect of personal considerations on conformity intentions was lower for the high PSC group than for the low PSC group.

For further information contact:
Randall L. Rose
Division of Marketing
College of Business
University of South Carolina
Columbia, SC 29208

A CROSS-CULTURAL STUDY ON THE EFFECT OF PRICE AND PERCEPTIONS OF PRODUCT QUALITY

Richard Sjolander, Lund University, Sweden and The University of West Florida

ABSTRACT

The relationship between the price cue and buyers' perceptions of product quality is examined in a cross-cultural environment. Poland and Sweden are chosen to explore the relationships in the construct between the newly emerging free market economies in Eastern Europe and traditional market economies. It is hypothesized that the price cue will have a significant effect on quality perceptions based on taste tests of ice cream. This relationship is not supported by the data. However, large differences are found in the level of quality perceived by different age cohorts in both Sweden and Poland. Preadolescent subjects consistently ranked the quality of all samples above their older cohorts.

INTRODUCTION

It is generally agreed in the literature that price and the perceived quality of goods and services have a high, positive correlation (Motes 1987). However, there is very little empirical evidence exploring this relationship, and the studies which have been done are limited to generalizing about the relationship within cultural boundaries (Garvin 1984).

Buyers' regularly face the task of estimating product quality under conditions of imperfect knowledge about the underlying attributes of the various product offers. Decisions are made with the aid of personal, self-perceived quality criteria (Bedeian 1971). This situation of actual buyer behavior in modern markets is far from the theoretical case of rational consumer decision making which forms the base for much economic theory, where free, competitive markets are composed of many buyers and sellers each of whom possesses

1. perfect information about all possible products and their respective utilities,

2. a well defined and explicit set of preferences, and

3. the ability to determine optimal combinations of the various products given their personal budget constraints.

It is further assumed,

4. that a knowledge of prices does not affect the subjective wants or satisfactions of the consumer (Monroe and Petroshius 1973).

Under these assumptions price merely represents the value of alternative goods and services. The price of a product has no intrinsic value of its own.

While these assumptions are of importance to the economist in the modeling of economic systems, they may place unnecessary constraints upon the development of buyer behavior models. The lack of perfect knowledge on the part of either buyers or sellers as to the exact content of products exchanged provides an explanation for much of the consumer protection legislation passed throughout Europe and North America during the 1960's and 1970's. Each of the other assumptions has also been questioned, and may be linked to the development of the perception of product quality by consumers. Clearly, each of the first three conditions may be affected by the forth, ie, shaped by pricing cues if we relax the assumption that consumer perception is not affected by price, per se.

Scitovszky (1945) identified a gap between the situation faced by consumers and the ideal, or theoretical case, as one in which they are confronted by the need to make consumption decisions under severe limitations of information. In such a case the use of price as an indicator of product quality is not irrational, but represents a belief that price is determined by the interplay of supply and demand forces in competitive markets. Thus, we would expect a strong positive relationship between price and actual, or objective, level of product quality (Dodds, Monroe, and Grewal 1991).

Various aspects of the relationship between price and quality have been a topic of study in marketing for decades. A number of these have been reported in the marketing literature (McConnell 1967, 1968; Ehrenberg and Charlton 1973; Motes 1987). These studies attempted to create situations similar to those occurring when consumers chose among various product offers for low involvement goods. One of the best known of these studies was published by McConnell (1968). Here the product was used was beer and a group of adult consumers in an American university setting were asked to choose from various product items, bottles of beer, distinguished only by price. Ehrenberg and Charlton conducted similar research in the United Kingdom in the early 1970's (1973). That study was replicated and partially validated by Motes (1987).

These experimental studies were longitudinal and principally concerned with the strength of brand preference when confronted with price differences. Thus, price was manipulated over time to observe the behavior of a group of experimental subjects. Others, such as Peterson

(1970), looked at the price quality relationship at a single point of time and manipulated the price cue, where product descriptions were given to the subjects. Enis and Stafford (1969), Wheatley, Chiu and Goldman (1981) carried this research further by including price cues and actual, or physical quality differences in the product. The products used in these studies were high involvement goods, ie. products associated with more extensive information gathering. In each of these studies subjects were exposed to one level of price and one level of physical quality in a 3 x 3 sampling frame. The results of these studies lent support to the hypothesis that price is a dimension of the concept of quality.

Each of these studies was conducted within the cultural boundaries of a single nation. Recent, rapid change in the way markets are perceived, often called international or global marketing perspectives, increases the importance of cross-cultural comparisons of consumer behavior (Levitt 1983; Ohmae 1989). It is difficult to expand the results of current studies into a cross-cultural dimension, The products and test methods used varied widely from study to study. This is one of the areas explored in the current study.

Changes in the market structure in Eastern Europe and what was the Soviet Republic add dynamic new dimensions to the whole area of consumer perceptions of products. In this respect the question of the price-quality perceptions of consumers is one dimension of a more general question of consumer reactions to market controllable cues in environments where such cues have been generally absent. Effects of the expansion of free markets into previously non-free-market economies on consumer behavior is a relatively new area of research. This is the area considered in the present research construct.

HYPOTHESES

The foregoing discussion suggests many interesting questions for cross-cultural consumer research in the area of the price-perceived quality relationship. Two have been chosen for attention in the current study. The first is to explore the relationship between price and the perception of quality in two diverse European cultures. This problem study can be formally stated in the following way:

What is the structure of the relationship between price and the perception of quality in a free market economy, such as Sweden, compared to a newly emerging free-market economy, such as Poland.

The choice of these two cultural regions was made to include one Western European country with a long history as a free market economy, and a country from the former Eastern European block with a recent history of centrally planned economic decision making. Poland is surrounded by former plan economies, East Germany,

Czechoslovakia, Hungary, and the Soviet Union. It was a plan economy during the period 1945 through 1990. The Polish economy can currently (1992) be characterized as one in transition to a market economy. The population of 37 million people now finds that there is a wide variety of goods available in all cities. The depth of assortment is less than that common to West European free market economies, such as Sweden, but is much greater than it was under the plan economy of the last 45 years. In the villages the change has been slower and more sporadic. The newness of the free market economy experience in Poland makes it an interesting test case.

Sweden, by contrast, is a highly industrialized North European economy. Its standard of living and per capita income are among the highest in the world. It is geographically near Poland, separated by the Baltic Sea. However, its history as a free market economy, similar to those throughout Western Europe and North America, sets it apart from Poland. The contrast between these economic and social systems may lead to significant differences in the way buyers use price cues to develop perceptions of product quality.

The first research hypothesis can be stated:

H1.   Is there a difference between the price-perceived quality relationship between the populations of Swedish and Polish youth.

This question is especially interesting for the emerging market economies, which Poland represents. The change from a plan economy was effected less than two years before the collection of the data. Very little is known about attitudes among the populations of these countries regarding product choice, except that a majority prefer to change over to a free market economic system (Wosinski 1987).

The second question relates to this first issue, as well as to much of the previous work which has been done on perceived quality. It concerns the issue of at what stage in development perceptions about price-quality are formed by consumers.

Much of the prior research in the area of price-perceived quality relationships has been done with student samples. They are easy to sample and will be representative of buyer behavior, at least among the higher income groups due to the predominance of the upper socio-economic groups among university students. There is an additional reason for using students in the present study. Poland has only recently changed from a command economy. It is assumed that students give a good indication of attitudes which may be diffusing through the society.

Little is known about possible differences in the price-perceived quality perceptions among pre-adolescents and young adults. Both of these groups represent increasingly important groups of consumers. The population for the present study is defined as youth and young adult students in Sweden and Poland and a stratified sample consisting of pre-adolescents and young adults is used.

Hypothesis two can be stated:

H2. Is the price/perceived quality relationship constant over the period from pre-adolescence to young adulthood.

RESEARCH METHOD

The approach used in the present study is similar to that used by Enis and Stafford (1969) to explore the price-perceived quality relationship with a stratified sample of consumers and retail sales personnel. However, here each subject will be given the product at three levels of price and asked to determine the level of perceived quality in each product.

Spontaneous judgments of quality based on one exposure to the product are studied, ie. without the added variable of "brand loyalty", such as in the case of repeated simulated 'purchases' over a period of time(McConnell 1968), or assuming brand attributes to a simulated product (Dodds, Monroe, and Grewal 1991). With control groups for each age cohort in each culture this will provide a 2 x 2 x 2 experimental design. The important quality perception rating question will be structured as a graphic rating scale to allow parametric statistical analysis.

The choice of product is critical for intercultural buyer perception studies. The use of pre-adolescents as one part of the stratified, random sample further truncates the set of products which fit the criteria for the experiment. The product must be familiar to the subjects and used in similar situations to provide similar satisfactions by both groups to be sampled, in each of the cultures included in the study. It must be a product which can be sampled without the subject either guessing the brand from physical characteristics of the product, or becoming suspect due to the absence of brand identification on products readily identifiable on the market, such as chocolate bars. Finally, the product must also occur at various price points in each cultural market, or only occur at one price level in all markets to avoid the unnecessary introduction of uncontrolled variation in the prior experience of the subjects. These factors caused the rejection of the products used in prior research, such as beer, potato chips, carpet, and business calculators.

Vanilla ice cream was chosen for this study after consideration of the market in both target countries, and with thought to the possible extension of the study into other markets at a later time. This product is well known, and frequently purchased. It is expected that the target population, children and young adults in each culture is experienced with the product and its purchase. The product exists at a wide range of prices in both markets. When the product is presented without its package brand identification from the physical characteristics of the product is very difficult.

A taste test was designed with the product price as the only distinguishing cue. Each subject was given three samples, and asked to judge the quality of the products on 5 point Likert scales, as well as making a comparative evaluation of a 7 point graphic rating scale. The true purpose of the experiment was disguised as a test of a new brand of ice cream being considered for introduction to the market.

The price levels used in the experimental condition in each market were chosen to approximate actual market prices on the basis of market surveys, and remain within the relevant (expected) price range for vanilla ice cream in each market. The absolute prices are thus market specific, and determined in each market. They cannot necessarily be translated among currencies at current exchange rates. It is important in this type of research not to fabricate the price levels (Wheatley, Chiu, and Goldman 1981).

Preparation of the questionnaire was a particular problem in the present case dealing in multiple cultures across language barriers. The document was designed simultaneously in Swedish and English for ease in translating the results into English for dissemination. This was done by using researchers fluent in both languages, but with their mother tongue and country of residence within each language group. This also provided the base for translation of the document into Polish. This was especially important as the author has no fluency in that language. Two, independent translations were made into Polish. These documents were then compared and formed the basis for the final questionnaire designed by a third translator. Extreme caution must be exercised to minimize the all too well documented problems of intercultural communication. Further, the script was prepared to indicate that this was a test being conducted by an international professor of business and read by to the subjects by nationals of the country being sampled, to avoid bias caused by the experiment originating in one of the test countries.

RESULTS

The tests were conducted during a two week period in December, 1991. There were no significant changes in the environments of either country to suspect that any change occurred during the sampling period. Classes of students of the appropriate ages were sampled from primary schools in both countries. As well college students from business classes at universities in each country provided the older samples. A total of 220 individuals were sampled in the eight cells of the research design. Cell size varied from 18 to 37 do to differences in the sixes of the classes sampled.

The three 'brands' were identified by the consonants 'M', 'L', and 'P'. Where prices were given, they were arranged so that 'M' was identified as the lowest price product. 'L' was identified with the highest price and 'P' occupied the middle position (McConnell 1968).

The study measured the influence of two independent variables, price and cultural background of the respondent, on one dependent variable, consumer perceptions of quality, under the controlled conditions of a taste test.

In order to minimize the interference of intervening variables only one identical level of physical product quality was used in the experiment. To control for variance between the cultural/geographical markets a leading brand, in terms of sales, among the higher priced ice creams was to be used in each case. This procedure was established to standardize the product, across cultural boundaries, and to minimize eventual problems with quality variations within each sample. However, in practice, the high priced market leader was used only in Sweden. In Poland, a medium priced ice cream was used due to availability.

Three brand labels were used in the study - L, M, and P. They have previously been used by McConnell (1968) for beer and Tucker (1964) for bread. They were chosen for ease of identification and memory, position as consonants from the middle of the alphabet, and as they have about the same frequency of use in English (McConnell 1968). These letters also occur in both the Swedish and Polish alphabets and are expected exhibit similar characteristics. Both the letters and the associated prices were used non-sequentially to avoid bias from respondents inferring differences from the positions of the letters in the test instrument.

The prices used were market prices for a 1/2 liter package of ice cream in Sweden and a scoop of ice cream (40-50 grams) in Poland. For each of the brands of ice cream the prices were:

Brand	Sweden	Poland
M	7 skr.	1000sz.
L	13 skr.	2000sz.
P	10 skr.	1500sz.

These prices were within the range of prices found in each market at the time the experiments were carried out. The price relevant range was defined by the retail prices of similar products in each country, ie. designer brands of ice cream were not included in the Swedish case, and only the most common Polish and German brands were in-

cluded with the Polish sample. The size of the reference product was also adapted to existing conditions in each country. In Sweden ice cream is typically purchased in supermarkets and convenience stores in half liter paperboard packages for consumption in the home. These packages are also sold for immediate consumption, usually being divided in two by the shop keeper and sold with disposable spoons. This purchase-consumption pattern is in contrast to conditions in Poland, where ice cream is typically purchased in ice cream shops by the scoop for immediate consumption.

The control groups were asked to compare three types of vanilla ice cream. The only additional information given to the subjects in the experimental groups was the price of each sample.

The results of the experiment, in terms of the treatment variable are shown in Tables 1 and 2. The student t-test for significant difference between the individual pairs of means. ANOVA was used to for analysis among the means in the data. The t-test is appropriate for comparing the results of individual experiment and control groups. Analysis of variance permits the examination of relationships between more than one independent variable and the dependent variable without requiring any assumptions about the nature of the relationship. The Scheffe method is an appropriate test to identify individually significant relationships where sample size varies. The requirements of the data for each of these statistical techniques were examined and found to be met.

The results of this cross-cultural examination of buyers' perceptions of product quality given the single characteristic of price to distinguish between the products lend only slight support to the link between price as a cue and buyers' perceptions of quality. Student t-tests of the differences in the means of the control and experiment groups in each country show only one relationship which is significant at the 5 percent level (Table 1). This is for the intermediate price level in Sweden. All of the other 5 test means lie within the range which could be expected from the control group.

The results for Poland do show a consistent increase in the perceived quality level as the price is increased. The Swedish level of perceived quality first rises with price to the medium level and then declines as the price is increased further. Analysis of variance for the experimental groups within each culture failed to show significant results (Table 1).

The data from this test do not support first hypothesis. There does not appear to be a difference between the price/perceived quality relationships in these two countries in the present study.

A highly significant difference wase found in the Polish sample between age groups (Table 2). Pre-adoles-

TABLE 1 - A
Perceptions of Product Quality Aggregated by Country

Poland	Average Responses (means)		
	(M)	(P)	(L)
Experiment Group	4.40	4.59	4.74
Control Group	4.58	4.95	4.68
t-test statistic	(0.54)	(1.00)	(0.18)

Sweden	Average Responses (means)		
	(M)	(P)	(L)
Experiment Group	4.86	4.94	4.87
Control Group	4.90	48.33	4.55
t-test statistic	(0.15)	(1.96)*	(1.23)

$p < 0.05$

Table 1 - B
Analysis of Variance of Mean Quality Perceptions In the Experiment Groups with Price Information

Dependent Variable : Quality Rankings of Ice Cream with Prices
Independent Variable: Price Cue
Levels of Variable : 3

Source	DF	Sum of Squares	Mean of Squares	F.	Probability
Poland					
Quality ranks	2	0.2985	0.1493	0.070	0.933
Residual	215	459.872	2.139		
Total	217	460.171			
Sweden					
Quality ranks	5	11.070	2.214	1.045	0.392
Residual	212	449.101	2.118		
Total	217	460.171			

cents perceived the quality of the ice cream to be higher than their older cohort at all price levels. However, when the cntrol group results are added to the analysis it becomes clear that there is a general difference in reported quality levels between the two age groups. Preadolescents attribute a higher level of qulity to the product in the absence of price information, too. This phenomenon was not observed in the Swedish sample.

Thus, the data failed to support hypothesis 2.

DISCUSSION AND LIMITATIONS

The experimental design chosen for this research included control groups for each experimental condition in each country. Student t-tests of the sample means showed significant differences for the price cues only in

TABLE 2
Perceptions of Product Quality Aggregated by Country and Age

Poland

Dependent Variable : Quality Rankings of Ice Cream with Prices
Independent Variable: Age of Respondent
Levels of Variable   : 6

Source	DF	Sum of Squares	Mean of Squares	F.	Probability
Quality ranks	5	104.412	20.882	9.6929	0.000
Residual	164	353.321	2.154		
Total	169	457.733			

Mean Responses Price Given

		Low (M)	Medium (P)	High (L)
Experiment	Pre-Adolescents	1 5.487	2 5.292	3 5.650
Groups	Adults	4 3.679	5 4.042	6 4.042

Scheffe Test for Significance ($p < 0.05$)

Group One	Group Two	Mean	Probability
1	4	1.808	0.0015
1	5	1.444	0.0259
1	6	1.444	0.0259
2	4	-1.613	0.0065
3	4	-1.971	0.0003
3	5	1.608	0.0068
3	6	1.608	0.0068

Sweden

Dependent Variable : Quality Rankings of Ice Cream with Prices
Independent Variable: Age of Respondent
Levels of Variable   : 6

Source	DF	Sum of Squares	Mean of Squares	F.	Probability
Quality ranks	5	11.070	2.214	1.045	0.392
Residual	212	449.101	2.118		
Total	217	460.171			

isolated cases. A more general analysis of variance test among groups did not support the hypotheses.Thus, ignoring for now the intercultural aspects,the present study is not in support the findings of much earlier research in this field. While it will be clearly noted that there was a generally positive relationship between price and perceived quality under the experimental condition in Poland, this relationship was not significantly different from the quality rankings of the control groups making their decisions about product quality without the price cue at the 0.05 level of significance. The relationship between the price cue and level of buyers' perceived quality proved to be much weaker in this study than it has been in much of the literature.

One surprising finding is that the lack of significant

difference exists both in Sweden and Polish samples. The author had expected a positive relationship between the price cue and perceived quality, and that this relationship would be stronger in a newly emerging market economy with less experience in dealing with free market price setting. As can be seen in Table 1-B, the data clearly do not support this hypothesis. Price information failed to be a significant predictor of perceived quality in either country.

The difference in the perception of quality between pre-adolescents and college age subjects offers material for many hypotheses (Table 2). The strength of the relationship in the Polish culture may indicate that considerable learning takes place during the intervening teenage years, undermining the faith of the consumer in the basic quality of goods. Although this relationship was not significant for the Swedish sample, a slight indication in the same direction as in the Polish sample, ie. that younger consumers tended to rank the quality of all samples of the product as possessing a higher level of quality than adults. It is interesting to find that these results show no difference between either age or cultural background and perceptions of quality on the basis of the price cue. Younger subjects ranked all samples higher than did their college age cohorts.

The reader should be reminded that this study used only one product, ice cream, in a controlled setting to study the relationship between price cues and buyers' perceptions of quality. Although it would be most interesting to see this type of research carried on with buyer behavior, it would be a mistake to extrapolate the results of the current study beyond limited perceptions of quality. There are many dimensions involved in the formation of perceptions of quality by buyers. This study attempted to isolate the price cue from its context and draw some conclusions from this partial analysis.

CONCLUSIONS AND DIRECTIONS FOR FUTURE RESEARCH

The results of this experiment offer only slight support for a direct link between the price cue and buyers' perceptions of quality. When compared with control groups, the experimental case results were very insignificant. This result is surprising for two reasons. First there is a growing literature in marketing, not to mention the theoretical economic basis for expecting this relationship between price and perceived quality to be both significant and positive.

Second, is the consideration of the countries studied in this experiment. One, Sweden, has a long history as a free market economy. Poland had a centrally planned economy until 1990. It was expected that differences in cultural backgrounds and learning would be reflected in buyers' perceptions of quality when given price cues. These effects were not supported by the data. More research is needed in the area of buyers' perceptions in various cultural settings to assist decision making as businesses expand into new markets.

What we did find was that subjects in both countries were not significantly affected by a knowledge of the prices of three types of vanilla ice cream when reporting their estimates of the relative quality levels of the products. It should be noted that the experimental design allowed the subjects to sample each of the three types of ice cream before making their decisions. This situation, thus, may be quite different from experiments where either product descriptions are presented to the subjects, or they are see a physical product without the chance for trial.

There is a need for much greater attention to cross-cultural research, especially with the newly emerging nations of Eastern Europe. These countries represent large markets of current and potential demand for world products. They also provide opportunities for longitudinal studies in the development of market systems to fill the vacuum left with the downfall of their plan economies. These topics are current and need to be addressed in the nearest future.

Considerable work needs to be done on refining the simple one factor relationships with buyers' perceptions of quality and price, as well as with more complex situations where brand, country of origin, etc. are also included. The rapid expansion of markets into international dimensions opens the whole area of cross-cultural consumer research.

Careful preparation and execution of questionnaire design and translation is obvious in cross cultural consumer behavior studies. Attention needs to be paid to the accurate translation of the intent of the questions. Literal, or verbatim translations will often lead to spurious results. The importance of native speakers to administer the experiment in each country was especially obvious with the pre-adolescents in this study. Cultural adaptation is a necessity for the gathering of cross-cultural data.

REFERENCES

Bedeian, A.G. (1971), "Consumer Perception of Price as an Indicator of Product Quality," *M S U Business Topics*, (Summer), 59-65.

Charlton, P. and A, A. C. Ehrenberg (1976), "An Experiment in Brand Choice," *Journal of Marketing Research*, 13 (May), 152-160.

Dodds, W. B., K. B. Monroe, and D. Grewal (1991), "Effects of Price, Brand, and Store Information on

Buyers' Product Evaluations," *Journal of Marketing Research*, 28 (August), 307-319.

Ehrenberg, A., and P. Charlton (1973), "An Analysis of Simulated Brand-Share Choice," *Journal of Advertising Research*, 13 (February), 21-22.

Enis, B.M., and J.E. Stafford (1969), "Consumers' Perception of Product Quality as a Function of Various Informational Inputs," AMA Fall Conference. Chicago: American Marketing Association, 340-344.

Garvin, David A. (1984), "What Does "Product Quality" Really Mean?" *Sloan Management Review*, (Fall), 25-43.

Gerstner, Eitan (1985), "Do Higher Prices Signal higher Quality?" *Journal of Marketing Research*, 22 (May), 209-215.

Levitt, Theodore (1983), "The Globalization of Markets," *Harvard Business Review*, (May/June), 92-102.

McConnell, J. Douglas (1967), "A Behavioral Study of the Development and Persistence of Brand Loyalty for a Consumer Product," Ph.D. Dissertation, Stanford University, #67-17459. Ann Arbor: Xerox University Microfilms.

_____ (1968a), "An Experimental Examination of the Price-Quality Relationship," *Journal of Business*, 41 (October), 439-444.

_____ (1968b), "The Price-Quality Relationship in an Experimental Setting," *Journal of Marketing Research*, 5 (August), 300-303.

_____ (1968c), "The Development of Brand Loyalty: An Experimental Study," *Journal of Marketing Research*, 5 (February) 13-19.

Monroe, K. B. and S. M. Petroshius (1973), "Buyers' Perceptions of Price: An Update of the Evidence," *Journal of Marketing Research*, 10 (February), 70-80.

Motes, William H. (1987), "Replication of Pricing Effects on Brand Choice Behavior," *European Journal of Marketing*, 21, 14-25.

Ohmae, Kenichi (1989), "Planting for a Global Harvest," *Harvard Business Review*, (July/August), 136-145.

Peacock, P. and H.L. Davis (1970), "The Alphabet as an Independent Variable: A Reply to J. Douglas McConnell," *Journal of Business*, 43 (April), 205-209.

Peterson, R.A. (1970), "The Price-Perceived Quality Relationship: Experimental Evidence," *Journal of Marketing Research*, 7 (November), 525-528.

Riesz, Peter C. (1978), "Price Verses Quality in the Marketplace 1961-1975," *Journal of Retailing*, 54 (Winter), 15-28.

Scitovszky, Tibor (1945), "Some Consequences of the Habit of Judging Quality by Price," *Review of Economic Studies*, 12, 477-485.

Tellis, G. J. and B. Wernerfelt (1988), "Competitive Price and Quality under Asymmetric Information," *Marketing Science*, 6, 240-253.

Wheatley, J. J., J. S. Chiu and A. Goldman (1981), "Physical Quality, Price, and Perceptions of Product Quality: Implications for Retailers," *Journal of Retailing*, 57 (Summer), 100-116.

Wosinski, Marek (1987), "A Model of Consumer Behavior in the Situation of Shortages," Research Paper No. 6326, The Economic Research Institute At the Stockholm School of Economics. Stockholm, Sweden: The Stockholm School of Economics.

STANDARDIZED GLOBAL MARKETING COMMUNICATION CAMPAIGNS ARE POSSIBLE, THEY'RE JUST HARD TO DO

Tom Duncan, University of Colorado-Boulder

ABSTRACT

For international marketers, there are many advantages of using a standardized global marketing communication campaign. Because of cultural differences, however, many experts feel that a standardized campaign is not feasible. This paper argues that a standardized campaign can be successful when marketers do three basic things: (1) use the concept of global stratification to segment and target, (2) use a creative strategy that is based on basic, cross-cultural needs, and (3) use executional techniques, such as those used in music, entertainment, and the arts, that are understood regardless of culture .

INTRODUCTION

A global marketing communication program can save millions in manufacturing, packaging, and advertising costs. When Colgate-Palmolive introduced its tartar control toothpaste in over 40 countries, the company used only two different campaigns (each country had its choice). The company estimated they saved between $1 and $2 million in each country by not having to produce customized campaigns. It also saved several millions by using a standardized package (Lipman 1988).

But there are several other advantages to using standardized global campaigns beside saving money. Some of these are:

- building a global brand which gives a brand more brand power/value
- maximizing a good creative idea
- faster response time when other global brands make a change
- take advantage of the growing number of global media

With the high cost of today's product development, most companies, especially those in medium and small countries, need to sell their new products internationally to insure a profitable return (*The Economist* 1989) But ask international marketers about standardized global campaigns, and most have a knee jerk reaction, saying it's ivory tower, contrary to marketing common sense, and virtually impossible unless you are Coca Cola or Marlboro.

Since Ted Levitt popularized the concept of global marketing (Levitt 1983) in 1983, his theory has received considerably more criticism than support. And the criticism has not let up with most focusing on national and cultural differences. Five years after Levitt's initial article was published, the lead story in an issue of the *Wall Street Journal* was headlined, "Marketers Turn Sour On Global Sales Pitch Harvard Guru Makes," (Lipman 1988) The article went on to state:

> For many, the global-marketing theory itself is bankrupt. In fact, the concept that once sent scores of executives scrambling to reconfigure their marketing strategies now has many feeling duped. Not only are cultural differences very much still with us, they say, but marketing a single product one way everywhere can scare off customers, alienate employees, and blind a company to its customers' needs."

Opponents of standardized global campaigns find it difficult to conceptually cross national borders with the same basic strategy and execution, pointing to such obvious differences as language, religion, climate, and food preparation. Critics of standardized advertising say that these cultural differences prevent marketers from:

1. identifying a global target market

2. using a creative strategy that has cross-cultural appeal

3. communicating this creative strategy in an execution that is understood by multiple cultures

The purpose of this paper is to show how these three things are both possible and practical, and therefore profitable.

Use Global Stratification to Identify Cross-Cultural Targets

Global stratification is the third generation of marketing segmentation. The first was demographics. This was followed in the 1960s by psychographics which pointed out that consumer attitudes and values could be used as a segmenting tool that could cut across demographic lines. But since different countries have different political structures, religions, and traditions, resulting in different attitudes and values, psychographics have been, by definition, culturally bound.

In searching for homogeneous groups, both demographic and psychographic segmenting has focused on **differences between groups**. Thus, when these traditional marketing tools were applied to international marketing communication, the goal was to identify groups of consumers with few differences. The conclusion has been, in most cases, to customize marketing programs country by country because of national and cultural differences. It is interesting to note that several leading international marketing textbooks don't even list market segmentation in their indices, suggesting they don't think it works at the international level or that global segmentation is an oxymoron.

Global stratification answers these needs because it focuses on **similarities rather than differences**. Global stratification looks at the world in layers, with each layer cutting across national boundaries and composed of a specific consumer characteristic such as new mothers, teenagers, farmers, computer technicians, business travelers. The fact that each of these groups has specific wants and needs resulting from their respective characteristics, is the basis on which each is stratified. This approach sees a national population as being composed of many layers or strata of consumers. The strata in different countries may vary in size and importance, as in a geological formation, but the layers themselves cut across national boundaries.

Global stratification is unlike the traditional process of segmentation which is to aim for a "bull's eye" target audience. In global stratification the **concept** of identifying potential users is the same, but the researcher needs to think of the bull's eye as being an elongated horizontal stratum that crosses national borders rather than a concentric circle.

Global stratification allows global marketers to identify what anthropologists refer to as *cross cultural cohorts*. These are people who have a distinct, common set of needs as a result of a common characteristic or role (regardless of their culture and nationality). Clifford Geertz, in his book, *The Interpretation of Cultures*, refers to these types of groups as "stratificatory realities within which men are everywhere contained..."(Geertz 1973). Some examples are: teenager, new mother, computer technician, business traveler, fashion conscious dresser, farmer, smoker, college student, retiree, athlete. Each of the above segments exists in countries as culturally diverse as China and France, India and Russia, Costa Rica, and the U.S., and in nearly every other country in the world (Geertz 1973). As Stanley Paliwoda states in *International Marketing*, "Segmentation of urban dwellers internationally may reveal greater similarities than between local nationals" (Paliwoda 1986).

As the hypothetical graph shows, the percent of each of these types of consumers will vary from country to country. While farmers, for example, may represent 3 percent of the US, 6 percent of the UK, 12 percent of Spain, 60 percent of China, the important point is, farmers exist in all these countries. These variances, however, are quickly narrowing as consumers and societies strive for what Levitt calls "modernity" and what others call the emergence of a global culture.

In his discussion of what a global cultural would look like, Smith makes several observations which helps explains the concept of global stratification:

A global culture, so the argument runs, will be eclectic like its western or European progenitor, but will wear a uniformly streamlined packaging. Standardized, commercialized mass commodities will nevertheless draw for their contents upon revivals of traditional, folk, or national motifs and styles in fashions, furnishings, music and the arts, lifted out of their original contexts and anaesthetized. So that a global culture would operate at several levels simultaneously: as a cornucopia of standardized commodities, as a patchwork of denationalized ethnic or folk motifs, as a series of generalized 'human values and interests,' as a uniform 'scientific' discourse of meaning, and finally as the interdependent system of communications which forms the material base for all the other components and levels (Smith 1990).

The concept of global stratification is endorsed by Marieke deMooij, Educational Secretary of the International Advertising Association. In her new book, *Advertising Worldwide*, De Mooij says "... there will be more and more homogeneous cross-cultural groups with similar needs, which can be approached in the same way" (DeMooij 1991).

Use Creative Strategies that Appeal to Basic Needs and Wants

The second "impossible" element a global marketing communication program must have is a selling proposition that has a cross-cultural appeal. Critics of global marketing again say cultural differences prevent this, pointing to the wide ranges of income, education, political structure, language, and traditions that exist among countries.

According to Edward Meyer, "Global marketing that is careful not to trample on local sensitivities is the wave of the future." He goes on to say, "On balance, the wants and needs of consumers of all ages are indeed more similar than not"(Meyer 1985).

After doing a cluster based analysis of 40 countries which looked at economic levels, media availability, and various other cultural factors, Sriram and Gopalakrishna concluded that multinational advertisers should view standardization "as a strategy that makes unified themes, images,and even brand names, possible"(Sriram and Gopalakrishna 1991).

Even though Abraham Maslow's hierarchy of needs has been around for over thirty years and considered as Psychology 101 by many, it has weathered well and should

FIGURE 1
Global Stratification

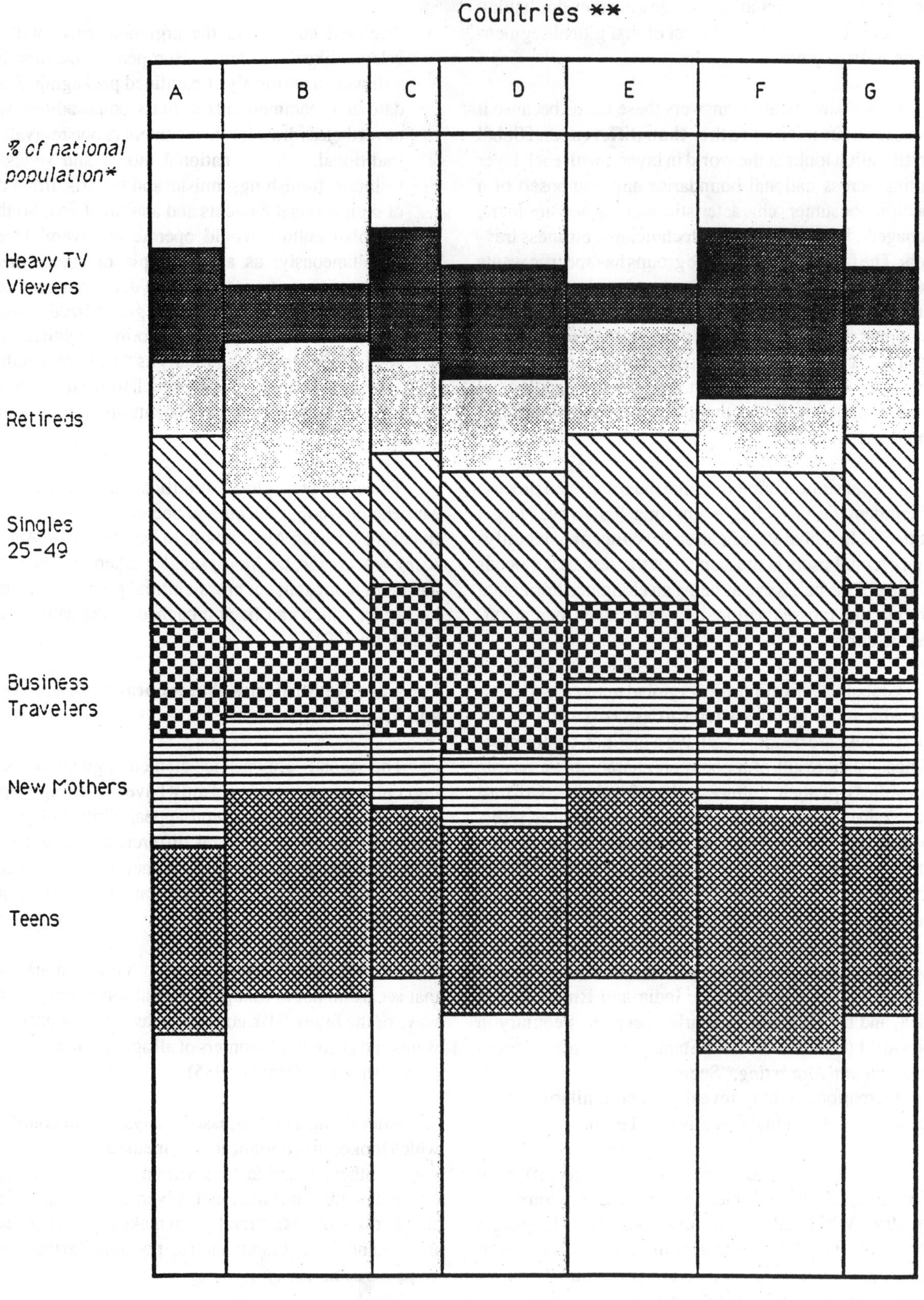

Countries **

% of national population*
Heavy TV Viewers
Retireds
Singles 25-49
Business Travelers
New Mothers
Teens

** "Width" of country's bar indicates relative differentiation in population

*These are not mutually exclusive groupings, (e.g. a person could be a single 25-49 and an aa business traveler or heavy TV viewer)

not be ignored. Frank Goble, in summarizing Maslow's theories, says "The human being is motivated by a number of basic needs which are species-wide, apparently unchanging, and genetic or instinctual in origin." Although Maslow admitted that these needs are often weak and can be repressed by one's culture, he felt that they cannot be killed (Goble 1970).

In his book, *Multinational Marketing Management,* Warren Keegan states that "much of the apparent cultural diversity in the world turns out to be different ways of accomplishing the same thing." He goes on to list over fifty "cultural universals" such as athletic sports, dancing, ethics, kin groups, sexual restrictions, superstitions. While each culture may have, for example, a dance that is unique to that culture, the basics of dancing - moving the feet, arms, body with a certain rhythm - is universal (Keegan 1984).

Teenagers around the world listen to rock music, drink Coke, wear trendy clothing, and eat McDonald's hamburgers. New mothers everywhere want their babies to be healthy, to laugh and respond, and to be admired by other people. Farmers in all cultures want their crops (not weeds) to grow, want their animals to be healthy, want top price for any extras they have to sell or barter, and they want to do their farming as quickly and easily as possible, regardless of whether they are farming a few acres or thousands of acres.

Critics of standardization would argue that the average US farmer uses a $100,000 combine while the average Chinese farmer uses an ox pulled hand plow. The fallacy of this argument is the word "average." The day of selling to the "average" person died with mass marketing. Today's strategic niche marketing along with the media ability to reach just those customers who have a need for a specific product, allows a John Deere to economically reach the 30,000 US farmers and the 2,000 Chinese cooperatives who can afford and who need a $100,000 combine.

Harris and Moran believe "Astute observers on the contemporary scene are well aware that modern society is in transition. . . (if they) witness the innovations in information, silicon, solar and space technologies that are causing a decline in traditional industries and pointing the way to tomorrow's work culture." They also say human migration is a catalyst to change, pointing to such forces as economic, social, political, religious causes which have prompted people to leave their native countries and enter alien cultures (Harris and Moran 1987). While these conditions are frequently thought of in a historical time frame, a look at the growing Hispanic population in the US, the millions of refugees in the mid-east and African countries, the growing Indian population in England, and the tens of thousands of Chinese students studying outside China, illustrate that these migrations continue to take place today.

Even if modern consumers never move out of their native country they will be subjected to changing cultural conditions. This is due to urbanization, the rapid expansion of educational programs (especially in developing countries), and the increasing availability of mass media. All of these changes, according to Verma and Bagley, mean that consumers "will not live out their lives in the same cultural circumstances as those in which they were initially raised" (Verma and Bagley 1988). Cultural anthropologists agree that acculturation (assimilation into another culture) takes place in the direction of the larger culture, which today is the pervasive modern or "developed" culture of the industrialized societies.

An example of how swift cultural change can take place can be seen in China. Following the fall of the Gang of Four in the mid 1970s, the vast majority of the population wore Mao suits. In less than ten years, the majority of these one billion people had switched to colorful shirts and blouses leaving the Mao suits to the very old. Another example of how basic cultural traditions are eroding is the changing eating habits of Europeans. They are not only changing what they eat but when they eat, even in the very traditional southern European countries (*The Economist* 1989).

When a culture is in transition, as most cultures are today, people see change happening all around them and thus can easily rationalize doing things that may be counter to tradition, according to Banton. (Any parent who has raised a typical teenager should be able to identify with this reality.) Banton points out that assimilation is often on an individual level and that the speed of the assimilation or adaptation can be directly related to the level of the reward offered (Blanton). A teenager in an Eastern culture, for example, may buy a pair of denim jeans to be "in" even if it is contrary to his traditional dress. The universal drive for social acceptance is stronger and more rewarding, than the respect and acceptance of his or her elders.

As the above examples illustrate, not only are there a broad range of common or basic wants and needs that ignore national and cultural boundaries as Ted Levitt has noted, but the differences that do exist are rapidly shrinking. Identifying which consumers have which common needs and wants, however, is only solving two of the three "impossible" criteria needed for having a successful global marketing program.

If *Time* Magazine and Dallas have Cross-Cultural Acceptance, Why Can't Ad Messages?

The third "impossible" thing to accomplish with a global campaign is putting the creative strategy into an advertising message that will attract the attention of, and be understood by, the global target audience.

While this may be more difficult than finding universal needs, it's being done everyday. Because message reception is culturally sensitive, marketers must look for what Schramm called "shared fields of experience" (Schramm 1954). The challenge is to find those universal cues and symbols and avoid the culturally bound idioms, metaphors, and words that don't translate clearly.

If full length magazines and a variety of TV series have global understanding and acceptance, why not a magazine ad or TV commercial? Advertising executions are no more than story lines, narratives, the verbal and visual "packaging" of the selling propositions. The critics have seemingly overlooked the fact that *Time* and *Reader's Digest* are successfully sold in nearly 200 countries using local language translation and localizing only a minority of the stories. The extensive international viewing of old TV series, such as Dallas and Gilligan's Island, has been so widespread that many Americans fear the world's perception of the US is being warped.

What makes these comparisons acid tests of universal receptivity of certain mass media "messages" is the fact that most of these magazines and TV shows were originally designed **just** for the U.S. market. The development of modern global advertising has the advantage of knowing - up front - that it has a cross-cultural audience.

Viacom has been selling MTV internationally for some time and soon plans to begin distribution of the children's channel, Nickelodeon. The desire for American programing has been so great that many developed countries, as well as the European Community as a whole, has taken steps or discussed legislation to limit the percent of programming that can be imported. If print and broadcast messages were as culturally bound as critics say, there would be no need for such regulations.

The cultural anthropologist provide more evidence of communication universals. In a study of body language, it was found that the people of literate and illiterate cultures, when shown pictures and video tapes of different expressions, identified the expressions with a high degree of accuracy. Eibl-Eklibesfeldt also found that the concept of gift exchange was universal and that the way people handled themselves in social situations had many universals. For example, it was found that when people want to be noticed or want to initiate a friendly meeting, they act in similar ways, despite their cultural heritage (Eible-Eibesfeldt 1979).

A cross-cultural study of facial expressions found that there is a relationship between these expressions and emotion. "Evidence for the universality of facial expressions supports the notion that they have an evolutionary biological basis and makes it reasonable to infer that they play some role in motivating adaptive actions" (Izard 1979). This is especially relevant to advertising since one of the standard scenes in many food ads is user satisfac-

tion, showing the consumer with a smile of approval after having just tried the product.

Closely linked to body language and expression is humor. Charlie Chaplin, for example, is widely recognized outside the US. More recently humor won top prize at one of the major international advertising competitions. London's DDB Needham received the 1988 Grand Prize for it's Volkswagon Passat commercial. The spot showed several competitive cars being dropped while the Passat was dropped and went through the floor demonstrating, in a humorous way, that the Passat was bigger and heavier than its competitors.

Studies of music (a basic ingredient in many broadcast ads) have found that below the surface of the many varieties of music, there are simple formal types of musical patterns that "recur over and over in repertories around the world and through history." Rahn goes on to suggests that this points to a "deep-seated cognitive or perceptual process" that is universal (Eger 1988). Classical music, for example, is universally appreciated.

The fact that the big rock stars are now quickly recognized and listened to around the world has lead Coke and Pepsi to sign these people to carry their universal messages. A point often overlooked, and of importance to marketers, is that the universal receptivity of popular music is not limited to developed countries. As a recent article in The Economist explained:

"The rock generation has grown up . . .(and) rock music is into moving the third world. . . . 'World music' records are selling more and more; artists from Mali (Salif Keita) or Panama (Ruben Blades) are becoming stars. Amnesty International's Human Rights Now tour last year went to places most 'world tours' ignore, such as India, Zambabwe, Ivory Coast and Argentina; and it was a tour where a Senegalese singer, Voussou N'Dour, could share the billing with Bruce Springsteen" (*The Economist* 1989).

Visuals, like music, also cut across cultures. The pervasiveness of international road signs, is one good example. Facial expressions and body language, as explained above, have been found to "say" the same thing to people in different cultures. The Marlboro cowboy has successfully symbolized, and differentiated, the Phillip Morris cigarette to make it the most popular cigarette in the world.

Other examples of the successful use of strong visuals which have been used in standardized advertising campaigns are:

- The Kraft TV commercials for its single-slice cheese showing how much milk is in each slice. Variations of this visual element are being used in North American, Europe, and Australia.

- The Snuggle laundry softener, which uses a traditional stuffed teddy bear to symbolize softness, has been used successfully throughout the Triad (US, Europe, Japan)

- Johnson & Johnson's new sanitary napkin, Silhouette, which was introduced in 1989 throughout western Europe, uses the same TV commercial (in English), the same brand name and the same package everywhere it's being distributed. The commercial is heavily visual using an absorbancy claim demonstrated with two paper birds, the same image that is on the package. The package carries brief product descriptions in four languages.

- Rolex watches use the same print ads throughout the EC and the U.S. The ads feature endorsements by internationally known sports figures such as Arnold Palmer. Layouts and copy of each ad are consistent, with copy translated into the local language.

To handle the language barriers, commercials can take advantage of "simulcasting." The newer satellites have the ability to send out one video and up to ten different audio tracks for that video. For example, a World Cup match can be broadcast live, with announcers for each major language sending out individual audio signals. The same technology, of course, can be applied to regular programing and commercials. Eger predicts that there will be an increasing number of global news specials which will be sponsored by advertisers with global brands (Eger 1988).

Arguments Against Global Advertising Don't Hold Up

While the eating patterns of Europe are changing, there are still big differences in favorite foods. The critics of global advertising, for example, point out that Italians eat bread three times as much as other Europeans, that the Spanish eat two times as much fresh fruit and vegetables while the Germans are heavy users of paprika. Such differences, however, are not that unusual and definitely don't negate, for example, developing a pan-European campaign for bread. In the U.S. it is not unusual for the category development index (CDI) to range from 65 - 250, as it does for processed meat (this means that the average household in the market with a 250 index consumes nearly four times the processed meat as does the average household in the market with a 65 index). Nevertheless, Oscar Mayer still does national advertising. The point is, EVERY product category has its strong and weak markets even within a country.

Another argument is that the trend is away from globalization and towards more local control of market-

ing budgets. An article in *Advertising Age* cited Pepsi as having recently divided the US into four regions so it could market locally. It also talked about Campbell Soup's 1986 restructuring in which it set up 22 regions so each could have its own marketing plan. The fact that McDonalds has 74 different agencies working with 150 U.S. ad cooperatives was also mentioned as evidence of "going local" (Lipman 1988). What this author overlooked was the fact that all these companies still spend considerable dollars on national advertising. The fact that they are giving more local control to **promotions** and **heavy-up spending** does not mean they are no longer taking advantage of the savings realized from doing as much as they can nationally. A global marketing effort does not, and should not, exclude regional and local heavy-ups and promotional drives, just as the major national marketers have been doing for years in the U.S.

CONCLUSION

Recognizing that there are cultural and national differences does not mean that a single message can't be effective against more than one nationality, especially when it's kept in mind that globally stratified consumers have the same basic needs.

Marketers can take advantage of the economies of scale offered by global marketing. They can do this by using global stratification in segmenting and analyzing the size of their respective targets in each country. They then need to develop a selling proposition that appeals to a common need of this cross-cultural cohort target. These are often basic physiological, sociological, and psychological needs as outlined by Maslow. Finally, they need to have executions of their selling propositions that use internationally recognized narrative elements.

"The question now for each business category is whether today there are greater variations in consumer need within countries than between them." according to David Miln, one of the original architects of Saatchi & Saatchi's global philosophy (Miln 1988).

As for the cultural difference criticism, it should be kept in mind that "differences do not necessarily mean barriers" (Harris and Moran 1987). Also, many of the cultural differences are rapidly eroding. And to some people like Mo Drake, "all this pious talk 'of deep seated differences' in national cultures is completely at variance with the facts" (Drake 1984).

Barry Day, vice-chairman of McCann-Erickson Worldwide, probably summed up the argument best when he said: "A lot of people tell me global advertising is impossible. It's not impossible - it's hard" (Cooper 1986).

REFERENCES

Banton, Michael , "Direction, Speed of Ethnic Change," in *Ethnic Change*, Charles F. Keyes, ed. Seattle: University of Washington Press, 81.

Cooper, Ann (1986), "Global Village," *Advertising Age*, (October 27), 46.

DeMooij, Marieke (1991), *Advertising Worldwide*. London: Prentice-Hall, 144.

Drake, MO (1986), "It's Product Culture That Matters," *Advertising Age's Focus*, (April), 36.

Eger, John (1988), "Ad Dollars Open As Rules Soften," *Advertising Age*, (September 19), 74.

Eible-Eibesfeldt (1979), "Universals of Human Expressive Behavior," *Nonverbal Behavior*, Aaron Wolfgang, ed. New York: Academic Press.

Falck, Robert and Timothy Rice (1982), *Cross-Cultural Perspectives on Music*. Toronto: University of Toronto Press.

Geertz, Clifford (1973), *The Interpretation of Cultures*. New York: Basic Books.

Goble, Frank (1970), *The Third Force*. New York: Grossman, 37.

Harris, Philip R. and Robert T. Moran (1987), *Managing Cultural Differences*, Houston: Gulf Publishing, 1987.

Izard, Carroll E. (1979), "Facial Expression, Emotion, and Motivation," *Nonverbal Behavior*, Aaron Wolfgang, ed. New York: Academic Press.

Keegan, Warren (1984), *Multinational Marketing Management*. 3rd ed., Englewood Cliffs NJ: Prentice-Hall, 98.

Levitt, Theodore (1983), "The Globalization of Markets," *Harvard Business Review*, (May/June), 92-102.

Lipman, Joanne (1988), "Marketers Turn Sour on Global Sales Pitch Harvard Guru Makes," *Wall Street Journal*, (May 12), 1.

Meyer, Edward H. (1985), "Consumers Around the World: Do They Have the Same Wants and Needs?," *Management Review*, (January), 26-29.

Miln, David (1990), "The Global Imperative: Remaining Competitive in the 1990's," Saatchi & Saatchi Company PLC.

Paliwoda, Stanley (1986), *International Marketing*. London: Wm. Heinemann Ltd, 181.

Schramm, Wilbur (1954), *The Process & Effects of Mass Communications*. 1st ed. Urbana: the University of Illinois Press, 6.

Smith, Anthony D. (1990), "Towards a Global Culture?" in *Global Culture*, Mike Featherstone, ed. London: Sage, 176.

Sriram, Ven and Pradeep Gopalakrishna (1991), "Can Advertising be Standardized Among Similiar Countries? A Cluster-Based Analysis," *International Journal of Advertising*, 10 (2), 137-150

The Economist (1989), "Fat Boys Have More Fun," (April 29), 65.

The Economist (1989), "Vox Pop," *The Economist*, (April 29).

Verma, Gajendra and Christopher Bagley (1988), *Cross-Cultural Studies of Personality, Attitudes and Cognition*. New York: St. Martin's Press.

WOMEN IN THE GLOBAL SALESFORCE: A CALL FOR RESEARCH

Laura M. Milner, University of Alaska-Fairbanks
Dale D. Fodness, University of Alaska-Fairbanks
Mark Speece, The Chinese University of Hong Kong

ABSTRACT

Research on women in the global salesforce is virtually nonexistent. In order to provide practical assistance to managers currently contemplating issues pertinent to women in international sales as well as to guide future research, studies in two related areas, women in "domestic" sales and women managers in cross-cultural work situations, are reviewed. Findings are then summarized within the context of four presumed myths about women in the global salesforce: women don't have what it takes; they won't go; they won't be accepted, and it won't work.

INTRODUCTION

Discussions of women in the context of sales management involve a variety of complex issues. For instance, how do women perceive personal selling? How do clients, colleagues, and sales managers perceive women who do personal selling? What factors favor or disfavor women in being selected, trained, retained, and promoted as sales representatives and sales managers? How do the answers to these questions differ for consumer or industrial sales? The added dimensions of cross-cultural and multinational factors make these complicated questions even more complex and, to date, research on women in a global sales context is virtually nonexistent.

The fact there is little research on this important and timely issue is not surprising. A recent review of gender positioning in global advertising, a phenomenon that has a greater "mass" existence than personal selling, revealed little existing research as well (Milner, in press). A literature review for the present paper indicated work on sales representative selection in international corporations that examined factors such as education, social class, ethnicity, and religious background (Gestetner 1974; Hill and Birdseye 1989; Ogbuehi, Abercrombie, Berl, and Rogers 1987; Still 1981); gender, however, thus far has been an excluded factor.

The related research itself is only a recent phenomenon and focuses on the following two general issues: women in "domestic" sales (Comer and Jolson 1985; Dubinsky and O'Connor 1983; Fugate, Decker, and Brewer 1988; Futrell 1984; Gable and Reed 1987; Jolson 1983; Muehling and Weeks 1988; Robertson and Hackett 1977; Russ and McNeilly 1988; Skolnik 1985; Swan, Futrell, and Todd 1978; Swan, Rink, Kiser, and Martin

1984) and women managers in a cross-cultural context (Adler 1987, 1986, 1984a, 1984b, 1984 c, 1979, Izraeli, Banai, and Zeira 1980; Mathison 1987; Taylor, Odjagov, and Morley 1975). Women entering professional sales and global management in numbers large enough to be noticed has only really occured within the last ten to twenty years. Little wonder then that nothing exists on the specific topic of women in global sales. The purpose of the present article will then be to glean insights from research in the relevant areas such as women in international management and women in domestic sales. Suggestions to the practitioner contemplating integration of women into international sales as well as the delineation of topics to guide future research are made by exploring the relevant research with the context of the following four presumed myths of women in the global salesforce: Women don't have what it takes; they won't go; they won't be accepted; and it won't work.

LITERATURE REVIEW

Women in "Domestic" Sales

The "domestic" literature on women in sales has tended to focus on the issues of recruitment and performance appraisal. Contrasting earlier literature on selection and performance appraisal for sales with later studies indicates that gender as an important criteria is waning. For instance, with reference to peer evaluation, Robertson and Hackett (1977) found that:

> Specifically, the males felt that women lacked professional expertise in the approach, set up, and closing of sales....[However], the fact that there is no perceived difference in the competency of saleswomen by salesmen would seem to illustrate that while women might utilize different methods and personalities in the sales environment, they still have been accepted as competent by their male peers in the profession of selling. (p. 70-71).

Regarding management attitudes, they note that "...a 'show me' attitude seems to permeate attitudes toward female sales representatives" (p. 71). Other earlier studies (Dipboye, Arvey, and Terpstra 1977; Hammer 1974; Swan, Futrell, and Todd 1978) also suggested that women did not receive good approval ratings.

More recent research however has indicated that women are interested in sales (Taylor 1980) and that companies are interested in having women in sales (Jolson 1983). Personal selling as a career path for women, particularly in professional sales, is a fairly recent phenomenon (Gable and Reed 1987; Jolson 1983; Kanuk 1978; Swan, Rink, Kiser, and Martin 1984). However, the increased interest of women in business in general and sales in particular is well documented. Taylor (1980) notes that within six years of being admitted to the here-to-fore "male only" sales and marketing fraternity, Pi Sigma Epsilon, women constituted 50 percent of the membership. Regarding performance, Swan, Rink, Kiser, and Martin (1984) found that "The results of our study hint that industrial purchasers may have perceived that performance from saleswomen has matched that of salesmen" (p. 115).

All is not rosy, however. There are large amounts of research pointing to still existing problems for women in sales. Fugate, Decker, and Brewer (1988) summarized recent research and found that the following factors are inhibitors for women in industrial sales:

women lack high self esteem (Epperson 1988); females seek feminine-oriented jobs (Comer and Jolson 1985); male sales managers [are] preferred over female managers (Futrell 1984); conflicting expectations result in career dissatisfaction, turnover (Raelin 1984); lack of managerial presence; unwillingness to exert authority (Epperson 1988; *Sales and Marketing Management* 1982); women carry around their own stereotypes of themselves (*Sales and Marketing Management* 1984); women are subjected to a new subtle sexism that is hard to fight (Schmidt 1987); women do not have [the] presumed credibility of men (Bertrand 1987; Kelley 1985). [See Table 2, p. 34]

Still, the best recommendation as to remedying these types of problems is offered by Russ and McNeilly (1988) who suggest that firms "... provide exposure to competent females in selling and sales management positions" (p. 43). Employment statistics cited by Fugate, Decker, and Brewer (1988) indicate that this is inevitable. Women in professional sales grew from 12 percent in 1970 to 23 percent by the early 1980's (1970 Census; Steinbrink 1986). Further, this trend will remain unabated. Consider that Kellerman (1987), reports "For the First Time, More Women than Men Earn Marketing Degrees."

International Female Managers

Literature on women and work, either in our culture or other cultures is quite extensive. [See for example, *Women and Work: An Annual Review*, Volumes 1, 2, and 3.] The existing literature on women and management may be subdivided into two categories, that of female managers, typically American, going abroad and studies of female managers within their own countries, including our own. The research on American female managers is

extensive and will not be reviewed here; however the reader is referred to some excellent reviews such as Brenner, Tomkiewicz, and Schein (1989). Rather, research on women managers going to other cultures as well as women managers in other cultures will be the focus.

The literature examining issues of women managers in a cross-cultural context is recent and very limited. For instance, Izraeli, Banai, and Zeira (1980) note that

"The subject of women executives in multinational corporation (MNC) subsidiaries has not received attention in the professional literature. Our survey of relevant research to the end of 1978 did not reveal a single study on the topic and hardly even a passing reference to women's presence as senior executives in international business. In his monumental review of research of management in international business, R. D. Robinson reports that women's place is almost never mentioned. The fact that he devotes only a single paragraph to the subject makes his book no exception" (p. 53).

Adler (1979) similarly observed, "A computerized search of the management, social science, psychological, sociological, anthropology, and women's literature revealed fewer than ten articles on women in international management" (p. 427).

Women Managers Overseas.

The most extensive program of research on women in international assignments has been carried out by Nancy Adler (1987, 1986, 1984a, 1984b, 1984 c; 1979). Her research has focused on three major questions, as follows: Do women want to pursue international careers?; Do companies send women on multinational assignments?; What happens when women go on overseas assignments? In order to determine whether women want to be international managers, Adler surveyed 1129 graduating MBAs from schools in Canada, Europe, and the U.S. and found no difference in the interest level of men and women to pursue international assignments. Ascertaining whether firms send women managers on overseas assignments was a second focus. She found that they do. Her survey of 686 Canadian and American firms indicated that of the 13,338 expatriates employed, 3 percent or 402, were women. Financial institutions send significantly more women overseas than any other industry.

Regarding what happens when women go overseas, Adler extensively interviewed 52 women placed in assignments in Asia. Ninety percent of the women were pioneers in that no other women managers had gone before them. Overwhelmingly (97%) the experiences reported indicate they were successful, not only in terms of subjective criteria but also by virtue of promotions for these women and the fact that most firms sent more women over after them. According to Adler (1987),

> Almost half of the women (42%) reported that "being female" served more as an advantage than a disadvantage. Sixteen percent found 'being female' to have both positive and negative effects, while another 22 percent saw it as 'irrelevant' or neutral. Only one woman in five (20%) found it to be primarily negative. (p. 182)

Among Her Conclusions,

> ...the Asians tended to assume that the women would not have been sent unless they were "the best," and therefore expected them to be "very, very good....A woman who is a foreigner (*gaijin*) is not expected to act like the locals. Therefore, the rules governing the behavior of local women which limit their access to management and managerial responsibility, do not apply to foreign women. Whereas women are considered the 'culture bearers' in almost all societies, foreign women in no way assume or are expected to assume that role. (p. 183, 187).

Similar results were found by Taylor, Odjagov, and Morley (1975) even though their survey tapped into different sample demographics. For instance, their sample was made up of representatives from mostly retailing and manufacturing who made trips abroad, as opposed to residing abroad, and included not only managers (95%) but also support staff such as secretaries (5%). They too found that at the time, very few companies had sent women. Their interviews with 32 of 34 women who had gone abroad revealed "...overwhelming satisfaction with their assignments....In addition, the organization's willingness to send a woman on a further assignment was judged to be objective proof of her success. Of 242 women on whom data is available, 137 made subsequent trips in the study period" (p. 454-455).

Parker and Hendon (1989) interviewed North American expatriate females in Taiwan and Singapore holding a variety of positions. They distinguished between firm-posted and voluntary expatriates, or those women who were sent abroad by a firm versus those who independently made the decision to move overseas. Their findings indicate what the other studies have found. Specifically, "Management does overlook women for foreign assignments, and women do face more discrimination among their countrymen than from local business people, most of whom are men" (p. 323).

Much of the research to date indicates a major obstacle to women working overseas is resistance by their own firms (Thal and Cateora 1979). However, research by Taylor and her colleagues (Taylor, Durrett, and Patterson 1981) suggests that firm support of international assignments for women may vary across industry. For instance, their survey of nearly 200 female executives from manufacturing, retailing and banking-consulting indicated that

> ...their company's attitude toward women traveling abroad on business was matter-of-fact (considers international assignment as a routine part of the job) or same as men. However, the retail industry women tend to feel their company's attitude toward their travel abroad is matter-of-fact or the same as towards men more frequently than the other two industries. (p. 65).

Taylor, et al. distinquished between short-term and long-term (more than three months) assignments. They found that "More than half of the women indicated they would accept such an assigment. However, over a third of the women in retailing indicate they would not while only 12 percent and 5 percent of the women in manufacturing and banking respectively indicated absolute refusal" (p. 65-66).

Women Managers in Other Countries

There is very little on women managers in other countries; however a recent emphasis in this limited literature has been on women managers in Asiatic countries, particularly Japan. Much of this interest can be attributed to the importance of Asiatic business to the United States, but also because of the conservative nature of the attitudes of these countries, particularly Japan, with regard to women, there is a fascination with women in the workforce and leadership roles, as though if "women can make it there, they can make it anywhere."

Certainly, while there are not incredible numbers of women in Japanese management, trends cited by Kaminski and Paiz (1984) indicate there will be an increased level of participation in the future. For instance, Japanese women are highly educated. One-third hold college degrees. "The number of women in management positions at larger companies doubled to 486,000 in 1987 from 239,000 a decade earlier" (Lehner and Graven 1989, p. 6). Adler (1987) also points out that because our statistics focus on large companies, we miss important data on entrepreneurial activity. Quoting Steinhoff and Tanaka (1986-1987), she notes that "...Japan has more than 25,000 female company presidents, all of whom manage small to medium-sized firms..." (p. 171). Similar figures are echoed by others. For instance, quoting the Japan Association for Female Executives, Lehner and Graven note that "Five out of six new businesses in Japan are started by women..." (p. 6).

However, a note of caution is in order in grouping Asiatic countries together. Mathison (1987) sums it eloquently,

There is not an Asian attitude toward women any more than there is an Asian way of thinking. To understand the present attitudes toward women requires an understanding of each nation's belief system. Japan may set the economic pace of Eastern Asia, but it does not influence the other Asian countries' culture. (p. 15).

CONCLUSIONS

The call for research is obvious. Data on the specific subject of women in the global salesforce needs to be collected. Thus far the limited research available suggests that women expatriates are succeeding, although problems do exist. Of course the practical reality of work force demographics dictates that women will work overseas even when sending women into other countries will be problematic. Naisbitt and Aberdeen (1990) note that "In business and many professions women have increased from a minority as low as 10 percent in 1970 to a critical mass ranging from 30 to 50 percent in much of the business world, including banking, accounting, and computer science" (p. 217). The trend is that more women will be entering the ranks of international management. As Adler (1984) says, "The current 3 percent should therefore be viewed as a *significant increase* and not as a poor showing" (p. 86). Several writers, including Adler (1987), note that we really cannot afford to depend on half the work force. Even Japan's increased desire for female labor is fueled by labor shortages (Lehner and Graven 1989). Given the implications of these trends, our recommendations for research and management to make the transition of female sales representatives into the global sales force easier are summarized by using four presumed erroneous suppositions about women in the global salesforce. These suppositions are probably more accurately labeled myths, and they are as follows: Women don't have what it takes; they won't go; they won't be accepted; it won't work.

Myth #1: Women Don't Have What It Takes

As alluded to previously in research by Fugate, Decker, and Brewer (1988) as well as others, women may have certain predispositions that some would consider handicapping. Even if we were to accept stereotypical characterizations of women in general as sensitive to the needs of others, understanding, compassionate, etc. (Bem 1974), Adler (1979) citing work by Haemmerli (1978) suggests that these "so-called feminine traits" which are usually perceived as drawbacks for women in American business may be useful attributes for working in the international arena since their empathy and sensitivity should make them more adaptable and capable of operating in others' cultures. Such a sentiment is emphatically echoed by Naisbitt and Aburdene (1990). Pointedly they state, "To be a leader in business today, it is no longer an advantage to have been socialized as a male...The

dominant principle of organization has shifted, from management in order to control an enterprise to leadership in order to bring out the best in people and to respond quickly to change" (p. 217-218). From the perspective of sales management, what could be better?

Myth #2: They Won't Go.

In seeking employees in the home-country, many might assume that women do not want to go or that only single women will. No objectively derived research supports these conclusions. For instance, Parker and Hendon (1989) found that "...the state of matrimony does not impose constraints on travel for these individuals" (p. 323). Further, it wasn't too long ago that assumptions of women not moving for jobs domestically abounded. *Business Week* (1980) notes that "The situation today is that women managers, newcomers to the corporate game, sometimes move more eagerly than men, savoring the delights of upward mobility with an enthusiasm that some male executives have lost" (p. 153). Certainly, not every woman will want to work overseas, but equally true, not every man will either.

Further, other sources of employees can be home-country women already present in the host country. For instance, Parker and Hendon (1989) suggest hiring voluntary expatriates:

The voluntary expatriates in this study show greater overall commitment to remaining in foreign cultures: they demonstrate this commitment by living on the local economy, making friends among locals, and by learning the language. Moreover, the average length of overseas experience is greater for the voluntary expatriates, who average 5.3 years abroad as compared to to 4.3 years for the firm-posted expatriates. Unlike the firm-posted women, voluntary expatriates expect to stay abroad and as a result, they may be more likely than firm-posted expatriates to accept deferred rewards and to demonstrate patience in order to earn the respect of local contacts. This suggests that they could be valuable employees for North American firms, especially as those firms develop locally trained managerial talent. (p. 325).

Myth #3: They Won't Be Accepted

Many might presume that attitudes of other cultures toward women in management are worse than the home country's. Izraeli, Banai, and Zeira (1980) found in their survey of European representatives of host country subsidiaries that "The majority of respondents (60.7%) agreed that a woman could successfully head and manage a MNC subsidiary" (p. 57). Adler (1979) notes that Eastern Bloc countries have a history of women in leadership in the working sector, and that in other countries such as Ghana, women are the traditional businesspeople. Indeed, even when a country's attitudes is more conservative, it may not matter. For instance, there are examples of businesswomen being successful in the Mid-East in general (Carter 1978) and in Saudi Arabia specifically (Cudaback 1979; Morgenthaler 1978). Other culture's biases against women may also prove to be advantageous. For instance, Lansing and Ready (1988) suggest hiring Japanese women for management, especially given the Japanese male taboo against working for foreigners.

Adler's research examining American women executives in Asia also presents some interesting implications. For instance, she concludes that their status as a *gaijin*, or foreigner, overrides their gender. That is, how they treat their own women is not a good predictor of how they will treat foreign women. An interesting question is what are the parameters of the gaijin concept? That is, would a Chinese woman in Japan be treated more as a foreigner, or given her Asiatic commonality, would she be treated more like Japanese businesswomen? How would an Asiatic sales woman be treated in the Latino culture? A Filipino woman in the U.S? The permutations are endless, but nevertheless the global business culture demands that we begin to seek the answers.

Indeed, a fundamental question is "what countries will be more difficult for saleswomen to work in?" Strategically, corporations need this information. Difficult cross-cultural situations would demand that companies send in their best; novice saleswomen could be sent to "easier" countries. In researching this question, Hofstede provides a possible framework to use. Specifically, Hofstede's research (1984a, b) categorizes countries along certain dimensions. One dimension he uses is the masculinity-femininity index. His measure examines differentiation between the genders. Specifically, "Some societies strive for maximum social differentiation between the sexes....Other societies strive for minimal social differentiation between the sexes" (1984b, p. 84). His categorization of 50 countries and regions along this dimension is a useful framework for contrasting countries on specific variables of interest relevant to the work place. Regarding work related consequences of the masculinity-femininity concepts, for instance, it would be expected that countries high on the index such as Japan (ranked #1) or the USA (ranked #14) would have a more difficult time accepting saleswomen than countries low on the index such as the the Netherlands (#47) or Norway

(#48).

Myth #4: It Won't Work

Research by Adler (1987), Parker and Hendon (1989), as well as Taylor, Odjagov, Morley (1975) suggests it will work. As with men, every resource should be made to ensure success. Adequate training, real support, and appropriate assignments with true possibilities of success should be present. If the business contacts begin deferring to a male colleague, it is that male's responsibility to make it clear he defers to his female superior. "Such behavior should not be interpreted as prejudice, but rather as the reaction to an ambiguous, atraditional situation...presume naivete, not malice" (Adler 1987, p. 189).

The assumptions guiding employment for working with male expatriates may not, however, be the same as working with female expatriates. For instance, Parker and Hendon (1989) note "Firms that employ the male spouse generally are unsupportive of female employment; they prefer that the spouse concentrate on the role of social asset, or fear that spouse employment will displease the local government" (p. 324). Obviously companies will need to consider the husband's role differently than they have traditionally for wives. Indeed a greater consideration of flexibility will be in order, as is usual in the global arena. For instance, Carter (1978) notes that short term assignments of eight months were quite frequent.

Further, it is important not to assume a failure is necessarily due to the expatriate being a female. Tung (1986) estimates that the failure rate for overseas assignments is 25 to 40 percent with developing countrys' figures probably being higher. Obviously factors beyond gender of the representative play a role in these types of figures.

Of course, given the right circumstances, much of the concern and lamentations over the issue of women in the global salesforce may be unnecessary. Adler (1987) quotes an American female manager in Hong Kong as saying, "It doesn't make any difference if I am blue, green, purple or a frog. If I have the best product at the best price, the Chinese will buy!" (p. 169). Under these conditions, it probably doesn't matter that she's a woman either.

REFERENCES

Adler, Nancy J. (1987), "Pacific Basin Managers: A *Gaijin*, Not a Woman," *Human Resource Management*, 26, 2 (Summer), 169-191.

_____(1986), "Do MBAs Want International Careers?" *International Journal of Intercultural Relations*, 10, 277-300.

_____(1984a), "Women in International Management: Where are They?" *California Management Review*, (Summer), 78-89.

_____(1984b), "Women Do Not Want International Careers: And Other Myths about International Management," *Organizational Dynamics*, 13 (2),

66-79.

_____(1984c), "Expecting International Success: Female Managers Overseas," *Columbia Journal of World Business,* (Fall), 79-85.

_____(1979), "Women as Androgynous Managers: A Conceptualization of the Potential for American Women in International Management," *International Journal of Intercultural Relations,* 3 (4), 407-435.

Bem, Sandra L. (1974), "The Measurement of Psychological Androgyny," *Journal of Consulting and Clinical Psychology,* 42, 155-162.

Bertrand, Kate (1987) "Women Break the Sales Glass Ceiling," *Business Marketing,* (November), 38.

Brenner, O. C., J. Tomkiewicz, and V. E. Schein, (1989), "The Relationship Between Sex Role Stereotypes and Requisite Management Characteristics Revisited," *Academy of Management Journal,* 32, 662-669.

Business Week, "Corporate Woman: Now Eager to Accept Transfers," (May 26), 153, 156.

Carter, Nancy (1978), "Womanpower Development: A New Personnel Goal in International Firms," *Business International,* (June 23), 196-197.

Comer, Lucette B. and Marvin A. Jolson (1985), "Sex Labeling of Selling Jobs and Their Applicants," *Journal of Personal Selling and Sales Management,* (May), 15-22.

Cudaback, David (1979), "Can a Woman Succeed in International Banking?" *The Institutional Investor,* (March), 52-61.

Dipboye, Robert L., Richard D. Arvey, and David E. Terpstra (1977), "Sex and Physical Attractiveness of Raters and Applicants as Determinants of Resume Evaluations," *Journal of Applied Psychology,* 62, (3), 288-292.

Dubinsky, Alan and P. J. O'Connor (1983), "A Multidimensional Analysis of Preferences for Sales Positions," *The Journal of Personal Selling and Sales Management,* 3 (November), 31-41.

Epperson, Sharon E. (1988), "Studies Link Subtle Sex Bias in Schools with Women's Behavior in the Workplace," *Wall Street Journal,* (September 16), 19.

Fugate, Douglas L., Philip J. Decker, and Joyce J. Brewer (1988), "Women in Professional Selling: A Human Resource Management Perspective," *Journal of Personal Selling and Sales Management,* VIII, (November 1988), 33-41.

Futrell, Charles M. (1984), "Salespeople's Perceptions of Sex Differences in Sales Managers," *Journal of Personal Selling and Sales Management,* (May), 19-23.

Gable, Myron and B. J Reed (1987), "The Current Status of Women in Professional Selling," *The Journal of Personal Selling and Sales Management,* 7 (May), 33-39.

Gestetner, David (1974), "Strategy on Managing International Sales," *Harvard Business Review,* 52, 5 (September), 103-107.

Haemmerli, A. (1978) "Women in International Business," Paper prepared for Women in International Business Conference, New York, (July 11).

Hammer, W. Clay (1974), "Race and Sex as Determinants of Ratings by Potential Employers in a Simulated Work-Sampling Task," *Journal of Applied Psychology,* 59, (6), 705-711.

Hill, John S. and Meg Birdseye (1989), "Salesperson Selection in Multinational Corporations: An Empirical Study," *Journal of Personal Selling and Sales Management,* IX (Summer), 39-47.

Hofstede, Geert (1984a), *Culture's Consequences: International Differences in Work-Related Values.* Beverly Hills: Sage Publications.

_____(1984b), "Cultural Dimensions in Management and Planning," *Asia Pacific Journal of Management,* (January), 81-99.

Izraeli, Dafna N., Moshe Banai, and Yoran Zeira (1980), Women Executives in MNC Subsidiaries, *California Management Review,* XXIII, 1 (Fall), 53-63.

Jolson, Marvin A. (1983), "Employment Barriers in Selling: Are Blacks and Females Welcome?" American Marketing Association Educators' *Proceedings,* 49, 267-270.

Kaminski, Marguerite and Judith Paiz (1984), "Japanese Women in Management: Where are They?," *Human Resource Management,* 23, 3 (Fall), 277-292.

Kanuk, Leslie (1978), "Women in Industrial Selling," *Journal of Marketing,* 42 (January), 87-91.

Kellerman, Bert J. (1987), "For the First Time, More Women than Men Earn Marketing Degrees," *Marketing News,* 21 (14) (July 3), 1.

Kelley, B. (1985), "Strictly for Salesmen and Women," *Industrial Distribution,* 74 (May), 91.

Lansing, Paul and Kathryn Ready (1988), "Hiring Women Managers in Japan: An Alternative for Foreign Employers," *Managing Human Resources,* (Spring), 112-127.

Lehner, Urban C. and Kathryn Graven, (1989), "Japan Women Rise in the Workplace, Challenging Mores," *Asian Wall Street Journal,* (September 11), 1-6.

Mathison, David L. (1987), "A Comparative Study of Attitudes Toward Women Managers in Five Asian Nations: A Preliminary Report," Presentation made at Annual Meeting of the Academy of Management.

Milner, Laura M. (in press), "Multinational Gender Positioning: A Call for Research," in B. Englis and F. Baker, eds. *Global and Multinational Advertising,* New York: New York: Lawrence-Erlbaum Associates.

Morgenthaler, E. (1978), "Women of the World: More U.S. Firms Put Females in Key Posts in Foreign Countries," *Wall Street Journal,* (March 16).

Muehling, Darrel D. and William A Weeks (1988), "Women's Perceptions of Personal Selling: Some

Positive Results," *Journal of Personal Selling and Sales Management,* VIII, (May), 11-20.

Naisbitt, John and Patricia Aburdene (1990), *Megatrends 2000: Ten New Directions for the 1990's.* New York: William Morrow and Company, Inc.

Ogbuehi, Alphonso, C. L. Abercrombie, Robert L. Berl, and Hudson P. Rogers (1987), "The Selection and Orientation of Salespeople for International Positions: A Contingency Framework," Southern Marketing Association *Proceedings ,* 33-36.

Parker, Barbara and Donald W. Hendon (1989), "Exported Work Discrimination: North American Women Expatriates in Taiwan and Singapore," *Advances in Marketing,* Proceedings of the Southwestern Marketing Association, 322-326.

Raelin, Joseph A. (1984), "An Examination of Deviant/Adaptive Behaviors in the Organizational Careers of Professionals," *Academy of Management Review,* 9 (3), 412-427.

Robertson, Dan H. and Donald W. Hackett (1977), "Saleswomen: Perceptions, Problems, and Prospects," *Journal of Marketing,* (July), 66-71.

Russ, Frederick A. and Kevin M. McNeilly (1988), "Has Sex Stereotyping Disappeared? A Study of Perceptions of Women and Men in Sales," *Journal of Personal Selling and Sales Management,* VIII, (November), 43-54.

Sales and Marketing Management (1982), "Advice and Discontent," (August 16), 45.

_____(1984), "Saleswomen Speak Out ,"[Panel Discussions], 132 (June 4), 76.

Schmidt, Peggy (1987), "Warning, Men at Work May be Hazardous to Your Career," *Mademoiselle,* (December), 179.

Skolnik, Rayna (1985), "A Woman's Place is on the Sales Force," *Sales and Marketing Management,* (April 1), 34-37.

Steinbrink, John (1986) "Sales Force Compensation—Dartnell's 23rd Biennial Survey," The Dartnell Corporation, 2.

Steinhoff, P.G. and K. Tanaka (1986) "Women Executives in Japan," *International Studies of Management and Organization,* (Fall-Winter 1986-1987), 108-132.

Still, Richard R. (1981), "Cross-Cultural Aspects of Sales Force Management," *Journal of Personal Selling and Sales Force Management,* 1, 2 (Spring/Summer), 6-9.

Swan, John E., Charles M. Futrell, and John T. Todd (1978), "Same Job—Different Views: Men and Women in Industrial Sales," *Journal of Marketing,* 42 (January), 92-98.

Swan, John E., David R. Rink, G. E. Kiser, and Warren S. Martin (1984), "Industrial Buyer Image of the Saleswoman," *Journal of Marketing,* 48 (Winter), 110-116.

Taylor, Thayer C. (1980), "The New Look at Pi Sigma Epsilon," *Sales and Marketing Management,* (May 19), 38-39.

Taylor, Marilyn L., Janice E. Durrett, and Carolyn Patterson (1981), "Cross-Industrial Comparison of Demographics, Supportiveness, and Overseas Assignments for Women," *Proceedings* for the Annual Meeting of the Academy of Management, 41, 64-68.

Taylor, Marilyn L., Marianne Odjagov, and Eileen Morley (1975), "Experience of American Professional Women in Overseas Business Assignments," *Proceedings* of The Academy of Management, 454-456.

Thal, Nancy L. and Philip R. Cateora (1979), "Opportunities for Women in International Business," *Business Horizons,* (December), 21-27.

Tung, Rosalie L. (1986), "Corporate Executives and Their Families in China: The Need for Cross-Cultural Understanding in Business," *Columbia Journal of World Business,* 22, 57-71.

WANT TO INCREASE STUDENT PARTICIPATION IN MARKETING CASE COURSES? TRY THE MICA METHOD

Gordon M. McAleer, Western New England College
Jesse R. Hale, Western New England College

ABSTRACT

The Harvard Case Method (HCM) has been an extremely successful teaching tool. However, even experienced teachers often have problems with the lack of active, intelligent, in-depth student participation. Many case classes have less than ideal, highly motivated students. Students who arrive in class with a thorough, analytical study of the assigned case are the exceptions.

The McAleer Interactive Case Analysis method (MICA) was initially conceived and implemented over 20 years ago and has been recently revised by the authors. *MICA techniques are readily transferable to other professors and do not require extraordinary skills beyond those required of any competent teacher.*

MICA may be used as a complement to the HCM or may replace it entirely. The method uses cases from standard sources such as textbooks and Harvard's Intercollegiate Case Clearing House. MICA can be applied to any course where the HCM is employed.

The method has three main components which are different than standard HCM procedures; (1) Students are evaluated on what they say at the time they say it. Scoring is based on the content and frequency of student comments and is subject to restrictions described in the paper. Scores are displayed to all immediately after the discussion period. (2) Class members score points by debating the advisability of adopting written "action steps" proposed by individual students. (3) Student teams are responsible for the <u>administration</u> (not the analysis) of the case.

The Administrative Team starts the case discussion by selecting one action step, and the process of discussion begins. The first author (multiple authors are normal) of the selected action step is called on to provide his/her rationale for the proposed course of action. Other students wishing to add to the rationale or argue against it and are called upon by the chairperson.

The professor selects a seat in the back row of the classroom where all students can be observed. The professor scores each student based on what he/she says at the time it is said, and records points on a seating chart. When scoring, the professor considers whether or not the comment(s) are (1) germane to the action step being discussed, (2) realistic, given the case facts and (3) not repetitive.

The class votes on whether to accept or reject the action step. If accepted, the action step becomes a fact of the case. Upon conclusion of the vote on the action step, the chairperson opens the floor for nominations of other action steps to be discussed.

The professor concludes the case by placing the score sheet in the front of the room. Some readers may be concerned that this procedure leads to undue debates over scores. The authors' experiences have been that arguments rarely occur and that scores once posted are agreed upon. We attribute this result to "coaching" in the early cases and to student self recognition (aided by peer comments during and after the cases) of the strength of the comments made.

The MICA method requires and achieves in-depth preparation. Since case facts are required to bolster arguments and gain points, students who try to skim the case very rarely earn more than token points.

The professor's presence is less visible since he/she is seated at the back of the room and ostensibly merely grades the discussion. Early indications are that the scoring, though subjective, is not a function of the individual instructor nor of the course content. Scoring, using MICA criteria, appears to be equitable and objective.

Professor Kenneth L. Bernhardt recently wrote (1991) "The case method offers many pedagogical advantages, but requires special skills for the instructor to use it effectively." The MICA method dramatically reduces the "special skills" required in HCM and enables the competent teacher to use his/her general teaching skills and techniques to effectively conduct cases.

Even the experienced instructor must make some adjustments; (1) be willing to listen to and objectively evaluate student comments, (2) have the courage to discriminate between students in terms of quality of performance, (3) publicly post scores after class, (4) be willing to perform an apparently passive role as opposed to being the center of discussion, and (5) have reasonable competence in the field of study concerned (i.e. marketing).

The advantage of the MICA Method which most observers first notice is a significant, often dramatic, increase in class participation. Another advantage is that it causes students to consider, evaluate, and adjust the marketing knowledge they have acquired to the compromises that are inevitably required when applying theory to specific situations.

For further information please contact:
Jesse R. Hale
Western New England College
School of Business
Springfield, MA 01119

BRING TODAY'S BUSINESS ENVIRONMENT INTO THE CLASSROOM THROUGH THE USE OF ELECTRONIC CASE STUDIES

William D. Harris, Quinnipiac College
John E. Stinson, Ohio University

ABSTRACT

This paper discusses the use of electronic cases and describes a sample electronic case, "Apple & IBM Joint Ventures 1991." After reviewing the appropriate goals for business education, the usefulness of living cases is discussed. Then the components of an electronic case are presented and the advantages and disadvantages of electronic cases, as opposed to paper cases, are reviewed.

INTRODUCTION

In recent years, the popular business press has published several reports critical of business education. Business schools have been chastised for being too theoretical and out of touch with business realities, for producing narrow-minded technicians who lack interpersonal and communication skills, and for concentrating on esoteric research which has little if anything to do with the business world.

While some of the reports are sensationalized and demonstrate a lack of understanding of both business schools and the business world, there is merit to the concerns expressed. Most business schools, including ours, have heard from members of their executive advisory boards, that graduates are not well prepared for the business world. They note that graduates do not have a realistic understanding of the business world, they criticize graduates for ineffective communication skills, they note the lack of leadership skills, and they comment on the need to train new graduates, teaching them concepts they supposedly learned in school.

Similar concerns were expressed in the Business-Higher Education Forum in its May 1985 report to President Reagan, *America's Business Schools: Priorities for Change.* After reviewing the concerns, the forum made several recommendations regarding curriculum and teaching methods. The following are of particular note:

"Objectives should be focused not only on the acquisition of a body of basic knowledge, but more importantly on the development of analytical and personal skills so that knowledge can be applied to detecting and solving managerial challenges."(pg.13)

These concerns were reiterated in the 1988 report of the futures project sponsored by the American Assembly of Collegiate Schools of Business. The report, *Management Education and Development: Drift or Thrust into the 21st Century?,* (Porter and McKibbin 1988) concludes that business schools must broaden their goals if they are to effectively prepare students for professional challenges.

What are the appropriate goals? If we are to prepare students to function effectively in the high-performing organizations of the future, business schools need to attempt to move toward a curriculum and a teaching-learning methodology which will: (Day and Stinson 1991)

*   help students develop a thorough understanding of the basic business disciplines and the ability to apply their knowledge to business situations.

*   help students develop the ability to analyze a business situation, (determining relevance of facts and information, further information or facts needed, and possible courses of action), organize their ideas regarding the situation, and communicate their ideas in a succinct and effective form.

*   help students develop the behavioral skills (e.g., oral and written communication, persuasion, leadership, and interpersonal relations) necessary to function effectively in the business world.

*   help students develop the ability to accept responsibility for directing their own activities, exercise initiative, function independently, take reasonable risks, and tolerate ambiguity.

*   help students develop a realistic understanding of the business world - its nature, functioning, and place in our society.

*   help students develop strategic thinking ability: the ability to understand the whole, to place it in perspective in the environment in which it is functioning, to understand and anticipate changes (external and internal) which may create problems or opportunities, and to foresee the consequences of actions.

Business schools are starting now to make many important adjustments in their curriculum. In particular, adjustments that will reflect these broader goals. They are starting to de-emphasize the narrow functional specialties and emphasize an integrated understanding of the enterprise as a whole. They are placing increased emphasis on world cultures, on morality, on social values, and on technology.

But, changing the curriculum alone is not sufficient; learning methodologies used must also be altered. As recent research indicates, it is impossible to effectively separate what is learned from how it is learned and used (Brown et al. 1989). Appropriate learning methodologies should encourage the development of the types of skills and personal characteristics needed in the business world as well as help students learn and be able to apply the required knowledge.

BUSINESS EDUCATION

Business education typically uses traditional didactic teaching methodology. At the undergraduate level, knowledge is divided into somewhat arbitrary disciplines and taught to students through lecture, sometimes with questions and answers, sometimes with discussion, and sometimes with simple problems to simulate application of knowledge. Students are expected to memorize concepts and techniques and regurgitate them on examinations, typically multiple-choice or true/false, sometimes with essay questions or problems. It is then assumed that students who score well on such exams have learned something relevant to the practice of marketing that they can apply in the world of work. People in high-performing organizations must not just know, they must be able to do. They must be able to apply knowledge to manage marketing functions in organizational situations. They must find problems, define problems, seize opportunities, obtain relevant information, and take action. They must confront and manage what Barrows calls ill-structured problems. (Barrows 1985) The education process described above does little to help students learn how to apply knowledge, and even less to develop the critical reasoning process.

In an attempt to move away from regurgitative learning, many teachers have turned to the use of case studies in their courses. However, frequently case studies at the undergraduate level are used simply for illustration purposes rather than the development of critical thinking. They are short incidents included at the end of a chapter in a textbook and require or allow little strategic analysis. They are an attempt to teach students how to apply knowledge by example, rather than by practice.

Even more complex cases, such as the typical Harvard case, limit the amount of reasoning development. While useful in developing problem solving skills, they do little to develop skills in problem finding. The problem is pre-framed and information is limited by the case writer. Thus, students are confronting a semi-structured problem rather than the ill-structured problem typical of business practice. In addition, students are generally discouraged from seeking information beyond that in the case. Thus, students do not develop the skill of unrestricted inquiry they will need to function effectively in their business careers.

More recently there has been increased use of a broader form of problem based or situated learning (Collins, Brown, and Newman 1990), a form that has been characterized as a "new apprenticeship" (Barrows 1985). This form of learning makes extensive use of "living cases."

In living cases, students are confronted with an ill-structured problem-situation, without the benefit of prior preparation, and challenged to define the problem and decide upon what actions to be taken. Some are real-life situations presented by cooperating companies, while still others are current situations reported in the business press. The critical element is that the problems are ill-structured and the information needed to manage the problem is not available at the outset and will have to be obtained through inquiry. Ackoff (1979) calls such problems "managerial messes." Further, it is critical that the students confront the problem without prior preparation. It is not the intent to have the student apply a predetermined theoretical model to an idealistically designed situation to obtain a "right" answer. (See Stinson 1990, for a more detailed description of the use of living cases.)

Living cases, however, are very time consuming. Students must do extensive research on the company and the industry. While it is important that they learn how to search public and private data bases to obtain and determine the relevancy of information, repeated searching of the same types of databases rapidly becomes busy work.

Electronic cases, sometimes referred to as computerized "microworlds," represent an alternative way to present ill-structured problems to students (*The Economist* 1991). Essentially, data relevant (and semi-relevant) to a particular problem situation is duplicated and made available to the students electronically. In essence, the computer becomes the "library." Thus the inquiry process can be done much more efficiently.

ELECTRONIC CASE DESIGN

The basic purpose of any case presentation is to provide a vehicle for the development a student's to apply knowledge to solve problems within a relevant contextual setting. This is equally true of an electronic case; however, the processes can be significantly enhanced by presentation methods. The electronic case assignment begins in much the same manner as a tradition case assignment with the presentation of a question or issue for the students to investigate. However, from this point on the two approaches begin to differ dramatical. The primary presentation method used in a written marketing strategy case is the linear narrative, where the case writer presents the business situation, industry historical background, major corporate players, and various exhibits.

In electronic cases the computer terminal serves as the student's gateway to the HyperMedia Learning System which contains the electronic case they have been assigned and other useful analytic tools. The students' first encounter with an electronic case is a menu or electronic table of contents. This menu can be thought of as a filing cabinet in which information has been stored that can be used to solve the assigned problem. Some of the information is in linear narrative format but much of the information is not. It is the students task to explore the filing cabinet, processing and extracting information as needed to find and solve problems. The information they require is available to them instantaneously in electronic form accompanied by computer-assisted learning modules containing relevant concepts and techniques. In addition, the case information and the learning modules are all linked together, so that the students can move back and forth between case exhibits and learning tools as they work through the assigned problem.

Invisible to the students are the programs that drive the various case modules. The authors' have found Claris' Hypercard running under System 7.0 on a Macintosh LC to be a very flexible design tool for creating electronic cases. Hypercard provides the driving engine for our electronic cases. It functions as an integrative mechanism for the separate sections of the case and the learning tools. In addition, to Hypercard the learning system contains copies of Excel 3.0 for spreadsheet analysis, WordPerfect 2.0 for electronic note taking, and Macromind Director's MoviePlayer for showing video clips. The notebook is accessed through a drop-down menu while the spreadsheet program is activated by clicking the mouse pointer on a button labeled financial analysis within the appropriate file drawer files. Also, video clips can be viewed by pointing and clicking the mouse pointer on Movie buttons found inside the various file drawer files. After viewing a movie, performing a calculation, or using the notebook the student is returned to point in the case were they were before they activated one of these special features. Built into each of the file drawers are navigation buttons which allow the student to probe progressively deeper into the current section or jump to other sections of the case materials as needed. Although the authors have not used them, it is our understanding that programs such as Asymertrix's ToolBook can perform similar tasks to Hypercard on IBM or IBM compatible computers using windows.

Apple and IBM: An Electronic Case

Recently the authors' developed an electronic case on the joint venture agreements between Apple Computer, Inc. and IBM. For this case a computer interface using Claris's Hypercard was built to resemble a filing cabinet containing eight drawers (see figure 1). Behind each drawer of the filing cabinet or main menu, the student will find varying amounts of information. For example, the "Background Information" drawer contains introductory information about the case highlighting what can be found in other sections of the case. The "Apple Corporation" and "IBM Corporation" drawers each contain several files of information including the president's letters from the past three years, five years of financial reports, sample advertisements, and a collection of corporate documents about their future plans. These corporate documents contain both text and video materials. The "Industry Forecasts" drawer contains descriptive information projections about the computer industry extracted from Industry Outlook, Standard and Poors, and other general corporate reporting services. Behind the "Environmental Scanning" drawer the student will find a collection of files containing articles, article summaries, and news clippings representing recent independent media information about the two companies and the computer industry. Once again, this information is presented as text or a video.

In addition to the case specific information described above the student will find three file drawers containing general case analysis resources. The first learning resource "Standard Analytic Questions" provides a group of folders which containing checklists of common questions one should ask/resolve in performing a strategic analysis. The "Information Sources" drawer provides a series of files on where to go to collect additional information not available electronically. (see Figure 2) Finally, the "Competitive Strategy" file presents a comprehensive overview of basic marketing strategy concepts and a glossary of terms used in the case.

The hypermedia contextual environment of an electronic case serves as an effective means of bridging the gap between a static written case and that of the dramatic living case. As can be seen from the above description, the information found in an electronic case is much closer to the natural state in which information is discovered when working on a living case. Because the case information has not been greatly refined by the case writer, the student is placed in the situation of having to use his/her learned knowledge base to follow leads and test hypotheses. Through the use of electronic magic in the form of digitized images and video the case comes alive with action and sound without the student having to leave the learning laboratory. These video and sound bites can contain information such as interviews with key players, news stories, site tours, or commercial messages. Through the use of electronic connections made to various application software embedded within the case materials the student can take notes in either text or video formats, perform spreadsheet calculations, conduct statistical analysis, or even connect to on-line databases such as Compuserve or the college's CD-ROM library reference tools.

FIGURE 1
Electronic Case Filing Cabinet

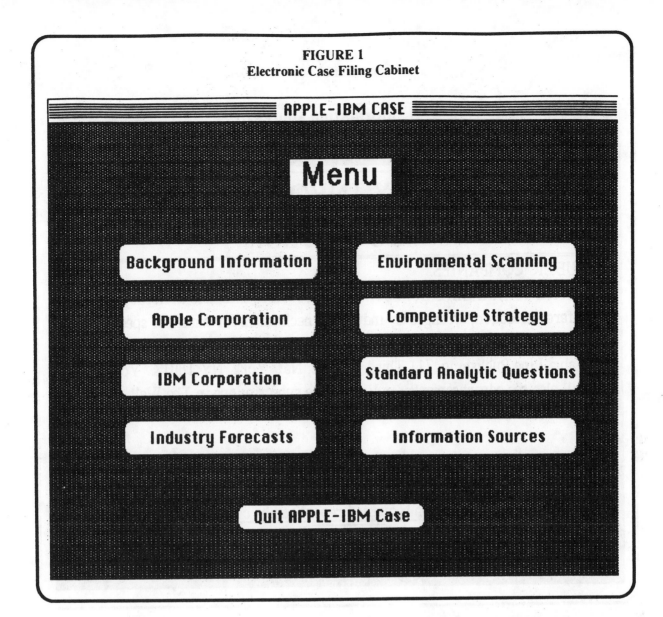

USING ELECTRONIC CASES IN THE CLASSROOM

We have found the taskforce setting to be most effective when using electronic cases. We assign four to five students to a taskforce for the purpose of addressing a particular ill-structured problem. The assignment given to students with regard to Apple Computer and IBM's joint venture case was to assess how these joint venture agreements are likely to effect the marketing strategy for Apple Computer and/or IBM over the next five years and what marketing actions should Apple Computer,Inc or IBM take as a direct result of these joint venture agreements. One set of teams viewed the case from Apple Computer's viewpoint while another set of teams tackled the problem from IBM's perspective.

After being confronted with the problem, the students immediately realize that they must make a decision in order to proceed with their inquiry. Specifically, they must answer the question, "Which drawer should we open first?" (see Figure 1) or more importantly "What information do we need to be able to solve the assigned problem?" The authors believe this is an important first step in learning how to approach ill-structure problems. Unlike the conventional written case were the student must generally wait until the end of the case to make any decisions, with the electronic case students are immediately placed into the role of problem finders.

To obtain help with the inquiry process, the taskforce might decided to start by accessing the file on Standard Analytic Questions (see Figure 3). After discussing what they found they might open the file on background information or begin framing an outline of the information they will need from the learning system to solve the problem.

As they work on their task over the next few days, they will continually access the case through the learning system. By opening the Apple Corporation or the IBM corporation drawers they can perform strategic analysis

FIGURE 2
Company Information Sources Folder

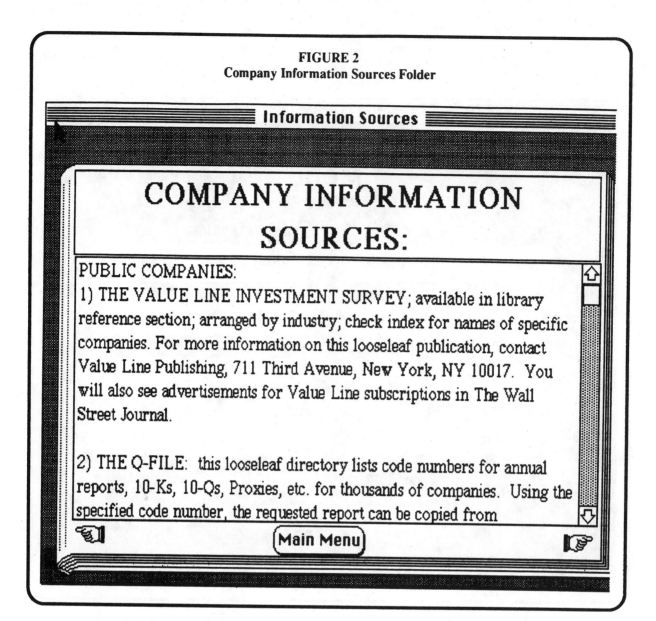

and financial analysis of the companies. They can view statements on each company's strategy given by the CEO. By accessing the environmental scanning drawer the students can review electronic copies of industry magazine articles or news stories to identify current trends in the electronic computer industry. Using the same information, they might conduct an analysis of the driving forces that represent future threats and opportunities to IBM or Apple Computer. When they need help to understand a concept or using a particular analytic technique, they can access the appropriate learning module found in the system. The taskforce will be forced to make decisions to investigate or not to investigate and to use or not use various bits of information as they investigate their case problem. Some of the information they find will to be extremely useful while other information material may be of very limited help. At times the information pieces will be redundant or they may even directly conflict with one another. Through making decisions and evaluating where their decisions take them, the students will find themselves progressively

refining their cognitive analytic abilities to resolve complex ill-structured problems. Each student will experience the frustration of pursuing nonproductive information and the excitement of discovering critical insights about issues central to the problem solution. Through both their failures and their successes, they will will learn important lessons about time management and critical thinking in today's information rich environment which will contribute to the their development as marketing managers with strong analytic abilities.

ELECTRONIC CASES AS EXTENSIONS OF EXISTING CASES

Another valuable use of electronic cases is in the development of extensions to existing cases in the form of electronic case updates. Once a business case about a major corporation is published it is out of date. Although the learning issues in the case may be timeless, the case environment will undoubtedly have changed from the time the case was written to time when the case is taught.

FIGURE 3
Standard Analytic Questions Folder

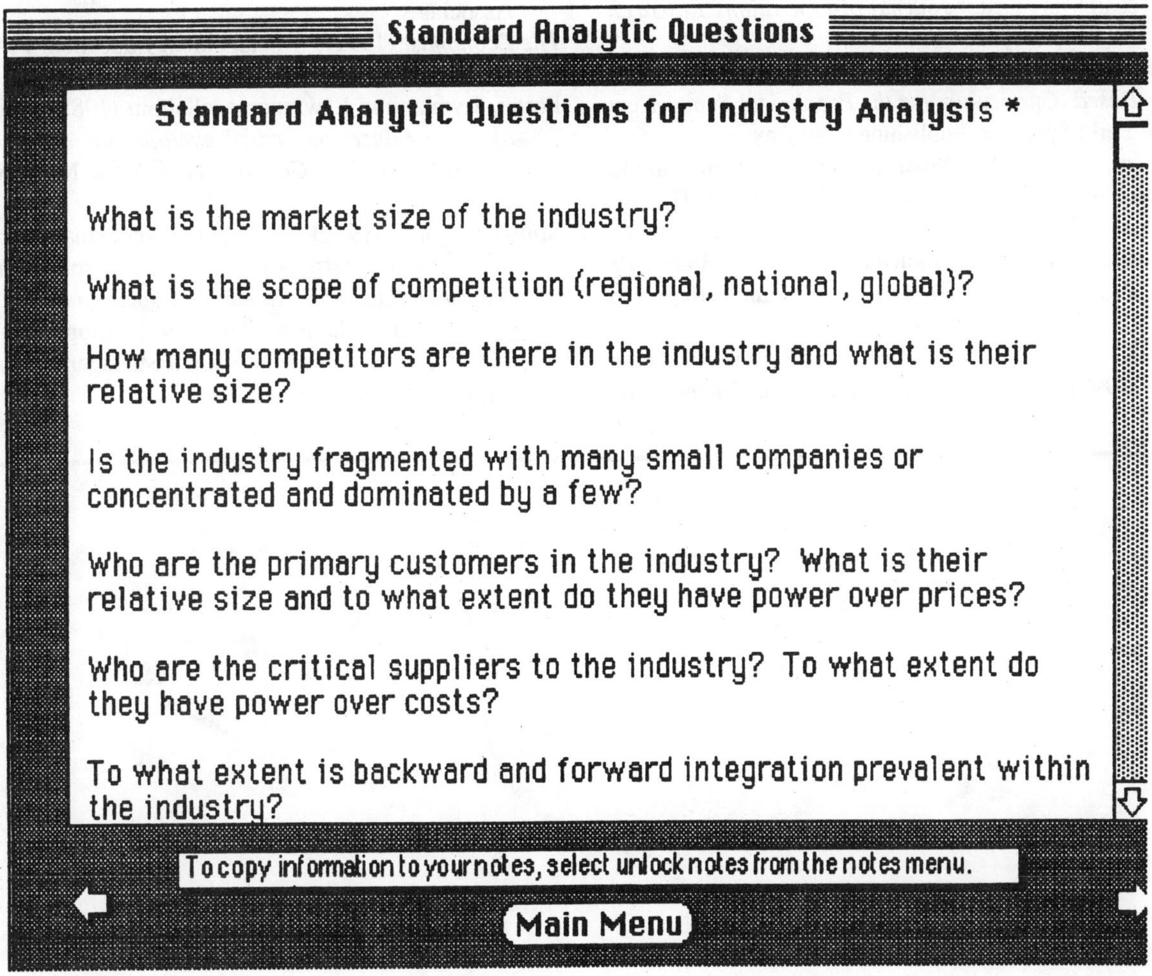

Standard Analytic Questions

Standard Analytic Questions for Industry Analysis *

What is the market size of the industry?

What is the scope of competition (regional, national, global)?

How many competitors are there in the industry and what is their relative size?

Is the industry fragmented with many small companies or concentrated and dominated by a few?

Who are the primary customers in the industry? What is their relative size and to what extent do they have power over prices?

Who are the critical suppliers to the industry? To what extent do they have power over costs?

To what extent is backward and forward integration prevalent within the industry?

To copy information to your notes, select unlock notes from the notes menu.

Main Menu

As a teacher of marketing strategy you can ignore the changes, wait for a case revision to appear, or attempt to update the case materials yourself. If you elect to do the later, the use of electronic cases can be very helpful. The authors have found that they can introduce the students to the historical case setting by assigning them to solve the written case using traditional case teaching methods. This initial case analysis is general conducted on an individual basis. After the class discussion of the written case, the instructor can then assign students to taskforces for the purpose of developing a strategic plan about what actions the company should take in the future with regard to a particular situation or problem based on the actually actions the company took and what has happened in the industry since the original case was written.

Included in this case update should be a brief background statement, current corporate data, recent industry forecasts, and relevant industrial periodical articles and news reports accompanied by the standard learning modules.

One of the major advantages of using electronic cases as extension to existing cases is that it allows the instructor cover the learning objectives of the original case while extended the students analytic abilities to addressing ill-structure problem situations that are truly future oriented. Electronic cases used in this manner can turn a learning environment locked in time into a dynamic future oriented instructional setting.

CONCLUSIONS

Our students upon graduation will most likely not be asked to solve yesterdays problems in a prior historical context. They will be asked by their company's to solve current marketing problems in an uncertain environment, the future. To be effective marketing managers they it is vitally important that our students develop the ability to create innovative future oriented solutions todays ill-structured business problems. The use of electronic case helps foster a creative learning environment that nurtures these talents.

REFERENCES

Ackoff, Russell (1979), "The Future of Operations Research is Past," *Journal of Operations Research Society,* 93-104.

Barrows, Howard S (1985), *How to Design a Problem-Based Curriculum for the Preclinical Years.* New York: Springer Publishing Company.

Brown, John Seely, Allan Collins, and Paul Duguid (1989), "Situated Cognition and the Culture of Learning," *Educational Researcher*, (January/February).

Business-Higher Education Forum (1985), *America's Business Schools: Priorities for Change.* Report to the President.

Collins, Allan, John Seely Brown, and Susan E. Newman (1990), "Cognitive Apprenticeship: Teaching the Craft of Reading, Writing, and Mathematics," in L. B. Resnick, ed. *Cognition and Instruction: Issues and Agendas,* Hillsdale NJ: Lawrence Erlbaum Associates.

The Economist (1991), "Management Education: Passport to Prosperity (1991)," (March 2), 4-26.

Porter, Lyman and Lawrence McKibbin (1988), *Management Education and Development: Drift or Thrust into the 21st Century.* New York: McGraw-Hill.

Stinson, John E. (1990), "Integrated Contextual Learning: Situated Learning in the Business Profession," *American Education Research Association.*

_____and William A. Day (1991), "Empowering Students to Become Empowered Managers,"*Eastern Academy of Management.*

LARGE-SCALE SIMULATION IN MARKETING EDUCATION

Frank Alpert, University of Missouri-St. Louis

ABSTRACT

For many years business people have been telling educators that business needs students with communication skills, students who can think, students who can tolerate ambiguity. Of late, business appears to have become increasingly disenchanted with business education--largely because business schools do not produce enough graduates with these qualities. (Chonko and Caballero 1991, p. 14.)

A large-scale marketing simulation can help remedy the problems cited above. Large-scale simulation is not a panacea, but adding it to the curriculum can provide substantial incremental value. This article provides an introduction to large-scale simulation for the undergraduate capstone marketing management and marketing strategy courses.

What is "large-scale simulation"? One dimension upon which simulations can be classified is their length. There are three levels of simulation: small scale, medium scale, and large scale. Small-scale simulations typically involve one or two students per team and take up less than half a class period per turn (if any). Examples are *Pharmasim* (James, Kinnear, and Deighan 1991) and *Product Manager* (Ayal and Zif 1989). Medium-scale simulations typically involve two to five member student teams and can take up full class periods for up to half of the course. For example, *Markstrat* (Larreche and Gatignon 1989) takes up about one-third of the course when course time is devoted exclusively to it. Large-scale simulations involve student teams of three to six players and can take up virtually the entire course (at minimum, half the course). Large-scale simulation is arguably the "next generation" of simulation software. *The Market Place* (Cadotte 1990) is the first large-scale simulation in marketing. This article is based on the author's experience with all four examples mentioned above.

Large-scale simulation is a strategic and tactical operationalization of all 4Ps of marketing. It has components addressing (1) promotion message design and promotion placement in media, (2) product feature design, (3) a multi-level channel (place) of distribution, and, (4) pricing decisions. Of these, pricing is the easiest to simulate, and channels of distribution are the most difficult to simulate. Therefore, one issue is whether a multi-level channel is necessary for a simulation to be classified as large-scale. Given the growing power and importance of distributors (see, for example, Felgner 1989, or Rao and McLaughlin 1990), it is highly desirable to include this aspect of marketing in the simulation. The large-scale simulation should also be as realistic as possible, using real products, real attributes, and real values (such as, in its mediagraphics, consumer demographics, U.S. and/or world geography, and consumer benefits). In contrast, many non-large scale simulations use abstract products (e.g., widgets) and abstract attribute (e.g., attribute A, attribute B, attribute C). Thus greater size and its drivers, greater comprehensiveness and greater realism, all define large-scale simulation.

The large-scale simulation is a comprehensive, indepth treatment of the marketing mix. Thus, such a simulation is most suitable in courses that are likewise comprehensive. The marketing principles course needs to introduce key theories of the marketing field, and so is not suited for a large-scale simulation. As Haas and Wotruba (1990) describe the "common objectives of the capstone marketing course" it is well-suited for large-scale simulation. Their list of objectives includes: integrating the marketing mix, translating concepts into practice, providing real-life marketing experience, stimulating more creative and flexible thinking, providing managerial experience, and interacting with peers. Simulations provide an alternative to the case method frequently used to achieve these objectives. Simulations are living, continuing cases. Simulations have the advantage that students have to live with the consequences of their decisions, which provides additional learning and motivational benefits.

This article discusses the benefits (pros) and issues (cons) of large-scale simulation in marketing. The purpose is not to describe the features of large-scale simulation in detail, as that information is contained in Burns' (1992) software review's description of *The Market Place* and in examination copies of instructor's manuals available from publishers. Rather, this paper is the first detailed analysis of large-scale simulation from the instructor's perspective. Faculty members considering using a large-scale simulation need to hear the "inside story" about large scale simulations in order to make an informed decision about whether or not to give large-scale simulation a try. Burns concludes that "as with most innovations, while it represents clear advantages over its competitors, it requires a new way of thinking." Thus, the worst thing that could happen is for an instructor to "walk into it blind." While large-scale simulation is tantalizing in theory, the instructor needs to know how well it really works in practice.

Eight benefits are discussed: communication skill, relationship management skill, holistic and strategic decisions under ambiguity, self-reliance, computer literacy, comprehensive and realistic tasks and issues, creativity and risk-taking, reliance on consumer preference instead of personal preference.

Eight issues are discussed: roughness of early products, computer problems, group grading issues, too time consuming?, unclear role of instructor, instructor start up costs, supplementation needs, "diffusion of innovation" and student and faculty resistance.

For further information please contact:
Frank Alpert
School of Business Administration
University of Missouri-St. Louis
8001 Natural Bridge Road
St. Louis, MO 63121

TOO MUCH OF A GOOD THING? - AN EMPIRICAL INVESTIGATION OF INFORMATION OVERLOAD IN PREDICTING MARKETING OUTCOMES

Subramanian Sivaramakrishnan, The Pennsylvania State University
W. Steven Perkins, The Pennsylvania State University

ABSTRACT

This experiment investigated the effects of manipulating the quantity of information on predictive accuracy. In the context of the MARKSTRAT simulation game, three groups received differing amounts of the available research reports—none, half, or all. The group receiving the most information forecasted the results of the game the least accurately. The results imply that a large quantity of information may be too much of a good thing, whereas a small quantity of good information may enhance managerial predictions.

INTRODUCTION

Marketing decision makers are increasingly faced with an abundance of information (Glazer 1991). Each year substantial resources are expended on marketing research, but there has been little research addressing what information and how much information to provide the decision maker. Studying the use of marketing research information by marketing managers, Deshpande and Zaltman (1982, 1984) found that managers used more market research information if it was deemed technically adequate, it confirmed prior expectations, and when the manager-researcher interaction was high. Though intuitively, it seems like more information use would result in better decisions, Jacoby, Speller, and Kohn (1974) showed otherwise in the case of consumer decision making. Keller and Staelin (1987) studied the effects of quality and quantity of information on consumer decision making and saw that while consumers made better decisions with increasing quality of information, their decisions became poor with increasing quantity. Glazer, Steckel, and Winer (1988) demonstrated that the presence of unrelated information encouraged managers to focus on those components of decision-making most clearly addressed by the information which may lead to poorer performance. In a related study, Glazer, Steckel, and Winer (1989) found that forecasts based on marketing research tended to be biased, but forecast errors were not related to the amount of available information. Considering the decision maker as a consumer of information, firms need to understand how prediction accuracy and decision effectiveness vary with information use in order to make the best utilization of their marketing research resources. Understanding decision making by marketing managers can provide insights which will help in building better tools for managers to use and lead to improved marketing decisions.

EFFECTS OF INFORMATION ON DECISION MAKING

Research has shown that information load affects human information processing (Schroeder et al. 1967; Newell and Simon 1972). In the area of consumer decision making, Jacoby, Speller, and Kohn (1974) studied the role of product information on decision making and noted that as the number of brand alternatives increased, satisfaction with the decision increased, and the desire not to have additional information regarding the new brand also increased. Their research was founded on the information overload paradigm which posits that consumers have finite limits to the amount of information they can assimilate and process. If these limits are exceeded, overload occurs and consumers become confused and make poorer decisions. Hence, too much information can lead to dysfunctional performance (Malhotra et al. 1982; Jacoby 1977). Russo (1974) reevaluated the research and concluded that more information aids the consumer in making decisions.

One major concern of policy makers and researchers interested in how individuals use available information is the determination of the maximum amount of information that a consumer can effectively process before experiencing decreased accuracy in assessing the value (utility) of available choice alternatives. Keller and Staelin (1987) demonstrated that consumers' decision effectiveness is adversely affected by increases in the quantity of information made available (holding quality fixed) and improved by increases in the quality level, at least up to a point (holding quantity levels fixed). They argued that information has two different components - quality and quantity, and that each component has a different and opposing influence on decision effectiveness. In their study, quality was operationalized as the cumulative score of individuals' importance weights for the attributes (information) provided and quantity as the number of attributes. Decision effectiveness was defined as a function of the utility assessment for the ideal choice and a choice error. Meyer and Johnson (1989) criticized Keller and Staelin's approach to identifying consumer error in a given choice, specifically, their use of inferred choice errors rather than objectively measured errors.

Several accounting researchers have examined the effects of accounting information load on decision making. Ashton (1974) suggests that more timely, relevant and useful information should be provided instead of just more information, because more information may not improve decision quality, but could result in reduced decision effectiveness. Casey (1980) demonstrated that accounting officers with the heaviest information load took longer and predicted no better than officers with lower information loads. Snowball (1980) studied the effects of information load on the confidence in and dispersion of predictions made from accounting reports and found that higher information loads tended to be associated with more confident and less varied predictions. Iselin (1988) showed that more diverse information resulted in lower decision accuracy and greater time usage by decision makers, when the decision task was structured. However, when the decision task was unstructured, Iselin (1989) found that increasing information diversity lead to information overload which resulted in greater time usage for decision making, but did not affect decision accuracy.

In marketing, although much attention has been given to consumer information processing and use, little study has been made of analogous issues in a managerial context (Deshpande and Zaltman 1984). In an effort to examine information use in managerial decision making and forecasting, Glazer, Steckel, and Winer (1987, 1988, 1989) have conducted a series of studies using MARKSTRAT (Larreche and Gatignon 1977). Glazer, Steckel, and Winer (1989) considered predictive accuracy in MARKSTRAT. Our study closely followed their procedures. For each time period in the game, 20 teams forecasted the number of brands in the market, the average price, and the total market size (in units sold) for the next time period. In 67 percent of the forecasts, teams were "unbiased" and in 85 percent of the forecasts, teams were "efficient." Defining these terms operationally, if the slope of the line between their predicted values and the actual values equalled one (and the intercept equalled zero), then a team was considered unbiased. If the difference between predicted and actual values was not related to the marketing research reports purchased, then a team was considered efficient. In general, teams that forecasted more accurately performed better in the game.

RESEARCH ISSUES

This exploratory study examined the effects of the quantity of marketing research information on managerial forecasting accuracy. Marketing managers often have to make good predictions in order to make good decisions. But, they may be overloaded with a number of market research reports, many of which may be of little use to the decision maker. On the other hand, marketing decision makers are sometimes not provided with those reports that would be most useful to them for a particular decision. Therefore, the effects of the two components of information, noted by Keller and Staelin - quality referring to the total utility of the reports and the quantity referring to the number - need to be considered when examining prediction accuracy. Marketing researchers

should provide both the right quantity and the right quality of information to the decision maker to make the most accurate prediction.

Suppose the decision task of the manager is to predict several variables such as sales, market share, and total number of competitors. Keeping the average quality of the information constant, if the quantity of the information is increased, two possibilities exist with reference to prediction accuracy. Going by the information overload paradigm, as the quantity of information is increased, the accuracy increases up to a point, beyond which it begins to decrease (an inverted U-shaped curve). The other possibility is that as the quantity of information is increased, the cumulative quality increases, and this in turn would improve prediction accuracy, at least up to a point. The terms 'cumulative quality' and 'average quality' are defined below. This study investigated how the prediction accuracy of decision makers behaves at different levels of quantity of information. In essence, we look at the information quantity as in Keller and Staelin (1987), but in the context of managerial prediction accuracy as in Glazer, Steckel, and Winer (1989).

Though some useful ideas are taken from their study, our study differs from that of Keller and Staelin (1987) in that the context is managerial decision making in the marketing simulation game MARKSTRAT, the decision makers are experienced in the decision making domain, the decision to be made is a prediction which can be evaluated by comparison to actuals, and the quality of the information is ascertained objectively.

METHODOLOGY

To research the issues stated above, we require a fairly realistic managerial environment in which a number of factors influence the outcomes, including the participants' use of marketing research information. This information should be 'good' - in the sense that it is reliable and valid and could be used to predict future market behavior. Ideally, the predictions based on this information can be compared to the actual results to measure accuracy. The computer simulation game MARKSTRAT is such an environment. It is considered to be among the most realistic simulation games used in management education (Glazer, Steckel, and Winer 1988). It has also provided data for other researchers in the area of forecasting and decision-making (Glazer, Steckel, and Winer 1987, 1988; Hogarth and Makridakis 1981).

MARKSTRAT

The game is typically played with students being divided into teams (3-4 per team), with five such teams (denoted A, E, I, O, and U) comprising a MARKSTRAT "industry." The number of "industries" depends on the total number of students. MARKSTRAT is played over a number of periods. At the start of the game, each of the five firms (teams) in each MARKSTRAT industry begins with different relative competitive positions. Each firm has two brands in the market place. Throughout the course of the game, firms are free to introduce new brands into the market, withdraw old ones and modify existing brands. In addition, firms make production, advertising, sales force, distribution, pricing, and product-positioning decisions for each of their brands in each period (however, this is only in the game and not in the experiment in this study, as is explained later). A team's performance (in terms of relative levels of sales, market share, and profits) is a function of its own decisions, its competitors' decisions, and general trends in the MARKSTRAT "economy." Decisions in subsequent periods are made after analyzing previous periods' results as well as any or all of the market research reports which firms can purchase. Since the MARKSTRAT market research studies are accurate reflections of the underlying response functions which determine marketplace behavior (i.e.. they have been generated by the same model), the ability to interpret information and use it in decision-making is a crucial requirement for successful performance in the MARKSTRAT simulation (Glazer, Steckel, and Winer 1988).

The following MARKSTRAT market research studies related to the "Sonite" market were used in the experiment:

1. Consumer Survey - brand awareness, purchase intentions, and shopping habit data in each of the five segments in the game.

2. Consumer Panel - market shares, based on units sold in each segment. The industry sales in each segment are also indicated.

3. Distribution Panel - market shares, based on units sold in each channel. The industry sales in each distribution channel are also indicated.

4. Semantic Scales - median scale values of different physical characteristics for each brand and for the segment ideal points.

5. Perceptual Mapping of Brands' Similarities and Preferences, - graphical representation of the perceptual positioning of the Sonite brands and the segments' ideal points.

6. Market Forecast - estimate of the market size, for the next period and a breakdown by segment.

Subjects received differing numbers of these reports during the experiment.

SUBJECTS AND STIMULI

Subjects were 17 students from an undergraduate course in MIS in which MARKSTRAT was used extensively as part of the course work. All students had one semester's (10 game periods) experience with the game. While a set of managers actually responsible for the decision investigated would have been ideal subjects, Babb et al. (1966) compared managers' and students game-playing behaviors (for a different simulation game) and concluded that managers and students behaved differently only if managers had experience in the actual market represented by the game. In this case, since all the students had 10 periods of experience with the MARKSTRAT industry, they represented a pool with sufficient ability to act as surrogates. Ashton and Kramer's (1980) literature review led them to the following summary observation: 'Studies which examined attitudes and attitude changes have found sizable discrepancies between students and other subjects, while studies which have focused on decision making have found considerable similarities in the decision and apparent underlying information processing behavior of student and non-student groups.' This observation supports the use of students in the experiment. The subjects were paid $4 for their participation.

To begin with, the percentage of times each market research report was purchased over the semester was obtained. The percentages (within parentheses) are as follows:

1. Consumer Survey, Market Sonite (78)

2. Consumer Panel, Market Sonite (46)

3. Distribution Panel, Market Sonite (41)

4. Semantic Scales, Market Sonite (73)

5. Perceptual Mapping of Brands' Similarities and Preferences, Market Sonite (92)

6. Market Forecast, Market Sonite (42)

These percentages represent to a great extent the perceived "usefulness" of the report, given that a firm would purchase a report only if it were useful. These percentages are henceforth referred to as the "weights" of the reports.

To keep the average quality of the information constant, information quality is operationalized as the average score of the weights of the reports. It should be noted that the quality here does not refer to the accuracy or reliability of the reports, but to it's "usefulness." Information quantity is operationalized as the number of market research reports (from those listed above) that a subject receives.

The market research reports were selectively chosen such that different subjects received the same average quality of information, but different quantities. Reports 2, 5, and 6 were chosen as the treatment for the low quantity of information group. These reports have an average quality of 60. The cumulative quality equalled 180. All 6 reports were selected for the high quantity of information group. These six reports have an average quality of 62 which is almost equal to that of reports 2, 5, and 6, and a cumulative quality of 372.

EXPERIMENTAL DESIGN

For the information quantity factor, there were three levels - 0 reports, 3 reports, and 6 reports. By selectively choosing the reports as described, subjects in each treatment were presented with market research reports corresponding to their treatment levels.

In order to ensure that no subject got the decisions, results and reports of their own firm in which he/she participated during the semester (in which case the subject could remember the sales their firm made), the following procedure was adopted: If a subject was in Industry 1, Firm x (where x could be 1 through 5), then he/she was given the decisions, results, and reports of Industry 2, Firm x and vice versa. This was done because, in MARKSTRAT, at period 0, firms do not start from the same base - each has a relative competitive position in comparison to other firms in the industry. This relative position is fairly similar in both industries. Therefore, to ensure that the decision makers are familiar with their decision making environment, they were given the scenario they were used to (in terms of relative positions), however with completely different figures.

In addition, by analyzing the usage of marketing research information by teams during the semester, teams could be placed into different semester groups based on whether they consistently used a high or low number of reports during the course of the game. In order to reduce variability due to being accustomed to a high or low quantity of information, subjects were assigned to experimental groups so as to balance their prior use of information across experimental treatments.

In sum, for the three experimental treatments, 5 subjects were assigned to the no-information group, 5 to the low-information group, and 7 to the high-information group. Their prior use of information during the semester was balanced across the three experimental groups.

PROCEDURE

The MARKSTRAT game is played by every firm in each industry making marketing decisions which form the input for the game simulation. The simulation then gives the output of the results which consists of a summary of the decisions taken by the firm followed by the financial and marketing results, an R&D report, a news-letter, and the marketing research reports which were bought by the firm.

As mentioned, the subjects participated in 10 periods (0 was the base period) of MARKSTRAT in their MIS course during Fall 1990. All decisions taken by them and subsequent financial and marketing results, and market research reports were available for each firm for each period. The output of the results from periods 1 to 5 were used for the study.

In the experiment, each subject got the actual financial results, marketing results, R & D report, and newsletter of a firm for period 0. In addition, the subject was provided with the decisions that firm took in period 1. Depending on which treatment the subject was assigned to, he/she was provided with the marketing research reports which corresponded to the quantity for that treatment. Using the marketing and financial results, market research reports, and decisions made, the subjects were asked to make the following five predictions for period 1:

— the total number of brands in the market in the next period,
— the average industry price,
— the total industry size (in units sold),
— their firm's market share, and
— their firm's sales in units.

This was repeated for periods 2 to 5. Therefore, each subject made 5 predictions in each of the 5 periods, giving 25 predicted values per subject. The questionnaire packets were arranged such that the subjects did not look at the actual data for a period before making the predictions for that period. The variables they forecasted were not shown on the reports for subsequent time periods, to ensure that subjects could not simply look ahead.

ANALYSIS AND RESULTS

The analyses examine the subjects' predictive accuracy given the different levels of information available to them in the experiment. The first two analyses generally follow the procedures in Glazer, Steckel, and Winer (1989) for testing forecasting unbiasedness and for testing forecasting efficiency. These analyses compare forecasted values to actual values for each type of forecast. The third approach considers the mean absolute percentage error (MAPE) between forecasted and actual values across all five types of forecasts.

If subjects are unbiased in their forecasts, the slope of the regression line between actual and forecasted values should equal one. That is, every change in observed values should be matched by an equal change in predicted values. By experimental group, actual values for each variable forecasted were regressed on their respective predicted values. Focussing on the estimated slope parameter, Table 1 presents the results of testing the slope of each regression equation. If the slope did not differ from 1.00, then the result is denoted as DNR (do not reject H_o) while it is denoted R (reject H_o) if the slope differed significantly ($p<.05$) from 1.00.

The low information group forecasted three of the five variables without bias. The other two groups per-

A repeated measures analysis of variance was run with experimental group, semester group, and their interaction as the independent variables and the MAPE values for each of the five forecasted variables as the dependent variables. The experimental group was significant ($p = 0.04$), showing that the quantity of information had an effect on the prediction accuracy. The semester group and the interaction term were not significant ($p = 0.14$ and $p = 0.12$ respectively). The results of the tests for between

---

TABLE 1
Testing Forecasting Unbiasedness
Ho B=1.00

| | Experimental Group | | |
Variable Forecasted	No reports	3 reports	6 reports
Brands	R	R	R
Price	R	R	R
Market Share	R	DNR	R
Market Size	DNR	DNR	R
Unit Sales	R	DNR	R

---

formed noticeably worse, with the high information group exhibiting biased forecasts of every variable.

The second analysis tested forecasting efficiency. If the subjects were efficient in their use of the available information, there should be no difference between actual and forecasted values on average. Table 2 presents the results of t tests comparing the difference between actual and forecasted values to zero. Again if the difference equals zero, then the result is denoted as DNR (do not reject H_o) while it is denoted R (reject H_o) if the difference between actual and forecasted differed significantly ($p<.05$) from zero.

Across the tests of unbiasedness and efficiency, the null hypothesis could not be rejected 30 percent of the time for the no-information group, 60 percent of the time for the low-information group, and 20 percent of the time for the high-information group. In other words, the group with a small number of research reports performed better than the other groups.

The measure selected for assessing the overall performance of the three experimental groups was the Mean Absolute Percentage Error (MAPE) between the predicted and actual values for the variables (see also for example Larreche and Moinpour 1983). Since the five variables which were predicted had different units, the MAPE was selected so as to make all the variables comparable. A larger MAPE indicated greater error in prediction and a MAPE of zero indicated an accurate forecast. Five values were calculated for each of the 17 subjects (averaging over the 5 time periods).

subjects effects are presented in Table 3.

The results of the univariate tests for within subjects effects are also presented in Table 3. The tests indicate that all within subjects effects were highly significant.

As shown in Table 4, for 4 out of 5 variables predicted, the group with the highest quantity of information had the greatest MAPE, meaning the least accuracy. From an analysis of the actuals, it was seen that the average percentage change from Period 0 to Period 5 was less for Price (8%) and Number of brands (30%) followed by Market Share (55%), Market Size (222%), and Unit Sales (242%). In the prediction of the variables Price and Number of Brands, which may be "easier" to predict since they have a lower percentage change, the group with no information performed the best. In the case of the more "difficult" variables, Market Size and Unit Sales, which have a high percentage of change, the groups with a high quantity of information predicted the worst. The group with moderate quantity of information performed the best in the case of Market Share and Market Size.

DISCUSSION

The findings of this study concur with the information overload paradigm in consumer behavior. In this study, it was seen that as information quantity increased from no research reports to a moderate number, the overall prediction accuracy generally increased. But, as the quantity was further increased to all research reports, the accuracy of the predictions fell sharply, indicating that the prediction accuracy takes an inverted-U path with

TABLE 2
Testing Forecasting Efficiency
Ho (Actual - Forecast) = 0

Variable Forecasted	Experimental Group		
	No reports	3 reports	6 reports
Brands	DNR	DNR	DNR
Price	R	DNR	R
Market Share	R	DNR	R
Market Size	R	R	DNR
Unit Sales	DNR	R	R

TABLE 3
Results of Repeated Measures Analysis

Between Subjects Source	df	F	PR>F
Experimental group	2	4.54	0.0365
Semester group	2	2.40	0.1363
Interaction	1	2.80	0.1222

Within Subjects Source	df	F	PR>F
Variable	4	7.58	0.0001
Variable * Experimental group	8	3.76	0.0020
Variable * Semester group	8	2.35	0.0336
Variable * Experimental group * Semester group	4	4.35	0.0048

TABLE 4
Mape Values for Forecasted Variables by Experimental Group

Variable	No reports	3 reports	6 reports	Mean
Brands		0.07	0.13	0.06
0.08				
Price			0.06	0.09
0.20	0.12			
Market Share	0.29	0.18	0.50	0.35
Market Size	0.28	0.17	0.32	0.26
Unit Sales	0.23	0.27	0.80	0.48
Mean	0.19	0.17	0.38	
Subjects	5	5	7	

increasing quantity of information. For "easy" variables, the quantity of information did not matter as much. But, for more "difficult" variables, a high quantity of information was seen to be more "dangerous" than having no information at all. While the no-information group did a little better than the some-information and high-information groups with the "easier" variables, their MAPE increased significantly with the "difficult" variables. This may suggest that managerial experience is sufficient when the task is easy. When the task gets more complex, relying only on intuition becomes inadequate. Information becomes necessary, but beyond a point too much information reduces predictive accuracy.

The group receiving three reports performed the best across the tests of unbiasedness, efficiency, and percent error. Though this group did not perform better than the no-information group with the "easier" variables, it performed better for the "difficult" variables. More importantly, the prediction accuracy did not drop as sharply with the other two experimental groups for the "difficult" variables.

As noted by researchers in consumer decision making (Jacoby, Kohn, and Speller 1973; Jacoby, Speller, and Kohn 1974; Jacoby, Speller, and Berning 1974; Jacoby 1984; Malhotra 1984), "too much" information leads to dysfunctional decision performance. While decision makers can develop mechanisms to regulate their intake of information, their limited information processing capacity can become overloaded if they attempt to process too much information. This can lead to confusion and cognitive strain resulting in poorer performance. Moreover, evidence from Jacoby, Kohn, and Speller (1973) suggests that increases in information load can make processing more time-consuming and can make decision makers pay less attention to relevant information. Increases in the quantity of information beyond the optimal point therefore leads to dysfunctional performance.

LIMITATIONS

The questionnaire packet which the subjects were given clearly encouraged them to analyze each of the marketing research reports and decisions made for the next period before making the predictions. However, since the subjects were allowed to take the packets home, there was no control on their actual nature and extent of use of the information. In addition, the quality of the reports was assessed based on how often the reports were bought by the teams in the game during the semester (which was almost the same when we also considered how often a report was bought given that it had been bought once). It is assumed that since in the game each report costs several thousand dollars, the teams would have been rational and bought the reports only if they did find them useful. Therefore, we had an objective measure of quality in terms of percentage of times purchased, but we do not know whether that accurately measures "usefulness."

FUTURE RESEARCH

As a follow-up study, it would be interesting to vary quality (the other component as per Keller and Staelin 1987) of the information and study the impact of different combinations of quality and quantity on the prediction of both the easier and the difficult variables used in this study. Another aspect to study would be the impact of information quantity on the learning curve of a decision maker. Does greater quantity of information shorten the curve ? Future research could also take into account differences in individual capability to process information. In addition, effects of information load on group decision making, considering variables such as attitude towards the task and level of effort (e.g. Glazer, Steckel, and Winer 1987) would be interesting research.

SUMMARY AND IMPLICATIONS

In this exploratory study, we have examined the effect of the quantity of marketing research information on the prediction accuracy of decision makers. The decision-making environment was MARKSTRAT. The primary criterion used for evaluating the predictions was the mean absolute percentage error. Subjects were assigned to different treatments and made predictions on several variables. The experimental treatment was significant, showing that the quantity of information has an effect on the accuracy of predictions. The treatment also seemed to have the same effect on forecasting unbiasedness and efficiency.

In conclusion, our results imply that a high quantity of information can do more harm than good. Having a few good reports is better than having no information or having too many reports. Particularly when the variable is a "difficult" one to predict, some good information is better than having too much or too little information. When the variable is "easy" to predict, little or no information may be adequate.

REFERENCES

Ashton, Robert H. (1974), "Behavioral Implications of Information Overload in Managerial Accounting Reports," *Cost and Management,* (July/August), 37-40.

_____ and Sandra S. Kramer (1980), "Students as Surrogates in Behavioral Accounting Research: Some Evidence," *Journal of Accounting Research,* 18 (Spring), 1-15.

Babb E. M., M. A. Leslie and M. D. Van Syke (1966), "The Potential of Business Gaming Methods in Research," *Journal of Business,* 39, 465-472.

Casey C. (1980), "Variations in Accounting Information Load: The Effect on Loan Officers' Predictions of Bankruptcy," *The Accounting Review,* (January), 36-49.

Deshpande, Rohit and Gerald Zaltman (1982), "Factors Affecting the Use of Market Research Information: A Path Analysis," *Journal of Marketing Research,* 19 (February), 14-31.

_____ and _____ (1984), "A Comparison of Factors Affecting Researcher and Manager Perceptions of Market Research Use," *Journal of Marketing Research,* 21 (February), 32-38.

Glazer, Rashi (1991), "Marketing in an Information Intensive Environment: Strategic Implications of Knowledge as an Asset," *Journal of Marketing,* 55

(October), 1-19.

_____, Joel H. Steckel, and Russell S. Winer (1987), "Group Process and Decision Performance in a Simulated Marketing Environment," *Journal of Business Research,* 15, 545-557.

_____, _____, and _____ (1988), "Locally Rational Decision Making: The Distracting Effect of Information on Marketing Performance," Columbia Business School Research Working Paper No. 88-AV-7.

_____, _____, and _____ (1989), "The Formation of Key Marketing Variable Expectations and Their Impact on Firm Performance: Some Experimental Evidence," *Marketing Science,* 1, (Winter).

Hogarth, Robin M. and Spyros Makridakis (1981), "The Value of Decision Making in a Complex Environment: An Experimental Approach," *Management Science,* 27, 93-107.

Iselin, Errol R. (1988), "The Effects of Information Load and Information Diversity on Decision Quality in a Structured Decision Task," *Accounting, Organizations and Society,* 13, 147-164.

_____ (1989), "The Impact of Information Diversity on Information Overload Effects in Unstructured Managerial Decision Making," *Journal of Information Science,* 15, 163-173.

Jacoby, Jacob (1977), "Information Load and Decision Quality: Some Contested Issues," *Journal of Marketing Research,* 14 (November), 569-573.

_____ (1984), "Perspectives on Information Overload," *Journal of Consumer Research,* 10 (March), 432-435.

_____, Carol A. Kohn, and Donald E. Speller (1973), "Time Spent Acquiring Information as a Function of Information Load and Organization," *Proceedings of the American Psychological Association's 81st Annual Convention,* Washington DC: 8, 813-814.

_____, Donald E. Speller, and Carol Kohn (1974), "Brand Choice Behaviour as a Function of Informa-

tion Load," *Journal of Marketing Research,* 11 (February), 63-69.

_____, _____, and Carol Kohn Berning (1974), "Brand Choice Behaviour as a Function of Information Load: Replication and Extension," *Journal of Consumer Research,* 1 (June), 33-42.

Keller, Kevin L. and Richard Staelin (1987), "Effects of Quality and Quantity of Information on Decision Effectiveness," *Journal of Consumer Research,* 14, 2 (September), 200-213.

Larreche, Jean-Claude, and Hubert Gatignon (1977), "MARKSTRAT: A Marketing Simulation Game," Palo Alto, CA: Scientific Press.

_____ and Reza Moinpour (1983), "Managerial Judgement in Marketing: The Concept of Expertise," *Journal of Marketing Research,* 20 (May), 110-121.

Malhotra, Naresh K., Arun K. Jain, and Stephen W. Lagakos (1982), "The Information Overload Controversy: An Alternative Viewpoint," *Journal of Marketing,* 46, 2 (Spring), 27-37.

_____ (1984), "Reflections on the Information Overload Paradigm in Consumer Decision Making," *Journal of Consumer Research,* 10 (March), 436-440.

Meyer, Robert J. and Eric J. Johnson (1989), "Information Overload and the Nonrobustness of Linear Models: A Comment on Keller and Staelin," *Journal of Consumer Research,* 15, 4 (March), 498-503.

Newell A. and H. Simon (1972), *Human Problem Solving,* Englewood Cliffs, NJ: Prentice-Hall.

Russo J. Edward (1974), "More Information is Better: A Reevaluation of Jacoby, Speller and Kohn," *Journal of Consumer Research,* 1 (December), 68-72.

Schroeder H. M., M. J. Driver, and S. Streufert (1967), Human Information Processing, New York: Holt, Rinehart, and Winston.

Snowball D. (1980), "Some Effects of Accounting Expertise and Information Load: An Empirical Study," *Accounting, Organizations and Society,* 323-338.

CONTROL AND COGNITION IN DECISION MAKING: IMPLICATIONS FOR THE ROLE OF INFORMATION IN MARKETING STRATEGY

David Prensky, Trenton State College

ABSTRACT

I propose a model of strategic decision making in marketing and the role that information plays in that process. Recognizing the importance, complexity, and uncertainty of such decisions, it proposes that the manager's desire for certainty and the firm's need to control the strategic decision process interact to create a mutually reinforcing procedural framework that becomes divorced from the environment. The procedural framework constrains the firm's strategic decisions to be consistent with past strategy and changes the role of information from true market intelligence to a symbol of rationality and a political tool.

A MODEL OF CONTROL AND COGNITION IN STRATEGIC DECISION MAKING

Strategic decisions are matters of importance, complexity, and uncertainty (Schwenk 1988b). In the face of such importance, complexity, and uncertainty, few firms are willing to allow a hit-or-miss approach to strategic decision making. The essence of marketing control (Jaworski 1988) is the firm's attempt to control the process by which marketing managers make strategic decisions. The firm's structure, culture, and politics all function to provide a framework for the decision making of the marketing managers. Given the nature of strategic decision making, controlling the output will be ineffective if not impossible, so the firm must control the process itself.

Marketing managers also want to arrange their decision making processes in a fashion that will reduce the complexity and uncertainty of the important task. They want to employ a framework for decision making that will simplify the complexity, reduce the uncertainty, and result in decisions that are acceptable to those in the firm who provide their rewards.

The result is that marketing managers use a procedural framework to guide their thoughts and actions about strategic decisions. Instead of thinking through every decision completely, such a framework provides an efficient resource to simplify decision making and ensure its consistency with the firm's goals. It includes categorizations of colleagues, customers, and competitors, and beliefs about the effects of alternative strategies. Cognitive heuristics are the rules of thumb that managers use to simplify decision making, while reasoning by analogy is the process by which managers use past decisions as guides for current decisions (Schwenk 1988a). However, heuristics and analogy are simplifications that are subject to bias. A manager may remember past events and their attendant strategic decisions because of individual cognitive reasons, or because of organizational structure, culture, or politics. Such memories will have little relevance or validity for the strategic decisions that must be made in today's rapidly changing environment.

The procedural framework acts as a constraint on the decisions that marketing managers make. Because of the biases that result from cognitive heuristics and application of analogies rooted in the firm's structure, culture, and politics, the manager's decision making is no longer directly responsive to the environment outside the firm. Instead, the procedural framework determines strategic decisions, reflecting cognitive limitations resulting from the firm much more than the effects of the environment. The procedural framework, which developed to give the firm control over strategic decisions made by individual managers and which managers welcomed because it simplified decision making, is now a constraint that divorces the firm from its environment (Levitt 1960; Barabba and Zaltman 1991).

The individual manager, in an attempt to deal with the complexity and uncertainty of the environment, has ceded his or her independent (and potentially rational) perceptions of the environment to the firm in exchange for the ones that are shared with other managers in the firm. The firm, because it is not capable of action that is independent of its managers, cannot be any more rational or objective in its decision making than its individual managers. Therefore, neither the firm nor the individual managers make strategic decisions about an objective environment.

IMPLICATIONS FOR THE ROLE OF INFORMATION IN MARKETING STRATEGY

The actual role of information in the procedural framework is far different from the one that it plays in conventional descriptions of strategic decision making as a rational process. In actual strategic decision making processes, information plays three major roles. It is a symbol that the manager has used rationality in his or her decision making, examining the environment as every good manager "should" (Feldman and March 1981). Information is also a political tool, used by the various groups in the firm to influence the decision making of others so that their procedural framework can continue to exist (Pfeffer, 1981a; b). Finally, there is the role that information "should" play: providing "objective" data about the environment that can shape strategic decision making. Sometimes the information gathered is so different from what the prevailing framework expects that it provokes a change in the procedural framework. (Huff and Schwenk 1990). This is the basis of many criticisms of American business as being too complacent until conditions deteriorate dramatically.

The procedural framework that I have described is the outgrowth of sound marketing control efforts by the firm and understandable attempts by the individual manager to make *better* strategic decisions. The dilemma that good marketing practice, both at the level of the firm and the individual manager, can result in such dysfunctional organizational arrangements is sobering. This strategic dilemma requires that we fully understand the management process of strategic decision making, not just the marketing content of those decisions. We must also access the impact of the information explosion on managers' procedural frameworks by asking ourselves whether these new sources of information are increasing the complexity of their tasks, making them even more likely to adopt simplifying cognitive structures, and therefore intensifying the dilemma that I have discussed.

For further information please contact:
David Prensky
School of Business
Trenton State College
Hillwood Lakes CN4700
Trenton, NJ 08650-4700

IN SEARCH OF THE MARKETING IMAGINATION: FACTORS AFFECTING THE CREATIVITY OF MARKETING PROGRAMS FOR MATURE PRODUCTS

Jonlee Andrews, Case Western Reserve University
Daniel C. Smith, University of Pittsburgh

ABSTRACT

Differentiation, a key factor in the success of new products, is also crucial for the ongoing success of mature products. However, marketing strategies for mature products are often characterized by incidental deviations from the status quo or me-too responses to competitors' actions. By simply suggesting that firms seek to differentiate their products from competitors, the marketing literature provides little guidance regarding factors which lead to the development of marketing programs that are successful in differentiating mature products. We propose relationships between several individual and situational factors and the creativity of marketing programs. Creativity is defined here as the degree of difference between a product's most recent marketing program and those of competitors. It is a necessary precursor to the continued differentiation of established products.

Main Effects Propositions

Broad and deep knowledge are essential to the development of creative solutions (Amabile 1983). In the context of marketing planning, critical "raw materials" include knowledge of the product domain, diversity of education, and diversity of experience.

P1:   The greater a product manager's (a) knowledge of the product domain, (b) diversity of education, and (c) diversity of experience, the greater the creativity of the marketing program.

The generation of creative ideas requires a great degree of effort and prolonged concentration on the problem. An individual must be motivated to put forth such concentrated effort (Amabile 1983; Hogarth 1980). A manager's intrinsic motivation to plan and willingness to take a risk are two motivational factors thought to be necessary to generate creative marketing programs.

P2:   The greater a product manager's (a) intrinsic motivation to plan and (b) propensity to take a risk, the greater the degree of creativity of the marketing program.

The environment in which marketing planning takes place should also affect the creativity of the marketing program. Formalization of the planning process, time pressure, a product's recent performance, and the degree of interaction with others are all expected to impact creativity of the marketing program.

P3:   Creativity of a marketing program will be greatest when planning process formalization is moderate.

P4:   The greater the time pressure experienced by a manager, the lower the creativity of the marketing program.

P5:   The more favorable a product's recent performance, the less creative the marketing program.

P6:   The more a manager interacts with members of other functional areas, the greater the creativity of the marketing program.

Factors Affecting the Relationship Between Knowledge and Creativity

Under certain motivational and situational conditions, a product manager may be unwilling or unable to fully utilize his or her broad and deep knowledge.

The effects of (a) knowledge of the product domain, (b) diversity of experience, and (c) diversity of education on creativity of the marketing program:

P7:   will be greater when intrinsic motivation to plan is high than when it is low.

P8:   will be greater when propensity to take a risk is high than when it is low.

P9:   will diminish as time pressure increases.

P10:   will be greater when recent performance is unfavorable than favorable.

However, interacting with others provides a forum through which combinations of ideas can be generated and considered, increasing the "value" of an individual's knowledge.

P11:   The effects of (a) knowledge of the product domain, (b) diversity of experience, and (c) diversity of education on creativity of the marketing program will be greater when interaction with others is high than when it is low.

Implications

There are a number of implications regarding hiring criteria, staffing levels, training policies, planning process structure, and so on. For example, the recent practice of downsizing middle management may adversely affect creativity by increasing the time pressure under which marketing managers must perform.

For further information please contact:
Jonlee Andrews
Weatherhead School of Management
Case Western Reserve University
Cleveland, OH 44106-7235

EXPLAINING CONSUMER COMPLAINT BEHAVIOR VIA THE LEARNED HELPLESSNESS PARADIGM

Victoria Bush, Memphis State University
Emin Babakus, Memphis State University

ABSTRACT

Although consumer complaints are increasingly recognized as a crucial element to retailer survival, in reality, very few consumers actually make the effort to complain. Most consumers either choose to do nothing or initiate negative word-of-mouth to others (Richins 1983b; Singh 1988; TARP 1986). This critical aspect of consumer complaint behavior justifies the need to understand the reasons behind various complaint or non-complaint actions that consumers demonstrate.

If a customer experiences repeated failures, say, inadequate auto repair, s/he may come to expect subsequent failures in the future. Further, these expectations of response independence may transfer across various situations. Thus, a valued customer may never complain because s/he expects the effort to be futile. Despite the apparent intuitive sense of the learned helplessness framework, very little research has been devoted to this alternative paradigm. The purpose of this study is to introduce and empirically examine a learned helplessness framework in further understanding complaint behavior.

Attribution theory in consumer complaint behavior (CCB) research has primarily focused on causal inferences that are situation specific. The learned helplessness paradigm is also based on attribution theory, however, this framework addresses the concept of attributional style. One's attributional style becomes a disposition that is not merely situation specific. Thus, learned helplessness is primarily cognitive in that mere exposure to an uncontrollable event does not produce characteristics of learned helplessness. Rather, an individual must learn to expect that outcomes are uncontrollable (Abramson, Garber, and Seligman 1980). It is these perceived expectations that determine the criticality of learned helplessness.

Three attributional dimensions have been developed that aid in further explanation of helplessness: internality, globality and stability. Internality refers to the belief that outcomes are caused by one's own response. Globality refers to the characteristic that expectations will recur across situations. Stability refers to a personal characteristic, such as ability, that is perceived with a certain degree of permanence. These causal attributions have implications as to the degree or severity of learned helplessness. Individuals who habitually attribute the causes of bad events as internal, stable and global are pessimistic in nature. Individuals who attribute causes of

are less prone to anxiety -- all of which also influence complaint intentions. The opposite was found for pessimistic individuals, i.e. those who attribute causes to internal, stable and global conditions. Pessimistic individuals have acquired learned helplessness traits and thus have learned that they have no control over outcomes. These people would thus believe that complaining is futile.

If marketers can understand these attributional dispositions within a learned helplessness paradigm, they may be able to better encourage future complaint behavior. Retailers might stress external, unstable, specific factors for consumer dissatisfaction. Thus, focusing away from possible attributions to the inadequacies of the consumer.

This study has been an initial exploration of the theoretical underpinnings of learned helplessness and its contribution to the CCB and retailing literature. Future research is needed to more rigorously test the relationships among variables involved.

For further information please contact:
Victoria Bush
Department of Marketing
Fogelman College of Business
Memphis State University
Memphis, TN 38152

FRAMING EFFECTS ON CONSUMERS' STORE CHOICE DECISIONS

Theresa DiNovo, University of Cincinnati
James J. Kellaris, University of Cincinnati

ABSTRACT

Prospect theory, rooted in the notion of bounded rationality, offers a positivistic view of decision making under uncertainty. The theory suggests that consumer choice depends on the way a problem is posed (i.e., "framed"), as well as the objective features of the problem (Kahneman and Tversky 1979; Tversky and Kahneman 1981). Decision making under uncertainty is conceptualized as a two-step process, including an editing phase and an evaluation phase (Burton and Babin 1989). During the editing phase, the decision maker "frames" the decision problem in a way that is consistent with his/her cognitive structure. For example, a consumer might recognize that she is able to purchase 65 percent of the items on her shopping list from a given store. In contrast, she might view the same situation as the inability to purchase 35 percent of the items on her list. Prospect theory would suggest that the perspective or "frame" adopted is likely to influence subsequent decisions and behaviors.

During the second phase, the decision maker assigns value to the edited prospect and chooses the prospect which offers the highest subjective utility. In a store choice context, this process might involve assigning probable values to the process, selection, and level of service expected (or not expected) at each store in each choice set.

To explore prospect theory in retail decision making, a series of three experiments was conducted. The purpose of the first study was to examine framing effects on preferences for risk versus certainty in a store choice context. The purpose of the second experiment was to replicate the first experiment using a different operation of framing. The third experiment explored the robustness of the framing effect by posing a decision problem in which the expected value of the alternatives was unequal.

In each experiment, subjects were exposed to a shopping decision scenario, then asked to select one of two alternative stores. The outcome of choosing "Store A" was expressed as a certainty ("you will definately get (or not get) the lowest price on 2 (or 4) out of the six books you need."), and the outcome of choosing "Store B" was expressed as a probability ("there is a 1/3 chance you will get (or 2/3 chance you will not get) the lowest price on all six books you need."). Framing was varied between-subjects. In each experiment, half the subjects were told what they would gain should they choose a given alternative, and half what they would lose. The scenarios were critiqued and revised by 15 graduate students (in a social cognition class) before use in the experiments.

Two-hundred two (N = 202) upper-level business students served as subjects. Each participated in only one experiment. Subjects were randomly assigned to a treatment condition (i.e., frame = gains or losses). Subjects were instructed to consider the problem thoughtfully and to indicate their preferred store choice.

Results were analyzed via cross-tabulation with chi-square statistical analysis. Framing effects were significant at the .05 level in all three experiments. Results indicated that preferences for risk-prone or risk-averse alternatives are influenced by how the consequences of a store choice are framed. Subjects tended to favor the risk-averse option when the store choice problem was framed in terms of potential gains, and the riskier option when the problem was framed in terms of potential losses.

The framing effect predicted by prospect theory would seem to be robust in the retail store choice decision context. Although the decisions we studied were hypothetical in nature, we believe our experimental results provide reasonably convincing, albeit preliminary, evidence.

While we have concentrated on decision framing at a theoretical level, managerial implications were also considered. These experiments suggest that a retailer might benefit by presenting "offers" to the consumer in different ways. Although consumers might not always think in terms of "probability of success" and "risk," a retailer could use these notions in advertising and promotion to take advantage of the framing effect. Our results suggest that a communication strategy which "guides" buyers' framing of store choice decisions (by supplying or suggesting an appropriate frame) may afford the retailer more influence over buyers' evaluation of decision criteria, and hence over store choices. For example, retailers with relatively strong competitive positions could capitalize on the framing effect by emphasizing certain (i.e., sure) gains and the risk of shopping elsewhere. Retailers in weaker competitive positions might benefit from using negative framing if they are perceived as a "riskier" shopping alternative.

For further information please contact:
Theresa DiNovo - ML 145
Department of Marketing
University of Cincinnati
Cincinnati, OH 45221-0145

ANTECEDENTS AND EFFECTS OF SERVICE CONSUMERS' PERCEIVED CONTROL: A THEORETICAL FRAMEWORK

K. F. Steve Cheng, University of Missouri-Columbia

ABSTRACT

The concept of perceived control is new to the marketing literature, but seems to be an interesting and a promising one to both researchers and practitioners. Bateson (1985) argues that the concept is intuitively appealing and managerially important. He urges the use of the perceived control approach to study service marketing.

The concept of control comes primarily from psychologists and has been defined as the need, activity, or capability of using one's resources (e.g., money, knowledge, competence) to influence his internal (mental) or external (both social and physical) environments. It can be broadly classified into two types: actual (objective) and perceived control. While the former refers to exercising particular overt responses to master an event, the latter refers to subjective appraisals or beliefs in one's capacity to master an event.

Empirical studies have shown that perceived control positively influences human physical and psychological well-being including tolerance of pain, frustration, distress, and anxiety, health, task involvement and performance, and job satisfaction. Based on the literature review, it is expected that perceived control will have direct and positive impact on service consumers' emotions (e.g., pleasure and arousal) and behaviors (e.g., approach-avoidance, purchase intention, and purchase behavior).

Because of the extreme settings used in most of the early studies on control, a question concerning whether or not the results of these studies can be generalized to service settings remains open. A recent study by Hui and Bateson (1991) seems to indicate that such generalization can be made. Further, that consumers often perceive high levels of uncertainty and risk when purchasing services could increase the importance of perceived control in the service transactions. Langer (1983) also argues that the findings of studies on control could be generalized across a variety of settings "because the belief in personal control may be essential to one's sense of competence and is basic to human functioning -- regardless of who the person is or where he or she may be" (p. 14).

As suggested by Wener (1985) and empirically supported by some researchers, physical environment factors, such as orientation and way finding (e.g., where we are, where we are going, and how things work), and the cues of a setting (e.g., cues to tell what behavior is expected from ourselves or from others) can affect one's perceived control and emotional responses. Factors in social settings can also affect one's perception of control including crowd density and role ambiguity and conflict. Some factors in service production and delivery process can affect perceived control as well. They include perceived choice, predictability, involvement, information sharing, etc..

As suggested by Bateson (1985), the underlying idea of perceived control is intuitively simple and appealing. If the ultimate purpose of research is to help managers in the design and management of services, an easy-to-understand concept is important to managers. However, the use of a perceived control approach to the study of service marketing is not without problems. The results from the studies conducted in laboratory settings must be interpreted cautiously before applying these results to the service contexts. The construct of perceived control needs to be investigated more thoroughly. Furthermore, how perceived control relates to other concepts such as perceived risk, trust, power, involvement, and others needs to be researched. Finally, many individual and situational factors which are left out in this article are worth exploring.

For further information contact:
K. F. Steve Cheng
Department of Marketing
214 Middlebush
University of Missouri
Columbia, MO 65211

THE EFFECT OF ORGANIZATIONAL AND ENVIRONMENTAL VARIABLES ON THE ROLE PERCEPTIONS AND JOB SATISFACTION OF SALESPEOPLE

Ravipreet S. Sohi, University of Nebraska - Lincoln

ABSTRACT

The success of a sales force depends to a large extent on the role perceptions and the satisfaction of its people. Because of the importance of these variables as determinants of sales force performance (Bagozzi 1980), a large body of literature has focused on the antecedents of role conflict, role ambiguity and job satisfaction. Most of these antecedents can be grouped into three categories (a) personal variables, (b) supervisory variables and (c) job related variables.

In addition to these variables, organizational and environmental factors play an important part in determining the role perceptions and job satisfaction of salespeople (Churchill, Ford and Walker 1990). Yet empirical research in the area is very limited (see for example Michaels et. al. 1987 and 1988). This paper extends the previous body of literature by looking at the effect of formalization, centralization, environmental dynamism and environmental heterogeneity on the role conflict, role ambiguity and the consequential job satisfaction of a salesperson. The hypothesized relationships between the variables are shown in Figure 1.

The data for this study was collected by a national

mail survey of salespeople belonging to six diverse industries; (a) food products, (b) furniture and fixtures, (c) chemical and allied products, (d) rubber and plastic products, (e) electronic computers, appliances and audio-visual equipment, and (f) toys and sporting goods. The response rate was 17.83 percent after adjusting for undeliverable letters. The final sample size was 230 salespeople, all belonging to different companies. To check for non-response bias, the early respondents were compared with the late respondents on a number of demographic and model variables. No significant differences were found between the two groups. Multi-item scales were adapted from existing literature for the constructs. Except for one, (coefficient alpha = 0.68) all the scales had alphas ranging between 0.75 and 0.90. The data was analyzed using OLS path analysis. The results are shown in Table 1.

The results indicate that the organizational and environmental variables included in this research affect a salesperson's job satisfaction indirectly through their effect on role perceptions. Role conflict and ambiguity have a negative effect on job satisfaction. This negative effect may be either enhanced or reduced by these organizational variables.

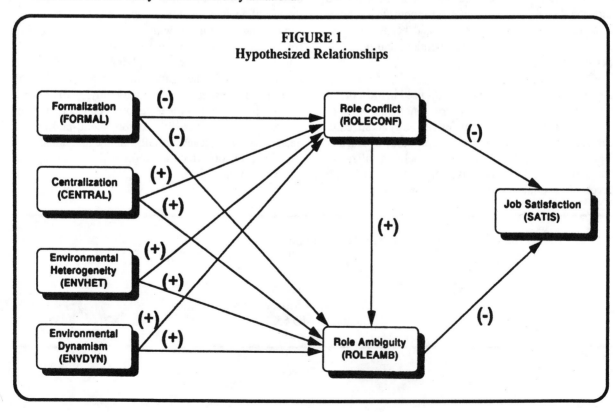

FIGURE 1
Hypothesized Relationships

TABLE 1
Results of the OLS Path Analysis

Dependent Variable	Predictor Variables	Hypothesized Sign	β	Std. β	t	p (2 tail)	R^2
ROLECONF	CONSTANT		1.572	---	---	---	
	FORMAL	-	-0.259	-0.172	-2.826	0.005	0.243
	CENTRAL	+	0.540	0.502	8.286	0.001	
	ENVHET	+	0.036	0.030	0.513	0.608	
	ENDVDYN	+	0.058	0.036	0.600	0.549	
ROLEAMB	CONSTANT		0.935	---	---	---	
	ROLECONF	+	0.321	0.395	6.502	0.001	0.390
	FORMAL	-	-0.186	-0.151	-2.721	0.007	
	CENTRAL	+	0.287	0.328	5.247	0.001	
	ENVHET	+	-0.011	-0.011	-0.203	0.839	
	ENVDYN	+	0.001	0.001	0.014	0.989	
SATIS	CONSTANT		5.293	---	---	---	
	ROLECONF	-	-0.186	-0.306	-4.744	0.001	0.353
	ROLEAMB	-	-0.278	-0.367	-5.701	0.001	

Formalization has a significant negative effect on role conflict and role ambiguity thereby implying that increased formalization within an organization may be beneficial in reducing role stress and improving job satisfaction. Centralization has a significant positive effect on role conflict and ambiguity. High degrees of centralization are likely to reduce job satisfaction through their adverse effect on role perceptions. By combining a high degree of formalization with decentralized decision making, organizations may be able to reduce the role stress of the salespeople and increase their overall job satisfaction. Formalization can be increased by laying down explicit rules and policies governing the channels of communication as well as the day to day operations of the salespeople.

Unlike formalization and centralization that can be managed by the organization, a salesperson has to work within the degree of dynamism and heterogeneity in the environment. It was hypothesized that environmental dynamism and heterogeneity would have an adverse effect on role perceptions. These relationships did not turn out to be significant. However, since these variables were adapted from organizational theory and haven't been used earlier in the sales force literature confidence in our findings is subject to future replication of these relationships with alternative approaches, measures and samples.

As is the case with every research, this study had a couple of limitations that the reader should be aware of. The first limitation concerns the generalizability of the results. Even though this was a multi-company, multi-industry study, the low response rate limits the extent to which the results of this study can be generalized to other situations. The second limitation is the possible existence of a self selection bias among the respondents. It is likely that the people who responded had a greater interest in this study. The tests for non-response bias only compared certain characteristics of the early versus late respondents. They did not address the self selection bias inherent in this type of study. Efforts were made to minimize this bias by randomly selecting the potential respondents from our mailing list. However, even this procedure could not eliminate the problem of self selection bias completely. All measures in this study were paper and pencil response questions. This could have resulted in some mono-method bias. The usual caveat regarding causation that accompanies all cross-sectional studies also holds here. The results should not be interpreted as proof of causal relationships, but rather as supporting or not supporting an *a priori* causal scheme.

For further information please contact:
Ravipreet S. Sohi
320 CBA
University of Nebraska
Lincoln, NE, 68588-0492

MARKETING CONTROLS, EMPLOYEE COMMITMENT, AND EMPLOYEE RESPONSES: AN EMPIRICAL INVESTIGATION

Sridhar N. Ramaswami, Iowa State University
Sanjeev Agarwal, Iowa State University

ABSTRACT

While formal controls are used to ensure that specified plans are implemented, they may lead to negative (e.g. job tension and dysfunctional behaviors) as well as positive employee responses (e.g., employee commitment toward the organization). This study examines the role that commitment plays in mitigating the occurrence of negative employee responses.

INTRODUCTION

During the last few years, marketing researchers have shown increasing interest in issues relating to control of marketing employees (Anderson and Chambers 1985; Anderson and Oliver 1987; Jaworski 1988; Jaworski and MacInnis 1989). One issue that has received much attention concerns the impact that different types of controls have on the psychological and behavioral responses of employees (Jaworski and MacInnis 1989). Basically, prior research has found that formal controls (such as output[1] and process[2] controls) lead to increased levels of job tension and dysfunctional behaviors among employees.

Though formal controls have been found to induce negative responses, one need not take the view that such controls are totally undesirable. In fact, such controls may produce positive responses (such as employee commitment toward the organization) that may mitigate the development of negative responses. For example, although process control has been found to lead to higher job tension and dysfunctional behavior, Anderson and Oliver (1987) posit that process control could induce salespeople to identify with and feel committed to their organization. This is based upon the argument that process controls free employees from short-term performance pressures. Because commitment is associated with positive work attitudes, the use of process control may have an indirect effect that reduces negative employee responses.

The study examines the direct impact that the two control forms--output and process--have on two types of negative employee responses--job tension and dysfunctional behavior, and one positive employee response--employee commitment. In addition, it examines the indirect impact that the two control forms have on negative employee responses through employee commitment. The hypothesized model is illustrated in Figure 1.

HYPOTHESES

Controls and Negative Employee Responses

Although the use of formal controls is intended to specify outcome measures and/or procedural measures to clarify the role of employees, its implicit role in deciding awards may lead to higher job tension and dysfunctional behaviors (Jaworski and MacInnis 1989; Merchant 1990).

Job Tension: Job tension reflects the extent to which the job, job evaluations, and the achievement of performance goals cause individual level stress. Use of output control imposes strict performance standards that must be met on time. This pressure can lead to development of stress. Past research suggests that the use of output control is associated with greater job tension (Hopwood 1974). Thus:

H1a: Greater the use of output controls, greater will be the incidence of job tension.

Use of process control imposes strict guidelines on which activities are to be performed and how the activities should be performed. Monitoring and correcting employee actions in an explicit manner is likely to offend their sense of autonomy and may result in disagreements over how different activities should be performed. This can lead to tension on the job (Hirst 1983). Thus:

H1b: Greater the use of process controls, greater will be the incidence of job tension.

Dysfunctional Behavior: Dysfunctional behavior reflects the tendency to engage in manipulative behaviors. Use of output control provides signals to employees that evaluation of output measures will influence their rewards. This means that they will put their energies in only the measured areas and direct efforts towards "game playing" to "beat the system" (Cammann and Nadler 1976). In other words, they may ignore performance measures that are not specified, but vital for the long term success of the organization. For example, those employees that are rewarded on the basis of market share, may engage in short term share capturing activities while ignoring activities that may have long term benefit for the organization.

H2a: Greater the use of output controls, greater will be the incidence of dysfunctional behaviors.

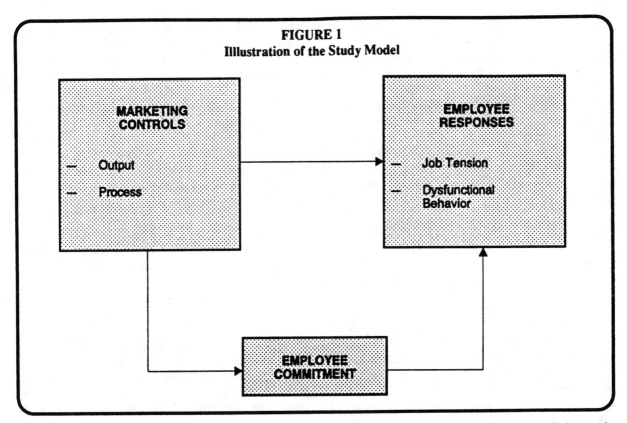

FIGURE 1
Illustration of the Study Model

MARKETING CONTROLS
— Output
— Process

EMPLOYEE RESPONSES
— Job Tension
— Dysfunctional Behavior

EMPLOYEE COMMITMENT

Use of process control has similar impact because of its strict requirement that a particular behavior be maintained. Thus:

H2b: Greater the use of process controls, greater will be the incidence of dysfunctional behaviors.

Controls and Employee Commitment

Research by sociologists (Etzioni 1975) and economists (Williamson 1975) has indicated that various forms of controls lead to differing levels of an employee's commitment toward the organization. Specifically, use of output control implies that employees must meet the specified performance goals, whatever way they choose to do so. Salancik (1977) indicates that when employees know what is expected of them, they tend to be more committed to the organization. The presence of output goals allows employees to get objective feedback on their performance and allows employees to feel responsible for achieving those goals.

H3a: Greater the use of output controls, greater will be the incidence of employee commitment toward the organization.

Use of process control, on the other hand, has a more complex impact on employee commitment. Use of process controls means that the managers evaluate employees on the means, behaviors, or activities that are thought to lead to a given outcome (Ouchi 1979). Total absence of process control means that managers have no idea about how an employee can carry out his/her job. Such a

working environment would lead to very little attachment to the organization. If, however, the managers are able to provide the procedural input and clarify roles, employees will develop attachment toward the organization. Excessive use of process control may, on the other hand, result in inflexible bureaucracy and limit employee flexibility and initiative (Hampton, Summer, and Webber 1978). If a supervisor takes an over-powering role in determining their subordinates' behaviors, the supervisor's presence may reduce the subordinates' perceived responsibility. For this reason, in fact, Chonko (1986) had recommended that managers can increase their employees' commitment by not closely monitoring their behaviors. Thus:

H3b: The relationship between process control and employee commitment is non-linear; employee commitment is likely to be low at the low and the high levels of process control and high at moderate levels of process controls.

Commitment and Negative Employee Responses

Higher commitment toward the organization implicitly assumes that employees have internalized the goals and values of the organization. This means that they take considerable responsibility for achieving the goals of the organization. Even though this may require additional work, they do not feel tense. In conditions where employees are not committed, research has found that they engage in considerable complaining and blaming if the goals are not achieved (Beck and Hillmar 1986). Such behaviors are usually a result of stress and frustration.

Thus:

H4a: Greater the commitment, lesser will be the incidence of job tension.

Internalization of goals and values induces a sense of what is fair and would, therefore, inhibit employees from engaging in any act that is not in the best interest of the organization. Research has shown that in situations where employee commitment is low, employees direct their energies toward coping with the output measures (Merchant 1990).

H4b: Greater the commitment, lesser will be the incidence of dysfunctional behavior.

Controls, Commitment, and Negative Employee Responses

The direct effects hypotheses indicated that both job tension and dysfunctional behaviors will be high when formal controls are high. A question this study attempts to address is how these effects are mitigated or strengthened by the effect of controls on employee commitment. Based on the arguments presented previously, we would expect that the effect of process controls on job tension and dysfunctional behavior will be strengthened. This is true because of negative effect of process control on commitment and negative effect of commitment on job tension and dysfunctional behaviors. On the other hand, the effect of output controls on job tension and dysfunctional behavior will be mitigated. This is true because of the positive effect of output control on commitment and negative effect of commitment on job tension and dysfunctional behaviors.

RESEARCH DESIGN

Sample and Data Collection

A survey questionnaire was developed with available measurement scales. After preliminary tests and some minor changes, the final questionnaire was mailed to a national sample of 1298 marketing personnel drawn randomly from a recent AMA roster. After two mailings, a total of 335 questionnaires were received. The usable sample turned out to be 1159 and usable questionnaires turned out to be 287, providing an effective response rate of 24.8 percent. A test for assessing the non-response bias, carried out using the procedure suggested by Armstrong and Overton (1977), suggested that non-response bias may not be a significant issue.

Measurement

The measurement scales for output control, process control, job tension and dysfunctional behaviors were drawn from Jaworski and MacInnis (1989). Due to the inadequate number of items in the job tension scale, it was expanded using items from a scale for job tension provided by Kahn, Wolfe, Quinn, Snoek, and Rosenthal (1964)[3]. The reliability coefficients for these scales were found to be 0.85, 0.85, 0.75, and 0.78, respectively.

Employee commitment was measured using the nine-item short-version of Porter, et al.'s 15-item measure (1974). A number of previous researchers have used this short version (Blau 1986; Reichers 1986). The coefficient alpha for this scale was found to be 0.90. The correlation matrix is presented in Table 1. High correlations between some of the variables casts doubt that multicollinearity may seriously impact the stability of parameter estimates. This was, however, tested by calculating variance inflation factors for each of the variables. The test was negative suggesting that multicollinearity is not be a serious problem here.

Analysis

The hypotheses were tested by estimating two recursive regression models. These include (1) job tension and dysfunctional behavior regressed against the two controls and employee commitment; (2) employee commitment regressed against the two controls. The beta coefficients and significance values for the different variables are reported in Table 2. The significant coefficients are used to estimate the indirect effects of controls on employee responses and are reported in the bottom part of this table.

RESULTS

The path coefficient results in Table 2 indicate that, contrary to the hypothesized expectation in H1a and H2a, output control has no significant effect on job tension (b = 0.044; p = 0.542) and dysfunctional behavior (b = 0.062; p = 0.375), respectively. Process control, on the other hand, shows the hypothesized positive effects (H1b and H2b) on job tension (b = 0.160; p = 0.020) and dysfunctional behavior (b = 0.184; p = 0.006), respectively.

The non-linear relationship hypothesized between process control and commitment was examined by introducing a quadratic term in the regression model. The incremental R-square was not found to be significant at the 0.05 level. Hence, the regression model between controls and commitment included only a linear term for process control. Results suggest that output controls have positive effect (b = 0.364; p = 0.000) on commitment, while process control shows no association (b = 0.021; p = 0.739) with commitment. These results support H3a, but do not support H3b.

Results also suggest that commitment does not influence job tension (thus not supporting H4a), but does have an inverse effect on dysfunctional behavior (thus supporting H4b).

TABLE 1
Correlation Matrix[1]

Variables	1	2	3	4	5
1 Output Control	0.85				
2 Process Control	0.55	0.85			
3 Job Tension	0.06	0.15	0.75		
4 Dysfunctional Behavior	0.07	0.17	0.22	0.78	
5 Employee- Commitment	0.37	0.20	-0.05	-0.19	0.90

[1] Diagonal entries include reliability coefficients.

Table 2

A. Standardized Parameter Estimates Using Ordinary Least Squares Method

Independent Variable	Dependent Variable								
	Employee Commitment			Job Tension			Dysfunctional Behavior		
	Beta	t	p	Beta	t	p	Beta	t	p
Output Control	.364	5.69	.000	.044	0.61	.542	.062	0.89	.375
Process Control	.021	.33	.739	.160	2.35	.020	.184	2.78	.006
Employee Commitment	-	-	-	-.069	-1.12	.262	-.239	-4.00	.000
R-Square	.141			.033			.077		
F-Value	24.84			3.39			18.37		
p	.000			.018			.000		

B. Direct and Indirect Effects of Controls on Employee Responses

Independent Variable	Dependent Variable					
	Job Tension			Dysfunctional Behavior		
	Direct Effect	Indirect Effect	Total Effect	Direct Effect	Indirect Effect	Total Effect
Output Control	-	-	-	-	-.087	-.087
Process Control	.160[1]	-	.160	.184	-	.184

[1] Only significant effects are reported.

DISCUSSION OF RESULTS

Controls and Negative Employee Responses

The study finds that though use of output controls didn't have any significant effect on increasing job tension and dysfunctional behaviors, process controls did. This result is in line with prior research which suggests that boundary spanning employees show lesser effectiveness with greater rules and procedures (Burns and Stalker 1961). The results clearly raise serious doubts about Lawler and Rhode's (1976) assertion that dysfunctional behavior is not necessarily a result of formal controls (p. 95).

Controls and Employee Commitment

The study finds that the use of output controls has positive effect on employee commitment, while use of process controls has no effect. The positive relationship between output controls and commitment suggests that employees consider availability of feedback about their work outcomes as salient for showing greater commitment toward the organization. This result supplements previous research findings that employees who have specific output goals tend to be more motivated than employees who have only broad definitions of their responsibilities (French, Kay, and Meyer 1966; Bryan and Locke 1967). The implication is clear that, for professional employees, managers should concentrate on achieving the clearest possible specification of output goals, rather than rely on exhorting employees to do well with vaguely defined objectives.

The lack of a relationship between process control and commitment indicates that they neither help nor hinder how people feel about and identify with their organization.

Commitment and Negative Employee Responses

The study finds that dysfunctional behaviors are less likely to occur when employees exhibit higher commitment toward their organizations. This relationship implies that an organization will get penalized for not developing a work environment that fosters greater commitment among its employees. Moreover, the significant coefficient implies that dysfunctional behavior can now be added to the repertoire of consequences of commitment that already includes variables such as turnover, intention to quit, absenteeism, etc.

Job tension, on the other hand, is unrelated to employee commitment, suggesting that commitment to the organization may not reduce tension-inducing stress on the job. Its importance to organizational designers derives from the argument that a positive attitude toward the organization is not sufficient to reduce feelings of tension on the job. This finding is consistent with previous findings that commitment to the organization may be unrelated to how marketing employees feel about their jobs (Ingram and Lee 1990). Tension on the job may possibly be effected by the satisfaction facets of the work environment such as the work itself, physical working conditions, extent of role ambiguity, etc.

Control, Commitment, and Negative Employee Responses

Results indicate that though output controls did not have any direct effect on job tension or dysfunctional behaviors, they had indirect influence on reducing dysfunctional behavior by invoking greater commitment toward the organization. This partially highlights the need for organizations to clearly specify goals and appraise employees of the progress they have made with respect to these goals on a continuous basis. Process controls, on the other hand, had significant direct effects. They don't seem to contribute to elicit positive employee responses like higher commitment and thus their impact is only negative for the employees.

CONCLUSIONS

The objective of this study was to develop a model for examining whether positive employee responses (employee commitment toward the organization) could mitigate the incidence of negative employee responses (job tension and dysfunctional behavior) of marketing controls. The empirical results, based on a survey of 287 marketing professionals, suggest that process controls lead to negative employee responses which cannot be mitigated by commitment. On the other hand, output controls did help reduce negative employee responses due to their ability to induce higher commitment toward the organization. These results provide useful and interesting insights on how marketing controls can enhance the commitment exhibited by employees toward their organization, and also suppress any negative reaction they may have to the controls imposed upon them.

Several key limitations of this study, however, should be noted. First, like most studies that depend on self-reported data, the results of this study may suffer from problems associated with common-methods variance. Second, the cross-sectional nature of the sample precludes causal conclusions. Third, the response rate for the study at 24.8 percent was somewhat low. Though the nonresponse bias analysis suggested that this response rate is adequate, more powerful tests are needed to ascertain that the study results can be generalized to the population of marketing professionals. Not withstanding these limitations, our study makes a unique and significant contribution to the control and organizational commitment literature.

ENDNOTES

[1] Output Controls are exercised when a given individual is evaluated in terms of the results of his or her performance relative to set standards of performance.

[2] Process Controls are exercised when managers attempt to influence how a given job is performed. It, therefore, centers on evaluating an individual in terms of the means, behaviors, or activities that are thought to lead to a given outcome.

[3] The scales can be made available upon request.

REFERENCES

Anderson, Erin and Richard Oliver (1987), "Perspectives on Behavior-Based Versus Outcome-Based Salesforce Control Systems," *Journal of Marketing*, 51 (October), 76-88.

Anderson, Paul F. and Terry Chambers (1985), "A Reward/Measurement Model of Organizational Buying Behavior," *Journal of Marketing*, 49 (Spring), 7-23.

Armstrong, J. Scott and Terry Overton (1977), "Estimating Non-Response Bias in Mail Surveys," *Journal of Marketing Research*, 14 (August), 396-402.

Beck, A.C. and E.D. Hillmar (1984), "What Managers Can Do to Turn Around Negative Attitudes in an Organization," *Management Review*, 73 (1), 22-25.

Blau, Gary J. (1986), "Job Involvement and Organizational Commitment as Interactive Predictors of Tardiness and Absenteeism," *Journal of Management*, 12 (4), 577-584.

Bryan, J.F. and E. A. Locke (1967), "Goal Setting as a Means of Increasing Motivation," *Journal of Applied Psychology*, 51, 274-277.

Burns, Tom and Graham M. Stalker (1961), *The Management of Innovation*. London: Tavistock.

Cammann, Cortlandt and David A. Nadler (1976), "Fit Control Systems to Your Managerial Style," *Harvard Business Review*, (January/February), 65-72.

Chonko, Lawrence B. (1986), "Organizational Commitment in the Salesforce," *Journal of Personal Selling and Sales Management*, 6 (November), 19-27.

Etzioni, A. (1975), *A Comparative Analysis of Complex Organizations*. New York, NY: Free Press.

French, J. R., E. Kay, and H. H. Meyer (1966), "Participation and the Appraisal System," *Human Relations*, 3-19.

Hampton, David R., Charles E. Summer, and Ross A. Webber (1978), *Organizational Behavior and the Practice of Management*. Glenview, IL: Scott Foresman and Company.

Hirst, Mark K. (1983), "Reliance on Accounting Performance Measures, and Dysfunctional Behavior: Some Extensions," *Journal of Accounting Research*, 21 (Autumn), 596-605.

Hopwood, Anthony (1974), *Accounting and Human Behavior*. London: Haymarket Publishing Ltd.

Ingram, Thomas N. and Keun S. Lee (1990), "Sales Force Commitment and Turnover," *Industrial Marketing Management*, 19, 149-154.

Jaworski, Bernard J. (1988), "Toward a Theory of Marketing Control: Environmental Context, Control Types, and Consequences," *Journal of Marketing*, 52 (July), 23-39.

_____ and Deborah J. MacInnis (1989), "Marketing Jobs and Management Controls: Toward a Framework," *Journal of Marketing Research*, 26 (November), 406-417.

Kahn, Robert L., Donald M. Wolfe, Robert P. Quinn, Jaap Diedrick Snoek, and Robert A. Rosenthal, (1964), *Organizational Stress*. New York, NY: John Wiley and Sons, Inc.

Lawler, Edward E. and John G. Rhode (1976), *Information and Control in Organizations*. Palisades, CA: Goodyear Publishing Company.

Merchant, Kenneth A. (1990), "The Effects of Financial Controls on Data Manipulation and Management Myopia," *Accounting, Organizations and Society*, 15 (4), 297-313.

Ouchi, William G. (1979), "A Conceptual Framework for the Design of Organizational Control Mechanisms," *Management Science*, 25 (9), 833-848.

Porter, Lyman W., Richard M. Steers, Richard T. Mowday, and Paul V. Boulian (1974), "Organizational Commitment, Job Satisfaction, and Turnover Among Psychiatric Technicians," *Journal of Applied Psychology*, 59 (October), 603-609.

Reichers, Arnon E. (1986), "Conflict and Organizational Commitments," *Journal of Applied Psychology*, 71 (3), 508-514.

Salancik, Gerald R. (1977), "Commitment and the Control of Organizational Behavior and Belief," in *New Directions in Organizational Behavior*, Barry M. Staw and Gerald R. Salancik, eds. Chicago, IL: St. Claire Press, 1-16.

Williamson, Oliver (1975), *Markets and Hierarchies*. New York, NY: The Free Press.

EVEN ROSES HAVE THORNS: FUNCTIONAL AND DYSFUNCTIONAL EFFECTS OF SALES CONTESTS ON SALES PERSONNEL

William H. Murphy, University of Wisconsin-Madison

ABSTRACT

Sales contests, short-term incentive programs designed to motivate sales personnel to accomplish specific sales objectives (Churchill, Ford, and Walker 1990), are widely used incentive tools used to direct salesperson efforts. Given the popularity of sales contests it is little wonder that they have received considerable attention in the trade and academic press.

From this attention we know that sales managers believe contests are effective at motivating salespeople and that contests apparently produce increases in contest-related sales goals. But do these short-term gains come with subtle yet significant costs? Hampton (1970) and others have suggested that peripheral salesperson responses may occur that have negative impacts on the company, customers and salespersons themselves. How prevalent are these responses? What conditions tend to make these responses more likely? Can management develop ways to counter these responses before harm results?

Whereas the focus of previous work has been on short term sales outcomes, this study focuses on the effects of sales contests on sales personnel. Specifically, this study examines the relationship between the attractiveness of a sales contest, captured in a construct called contest appeal, and the ensuing responses of salespersons (e.g., pursuit, neglect of other duties, lessening of cooperation, unprincipled behaviors). Definitionally, contest appeal represents a salesperson's predisposition to respond to a given sales contest. This predisposition arises from salespersons' perceptions about the clarity, competitiveness and difficulty, award valence, and goal appropriateness of the contest.

Additionally, since sales personnel are not likely to respond to a sales contest in the same way, this study also examines the extent to which the contest appeal-salesperson responses relationship is moderated by various individual and situational factors. These include personal factors (e.g., advancement desire, contest related self-esteem, customer orientation, intrinsic motivation) and situational factors (e.g., relationship to manager, super-visory involvement in the contest, organizational commitment).

To summarize, the following two questions are addressed: (1) How does contest appeal affect contest-related responses?; (2) What factors moderate the relationships between contest appeal and contest-related responses?

Main Effect Hypothesis

H1. As contest appeal increases, (a) pursuit increases, (b) neglect of other duties increases, (c) cooperation lessens and (d) unprincipled behaviors increases.

A Moderator Hypothesis

Advancement desire is associated with wanting to draw positive managerial attention. Sales contests provide an avenue for this attention. Thus, to gain the publicity value of winning, high advancement desire salespeople are more likely to pursue. Still, since most salesperson behaviors are outside the attention of management, peripheral responses are also more likely, leading high advancement desire salespeople to take more "liberties" with their behavioral responses.

H2. The effects of contest appeal on (a) pursuit, (b) cooperation, (c) neglect and (d) unprincipled behaviors will be greater under high advancement desire than under low advancement desire.

Contributions

The specific contributions of this research will be (1) managerial insights and direction for the design and implementation of more effective sales contests; (2) step towards the development of a theory base for understanding the effects of sales contests on salespersons; (3) theoretical step beyond the current "contests motivate" mentality; (4) theoretical change toward treating particular contest perceptions as components of a construct called contest appeal.

For further information please contact:
William H. Murphy
1155 Observatory Dr.
University of Wisconsin-Madison
Madison, WI 53706

A HIGH-TECHNOLOGY MARKETING CURRICULUM: AN ACADEMIC RESPONSE TO "WORLD-CLASS" INDUSTRIAL EVOLUTION

Roger Gomes, Clemson University
Gregory Pickett, Clemson University
Charles Duke, Clemson University

ABSTRACT

This paper suggests that the strategies being employed by American industry to regain its "world class" competitive stature result in basic changes in how organizations function. For the High-Technology business segment, these changes tend to result in an increase in the technical integration of the marketing function. The extensive cross-disciplinary expertise required by this technical integration argues for increased academic exposure to science and technology in education programs which train this segment's future marketing managers. To provide this training, universities should evaluate the market's changing needs and consider modifying curriculums.

This research surveyed the extent to which businesses agree that the work environment is changing, the direction of that change, and the response institutions of higher education might take to better equip new college marketing graduates to compete in tomorrow's business world. Particular attention was paid to the employers' views of the need for broadening the training of marketing graduates to include more than the AACSB mandated minimums in science and technology. Additionally, this study investigated employers' response to a proposed program to integrate business and science within a marketing education.

Data were collected for this study through telephone surveys of 600 firms that maintained a recruiting presence at a major southeastern university during the 1990-1991 academic year. Firms were qualified for participation in this investigation if their hiring efforts involved recruitment of recent college graduates for non-clerical entry-level marketing or sales positions.

Most of the firms in the sample felt that the marketing of their firm's products required a "high" level of technical expertise (44%) with only 14 percent indicating a "low" technical orientation. Over 86 percent of the sample agreed or strongly agreed that changes in the work environment would require more broadly trained college graduates in the future. Over 44 percent of the respondents felt that a "broader education" should incorporate more hands on experience for the students (39% listed "experience/internships" while 5% suggested "application-type" courses).

The major objective of this research involved the investigation of recruiters' responses to a proposed marketing curriculum reorientation toward a "technical" emphasis. A "technical marketing" concentration was briefly described to the respondents and they were asked a series of questions related to it. Specifically, this proposed technical option was defined for the sample as a program which would require that marketing students take "three business-to-business marketing courses and three technical courses in either engineering, the physical sciences, or the biological sciences in addition to the normal degree requirements."

Relatively strong support seemed to exist for a marketing concentration emphasizing technical issues. Over 75 percent of the sample strongly agreed or agreed that a person graduating with the proposed technical marketing concentration would have an advantage in marketing their firms products over a general marketing degree graduate. Additionally, almost 65 percent of the sample agreed that a technical marketing graduate would be able to sell their firm's products "at least as well" as someone possessing a technical science degree. Respondents seemed to agree that this type of program had the potential to add to a new employee's skill level beyond that which might be attained through job training alone. Finally, 61 percent of the sample agreed that the technical marketing degree would be an important decision factor in the hiring process for entry level marketing job applicants.

To some extent, marketers have always been considered "boundary spanners" operating across internal functional areas and across channel interfaces, but now the emphasis and contribution expectations are even greater. It has been posited that the integrated knowledge required by world-class marketing decision makers could best be developed by additional credit-hours of exposure to advanced material in technical areas. The survey results indicated that many recruiting decision makers agree.

For further information please contact:
Roger Gomes
Department of Marketing
Clemson University
Clemson, SC 29634

SALES MANAGEMENT COURSE DESIGN INCORPORATING STUDENT PREFERENCES

Khalid M. Dubas, St. John's University
Venkatapparao Mummalaneni, St. John's University

ABSTRACT

To better prepare our students for sales careers, we need to understand their needs and those of their employers. The courses that we teach should incorporate the needs and preferences of our immediate and ultimate customers, i.e., the students and their employers. Conjoint analysis is used to design two courses in sales management for the undergraduate and graduate students. Zufryden (1983) and Dubas and Strong (1992) describe and illustrate the use of conjoint analysis to incorporate student preferences in curriculum design.

In order to design an optimal course, five salient attributes of a course on sales management were identified through discussions with students and instructors. One attribute was measured at two levels while the other four were measured at four levels each. These attributes and their levels are: Course Content (Sales Mgt; Sales Mgt + Ethics; Sales Mgt + Selling Process; Sales Mgt + Ethics + Selling Process), Class Format (Lectures; Lectures + Cases; Lectures + Simulation; Lectures + Cases + Simulation), Teaching Aids (None; Guest Speakers;

employed either part-time or full-time. Six out of ten undergraduates and five out of ten graduate students had worked as a salesperson. Undergraduates had worked as a rep for about 3 years on average, while the graduate students had worked as a rep for about 4 years.

A conjoint analysis using linear additive model based on main-effects only was performed. The most preferred courses for the undergraduate and graduate students are listed in Exhibit 1. The attributes for the pooled model for the undergraduate students are ranked from the most important to the least important as follows: real world experience, teaching aids, assignments, class format, and course content. The attributes for the pooled model for the graduate students are ranked from the most important to the least important as follows: teaching aids, course content, assignments, class format, and real world experience.

Future research must explore the views of practicing sales executives and faculty members teaching courses in sales management. It is imperative that the preferences of the practitioners and faculty groups be identified for the

---

EXHIBIT 1
Attributes and Levels for the Most Preferred Courses

Class	Course Content	Class Format	Teaching Aids	Assignments	Real World Experience
Undergraduate	Sales Mgt	Lectures + Cases	Visual Aids + Guest Speakers	Projects With Company Information	A Day in the Field With a Salesperson
Graduate	Sales Mgt + Selling Process	Lectures + Cases + Simulation	Visual Aids + Guest Speakers	Projects With Library Research	No Field Trip

---

Visual Aids; Visual Aids + Guest Speakers), Assignments (None; Projects with Library Research; Projects with Company Information; Projects with Library Research + Presentations), and Real World Experience (A Day in the Field with a Rep; No Field Trip). A full-profile design was used based on five attributes. Sixteen profiles were used for model calibration and six profiles were used for cross-validation. Students were asked to evaluate each course concept against their ideal course.

The sample for this study was students enrolled in five different classes in sales management. A total of 71 questionnaires were filled out. There were 47 (32 males, 15 females) undergraduate students and 24 (17 males, 7 females) graduate students. Nine out of ten (43 students) undergraduates were in the 21-25 year age group while only 4 out of 10 (9 students) graduate students were in the same age bracket. All the remaining students were between 26-35 years of age. About 8 out of 10 students were

first group constitutes the ultimate consumers of our products (courses) and the latter is the producers. Whatever differences might exist among these multiple perspectives (of students, faculty and sales managers) must be reconciled or discussed at least, with a view to improving the product.

For further information please contact:
Khalid M. Dubas
St. John's University
Jamaica, NY 11439

MOVING MARKETING EDUCATION INTO THE NEXT CENTURY: RELEVANCY, COMPETENCY, AND MASTERY

Jeffrey Stoltman, Wayne State University
Attila Yaprak, Wayne State University
James Gentry, University of Nebraska

ABSTRACT

This paper focuses on the basic basic criticisms that students are not receiving relevant instruction, nor are they learning what is being taught. Changes presently being debated serve to frame the discussion, and we find sufficient justification to expand the current debate. Three levels of change (institutional, programmatic, and pedagogical) are discussed, and their interrelationships are identified. This perspective is based on literature regarding instructional design, instructional psychology, and the nature of human intelligence. We focus on how students learn and achieve levels of mastery (or expertise).

INTRODUCTION

There has been a steady stream of criticism directed at business education (cf. Deutschman 1991; Fuchsberg 1991). Large-scale studies by Porter and McKibben (1988) and the Graduate Management Admissions Council (see Fuchsberg 1990) have concluded that business schools are not producing what is needed: students are primarily number crunchers, weak on interpersonal, communication, and decision making skills; the curriculum and research activity of the professoriate is largely irrelevant to business practitioners; and there has been a failure to incorporate technological advances and global perspectives on business. There is also the belief that students have not been retaining what they are being taught. While the discussion has primarily focused on MBA programs, undergraduate programs and specific disciplines, such as marketing, are obviously implicated.

The attention given to business schools comes at a time when the entire educational system is being examined (Hirsch 1987; Governors' Report 1991). The evolution of this society and the U.S. economy has steadily moved toward the creation of what Drucker (1989) and others have called "knowledge workers." Drucker (p. 18) notes that "...knowledge is rapidly becoming our true capital base and premier wealth-producing resource." He feels that changes in the educational system responsible for creating this wealth have been slow to develop, and that several changes are required, including better teaching of both basic skills (verbal, mathematic, scientific) and general abilities to reason and make morally sound decisions. He has concluded that (p. 19): *"No educational system, not even the graduate business schools, tries to equip students with the elementary skills...the ability to present ideas orally and in writing, briefly, simply, clearly; the ability to work with people; the capacity to shape and direct one's own work, contribution and career..."*

A *zeitgeist* has been created by the face validity, persistency, and the cumulative strength of the criticism directed toward business education. There are fundamental issues that require sustained critical discussion and empirical study. There is no compelling evidence to support or refute the claims or counter-claims. There are unresolved practical and philosophical issues that require thoughtful response. In marketing, the response has been rather limited. The AMA Task Force Report (1988) and some of the commentary it provoked (cf. Garda 1988) has recognized this *zeitgeist*. Recommended changes in doctoral programs to address deficiencies in pedagogical training and ideas for achieving greater relevancy in the classroom and in research address the criticisms at a general level (cf. Ferrell 1990; Hair 1990; Mason 1990; Miller, Chamberlain, and Seay 1991; Woodruff and Cravens 1990). Examining the current discourse, the following requirements for marketing education emerge. Marketing education must: (1) be relevant. The substance of the educational experience must be of practical value; (2) create competencies which represent the "how," not just the "what" of marketing; (3) create a certain minimum level of competency which extends beyond awareness to include demonstrable levels of mastery and ability; and, (4) be integrated both internally (i.e., within and across the marketing program elements), and externally (within and across the entire educational experience).

Specific aspects of each of these requirements may be arguable, but agreement on the logic and the purpose of these orienting principles should be easy to reach. For example, Glazer's (1991) observations strongly support the need to take an integrative, rather than a functional perspective. What is not so easily accomplished is significant movement toward creating marketing programs that embody these principles. This would require a sustained and objective assessment of the many facets of the curriculum. Marketing educators must become full participants in this activity. There is a clear opportunity to help shape the issues, the criteria, and the directions that change will take. Importantly, pedagogical issues and the basic aspects of instructional design will need to be more specifically discussed. The purpose of this paper is to fuel critical discussion of these issues by marketing educators by providing a framework for this discussion. A critical mass is needed in order to marshall significant resources to be allocated to this effort.

There are clear signs that change is expected and that significant improvements are possible. Porter and McKibben (1988) feel that U.S. business will drift into the next century in a far weaker competitive posture unless there is a concerted and more purposeful effort to change, and Drucker (1989) sees one of our greatest assets presently at risk (see also Fuchsberg 1990, 1991). Whether business schools can do better is not really a matter of dispute. Most concede that we can be and are expected to do better. Recent reports discuss changes being made in the curricula of several business schools (see Blum 1991 for an overview; see also Bryne 1991; Konrad 1991; Main 1989; Narisetti 1991). However, there is a sense that change is not occurring rapidly enough or on a broad enough scale. Many also feel that these changes are not addressing fundamental issues. For example, Oviatt and Miller (1989) note the strong opinions regarding the irrelevancy of teaching and research stemming from, and contributing further to, a widening gap between practitioners and academicians. Though there are several plausible explanations for the "intransigence" of faculty, university culture is a significant factor. They observe that the influx of faculty with doctoral degrees, the heavy research orientation, and the emphasis on quantitative methods have created a culture "detached from the very activity that is their focus of study" (p. 308). In expressing a view that is shared by many, Mason (1990) sees the same developments of the past 30 years in a decidedly positive light.

Clearly, given the evolutionary status of the change occurring, there is ample opportunity to shape the debate. A diversity of viewpoints will enrich the debate considerably. Disagreements should be expected regarding the magnitude of the problem, the underlying causes, and the appropriate and viable responses. These differences of opinion are crucial because they will shape the boundaries of debate and will determine the strength of the effort to participate in the discussion and to implement change. Positive change will be more likely if a framework that contains a diversity of perspectives can be developed and employed in the coming debate. As noted in a recent *Wall Street Journal* report (1990, p. 1), "Better corporate training may serve as a stop gap. But ultimately the burden of change rests with our schools. While the debate rages about how change should come, almost everybody agrees that something has to be done. And quickly." The level of attention must increase and discussion must be focused on what the nature of the change will be. Accordingly, a more expanded view of the possible changes in marketing curricula is introduced here.

FOCUSING THE DISCUSSION REGARDING CHANGE

The following discussion is organized around two deceptively simple, but vital questions that a wider audience of academics and practitioners must begin to discuss on a sustained and critical basis. First, what should we examine or consider changing? Second, what should we change to? These questions must be taken up or others will be deciding for us. Already there are legislative initiatives to mandate certain types of programmatic changes in the educational system, including competency-based assessments (cf. Miller, Chamberlain, and Seay 1991).

As to the first question — what to examine and consider changing — the position advocated here is that every aspect and every layer of the curriculum must be considered. The lessons, modules, intra- and inter-module and course sequences, the range of course offerings, the programs of study — everything related to basic aspects of pedagogy as well as the educational mission of a university must be audited. Fundamentally, this inquiry must be better informed by the principles and methods of instructional design and instructional psychology. The second question — what to change to — tests whether there has been a full examination of not only what we teach, but also how we teach. Anything less than a systemic appraisal of each of these issues risks leaving in place certain features (constraints, policies, etc.) that may doom any given initiative to at least some measure of failure. As argued below, the changes being discussed do not take this systems view.

Current discussions of business education reform are preoccupied with the question of "what" we should teach. The views appear to be shaped by a dated and narrow model of learning. By taking up the companion question "how should we teach" necessary improvements will be more likely, and the bottom-line question that emerges from the criticisms will come into focus: *How do students learn what it is we decide is worth teaching?* We do not believe that business educators have chosen to employ outdated models of learning. Rather, because of inadequate training and the low relative importance given to teaching, there isn't a sound basis for keeping abreast of the changes in education. Hopefully, this discussion can help address this situation as well.

WHAT TO CHANGE AND CHANGE TO: ANALYSIS OF SOME CURRENT INITIATIVES

There has not been any consensus on the two driving questions posed here, but the responses that some schools have been discussing and/or implementing provide a good starting point. It is important to note that there have been corresponding concerns about the need for change and the type of change. Exhibit 1 presents a synthesis of recent reports of both changes and the resistance to these initiatives (see Blum 1991; Bryne 1991; Konrad 1991; Main 1989; Narisetti 1991). It may be safe to assume that these innovations represent effective responses to the criticisms that have been raised. The prestige of the institutions involved should not be discounted; some have clearly devised a strategic response to the critics and the educational needs of the corporate sector as a way to take (or maintain) their place among the elite schools (cf. Konrad 1991; Narisetti 1991). It appears that most schools examine their present program offerings (content areas), survey their constituencies (e.g., corporate recruiters, students, faculty), and make changes based on various resource and operating constraints. The changes represent a good faith effort to respond to the concerns of critics.

Change is occurring slowly and in a fragmented manner. In part, this is because there are many obstacles to change, in part because a unifying set of issues and criteria have not been developed. Importantly, most of the remedies seem to reflect a general level of analysis. Thus, there is an open question as to whether these changes will be sufficient or effective. A number of more specific problems can be identified. First, it is apparent that the types of change noted above are not systemic and tend to be piecemeal. Primarily, only MBA programs are targeted for change, leaving continuing problems in other areas. Additionally, the institutions involved are only making some of these changes. Secondly, the changes are basically substitutions in the curriculum. The fundamental assumptions and the design of a curriculum do not appear to be tested or changed.

Third, on a more fundamental level, these changes do not insure greater relevancy or better learning. For example, when international marketing is made a required course, there is no indication that this achieves the goal of providing students with relevant, usable knowledge in this area. Simply exposing students to certain domains or experiences provides no assurance that the information is learned, retained, or ready to be applied in decision contexts. Clearrly, exposure is a neccessary but not sufficient condition for learning to take place. A fourth, related, set of issues pertain to the tradeoffs that are being made. Without an expansion in the number of classes and/or faculty, other coursework has become expendable. The interests of the faculty can easily be threatened by such changes and, in the absence of evidence that the changes will achieve the desirable objectives, resistance can be expected. Finally, there is no indication that these changes will establish the broad, general knowledge and abilities pertaining to critical thinking, informed judgment, and effective communication. The changes being contemplated do not focus on the enhancement of performance competency that stems from fluid abilities such as synthesizing, generating

creative solutions, or efficient response to complex situations (cf. Bloom et al. 1956). Thus, a dual problem is created: The foundation upon which we presume to build professional expertise will be hollow and we will have failed to respond to the basic criticisms raised.

Clearly, there are a number of other options available to those interested in revising a curriculum. One is to shift the obligation to other phases of the students' educational program (e.g., general education requirements) or to post-graduate and on-the-job training experiences. An alternative is to take these requirements into the marketing curriculum, i.e., devise lessons and programs that will instill and nurture mastery of general knowledge and abilities, thus achieving greater relevance and providing a basis for effective job performance and life-long learning. This is the view advanced below. Importantly, however, the effort must extend beyond claims or rhetoric. The era that is upon us requires evidence that such aims are being successfully managed, i.e., that we are, in fact, getting the job done (see Miller et al. 1991). We now turn our attention to various levels of response that represent a continuum from macro to micro-learning issues. The greatest gains are expected to be found at the micro end of this continuum. It is in this area that performance is most readily assessed and remedied.

Institutional Options: Attempts to implement change must overcome the powerful counter-force of inertia, as well as several specific problems that have been noted (see Cheit 1985; Oviatt and Miller 1989; Porter and McKibben 1988), including: the misalignment of the corporate and academic cultures; the fact that teaching is of low institutional value on many campuses; the vested interest of the faculty who have prospered in the present context; and difficulty deciding which areas of breadth and depth of coverage are essential, and whose turf will be challenged. Institutions, can elect to wait for the forces of change to gain sufficient momentum. Some may prefer to give the appearance of change and/or participate in providing direct opposition to any such notions. Retreating to discussions about a "lack of empirical evidence," shifting the blame to various other facets of the educational system (primary and secondary schools, liberal arts, other functional areas, or departmental colleagues), or to the students themselves, are all responses we have observed. These attitudes and obstacles will be encountered, but should not be regarded as just cause for failing to act or settling for compromise solutions.

Changes in the institutional culture are conceivable and desirable (cf. Cheit 1985; Hair 1990; Mason 1990). Reportedly, the AACSB is moving in this direction by requiring greater explicit recognition of the importance of teaching, requiring doctoral students to be trained in instructional design, and by requiring significant movement toward co-operative education requirements (see Mason 1990). Additionally, there must be institutional

```
╔══════════════════════════════════════════════════════════════════════════════╗
║                                   EXHIBIT 1                                     ║
║                       Anticipated Changes and Counterpoints                     ║
║                                                                                 ║
║   Changes                                  Counterpoints                        ║
║   Incorporate new material                 Some of the changes are superficial, cosmetic ║
║   Introduce new specialities               The changes dilute the offering, no focus ║
║   Emphasize certain domains                In flexibility, we lose consistency, structure ║
║   Emphasize certain skills                 The changes are reactive              ║
║   Evaluate student & tailor program        The changes divert resources and attention ║
║       to strengths and weaknesses              fundamentals (blocking and tackling) ║
║   Integration - across time periods and    The changes are short-term, will create problems ║
║       across different contexts.               planning and in teaching loads   ║
║   Integration - across functional areas    The changes are short-term and faddish ║
║   Develop smaller program modules                                               ║
║   Develop extended programs (e.g. re-certify)                                   ║
║   Introduce/Increase Experiential Components                                    ║
╚══════════════════════════════════════════════════════════════════════════════╝
```

value attached to research focused on matters of pedagogy and marketing practice. Faculty members are still required to maintain a high level of research productivity, and many make direct tradeoffs between teaching and research. Often, teaching effort is reduced in favor of what Haynes (1991) calls "academically fashionable" research. While research on pedagogy may not be able to attain equal status, it can certainly be given far greater weight in performance reviews and funding decisions.

Eventually, the attitudes of marketing academics will need to change as well. Institutional change is slow to occur and complicated by many other issues; it is not generally an arena that faculty members choose or are permitted to operate in. Professors will need to find intrinsic rewards until these institutional changes come about. Within their span of control, professors can bring about "grass roots" changes by focusing on the gap between themselves and the practitioner community, participating in faculty internships, bringing practitioners into the classroom, etc. (cf. Ferrell 1990). In general, the changes that are more readily implemented by individual educators are probably best accomplished at the program and pedagogical levels of response.

Program-Level Options: Programmatic responses have not been systemic. Selected facets of the curriculum are revised and the common change is to offer new specialties or emphasis. The institutional culture and the pedagogical features of the curriculum tend to remain intact, and new programs or emphases will tend to be less effective and may appear opportunistic. Significant programmatic change requires that all aspects of the present curriculum be examined. The examination would include both obvious candidates for change as well as those that appear to be or are regarded as "untouchable." This includes all courses, course sequences, concentrations, and other features (such as capstone courses, or the insistence on a case format). The operating constraints,

policies, assumptions, untested philosophies, and our own belief systems that produced the current program can certainly be challenged. Deficiencies can only be addressed if they are subjected to critical analysis, and the analysis must include mundane matters of pedagogy, i.e., to the matter of instructional design. If instructional design principles are followed, far greater attention will be given to the basic question "how do students learn best." This question should assume a central place in future discussions of changes in the programs of a business curriculum.

Drucker (1991, p. 19) identifies a programmatic level of response that is not evident in options presented in Exhibit 1 (above): "...we must discard the notion that schools can teach students everything they need to know through life. Instead, educators must recognize that learning is now a lifelong process...the most pressing task is to teach people how to learn" (emphasis added). This idea is echoed by Haynes (1991, p. 4), who notes that: "Business challenges are always changing. If management education is to be of real use to companies in future, it will (like many of those companies) have to undergo radical restructuring. It will have to move...towards what might be called 'continuous learning'." Whether this is truly programmatic, or rises to the level of an institutional change, is arguable. We place it here because it is a transition issue; it links the institutional level of analysis with the pedagogical level of analysis.

Pedagogical Changes: The focus on both "what" we should teach and "how" we should teach is far and away the most significant change that can be made. To understand how people learn (a requirement if we are to teach them how) we will need to recognize the different levels and types of learning that humans are capable of. Hirsch (1987) demonstrated the value of two general shifts in pedagogy. The first requires us to distinguish between declarative (content) knowledge — knowledge of facts, concepts, terms, etc. — and procedural (process) knowledge — knowledge of what to do and how to do it. Business students should be expected to develop both. Second, Hirsch (1987) persuasively demonstrates how these aspects of knowledge are intertwined. Knowledge of the world (cultural literacy) provides the foundation for "know how." The strength of each type of knowledge, and of their integration, provides a foundation for effective functioning in society and for continuous learning. Several additional steps are also in order.

We must begin to accommodate the diversity of talents and learning styles (or paces) that students possess (cf. Drucker 1989; Finn 1990; Haynes 1991). As Sternberg (1986) notes, the concept of learning styles can help to explain why students exposed to the same programs of education often retain different knowledge. Additionally, given the a paradigm shift already taking hold in education, we must begin to focus on measuring progress and providing specific feedback to our students: *"Under the new definition, now struggling to be born, education is the result achieved, the learning that takes root when the process has been effective. Only if the process succeeds and learning occurs will we say that education happened. Absent evidence of such a result, there is no education — however many attempts have been made, resources deployed, or energies expended"* (Finn 1990, p. 586). This emphasis is evident in the increasing pressure to perform outcome assessments (see Miller et al. 1991; Woodruff and Cravens 1990). Third, and most importantly, each student must be assisted in reaching a desired level of competency. This requires an adjustment to their interests and learning styles. Presently, students are required to adjust to our programs and pedagogy, and the initiatives being discussed still reflect this outdated notion. Caution should be exercised, however, because we must adjust to learning styles an help students learn how they will need to adapt to corporate culture.

INTEGRATION FOR MEANINGFUL CHANGE IN CURRICULA

Three concepts can be examined as a means to integrate the preceding discussion. A detailed discussion of each concept can be found in the instructional design and instructional psychology literature (cf. Gagne and Dick 1983; Gagne and Bassok 1989). First, we must begin to make specific use of design principles. Design principles help to operationalize the systems orientation and recognize the central principles of types, levels, and styles of learning. As discussed in Gagne and Briggs (1979), instructional design separates program and pedagogical features. Following a detailed analysis of the concepts, skills, and tasks to be mastered, the status of essential and supporting prerequisite concepts and skills is determined. Then, with considerable latitude guided by the central principles, the instructor develops a specific plan constructed around issues such as the number and

nature of instructional events, the role of various instructional media, the number of repetitions, the time on task, the sequence of tasks, the role of the learner and the teacher, the degree and timing of feedback, and the amount of active participation required.

A second way to integrate change is to emphasize mastery and competency (and the related notions of assessment and feedback). These are also central principles in contemporary design theories (see Gagne and Dick 1983). Significantly, current views support the idea that mastery can be achieved by focusing on the use of knowledge, i.e., application (cf. Perkins 1986). The third basis for integrated change in the curriculum is to focus on recent developments regarding the nature and acquisition of practical intelligence and expertise (cf. Ford 1986; Sternberg and Wagner 1986). Many of the changes the critics have called for are embodied in these related concepts.

In Neiser's (1976) view, formal education stresses "academic intelligence," which differs from the intelligence required for performance in natural settings. The latter consists of "responding appropriately in terms of one's long-range and short-range goals, given the actual facts of the situation as one discovers them" (p. 137). While, business education moves a step closer to the real-world requirements than, say, a liberal arts education, the critics are challenging how close we have come in this regard. Significant attention must be given to the specific facets of practical intelligence if we are to begin making meaningful changes in the marketing curricula. The best approach to identifying facets of practical intelligence is on a case- or context-specific basis. A point of entry will be useful, and we suggest application of the conceptual and operational scheme provided by Wagner and Sternberg (cf. Wagner and Sternberg 1985).

Based on a number of developments in cognitive and developmental psychology, these authors propose that practical intelligence can be analyzed both in terms of its scope and its structure, and there are three basic dimensions which they have delineated. Content can pertain to managing oneself, others, or tasks. All three areas are of importance, and competency should be demonstrated in each area. Many of the more recent criticisms, and the changing nature of the business environment clearly identify the need to focus specifically on managing (or simply working with) others. Context is either local (short- range, self-contained), or global (long-range, big picture). This facet of the framework provides a means to begin examining and addressing the criticism that MBA students are preoccupied with short-term consequence at the expense of long term advantages. Orientation (representing both a behavioral and a motivational force) can be either idealistic or pragmatic. To isolate these dimensions, we must become involved in the challenging and complex task of exploring the knowledge demands of real-world job settings. Many avenues can be taken, including practitioner involvement in course design, depth interviews with practitioners, case studies, and faculty internships. Our ability to deliver programs of importance and our ability to assess progress in this regard depends on the navigation of this fundamental step.

Another useful distinction supersedes the concept practical knowledge, namely the difference between an expert and a novice. Experts not only know what to do, but they are able to do it. Glaser and Bassok note (1989, p. 635): *"Novices can know a principle, or a rule or a specialized vocabulary without knowing the conditions of effective application. In contrast, when experts access knowledge, it is functional or bound to conditions of applicability. Moreover, experts' knowledge is closely tied to their conceptions of the goal structure of the problem space. Experts and novices may be equally competent at recalling specific items of information, but experts chunk these items in memory in cause and effect sequences that relate to the goals and the sub-goals of problem solution and use this information for further action. The progression from declarative knowledge to well-tuned functional knowledge is a significant dimension of developing competence."*

From our view, as we begin to identify what should be learned and how it will be learned, critical guidance is provided by the fundamental question: "How do we bring about and measure the progression or transition from novice to expert?" In this question, one implicitly acknowledges two things. First, that gradations exist, and second, that a progression is identifiable and important. The transition or progression from declarative to procedural knowledge has been mapped and studied under several headings such as reasoning (Galotti 1989; Hunt 1989; Nummendal 1987; Rips 1990), analogical transfer (Glass and Holyoak 1986; Halpern 1987; Holyoak 1984), and problem solving (cf. Mayer 1987). Each represents a basic skill that critics have claimed is lacking in business school graduates. Self-regulatory competencies also seem to distinguish experts from novices: "The experience of experts enables them to develop executive skills for monitoring performance; they rapidly check their work on a problem, accurately judge its difficulty, apportion their time, assess their progress, and predict the outcomes of their performance..." (Glaser and Bassok 1989, p. 641). The skills involved are implicated both in the process of knowledge acquisition, and in the process of knowledge application. In the latter case, what is at issue is the individuals' ability to stay on top of things as the learning experience unfolds. It believed that individuals differ in their ability to monitor, and that this ability can be improved through several instructional methods (see (Glaser and Bassok 1989, and Pintrich, et al. 1986). Thus, greater attention to differences between novices and experts can offer great insights into more responsive curricular change.

CONCLUSION

The range of issues introduced here is summarized in Exhibit 2. Using these parameters to assess the scope of the marketing curriculum a sound basis for meaningful and effective change can be discovered. These parameters can be tailored to meet the situation faced by a specific institution and can provide a coherent framework for scholarly debate and research. The systems view will permit interested parties to become aware of the interrelationships among various issues and to acknowledge the obstacles to optimal performance. The following questions can be derived from the framework that emerges: *Will the change achieve learning is beyond the level of awareness? Will knowledge applicability be achieved? Will students learn when to transfer and apply certain knowledge? Will a problem solving orientation be learned? Will the diversity of learning styles be accommodated?* Such questions present challenges that are quite unlike the ideas in Exhibit 1.

EXHIBIT 2
Parameters of A Framework for Assessing Marketing Curricula

Levels of Analysis: Institutional, Programs, Pedagogy
Foci: Breadth vs Depth Tradeoffs
Core vs Peripheral Knowledge
Knowledge-Of vs Know-How
How to Learn — Types and Levels
Instructional Design
How to Learn — Process
Fulfilling Requirements of Relevance and Integration Via:
Recognition of Levels of Human Learning
Preparation for Life-Long Learning
Recognition of Learning Styles / Individual Differences
Pedagogy that Establishes Progression from Competency to Mastery
Pedagogy Based on Practical Intelligence
Pedagogy that Develops Expertise
Pedagogy that Requires and Fosters Self-Regulated Competencies

---

Clearly, there is nothing sacred about the types of changes being discussed. They have not diffused widely or rapidly, and some regard them as "hazy and fragile" (see Oviatt and Miller 1989). What is needed is a sustained, critical discussion of the kinds of questions raised here. Alternative ways of accomplishing alterations in the present curriculum should be examined. Relevance provides a one-word directive for both institutional and programmatic change. However, relevance is only going to be insured if we study and facilitate learning itself, including the concept of learning styles. That is, the micro-issues that have not been encountered in previous debates must be attended to. Additionally, assuming a systems orientation is clearly warranted, at least in the examination phase. This perspective, shaped by the principles and methods of instructional design, will bring to light the fundamental flaws in the current curriculum. By seizing the initiative during this period of heightened awareness and by participating in the discussions and raising the level of debate marketers can help shape the landscape of business education. Programmatic study can help clarify the issues, help us achieve consensus on assessment issues, etc., but the definition of permissible research and publication activity needs to be changed. Research should focus on measuring and explaining the best way to ensure that we are delivering on the requirements of marketing education: relevance, competency, and mastery. We should begin to study how learning

occurs. How knowledge is acquired and how it is applied must become keystones of our pedagogy as well. Finally, by zeroing in on practical intelligence we can instill the interpersonal and general problem solving skills that students are expected to have. We see the failure to achieve meaningful education in each of these areas as being indisputable. Significant room for improvement exists as the gap between what is and what might becomes into greater focus.

REFERENCES

AMA Task Force (1988), "Developing, Disseminating, and Utilizing Marketing Knowledge," *Journal of Marketing*, 52 (October), 1-25.

Bloom, B.S., M.D. Englehart, E.D. Furst, W.H. Hill, and D.R. Krathwohl (1956), *Taxonomy of Educational Objectives: The Classification of Educational Goals*. New York: David McKay Company.

Blum, Debra E. (1991), "Business Schools Rush to Revise Curricula in Response to Critics and Competition," *Chronicle of Higher Education*, (December 4), A23, A28-29.

Bryne, John A. (1991), "Wharton Rewrites the Book on B-Schools," *BusinessWeek*, (May 13), 43.

Cheit, Earl G. (1985), "Business Schools and Their Critics," *California Management Review*, 27 (3), 43-62.

Deutschman, Alan (1991), "The Trouble With MBAs," *Fortune*, (July 29), 67-78.

Drucker, Peter F. (1989), "How Schools Must Change," *Psychology Today*, (May), 18-20.

Ferrell, O.C. (1990), "Improving Marketing Education in the 1990s: A Faculty Perspective," *Marketing Education Review*, 30-33.

Finn, Chester E. (1990), "The Biggest Reform of All," *Phi Delta Kappan*, 585-592.

Ford, Martin E. (1986), "For All Practical Purposes: Criteria for Defining and Evaluating Practical Intelligence," in *Practical Intelligence*, Robert J. Sternberg and Richard K. Wagner, eds. London: Cambridge University Press.

Fuschberg, Gilbert (1991) Under Pressure, Business Schools Devise Changes, *Wall Street Journal*, (April 23), B1 + B3.

_____ (1990), "Business Schools Get Bad Grade," *Wall Street Journal*, (June 6), B1-2.

Gagne, Robert M. and Leslie J. Briggs (1979), *Principles of Instructional Design*. New York: Holt, Rinehart and Winston.

_____ and Walter Dick (1983), "Instructional Psychology," *Annual Review of Psychology*, 34, 261-295.

_____ and Miriam Bassok (1989), "Learning Theory and the Study of Instruction," *Annual Review of Psychology*, 40, 631-666.

Galotti, Kathleen M. (1989), "Approaches to Studying Formal and Everyday Reasoning," *Psychological Bulletin*, 105 (3), 331-351.

Garda, Robert A. (1988), "Comment," *Journal of Marketing*, 52 (October), 32-41.

Gardner, Howard (1983), *Frames of Mind: The Theory of Multiple Intelligences*. New York: Basic Books.

Glaser, Robert and Miriam Bassok (1989), "Learning Theory and the Study of Instruction," *Annual Review of Psychology*, 40, 631-666.

Glass, Arnold L. and Keith J. Holyoak (1986), *Cognition*, 2nd Ed. New York: Random House.

Glazer, Rashi (1991), "Marketing in an Information-Intensive Environment: Strategic Implications of Knowledge as an Asset," *Journal of Marketing*, 55 (October), 1-19.

Governor's Report (1991), *Time for Results: The Governors' 1991 Report on Education*. Washington DC: National Governors' Association.

Guilford, J.P. (1967), *The Nature of Human Intelligence*. New York: McGraw-Hill.

Hair, Joseph F. (1990), "Improving Marketing Education in the 1990s: A Chairperson's Perspective," *Marketing Education Review*, 23-29.

Halpern, Diane F. (1987), "Analogies as a Critical Thinking Skill," in *Applications of Cognitive Psychology: Problem Solving, Education, and Computing,*, D.E. Berger, K. Pezdek and W. Banks, eds. Hillsdale, NJ: Lawrence Erlbaum Associates, 75-86.

Haynes, Peter (1991), "Management Education," *The Economist*, (March 2), 3-26.

Hirsch, E.D., Jr. (1987), *Cultural Literacy: What Every American Needs to Know*. Boston: Houghton Mifflen

Holyoak, Keith J. (1984), "Mental Models in Problem Solving," in *Tutorials in Learning and Memory*, J.R. Anderson and S.M. Kosslyn, eds San Francisco: W.H. Freeman, 193-213.

Hunt, Earl (1989), "Cognitive Science: Definition, Status and Questions," *Annual Review of Psychology*, 40, 603-629.

Konrad, Dennis (1991) "Can Tennessee Put Its B-School on the Map?" *BusinessWeek*, (March 11), 74.

Main, Jeremy (1989), B-Schools Get a Global Vision, *Fortune*, (July 17), 78-86.

Mason, J. Barry (1990), "Improving Marketing Education in the 1990s: A Dean's Perspective," *Marketing*

Education Review, 10-22

Mayer, Richard E. (1987), "Learnable Aspects of Problem Solving: Some Examples," in *Applications of Cognitive Psychology: Problem Solving, Education, and Computing*, D. E. Berger, K. Pezdek, and W. Banks, eds. Hillsdale, NJ: Lawrence Erlbaum Associates, 109-122.

Miller, Fred, Don Chamberlain, and Robert Seay (1991), "The Current Status of Outcomes Assessment in Marketing Education," *Journal of the Academy of Marketing Science*, 19 (4), 353-362.

Narisetti, Raju (1991), "Business Schools Revamp to Win Students,"*Wall Street Journal*, August 21, B1 + B4.

Neisser, Ulrich (1976), "General, Academic, and Artificial Intelligence," in*The Nature of Intelligence*, L. Resnick , ed. Hillsdale, NJ: Lawrence Erlbaum Associates, 135-144.

Nummendal, Susan G. (1987), "Developing Reasoning Skills in College Students," in *Applications of Cognitive Psychology: Problem Solving, Education, and Computing*, D. E. Berger, K. Pezdek and W. Banks, eds. Hillsdale, NJ: Lawrence Erlbaum Associates 87-97.

Oviatt, Benjamin M. and Warren D. Miller (1989), Irrelvance, Instransigence, and Business Professors, *Academy of Management Executive*, 3 (4), 304-312.

Perkins, D.N. (1986), *Knowledge as Design.* New Jersey: Lawrence Erlbaum Associates.

Pintrich, Paul R. David R. Cross, Robert B. Kozma and Wilbert J. McKeachie (1986), "Instructional Psychology," *Annual Review of Psychology*, 37, 611-651.

Porter, Lyman W. and Lawrence E. McKibbin (1988), *Management Education and Development: Drift or Thrust into the 21st Century?*, New York: McGraw-Hill.

Rips, Lance J. (1990), "Reasoning," *Annual Review of Psychology*, 41, 321-353.

Sternberg, Robert J. (1986) *Intelligence Applied.* San Diego, CA: Harcourt Brace Jovanovich.

_____ and Richard K. Wagner (1986), *Practical Intelligence*, London: Cambridge University Press.

Wagner, Richard K. and Robert J. Sternberg (1985), "Practical Intelligence in Real-World Pursuits: The Role of Tacit Knowledge," *Journal of Personality and Social Psychology*, 49 (2), 436-458.

Wall Street Journal (1990), Education, (February 9), 36 page Special Section.

Woodruff, Robert F. and David W. Cravens (1990), "Challenges for Graduate Marketing Education in the Twenty-First Century," *Marketing Education Review*, 34-44.

HOW ACCURATE ARE THE "SURVEY OF BUYING POWER" PROJECTIONS?

W. E. Patton, III, Appalachian State University

ABSTRACT

The study reported here examines the accuracy of the projections published in *Sales and Marketing Management* magazine's "Survey of Buying Power". The study compares demographic and economic projections for 1990 with the actual 1990 figures in the aggregate and for a sample of 367 Metropolitan Statistical Areas and counties. Results indicate that the SBP demographic projections and projections in the aggregate are very accurate, but projections for economic variables and for individual areas are not as accurate and accuracy varies by region of the country.

INTRODUCTION

For over six decades, the "Survey of Buying Power" (SBP) has been published by *Sales and Marketing Management* magazine, and it has become of the most widely recognized sources for demographic data in the country. In the seventies, Charles Waldo and Dennis Fuller (1977) speculated that nearly all marketers were familiar with the SBP, and furthermore the SBP was one of the primary sources of demographic data for use in planning and forecasting. These statements continue to be true in the 1990's.

Many principles of marketing and marketing research texts of the 1980's and 1990's feature the "Survey of Buying Power" as widely available and widely used, particularly in developing marketing plans for consumer goods companies (cf Tull and Hawkins 1987; Parasuraman 1986; Kotler and Armstrong 1989; and Churchill 1991). The applications suggested for the SBP range from identifying target markets and allocating advertising funds (Tull and Hawkins 1987) to measuring inter-market retail sales flows (Young 1990). Other uses for the data in the Survey of Buying Power include store location analysis (Lusch and Dunne 1990), sales territory identification and assignment (Wotruba and Simpson 1989) and developing estimates of market potential and sales forecasts (Stanton, Buskirk, and Spiro 1991). Each issue of the "Survey of Buying Power" provides examples of the use of the data for these and other applications.

Of particular value in forecasting and estimating future market potentials are the five year projections included in the Survey's "Part II" (Now the "Survey of Media Markets") published by *Sales and Marketing Management* in the fall of each year. These projections for population, number of households, retail sales, effective buying income (EBI) and Buying Power Index (BPI) are particularly important in attempts to identify the relative attractiveness of markets and relative market potentials for the future (Levison and Delozier 1989).

While the SBP appears to be a widely accepted tool with many applications, questions arise from time to time about just how accurate the figures in the SBP are. In one of the few independent examinations of the accuracy of SBP, Waldo and Fuller (1977) discovered that the SBP data was quite accurate indeed, at least in the case of current population estimates. In fact, Waldo and Fuller found the SBP 1975 population figures to be even more accurate than the SBP users thought they were. The users surveyed felt that an error range of 10 percent from actual was acceptable, but the authors found the SBP to be generally much more accurate than that.

The Waldo and Fuller study is now 15 years old, and it only examined current estimates rather than projections. Since then, however, *Sales and Marketing Management* magazine has conducted two studies of its own to examine (and promote) the accuracy of its projections. In 1985 the magazine found that its population projections for 1983 (made in 1979) were quite accurate (Kern 1985). The total 1983 population for the United States had been under-predicted by less than 2 percent, and most population projections for regions and states were well within the plus-or-minus-10 percent acceptance range.

The magazine conducted another such study in 1987, expanding the study to include an examination of the accuracy of the projections for Effective Buying Income (EBI) and Retail Sales as well as projections of population ("Projections" 1987). The study compared the projections for 1986 (made in the 1982 SBP) with the 1986 actual figures, and found the population projections to be even more accurate than in the previous study. Unfortunately, the projections for EBI and Retail Sales were well wide of the target - many of the income estimates were off by over 20 percent (one as much as 44%) and the retail sales projections were even worse. The article addressed these problems and warned readers about the problems in projecting sales and income.

It has now been nearly five years since *Sales and Marketing Managements'* own assessment of the accuracy of its projections, and nearly fifteen years have passed since Waldo and Fuller's independent assessment of SBP accuracy. Furthermore, the latest "Survey of Buying Power" (1991) now includes data for 1990 updated from the 1990 census. It would appear that now is an appropriate time for another assessment of the accuracy of the "Survey of Buying Power's" projections, and in particular to examine just how good the projections for 1990 were.

The purpose of the study reported in the remainder of this paper is to conduct just such an examination of the accuracy of the SBP projections for 1990 that were published back in 1986. The study compares the projections with the census-updated 1990 actual figures and thus replicates the *Sales and Marketing Management* study of 1987 to some extent. The study then goes a step further by examining the accuracy of the projections for a sample of metro areas and counties instead of just the aggregates for states, regions, and large markets.

METHOD

The projections of population, number of households, total effective buying income (EBI), total retail sales, and the Buying Power Index (BPI) for 1990 were taken directly from the 1986 "Survey of Buying Power: Part II" (SBP:II 1986). The actual 1990 figures for these same variables were taken from the 1991 "Survey of Buying Power" (SBP 1991) which included the 1990 census updated figures.

First, data was collected for the total United States, for each of the nine major regions adopted by the "Survey of Buying Power," the nine largest states, and the nine largest metro markets. Then a random sample of 367 Metropolitan Statistical Areas (MSA's) and counties for which projections were made was drawn from the 1986 "Survey of Buying Power." The sample was selected in a manner that precluded "double-counting" of counties imbedded withing MSAs. This sample was then matched unit-for-unit with the 1991 "Survey of Buying Power to assure that all units were included in each survey and included the same geographical areas in both surveys.[1] The result was a matched-pairs, repeated measures design that included 117 MSA's and 250 counties.

Before data comparison was conducted, the 1990 figures for Effective Buying Income (EBI) were adjusted to reflect a 1989 modification in the composition of EBI. The adjustment involved the treatment of pension contributions and imputed interest and rentals and resulted in an approximate 11 percent reduction in the EBI figures after 1989, and the 1990 figures were adjusted appropriately to reflect the change. Then raw differences and percentage differences between projections and actual figures were calculated, with the percentage variation expressed as a percentage of the 1990 actual figures.

Finally, the MSA's and counties were rank ordered on each of the variables for the projection and actual figures. The rank order projected and the actual rank orders were then compared, and raw differences were calculated to measure the shifts in rank ordering between projected and actual 1990 rankings.

FINDINGS

Accuracy of Aggregate Projections

The analysis of the accuracy of the aggregate 1990 Survey of Buying Power (SBP) for the total United States, the nine regions, the nine largest states, and the nine largest metro markets is shown in Table 1 which shows the percentage variation between the SBP projections and the actual figures for population, total Effective Buying Income (EBI), and total retail sales.

The data in Table 1 suggests that the Survey of Buying Power population projections for 1990 are all within the plus-or-minus 10 percent acceptable range suggested by Waldo and Fuller (1977). The projection for total 1990 U.S. population was within 1 percent of the actual census-supported figures, and 21 of the 27 other population projections were within plus-or-minus 5 percent. The only troublesome areas seemed to be the West South Central (off by 9%), which includes Texas (off by 7%) and, of course, Houston (off by 9.2%).

The projections for 1990 Effective Buying Income and total retail sales were not nearly as accurate as were the projections for population, but the projections for total EBI for the entire country was well within the 10% acceptable range, as were 75 percent of the regional, state, and metro projections for EBI. The projections for retail sales were well off the mark, however, with only two of the projections within 10 percent of the actual 1990 sales figures, and these two were just barely within the acceptable range.

Two general patterns emerge from the data in Table 1. One pattern is that in virtually all cases, the population projections are considerably more accurate than are the projections for EBI and retail sales, and the EBI projections are typically more accurate than those for retail sales. The other pattern is that regional, state, and metro market projections are not universally as accurate as are the projections for the country as a whole and there tends to be an increase in variability as the projections move from macro to micro.

Finally, there also appear to be some strong regional differences in prediction accuracy. The predictions for the West South Central region (including Texas and Houston) are typically the most troublesome in accuracy, followed by predication for the Mountain region. Projections seem to have been generally most accurate for the Middle Atlantic region (New York, New Jersey, and Pennsylvania).

---

[1] The author gratefully acknowledges the efforts of John Ketner and Karsten Schroer in collecting the data.

American Marketing Association / Summer 1992

TABLE 1
Analysis of Accuracy of Aggregate SBP Projections: Percentage Variation Between SBP Projections and Actual Figures*

		Population	Total Effective Buying Income (EBI)	Total Retail Sales
Total U.S.		+0.9%	7.5%	+15.4%
Region:	New England	-2.1	+2.2	+16.1
	Middle Atlantic	+1.3	+1.0	+11.5
	East North Central	+0.7	+11.3	+13.3
	West North Central	+2.7	+14.1	+23.6
	South Atlantic	-1.3	+3.6	+12.9
	East South Central	+3.8	+13.6	+15.5
	West South Central	+9.0	+25.7	+24.5
	Mountain	+4.6	+17.1	+25.4
Big States:	California	-5.4%	-2.1%	+14.4
	New York	+1.4	+0.7	+11.4
	Texas	+7.0	+23.5	+24.8
	Florida	-2.4	+2.9	+10.9
	Pennsylvania	+1.7	+4.2	+10.5
	Illinois	+3.0	+10.3	+9.4
	Ohio	-0.4	+11.7	+20.0
	Michigan	-0.7	+11.6	+11.7
	New Jersey	+0.7	-2.2	+13.0
Big Metros:	New York	-3.7%	-0.3%	+21.6
	L.A./Long Beach	-0.3	-2.4	+14.0
	Chicago	+1.6	+10.6	+9.9
	Philadelphia	-0.1	+1.2	+16.9
	Detroit	-0.8	+7.8	+13.3
	Boston	-1.4	+1.5	+24.6
	Washington, DC	-7.1	-1.4	+17.8
	Houston	+9.2	+28.9	+31.5
	Nassau/Suffolk, NY	+6.5	+3.2	+10.6

*Calculated by comparing projections for 1990 published in 1986 *SMM Survey of Buying Power Part II* with figures for 1990 published in 1991 *SMM Survey of Buying Power*. Plus figures indicate that the projection was higher than the actual figures and vice versa.

Accuracy of Projections for Sample MSA's and Counties

Table 2 presents a basic analysis of the accuracy of the *Survey of Buying Power's* projections for 1990 for the 367 MSA's and counties randomly selected for this study. The table shows the percentage of projections that fell within each of the variation categories indicated. Projections for the number of households and the Buying Power Index are included in addition to projections for population, total Effective Buying Income, and total retail sales.

The projections for population and number of house-

holds are reasonably accurate, with a mean absolute variation of under 6 percent and a vast majority of the projections falling within plus-or-minus 10 percent of the actual 1990 figures. It should be noted, however, that while none of the aggregate population projections shown in Table 1 were outside the 10 percent "acceptable" range, fully 15 percent of the projections for individual MSA's and counties were wrong by more than 10 percent.

The projections for the EBI and retail sales for the sample MSA's and counties indicate some serious problems with accuracy. The <u>majority</u> of projections for each variable were off by more than 10 percent, the average

TABLE 2
Analysis of Sample Data: Variation of SBP
Projections for 1990 from Actual 1990 figures

Percentage of Sample Projections in Each
Variation Category (n=367)

Percent Variation*: Projection vs. Actual	Population	No. of House-Holds	Total Effective Buying Income	Total Retail Sales	Buying Power Index
			Variable Projected:		
Over + 20%	1.4%	2.5%	23.4%	29.6%	5.7%
+15.01% to 20.0%	4.1	2.5	10.4	14.2	3.8
+10.01% to 15.0%	6.0	6.5	14.2	15.6	8.5
+5.01% to 10.0%	18.3	17.7	17.2	9.5	12.3
0% to 5.0%	23.4	26.4	13.4	11.2	19.9
-0.01 to -5.0%	27.2	27.8	11.4	6.0	23.1
-5.01% to -10.0%	15.5	12.0	4.9	5.4	15.0
-10.01 to 15.0%	3.3	2.7	3.0	3.5	8.7
-15.01 to -20.0%	0.3	0.8	1.4	2.8	1.9
More than -20% Variation	0.5	1.1	0.8	2.2	1.1
Percentage within +/- 10%	84.4%	83.9%	46.9%	32.1%	70.3%
Mean Variation	1.41%	1.50%	10.63%	14.82%	1.43%
Mean Absolute Variation	5.87%	5.93%	13.44%	18.88%	8.00%
T-Test Probability**	.489	.305	<.001	<.001	.010

*Plus figures indicate the 1990 projection was higher than the actual 1990 figures and minus figures indicate that the 1990 projection was under the actual 1990 figures

**Probability generated from application of pairwise T-Test for repeated measures, comparing projected with actual figures

error in prediction was well above the acceptable range, and a significant proportion of the projections were wide of the mark by over 20%. In addition to a substantial error rate, there is an obvious upward bias in the projections since the vast majority of the projections over-predicted the Effective Buying Income and retail sales for the sample MSA's and counties.

Not surprisingly, the accuracy of the projections of the Buying Power Index (BPI) for 1990 falls somewhere in between that of the projections for population and for

EBI and retail sales, since these three elements are utilized in generating BPI. The relative accuracy of the survey in projecting demographics is obviously offset by the serious problems in projecting the economic variables, and the accuracy of the BPI projections was thus diminished to the point that nearly 30 percent of the projections were more than 10 percent away from the actual 1990 BPI ratings.

The effects observed in Table 2 appear to hold regardless of whether the projections are for full Metro-

TABLE 3
Analysis of Sample Data: Variation of SBP 1990 Projections from 1990 Actual Figures by Region

REGION	PERCENTAGE OF 1990 PROJECTIONS WITHIN PLUS OR MINUS 10% OF 1990 ACTUAL FIGURES					MEAN PERCENTAGE VARIATION*					MEAN ABSOLUTE PERCENTAGE VARIATION				
	POP.	HSHLDS	EBI	SALES	BPI	POP.	HSHLDS	EBI	SALES	BPI	POP.	HSHLDS	EBI	SALES	BPI
N. EAST	100.0%	100.0%	100.0%	46.2%	84.6%	-2.8%	-2.0%	-0.4%	+13.8%	-4.9%	3.8%	3.7%	4.0%	13.8%	5.2%
MID. ATL.	93.2	95.5	79.6	52.3	68.2	+1.2	+1.9	+1.8	+6.0	-5.0	4.0	4.3	6.9	9.3	6.7
E.N. CNT.	92.3	96.9	32.3	27.7	84.6	+0.8	+1.0	+13.9	+13.4	+2.0	4.1	3.8	14.1	17.5	5.7
W.N. CNT.	84.2	71.0	31.6	21.0	65.8	+0.8	-0.6	+12.4	+14.6	+2.6	6.3	6.6	15.4	17.8	7.9
S. ATL.	89.0	92.7	57.3	30.5	75.6	-.06	-2.0	+5.5	+13.7	-1.7	5.4	5.7	9.4	15.7	7.0
E.S. CNT.	82.9	91.4	31.4	20.0	80.0	+2.6	+1.5	+12.7	+14.3	+3.2	5.5	5.0	14.4	21.0	6.3
W.S. CNT.	53.9	48.7	5.1	23.1	33.3	+10.5	+10.4	+29.4	+30.0	+15.8	11.1	11.1	29.4	33.9	16.9
MTN.	70.0	65.0	35.0	15.0	60.0	+3.8	+5.5	+17.4	+19.7	+6.6	8.3	8.8	19.4	22.6	9.9
PACIFIC	87.1	83.9	77.4	64.5	70.9	-3.5	+1.5	+2.1	+12.2	-4.5	6.3	6.1	8.5	15.7	8.3
TOTAL SAMPLE	84.5%	83.9%	46.9%	32.1%	70.3%	+1.4%	+1.5%	+10.6%	+14.8%	+1.4%	5.9%	5.9%	13.4%	18.9%	8.0%

*Plus figures indicate that the 1990 projection was higher than the actual 1990 figures and vice versa.
NOTE: All anova probabilities testing for differences among regions in mean percentage variation and mean absolute percentage variations were <.001. All Chi-Square probabilities testing for differences among regions in proportions within +/-10% were <.0001.

TABLE 4
Analysis of Sample Data: Differences in Rank Order Between SBP Projections for 1900 and Actual 1990 Rank Order

Percentage of Sample in Each Rank Order Difference Category

DIFFERENCES IN RANK ORDER	Population	Number of Households	Total Effective Buying Income	Total Retail Sales	Buying Power Index
More than +10 Places	5.7%	7.4%	13.4%	18.5%	10.4%
+6 to +5 Places	12.8	10.1	11.2	9.0	12.0
+1 to +5 Places	28.3	30.5	21.5	21.3	25.6
Same Rank	11.7	10.1	9.3	6.5	9.8
-1 to -5 Places	27.0	25.9	18.3	18.0	21.8
-6 to -10 Places	7.9	10.1	13.6	9.5	11.4
More than -10 Places	6.5	6.0	12.8	17.2	9.0
Percentage within +/- 5 Places	67.0%	66.5%	49.1%	45.8%	57.2%
Percentage within +/- 10 Places	87.7%	86.7%	73.9%	64.3%	80.6%
Mean Absolute Variation Rank	4.9	5.1	8.0	9.5	6.6
T-Test Probability*	<.001	<.001	<.001	<.001	<.001

*Probability generated testing the mean absolute variation in rank against a zero mean variation.

politan Statistical Areas (MSA's) or counties (All p >.45), but there are significant differences in the accuracy of the projections by region. Table 3 presents an analysis of the SBP 1990 projection accuracy by region and includes the proportion of projections within the plus-or-minus 10 percent range, the mean percentage variation, and the mean absolute percentage variation (disregarding direction of error).

The patterns in Table 3 mirror to a large extent the patterns that were evident in the aggregate projections shown in Table 1. As suspected, there are significant variations in projection accuracy among the nine regions of the country. Projections for the Northeast and the Mid-Atlantic are typically quite accurate across the board, as are most of the projections for the Pacific region. Again, the real problem appears to be in the projections for the sample units in the West South Central, although there are also problems in projections for other areas such as the Mountain region.

It should be noted that although the Survey's projections for the total population of the nation was within 1 percent, and the projection for 1990 Total EBI was within 7-1/2 percent, this level of accuracy is not even closely approximated for the sample MSA's and counties in several regions of the country. Although projections for the West South Central are certainly the least accurate, one can take little solace in the fact that 35 percent of the projections for the number of households are off by more than 10 percent or that only 20 percent of the retail sales projection for the MSA's and counties in the East South Central are within the acceptable range.

The patterns in Tables 2 and 3 mirror the patterns identified in Table 1 in that the projections for the economic variables are considerably less accurate than those for the demographic variables. This tendency has been recognized by *Sales and Marketing Management* magazine on a number of occasions, and the producers of the projections have taken great care to warn readers that the numbers are projections and not forecasts and that the economic projections are particularly susceptible to error ("Projections" 1987). The Survey and others have regularly warned readers that the projections may well be off and that users should compare markets relatively rather than absolutely (cf. Lewison and Delozier 1989, SBP 1991). This suggests the need for the analysis of projected market rankings presented in the following section.

Accuracy of Projected Relative Rankings

Tables 4 and 5 present an analysis of the differences between the rank orderings of the 367 MSA's and counties in the sample. The analysis is similar to that presented in Tables 2 and 3 in the previous section except that simple rank orderings are utilized rather than raw data, and the difference measure is stated in terms of rank order "places" rather than percentage difference from actual. For example, if a MSA projected to be in 95th place in

1990 actually emerged in 100th place, the difference would be 5 places rather than 5 percent.

The data in Table 4 suggests that considering projections in relative terms rather than absolute terms does not remove the problem of error in projection, but it does make the amount of error a bit more consistent across variables. The proportion of ranks that were the same in 1990 as projected is quite low regardless of the variable under consideration, and there is no significant difference among the variables in the proportions of MSAs or counties that were ranked the same in 1990 as predicted. It would also seem that at least a third, and as many as a half, of the MSA's and counties would be mis-ranked by more than five positions, and well over 10 percent were mis-ranked by more than 10 places.

As with the accuracy of the raw projections, the accuracy of rank order projections differed significantly by region, with the exception of the rank order projection accuracy for retail sales. Table 5 contains the analysis of rank order projection accuracy by region.

The patterns exhibited in Table 5 should be familiar by now. Again, it appears that the projections for the West South Central are the most troublesome, followed by some of those in the Mountain region. Also, it appears that the accuracy of ranking projections for EBI and retail sales seems to more closely approximate the accuracy of the demographic projections than was the case with the absolute projections. Finally, projections seem more accurate in the populous Northeast, Mid-atlantic, and East North Central regions.

In even the best regions, however, there appears to be a substantial proportion of the MSA's and counties that are mis-rated by more than five places - and some of these mis-rankings can be substantial. For example, the projection for Oklahoma City's EBI ranked it 17 places higher than it actually achieved in 1990, and the projection for the Santa Barbara MSA's retail sales was overprojected by 30 places. Relying on projected rankings or projected relative positions obviously does not remove the risk of some substantial error, and this error may be more severe in some regions than others.

Summary of Findings

The answer to the question "How accurate are the 'Survey of Buying Power's' projections?" is: It depends. The projections for the demographic variables in the aggregate are quite accurate. One can generally rely on the projections for population and households for the total U.S. and its nine regions to be within the acceptable 10 percent margin of accuracy. The accuracy is considerably less for the economic variables (EBI and retail sales) and for the Buying Power Index. Furthermore, the accuracy is considerably lessened when projections for individual MSA's and counties are examined. Finally, pro-

TABLE 5
Analysis of Sample Data: Variations in SBP 1990
Projected Rankings and Actual 1990 Rankings by Region

	Percentage of 1990 Projected Rankings within Plus or Minus Five Ranks of Actual 1990 Rankings						Mean Absolute Variation Between Projected 1990 Ranking and Actual 1990 Rankings				
Region	Pop.	No. of Hshlds	Total EBI	Total Retail Sales	Buying Power Index		Pop.	No. of Hshlds	Total EBI	Total Retail Sales	Buying Power Index
N.East	76.9%	61.5%	53.8%	69.2%	61.5%		3.54	3.77	8.15	5.46	4.62
Mid. Atl.	68.2	79.5	40.9	50.0	59.1		3.34	3.66	8.07	7.82	5.84
E.N. Cnt.	78.5	76.9	56.9	38.5	63.0		3.69	3.86	5.88	9.75	4.85
W.N. Cnt.	68.4	68.4	39.5	44.7	65.8		5.00	5.21	8.21	8.42	6.11
S. Atl.	65.8	60.9	51.2	51.2	56.1		5.04	5.48	7.30	7.26	6.10
E.S. Cnt.	65.7	71.4	68.6	48.6	74.2		4.60	4.23	4.89	9.37	4.06
W.S. Cnt.	41.0	38.5	15.4	33.3	35.9		7.97	8.23	13.77	15.67	12.41
MTN.	70.0	65.0	45.0	50.0	45.0		6.30	7.15	9.95	11.55	9.20
Pacific	58.1	70.9	54.8	41.9	48.4		5.10	4.97	8.68	11.10	7.94
TOTAL SAMPLE	67.0	66.5	49.1	45.8	57.2		4.88	5.11	7.97	9.48	6.59
PROBA-BILITIES*	.0013	.0044	.0037	.3894	.0443		.0098	.0316	.0001	.0706	.0009

*Probabilities resulting from Chi-Square test for differences in proportions within +/-5 ranks and Kruskal-Wallis analysis of variance for differences in mean absolute variation in rank.

jection accuracy differs sharply depending upon the region of the country under consideration. It would appear that projections for regions may "wash out" many of the errors that may be embedded within the regions, but projections for the "oil patch" may be so affected by the volatile energy-related economies that the errors are not "washed out" but compounded instead.

CONCLUSION

As Waldo and Fuller (1977) concluded, "SBP isn't 'Holy', but it does deserve its place on the market researcher or planner's bookshelf." That statement is still true. This study has shown that the projections published by the "Survey of Buying Power" are more likely to be accurate within an acceptable range than not. In the aggregate and for large areas, the demographic projections are remarkably accurate. As long as the user doesn't need exact figures for precise markets, the projections can be quite accurate and quite useful.

But let the user beware. As the publishers of the

survey themselves point out, the projections are just that: Projections. They are not forecasts and the projections for the economic variables are subject to a larger number of factors than are the demographic variables and thus subject to more chance for error. Similarly, projections for large, inclusive areas tend to cancel out many errors in individual smaller units. Blind reliance on precise projections for individual metro or county markets is inviting trouble.

Instead, users of the "Survey of Buying Power: Part II" (now the "Survey of Media Markets") projections should do so with the understanding that the projections may vary sharply in accuracy, depending on the part of the country, the variable under consideration, and other factors. A check of the "track record" for the last several projections for the markets of interests (using the same methods used in this study, perhaps) may well point out problems in accuracy or conversely give the user additional confidence in the projections.

Finally, the worst thing a marketing planner or

market researcher can do with the "Survey of Buying Power" is to ignore it and leave it in the bookshelf. The SBP is not perfect and does not pretend to be, but it can be extremely useful if used with an understanding of its strengths and weaknesses.

REFERENCES

Churchill, G.A. (1991), *Marketing Research*. Chicago: Dryden Press.

Kern, R. (1985), "How We Do It, And How Well," *Sales and Marketing Management,* (July 22), A7-A20

Kotler, P. and G. Armstrong (1989), *Principles of Marketing*. Englewood Cliffs, NJ: Prentice Hall

Lewison, D. M. and M. W. DeLozier (1989), *Retailing*. Columbus, OH: Merrill Publishing Co.

Lusch, R.F. and P. Dunne (1990), *Retail Management*. Cincinnati, OH: South-Western Publishing.

Parasuraman, A. (1986), *Marketing Research*. Reading, MA: Addison-Wesley.

"Projections: Just how reliable are they?" (1987), *Sales and Marketing Management*. (October 26), 8-38.

Stanton, W. J., R. H. Buskirk, R. L. Spiro (1991), *Management of a Sales Force*. Homestead, IL: Irwin.

"Survey of Buying Power: Part II" (1986), *Sales and Marketing Management,* (October 27).

"Survey of Buying Power" (1991), *Sales and Marketing Management,* (August 19).

Tull, D. J. and D. I. Hawkins (1987), *Marketing Research*. New York: MacMillan Publishing.

Waldo, C. and D. Fuller (1977), "Just How Good is the Survey of Buying Power?," *Journal of Marketing,* (October), 64-66.

Wotruba, T. R. and E. K. Simpson (1989), *Sales Management,* Boston: PWS-Kent.

Young, M.R. (1990), "Measures of Intermarket Retail Sales Flows," *Progress in Marketing Thought,* Orlando, FL: Southern Marketing Association, 363-365.

THE STRATEGIC PRICING CENTER: INTEGRATING CUSTOMER, COMPETITOR AND COMPANY INFORMATION IN THE PRICING DECISION

Robert R. Harmon, Portland State University
Thomas R. Gillpatrick, Portland State University

ABSTRACT

One of the most vexing problems facing multi-line manufacturing companies is how to price components in a highly competitive market environment. Frequently, fullservice component manufacturers participate in markets that are characterized by highly diverse segments ranging from lowvolume custom manufactured components to highvolume commodity products. The segments may be characterized by widely diverse customer needs, organizational size, purchasing behavior, volume and delivery requirements and sensitivity to price. Often, because of competition, prices are set in a rather fluid manner and vary not only between segments but within segments over time.

The complexity of the pricing decision demands coordinated information sharing and concerted effort between marketing, engineering and manufacturing to ensure the implementation of effective pricing strategy. Although a growing body of literature has looked at the various aspects of the marketing, engineering, and manufacturing interface in the innovation process (Gupta et. al. 1986; Moenaert and Souder 1990a,b; Hise et al. 1990; Souder 1988; Gupta and Wilemon 1988a,b), the nature of their roles in the pricing process remains largely unexplored. It is the purpose of this article to discuss how marketing, engineering, and manufacturing as participants in the pricing process, can, through the use of techniques such as economic value to the customer (EVC) analysis, competitor analysis, value engineering, design for manufacturability and Quality Function Deployment (QFD) concepts, contribute to the development of effective pricing strategies. The concept of the "pricing center" is introduced as the organizational framework for the development of pricing strategy.

THE PRICING CENTER

The three major inputs to pricing strategy are customer and market analysis, competitor analysis, and cost analysis. Input from marketing, engineering, manufacturing, and accounting should be considered in each pricing decision. Individuals from these functional areas, in addition to corporate or division management, that share responsibility for the price decision-making process are members of the pricing center of the firm. From a company perspective, the members of the pricing center constitute a team that shares common goals and risks arising from the pricing decision. Effective pricing will contribute to the attainment of organization and individual goals, while improper pricing can result in missed sales opportunities, reduction in profitability and mispositioning in the market. It is important to recognize that the pricing decision is a process that has several players. The size and composition of the pricing center will vary depending on the factors such as the: type of product, size of firm, industry, and importance of the product to the firm. The organization of the pricing center will vary depending on whether the firm is product cost-driven or market-driven in its approach to the pricing decision (Nagle 1987; Abell 1980).

The product cost-driven approach leads to a focus on cost-based pricing such as markup pricing and target return pricing. The price decision maker, perhaps the accounting manager or division general manager, views the product configuration as given and not subject to change. The goal is to set the price at a level to recover costs and provide a desired return. This cost-oriented approach is simplistic since there is no provision for customer input, competitive information, or an understanding of how price relates to value. Costs are indicative of whether a product can be sold at a profit, but yield no information on what margin buyers will be willing to accept (Monroe 1990; Nagle 1987).

The market-driven pricing center might feature the marketing manager as the principal price decision maker. Market information on price-value relationships and competitor positioning are used to develop potential pricing strategies. This information is then integrated with the cost information in order to determine whether the product can be profitably sold at the specified price. Product features are viewed as being subject to change. Market information allows engineering to adapt the product configuration to better match customer demand (Nagle 1987).

Of particular interest is the roles played by marketing, engineering and manufacturing in the pricing process. Each function can influence the final price. Engineering and manufacturing can influence price internally through the impact of product design and manufacturing processes on costs. Marketing's influence is primarily through its knowledge of how the customer perceives value and how competitors are positioned on price. The use of this information by engineering can influence costs as products are adapted to market requirements (Cooper and Kaplan 1988). We also discuss briefly the role of the accountant in the pricing process. The choice of cost accounting method may greatly impact the representation of product costs.

Quality Function Deployment

A management approach known as QFD is a set of management and communications procedures that facilitate the coordination of effort between marketing, engineering and manufacturing in order to ensure that goods are designed, manufactured and marketed to meet identified customer needs. The inter-disciplinary nature of the QFD team mirrors the functional needs of the pricing center. With the addition of the accounting function, QFD provides an excellent framework for supporting the pricing decision process. Market-driven pricing strategy is dependent on customer perceptions of value. The object of QFD is to deliver quality through improved product value and customer satisfaction. Fortuitously, these results are key to gaining differential competitive advantage and influencing the price the customer is willing to pay.

QFD also focuses on the cost side of the pricing equation. It can provide a vehicle for implementing value engineering, design for manufacturing, and other cost-saving strategies. Combined with activity-based costing, the QFD framework has the potential to provide better cost data for supporting pricing decisions. As a vehicle for integrating the market and cost information necessary for effective pricing, the QFD process holds great promise for institutionalizing the interfunctional cooperation and communication necessary for carrying out the pricing center's activities.

CONCLUSION

The development of effective pricing strategy in the highly competitive market environments faced by most component suppliers has become an issue that is central to the firm's viability. With the evolution toward more customer-driven approaches to pricing strategy, the benefits of a coordinated multidisciplinary approach to pricing are becoming more pronounced. The pricing center is a concept that facilitates cooperation and coordination of efforts by marketers, engineers, manufacturers, and accountants that are relevant to the development of effective pricing strategy. Product-cost based pricing strategies are naive in that they are silent on the critical issues of customer perceptions of value and competitor market positions. Market-driven pricing strategies, although conceptually more justifiable from a marketing perspective, are silent on product costs and profit considerations. It is the integration of these two approaches, through the workings of the pricing center, that should provide the firm with the framework for profitably delivering customer satisfaction. The QFD process provides a useful model which can be extended to support the integrated decision making necessary in the development of effective price strategy. More research is needed on how the structure of the pricing center may change under different product/industry situations.

For further information please contact:
Robert R. Harmon
School of Business Administration
Portland State University
P.O. Box 751
Portland, Oregon 97207

USING PERSONAL INVESTMENT THEORY AS A BASIS FOR MARKETING STRATEGY

Jason W. Gray-Lee, University of Utah
Kent L. Granzin, University of Utah

ABSTRACT

Maehr and Braskamp's Personal Investment Theory (PIT) suggests that people invest personal time, energy, and finances to gain anticipated benefits. This study investigates the efficacy of adapting for marketing strategy Maehr and Braskamp's PIT model within the context of fitness-related market choices. We focus on the fitness industry because of its intensely competitive and volatile nature and the clear connection between exercise-related investment and long-term benefits.

PIT holds that people are motivated to invest in certain courses of action because of the meaning they have derived from a situation that requires a behavioral choice. Thus, to understand the choices people make, it is important to understand what meaning they derive from the decision situation and the antecedent forces that influence that meaning. In the model, Meaning comprises the components of Personal Incentives, Sense of Self, and Perceived Options, which PIT maintains determine the behavioral choice one makes from the set of available, alternative courses of action. Meaning is influenced by five antecedent components: Social Expectations, Task Design, Personal Experiences, Information, Age/Lifestage, and Socio-cultural Context.

Personal Incentives for exercise and purchase of fitness-related products and services may be Task, Ego, Social, or Health incentives, or Extrinsic Rewards. Second, the Sense of Self affects investment through the constructs of Sense of Competence, Goal-directedness, Self-reliance, and Social Identity. Third, Perceived Options represents the effect on investment caused by Perceived Barriers to and Perceived Opportunities for exercise-related behavior.

Data came from a quota sample of 213 adult residents of a major western metropolitan area. Trichotomous measures of exercise and fitness-related apparel expenditures, and importance ratings on six purchase criteria served as three criterion variables. Composites formed from 6-point Likert scales operationalized the fifteen PIT constructs functioning as the continuous explanatory variables. Although not reported here, demographic measures operationalized Age/Lifestage and Socio-cultural Context.

Discriminant analysis, supplemented by univariate ANOVA, suggested that twelve of the fifteen predictor variables were important contributors to explaining exercise participation. First, individuals' exercise habits are directly related to past experience and perceptions of health status and physical ability. Second, individuals exercise to the degree that they enjoy exercise, perceive opportunities, and are task motivated and goal-directed. Third, those who are socially motivated tend to exercise heavily or not at all.

Marketing managers should be able to enhance long term markets by creating opportunities for customers to acquire experience. The appropriate marketing mix should focus on supporting identifiable extensions of customers' past experiences and reinforced perceptions of opportunities and ability to perform and enjoy the exercise task while developing new skills and reaching personal goals. For some customers, the marketing mix should also highlight social benefits.

The second discriminant analysis tested the proposed relationship between exercise clothing expenditures and the same predictors. Twelve variables were important to the function and univariate tests and indicated that expenditures were positively related to increased long-term, internally-motivated commitment, competence, and awareness of opportunities for goal achievement. Interestingly, Light, but not Heavy, purchasers are better characterized by exercise enjoyment and belief in and value of the efficacy of exercise for improving health.

These results, when compared with the previous analysis, reaffirm the importance of experience, perceived competence, and opportunities. Marketing strategies aimed at increasing sales to customers more likely to purchase higher ticket items should target individuals who are already active, informed, and consider themselves competent; should capitalize on established social networks; and should enhance perceptions of opportunities for exercise activities. Strategies should also consider light purchasers who enjoy exercise and its health benefits.

A canonical correlation examined the proposed relationship between a set of importance ratings for seven clothing purchase criteria and the same predictors. Here, the social and other-directed aspects of motivation are strongly related to customers' purchase decision criteria. This finding suggests that there is an identifiable segment of exercise apparel purchasers who are heavily dependent upon others for incentives, approval, and identity and who also place higher value on brand, attractiveness, and others' advice. Promotion strategies for these customers should feature the security and social acceptance benefits resulting from purchase of attractive and identifiable brands.

These analyses provided several important implications. First, all PIT constructs were important contributors to understanding results from at least one analysis, giving evidence of the model's applicability to the study of fitness-related market behavior. Second, PIT provides a means by which marketers can identify current and potential market segments. Third, PIT yields information which can be used to develop marketing strategies.

For further information please contact:
Kent L. Granzin
David Eccles School of Business
University of Utah
Salt Lake City, Utah 84112

MARKETPLACE DIFFERENTIALS AND THEIR IMPACT ON MARKETING INFORMATION SYSTEMS

David J. Good, Central Missouri State University
Robert W. Stone, Georgia Southern University

ABSTRACT

The premise of this paper is to examine operational Marketing Information Systems (MkIS) as they are influenced by different environmental constraints. The study includes a survey of 131 marketing managers' perspectives of the influence of the environment on the Marketing Information System.

INTRODUCTION

Due to increases in the levels of competition, there is an escalating need for marketplace intelligence (Gilad 1991; Fuld 1991; Roush 1991; etc.). The transformation of the marketplace environment to a highly competitive structure has created the condition where the ability of a firm to gather, analyze, and communicate strategic information is vital to managerial decision making and organizational success (Giordanella 1989). Information therefore, is an important determinant in maintaining a competitive advantage (D. Cravens 1991; Porter and Millar 1985; etc.). The management of information is probably most visible in a marketing organization through marketing information systems (MkIS).

Marketing information systems continually monitor the environment for the purpose of providing managers the appropriate information to construct anticipatory and responsive strategies. Yet, despite the widely accepted perceptions regarding the importance of marketing information systems (Mayros and Dolan 1988), there has been little research on their actual implementation and operation in marketing organizations. Instead, existing research has focused on potential, theoretical, and hypothesized propositions concerning operative conditions.

Research in this area is frequently grounded in Montgomery and Weinberg's (1979) informational elements proposed to be important in a marketing organization. Later research has reported that these same elements are typically under utilized in operational marketing information systems (Stone and Good 1989). That is, managers perceive the Montgomery and Weinberg (1979) elements to be more important to the marketing role than their actual utilization indicates. Given that differences in perceived importance and utilization of the elements in a marketing information system exist, a logical exploration is to determine what factors influence these differences. Such an exploration is the focus of this study.

In Chandler's (1962) classic study of strategy and organizational structure, it was concluded that differences in how firms implement similar administrative activities is important. It is also accepted that organizations operate under a variety of environments, each providing unique constraints and managerial considerations. Successful firms require management skills and tools which reflect the situational nature of a particular environment (Hofer 1975). As part of the management of unique situations, marketing managers typically employ marketing information systems to provide timely market data about their environment.

The perceived importance and actual use of a marketing information system should vary when comparing different managerial situations as those provided by unique markets or environments. The purpose of this article is to examine differences in the operational and preferred traits of marketing information systems when firms are confronted with distinctive managerial environments across unique marketplaces.

BENEFITS OF STRATEGIC INFORMATION

Although specific benefits of information reside in the perceptions of the user (Hawes 1987), it is generally acknowledged that the possession of information provides the "owner" a significant competitive advantage (Porter and Millar 1985; Kim and Michelman 1990). While the advantages of information ownership are quite numerous, it can be expected that the benefits to the organization will increase as technological capabilities provide more extensive information options. The advantages of information ownership include a reduction in operating costs, improved decision making, and the ability to create new market opportunities (K. Cravens 1991).

These advantages represent the premise for managers generally accepting the escalated importance of information to the organization (Goodhue, Quillard, and Rockart 1988). In fact, the possession of information can be so important to the organization that its strategic value now represents a distinctive corporate asset (Higgins, McIntyre, and Raine 1991). Such an asset confirms that information frequently is being used strategically to gain a competitive advantage (Porter and Millar 1985).

MARKETING INFORMATION SYSTEMS

Increases in the difficulty and complexity of decision making in the last decade have placed greater emphasis on the depth and timeliness of the information required by managers (Raphael and Parket 1991). Coupled with the need for an active intelligence system (Grabowski 1987), marketing information systems have begun to develop and grow in importance.

A marketing information system is a collection of components which monitor both the internal workings of the organization and its environment (K. Cravens 1991). This monitoring is done through the collection of data and its transformation into information. The information is distributed to the marketing organization and its managers. Ideally, this is done quickly, thereby assisting managers in making timely decisions.

Marketing information systems were initially hypothesized to provide marketing managers information in six major areas of coverage (Montgomery and Weinberg 1979) that have subsequently been found to be representative of the elements of an effective MkIS (Stone and Good 1989).

Since the environment typically represents a significant obstacle to the marketer, the ability to understand organizational surroundings through a marketing information system can be crucial to the success of the organization. Increasing levels of marketplace uncertainty have subsequently created even greater demands on organizations to have marketing information systems in operation (Evans and Schlacter 1985).

Because of inherent environmental differences within marketplaces, it is reasonable to hypothesize that marketing managers need to evaluate, and subsequently respond to their surroundings differently. The importance and use of the elements in a marketing information system should therefore vary by specific marketplace challenges. It is proposed that when the surroundings of firms are not consistent with one another in a meaningful fashion, the differences between perceived importance and use of the elements in a marketing information system will vary.

Variance in marketplaces are likely candidates for these environmental and marketing information systems differences. Specifically, the differences between utilization and perceived importance of the elements in a marketing information system should differ based upon environmental or marketplace distinctions. An important marketplace difference proposed to exist in this study is across different product lines.

THE EMPIRICAL STUDY

The empirical study is based upon a questionnaire which was developed and mailed to the marketing managers of 281 randomly selected firms. Each questionnaire asked the respondent to answer a series of questions regarding the individual's perceived importance of a variety of elements in an effective marketing information system. These elements were rated by the respondents using a five-point system of scales and weights. The scale and weights were; 1-very unimportant; 2-unimportant; 3-neutral; 4- important; 5-very important. Marketing managers were also asked to respond to their perception of the degree that their firm utilizes the same elements in its marketing information system. The scale and weights used to rate utilization were; 1-no utilization; 2-low utilization; 3-neutral; 4-high utilization; 5-extensive utilization.

The questionnaire was sent directly to marketing managers for a number of reasons. First, marketing managers are likely to have an important need for a marketing information system as well as operating knowledge about this system. Such an approach is consistent with similar information systems survey research which has been directed to the "user manager" (Alloway and Quillard 1983). Further, the marketing manager is likely to have a controlling and vested interest in the marketing information system. Finally, since it has been found that middle managers are provided the most support from a marketing information system (McLeod and Rogers 1982), it is probable that the marketing manager would actively use the marketing information system.

There were 131 usable questionnaires returned, producing a response rate of 46.62 percent. The responding firms had annual sales ranging from under $25 million to over $350 million. These data were used to examine whether or not any differences between perceived importance and use of the elements in a marketing information system differ systematically across firms' product lines. Each of the six elements defined by Montgomery and Weinberg (1979) were measured by a variety of questions on the questionnaire. Similar questions were used for both perceived importance and actual use of each element. These questionnaire items measuring the six Montgomery and Weinberg elements are displayed in Table 1.

In order to measure the competition element regarding perceived importance, the respondent's answers to three questions were summed. These three responses were to the questions concerning the perceived importance of "strategic programs on competitors," "prices of competitors," and "geographic coverage of competition." The answers by each respondent to these similar questions regarding the utilization of the information elements of "strategic programs on competitors," "prices of competitors," and "geographic coverage of competition" were summed to measure the competition element with respect to its use in a marketing information system.

This process was repeated for each of the remaining groups of questionnaire items measuring the Montgomery and Weinberg (1979) elements. The technology element was measured by a question concerning the perceived importance and use of information regarding "new technological advances in the industry." The cus-

```
                            TABLE 1
        The Questionnaire Items Representing the Elements
               in a Marketing Information System_a

   *    Competition
   *    Strategic programs on competitors.
   *    Prices of competitors.
   *    Geographic coverage of competition.
   *    Technology
   *    New technological advances in the industry.
   *    Customer
   *    Existing customers.
   *    Past customers.
   *    Economic
   *    Economic conditions in the USA.
   *    Political and Regulatory
   *    Political climate in the USA.
   *    Regulatory environment in the USA.
   *    Social
   *    Social climate in the USA.
   *    Public attitude with respect to your firm.
```

_a_Each item was asked of respondents twice. First, the respondent was asked to rate the perceived importance of each item in a Marketing Information System. The second time, the respondent was asked to rate the use of each item in the marketing information system of the respondent's firm.

tomer element was measured by summing responses to the questions regarding "existing customers" and "past customers." A question regarding "economic conditions in the USA" was used to measure the perceived importance and use of the economic element. The political element was measured by summing responses to questions about the "political climate in the USA" and the "regulatory environment in the USA." The social element was measured by summing the scores to questions regarding the "social climate in the USA" and the "public attitude with respect to your firm."

The twelve constructs built by summing the questionnaire items for perceived importance and utilization were examined for their reliability using Cronbach's Alpha. The reliability of all 22 questionnaire items which were summed to form these constructs was also examined using Cronbach's Alpha. Cronbach's Alpha measures were computed for each pair of summated scores of questionnaire items. The pairs were formed by matching the summated score for perceived importance with the summated score for utilization for each Montgomery and Weinberg element. These Cronbach's Alpha measures were, using standardized variables, competition 0.84; technology 0.82; customer 0.82; economic 0.63; political and regulatory 0.82; social 0.82. The Cronbach's Alpha for all 22 questionnaire items was 0.84. These results indicate that the questionnaire responses provided more than a minimum level of reliability.

Given these summated scores, differences in their values

were computed by subtracting the utilization score from the perceived importance score. Throughout the process to compute the differences between perceived importance and utilization, any respondent who failed to answer all the needed questions was eliminated from the study. These differences were then collected into 13 different product line groups. These product lines were: computer hardware and software; telecommunication equipment and services; electronic components; home appliances; aerospace products; electricity; natural gas; automotive products; transportation services; industrial equipment and materials; printing and paper materials; information services; and health and beauty products.

The differences between perceived importance and use for the six different elements in a marketing information systems across the thirteen product lines were examined using multiple analysis of variance (MANOVA). The results from this analysis are shown in Table 2.

From the differences shown in Table 2, it can be seen that each element was perceived as more important than its degree of utilization. Also from the results shown in Table 2, it can be seen that there exist meaningful product line distinctions between the perceived importance and use of the elements in a marketing information system. This result is shown by the statistical significance of the "Effect for All Elements" line in Table 2. Further, the differences for the elements of competition and technology were found to be individually statistically significant for at least a 3 percent significance level.

TABLE 2
Differences in the Perceived Importance and
Use of the Elements in a Marketing Information System

| Element | Difference[1] | | Degrees of | F-Value | Significance |
	Mean	STD[2]	Freedom		Level
Competition	0.94	1.63	10;99	2.14	0.03*
Technology	0.24	0.63	10;99	3.13	0.01**
Customer	0.52	1.23	10;99	1.82	0.07
Economic	0.35	0.83	10;99	1.75	0.08
Political	0.67	1.29	10;99	0.90	0.54
Social	0.59	1.22	10;99	0.89	0.54

[1]The difference was computed by subtracting the utilization score from the perceived importance score on each element.
[2]STD denotes the standard deviation.

	Wilk's Criterion	Degrees of Freedom	F-Value	Significance Level
Effect for All Elements	0.34	60;498	1.78	0.01**

* Significant at $p < .05$.
** Significant at $p < .01$.

MANAGERIAL IMPLICATIONS AND CONCLUSIONS

Relationships have previously been found to exist between the objectives of an organization and the method in which information is collected (Zviran 1990). Despite such a linkage, organizations are traditionally poor at understanding environmental changes (Foster and Pryor 1986). Yet, marketing personnel have the unique charter of producing profitable revenue under these conditions. As a result, the marketer's mission can partially explain the importance of information collection and usage. Further, it therefore is logical that managers in distinct environments (e.g., firms marketing separate product lines) visualize the use, and importance of marketing information systems differently.

The differences in perceived importance and actual use of marketing information systems can be marketplace driven. Different markets require different information from the marketing information systems of firms. These market forces drive executives' perceptions of the worth and usefulness of the information generated by the marketing information system.

From the marketer's perspective, this finding suggests that managers in different industries (e.g., market-places) do not visualize the value of marketing information systems identically. This would result in organizations providing varying degrees of usage and support for information systems. It supports the proposition that environments are different, and managers and organizations must provide and accept different levels of support for the information system they have selected to utilize.

Another implication of the study involves the lack of cross culturalization of marketing information systems that apparently exists. Each industry's uniqueness indicates that the experience of a manager in one type of environment may not sufficiently prepare this manager for another distinctively unique environment. Further, it suggests that those responsible for the construction and implementation of marketing information systems need to be extremely sensitive to the environmental parameters and operational definitions used to design and implement each organization's marketing information system.

The evolution of marketing information systems would logically seem to correlate with the integration of a firm's acceptance of computers. It is therefore apparent that computer-based information systems have become vital to businesses (Lederer 1990). The capabilities (Steinberg and Plank 1990) and use of these systems will continue to expand in sales and marketing organizations (Manssen 1990; Mentzer, Schuster and Roberts 1987; Buckner and Shah 1991) in the future. Yet, the spread of information technology in business comes with a price to the firm and its employees (Barlow 1991). One such potentially negative impact includes managerial perceptions that the construction of a marketing information system was designed to reduce human authority in decision making. This conclusion suggests that it may be that managers and firms need to more carefully consider "human elements" as well as more obvious factors (e.g., financial costs), when considering how and where to use marketing information systems.

Because the business environment is the most competitive and complex in history (Herring 1988), the marketer's need for information has exploded. This need has been forecast to continue in its importance to marketers well into the future (Laczniak and Lusch 1987). The need for information indicates that it is not enough for firms to automate, they must inform as well (Zuboff 1985). The process is compounded because environments rapidly change. In states of alteration, firms must utilize innovation to survive. Innovation in turn, requires sound information (Dyer and Forman 1991). Finally, since information can be used to establish and sustain a competitive advantage, this can only be accomplished when an organization is able to respond to environmental threats (Barney 1991). As a result, the importance of marketing information systems will likely become more vital in the future.

REFERENCES

Alloway, Robert and Judith A. Quillard (1983), "User Managers' Systems Needs," *MIS Quarterly,* 7 (June), 27-41.

Barlow, John F. (1991), "Group Decision Making In Computer Project Justification," *Journal of Systems Management,* 42 (June), 13-37.

Barney, Jay (1991), "Firm Resources and Sustained Competitive Advantage," *Journal of Management,* 17 (March), 99-120.

Buckner, Gary D. and Vivek Shah (1991), "Management of Knowledge-Based Organizations," *American Business Review,* 9 (June), 70-78.

Chandler, Alfred (1962), *Strategy and Structure.* Cambridge: MIT Press, Massachusetts Institute of Technology.

Cravens, David W. (1991), *Strategic Marketing.* Homewood, Il.: Irwin.

Cravens, Karen S. (1991), "The Strategic Role of Information," in *Strategic Marketing,* David W. Cravens, ed. Homewood, Il.: Irwin, 593-617.

Dyer, Robert F. and Ernest H. Forman (1991), *An Analytic Approach To Marketing Decisions.* Englewood Cliffs, NJ: Prentice Hall.

Evans, Kenneth R. and John L. Schlacter (1985), "The Role of Sales Managers and Salespeople in a Marketing Information System," *Journal of Personal Selling & Sales Management,* 5 (November), 49-58.

Foster, William K. and Austin K. Pryor (1986), "The Strategic Management of Innovation," *The Journal of Business Strategy,* 7 (Summer), 38-40.

Fuld, Leonard (1991), "A Recipe for Business Intelligence Success," *The Journal of Business Strategy,* 12 (January/February), 12-17.

Gilad, Benjamin (1991), "U.S. Intelligence System: Model for Corporate Chiefs?," *The Journal of Business Strategy,* 12 (May/June), 20-25.

Giordanella, Richard (1989), "Choosing an Executive Information System," *Journal of Accounting and EDP,* 5 (Spring), 10-16.

Goodhue, Dale L., Judith A. Quillard, and John F. Rockart (1988), "Managing the Data Resource: A Contingency Perspective," *MIS Quarterly,* 12 (September), 373-392.

Grabowski, Daniel P. (1987), "Building an Effective Competitive Intelligence System," *Journal of Business & Industrial Marketing,* 2 (Winter), 39-43.

Hawes, Douglas K. (1987), "The Role of Marketing in Facilitating the Diffusion of Microcomputers and 'The Information Society,'" *Journal of The Academy of Marketing Science,* 15 (Summer), 83-90.

Higgins, Lexis. F., Scott C. McIntyre, and Cynthia G. Raine (1991), "Design of Global Marketing Information Systems," *The Journal of Business and Industrial Marketing,* 6 (Summer/Fall), 49-58.

Herring, Jan P. (1988), "Building a Business Intelligence System," *The Journal of Business Strategy,* 9 (May/June), 4-9.

Hofer, Charles W. (1975). "Toward a Contingency Theory of Business Strategy," *Academy of Management Journal,* 18 (December), 784-808.

Kim, K. Kyu, and Jeffrey E. Michelman (1990), "An Examination of Factors for the Strategic Use of Information Systems in the Healthcare Industry," *MIS Quarterly,* 14 (June), 201-214.

Laczniak, Gene R. and Robert F. Lusch (1987), "Environment and Strategy in 1995: A Survey of High-Level Executives," *Journal of Business & Industrial Marketing,* 2 (Winter), 5-23.

Lederer, Albert L. (1990), "Making Strategic Information Systems Happen," *Academy of Management Executive,* 4 (August), 76-83.

Manssen, L. Brent (1990), "Using PCs to Automate and Innovate Marketing Activities," *Industrial Marketing Management,* 19 (August), 209-213.

Mayros, Van and Dennis J. Dolan (1988), "Hefting the Data Load: How to Design the MkIS that Works for You," *Business Marketing,* 73 (March), 47-69.

McLeod, Raymond, Jr. and John Rogers (1982), "Marketing Information Systems: Uses in the *Fortune 500*," *California Management Review*, 25 (Fall), 106-118.

Mentzer, John T., Camille P. Schuster, and David J. Roberts (1987), "Microcomputers Versus Mainframe Usage by Marketing Professionals," *Journal of The Academy of Marketing Science*, (Summer), 1-9.

Montgomery, David B. and Charles B. Weinberg (1979), "Toward Strategic Intelligence Systems," *Journal of Marketing*, 43 (Fall), 41-52.

Porter, Michael E. and Victor E. Millar (1985), "How Information Gives You Competitive Advantage," *Harvard Business Review*, 63 (July-August), 149-160.

Raphael, Joel and I. Robert Parket (1991), "The Needs for Market Research in Executive Decision Making," *Journal of Business and Industrial Marketing*, 6 (Spring), 15-21.

Roush, Gary B. (1991), "A Program for Sharing Corporate Intelligence," *The Journal of Business Strategy*, 12 (January/February), 4-7.

Steinberg, Margery and Richard E. Plank (1990), "Implementing Expert Systems Into Business-to-Business Marketing Practice," *Journal of Business & Industrial Marketing*, 5 (Summer/Fall), 15-26.

Stone, Robert W. and David J. Good (1989), "Theoretical and Operational Marketing Information Systems," *Review of Business*, 11 (Winter), 23-28.

Zuboff, Shoshana (1985), "Automate/Informate: The Two Faces of Intelligent Technology," *Organizational Dynamics*, (Autumn), 5-18.

Zviran, Moshe (1990), "Relationships between Organizational and Information Systems Objectives: Some Empirical Evidence," *Journal of Management Information Systems*, 7 (Summer), 65-84.

SOME METHODOLOGICAL AND EMPIRICAL FINDINGS REGARDING SELF-EXPLICATED PREFERENCE MODELS

Paul E. Green, University of Pennsylvania
Abba M. Krieger, University of Pennsylvania
Catherine M. Schaffer, University of Denver

ABSTRACT

Recently, self-explicated preference models have become a subject of considerable research activity on the part of consumer researchers.

This paper reports some findings that may increase researcher interest. First, we show analytically, and via simulation, why self-explicated models often perform well against conjoint models. Second, we describe some empirical results showing that the common industry practice of rescaling attribute desirability judgments to equate ranges actually reduces cross validity.

Self-explicated models assume that preference is a simple additive function of attribute importances times attribute level desirabilities. A recent review of conjoint analysis (Green and Srinivasan 1990) devotes considerable space to this class of models. Renewed interest in the self-explicated model has proceeded along several fronts.

At the academic research level, new classes of models, such as hybrid conjoint (Green, Goldberg, and Montemayor 1981; Cattin, Hermet, and Pioche 1982; Akaah and Korgaonkar 1983), have utilized self-explicated data as a first stage in the development of a compositional/conjoint model.

At the industry application level, Sawtooth Software's Adaptive Conjoint Analysis (Johnson 1987) incorporates self-explicated data as a first step prior to "Bayesian" updating, based on individuals' evaluations of paired comparisons stimuli. M/A/R/C, a national marketing research firm, has developed CASEMAP (Srinivasan and Wyner 1989), a telephone interviewing method that collects only self-explicated data for preference modeling (i.e., there is no conjoint data collection stage).

Self-explicated preference models frequently predict conjoint-based profile responses reasonably well (Leigh, MacKay, and Summers 1984; Srinivasan 1988). Of course, one could describe sets of conditions (e.g., preference evaluations of "holistic" stimuli such as food/beverage formulations, package designs, and physical stimuli in general) where the collection of self-explicated data would not make much sense. Still, there do appear to be contexts where self-explicated preference models perform well.

OBJECTIVES OF THE PAPER

The objectives of this paper are two-fold. First, we show, both theoretically and by computer simulation, that self-explicated preference models exhibit considerable robustness to ordinal transformations in subjects' attribute-level desirabilities and importance weights. Second, we report empirical findings regarding the appropriateness of translating and stretching original attribute-level desirability ratings, within attribute to equate ranges across attributes. This transformation sets the lowest desirability scale value at 0 and the highest at 1 for each attribute. (Intermediate scale values are interpolated within these end points).

Our empirical findings suggest that such a transformation should be questioned. We show in three different studies that self-explicated models based on the original desirability ratings cross validate better than those that incorporate the transformation suggested by conventional industry practice.

THE SELF-EXPLICATED PREFERENCE MODEL

The self-explicated preference model has been described by Green (1984). Following his notation, we let:

$$\underset{\sim}{i} = (i_1, i_2, ..., i_j, ... i_J)$$

denote a multiattribute profile in which the vector component i_j denotes level i_j ($i_j = 1, I_j$) of attribute j ($j = 1, J$). Next, we let

u_{ijk} = respondent k's (k = 1, K) self-explicated desirability (or acceptability) score for level i of attribute j,

w_{jk} = respondent k's self-explicated importance weight for attribute j; w_{jk} 0;

$$\sum_{j=1}^{J} w_{jk} = 1.0$$

Then,

$$U_{i_1, i_2, ..., iJ, k} = \sum_{j=1}^{J} w_{jk} u_{ijk}$$

denotes respondent k's overall preference score, or utility U, for profile a as a weighted sum of the desirability scores u_{ijk}.

The u's are usually obtained as rating scale values on (say) a 0 to 10 scale. Depending upon the number of attributes, the w's may be obtained from constant sum tasks or from rating scales (where the importance ratings are later normalized to sum to unity). However, Johnson (1987) obtains desirability scores as integer rank numbers across the levels of each attribute (which are later normalized to range between 0 and 1) and importance weights as ratings on a 4-point scale.

SOME ROBUST PROPERTIES OF SELF-EXPLICATED DESIRABILITIES AND ATTRIBUTE IMPORTANCES

The first problem considered here assumes that a subject has a "true" set of part-worths, expressed as the product of a self-explicated desirability score by a self-explicated importance score. We first assume that the decision maker's stated desirability ratings (of levels within attribute) at least preserves the ordering of her true desirabilities.

However, we assume greater uncertainty surrounding the decision maker's reliability in estimating these true attribute importances.[1] For example, attribute importances may be more sensitive to decision contexts (i.e., product use scenarios) or to the attribute-level composition of the stimuli being evaluated. Four possible relationships between derived importance and true importance scores are examined:

1. The decision maker is unable to be more precise than giving equal scores to all attribute importances.

2. The decision maker is unable to do better than randomly order all of the attributes with respect to importance.

3. The decision maker's complete ordering of the estimated importance scores is the same as the ordering of her true importance scores.

4. A partial ordering of the estimated scores is the same as the true importance scores. For example, the decision-maker gets the top two importances correctly ordered but not the rest. (Lesser importances are randomly assigned across attributes.)

In sum, the decision maker's derived desirabilities are assumed to maintain the ordering (but not necessarily the spacing) of the true desirabilities. The decision maker's derived attribute importance ranking can range anywhere from agreeing completely with the ranks of the true importance scores to an ordering that is essentially random, with respect to the true ordering.

Some Analytical Results

We study the problem analytically by considering the correlation between the true and predicted (i.e., estimated) part-worths. We use the following notation:

A = number of attributes

L = number of levels for each attribute; we assume that the number of levels across attribute is constant (to simplify the exposition)

d_{ij} = true desirability score for level j of attribute i

W_i = true importance score for attribute i

e_{ij} = predicted desirability score for level j of attribute i, and

V_i = predicted importance score for attribute i.

The correlation between the true and predicted part-worth vectors is given by

$$R \equiv (C - \bar{X}_t \bar{X}_p)/[(\bar{S}_t - \bar{X}_t^2)(\bar{S}_p - \bar{X}_p^2)]^{\frac{1}{2}}$$

$$\text{where} \quad C = \frac{\sum_{i=1}^{A} \sum_{j=1}^{L} W_i d_{ij} V_i e_{ij}}{AL}$$

$$\bar{X}_t = \frac{\sum_{i=1}^{A} \sum_{j=1}^{L} W_i d_{ij}}{AL}$$

$$\bar{X}_p = \frac{\sum_{i=1}^{A} \sum_{j=1}^{L} V_i e_{ij}}{AL} \qquad (1)$$

$$\bar{S}_t = \frac{\sum_{i=1}^{A} \sum_{j=1}^{L} (W_i d_{ij})^2}{AL}$$

$$\bar{S}_p = \frac{\sum_{i=1}^{A} \sum_{j=1}^{L} (V_i e_{ij})^2}{AL}$$

We study the behavior of R by assuming that the true desirabilities and weights, d_{ij} and W_i, are independently chosen from a uniform distribution on (0,1). (However, it would be straightforward to extend the results about the behavior of R to other distributions.) Without loss of generality, we label the attributes in decreasing order of W_i and the levels within each attribute in decreasing order of d_{ij}.

The predicted desirabilities are generated by taking independent uniforms on (0,1); we then reorder the uniforms, within attribute, from highest to lowest so that the order of e_{ij} agrees with the order of d_{ij}. As mentioned above, we consider four cases:

1. The V_i are all set equal to .5 to agree in expectation with the true weights

2. The V_i are randomly generated from a uniform (0,1)

3. Independent uniforms (0,1) are generated and ordered from highest to lowest so that the W_i and V_i are in the same order

4. Independent uniforms (0,1) are generated. The k largest values of V_i are assigned in decreasing order to agree with the first k attributes of W_i and the remaining A - k are randomly assigned.

We consider the behavior of R in probability as the number of attributes, $A \to \infty$.

1. Equal Weights

Since the expectation

$$E(C) = \frac{1}{2} \sum_{i=1}^{A} \sum_{j=1}^{L} \left(\frac{L+1-j}{L+1}\right)^2 \frac{A+1-i}{A+1} \Big/ AL = \frac{2L+1}{24(L+1)},$$

then

$$R \to \frac{\left(\frac{2L+1}{24(L+1)} - \frac{1}{16}\right)}{\left[\frac{7}{144} \times \frac{4}{144}\right]^{1/2}} = \frac{L-1}{L+1} \frac{3}{\sqrt{28}} \qquad (2)$$

2. Random Weights

Since E(C) is the same here as in the previous case,

$$R \to \frac{\left(\frac{2L+1}{24(L+1)} - \frac{1}{16}\right)}{\left[\frac{7}{144}\right]} = \frac{3(L-1)}{7(L+1)} \qquad (3)$$

3. Completely Ordered Weights

Since

$$E(C) = \sum_{i=1}^{A} \sum_{j=1}^{L} \left(\frac{L+1-j}{L+1}\right)^2 \left(\frac{A+1-i}{A+1}\right)^2 / AL$$

$$= \left(\frac{2L+1}{6(L+1)}\right)\left(\frac{2A+1}{6(A+1)}\right) \to \frac{2L+1}{18(L+1)}$$

as $A \to \infty$,

$$R \to \frac{\left(\frac{2L+1}{18(L+1)} - \frac{1}{16}\right)}{\frac{7}{144}} = \frac{(7L-1)}{7(L+1)}. \qquad (4)$$

4. The Top k Ordered Set

It should be noted that if k is fixed, then as A this case would reduce to the one with random weights. Therefore, we assume that k gets larger with A, where f=k/A (i.e., we fix the fraction f of top ordered choices).

Since

$$E(C) = \frac{\sum_{j=1}^{L}\left(\frac{L+1-j}{L+1}\right)^2 \left\{\sum_{i=1}^{k}\left(\frac{A+1-i}{A+1}\right)^2 + \sum_{i=k+1}^{A}\left(\frac{A+1-i}{A+1}\right)\left(\frac{A-k+1}{2(A+1)}\right)\right\}}{L \qquad A}$$

$$= \frac{2L+1}{6(L+1)}\left\{\frac{A(A+1)(2A+1)-(A-k)(A-k+1)(2A-2k+1)}{6}\right.$$

$$\left. + \left(\frac{A-k+1}{2}\right)^2 (A-k)\right\} / A(A+1)^2$$

$$\to \frac{2L+1}{6(L+1)}\left\{\frac{1}{3} - \frac{(1-f)^3}{12}\right\} \text{ as } A \to \infty.$$

Hence,

$$R \to \frac{7L-1-2(1-f)^3 (2L+1)}{7(L+1)}. \qquad (5)$$

We note that results are in accord will intuition. For example, the correlation R is higher with equal weights than with random weights. The value of R is highest in case 3, lowest in case 2 and intermediate in cases 3 and 4. Case 4 reduces to case 2 when f=0 and to case 3 when f=1, as it should.

SIMULATION RESULTS

While the analytical findings in the preceding section show asymptotic results, from a practical standpoint one would be interested in how well the derived importance and desirabilities scores "recover" the true partworths in problem sizes likely to be encountered in real applications.

A factorial experiment was set up in which the following characteristics were varied in a set of simulations:

1. Importance score order agreements with the true importance ordering
   a. Complete ordering agreement
   b. Top two importances correctly ordered
   c. Top one correctly ordered
   d. Equal importance scores are estimated
   e. Random ordering of estimated importance scores

2. Number of attributes
   a. 4
   b. 8
   c. 12
   d. 16

3. Number of levels within attribute (assumed equal across attributes)
   a. 2
   b. 4
   c. 6
   d. 8

A simulation design was set up with 80 combinations (i.e., a full factorial). Each simulation was based on 400 replications. The response measure was the product moment correlation between the true part-worths and the estimated part-worths. In all cases, the true attribute-level desirabilities orderings were respected.

Table 1 shows the main effects results of the experiments.[2] As noted from the table, the ordering of each effect is in the anticipated direction. For example, if the decision-maker is able to estimate the true order of both desirability and importance scores, on average the correlation between true and estimated part-worths in 0.73. This is rather good, given that only rank orders are preserved.[3]

As the number of attributes increase, the correlation decreases, on average, but the decline is not marked (as is confirmed by the relatively small sum of squares

TABLE 1
Results of Simulation

Main Effect	Average Correlation	Sum of Squares Accounted for
Importance score ordering		
Full ordering	.73	1.672
Top two	.53	
Top one	.44	
Equal weights	.43	
Random	.30	
Number of attributes		.120
4	.55	
8	.49	
12	.46	
16	.45	
Number of levels within attribute		.639
2	.34	
4	.48	
6	.54	
8	.58	

accounted for by this experimental factor). As the number of levels increase, the correlation also increases.

Conclusions

Analytical and simulation results support the notion that the simple self-explicated part-worth model described here is fairly robust. For example, assume that a decision maker is able to come up with the correct ordering of desirabilities within attribute and importance scores in a problem involving eight attributes, each at four levels. If so, the resulting correlation between true and derived part-worths is 0.73. This is quite respectable,

given past cross-validation findings on real data.

Our results are in the same spirit as those reported by Dawes and Corrigan (1974) in the context of linear, additive functions used in policy capturing models. We also note that even using equal importance weights in the simulation results in a correlation of 0.42 for the same conditions noted above.

TRANSFORMATIONS OF SELF-EXPLICATED DESIRABILITY SCORES

It is common practice in industry applications of self-explicated preference modeling to rescale the original attribute desirability ratings to vary between 0 and 1. This transformation entails both a translation (to zero) and a subsequent rescaling of the original ratings. M/A/R/C's CASEMAP procedure incorporates this idea (Srinivasan and Wyner 1989). Also, Sawtooth's ACA package (Johnson 1987) scales the original attribute-level desirabilities (originally expressed as a strict rank order), to range between 0 (lowest) and 1 (highest).

Recently, Green and Schaffer (1991) reported the rather surprising result that this common practice leads to lower cross validation than that obtained from the original self-explicated desirability scores. Their study employed apartment descriptions varying on six attributes (see Table 2). The sample size was 177 respondents; all were business school students, planning to rent an apartment near campus.

The original attribute-level desirabilities were first rated on a 0 to 10 scale, ranging from 0 (described as completely unacceptable) to 10 (described as completely acceptable). Attribute importance scores were obtained from a constant sum task in which the respondent allocated 100 points across the six attributes, so as to reflect their relative importance. Following these tasks, each respondent rated 18 full profiles on a 0 to 100 likelihood-of-renting scale. First, the subject sorted the 18 profiles into three piles: low interest, medium interest, and high interest. Then, the respondent rated the high interest profiles first, followed by the medium, and finally by the low interest stimuli.

The 18 (orthogonally designed) profiles constituted the validation set. Two self-explicated prediction models were formulated, one with untransformed desirabilities and the other with desirabilities normalized by translation and scaling, so as to range between 0 and 1, for each attribute.

The first section of Table 3 shows the results. All predictions were carried out at the individual respondent level. The validation coefficients (product moment correlations) were then averaged across subjects. As noted for the apartment study (entailing one validation sample), the cross validation for the self-explicated model

TABLE 2
Attributes and Levels Used in Apartment Study

A. *Walking Time to Classes*
1. 10 minutes
2. 20 minutes
3. 30 minutes

B. *Noise Level of Apartment House*
1. Very quite
2. Average noise level
3. Extremely noisy

C. *Safety of Apartment Location*
1. Very safe location
2. Average safety
3. Very unsafe location

D. *Condition of Apartment*
1. Newly renovated throughout
2. Renovated kitchen only
3. Poor condition

E. *Size of Living/Dining Area*
1. 24 by 30 feet
2. 15 by 20 feet
3. 9 by 12 feet

F. *Monthly Rent (Utilities Incl.)*
1. $540
2. $360
3. $225

TABLE 3
Cross Validation Correlations, by Study Model

Study	First Cross Validation		Second Cross Validation	
	Untransformed Desirabilities	Transformed Desirabilities	Untransformed Desirabilities	Transformed Desirabilities
Apartments	.712	.538	—	—
Cars	.349	.275	.303	.282
Jobs	.447	.442	.288	.271

TABLE 4
Attributes and Levels in Car Study

A. *Body Style*
1. Sedan
2. Station wagon
3. Van
4. Convertible

B. *Country of Manufacture*
1. U.S.-made
2. German-made
3. Japanese-made
4. Swedish-made

C. *Fuel Economy*
1. 20 MPG average
2. 25 MPG average
3. 30 MPG average
4. 35 MPG average

D. *Base Price*
1. $10,000
2. $13,000
3. $16,000
4. $19,000

E. *Engine Type*
1. 4-Cylinder
2. 4-Cylinder Turbo + $500
3. 6-Cylinder + $600
4. 6-Cylinder + $1000

F. *Exterior Color*
1. Maroon
2. Silver
3. White
4. Light blue

G. *Radio*
1. AM only
2. AM/FM + $100
3. AM/FM stereo +250
4. AM/FM stereo, tape deck + $350

H. *Warranty*
1. 1-year
2. 6-year + $600

TABLE 5
Attribute and Levels Used in Jobs Study

A. *Starting Salary Compared to Market*

1. 15% below
2. Equals
3. 15% above
4. 20% above

B. *Job Security*

1. Lifetime employment not company policy
2. Lifetime employment is company policy

C. *Organization's Friendliness*

1. Unfriendly
2. Indifferent
3. Somewhat friendly
4. Very friendly

D. *First Pay Raise/Promotion*

1. 18-24 months
2. 12-18
3. 6-12
4. Within 6 months

E. *Personal Development Opportunities*

1. Almost none
2. Few
3. Moderate
4. Considerable

F. *Job Prestige*

1. Almost none
2. A little
3. Moderate
4. High

G. *Recognition*

1. Very little
2. Considerable

H. *Responsibility*

1. Almost none
2. Little
3. Moderate
4. Considerable

J. *Location*

1. Rural
2. Small town
3. Medium size city
4. Major city

K. *Medical/Vacation Benefits*

1. Average
2. Considerably above average

L. *Nights away from home*

1. About two nights/month
2. About six nights/month

---

based on the unstretched desirabilities (0.712) well exceeded that (0.538) for the model utilizing desirabilities

ADDITIONAL STUDIES

More recently, one of the authors (Schaffer) conducted two additional studies with business school students drawn from a midwestern university. The first study involved car attributes (see Table 4); the sample size was 160. The second study entailed job attributes (see Table 5); the sample size was 169.

Desirability ratings and importance allocations were implemented in the same way as illustrated in the apartment study. In the first validation task of each study, each respondent received a balanced block of eight full profiles drawn from an orthogonal design of 32 profiles. After looking at (and sorting) the eight profiles, the respondent rated each on a 0 - 100 likelihood-of-intent scale.

One week later the respondent received a second (and different) block of eight profiles, also drawn from the master orthogonal array. Again, the subject rated each profile on a 0 - 100 likelihood-of-interest scale. The same self-explicated models (original and transformed) were used in this second validation exercise for both studies.

RESULTS

Study results for the automobile and job studies are also shown in Table 3. We first note that the more complex tasks (eight attributes for cars and twelve attributes for jobs) lead to lower cross validations than noted for apartments. The car study validations are particularly poor and reflect the difficult job of evaluating profiles where prices are covarying with car option enhancements.

Still, we note that the stretched desirabilities again lead to *lower* cross validations for both stimulus sets, in both time periods: current and one week later.

In the case of the car study, the cross validation is significantly higher for the unstretched desirabilities in the current period. However, in the one-week later case, the cross validations are both so low that no significant difference is found. No significant differences are found across the jobs study either, although the sample averages suggest that no transformation of desirabilities is preferable, in terms of cross validation.

CONCLUSIONS

The prevailing industry practice of stretching attribute-level desirabilities to range between 0 and 1, within each attribute, may lead to information loss. The results of Table 3, across three separate studies, suggest that information regarding attribute importance may be lost by assuming that self-explicated importances convey *all* of the input to this question.

The studies reported have suggested that attribute importance information is contained in the range of self-explicated desirabilities. Larger ranges convey greater attribute importance. Equalizing all such ranges to vary between 0 and 1 removes this source of attribute differentiation, which is not entirely compensated for in the respondent's subjective judgments of attribute importance.

ENDNOTES

[1] There are some empirical results supporting the intuitive view that desirability scores are more reliable on a test/retest basis than importance scores. For example, a recent study by the authors, using Sawtooth's Adaptive Conjoint Analysis procedure, showed that test/retest reliabilities of desirabilities averaged 0.89, versus only 0.63 for importance ratings.

[2] Main effects alone accounted for over 95% of the total sum of squares in the dependent variable.

[3] Interestingly, the .73 correlation result is not much different from the value of .75 that is representative of full profile conjoint's cross-validation ability in real studies (Bateson, Reibstein and Boulding 1987).

[4] Two additional validation sets were also employed. However, these sets were not comparable to the initial set since they used only the first and third levels of each attribute.

REFERENCES

Akaah, Ishmael, P., and Pradeep K. Korgaonkar (1983), "An Empirical Comparison of Predictive Validity for the Self-Explicated, Huber-hybrid, Traditional Conjoint and Hybrid Conjoint Models," *Journal of Marketing Research,* 20 (May), 187-97.

Bateson, John E.G., David J. Reibstein, and William Boulding (1987), "Conjoint Analysis Reliability and Validity: A Framework for Future Research," in *Review of Marketing,* M. J. Houston, ed. Chicago: American Marketing Association, 451-81.

Cattin, Philippe, Gerard Hermet, and Alan Pioche (1982), "Alternative Hybrid Models for Conjoint Analysis: Some Empirical Results," in *Analytical Approaches to Product and Market Planning,* The Second Conference, Raj Srivastava and Allan D. Shocker, eds. Cambridge, MA: Marketing Science Institute, (October), 142-52.

Dawes, Robyn M. and Bernard Corrigan (1974), "Linear Models in Decision Making," *Psychological Bulletin,* 81, 95-106.

Green, Paul E. (1984), "Hybrid Models for Conjoint Analysis: An Expository Review," *Journal of Marketing Research,* 21 (May) 155-9.

_____, Stephen M. Goldberg, and Mila Montemayor (1981), "A Hybrid Utility Estimation Model for Conjoint Analysis," *Journal of Marketing,* 45 (Winter), 33-41.

_____ and V. Srinivasan (1990), "Conjoint Analysis in Marketing Research: New Developments and Directions," *Journal of Marketing,* 54 (October), 3-19.

_____ and Catherine M. Schaffer (1991), "Importance Weight Effects on Self-Explicated Preference Models: Some Empirical Findings," *Advances in Consumer Research,* 18 Provo, UT: Association of Consumer Research, 476-482.

Johnson, Richard M. (1987), "Adaptive Conjoint Analysis," *Sawtooth Software Conference on Perceptual Mapping, Conjoint Analysis, and Computer Interviewing,* Ketchum, ID: Sawtooth Software.

Leigh, T. W., David B. MacKay, and John O. Summers (1984), "Reliability and Validity of Conjoint Analysis and Self-Explicated Weights: A Comparison," *Journal of Marketing Research,* 21 (November), 456-462.

Srinivasan, V. (1988), "A Conjunctive-Compensatory Approach to the Self-Explication of Multiattributed Preferences," *Decision Sciences,* 19 (Spring), 295-305.

Srinivasan, V., and Gordon A. Wyner (1989), "CASEMAP: Computer-Assisted Self-Explication of Multi-Attributed Preferences," in New *Product Development and Testing,* W. Henry, M. Menasco, and H. Takada, eds. Lexington, MA: Lexington Books, 91-111.

OUTDOOR ADVERTISING OF SERVICES

Naveen Donthu, Georgia State University

ABSTRACT

Outdoor advertising is changing from traditional heavy use by liquor and cigarette manufacturers. Now outdoor advertising is used routinely by marketers of consumer goods and services. As outdoor advertising becomes increasingly acceptable for product and services, there is pressure on media agencies to prove that outdoor advertising is effective, can help create awareness, and provide information (such as price or direction).

Several studies have been conducted to measure the effectiveness of outdoor advertising in general. The effectiveness of the media has been compared using recall, awareness levels and sales response. All of these studies have concentrated on analyzing the effectiveness of outdoor advertising in general, and have shown that outdoor advertising is a very effective media. However, there have been no studies testing the effectiveness of outdoor advertising of services and comparing this effectiveness with that of outdoor advertisements of consumer goods. As the role of services industry in our economy increases, studies investigating the effectiveness of outdoor advertising of services will be necessary to help marketers and advertisers of services understand the importance and effectiveness of outdoor campaigns.

In this paper we analyze the effectiveness of outdoor advertising of services and compare its effectiveness with effectiveness of outdoor advertisements of consumer goods. In addition to billboard related factors such as color and directional information, factors such as respondent involvement with outdoor advertisements, and respondent attitude towards advertising are also investigated. We use respondent recall (unaided and aided) as a measure of outdoor advertising effectiveness.

Data for this study was collected via telephone interviews of 142 adult residents of a suburb in a large U.S. city. Respondents were included in the study only if they commuted on a certain highway while traveling downtown and passed the ten outdoor advertisements that were selected for this study. Ten new billboard ads went up between 45 to 60 days before the telephone interview on a certain 30 mile stretch between the suburb and a particular exit in downtown. This provided a natural experimental design setting to test the effectiveness of outdoor advertising.

Analysis of variance was performed using the general linear model procedure. The five independent variables: product type (services [6 advertisements] or consumer goods [4 advertisements]), color (black & white [3 advertisements] or color [7 advertisements]), directional information (yes [2 advertisements] or no [8 advertisements]), respondent involvement (high [50 respondents] or low [92 respondents]), and respondent attitude towards advertising (positive [58 respondents] or negative [84 respondents]), captured the variations in the ten outdoor advertisements and the respondents. The dependent variable, recall, was dummy coded where 0 represented not recalled and 1 represented recalled.

The results showed that black & white ads of services with directional information were more effective than color ads of consumer goods or color ads of services with no directional information. Respondents who were involved with outdoor advertisements and had a positive attitude towards advertising seem to recall more ads than respondents who were not involved with the task of viewing outdoor ads and had a negative attitude towards advertising.

Given that there are no published studies on outdoor advertising of services, this exploratory study makes a significant contribution to the knowledge in this area. Future studies should investigate the effect of other ad related and respondent related factors on the effectiveness of outdoor advertisements of services. The next logical step is to understand the effectiveness of outdoor advertising of services when used in conjunction with other media such as television and print media. The primary goal of advertisements is not just ad recall. The ultimate goal is to change consumer attitudes and induce purchase. Future work should investigate how successful outdoors ads of services are in changing consumer attitude and purchase intentions.

For further information please contact:
Naveen Donthu
Department of Marketing
Georgia State University
Atlanta, Ga 30303

A MERTONIAN APPROACH TO THE ANALYSIS OF ADVERTISING'S ROLE IN SOCIETY: FROM POLEMICS TO DISCOURSE

Stephen J. Grove, Clemson University
William E. Kilbourne, Sam Houston State University

ABSTRACT

The debate over the nature and impact of advertising is not a new one. Recently, Pollay (1986) and Holbrook (1987) exchanged views reflecting differing interpretations of the social consequences of advertising. Pollay adopts the modeling perspective which suggests advertising provides a model for behavior. Holbrook assumes the mirroring perspective which suggests advertising simply reflects behavioral characteristics already evident in society. In adopting these diverse perspectives, the authors seem more to talk past each other rather than engaging in discussion. The reason for this is the lack of a common framework relating the two perspectives.

The purpose of this paper is to provide a sociological framework for the analysis of the social effects of advertising. To date, most of the discussion has been polemical with traditional advertisers addressing their version of advertising and critics addressing their version. To the observer, it would appear that the two camps are talking about different phenomena. This is not the case, however, as this paper will point out.

The framework suggested in this paper is Mertonian functionalism which suggests that social phenomena, like advertising, generally serve a function in society. More importantly, the function(s) can be categorized as manifest (the social element's objective consequences that contribute to its adoption and are intended) or latent (the element's unintended and generally unrecognized consequences). As to the consequences themselves, they may be functional (a positive social consequence) or dysfunctional (a negative social consequence).

For example, a manifest function of advertising is to inform consumers about product offerings. Few would disagree that consumers need to know information about availability and product features. A manifest dysfunction of advertising would be characterized by intentionally deceptive ads. Here again, there is little disagreement among supporters or critics that intentionally deceiving consumers is not in the interest of society. With latent functions, the analysis is subject to greater disagreement, however.

An example of a latent function would be the development of new products. Since the individuals investing in research and development of new products know that advertising is available to sell the product once developed, they would be more willing to invest since advertising reduces the risk of failure. A latent dysfunction of advertising would be the development of crass commercialism and irrational consumption behavior. By consistently promoting unnecessary consumption, critics argue that uncritical consciousness, passivity and powerlessness develop in the consumer.

As can be seen from the limited examples, the perspective one chooses to adopt in the analysis of the social consequences of advertising practically determines the nature of the conclusions that will be drawn. From this, the polemical nature of the debate over the social consequences of advertising is not surprising. Each member of the debate brings a unique and potentially conflicting perspective to the discussion. Each is conditioned by their particular background to see the debate in their own terms and not those of the other.

When advertising is analyzed in the Mertonian framework, it provides a basis for understanding the polemical nature of advertising debates. The traditional approach to assessing the effects of advertising taken by its supporters considers primarily the manifest/functional dimension of advertising. Critics, on the other hand, generally refer to the latent dysfunctions of advertising. The polemical nature of the debate ensues because the viewpoints expressed come from non-overlapping subsets of the advertising phenomenon. When this is true, discourse cannot develop since there is no common ground to discuss. Once the problem is defined within the Mertonian framework and the different dimensions are established, discourse is possible. Without this recognition, the polemical character of the debate on the social function of advertising will continue to the detriment of both sides and the public at large.

For further information please contact:
William Kilbourne
Sam Houston State Univ.
Department of Management
Huntsville, Tx 77341

A THEORETICAL FRAMEWORK FOR ADVERTISING

Arjun Chaudhuri, Fairfield University

ABSTRACT

An "Advertising Differentiation Matrix" is proposed as a theoretical framework from which to draw normative implications for advertising strategy. The matrix encompasses within its scope the major elements within a typical advertisement and attempts to determine their effect on two types of psychological outcomes - analytic and syncretic cognitions.

INTRODUCTION

My great religion is a belief in the blood, the flesh, as being wiser than the intellect. We can go wrong in our minds. But what our blood feels and believes and says is always true. The intellect is only a bit and a bridle. What do I care about knowledge? All I want is to be able to answer to my blood, direct, without fribbling intervention of mind or moral, or what not. (D. H. Lawrence in Blanshard 1962, p. 47)

The role of emotion has recently been addressed in advertising, marketing and consumer behavior theory (Edell and Burke 1987; Holbrook and Hirschman 1982). There is no doubt that consumers use emotions in their evaluation of advertisements. On the other hand, under the traditional information processing paradigm (Bettman 1979), there are advertisements which are processed largely on the basis of "rational" criteria. Such advertisements solve consumer problems and are capable of brand differentiation on the level of product attributes. Consequently, advertising research emphasizes both emotional and rational outcomes that are created by advertising stimuli.

This paper attempts to develop a matrix of advertisement categories, based on emotional (syncretic cognitions) and rational (analytic cognitions) outcomes and suggests normative implications for advertising planning and strategy. Previous classifications, such as the FCB grid (Vaughn 1980), have considered emotional and rational outcomes to be two ends on a single continuum. However, Pechmann and Stewart (1989) have pointed out that feeling and thinking are separate and independent dimensions which cannot realistically be used as opposite ends of a single continuum. Unfortunately, Pechmann and Stewart (1989) suggest an alternative continuum (systematic - heuristic) which, in turn, suffers from the same limitation, since heuristic processing may lead to emotional outcomes. The attempt here will be to classify advertisements on separate dimensions of emotional and rational outcomes. In order to arrive at normative implications for advertising practitioners, this paper will also investigate the sources in the advertising environment (media, product category and advertising strategy) which account for analytic and syncretic cognitions.

ANALYTIC AND SYNCRETIC COGNITIONS

Buck (1988) discusses two separate types of cognition: syncretic cognition, which is knowledge by acquaintance and analytic cognition, which is knowledge by description. In the former, processing is right hemispheric in origin, emotional, spontaneous and non-propositional in nature. In the latter, evaluation is left hemispheric in origin, rational, symbolic and propositional. Syncretic cognition or knowledge by acquaintance is immediate and subjective emotional experience that is known directly by the individual and cannot be described. This is the process that Bertrand Russell described as "direct sensory awareness without the intermediary of any process of inference or any knowledge of truths" (in Buck 1988, p. 398). In contrast, analytic cognition, or knowledge by description, involves the interpretation of sense data resulting in cognitive judgements about phenomena.

PRODUCT INVOLVEMENT

On the level of product categories, we can, therefore, also conceive of two types of consumer knowledge - one that is acquired by direct sensory experience with the product and another that is ratiocinative and involves analysis and judgement. The first is described here as the syncretic value of a product, that is known directly through immediate and subjective experience with the product and that results in a sensation of affect or pleasure; the second, as the analytic value of the product which can be described in terms of judgements concerning the functional attributes of the product. Since consumers, today, are faced with many competing versions of the same product, these judgements are further seen to relate to the perceived differences between brands.

Laurent and Kapferer (1985) identified four different aspects of product involvement. Two of these aspects ("imporisk" and "risk probability") correspond with the notion of "analytic value" described earlier, since perceived risk is a function of perceived quality differences between brands (Bettman 1973) and leads to active information search and evaluation. The other two aspects ("sign value" and "hedonic value") identified by Laurent and Kapferer are affective aspects, akin to the notion of "syncretic value."

The empirical evidence cited by Laurent and Kapferer (1985, p. 45) indicates that involvement with the product category is arguably a function of syncretic and analytic values and their analysis reveals four types of products: (1) products, such as irons and vacuum cleaners, in which the analytic characteristics of the product allow differentiation between brands, derived from consumers' ability to perceive actual differences between brands. (2) products, such as chocolate and yogurt, in which to the extent that the product conforms to the consumer's sense of what provides happiness, joy and other affects, syncretic value is obtained. (3) products, such as TV sets and champagne, in which the relative importance of syncretic and analytic criteria is about equal (4) products, such as detergents and toothpaste, in which neither syncretic nor analytic criteria have much importance.

ADVERTISING STRATEGY

Preston (1968) differentiated between "sign-relevant" ads, which rely on tangible, inherent aspects of the product, and "arbitrary" ads, which depend on other factors such as the aspects of the celebrity used in the ad. Such arbitrary ads were found to be rated lower in rational appeal than sign-relevant ads, but higher in emotional appeal. Thus, aspects of advertising strategy, specifically emotional and rational advertising strategies, may account for syncretic and analytic responses.

Emotional advertising can be defined, as the communication form in which a consumer experiences his/her evaluation of the affective relationship of a brand to him/her. Further, affect with the product should be distinguished from affect derived from the advertisement. Though both are affective techniques, "product induced affect" is affect depicted in advertising as arising from the product itself, while the effect in "ad induced affect" is derived from the presentational elements of the ad. The latter strategy (or classical conditioning) is specially relevant for "low involvement" items that possess little inherent hedonic value. This conditioning process is a fundamental advertising technique and has been well documented (Gorn 1982; Mitchell and Olsen 1981).

In contrast, rational advertising can be described as the communication form in which a consumer experiences his\her evaluation of the consequences of choosing the wrong brand or the analytic relationship of a brand to him/her. Accordingly, rational advertising emphasizes the differences between brands and suggests the lowering of perceived risk through the unique attributes of the advertised brand.

The conditions under which analytic and syncretic cognitions may occur are equally important. For instance, in the same experiment cited above, Preston (1968) found that the nature of the product affected the emotionality of the message but not the rationality of the message and he concluded that emotionality may be more topic (product category) centered than message (ad strategy) centered. Thus, it must be considered that outcomes such as analytic and syncretic cognition are dependent on the interaction of advertising strategy, product category and media class.

MEDIA CLASS

Buchholz and Smith (1991) have found significant interaction effects between media type and the level of involvement. Golden and Johnson (1983) also found a significant interaction effect between product category and person's preferred sensory modes (aural/visual) with regard to five measures of advertising effectiveness. Thus, it is suggested:

1. that the advertising of products high in analytic involvement in the print media, especially, serves to engender analytic cognitions, since print allows readers the opportunity to process information that reduces the inherent risk in such product categories.

2. that the advertising of products high in syncretic involvement in the broadcast media, elicits syncretic cognition by the use of non verbal cues.

Some non verbal cues, such as music, are available only in the broadcast media and this is one reason for suggesting that broadcast media generates syncretic cognitions. Chaudhuri (1985) found that music is significantly related to happiness responses in radio commercials. On the other hand, Park and Young (1986) found that music in television commercials had a distracting effect during analytic cognitive situations. The lack of such cues as music in print media may thus encourage analytic cognitive responses, at least in comparison to broadcast media.

Further, Wright (1974) showed that print media moderate analytic cognitive responses to advertising, such as source derogation and counterarguing. While Wright did not examine syncretic cognitions, another study by Chaudhuri and Buck (1990), using a repeated measures design, found significant differences in the effects of television, radio and magazines across eleven of fourteen syncretic responses, such as happiness, fear, surprise, etc. Significant differences in the three media formats were also noted for reactions to the cognitive content of the ads.

ADVERTISING DIFFERENTIATION MATRIX[1]

Figure 1 presents an "Advertising Differentiation Matrix" that uses the dimensions of analytic and syncretic responses to categorize advertisements into four classes. The general implication, for advertising strategy, that derives from this conceptual approach, is that emotional advertising is viable for all product categories. For

---

[1] Some of the points made in this section are taken from Chaudhuri (1992).

FIGURE 1
Advertising Differentiation Matrix

SYNCRETIC
COGNITION

HI   **LO**

1. Products: High in syncretic value <u>and</u> high in analytic value (autos, airlines, televisions)

   Strategies:
   - Brand Differentiation using Print media
   - Product Induced Affect using Broadcast media
   - Ad Induced Affect using Broadcast media

2. Products: Low in syncretic value <u>but</u> high in analytic value (banks, appliances, industrial products)   **HI**

   Strategies:
   - Brand Differentiation using Print media
   - Ad Induced Affect using Broadcast media

ANALYTIC COGNITION

4. Products: High in syncretic value <u>but</u> low in analytic value (chocolate, beer, sodas, yoghurt)

   Strategies:
   - Product Induced Affect using Broadcast media
   - Ad Induced Affect using Broadcast media

3. Products: Low in syncretic value <u>and</u> low in analytic value (tissues, detergents, fabric softeners)   **LO**

   Strategies:
   - Ad Induced Affect using Broadcast media

---

instance, ad induced affect (classical conditioning) is used in all four classes. In the low/low category, however, it is not accompanied by brand differentiation or product induced affect. Conversely, in the high/high category all three ad strategies are used. In the other two categories, either brand differentiation or product induced affect can be evidenced along with ad induced affect.

Quadrant 1: Certain products, such as automobiles, airlines and televisions are high in syncretic value <u>and</u> high in analytic value. A product that has sufficient affective potential generates syncretic cognition and leads to appraisal of the product category in terms of brand differences and other analytic cognitions that understand and describe the product. The advertising of such products emphasizes brand differences and <u>also</u> elicits "product induced affect" by delineating the enjoyment that can be derived from the advertised product. In addition, ads for such products utilize classical conditioning strategies to derive "ad induced affect". Product induced affect in this category serves to increase consumers' existing high involvement while brand differences and ad induced affect serve to differentiate the advertised brand from competition. An obvious failing of the FCB grid is its contention that products like automobiles are purchased solely on "thinking". A cursory look at auto ads on TV will reveal the insistent use of "feeling" techniques (jingles, etc.).

According to McLuhan (1964), print media emphasize the visual aspect of the senses leading to an analytic cognitive style of information processing that is logical and sequential. Electronic media, on the other hand, encourage a holistic style of processing that is synthetic and involves all of the senses. Krugman (1965) also noted that television communicates very differently from the active, "working to learn" mode of communication used in print. In keeping with this and the earlier discussion in the "media" section, it may be expected that for products high in syncretic <u>and</u> analytic involvement, broadcast media will produce syncretic cognition while print media will produce analytic cognition.

H1: For products high in both analytic and syncretic involvement, broadcast media will produce greater <u>syncretic</u> cognitive response than print media.

H2: For products high in both analytic and syncretic involvement, print media will produce greater <u>analytic</u> cognitive response than broadcast media.

Quadrant 2: Industrial products, services like banking and household appliances are low in syncretic value and high in analytic value. The advertising of such products emphasizes brand differences and analytic cognitive responses. In addition, ads for such products utilize classical conditioning strategies to derive ad induced affect and thereby further differentiate the advertised brand. The attempt is to generate syncretic value through the advertisements for products, which otherwise possesses very little inherent affective potential.

Bowen and Chaffee (1974) found that "pertinent" ad appeals, in which objective brand information was given, were more effective (in terms of ad evaluation and willingness to buy) than non-pertinent or "arbitrary" ad appeals, under conditions of high involvement with the product category. Thus, a greater level of involvement motivates the consumer to process brand information. Product information is also likely to generate greater analytic cognitive responses when it is used in the print media, since print allows greater opportunity to process such information (Wright 1974).

H3: For products high in analytic involvement but low in syncretic involvement, brand differentiation strategies will produce greater analytic cognitive response than other strategies.

H4: For products high in analytic involvement but low in syncretic involvement, brand differentiation strategies in print media will produce greater analytic cognitive response than brand differentiation strategies in broadcast media.

Quadrant 3: The FCB grid does not accomodate products that may be low in both thinking and feeling, but certain products, such as tissues, fabric softeners and detergents are low in syncretic value and low in analytic value. Ads for such products utilize classical conditioning strategies to derive ad induced affect, thereby differentiating the brand from competition.

At first glance it would appear that industrial products and tissues could not possibly benefit from emotional advertising. However, ads for industrial products do not only develop beliefs and ads for tissues do not only repeat the brand name. In both classes there is classical conditioning through the subtle use of symbols. The attempt is to create involvement with the ad by using, say, puppies in an ad for toilet tissues. Affection for trade characters (Snuggle, Pillsbury Doughboy, etc.) also translates into affection for the product. Of particular interest is the interaction, if any, between such thematic elements and different media. For instance, it is entirely possible that humor on broadcast media produces greater affect than in print due to the "vividness" effect, described by Chaiken and Eagly (1983).

Music is another spontaneous cue in classical conditioning strategies and one that can obviously be used only in broadcast media. Gorn (1982) found that positive attitudes towards a product could develop as a result of the association of the product with music that had a positive effect on the listener. Hearing liked or disliked music directly affected product choice in his experiment.

Gorn argues that the positive emotions generated by music become associated with the advertised product through classical conditioning. The liking for the ad gets conditioned to the brand itself and becomes part of the brand. This can take place in the total absence of analytic cognitions or beliefs, since product information was kept at a minimal level in the experiment.

In general, broadcast media can be expected to function more effectively in this quadrant than print, since broadcast contains more sensory elements and thus allows for greater arousal and greater affective response. In sum, it is suggested that low involvement products in the broadcast media produce syncretic cognitions through the use of classical conditioning (ad induced affect) strategies.

H5: For products low in both analytic and syncretic involvement, classical conditioning strategies will produce greater syncretic cognitive response than other strategies.

H6: For products low in both analytic and syncretic involvement, classical conditioning strategies in broadcast media will produce greater syncretic cognitive response than classical conditioning strategies in print media.

Quadrant 4: Certain products, such as chocolate, alcoholic beverages and sodas, are high in syncretic value but low in analytic value. The advertising of such products elicits product induced affect by delineating the pleasure that can be derived from the advertised product and serves to increase consumers' existing involvement with these products. Unlike the FCB grid, the matrix does not consider these categories to be low involvement. Involvement here is increased by the use of emotional treatments, which enhance the perceived value of the product. Further, actual differences are hard to come by in these product classes and advertising is the "real" difference induced through classical conditioning strategies.

Television is crucial for the success of such high involvement products, since the emotional or pleasurable stimulus is presented in the most lifelike and realistic way. Moreover, the facial expressions of the models on television using the product (say, ice cream) convey the rewards of product usage and generate greater affect.

H7: For products high in syncretic involvement but low in analytic involvement, product induced affect strategies will produce greater syncretic cognitive response than other strategies.

H8: For products high in syncretic involvement but low in analytic involvement, product induced affect strategies in broadcast media will produce greater syncretic cognitive response than product induced affect strategies in print media.

CONCLUSION

The implications for advertisers is clear. For "high" involvement products, high in analytic value, print ads should emphasize brand differentiation strategies based on the attributes of the brand. At the same time, it behooves advertisers to derive affect based differentiation with their ads which may in time be transferred to the brand itself. A complete and sound brand image requires that both analytic and syncretic cognitions be elicited in the advertising of these types of products.

For "high" involvement products, high in syncretic value, ads should show the affect that can be derived from the product, while for "low" involvement products, low in both analytic and syncretic values, ads should produce ad induced affect from the presentational elements in the ad, since such products lack the inherent motivational potential to produce affect. In either case, emotional communication is always relevant. Moreover, as emphasized throughout, such communication is best achieved through the broadcast media which present sensory information in more vivid, life like and dynamic images than print and thereby produce greater syncretic cognitive response.

REFERENCES

Bettman, James R. (1973), "Perceived Risk and Its Components: A Model and Empirical Test," *Journal of Marketing Research,* 10 (May), 184-90.

_____(1979), *An Information Processing Theory of Consumer Choice.* Reading, MA: Addison-Wesley.

Blanshard, Brand (1962), *Reason and Analysis.* La Salle, IL: Open Court.

Bowen, Lawrence and Steven H. Chaffee (1974), "Product Involvement and Pertinent Advertising Appeals," *Journalism Quarterly,* 51 (Winter), 613-621.

Buchholz, Laura M. and Robert E. Smith (1991), "The Role of Consumer Involvement in Determining Cognitive Response to Broadcast Advertising," *Journal of Advertising,* 20 (1), 4-17.

Buck, Ross (1988), *Human Motivation and Emotion.* New York, NY: John Wiley.

Chaiken, Shelly and Alice H. Eagly (1983), "Communicator Modality as a Determinant of Persuasion: The Role of Communicator Salience," *Journal of Personality and Social Psychology,* 45 (2), 241-256.

Chaudhuri, Arjun (1985), "Attributes in Radio Commercials That Predict Emotional Responses," Masters thesis, University of Connecticut.

_____(1992), "Advertising Implications of the Pleasure Principle in the Classification of Products," presented at Association for Consumer Research Conference, Amsterdam, (June), 11-14.

_____and Ross Buck (1990), "Media Differences in Emotional Responses to Advertising," Unpublished study, University of Connecticut.

Edell, Julie A. and Marian C. Burke (1987), "The Power of Feelings in Understanding Advertising Effects," *Journal of Consumer Research,* 14 (December), 421-433.

Golden, Linda and Keren A. Johnson (1983), "The Impact of Sensory Preference and Thinking Versus Feeling Appeals on Advertising Effectiveness," in *Advances in Consumer Research,* Alice M. Tybout and Richard P. Bagozzi, eds. Ann Arbor, MI: Association for Consumer Research, (10), 203-208.

Gorn, Gerald J. (1982), "The Effect of Music in Advertising on Choice Behavior: A Classical Conditioning Approach," *Journal of Marketing,* 46 (Winter), 94-101.

Holbrook, Morris B. and Elizabeth C. Hirschman (1982), "The Experiential Aspects of Consumption: Consumer Fantasies, Feelings and Fun," *Journal of Consumer Research,* 9 (September), 132-140.

Krugman, Herbert E. (1965), "The Impact of Television Advertising: Learning Without Involvement," *Public Opinion Quarterly,* 29 (Fall), 349-356.

Laurent, Gilles and Jean-Noel Kapferer (1985), "Measuring Consumer Involvement Profiles," *Journal of Marketing Research,* 22 (February), 41-53.

McLuhan, Marshall H. (1964), *Understanding Media: The Extension of Man.* New York: McGraw-Hill.

Mitchell, Andrew and Jerry C. Olson (1981), "Are Product Attribute Beliefs the Only Mediator of Advertising Effects on Brand Attitude ?" *Journal of Marketing Research,* 18 (August), 318-332.

Park, C. Whan and S. Mark Young (1986), "Consumer Response to Television Commercials: The Impact of Involvement and Background Music on Brand Attitude Formation," *Journal of Marketing Research,* 23 (February), 11-24.

Pechmann, Cornelia and David W. Stewart (1989), "The Multidimensionality of Persuasive Communications: Theoretical and Empirical Foundations," in *Cognitive and Affective Responses to Advertising,* Patricia Cafferata and Alice M. Tybout, eds. Lexington, MA: Lexington Books.

Preston, Ivan L. (1968), "Relationships Between Emotional, Intellectual and Rational Appeals in Advertising," *Speech Monographs,* 35, 504-511.

Vaughn, Richard (1980), "How Advertising Works: A Planning Model," *Journal of Advertising Research,* 20 (5), 27-33.

Wright, Peter L. (1974), "Analyzing Media Effects on Advertising Responses," *Public Opinion Quarterly,* 38 (Summer), 195-205.

ORGANIZATION AND SUPPLIER EVALUATION IN MERCHANDISERS

Richard Germain, Oklahoma State University
Dale S. Rogers, University of Nevada

ABSTRACT

The study examines empirically how structure, technology adoption and context affect use of supplier evaluation criteria in merchandisers. Formal supplier evaluation was found to be associated with formal information control and electronic data interchange (EDI) adoption, and inversely related to size and the central consolidation of distribution activities in a single hierarchy.

INTRODUCTION

An important aspect of organizational buyer behavior is supplier evaluation. Supplier evaluation provides a formal basis for tracking alternative supplier performance, for providing feedback to suppliers on how well they are meeting expectations and standards, and for reducing the number of suppliers. In practice, relational exchange with a reduced number of suppliers has been dependent on formal supplier evaluation programs (Harrington, Lambert and Christopher 1991; Spekman 1988). Major corporations including Xerox and Chrysler have decreased the number of suppliers dealt with over the last decade to fuel performance. It is the link between supplier evaluation and performance (Nilsson 1977) that has spurred interest in the topic.

Given the performance implications of supplier evaluation, the current study seeks to expand our knowledge of the phenomenon in merchandise organizations. The study's underlying premise is that supplier evaluation is a formal organizational process. Given such, it should, just like any other formal process, be related to the firm's structure, technology and operating context. The study's setting is primarily one of distribution (used interchangeably with logistics and operations). Thus the dimensions of structure and many of the supplier evaluation criteria in the study relate to distribution.

In the section that follows, supplier evaluation is discussed in more detail. The structure, technology and context variables are introduced, and general expectations as to why they should relate to the extent of supplier evaluation are presented. An empirical study is described, and dimensions of supplier evaluation are derived using factor analysis. Results relating the predictor variables to the supplier evaluation dimensions are presented and discussed.

BACKGROUND

Supplier Evaluation

According to Spekman (1988), two broad types of supplier evaluation criteria exist: supplier efficiency and relationship quality criteria. Supplier efficiency criteria are the traditional ones of price, product quality and delivery capability. On-time delivery, an element of supplier efficiency, allows a buying firm to reduce safety stocks and financing requirements while maintaining the same stock out rate to customers. This underlies the importance of on-time delivery in a just-in-time manufacturing environment. All too often efficiency criteria are used in an adversarial context: "although these are important concerns [price, quality, delivery capability], they do not cover all the issues upon which a good long term relationship should be based" (Spekman 1988, p.80). Many buyers use efficiency criteria to play suppliers off against one another, thereby gaining price, product quality and delivery concessions.

Relationship quality evaluation criteria have long term, strategic implications. Supplier technical support, management capability, management support and flexibility to meet changing needs provide bases for relational exchange. Managers use relationship quality criteria in conjunction with efficiency ones to formulate long term plans and goals. They allow managers to better understand and control tradeoffs between supplier efficiency and relationship quality. They also provide a rational basis for reducing the number of suppliers and for creating strategic supplier relationships. When Xerox reduced its suppliers by 50 percent during the 1980s, the key criteria of supplier quality commitment, innovativeness and ability to reduce costs blended efficiency and relationship quality concerns (*Purchasing* 1985).

Past research has identified a number of variables that affect the use of supplier evaluation criteria. Shipley (1985) reported that merchandisers' use of supplier evaluation criteria varies with whether the product under consideration is a convenience versus shopping good. Use also varies with the purchase of major capital items versus component parts (Jackson, Keith, and Burdick 1986). The industry itself also has an effect (Dempsey 1978).

Few if any studies have examined how the use of supplier evaluation criteria vary with respect to the structure, technology and context of the firm. These issues are examined in the following sections.

Structure, Technology and Context

The first structure variable in the study is the extent to which responsibility for logistics activities are centrally consolidated in a single hierarchy. This issue has been subject to considerable debate in the distribution literature (Bowersox et al. 1989; Glaskowsky, Hudson, and Ivie 1992; Johnson and Wood 1990). Centralized consolidation is thought to provide the firm with a greater base of logistics expertise that fosters technology adoption, efficiency and functional integration. For instance, the consolidation of outbound transportation from a marketing hierarchy and inbound transportation from a purchasing one may increase negotiating leverage against transportation carriers, and may allow the firm to balance inbound, outbound and intra-firm shipments through computerized vehicle scheduling.

One of the benefits of central consolidation of logistics responsibilities in a single hierarchy may be greater evaluation of suppliers on various criteria, especially distribution criteria. For example, a hierarchy that controls many logistics activities may be better positioned to understand the impact of alternative supplier on-time delivery performance.

The second and third structure variables are the extent of formal information from internal and external sources used to gauge operations and performance, respectively called formal internal control and formal environmental control. The potential relationships between formalized control and use of supplier evaluation is grounded in the belief that supplier evaluation is a formalized control process. If it is a formal control process that evaluates supplier performance, then it is similar, at least conceptually, to a formalized control process that evaluates the performance of the firm relative to the competition (i.e., formal environmental control) or that evaluates the firm on internally generated performance standards such as return on investment or fill rate to customers (i.e., formal internal control). In addition, both internal and environmental control heighten management awareness of organizational performance, which may mean that managers look to suppliers to fulfill performance objectives. Simply put, a firm that is more aware of its own performance, either through internal or external sources, should be more aware of alternative supplier performance.

The technology variable in the study is EDI. The adoption of this technology in particular is a signal that the firm is forging strategic links with suppliers. Furthermore, EDI systems have the capability to provide management with hard facts concerning alternative supplier

performance (Benjamin, de Long, and Morton 1990). Information systems can filter through purchasing records and freight bills to provide managers with performance estimates on supplier fill rates, on-time delivery and order cycle variance. Greater adoption of EDI technology should be related to the extent of supplier evaluation.

Finally, size, a context variable, is included in the study. Research findings have consistently reported that larger firms are more formalized, decentralized and specialized (Miller and Dröge 1986), and adopt greater levels of technology (Carter 1984). If supplier evaluation is a formal process, it should be related to size.

HYPOTHESES

Based on the previous discussion, the following hypotheses are proposed:

H_1: Centralization of logistics responsibilities in a single hierarchy is related to use of supplier evaluation criteria.

H_2: Formal internal controls are related to the use of supplier evaluation criteria.

H_3: Formal environmental controls are related to the use of supplier evaluation criteria.

H_4: Adoption of EDI technology is related to the use of supplier evaluation criteria.

H_5: Size is related to the use of supplier evaluation criteria.

The above hypotheses are universalistic in that they do not differentiate between types of supplier evaluation criteria. Little reason exists to suspect that size, for instance, would be more related to the use of delivery capability criteria than to relationship quality criteria. On this basis, the following hypotheses is proposed.

H_6: The effect of the predictor variables in H_1-H_5 is the same regardless of the type of supplier evaluation criteria.

METHOD

Sample

A panel of academicians and industry executives developed a self-administered questionnaire. A sampling frame of 6,678 U.S. and Canadian wholesalers and retailers was purchased from Dunn and Bradstreet. After pretesting, a questionnaire was mailed to the CEO in each firm and a total of 367 (5.5%) were returned. Respondents were asked to select from as many as were appropriate from wholesaler, retailer and manufacturer. This study concentrates on the 286 wholesalers, retailers and vertically integrated wholesale-retailers. Firms indicating a manufacturing orientation in addition to a merchandising one were excluded to create a more homogeneous class of respondents. CEOs, presidents and vice presidents completed about two-thirds of the questionnaires, while the remainder were completed by directors or managers, most with responsibility for operations or distribution.

Mean annual sales were $1.02 billion with a standard deviation of $2.76 billion and a median of $160 million. The class of trade distribution was: food, 23.2 percent; building materials, hardware and garden supply, 16.5 percent; furniture and home furnishings, 13.7 percent; general merchandise, 11.2 percent; automotive (no dealers), 9.1 percent; apparel and accessory, 8.8 percent; fuel, 5.6 percent; drugs, health and beauty aids, 5.6 percent; paper and office supplies, 3.9 percent; and "other," 2.4 percent.

Scaling: The Independent Variables

The centralization of logistics responsibilities in a single hierarchy was measured on a 5-point scale with endpoints of "completely decentralized" and "completely centralized" (mean = 3.57; sd = 1.15).

Formal internal control was operationalized as the number of information items out of a list of 38 that respondents indicated they used to formally monitor operations (mean = 23.30; sd = 8.01). The list included a wide array of items relating to asset management (inventory turns, obsolete inventory) costs (warehouse costs, inbound and outbound freight costs), customer service (fill rate, on-time delivery, cycle time), claims (dollar amount of damage, credit claims), and productivity (units shipped per employee, goal programs). Formal environmental control was operationalized as the number out of a list of 10 areas that the firm compared itself to against competitors (mean = 3.77; sd = 3.10), and included customer service, transportation operations, logistics strategy and logistics costs.

The adoption of EDI technology was operationalized as the number of entities out of a list of eight that the firm had forged telecommunication links with (mean = 1.43; sd = 1.44). The entities included public warehouses, transportation carriers and manufacturers.

Size was measured by the natural logarithm of annual sales (mean = 19.20; sd = 1.71). Reliability of the summed yes/no scales was estimated using the Kuder Richardson 20 formula. Respective KR_{20} estimates of .94, .85 and .58 for formal internal and environmental control and EDI adoption are acceptable.

Scaling: The Dependent Variables

Respondents were asked to rate the use of each of the 15 supplier evaluation criteria shown in Table 1. Five-point scales with endpoints of "never use" and "always use" were employed.

The 15 criteria were factor analyzed using the maximum likelihood approach. Empirical indicators and factor interpretability concerns suggested a three factor solution was appropriate. Table 1 presents the promax rotated factor pattern matrix. With the exception of short order cycle, all the criteria load on one and only one factor at .50 or greater. Most load on at least one additional factor near zero.

The first factor, relationship quality, which has nine variables loading on it, addresses the quality of buyer-supplier trading relations and includes good communications, supplier management quality, supplier positive attitude and early notification of disruption. The second factor, packaging/cycle quality, addresses quality and variance in the supplier's order cycle and packaging. Distribution performance, the third factor, addresses on-time delivery and percent of orders shipped complete, two key delivery capability variables.

Several observations should be made concerning the factor analysis. The emergence of the second and third factors suggests that delivery capability, as one of three evaluation criteria areas suggested by Spekman (1988), is not a unidimensional construct, but is multidimensional and composed of at least two distinct dimensions. The distinction between factors two and three is subtle but important. The level of on-time delivery and percent of orders shipped complete by a supplier may immediately affect the buyer's performance and the effect may be readily apparent. Late deliveries and incomplete shipments may lead to a merchandiser confronting its own stockout situation. The second factor, on the other hand, is primarily concerned with variance. If quality is in part a variance problem, then cycle variance is a quality issue, and merchandisers therefore conceptualize packaging quality and cycle variance as elements of the same dimension.

RESULTS

Three multiple regression models were estimated. Each model predicts one of the three factor scored dimensions underlying supplier evaluation. The independent variables in each model are centralization, formal internal and environmental control, EDI technology adoption and size. The results of the regression models are summarized in Table 2. The percent of variance explained by the models is modest and ranges from 13 percent to 23 percent. All three models are significant at the 1 percent level.

Twelve of the fifteen parameter estimates in the models are significant at the 10 percent level. Centralization is inversely related to relationship quality (F1), packaging/cycle quality (F2) and distribution performance (F3). Formal internal control and EDI technology

TABLE 1
Summary of Maximum Likelihood Factor Analysis

Variable and Factor	Promax Rotated Loadings		
	F1	F2	F3
F1: Relationship quality			
flexible	.90	-.01	-.04
positive attitude	.84	.13	-.10
management quality	.83	-.04	-.01
good communications	.78	-.04	.14
easy to work with	.75	.07	.05
service quality	.72	.04	.14
customized service	.70	.05	.02
customer support	.69	.08	.04
early notification of disruption	.63	.01	.17
F2: Packaging/cycle quality			
shelf unit package quality	.03	.90	-.06
master carton package quality	-.05	.89	.03
consistent order cycle	.29	.50	.14
short order cycle	.26	.36	.21
F3: Distribution Performance			
on-time delivery	.21	-.05	.75
percent of orders shipped complete	-.22	.29	.63

adoption are related to all three dimensions of supplier evaluation criteria. Formal environmental control is associated with the use of relationship quality (F1) criteria. Finally, size is inversely related to the use of relationship quality (F1) and distribution performance (F3) criteria.

To address H_6, a multivariate multiple regression model was estimated. The overall model was significant (Wilks' lambda = .69; F = 6.77; p < .01) indicating that not all parameter estimates equal zero. Individual F-tests for the equality of each unstandardized parameter estimate are reported on the right hand side of Table 2. The only significant F-statistic is the one for centralization of logistics responsibilities. This means that the unstandardized parameter estimates of formal internal and environmental control, EDI technology adoption and size are equal across regression models. The unstandardized parameter estimates of centralization of logistics responsibilities are unequal across regression models however. With the exception of centralization, H_6 is supported.

Four broad conclusions can be drawn. First, formal internal control and EDI technology adoption each alone equally affect the use of all three dimensions of supplier evaluation (respectively supporting H_2 and H_4). Second, centralization inversely affects all three dimensions of supplier evaluation (contradicting H_1), but the magnitude of the effect dependents on the particular criteria under consideration. Third, size has an inverse and equal effect on all three dimensions of supplier evaluation (contra-

dicting H_5). While only two of the size parameters estimates are significant, the signs of all three are negative and statistically equal. Finally, the overall role of formal environmental control is marginal since only one parameter estimate is significant, but all three are equal (not supporting H_3).

LIMITATIONS

Two limitations in particular are worthy of mention. First, the low survey response rate raises the issue of external validity. The reader is cautioned to infer the results to the population with extreme care.

Second, the list of supplier evaluation criteria did not include product price and product quality. We can speculate that their inclusion in the factor analysis may result in a fourth factor emerging: a value dimension containing price and product quality. On the plus side, several evaluation criteria including packaging quality have not been included in previous studies.

Both limitations point out the importance of conducting further research to validate the dimensions underlying supplier evaluation criteria and the relationships between organization and supplier evaluation.

DISCUSSION AND CONCLUSION

Several results warrant discussion. The major contribution of the study is that structure, technology and

TABLE 2
Summary of Regression Models

Independent Variable	Dependent Variables Standardized Coefficients (t-values)			Multivariate Tests Wilks'	
	F1	F2	F3	Lambda	F
Centralization of logistics Responsibilities	-.20a (-3.55)	-.12b (-2.15)	-.11c (-1.95)	.98	4.74b
Formal internal Control	.19a (3.00)	.39a (6.42)	.19a (2.96)	.99	0.01
Formal environmental Control	.17a (2.66)	.06 (1.06)	.10 (1.56)	.99	2.26
EDI technology Adoption	.17a (2.77)	.13b (2.22)	.18a (2.90)	.99	0.01
Size (log of sales)	-.19a (-3.31)	-.06 (-1.01)	-.15b (-2.46)	.98	1.45
R-square	.18	.23	.13		
Model F	11.58a	15.76a	7.62a		

a = significant at 1%; b = significant at 5%; c =s ignificant at 10%
F1= relationship quality; F2 = packaging/cycle quality; F3 = distribution performance.

context are related to the extent to which merchandisers' evaluate suppliers. The results concerning formal information control and EDI technology adoption suggest that supplier evaluation can be thought of as an extension of the firm's formal control and technology system. To our knowledge, this is the first time that such a finding has been reported in the literature.

Two of the findings contradicted expectations. First, centralized consolidation of logistical responsibilities in a single hierarchy detracted from merchandiser efforts to evaluate alternative suppliers. Central consolidation may result in the distribution hierarchy retaining control over the dissemination of internally generated distribution performance information. An understanding of the impact of alternative supplier performance may be centralized in the department, and this may stifle supplier evaluation. From the opposite perspective, dispersed logistical responsibilities may mean that supplier performance is a concern of many hierarchies and many managers, and this may spur the evaluation of alternative suppliers.

Second, size was inversely related to the extent of supplier evaluation efforts. If supplier evaluation is really

a type of formalized control, then a positive relationship should have been reported between it and size. It is possible that as size increases, merchandisers become more concerned with value (price and product quality) as the criterion of primary interest and less concerned with delivery capability and relationship quality. Size provides the marketplace muscle to gain steep price concessions that in total may outweigh the financial gains obtained from delivery concessions and enhanced relationship quality.

As a case in point, Wal-Mart, which competes heavily on price, recently wrote to suppliers and told them that they wanted to deal directly with manufacturers and not with manufacturers' representatives or independent brokers. While increased communication and improved reaction time were factors Wal-Mart cited as precipitating the strategy, the industry saw it as an attempt to "eliminate a layer of costs, a logical desire for a retailer that brags about its everyday low prices" (Blumenthal 1991, p. A3). Of course, representatives and brokers are displeased with the plan, as well as many small manufacturers that cannot afford a full time salesforce. Several brokers are threatening to sue since anti-trust laws clearly state that it is illegal for a retailer

competitive" (Blumenthal 1991, p. A3). In addition, Sears just announced that they want suppliers to cut packaging materials by about one-quarter over the next couple of years which is projected to save several millions of dollars each year in shipping costs.

The point of these examples is that large merchandisers have the marketplace presence to aggressively seek price/cost concessions from suppliers. They may very well be trading relationship quality and delivery capability against price. And we can speculate that this explains the inverse relationships between size and the supplier evaluation dimensions included in this study. A study addressing size and supplier evaluation that includes price and product quality would be a welcomed addition to the literature.

With the exception of central consolidation of logistics, the magnitude of the predictor variable effects did not vary significantly across the dimensions of supplier evaluation criteria. Further research should also address this issue.

A number of additional variables can be identified for inclusion in future research. Aside from value supplier evaluation criteria, additional structure, technology and context as well as strategy variables should be studied. Environmental stability, for example, may be conducive to evaluating suppliers. Merchandisers that supply products where the products themselves undergo frequent change (e.g., electronics) or that operate in industries where consumer tastes change quickly (e.g., fashion) may not want to evaluate suppliers with the goal of limiting the supplier base. Such could decrease the firm's ability to respond to environmental variability. A discount retail strategy in addition to size may engender increased use of a price criterion, and decreased use of other criteria.

CONCLUSION

The study provides several insights for managers. The most important centers on the role of supplier evaluation in the firm. Supplier evaluation is more than an isolated activity implemented by purchasing to gain concessions from suppliers, to reduce the number of suppliers, or to forge long term strategic supplier relations. It is an extension of the merchandiser's formalized control system. It is linked to purchasers' formal internal information system and to the level of EDI technology. As merchandisers increasingly formalize control over operations, as they become increasingly aware of their own performance in terms of, for example, customer service, they increasingly monitor suppliers on distribution performance, packaging and cycle quality, and supplier relationship quality. The role of EDI technology may be less direct than that of formal internal control: aside from service implications, EDI provides a means of data collection on alternative supplier performance.

Central consolidation of logistical responsibilities and size both have a negative impact on the level of supplier evaluation. Managers should be aware that while functional integration and the total cost concept remain key considerations when designing a structure for the firm (Bowersox et al. 1989), centralizing logistical responsibilities is apparently not a route that integrates supplier performance with that of the firm. Size as well detracts from evaluation efforts, possibly because larger merchandisers focus more on value and price than on relationship quality and delivery capability.

In summary, the study demonstrated an important linkage between supplier evaluation and organization in merchandisers. They key implication is that distribution operations and supplier evaluation are related to one another, and that together they form a coordinated planning and control system that links suppliers to customers and to performance.

ENDNOTE

The authors thank Donald J. Bowersox for providing the data and A.T. Kearney and Digital Equipment Corporation for their financial assistance.

REFERENCES

Benjamin, Robert I., David W. de Long and Michael S. Morton (1990), "Electronic Data Interchange: How Much Competitive Advantage?" *Long Range Planning,* 23 (February), 29-40.

Blumenthal, Karen (1991), "Wal-Mart Set to Eliminate Reps, Brokers," *The Wall Street Journal,* (December 2), A3+.

Bowersox, Donald J., Patricia J. Daugherty, Cornelia L. Dröge, Dale S. Rogers, and Daniel L. Wardlow (1989), *Leading Edge Logistics: Competitive Positioning for the 1990s.* Oak Brook, IL: Council of Logistics Management.

Carter, Nancy M. (1984), "Computerization as a Predominant Technology: Its Influence on Structure of Newspaper Organizations," *Academy of Management Journal,* 27 (June), 247-270.

Dempsey, William A. (1978), "Vendor Selection and the Buying Process," *Industrial Marketing Management,* 7 (August), 257-267.

Glaskowsky, Nicholas A., Jr., Donald R. Hudson, and Robert M. Ivie (1992), *Business Logistics.* New York: The Dryden Press.

Harrington, Thomas C., Douglas M. Lambert, and Martin Christopher, (1991), "A Methodology for Measuring Vendor Performance," *Journal of Business Logistics,* 12 (1), 83-104.

Jackson, Donald W. Jr., Janet E. Keith, and Richard K. Burdick (1986), "Examining the Relative Importance of Physical Distribution Service Elements," *Journal of Business Logistics,* 7 (2), 14-32.

Johnson, James C. and Donald F. Wood (1990), *Contemporary Logistics.* New York: Macmillan.

Miller, Danny and Cornelia Dröge (1986), "Traditional and Psychological Determinants of Structure," *Administrative Science Quarterly,* 31 (December), 661-674.

Nilsson, Jerker (1977), "Purchasing by Swedish Grocery Chains," *Industrial Marketing Management,* 6 (2), 317-328.

Purchasing (1985), "Xerox Preaches the Gospel of Just-in-Time to Suppliers," 32 (October 24), 21-22.

Shipley, David D. (1985), "Resellers' Supplier Selection Criteria for Different Consumer Products," *European Journal of Marketing,* 19 (7), 26-36.

Spekman, Robert E. (1988), "Strategic Supplier Selection: Understanding Term Buyer Relationships," *Business Horizons,* 31 (July/August), 75-81.

USE OF CREDIT BY OLDER ADULTS

Anil Mathur, Hofstra University
George P. Moschis, Georgia State University

ABSTRACT

In 1989, households headed by individuals age 55 and older spent a total of $730 billion on goods and services, or 27 percent of expenditures of all U.S households. This figure is approximately 10 percent greater than what the average household spends on a per capita basis, according to U.S Bureau of Labor Statistics (1989). Credit is not only a common method of payment (Stanley, Sewall and Moschis 1982), but also one of the most important determinants of store patronage (e.g., Hirschman 1979). Given that a large portion of older adults may use credit to purchase products and services (e.g., Bartos 1980, Stanley et al. 1982), patterns of credit use among the mature market should be of particular interest to retailers, businesses selling directly to consumers, and marketers of financial services.

This study examines several issues related to actual use of credit and the reasons for age related differences in credit card ownership, use, or attitudes toward credit. For example, how dose credit card ownership relate to actual credit use? Are older people less likely to use credit or do they have fewer opportunities to use credit? What are the reasons for the age-related differences and inconsistencies in previous research findings? Do age differences in credit use reflect changes in lifestyles or possibly attitudes toward credit as a result of early life experiences (e.g., the Great Depression years)?

Six factors were used as alternative explanations for lower credit use: number of credit cards owned, frequency of purchasing products at stores (other than food or drug items), frequency of buying direct, number of major purchases made, employment status, and family income. These variables were expected to explain difference in frequency of credit use commonly attributed to age.

The study consisted of 1,305 telephone interviews conducted in December 1990 by Market Facts' National Telephone Center in Evanston Illinois. The sample for the survey was selected from Market Facts' weekly omnibus telephone survey, TeleNation. To facilitate comparison across age groups quotas were set for five age groups: 25-49 (300), 50-64 (302), 65-74 (301), 75-84 (202), and 85+ (200). Within each age groups, interviews were conducted for males and females proportionate to their distribution in the population.

This study found that older adults use credit as frequently as younger adults when needs and opportunities for consumptions in both groups are similar. Age declines in use of credit may reflect changes in lifestyles and other circumstances associated with age, not age per se. The results further suggest that credit vehicles should be positioned as means of making purchases convenient rather than as instruments for financing purchases.

Taken together, these results dispel the conventional wisdom that older people do not use credit because they have been sensitized to negative connotations of credit due to, for example, the Great Depression years. A major finding that emerges from these data is that older people may use credit less frequently due to changes in lifestyles and other circumstances associated with age, not age per se. Thus, it may not be the older person's attitude toward credit but rather needs and circumstances which create or suppress opportunities to use credit. These findings have important implications for retailers and consumer credit lenders.

For further information please contact:
Anil Mathur
Assistant Professor
Department of Marketing and International Business
Hofstra University
Hempstead, New York 11550

IN QUEST OF WHAT SHAPES A UNIVERSITY'S IMAGE: AN EXPLORATORY ANALYSIS

Ravi Parameswaran, Oakland University
Aleksandra E. Glowacka, Oakland University

ABSTRACT

The declining number of university age students in the demographic make-up of the United States in the 90's and the early part of the next century, decreases in federal and state funding for higher education and the intense competition for the consumer's discretionary dollars, are all contributing to the need for institutions of higher education to restructure and strategically reposition their organizations. Among the trends already evident, as higher education copes with these dynamic changes, is the increasing use of advertising, promotion and other strategic marketing tools. Consistent with the characteristics of organizations facing increased competition, institutions of higher education will need to create, mold, disseminate, and maintain a rather distinctive image as a means to maintain competitive advantage in the marketplace. Towards this end, colleges and universities will have to determine what is their current image (if any), where do their strengths lie, what can they do best, rethink their mission and develop strategies for positioning and repositioning.

An extensive computer literature search did not reveal any studies on the development or the basis for such development of university images. The current study offers useful insight on the existence of distinct university images. We then examine such images in light of information processing theories relative to consumption decision-making and offer it as a theoretical base through which the structure of university images may be examined.

A considerable research effort has been devoted to examining the consumer problem-solving, information processing and decision-making behaviors. Much has been learned from these research studies. Of particular interest are theories pertaining to explanations of how consumers process relevant information when evaluating and selecting product brands. Researchers have also been interested in the order in which product-attribute information is acquired. It is generally accepted that consumers may follow a brand search sequence (*processing by brand*), where each brand is evaluated against all criteria before search proceeds to the next brand. An alternative approach involves an attribute search sequence (*processing by attribute*), where brand information is collected by examining all brands simultaneously on an attribute-by-attribute basis. Reliance on a well-known brand name with a reputation for outstanding quality can be an effective way of reducing risk, especially when consum-

ers lack personal experience with a product. In this case, a brand image serves as a halo and influences consumer beliefs about attribute performance. In contrast, as consumers become familiar with a product, image can serve as a summary construct which summarizes consumers' beliefs about product attributes and directly affects their brand attitude. The summary construct view is based on the notion of information chunking. Studies on categorization provide additional insight into our understanding of the type of information processing a consumer might engage in order to arrive at final judgment. Their underlying assumption is that people divide the world of objects around them into categories (*category based approach*), which enables them in understanding and processing information from the environment in an efficient manner. An alternative approach to the category-based model is processing by attributes (*piecemeal approach*). Its basic premise is that consumers combine the pieces of attribute information (usually by adding or averaging, viz. summarizing) to arrive at the overall value of the object under consideration. We examine the structure of university images in the context of such information processing generalizations.

Two hundred and forty three human resource managers were interviewed in a large midwestern metropolitan area to gauge their perceptions of graduates from nine area colleges and universities. The managers represented a broad spectrum of firms in various industries characteristic of the region and included managers from small, medium and large firms. Based on the literature relating to personnel selection and evaluation, six categories of attributes were considered important in the employee selection and retention process: knowledge, skills, productivity, employability, personality, and motivation. These six attribute domains were further elaborated into 40 specific attributes which were considered germane in differentiating among employees or potential employees. Respondents rated graduates from relevant colleges/universities on each of these attributes based on actual experience or perceptions as a proxy measure for the university's image. A total of 729 university image evaluations were obtained. In this preliminary analysis, we decided to use *exploratory* rather than *confirmatory* techniques. That is, we considered the research to be primarily exploratory in nature. Exploratory factor and discriminant analyses were the main analytic procedure that we employed in the analysis of the data.

The findings reveal that perceptions of the quality of graduates from an institution of higher education are indeed formed on the basis of a relatively small number of criteria (one to nine) rather than by the dozens. These criteria are, however, attribute aggregates (chunks) suggesting that choice processes in college recruitment occur at a higher level of abstraction. This result is consistent with general findings in consumer research which suggest that six or fewer evaluative criteria are likely to be used by most consumers. There is strong evidence that choice processing in this domain is by brand rather than attribute. Of the 35 factors extracted in the nine factor analyses, 25 (71%) were linear composites of five or more variables. The above finding is further strengthened when we compare factor solutions from different colleges/universities. Each college/university had a distinct factor solution. The number and/or the composition of the factors varied from institution to institution. As a result of this study, there is compelling evidence that, in college recruiting, each institution is perceived as a unique entity with a "personality". Of the nine colleges/universities examined in this study, the factor analytic results identified two or more factors in seven of the cases. This finding suggests that "image" serves as a *summary*, rather than as a *halo*, construct in higher education where the consumer is familiar with the "product". Finally, using multiple discriminant analyses, there is evidence that university images are formed through a piecemeal, rather than a category-based, process.

REFERENCES

Bettman, James R. (1979), *An Information Processing Theory of Consumer Choice*. Reading, MA: Addison-Wesley.

Biehal, Gabriel and Dipankar Chakravarti (1983), "Information Accessibility as a Moderator of Consumer Choice," *Journal of Consumer Research*, 10 (June), 1-14.

Sujan, Mita (1985), "Consumer Knowledge: Effects on Evaluation Strategies Mediating Consumer Judgments," *Journal of Consumer Research*, 12 (June), 31-46.

For further information please contact:
Ravi Parameswaran
Oakland University
School of Business Administration
Rochester, MI 48309-4401

INDUSTRIAL BUYER ' CHOICE CRITERIA' IN DEVELOPING COUNTRIES

Srivatsa Seshadri, University of Arkansas
C.P. Rao, University of Arkansas

ABSTRACT

Industrial marketers operating in the world market have two strategies -- global or multi-national - to choose from. This study explores and compares the attributes emphasized by industrial purchasers, in India and Nigeria, in supplier selection to suggest the latter as more appropriate. The study suggests that knowledge of the perceptual/conceptual differences in choice criteria between purchasers of developing countries, even though within homogeneous blocks, is crucial in developing an appropriate marketing strategy in an international context.

There is a general tendency to adopt a global strategy, within prior defined blocks of countries, to market industrial goods in marked contrast to marketing consumer goods. For example developing countries are implicitly treated as a homogeneous block, with each country in the block assumed to have similar procurement criteria, an ecological fallacy, and a single strategy adopted. The appropriateness of this approach is the focus of this paper.

"Supplier attributes" emphasized by industrial buyers in the aforementioned developing countries are investigated by comparing the dis/similarities in the attributes. Two research hypotheses were formulated:

H1: The industrial purchasers of standard products in India and Nigeria perceive 'supplier attributes' differentially.

H2: The industrial purchasers of special products in India and Nigeria perceive 'supplier attributes' differentially.

The respondents were allowed to think of relevant products in these two categories within their own contexts. An exhaustive list of 'choice criteria' was developed using previous research work (Bertrand 1961; Dickson 1966; Rao and Kiser 1974b; Rao and Kiser 1977) and consultations with other researchers and a limited number of industrial buyers in both the countries. Fifty one choice-criteria were finalized and 7-point Likert-scales anchored at 'little or no importance' (1) and "very important' (7) were created. Questionnaires were sent to a random selection of 500 Indian and 300 Nigerian companies. Responses were received from 172 Indian firms and 84 from Nigerian companies, yielding response rates of 34.4 percent and 28 percent respectively.

Four sets of data were thus collected, for (1) India - Standard Products, (2) Nigeria - Standard Products, (3) India - Special Products, and (4) Nigeria - Special Products. The hypotheses were tested by a Factor Analysis procedure employing oblique rotation, using the method of Principal Components. Factors (supplier attributes) were extracted Velicer's criteria of Minimum Average Partials (off-diagonals) (Velicer 1976), since the latent root criterion is known to overextract the number of common factors (Velicer 1976; Velicer and Jackson 1990; Hubbard and Allen 1987). In the context of Indian firms three common factors were extracted for both standard and special products. These were named CONVENIENCE, CALIBER, and COMPETENCE for standard products and IMAGE, ACCOMMODATION and PROFICIENCY for special products. Five factors were extracted for both standard and special products in the context of Nigerian companies. These were INFRA-STRUCTURE, RELIABILITY, RELATIONSHIP, SERVICE and FINANCIAL TERMS in the context of standard products and DEPENDABILITY, SUPPORT, FINANCIAL TERMS, FIRM-IMAGE and FACILITIES for special products.

The number of common factors extracted differed between the two countries indicating of divergence in the valence of the choice criteria in selecting the supplier. In the context of standard products Indian purchasers considered CONVENIENCE in contrast to the Nigerian Buyers, who weighed both FINANCIAL TERMS and the vendor RELATIONSHIP. What was considered by Indian purchasers as CALIBER, is perceived, in contrast, by Nigerian industrial buyers as related to vendors' INFRA-STRUCTURE, and some aspects of RELIABILITY and SERVICE. In the context of special products Indian purchasers considered ACCOMMODATION, a vendor attribute which roughly corresponded to FINANCIAL TERMS and SUPPORT that Nigerian buyers considered separately. IMAGE, as considered by Indian industries, appeared different to Nigerian buyers' understanding of it. A between countries comparison of the factor patterns, for each product category, indicated that most choice variables loaded differentially, and some choice criteria considered by one country were not considered by the other. The correlation matrices generated supported the research hypotheses by revealing very low correlations between factors of the two countries for each product-type. These seem to indicate significantly different perceptions of the importance of choice criteria, though part of the divergence could be attributed to measurement issues.

The study demonstrates that industrial marketers with an international perspective need to emphasize different aspects of the purchasers' choice-criteria depending on the target country. Understanding the perceptions of the industrial purchasers of a country about such constructs as IMAGE, SERVICE, CALIBER, etc. is critical. Choice criteria considered important by the buyers in one country need not necessarily be considered important by industrial purchasers of another country, even though they may be in the same stage of development.

For further information contact:
Srivatsa Seshadri
College of Business
BADM 302
University of Arkansas
Fayetteville, AR 72701.

A CROSS CULTURAL ANALYSIS OF ENVIRONMENTAL BUYER BEHAVIOUR

Hazel T. Suchard, Australian Catholic University
Michael J. Polonsky, University of Newcastle
David Bejou, Memphis State University
Emin Babakus, Memphis State University

ABSTRACT

Studies in consumer behaviour examine a broad range of issues. Two types of issues often examined in the literature are those that attempt to determine the important factors in the consumer decision making process and how important these factors are.

One of the most pressing issues facing marketers at all levels is how the increased general interest in the environment affects the consumption pattern of consumers. Researchers have tried to quantify consumer interest in a variety of ways. They have examined attitudes, perceptions, knowledge and behaviour of various groups to a range of environmental issues. These studies have gone on to examine the "causality" of factors such as demographics, psychographics, socio-economic variables on consumers environmental attitudes, perceptions, knowledge and behaviour. In all these cases, there have been few, if any, models of consumer behaviour put forward that are generalisable to all groups. In fact, many of the studies compare the environmental behaviour for two different groups, usually highlighting the differences between the groups examined. Given that differences exist between groups, it is not unusual to find that cross-cultural studies also produce differences between the consumer groups in the different countries studied.

Cross-cultural environmental behaviour studies are exceedingly rare, though there exist numerous studies examining other behaviour cross-culturally. This study examines the environmental attitudes and perceptions of Australian and American consumers for a number of issues. It also examines the consistency of these two groups between their perceptions and prepurchase consideration (a proxy for intention and environmental action).

The paper extends earlier work (Suchard and Polonsky 1991). In that earlier paper a model is developed, based on Ajzen and Fishbein's model of consumer behaviour. In the model (see Figure 1), the various types of risk that consumers face are incorporated into the decision process. The earlier paper added environmental risk into the model and was based on a study of Australian consumers.

The present study is a crosscultural one which compares consumers in Australia and the U.S.A. The study compares two set of consumers, who do the regular non-food shopping for themselves or their family. In the US sample there are 302 respondents and in the Australian sample there are 275 respondents. The respondents were interviewed outside retail shopping centres which contained a supermarket. Both samples used the same survey instrument, though the US data was collected approximately 18 months after the Australian data.

A number of issues are examined. These include, inter alia, consumers attitudes towards the affect of a number of product groups on the environment, the consumers pre-purchase consideration of these effects prior to purchase of these product groups, the consistency between these two factors, the impact of various publics on consumer decisions to purchase environmental products and various other environmental issues relating to purchase. The product groups examined were; Wood (for building); Pesticides; Plastics including Packaging; Cosmetics; Aerosols; Petrol; Power; Paper Products including Newspapers; Household Cleaning Agents; and Laundry Liquids and Powders.

In all cases, US consumers perceived the detrimental impact of the various product types to be less that of the Australian consumers. In all cases except one, these responses were also statistically different. In terms of the pre-purchase consideration given towards the detrimental impact of the product groups on the environment, the Australian consumers gave the environmental impact more pre-purchase consideration, in six cases. In the other four cases, the US consumers gave the environmental impact more pre-purchase consideration. Responses for five of the product categories were statistically different, usually the Australian consumers gave the environmental impact more pre-purchase consideration, though this was not always the case.

It appeared that often the consumers in the two countries were inconsistent in their views that the products were detrimental to the environment and with regard to the amount of pre-purchase consideration of the detrimental environmental impact the products had. The degree of inconsistency differed between countries as well.

This study looked at the relationship between perception of detrimental impact and the amount of pre-

FIGURE 1
A Theory of Environmental Buyer Behavior

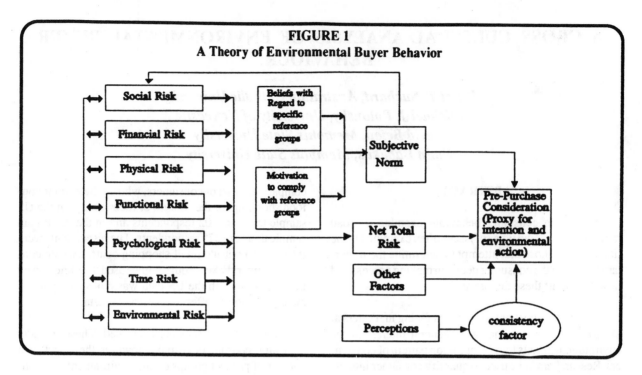

purchase consideration given for the various product groups. It was found that there was some relationship between the two variables and the relationship was stronger for US consumers than Australian consumers. In some cases the US correlations were twice as high as the corresponding Australian correlations. Using the proportion of variation explained by the correlations (R-squared) the differences in the relationship between perception of detrimental impact on the environment and pre-purchase consideration even vary further. In all cases, the relationship is almost always twice as strong for American consumers as Australian consumers.

In examining the impact of various publics on consumers purchasing patterns, it was found that they both tend to be influenced by the same groups, children and family being the most important, with political parties and government being the least important. In all cases, the mean responses were not significantly different, except for government, which was rated as being more important by US consumers than Australian consumers.

Responses of consumers to giving certain other factors prepurchase consideration were also examined and in a majority of cases the Australian consumers responded more positively than the American consumers in terms of their environmental behaviour or consideration of the environmental impact of various factors, although they were not as consistent as the Americans. It possible that Australian consumers are more concerned in general, but do not believe that they can have an impact on the resulting environmental consequences or they do not believe their behaviour will make a difference.

The paper then goes on to examine some of the broader issues involved with the general buyer behaviour

model. Physical risk is incorporated as individuals responded that they were most concerned with the impact on their health when purchasing goods. From a financial risk perspective, consumers are still concerned with paying more for goods, though overall they are willing to pay more. A larger proportion of the Australian respondents than the American respondents indicated that they would be willing to pay more for environmentally safe goods, though a majority of all consumers believed that environmental goods must perform as well as competitively priced goods. This implies that functional risk will be an important factor in the decision to buy environmentally "friendly" goods. Societal risk was demonstrated when the reference groups were examined. Given the rankings, all those groups, which consumers directly relate to, have the greatest influence on their purchasing behaviour of environmental goods.

Though the model structure was not stringently tested it appears that many of the components are indeed important. There needs to be further research to determine if this general model holds for different types of buyer behaviour, aside from that of environmental buyer behaviour. Additionally, can the model be generalized to other types of environmental behaviour, for example, recycling and voting behaviour.

The paper found that there were differences between American and Australian consumers. It appeared that Americans are more consistent in their perceptions and behaviour, though the Australian consumers believe environmental problems are more important. This implies that Australian consumers do not believe they have the ability to change the environment they live in. Marketers need be aware that any environmental marketing activities, while important, may have varying success in different countries. Given the results of this study, it could be inferred that Australians would be more likely to join environmental action groups rather than change their purchasing behaviour, while in the US, consumers may take the opposite route. Understanding the weighting of the variables in the general model would assist marketers to determine which factors are the most important in that country. They must then determine the most appropriate marketing strategy to take given these differences.

For further information contact:
Hazel T. Suchard
Division of Business
Australian Catholic University
40 Edward Street
NORTH SYDNEY   NSW   2060
AUSTRALIA

CONVENIENCE-ORIENTED CONSUMPTION IN GLOBAL MARKET SEGMENTATION AND PLANNING

Mushtaq Luqmani, Western Michigan University
Zahir A. Quraeshi, Western Michigan University
Ugur Yavas, East Tennessee State University

ABSTRACT

The bases for the segmentation of international markets by classifying countries have mainly centered on the use of macro environmental factors such as economic, geographic, political, cultural or religious. The effectiveness of these classifications is influenced in some measure by micro-variables such as the objective(s) of segmenting markets (Jain 1990), by the nature of the company's product (Pryor 1965) and by the individual purchase orientation of customers. This signals a need to complement or build on macro classifactory variables by examining specific variables that have a direct influence on consumer and product preferences and yet are useful in the delineation of international markets. A specific segmentation variable that could be useful in accomplishing this purpose is the convenience-orientation of customers. A convenience-orientation is expressed in the value placed on, and the active search for, products, facilities and processes that will either provide personal comfort and/or save time in performing necessary activities. Using convenience-orientation as a variable in segmenting international markets has merit for several reasons:

1. The construct can be reasonably-defined and adequately measured in equivalent terms across cultures.

2. Convenience as a product specific variable is known to have a direct and substantive influence on consumer preferences (Kargaonkar 1984).

3. Worldwide, convenience-oriented consumption is on the rise with no signs of abating (Benway et al. 1987).

4. Since consumers in different countries may demand varying levels of convenience, charting a worldwide convenience-orientation can be assumed to have the characteristics of a continuous variable.

Also the consumption patterns corresponding to convenience are not inconsistent with the patterns of consumption reflected in the conventional classification of developed versus less developed countries, and suggests that a convenience classification can be used as a complement to existing schemes.

The literature on convenience can be partitioned into two research streams pertaining to: (1) Dimensions of Convenience and (2) Determinants of Convenience. The dimensions of convenience can be factored into either a time-oriented or a comfort-oriented basis. A perspective on the literature on convenience can also be gained by a discussion of its determinants. For the most part, the demand for convenience stems from (a) the value placed on time and comfort, (b) the extent of economic affluence and industrialization and (c) cultural influences.

Convenience as a common factor of consumption among countries may be used to provide global strategic planning insights. A convenience in each nation. In this matrix, countries that are high on both dimensions can be viewed as innovator countries. These countries could be studied for lead indicators on how consumption and demand patterns may change in the future as a result of an increasing convenience orientation. They would also serve as useful models for evaluating other follower countries progressing toward more convenience.

The ability-to-buy factor is important for eventual consumption. A particular group may desire convenience only to find that the added costs to service the requisite convenience are prohibitive. The two dimensions, a convenience orientation (high vs. low) and ability to pay (affordable vs. unaffordable), when combined offer four potential scenarios in terms of opportunities.

Insights can also be gained from a careful examination of the convenience continuum. In terms of product planning the same product could be marketed simultaneously in several countries to groups with similar levels of convenience. Additionally, product that are presently in demand because of convenience factors in one country can at a future time be targeted to countries that are presently low on the convenience continuum scale. In terms of promotional strategies, basic appeals can be centered on the need for convenience. In terms of distribution, the availability and mix of products that match varying levels of convenience would need to be determined for various countries. Just as with promotional appeals, a proper match ought to be accomplished between the convenience oriented consumers and the offer of convenience in distribution channels.

Also, it may be essential to incorporate convenience

as a new dimension to the traditional price-quality-service set of evaluative factors. Similarly, prestige and status-oriented approaches may be complemented with a convenience-oriented pricing approach.

For further information please contact:
Dr. Mushtaq Luqmani
Western Michigan University
Haworth College of Business
Kalamazoo, MI 49008

IDENTIFYING DIFFERENTIAL COMPETITIVE ADVANTAGES USING AN EXTENDED GAP ANALYSIS MODEL

Jay U. Sterling, *University of Alabama*
Robert A. Robicheaux, *University of Alabama*
Carl E. Ferguson, Jr., *University of Alabama*

ABSTRACT

Parasuraman, Zeithaml and Berry (1985) identified that significant barriers frequently prevent the successful implementation of the marketing concept, namely discrepancies (or gaps) between buyer and seller perceptions of both service quality levels and expectations. Lambert, Stock, and Sterling (1990) expanded the five gaps identified by Parasuraman, to include an additional four gaps, covering all four components of the marketing mix in a manufacturing environment. This paper modifies the gaps of these previous authors and uses them to identify future intentions and overall satisfaction levels of customers as well as those "threshold" marketing services that must be provided to maintain current business and "value added" services that will most likely lead to incremental business.

The gaps proposed by Parasuraman, et al. and Lambert, et al. were refined to a set of six gaps that were developed from an external survey of customers and an internal audit of a sponsoring firm's perceived and actual performance levels. Customers' expectations and their perceived evaluations of how major vendors were performing on the various marketing services were matched with the provider's perceptions of customer expectations and performance levels, as well as actual performance levels as determined from an audit of company (provider) records. By matching the output from these various measurements it was possible to identify and predict key measurements of overall firm performance: (1) current market share of each vendor, (2) future intentions of customers; (3) overall satisfaction evaluations by customers; and (4) differences between "A" (primary) versus "B" (secondary) vendors. The resulting gaps that emerged as predictors or determinants of these global measurements were also used as the basis for: (1) segmenting markets; (2) developing channel specific marketing programs; (3) identifying options to gain differential advantage over competitors; and 4) developing specific action programs across each of the components of the marketing mix.

METHODOLOGY

The premium pet food industry was selected to test the validity of the extended model. A total of 208 marketing services (attributes) were identified. Four thousand names, were randomly extracted from a purchased mailing list of active U.S. veterinarians. 2,406 eligible respondents were identified by personal telephone calls from MBA students. The process used to construct the sample in this study reemphasized the importance of both qualifying and incenting prospective respondents. Of the 2406 persons sampled, 1365 responded, representing a response rate of 57 percent. Surveys identical to the ones mailed to veterinarians were also mailed to 355 managers of a co-operating manufacturer.

Respondents were asked to evaluate the importance of the 208 marketing mix elements that they considered when selecting a new brand or evaluating the performance of current brands. Seven point scales of importance were anchored on each extreme. Participants were also requested to provide evaluations of their two primary vendors using a 7-point scale with 1 = very poor to 7 = excellent/outstanding.

RESULTS

The 208 marketing services in the questionnaire were factor analyzed. These factors were used to identify determinant marketing services. Multiple discriminant analysis was used to predict whether a manufacturer was a primary (A) or secondary (B) vendor, based on performance factor gaps. For example, the discriminant analysis procedure produced a statistically significant discriminant function that correctly classified 90% of the cases (respondents) where the co-operating manufacturer was the "A" versus the "B" vendor. The factor scales used in this analysis represented composite scores of the gaps between customers' perceptions of importance and their evaluations of the manufacturer's performance. This analysis identified two distinct classes of influential marketing services. One set contained positive discriminant coefficients, suggesting that superior relative performance on these factors would increase the likelihood that the manufacturer would continue as/become the "A" vendor. These factors were labeled "Value Added" attributes. The second set of factors had negative coefficients in the discriminant functions, indicating that failure to meet or exceed competitive performance levels on these factors could relegate the manufacturer to "B" vendor status. These factors were labeled "threshold" attributes.

The final phase of the model involved the identification of a parsimonious set of variables that management could use to build and operationlize a strategic marketing plan. The framework for identifying these attributes was derived by computing the significant gaps for each of the variables contained in the nine significant discriminating factors.

For further information contact:
Jay U. Sterling
Department of Management and Marketing
University of Alabama
College of Commerce & Business Administration
Tuscaloosa, AL 35487-0225

DEFENDING MARKET LEADERSHIP: CHARACTERISTICS OF COMPETITIVE BEHAVIOR

Stanley F. Stasch, Loyola University of Chicago
John L. Ward, Loyola University of Chicago

ABSTRACT

A study of some three dozen case histories was used to classify the competitive behavior characteristics exhibited by firms which aggressively attacked market leaders and by the market leaders which were attacked. The study resulted in a three-part model consisting of (1) the attack, (2) the leader's defense, and (3) the attacker's counter response.

INTRODUCTION

Although a market leader is in the enviable position of holding the largest share of the market, other competitors in the market tend to look at the leader's share with covetous eyes. Each year the business press reports a number of examples where a competitor makes a serious attempt to capture a significant portion of the leader's market share. Sometimes such attempts succeed, but often they do not appear to be more than marginally successful, or even to enjoy any success at all. On the surface of it, because such situations involve market leaders, one would expect the marketing literature to abound with both theoretical and empirical studies addressing the following issues:

How do market leaders successfully defend their leadership positions?

What marketing strategies can a challenger firm use to take significant market share away from the market leader?

Yet a search of the literature does not bring the expected reward. Instead, the researcher finds that there exists only three substantive articles which address the issues of market leadership strategies or attacking market leaders. Bloom and Kotler (1975) authored an article which addressed "Strategies For High Market Share Companies". Ten years later *Fortune* magazine published "How To Attack The Industry Leader," by Porter (1985). A year later, Ward and Stasch (1986) analyzed the question of "When Are Market Leaders Most Likely To Be Attacked?" The literature search did not uncover any empirical studies addressing either of the two issues noted above. Neither did it uncover any articles concerned with the competitive behavior of market leaders when they are attacked, or any articles concerned with the competitive behavior of firms that attack market leaders.

PURPOSE OF THE PAPER

For several years we have been compiling case histories of marketing strategies actually used by firms, in order to gain insights into why they are successful or unsuccessful. Our research approach is based upon case histories of marketing strategies which are both visible to an interested observer and well-documented in publications. In each case history we classify the market and competitive situation faced by the brand or firm which is the subject of the study, and we do so according to twenty-three different categories of situational factors. (See Ward and Stasch 1980.) We also identify the specific details of the marketing strategy employed by the firm, and these details are broken down into twelve marketing strategy elements. Finally, we typically use changes in market share to record the results of the strategy, but we also use other measures, such as profitability, when such information is available.

Of the eighty-odd cases compiled to date, more than three dozen involve an aggressive attack upon a market leader by a competitor who had not recently demonstrated above-normal aggressiveness toward the market leader. (Table 1 shows a select list of such attacks on market leaders.) We considered a competitor's attack to be "above-normal" in aggressiveness if it was noticeably stronger than the marketing activities engaged in by that competitor during the previous year or two. Examples of such above-normal aggressiveness included: moving into new geographic markets where the competitor previously had not had distribution, but which the leader traditionally had dominated; introducing a new product into direct head-to-head competition with the market leader's brand and then using comparative advertising to encourage trial of the new product; dramatically increasing advertising expenditures far above the market leader's and the industry's norm, thus forcing an increase in the industry's expenditures on advertising; entering for the first time into the market with a new product that is very competitive with the leader's product and is supported by large marketing programs.

While analyzing these case histories, we saw that all of them displayed competitive behavior characteristics which were very similar. Most of the case histories had a few minor competitive behavior characteristics which were shared by some, but not all, of the other case histories. Because these minor competitive behavior characteristics seemed to logically fit with the characteristics displayed by all of the cases, we combined both sets of characteristics. We believe that the resulting composite represents a classification--or"model"--of the full range of competitive behavior characteristics which can be exhibited by firms which aggressively attack market leaders and by the market leaders which are aggressively attacked. The purpose of this paper is to describe that "model" of competitive behavior characteristics.

We believe this "model" can be useful to both marketing academicians and practitioners for the following reasons.

1. It represents necessary input information if we are to begin building a theory associated with what strategies market leaders should use when they are aggressively attacked, and what strategies firms can use to attack market leaders.

2. It helps marketers understand the competitive interaction and dynamics of an attack on a market leader and the market leader's response, and the nature of the competitive behavior used by the two combatants.

3. It provides a framework which marketers can use when studying which strategies can be used by market leaders to successfully defend their leadership positions, as well as which strategiesare not likely to be successful.

4. Conversely, it can help marketers study the strategies used by attacking firms in order to identify why some strategies are successful while others are not.

CHARACTERISTICS OF COMPETITIVE BEHAVIOR

Our analysis suggests that a three-part model best describes the behavior characteristics of competitors when a market leader is being attacked. The three parts consist of (1) the attack, (2) the leader's defense or response, and (3) the attacker's counter response. Each part consists of four or five major elements which can be used to describe the behavior of the two competitors. Each major element further consists of approximately four to six sub-elements which help describe the competitors' behavior. Table 2 outlines the three-part model with all its major elements and sub-elements.

The following discussion presents the major elements associated with each part of the model. In the discussion, each of the major elements is presented as a question. The discussion then addresses some of the "different ways" the question can be answered. The "different ways" the question can be answered are based on the sub-elements associated with each major element of the model (see Table 2). In the discussion, the case histories listed in Table 1 are used to illustrate the model's major elements and some of its sub-elements.

The Attack

1. **Does the market leader see the attack coming?** Our research indicates that there are several possibilities here, and each is likely to have a differing effect on competitive behavior. The attack can be a complete surprise, and it can come either from a logical rival or from an unexpected one. Our research suggests that the competitive behavior of an unexpected rival is likely to be different from that of a logical rival. Rather than being a surprise, some attacks are well-signaled. For example, Johnson and Johnson was alerted to expect a new competitor in the sutures market when U.S. Surgical petitioned the FDA for permission to begin testing their new sutures.[1] Sometimes the market leader can see that an attack is evolving and is likely to emerge sometime in the future. When Bic expanded its disposable razor out of the European market into Canada, Gillette saw that it was highly probable that Bic would soon be introducing its disposable razors into the U.S.

2. **What is the form of the attack?** Attacks can be categorized four ways: innovative, power-oriented, based on one or more of the attacker's strengths, or "copy the leader." Each is likely to result in different competitive behavior.

By definition, an innovative attack will introduce some type of competitive behavior which is new to that marketplace. Power-oriented attacks are most likely to involve the use of lower prices to compete and/or heavy expenditures on advertising and promotion. Not surprisingly, some attacks are based on the attacker's current strengths, as when Procter & Gamble utilized its distribution strengths to achieve good distribution for its Citrus Hill orange juice against strong competitors Minute Maid and Tropicana. The fourth type of attack, perhaps the most commonly used one, occurs when the attacker merely tries to duplicate the marketing efforts being used by the market leader (i.e., "copy the leader".)

3. **What is the attacker's market definition strategy?** Competitive behavior can also be influenced by how the attacker defines its market. After all, an attacker may choose not to define the market in the same manner as the market leader. When Hanes introduced its L'eggs product, they choose not to define their target market in the traditional manner used by the leading marketer of women's hosiery. Rather, they defined their market differently: working women who wanted to purchase good hosiery as a convenience product where they shopped for food and cosmetics. Sometimes an attack may be based on attempting to simultaneously serve two traditional, but different, segments with a single offering. When Quaker Oats introduced its soft-moist dog food, Tender Chunks, this one product served as a substitute for both traditional canned dog food and dry dog food. A company may utilize their reputation or brand name as the basis for defining their market. Anheuser-Busch was

TABLE 1
Selected Cases Of Attacks On Market Leaders

Market	Years	Market leader	Attacker
Sutures	'87-91	Johnson & Johnson	U.S. Surgical
Disp. razors	'76-79	Gillette	Bic
Orange juice	'82-85	Minute Maid	Citrus Hill
Hosiery	'68-70	Burlington Ind.	Hane's L'eggs
Dog food	'77-79	Ralston Purina	Tender Chunks
Light beer	'77-83	Miller Lite	Bud Light
Oatmeal	'87-88	Quaker Oats	General Mills' Total
Ath. shoes	'87-90	Nike	Reebok
Disp. diapers	'80-84	P & G's Pampers	Huggies
Pickles	'65-70	Heinz, Borden	Vlassic
Mouthwash	'76-77	Listerine	P & G's Extend
Batteries	'86-89	Eveready	Kodak
Toothpaste	'78-80	P & G's Crest	Beecham, Lever
Bran cereal	'85-86	Kellogg All Bran	Fiber One
Chewing gum	'75-80	Wrigley	American Chicle
Pkg. delivery	'82-85	Federal Express	UPS, others
Coffee	'74-78	Maxwell House	Folgers

Pump is an example of a highly differentiated counter response which, because of the relatively good timing of its introduction, suggests that Reebok was well-prepared for Nike's defense. General Mills' quick reformulation of its Fiber One to a higher fiber content represented an attempt on their part to deny Kellogg an advantage based on at least some differentiation. Again, the relatively good timing of General Mills' counter response suggests that they also were reasonably well-prepared for Kellogg's defense. Often counter responses appear to be based on the attacker trying to "just match" the leader's defense, as when American Chicle made some attempts to introduce new chewing gums similar to those used by Wrigley to defend its leadership position.

4. What marketing mix strategy is used in the counter response? When Folger's coffee aggressively entered Maxwell House's traditional eastern markets, Maxwell House put up strong defenses, including changes in their traditional marketing mix. In their counter response, Folgers made changes in their marketing mix strategy to attempt to match the leaders' defensive moves relative to advertising, promotion, or price. As reported above in the American Chicle example, a counter response may include modifying the product line to match the product line changes the leader made when defending against the attack. Or, a counter response may include a somewhat, or even a highly, differentiated product--such as the Pump, in the case of Reebok's counter response after Nike had regained market leadership. In their counter response, Reebok also changed their advertising message from a product-oriented one to a lifestyle theme when they employed their "U. B. U." campaign. The evidence indicates that when an attacker does counter respond to the leader's defense, the attacker may change their marketing mix to match the leader's defense, or they may

TABLE 2
Three-Part Model of Competitive Behavior
Characteristics When Market

A. **THE ATTACK**

1. Does the Market Leader see the attack coming?
   a. Well signaled
   b. Evolutionary emergence
   c. Surprise, but from logical rival
   d. Surprise, from unexpected rival

2. What is the form of the attack?
   a. Copy the leader: help fill market void
   b. Emphasize current strengths
   c. Power play: compete on price or marketing dollars
   d. Innovate: do something better/different

3. What is the attacker's market definition strategy?
   a. New users category/segment identified
   b. New form of segmentation
   c. Straddle two or more segments
   d. Utilize reputation and resources from a related business (e.g., brand extension)
   e. Change product-market coverage definition

4. How differentiated is the attack?
   a. How much differentiated?
   b. Improved features?
   c. New features?
   d. New price-quality (value) relationship?

5. What is the attacker's marketing mix strategy?
   a. Spending trend relative to market share
   b. New mix variables emphasized? (e.g., direct sales)
   c. New tactics?

B. **LEADER'S DEFENSE**

1. Is the leader well-prepared for the attack?
   a. Very high: anticipated attack and was prepared (e.g., fighting brand ready)
   b. High: anticipated attack and counterattacked almost immediately
   c. Didn't anticipate attack, wasn't prepared, took a short period of time to respond (e.g., 3-6 months)
   d. Wasn't prepared, didn't respond

2. What is the form of the leader's defense?
   a. Pre-emptive (i.e., see attack coming and beat them to the market)
   b. Aggressive (i.e., one-up them to punish them or to increase share aggressively)
   c. Responsive (i.e., increase the competitive stakes or arena)
   d. Reactive (i.e., try to cope with your deficiency, make some defensive effort)
   e. Ignore the initial attack (i.e., do nothing at first)
   f. Evolutionary response
   g. No response or defense at all

3. How differentiated is the leader's defense?
   a. How much differentiated?
   b. Improved features?
   c. New features?
   d. New price-quality (value) relationship?

4. Did the leader change its marketing mix strategy?
   1. Spending trend relative to market share?
   2. New mix variables emphasized? (e.g., direct sales)
   3. New tactics?

C. **THE ATTACKER'S COUNTER RESPONSE**

1. Is the attacker prepared to respond to the leader's defense?
   a. Well prepared to respond?
   b. Evolutionary counter response?
   c. Attacker was not prepared

2. What is the form of the attacker's counter response?
   a. A delayed response?
   b. A more reactive response?
   c. A more responsive response?
   d. A more aggressive response?

3. How differentiated is the attacker's counter response?
   a. How much differentiated?
   b. Improved features?
   c. New features?
   d. New price-quality (value) relationship?

4. What marketing mix strategy is used in the counter response?
   a. Increased spending trend relative to market share?
   b. New mix variables emphasized? (e.g., direct sales)
   c. New tactics?

unable to make significant inroads into Miller Lite's share of market with either Anheuser-Busch Natural Light or Michelob Light. It was only when they used their most well-known brand name as a brand extension (Bud Light) that they were able to take noticeable market share from Miller Lite.

4. How differentiated is the attacker's offering? An attack on the market leader may be based on a "me-too" product, on a product with some or much differentiation, or on a completely new product. The level of the competition between the competitors varies greatly over this range of possibilities.

Procter & Gamble essentially introduced a me-too product when it introduced Citrus Hill against Minute Maid and Tropicana, and General Mill did likewise when it introduced Total Oatmeal against Quaker Oat's Oatmeal. The lack of differentiation in these attacks undoubtedly made it easier for the market leaders to defend their positions. Reebok used a differentiated product (a fashionable aerobics shoe designed for women) to take share away from Nike in the athletic shoe market. Kimberly Clark used shape and fit to differentiate its disposable diaper (Huggies) from those offered by leader Procter & Gamble. Because both Reebok and Kimberly Clark used differentiated products, they raised the level of competitive activity in their attacks.

5. What is the attacker's marketing mix strategy? There appears to be four options available to an attacker when deciding on a marketing mix strategy. One is to use the same marketing mix and the same spending levels traditionally used by the market leader. A second option is to use the same marketing mix at an increased spending level, thus intensifying the competitive activity. A third option is to emphasize a new marketing mix variable, one which has not been used by the market leader. When they attempted to improve their market position, Vlassic made heavy use of trade promotions and in-store promotions, two marketing mix elements little used by market leaders Heinz and Borden. A fourth option open to an attacker is to use a completely new marketing mix, one that essentially "changes the rules" of marketing. Hanes moved from third place to first place in the women's hosiery market when it introduced L'eggs, and used a completely new marketing mix when doing so, e.g., television advertising, direct distribution to grocery stores, and consignment pricing. Clearly, an attacker can significantly raise the level of competitive activity by moving away from the first option noted above to any of the other options.

The Leader's Defense

1. Is the leader well-prepared for the attack? Our research indicated that market leaders demonstrate varying degrees of alertness to, and preparation for, an aggressive attack. In general, higher levels of preparation seem to result in more intense competitive activity.

The Gillette Company anticipated that Bic would soon be introducing its disposable razor into the U.S., but rather than wait for Bic to act, Gillette pre-empted Bic's introduction by introducing its own disposable razor (Good News). When Procter & Gamble used a new mouthwash (Extend) to directly attack Warner-Lambert's market leader Listerine, Warner-Lambert immediately counterattacked with its own new brand (Depend), which was used as a fighting brand to destroy the effectiveness of P & G's introduction of its new mouthwash. Both Eveready and Duracell introduced heavy trade and consumer promotions as soon as Kodak entered the replacement battery market.

Some of our cases involve market leaders who did not exhibit alertness and preparation when attacked. Within a relatively short period of time, Beacham introduced Aqua-Fresh toothpaste and Lever introduced Aim and CloseUp toothpastes, all three of which took share from market leader Crest. Procter & Gamble did not, or could not, come up with an effective response to these attacks for almost two years, by which time all three of the new brands had become quite well established.

2. What is the form of the leader's defense? A leader's defense can take on one of several forms. It can be pre-emptive, as Gillette was when it introduced its Good News razor before Bic could introduce its disposable razor. It can be very aggressive, as when Warner-Lambert used a fighting brand to counter Procter & Gamble's introduction of its new mouthwash (Extend). A market leader may also do something to increase the level of competition above that brought about by the attacker. For example, General Mills' Fiber One directly attacked Kellogg's All Bran by claiming its brand had a higher fiber content than the Kellogg brand. Within a few months, Kellogg's All Bran was reformulated to have a greater fiber content than that claimed by Fiber One, thus eliminating Fiber One's main advertising claim.

3. How differentiated is the leader's defense? Just as an attacker can use differentiation to gain an advantage, so also can the market leader use differentiation in its defense. When Gillette used its Good News razor to defend against Bic's disposable razor, they had the advantage of a "twin blade" offer compared with Bic's "single blade" offer. The fighting brand Warner Lambert used (Depend) to fend off Procter & Gamble's attack on Listerine mouth-wash was very different from Listerine but very similar to the new brand P & G was introducing (Extend). After Reebok began making strong gains in the athletic shoe market, one of the factors strongly contributing to Nike's successful counterattack was its very popular Air Jordan basketball shoe. In the example described in the preceding paragraph, when General Mills attacked Kellogg's All Bran, Kellogg responded by differentiating their product even more than the attacker had differentiated Fiber One. These examples suggest just some of the ways a leader can use differentiation in their own defense; clearly, the use of some kind of differentiation by the leader will represent an escalation in the level of competitive behavior.

4. Did the leader change its marketing mix strategy?

An option that may be available to a leader under attack is that of altering its marketing mix in a way that will be advantageous to their defense. Expansion or modification of its product line is one way leaders may enhance their defense. In the attack on Listerine, Warner-Lambert used an addition to its product line to defend against the attack. When American Chicle began making inroads into Wrigley's share of the chewing gum market, Wrigley responded with a series of successful new product introductions over a three-to-four year period. To fend off encroaching competitors, Federal Express guaranteed that overnight packages would be delivered by 10:30 AM the next morning and started using computers to be able to inform customers of the exact locations of their packages at any time.

Leaders can also use advertising, promotion, price, and distribution to alter their marketing mix. After Reebok made inroads into Nike's market share, Nike realized it could no longer ignore the use of mass media in its marketing efforts and, accordingly, began strongly using media advertising. At the same time, Nike also introduced more efficient ordering procedures, shortened delivery cycles, and greatly improved relationships with their dealers. When Maxwell House coffee was attacked by Folgers, when Eveready batteries was attacked by Kodak, and when Quaker Oats Oatmeal was attacked by Total Oatmeal, all of the leaders put increased emphasis on media advertising and/or consumer promotions in order to offset the effect of the attacker's marketing efforts.

The Attacker's Counter Response

Our research showed that almost all market leaders made some effort to defend themselves against their attackers. Most of the leaders responded fairly quickly to the attacks, but some leaders did not respond until three to six months after being attacked, in some cases even longer. If the market leader puts up a reasonable or strong defense against the attack, occasionally the attacker will offer a counter response to the leader's defense. In order to understand the character of competitive behavior when a market leader is attacked, it is necessary to investigate also the characteristics of these counter responses when they occur.

Because we observed fewer cases which demonstrated the full sequence of (1) an attack on the market leader, (2) the market leader's defense against the attack, and (3) the attacker's counter response, the amount of evidence we have on which to base a description of attackers' counter responses is less than that we have regarding both the attack and the leader's defense. The

evidence from cases which exhibited all three types of competitive behavior suggests that an attacker's counter response can consist of the same kinds of characteristics as the leader's defense. This seems to be a valid observation, especially when one recognizes that the attacker's counter response is essentially the attacker's defense against the leader's defense of the original attack. Consequently, even though we were not able to observe as many cases of attackers' counter responses, we believe the following four characteristics can be used to describe this aspect of competitive behavior when market leaders are attacked.

1. Is the attacker prepared to respond to the leader's defense?

Approximately twenty to thirty percent of the attackers showed some kind of counter response after the leader defended against the attack. Only a few of the counter responses could be characterized as being very aggressive or fairly aggressive. If there is such a thing as a more typical counter response, it would appear to be where the attacker would try to do what was necessary to "match" the leader's defense. The relatively few cases of attackers counter responding to the leaders' defenses suggest that often the attackers were not prepared, or were poorly prepared, for the leaders' defenses.

Regarding the timing of the counter responses, only one or two attacker counter responses occurred shortly after the leader's defense was established. It seems more common for a counter response to be developed over time, as the attacker sees and under-stands the nature of the leader's defense and figures out how to formulate a counter response. When the length of the time delay associated with attackers' counter responses are taken into considered along with the relatively few number of counter responses we observed, one can probably conclude that attackers tend not to be well-prepared for the leaders' defenses.

2. What is the form of the attacker's counter response?

Like a leader's defense, a counter response can be very aggressive. For example, after Nike regained its market leadership from Reebok, Reebok introduced its innovative air-inflated athletic shoe, the Pump. This new product significantly increased the level of competitive behavior between the two firms. When General Mills introduced Fiber One, Kellogg responded by increasing the fiber content of its All Bran brand. General Mills' counter response was to increase the fiber content of its Fiber One brand to match the fiber content level of the reformulated All Bran. Probably this is the most common form of counter response--where the attacker attempts to match the leader's defensive moves item by item.

3. How differentiated is the attacker's counter response?

A counter response can use differentiation ranging from little to very high, but the latter is likely to be more difficult to achieve because of the time required to come up with a much differentiated product. Reebok's

change their marketing mix in some other way. In either case, the result is likely to be an escalation in competitive behavior.

CONCLUDING COMMENTS

Although attempts to take significant share from market leaders are commonplace occurrences, there is very little in the literature which deals with this type of competition. Using some three dozen case histories of such competitive engagements, we have attempted to study and classify the competitive behavior characteristics exhibited by firms which aggressively attack market leaders and by the market leaders which are attacked.

The analysis of these case histories resulted in a three-part model of such competition: (1) the attack, (2) the leader's defense, and (3) the attacker's counter response. Each of these three parts consists of four or five major elements which represent important categories of the behavior of the two competitors. Each of the major elements further consists of four to six sub-elements which represent more descriptive details of this type of competitive behavior. We believe this model represents the range of competitive behavior characteristics which can be exhibited by firms which attack market leaders and by the market leaders which are attacked.

We feel the model can be helpful in building a theory of market leadership attack and defense. It can help marketers understand the competitive behavior dynamics of, and the interaction between, the antagonists in this type of confrontation. The model should also be of help to researchers who are interested in studying the marketing strategies used in these types of situations in order to gain a better understanding of why some are successful and others are not.

ENDNOTE

[1] Because of the numerous sources associated with each case example referred to in this paper, it is not practical to list references for these cases. References can be supplied upon request.

REFERENCES

Bloom, Paul and Philip Kotler (1975), "Strategies For High Market-Share Companies," *Harvard Business Review,* (November/December), 62-68.

Porter, Michael (1985), "How To Attack The Industry Leader,"*Fortune*, (April 29), 152-166.

Ward, John and Stanley Stasch (1980), "A Conceptual Framework for Analyzing Marketing Strategy Cases," *Journal of Marketing Education,* (April), 57-63.

_____and_____(1986), "When Are Market Leaders Most Likely To Be Attacked?," *The Journal of Consumer Marketing*, 3, 4 (Fall), 41-48.

THE TRANSVECTION AND THE VALUE SYSTEM: A COMPARISON OF ALDERSON AND PORTER

Richard L. Priem, The University of Texas at Arlington
Shahrzad Amirani, The University of Texas at Arlington

ABSTRACT

Alderson's (1965) concept of the transvection and Porter's (1985) concept of the value system exhibit remarkable similarities. Both are at the macro (i.e., marketing system) level of analysis, conceptualized as the "activities" required to move from raw materials to finished goods in the hands of consumers. Both are suggested as useful planning tools for achieving sustainable competitive advantage (Alderson 1965, p. 22; Porter 1985, p. 63). Both were influenced by economic theory. Alderson (1965), for example, acknowledges the influence of Chamberlin's (1933) theory of imperfect competition on the development of Alderson's ideas on differential advantage (Grether 1967; Savitt 1990). Similarly, Porter's recent ideas were influenced by his training in industrial organization economics (e.g., Caves and Porter 1977; Porter 1974).

The degree of influence each author's work has had on practitioners and scholars has, however, been quite dissimilar. Barksdale has noted that Alderson's "theoretical system never became the organizing concept for the mainstream of marketing thought" (1980, p. 3). Few of the 150 falsifiable propositions offered in Alderson's 1965 work have been tested (see Shapiro 1964, for an exception), and little conceptual work has been undertaken to refine or extend his general theory (Barksdale 1980; Dawson and Wales 1979).

Porter's work (1980, 1985; 1990), on the other hand, has had considerable influence on practitioners and scholars. *Business Week* notes, for example, that "Porter's model of the 'value chain' has become one of the bag of tools every MBA should graduate with... Management consultants have made millions by applying the author's competitive logic to one company after another" (1990, p. 12). Management researchers have undertaken empirical work to evaluate Porter's generic strategies (e.g., Dess and Davis 1984; Miller and Friesen 1986 a and 1986b), and have extended Porter's ideas via the "resource-based" approach to strategic management (e.g., Barney 1989; Dierickx and Cool 1989; Rumelt 1984). Marketing researchers have also begun to make use of Porter's concepts (e.g., Wright et al., 1991).

This paper evaluates Porter's (1985) value system concept as a possible platform for the further conceptualization and justification of Alderson's (1965) transvection ideas. First, the transvection and value chain concepts are compared. Then, Alderson's (1965) and Porter's (1985) use of these ideas in describing sources of sustainable competitive advantage are contrasted. Finally, the potential for future research based on the interaction of Porter's and Alderson's conceptualizations is discussed.

Barksdale (1980) speculated that the theoretical contribution of Alderson would be rediscovered at some point in the future and be incorporated into the mainstream of marketing thought, but that such an occurance would be unlikely. As illustrated throughout this paper, the similarities between Porter's recent value system concept and Alderson's notion of the transvection may lead one to conclude that Barkesdale's speculation has been realized and that Porter could be regarded as the rebirth of Alderson.

The strong similarlties between the concepts of the transvection and the value system may be useful for extending and justifying Alderson's (1965) general theory of marketing. The resource based approach to strategic management, for example, takes its lead from Porter (1980, 1985) in arguing that "strategic resources are heterogeneously distributed across firms... that these differences are stable over time," and examining "the link between firm resources and sustained competitive advantage" (Barney 1991, p. 99). Such conceptual efforts may, given the similar conceptual foundations, ultimately inform Alderson's general theory, while Alderson's (1965) emphasis on product markets may extend the work of the strategic management theorists. Porter's (1990) recent work examining sources of the competitive advantage of nations may be similarly useful in potentially extending Alderson's (1965) theory to encompass a global macromarketing perspective. Alderson's transvection concept may be useful in addressing disputes among management scholars over whether the cost leadership and differentiation business-level strategies may be successfully pursued simultaneously, or whether they represent ends on a continuum (e.g., Murray 1988). Given the similarities between Alderson (1965) and Porter (1985), Porter's many prescriptions may be of substantial interest to marketing practitioners. While the similarities may be helpful to practioners, however, the differences may be most useful to scholars in stimulating further theory building.

For further information contact: Richard L. Priem
University of Texas at Arlington
Arlington, Texas 76019

ECOLOGICAL RESEARCH ON PRICING DECISIONS IN MANUFACTURER-DISTRIBUTOR CHANNELS

Arch G. Woodside, Tulane University

ABSTRACT

Ecological research is the employment of ethnomethodologies to learn how the logic and realities of real-life decisions are made and implemented. An application of ecological research in pricing decisions is presented in this paper. A contingency decision map is described for manufacturer-distributor pricing decisions in the office furniture industry in the United States. The study is used to illustrate the research approach. The preparation of valid contingency maps of real-life decisions may help pricing strategists plan better decisions in competitive bid situations.

INTRODUCTION

Ethnomethodology includes the laying out of reality from the perspectives of all actors participating in creating and living in a particular situational reality. The ethnomethodologist believes that we can reach deep understanding and multiple truths by collecting and combining the perceptions of several participants in a reality framed in a given situation (see Mehan and Wood 1975). Research applications of ethnomethodology involve direct observation and interviews of multiple participants through several time periods as the participants' decisions and behaviors unfold. Ecological research is a branch of ethnomethodology that is particularly concerned with understanding the logic (rules) used in making decisions related to a stream of related steps. An ecological approach was employed in the study reported here on how manufacturers and distributors interact in making pricing decisions for large-order jobs in the office furniture industry.

Ecological research on marketing decisions has been reviewed by Hulbert (1981). The most well known application of the applying this ethnomethodology in pricing decisions is the work of Howard and Morgenroth (1968); these researchers demonstrated that competitive pricing decisions are contingent on the perceptions of realities by senior and local, district, managers. The research setting was gasoline pricing by Gulf Oil. A key finding in the study was that price decreases were more complex (i.e., contingent on more factors) and involved more time than price increases because of senior management's desire to limit the spread of lost margins, avoid price wars, and to signal competitors (Howard and Morgenroth (1968).

The use of ecological research on studying responses to competitive price decreases situation is illustrated by Raymond J. Trapp in a study reported by Kotler (1991, p.

502). A key finding of the Trapp study is that responses to competitor price decreases are contingent upon the answers to multiple issues: the impact of the competitor Y's lower new price on X's sales, whether or not X views Y's lower new price as permanent, and how much has the price been cut.

Both Trapp's study (Kotler 1991) and the work by Howard and Morgenroth (1968) are examples of inductive case study research that attempt to bridge field observations, interviews, and document analyses to build and test theory, and to generalize to theory, versus more well-known deductive attempts to build theory followed by testing theory to a convenience or representative sample of population units. The argument for generalizing to theory in case study research has been made in psychology by Campbell (1966; 1975), case study research by Yin (1989), buyer behavior by Wilson and Wilson (1988), and in anthropology by Gladwin (1989).

> "A common complaint about case studies is that it is difficult to generalize from one case to another. Thus, analysts fall into the trap of trying to select a 'representative' case or set of cases. Yet no set of cases, no matter how large, is likely to deal satisfactory with the complaint. The problem lies in the very notion of generalizing to other case studies. Instead, an analyst should try to generalize findings to 'theory,' analogous to the way a scientist generalizes from experimental results to theory. (Note that the scientist does not attempt to select 'representative' experiments." (Yin 1989, p. 44)

Unfortunately, Campbell and Stanley's (1963) and strong attack against "one-shot case studies" as being "of almost no scientific value" are much more well known than Campbell's revised views on case study research (Campbell 1966; 1975; 1979). In his revised view, Campbell (1979, p. 57) emphasizes that "I have overlooked a major source of discipline (i.e., of degrees of freedom if I persist in using this statistical concept for the analogous problem in non-statistical settings). In a case study done by an alert social scientist who has thorough local acquaintance, the theory he uses to explain the focal difference also generates predictions or expectations on dozens of other aspects of the culture, and he does not retain the theory unless most of these are also confirmed. In some sense, he has tested the theory with degrees of freedom coming from the multiple implications of any one theory. The process is a kind of pattern-matching in which there are many aspects of the pattern demanded by theory that are available for matching with his observations on the local setting."

The study by Howard and Morgenroth (1968) is an example of creating theory from case study research and testing the theory in the same case study setting. A triangulation of research methods (observations, document analyses, and interviews) was used to construct binary flow diagrams (an information processing and decision theory) of pricing decisions within one firm. The units of analysis was not the one firm examined but rather the population of pricing decisions made within the firm. Howard and Morgenroth (1968) were able to test and generalize their inductive theory to a sample of these population units: the information processes and paths taken in making 32 pricing decisions were used to test the decisions predicted from the inductive theory to actual decision outcomes; the model predicted correctly 100 percent of the 32 decision outcomes (also, cf. Morgenroth 1964). Even though only directions (up, down, and no change) were predicted by the model, the case study research, theory construction, and theory testing by Howard and Morgenroth (1968) is an early empirical example of the substantial value of case study research for both building and testing grounded theories of marketing decisions-behaviors.

In the present paper, we report the pricing decisions, and contingencies involved in pricing high versus low, in one business-to-business industry in the Unites States: the office furniture industry. The aim of the study was to develop a descriptive model, that is, a contingency map, of the dynamics of pricing decisions in situations involving two levels of a business-to-business marketing channel when planning competitive bids. Contributions of the study include the reporting of the specific contingencies involved in relatively docile versus highly aggressive bidding situations and the integration of bid renegotiation requests made by customers in deciding on final bids.

Pricing decisions in business marketing often are made on a case-by-case basis; thus, in the case study reported here and similar to Howard and Morgenroth (1968), the unit of analysis is the pricing decision with respect to one market or individual customer within one time period. A local distributor's price sometimes depends on: the customer's negotiations skills; the distributor's own price requests; how important the customer is to both the distributor and the manufacturer; how aggressive the competitors are for this customer's business; and the working relationship the distributor has with manufacturer related to the product meeting the customer's specifications.

The contingency pricing model described here differs from the previous work of Howard and Morgenroth (1968) and Trapp (Kotler 1991) in several ways. Unlike the previous studies, competitive bids are submitted by competing office furniture distributors and customers are involved actively in influencing the final pricing decision; thus, modelling of marketing decisions in such settings involves the integration of marketing and buying

contingencies within one set of decision rules and flow diagram. In many cases (specific pricing decisions), the realities of competitive bidding include customer's attempts to renegotiate marketers' bids and multiple attempts to set a price to profitably win a customer's business. A key issue in "big-job" pricing decisions is whether or not the distributor and the manufacturer want to go-to-the-mat with the competing manufacturer-distributor channels to get the contract.

Preparing contingency maps of real-life price decisions in different contingency conditions may help strategists understand and predict what is going to happen next, if certain events turn-up during specific marketing and buying scenarios. Such maps provide a theory-in-use approach for learning the choice criteria and heuristics in use by each channel member in the pricing process: the manufacturer, the distributor, and the customer. The multiple paths to a competitively high, parity, and low price can often be summarized elegantly in one map.

A detailed contingency map is described here of the pricing strategies that occur frequently in the office furniture industry in the U.S. The map involves the pricing strategies for one major category of customers: large customers bidding large jobs. For example, the map fits the situations of a state-wide bank buying furniture for several planned new local branches or a manufacturer buying furniture and design services for remodeling its national headquarters.

METHOD

The office furniture pricing map and discussion are based on in-depth direct field research and observations of distributor relationships with manufacturers, and distributor relationships with their customers. The occurrence of each path and the contingencies involved were confirmed by direct observations of the bidding processes, and contract awards lost and won, and by multiple interviews with the same respondents. A total of 80 bidding processes were examined involving 13 manufacturers and 7 office furniture distributors, and one to three persons in each of the 80 customer buying centers.

To gain trust among distributors and customers, and deep knowledge of pricing decisions, takes time. Living with decision makers, that is, doing multiple interviews, once and twice each week, for several months is necessary to learn why a distributor makes a special pricing request to a manufacturer, when the manufacturer grants the request, and when a customer attempts to renegotiate a bid. Before building and attempting to generalize descriptive pricing models, such ethnographic research studies need to be completed in many industries.

Access to the individual decision makers included in the study was gained by first approaching the senior managers of the firms involved. Initial contact included three steps: letter, telephone call, and initial personal interview. The rationale for the study included explaining that most marketing and buying decisions involve several steps made in a time period of days and weeks and that little is known about the day-to-day activities of how executives make such decisions in the office furniture and other industries. Confidentiality and a copy of the findings of the study were offered to the executives of the participating firms; no other incentives were offered.

A total of 4 to 12 face-to-face interviews were completed with each of the marketing decision makers among the distributors in the study. In the customer organizations, one person was interviewed one time in 47 of the cases; one person was interviewed twice in 13 cases; two persons in the same buying organization were interviewed in the same day in 12 cases; and for 8 cases, three persons were interviewed in one or more days each. Working 2 to 3 workdays per week, a total of nine months was taken to complete the field work for the study.

Part of the research process is showing early and later revisions of contingency maps to individuals participating in the decision process; and asking for comments on important missing features, and how the map might be improved to better reflect reality. Several rounds of re-interviews with the same persons are required before they agree that all the important contingencies are included. So like Colombo, the pricing researcher needs to be a detective who interviews key participants several times to learn what really is happening and why it is happening.

Bonoma (1985a, 1985b) has been a strong advocate for greater use of such case research approaches illustrated by decision maps. He points out that many currently underspecified marketing phenomenon are well suited for case-based investigation. "The management of distributor relationships, sales management, and the general question of what constitutes effective marketing management are three illustrative areas where case research could lead to substantial theoretical advances" (Bonoma 1985a).

MARKETING TO LARGE CUSTOMERS IN THE OFFICE FURNITURE INDUSTRY IN THE UNITED STATES

No one manufacturer has a dominating market share in the $55 billion office furniture industry in the U.S. However, Steelcase is the largest office furniture manufacturer in sales. Steelcase is a competitor often pricing aggressively to seek increases in market share and to become the dominant supplier of large customers. Herman Miller and Haworth are competitors to Steelcase; these two competitors follow high-price, high-product and design quality, marketing strategies, but they sometimes offer their distributors special price deals depending on the immediate situation.

In the U.S. over 70 percent of office furniture is sold in local markets through distributors. Most distributors offer office design, free-standing and open-system furniture, credit, warehousing, installation and repair, as well as ordering and transporting services to their customers. In any given state, no one distributor usually dominates the state-wide market, although a few (4 to 8) large competing distributors have most of the available business within a specific metropolitan area.

In the U.S. office furniture industry, local distributors do not have exclusive sales territories. Competing distributors often have sales offices in two or more major cities in the same state. A manufacturer often identifies different distributors as principal distributors for different cities. To limit channel friction, manufacturers prefer not to use two distributors located principally in the same city.

Thus, in responding to a large customer's request for quotation (a customer with furniture purchases annually often more than $100,000), a distributor may face competing distributors who carry the same manufacturer's product lines. That is, a Herman Miller distributor headquartered in Nashville may be competing against a Herman Miller distributor headquartered in Memphis, as well as competing against a Steelcase and other distributors, for the same job.

MAPPING CONTINGENCY PRICING STRATEGIES FOR LARGER-ORDER BIDS FOR OFFICE FURNITURE

The head of purchasing at Highland Bank (Name and location disguised) in Memphis, Tennessee, requests several in-state office furniture dealers to bid on furniture requirements of four new branch locations planned by the bank for 1992. Two dealers headquartered in different cities and representing Herman Miller, one Westinghouse, one Steelcase, and three dealers representing other manufacturers' product-lines are planning to bid on the work. How will each bid the job? Who will be awarded the contract? Why?

The Figure is a summary map of the contingencies and paths that often occur in the pricing decisions in manufacturer-distributor channels when biding on large jobs. The initial question raised between the distributor's senior pricing manager and the firm's account rep is whether or not an extra price quantity discount should be sought from the manufacturer (box 2).

Most distributors will only make such requests under certain conditions and usually not often (less than once a month). The distributors do not want to jeopardize their working relationships with manufacturers by always asking for special price concessions (to pass on to customers to get the business). The distributors do not want to "use-up" their special-pricing favors they have built-

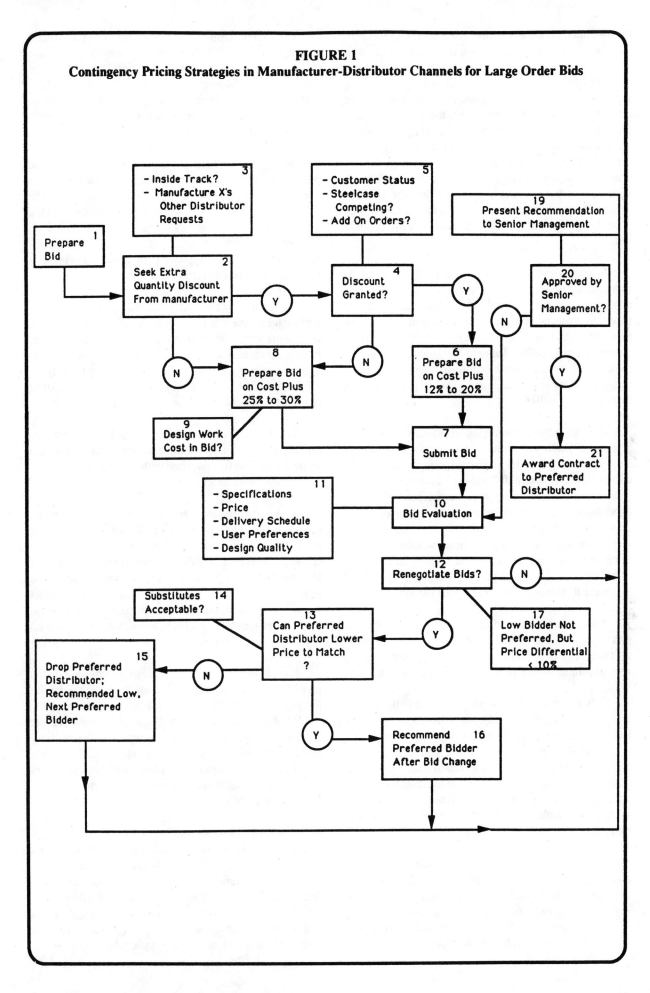

FIGURE 1
Contingency Pricing Strategies in Manufacturer-Distributor Channels for Large Order Bids

up with manufacturers (earned by responding favorably to previous special requests from these manufacturers).

The key issue early in the distributor's pricing decision are the distributor's long-term relationship with the customer. If it is a new customer, the distributor may make an extra effort to bid low--because large customers seldom move their major, long-term, accounts between distributors. When a strategic window opens up, such as a bid request from a large customer new to the state, a distributor's bid is made with much thought given to building a long-term relationship with this customer. The chance to gain the account may not occur again for some time.

A second issue is whether or not another distributor representing the same manufacturer (say firm X) is competing for the job and this second distributor is receiving a special price deal from the manufacturer. For example, a Herman Miller dealer in Nashville learns that another Herman Miller dealer in Memphis is bidding on the same job for a customer location in Memphis, and that this second dealer has requested a special price discount from Herman Miller.

How the manufacturer responds to such dealer price requests depends often on whether or not Steelcase is another approved vendor that is competing for the job and the amount of potential "add-on" business that will follow the initial awarding of a contract (boxes 4 and 5). Other manufacturers often become more aggressive when they learn Steelcase is likely to be a bidder on a large job; they know coming close or beating Steelcase's bid is often tough to do. Some of the small market share distributors are known to give-up without a fight if the Steelcase distributor is competing for the job.

Add-on business is additional furniture and design purchases that are often not covered in the original purchase requirements being bid; add-on business can be very profitable for both the distributor and manufacturer.

Office furniture is (almost) never sold in the U.S. at list price. Bid prices are decided on a distributor cost-plus basis. If a distributor requests, and is granted, a price deal by a manufacturer because of the contingencies described, then the bid is usually prepared on the basis of cost-plus 12 to 20 percent (box 6). If the distributor does not make the request or the manufacturer does not grant the request if made, then the bid is prepared usually on the basis of cost-plus 25 to 30 percent (box 8).

In preparing cost-plus 25 to 30 percent bids, some amount of the costs to do office layout design-work (if required for the job and done by the distributor) will be itemized in the bid (box 9). In very aggressive cost-plus 12 to 20 percent bids, the cost of any necessary design work is often absorbed by the distributor.

Customer Responses to the Bids. The customer's response to the bids depends on whether or not the preferred distributor is the low bidder. If not, the issue becomes one of how much is the spread in the prices bid? If the spread is too great to ignore, such as 10 percent or more, then the preferred distributor is often given a chance to bid a second time (box 13).

In response to this second-bid customer request, the preferred distributor often asks the customer if substitutes can be made to a few of the requirements specified in the original bid request (box 14) in order to lower the total bid price. If the customer agrees, the tentatively accepted bid is submitted to senior management for approval (box 19). If the changes are not approved, the preferred supplier's bid will likely be rejected at this point (box 15).

It is not a done deal until the contract receives approval by senior management in the customer's firm. If certain events occurred along the way, such as substitutes were requested and initially approved, senior management may reject the recommendation by the buying center and another round of bid evaluations will occur or request for new bids may be sent to the distributors.

The five principal decision paths found most frequently among the 80 pricing decisions are summarized in the Table. The five decision paths represent 74 percent of the total cases examined.

Comparing the average accepted bid dollar amounts (and standard deviations) in the Table indicates the inside track, no renegotiation, decision path leads to a significantly lower average bid ($53,500) in comparison each of the other decision paths ($p < .05$, two-tailed tests). The other four decision paths summarized in the Table reflect for aggressive bidding situations which are likely to be found when the stakes are high, that is, bidding situations involving very large orders.

Note in the Table that two decision paths include the identification of a distributor having an inside track with the customer (the first and third decision paths in the Table). The inside track distributors were awarded the contract in these cases. Such cases represent the majority (58%) of the 80 pricing decisions examined. Such findings likely reflect successful attempts of both suppliers and buyers to build and maintain long-term marketer-client relationships.

Note that when the inside track distributor is unsuccessful when renegotiating the bid the average contract awarded is very high ($117,300). One speculative rationale for this finding is that very large orders cause "outsuppliers" (i.e., bidders not having received previous orders from a given customer) to become very aggressive in their initial bids to overcome the bias of customers to award the contract to a favored supplier. Such aggressive,

TABLE 1
Summary of Main Contingent Pricing Decisions
For Large Order Bids

Pricing Decision Summary	Decision Path	Average Accepted Bid (s)	Frequency in Percent (n=80)
Inside track, no n=renegotiation	1-2-8-7-10-12-19	$ 53,500 (17,000)	35%
Two distributions representing some manufacturing with Steelcase active, plus other bids	1-2-4-6-7-10-12-13-16-19-20-21	$ 92,000 (28,000)	9%
Inside track, renegotiation successful	1-2-8-7-10-12-13-16-18-20-21	$ 80,400 (35,400)	23%
Inside track, renegotiation unsuccessful	1-2-8-7-10-12-13-15-19-20-21	$117,300 (19,500)	6%
Two distributions representing some manufacturing with Steelcase inactive, plus other bids	1-2-4-8-7-10-12-13-16-19-20-21	$ 83,800 (19,700)	14%

initial, bids may be close to 12 percent and not cover full costs of installing and servicing the contract. However, the vendor (a previous outsupplier) may rationalize the situation with the belief that future add-on business from the customer (by achieving inside track status) will justify the low margin necessary to achieve the contract.

None of the distributors included in the study had considered estimated the discounted net cash flow value of their long-term relationships with customers. Whether or not inside track suppliers are making suboptimal decisions in failing (or succeeding) to renegotiate bids when requested by customers needs to be examined in future research.

LIMITATIONS

Very limited objectives were set for the present study. The major objective was to learn the contingencies involved in large-order pricing strategies for business-to-business price decisions. The results are limited to one industry and to a small sample of firms within this industry. Additional research is needed before attempting to generalize the results to a population of pricing decisions and to the office furniture industry, or other industries. The results presented here are intended to be exploratory only.

Strategic Pricing Implications

Knowing what contingencies are likely to affect price decisions, and knowing when and why they occur,

aids in doing "what if" pricing and cost analysis for manufacturers, distributors and customers. Without referring to an accurate pricing blueprint, a contingency map, manufacturers and distributors are more likely to bid a price too high or unnecessarily too low to get the contract award.

From a middle-range theory-in-use perspective, pricing decisions in manufacturer-distributor channels may be viewed best as a series of connected binary choice rules, with more than one path existing to reach unfavorable or favorable outcomes (boxes 15 and 21). The occurrence of certain contingencies act as on/off switches, or gates, to allow a pricing path to be taken or not taken.

What Happened in Memphis on the Highland Bank Furniture Bids?

Two of the office furniture dealers planning to bid on the Highland Bank job decided not to prepare bids when they learned that the Steelcase would be a competitor. The Herman Miller dealer not headquartered in Memphis requested and received a special price for bidding the job, because of Steelcase's likely low bid and the importance of the customer to both the dealer and Herman Miller.

The other Herman Miller dealer asked the Herman Miller district manager if such a price request had been made and granted. The affirmative answer he heard was followed by the second dealer's request for the same special price deal which was granted.

Both these dealers put in bids above Steelcase's bid price and close to the bid made by the Westinghouse dealer; the customer judged the products bid of the other dealers not to meet the specifications described in the request for proposals. Senior management at the bank decided to go with the local Herman Miller dealer because this dealer's bid "was close enough" (within 10% of the Steelcase bid), the Herman Miller product line was judged to be slightly better than the competing lines, and local dealer "will probably respond a little quicker if we have installation problems."

REFERENCES

Bonoma, Thomas (1985a), "Case Research in Marketing: Opportunities, Problems, and a Process," *Journal of Marketing Research,* 22 (May), 199-205.

_____(1985b), *The Marketing Edge: Making Strategies Work.* New York: The Free Press.

Campbell, Donald T. and Julian Stanley (1963), "Experimental and Quasi-Experimental Designs for Research or Teaching," in *Handbook on Research on Teaching,* N. L. Gage, ed. Chicago: Rand McNally and Company, Chapter 5, 171-246.

_____(1966), "Pattern Matching as an Essential in Distal Knowing," in *The Psychology of Egon Brunswik,* K. Hammond, ed. New York: Holt, Rinehart, and Winston, 81-106.

_____(1975), "'Degrees of Freedom' and the Case Study," *Comparative Political Studies,* 8 (July), 178-193.

_____(1979), "'Degrees of Freedom' and the Case Study," in *Qualitative and Quantitative Methods in Evaluation Research,* Thomas D. Cook and Charles S. Reichardt, eds. Beverly Hills, CA: Sage.

Gladwin, Christina (1989), *Ethnographic Decision Tree Modelling.* Newbury Park, CA: Sage.

Howard, John A. and William M. Morgenroth (1968), "Information Processing Model of Executive Decisions," *Management Science,* 14, 416-428.

Hulbert, James M. (1981), "Descriptive Models of Marketing Decisions," in *Marketing Decision Models,* R. L. Schultz and A. A. Zoltners, eds. New York: North-Holland, 19-53.

Kotler, Philip (1991), *Marketing Management,* 7th Edition. Englewood Cliffs, NJ: Prentice-Hall.

Morgenroth, William A. (1964), "A Method for Understanding Price Determinants," *Journal of Marketing Research,* 1, 17-26.

Mehan, Hugh and Houston Wood (1975), *The Reality of Ethnomethodology.* New York: Wiley.

Wilson, Elizabeth J. and David T. Wilson (1988), "'Degrees of Freedom' in Case Research of Behavioral Theories of Group Buying," *Advances in Consumer Research,* 15, 587-594.

Yin, Robert K. (1989), *Case Study Research: Design and Methods.* Newbury Park, CA: Sage.

A SEQUENTIAL AND DYNAMIC TESTING METHODOLOGY FOR VALIDATING AN INTELLIGENT DATABASE SYSTEM

Cuneyt Evirgen, Michigan State University
Mike Mitri, Michigan State University
Vivek Bhargava, Michigan State University
S. Tamer Cavusgil, Michigan State University

ABSTRACT

Artificial intelligence techniques are increasingly being used in business applications. Their use necessitates rigorous validation methodologies since they are designed as decision support systems to enhance decision making. In this paper, the authors propose such a validation methodology for a particular international marketing decision support system called the Country Consultant.

INTRODUCTION

The emergence of artificial intelligence (AI) systems in the business world results in a need for validation of these systems. There is extensive literature on validation of *expert systems* (e.g. see Gaschnig et al 1983; O'Keefe 1989). Most authors describe the following characteristics that should be measured in an expert system: quality of decision and advice, correctness of reasoning techniques, quality of human-computer interaction, and efficiency and effectiveness of the system.

Although the literature has concentrated primarily on expert systems validation, there is also a need for validation of other AI-related software. For example, *intelligent databases* are increasingly used in business applications, necessitating validation of their content and structure. The term "intelligent database" refers to a class of database structures and querying methods that employ AI techniques to deal with uncertainty and incompleteness in the content of the database. Thus, intelligent databases commonly *infer* responses to queries for which there is no explicit data (Frisch and Allen 1989).

This article presents a validation method for assessing content- and structural-validity of an intelligent database, called the Country Consultant, developed at the International Business Centers (IBC) of Michigan State University (MSU). The Country Consultant is designed to aid international marketing executives in market analysis and selection.

The paper is divided into three sections. First, we present a brief description of the Country Consultant. In the second section, we describe our validation method vis-a-vis the Country Consultant. Finally, we present concluding remarks and implications.

THE COUNTRY CONSULTANT[1]

The Country Consultant (CC) is an intelligent database that contains information on foreign markets. Its "intelligence" stems from a capability to infer evaluative judgements on foreign market characteristics based on other information stored in its database when direct information is not available.

CC is structured along four components, called *concept types*: which include feature, industry, entry mode and market. Each concept type includes a number of concepts. Any particular combination of these concepts is called a *concept combination*. An example of a concept combination is regulations (feature) for licensing (entry mode) computers and peripherals (industry) in Germany (market).

A *feature* is an evaluation criterion of a country or market. Examples include economic environment, commercial environment, intellectual property protection, tariffs, etc. *Industries* are product/service classifications which are used by CC. Computers and peripherals, automotive parts and accessories, and medical equipment are examples of the industries listed. *Entry mode* refers to the way by which companies can enter foreign markets, such as export or foreign direct investment. *Markets* are countries or regional groupings to be analyzed. All of these concepts have their own hierarchical structures.

The features, industries and entry modes can be viewed either alphabetically or in parent-child (hierarchical) order. In a parent-child relation, each concept type is divided into macro (parent) and micro (child) concepts. For example, in the parent-child listing of the feature concept, commercial environment is a macro feature, or "parent" under which features such as demand, competition, distribution infrastructure are micro features, or its "children". Distribution infrastructure is further subdivided into rail, communication, sea, air and road infrastructures. Thus, distribution infrastructure will act as both a parent and a child. Parent-child relationships play an important role in the inference process in the Country Consultant.

CC's data records are of two types: *judgements* and *guidelines*. Each judgement or guideline is indexed by a particular concept combination. Judgements are evaluative in nature, i.e. they provide evaluative information for the concept combination they are related to. Hence, the data used in arriving at the judgement must be concrete enough to derive a conclusion about the particular concept combination. A judgement includes the current state (excellent, good, fair, poor, terrible) and its foreseen future direction (rapidly improving, improving, stable, deteriorating, rapidly deteriorating).

Guidelines, on the other hand, provide descriptive information which would assist in conducting business in a foreign country, but which is not necessarily evaluative in nature. For example, they may contain a how-to guide or some statistical information.

Information can be searched in CC by specifying a concept combination. The system responds to such a query by finding the related judgement and guideline both of which are easily and immediately accessible to the user. If no judgement exists in CC that is related to the chosen concept combination, the system can *infer* a judgement, using AI techniques, based on judgements available for other "closely" related concept combinations. The definition of "close" is at the user's discretion since s/he can define the *inference strategy* to be followed.

The method used to infer in the Country Consultant combines techniques from AI with ideas from *multi-attribute utility theory* (MAUT) (Von Winterfeldt and Fischer 1975). The hierarchical structure of the four concept types comprise a *semantic network*, which allows the use of *spreading activation* (Quillian 1985) by which the system can search for concepts that are related to the user's query. In inferring a judgment, CC uses a weighted linear model to combine the judgments found via spreading activation. Each judgment's weight of influence is based on its "conceptual closeness" to the query judgment and on the confidence level assigned to the judgment. Detailed descriptions of CC's inference process can be found in Mitri (1992) and Mitri et al. (1991).

VALIDATION OF THE COUNTRY CONSULTANT

The methodology described below was developed for validating CC's content and structure. We believe the ideas and processes described below are applicable to the validation of other databases using similar indexing structure: namely a semantic network combined with multi-attribute utility inferencing.

Our validation method is a sequential process, taking place in consecutive stages with each stage serving a different purpose. The process is dynamic and iterative in that the validation is not a one-time project, but rather a continuous, on-going process. This is due to the dynamic nature of CC itself, where judgements and guidelines are continuously added, deleted, and updated. Hence, it is necessary to validate all the new information entered into the database as well as to delete redundant or out-of-date information. Note the discrepancy between this sort of validation and the normal, one-time efforts required for most expert systems, whose knowledge tends to be more static.

There are two issues of validating CC: internal and external validity of the information. The former refers to a validation process within CC itself, whereas the latter refers to validating the information against outside sources. We will come back to the distinction between the two in our description of the stages in the validation methodology.

CC's validation method incorporates both qualitative and quantitative tests for the structure and the information content of the Country Consultant. The full picture of the stages in the proposed validation methodology and the processes involved at each stage are shown in Figure 1. Now we will go on to describe each stage and the processes involved in more detail.

Stage 1: Initial Screening and Structural Development

Stage 1 has two components: initial evaluation of the information *content* of CC and validation of its *structure*. The first component mainly involves evaluation of the individual judgements and guidelines in the database.

In content analysis, records are checked to ensure that judgements are indeed evaluative and guidelines are indeed descriptive in nature. This process may necessitate completely or partially changing a judgement to a guideline or vice versa, or deleting parts of irrelevant information from either a judgement or a guideline. In addition, information in each of the judgements and guidelines is also reviewed to make sure that it is appropriate for the assigned concept combination. For example, comments made for the concept combination of patent protection (feature) for licensing (entry mode) medical equipment (industry) to India (market) is checked to see if they actually relate to that particular concept combination. If the comments do not relate to the concept combination, then the combination is changed to get the best fit for the information.

The second main process in Stage 1 involves CC's structure. This includes validating the comprehensiveness of the features, industries and entry modes used, as well as validating their respective hierarchical structures. The validation of the features used and their hierarchical structure was accomplished through a review of the related literature and consulting experts in the area[2].Categories included under the industry concept correspond to the industry classifications suggested by the U.S. Chamber of Commerce. Various forms of entry to foreign markets are included under the entry mode concept. Finally, markets are the countries that the U.S. has international business relations with.

Additional issues pertaining to the structure validation of stage one involve the validation and enhancement of the computer program itself. This includes evaluation of the format of screen displays, and of the user-query capabilities in Country Consultant described earlier. The main issue here is to determine the ease of use and understandability of the displayed information. This is accomplished, in the initial screening, by the developers themselves analyzing the content and display of information, and making subsequent changes to the program code as deemed necessary. Note that the structural validation is relatively static compared to content validation. Judgments and guidelines will continuously be changed, but the index structure and screen displays will remain in place. This again points to the difference in validation between intelligent databases and expert systems.

Stage 2: Expert Opinion - Qualitative Testing

At this stage, the Country Consultant is put through a rigorous in-house testing process. A group of in-house professors and researchers, knowledgeable in the information requirements in foreign market assessment, are used as the experts to judge various aspects of CC. Hence, this stage represents a qualitative validation CC with respect to the compatibility of its information content with its structure.

The first process at this stage is to check for the internal consistency of the information in the parent-child links. As noted before, CC provides information in the form of judgements and guidelines for specific concept combinations. Hence, it is very important to make sure that the judgements made at each level in the structural hierarchies built into the system are consistent with other judgements at higher or lower levels. Let us illustrate the process with an example.

When the internal consistency of the judgements made on the feature *intellectual property protection* is checked, a tree diagram of the links between that feature and its children was formed. That particular feature has four children, namely *copyrights, patent protection, royalties, and trademarks*. Hence, including intellectual property protection itself, a total number of five features are involved in this case. A tree diagram of these features is shown in Figure 2.

Through CC's various query options, all of the stored judgements related to the concept combinations having either of the five features mentioned above as their feature component and any industry or entry mode as their other two components are obtained for a particular market. Then, the judgements are entered into the tree diagram under their feature. Thus, the tree diagram provides a visual presentation of all of the related judgements stored CC regarding the five features of the particular country for which the query was made. The experts have the opportunity to see the different judgements made along the parent-child links and analyze them to diagnose any inconsistencies. This process is repeated across all countries. Hence, in addition to diagnosing any inconsistencies that might exist along the structural links for an individual country, the experts are also able to analyze the judgements across countries. This is to make sure that consistent criteria were used in arriving at the judgements for different countries. In doing so, the comments provided to support each judgement are also analyzed.

A second process involves checking for the reliability of the information given. In other words, the experts analyze both the judgements made and the supporting comments given to make sure that reliable information is provided. This is a qualitative and subjective assessment of the experts of the reliability of the information.

Closely related to the second process is the evaluation of the information by the experts. This involves evaluating the information in terms of its content, quality, relevance, etc. A specific task of the experts in this process is to check for the correspondence between the judgements/directions and the supporting comments given for them. That is, they check to see if the particular judgement made (e.g. good, poor,etc.) or the particular direction given (e.g. improving, deteriorating, etc.) is indeed well supported by the comments provided. In doing so, they also consider the credibility of the source(s) cited to back up the comments.

Another process involved in stage 2 is to identify the gaps in CC's database. Through the analyses of the tree diagrams referred to above, experts are able to diagnose features, industries or entry modes for which there is little or no information. This helps to identify the areas where future market research activities are needed. As noted before, CC has the inferencing capabilities to compensate for lack of judgements related to particular concept combinations. However, we want to make sure that the database has enough judgements stored in it covering the critical domains so that: (1) more direct information will be available, and (2) the effectiveness of the inferencing process will be enhanced.

Finally, the experts also have focus group meetings to design other testing procedures. Specifically, they discuss what needs to be done next and also concentrate on particular empirical tests that can be conducted to test the internal and external validity of the CC quantita-

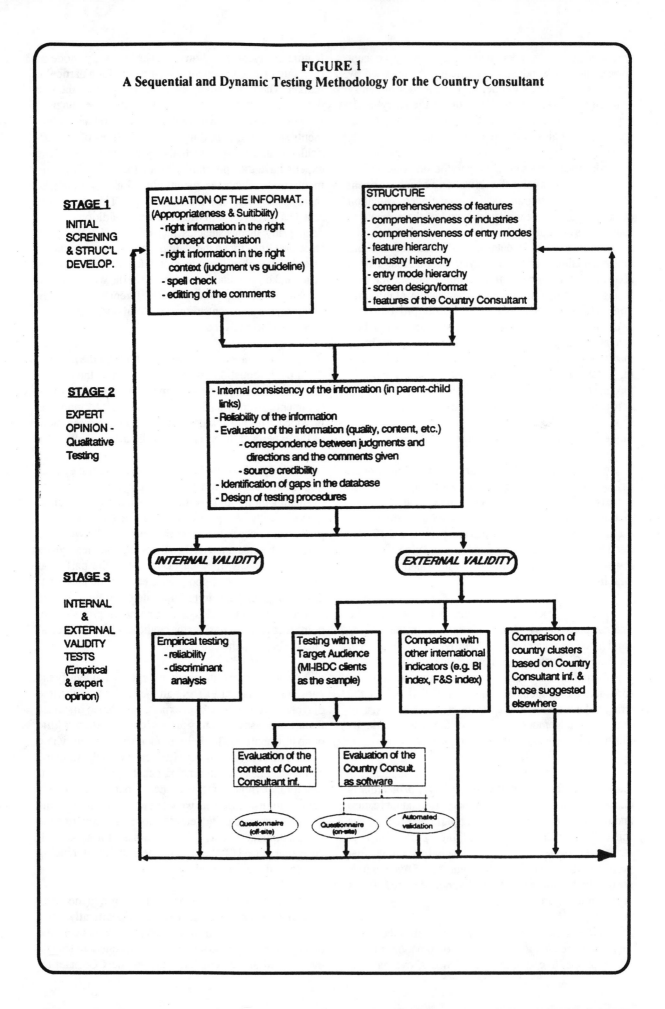

FIGURE 1
A Sequential and Dynamic Testing Methodology for the Country Consultant

STAGE 1

INITIAL SCREENING & STRUC'L DEVELOP.

EVALUATION OF THE INFORMAT.
(Appropriateness & Suitibility)
- right information in the right concept combination
- right information in the right context (judgment vs guideline)
- spell check
- editting of the comments

STRUCTURE
- comprehensiveness of features
- comprehensiveness of industries
- comprehensiveness of entry modes
- feature hierarchy
- industry hierarchy
- entry mode hierarchy
- screen design/format
- features of the Country Consultant

STAGE 2

EXPERT OPINION - Qualitative Testing

- Internal consistency of the information (in parent-child links)
- Reliability of the information
- Evaluation of the information (quality, content, etc.)
  - correspondence between judgments and directions and the comments given
  - source credibility
- Identification of gaps in the database
- Design of testing procedures

STAGE 3

INTERNAL & EXTERNAL VALIDITY TESTS (Empirical & expert opinion)

INTERNAL VALIDITY

EXTERNAL VALIDITY

Empirical testing
- reliability
- discriminant analysis

Testing with the Target Audience (MI-IBDC clients as the sample)

Comparison with other international indicators (e.g. BI index, F&S index)

Comparison of country clusters based on Country Consultant inf. & those suggested elsewhere

Evaluation of the content of Count. Consultant inf.

Evaluation of the Country Consult. as software

Questionnaire (off-site)

Questionnaire (on-site)

Automated validation

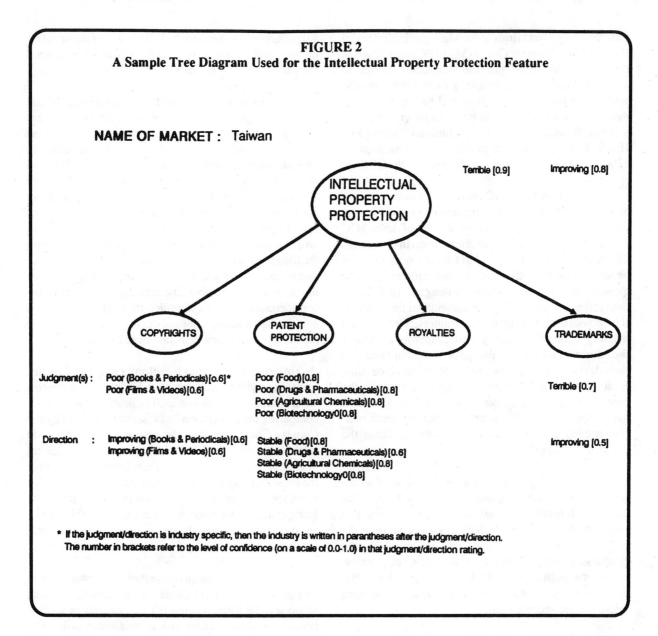

FIGURE 2
A Sample Tree Diagram Used for the Intellectual Property Protection Feature

NAME OF MARKET : Taiwan

Terrible [0.9]   Improving [0.8]

INTELLECTUAL PROPERTY PROTECTION

COPYRIGHTS   PATENT PROTECTION   ROYALTIES   TRADEMARKS

Judgment(s) :   Poor (Books & Periodicals) [o.6]*   Poor (Food) [0.8]   Terrible [0.7]
                Poor (Films & Videos) [0.6]   Poor (Drugs & Pharmaceuticals) [0.8]
                                                     Poor (Agricultural Chemicals) [0.8]
                                                     Poor (Biotechnology0 [0.8]

Direction   :   Improving (Books & Periodicals) [0.6]   Stable (Food) [0.8]   Improving [0.5]
                Improving (Films & Videos) [0.6]   Stable (Drugs & Pharmaceuticals) [0.6]
                                                         Stable (Agricultural Chemicals) [0.8]
                                                         Stable (Biotechnology0 [0.8]

* If the judgment/direction is industry specific, then the industry is written in parantheses after the judgment/direction.
  The number in brackets refer to the level of confidence (on a scale of 0.0-1.0) in that judgment/direction rating.

tively. This again points to the iterative process of the validation process.

Stage 3: Internal and External Validity Tests - Empirical Validation Coupled With Expert Opinion

This final stage in the sequential validation process serves the dual purpose of validating CC internally and externally in an empirical sense. In order to empirically test the Country Consultant, a coding schema needs to be developed to extract the judgmental and directional information stored. Since the judgements and the directions are given on a five-point Likert type scale, a coding schema related to that scale is used to extract the data points needed for the empirical analyses. The sample is determined by the number of countries included in CC.

Since we have a coded data set for input, various statistical tests can be done for internal validation of the judgements and directions. For instance, reliability esti-

mates can be obtained for the data. Cronbach's alpha can be used for the internal consistency reliability estimation (Carmiens and Zeller 1982). Furthermore, discriminant analysis can be done to see whether the concepts used in the structure of the Country Consultant have discriminatory power. Currently, we are still in the process of designing empirical tests for internal validation.

For external validation, we pursue two routes. First, we test CC with potential users in our target audience. Second, we compare the information in CC with information available through other sources, including databases, reports, and consulting firms.

CC's target audience of intended end users includes consultants, academicians, international business executives, and government agencies. CC has already been demonstrated to many visiting scholars and businessmen during its development process, and feedback received from them has guided the development process. For formal testing, client firms of the Michigan International Business Development Center (MI-IBDC) are chosen as the sample. MI-IBDC provides consulting service to small- and medium-sized businesses in Michigan who want to get involved in international business. Most of these clients are at the initial stages of internationalization and, therefore, need a lot of preliminary information. Hence, they form an ideal sample to test the effectiveness, relevance, usefulness and efficiency of the CC data.

Testing with MI-IBDC clients is performed in two ways, using two different questionnaires. In the first process, called *off-site testing*, hardcopies of desired CC information is provided to the clients upon their request. The clients are then requested to fill out a questionnaire about a week after they receive the information. The questionnaire for these clients is designed to measure their responses to the following attributes of the information provided to them: quality, usefulness, relevance and quantity of the information provided, appropriateness of the information for particular concept combinations and their level of satisfaction with the information they received. This first process will help us to evaluate the content of information entered, identify the information gaps in the Country Consultant and the type of information needed by the clients, and finally, facilitate the external validation process.

Off-site testing has helped to identify areas of weaknesses and steps needed to improve them. The strategy for entering information into the Country Consultant has also been modified based on the feedback received from the clients. For example, the main focus of data entry in the past was to enter macro level data (e.g. economics, commerce, politics, etc.) for individual countries. The focus has now been changed to industry specific and more micro feature specific entries.

The second process, called *on-site testing*, evaluates the software of the Country Consultant. For this purpose, clients are invited to the MI-IBDC office. A preliminary information packet is provided to the clients beforehand. Clients are taken through a brief presentation of using the Country Consultant after which they use the system for 15-20 minutes. After working on the system, they are asked to evaluate the software by filling out a questionnaire. Since the clients actually have the opportunity to work with the software, the questionnaire is designed to measure their responses to the following attributes of the CC: user-friendliness, screen layout and general design, functions available in the software and their level of satisfaction with working on the CC.

In addition to evaluating the above mentioned factors, the questionnaire also measures the client's familiarity with computers and his/her prior experience(s) with expert systems. The responses obtained in this process will be used as feedback to improve the Country Consult-

ant program. The data will be collected over the next few months, and then statistical analyses will be performed for validity studies on the CC.

Because of the need for iterative, dynamic validation, we recognize the wisdom of automating this process as much as possible. Therefore, there is much effort underway to enhance the software of CC in order to provide automatic validation in several respects. First, AI techniques of text analysis will be incorporated to ensure that judgement/guideline comments are appropriately categorized to their proper concept combinations. Second, the inferential mechanism of the Country Consultant will be used to test for consistency of judgements. Third, the distribution of judgements will be checked to ensure that country comparisons are meaningful. For example, it makes no sense to give all countries a "fair" rating for commercial environment; rather, the judgements should be distributed along a normal curve, similar to the way grades are distributed in a class of students.

In terms of comparing the information in the Country Consultant with information available from other sources, we are pursuing two processes. The first process involves comparing the foreign market assessments given by the Country Consultant with the assessments of the same markets as presented by widely known international market indicators (e.g. the Business International index, the Frost and Sullivan index). A LISREL model has been developed for this purpose which is in the process of being tested. If the model holds as expected, this will be an important accomplishment in terms of the external validation of the Country Consultant.

The second process involves running cluster analysis on our data set to form clusters of countries. A focus group will be formed comprising of experts in foreign country assessment. One task of this group will be to analyze the clusters formed and critique them. At the same time, country clusters suggested elsewhere (in academic or non-academic literature) will be searched. The second task of the focus group will be to compare the clusters formed from the information in the CC with the clusters suggested elsewhere. These processes will further facilitate external validation of the CC.

CONCLUSIONS AND IMPLICATIONS

In this paper, we presented a method for validating an intelligent database application in international business. This program, called the Country Consultant, contains judgements and guidelines about foreign markets, together with a capacity to infer information that is not explicitly stored in its database.

The proposed methodology suggests that the validation procedure must involve a dynamic and iterative process. Knowledge engineering in general is an iterative process whereby the system is continuously revised and upgraded based on its performance.

It is also suggested that a sequential process must be followed in the validation. First, the structure of the system must be validated. Second, the content of the system must be qualitatively tested using expert opinion. Finally, quantitative techniques must be used to test the internal and external validity of the system.

Although some of the specifics of the methodology would relate only to the Country Consultant, the ideas and processes presented are in general applicable to validating other types of intelligent database applications. In particular, databases utilizing a combination of semantic network/spreading activation techniques and MAUT utility assessment can benefit from the validation method described above.

ENDNOTES

[1] For more information on the Country Consultant, see Mitri et al. (1991).

[2] See Mitri et al (1991) for a thorough review of the literature.

REFERENCES

Carmiens, Edward G. and Richard A. Zeller (1982), *Reliability and Validity Assessment.* Newbury Park, CA: SAGE Publications, Inc..

Evirgen, Cuneyt (1990). Information Need Assessment for Exporters. Unpublished Master's thesis, Istanbul, Turkey: Bosphorous University,

_____ (1992), "A Causal Model for Foreign Market Attractiveness and Use of a Decision Support Tool as the Knowledge Base." Accepted for publication in *Proceedings of the AMA 1992 Summer Educator's Conference (forthcoming).*

Frisch, A. and J. Allen (1988), "Knowledge Retrieval as Limited Inference," in *Readings in Artificial Intelligence and Databases,* Mylopolopus and Brodie, eds. Los Altos, CA: Morgan Kaufmann Publishers, Inc. 444-451.

Gaschnig, J., P. Klahr, H. Pople, E. Shortliffe, A. Terry (1983), "Evaluation of Expert Systems: Issues and Case Studies," in *Building Expert Systems.* F. Hayes-Roth, D. Waterman, D. Lenat, Reading, MA: Addison-Wesley Publishing Co., 241-280.

Mitri, Michel (1992), "Candidate Evaluation: A Task Specific Architecture Using Multiattribute Utility Theory With Applications in International Marketing," *Unpublished PhD Dissertation,* Computer Science Department. Michigan State University.

Mitri, Mike, Cuneyt Evirgen, and S.Tamer Cavusgil (1991), "The Country Consultant: An Expert System for the International Marketing Executive," *Proceedings of the 1991 AMA Microcomputers in the Marketing Education Conference,* (August), 21-33.

O'Keefe, R.M. (1989), "The Evaluation of Decision-Aiding Systems: Guidelines and Methods," *Information and Management: The International Journal of Information Systems Applications,* 17, 4 (November), 217-226.

Quillian, M. R. (1985), "Word Concepts: A Theory and Simulation of Some Basic Semantic Capabilities," in *Readings in Knowledge Representation,* Brachman and Levesque, eds. Los Altos, CA: Morgan Kaufmann Publishers, Inc., 97-118.

Von Winterfeldt, D. and G. W. Fischer (1975), "Multi-Attribute Utility Theory: Models and Assessment Procedures," in *Utility, Probability, and Human Decision Making,* D. Wendt. ed. Dordrecht, The Netherlands, 47-86.

WHO SPENDS MORE DOLLARS? AN INVESTIGATION INTO CONSUMER SHOPPING BEHAVIOR

Srini S. Srinivasan, The University of Texas-Austin

ABSTRACT

Both manufacturers and retailers are interested in consumers who spend more dollars during their shopping activities. It is essential for store managers to know the characteristics of frequent shoppers and heavy spenders so that promotional efforts can be targeted to these segments of the population. This research studies the impact of demographics and dealing characteristics of households (like size of the family, income, time availability and coupon proneness) on the total dollars spent and total trips made by the various households.

Conceptual framework:

These are several factors which determine the frequency of shopping trips made by consumers. Consumers who are coupon prone are willing to invest their time in cutting and collecting coupons to save money. These coupon prone consumers are likely to frequent various retailers to take advantage of the deals available in different stores. Therefore it is hypothesized that:

H1: Consumers who are coupon prone tend to make more shopping trips/year than non users of coupons.

In order to take advantage of the deals in various stores, it is essential that the households be able to spend the necessary time to visit these stores. The decision to shop around in different stores to take advantage of deals depends on the time demands facing the household. As the number of family members in a household increases the time pressure also increases. Hence it is hypothesized that:

H2: The higher the number of members in the household the lesser will be the number of shopping trips made by the household.

Also the number of hours worked by the male and female heads of the household will have an impact on the free time available for shopping trips. Hence it is hypothesized that:

H3: The higher the total number of hours worked by the male and female heads of the households the lesser will be the shopping trip frequency.

Mackay (1973) demonstrated that the number of shopping trips made by consumers is positively related to the demand for super market products. As demand for groceries increases with the number of members in the

household it is hypothesized that:

H4: Households that spend more dollars per year make more shopping trips than households that spend fewer dollars.

One important variable explaining the total dollars spent by the household is the number of members present in the household unit. As the number of household members increases the household consumes more items. Hence it is hypothesized that:

H5: The bigger the number of members present in a household the higher the total dollars spent by the household unit.

Households making more number of trips are exposed to more retailer promotions and have greater opportunity to spend more dollars. Hence it is hypothesized that:

H6: The higher the number of shopping trips made, the higher the total dollars spent by the household.

Total dollars spent depends both on the quantity and unit price of goods purchased. People with higher income are likely to purchase premium brands costing more than the ordinary brands (Frank, Green, and Sieber (1967). Also higher household income means more money to spend on shopping trips. Hence it is hypothesized that:

H7: The higher the household income the higher the total dollars spent on shopping trips.

Data used:

The study was conducted using panel data supplied by A.C. Nielson. The household data was collected in two markets - Sioux Falls, SD and Springfield, MO.

Analysis:

Four hypotheses 1-4 the endogenous variable is total trips made per year (TTRPYR) and the exogenous variables are coupon proneness (CPNPRN), number of members in the household (MEMBERS), total hours worked (TOTHOURS) and total dollars spent per year (TDOLYR). The relationships postulated in these hypotheses are given by equation 1.

$$TTRPYR = \beta_{10} + \Gamma_{12TDOLYR} + \beta_{11MEMBERS} + \beta_{12TOTHOURS} + \beta_{13CPNPRN} + \varepsilon \quad (1)$$

For hypotheses 4-7 the endogenous variable is total dollars spent per year (TDOLYR) and the exogenous variables are number of members in the household (MEMBERS), total number of shopping trips per year (TTRPYR), and the household income (two dummies, INCOME1 and INCOME2 captures the three levels of income). The relationships postulated in these hypotheses are given by equation 2.

$$TODLRY = \beta_{20} + \Gamma_{21TTRPYR} + \beta_{21MEMBERS} + \beta_{22INCOME1} + \beta_{23INCOME2} + \varepsilon \qquad (2)$$

The above equations are inter dependent in the sense that the endogenous variable of each equation is one of the exogenous variables in the other. Hence doing independent OLS estimates on the above two equations will result in biased and inconsistent estimated (Judge et al. 1982, pages 610). The parameters of the above system of equations were estimated using a 2SLS procedure.

Results

The structural equation estimates confirm six out of the seven hypotheses. All the hypotheses excepting H2 are confirmed in both the markets.

For further information please contact:
Srini S. Srinivansan
Department of Marketing
The University of Texas
Austin, TX 78712

UNDERSTANDING AND MEASURING COMPETITIVE ADVANTAGE: A GENERAL METHOD AND AN EMPIRICAL TEST

Brien Ellis, University of Kentucky

ABSTRACT

The concept of competitive advantage as a key to understanding the long-term survival and success of a firm has become central to marketing and strategic management research. The idea of competitive advantage seems simple enough: acquire a sustainable edge over competition in the marketplace and the firm prospers. However, identifying, measuring, and understanding such an advantage have proved particularly troublesome for marketing practitioners and researchers because competitive advantage is not a single entity, but a complex concept consisting of many disparate parts (Day and Wensley 1988). This premise is usually based on Porter's (1985) conceptualization of competitive advantage and the supposition that it may be acquired by the firm achieving either a cost or differentiation advantage. The outcome of successfully implementing these approaches is then reflected in a variety of performance indicators. This study offers a viable measurement process for competitive advantage that is demonstrated and described in the context of the retail drugstore industry.

A competitive advantage is defined as a significant edge over one's rivals in the marketplace in cost, differentiation, or the outcomes that result from these positional strategies (Day and Wensley 1988). A cost advantage is achieved by performing important activities at a lower cost than competitors and can lead to a superior competitive position. However, just establishing that a firm attempts to achieve or achieves a cost advantage over a competitor tells little about the advantage: specific costs must be analyzed. Retail costs may be broken down into two broad categories: cost of goods and operating expenses. Cost of goods in this study was measured by a market basket of 15 top selling items as determined by trade literature surveys. Two key operating expenses were also measured: rent or mortgage and advertising expense. Both of these expenses were measured as a percentage of sales. Differentiation can encompass all activities and relationships in a business (Day and Wensley 1988). Conceptually, retail differentiation at the store level concerns significant variance as compared to the competition with respect to the retailer's physical facilities, products, services, promotions, and/or prices that are perceived as valuable by the buyer. Operationally, for a retail drugstore, differentiation should be measured relative to the competition in each of the above areas to be meaningful in the assessment of competitive advantages. The differentiation construct contained 24 items comprising five scales: product (e.g., brands, lines, private label), promotion amount and effectiveness (e.g., cou-

pons, health promotions, newspaper), distribution (e.g., hours open, location, delivery), and customer service (e.g., speed, friendliness, availability, knowledge). The following measures of outcomes of competitive advantage were chosen for the study: sales volume, gross margin, and net profit. Respondents were asked to indicate each of these outcomes for their most recent fiscal year.

Measurement Process

The measurement process offers a systematic approach to measuring competitive advantage which can be applied to many different types of business and industries. The first step simply states that the firms or types of firms studied must be in competition with one another. The second step requires measurement of two firms or two types of firms simultaneously and consideration of the necessary logistical steps (e.g., preparation of two surveys and sampling frames) needed to implement the procedure properly. The measurement must be concurrent because any change in the environment or in the variables studied can shift the competitive equilibrium. In the third step, study as many variables as possible because each different competitor who survives must have a distinct advantage over the other (Henderson 1983). Once the above steps are complete, one can then define the relative "position" of a firm in relation to competitors.

Results and Conclusion

The study population consisted of a chain of drugstores with approximately 75 units in 56 cities and independent drugstores located in the same cities as the chain outlets. Surveys were mailed to 191 independents; 96 surveys were returned within six weeks for a response rate of 50.3 percent. For the chain, 63 out of 73 stores (86 percent) returned the surveys within the same six-week period. Univariate t-tests were used to determine differences and advantages between the two types of firms. Chains had a significant (p<.05) edge in cost of goods, sales, and differentiation, independents maintained an advantage in terms of customer service and net profit. Neither type of firm had a significant advantage in gross profit, although independent stores did charge significantly higher prices. For the differentiation subscales, the chain offered more product differentiation, had more promotion, and greater promotion effectiveness. The advantage of the distribution scale was dependent on delivery. Since the chain does not deliver, when this variable was included, chain advantages in hours open and location were lost. Finally, the greater promotion of the chain and more desirable location also meant higher advertising and rent expenses which may have affected profits.

While a retailer may not know a competitor's cost or profit structure, the assessment of competitive advantage is still possible and important. Competitive information can be obtained from industry sources, advertising, as well as first-hand knowledge of products and prices gathered through observation. In addition, the present study used a competitor-centered approach to measurement, a combination of competitor-centered and customer-focused approaches could be utilized when assessing competitive advantage. Thus, by knowing and understanding advantages and disadvantages relative to a key competitor, a retailer can better formulate and implement an effective marketing strategy.

Several managerial and research implications can be derived specifically from the findings of this study. First, if a retailer chooses a differentiation strategy, the retailer must be prepared to accept the resulting costs which may lead to lower profits. Second, the importance of price cannot be overstated. Although the independents have higher costs for goods and offer less differentiation, they are able to charge a higher price, which results in larger margins and greater profitability. One explanation for this phenomenon is the higher level of service offered by independents and the use of delivery to overcome a distribution disadvantage.

For researchers, the measurement process presented outlines the steps needed to identify and measure competitive advantages. This method allows researchers to measure competitive advantage and analyze strategies for different types of firms in different industries. Additionally, by measuring competing perceptions of strategies relative to one another, a measure of consistency can be obtained. Finally, measurement of customer-related variables, such as differentiation and customer satisfaction, should be done from a customer as well as a managerial perspective.

For Additional Information, contact:
Brien Ellis
Department of Marketing
College of Business and Economics
University of Kentucky
Lexington, KY 40506-0034

ROLES, PERCEPTIONS, AND RESPONSES IN THE FRANCHISE TRIAD: IMPLICATIONS FOR OVERALL FRANCHISE PERFORMANCE

Van R. Wood, Texas Tech University
Pamela Kiecker, Texas Tech University

ABSTRACT

While franchising may be considered one of the major success stories of our time, it is today facing new challenges brought on by its own maturity. Once stable, channel relationships are now in flux as the demands of experienced franchisees reflect their desire to have a significant say in how their businesses will operate. Docile receptivity to standardized procedures is no longer the norm among franchisees, especially mature franchisees. Over the years, learning has taken place, skills have been gained, confidences have grown, and markets have changed. As a consequence, many experienced franchisees believe they know how to run their business and respond to their markets better than their franchisors. More and more, they are balking at being told what, when, and how to operate their outlets. Franchise maturation has also altered the relationship with franchise customers. Now, more than ever, franchise consumers have patronage choices, ranging from other retail options (franchising being but one option), to a multitude of similar franchise operations that offer a wide variety of competing products and brands. This explosion of alternatives has created a new franchising environment, one in which customer power/ability to demand and receive satisfaction is growing, further impacting franchise relationships.

The evolution of franchising has given rise to considerable diversity in individual franchisees' experience and corresponding expertise. It is no longer the case that all franchisees require (or want) the type of leadership exercised by the franchisor at the onset of a franchise relationship. On one hand, more and more mature franchisees with high levels of perceived expertise are telling franchisors: "Don't tell me what to do," or are asking them to "just support me." On the other hand, new or less experienced franchisees with lower levels of perceived expertise, need and will continue to want more guidance from the franchisor. They are characterized by their requests to "tell me what to do, and tell me how I'm doing."

Many observers now contend that franchising is undergoing a metamorphosis as new relationships replace old ones. While the original methods of structuring franchise operations may still be applicable, particularly where newer, less experienced franchisees are operating in markets having relatively little competition, such is not the case for the growing number of mature, highly experienced franchisees operating in very competitive markets. However, these contentions are based largely on speculation and isolated pieces of anecdotal evidence. Our theoretical and empirical knowledge of this "maturing" phenomena in franchising and its implications for future franchisor, franchisee, and franchise customer relationships is woefully inadequate. We have little insight into some very fundamental questions. For example, why is conflict high in some franchise operations and low in others when the policies and procedures of all have been standardized? Why does franchisor guidance produce different franchisee responses (ranging from cooperation to hostility) in standardized franchise operations? Why are customers satisfied by some franchise operations, but dissatisfied by others, even when all operations have been standardized?

This paper addresses these questions by examining roles, perceptions, and responses in franchise operations. In doing so, the issue of overall franchising performance is viewed from a broader perspective than here-to-fore presented in the literature, one that includes relationships and interactions between the franchisor, the franchisee, and the franchise customer. Franchisor leadership style, franchisee perceived expertise, and franchise customer actions and reactions are considered in a nomological model that relates these constructs to franchisor-franchisee conflict, franchisee satisfaction, and overall franchise performance (see Figure). Twelve research propositions suggested by the model are offered for future empirical testing.

In general, franchisors' must select an appropriate leadership style relative to their franchisees' perceived expertise. That is, franchisors interested in creating and sustaining franchise harmony must employ a supportive and/or participative leadership style with mature and experienced franchisees, and a directive leadership style with new and less experienced franchisees. Likewise, while the relationship between the franchisor and franchisee is clearly an important determinant of overall franchise performance, recognition of franchise customer satisfaction in determining overall franchise success is also critical. As emphasized here, a key ingredient in achieving high customer satisfaction and, subsequently, favorable customer responses, is to achieve and sustain franchisor-franchisee harmony. Clearly, a dissatisfied franchisee, or one that is in conflict with his or her franchisor, will be less likely to produce a franchise atmosphere that meets customer needs and delivers cus-

FIGURE 1
A Model of Franchise Performance

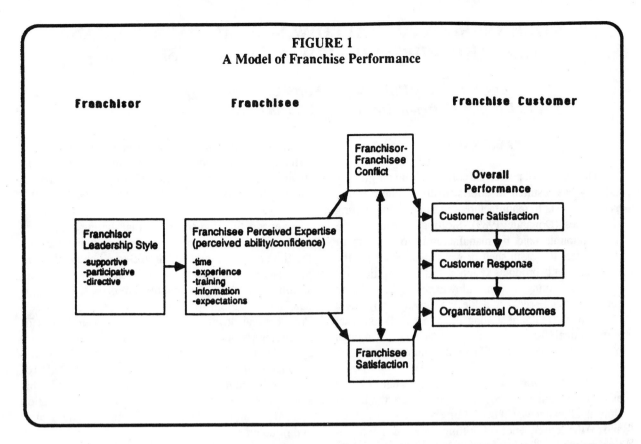

tomer satisfaction. In short, when a franchisor selects a leadership style appropriate for his or her franchisees, dyad conflict can be effectively managed, increasing both franchisee and franchise customer satisfaction, which ultimately enhances the probability of heightened overall performance. The key is to recognize and understand the ever changing roles, perceptions, and responses in the franchise triad.

For further information contact:
Van R. Wood or Pamela Kiecker
Texas Tech University
P.O. Box 4320
Lubbock, Texas 79409

THE ROLE OF SLOTTING ALLOWANCES IN RETAIL CHANNEL RELATIONSHIPS: REVIEW AND PROPOSITIONS

Judy A. Siguaw, University of North Carolina at Wilmington
K. Douglas Hoffman, University of North Carolina at Wilmington

ABSTRACT

The transfer of power and control within the grocery industry has resulted in efforts to divert intermediary overhead costs to manufacturers in the form of slotting allowances (Donahue 1989). Slotting allowances are those amounts paid by manufacturers to retailers or wholesalers to obtain shelf or warehouse space for the manufacturers' products (Fannin 1987). Empirical research concerning slotting allowances is limited. As such, this article seeks to achieve a threefold objective: (1) define the realm of slotting allowances, (2) construct a theoretical framework, and (3) generate a related propositional inventory to facilitate future research.

The framework consists of three categories: (1) antecedent elements whose presence fosters the use of slotting allowances, (2) the slotting allowance variable, and (3) the consequences of slotting allowances. Integrative growth, market information, private label development, product proliferation, and a desire for higher profits are posited as antecedents of the shift in channel power and the subsequent practice of slotting practices. Channel conflict, reduced competitiveness, poorly conceived products, reduced customer orientation, and legal violations are posited as consequences of slotting allowances.

The requirement of slotting allowances in exchange for shelf or warehouse space potentially appears to be predominately associated with negative consequences. However, as long as manufacturers are willing and able to pay slotting allowances, little motivation exists for middlemen to discontinue this practice. In fact, middlemen who do not charge slotting allowances at this point in time may actually be competitively disadvantaged.

Although short-term profits may be derived via slotting allowances, the long-term effects are proposed to be detrimental to individual companies. Moreover, practices stemming from the use of slotting allowances may result in laws and regulations that will harm the industry in the long-term. Hence, serious consideration needs to be given to self-regulation.

Managerial Implications

The propositions developed in this study have direct managerial implications. First, this research suggests that the practice of slotting allowances can be attributed to a shift in channel power. Manufacturers must forge new relationships within this changing framework. To re-cover some of their former channel power, manufacturers will require enhanced negotiating skills and greater agility at responding to the retailers' computerized market information (*Sales and Marketing Management* 1989).

Second, this study proposes that slotting allowances are beneficial to influential middlemen at the outset, but the final outcome may be harmful to all channel members. Hence, the industry would benefit by abolishing slotting allowances, but manufacturers must first eliminate some of the justifications for slotting allowances. Producers can do this by establish stringent guidelines for product introductions--including research, testing, strategy, planning, and promotion (*Sales and Marketing Management* 1989) --and suspending the introduction of "me too" products that are destined to be "dogs." This step would alleviate the problem of product proliferation and reduce failed product costs for both the manufacturer and middlemen.

Additional strategies exist for eradicating the utilization of slotting fees. Manufacturers and channel intermediaries must form a cooperative venture that balances the needs of both. This may require a greater focus on trade marketing and the use of team selling. Manufacturers must also be more proficient at acquiring and utilizing computerized information. The goal is to become the category leader through strategic selling, category analysis, negotiation, customer orientation, and a greater understanding of retail account management and financing (*PROMO* 1991; *Sales and Marketing Management* 1989).

Suggestions for Future Research

Due to the sensitive nature of the subject matter, empirical research concerning slotting allowances is limited. The research which does exist is principally comprised of (1) descriptive essays documenting the existence of slotting fees while estimating the degree of utilization (e.g., Fannin 1987; Gibson 1988; *Progressive Grocer* 1991; Thompson 1990), and (2) discussions of the legality of slotting allowances (e.g., Aalberts and Judd 1991). Hence, it would be beneficial to the marketing discipline to extend theory through empirically based research on slotting allowances.

The propositional inventory presented in this study is intended to provide a foundation for empirical and theoretical research regarding slotting allowances. However, given the possible illegality of slotting allowances and social desirability bias (Nederhof 1986), there may be a tendency for respondents to deny the existence of slotting requirements/payments within their organization. Consequently, researchers may have to develop innovative methods for collecting this data. One such method involves surveying channel members' perceptions of their own, as well as other members, participation in slotting allowances. This method should provide an accurate assessment of slotting activity within the industry.

For further information please contact:
Judy Siguaw
University of North Carolina at Wilmington
Cameron School of Business Administration
Wilmington, NC 28403-3297

TYPE OF EXCHANGE AND ENVIRONMENTAL UNCERTAINTY WITHIN A MARKETING CHANNEL

Thomas L. Baker, University of Akron
Jon M. Hawes, University of Akron

ABSTRACT

This paper examines the two types of exchange, discrete and relational, proposed by Macneil (1978) in relation to executive perception of environmental uncertainty within a marketing channel. The distributor's perspective is used to consider both up-channel, or input sector environmental uncertainty, as well as the down-channel, or output sector type. By juxtapositioning these two important concepts, greater insight into the distributor's strategic focus of flexibility versus stability may be possible.

INTRODUCTION

One can argue that the dominant framework in marketing channels research is the political economy framework introduced by Stern and Reve (1980). While this paradigm has greatly contributed to our understanding of the workings of channels of distribution, it does not directly address an important concept that is the central focus of this paper--the choice between stability versus flexibility which is inherent in all decisions about channel relationships.

This important strategic decision is one which all channel participants must make. Macneil (1978, p. 854) characterized this issue as the "constant clash in modern economic structures between the need for stability and the need to respond to change." He developed a taxonomy of two types of exchange, discrete and relational, which allow for differing degrees of stability and flexibility. Discrete exchange provides for the greatest flexibility because there is absolutely no assumption, expectation, or requirement for continuity of the relationship between exchange participants after the one transaction under consideration is completed.

Relational exchange, on the other hand, enhances stability because the firms make a commitment to exchange goods with each other over a specified period of time. While this leads to lower levels of uncertainty, it reduces the firm's range of strategic choice during the contract period--thereby potentially limiting its ability to take advantage of unexpected opportunities or to deal with unforeseen problems.

One of the implications of the conflict between stability and flexibility (and therefore discrete and relational exchange) is the possible effect on the short- vs. long-run orientation of the firm. One of the criticism of many American companies, especially the "Big Three" auto firms, has been a focus on short-run profitability rather than long-run effectiveness. While it is true that choosing flexibility over stability may be a short-run response to uncertainty, the choice of stability is not inherently better since this strategy does not allow the firm to take advantage of changes which occur in the environment. In essence, one should not look at flexibility or stability as being disadvantageous in and of themselves. It is not the choice of stability or flexibility that is of paramount importance, but rather is the strategy pursued consistently given the environmental conditions faced by the firm.

While the conflict between the need for stability and flexibility (or the choice between relational and discrete exchange types) appears to be a fundamental issue within the discipline, it has not received much attention in the literature. Although Dwyer, Schurr, and Oh (1987) recently examined Macneil's (1978) distinction between discrete and relational transactions in a buyer-seller context, there are few other applications of this very useful framework in the marketing channels literature. This is particularly unfortunate in view of the extensive recent attention devoted to the related concept of environmental uncertainty. Organizational theory researchers have concluded that such uncertainty is a major determinant of various organizational actions (e.g., Dill 1958; Duncan 1972; Emery and Trist; Lawrence and Lorsch 1967; and Thompson 1967). This would include, of course, the type of exchange relationship sought by firms within the marketing channel.

The importance of studying environmental uncertainty within a channel's context is without question. Recently, channel of distribution researchers have investigated: the effect of environmental uncertainty on channel dyads (Achrol, Reve, and Stern 1983), the interorganizational responses to uncertainty by channel members (Dwyer and Welsh 1985), and the determinants of decision-making uncertainty (Achrol and Stern 1988). In fact, this latter study concluded that uncertainty is a "key organizing concept" for analyzing channel environments (Achrol and Stern 1988, p. 37).

Consequently, the purpose of this paper is to examine the concept of environmental uncertainty within the context of Macneil's (1978) exchange taxonomy (discrete versus relational). A concurrent examination of these inherently related theoretical concepts could offer considerable insight into channel strategy and management. In particular, a series of propositions relating to a distributor's preference for flexibility verses stability under various conditions of environmental uncertainty will be presented. The political economy framework's distinction between input and output sectors of the external environment and the corresponding levels of uncertainty will be incorporated into the propositions.

The paper will first present a more thorough discussion of Macneil's (1978) distinctions between discrete and relational exchange transactions and the corresponding relation to flexibility and stability. Following this, a brief presentation of the political economy paradigm will be offered. The propositions will then be presented.

TYPES OF EXCHANGE RELATIONSHIPS

Macneil (1978) states that organizations can maximize flexibility by entering into discrete transactions and maximize stability by entering into more relational exchange relationships. Both discrete and relational transactions will be reviewed.

Discrete Transactions

A purely discrete transaction would be "entirely separate, not only from all other present relations, but (also) from all past and future relations as well" (Macneil 1978, p. 856). A purely discrete transaction would take place between two parties when all of the following conditions are met: (1) neither party has previously seen the other, (2) both are completely sure of never seeing the other again, and (3) they were brought together by chance. Barter is necessary rather than the use of money which is acceptable to both parties, because the latter would indicate a common social structure.

As is evident by the above description, purely discrete transactions very rarely, if ever, occur. Purely discrete transactions certainly would not be expected between channel intermediaries since most of these exchange relationships are planned to occur over a period of time (Dwyer, Schurr, and Oh 1987). However, some "pseudo-discrete" transactions can and do occur. These transactions may involve exchange relationships which occur between two parties over time, but each transaction is viewed as being separate from all others. For example, a distributor who purchases a large percentage of a particular product from Manufacturer A may occasionally have to purchase some of the product from Manufacturer B, if Manufacturer A is unable to meet demand at that particular time. Since the distributor would intend for the transaction with Manufacturer B to be a one-time-only transaction (even though there may actually be many such transactions over a period of time), it could be classified as a discrete transaction, based on the intention.

The flexibility afforded by discrete transactions comes from outside the "focal" transaction, not from

within it. In other words, the flexibility inherent in discrete transactions arises from the fact that the exchange which occurs between the parties is of short duration. Both parties can then do whatever they chose in subsequent periods.

The terms of a discrete transaction may be rigid with little or no opportunity for variation through negotiation. But by only contracting once and for only a small quantity of goods, a distributor is then free to purchase from any other manufacturer in the future, thus assuring flexibility. For example, a small distributor not having an adequate financial base to enter into a long-term contract with a manufacturer for a specified quantity of goods might choose to engage in "pseudo-discrete" transactions. Consequently, the distributor would enter into a series of individual purchase agreements with one or more manufacturers for the desired goods, thus providing greater flexibility than would be the case with a single, binding long-term contract. Of course, the lack of a long-term contract would severely reduce stability and the assurance of a continuity of supply for the distributor. If stability is of greater interest, exchange participants would instead focus on relational transactions.

Relational Transactions

In comparison to discrete transactions, relational transactions occur repeatedly over an extended period of time between two exchange partners. Dwyer, Schurr, and Oh (1987) point out that trust plays an important role in the development of relational exchanges. Trust is both a necessary prerequisite in order for this type of exchange to occur and an expected outcome, given at least reasonable compliance with the terms of the exchange agreements by the other party.

Relational exchange relationships are, by definition, more stable than purely discrete transactions since both exchange partners must agree to abide by the terms of the exchange agreement (contract) for a specified period of time. For instance, a medium sized distributor which having a fairly stable customer base may enter into a long-term contract with a large manufacturer in order to obtain a more reliable source of supply.

This is not to say that relational exchange relationships cannot have some degree of flexibility. On the contrary, most relational exchange relationships explicitly allow for some variability in the exchange (Macneil 1978). He presented four major ways in which flexibility can be planned into relational exchanges: (1) the use of a predetermined, variable standard not controlled by either party (e.g., a variable rate of interest on finance charges tied to the prime rate), (2) direct third-party determination of performance, (3) one party control of terms, and (4) an agreement to agree (in sports, for example, the popular "player to be named later" concept).

In summary, discrete transactions allow the greatest degree of flexibility since there is no binding long-term agreement on the part of either party to continue to exchange goods over a period of time. Even though, however, the terms of any particular discrete transaction **can**, at times, be quite rigid (Macneil 1978). On the other hand, relational transaction occur over time and provide a greater degree of stability. Nevertheless, flexibility **can**, to a certain degree, be built into relational exchange contracts.

THE EXTERNAL ENVIRONMENT OF THE POLITICAL ECONOMY PARADIGM

As mentioned in the first part of the paper, a fundamental issue for distributor is the choice of flexibility or stability. It has been posited in this paper that a key factor impacting that choice is uncertainty concerning the external environment. In this section, a brief review of the external environment as conceptualized by the political economy paradigm will be presented.

In the most basic sense, the political economy framework consists of four "areas": (1) the internal and (2) external polity, as well as the (3) the internal and (4) external economy (Stern and Reve 1980). The internal polity concerns the internal sociopolitical structure and processes of the firm, while the external polity refers to the sociopolitical environment facing, but outside, the firm. Likewise, the internal economy is concerned with the internal economic structure and processes of the firm. The external economy is concerned with the macroeconomic environment confronting the firm.

Achrol, Reve, and Stern (1983) extended Reve and Stern's (1980) conceptualization of the political economy by suggesting a framework which takes into account the environment faced by channel members. In essence, the environment faced by a distributor can be analyzed in terms of the: (1) primary task environment, (2) secondary task environment, and (3) macro environment. The primary task environment is simply the immediate suppliers and customers of the distributor, while the secondary task environment is comprised of suppliers to immediate suppliers and customers of immediate customers.

The primary and secondary task environments may be further subdivided into: (1) an input sector, consisting of "up-channel" relationships, (2) an output sector, involving "down-channel" interactions, (3) a competitive sector, and (4) a regulatory sector. The input and output sectors are examined in this paper as the major sources of uncertainty facing the distributor. While the competitive and regulatory sectors are certainly also sources of uncertainty, this paper concentrates on "market" uncertainty (i.e., uncertainty emanating from suppliers or customers), rather than these other types.

As one would expect, up-channel relations with immediate suppliers as well as suppliers to immediate suppliers represent input sector issues. Therefore, <u>environmental uncertainty concerning the input sector involves the availability of goods</u>. The output sector consists of down-channel relations with immediate customers and customers of customers. Accordingly, <u>environmental uncertainty in the output sector concerns the ability of the distributor to sell the products purchased from organizations in the input sector</u>. It should be recognized that this demand uncertainty can emanate from demand which is either "in excess or short of forecasted sales for a time period" (Speh and Wagenheim 1978, pg. 96).

It is expected that environmental uncertainty in the input and output sectors will impact a distributor's strategic focus of flexibility verses stability. In the next section of this paper, a series of propositions will be presented explaining which strategy might be expected for different combinations of environmental uncertainty.

THE PROPOSITIONS

Figure 1 shows the matrix which summarizes the propositions to be presented in this section. Environmental uncertainty in the output sector represents the horizontal dimension and is characterized as being either "high" or "low." Two types of input sector uncertainty (high and low) are shown on the vertical dimension. This results in a two-by-two matrix of environmental uncertainty.

One of the key assumptions inherent in this discussion is that uncertainty in the output sector will be viewed by distributors as a more severe problem than uncertainty in the input sector. This is because the real economic loss from buying and then being unable to sell the goods is considerably more significant for the distributor than the opportunity costs of not being able to generate gross margin from the sales of goods because they were not available in the first place. Even in situations of high input uncertainty, distributors should be able to secure products from some source. In the event no supplier is found, competitors are probably in no better position and the distributor's out-of-pocket costs are not greatly increased because of the problem.

On the other hand, in situations of high output uncertainty, distributors face difficulty in finding buyers and may incur considerably increased warehousing, storage, promotional, financing, and other costs until a qualified buyer is found. And there is always a chance that the goods will lose value before the sale is made--or that the sale will never be made.

Quadrant One

This quadrant is characterized by a high degree of uncertainty in both the input and output sectors. Consequently, the distributor's primary concern will be to

FIGURE 1
A Distributor's Strategic Focus Under Various Conditions of Environmental Uncertainty

Environmental Uncertainty in **Output** Sector

Environmental Uncertainty in **Input** Sector

	High	
	Quadrant I Stability	Quadrant II Flexibility
	Quadrant III Stability	Quadrant IV Flexibility
	Low	

achieve a stable operating situation (or at least as stable a situation as is possible in such a highly uncertain environment). It is in this quadrant that a distributor is most likely to attempt to focus on relational exchange with both suppliers and customers. If such long-term agreements can be secured, these relational exchange relationships will allow the distributor to at least partially insulate itself from the turbulence occurring in the input and output sectors by contractually guaranteeing a relatively constant supply of goods as well as a reliable source to whom these goods can be sold.

Proposition 1: Under conditions of high input and high output uncertainty distributors will strategically focus on stability over flexibility. Accordingly, distributors will seek to enter into relational (long-term) agreements with both suppliers and customers.

Quadrant 2

Quadrant 2 is characterized by low output uncertainty and high input uncertainty. While confident of the ability to sell, they expect to face difficulty in finding a source of supply. Distributors in this quadrant are expected to prefer flexibility over stability as a strategic focus. Accordingly, they are likely to enter into shorter, more discrete transaction agreements with customers in their down-channel relations in order to improve their ability to take advantage of opportunities which may develop in the output sector.

For example, take the case of a small distributor who is able to secure a only a minimal quantity of a particular

product from a manufacturer. If all of this is guaranteed to a certain customer through a long-term contract, the distributor will be unable to offer the product to other customers at possibly (and likely) higher prices if the demand should rise.

Due to high input sector uncertainty, distributors will attempt to enter into relational agreements with suppliers. However it is expected that distributors will still seek flexibility over stability as the firm's comprehensive strategic focus since the model assumes that output certainty concerns will take precedence over input certainty concerns.

Proposition 2: Under conditions of low output uncertainty and high input uncertainty, distributors will place a premium on flexibility. Consequently, distributors will enter into more discrete transactions with customers, although they may enter into long-term transaction agreements with suppliers in order to counter the high input sector uncertainty.

Quadrant 3

Owing to the high output uncertainty, it is expected that distributors in this quadrant will prefer a strategic focus of stability over flexibility. In order to assure itself of a constant source of customers, the distributor may enter into a long-term transaction agreement with a particular customer or customers to supply a particular product. This will enable the distributor to buffer itself from the effects of the output uncertainty. An example might be a supplier of building products. Given the uncertainty in demand for products due to variability in the building of new houses, this distributor may enter into an agreement with one of more builders to supply certain materials, thereby assuring a contributing to the stability of sales revenue during such volatile times.

The low input sector uncertainty will enable the distributor to enter into more discrete transaction agreements with suppliers. This flexibility arising from discrete transactions with suppliers should enable the distributor to find the best terms for the products purchased, thereby enhancing margins for the sale of products to down-channel firms in the output sector.

Proposition 3: In situations of high output sector uncertainty and low input sector uncertainty distributors will seek stability over flexibility. In order to achieve this strategic focus, distributors will enter into relational transaction agreements with customers, but engaging in discrete transactions with the many qualified and readily available suppliers.

Quadrant 4

In this quadrant the low degree of input as well as output uncertainty allows the distributor to pursue a strategic focus of flexibility over stability. Since the distributor achieves this flexibility by entering into discrete transactions, the distributor is able to constantly search for the most favorable exchange relationships with both suppliers and customers.

Proposition 4: Under conditions of low input as well as low output sector uncertainty, distributors seek flexibility over stability and will achieve this strategic focus by entering into discrete exchange relationships.

SUMMARY

This paper has argued that a channel member's strategic focus is influenced by the environmental uncertainty in both the input as well as output sectors which it confronts. Macneil's (1978) taxonomy of exchange type (discrete verses relational) provides the firm with a choice of flexibility or stability in its interaction with exchange participants. By concurrently examining these two inherently related concepts, four propositions relating to a distributor's choice of strategic focus were offered.

Future research should subject these propositions to empirical testing. Ideally, a longitudinal study could be conducted in which distributor's perceptions of environmental uncertainty could be surveyed over periods of time. In addition, strategic behavior could be either surveyed and/or observed to test the propositions presented in this paper. Failing this, a quasi-experimental design could be utilized. In this case, distributor's would be presented with different combinations of scenarios regarding input/output uncertainty. They would then be asked what type of strategy (flexible or stable) they would be most likely to pursue. Finally, a market simulation such as The Marketplace (Cadotte 1990) might be utilized.

Such studies would greatly contribute to our understanding of channel member behavior as well as our ability to predict the nature of exchange interactions among participants in the marketing channel. Given that discrete exchange may sometimes be preferred because of the flexibility it offers, we may also gain some insight into why the marketing concept, with its focus on long-run profit maximization through customer satisfaction, has not yet been universally adopted.

REFERENCES

Achrol, Ravi Singh and Louis W. Stern (1988), "Environmental Determinants of Decision-Making Uncertainty in Marketing Channels, *Journal of Marketing*, 25 (February), 36-50.

_____, Torger Reve and Louis W. Stern (1983), "The Environment of Marketing Channel Dyads: A Framework for Comparative Analysis," *Journal of Marketing*, 47 (Fall), 55-67.

Cadotte, Ernest R. (1990), *The Marketplace: A Strategic Marketing Simulation.* Homewood, IL: Irwin.

Dill, W. R. (1958), "Environment as an Influence on Managerial Autonomy," *Administrative Science Quarterly*, 2 (March), 407-443.

Duncan, R. B. (1972), "Characteristics of Organizational Environments and Perceived Environmental Uncertainty, *Administrative Science Quarterly*, 17 (September), 313-327.

Dwyer, F. Robert, Paul H. Schurr and Sejo Oh (1987), Developing Buyer-Seller Relationships," *Journal of Marketing*, 51 (April), 11-27.

_____ and M. Ann Welsh (1985), "Environmental Relationships of the Internal Political Economy of Marketing Channels," *Journal of Marketing Research*, 22 (November), 397-414.

Emery, F. E. and E. L. Trist (1965), "The Causal Texture of Organizational Environments," *Human Relations*, 18 (February), 21-32.

Lawrence, P. and J. Lorsch (1967), *Organizations and Environment.* Cambridge, MA: Harvard Business School.

Macneil, Ian R. (1978), "Contracts: Adjustment of Long-Term Economic Relations Under Classical, Neoclassical, and Relational Contract Law," *Northwestern University Law Review*, 72, 854-902.

Speh, Thomas W. and George D. Wagenheim (1978), "Demand and Lead-Time Uncertainty: The Impacts on Physical Distribution Performance and Management," *Journal of Business Logistics,* 1 (1), 95-113.

Stern, Louis and Torger Reve (1980), "Distribution Channels as Political Economies: A Framework for Comparative Analysis," *Journal of Marketing*, 44 (Summer), 52-64.

Thompson, J. D. (1967), *Organizations in Action*. New York:McGraw-Hill.

DATABASE MARKETING FOR COMPETITIVE ADVANTAGE IN TRAVEL SERVICES

Richard K. Robinson, Marquette University
Terrence J. Kearney, Marquette University

ABSTRACT

If there is one particular service sector in which information technology, marketing, and cross-industry alliances have converged to impact the environment for both providers and customers, it is that of travel services. Within this arena, the effects are most visible in the airline market. Computer reservation systems and frequent flyer programs have merged in a profitable application of database marketing.

This paper assesses the impact of information technology and micro-marketing developments in the competitive environment of travel services. The focus is the application of database marketing in airline-related travel and its role in the pursuit of competitive advantage. Kotler (1991, p. 627) defines a marketing database as "an organized collection of data about individual customers, prospects, or suspects that is accessible and actionable" for marketing purposes such as product/service sales or maintenance of customer relationships. Database marketing gives service marketers an edge in learning more about their regular customers, as well as an opportunity to build customer loyalty through improved service (Francese and Renagban 1991). Moreover, in contributing to long-term strategy, it can reduce the cost of marketing by increasing overall marketing precision. While many service firms are working to build effective marketing database systems, the travel industry has led the way in systems development. Airlines, hotels, and travel agencies have moved well along the learning curve in exploiting database systems.

Three Marketing Tools for Competitive Advantage

During the period since deregulation, airlines have developed three database marketing tools that are being used to achieve competitive advantage. These three tools--computer reservation systems, frequent flyer programs and yield management programs-- are employed throughout the industry and by a number of other service industries. Deregulation of the airline industry has increased the importance of computer reservation systems (CRSs) since they make it easier for travel agents to review the proliferation of data on airline flights and fares. Information technology has increased CRS efficiency and opened the door to cross-industry data shar-ing. CRSs now display information for a wide range of travel and leisure services. Beyond this, CRSs have directly influenced the pursuit of competitive advantage in the airline industry. Since many travelers do not have particular airline preferences, travel agencies can determine the carrier-selection decisions of substantial numbers of business and leisure travelers.

Closely tied to CRSs are frequent flyer programs, which are central to a strategy to develop brand loyalty in a service class that is not naturally suited to high degrees of loyalty. Frequent flyer programs (FFPs) have been recognized as one of the most effective marketing practices yet devised for differentiating airline services (U.S. DOT 1990). Coupled with effective yield management, FFPs have increased airline productivity and efficiency. Yield management is the process of determining the optimal mix of seats that will be offered to discount customers versus seats that will be reserved for full-fare passengers. The nature of business travel has led the airlines to use advance purchase requirements as a barrier against potential full-fare passengers shifting into discount fares. Since yield management programs can be employed to funnel frequent flyers awards to fill empty seats, the cost of FFPs can be kept low. This represents a key competitive advantage in the battle to retain business travelers as loyal customers.

Conclusions/Managerial Implications

The number of products suitable to mass marketing has been declining. Business is targeting smaller and smaller groups of customers in multiple target-market strategies. The travel industry has been very successful in designing and employing database marketing programs to get close to the customer. CRS, FFP and reservations data have been put to good use not only by airlines, but also by hotels, rental car companies and travel agents. These industries have always been knowledge-intensive and dependent upon accurate and extensive record keeping. Other service providers, from banks and insurance firms to hospitals, have similar characteristics. Many of the cutting-edge marketing practices employed in the transportation industry could be applied in these sectors. As technology develops and managers further exploit the capabilities of database marketing, the practice of marketing in many industries will change in dramatic ways.

For further information please contact: Richard K. Robinson
Department of Marketing
Marquette University
Milwaukee, WI 53233

RESALE PRICE MAINTENANCE AND THE RULE OF REASON: A FRAMEWORK PROPOSED TO ELIMINATE FREE RIDERS

Abhay Shah, University of Southern Colorado

ABSTRACT

Resale Price Maintenance (RPM) has remained controversial to this day. Some scholars support the "per se legal" view, some support the "per se illegal" view, while others support the "rule of reason". This paper examines the three arguments and provides a framework that may help solve the confusion in RPM.

INTRODUCTION

The recent scandal in price fixing and the ultimate conviction involving Nintendo games has brought the issue of Resale Price Maintenance (RPM) back to the limelight again. RPM, also referred to as vertical price fixing, is one of the many subjects in anti-trust that has been much misunderstood and has remained controversial to this day (Miller 1984). Recently, Cady (1982); Kaufmann (1988); Maurer and Ursic (1987); and Sheffet and Scammon (1985), pointed out the importance of RPM and how it affects manufacturers as well as retailers of certain goods.

Beginning in 1911 with the case of Dr. Miles Medical Company v. John D. Park & Sons Company, until recently with the case of Monsanto Company v. Spray Rite Service Corporation (1984), the judgments passed by the courts can be best described as, "RPM has taken a roller coaster ride..." (Sheffet and Scammon 1985, pg 82).

The courts have maintained that a manufacturer can not dictate resale prices to its distributors and violation of this is deemed illegal since it constitutes an unreasonable restraint of trade. In evaluating RPM, the courts opined that RPM had the same impact as a horizontal price agreement between dealers (and this has also been deemed illegal). The courts have also expressed that resale price fixing did not provide any real benefits to the manufacturer. Once the product is sold, the manufacturer should have no interest in what happens at the retail level, and the consumers are entitled to any advantage that may result down the distribution chain.

A manufacturer can also not dictate maximum resale prices as was seen in the Albrecht v. Herald Company case and the Kiefer-Stewart Company v. Joseph E. Seagram and Sons Inc., case. In both these cases, the Supreme court declared "per se illegal" a manufacturer's attempt to fix maximum resale prices. The court has maintained that a manufacturer can not suggest minimum resale prices or, for that matter, maximum resale prices.

In fall 1983, the Justice department along with the Federal Trade Commission proposed that the "illegal per se" rule for RPM be replaced by the "rule of reason", whereby each case could be judged on its impact on competition and RPM should be legal even though it may prevent intrabrand competition as long as it did not restrict inter-brand competition between manufacturers. This was advocated in the Continental T.V v. GTE Sylvania case. However, this was not followed, and the 1984 decision on Monsanto showed that the courts still favored the "illegal per se" rule.

The courts have, with a broad brush, made RPM "illegal per se" without realizing that their judgments may promote unfair competition and also free-ridership which may benefit a certain class of distributors at the expense of another class. Free riders are those resellers who are able to increase their own sales by lowering prices but they do not provide the desired services that a manufacturer wants them to provide to buyers of that product. A customer may also be considered to be a free rider if he/she is able to get all the knowledge about a technically complex product like a computer from a full service store, but purchases the computer from a lower priced no service store or mail-order. Free riders are able to benefit from the services rendered by others without paying for them.

Scholars have cited a number of reasons for the use of RPM, some reasoning that RPM improves distribution efficiency (Bork 1965) while others assert that RPM inhibits competition between distributors (Marvel and McCafferty 1987). A Manufacturer may use RPM for enforcing retailers to provide special services and eliminating free riders (Springer and Frech 1986).

RPM should be judged using the "rule of reason" in order to prevent retailers from free riding on the services provided by others, to gain distributor support, enter new markets and increase market coverage (Cady 1982; Ornstein 1985; Pitofsky 1984; Turner 1962). However, Cady and Pitofsky both think that the ill defined "rule of reason" could be responsible in increasing litigation costs and other costs to enforce RPM over those incurred under the "per se illegal" rule. The failure of the Miller Tydings Act and the McGuire Act (which were repealed in 1975) was due to the absence of such a framework which would otherwise have provided judges with the basis for enforcing the "rule of reason".

This paper attempts to show that a blanket ban on RPM (illegal per se) could be construed as an unfair and discriminatory anti-trust law. Section I of the Sherman act imposes a blanket ban on RPM under the assumption that the "illegal per se" rule will be procompetitive and weed out those who are attempting to monopolize. However, Bork (1965) and Miller (1984) point out that the courts have failed to realize that markets, consumers and products are heterogeneous and not homogeneous, and the "illegal per se" rule is not practical.

This paper is in complete agreement with Cady's, Miller's and Pitofsky's proposition and suggests a stricter framework to enforce the rule of reason by using the classification scheme of goods proposed by Copeland (1925); Bucklin (1963); and Murphy and Enis (1986); in order to eliminate free riders. The framework can also be used by judges when judging RPM on the basis of the "rule of reason."

THE THREE VIEWS ON RESALE PRICE MAINTENANCE

As stated earlier, there are three distinct views on RPM - the "per se legality" of RPM, the "per se illegality" and the "rule of reason" for RPM. Supporters of the "per se illegality" of RPM firmly believe that RPM is anticompetitive and encourages a manufacturer's attempt to monopolize. Proponents of the "per se legality" of RPM maintain that RPM should be made legal under all circumstances. They argue that it is procompetitive and everyone involved stands to gain through this rule. Finally, supporters of the "rule of reason" think that RPM should be judged on a case by case basis since products are heterogeneous. The use of RPM by manufacturers is justified under certain circumstances, but may not be justified and may lead to monopoly power under other circumstances.

Arguments Supporting the "Per Se Illegality" of RPM

Starting with the Dr. Miles case (1911) to the Monsanto case (1984), the courts have maintained (with the exception of the GTE Sylvania case in 1977) that RPM is, and should be treated illegal per se, and a manufacturer can not force its distributors to adhere to a maximum or minimum resale price. One of the proponents of this view, Areeda (1984) defends the Supreme Court's Dr. Miles decision and says, "...Though economically wrong, it was probably historically correct." (p. 20). Although Areeda agrees that the intention of supporters of RPM is to eliminate competition, he goes on to say, "I am willing to make the broad brush judgment that their main purpose was to eliminate competition among themselves." (p. 20).

Telser (1960) and Comanor (1968), support the "per se illegality" of RPM and maintain that RPM creates product differentiation which enhances market power and may lead to a dealers' or manufacturers' cartel, price

discrimination and restriction of output. Pitofsky (1984) also supports the view that RPM should be "illegal per se" and believes that although debaters agree on the basic premise, they disagree on major conclusions. Pitofsky thinks that the seller with the lowest price does not necessarily offer the least service. Discounters are usually quite efficient and they pass that efficiency along to consumers. A rule supporting the "per se illegality" would deny dealers to pass these efficiencies along to the consumer.

Flaws with this viewpoint. Most of the arguments put forward by proponents of the "per se illegality" appear to be sound at first glance, but they fail to hold ground on closer examination. What they have overlooked is that the reason a manufacturer may need to use RPM is because of the need for control at the retail level which arises due to the differences in products, i.e. products are heterogeneous and not homogeneous. The "per se illegality" would actually hurt manufacturers of those products where consumers of those products need extra services in the form of explaining, how to install and properly use the product, maintaining image, etc. One of the best ways a manufacturer can be certain that these services are provided is by using RPM, where the retailer provides the desired services.

The "illegal per se" rule has given birth to free-riders. To promote fair competition, eliminate free-riders, and preserve the interests of the retailers, the manufacturer's best option may be the use RPM as the controlling tool. This would force retailers to provide the desired level of before and after sales service. RPM, in such cases, should be considered procompetitive since it helps in eliminating free riders.

Views of the "Per Se Legality" Rule for RPM

Bork (1978), and Easterbrook (1984) maintain that RPM should be "legal per se". Cartels and restricted dealings (also regarded as RPM) should not be lumped together, since restricted dealings benefit consumers while cartels hurt consumers (Bork 1978). Just like there is cooperation within a firm, there can also be cooperation across firms, and restricted dealing should be considered a form of cooperation between retailers, since it does not restrict competition between manufacturers (Comanor 1968; Easterbrook 1984). A manufacturer may be unable to enforce the service standards without RPM. A customer may take advantage of the services and time of a salesperson in a full service store and may then order from a mail order or discount store, encouraging free riders. RPM should then be used to force and maintain those standards and eliminate free-riders.

Manufacturers, almost always, desire product differentiation and one way to do this is through a manufacturer-dealer relationship where the dealer is also involved in helping to create product differentiation which would in effect maximize sales. The manufacturers may desire these types of product differentiation over price competition because, unlike price competition, they are difficult to duplicate by competitors.

The confusion in RPM today is due to the incorrect premise laid down by Justice Hughes in the Dr. Miles case (Bork 1978). According to Bork, a manufacturer imposes RPM only to achieve distributive efficiency, not eliminate competition or restrict output. A manufacturer will never use RPM to let resellers gain a more than competitive return, which may make the manufacturer's brand uncompetitive in terms of price. The manufacturer or supplier chooses the RPM criteria to enhance consumer welfare by providing the consumer with the needed pre-sale and after sale service. A retailer whose price is controlled by a manufacturer will be forced to compete for business through increased service.

Enforcing RPM would lead to the elimination of free riders and increased services by retailers. It may also provide some form of quality certification by retailers since customers care that a particular product is being sold by leading retailers. If RPM leads to a decrease in output, then the conclusion would be that it is anticompetitive, leading to a drop in social welfare, but if it leads to an increase in output (sale) due to the increased services, then it can clearly be considered procompetitive and will lead to increased social welfare (Comanor 1965; Marvel and McCafferty 1985). The higher margins ensured to distributors, if a manufacturer uses RPM, will encourage more dealers to carry the manufacturer's goods, thus increasing distribution and availability of the good to the public (Bittlingmayer 1983).

If those who view the services as a very important and integral part of the product outweigh those who think that services are unimportant in the purchase of the product, then a loss in social welfare will occur if RPM is considered illegal. RPM should therefore be seen as a tool that can raise consumer welfare for products that need extra sales services and RPM would not be used for products where consumers do not need such extra sales services.

Consumer welfare will increase due to RPM as long as it is motivated by service provisions (Marvel and McCafferty 1985). Marvel and McCafferty found that the use of RPM was concentrated in urban areas and inhibited entry by free riders and was not simply used to preserve dealer cartels forced by the manufacturer. Springer and Frech (1986) found that in the absence of RPM, retailers used misleading prices and higher mark-ups, while Bittlingmayer (1983) thinks that RPM is used as a socially beneficial method of price control to avoid instability and chaos among retailers.

Flaws with this viewpoint. One of the big problems with the "per se legality" view is that a manufacturer can (explicitly or implicitly) force dealers to honor price agreements or face being cut off as the manufacturer's dealer. The manufacturer can also police a dealers' cartel where retailers may demand that the manufacturer force all dealers to adhere to the agreement or face termination (boycott).

Like the supporters of RPM's "per se illegality" view, supporters of this view have failed to realize that the "per se legality" of RPM may give an undue advantage to a large corporation if consumers of its products do not need services. A simple example should suffice in explaining this. Legalizing RPM is appropriate for products where the customers need service before or after purchase of the product. However, making RPM legal across the board could also give a giant corporation the power to dictate prices irrespective of the nature of the product. A large company could drive out smaller competitors by suggesting maximum retail prices to its retailers which could be lower than what a competitor could afford to stay in business. The company could later raise its price after the departure of the competitor. Similarly, a corporation could refuse to deal with a distributor who did not wish to adhere to its suggested minimum or maximum price and thus exercise discriminatory power.

The "Rule of Reason" and why it is the Most Suitable Rule

The decision on the Continental T.V. v. GTE Sylvania case was the only one that advocated the rule of reason. The court opined that although GTE's act of terminating Continental prevented intrabrand competition, it did not prevent interbrand competition, and therefore it was justified. The ruling of the Monsanto case advocates the "rule of reason" for RPM (although the decision on the Monsanto case was based on the "per se illegality" rule). Later, in the Business Electronics v. Sharp Electronics case, the Supreme Court used the "rule of reason" and supported Sharp's position of terminating its dealings with Business Electronics because Business Electronics was cutting prices below Sharp's list price. However, this ruling violates HR 585 and S.430, the proposed amendment to the Sherman Act.

This author is in unison with those who advocate the "rule of reason" since it recognizes the fact that products and markets are heterogeneous, not homogeneous. RPM is procompetitive and it could be good or bad depending on the circumstances, and legislators should tailor laws accordingly (Miller 1984). If a manufacturer could not impose market restrictions in the form of exclusive territories, the distributors would have no incentive to provide costly selling services (eg, educated and well trained salespeople), but will free ride on the services provided by others. On the other hand, if the reseller's price is maintained, the retailer will be forced to provide such services thus eliminating the temptation to free ride on the services provided by others.

However, a problem with using the "rule of reason" may occur while differentiating between the use of RPM for preserving fair competition and the use of RPM which may turn out to be anticompetitive. Clearly, the objective should be to discourage the use of RPM where it stifles competition and promotes attempts to monopolize. For this, the legislators and the courts should be made to realize that products and markets are heterogeneous, and different products may need different treatment.

The inherent heterogeneity of products calls for using the "rule of reason." Using the "per se illegality" (as is the case now), or the "per se legality" rule as proposed by others will not serve the purpose that the anti-trust acts wish to achieve. The former, while attempting to preserve competition, unfortunately encourages free riders and may lead to unfair competition. Although the latter attempts to preserve competition by trying to eliminate free riders, it offers no solution if RPM is used by a firm attempting to monopolize or discriminate. Using the classification of goods proposed by Copeland (1925); Bucklin (1963); and Murphy and Enis (1986); the following section suggests a framework for judging RPM.

HETEROGENEITY BETWEEN PRODUCTS - A FRAMEWORK FOR APPLYING RESALE PRICE MAINTENANCE JUDGMENTS

The premise of the "rule of reason" is based on the fact that products and markets are not homogeneous. The inherent heterogeneity between products advocates the "rule of reason" and the application of RPM should be viewed according to that. RPM should be made legal for those products where customers need certain types of services (eg, explaining product features, how to install and use the product, etc.,) before and after the purchase of the product, and illegal for those products where customers do not need such services. Classifying consumer goods as convenience, shopping and specialty, based on travel, brand comparison, and brand loyalty as suggested by Copeland (1925), shopping effort and prepurchase preference as suggested by Bucklin (1963), and degrees of effort and risk as proposed by Murphy and Enis (1986) will help in this analysis. The following section shows how the "rule of reason" can be justified using this classification.

Convenience Goods

Copeland (1925) defines convenience goods as: "...those customarily purchased at easily accessible stores." (p. 14). These are low in effort and risk, and consumers do not spend much time or money when shopping for them (Murphy and Enis 1986), or expend much shopping

effort (Bucklin 1963). Examples are grocery staples, canned soup, magazines, laundry soap, etc.

Relying on the above descriptions of convenience goods, it is quite clear that none of the goods that would fall in this category need any special attention in terms of explanation or other such services that consumers (and manufacturers) may desire before or after purchase of the product. Why, then, would a manufacturer of such a product use RPM? Simple logic dictates that a manufacturer of such a product will not use RPM for such a product, since it would hurt the sales of its own products against competitors (if minimum prices are dictated using RPM).

However, this does not rule out the fact that a manufacturer could use RPM, especially if its motives are to prevent competition or discriminate against a dealer. The attempt to compete unfairly could happen, especially if there is a large corporation which is in a position to dictate prices merely through coercion despite the fact that it is engaged in selling a convenience good. The case of Dr. Miles is a classic example of this and legalizing RPM in a case like this will undermine the effectiveness of RPM. A manufacturer could drive out its competitors by forcing its distributors not to sell above the suggested price. Free-riding seems very unlikely in such a situation and the use of RPM seems unjustifiable. RPM should, therefore, be considered illegal for convenience goods and a manufacturer should be penalized if caught enforcing RPM for convenience goods. Consequently, the following hypothesis is proposed.

H1: Manufacturers and resellers of convenience goods will not want to use Resale Price Maintenance.

Shopping Goods

Copeland (1925), defines shopping goods as, "...those for which a consumer desires to compare prices, quality, and style at the time of purchase" (p. 14). Consumers perceive high levels of risk and thus spend a fair amount of time and money when searching and evaluating alternatives (Murphy and Enis 1986). Examples of these are furniture, clothing and major appliances.

Consumers of some shopping (homogenous) goods have been considered to be price sensitive since consumers consider the different brands in this category to be quite uniform in quality, etc. Consumers of heterogeneous shopping goods are not price sensitive and may shop for styles, design, etc. Consumers usually need services in the form of presale education and they will acquire this through rational shopping behavior encouraging low price-low service dealers to free ride at the expense of the high-priced high-service stores (Kaufmann 1988). Marketers should emphasize personal selling when marketing these goods (Murphy and Enis 1986). In order to provide certain before and after sales service, the manufacturer may want to use RPM. However, the "illegality per se" rule of RPM has seen rampant free riding for such products.

Pitofsky (1984), argues that shopping goods like jeans do not need any special effort to sell. A store like Bloomingdale's will lay down jeans on a rack in the same way as K-Mart does. The decision on Levi Strauss & Company similarly reinforces this belief. Levi's had refused to sell to discounters. A suit was filed against Levi's and the court decided that Levi's could not do so, thus supporting the "rule of reason" for shopping (homogeneous) goods, i.e. RPM Should be legal for heterogeneous shopping goods and illegal for homogeneous shopping goods. Based on the above arguments, the following hypotheses are proposed.

H2a: Manufacturers and resellers of homogeneous shopping goods will not want to use RPM. Exceptions being those manufacturers who want to project and preserve an image of their brand or company.

H2b: Manufacturers and resellers of heterogeneous shopping goods who want to ensure that the required before and after sales service are made available to consumers will want to use RPM.

H2c: Resellers like discount stores, catalogue showrooms and mail-orders would not want manufacturers to use RPM since this category of resellers do not provide the services that may be required of them and are most likely to free ride on the services provided by others.

Specialty Goods

This category of consumer goods is the one where unfair competition in the form of free riders may be most prevalent. Copeland (1925) defines it as:

..those which have some particular attraction for the consumer, other than price, which induces him to put forth special effort to visit the store in which they are sold and to make a purchase without shopping (p. 103).

These are also very high in terms of risk and effort, the big difference between shopping and specialty goods is in terms of effort, not risk (Murphy and Enis 1986). Examples are cars, hi-fi equipments, photographic equipment. Getting information on these goods is very important to consumers.

Easterbrook (1984), Pitofsky (1984), and others have used the much common example of computers while defending the legalizing of RPM. Personal computers, like cameras, hi-fi equipments and cars need a lot of attention and patient explaining by salespeople. Marketers should emphasize personal selling while selling specialty goods (Murphy and Enis 1986). Service doesn't just stop there. Most customers need service even after the purchase of such products and it is here that a free rider like a discount store, catalogue showroom or a mail order service (providing no services) will benefit from services provided by the full service stores. The objective of RPM in this case is to preserve the physical product-service combination and preserve fair competition by eliminating free riders. Before one attempts to justify the "per se illegality" rule, one should ask the question, "Would the free riders be able to sell their products in the absence of the full service stores?." The answer to this will be a qualified "No."

The free riders in the case of specialty goods are discount stores, catalogue showrooms, mail orders, etc. These retailers do not provide the services desired before the purchase of specialty goods. Most customers buying through these types of outlets usually do so after soaking up the knowledge about the product from other full service stores, thereby benefiting the free riders (both consumers and distributors) at the expense of the full service stores.

The "rule of reason" for RPM would discourage efficiency and also harm consumers since the dealers would not be able to pass the cost benefit down to consumers (Pitofsky 1984). However, this author believes that Pitofsky's arguments are not correct. If a store is cost efficient, it may still be able to gain in the face of RPM. Price is not the only way to compete, and a retailer may be able to gain if it can increase its quality of services and attract customers on the basis of these enhanced services rather than lower prices. On the other hand, if the retailer does not wish to follow this choice, it can still come out a winner by merely pocketing the difference resulting out of this efficiency. In both cases, the retailer stands to gain without lowering prices. Subsequently, the following hypotheses are proposed.

H3a: Manufacturers and resellers of specialty goods which need extra services would want to use RPM.

H3b: Resellers like mail-order and catalogue showroom and other types of no-service stores would not like to see manufacturers dictate resale price. This category is considered free-riders.

CONCLUSION

This paper provided an overview of RPM and the different views held on it. It also showed that the arguments put forth by supporters of the "per se illegality" and the "per se legality" suffered from some logical and practical deficiencies and that the "rule of reason" is the most ideal rule to judge RPM. Using the "per se legality" or the "per se illegality" rule to judge RPM would lead to a loss of social welfare either through turning a blind eye to attempts to monopolize or encouraging free-riders.

A framework, using Copeland's (1925); Bucklin's (1963); and Murphy and Enis's (1986); classification of goods, along with some hypotheses, was proposed as a guideline that could be used while judging RPM. Using this framework, judges can implement the "rule of reason" whereby each case could be judged based on its own merit. This would ensure a marketplace where competition is fair, where a manufacturer would not be able to discriminate against any intermediary and where free riders would no longer be able to take a free ride on the services offered by other intermediaries.

REFERENCES

Albrecht v. Herald Co. dba Globe Democrat Publishing Co. (1968), 390, U.S. 145.

Areeda, Phillip (1984), "The State of the Law," *Regulation,* (January/February), 19-22.

Bittlingmayer George (1983), "A Model of Vertical Restriction and Equilibrium in Retailing," *Journal of Business,* 56 (October), 477-496.

Bork, Robert H. (1965), "The Rule Of Reason And The Per Se Concept: Price Fixing and Market Division," *The Yale Law Journal,* 74 (5), 373-399.

_____(1978), *The Antitrust Paradox - A Policy At War With Itself.* New York: Basic Books Inc., Harper Torchbooks.

Bucklin, Louis (1963), "Retail Strategy and the Classification of Consumer Goods," *Journal of Marketing,* 27 (January), 51-56.

Business Electronics Corp. v. Sharp Electronics Corp. (1988), 56 LW 4387.

Cady, John F. (1982), "Reasonable Rules and Rules of Reason: Vertical Restrictions on Distributors," *Journal of Marketing,* 46 (Summer), 27-37.

Comanor William S. (1965), "Vertical Territories And Customer Restrictions: White Motor And Its Aftermath," *Harvard Law Review,* 81, 1419-1438.

Continental T.V., Inc. v. GTE Sylvania (1977), 433 U.S. 36.

Copeland, Melvin T. (1925), *Principles of Merchandising.* Chicago: A. W. Shaw Co.

Dr. Miles Medical Co. v. John D. Park & Sons Co. (1911), 220 U.S. 373.

Easterbrook, Frank (1984), "Restricted Dealing Is A Way To Compete," *Regulation,* (January/February), 23-26.

House of Representatives Committee on the Judiciary (1987), "Report on HR 585, the Freedom From Vertical Price Fixing Act of 1987," *Report,* 100-421.

Kaufmann Patrick J. (1988), "Dealer Termination Agreements and Resale Price Maintenance: Implications of the Business Electronics Case and the Proposed Amendment to the Sherman Act," *Journal of Retailing,* 64 (Summer), 113-124.

Kiefer-Stewart Co. v. Joseph E. Seagram & Sons, Inc. et al. (1951), 340 U.S. 211.

Marvel, Howard P. and S. McCafferty (1985), "The Welfare Effects of Resale Price Maintenance," *The Journal of Law & Economics,* (May), 363-379.

Maurer, Virginia G., & Michael Ursic (1987), "Resale Price Maintenance: A Legal Review," *Journal of Public Policy & Marketing,* 171-180.

Miller, James C. (1984), "An Analytical Framework," *Regulation,* (January/February), 31-32.

Monsanto Co. v. Spray-Rite Service Corporation. (1984) 775 U.S. 104.

Murphy Patrick E., & Ben M. Enis (1986), "Classifying Products Strategically," *Journal of Marketing,* 50 (July), 24-42.

Ornstein, Stanley I. (1985), "Resale Price Maintenance and Cartels," *The Antitrust Bulletin,* Summer, 401-432.

Pitofsky, Robert (1984), "Why Dr. Miles Was Right," *Regulation,* (January/February), 27-30.

Senate Committee on the Judiciary (1988), "Report on S.430, the Retail Competition Enforcement Act of 1987," *Report,* 100-280.

Sheffet, Mary Jane & Debra L. Scammon (1985), "Resale Price Maintenance: Is It Safe To Suggest Retail Prices?," *Journal of Marketing,* 49 (Fall), 82-91.

Springer Robert F. and H. E. Frech (1986), "Deterring Fraud: The Role of Resale Price Maintenance," *Journal of Business,* 59 (July), 433-449.

Telser, Lester G. (1960), "Why Should Manufacturers Want Free Trade ?," *The Journal of Law and Economics,* (May), 86-105.

Turner, Donald F. (1962), "The Definition of Agreement Under the Sherman Act: Conscious Parallelism and Refusal to Deal," *Harvard Law Review,* 75, 655-706.

A CROSS-NATIONAL STUDY OF U.S. VERSUS RUSSIAN BELIEFS AND ATTITUDES TOWARD ADVERTISING IN GENERAL

J. Craig Andrews, Marquette University
Srinivas Durvasula, Marquette University
Richard G. Netemeyer, Louisiana State University

ABSTRACT

The primary purpose of our study was to conduct an initial cross-national comparison of beliefs and attitudes toward advertising in general between samples from the U.S. and Russia. The study also emphasized the recommended procedures for testing the cross-national applicability of constructs and measures (cf., Irvine and Carroll 1980). Based on previous research in the U.S. on beliefs and attitudes toward advertising (Bauer and Greyser 1968; Muehling 1987), views on Russian fascination with executional advertising qualities, and problems with the Russian economy, it was expected that U.S. respondents would exhibit more favorable beliefs toward the economic effects of advertising and have a more favorable attitude-toward-the-institution of advertising than would Russian respondents. On the other hand, Russian respondents should exhibit more favorable beliefs toward the social effects of advertising and have a more favorable attitude-toward-the-instrument of advertising and more favorable attitude-toward-advertising-in-general than U.S. respondents.

A total of 212 business and economics students with similar age and gender characteristics provided complete responses to the study's survey. Of this total, 148 students were from a major, Midwestern university in the U.S., while 64 students were from two major universities in the Russian Republic. The Russian sample received a carefully translated version of the questionnaire drafted with a bilingual expert not only fluent in both English and Russian, but familiar with the cultural nuances and meanings of the words used. The questionnaire was also carefully back-translated into English to ensure correct meaning and the cross-cultural equivalence of measures. Based on previous advertising belief and attitude research, the questionnaire included: seven Bauer and Greyser (1968) belief items assessing advertising's economic and social effects, a four-item summed scale of attitude-toward-the-institution of advertising, a three-item summed scale of attitude-toward-the-instrument of advertising, and a three-item summed scale of attitude-toward-advertising-in-general. A set of confirmatory factor analyses and a multiple group analysis provided general support for the dimensionality, discriminant validity, and reliability of all measures for both the U.S. and Russia. However, due to low composite reliabilities for the separate economic and social belief dimensions in the U.S. and Russia, the belief items were then treated separately (and not summed) for mean comparisons. Given the general support for the cross-national equivalency of the measures, a set of mean comparisons was then made via MANOVA to examine study predictions. The MANOVA results first indicated that the U.S. respondents were <u>not</u> more agreeable to the economic beliefs about advertising, contrary to predictions. In fact, the Russians exhibited significantly greater agreement versus U.S. respondents that "Advertising is essential." This may be due in part to the view that advertising is a necessary part of their change to a market-driven economy. The results for the social belief items were as predicted, demonstrating the U.S. sample's more negative view of the social impact of advertising. The results were also as expected for attitude-institution (i.e., advertising's purpose and effects), with U.S. respondents being more favorable than Russian respondents. However, support was not found for Russians being more favorable to attitude-instrument (i.e., advertising's practices and methods) than U.S. respondents. It may be that U.S. respondents were just as favorable as the Russians due to their common academic background (i.e., business) and future employment possibilities with advertising-related businesses. Finally, the Russians had a more favorable attitude-toward-advertising-in-general than U.S. respondents, as predicted. It is likely that the U.S. respondents' negative reactions to the social effects of advertising played a part in this result, whereas Russian respondents were likely to view advertising positively as "the engine of trade." While these results should be viewed in light of the business student sample employed and different historical, economic and advertising backgrounds in the countries, it provides the first comparative study (to our knowledge) assessing Russian beliefs and attitudes toward advertising. It is hoped that the present study and its recommended methodology will encourage other studies of advertising in Russia and contribute to our knowledge of how advertising affects individuals throughout the world.

REFERENCES

Bauer, Raymond A. and Stephen A. Greyser (1968), *Advertising in America: The Consumer View.* Boston: Harvard University.

Irvine, Sid H. and William K. Carroll (1980), "Testing and Assessment Across Cultures: Issues in Methodology and Theory," in *The Handbook of Cross-*

Cultural Psychology, Harry C. Triandis and John W. Berry, eds. Boston, MA: Allyn and Bacon, Inc., 2, 127-180.

Muehling, Darrel D. (1987), "An Investigation of Factors Underlying Attitude-Toward-Advertising-in-General," *Journal of Advertising,* 16 (1), 32-40.

For further information please contact:
J. Craig Andrews
Department of Marketing
Marquette University
Milwaukee, WI 53233

A CROSS-CULTURAL COMPARISON OF CONSUMER ETHNOCENTRISM IN THE UNITED STATES AND RUSSIA

Srinivas Durvasula, Marquette University
J. Craig Andrews, Marquette University
Richard G. Netemeyer, Louisiana State University

ABSTRACT

An important contribution to consumer research has been the development and international application of the CETSCALE, measuring consumer ethnocentrism. This scale, comprised of 17 items, was first applied by Shimp and Sharma (1987, p. 280) to represent "the beliefs held by American consumers about the appropriateness, indeed morality, of purchasing foreign-made products." Consumer ethnocentrics are said to view purchasing foreign products as wrong because it hurts the domestic economy, causes a loss of jobs, and is simply unpatriotic. For nonethnocentric consumers, foreign products should be evaluated on their own merit, rather than based on where they are produced.

After providing support for the psychometric properties of the scale in the U.S., Shimp and Sharma (1987) suggested several potential applications of the scale to population groups in other countries. However, researchers were first cautioned to provide an accurate translation and assessment of the scale's psychometric properties. In response, Netemeyer, Durvasula, and Lichtenstein (1991) found strong support for the psychometric properties and nomological validity of the scale across four different Westernized countries (i.e., the United States, France, Japan, and West Germany). However, Netemeyer et al. (1991, p. 326) also recommended that researchers translate and apply the CETSCALE in other countries, such as in the former Soviet-bloc countries.

Therefore, our study examined the psychometric properties and mean values of the CETSCALE in Russia and compared the findings with those in the U.S.. Given that many U.S.-multinationals such as Eastman Kodak and Johnson & Johnson are actively promoting the U.S. brands in Russia (cf. Newman 1988), it is important for marketers to first understand the extent to which consumers in Russia exhibit ethnocentric tendencies. It was hypothesized that the CETSCALE would exhibit a unidimensional factor structure and a high level of reliability for both the U.S. and Russian samples. Next, the scale should have a positive correlation with general attitude toward the home country and thereby offer evidence of discriminant validity. To assess nomological validity, the CETSCALE was expected to be significantly and positively correlated with the importance of buying domestic products and significantly negatively correlated with measures of general attitude toward buying the "other" country's products as well as with general beliefs about the quality of products from the "other" country. Given the fascination for foreign products coupled with a bleak outlook for the domestic economy and products in Russia, it was hypothesized that the mean scores on CETSCALE will be higher for the U.S. sample than for the Russian sample. In contrast, the mean values for the measures of beliefs and attitudes toward "other" country's products were expected to be higher for the Russian sample than for the U.S. sample.

A total of 144 business and economics students from a major, Midwestern University in the United States and 60 such students from two major Universities in Russia provided the necessary data. Subjects in both samples were similar in age and male/female ratio. The Russian version of the questionnaire was developed with the assistance of two bilingual experts; one of which translated the English version to Russian. The other expert compared both versions to check for accuracy in translation. A series of confirmatory analyses was performed and the results generally supported the unidimensionality, reliability, discriminant validity, and nomological validity of the scale. (Contrary to expectations, U.S. respondents' general beliefs and attitudes toward Russian products were unrelated to their CETSCALE scores.) Next, a multivariate analysis of variance was performed with country as the independent variable. CETSCALE and other belief and attitude variables served as the dependent measures. A significant overall effect provided evidence for mean differences between the two samples. Tests for individual mean differences supported all other hypotheses.

Since both samples were comprised of students, the results must be evaluated with caution. Further, the U.S. respondents' relatively less favorable attitudes toward "other" country's (i.e., Russian) products may not be generalizable across all product categories and other countries of origin. For the U.S. respondents, the strength of relationship between CETSCALE and attitude toward "other" country's products may also vary depending on what the "other" country is. These caveats notwithstanding, this study supports the applicability of the CETSCALE to Russia.

REFERENCES

Netemeyer, Richard G., Srinivas Durvasula, and Donald R. Lichtenstein (1991), "A Cross-National Assessment of the Reliability and Validity of the CETSCALE," *Journal of Marketing Research*, 28 (August), 320-327.

Newman, Barry (1988), "Perestroika Pitch: The Spirit of Glasnost Has Admen in Moscow Sharpening Up Copy," *The Wall Street Journal*, (July 8), A1, A9.

Shimp, Terence A. and Subhash Sharma (1987), "Consumer Ethnocentrism:Construction and Validation of the CETSCALE," *Journal of Marketing Research*, 24 (August), 280-289.

For further information contact:
Srinivas Durvasula
Marketing Department
Marquette University
Milwaukee, WI 53233

OBSERVATION OF MARITAL ROLES IN DECISION MAKING: A THIRD WORLD PERSPECTIVE

Cynthia Webster, Mississippi State University

ABSTRACT

Patterns of interaction between Indian husbands and wives were unobtrusively observed as they shopped for products within several categories. This exploratory investigation sought to determine which spouse initiates the product selection, how the other spouse responds, the content and tone of communication, and occurrence of unpleasant consequences such as arguments or heated debate.

INTRODUCTION

In spite of the ongoing interest among researchers regarding marital roles in decision making, most of the studies continue to focus on theory-laden, self-reports of spouses living in industrialized countries. By utilizing such scales as the constant-sum scale (Haley and Overholser 1975) and the popular 5-point scale of relative influence (Davis 1970), the family decision-making literature has focused mainly on who is influential (i.e., Ekstrom et al. 1987; Foxman et al. 1989) and who makes the decisions about purchases within families (Brinberg and Schwenk 1985; Imperia et al. 1985). This study attempts to broaden our understanding of husband/wife relative influence in decision making by deviating from the standard practices utilized in past studies.

This study differs from past related studies in two major ways. First, theory-free, unobtrusively observation will be conducted of couples as they shop for various products. Thus, this study follows the thought of many anthropologists and qualitative researchers who espouse an inductive research posture. This posture insists that research questions framed during initial work are generally misleading; meaningful questions must be formed after considerable research is complete (Everhart 1976). Kuhn (1962) thought that value-free and unbiased knowledge in natural sciences was a result of, at least in part, their great reliance on theory-free observations and concluded that researchers' "paradigms" or "World Views" determined what they "saw." Indeed, objectivity in science has been deemed impossible because theories and paradigms precede and determine facts and observations (Hudson and Ozanne 1988; Kuhn 1962; Mick 1986; Peter and Olson 1983).

Secondly, the data will be collected from various regions in India, a cultural environment vastly different from those in which past related studies were conducted. It is possible that theory-free data derived from a culture that has an extended family concept, arranged marriages

by elders, and hence, is quite different from Western cultures, will provide a unique context for enhancing our understanding of marital roles in decision making.

BACKGROUND

Importance Of Marital Role Research

Husband/Wife influence in family decision making is of considerable interest to researchers from various disciplines who share an interest in consumer behavior (Putnam and Davidson 1987). For example, psychologists are concerned with the roles played by spouses in decision making and the dependence of these roles on various psychological factors (Holloman and Hendrick 1973). By comparing problem-solving behavior within families to that already explored within the laboratory, sociologists can better assess the external validity of small group research using ad hoc groups. For economists interested in studying household economic decisions, this topic would be relevant in determining whether information about family interaction needs to be explicitly considered in predicting consumer choices (Ferber 1973).

Information about the roles played by the spouse throughout the decision-making process in relevant in assessing the feasibility of using marital roles in addition to sex roles as a basis for market segmentation. This information is also beneficial to any organization--private or public--interested in communicating with the appropriate decision-maker(s) in the family or obtaining valid data about household preferences, intentions, or behavior. In other words, to maximize the effectiveness of limited budget allocations, the marketing manager must know which spouse in the household has the dominant influence in decision making so that the marketing and promotional strategy can be oriented accordingly (Menasco and Curry 1989).

The Indian Market

Though considerable research effort has been expended on family decision making in developed western countries, hardly any published work exists on this topic in the Indian cultural context. This lack of research is unfortunate in that economic anthropologists have long recognized the potent source of Third World cultural change that the evolving world market system represents (Sherry 1987b). World-systems analyses show that Indians as a Third World country, has great potential of becoming well integrated into the world economy. As a country predicted to become the largest in the world, India is attracting worldwide interest among marketers. This vast country is rich in resources, is becoming more materialistic, and is desperately searching for ways to improve its economic situation (Crook 1991). Though poor by western standards, the attractiveness of India is based upon its infrastructure, well-developed legal system, and large numbers of well-educated doctors, engineers, and other needed for growth of a thriving middle class (Engel et al. 1990). Indeed, the middle class is the key to understanding India's consumer markets. Some economists estimate the number in the class at 7 to 12 percent of the population or a market range from 60 million to 100 million, larger, for instance, than that of France. Consequently, the demand for consumer goods is rising rapidly, making India a very attractive market (Spaeth 1988).

In contrast to the U.S., India more closely resembles a continent in which each state is like a separate nation, complete with different languages, religions, and ethnic groups (Fisher 1980, p. 23). Associated with these differences are variation in architecture, cuisine, dress, rituals, music, and traditions. Despite constitutional prescriptions, the caste system remains evident among the Hindus, who account for over 80 percent of all Indians. In part because of Muslim influence, however, caste hierarchy in north India is mostly confined to rural areas, with social class hierarchies more significant than caste in urban areas (Dutt and Noble 1982). Cities such as Bombay and Delhi have a strong urban social class system, and the caste hierarchies are not strictly followed.

Caste-independent social classes are most evident in Indian towns and cities, where only 20-25 percent of the population reside. Despite a per capita income of only $240 for all of India, a relatively affluent upper class exists in urban India. This upper class constitutes under 10 percent of the total Indian population but accounts for approximately 50 percent of the Indian gross national product (Mehta and Belk 1991).

The cities of India are growing faster than towns and villages. One effect of the urban lifestyle of larger cities is to disrupt the occupational prescriptions of caste that are still found in the towns and villages from which the many new large-city residents have migrated (Conlon 1977). The pursuit of economic riches in the city also tends to weaken kinship ties and lessen the frequency of joint or extended families (Lannoy 1971).

On the other hand, the great majority of India's population resides in villages. Three fourths of the world's population live in villages; one seventh of the world's population live in the 560,000 villages in India. The "typical" Indian woman, representing about 75 percent of the 400,000,000 women and female children in India, lives in a village. She comes from a small peasant family that owns less than an acre of land, or from a landless family that depends on the whims of big farmers for sporadic work and wages. Her occupation is field work, chiefly harvesting, planting and weeding, for which she often receives less than fifty cents a day--in many cases, half the wage that a man receives for the same amount of work (Bumiller 1990, p.11).

Power is gender related in India under the predominant patriarchal and patrilocal system. Alexander and Jayaraman (1977) find that, while the status gap between men and women is narrowing in upper castes as industrialization and urbanization create greater opportunities, sex inequality is growing in lower castes where these same trends have tended to take women out of production rather than provide them opportunities.

Marriage in India traditionally occurs just after puberty, although the age of marriage is now increasing, especially in cities. Arranged marriages remain dominant. Because daughters require costly dowrises and do not carry on the family name or remain in the home, they are less esteemed than sons. (Mehta and Belk 1991).

The purpose of this paper is to work towards enhancing the understanding of marital roles in decision making by unobtrusively observing the interaction of husband and wife from various regions in an environment which is quite different from Western cultures.

METHOD

The observations were conducted in both cities and villages within five states in India: Kerala (in the southern tip of India), Rajasthan (northwest), Karnataka (south), Uttar Pradesh (north), and Maharashtra (west). Data were collected in the respective cities of Coimbatore, Jaipur, Mysore, Delhi, Aurangabad and in ten villages surrounding these larger cities. The target population was defined as married couples[1] who were considering small appliance, furniture, and clothing purchases. A total of 168 spousal shopping units were observed during the latter part of 1990 and the early part of 1991. Seventy-one couples were observed in cities and 97 in villages. Approximately 34 percent of the couples were lower or labor class, 39 percent middle class, and 27 percent upper class.[2] About 83 percent of the couples were Hindu, 12 percent Muslim, and 5 percent Sikh.[3]

Five students from area Indian universities and the author observed the couples in the shopping environment. In order to closely observe yet not contaminate the behavior of the shoppers, the students stood near the couple and tried to present the appearance of a fellow customer; the author also stood near the shopping couple and tried to present the appearance of a mere tourist. The observers were successful in attaining an unobtrusive vantage point for listening to all the communication and furtively watching much of the behavior. The primary responsibility of the observers was to record a verbatim description of the sequence of husband-wife exchanges.

After the field work, the observation notes were coded by two independent codes, who summarized the chain of communications into an essential initiation-response categorization (Atkins 1978). First, the coders determined which party took the initiative in the product selection aspect of the interaction and rated the tone of the message: if the wife initiated, did she ask her husband's permission for the product (Request) or did she more forcefully tell her husband that she wanted the product (Demand); if the husband initiated, did he ask his wife what she wanted or tell her to pick her choice (Invite), or did he more forcefully tell his wife that he wanted a particular product (Demand).

The classification of the response was based on the action eventually taken by the other party: if the wife made a request, the husband could agree, deny outright, or suggest another alternative (brand); if the wife made a demand, her husband could yield, reject outright, or suggest another. On the other hand, if the husband invited selection, his wife could select or decline; and if the husband made a demand, his wife could agree, reject outright, or suggest another alternative. In two situations, the sequence was coded one step further: if the husband invited selection and the wife made a selection, his response of agreeing to the selection or denying the selection was scored; if the husband demanded a certain product and his wife suggested another, coders rated whether the husband agreed or denied the wife's counter-nomination.

FINDINGS

First, no apparent variation in husband/wife interaction was revealed among the ethnic groups (Sikhs, Hindus, and Muslims), between couples from villages and cities, and among couples residing in the various regions or states in India. Thus, the data from the three ethnic groups, the cities and villages, and the various states were combined.

In approximately 60 percent of the shopping episodes observed and studies, the wife initiated the interaction sequence by expressing a desire for the product. Table 1 shows that 41 percent of the wives requested or asked for a particular product, and an additional 20 percent of the wives made a more assertive "demand." The Indian husband is much more likely to agree with the purchasing desires of his wife when she is less assertive. Interestingly, the percentage of cases in which the husband either denies outright or suggests an alternative product/brand is very similar for both "request" and "demand" instances.

Table 1 shows that when the husband initiates a particular purchase, he either invites his wife to make a selection, or much more likely, he makes a demand for a specific product. When he does invite selection, she is likely to take the opportunity to select a product, and he is likely to agree with her selection. However, the data in Table 1 indicates that his inviting her to select does not mean he will yield to what she wants. As previously mentioned, the Indian husband is most likely to demand a certain product if he initiates. In the majority of cases, his wife agrees or yields to his demand; she never denies. However, in a minority of cases, she will suggest an alternative product, but he is not likely to agree with her suggestion.

Table 2 reveals the nature of husband/wife interaction and the outcomes of the interaction, by both product category and social class. Several observations can be made regarding the data in Table 2. First, in approximately 46 percent of the cases, the wife initiates and the husband's response is positive. However, it should be noted that this finding, surprising for a patriarchal culture, is due to the wife's dominance regarding clothing purchases. In nearly 27 percent of the cases, the husband initiates and the wife's response is positive. The other major interactions involve the wife initiating and the husband responding negatively (14%) and the husband initiating and the wife responding negatively (12%).

Second, the data in Table 2 show that the nature of husband/wife interaction varies by product category and social class. For example, for both small appliance and furniture purchases, the husband of the lower class couples; definitely has more power; among the middle class couples; the power shifts to the wife; and among the upper class couples, the decision making appears to range from equal decision making to husband dominance. For clothing purchases, on the other hand, the Indian wife has dominance; this holds true for each of the classes.

Third, the data in Table 2 reveal several interesting relationships. The chi-square results indicate a significant relationship between interation and product category, interation and social class, and husband/wife conflict and social class. The husband is much more likely to initiate and the wife react positively for small appliance and furniture purchases. On the other hand, the wife is likely to initiate and the husband react positively for the clothing purchases. Regarding the interaction/social class relationship, the husband initiating and the wife responding positively is much more likely among the lower class couples, where the husband initiating and the wife reacting negatively is much more likely among the upper class couples. The wife initiating and the husband responding positively is much more likely among the middle class couples, and the wife initiating and the husband reacting negatively is more likely among the lower and upper class couples. Finally, there appears to be a positive relationship between marital conflict and social class; that is, the likelihood of conflict and social class; that is, the likelihood of conflict increases as class position increases.

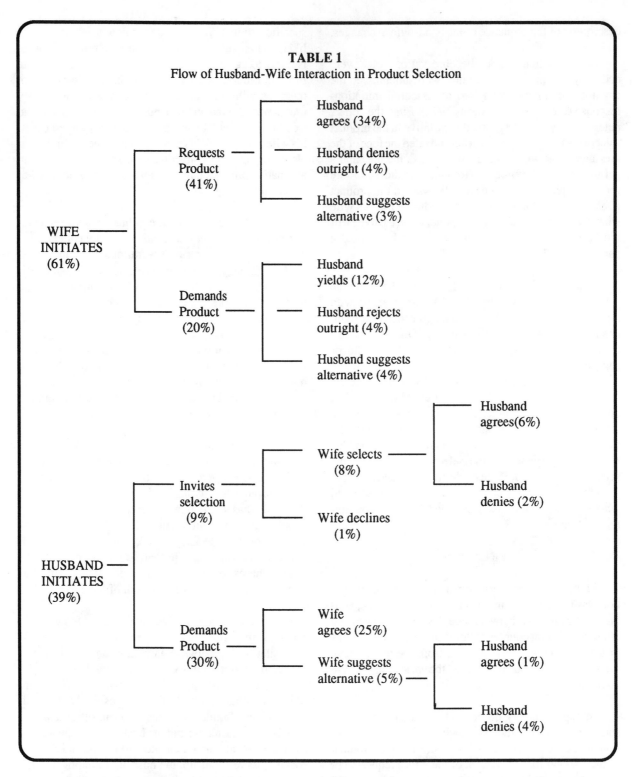

TABLE 1
Flow of Husband-Wife Interaction in Product Selection

WIFE INITIATES (61%)
- Requests Product (41%)
  - Husband agrees (34%)
  - Husband denies outright (4%)
  - Husband suggests alternative (3%)
- Demands Product (20%)
  - Husband yields (12%)
  - Husband rejects outright (4%)
  - Husband suggests alternative (4%)

HUSBAND INITIATES (39%)
- Invites selection (9%)
  - Wife selects (8%)
    - Husband agrees (6%)
    - Husband denies (2%)
  - Wife declines (1%)
- Demands Product (30%)
  - Wife agrees (25%)
  - Wife suggests alternative (5%)
    - Husband agrees (1%)
    - Husband denies (4%)

DISCUSSION, IMPLICATIONS, AND DIRECTIONS FOR FUTURE RESEARCH

Though exploratory, this study revealed some interesting findings regarding husband/wife interaction while engaged in the actual shopping task. Although other studies have either implicitly or explicitly made the point that husbands in relatively patriarchal cultures have the dominant role and their wives the submissive role (i.e., Cromwell et al. 1973, Kumar and Rao 1987), the unobtrusive observational technique utilized in this study revealed that the Indian wife is not completely submissive in shopping behavior.

However, it does appear that the nature of husband/wife interaction depends on the importance of the product. For example, the Indian male may not become involved significantly with clothing purchases because of their relative unimportant nature. Since appliances and furniture require a more significant monetary outlay, he may feel compelled to dominate in making the decisions.

TABLE 2
Husband-wife Interaction and Consequences, by Product Category and Class

	Small Appliances Class			Product Category Clothing Class			Furniture Class		
	Lower (n=18)	Middle (n=15)	Upper (n=13)	Lower (n=28)	Middle (n=32)	Upper (n=17)	Lower (n=12)	Middle (n=18)	Upper (n=15)
Husband-Wife Interaction									
Husband initiates, wife positive	56%	20%	31%	14%	16%	12%	75%	17%	33%
Husband initiates, wife negative	11	13	31	11	6	12	0	17	20
Wife initiates, husband positive	11	53	23	64	72	65	8	50	20
Wife initiates, husband negative	22	13	15	11	6	12	17	17	27
Husband-Wife Conflict									
Yes	6%	10%	15%	10%	16%	23%	7%	22%	27%
No	94	90	85	90	84	77	93	78	71

These relationships are significant at the $p \leq .05$ level by chi-square test: husband/wife interaction by product category ($x^2 = 27.8$, df = 6), interaction by class $x^2 = 31.4$, df = 6), and conflict by class ($x^2 = 12.4$, df = 2).

Another finding resulting from this research is the nonlinear relationship between social class or income (or "well-offness") and the relative influence of the husband in decision making. Though other studies (i.e., Huszagh and Murphy, Komarovsky 1961, Wallendorf and Reilly 1983) have implied a negative linear relationship between income or social class and the husband's power (i.e., as income or social class increases or become higher, the influence of the husband decreases), this study found that, among Indian couples, the husband has the dominant role among the lower class couples; however, the dominance shifts to the wife among the middle class couples, and then the influence tends to balance between husband and wife among the higher-class couples.

Although a substantial minority of husband/wife dyads exhibit arguments, open-end observations indicate that the conflict is seldom intense or persistent. Displays of spouse anger or disappointment appear to be short-lived in most cases.

These findings seem to suggest several potentially valuable implications for marketers. Probably the most important implication of these findings is that the fast-growing Indian market should not be viewed as being homogenous with respect to marital roles in decision making. The finding of role differences indicates that separate marketing mixes and programs be targeted toward these class-based segments.

Given the patriarchal nature of the Indian culture, one would probably expect the husband to be dominant, regardless of the social class. This was indeed the case for the lower-class families. Thus, promotional messages should be targeted to the husband. However, the role of the Indian wife becomes more dominant in the middle-class families; therefore, she is the one who should be the target of a firm's communications. When joint or equal decision making exists (as it does for the upper-class families), advertising and promotion cannot effectively be geared to just one sex.

While these findings are interesting and yield valuable implications and insight into the area of marital roles in decision making, they were derived from an investigation that was exploratory in nature. Because of both the qualitative and exploratory thrust of the research, there are several limitations which should be improved in future studies. First, this study focus on only three product categories; future work should examine husband/wife influence in decision making across several product categories. Second, other data collection techniques should be used rather than relying solely on observation. Although there are several propositions and theories of family decision making (Zaltman and Wallendorf 1982), they are based on research conducted in developed Western countries such as the U.S. and Canada (Kumar and Rao 1987). Thus, future research might attempt to broaden the theory of family decision making by presenting ethnographic case materials from different states in India. These materials will provide a check on the construct validity or generality of standard propositions for decision-making research (Sheth 1974). India will provide a unique context for reconsidering models of family decision making. Analysis of the case materials will suggest elements of an improved, multicultural model for family decision making, and will help transform the metaphorical of descriptive mission of anthropology for consumer research into a paradigm-building one (Sherry 1987a).

ENDNOTES

[1] Based on their physical proximity to one another and the symbols of marriage displayed by the female.

[2] Based on dress, demeanor, neighborhood, and store.

[3] Based on dress (including headwear).

REFERENCES

Alexander, Sue C. and Raja Jayaraman (1977), "The Changing Status of Women in India," in *Indian Urbanization and Planning: Vehicles of Modernization*, Allen G. Noble and Ashok K. Dutt, eds. New Delhi: Tata McGraw-Hill, 150-158.

Atkin, Charles K. (1978), "Observation of Parent-Child Interaction in Supermarket Decision-Making," *Journal of Marketing*, (October), 41-45.

Brinberg, David and Nancy Schwenk (1985), "Husband-Wife Decision Making: An Exploratory Study of the Interaction Process," in *Advances in Consumer Research*, 12, E.C. Hirschman and M.B. Holbrook, eds. Provo, UT: Association for Consumer Research, 487-491.

Bumiller, Elizabeth (1990), *May You Be the Mother of a Hundred Sons*. New York: Random House.

Conlon, Frank F. (1977), "Urbanism and Indian Society: The Aspect of Caste," *Indian Urbanization and Planning: Vehicles of Modernization*, Allen G. Noble and Ashok K. Dutt, eds. New Delhi: Tata McGraw-Hill, 126-140.

Cromwell, Ronald E., Ramon Corrales, and Peter M. Torsiello (1973), "Normative Patterns of Marital Decision Making Power and Influence in Mexico and the United States: A Partial Test of Resource and Ideology and Theory," *Journal of Comparative Family Studies*, 4 (2) (August), 177-196.

Crook, Clive (1991), "A Survey of India," *The Economist*, (May 4), 3-18.

Davis, H. L. (1970), "Dimensions of Marital Roles in Consumer Decision-Making," *Journal of Marketing Research*, 7 (May) 168-177.

Dutt, Ashok K. and Allen G. Noble (1982), "The Culture of India in Spacial Perspective: An Introduction," in *India: Cultural Patterns and Processes*, Allen G. Noble and Ashok K. Dutt, eds. Boulder, CO: Westview, 1-28.

Ekstrom, Karin M., Patriya S. Tansuhaj, and Ellen R. Foxman (1987), "Children's Influence in Family Decision and Consumer Socialization: A reciprocal View," in *Advances in Consumer Research*, M. Wallendorf and P. Anderson, eds. Provo, UT: ACR, 14, 283-87.

Engel, James F., R.D. Blackwell, and P.W. Miniard (1990), *Consumer Behavior*. 3rd ed., New York: Holt.

Everhart, Robert B. (1976), "Ethnography and Educational Policy: Love and Marriage or Strange Bedfellows?" *Anthropology and Education Quarterly*, 7, 17-25.

Ferber, R. (1973), "Family Decision Making and Economic Behavior," *Family Economic Behavior: Problems and Prospects*, E.B. Sheldon, ed. Philadelphia: J.B. Lippincott Co.

Fisher, Maxine P. (1980), *The Indians of New York City: A Study of Immigrants from India*. Colombia, MO: South Asian.

Foxman, Ellen R., P.S. Tansuhaj, and K. Ekstrom (1989), "Family Members' Perceptions and Adolescents' Influence in Family Decision Making," *Journal of Consumer Research*, 15 (March), 482-491.

Haley, Russell and C. C. Overholser and Associates (1974), *Purchase Influence: Measures of Husband/Wife Influence in Buying Decisions*. New Canaan, CT: Haley, Overholser, and Associates, Inc.

Holloman, Charles R. and Hendrick, Hal W. (1973), "Effects of Status and Individual Ability on Group Problem Solving," *Decision Sciences*, 4 (July), 55-63.

Hudson, Laurel A. and Julie L. Ozanne (1988), "Alternative Ways of Seeking Knowledge in Consumer Research," *Journal of Consumer Research*, 14 (March), 508-521.

Huszagh, Sandra M. and Arthur D. Murphy (1982), "Patterns of Influence in the Purchase of Consumer Durables by Mexican Households," *Educators' Conference Proceedings*, B. J. Walker et al., ed. Chicago: American Marketing Association, 1-6.

Imperia, Giovanna, O'Guinn, Thomas C., and MacAdams, Elizabeth A. (1985), "Family Decision Making Role Perceptions Among Mexican-American and Anglo Wives: A Cross Cultural Comparison," in *Advances in Consumer Research*, E.C. Hirschman and M.B. Holbrook, eds. Provo, UT: Association for Consumer Research, 12, 71-74.

Komarovsky, Mirra (1961), "Class Differences in Family Decision-Making on Expenditures," in N.N. Foote, ed. *Household Decision-Making*, New York: University Press, 255-265.

Kuhn, Thomas S. (1962), *The Structure of Scientific Revolutions*. Chicago: The University of Chicago Press.

Kumar, K. Ambarish and C.P. Rao (1987), "Problems of Researching Household Consumer Behavior in India," *World Marketing Congress Proceedings*, 3, 37-40.

Lannoy, Richard (1971), *The Speaking Tree: A Study of Indian Culture and Society*, London: Oxford University Press.

Mehta, Raj and Russell W. Belk (1991), "Artifacts, Identity, and Transition: Favorite Possessions of Indians and Indian Immigrants to the United States,"

Journal of Consumer Research, 17 (March), 398-411.

Menasco, Michael B. and David J. Curry (1989), "Utility and Choice: An Empirical Study of Wife/Husband Decision Making," *Journal of Consumer Research,* 16 (June) 87-97.

Mick, David Glen (1986), "Consumer Research and Semiotics: Exploring the Morphology of Signs, Symbols, and Significance," *Journal of Consumer Research,* 13 (September), 196-213.

Peter, J. Paul and Jerry C. Olson (1983), "Is Science Marketing?" *Journal of Marketing,* 47 (Fall), 111-125.

Putnam, Mandy and William R. Davidson (1987), *Family Purchasing Behavior: II Family Roles by Product Category.* Columbus, Ohio: Management Horizons, Inc., A Division of Price Waterhouse.

Sheth, J.N. (1974), "A Theory of Family Buying Decisions," *Models of Buyer Behavior,* Harper and Row, 17-33.

Sherry, John F., Jr. (1987a), "Heresy and the Useful Miracle: Rethinking Anthropology's Contribution to Marketing," *Research in Marketing,* J. Sheth, ed. Greenwich, CT: JAI, 9, 285-306.

_____(1987b), "Cultural Propriety in a Global Marketplace," *Philosophical and Radical Thought in Marketing,* A.F. Firat, et al., eds. Lexington, MA: D.C. Heath, 179-192.

Spaeth, Anthony (1988), "A Thriving Middle Class Is Changing the Face of India," *The Wall Street Journal,* (May 19), 22.

Wallendorf, Melanie and Michael D. Reilly (1983), "Ethnic Migration, Assimilation, and Consumption," *Journal of Consumer Research,* 10 (December), 292-301.

Zaltman, Gerald and M. Wallendorf (1982), *Consumer Behavior.* 2nd. ed., New York: John Wiley and Sons.

THE NONINTEGRATED EXPORT CHANNEL: ANTECEDENTS OF PERFORMANCE

Daniel C. Bello, Georgia State University
Li Zhang, Georgia State University

ABSTRACT

Drawing upon transaction cost analysis (TCA) and internationalization theory (INT), this research develops and tests a model of the antecedents to financial and operational performance in indirect export channels. Specifically, the model posits that transaction characteristics (asset specificity and environmental uncertainty) and firm characteristics (knowledge and resources) impact export performance through two key mediators--monitoring behavior and continuity commitment.

INTRODUCTION

In contrast to integrated channels (foreign salesforce or subsidiary), nonintegrated channels (independent agents or distributors) provide a relatively easy, low-cost form of foreign market entry. Experts note that the majority of world trade is handled through independent middlemen and that these export intermediaries possess superior local market knowledge, crucial contacts with foreign buyers, and the ability to provide sophisticated marketing services.

Despite these advantages, research on nonintegrated international channels show that relationships with middlemen are hard to manage and high performance is difficult to achieve. There are two major reasons for poor performance in nonintegrated export channels: (1) middlemen may not adequately invest in the task-specific assets necessary to market a manufacturer's brand because they fear future termination, and (2) they may engage in dependence-balancing activities with foreign buyers. These problems mainly arise from the separation of ownership and profit centers associated with independent trading firms, and give rise to the major inhibitors of export performance.

In this research, it is argued that middlemen opportunism is dampened by manufacturers' monitoring efforts, and the problem of underinvestment is alleviated by manufacturers' continuance commitment to middlemen. Further, four major conditions that antecede monitoring and commitment are also specified by applying the explanatory mechanisms of TCA and INT. Specifically, transaction specific assets and environmental uncertainty motivate manufacturers to monitor the middleman, and these two conditions also lead manufacturers to have continuance commitment to the middleman. Firm knowledge and firm resources, on the other hand, empower manufacturers to monitor the middleman, but they tend to reduce manufacturers' continuance commitment to the middleman.

METHOD

Data was collected from a national sample of manufacturers that export through middlemen. Twenty in-depth field interviews and a pretest of 100 firms were conducted to develop questionnaire items and examine their psychometric properties. The multi-step approach for confirmatory measurement and structural equation modeling was adopted using LISREL 7 to analyze data for the main data collection effort. First, a confirmatory indicator measurement or factor analysis model specifies the relationship between an initial pool of questionnaire items and their posited, underlying first-order indicators. Second, a confirmatory construct measurement or factor analysis model relates the first-order indicators defined in the prior model to their posited, underlying theoretical constructs. Finally, a confirmatory structural model tests the hypothesized relationships among the theoretical constructs.

RESULTS AND CONCLUSIONS

The first order indicator measurement model becomes acceptable after minor respecifications. The second order construct measurement model is acceptable without any respecifications. All the hypothesized relationships, except one, in the structural model are supported. As a result, an alternative structural model is respecified by dropping an unsupported path and adding a supported path. This final model fits the data well.

This research highlights the need to elaborate upon the roles of monitoring and commitment in the nonintegrated channel. The findings show a strong association between these two constructs and the level of export performance derived from the use of export middlemen. These results suggest that future research should devote more attention to implementation details as well as strategic integration issues addressed by TCA and INT theories. That is, performance outcomes are directly related to implementation details such as whether the firm actively monitors the middleman and desires continuity with its independent trading partner.

For further information please contact:
Daniel C. Bello
Department of Marketing
Georgia State University
Atlanta, GA 30303

EXPORT MARKET CHARACTERISTICS AS DETERMINANTS OF PRODUCT ADAPTATION: AN EMPIRICAL STUDY

Wiboon Arunthanes, Washington State University at Tri-Cities
Jean L. Johnson, Washington State University

ABSTRACT

Increasing pressure from global competition has prompted marketing practitioners and researchers to seriously consider the issues involved in the design of marketing strategy for foreign market entry. At one end of the spectrum, advocates of standardization argue that although differences between countries and/or cultures may exist, basic human needs are the same throughout the world. Therefore, marketers need not address these differences specifically in their marketing programs. At the other end of the spectrum, advocates of adaptation or local adaptation, acknowledge that basic human needs may be similar everywhere, but argue that differences in cultural and other environmental factors may significantly influence the buying behavior of people in different countries.

In an effort to gain a better understanding of the adaptation decision and offer practitioners some guidance, we explore the factors in foreign markets that drive U.S. exporters' decisions to adapt products. Six hypotheses are posited.

H1: The degree of product adaptation varies by product type: a. consumer nondurables show the highest level; b. consumer durables show midlevels; c. industrial products show the lowest level.

H2: Export market government regulation positively affects the amount of adaptation: a. more for consumer nondurables; b. less for consumer durables; c. the least for industrial products.

H3: Marketing infrastructure limitations increase product adaptation: a. more for consumer nondurables; b. less for consumer durables; c. not at all for industrial products.

H4: Differences in market lag between the domestic and local markets positively affect product adaptation: a. the most for consumer nondurables; b. midlevels for consumer durables; c. the least for industrial products.

H5: When competition is intense in the export market, cultural differences between the domestic and export markets positively affect product adaptation: a. more for consumer nondurable products; b. less for consumer nondurables; c. not at all for industrial products.

H6: When competition is intense in the export market, product preferences and tastes in the export market positively affects adaptation: a. more for consumer nondurables; b. less for consumer durable and industrial products;

The exporting firms used in this study were randomly drawn from a list of U.S. exporters in the United States Importers and Exporters Directory 1990. Hypotheses were tested by t-tests, multivariate analysis of variance with product adaptation as the dependent variable. Follow-ups investigating the detailed effects of export market characteristics were performed with multiple regression with dummy variable coding.

MANOVA results suggest that both H1 and H2 are partially supported. Because consumer durables and nondurables exporters did not report significantly different levels of adaptation, they were collapsed into one group for subsequent analysis. Tests of H2 through H6 now involve only two product types, consumer products and industrial products. For H2, MANOVA results indicate that government regulations significantly affect product adaptation. Regression follow-ups, however, indicate that the degree of influence by product type is not discernably different in these data. For H3, MANOVA results indicate that infrastructure differences significantly affect product adaptation. Regression follow-ups suggest that the levels of adaptation differ significantly by product type. We find no support for H4 through H6.

One major conclusion of this study is that the U.S. firms examined adapted products for export only when, and to the extent that local government regulation and constraints in the marketing infrastructure forced them to do so. That is, these firms seemed to turn a blind eye to the individual needs and wants of various markets they were attempting to serve.

This lack of attention to export markets is often the case when a firm's predominant concern is the domestic market and commitment to export activity is low. The fact that for nearly all of the firms surveyed in this study, less than 20 percent of the exported product's total sales came from foreign markets demonstrates this tendency. A firm may extend a standardized product because it views export markets as a bonus beyond the main domestic market. Such views result in an unwillingness to invest time and resources into product adaptation. However, U.S. exporters may be neglecting untapped market potential. With some exploration into the adaptation decisions, firms could realize considerable gains.

With regard to differences between adaptation levels of product types, results of this study suggest that local governments regulate both consumer and industrial markets to a significant degree. Firms seeking to minimize the bureaucracy and physical requirements for exporting may not be able to do so by confining their activities to industrial markets. This implies that U.S. exporters must be willing to devote resources and assume most marketing functions. In exploring export market opportunities, managers should be aware of these limitations and count them into costs initially.

For further information please contact:
Jean L. Johnson
Department of Marketing
Washington State University
Pullman, WA 99164-4730

STRATEGIC ALLIANCES IN INTERNATIONAL TOURISM MARKETING

Tracey Hill, Griffith University
Robin N. Shaw, Griffith University

ABSTRACT

An exploratory study was conducted into the criteria for the successful cooperative marketing of two countries' tourism industries, and the opportunity for strategic alliances to be formed.

Key variables in the decision making process were identified, including country-pair destination elements such as mutual proximity, the similarity of attractions, the existence of multinational ownership and management links, the standards of infrastructure, and the convenience of air links; and the nature of the origin target market.

The relative importance of these attributes was tested via a mail questionnaire sent to a sample of knowledgeable people from within the tourism industry. Several questioning techniques were utilized, including conjoint analysis, elicitation, and direct rating.

The preference structure derived from the conjoint exercise suggested that the respondents perceived each of the variables to be important, although convenient air links and infrastructure were the most influential variables in the decision making process. The correlation between the holdout data and the predicted scores for 372 observations (two holdout profiles) was 0.78, with the mean absolute difference between these scores being 1.24 on a scale of 1 to 10.

The open-ended exercise gave respondents the opportunity to list any variables they believed were important in the consideration of a cooperative alliance. When closely related concepts were collapsed into broader variables, there was substantial agreement between these results and those achieved in the conjoint exercise.

The direct rating task differed from the other two exercises in that it identified specific target markets and named specific country combinations. The exercise used multiple regression in which the five key variables were regarded as the independent variables, and the combination of specific country-pair and target market as the dependent variable.

The results of this were varied, with regression R-squared values ranging from 0.06 to 0.44, with a median of 0.27. The predictor variables were not as useful in estimating the desirability of the country combinations as they were in the conjoint exercise. In some country combinations the association between the dependent variable and the independent variables was not statistically significant.

When these results were compared to the results achieved in the other two exercises, the contrast was intriguing. By naming specific country combinations and particular target markets the strength of association between the prominent variables originally proposed and the desirability of cooperation was decreased. This suggested that other variables may be important in the process of determining whether two named countries should cooperate, and yet they did not appear in the open-ended responses.

Additional research is required to isolate the contribution to the observed results of, first, the differing questioning techniques, and second, the influence of past experience when countries are named rather than anonymous stimuli. In the present exploratory study, it was not possible to separate the interacting effects unequivocally.

For further information contact:
Robin N. Shaw
Commerce and Administration
Griffith University
Nathan, Queensland 4111
Australia

ANTECEDENTS OF STUDENT SATISFACTION: A CAUSAL ANALYSIS

Sundar A. Bharadwaj, Texas A&M University
Charles M. Futrell, Texas A&M University
Donna M. Kantak, Georgia State University

ABSTRACT

This study seeks to look at major dimensions that influence students' course satisfaction. Specifically, the research sought to (1) identify the factors influencing student satisfaction; (2) develop and test a model of student satisfaction, (3) develop and test a causal model of changes in factors influencing the model of student satisfaction over the course of a semester.

SAMPLE AND METHODOLOGY

Undergraduate students in four different senior marketing classes at a large state university participated in this study. The classes were taught by five instructors teaching a total of seven sections. Data was collected two times during the course: (1) the third week after the course began; and (2) at the end of the semester, one week before the final examinations. There were 519 students participating in time 1 and 320 in time 2. The lower number of students in time 2 resulted from using only "matched" responses to form the cohort for analysis purposes.

The Student Instructional Report (SIR) developed and tested by the Educational Testing Service (Centra 1972a, 1972b, 1976) was used to measure the variables in the hypotheses developed. Twenty-two of the instrument's 39 likert scale questions were used in this study--the 17 questions not used were demographic in nature.

Structural equations with unobservable or latent constructs were used to test the hypothesis. This statistical method, which is ideal for analyzing causal models, allows the researcher to assess the measurement constructs and the structural relationship between the constructs.

RESULTS

The results suggest that the role of the instructor and the course quality strongly and significantly influenced student satisfaction. However, although in the positive direction hypothesized, the teacher-student relationship influence on satisfaction was not statistically significant.

The direct positive impact of role of the instructor suggests that making course objectives clear, achieving the set objectives, using class time well, being available to the student, preparing well for class, informing students of the evaluation process, and other similar activities increases the student satisfaction. The construct that we labelled "course quality" also had a direct, positive and significant impact on student satisfaction. Thus, the student rating of the textbook, supplementary reading, lectures, exams, and discussions has an impact on his/her satisfaction with the course. Although, the construct of student-teacher relationship did not have a statistically significant relationship with student satisfaction, its impact was direct and positive. The instructor's understanding and gauging student's progress in the class, being open to other opinions, raising challenging questions, and encouraging students to participate, seemed to impress the students favorably and impact on their satisfaction with the course.

Examination of the changes over the course of the semester revealed two significant relationships among the exogenous and endogenous constructs. Among the exogenous constructs, teacher-student relationship and course quality affected student satisfaction. In other words, the changes in student perception of course quality and the teacher-student relationship influenced student satisfaction. On the other hand, changes in the student perception of the role of the instructor in the classroom did not influence the satisfaction of students.

CONCLUSION

Examining the satisfaction of students and trying to increase student satisfaction has been a topic of growing interest among academicians. A recent novel effort by an academician to offer a money-back guarantee to "dissatisfied students" introduced a flurry of opinions from other academicians in an electronic mailing group to which one of the authors subscribed. The overwhelming consensus was the need for academics to view students as "customers," rather than "students" per se. Further, as marketing academicians, we teach students the importance of customer satisfaction and thus it is in our own best interest to focus on and attempt to achieve customer satisfaction.

For further information contact: Charles Futrell
Professor of Marketing
Texas A&M University
College Station, Texas 77843-4112

COMPREHENSIVE EXAMINATIONS IN MARKETING DOCTORAL PROGRAMS: PROCESS, CONTENT, PURPOSE, AND OUTCOMES

George R. Franke, Virginia Polytechnic Institute and State University
Kenneth B. Kahn, Virginia Polytechnic Institute and State University

ABSTRACT

This study investigates the use of comprehensive examinations in U.S. and Canadian doctoral programs in marketing. In addition to providing current information on the process and content of such exams, the study also examines the purpose and outcomes of the examination process. The two outcomes considered are the proportion of students failing different numbers of questions, and the faculty's degree of satisfaction that the examination process is meeting its objectives. The paper presents the results of a survey of marketing doctoral programs and offers suggestions for improving the comprehensive examination process.

SURVEY METHOD

A four-page questionnaire was developed consisting mostly of fixed-response questions along with a request for respondents to expand on their answers as necessary. Cover letters and questionnaires were sent to the marketing departments at 74 U.S. and 6 Canadian universities. As in Jackson, Mokwa and Buckles (1986), the survey was sent to the department head at each institution with a request to direct the questionnaire to the person in his or her department most familiar with the comprehensive examination process. Including the authors' institution, questionnaires were returned from 43 of 75 U.S. programs and 4 of 6 Canadian programs for an overall response rate of 58 percent.

SELECTED RESULTS

The process and content of comprehensive examinations in marketing are described in the full paper and in studies by Jackson, Mokwa and Buckles (1986) and by Kardes (1991). This abstract focuses on results pertaining to the use and purpose of and satisfaction with the exam process.

Of the 47 schools responding to the survey, 45 (96 percent) require students to take a written comprehensive exam. Of these 45, 24 require an oral exam of all students. Another 10 require an oral exam when a student's performance on the written exam is marginal or shows specific weaknesses. Two schools require neither written nor oral exams.

Respondents were asked to indicate what they hope to accomplish with their (written) examination process by allocating 100 points among 6 categories. The most important purpose (mean = 35.4) is to test students' ability to synthesize information in developing research ideas. Obtaining other diagnostic information about students' development receives considerably less weight from most schools (mean = 10.5). Many schools intend that the exam function as a learning experience: Forcing students to review previously-covered material and to broaden their exposure to new material receive average weights of 22.0 and 17.2, respectively. Finally, eliminating deficient students from the program is a major thrust at a few schools, with weights of 50 or more, but on average this category receives a lower weight of 14.0.

Of the 47 schools responding to the survey, 15 (32 percent) are "quite satisfied" that the evaluation method they use "meets its objectives." Almost half (47 percent) are somewhat satisfied, six (13 percent) are somewhat dissatisfied, and the remaining four (9 percent) are quite dissatisfied.

The respondents' open-ended comments indicate several common areas of concern. Unclear or disputed objectives for the process are one important source of dissatisfaction. Dissatisfied respondents also tend to feel that their exams place too much emphasis on recall and not enough emphasis on integration of concepts. Grading standards that vary across graders and over time also cause problems. Although no comments specifically indicate that graders are too lenient, respondents reporting lower failure rates among test-takers tend to be less satisfied with the exam process.

DISCUSSION AND RECOMMENDATIONS

The survey results suggest that almost any evaluation process that might reasonably be adopted will have a precedent at another marketing program. Furthermore, it seems that almost any procedure that might be used will satisfy some schools and frustrate others. Therefore, there are few absolute "musts" or "must nots" in the comprehensive examination process.

One place to start in reviewing the evaluation method is to determine whether it produces any surprises. Murray (1973), for example, points out that an exam that merely confirms what the faculty already know about the students is essentially worthless. If it is determined that the evaluation process could be improved, an important step—probably the most important—is to decide what the process is supposed to accomplish. Until the objectives for the examination process have been determined, any modifications in the procedure will be haphazard at best.

For further information please contact:
George R. Franke
Virginia Polytechnic Institute & State University
Department of Marketing
Blacksburg, VA 24061-0236

ON INCREASING MBA COURSE SATISFACTION

Ruth Lesher Taylor, Southwest Texas State University

ABSTRACT

As business schools rush to revise their MBA courses and curricula in response to critics and competition, there is a need to ensure that the MBA student, as a consumer, is not lost in the shuffle. Critics, the corporate world and the competitive market for students have pressured many of the nation's 700 graduate business schools to rethink marketing strategies. MBA course content and environmental settings are being reconsidered.

The ideal pedagogical goals of transmitting knowledge to students and motivating students to learn business principles and applications are many times not met because what is being provided by the instructor is not consistent with student expectations. The MBA student is constantly changing (i.e. becoming older and more experienced). What is expected in a MBA course/professor changes accordingly. Traditional pedagogy needs to be altered to meet the changed and changing student.

A literature review revealed several studies concerning the design of MBA programs but relatively few studies directly related to the experienced adult learner in individual MBA courses. No research was found where MBA student course/professor expectations and the relative importance of these expectations have been studied. This paper suggests structural characteristics of MBA courses that help increase the probability of MBA student satisfaction.

The study provides insights into MBA student course/professor satisfaction levels and expectations, commonalities of expectations among diverse groups, and measures the relative importance of these expectations. The study further provides ideals useful in designing MBA courses with student satisfaction as a priority.

MBA marketing and management students were systematically drawn from two southwestern universities located in two different southwestern cities. Participating MBA students were place in three groups according to their employment status: high-tech employed part-time students, diverse employed part-time students, and full-time non-employed students. Data relative to present program satisfactions, rank-ordered desirable course/professor characteristics, and demographics were collected. Descriptive, Kruskal-Wallis one-way ANOVA and crosstab analyses were used to analyze the non-parametric ordinal-scaled data.

Findings show that more of the high-tech group were more satisfied (35.7%) with their present program than were the diversified (17.9%) or the full-time student group (20.8%). The most frequently requested change was to add a real-world orientation. Individually: (1) the diverse group requested more specialized courses and increased rigor, (2) the high-tech group requested more time on assignments, and (3) the full-time student group requested professors with improved teaching skills. When rank-ordered preferences were tested for significant differences between the groups, one of the fifteen ideal COURSE characteristics was found to be significantly different, whereas significant differences were found in ten of the eighteen ideal PROFESSOR characteristics.

Findings showed that different groups desire different course resources and pedagogy. Findings further indicated that MBA courses designed with certain structural characteristics increased the probability of MBA course satisfaction: (1) popular press texts, (2) leveled critical thinking exercises, 3) leveled oral presentations - dependent on past experience, (4) a combination of student-led and professor-led pedagogy, (5) a combination of common and flexible due dates, (6) peer evaluations, and (7) professor/student selected texts, projects and evaluation techniques.

This study, an initial step in evaluating diverse MBA student needs and expectations, encouraged letting MBA students custom design learning experiences to strengthen felt weakness. Though this customizing was encouraged, commonality of structure and content were not to be sacrificed. Further instructional research is needed concerning the blending of custom and common features in the structure of MBA courses to meet diverse student needs.

For further information contact:
Ruth Taylor
Southwest Texas State University
Department of Management and Marketing
San Marcos, Texas 78666

CHANNEL STRUCTURE AND STRATEGIC CHOICE IN MARKETING CHANNELS

Brent M. Wren, Memphis State University

ABSTRACT

Though marketing in general has begun to adopt a strategic orientation, little attention has been given to strategy within marketing channels. The present paper examines how one strategy concept, choice of a generic strategy, can be applied in a channels context. Propositions are developed to stimulate interest in this area.

INTRODUCTION

During the late 1970's and early 1980's the position of marketing within most firms was eroded or displaced by developments in strategic planning (Day and Wensley 1983). The cause of much of this deterioration can be attributed to multiple factors, including: marketing's short-run orientation, a fixation on the brand-unit level of analysis, lack of rigorous competitive analysis, and the lack of an integrated strategic framework (Anderson 1982; Day and Wensley 1983; Wind and Robertson 1983). The advent of the eighties has required a significant evolution in planning practices that present an opportunity for marketing to reassert itself as an influence in organizational development (Gluck, Kaufman, and Walleck 1980). The emergence of this opportunity is due in part to marketing's adoption of a strategic management perspective.

The essence of the strategic management perspective is an integrated organizational emphasis on securing and sustaining a competitive advantage (Day and Wensley 1983). Researchers in the marketing discipline have begun to adopt this perspective, as evidenced by the emergence of research on environmental management (Zeithaml and Zeithaml 1984), strategic planning (Anderson 1982), competitive advantage (Day and Wensley 1988), the implementation of business strategies (Ruekert and Walker 1987), and strategy-performance relationships (McDaniel and Kolari 1987; McKee, Varadarajan and Pride 1989). This growing body of research suggests that the field of marketing is starting to realize its strategic role in ensuring the long-run success of firms.

Though the field of marketing in general has begun to adopt a strategic perspective, one particular area, marketing channels, has been relatively slow to embrace this perspective. Aside from research on the manipulation of power and influence attempts, little attention has been given to the study of channel strategies. The importance of marketing channel strategy decisions is highlighted by (1) their inherent long-term consequences and (2) the constraints and opportunities that they represent (Dwyer and Welsh 1985). The development of relation-

ships in a marketing channel often takes a great deal of time and effort, therefore any decisions made concerning these relations take on added strategic importance. Given this importance, the incorporation of strategic management theory is very relevant to the study of marketing channels.

The intent of the present paper is to examine how one strategy concept, choice of a generic strategy, can be applied in a channels context. This will be accomplished by examining the contingent relationship between channel structure (e.g., transactional and bureaucratic form) and subsequent choice of a generic strategy. The basis of the discussion of strategy will be Porter's (1980) strategy typology, though supporting literature will also be used. It is hoped that the propositions developed within the paper will stimulate interest in applying strategy concepts in this complex area. The paper will first provide a brief discussion of the literature on channel structure. Next, I will provide an introduction to Porter's generic types, as well as a "combination" strategy which has emerged within the management literature. I will then develop propositions based on relevant theoretical considerations and discuss the implications of the study.

DEVELOPMENT OF CHANNEL STRUCTURE

The marketing channels literature has given considerable attention to the study of channel structure. Early researchers discussed channel structure in terms of the functions performed by channel members (Mallen 1973). The basic idea was that these functions could be allocated in different mixes among the various channel members depending on the characteristics of the channel. As structure research evolved, several common elements emerged which were seen as varying across different channels, including: the number of channel levels (i.e., number of intermediaries involved), the intensity at the various levels (the number intermediaries at each level of distribution), and the types of intermediaries at each level (i.e., retailers, wholesalers) (Rosenbloom 1987). Thus, channel structure was essentially treated at a micro level, rather than examining the more macro issues such as: how firms decide who will perform what activities, the costs and trade-offs involved in using various channel strategies, and various extraneous factors affecting channel relations.

More recent research in channel structure examines both macro and micro issues. The majority of the current research on channel structure focuses on one of two broad operationalizations of structure: transactional form and bureaucratic form. Though it could be argued that the degree of relationalism also reflects the structure of the relationship, transactional form and bureaucratic form are the most widely accepted.

Transactional form. Transactional form research flows from work done in the transaction costs analysis (TCA) area. Largely attributed to work done by Williamson (1979, 1981), this research is concerned with appropriate governance structures and whether particular activities should be performed internally or externally. For example, part of Stern and Reve's (1980) political economy paradigm examined the internal economic structure of the channel. This operationalization was concerned with decisions about the level of vertical integration present in a channel relationship. Several researchers have examined the costs and benefits of using vertically integrated channels (cf. Dwyer and Oh 1988; Heide and John 1988; Noordewier, et al. 1990). These researchers have shown that external (market) transactions are superior to internal ones when: environmental uncertainty is low, there are low levels of transaction-specific assets required, there is large numbers bargaining condition, and when performance assessment is straight-forward (Reukert, Walker, and Roering 1985; Dwyer and Oh 1988; Heide and John 1988; Noordewier, et al. 1990).

Bureaucratic form. The second commonly used operationalization of structure involves the examination of the bureaucratic form of the channel. Developed from Weber's (1974) notion of bureaucracy, this perspective examines such structural dimensions as centralization, formalization, and specialization/differentiation as they relate to the performance of the channel (Reukert, Walker, and Roering 1985; Dwyer and Oh 1988; Stern and Reve 1980). The focus of this approach is on the power, authority, and control of the channel. It is generally hypothesized that the effectiveness, efficiency, and adaptiveness of the channel can be improved by increasing centralization, formalization, and specialization respectively. Centralization refers to the extent to which decisions are shared within the channel system. Formalization involves the degree to which activities and social relationships are governed by rules, procedures, and contracts. Specialization/differentiation represents the degree to which tasks are divided into unique elements (Reukert, Walker, and Roering 1985).

Though this discussion of channel structure has presented each perspective separately, the most useful research effectively combines both perspectives (cf., Stern and Reve 1980; Dwyer and Oh 1988; and Reukert, Walker, and Roering 1985). Though this research is generally more explanatory in nature, it provides greater understanding of channel structure. Thus, the present paper will utilize aspects of both perspectives in developing propositions. Specifically, I will be concerned with how varying levels of vertical integration and power/control within the channel affect the choice of a generic strategy. Before developing propositions, I first need to provide of brief review of the strategy framework to be utilized.

THE STRATEGIC FRAMEWORK

The work by Porter (1980, 1985) defines three generic strategies which firms might choose to pursue in order to establish a competitive advantage: overall low-cost leader (OLC), differentiation, and focus. Competitive advantages accrue from the combination of firm strengths, industry structure, and the firm's ability to cope with five competitive forces (threat of new entrants, threat of substitutes, bargaining power of suppliers, bargaining power of buyers, and rivalry among existing firms). According to Porter, a firm's competitive advantage combines with its scope of activities (competitive scope) to determine which of the three generic strategies the firm will choose. The generic strategy then affects the performance of the firm.

Overall Low-Cost Leader

The OLC strategy stresses economies of scale, proprietary knowledge, preferential access to raw materials, aggressive pricing policies, cost minimization, stable product lines and other factors which lead the firm to become "the" low-cost producer or supplier in its industry (Porter 1980). Low-cost leaders tend to "concentrate on standard, no-frills products and place considerable emphasis on reaping scale or absolute cost advantages from all sources" (Porter 1985, p. 13).

Differentiation

Firms stressing the differentiation strategy seek to be unique in their industry along some dimensions that are widely valued by buyers (Porter 1985). The means of differentiation might include such things as emphasis on quality, product durability, service, and/or product or brand image. Firms which succeed at differentiation often are able to charge premium prices, thus becoming an above average performer within the industry.

Focus

The focus strategy rests on the choice of a narrow competitive scope within an industry (Porter 1985). The firm following this strategy selects a segment or subsection of an industry and sets a strategy to serve it better than anyone else in the industry. This focus on serving a particular segment well often come at the expense of not serving other segments. Thus, by exploiting a narrow segment of the industry, the firm must sacrifice potential earnings from the balance of the industry.

Combination Strategies

Porter (1985) states that each of his strategies is a "fundamentally different approach to creating and sustaining a competitive advantage". He also states that firms must choose between pursuing the over low-cost strategy and the differentiation strategy because the two are generally incompatible. More recently, there has been a good deal of research concerning the potential for a combination strategy (e.g., Hall 1980; Phillips, Chang, and Buzzell 1983; Wright, Kroll, Tu, and Helms 1991). This emergent research suggests that the OLC and differentiation strategies may not be incompatible, but synergistic.

Hall (1980) observed that in certain cases (though very rarely), the most successful firms simultaneously pursued both a differentiation and an OLC strategy. This study was supported by Phillips, Chang, and Buzzell (1983). These researchers found that stressing quality (a differentiation strategy) is not inconsistent with low costs. In fact, as quality increases, the firm may lower costs either through improved efficiency or through achieving economies of scale. Further support for a combination strategy is found in Wright, Kroll, Tu, and Helms (1991). These authors examined the performance of firms stressing either differentiation, OLC, or some combination of the two. They found that when firms attempted a low-cost strategy and were unsuccessful, they tended to have the lowest performance. Interestingly, the firms with the highest performance, followed a combination strategy. It appears that following a combination strategy allows firms to cope with changes in the industry better than those were who focus on a single strategy.

The literature just discussed provides evidence that organizations may pursue more than one strategy at a time, thus allowing for a combination strategy. Therefore the current paper will include four potential strategies from which firms might choose: OLC, differentiation, focus, and combination. The following section will develop propositions relating contingent channel conditions (differing structural issues) to the choice of a generic strategy.

DEVELOPMENT OF PROPOSITIONS

A number of management researchers have put forth contingency approaches, identifying under what conditions each generic strategy is appropriate. For example, researchers have examined the contingent effects of industry type (Hambrick 1983; Hill 1988), firm size within an industry (Wright 1987), and ability to differentiate products (Hill 1988) on the success of a chosen strategy. Many of these articles provide support for the propositions developed here.

Vertical Integration and Strategy

As mentioned earlier, the decision of whether to perform tasks internally or externally is central to the development of channel structure. Here, it is argued that this decision is also crucial to the selection of a generic strategy. Research has shown that an external focus (i.e., low vertical integration) will be chosen when there is low environmental uncertainty, low levels of transaction-specific assets, and when performance assessment is straight-forward (Dwyer and Oh 1988; Heide and John 1988; Noordewier, et al. 1990; Reukert, et al 1985). It is felt that under these circumstances, the external orientation allows for more flexibility and efficiency, with minimal risk. However, when the environment is highly volatile and more prone to asset risk from things such as opportunism (Williamson 1979), the literature suggests that firms will become more internally oriented. The rationale for this is that risks can be reduced or offset by taking control of as many processes as possible. For example, by vertically integrating, firms can reduce the risk of resource shortages.

Research from the strategic management area can provide insight into what this means in terms of strategic choice. Wright, Kroll, Chan, and Hamel (1991) view organizational strategy as a spectrum ranging from internal orientation to external orientation. On the internal end, are the cost minimization, low cost leader, and defender strategies, consistent with the vertically integrated firm. At the other end of the continuum, are maximizing, prospecting, and differentiating strategies, consistent with the non-integrated firm. This research indicates that when firms are internally focused, they incur lower costs due to the emphasis on stable technologies and efficient operations (Wright, Kroll, chan, and Hamel 1991; Segev 1989). The emphasis on lower costs allows the firm to establish itself as the low-cost leader in the industry. Thus, internally focused (highly integrated) firms are more likely to exhibit characteristics of a low-cost leader.

On the other hand, firms which are externally focused tend to be more technologically active, with higher costs and more innovative outputs (Wright, Kroll, Chan, and Hamel 1991; Segev 1989). This emphasis on technological advancement and innovative outputs allows a firm to position itself in many different ways. Firms might choose to differentiate itself in terms of high quality, premium features, technological leadership, etc. When the firm achieves this sort of differentiation, it is better able to attain higher returns. Thus, firms which are externally focused are better able to concentrate on differentiating themselves from the rest of the industry.

In terms of a combination strategy, there is evidence to suggest that firms which generate high growth and high profits are better able to use both a differentiation and an OLC strategy (Hambrick 1983; Hill 1988). For example, Wright (1987) suggests that larger firms in an industry are in a better position to choose between OLC and differentiation strategies. In other words, both OLC and differentiation strategies are available to firms with high profitability and market share (Wright 1987). If we look at this in relation to the degree of vertical integration, one would expect that firms which are moderately integrated would be better able to implement a combination strategy than firms at either extreme. The reason is that firms which have the low cost focus of an integrated firm and the ability of the non-integrated firm to differentiate, are able to reap synergistic benefits (Phillips, et al. 1983). Research suggests that firms stressing high quality are able to minimize costs through improved efficiency, while simultaneously differentiating themselves as a premium product. When combined, these strategies produce enhanced economies of scale and improved ROI. The end result being stronger market positions. Thus, firms which are moderately integrated are better able to implement a combination strategy. On the basis of this discussion, the following propositions are developed:

P1: Firms which are highly vertical integrated are more likely to choose an OLC strategy.

P2: Firms with low levels of integration are more likely to choose a differentiation strategy.

P3: Firms which are moderately integrated are better able to choose a combination strategy.

Power/Control and Strategy

The phenomenon of power and control is one of the most frequently examined topics in the marketing channels literature. Researchers have long sought to understand how different relationships and power structures within the marketing channel affect the decisions of channel members (cf. Bucklin 1973; Gaski 1984; Pondy 1967). Power is generally seen as the ability of one channel member to change another's behavior, thereby controlling the decision variables of the other member (Gaski 1984; Stern and El-Ansary 1977). Some researchers take the position that power is necessarily a negative aspect in that, those who possess it will attempt to influence exchange partners by use of coercive influence strategies (Frazier and Summers 1986; Robicheaux and El-Ansary 1975). Other researchers stress that power can be a good thing in that it creates natural divisions and coordination among channel members (Frazier and Summers 1986).

It is clear from a review of the literature that the distribution of power in the channel is seldom symmetrical. It is generally the case that one side of the exchange possesses some degree of power or control over the other. This power rests explicitly on the fact that the partners are not always equally dependent on one another. Although the partners are mutually dependent to some degree, one partner will generally be more dependent than the other. When this asymmetrical situation arises, the decisions of both parties will be affected.

Porter (1980) suggests that when buyers have power over suppliers (as in the case of retailing giant Wal-Mart over its suppliers), they will attempt to play suppliers against each other, inducing price competition. When suppliers have no alternative outlet for their products (e.g., transaction-specific assets), Williamson (1979) says that buyers will take advantage and seek maximal personal gain. When this occurs, the supplier has two alternatives: focus or differentiation.

If the firm chooses a focus strategy, it will attempt to "own" a particular market segment either through price leadership or differentiation (Porter 1980). If the firm chooses to focus on price, it will attempt to offer the lowest prices for a specific segment. If the supplier chooses a differentiated focus, it will attempt to serve a particular segment especially well (e.g., service quality). The second alternative is to attempt an industry-wide differentiation strategy. Here the firm would attempt to position itself as a premium product relative to competition by emphasizing such value enhancing factors as quality, service, innovation, and/or brand image. The difference between this strategy and the focus strategy is the fact that focus concentrates on a particular segment, while this strategy is industry-wide.

The choice between these two strategies is likely to depend on the scope of the supplier's activities (Davis, Robinson, and Pearce 1991). Small firms which are essentially regional in competitive (market) scope will have a hard time creating any sort of differentiation for themselves on a national level. For example, a small aerospace firm may be unable to differentiate itself in such a large, capital intensive industry. However, it can do quite well as a supplier of high quality, precision machine work to national suppliers. Davis, Robinson, and Pearce (1991) suggests that these firms should follow an OCL strategy in order to facilitate growth, eventually leading to the ability to compete on a national basis. In other words, due to lack of breadth and the inability to achieve economies of scale small firms will be more effective at concentrating on a particular segment of the industry.

Supplier firms with a national competitive scope, on the other hand, will be much better able to differentiate themselves in the overall market. Due to their ability to achieve economies of scale, they will be able to compete on the basis of differentiation (Davis, Robinson, and Pearce 1991). While these firms are able to compete on an OLC strategy, there is not much incentive to do so. The reason is that, with rare exception, most of the firms which compete on a national level in a given market are equally capable of competing on price. However, firms are generally reluctant to undercut the competition due to the fact that any gains realized will be short-lived due to counter actions by competitors. When competing firms counter the low cost leader strategy, firms must eventually turn to some form of differentiation or suffer long-run consequences for the industry (the "cola wars" are an excellent example of this). Thus, once meeting some minimum level of price competition, firms will choose a differentiation strategy. For example, in the highly competitive market for military aircraft, price is usually fairly close for all suppliers. Therefore, the only way that a large supplier of military aircraft can combat the power of military buyers is to differentiate itself is on the basis of technology. Given this logic, the following propositions are developed:

P4: When faced with the superior power of buyers, suppliers with a national competitive scope will attempt to combat the power of buyers by choosing a differentiation strategy.

P5: When faced with the superior power of buyers, suppliers with a regional competitive scope will attempt to combat the power of buyers by choosing a focus strategy.

In asymmetrical power settings, it is also possible for suppliers to have control over buyers, as in the case of suppliers of scarce natural resources to buyers. This power is based on the supplier's ability to charge higher prices, reduce service, and/or govern contracts. When buyers have no alternative sources for the resources mediated by suppliers or when asset-specific investments make switching costs prohibitively high (Williamson 1979) buyer dependency on the supplier is increased. Thus, buyer dependency leads to enhanced supplier control.

Davis, Schul, and Hartline (1991) suggest that firms dealing with high supplier power tend to look toward vertical integration, elimination of switching costs, and maximization of throughput in order to reduce the dependency on specific suppliers. Research on the reduction of opportunism in marketing channels supports this contention (Dwyer and Oh 1988; John 1984; Williamson 1979). The general consensus is that a firm must either vertically integrate or make offsetting investments in order to protect itself from opportunistic behavior (such as price gouging) by exchange partners.

As discussed in the section on vertical integration, the pursuit of tactics such as integration, cost reductions, and reliance on standardization of practices, is consistent with an OLC strategy. In fact, Davis, Schul, and Hartline (1991) and Jackson (1985) both suggest that by standardizing inputs, the cost leader can substantially reduce its switching costs and thus, reduce its dependency on a particular supplier (Davis, Schul, and Hartline 1991; Jackson 1985). However, it would seem impossible to implement a low-cost leadership strategy while being subject to potential supplier pressures in terms of price gouging and restriction of supply. In other words, if suppliers charge high prices there is no way for buyers to pursue a low-cost strategy and remain profitable.

A more feasible alternative for buyers is to make themselves more desirable to suppliers. The channels literature suggest that the superior power of suppliers can be offset when there are munificent (rich) markets (Dwyer and Oh 1987). The reason for this is that in high growth markets, with high profit potential, suppliers see dealers as a means of enhancing their own performance, and are willing to work more closely with dealers to reap greater rewards. Additional support for this contention is provided by Heide and John (1988). These authors suggest that when vertical integration is not feasible, firms can offset the risk of opportunism by developing relational ties with the stronger firm. When such offsetting investments are used, power becomes more symmetrical. Based on these considerations, it seems that the best alternative for weak buyers would be to focus on creating a munificent market to serve. The only way to do this would be through a differentiated focus strategy. Dwyer and Oh (1988) suggest that small firms (analogous here to weak buyers) are relatively incapable of vertical integration and price competition on a national basis. However, these firms can focus on a the development of highly profitable market niches. Based on the findings of Dwyer and Oh (1987), creation of these high profit niches should then make the buyer more desirable to suppliers, thereby offsetting the power imbalance. Based on this logic, the following proposition is developed.

P6: When faced by high levels of supplier power, buying firms will emphasize an a differentiated focus strategy.

CONCLUSIONS

The literature on marketing channels has given a good deal of time and effort to understanding the many interrelationships which develop between channel members. In this effort, topics such as channel structure, power/conflict, environmental issues, and relational dimensions have been studied thoroughly. However, the concept of channel strategy has received little attention. This paper has attempted to show how the concepts developed in strategic management can be used in a marketing channels context. In this endeavor, I have discussed relevant channel structural issues which affect the generic strategy choices of channel members. Specifically, the contingent effects of channel power/control and the degree of vertical integration have been examined as they affect the choice between the generic strategies of overall cost-leadership, differentiation, focus, and combination strategies.

The development of contingent propositions is meant to show the interrelationship of channel structure and subsequent channel strategies. The implication to be drawn from this paper is that firms will choose different strategies under different channel conditions. Though this appears fairly intuitive, it has not been addressed in the channels literature. This is unfortunate because it might hold insight as to why firms within the same channel behave differently. The choice of a generic competitive strategy could offer additional understand- ing in this area. Though this paper is only a starting point in the merger of channels and strategic management, I hope that the paper has provided some degree of progress towards its intended purpose.

REFERENCES

Anderson, Paul F. (1982), "Marketing, Strategic Planning and the Theory of the Firm," *Journal of Marketing,* 46 (Spring), 15-26.

Bucklin, Louis (1973), "A Theory of Channel Control," *Journal of Marketing,* 37 (January), 39-47.

Davis, Peter S., Richard B. Robinson, and John A. Pearce, II. (1991), "The Moderating Effects of Strategic 'Focus' on Environment-Strategy-Share-Performance Relationships," (working paper).

_____, Patrick L. Schul, and Michael D. Hartline (1991), "A Path-Analytic Test of Competing Paradigms of Environment-Organization Relations," (working paper).

Day, George S. and Wensley (1983), "Marketing Theory with a Strategic Orientation," *Journal of Marketing,* 47 (Fall), 79-89.

Dwyer, Robert F. and Sejo Oh (1988), "A Transaction Cost Perspective on Vertical Contractual Structure and Interchannel Competitive Strategies," *Journal of Marketing,* 52 (April), 21-34.

_____ and _____ (1987), "Output Sector Munificence Efforts on the Internal Political Economy of Marketing Channels," *Journal of Marketing Research,* 24 (November), 347-358.

_____ and M. Ann Welsh (1985), "Environmental Relationships of the Internal Political Economy of Marketing Channels," *Journal of Marketing Research,* 22 (November), 397-414.

Frazier, Gary L. and John D. Summers (1986), "Interfirm Influence Strategies and Their Application Within Distribution Channels," *Journal of Marketing,* 48 (Summer), 43-55.

Gaski, John F. (1984), "The Theory of Power and Conflict in Channels of Distribution," *Journal of Marketing,* 48 (Summer), 9-29.

Gluck, Frederick, Stephen P. Kaufman, and A. Steven Walleck (1980), "Strategic Management for Competitive Advantage," *Harvard Business Review,* 58 (July/August), 154-161.

Hall, W.K. (1980), "Survival Strategies in a Hostile Environment," *Harvard Business Review,* 58 (5), 75-85.

Hambrick, Donald (1983), "High Profit Strategies in Mature Goods Industries: A Contingency Approach," *Academy of Management Journal,* 26 (4), 687-707.

Heide, Jan B. and George John (1988), "The Role of Dependence Balancing in Safeguarding Transaction-Specific Assets in Conventional Channels," *Journal of Marketing,* 52 (January), 20-35.

Hill, Charles W. L. (1988), "Differentiation Versus Low Cost or Differentiation and Low Cost: A Contingency Framework," *Academy of Management Journal,* 13 (3), 401-412.

Jackson, Barbara B. (1985), *Winning and Keeping Industrial Customers: The Dynamics of Customer Relationships.* Lexington, MA: Lexington Books.

John, George (1984), "An Empirical Investigation of Some Antecedents of Opportunism in a Marketing Channel," *Journal of Marketing Research,* 21 (August), 278-289.

Mallen, Bruce (1973), "Functional Spin-off: A Key to Anticipating Change in Distribution Structure," *Journal of Marketing,* 37 (July), 18-25.

McDaniel, Stephen W. and James W. Kolari (1987), "Marketing Strategy Implications of the Miles and Snow Strategic Typology," Journal of Marketing, 51 (October), 19-30.

McKee, Daryl O., P. Rajan Varadarajan, and William M. Pride (1989), "Strategic Adaptability and Firm Performance: A Market-Contingent Perspective," *Journal of Marketing,* 53 (July), 21-35.

Noordewier, Thomas G., George John, and John R. Nevin (1990), "Performance Outcomes of Purchasing Arrangements in Industrial Buyer-Vendor Relationships," *Journal of Marketing,* 54 (October), 80-93.

Pondy, Louis R. (1967), "Organizational Conflict: Concepts and Models," *Administrative Science Quarterly,* 12, 296-320.

Phillips, Lynn W., Dae R. Chang, and Robert D. Buzzell (1983), "Product Quality, Cost Position, and Business Performance: A Test of Some Key Hypotheses," *Journal of Marketing,* 47 (Spring), 26-43.

Porter, Michael E. (1980) *Competitive Strategy: Techniques for analyzing Industries and Companies.* New York: Free Press.

_____ (1985), *Competitive Advantage: Creating and Sustaining Superior Performance.* New York: Free Press.

Reukert, Robert W., Orville C. Walker, Jr., and Kenneth J. Roering (1985), "The Organization of Marketing Activities: A Contingency Theory of Structure and Performance," *Journal of Marketing,* 49 (Winter), 13-25.

_____ and _____ (1987), "Marketing's Interaction with other Functional Units: A Conceptual Framework and Empirical Evidence," *Journal of Marketing,* 51 (January), 44-58.

Robicheaux, Robert and Adel El-Ansary (1975), "A General Model for Understanding Channel Member Behavior," *Journal of Retailing,* 52 (Winter), 13-29.

Rosenbloom, Bert (1987), *Marketing Channels: A Management View.* 3rd ed., New York: The Dryden

Press.

Segev, Eli (1989), "A Systematic Comparative Analysis and Synthesis of Two Business-Level Strategic Typologies," *Strategic Management Journal*, 10, 487-505.

Stern, Louis W. and Adel El-Ansary (1977), *Marketing Channels*. Englewood Cliffs, NJ: Prentice-Hall, Inc.

_____ and Torger Reve (1980), "Distribution Channels as Political Economies: A Framework for Comparative Analysis," *Journal of Marketing*, 44 (Summer), 52-64.

Weber, Max (1974), *The Theory of Social and Economic Organizations*. translated by A.M. Henderson and Talcott M. Parsons, New York: The Free Press.

Williamson, Oliver E. (1979), "Transaction-Cost Economics: The Governance of Contractual Relations," *Journal of Law and Economics*, 22 (October), 233-261.

_____ (1981), "The Economics of Organization: The Transaction Cost Approach," *American Journal of Sociology*, 87, 548-577.

Wind, Yoram and Thomas S. Robertson (1983), "Marketing Strategy: New Directions for Theory and Research," *Journal of Marketing*, 47 (Spring), 12-25.

Wright, Peter (1987), "A Refinement of Porter's Strategies," *Strategic Management Journal*, 8, 93-101.

_____, Mark Kroll, Howard Tu, and Marilyn Helms (1991a), "Generic Strategies and Business Performance: an Empirical Study of the Screw Machine Products Industry," *British Journal of Management*, 2, 57-65.

_____, _____, Peng Chan, and Karin Hamel (1991b), "Strategic Profiles and Performance: An Empirical Test of Select Key Propositions," *Journal of the Academy of Marketing Science*, 19 (Summer), 245-254.

Zeithaml, Carl P. and Valerie A. Zeithaml (1984), "Environmental Management: Revising the Marketing Perspective," *Journal of Marketing*, 48 (Spring), 46-53.

EXCHANGE GOVERNANCE: EXPLORING PLURAL FORMS

Gregory T. Gundlach, University of Notre Dame
Ravi S. Achrol, University of Notre Dame

ABSTRACT

The nature and combined use of multiple mechanisms for governing exchange relationships is investigated. Focus is given to the use of authority extending from legal contract and social norms within market channel relationships. Drawing from theories of Transaction Cost Economics (Williamson 1985) and Relational Exchange (Macneil 1980), how these governance modes are employed to regulate the conduct of exchange parties is examined. A simulated channel environment is used to test hypotheses relating to the effect of environmental uncertainty, relational interaction and performance outcomes.

A central theme in marketing channels research emphasizes the governance of longer-term relationships among exchange participants. Conventional concepts of channel structure (Stern and El-Ansary 1990) have been enriched by theoretical insight obtained from Transaction Cost Economics (Williamson 1985) and Relational Exchange Theory (Macneil 1980). Governance as defined within relational exchange theory posits a set of contracting norms or shared expectations regarding behavior from which a continuum of exchange types may be distinguished. Depending on the manifest nature of these norms, a continuum of governance extending from discrete transacting to relational exchange is specified. In contrast, governance as characterized within the transaction cost economics framework focuses on ownership and control underlying a decision to vertically integrate. This approach distinguishes governance based on markets versus hierarchies (Williamson 1975). Hybrid forms of trilateral (third party) and bilateral governance are thought to provide alternatives between these polar archetypes (Williamson 1979, 1985). In an attempt to further distinguish between these hybrid forms, researchers (Williamson 1979, 1985; Noordeweir, John, and Nevin 1990) have used the discrete transaction -- relational exchange continuum implied within relational exchange theory (Macneil 1980) to further distinguish bilateral and trilateral governance classifications.

An important research question is whether exchange relationships can be properly understood as being governed by mutually exclusive forms of governance arrayed along such a continuum. Conceptually, the content underlying markets and hierarchies is distinguishable from discrete transactions and relational exchange. Although similarities exist between market-mediated exchanges and discrete transactions, relational exchanges do not resemble hierarchy governed relationshps (cf. Dant and Kaufmann 1992). Hierarchy implies a heightened level of monitoring and active supervision by one party. In contrast, norms underlying relational exchange reflect a bilateral longer-term orientation accompanied by shared decision making. Thus, incorporation of the governance continuum envisioned under relational exchange theory within transaction cost's governance framework appears conceptually problematic.

Further insight regarding the complexity of exchange governance and theoretical distinctions of the governing modes envisioned within transaction cost economics and relational exchange theory is provided by scholars who emphasize "plural forms." Bradach and Eccles (1989) and others (Eccles 1985; Stinchcombe 1985; Kaufmann and Dant 1992; Heide and John 1992) argue exchange transactions may be better understood as embedded within a complex matrix of other transactions and social context. Citing evidence which suggests exchange relationships often combine elements of markets and hierarchies and relational exchange, they posit the presence of distinct organizational control mechanisms operating simultaneously and complementary to govern exchange. Arguing exchange rarely is governed solely by one mechanism of governance, they suggest a variety of differing governance mechanisms serve as the building blocks for complex governance structures underlying and so common in exchange relationships.

Together, the similarities as well as the theoretical differences underlying the transaction cost approach and relational exchange theory and emergent alternative perspectives (i.e. plural forms) point to an important area of investigation and the objective of the current research. We propose and investigate the presence and simultaneous use of multiple governance mechanisms within market channel exchange relationships. In particular, we examine the use of governance guided by authority (i.e. hierarchy by contract) and governance through norms of relational exchange. Focus is given to the effects of environmental uncertainty and exchange interaction on these mechanisms and their combined nature and impact on performance. This paper reports on the conceptual foundations and methodology employed in this research. Key results are discussed and suggestions for further research indicated.

For further information please contact:
Gregory T. Gundlach
University of Notre Dame
Notre Dame, IN 46556

APPLYING A GESTALT APPROACH IN EXAMINING ADAPTIVE BEHAVIORS IN CHANNELS OF DISTRIBUTION

Patrick L. Schul, Memphis State University
Rajiv P. Dant, Boston University
Brent M. Wren, Memphis State University

ABSTRACT

A good deal of effort and research in distribution channels has been given to examining how channel organizations deal with various internal and external environments (cf. Achrol and Stern 1988; Dwyer and Oh 1987; Dwyer and Welsh 1985; Heide and John 1988, 1990). In this pursuit, many researchers are focusing on how certain variables interact to affect organizational adaptation, a concept known as the contingency approach (cf. Achrol, Reve, and Stern 1983; Heide and John 1988; Stern and Reve 1980). The basic idea behind contingency theory is that, depending on the situation, certain approaches are better at explaining organizational functioning (e.g., adaptation, survival) than others (Galbraith 1973). Thus organizational effectiveness becomes dependent upon the appropriate matching of contingency variables (i.e., situational characteristics) with particular internal organizational designs that allow for appropriate responses to the environment (Zeithaml, Varadarajan, and Zeithaml 1988).

While the use of contingency theory to explain relationships between environmental, structural, and behavioral (strategic) variables seems useful, problems have been identified in the normative and descriptive approaches being adopted in examining such contingent relationships. Research has identified five general weaknesses in the underlying assumptions of contingency theory which often lead to fragmented and conflicting findings: (1) the search for "the one correct path" for dealing with a particular occurrence, (2) the general reliance on linear models and correlation methods to assess relationships between variables, (3) the use of measures which are generally cross-sectional in nature, (4) researchers often fail to address the interaction between contingency variables, and (5) the approach limits the researcher's ability to develop parsimonious descriptions of complex contingency relationships between the involved variables (Miller 1981; Miller and Friesen 1980, 1984; Schoonhoven 1981). Thus, it appears that the contingency approach might be overly restrictive, concealing much of the complexity of distribution channels. We need to be able to consider the multiplicity of environmental, structural, and behavioral attributes that will interact to influence organizational responses. The present paper discusses Gestalt theory as an alternative for dealing with the weaknesses of the contingency approach.

The gestalt approach was introduced in the strategic management literature by Miller and Friesen (cf. Miller 1981; Miller and Friesen 1980, 1984). This approach is holistic, in that it attempts to assess the influence of a large number of variables that "collectively define a meaningful and coherent slice of organizational reality" (Miller 1981, p. 8). In fact, Miller and Friesen (1984) outline four characteristics of Gestalts: (1) a large number of qualities (e.g., states, processes, and situations) are studied in order to yield a detailed, holistic, integrated image of reality; (2) data analysis and theory building are geared to finding common natural clusters among the attributes studied; (3) causation is viewed in the broadest possible terms; and (4) time and process are taken into account whenever possible (favors longitudinal research). The goal of the researcher is to use taxonomic procedures to box or cluster given sets of organizational factors so as to provide a means of identifying remaining features. These natural clusters or "configurations" of variables (i.e., environmental, structural, and/or behavioral dimensions) are then tested for predictive utility.

Gestalt methodologies seek to derive a parsimonious set of categories encompassing a large proportion of the population of organizations and to develop a taxonomy of configurations that are sufficiently restrictive (i.e., tightly defined) to allow meaningful descriptions of their members (McKelvey 1975). Thus, a parsimonious taxonomy with high predictive ability will be needed to validate the superiority of Gestalt approach over the contingency-based approach. McKelvey (1975) distinguishes between two types of configurations: taxonomies and typologies. Taxonomies are empirically driven approaches which start with broad, representative random samples and use multivariate analysis techniques such as cluster analysis, hierarchical clustering, factor analysis, and/or multidimensional scaling, to generate configurations. Typologies, on the other hand, are conceptual configurations which are developed intuitively on the basis of their detailed descriptions. Once this has been done across a number of categories or types of channels, the descriptions can be used to build a parsimonious set of predictive typologies. Most researchers seeking to develop Gestalts will use a combination of these two approaches so as to ensure both the theoretical foundation, and the empirical stability of the clusters. McKelvey (1975) recommends several useful guidelines for the development of configurations.

The evidence for gestalts has been provided by

researchers in the strategic management literature (e.g., Chenhall 1983; Dess and Davis 1984; Galbraith and Schendel 1982). Based on the literature suggesting similarities between simple and complex organizations (Stern and El-Ansary 1988), one would logically assume that potential exists for predictively useful configuration or Gestalts that describe behaviors in channel organizations. Similar to simple organizations, in channel organizations the environment will restrict the number of possible strategies and structures available in that environment. Further, there will be ties that unite certain channel structures and behavioral repertoire. In other words, given a particular structure, there will be only a limited number of suitable behavioral/strategy alternatives which lead to desirable outcomes. Finally, channel organizations have been shown to exhibit relatively stable attributes (Stern and Reve 1980), which leads to the expectation of somewhat stable patterns of organizational functioning. Given these observations it is logical to extend the Gestalt approach, as utilized in other settings, to the channel environment. Following the suggestions outlined by McKelvey (1975), we provide an example to illustrate the application of the gestalt approach in marketing channels. Though gestalt theory may not always be applicable, we show that it is often a useful tool for understanding the adaptive processes in channel systems.

For further information contact:
Patrick L. Schul
Memphis State University
Fogelman College of Business and Economics
Memphis, TN 38152

A CATEGORICAL FRAMEWORK OF RESEARCHER INTERACTION BIASES IN MARKETING RESEARCH DATA COLLECTION

Anthony D. Miyazaki, University of South Carolina

ABSTRACT

As the study of marketing shifts toward new theories and more rigorous analyses, researchers necessarily remain concerned with the investigation of human beings as marketers and consumers. Although some modes of study shy away from personal contact (e.g., electronic data collection), interaction of some kind with human subjects (respondents, informants, etc.) endures as the central method of inquiry.

Systematically biased responses, which may occur when researchers interact with their subjects, have long been a concern. Although some researchers (particularly in data collection capacities) may bias data by misrecording or misinterpreting responses, other biases occur when a subject's actions or responses are influenced by the introduction of researchers into the subject's contextual environment. This paper presents an organizational framework of these researcher interaction biases, a review of studies in this area, and methods to identify and reveal potential biases.

A categorical framework

Most methods of data collection are susceptible to a variety of researcher interaction effects, including (but not limited to) personal interviews, focus groups, telephone surveys, mall intercepts, naturalistic inquiries, laboratory experiments, and even mail surveys. An organized framework of these biases helps researchers examine and evaluate their studies in order to identify, and subsequently explain or eliminate, potential biases.

A review of past literature reveals a categorical framework of potential researcher interaction biases. Most of these biases can be classified into one of three categories, based on the various researcher characteristics to which subjects may react, namely, psychological traits, physical characteristics, and perceived background characteristics. Clearly, a number of effects may bias the collection of data at any one time, and ultimate control over all effects is typically impractical.

A number of studies have investigated the psychological traits and attributes of researchers in the context of researcher interaction biases, including research on personality differences, intimacy, attitudes, expectations, and enthusiasm.

Differences in researchers that are more easily detected are those that are physical in nature. While psychological attributes and background characteristics may be "hidden" from the subjects (to some degree), physical characteristics are more difficult to conceal. Key physical characteristics that have been studied with respect to researcher interaction biases are researcher sex, race, and age. Other physical characteristics that may influence subject reactions include body size and shape, physical attractiveness, physical disabilities, and researcher-subject similarities.

Some subjects may perceive researchers to have certain background characteristics, or may associate researchers with a particular societal subgroup. If these perceptions or associations (whether inferred correctly or not), systematically influence the actions or responses of the subjects, biases may result. Examples of these perceived background characteristics are the researcher's social class, level of education, extent of training, political, religious, or social affiliations, and ethnic identification or orientation. These characteristics differ from physical characteristics in that background characteristics are less obvious and may be controlled or disguised in most instances. While both psychological and background characteristics may be inferred through verbal or nonverbal cues of the researcher, background characteristics often represent part of an experiential or perhaps cultural aspect of life.

A review of methods to prevent or minimize the impact of researcher interaction biases is presented. In addition, role-playing, pretesting, and post-pretest debriefing are recommended as methods of identifying potential researcher interaction biases before studies are conducted. Ultimately, if these biases are not controlled, the researcher must decide whether to explain, adjust or discard the data.

For further information contact:
Anthony Miyazaki
Department of Marketing
University of South Carolina
Columbia, SC 29208

THE INFLUENCE OF MODERATOR PHILOSOPHY ON THE CONTENT OF FOCUS GROUP SESSIONS: A MULTIVARIATE ANALYSIS OF GROUP SESSION CONTENT

William J. McDonald, Hofstra University

ABSTRACT

This paper is about the influence of moderator philosophy on the content of focus group sessions. The group session transcripts of 66 moderators were tabulated for 23 content categories, factor analyzed, and used in a discriminant analysis, with moderator philosophy serving as the dependent variable. The research shows that focus group content is significantly influenced by the moderator's approach to managing group session dynamics.

INTRODUCTION

Group interviews, or focus groups, are among the most widely used tools in marketing research. The contemporary focus group interview involves the discussion of a particular topic under the direction of a moderator, who promotes group participant interaction and manages the discussion through a series of topics. The moderator is the key to assuring that the group session is productive and relevant to the marketing problem being researched. His management of group dynamics determine the outcome of the sessions, influencing the types and quality of information obtained.

Given the significance of the moderator's role in the focus group process, it becomes important to understand how moderator characteristics affect group session dynamics. Specifically, the issue is whether a moderator's philosophical approach to managing focus group sessions significantly changes the nature of the session content. One way to address this issue is to conduct a context analysis of the words used during the groups to determine if specific verbal patterns emerge.

This paper describes research about the impact of focus group moderator philosophy on the content of the research sessions. It applies content analysis and multivariate statistical methods to a collection of transcripts to show whether is it possible to identify distinctive verbal themes that vary by who conducts the group sessions.

BACKGROUND

Focus group moderators. The effectiveness of focus group moderators is a function of personal characteristics, education and training, experience, and situational factors (Stewart and Shamdasani 1991). Personal characteristics include age, personality, and gender. Educa-

tional background and training include formal schooling and training in a specific discipline such as psychology or sociology. Moderators also are a product of their moderating experience. The substantial literature on interviewer effects and interviewing provides support for the idea that the factors above are critical to understanding the role of the focus group moderator (see Fowler and Mangione 1990).

Among practitioners and commissioners of focus group research, there is a wide divergence of opinion about the qualifications a moderator should possess (McDaniel 1979; McDonald 1980). Stewart and Shamdasani (1991) note that an educational background in marketing, psychology, or other social science or training in psychotherapy, is not a necessary or sufficient qualification for effective moderating. Also, given similar training and experience, variations in moderating style are primarily a function of personality. Is moderating a creative art related to some intangible beyond just years of training and experience? Generally, there are no professional requirements for being a focus group moderator.

Focus group research philosophies. Utilizing a philosophy of science perspective that separates everyday from scientific discourse, Calder (1977) addressed the issue of focus group objectives and related moderator qualifications. In his description of the clinical, exploratory and phenomenological approaches to qualitative research, he makes assumptions about the rationales and goals for conducting the process of knowledge acquisition using qualitative research. According to Calder, first degree constructs based on the social construction of reality are the purview of everyday knowledge. In contrast, second degree constructs are generally highly abstract and subject to scientific methods.

Comparisons can be made between how various qualitative research approaches relate to the type consumer or market knowledge desired. Some qualitative researchers are first degree construct focused, while others are able to understand and describe consumer behavior and market dynamics in first and second degree terms. Calder notes that clinical and exploratory work require a qualitative researcher with a high degree of sophistication with scientific theory. In contrast, phenomenological work requires a researcher whose experiences are highly compatible with those of the group session participants.

In support of Calder's concepts, McDonald (1992) found a significant interaction between different knowledge acquisition objectives and moderator philosophies in the ratings of group sessions and their associated project reports. The research encourages the use of a moderator's scientific training as a criterion in project planning. In contrast, McQuarrie and McIntyre (1990) advocate that consumers are best understood in their own terms, with a good phenomenologist avoiding assumptions and abstractions because they interfere with an ability to discover the consumer experience.

Content analysis in consumer research. Content analysis is a method for studying and analyzing communications in a systematic, objective, and quantitative manner. It is a method of observation, a way of categorizing and summarizing communications to understand the nature of verbal and written materials. Although it can be used for many purposes, one significant area in marketing research involves the analysis of qualitative research.

Kassarjian (1977) conducted the first major review of content analysis in consumer research. Most recently, Kolbe and Burnett (1991) provided a review and synthesis of published studies that have used content analysis methods. General, comprehensive reviews of the theories, methods, applications in content analysis research can be found in Weber (1990) and Krippendorff (1990).

The work of Grunert and Bader (1986) used a keyword-in-context (KWIC) approach to developing an interactive tool for designing a customized dictionary of categories. The research illustrated their procedure with focus groups designed to explore the way lay persons and experts talk and think about cameras. Richer associative structures emerged among experts than among lay persons. This demonstrated the power of the computer as a data reduction tool for uncovering relationships that might otherwise go undiscovered.

Computer-based content analysis. Quantitative computer-based content analysis can take several forms. Techniques range from detailed analysis of word or phrase usage (KWIC lists and concordances) to multivariate analyses based on quantification (Krippendorff 1990). While all counts and listings take words out of their original linguistic environment and make their context-dependent meaning no longer recognizable by the analyst, a KWIC approach does just the opposite. It lists occurrences of selected words with the linguistic environment in which they occur and, therefore, gives the researcher an idea of how each key word is used.

Computer-aided content analysis has the advantage of providing explicit rules for coding text and perfect coder reliability in the application of a coding scheme. Computational efforts consist of developing data and applying analytical constructs. There is a need to discover patterns within the data and, ideally, to relate the data to some exogenous factor.

METHOD

Research Materials. Over the last ten years, this author collected hundreds of focus group session tapes. This occurred as part of his consulting activities and because of professional associations with numerous moderators. This group research resource represents the work of 66 moderators. All materials came with the condition that they would not be used for any commercial purpose and that the confidentiality of the moderator, client, and research subject would be strictly maintained. The group session topics mostly involved consumer-goods marketing issues, including work on new product ideas, advertising strategies, questionnaire preparation, marketing programs, and many others.

0For the purposes of this analysis, one tape was selected at random from work of each moderator. The tapes were transcribed into a format suitable for a computerized content analysis by a stenographer who created verbatim computer files of the group sessions. The typed transcripts averaged 20 to 30 pages of single-spaced text.

The Content Analysis Categories. Certain problems can arise in the creation of any content category or set of categories. These problems stem from the ambiguity of both the category definitions and the words assigned to categories. The category scheme here assigns words to "first-order" categories (see Dunphy, Bullard, and Crossing 1989). This first-order classification scheme insures that the categories are mutually exclusive, a requirement for the application of multivariate statistical methods where there is a need for statistical independence.

Even with precise category definitions, the decision to classify a particular word in a category often is difficult because of ambiguities in word meaning. Word ambiguity poses problems because a word may have multiple meanings. Sometimes, certain words clearly belong to a particular category. Other words represent a category less strongly; still others seem to belong in more than one category. Many proposals exist to solve these problems (see Weber 1990), but none are entirely satisfactory. If there was sufficient ambiguity, a word was dropped from a category and, sometimes, if necessary, from the analysis.

KWIC lists are important aids to developing categories of meaning such as required for dictionary construction (Krippendorff 1990). This author created a KWIC analysis system to produce a dictionary of words and categories. Guidance for category creation also came from the work of Roget (see Dutch 1965) who originated the thesaurus approach to language classification by indexing words into logical groupings.

The final context analysis dictionary included category names and the rules for assigning words to categories, including approximately 39,500 words belonging to 23 categories. To illustrate, a "personal" category contains such words as joy, relief, amusement, among many others. A "reasoning" category contains judgments, beliefs, knowledge, evidence, and so on. Broad dictionary categories are necessary to cover with a wide range of topics, contexts, and products and services. Reliability was evaluated by interactively scanning several group session files to confirm the membership of words in their intended classification categories.

Everyday versus scientific moderators. In this research, moderators are differentiated by their espoused focus group research philosophy. Given this criterion, two types of moderators emerge: (1) everyday moderators, defined as those individuals who take a conversational approach to conducting and reporting group sessions, and (2) scientific moderators, defined as users of motivational theories or other social science concepts in group session dynamics management and reporting. The distinction is between those moderators who have a high degree of sophistication with scientific theory versus those who are more like everyday people. In general, everyday moderators have more in common with focus group participants than their scientific counterparts. They rely much less on psychological and sociological theories for interpretative analysis and much more on a common sense understanding of human behavior. Everyday moderators are members of the focus group; they are more like participant leaders than observers. Some call this the "personality school" of moderating (McDaniel 1979).

The Analysis Approach. Much of the content analysis worked that occurs on focus group data is descriptive, but this need not be the case. Indeed, although focus group data is regarded as qualitative, proper content analysis of the data can make it amenable to the most sophisticated quantitative analysis.

An application of the dictionary and categories created specifically for this research produced word and category frequency counts, resulting in a computer record for each group session transcript. The category counts were then factor analyzed using a varimax rotation. The factor analysis themes were subsequently used in a discriminant analysis, with moderator type as the dependent variable.

FINDINGS

Before the content and multivariate research began, the focus group session tapes were examined on overall session characteristics, comparing groups conducted by everyday versus scientific moderators. Table 3 profiles the tapes on three dimensions: (1) gender of group participants, (2) group purpose, that is, type of group according to the Calder (1977) framework, and (3) aver-

age group session length. First, of the 66 tapes in the analysis, 42 are from sessions conducted by everyday moderators and 24 are from the work of scientific moderators. Statistical tests on the gender, group purpose, and group length variables did not reveal any significant differences. Thus, this initial profiling of the tapes indicates that the few tape variables available to this researcher do not define differences that need to be considered during the multivariate analysis.

TABLE 1
A Profile of the Focus Group Session Tapes

	Moderator Philosophy	
	Everyday	Scientific
Group session gender: Male	(42)	(24)
	29%	33%
Female	55	54
Both	17	13
	100%	100%
Group session approach:		
Phenomenological	52%	33%
Exploratory	19	29
Clinical	29	38
	100%	100%
Average group length:	101 min.	97 min.

Note: No statistically significant relationships above.

Table 2 compares the two types of moderators on demographics. What stands out most are significant differences on gender, years of group research experience, and education. The majority of everyday moderators are women, while the majority of scientific moderators are men. Although the everyday moderators have significantly more experience, the scientific moderators are, not surprisingly, more highly educated.

TABLE 2
A Comparison of Everyday Versus Scientific Moderators

Variables	Everyday (42)	Scientific (24)
Average age:	38.1	40.3
Gender: Male	33%	75%*
Female	67	25
Average years of experience in group research:	8.8	7.1*
Average years of college level education:	4.7	7.6*
Advanced degrees:	42.9%	100.0%*

* Significant at the P=.05 level.

Content analysis categories and group session themes. The content analysis produced a frequency count for each of the 23 categories. These frequencies were factor analyzed, resulting in four factors or themes. Referring to

Table 3, the total factor structure accounts for 62 percent of the total variance. Of the 23 categories, 17 formed into factors. Categories not in factor structure include action, dimension, existence, form, motion, and quantity.

The first theme is descriptive of cause and effect categories. It includes causation as well as change, relations, order, volition, and thought. This first factor accounts for some 24.1 percent of the variance. The second theme is more emotional in nature. It contains sympathetic, sensation, personal, and moral loadings, and a negative association with reasoning. The third theme is object oriented. This list of categories is linguistically a collection of references to nouns. Finally, theme four is a cognition factor, including categories that refer to ideas, reasoning, and thought.

Discriminant analysis. The results of the factor analysis were used in a discriminant analysis, along with years of experience as a moderator. They became the independent or predictor variables, while the two moderator categories became the dependent variable. All factor analysis coefficients in Table 4 are significant at the P=.05 level. They show that the cause and effect theme is most influential. However, the coefficients also show that the other themes play an important role in the discrimination. While scientific moderators generate more cause and effect and emotionality themes in their group sessions, everyday moderators produce more cognition and objects references. Years of experience moderating is not a significant predictor.

The overall F-value for the discriminant model is 25.51, with 5 and 60 degrees of freedom. It is significant at the P=.05 level. The statistical significance of the discriminant analysis provides answers about if the themes discriminate the moderator types, and if they help to describe differences between the moderator types.

A confusion matrix, indicating the predictive efficiency of the discriminant analysis model, produced a prediction level of 68 percent. Clearly, however, the predictive efficiency of the model is biased by the fact that the same data used to estimate the discriminant function model was used to test its predictive efficiency. Given a larger database, the model would have been applied to a holdout sample to test its true predictive power.

A separate discriminant analysis using moderator gender as the dependent variable and the factors and years of experience as independent variables did not produce a statistically significant discriminant function. Thus the gender differences apparent in Table 2 are not relevant to an understanding of group session content.

DISCUSSION AND CONCLUSIONS

The content analysis and multivariate modeling clearly show that focus group moderator philosophy has a significant influence on the content of group sessions. The findings reinforce the idea that the moderator is critical to the research process by proving that the nature of group session content is affected by the moderator.

However, this is a study of differences and not a study

TABLE 3
Factor Analysis of Content Categories

Theme 1: Cause and effect

Categories	Loading
Relations	0.888
Causation	0.734
Change	0.601
Order	0.588
Volition	0.502
Thought	0.475

Explained variance: 24.1%

Theme 2: Emotionality

Categories	Loading
Sympathetic	0.881
Sensation	0.808
Personal	0.534
Reasoning	-0.481
Moral	0.475

Explained variance: 16.8%

Theme 3: Objects

Categories	Loading
Things	0.704
Persons	0.659
Institutions	0.579
Affiliations	0.556
Time	0.445

Explained variance: 12.7%

Theme 4: Cognition

Categories	Loading
Ideas	0.744
Reasoning	0.557
Thought	0.402

Explained variance: 8.7%

Minimum factor loading level = .400

Total variance explained = 62.3%

TABLE 4
A Discriminant Analysis of Content Themes and Moderator Types

	Mean values of predictor variables				
	Everyday	Scientific		Normalized	
Predictor variables	(42)	(24)	Diff.	coefficients	Rank
Cause and effect	-0.51	0.89	1.40	-2.00*	1
Emotionality	-0.74	0.43	1.17	-1.69*	2
Cognition	0.21	-0.37	0.58	0.77*	3
Objects	0.30	-0.25	0.55	0.71*	4
Years of experience	8.8	7.1	1.7	-0.03	5

* Significant at P=.05 level as predictor.

Note: Overall F-value of 25.51, 5 and 60 d. f., significant at P=.05 level.

of relative effectiveness. It does not tell us if having more cause and effect and emotional content is better or worse than having more cognition and objects content. One could assume that the explication of cause and effect and emotionality is more characteristic of motivational discourse. One also could assume that discussions about cognition and objects represent a less complex level of discourse more similar to everyday conversation.

Fundamentally, the issue of appropriate focus group session content goes back to the intended nature of the group process itself. If group interviews are supposed to stimulate free and spontaneous discussions that provide insights into consumer motivations, then the attributions of cause and effect and their emotionality seem important. Cause and effect discussions go to the heart of the inquiry into the why of consumer behavior. At another level, so does the discussion of feelings about buyer behavior. This is particularly true when we realize that sympathetic, sensation, personal, non-reasoning, and moral categories dominate the emotionality theme.

Cognition, as defined in this research, appear to represent logical explanations for consumer behavior. They have a distinctly rational flavor. Ideas, reasoning, and thought sound like the "intellectualized" aspects of the consumer experience. Discussions of nouns such as persons, things, ideas, affiliations, institutions, and time are important in framing the discussion of consumer behavior. However, they do not constitute explanations in and of themselves.

Calder's (1977) discussion of focus group objectives and moderator qualifications is relevant here. Consistent with his analytical structure, different types of moderators do appear to bring different skills to the research process. Evidently, advanced training in scientific principles and methods does separate moderators on how they conduct qualitative research. An avowed reliance on psychological and sociological theories for interpretative analysis rather than on common sense understandings of

human behavior influences the content of qualitative work. Thus, the pursuit of second degree constructs does result in differences in what is said during the focus group sessions.

Clarity in this area may result from a recognition that all types of group research work benefit from an understanding of consumers and markets in both first degree and second degree terms. But it is also worth noting that if focus group research contributes to the creation of competitive advantages, it is unlikely to be based only on everyday explanations. Everyday knowledge is too close to common sense to provide one firm a real advantage over another firm.

Nevertheless, regardless of philosophy, moderators are just as likely to conduct qualitative research projects that have exploratory, phenomenological, or clinical knowledge acquisition objectives (also Fern 1982). The lack of a significant association between moderator selection and focus group research objectives, as defined by Calder, leads to questions about whether his framework is correct. However, this research also confirms the work of McDonald (1992) who found an interaction between group session objectives and moderator philosophy that added to our understanding of how moderators may be evaluated.

It is important to note that the findings of this research are based on some methodological weaknesses. Clearly, the study depends on a small sample of focus group sessions. Since the tapes used in this research represent a convenience sample, there is also no guarantee that there may not be other significant group and moderator differences in a replication study. The research does not address any questions about what moderator qualifications should be. It just shows that differences exist. A study is now being conducted by this author to relate moderator philosophy to group session effectiveness and report impact on the marketing decision-making process.

REFERENCES

Calder, Bobby J. (1977), "Focus Groups and the Nature of Qualitative Marketing Research," *Journal of Marketing Research,* 14 (August), 353-364.

Dunphy, Dexter. C., C. G. Bullard, and E. E. M. Crossing (1989), "Validation of the General Inquirer Harvard IV Dictionary," in Computer-assisted Text Analysis for the Social Sciences: The General Inquirer III, Cornelia Zuell, Robert P. Weber, and Peter Mohler, Mannheim, FRG: Center for Surveys, Methods, and Analysis (ZUMA).

Dutch, Robert A. (1965), *The Original Roget's Thesaurus of English Words and Phrases.* New York: St. Martin's Press.

Fern, Edward F. (1982), "The Use of Focus Groups for Idea Generation: The Effects of Groups Size, Acquaintanceship, and Moderator on Response Quantity and Quality," *Journal of Marketing Research,* 19 (February), 1-13.

Fowler, J. Floyd and Thomas M. Mangione (1989), *Standardized Survey Interviewing: Minimizing Interviewer-Related Error.* Beverly Hills: Sage Publications.

Grunert, K. G. and M. Bader (1986), "A Systematic Way to Analyze Focus Group Data," in *1986 Summer Marketing Educator's Conference Proceedings,* Terence A. Shimp et al., eds.Chicago: American Marketing Association, Series 52, 381.

Kassarjian, Harold H. (1977), "Content Analysis in Consumer Research," *Journal of Consumer Research,* 4 (June), 8-18.

Krippendorff, Klaus (1990), *Content Analysis: An Introduction to its Methodology.* Beverly Hills: Sage Publications.

Kolbe, Richard H. and Melissa S. Burnett (1991), "Content-Analysis Research: An Examination of Applications with Directives for Improving Research Reliability and Objectivity," *Journal of Consumer Research,* 18 (September), 243-250.

McDaniel, Carl. (1979), "Focus Groups - Their Role in the Marketing Research Process," *Akron Business and Economic Review,* 10 (June), 14-19.

McDonald, William J. (1980), "Group Research: Applications and Philosophies," unpublished working paper, Marketing Department, University of Illinois at Chicago Circle.

_____, (1992), "Focus Group Research Dynamics and Reporting: An Examination of Group Objectives and Moderator Influences," unpublished working paper, Department of Marketing and International Business, Hofstra University.

McQuarrie, Edward F. and Shelby McIntyre (1990), "What the Group Interview Can Contribute to Research on Consumer Phenomenology," in *Research in Consumer Behavior,* Elizabeth C. Hirschman, ed. Greenwich: JAI Press, 165-194.

Stewart, David W. and Prem N. Shamdasani. (1991), *Focus Groups: Theory and Practice.* Beverly Hills: Sage Publications.

Weber, Robert P. (1990), *Basic Content Analysis.* Beverly Hills: Sage Publications.

MAGNITUDE ESTIMATION FOR THE ASSESSMENT OF CONSUMER PERCEPTIONS OF PRODUCT QUALITY AND PRICE

Noel Mark Lavenka, Loyola University of Chicago

ABSTRACT

Introduction: Research suggests that consumers, lacking other obvious cues, will impute quality on the basis of price. The quantity of this research lends support to the general acceptance of a "price-quality" relationship (Monroe and Krishnan 1985). However, given the present constraints for evaluating perceptions of product quality, little is known if consumers can submit a correspondingly applicable price <u>after</u> assessing the level of product quality. Since previous price-quality research has been correlational by nature, it remains unclear whether the causal source of this relationship starts with establishing a price level or with that of a quality level (Monroe and Dodds 1988).

Consumer judgments about product quality usually take place in a comparison context among other related brands. The instruments we presently use to measure consumer judgments about products allow for only ordinal, or equal-appearing-interval ratings. These scales require the use of defined attributes to determine the construct for quality. The major problem that arises is that brands within a competitive product category may or may not share similar attributes distorting direct brand comparisons. Secondly, measurements of product quality collected on a rank order scale can only result in rank order interpretation.

Measurement Scale: The application of the magnitude estimation procedure was chosen to assess both product quality and price. Two sensory measures are validated according to Steven's Power Law (Stevens 1975). This Law asserts that sensation (S) is proportional to stimulus intensity (I) raised to some power (b):

$$S = k\,I^{\,b}$$

where k is simply a constant that depends on the unit of measurement being used (Lodge 1981).

Recent advances in the validity, application, and generalization of the magnitude estimation approach to the measurement of marketing related phenomena specifically address the issues that concern product quality assessment. Research findings indicate strong support for the validity of magnitude scaling methods for aggregate data over that of the category rating scale (Crask and Fox 1987, Teas 1987). The magnitude scale is found to be more sensitive to perceptions and preferences, providing a means to present product quality judgments on a linear, ratio determined scale (Lavenka 1989).

Experimental Setting: A convenience sample of 30 student respondents age 18 to 25 was chosen during a one week period. A sample of heavy users (who purchased 10 or more bars a week) was selected to profile the buyer and consumer of these confectionery products. The sample was used for illustrative use of the procedure and should not be considered representative of the entire population. The product category of chocolate candy bars presents a convenient illustration of consumer judgments about product quality and price. This product category offers a wide selection of competitive brands for comparison along with varied intrinsic differences. Furthermore, candy bars share the <u>same</u> reference price-point of about 50 cents within a retail setting. This isolates any previous price-quality judgments that may have a predetermined influence on consumers' perceptions (Monroe and Dodds 1988). The complete study involved a 35 minute personal interview to evaluate 14 candy-bars in an experimental setting.

Results: The results support the hypotheses that the respondents' judgments about product quality and price are a valid application of the magnitude estimation procedure according to Steven's Power Law (Lodge 1981). The respondents' judgments about product quality comparisons are determined to have a positive ($R^2 = .923$) influence on their price assessment. Analysis of variance indicates no significant difference between their judgments of quality with the assessment of the price they would expect to pay based on their quality judgments.

For further information please contact:
Noel M. Lavenka
333 E. Ontario #4201 - B
Chicago, Illinois 60611

THE THEORY OF REASONED ACTION REVISITED: A CASE OF HIGHLY INVOLVED, LONG-TERM VOLUNTARY BEHAVIOR

Mark R. Young, Winona State University
Rosemary R. Lagace, University of South Florida

ABSTRACT

This study tests the Fishbein-Ajzen theory of reasoned action and replicates the Shimp and Kavas (1984) examination of extensions of the theory. Multidimensional rather than unidimensional cognitive and normative structures are examined in addition to the direct effects of A_{act} and SN on behavior. The theory is applied to the highly involved long-term voluntary behavior of the Big Brother/Sister program.

INTRODUCTION

Since the social-awareness era of the 1960's and 1970's the number of nonprofit organizations has increased significantly. It has been estimated that there are over 780,000 nonprofit groups in the United States (Kotler and Andreasen 1987). Many of these organizations rely on volunteers to assist with the fulfillment of their objectives. In 1985, 89 million citizens of the U.S. contributed over 16 billion hours of voluntary services to nonprofit organizations (*American Volunteer* 1986). The United Way organization alone involves 11 million volunteers (Wilkinson 1989). The important role of volunteers and other forms of donating has prompted researchers to examine a variety of helping behaviors (e.g. Batson, Bolen, Cross, and Neuringer-Benefiel 1986; Campbell 1975; Hoffman 1981). Much of this research focuses on behavior such as blood or money donating (Bagozzi 1981, 1982; Burnkrant and Page 1982).

However, many donating activities require some time commitment. In an era where time poverty is increasing at a dramatic rate (Schiffman and Kanuk 1983), it is imperative that the managers of these institutions fully understand the motivations and behaviors of the volunteer sector.

One area which has been investigated in the nonprofit research is the volunteers' attitude toward the behavior. Webster (1975) and Andreasen and Belk (1980) have suggested attitudes be used as market segmentation criteria for the socially-responsible individuals. Attitude measures investigate the nature and value of various outcomes that an individual expects from a specific behavior. Fishbein's extended model (Fishbein and Ajzen 1975) also incorporates the extent to which significant others believe that the individual should engage in that specific behavior.

However, Fishbein and Ajzen's model (the Theory of Reasoned Action) has rarely been investigated in the nonprofit area, especially in an organization as focused as the Big Brother/Sister program. The Big Brother/Big Sister organization relies on long-term time commitments (typically more than one year) and the volunteers become highly involved (parent/child relationship) with their little brother/sister. This highly involved, long-term voluntary behavior has received little research attention and is the focus of this study. The purpose of this study is to empirically test the theory of reasoned action (Ajzen and Fishbein 1980), comparing the specification of the cognitive and normative components as unidimensional versus multidimensional, and examines the direct influence of attitude and subjective norm on behavior.

BACKGROUND

This partial replication of the Shimp and Kavas (1984) study is based on the premise that volunteering to be a Big Brother/Sister is thoughtful rational behavior and not impulsive. This is critical for testing the Theory of Reasoned Action, and also conforms to the dimensions of helping behavior suggested by Smithson, Amato and Pearce (1983), those being planned, serious, and direct help. Three models presenting variations of the theory of reasoned action are examined in this study and are diagramed in Figures 1, 2, 3. Model A (Figure 1) is the traditional Fishbein-Ajzen model of reasoned action. Behavior is directly influenced by behavioral intentions that result from an attitude toward the act (A_{act}) and from subjective norms (SN). A_{act} results from the consequences of the behavior and the evaluation of these consequences, where $\Sigma b_i e_i$ is a unidimensional concept. SN represents normative beliefs about the behavior and the motivation to comply with important others' expectations, $\Sigma NB_j MC_j$ is also unidimensional. In addition, behavioral intentions mediates the influence of A_{act} and SN on behavior. Detailed explanation of the theory can be found in Ajzen and Fishbein 1980.

Models B and C are variations of the traditional Fishbein model. Model B utilizes a multidimensional portrayal of the expectancy-value components in contrast to the unidimensional $\Sigma b_i e_i$ in Model A. Model C includes direct effects of A_{act} and SN on behavior rather than strictly being mediated through behavioral intentions. Full justification for these modifications and relevant literature cites can be found in Shimp and Kavas (1984).

The Shimp and Kavas study found support for the

multidimensional representation of the cognitive component, was inconclusive on the dimensionality of the normative component and supported the mediating effect of behavioral intentions.

METHODOLOGY

Subjects

Data were collected in two waves from current adult members of a Big Brother/Sister program. A mail questionnaire was utilized to collect information on attitudes, subjective norms and behavioral intentions. A follow-up was conducted 12 months later to determine actual behavior (program participation). The data set in this analysis is based on 134 responses representing a 63 percent response rate. Subject demographics are shown on Table 1.

A nominal group technique (Claxton, Ritchie and Zaichkaivsky 1980) utilizing current Big Brothers/Sisters, was employed to develop the items for behavioral consequences and important normative influences. The questionnaire was pretested on MBA students and a subsample of Big Brothers/Sisters before being administered to the study group.

Measures

The measurement of the variables used to operationalize the various constructs of the theory of reasoned action are:

Beliefs (b_i) : seven salient beliefs were measured on 7-point scales anchored with "very likely" (+3) and "very unlikely' (-3) (e.g., "Being a Big Brother/Sister allows me to make a positive impact on a young persons life").

Evaluations (e_i) : the evaluative component corresponding to the salient beliefs was measured by asking respondents to evaluate the consequence of each belief on a 7-point scale anchored with "very good" (+3) and "very bad" (-3) (e.g., "Making a positive impact on a young persons life is:").

Attitude toward the act (A_{act}) : 7-point semantic differential scale (e.g., important/unimportant, helpful/unhelpful, wise/foolish, valuable/worthless).

Normative Beliefs (NB_j) : 7-point scaled anchored with "very likely" (+3) and "very unlikely" (-3) for 'significant other', 'immediate family' and 'friends' (e.g., "My 'significant other' (wife/husband, girl/boy friend) thinks I should be a Big Brother/Sister").

Motivation to comply (MC_j) : the MC component corresponding to each NB was measured on a 7-point "very much" (+3) to "not much" (-3) scale (e.g., "I want to do what my "significant other" thinks I should do regarding being a Big Brother/Sister").

Subjective Norm (SN) : four bipolar 7-point scales (important/unimportant, helpful/unhelpful, wise/foolish, valuable/worthless) in response to: "People who are important to me and whose opinion I value think my being a Big Brother/Sister would be:"

Behavioral intentions (BI) : 9-point scale anchored with "highly likely" (9) and "highly unlikely" (1) in response to: "Indicate the likelihood that you will stay in the Big Brother/Sister program for at least one additional year."

Behavior (B) : One year after initial questionnaire was completed the Big Brother/Sister organization provided program participation status for each respondent.

Analysis

Maximum likelihood estimation, calculated by EQS (Bentler 1989) was used in the measurement and model testing phases of this study. This analysis provides a simultaneous test of model relationships as well as estimates of measurement error in the constructs. The indicators for the latent factors are presented in Table2.

RESULTS

Parameter estimates for the standard Fishbein representation (model A) are presented in Figure 4. Whether one uses the .90 heuristic offered from Bentler and Bonett (1980) or the .95 value suggested by Bearden, Sharma and Teel (1982) the normed fit index and the comparative fit index indicate a reasonable model fit with values of .992 and .997 respectfully. The chi square goodness of fit statistic did not support the model fit; however, as Bentler (1989) points out acceptance or rejection of the null hypothesis based on this statistic may be inappropriate.

All indicators showed significant loadings as well as the paths from Σbe to A_{act} and BI to B. Even though the paths leading to behavior intentions were not statistically significant the standardized coefficient from A_{act} was twice the magnitude as the coefficient from subjective norm. This may indicate the intention of remaining in the Big Brother/Sister program is more dependent on cognitive thoughts than on influences from others.

Model B (Figure 5) represents the multidimensional rather than the unidimensional portrayal of the cognitive and normative components leading to A_{act} and SN. Overall model fit seems reasonable with a normed fit index of .99 and a comparative fit index of .995. The path from Aact to BI is now significant while the path from SN to BI is not. None of the paths from the cognitive nor normative components are significant. However, it can

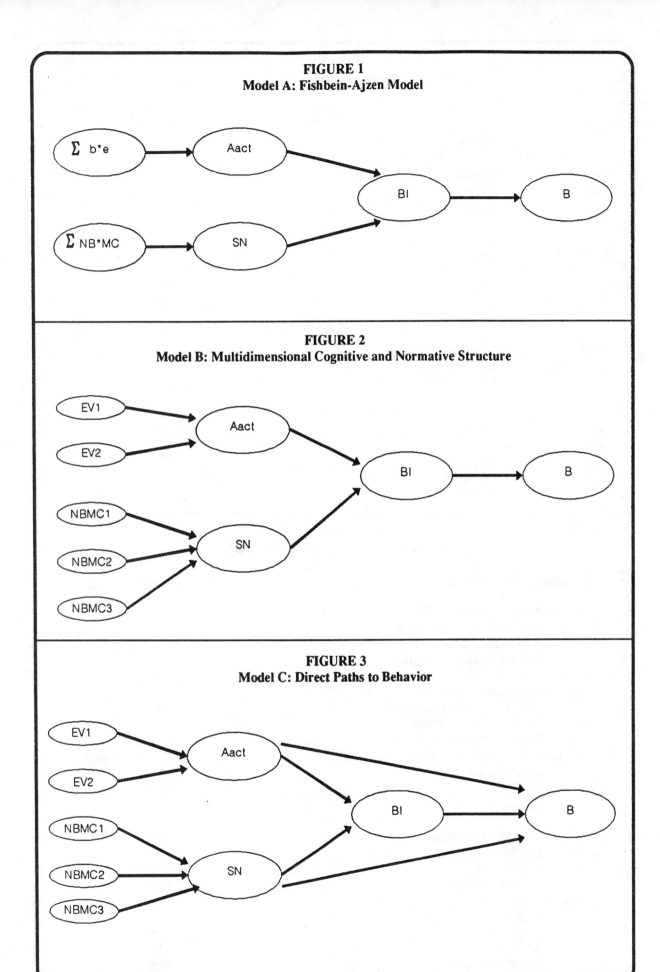

FIGURE 1
Model A: Fishbein-Ajzen Model

FIGURE 2
Model B: Multidimensional Cognitive and Normative Structure

FIGURE 3
Model C: Direct Paths to Behavior

TABLE 1
Subject Demographics

PERCENT

		PERCENT
Gender	Male	42
	Female	58
Marital Status	Married	38
	Single	56
	Other	6
Age	18-24	38
	25-34	43
	35-49	18
	50+	1
Education	Some High School	0
	High School Graduate	8
	1-3 Years College	25
	College Graduate	67
Family Income	<10,000	8
	10-19,999	20
	20-34,999	27
	35-49,999	14
	50,000+	31

TABLE 2
Operationalization of Latent Constructs

Construct and Indicators	Notation
Positive Expectancy-Value (+EV)	
Positive impact on child's life	V1
Help children develop values	V2
Develop trusting relationship	V3
Like adding member to family	V4
Negative Expectancy-Value (-EV)	
Must give up a lot of activities	V5
Gives me more problems	V6
Requires spending a lot of money	V7
Normative Beliefs & Motivation to Comply (NBMC)	
Significant other	V8
Family	V9
Friends	V10
A_{act}	
Important/unimportant	V11
Helpful/unhelpful	V12
Wise/foolish	V13
Valuable/worthless	V14
Subjective Norm (SN)	
Important/unimportant	V15
Helpful/unhelpful	V16
Wise/foolish	V17
Valuable/worthless	V18

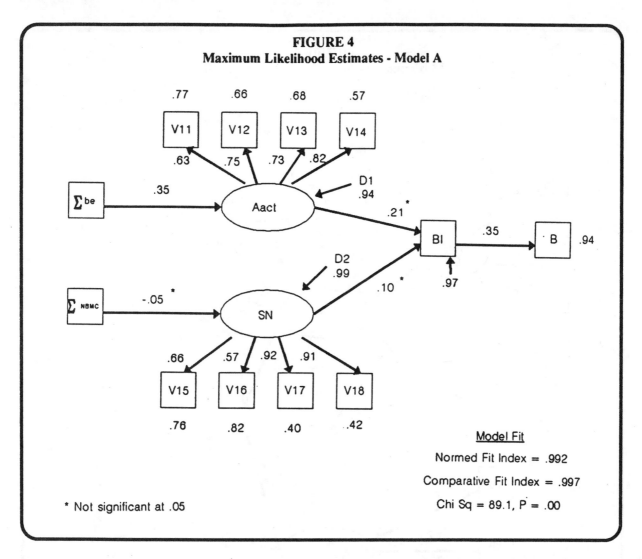

FIGURE 4
Maximum Likelihood Estimates - Model A

Model Fit
Normed Fit Index = .992
Comparative Fit Index = .997
Chi Sq = 89.1, P = .00

* Not significant at .05

be seen that the negative expectancy-value component has a larger standardized loading than the positive expectancy-value component. Suggesting that what one must give up or put up with may be more influential in forming the overall attitude toward remaining in the program than the positive aspects.

Model C (Figure 6) is the extension of model B to include direct paths from A_{act} and SN to Behavior. The overall fit and individual parameters are essentially the same as in model B. The two additional direct paths to Behavior were not significant.

DISCUSSION

Our findings tend to support the unidimensional nature of the cognitive component in the theory of reasoned action. Neither coefficient in the multidimensional expectancy-value representation were statistically significant, where as, the unidimensional $\Sigma b_j e_j$ coefficient did achieve statistical significance. The nonsignificant coefficients relating normative indicators to SN both in the unidimensional model and in the multidimensional model leave this issue inconclusive. The direct paths from Aact and SN to Behavior were nonsignificant,

thereby supporting the original theory in addition to the Bagozzi (1981, 1982) and Shimp & Kavas (1984) findings. The insights gained from this study support the conventional representation of the theory of reasoned action.

Of managerial interest in this particular application of the theory is the stronger influence of the attitude over the normative component on behavioral intention and behavior. The high degree of involvement and the long time commitment may lead individuals to base their actions on their past experiences of what they individually were able to give and receive from their participation in the program and less on what others may think. This may suggest additional research comparing new applicants attitudes and subjective norms to current members. Individuals motivated more from normative influences may be less likely to continue in the program.

In the multidimensional expectancy-value representation it was found that negative expectancy-values were of greater influence on A_{act} than were positive expectancy-values. In particular 'giving up a lot of activities' and 'gives me more problems' were key influences on the attitude toward the act of remaining in the program. This

FIGURE 5
Maximum Likelihood Estimates - Model B

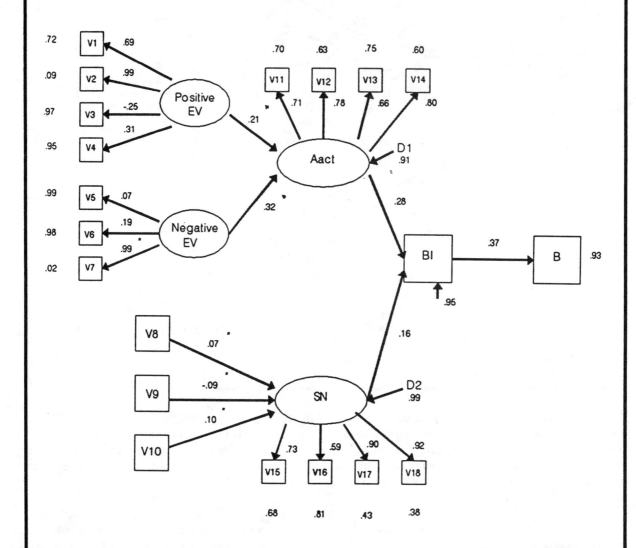

* Not Significant at .05

Model Fit

Normed Fit Index = .99

Comparative Fit Index = .995

Chi Sq = 263.5, P = .00

FIGURE 6
Maximum Likelihood Estimates - Model C

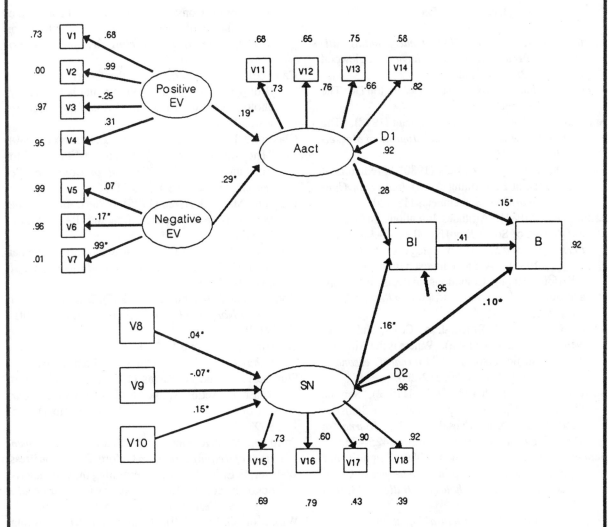

* Not significant at .05

Model Fit

Normed Fit Index = .99

Comparative Fit Index = .995

Chi Sq = 262.1, P = .00

may suggest providing the Big Brothers/Sisters with ways of incorporating the activities of the Little Brother/Sister into their current activities so that less is given up. Additional support in problem handling and counseling may be necessary to overcome some of the negative cognitions. The strongest positive expectancy-value was 'helping children develop values'. This should be stressed in communications about the program (recruitment) and in reinforcing current participants.

In summary, the conventional representation of the theory of reasoned action was supported in terms of unidimensional components and the mediating effect of behavioral intentions on behavior. The application to the Big Brother/Sister volunteers proved managerially useful and insightful.

REFERENCES

Ajzen, I. and M. Fishbein (1980), *Understanding Attitudes and Predicting Social Behavior*. Englewood Cliffs, NJ: Prentice-Hall.

Americans Volunteer 1985 (1986), Washington DC: The Independent Sector.

Anderson, W. T. and W. H. Cunningham (1972), "The Socially Conscious Consumer," *Journal of Marketing,* 36 (July), 23-31.

Andreasen, A. R. and R. W. Belk (1980), "Predictors of Attendance at Performing Arts," *Journal of Consumer Research,* 7 (September), 112-120.

Bagozzi, R. P. (1981), "Attitudes, Intentions, and Behavior: A Test of Some Key Hypotheses," *Journal of Personality and Social Psychology,* 41, 607-627.

_____(1982), "A Field Investigation of Causal Relations Among Cognitions, Affects, Intentions and Behavior," *Journal of Marketing Research,* 19, (November), 562-584.

Batson, C. D., M. H. Bolen, J. A. Cross, and H. E. Neuringer-Benefiel, (1986), "Where is the Altruism in the Altruistic Personality?," *Journal of Personalty and Social Psychology,* 50, 212-220.

Bearden, W., S. Subhash, and J. E. Teel (1982), "Sample Size Effects Upon Chi-Square and Other Statistics Used in Evaluating Causal Models," *Journal of Marketing Research,* 19 (November), 425-430.

Bentler, P. M. and D. G. Bonett (1980), "Significance Tests and Goodness of Fit in the Analysis of Covariance Structures," *Psychological Bulletin,* 88, 588-606.

_____(1989), *EQS Structural Equations Program Manual.* BMDP Statistical Software, Los Angels, CA.

Burnkrant, R. E. and T. J. Page, Jr. (1982), "An Examination of the Convergent, Discriminant and Predictive Validity of Fishbein's Behavioral Intention Model," *Journal of Marketing Research,* 19 (November), 550-561.

Campbell, D. T. (1975), "On the Conflicts between Biological and Social Evolution and between Psychology and Moral Tradition," *American Psychologist,* 30, 1103-1126.

Claxton, J. D., J. R. Ritchie, and J. Zaichkaivsky (1980), "The Nominal Group Technique. Its' Potential for Consumer Research," *Journal of Consumer Research,* 7 (December), 308-313.

Fishbein, M. and I. Ajzen (1975), *Beliefs, Attitude, and Intentions, and Research.* Reading, PA: Addison-Wesley.

Hoffman, M. L. (1981), "Is Altruism Part of Human Nature?" *Journal of Personality and Social Psychology,* 40, 121-137.

Kotler, P. and A. R. Andreason (1987), *Strategic Marketing for Nonprofit Organizations.* Englewood Cliffs, NJ: Prentice-Hall.

Schiffman, L. G. and L. L. Kanuk (1983), *Consumer Behavior.* Englewood Cliffs, NJ: Prentice-Hall.

Shimp, T. A. and A. Kavas (1984), "The Theory of Reasoned Action Applied to Coupon Usage," *Journal of Consumer Research,* 11, (December), 795-809.

Smithson, M., P. R. Amato and P. Pearce (1983), *Dimensions of Helping Behavior.* Oxford: Pergamon Press.

Webster, F. E. Jr. (1975), "Determining the Characteristics of the Socially Conscious Consumer," *Journal of Consumer Research,* 2 (December) 188-196.

Wilkinson, G. W. (1989), "Getting and Using Information, the United Way," *Marketing Research: A Magazine of Management and Applications.* 1 (September) 5-12.

THE INFLUENCE OF ACCESS-AND RESOURCE-RELATED VARIABLES ON CONSUMER SATISFACTION WITH HEALTH CARE

Venkatapparao Mummalaneni, St. John's University
Pradeep Gopalakrishna, Hofstra University

ABSTRACT

Services marketers including health care providers continue to consider consumer satisfaction the key to market share and long-term profitability. Interest in consumer satisfaction with health care however, extends beyond marketing to such varied disciplines as sociology (Mechanic 1990) and economics (Fuchs 1988). Marketing scholars continue to build upon the contribution of these pioneering disciplines in exploring the dimensions and sources of consumer satisfaction (Singh 1990).

Excellent reviews of the health care literature that appeared in recent years (Pascoe 1983; Singh 1991) indicate what we know about consumer satisfaction and what aspects of it elude clear understanding. Despite the considerable progress made in the last few decades, the research to date has several drawbacks, especially from a marketing point of view. While the contributions of numerous provider-related variables to consumer satisfaction have been examined, scarcely ever is the distinction made between administratively-controllable (parking facilities, waiting time) and uncontrollable or less controllable (such as physicians art of care); further, true comparative studies contrasting the performance of HMO's and fee-for-service (FFS) health care plans on these variables have been rare (Luft 1991). The present study attempts to address these drawbacks in the existing literature. Also, consumer satisfaction is tracked over time and the stability of the contributions made by various administratively controllable factors is examined here.

Adapting a framework developed by Aday et. al. (1980) for the study of access to health care, a conceptual model is developed. The model posits that consumer satisfaction is influenced by access and resource related characteristics of the health care delivery system (convenient location, waiting time etc.). This relationship is moderated in our model by the structure of the delivery system (HMO's Vs. FFS) as well as time.

Secondary data made available by a major research agency are used to test the model. Data were gathered as part of a large study designed to address several issues relating to the consumption of health care services, including consumer attitudes toward care received as well as health outcomes. The data employed in the present study were collected in a Northwestern city in the United States. The study population of 602 HMO enrolles and 1833 conventional care seekers were surveyed twice, at a time interval in excess of two and a half years and the response rates ranged from 57 per cent to over 85 per cent.

The model proposed here was tested through multiple regression analysis. The data from both sets of study participants (HMO and FFS) at the time of second measurement indicate that a modest 19 per cent of the variance in consumer satisfaction is accounted for by the nine access-and resource-related characteristics of the health care delivery system employed in the study. Next, to test the moderating influence of care delivery system structure (health plan type: HMO Vs. FFS) as well as time variable, sub-group analysis was performed. To test whether two regression relationships were of the same form (Arnold 1992) the Chow statistic was computed. Our results indicate that for HMO enrolles, the form of regression relationship remained the same over time, whereas for the FFS participants, it has changed. That is, the contributions made by access-and resource-related variables to consumer satisfaction remained stable for the HMO group by changed overtime for the other group. The variance explained in consumer satisfaction has gone down from 28 percent to 19 per cent in this latter group, whereas an increase (from 15 to 30 percent) has been observed for the HMO group.

At a time when cost and quality of care concerns are intensifying the debate regarding the performance of HMO's and FFS health care plans, our results indicate that consumers remain well-satisfied with the HMO's. Further, our results identify the magnitude of the contributions made by access-and resource-related variables to be significant enough to warrant the attention of hospital administrators.

In both HMO's as well as conventional care arrangements, these variables account for a moderate amount (15 to 30 per cent) of the variance in overall consumer satisfaction and more importantly, continue to exert their influence over an extended period of time. The implications are that the access-and resource-related variables are fairly stable sources of consumer satisfaction and that hospital administrators can retain the loyalty of the consumers through continued attention to these variables.

For further information contact:
Venkat Mummalaneni
Asst. Professor of Marketing
St. John's University
Jamaica, N.Y. 11439

MANAGED CARE AND THE PHYSICIAN: AN EXPLORATORY STUDY

Ronald Paul Hill, Villanova University
Maria Cacia, Medical College of Pennsylvania
John Shamsey, Upjohn

ABSTRACT

The purpose of this paper is to provide the results of an investigation of physicians' attitudes, beliefs, and feelings towards the changing health care environment spawned by managed care. The opening sections frame this issue within the context of managed care as a possible solution to the escalating cost of medical treatment in this country. Then, a qualitative study involving physicians is described and results are presented focusing on emergent themes. Finally, future directions for health care marketers are discussed with special attention given to the consumer interface problem identified.

INTRODUCTION

It would be an understatement to say that health care costs in the United States are out of control. Americans pay approximately $700 billion a year for health care, representing approximately 12 percent of GNP and more than $2500 per person (Hilts 1991). Most estimates report that health premiums increased 20 percent to 30 percent in 1989 and 1990, and the percent of GNP dedicated to health care is predicted to rise to 15 percent or 16 percent by the year 2000 (*Federation of American Health Systems Review* 1988b; Luthans and Davis 1990). Between 1960 and 1990, businesses' costs for health care went from 4 to 8 cents to an unbelievable 25 to 50 cents of each dollar of profit (Hilts 1991). No wonder 92 percent of top executives in a recent poll stated that they were "very concerned" about rising health insurance premium costs (*Business and Health* 1990).

While the causes of this escalation are multifaceted and complex, most sources suggest that the following constituencies have been major contributors. One party that is often indicted is the consumer. The American public believes that all persons have the right to the best possible health care regardless of cost (Luthans and Davis 1990). According to J. Alexander McMahon, former president of the American Hospital Association, Chicago, "We still have a system that encourages people to seek all the [medical] help they want ... not that they need. That can't do anything but lead them to seek more care" (Tokarski 1990, p. 51). Another group that receives blame is corporate executives. The private, job-tied, employer-paid insurance, that remains the cornerstone of America's health system, was created by business during World War II to evade government-imposed limits on wages (Reinhardt 1990). After the war, this insurance system became an important part of the compensation package provided by firms, and has resulted in bitter struggles of costs versus benefits between management and labor. On the other hand, many corporate officers blame these troubles on the government. According to their perspective, health care costs became a problem after the federal government instituted the Medicare program which "threw the normal supply and demand market out of whack, driving up costs" (CE Roundtable 1990, p. 54).

These causes notwithstanding, the most widely discussed culprits are physicians who are often characterized as strongly favoring "a fee-for-service health care system that pays providers more for delivering costly care, whether or not it is appropriate or beneficial" (Freedman 1990, p. 172). Critics estimate that up to one-fifth of all delivered health care is unnecessary (*Modern Healthcare* 1989). Some of this "excess" may be the result of defensive medicine "which has more to do with the doctor's self-interest than his or her concern for the patient" (Luthans and Davis 1990, p. 25). The American Medical Association estimates that approximately $15 billion is spent annually for this purpose. Other causes of growing costs that are tied to the role of physicians are the extensive use of costly medical technology, the continuous rise of malpractice premiums, and the significant increase in outpatient treatment during the 1980s (see Freedman 1990; Schramm 1990).

One of the primary ways to control costs and restrain the activities of physicians has been managed care (Kramon 1991). Projections indicate that up to 90 percent of the insured population in this country will belong to some form of managed care organization by the year 1995 (Buckner 1990). The purpose of this paper is to provide the results of an investigation of physicians' attitudes, beliefs, and feelings towards this changing health care environment as well as their perceptions of their ability to provide quality care to patients within its constraints. The next section briefly discusses the current dimensions of managed care with an emphasis on the quality of care provided to consumers of health services. Then, a qualitative study involving physicians is described and results are presented focussing on emergent themes. Finally, future directions for health care marketers are discussed with special attention given to problems identified.

THE CURRENT MANAGED CARE ENVIRONMENT

The growth of managed care since 1980 has been nothing short of phenomenal. Over one-fourth of all Americans now receive health care through some form of managed care, and there exists more than 600 HMOs and 700 PPOs nationally to serve their needs (Kenkel 1990). While the purpose of these organizations is to control health-related costs (see Signorovitch 1990), most advocates believe that the provision of quality care is just as essential. For example, Gagliardi and Freedman (1987, p.360) state that: "Managed care is a business process applied to health care. The goal is to ensure that the appropriate quality and quantity of care is delivered to a patient at an affordable cost."

The backbone of managed care has been the HMO (Coile 1990). An HMO provides health care for its consumers for a predetermined and fixed periodic payment (Gilman and Bucco 1987). HMOs operate within a budget determined by these payments, and are responsible for providing contracted services for their consumers. In contrast to the traditional fee-for-service system, HMOs create a financial incentive for providers to control costs since their pay is independent of the amount of service rendered.

PPOs differ from HMOs in two principle respects (Fox 1989). First, PPO consumers are free to use nonparticipating providers, although their financial liability is often higher when they exercise this option. Second, unlike the HMO, the PPO does not accept monetary risk since the provider is paid on a reduced fee-for-service basis. This more flexible approach has become very popular among consumers, and has caused the development of a "hybrid" often called the open-ended HMO or the point-of-service plan (Frieden and Traska 1989). Such programs provide the organizational structure of an HMO with the ability to go outside the network of providers if consumers so desire.

Regardless of the type of managed care organization, one of the essential ingredients to controlling costs is case management and utilization review (Curtiss 1989; Kittrell 1986). Using this tactic, a health care professional (often a registered nurse) reviews proposed medical treatment plans to determine their appropriateness (Fuller 1989). Such reviews include hospital pre-admission certification/continued stay review, hospital discharge planning, and comprehensive medical case management for complex or catastrophic illnesses and injuries (Anderson 1990).

Recently, the ability of such managed care programs to provide high quality health care has come under fire. According to AHSM's *The Academy Bulletin* (Howgill 1991, p.1):

First, a focus on quality means a focus on the customer. It is the health care provider's patients and other customers who define quality in terms of their everchanging requirements and expectations.

Unfortunately, greater consumer awareness of "the financial incentive to underserve [and] the publicity surrounding cases, however isolated, of patients being discharged `quicker and sicker'" (Fox 1989, p. 104) has jeopardized managed care's ability to provide quality care (also see Caldwell 1989). Further, an adversarial relationship between managed care organizations and physicians is developing that is affecting medical doctors' perceptions of their ability to serve consumers (Kertesz 1990; Kuriyan 1989). One angry physician stated that managed care firms "must come off their arbitrary computer pedestals and recognize that they have a moral obligation that goes beyond their need or promise to an insurance company to save X number of dollars" (*Federation of American Health Systems Review* 1988a, p.41). Nonetheless, the result is that the prestige and professional autonomy of the physician has been compromised, further eroding judgments of quality by consumers (Kenkel 1989).

AN EXPLORATORY STUDY OF PHYSICIANS

Methodology

Because of the exploratory nature of this investigation, the focus group was selected as the data collection method. According to Stewart and Shamdasani (1991, p. 15), "focus groups ... are particularly useful for exploratory research where rather little is known about the phenomenon of interest." Further, this technique, if properly used, will produce "a very rich body of data expressed in the respondents' own words and context" (p. 12). Thus, this research method was selected in order to understand the range (rather than representativeness) of possible reactions of physicians to the managed care environment using an emic (i.e., physician-oriented) perspective.

A major issue faced in the formation of any focus group involves interpersonal dynamics. According to Stewart and Shamdasani (1991, p. 33), group dynamics can affect "the extent to which participants feel comfortable about openly communicating their ideas, views or opinions." Therefore, care must be exercised to ensure that the demographic, physical, and personality makeup of the group facilitates honest discussion, usually requiring the recruitment of participants who are more similar than different.

However, the goal of focus group research is to examine the diversity of opinions, beliefs, and attitudes that exist within the environment of interest. Thus, to meet these two often conflicting requirements, six focus groups were conducted in three major cities that differed significantly in the extent to which managed care dominates the health care marketplace - Miami, Philadelphia, and Washington, D.C. Further, diversity in specialty (e.g., family practice, obstetrics/gynecology, pediatrics, cardiology, rheumatology, gastroenterology), length of practice (five to thirty or more years), and current and previous relationships with managed care organizations (ranging from 0 to 100% managed care patients in practice) among participants was maximized across rather than within groups of between eight and twelve physicians.

The moderator's guide was developed by the authors in conjunction with an expert in the health care marketplace as well as representatives of the marketing and marketing research departments at SmithKline Beecham which funded this project. Each session was described to the participants as focussed generally on managed health care. Respondents were given wide latitude in the nature and direction of their comments, and the discussion was loosely organized around the following topics: the meaning of the term managed care, personal experiences with managed care, influences on their orientations and attitudes toward managed care, and satisfactions/dissatisfactions and growth opportunities/constraints due to managed care. All sessions were videotaped with the consent of the participants.

Emergent Themes

In order to identify the major themes and issues that emerged across groups, two researchers content analyzed the videotapes of all focus group sessions (see Stewart and Shamdasani 1991 for more details on this procedure). After this task was completed, the senior researcher on this project took these results and organized this information into distinct interpretive categories. Finally, an independent auditor from the health care community reviewed the materials and made additional suggestions for change. Emergent themes are described in the following subsections, and verbatim comments by respondents are used to provide relevant examples of statements that led to these conclusions.

The Physician-Patient Relationship

The general consensus across groups was that managed health care is detrimental to the physician-patient relationship. For example, the current movement from traditional fee-for-service health care to HMOs and PPOs has led to a massive exodus of patients from long-standing relationships with physicians:

> "There is no loyalty of patient-physician relationship. You can go to a doctor for 20 to 25 years and then your employer changes insurance and you have to leave so you choose the doctor closest to [mass transportation] without knowing his skills."

These alliances are being replaced by physician-patient pairings that have considerably weaker bonds due to their recency, the mode of selection ("A lot of people pick you from a book [a list provided by the managed care organization]. You're not a referral from their friend or from another physician."), and the economic incentives to physicians to handle large numbers of managed care patients which limits their availability ("HMOs are sort of like my experience in the Army seeing 200 soldiers in two hours."). The result is often a lack of trust by managed care patients for physicians and an increase in the likelihood of malpractice lawsuits:

> "Knowing the patient [for a longer period of time] makes a difference in my ability to feel what they might need in that point in time. You have a better relationship and [are] less likely to end up in law suits."

An additional strain on this relationship involves an increase in patient demands. While the expanding number of managed care patients a practice must maintain to be profitable restricts physicians' availability, patients often expect more services because of the promises made by health care marketers. Thus, our participants, especially primary care physicians, found that patients over-utilized office visits because of the low cost, and requested access to specialists or expensive testing despite their objections. However, even when these physicians agreed that more extensive treatment was necessary, they were often restricted by managed care organizations. Nonetheless, the patients tended to place the blame on physicians who played the role of "gatekeeper":

> "You end up being the `gatekeeper' and you wind up fighting with the patients, which is the last thing you want to do. You're painted as the evil one! They were told they could do whatever they want if you told them they could go."

Quality of Care

The consensus opinion among the physicians was that the quality of care for patients suffered under managed care: "The American public is not benefiting from [managed care]. They really aren't. It's a sad thing." First, restrictions on their authority to make referrals or perform tests combined with various economic incentives were believed to limit physicians' ability to make adequate diagnoses and recommend appropriate treatments:

> "If I have to send a patient to a specific radiology group because that's what they [administrators] dictate, then I am compromising and diminishing my own ability. ... I don't want to [use] a radiologist who underbid someone else. That doesn't mean he is better, just cheaper."

"It's a screwball system, but the physicians who put patients off by avoiding doing the expensive tests, avoid doing the consultation, avoid giving a referral at all costs unless it is a life threatening illness can maximize income."

Second, the restricted access to physicians mentioned earlier limited the amount of emotional support provided to patients:

"Bedside manner, relationship, care and love, etc. is very different for managed care patients. Relationship does not exist in a managed care program. I went into family practice because I wanted to know my patients well and be part of their families. Thirty years ago I was, now I'm not."

Third, the need for approval for certain procedures and centralized testing tended to slow down the process of healing, causing patients to be inconvenienced and remain in pain for longer periods of time:

"I was put in a very precarious situation when a woman had a ruptured tubal pregnancy and I needed an obstetrician but could not find one that was in the HMO. This was dangerous for the patient. I finally had to use someone who was not in the HMO and fight with the HMO to honor the fee the next day!"

Finally, managed care patients were often viewed differently by physicians, almost like "second-class citizens" who were resented because of the reduced fees paid for services rendered or the possible negative impact of treatments upon physicians' end of the year bonuses:

"I'm gonna get my eight dollars a month [capitation fee] whether I go tonight or not. If I leave now, I'll have dinner with the kids and family. If I go to the hospital, I'll get home at 7:30, so I'm gonna go home."

"A minority of physicians will very skillfully put people off who don't have life threatening problems in hopes of avoiding the cost of an expensive evaluation that comes out of the pools or their bonuses."

The Physician-Managed Care Organization Relationship

While some participants felt that a positive relationship existed currently, the majority expressed a highly negative opinion of this association:

"The attitude of administration of HMOs is adversarial and instead of incorporating us into the solution, we are looked on as the problem. Instead of getting our input and form policies together, our policies are ignored. They know best and we screwed it up!"

For instance, these physicians expressed concern over the constraints placed on them by managed care organizations. One physician defined managed care as "render care under certain significant constraints issued by [a] third party payer." Thus, respondents resented the restrictions on their ability to make referrals to well-know colleagues and established lab facilities. Further, the consultants that reviewed medical care and hospital utilization were seen as less capable and without appropriate knowledge of the cases under discussion:

"If someone does not have any kind of health degree, it is ludicrous for them to ask why I had someone in the hospital one or two days!"

The respondents were also critical of the economic split, particularly when capitation arrangements existed. The feeling was that the vast majority of the monies paid by patients were spent on marketing and administration to the neglect of medical treatment. For example, HMO executives were characterized as "making six figures" or their organizations were believed to be "making a healthy profit" while the health care provider received a nominal share: "These [managed care] companies are making money hand-over-fist, yet what they're reimbursing the physician has not kept pace." As a result of this negative relationship, respondents were left feeling insecure about future opportunities with current managed care employers:

"I've heard stories where doctors who had major economic income controlled by managed care and then all of a sudden they were starting all over again ... [because] they [administrators] decided they weren't going to renew them."

Current Perceptions and Future Expectations of the Role of Physicians

The consensus was that the status of the physician in our society has been eroded ("Managed care is creating the doctor into a lower social stratum in our society."), and the financial and personal rewards of the occupation have been reduced greatly. The end result of these changes is lower job satisfaction: "As far as I'm concerned, there is very little personal satisfaction for the doctor [anymore]."

While many factors have contributed to this decline, the loss of personal autonomy due to managed care was viewed as the primary culprit: "Management and `Big Brother' telling us what we must do. I just don't like it." Further, respondents also felt that this current environment has caused the "best and brightest" students to shun medical schools in favor of careers in business or engineering:

"[This] environment is swaying people to go to other

professions, and they're forecasting that better minds (3.4 averages) are going into other fields and, consequently, medical care will decline."

Most agree with this assessment and have not recommended the occupation to their own children: "My son who is 26 has decided to go to medical school. I don't think this is a wise decision."

Respondents' long-term outlook for the profession is also bleak. Managed care, the embodiment of many of these negative changes, looms large on the horizon, and was predicted to dominate medicine in the future. Some anticipate a two-tier system, where the wealthy have the luxury of selecting private physicians who can prescribe necessary treatments while the middle and lower classes will be subjected to a form of ineffective "social medicine":

"Are we going to end up with a two-tiered English medical system where one [is] for everybody in the lower classes and the other for people who can afford it - aristocrat and common?"

The only hope is that patients become aware of the injustices within the managed care system, and demand a move back to fee-for-service medical treatment: "[Hopefully] by the year 2010, people will be fed up [with managed care] and it will be all fee-for-service!"

DISCUSSION

The results of this exploratory investigation show that negative reactions dominated our focus group participants' responses to the health care environment created by managed care. First, they believed that the bond that existed previously between patients and medical doctors has been severed, decreasing consumers' trust and confidence in medical decisions and, consequently, increasing the likelihood of malpractice suits. Second, the consensus opinion was that the quality of medical care provided to managed care patients is significantly lower than fee-for-service patients due to various organizational restrictions and "bureaucratic" procedures as well as physicians' unhappiness over lower economic rewards. Third, the physician-managed care organization relationship was viewed as adversarial and inequitable, resulting in feelings of insecurity about the long-term possibilities of this relationship. Finally, their perceptions of the profession suggested a loss in status, with expectations for the future equally bleak.

Future Directions for Health Care Marketers

These findings are the result of a study taken from an emic or physician-oriented perspective, and, therefore, represent only one very subjective viewpoint. Nonethe-

less, as a marketer, consider the possible negative effects of a representative of the firm to the consumer with the following opinion of your organization: "These things [managed care organizations] came and they spread like cancers."

As with many service-oriented and market-driven organizations, managed care firms are judged by consumers using the experiences they have with agents of these companies as the primary input. While our participants accepted some of the blame for the current health care crisis ("We brought some of this on ourselves."), they felt that the effects of their negative feelings towards managed care as the solution to this problem impacted the way they interacted with patients:

"Doctors get frustrated and get angry with the [managed care] system and some of that spills over to the patient."

Some attempted to solve this problem by voicing their concerns to their patients. However, this tactic may cause these consumers to develop a negative attitude towards managed care organizations: "I try to educate my patients, and when I do they say `My God, I didn't know that this doctor loses money when I go to see someone else [a specialist on referrals]!'"

In the long-run, few organizations are able to survive when their primary consumer interface (whether salesperson or retail clerk) fails to present a positive image consistent with marketing communications used by the firm. While there are no easy solutions, the ultimate goal is clear - managed care organizations must either recruit health care providers who feel that their role is economically and professionally rewarding or change the current system so that it is consistent with physicians' needs. If the latter approach is selected, one tactic marketers might use is to increase the level of involvement of physicians in decision making processes regarding important issues such as the establishment of fees, approved medical procedures, and drug formularies. Such a step may increase physicians' feelings of ownership of these decisions and reduce the possibility of the kind of frustration that negatively impacts their relationships with patients.

There are two important avenues for future study. First, researchers should determine the extent to which the negativity of these results are representative of various physician subpopulations. Survey data collected from diverse geographic sites that include physicians of a variety of ages and specialties seems appropriate. Second, if these results are consistent with our findings, an additional investigation that looks at the impact of this negativity on the quality of care from the patients' point of view should be conducted.

REFERENCES

Anderson, Richard A. (1990), "Handling Health-Care Costs in the '90s," *HR Magazine,* (June), 89-94.

Buckner, Jean (1990), "Guest Editorial: The Managed Care Marketplace," *Journal of Health Care Marketing,* 10 (March), 2-5.

Business and Health (1990), "The 1990 National Executive Poll on Health Care Costs and Benefits," (April), 25-26, 30-31, 34, 36-38.

Caldwell, Bernice (1989), "Health Lawyers Probe The Cost and Quality Nexus," *Employee Benefit Plan Review,* (August), 30-31.

CE Roundtable (1990), "Can Health Care Costs Be Cured?" *Chief Executive,* (June), 54-71.

Coile, Russell C. (1990), "The Megatrends -- And the Backlash," *Healthcare Forum Journal,* (March/April), 37-41.

Curtiss, Frederic R. (1989), "How Managed Care Works," *Personnel Journal,* (July), 39-53.

Federation of American Health Systems Review (1988a), "AMA Trustee Advises: Fight Improper Application of Managed Care Principles," (July/August), 41-43.

Federation of American Health Systems Review (1988b), "HHS Chief of Staff Burke Urges Industry to Face Up to the Economic Facts of Life," (March/April), 12-20.

Fox, Peter D. (1989), "The Future of HMOs," *Compensation and Benefits Management.* (Winter), 101-106.

Freedman, Marian (1990), "In Search of Health Care Access and Affordability," *Best's Review,* (June), 172-181.

Frieden, Joyce and Maria Traska (1989), "Managed Care: It's Everywhere, But What Is It?" *Business and Health,* (December), 22, 24.

Fuller, Warren E. (1989), "Another Perspective: Allies in Containing Healthcare Costs," *National Underwriter,* (July 10), 27, 30.

Gagliardi, Margaret M. and Edwin E. Freedman (1987), "Managed Care: The Ultimate Health Care Solution," *Journal of Compensation and Benefits,* (May-June), 360-362.

Gilman, Thomas A. and Cynthia K. Bucco (1987), "Alternative Delivery Systems: An Overview," *Topics in Health Care Financing,* 13 (Spring), 1-7.

Hilts, Philip J. (1991), "Say Ouch: Demands to Fix U.S. Health Care Reach a Crescendo," *The New York Times,* (May 19), Section 4, 1, 5.

Howgill, Martyn (1991), "Focus on `Quality' Changes the Marketer's Role," *The Academy Bulletin,* (March), 1, 4.

Kenkel, Paul J. (1989), "Physicians' Changing Roles," *Modern Healthcare,* (November 10), 48.

_____ (1990), "Managed-Care Organizations on the Rebound," *Modern Healthcare,* (May 21), 82-88.

Kertesz, Louise (1990), "At Long Last, Doctor Finds Health Care's `Prince'," *Business Insurance,* (June 25), 17-18.

Kittrell, Alison (1986), "Employers Turn to Managed Care, Utilization Review to Control Costs," *Modern Healthcare,* (May 9), 96, 98.

Kramon, Glenn (1991), "Insurers Move Into the Front Lines Against Rising Health-Care Costs," *New York Times,* (August 25), 1, 28.

Kuriyan, Jacob G. (1989), "Physicians: Managed Care Allies or Adversaries?" *Computers in Healthcare,* (September), 20-23.

Luthans, Fred and Elaine Davis (1990), "The Healthcare Cost Crisis: Causes and Containment," *Personnel,* (February), 24-30.

Modern Healthcare (1989), "Cost Control: Still an Uphill Battle," (January 13), 27-28.

Reinhardt, Uwe (1990), "Health Care: Business Forgets It Created the Mess; Now It Must Own Up to Its Mistakes and Help Find a Cure," *Business Month,* (October), 56-57.

Schramm, Carl J. (1990), "Healthcare Industry Problems Call for Cooperative Solutions," *Healthcare Financial Management,* (January), 54, 56, 60-61.

Signorovitch, Dennis J. (1990), "U.S. Health Costs: A Communication Challenge for the 90s," *Executive Speeches,* (October), 31-34.

Stewart, David W. and Prem N. Shamdasani (1991), *Focus Groups: Theory and Practice,* Newbury Park, CA: Sage Publications.

Tokarski, Cathy (1990), "1980s Prove Uncertainty of Instant Cures: Cost Containment, Competition Fail to Cap Rising Cures," *Modern Healthcare,* (January 8), 51-52.

SERVICE SELLING AND BUYING:
THE IMPACT OF SELECTED SELLER AND BUYER CHARACTERISTICS

Avraham Shama, The University of New Mexico

HEADNOTE

While much research exists about the impact of seller and buyer characteristics on sales of tangible products, this study addresses such influences in the process of selling a service. The study reports that, when selling a service, the attractiveness, sex, and ethnicity of the salesperson were not found to play a significant role in persuading potential customers to buy that service, nor were the ethnicity, sex, and age of the potential customers.

INTRODUCTION

The U. S. economy, and indeed the global economy, have increasingly become service economies. In fact, the service economy of the U.S. is far larger than the non-service economy which centers on tangible products. For example, Kotler (1988) reports that the service sector constitutes 70% of the U.S. Gross National Product and employs 77% of its labor force (p. 476). Furthermore, this trend of an increasing share of service economy in the U.S. and the world is expected to continue for the foreseeable future.

Equally important is that the marketing of services created some controversy pertaining to the applicability of marketing techniques and findings, which center on tangible products, to the marketing of services. Some argue that services marketing is different (see, for example, Berry 1980, Langeard et al. 1981), while others argue that product marketing and services marketing may be quite similar (Levitt 1972). Both groups, however, rarely provide scientific data to support their propositions.

And while this controversy will undoubtedly continue for years to come, this paper investigates the impact of salespeople's physical attractiveness, sex, and ethnicity in persuading potential service buyers, as well as the impact of buyers' sex, ethnicity, and age on their attitudes toward the service presented to them.

LITERATURE REVIEW

Studies by psychologists generally report that physically attractive people elicit more positive responses than less attractive people (See, for example, Adams 1977, Efran and Patterson 1976, Dion et al. 1972, Stewart 1980, Sigall and Ostrove 1975). Focusing on the relationship between attractiveness and persuasion, Chaiken (1979) reported that attractive communicators had a significantly higher degree of success in persuading others than did unattractive communicators. Chaiken concluded that "Physical attractiveness can significantly enhance communicator persuasiveness" (p. 1394).

Also, the psychology literature generally reports that women generate more positive results than do men (see, for example, Benson, Karbenick and Lerner 1976), and that ethnicity is not significantly related to persuasion (see, for example, Atkinson, Ponce, and Martinez 1984, Atkinson, Winzelberg and Holland 1985).

On the other hand, sales and marketing literature portray a more complicated picture pertaining to the relationship between attractiveness, sex, ethnicity and persuasion. Studies of the effectiveness of using physically attractive and sexually suggestive people in print advertising by Peterson and Kerin (1977), Smith and Engel (1968), and Steadman (1969) reported that the use of physically attractive and sexually suggestive people in advertising, when compared to using less attractive and less suggestive people, did not increase consumer brand name recognition. On the contrary: it may have decreased brand name recall by taking attention away from the product. Consistent with this, Baker and Churchill (1977) argue that physical attractiveness is essentially a decorative, functionless aspect of the message about the product.

In another case, investigating the effectiveness of attractiveness and sex in direct mail advertisements, Caballero and Pride (1984) report that while attractiveness per se does not affect sales, attractive females generate significantly more sales through mail order. One would therefore expect the exploitation of such a finding in sales and marketing by using more and more women as salespeople. However, research findings thus far indicate that the attribute of sex may work differently and evolve more slowly in the practice of sales and marketing. Hence, Kanuk (1978) argues that for many years, women's role in the sales field was to "soften" prospective buyers. However, Kanuk demonstrates that as values change, women are increasingly performing full sales functions, from softening the buyer (who is increasingly apt the be a woman) to closing the sale.

In line with the above, Swan, Rink, Kiser and Martin (1984) report that the industrial buyer's image of saleswomen is quite similar to his/her image of salesmen. The authors conclude by saying that "Female members of the sales force will be accepted by industrial buyers." (p. 114)

Finally, Shama (1974) reported that the ethnicity of a presenter or salesperson does not significantly affect his persuasion level as measured by the listener or customer attitude toward him/her and toward the product or idea presented.

But perhaps one of the most comprehensive studies with regard to the impact of personal factors such as attractiveness, sex, and ethnicity on the performance of salespeople was reported by Churchill et al. (1976 and 1985). The authors used metanalysis techniques to analyze all 116 articles on the topic which existed in 1985, asserting that of six different factors (role variables, skill, motivation, personal factors, aptitude, and organizational/ environmental) personal factors produced "the second largest category of association, accounting for approximately 25% of all reported correlations" (p. 109). Moreover, personal factors make the most difference when salespeople are selling services (p. 113; see also Enis and Chonko 1978, and Weitz 1979).

The hypotheses below regarding the personal factors of attractiveness, sex, and ethnicity of salespeople (H1-H3) reflect the null hypothesis which is generally reflected in the marketing literature.

Respondent background

The background of the respondents, like their age, sex and ethnic identification, may affect their perceptions of salespeople and hence the effectiveness of the salespeople. For example, Atkinson et al. (1985) reported that the ethnic background of a respondent does not affect his/her attitudes to family planners. On the other hand, Caballero and Pride (1984) suggest that women generally respond more positively than do men, while Swan et al. (1984) suggest that older industrial buyers rate salesmen somewhat more positively than saleswomen.

However, in the pretests associated with this study (see below) we found more support for the null hypothesis, that is that the respondents' age, sex and ethnic identification do not significantly affect their responses to a salesperson's presentation. This is reflected in H4-H6 below.

Hypotheses

H1: Attractiveness does not influence persuasion significantly; that is, more and less attractive salespeople are equally persuasive.

H2: Gender does not influence persuasion significantly; that is, male and female salespeople are equally persuasive.

H3: Ethnicity does not influence persuasion significantly; that is, Anglo and Hispanic salespeople are equally persuasive.

H4: Respondents' ethnicity does not significantly influence their response to salespeople; that is, Anglos and Hispanics respond to salespeople in the same manner.

H5: Respondents' gender does not significantly affect their response to salespeople; that is, men and women respond to salespeople in the same manner.

H6: Respondents' age does not significantly affect their response to salespeople; that is, respondents of different ages respond to salespeople in the same manner.

METHOD

The hypotheses of this study were tested by the use of a 2 x 2 x 2 balanced quasi experimental design. Depicted in Figure 1, this design used eight equally experienced, college-educated salespeople between 26 and 30 years old. Four of these salespeople were male and four were female. Four were attractive and four were average-looking. Similarly, four of them (two male and two female) were Anglo and four (two male and two female) were Hispanic.

The attractiveness of each salesperson was determined by a separate pretest asking a group of five judges of the opposite sex to classify a salesperson as "attractive" or "average looking." Thus, altogether there were five men and five women judges, judging on a two-point scale. A person was judged attractive or average-looking, and chosen to be a presenter in this study, only if there was a consensus among all five judges. Hence, the likelihood of classifying an "average looking" presenter as "attractive" or vice-versa was very

564

remote (in fact, the probability for this to happen was .0625 = .5 x .5 x .5 x .5 x .5).

Likewise, ethnicity was operationalized by a combination of three factors: surnames, which were used by the salespersons to introduce themselves, facial complexion and facial characteristics. Again, in a pretest using another group of six judges, three of whom were Anglo and three Hispanic, it was determined that all four Anglo salespeople were perceived as such and all four Hispanic presenters were perceived as Hispanic. A salesperson was classified as Hispanic or Anglo only if all six judges so classified him/her.

Finally, sex was communicated through name and gender-consistent dress code. Salesmen were neatly groomed and wore suits and ties of similar colors. Similarly, saleswomen wore two piece suits of similar colors and had professional demeanor. Again, a consensus of six judges (three men and three women) had to be achieved concerning gender-consistent dress code and professional look before a presenter could be used in this study. As a result, of 24 salespeople, eight were chosen to take part in this study.

Each of the salespeople made a sales presentation about a new employment agency, Execu-Search, to a different group of about 30 people in the job market. Execu-Search was a new executive search company in town, centering on placing the college-educated in the job market. The salespeople were randomly assigned to the eight groups of job-seekers. These job-seekers were both men and women, all of whom had at least a college education (some had a Ph.D) and were between 20 and 45 years old (mode of 35 years). Job-seekers were not charged any fee for the services of Execu-Search.

The presenters, each of whom had 10-12 years experience in service selling, were given a copy of the sales presentation to rehearse. The presentation was then made before a group of two judges whose role was to ensure that, in addition to the information about Execu-Search, only the factors of attractiveness, sex and ethnicity were being communicated during the presentation to the job-seekers.
None of the judges or presenters was informed of the hypotheses to be tested. If they asked, they were told that the purpose of the study was to present a new employment service to potential job-seekers in

town. Each presenter was paid an honorarium of $50. Judges did not receive any payment.

After each presentation, respondents were given a one-page questionnaire to fill out. The questionnaire included two parts. The first part had 12 four-point Likert scale items (strongly agree . . strongly disagree) which asked the respondents to rate the presenter, the presentation, and their intention to use the Execu-Search service and recommend it to their friends. Together, these twelve scale items were the operational measures of persuasion. The second part included background questions about the respondents, such as age, sex and ethnic identification.

The hypotheses of this study were tested by t-tests and analysis of variance which yielded the same results. For purposes of simplicity, only t-test findings are reported below.

RESULTS

Table 1 presents the frequency distribution of the respondents by the attractiveness, sex and ethnicity of the presenter. As can be seen, a total of 287 job-seekers took part in this study. They were quite evenly distributed along the variables of the hypotheses: attractiveness, sex, and ethnicity.

Table 2 provides the results of the test of H1, H2 and H3. It presents the combined mean response to the 12 questions (rating the presenter, the presentation, and intention to use Execu-Search and recommend it to friends) for attractive and average-looking presenters, for men and women presenters, and for Anglo and Hispanic presenters. Results of t-tests, which test whether the difference between every two means (attractive vs. average-looking, females vs. male, Anglo vs. Hispanic) is statistically significant and must be attributed to the difference between the presenters, or statistically insignificant and must be attributed to chance, are also presented.

Table 3 presents the mean response and t-test results for each of the 12 questions along the variables of H1, H2, and H3.

As can be seen in Table 2, the attractiveness, sex and ethnicity of a salesperson did not significantly affect the respondents' rating of the salesperson and his/her presentation, nor did it significantly affect intention to use the employment service on at least

.05 significance level. These results confirm the first three hypotheses of this study,-- that is, that salesperson attractiveness, sex and ethnicity do not make a significant difference in persuading respondents. It should also be noted that ANOVA's interaction effects among attractiveness, sex and ethnicity were tested and found insignificant.

Question-by-question comparisons provided in Table 3 further support these findings for H2 and H3. As can be seen, none of the 12 questions produced a significant difference on the .05 level between salesmen and saleswomen or between Anglo and Hispanic salespeople. When it comes to H1, however, a significant difference is found in the responses to attractive and average-looking salespeople along items 4, 6, and 7 (printed in bold) of a total of twelve items listed in Table 3. However, a closer look at these three items shows that the mean response to the average-looking salesperson was more positive in items 4 and 6, and the contrary was true for item 7. This means that average-looking salespersons are perceived as significantly more knowledgeable and confident than are attractive salespeople. This is further supported by the responses to items 1, 5, and 8, which were significant at the .1 level. On the other hand, attractive salespeople are perceived as significantly more persuasive than average-looking salespeople as indicated by the t-test results of item 7. Finally, when it comes to intentions to use or recommend the service (item 10), there were no significant differences between attractive and average-looking salespeople.

Table 4 presents the results of the test of H4, H5, and H6 pertaining to the background of the respondents, as did Table 2 for the salespeople. As can be seen, respondents' ethnicity, sex, and age do not significantly affect their responses to salespeople. Therefore, one may accept H4, H5, and H6.

SUMMARY AND CONCLUSIONS

This study has reported that in selling a service by the college-educated to the college-educated the attractiveness, sex and ethnicity of the sales force do not play a statistically significant role in the selling process nor do the ethnicity, sex and age of the buyers play such an important role in their perceptions of salespeople. By implication, then, what matters may be the quality of the product or service being sold, as perceived by potential customers.

More importantly, however, is that the findings of this study suggest that when selling a service, the attributes of personal attractiveness, sex, and ethnicity of both the sales force and the prospective customers have no significant impact on the persuasiveness of the sales force. In these respects, selling a service is the same as selling a product.

BIBLIOGRAPHY

Adams, G.R. (1977). Physical attractiveness research: Toward a developmental social psychology of beauty. *Human Development, 20,* 217-239.

Atkinson, D.R., Ponce, F.Q., & Martinez, F.M. (1984). Effects of ethnic, sex, and attitude similarity on counselor credibility. *Journal of Counseling Psychology, 31* (4), 588-590.

Atkinson, D.R., Winzelberg, A. & Holland, A. (1985). Ethnicity, locus of control for family planning, and pregnancy counselor credibility. *Journal of Counseling Psychology, 32* (3), 417-421.

Baker, M.J. & Churchill, G.A. Jr. (1977, November). The impact of physically attractive models on advertising evaluation. *Journal of Marketing Research, 14,* 538-555.

Benson, P.L., Karbenick, S.A., & Lerner, R.M. (1976). Pretty pleases: The effects of physical attractiveness, race, and sex on receiving help. *Journal of Experimental Psychology, 12,* 409-415.

Berry, L. (1980, May-June). Services marketing is different. *Business,* 24-30.

Caballero, M.J., & Pride, W.M. (1984, Winter). Selected effects of salesperson sex and attractiveness in direct mail advertisements. *Journal of Marketing, 48,* 94-100.

Chaiken, S. (1979). Communicator physical attractiveness and persuasion. *Journal of Personality and Social Psychology, 37* (8), 1387-1397.

Churchill, A.G. & Ford, N.M. (1976). *Motivating the Industrial Sales Force: The Attractiveness of Alternative Rewards.* Cambridge, MA: MSI.

Churchill, A.G., N.M. Ford, S.W. Hartley & O.C. Walker Jr. (1985). The determinants of sales force performance: A meta-analysis. *Journal of Marketing Research,* 103-118.

Dion, K., Berscheid, E., & Walster, E. (1972, December). What is beautiful is good. *Journal of Personality and Social Psychology, 24,* 285-290.

Efran, M.G. & Patterson, E.W.J. (1976). *The Politics of Appearance.* Unpublished manuscript, University of Toronto.

Enis, B.M. & L.B. Chonko (1978). A review of personal selling: Implications for managers and researchers. *Review of Marketing 1978.* Chicago: American Marketing Association, 276-302.

Kanuk, L. (1978, January). Women in industrial selling. *Journal of Marketing, 42,* 87-91.

Kotler, P. (1988). *Marketing Management Analysis Planning, Implementation and Control* (6th ed.). Englewood Cliffs NJ: Prentice Hall.

Langeard, E., Bateson, J.E.G., Lovelock, C., & Eiglier, P. (1981). *Service Marketing: New Insights from Consumers and Managers.* Cambridge MA: Marketing Science Institute.

Peterson, R.A. & Kerin, R.A. (1977, October). The female role in advertisements: Some experimental evidence. *Journal of Marketing, 41,* 59-63.

Shama, A. (1974). *Candidate image and voter preference.* Presented before the American Marketing Association, Portland OR.

Sigall, H. & Ostrove, N. (1975). Beautiful but dangerous: Effects of offender attractiveness and nature of the crime on juridic judgment. *Journal of Personality and Social Psychology, 31* (3), 410-414.

Smith, G. & Engel, R. (1968). Influence of a female model on perceived characteristics of an automobile. *Proceedings of the 76th Annual Convention of the American Psychological Association,* 681-682.

Steadman, M. (1969, March). How sexy illustrations affect brand recall. *Journal of Advertising Research, 9,* 15-19.

Stewart, J.E. II (1980). Defendant's attractiveness as a factor in the outcome of criminal trials: An observational study. *Journal of Applied Social Psychology, 10* (4), 348-361.

Swan, J.E., Rink, D.R., Kiser, G.E., & Martin, W.S. (1984, Winter). Industrial buyer image of the saleswoman. *Journal of Marketing, 48,* 110-116.

Weitz, B.A. (1979). A critical review of personal selling research: The need for contingency approaches. In G. Albaum & G. Churchill (Eds.), *Critical Issues in Sales Management: State-of-the-Art and Future Research Needs.* Eugene: College of Business Administration, University of Oregon, 10-75.

Figure 1.   Quasi Experimental Design Used in the Study

Group Number	Size	Presenter Name	Ethnicity	Sex	Attractiveness
1	46	C. Wooten	Anglo	F	Attractive
2	33	G. Smothermon	Anglo	M	Attractive
3	34	Y. Baca	Hispanic	F	Attractive
4	30	F. Paz	Hispanic	M	Attractive
5	33	R. Minton	Anglo	F	Average
6	32	B. Richardson	Anglo	M	Average
7	44	A. Silva	Hispanic	F	Average
8	35	J. Romero	Hispanic	M	Average

Table 1.   Frequency Responses by Presenter's Attractiveness, Sex and Ethnicity

Presenter	Job-seekers (N=287)	Percent
Attractiveness		
Attractive	157	54.7
Average	130	45.3
Sex		
Male	144	50.2
Female	143	49.8
Ethnicity		
Anglo	143	49.8
Hispanic	144	50.2

Table 2. Result of T-tests by Salesperson Attractiveness, Sex and Ethnicity

Sales person	Number of Responses	D F	Mean Response	Standard Deviation	F. Value	Significance at P.<
Attractive	132	131	24.86	6.47		
Average	113	112	24.22	5.57	1.35	.11
Female	121	120	23.87	6.00		
Male	124	123	25.24	6.08	1.03	.88
Anglo	124	120	25.06	5.70		
Hispanic	121	123	24.04	6.41	1.26	.20

Table 3: Mean Responses[a] by Salesperson's Attractiveness, Sex and Ethnicity

Statement[b]	Attractive	Average	Male	Female	Anglo	Hispanic
1. The presentation was easily understood	1.71[c]	1.61[c]	1.66	1.66	1.72	1.62
2. The presentation was a productive use of my time	2.05	2.04	2.13	1.96	2.06	2.03
3. The salesperson was friendly	1.72	1.57	1.67	1.63	1.70	1.61
4. The salesperson was knowledgeable	**1.95**	**1.76**	1.94	1.78	1.97	1.74
5. The salesperson provided valuable information	1.95[c]	1.92[c]	1.98	1.89	1.97	1.90
6. The salesperson was confident	**2.19**	**2.08**	2.29	2.08	2.29	2.08
7. The salesperson was persuasive	**2.39**	**2.45**	2.52	2.31	2.46	2.37
8. The salesperson captured my attention	2.31[c]	2.23[c]	2.37	2.18	2.32	2.23
9. Execu-Search sounds like a good idea	1.74	1.69	1.74	1.69	1.70	1.73
10. I intend to get more information about Execu-Search	2.26	2.27	2.32	2.22	2.28	2.26
11. I will apply with Execu-Search	2.41	2.48	2.49	2.39	2.24	2.44
12. I will recommend Execu-Search to friends	2.33	2.22	2.25	2.31	2.29	2.27

a Mean responses in bold display a significant different at the 0.05 level among the respondents to the salesperson.
b Each statement was scaled on a 4-point scale, with 1 = strongly agree and 4 = strongly disagree.
c Means a significant difference on the .1 level.

Table 4. Results of T-tests by Respondent Sex, Age, and Ethnicity[a]

Respondent	Number of responses	DF	Mean response	Std. Dev.	F. value	Significance at P.<
Female	127	126	24.25	6.05		
Male	105	104	24.57	5.67	1.14	.49
Anglo	174	173	25.02	5.90		
Hispanic	72	71	24.76	6.37	1.12	.45
< 30	177	176	23.60	6.41		
≥ 30	105	104	24.01	5.53	1.09	.39

a   Only the responses of Anglo and Hispanic respondents were analyzed.

571

AUTHOR INDEX

Stinson, John E.	368
Stoltman, Jeffrey J.	257, 407
Stone, Robert W.	427
Subramanian, Suresh	300
Suchard, Hazel T.	459
Sullivan, Jeremiah J.	56
Szymanski, David M.	309
Talarzyk, W. Wayne	205
Taylor, Ruth Lesher	528
Ueltschy, Linda C.	297
Urban, David J.	313
Varadarajan, P. Rajan	309
Waheeduzzaman, A.N.M.	109, 121
Ward, John L.	466
Wayland, Jane P.	313
Webster, Cynthia	513
Weiss, John E.	211
Widgery, Robin	117
Widing, Robert E II	205
Wood, Van R.	492
Woodside, Arch G.	474
Wooldridge, Bill	151
Wren, Brent M.	529, 537
Yadav, Manjit S.	282
Yalch, Richard F.	56
Yaprak, Attila	407
Yavas, Ugur	462
Yeoh, Poh-Lin	43
Yoo, Yangjin	28
Young, Mark R.	547
Zhang, Li	520
Zhou, Nan	119

ADDENDUM

Shama, Avraham	563